1979

A
SHORT HISTORY
OF
PHILOSOPHY

N° 645

F.-J. THONNARD, A. A.

PROFESSOR OF PHILOSOPHY

A
SHORT HISTORY
OF
PHILOSOPHY

TRANSLATED FROM THE
REVISED AND CORRECTED EDITION

BY

EDWARD A. MAZIARZ, C. PP. S., M. S., PH. D.

SOCIETY OF ST. JOHN THE EVANGELIST

DESCLÉE & CIE

PUBLISHERS TO THE HOLY APOSTOLIC SEE

PARIS — TOURNAI — ROME — NEW YORK

1955

Printed in Belgium

Imprimi potest.

S. W. Oberhauser, C. PP. S.

L.C. #56-3056

Imprimatur.

✠ John G. Bennett

Bishop of Lafayette in Indiana

SANCTO PATRI AUGUSTINO

DIVOQUE THOMÆ

MAGISTRIS

AUTHOR'S PREFACE TO THE SECOND EDITION.

The first edition of this history of philosophy was favorably received. Wide acclaim was especially given to its method, which includes a review of the great doctrinal currents along with a presentation of the more important thinkers. " The master ideas of each system are brought out clearly and the filiation of systems is carefully analyzed. In a general way, the author can be said to sympathize with each philosopher who is studied, for his criticism is intelligent and benevolent, and yet strong enough to point out and to condemn errors " [1]. If it has been found necessary on occasion "to replace the sinuous forms of historical development by sharp and well defined constructions " [2], one can readily indulge this practice which is inevitable in a short history and which readily finds compensation in the pedagogical advantages of clearness and simplicity.

This new edition of the book is revised, and, in part, recast. It aims to take advantage of the suggestions of kindly critics, and yet to keep the characteristics which made its first appearance so welcome. In this way, it is hoped that it will be useful to a larger number of readers.

One of the main purposes of this history is to serve as an introductory manual for the use of ecclesiastical students. It thus completes the set on theology and on patrology published for the same purpose [3]. This fact explains the care and detail given to the thought of the Scholastic masters. In this latter section, the treatment of St. Bonaventure and of Suarez has been carefully done over.

---

[1] Quoted from a review by M. FESTUGIÉRE in *Revue Bénédictine*, XI, 1938.

[2] Quoted from a revue by F. Jansen in *Nouvelle revue théologique*, February, 1938. The same author writes, " The pearl of the work is the section on St. Augustine which is written with devotion, excellent though these latter pages are, those dealing with Bergson, Plotinus and Saint Thomas are likewise filled with admiration and ardor".

[3] Reference is being made here to a Latin treatise on theology written by F. Diekamp, to a Latin work on moral theology and another on dogmatic theology written by A. Tanquerey, and to a French work on patrology written by F. Cayré; the latter work has been translated into English by H. Howitt as *Manual of Patrology and History of Theology* (2 vols., Desclée, 1936-40).

A second aim in writing this work has been to be of service to college students majoring in philosophy, those taking courses in the history of philosophy, or those preparing for comprehensive examinations. An exposition of the opinions defended by the various philosophical schools, presented in their historical connectedness as a living and coherent unity, can be helpful to such students. Already in the first edition, particular attention was given to modern philosophy, especially in its positivistic aspect; in fact, the *Doctrinal Table* at the end of this history helped to make the whole treatment of modern philosophy meaningful and practical. This new edition attempts to treat more fully the results of research into such modern authors as Francis Bacon, Spinoza, Locke, Hume, John Stuart Mill and others. The various branches and ramifications of experimental psychology — whether English, French or German — and the main directions of this branch of learning are also included in this revised edition [1].

This history of philosophy is also directed toward the cultured public in order to acquaint them with the various aspects of philosophical thought, especially that of the modern era. It seems more necessary now than ever before that a man be better informed on such matters, in order that he be not led astray in fulfilling his duties in an age as troubled as our own. It is more clear today that " ideas rule the world ". Reasons like these have prompted a more complete treatment of modern philosophy, whose spirit has quietly slipped into men's minds.

The broad divisions used in the first edition have been kept. They give some measure of order and clarity to the multitude of systems. Each current of thought has been traced, as much as possible, into modern times. The chapter on positivism, for instance, has been enlarged with a treatment of socialism and of communism. The pages devoted to Bergsonianism have been completed by a treatment of contemporary views that is better ordered. It is not possible to give a definitive treatment to thought which is still in process of formation. Accordingly, an attempt has been made to fix the orientations of contemporary thought and to give some estimate of them in the light of Christian philosophy.

---

[1] Most of these new sections are distinguishable from the original edition by being placed in smaller print or by adding to the original paragraph numbering.

The history of philosophy is but an aspect of the history of human thought. Inasmuch as Philosophy is superior to the more particularized sciences, and yet inferior to the supernatural and religious doctrines which belong to the realm of Revelation, its history is the most interesting, and invites the attention of both believers and nonbelievers. This history is addressed to both types of thinkers in the hope that as they follow the efforts and struggles of reason in the pursuit of truth, they will see more clearly the plan of Providence, which gave man the precious light of natural reason in order that he might find the brilliant light of grace and of the Catholic faith.

November 21, 1940.

F. J. THONNARD, A. A.

Note for the 1948 edition.

The bibliography has been gone over and brought up to date. It makes no pretense at being complete, but of giving a preliminary acquaintance with the following :

1º The best editions of the works of philosophers and the best and most accessible French translations of them;

2º The more important studies on various men or periods, especially those universally known, and those which were written or have been translated into French.

A work of this sort is constantly capable of being corrected and perfected. The author willingly accepts any suggestions from his readers.

F. J. THONNARD, A. A.

TRANSLATOR'S PREFACE.

There is an increasing number of histories of philosophy in English which include some evaluation and criticism along with the presentation of philosophical thought. This translation adds to these books a sufficiently short but complete work which views the history of philosophy in the light of both natural and Christian truth. The appearance of this work in English, then, fulfills a definite need on the part of English-speaking students and readers [1] for a critical work in the history of philosophy.

Father Thonnard is objective in his presentation and is sympathetic to even the slightest suggestion of truth which a thinker may have proposed. His work is well organized and is easily seen to stem from the mind of a man who is both an historian and a logician. In addition, the author has the rare quality needed in a good historian of philosophy — he is a metaphysician who succeeds in presenting the history of thought as a living actuation of truth in the minds of men.

When the translation was undertaken, a portion [2] of the work had already been done by another hand. This part was checked for accuracy. In the remainder of the work, a constant attempt was made to be exact, faithful to the author's presentation, and yet to make the reading of the work in English as idiomatic as possible. Similarly, while the original bibliographies and references have, in large part, been retained, a certain amount of editing was considered necessary in order to accommodate

---

[1] William Turner's *History of Philosophy* (New York, 1929), though a good work in the field, is now out of date. The work of F. Copleston (*A History of Philosophy*, Westminster, Md., 1946 ff.), of which three volumes have thus far appeared is an excellent work but quite long. The *History of Christian Philosophy in the Middle Ages* (New York, 1955) by Etienne Gilson, *A History of Modern European Philosophy* (Milwaukee, Wis., 1954) by James Collins, and the *History of Medieval Philosophy* (currently being reprinted in the United States and Great Britain) by Maurice De Wulf, are superb works but they deal with special periods in the history of philosophical thought.

[2] The translation of the first eighty-two paragraphs had been done and set into print (to page 115).

the work to an English audience. Some references have been omitted, and the bibliography has been expanded with a number of standard works, especially those appearing in English. The author's selections and method of presentation have not been substantially altered, however, and the bibliographies will be found to contain a select but adequate list of the more important works in the field. An evaluation of how well all of this has been done is left to the experience of the cultured reader and the student — whose suggestions will be gratefully accepted.

The great Aristotle once said that a man can do little without the help of friends. My thanks are due to the administration of Saint Joseph's College, to the many friends who encouraged and assisted me, to Father Cletus G. Kern for help in reading the manuscript, and to Messrs. Edmund F. Byrne and James J. Brophy for their painstaking work in reading and correcting proofs.

March 7, 1955

Rev. Edward A. Maziarz, C. PP. S.
Saint Joseph's College
Collegeville, Indiana.

INTRODUCTION.

I. — DEFINITION.

1. *By the term " history of philosophy " is meant a reasoned study of the attempts made by the mind of man throughout the ages to reach the truth concerning the ultimate and most general causes of things.*

We may indicate the scope of this study by starting from the commonly accepted notion of philosophy as a body of doctrine conceived by the human mind, acting in its own particular sphere with the aim of solving the more general problems of the universe and of man. In such a study there is no place for literature, mathematics, or any of the special branches of knowledge such as astronomy, physics, chemistry, etc. These subjects, classified by the moderns under the general name of *Science*, deal with the immediate causes of things. The explanations given by them are in terms of mathematics. Religions are also excluded from the history of philosophy, together with divinely revealed truths and all knowledge based on them, such as theology : these are concerned with a supra-rational order of things.

All philosophers are by no means agreed as to the precise limits of their field of research. In ancient times, and up to the medieval period, philosophy was held to embody all known branches of learning. Cicero's definition aptly conveys this view : " Philosophia est rerum divinarum et humanarum, causarumque quibus hæ res continentur, scientia " [1]. In the philosophico-theological mind of the Christian scholar there has not always been a clear line of distinction between the domain of faith and that of reason; while among the moderns there is the greatest diversity of opinion [2].

---

[1] CICERO, *De Offic.*, Book II, Ch. II.
[2] A. COMTE, for instance, holds that philosophy covers the whole range of positive sciences. For BERGSON its object is " *the purely durational* " which is not attained by the deductions of those same sciences.

However by taking a broad view of the scope of philosophy and by making an occasional appeal to the scientific systems connected with it for the elucidation of certain questions, it is possible to select for special study, without falsifying them, the purely philosophical theories of the various thinkers. Thus it is that the great names and outstanding systems dealt with in this manual are studied by all those concerned with the history of philosophy.

2. On the other hand, the work undertaken here must be, like all true history, rational and scientific. It cannot be a mere index of names and systems. We shall have both to understand these systems and to estimate their value.

a) We must first *understand* them. This implies a clear grasp of the key thought, of what might be called the *fundamental principle* of a given philosophy. We must note the connection between the genesis of a doctrine and the historical background and character of the philosopher, together with his physical, and more especially his moral and intellectual environment. Along these lines, at once objective and impartial, our mind in harmony with his, we should consider the internal growth of his system and the breadth and coherence of the conclusions drawn from its first principles. This combination of wealth and fertility in the development with unity of principle is the unmistakable sign of true genius. Furthermore, history can show with varying degrees of certainty the influence that successive systems of thought have had one upon another, and so lead us to see the logical connection between them. Such a conception of the history of philosophy was expressed by De Wulf when he defined it as : " the history of the filiation of systems " [1].

b) Once we have understood a philosophy, we must *estimate its value*. Obviously nothing would be more contrary to the true historical method than to make of each and every philosophy a more or less forced interpretation with a view to establishing a preconceived thesis [2]. But truth is *one;* and

---

[1] *Histoire de la philosophie médiévale*, 5th ed., preface, p. 1.

[2] CONDORCET, in his *Esquisse d'un tableau historique des progrès de l'esprit humain* (written in 1793) sets out to prove the theory of progress. HEGEL formulates the law of progress according to the universal, rhythmic movement of *thesis, antithesis* and *synthesis;* A. COMTE studies it in the light of the law of the three states (theological, metaphysical, positive). For the various conceptions of philosophical authors, see BRÉHIER : *Hist. de la phil.* 1, Introd., pp. 12-33.

there is truth to be found everywhere, either pure or mingled with error, profound or superficial, whole and entire or fragmentary. Hence the necessity for the full comprehension of a philosophical system, of discerning the element of truth it must contain. Truth is *one;* but it shows itself in a multiplicity of forms. There is no such thing as pure error. No sincere thinker who has any talent can fail to reveal one or other of the many aspects of truth. Falsehood itself will be a guide; for falsehood is, for the most part, merely the result of giving a disproportionate value to an otherwise sound point of view. Under much diversity of expression we shall therefore find a steady current of thought nourished by sound judgment, a common heritage of truth to which every philosopher worthy, of the name has contributed. This was clearly the view that Leibnitz took when he spoke of the *perennial philosophy:* " Philosophia perennis " [1].

c) To realize this double aim we shall combine in the present manual the chronological method with the logical. In every age are to be found a few creative minds who add something new to the doctrines previously elaborated, whose teachings attract a number of disciples, and who in turn prepare the ground for the construction of a new system of thought. It is possible therefore to maintain a broadly chronological sequence of names and to insist at the same time on the inter-dependence of the various lines of thought. With this in view, the space devoted to secondary authors has been intentionally limited, and stress laid on those whose names stand for a school of thought, or whose writings have a markedly original value. For less important names some more fully developed history should be consulted [2].

Corollaries.

a) This conception of the history of philosophy in no way leads to scepticism. It is on the contrary most valuable as a complement to the study of philosophy itself. Such was the

---

[1] Cf. n. 270.

[2] We may note here that the case is different for students of Patrology. It was not merely in their own name that the Fathers of the Church wrote. They were witnesses to the divine revelation as conveyed in tradition. Hence the importance of even the minor writings. In the domain of philosophy the merit of a work depends above all on its doctrinal value and on the radiating influence of the philosopher's mind.

opinion of St. Thomas himself. Aquinas holds no doubt as an essential that : " philosophy is concerned not with the opinions of men, but with truth and reality " [1] but he adds that " the mind of man has proceeded step by step in the discovery of the origin of things " [2], and we should make use of these endeavors. Elsewhere he says : " No doubt the contribution that the labors and talents of one man can make to the progress of truth is not much compared with the sum total of knowledge; yet from the coordination of all the individual contributions, selected and put together, something great has resulted; witness the various sciences which, thanks to the efforts and discernment of several men, have reached a wonderful development " [3]. Therefore, " the opinion of the ancients, whoever they may be, is worthy of our consideration. It has a twofold utility : in so far as it is sound we shall accept it, and in so far as it is faulty we shall beware of it " [4].

b) It may be added that this subject is of interest to the historian, to the apologist and to the theologian.

1. **Historical interest.** Human activity finds its true explanation in the ideal which is its goal. The history of events cannot be reasonably separated from the history of ideas; and if philosophical ideas have not alone been responsible for leading the world, (the Gospel may be instanced as another guiding factor) they have nevertheless played their part.

2. **Apologetic interest.** Reason left to itself has fallen into many errors in the field of philosophical discovery. Some sort of natural explanation is undoubtedly to be found in the complex nature of the subject, in the difficulty of the method, and in the moral consequences that follow from it. But the doctrine of original sin offers the only true solution of this historical paradox; and this study is truly a commentary on the following pronouncement of the Vatican Council : " Divinæ revelationi tribuendum est, ut ea quæ in rebus divinis humanæ rationi per se impervia non sunt, in præsenti quoque generis humanæ conditione, ab omnibus, expedite, firma certitudine et nullo admixto errore cognosci possint " [5].

---

[1] *De cælo et mundo*, i, lect. 22.
[2] *De substantiis separatis*, Q. 7.
[3] II. *Met.*, lect. 1.
[4] I. *De Anima*, lect. 2.
[5] Sess. III, Ch. 2, Denzinger-Bannwart, n. 1786.

3. **Theological interest.** In the writings of the Fathers there are frequent references to the different schools of philosophy. For instance, there is a strong current of Platonism in the primitive Fathers : St. Justin, Origen, etc. Many a chapter of St. Augustine should be interpreted with reference to Plotinus; St. Thomas appeals constantly to Aristotle. Indeed theology has always implied an effort to understand and systematize, in the light of a philosophy, the truths obtained by revelation. So, although complete in itself, this treatise is at the same time a most useful complement to that on *Patrology* [1].

II. — GENERAL VIEW AND DIVISION OF THE SUBJECT.

3. A general survey of the whole history of philosophy shows its development not as a regular, undeviating line of progressive evolution, but as the alternate ebb and flow of a triple current of ideas.

1. The main philosophical problems are stated very early, and are solved according to a rudimentary formula which is gradually improved upon, until at last the impulse given by Socrates enables Plato and Aristotle to construct the first relatively complete systems of philosophy. These three however offer only vague answers to several questions of the first importance. Moreover, their disciples who carry on their work are much less significant than they. With the later scholars of ancient Greece and those of pagan Rome, philosophical thought is on the whole marked by a decline. Neo-Platonism sheds a last glory on the philosophy of the ancients, which fails to survive paganism and so may well be called *pagan philosophy*.

2. Christianity now infuses a new vigor into the activity of the human mind. Its influence first affects Platonism, a system dear to the early Fathers and above all to St. Augustine. The ground is thus prepared for the organic doctrinal structures realized particularly in the twelfth and thirteenth centuries by the schoolmen who accepted the beneficial guidance of Christian belief. Here again, however, the great conceptions

---

[1] F. CAYRÉ, *Manual of patrology and history of theology*, 2 vols., Desclée, 1936-40.

of the master minds, St. Thomas Aquinas, St. Bonaventure and Duns Scotus, are much superior to those of their followers and another decline is inevitable. Now it will be noted particularly during this period that men are concerned with harmonizing reason and Revelation. Christian influence pervades the whole range of thought and we are justified in applying to this second phase the name of *Christian philosophy* [1].

3. With Descartes, philosophical thought receives a fresh impulse and, at the same time, frees itself from dependence on theology and faith. Notable achievements in the domain of natural science, and an inquiring attitude with regard to the value of human knowledge, provide reason with a new source of energy and inspiration. This phase may be qualified as rationalist, critical, and scientific: three characteristics which are admittedly distinctive of *modern philosophy* [2].

However it is not normal that there should exist opposition between the faith of the Catholic and the wisdom of the philosopher. In recent times, thanks to the initiative of Leo XIII, they have been brought together once more. The great Scholastic system has been revived in a form more consciously rational, less directly influenced by theology, than it was in the Middle Ages, and perfect in its kind [3]. This new scholasticism interprets chiefly the Thomist conception. This last period will therefore include both *modern and neo-Thomist philosophy.* Hence the three main divisions of this book:

I.   THE GREEK AND ROMAN ERAS. Pagan Philosophy. (6th Cent. B. C. — 6th A. D.)

II. THE PATRISTIC AND MEDIEVAL ERAS. Christian Philosophy. (2nd Cent. — 16th Cent.)

III. THE MODERN ERA. Modern and neo-Thomist Philosophy. (17th Cent. — 20th Cent.)

---

[1] The word *Christian* is taken here in a purely historical sense. We shall see that we are dealing, not with theological systems, but with philosophy in the true meaning of the word.

[2] Although there are *modern* philosophers whose outlook is sincerely Christian, their *philosophy* can no longer, as in the previous period, be called Christian. Cf. n. 312.

[3] Although the neo-Thomists accept the Revelation and although their system is in perfect agreement with Christian doctrine, it cannot strictly speaking be termed a Christian philosophy. Cf. nn. 178 and 244.

GENERAL BIBLIOGRAPHY.

For a recent, English summary of bibliographical detail, see LOUIS DE RAEYMAEKER, *Introduction to philosophy*, Translated by Harry Mc Neill, New York, 1948, pp. 183-258.

BARBEDETTE, D., *Histoire de la philosophie*, 8e édit., Paris, 1938. — BLANC, E., *Histoire de la philosophie*, 3 vols., Paris-Lyons, 1896. — BRÉHIER, E., *Histoire de la philosophie*, 2 vols., Paris, 1932. — BROCHARD, V., *Etudes de philosophie ancienne et de philosophie moderne*, nouv. édit., Paris, 1926. — BRUCKER, J. J., *Historia critica philosophiæ*, 5 vols., Lipsiæ, 1742-4. — COPLESTON, F., *A history of philosophy*, 3 vols. completed, Westminster, Md., 1946. — COUSIN, V., *Histoire générale de la philosophie*, 5 vols., 4e édit., Paris, 1867. — DE WULF, M., *Précis d'histoire de la philosophie*, 8e édit., Louvain, 1938. — ERDMANN, J., *History of philosophy*, 2nd ed., 3 vols., New York, 1892. — FERM, V., *History of philosophical systems*, New York, 1950. — FULLER, B. A. G., *A history of philosophy*, 2 vols., rev. éd., New York, 1945. — JANET, P. A. R., and Seailles, G., *History of the problems of philosophy*, 2 vols., New York, 1923. — JONES, W. T., *History of western philosophy*, 2 vols., New York, 1952. — PALHORIES, F., *Vies et doctrines des grands philosophes à travers les âges*, 3 vols., Paris, 1939. — RADHAKRISHNAN, S. (ed.), *History of Philosophy : Eastern and Western*, 2 vols., London, 1952. — SARTON, G. *Introduction to the history and method of science*, 3 volumes in 5° — BALTIMORE, Md., 1927-48. *A history of science*, Cambridge, Mass., 1952. — STALLKNECHT, N. P., and BRUMBAUGH, R. S., *Spirit of western philosophy*, New York, 1950. — TENNEMAN, W. G., *Geschichte der philosophie*, 11 vols., Leipzig, 1798-1818. — TURNER, W., *History of philosophy*, New York, 1929. — UEBERWEG, F., *Grundriss der Geschichte der philosophie*, 5 vols., Berlin, 1923-8. — WALSHE, T. J., *The quest of reality*, St. Louis, Mo., 1933. — WINDELBAND, W., *History of philosophy*, 2nd ed., New York, 1893.

Studies on various philosophers and on their doctrines are also treated in numerous reviews and periodicals; for a quite complete listing of these, see the work of Louis de Raeymaeker listed above (pp. 242-52). In the same work (pp. 204-231), will be found a long list of the various editions of philosophical texts in English.

For current bibliography of philosophy, see one of the following : *Répertoire bibliographique* (1934, *ff.*), quarterly supplement of *Revue philosophique de Louvain; Bibliographia philosophica*, (G. A. DE BRIE, ed.) Brussels, 1934, *ff.; Philosophic Abstracts*, New York, 1939, *ff.*

PART ONE.

GREEK AND ROMAN ERAS.

PAGAN PHILOSOPHY.

---

4. Greek philosophy will be the first object of our study The history of the highly civilized nations of the East would no doubt bring us into contact with doctrinal systems of no little interest. Besides the ancient Egyptian moralists, the Brahmins and the Buddhists of India, and Confucius and Lao-Tse in China had formed partly philosophical notions about the universe, the soul, and God. But these sages were primarily founders or reformers of religion; it was in God's name rather than in the name of reason that they taught [1].

It seems clear that, alone among the pagans of antiquity, the Greeks and the Romans produced thinkers who were able to pursue a rational inquiry independently of their religious beliefs. Two reasons may be given for this : the naturally curious and speculative genius of these two peoples, and the peculiar nature of their religions, which made more of cult than of the doctrine. The Greeks, more easily than any other pagan race, could rationalize the teachings of their mythology while maintaining the traditions of their worship [2].

The result has been to give philosophy an all important part in that distinctive mold of human life, in its moral,

---

[1] This was truer still of the Jews who, unconcerned with the wisdom of men, kept faithfully the precious teachings entrusted to them by God Himself.

[2] Note too the difficulty of obtaining now any knowledge of oriental philosophies, e. g. of the Mesopotamian civilization, which certainly left its mark on the minds of the early Greek philosophers. BRÉHIER stresses this fact, (*Hist. de la philosophie*, Introd., pp. 5-7) but he too begins his history with Greek philosophy.

aesthetic and intellectual aspects, which we know as *Hellenism*. The Greek sage took upon himself to provide for the individual, frequently for the whole nation, a moral code which would answer a rational conception. We may therefore use the general appellation : *philosophical Hellenism.*

This system reached its full development in the masterly syntheses of Plato and Aristotle during the 5th and 4th centuries. The climax was preceded by two centuries of gropings after truth, and it was followed by nine centuries of decline during which works of great merit occasionally appeared. This last period was a natural transition from pagan to Christian philosophy.

The division of this first epoch is therefore threefold :

FIRST   PERIOD : The Dawn of philosophical Hellenism. (6th and 5th Cent. B. C.)

SECOND PERIOD : The Climax of philosophical Hellenism. (5th and 4th Cent. B. C.)

THIRD   PERIOD : Decline and transition. (4th Cent. B. C. — 6th Cent. A. D.)

GENERAL BIBLIOGRAPHY FOR THE PAGAN PERIOD.

ARMSTRONG, A. H., *Introduction to ancient philosophy*, 2nd rev. ed., London, 1949. — BENN, A. W., *The greek philosophers*, 2 vols., London, 1914. — BURNET, J., *Early greek philosophy*, 3rd ed., London, 1930. *Greek philosophy Thales to Plato*, London, 1928. — DIOGENES LAERTIUS, *Lives of eminent philosophers*, 2 vols., New York, 1925. — FULLER, B. A. G., *History of greek philosophy*, 3 vols., New York, 1923-31. — GOMPERZ, T., *Greek thinkers*, 4 vols., 4th ed., London, 1930. — JAEGER, W., *Paideia, The ideals of greek culture*, 3 vols., 2nd ed., New York, 1945. — MARITAIN, J., *An introduction to philosophy*, New York, n. d. — MAYER, F., *History of ancient and medieval philosophy*, New York, 1950. — RIVAUD, A., *Les grands courants de la pensée antique*, Paris, 1929. — ROBIN, L., *Greek thought and the origin of the scientific spirit*, London, 1928. — STACE, W. T., *A critical history of greek philosophy*, London, 1920. — VERBEKE, G., *L'évolution de la doctrine du Pneuma, du stoïcisme à saint Augustin*, Paris, 1945. — WERNER, C., *La philosophie grecque*, Paris, 1938. — ZELLER, E., *Outlines of the history of greek philosophy*, New York, 1931.

FIRST PERIOD.

Dawn of Philosophical Hellenism.

(6TH AND 5TH CENTURIES B. C.)

5. Towards the end of the 7th century B. C. the early Greek scholars, in search of a rational explanation of things, abandoned the teachings of poetry and mythology and founded philosophy. The movement began in the Ionian colony of Asia Minor, at Miletus, an important trading center connected with Chaldea and Egypt. Miletus was one of the cities where new learning was the most eagerly received. Geography, astronomy and the other sciences were held in high repute. The Greeks who dwelt there took from the Egyptians and the Chaldaeans the results of their researches; but their originality consisted in drawing from those conclusions a solution to the general problems of the natural world.

Miletus was destroyed in 494 B. C., after the Persian conquest, and the seat of philosophy was then transferred to southern Italy and to Sicily, which was known as Greater Greece because of the Greek colonies that dotted its coast. It was not until the end of this period that the Greeks of the continent were initiated to the movement.

The inquiries of the first philosophers bore, not on the inner world of the mind, but on the *outer, visible world* [1]. They were lacking in experience and bothered little about a logical sequence of questions, but they had in mind nothing less than a comprehensive solution of the world's problems. Aristotle correctly names them *Physicists*.

What first struck them was the unceasing evolution of nature which, as if moved by some hidden power, is constantly renewing itself. Faced with the fact of the world's existence they set out to explain the changes at work in it. In other

---

[1] The usual occupations of these traders and hardy navigators would naturally lead them to seek for a solution of the puzzles of the exterior world. One may nonetheless see here an instance of the psychological law expressed by the axiom: " *Nihil est in intellectu quin prius fuerit in sensu* ".

words, what needs an explanation in their eyes is not Being or creation, but the perpetual *becoming* of things. Now this is one of the root problems of philosophy. An adequate solution supposes a system of metaphysics whereby the principle of identity perceived in a thing by the intellect may be reconciled with the fact of movement to which the senses bear witness. Such a system is not possible without an attentive examination, at once psychological and critical, of our faculties of understanding. It is thus in the light of the Aristotelian theory of potentiality and actuality that a coherent answer is to be formulated.

The efforts of the early thinkers reveal the gradual outlining of this basic principle of the Peripateticians. The two contradictory solutions they propose go far towards defining the question by stressing the two terms involved : on the one hand we have the *sensualist solution* put forward by the *Ionians*, who were impressed by the palpable evidence of movement; on the other, the *rationalist solution* as stated by the *Eleatics*, who laid stress on the absolute element of reality. The *Atomists* attempted a conciliatory theory, but without success. Finally the *Sophists*, disheartened by so many futile endeavors, gave up speculation in favor of action and took refuge in scepticism. Their teaching was, however, in reality another effort towards conciliation, not on the objective or physical plane, but in the subjective or psychological order.

We have, then, four phases in this first period :

I.   *Sensualist solution :* the Ionians (6th cent. and early 5th cent. B. C.)

II.   *Rationalist solution :* the Eleatics (same period.)

III. *Via media — physical :* the Atomists (late 5th cent. and 4th cent. B. C.)

IV.   *Via media — psychological :* the Sophists (same period.)

BIBLIOGRAPHY (for the first era).

ADAMSON, R., *The development of Greek philosophy*, London, 1908. — BAKEWELL, C. M., *Source book in ancient philosophy*, rev. ed., New York, 1939. — BENN, A. W., *History of ancient philosophy*, London, 1936. — BURNET, J. *Early Greek philosophy*, 5th ed., London, 1945. — CHERNISS, H., *Aristotle's criticism of presocratic philosophy*, Baltimore, Md., 1935. — CORNFORD, F. M., (ed.),

Greek religious thought from Homer to the age of Alexander, new ed., Boston, 1950. — FREEMAN, K., *Ancilla to the pre-socratic philosophers : A complete translation of the fragments in Diels' Fragmente der Vorsokratiker*, New York, 1948. *The pre-socratic philosophers*, New York, 1946. — GUTHRIE, W., *Greek philosophers from Thales to Aristotle*, New York, 1950. — LECLÈRE, A., *La philosophie grecque avant Socrate*, Paris, 1908. — LEE, H. D. P., *Zeno of Elea*, London, 1936. — RAVEN, J. E., *Pythagoreans and eleatics*, London, 1948. — SCOON, R. M., *Greek philosophy before Plato*, Princeton, 1928. — TANNERY, W., *Pour l'histoire de la science hellène*, Paris, 1887.

ARTICLE ONE.

SENSUALIST SOLUTION : THE IONIANS.

I. THE EARLY IONIANS.

6. The first sages, rising above the anthropomorphism of mythological theogonies, seek a principle of unity for the ever changing multiplicity of phenomena. Thus they are rightly given a place in the company of philosophers. The earliest were :

THALES OF MILETUS, (circ. 640-550); ANAXIMANDER, (611-546); ANAXIMENES, (588-524) : all three of the city of Miletus.

We know little of the lives of these early philosophers, or of their teachings. It is sure that Thales, before lecturing at Miletus, travelled in Egypt and the East. Diogenes Laertius commended his knowledge of astronomy; and he is known to have foretold the total eclipse of the sun which took place on May 28th, 585 B. C. [1]. He left no writings, but it was his disciple, Anaximander, who first elaborated a treatise *On Nature* (Περὶ φύσεως); only fragments of it remain. We have, however, abstracts of their discoveries, principally in the domain of science, astronomy or meteorology. They had not yet freed themselves entirely from poetical superstitions and had no scruples about introducing a soul or a god when other explanations failed them. From what Aristotle tells us of their views on things distinctively philosophical we may draw the following conclusions :

Excessively influenced as they were by sense perception, and conscious of the universal transformation of things into other things (bread into flesh, wood into fire, etc.) they groped among

---

[1] RIVAUD, *Les grands courants de la pensée antique*, p. 22.

these sensible elements for the principle of unity, which, they imagined, was the source of all reality [1].

THALES selects *water*, which readily adapts itself to any form, is necessary for the existence of all beings, and is found in all nourishment and in all germs.

ANAXIMANDER finds something prior to water: it is the " *Indeterminate* " or " *Infinite* " (ἄπειρον), which is a compound of all contrary elements. All things originate from it and return to it [2].

ANAXIMENES chooses *air*. It is just as necessary as, and more rarefied than, water; and it can take any form by condensation or by expansion.

Finally we learn from Aristotle that they upheld *hylozoism*, maintaining that there is life in matter. " According to them ", he says, " there are gods in everything " [3].

Remark. **7.** These philosophers are justly called *sensualists* because they rarely see beyond the objects of sense perception. It is not that they deny the existence of the intelligence; they are ignorant of it. They are not yet aware that there is an intelligible object distinct from that of the senses. Their knowledge is in a rudimentary and vague state. We may say that they are more important as pioneers in the world of natural science than as philosophers.

II. HERACLITUS OF EPHESUS. (Between 540 and 475).

8. Heraclitus was a descendant of Androcles, the founder of Ephesus. His love of philosophy caused him to refuse the position of Basileus. " His was a haughty and solitary genius ", says Maritain. " He had no use for the crowd or for the popular religion. By him the ideas of the Ionian philosophers were nobly carried to their first metaphysical principles, and thus was fixed once and for all one of the landmarks of specu-

---

[1] In Thomist language, they tried to explain everything with reference to a *material cause*, a permanent element underlying all change; with this they mingled the notion of an *efficient cause* in the form of some vital force which governs the evolution of things. In reality they were laboring with a very vague idea of the *causa explicativa*.

[2] There is nothing very clear in this *Infinite*. Others see in it a kind of vast container from which worlds emerge only to sink back into it (RIVAUD, *op. cit.*, p. 24).

[3] *De Anima*, Book I, Ch. III.

lative thought and of error " [1]. He founded the philosophy of the *durational*. Important too was his effort to establish a fundamental principle and to draw from it its main conclusions and applications.

1. *The fundamental principle.*

What exists is not Being but Becoming; change is the only reality.

Proof : What Heraclitus does is to assert his principle with much vigor, as a manifest result of sense perception. " All things pass ", he says; " everything flows on and nothing remains " (πάντα ρεῖ καὶ οὐδὲν μένει). The universe is like a river, and no man bathes twice in the same river. In a word, *that which is*, is what it is in virtue of its ceaseless change.

Underneath these unconditional assertions lies the well-known dilemma : admit Being and you make change impossible; for whatever becomes cannot come from Not-Being — " ex nihilo nihil fit " — nor from Being — " ex ente non fit ens quia jam est ens ". But since either Being or change must be admitted, Heraclitus, consistent with Ionian thought, accepts the evidence of the *senses* and rejects Being in favor of change. However he never formulates explicitly this a priori deduction and it will not be given full prominence until it is used against him by Parmenides.

2. *Conclusions and applications.*

9. *a)* **Monism.** If change is the only reality, then all things though differing in appearance are radically identical : *monism* is necessarily inferred. Heraclitus gives a part in his theory to the imagination by selecting *Fire* as the sole material of this universal Becoming, since fire is at once the most elusive and the most active of elements, and is perpetually in movement.

b) **Evolutionism.** Heraclitus sets out to explain everything with reference to this ever-evolving fire. " In his wonderfully vigorous and concise prose ", says Croiset, " the pithy sentences of which draw a certain majesty from their very obscurity, he tells how fire is changed into air, air into water and water into earth, and how by a simultaneous and inverse process

---

[1] J. MARITAIN, *An introduction to philosophy*, p. 50.

earth is transformed into water, water into air and air into
fire ". The worlds themselves follow individual realities in
obedience to this law of alternation and are now grouped in
unity, now distributed in parts and again, by the same evolution,
brought into one whole [1]. " Unceasing oscillation ", concludes
Croiset, " an unlimited succession of deaths resulting in as many
births, of related movements *upward* and *downward;* all this
according to a rhythm, an inner Logos, formed of equivalences
and compensations " [2].

c) **Pantheism.** The presence of this Logos (or rational
principle) in the process of Becoming leads to the conception
of the original fire as of something *living* and *godlike.* In the
world it is the supreme but impersonal and indwelling principle;
the ever-flowing fountain of life. And everything that we see
is a particle of this fire, everything is divine. The human soul,
itself a spark from the all animating flame, has but an impersonal
immortality; it emerges from the vast whole and will be absorbed
into it again. Heraclitus is thus the founder of *pantheism.*

d) **Anti-intellectualism.** Rigorous adherence to his evolutionist principle leads Heraclitus to assert that *whatever is,
in so far as it is, is not,* since it is subject to change. In other
words he denies the law of identity, and with it all understanding. He claims that the Logos, origin of all things, is
contradiction itself, the identification of contraries, represented
by the concept of war or of discord : ὁ πόλεμος πατήρ πάντων.
" We go down, and we do not go down, into the same river;
we are, and we are not; sea water is at once the purest and the
most tainted; good and evil are one and the same thing ".
The idea of anything substantial is abandoned, and hazard
is the only law of evolution : " like to a boy amusing himself
at an aimless game of backgammon ".

3. *What the system is worth.*

10. The Greek genius was too sober to be misled by so
paradoxical a system. An early refutation of it is found in the
fourth book of the Metaphysics.

A) Aristotle first shows the absurdity of its conclusions :
1. No one can possibly conceive the same thing as existing

---

[1] We shall come across this notion again in connection with the Stoics.
See n. 99.

[2] A. CROISET, *Histoire de la littérature grecque,* 5 vols., Paris, 1914-29,
Vol. I, p. 47.

and not existing. Heraclitus, according to some, thinks otherwise. But a man does not necessarily think everything he says. 2. Such a conception is equivalent to doing away with all language and then affirming the possibility of speech. 3. It implies that all words are synonyms and all things identical : a galley, a wall and a man would not be distinguishable. 4. It leads one to deny the existence of anything substantial and to assert that all things are accidents. But change without a permanent substratum would cease to be a *change* and would be merely an endless succession of destructions and creations [1]. (ch. 3 and 4.)

B) Chiefly important is Aristotle's denunciation of the root error of the whole system. " The reason why these philosophers went astray ", he says, " is that they admitted as real only objects of sense perception. And as they saw these objects in ceaseless evolution, some of them, such as Cratylus [2], considered all speech superfluous and merely wagged their fingers ". (ch. 5.) Philosophy, on the contrary, should interpret the facts of experience and of conscious perception by the intelligence, recognized as the sovereign faculty in the domain of being and reality.

However, in order to correct Heraclitus without falling into the opposite error, we must know exactly what is the rôle ascribed to *our intelligence*. Parmenides will turn our considerations to this point.

---

[1] BERGSON's philosophy of the *purely durational* revives the principle put forward by Heraclitus. But there is an attempt to evade these conclusive refutations by the introduction of another cognitive faculty : *intuition*. Cf. Inf. nn. 538-540.

[2] CRATYLUS was Plato's first teacher. Cf. inf. n. 39.

ARTICLE TWO.

RATIONALIST SOLUTION : THE ELEATICS.

I. FORERUNNERS.

11. Between the Ionians with their sensualist view and the Eleatics with their metaphysical solution, we may conveniently consider :

PYTHAGORAS OF SAMOS (Between 580-500).

His life is wrapped up in legend. It is certain that he travelled extensively and made a fruitful contact with Egyptian learning. Returning to Samos, his native land, he found the island under the despotic rule of Polycrates and migrated to Croton, a Dorian colony in southern Italy. Here he founded a brotherhood of which the aims were at once religious, philosophical and political. Such communities became more and more numerous until the day when the colonists, weary of their domination, trampled them out. It was then, probably, that Pythagoras met with his death at Metapontium.

He left no writings. We know his teachings through his disciples, in whom his influence lived on until the 2nd century of the Christian era. He was the first to assume the name of *philosopher*, or *lover of wisdom*. God alone, he thought, could be properly called wise [1]. He was also the first to apply the term χόσμος to the world, as expressing the harmony and beauty of things. From the sages of Egypt or of India he held his theory of transmigration *(metempsychosis)* according to which the soul, admittedly immortal, can leave one body and enter another, whether of man or beast. But the most important of Pythagorean doctrines are those concerned with music, geometry and arithmetic [2] containing as they do in a definite form the basic laws of these sciences : the elementary relations and divisions of numbers. Pythagoras showed in particular the dependence of musical intervals on certain arithmetical ratios of length of string at a given tension [3].

His philosophy is closely connected with this mathematical learning. Two things impressed Pythagoras : the regulation of

---

[1] Cf. CICERO, *Tusculan Disp.*, Vol. VIII.

[2] The Pythagorean astronomy also contains much that is sound. Philolaus (5th cent.) described the earth and the other planets as revolving round a central fire.

[3] To Pythagoras also is attributed the theorem of the square on the hypotenuse.

movement, and the harmonious proportions of things. He teaches that in the numbers expressing these proportions consists the whole of reality, the principle of all existing things. Their unvarying nature shows that they are prior to things that change. They are, as it were, the ideal types of all beings. Pythagoras claims even, according to Aristotle, that these numbers constitute the very essence of things and, in some way, their substance [1]. Thus the principles of numbers are the principles of all existing things. To each essence corresponds a number (number 4, for instance, is not merely a symbol; it is to be identified with justice, number 3 with holiness, 7 with time, 10 with perfection... [2]) and all inquiry into the origin and nature of reality merges into a speculation on the origin and properties of numbers [3].

Value and influence. 12. Pythagoras glimpses a reality of a higher order than sensible phenomena. He sees beyond the sensualist horizon of the Ionians, and reaches the second degree of abstraction, but he fails to perceive the true object of the intelligence : Being, as including both the spiritual and the corporeal worlds [4]. His mistake lies in applying to all things indiscriminately the enlightening but narrow principles of mathematics. Much in the same way Descartes will confuse bodily substance with quantity.

The Pythagorean method, it must be added, can hardly be called philosophical. In the place of rational inquiry it introduced the rule of the *Magister dixit* (αὐτὸς ἔφη) which was consecrated by an initiation and ritual practices [5]. In spite of its lasting influence the Pythagorean school is of little importance in the history of philosophy; it counts for much more in the realm of mathematics.

---

[1] METAPHYS., Book I, Ch. III.

[2] This explains why the Pythagorean astronomers, having discovered only nine planets, perfected their conception of the universe by imagining the " counter-earth ".

[3] J. MARITAIN, *op. cit.*, p. 57.

[4] Pythagoras, however, apparently accepts God, the sovereign unity and source of all things. He sees Him as a kind of universal soul, fountain of all harmony, just as our soul is the principle of harmony, the constitutive number of our human being. Thus he foreshadows confusedly the discoveries of Anaxagoras and Plato.

[5] It was not long before the Pythagorean initiations were absorbed into the Orphic mysteries which became known in Greece towards the 5th century. Their influence is perceptible in neo-Platonism. The study of these tendencies belongs to the history of religions and of pagan " mysticism ".

13. With Pythagoras comes another Asiatic Greek, his contemporary, XENOPHANES (570-478). He was born at Colophon and according to tradition founded the Eleatic school. All the cities of Sicily and southern Italy heard this rhapsodist reciting his poems on different themes, historical, satirical and philosophical. He boldly ridiculed the popular mythology and opposed it with his pantheistic conception of God and the Cosmos forming an absolute unity : the ONE and the ALL : Ἕν καὶ πᾶν.

Two philosophers, however, are mainly representative of this school : Parmenides as its metaphysician and Zeno as its apologist.

II.   PARMENIDES OF ELEA (Between 530-444).

14. Parmenides knew Xenophanes at his native town of Elea. His system is set forth in the poem : Περὶ φυσέως, which embodies in its first part, Τὰ πρὸς ἀλήθειαν, a rudimentary treatise on metaphysics. He proceeds, like Heraclitus but in a contrary direction, from a root principle to the unfolding of its consequences.

A) **Fundamental principle.** *Only what is, is real.* " We must admit either Being or Not-Being. The whole question to be decided lies in the terms : existence or non-existence. But the non-existent is not, nor can it come to be. Then, only what is, is ".

Thus Parmenides' starting point is a forceful statement of the real object of man's intelligence and of its objective value. It implies a clear view of the first principle governing all our scientific processes : the principle of identity and of contradiction. The proof given — the only possible one — is the direct and necessary evidence of a rational assertion independent of sense perception : " What is, is; what is not, is not. This truth is undeniable ". Plato appreciated the soundness of this basis; he used to speak of the " great Parmenides " [1].

B) **Conclusions.** Full of the notion of Being, as Heraclitus was of that of Becoming, Parmenides kept strictly to the a priori method, disregarding the value of sense-data, and deduced

---

[1] PLATO, *Sophistes*, 237, a.

a series of conclusions containing the outline of a treatise on the transcendentals :

1. **The Absolute.** Being, or reality, is eternal, unchangeable, uncreated and imperishable. For if it were produced it would come either from Ens or from Non-Ens. But nothing can come from Non-Ens : " Ex nihilo nihil fit " ; nor can it come from that which is already : " Ex ente non fit ens, quia jam est ens ". Hence no Becoming or mutation is possible ; what is, is absolutely and eternally. " Fate prevents Being from acquiring or losing existence, and keeps it free from change ".

2. **Unity.** Being, or reality, is one, and is of itself indivisible and homogeneous. Apart from Being there is only the non-existent (which is not real). There is, then, no cause which could bring plurality or diversity of parts into what exists. " What is, is " one and equal in all its parts.

3. **Truth.** Being, or reality, is one with truth and thought. " Thought ", says Parmenides, " is the same as Being ; thought is identified with its object " [1]. It could not be otherwise since nothing is real except Being. Thought and truth are real and must therefore be identified with what is.

4. **Goodness.** Being is, finally, perfect or complete. It alone possesses all reality, free from change and destruction. It alone has every quality and perfection beyond which there is nothing.

Yet, strongly impressed as he was by the intelligence and its specific object, Parmenides was still held by his imagination. His one, eternal reality was a material being whose perfection took the form of a smooth sphere, complete and continuous. Such was his notion of the universe or κόσμος.

In brief, this is the true conclusion reached by the intelligence : the universe, made of matter and evenly extended, is the only reality, eternal and immutable ; the ONE and the ALL, without generation, destruction, change or plurality.

C) The *facts of experience*, in glaring opposition with this theory, are considered in the second part of the work : Τὰ πρὸς δόξαν. Sense perception is declared to be illusory, scientifically speaking, though not without practical significance since in our daily existence we are satisfied with appearances.

---

[1] Cf. FOUILLÉE, *Extraits des grands philosophes*, p. 34.

15. The two essential problems of philosophy are now before us : the metaphysical problem of the compatibility of being and coming-to-be; and the psychological problem of the value of our twofold cognition. The two solutions are inter-dependent and it was neglect of the latter that led the early philosophers into error concerning the former.

The ultimate metaphysical confusion was the same for both Heraclitus and Parmenides : pantheistic monism. Heraclitus over-estimated the value of sensible experience and rejected that of the intelligence; Parmenides stood for a strict and unqualified realism and disregarded the function of the senses in mental processes. During the two subsequent centuries, philosophers sought truth in the conciliation of these two errors. They found it when, under the influence of Socrates, they turned from the physical (objective), to the psychological standpoint. An adequate solution is found in the two great Aristotelian theories : actuality and potentiality, and the analogical value of the abstract notion of being.

Thus all the difficulties raised by Parmenides could easily be solved by dividing Being into two kinds, two realities, two essentially different realizations (rationes simpliciter diversæ secundum quid eædem) of the same analogical idea of Being :

1. Being realized in a supreme and infinite degree, i. e. the essentially existent, the purely actual — *ipsum esse subsistens* — to which are applicable all Parmenides' metaphysical inferences, provided all material elements be excluded.

2. Being realized in varyingly limited degrees, in things affected more or less with potentiality, the objects of sense experience. In regard to beings of this kind, the Eleatic arguments have no validity.

III. ZENO OF ELEA [1] (circ. 490).

16. The lofty theories of Parmenides, opposed as they were to common sense, raised many objections. But they were zealously defended by the subtle-minded Zeno. To prove the impossibility of movement Zeno attempted to convict his

---

[1] For Zeno's paradoxes see BROCHARD, *Etudes de phil. ancienne.* pp. 3-23. — F. CAJOU, *Hist. of Zeno's arguments against motion*, (1915). — SERTILLANGES, *Saint Thomas*, I, pp. 94-102. — NYS, *Cosmologie*, 2nd ed., Paris-Louvain, 1906, pp. 243-247.

opponents of absurdity by placing them in the following dilemma :

The continuous (space and time) is either divisible to infinity, or it is made up of indivisible parts.

In both hypotheses movement is impossible.

1. If the continuous is taken as divisible to infinity, then we are faced with the following arguments :

a) Dichotomy. Before a moving body can reach a given point it must attain the middle of its course; and before it can reach the middle it must come to the middle of the first half, and so on *ad infinitum,* since the course is by hypothesis infinitely divisible. Consequently the goal is unattainable and movement is impossible.

b) The Achilles. The quickest pursuer can never catch up with the slowest quarry. For the former must first reach the latter's starting point, that is, it must cover an infinite number of divided parts, and the fugitive will always be ahead. The fleet-footed Achilles may run *ad infinitum* without overtaking the tortoise. In other words, he cannot move.

Summary. To cover a distance it is necessary to traverse each intermediary stage.

But if the distance is divisible *ad infinitum,* the number of intermediary stages is unlimited.

In this hypothesis, then, distance cannot be covered.

2. If, on the contrary, it is asserted that the continuous is made up of non-divisible parts, time is then a succession of indivisible instants and space a succession of indivisible points. And since movement cannot occur in any of these instants or points, it is still inadmissible. Zeno proves it by two more paradoxes :

a) The arrow. At any given instant of the time which measures its so-called movement, the arrow is either moving or still.

Now it cannot be in motion since it cannot change its position in an instant indivisible by hypothesis. At least two divisions would be required : one for the start and another for the arrival, because the arrow cannot leave one point and reach another in the same instant without remaining motionless.

Therefore at each instant the arrow is at rest.

b) The Stadium is a more complex form of the same argument :

Fig. I

A B

A C D —>

<— E F G

Fig. II

A B

A C D

E F G

Suppose in *Fig. I* three lines of indivisible points, the first being motionless A B and the other two moving in opposite directions. After the first indivisible instant of time the points will occupy the position shown in *Fig. II.* Then one of two things must be admitted : either D and E did not cross, and there was no movement; or else they crossed, and since they must have met in the middle of the instant A B, we must admit a *divisible* instant. But this is against the hypothesis.

Summary. In each indivisible point of time or space, the body is at rest (since all motion would require a distinction of parts, one point being lost and another gained).

But movement cannot result from rest.

Therefore through indivisible time or space there can be no movement.

CONCLUSION. **17.** Zeno's paradoxes became famous and helped to turn philosophical thought to the problems of continuity, and space and time. The true solution is again found in the theory of *actus* and *potentia*. The continuous — space or time — must be conceived as mathematically divisible to infinity and cannot be composed of indivisible parts. But Zeno took for granted not merely divisibility but real division, so that a moving body had an **actually** infinite number of points to traverse, which is clearly impossible. In fact, the continuous has no actual, but merely potential, parts; so also time and space. To an actually finite space correspond motion and time of the same order; to a potentially infinite space correspond motion and time also potentially infinite. The difficulty is eliminated.

Thus Aristotle's leading principle harmonizes the contradictory theses of Heraclitus and Parmenides, and disposes of all objections. But this final solution was preceded by several fruitless attempts at conciliation.

ARTICLE THREE.

VIA MEDIA—PHYSICAL : THE ATOMISTS.

18.   The Atomists (first half of the 5th century) were the first to attempt a common sense solution of the problem of change, with an eye to all the data and an effort to harmonize the facts of experience with intellectual knowledge.

1.   LEUCIPPUS founded a school about the year 500 B. C. at Abdera, on the coastal frontier of Thracia and Macedonia. There he elaborated the Atomic system.

2.   DEMOCRITUS (circ. 460-400) was his best known disciple. Like Thales and Pythagoras he travelled extensively, visiting Egypt and Asia.   In numerous writings he developed the theories of Leucippus and his work absorbed that of the founder.

3.   EMPEDOCLES of Agrigentum (Sicily), philosopher, physician and magician, taught at Athens towards the year 445 [1].

4.   ANAXAGORAS of Clazomenæ, near Smyrna, (between 500 and 428) also came to teach at Athens under the patronage of his friend Pericles (494-429).   Condemned for dangerous innovations, he was exiled and died at Lampsacus.

The two last named were contemporaries but the extent of their mutual influence cannot be clearly determined.   Anaxagoras was the more advanced thinker.

We shall deal with the basis of the system, with the individual contribution of each philosopher and with a special theory due to Anaxagoras.

1.   *The basis of the system.*

19.   This group accepted the notion of a reality in some way unchanging and undivided (atomism), and the Ionian assertion of movement in space (mechanism).   Their somewhat superficial

---

[1] The manner of his death is unknown.   He has been accused, unjustly it seems of flinging himself into the crater of Etna in order to prove himself a god.

theories were built up on an effort to explain the universe in the light of this **basic principle.** Two essential propositions summarize their doctrine.

A) **Movement is real,** as is shown by experience. Hence, a threefold conclusion :

1. The one perfect being conceived by Parmenides is divided into a plurality of beings (atoms) which — no doubt because of Zeno's infinite divisibility — are infinitely small and infinitely numerous. This is necessary to explain the variations of movement.

2. Each atom is surrounded by vacuum, a kind of real non-being existing on the same plane as being. This again is postulated as the theater of movement.

3. The atoms are set in motion by a power which, for the early Atomists, seems to have been mere chance or fatality, or else the energy of movement itself.

B) **But that which is real pertains to being,** consequently the atoms have the properties of Being in the Eleatic sense:

1. They are eternal, complete and perfect, each in its own order.

2. They are physically indivisible and homogeneous (whence the name " atom ").

3. They even have a certain immutability in the sense that in their various combinations they keep the same nature. Moreover the early Atomists held that this nature was the same for every atom.

Such is the Atomist explanation of the universe : a mass of atoms falling incessantly through vacuum, clinging to one another, (they are of divers shapes and possess hook-like members) uniting in numerous combinations and thus forming all physical bodies and all changes in the universe and in history. Souls and even gods are nothing but atomic groups, more consistent no doubt, but always perishable according to the laws of necessity.

2. *Complementary theories.*

20. Leucippus was satisfied with these essential propositions. A few other noteworthy theories are due to his disciples:

1.   DEMOCRITUS [1] sought an **atomic explanation of knowledge:**

He sets out with an excellent principle: " Knowledge supposes similarity or identity between the subject and the object of knowledge ". This is true in the spiritual order of things to which knowledge properly belongs. But Democritus knew nothing of that order [2] and understood his principle in a physical sense. He imagined that every object radiates atoms similar to those of which it is itself composed, but of a more tenuous nature. These images or " **idols** " ($\varepsilon\iota\delta\omega\lambda\alpha$) implant themselves in the cognitive faculty and make it one with its object. This was, in a crude and materialistic outline, the theory of the " species impressæ ".

2.   EMPEDOCLES modified the theory of **homogeneous matter.** He saw different objects and inferred a minimum of diversity in the composition of matter. He distinguished four elements : water, earth, air and fire. These were no longer however, as for the Ionians, passing states of a single substance, but four eternally separate substances.

He shed light also on the **driving force** of movement by distinguishing attraction (**love**) from repulsion (**hate**). With a poet's vision he imagined the four kinds of atoms ceaselessly revolving and combining under the impulse of Hate or of Love to form an endless cycle of aggregations and disintegrations.

3.   ANAXAGORAS makes another adjustment to the theory of homogeneous matter by his conception of the " **simple substances** " or $\dot{o}\mu o\iota\omega\mu\dot{\varepsilon}\rho\alpha\iota$ [3]. The difference of perfection in things is consistent with their transformations on the supposition that matter is atomic dust composed of all the substances that form different bodies. Thus everything has particles of everything else and objects can become other objects without substantial change. In this notion is vaguely foreshadowed Aristotle's conception of " prime matter ".

There remains to expose the theory for which Anaxagoras is chiefly famous; but as it belongs to a different order, it will be preferable to give first an appreciation of Atomism.

---

[1] See BROCHARD, *Etudes de phil. anc. et mod.*, Ch. III.

[2] In scholastic terms, the " *ordo intentionalis* " because it implies that the subject, admittedly a physical reality, is *carried out of itself* to be identified (as *cognoscens*) with the *cognoscibile*.

[3] From $\dot{o}\mu o\iota o\varsigma$, like, and $\mu\dot{\varepsilon}\rho o\varsigma$, part.

3. *Atomism deficient as a philosophy.*

21. The great weakness of the Atomists as philosophers was their shallowness. The solution they offered was short-sighted and totally incomplete. They sought to harmonize the idea of stability and unity with that of movement and plurality by simply rejecting two of Parmenides' conclusions : the oneness and the immutability of being. **Experience** no doubt justified their attitude, but the true philosopher must solve the difficulties put to him.

Above all it is to be noted that their appeal to experience was very superficial and passed over many facts essential to the explanation of the world. They admitted motion in space only, and maintained the Eleatic notion of quality and substance as unchangeable.

Consequently:

a) They could not explain the immaterial movement of thought. They had materialistic tendencies, acknowledged no spiritual soul, and barred themselves from all knowledge of God.

b) Even in the world of matter they rendered inexplicable many changes which suppose either qualities really distinct from quantity, or, in the case of deeper changes, real substances specifically distinct.

c) Finally, by rejecting the final cause in favor of the merely mechanical antecedent, or efficient cause [1], they left unexplained the ordered universe and those natural activities which, working for the general good, prove the existence of an internal finality.

In brief, the Atomists never penetrated beneath the surface. They realized that changes could not be explained without an element of stability, but, failing even to conceive an underlying principle of the intelligible and metaphysical order, (such as *prime matter* and *substantial form* in Aristotle) they adopted an imaginary element, a secondary matter, (quantity and

---

[1] One recognizes the modern mechanist theory, regarding as *efficient cause* the antecedent necessarily implied in any consequent movement by the determinism of things. Descartes developed this notion put forth by the Atomists of old.

shape) which reason could never accept as an explanation of the universe.

These criticisms apply to atomism considered only as a **philosophy** claiming to give the ultimate reason of things. The **scientific** value of the system remains unaffected. As an hypothesis it has been of good use to mathematicians in modern times. Chemists find in it a practical and fruitful system of notation. Moreover the existence of atoms has been conclusively proved [1]. For this reason some of the moderns have looked back with favor on the theories of the ancient Atomists. But although the latter may appear to lead the way in the field of scientific research, their philosophy is none the less deficient and false [2].

4. *Anaxagoras and the* Nous.

22. Anaxagoras has gained a place of honor among the first philosophers by a new contribution to speculative thought. So far Fate, as the immanent power regulating all movement, had been considered as governing the world in formation.

Anaxagoras, on the contrary, struck by the orderly organization of the universe, attributed it to an absolutely distinct and superior power which he calls " Nous " i. e. Mind or Reason. Order, he concluded, postulates a supreme intelligence. This principle suggests to him the chief properties of the *Nous*.

1. *Spirituality.* Reason is the purest and most subtle of things. It cannot be composed of *homoeomerai* like other realities for that would make it imperfect like them and unsuited to rule all things. Therefore " Reason is infinite, independent (αὐτοκράτης) and free from mixture. It exists by itself and of itself ". Its essence is simple and separate : in a word, it is truly immaterial or spiritual.

2. *Knowledge.* Reason cannot regulate things without knowing them. " It has a complete knowledge of the whole world; nothing escapes it ".

3. *Providence.* The particular function of the *Nous* is to produce order. It disentangles the primitive chaos, builds the

---

[1] For discussion on this point, see J. PERRIN, *Atoms*, 2nd eng. ed. rev., London, 1923.

[2] While rejecting these errors the Thomist willingly accepts the stimulating developments of modern thought. His doctrine is in full agreement with them provided they do not assume undue importance. See NYS, *Cosmologie.*— MARITAIN, *Les Degrés du Savoir*.

cosmos and keeps it in order. Its power is therefore unlimited. " The Mind moves and ordains all things : what was to be, what has been, what is, and what will be " [1].

Aristotle warmly admired this doctrine. " When there came a man ", he says, " proclaiming that the order and regularity everywhere evident in the world is caused both in nature and in living things by an intelligence, that man alone appeared sane in spite of the absurdities of his predecessors : *velut sobrius inter ebrios* " [2].

No doubt Anaxagoras left many imperfections in his teaching. He had no clear idea of a personal Mind with freedom of action. When defining the organizing power of the *Nous*, he seemed to conceive it as being in contact with matter, like a soul or an inherent energy. He was yet too subject to the imagination to reach the notion of a purely causal influence without contact in space. For this reason, perhaps, he restricted notably the Mind's field of action. Aristotle reproached him with making of his *Nous* a " deus ex machina " to be called upon when material explanations were lacking.

But Anaxagoras is chiefly deserving for having first approached the problem of the intelligence from a scientific angle, thus laying the foundation of a rational system of theodicy and of psychology, and paving the way for Socrates [3].

ARTICLE FOUR.

VIA MEDIA—PSYCHOLOGICAL :
THE SOPHISTS. [4]

23. Sophistry links up the early Phycisists with the master minds of the golden age, and forms an historical background for Socrates and his work. To gain a clear idea of its nature we shall study : 1) the genesis of Sophistry; 2) the characteristics

---

[1] ARISTOTLE, *De Anima*, Book I, Ch. III; FOUILLÉE, *Extraits des grands phil.*, p. 23.

[2] *Metaphys.*, II, 13. It was no less than a revolution. Until then human life and thought had been considered physical phenomena. Anaxagoras on the contrary referred the whole of nature and its elements to reason as to their original source.

[3] Socrates was forty when Anaxagoras died, and may have seen and heard him at Athens. He was certainly acquainted with the Atomist's doctrine.

[4] See PIAT, *Socrate*, Ch. I. — BROCHARD, *op. cit.*, Ch. III : Protagoras et Democrite. — G. GROTE, *History of Greece*, Ch. LXVII.

of the school; 3) the known teachings of the most prominent Sophists.

I.   *Genesis of Sophistry.*

Towards the end of the fifth century, under Pericles (494-429) Athens, politically the most powerful of the Greek republics, became the centre of the intellectual life of the country.   To Athens flocked all those thinkers who had ambition.   This simultaneous contact of all the different schools of thought to which the past century had given birth revealed in a striking way their deficiencies and their contradictions.

1.   **Their deficiencies.**   None had as yet probed deeply into the study of man and of human understanding.   This fundamental defect vitiated inevitably the solutions presumptuously put forward by these philosophers in answer to the vast problem of the universe.

2.   **Their contradictions.**   Even within the limits of the material world each one saw only one aspect of the question. Since the principles were too narrow to apply to the whole of reality, the solutions, when compared, were bound to clash. And in fact, the concourse of all the hypotheses resulted in a deplorable and fruitless casuistry.   Then, amid the most pretentious and most depressing of philosophical babels, appeared the *Sophists.*

2.   *Characteristics of the Sophists.*

The name was first given to men remarkable for their superior knowledge.   In the 5th century it designated those who taught by profession and for payment : travelling teachers, lecturers, encyclopedists or dilettanti.   They claimed universal knowledge. The Athenian youth who sought distinction in public life, or who merely wished to extend his learning, could be instructed by them in ethics, law, economics, politics, rhetoric and philosophy.   The work brought them honour and filled their purses.   They were, in reality, everything except true philosophers.   As Maritain says : " They loved science for the profits it brought, but they were indifferent to truth [1] ".

1.   **They were indifferent to truth.**   Noting the contradictions of their predecessors they despaired of finding truth.   All their intellectual talent is spent in negative and destructive criticism, " because, for men as for children, destruction is the easiest way of showing strength " [1].

---

[1] J. MARITAIN, *op. cit.*, p. 66.

a) They were at one with the poets and the comedians (like Aristophanes) in discrediting religion and the old morality which was firmly rooted in the acceptance of a universal law, of an absolute will powerful enough to impose it with sanctions, and of a life to come. Their arguments led to a naturalist view of religion, destroyed belief in the gods and in their providential action, and showed every obligation imposed on humanity as an arbitrary convention. Virtue for them was nothing more than the art of succeeding in life.

b) The special object of their attacks was the work of earlier philosophers from whose principles they strove to draw the most contradictory conclusions. They themselves, while not explicitly admitting scepticism, devised a relativist system which clearly showed their contempt for philosophical inquiry. They had, in fact, a more fruitful aim.

2. **They looked on science as a source of gain,** for themselves and for their pupils. This explains their method and their object.

a) *For themselves* success is the thing that counts. Their method was to attract as many as possible to their lectures by their claim to omniscience. They gave apparently lucid answers to all kinds of questions, particularly to the doubtful and complex problems of human life because these brought in the richest gains. To guarantee for themselves a constantly interested audience these quack-professors travelled from place to place offering in a few lessons a compendium of all that a scholar should know. Naturally enough this instruction had no scientific value.

b) Besides, nothing in their *aim* justified a prolonged and patient search for truth. Knowledge was merely a means to power, to intellectual mastery or mental enjoyment. Their pupils learned the secret of " civic excellence " in the study of law and of history, and chiefly in that of oratory and of other practical formulæ. The Sophists were experts in the art of succeeding.

To sum up, " Of all that had inspired the high doctrinal ambitions of the previous era, the Sophists had retained intellectual arrogance but no love of truth. Neglecting reality they sought more than ever to attain greatness by their learning... They believed in knowledge but not in truth " [1]. Hence the discredit that attaches to their name.

3. *Two prominent Sophists.*

24. Plato has left sketches of several Sophists. The two leading names are Protagoras and Gorgias from whom we may borrow typical examples of *Sophisms*.

---

[1] *Ibid.*, p. 67.

A) PROTAGORAS OF ABDERA (between 480 and 410) protégé of Pericles.

To make apparent variation agree with unchanging reality, Protagoras appeals to the conscious subject. " Man ", he says, " is the measure of all things; of what is, that it is; of what is not, that it is not ". In other words, truth is immutable only in relation to man; for if change is universal objectively, human nature alone can provide the basis of a knowledge that remains.

Socrates will find in this theory the way to a sound solution by studying the nature of our abstract ideas, of their objective value and of their connection with concrete realities whence they are obtained by induction. Protagoras considers all this superficially and concludes merely that " truth is what appears to each one ", so that the same object may be white for one and black for another. He says also : " About any one thing two contradictory statements may be made ". And again : " Concerning the gods, I cannot say that they are, or that they are not. There is much to prevent me from knowing it, above all the obscurity of the question and the shortness of human life ".

B) GORGIAS OF LEONTINI (Sicily), ambassador and orator of fame. He came to Athens in 427 and died a centenarian at Lerissa (Thessalia) in 375.

He is known for his *threefold assertion* and for the sophisms which support it :

1. " **What is, is not** ", or " **nothing is real** ".

Proof.   Non-being *is* certainly non-being.

But whatever *is*, is real, and exists.

Therefore non-being is real, and exists.

And since non-being is opposed to being, if the former is, then the latter is not.

2. " **If anything is, it cannot be known** ".

Proof.   Our thought is naturally opposed to reality since *a*) thought is fixed while things are in flux, and *b*) thought can conceive things impossible to realize, such as a chariot travelling on the sea.

Therefore thought cannot give knowledge or represent things with any sureness.

N° 645. — 2

3. If anything is known, it cannot be expressed in speech.

Proof. Words, the instruments of expression are also opposed to thought. Words are fugitive and are perceptible to the ear, whereas an object of thought may be something stable, free from sound : e. g., number, silence, etc.

CONCLUSION. **25.** By his sophistic reasoning Gorgias, even more than Protagoras, led men to reflect on the value of abstract thought with reference to objective reality. The Sophists had thus at least one merit : that of putting before the minds of their contemporaries man and the things that concern man.

It is true that this merit was almost accidental. It was the reaction they occasioned that was beneficial to philosophy. As far as can be judged by the fragments that remain, it seems clear that their teaching was destined to kill whatever speculative knowledge existed at the time, without offering a substitute [1]. Under their influence Greek thought was fated to become the victim of scepticism, subtlety and paradox, unless there could be found a philosopher able to define both the true object of thought and the method of conceiving it. For the salvation of pagan learning Providence sent SOCRATES.

---

[1] Valuable no doubt were their contributions to grammar, rhetoric and general learning. But this does not justify their rehabilitation by some modern thinkers, such as GOMPERTZ. See his *Greek thinkers*, Vol. II.

SECOND PERIOD.

Golden Age of Philosophical Hellenism.

26. This period is sometimes called the " Socratic Period " or " Socratic Restoration ", because historically it was dominated by Socrates and his work. Its doctrinal tendencies have earned for it the name of **" anthropological "** period : during this age an incentive was given to those branches of knowledge that concern man : ethics and sociology, psychology, dialectic and logic. Above all it was the **golden age** in which three great minds, working in chronological sequence, influenced each other as masters and disciples in the task of guiding reason towards truth and of constructing the first substantial synthesis of human learning in the form of a true philosophy. In its most perfect form this philosophy is known as **Peripateticism.**

The period is covered in three chapters dealing respectively with Socrates, Plato and Aristotle.

CHAPTER ONE.

SOCRATES (470-399).

SPECIAL BIBLIOGRAPHY.

1⁰ **Texts :** XENOPHON, *Memorabilia Socratis dicta*, translated by E. C. Marchant, New York, 1923. — TAYLOR, A. E., *Varia Socratica*, Oxford, 1911.

2⁰ **Studies :** CORNFORD, F. M., *Before and after Socrates*, New York, 1932. — CRESSON, A., *Socrate, sa vie, son œuvre*, Paris, 1947. — DIÈS, A., *Socrate*, (dans *Autour de Platon*), Paris, 1927. — FESTUGIÈRE, A. J., *Socrate*, Paris, 1934. — FOUILLÉE, A., *La philosophie de Socrate*, 2 vols., Paris, 1874. — MAIER, H., *Sokrates*, Tübingen, 1913. — MEUNIER, M., *La légende de Socrate*, Paris, 1926. — PIAT, C., *Socrate*, Paris, 1900. — TAYLOR, A. E., *Socrates*, London, 1935.

27. Socrates was an Athenian of humble condition, son of Sophroniscus, a sculptor, and of Phaenarete, a midwife. Eminent by his moral and intellectual qualities, by his thirst for knowledge, and above all by his ardent love of truth and goodness, he gained great influence over the Athenians.

In his day the Athenian civilization was on the wane. A triple cause had led to its disintegration : demagogy and its consequent immorality; the Peloponnesian war with its disastrous legacy of hatred and dissensions; and the destructive theories of the Sophists. Socrates noted all this and, at the age of forty, undertook to work for the moral regeneration of his fellow-citizens. An internal voice which he regarded as that of Providence and which he calls his " *demon* " (δαίμων) [1] strengthened him in his vocation. Heedless of all else, despising money and refusing to take a salary for his lessons, he spent his days in the streets of Athens, conversing with the people and quietly imparting to all his ideas on virtue and wisdom. He left no writings : we know his doctrine by the works of his disciples : Xenophon's *Memorabilia* and Plato's *Dialogues*. As for Socrates, he **lived** his doctrine and, pagan though he was, gave the example of the highest virtues : generosity, self-control, and patience in dealing with his wife Xanthippe. Though he would accept no public charge which might interfere with his work, he was a conscientious citizen and as a soldier gave proof of courage and endurance in war.

His importance in the philosophical sphere results from the **purely intellectual** conception he had of his reforming mission. He was convinced that men would be virtuous if they were taught the science of virtue. His aim was to reform the lives of his contemporaries, and for that he sought merely to reform their minds and to turn them towards the truth for which they were ordained. Such was the principle on which Socrates worked. It involves four points which we shall treat in the following paragraphs :

1. The aim of his philosophy, and his attitude towards his predecessors with regard to the scope of philosophy.

2. His particular method of teaching.

3. His ethical science in outline, supplemented by

4. Considerations of the psychological and theological orders.

---

[1] *Demon* (or *Daemon*) in the Socratic sense has no implication of evil. See n. 37.

I. Object of Socratic philosophy.

28. Intellectual confusion was, in the eyes of Socrates, the chief, or rather the sole obstacle to the conversion of his fellow men. For this confusion he held responsible his predecessors, the Physicists and the Sophists.

The former, concerned only with nature, followed a truly scientific method and sought for a single and immutable principle to explain the changing multiplicity of things. The Sophists, on the other hand, study mainly the realities that concern man, but their method was by no means scientific. Intellectual culture was the theme of their discourses; but they failed to impart that culture. What they taught was the science of success.

The fault of both schools, thought Socrates, was that they misused the good elements of their philosophy. The process of thought followed by the Physicists could have brought consistent and communicable knowledge within their reach, but they applied it to the wrong object. Socrates condemned their physical science for three reasons : 1) it was **impossible**, since the problem of the universe is beyond us and the study of it leads to contradictions; 2) it was **impious,** since the gods have made of it their special domain; 3) it was **useless,** since it could do nothing towards making man good and happy.

The Sophists on the contrary found an object truly proportioned to the human intellect, teaching as they did virtue, eloquence, politics and other human sciences. But their method, purely empirical and utilitarian, had to be rejected.

Socrates, therefore, abandoned physical research, in which he had been passionately interested. If he ever took it up again, it was but incidentally, as a means of schooling his mind and that of his audience in order to increase their capacity for knowledge and for virtue. Thus the object he pursued was that of the Sophists, but his method was the scientific method of the Physicists, and his aim was to construct a science useful like art and, like knowledge, universal and communicable. Hence the importance of the Socratic method.

II. The Socratic Method.

29. Socrates suited his method to his aim and to his audience. His disciples could not reach a truly scientific knowledge of the moral life until he had freed them from the errors and prejudices of Sophistry. This explains the general nature of his method and its twofold phase.

A) **General features.** It may be broadly defined as a Dialogue, composed of a series of brief questions and precise answers. Its aim is to excite attention and, the needs of each individual being considered, to lead the mind by degrees towards truth. The Sophists with their fine speeches focussed attention on their own qualities; too frequently they were only half understood and in any case they took the doctrine for granted. Socrates declares himself ignorant of everything, hoping in this way to bring home to others their ignorance and to lead them to true knowledge. The dialogue was for him a necessary means of establishing direct contact between master and disciple, especially as he looked upon all the citizens of Athens as his disciples.

B) **The two phases.** The complete dialogue includes two parts;

1. Socratic Irony : Socrates seeks first of all to empty the mind by forcing the disciple to contradict himself. Pleading ignorance himself, he puts questions apparently to obtain information but in reality to perplex his interlocutor and bring him to confess ignorance also. Simple minds profit little by this method. It was useful, above all, for the Sophists and for the cultured minds formed by them. Sometimes the Master went no further than this preliminary stage; more often he rouses the disciple to reflection and passes on to the constructive work.

2. Maieutic [1]. This is the second stage. The problem has been set : a conclusion must be reached. Without making any authoritative statement, Socrates helps the student to **conceive** a solution by means of personal reflection. He holds that only a perversion of the moral sense (such as would result from

---

[1] From μαιεύω, to deliver; the art of delivering the mind, to enable it to conceive and give birth to truth.

inveterate habits of vice) can deprive a man of those innate moral concepts necessary for the good guidance of his life. " The soul ", he says, " is pregnant with truth " [1]. Thus he is following his mother's profession; but while she delivers bodies, he liberates minds. Now the movement of the mind towards truth is **reasoning,** and Socrates uses it in both its forms : induction and deduction.

a) **Socratic induction.** That the countless variety of individual cases should be reducible to the unity of one concept applicable to an indefinite number of like instances : such is the condition of an ethical science free from the relativism of Sophistry and acceptable to all men. Facts of experience rightly interpreted by common sense or by reason should lead to the **definition** of the object under investigation. In a word the philosopher must take into account the rules of induction which will furnish a sound basis for discussion and will give, according to Socrates, a principle full of significance for the consistently good guidance of conduct.

Thus the Athenian reformer, faithful to his mission, is interested only in **moral science.** He based his inductions not on any fact of experience, but generally on the current opinions of men of good judgment and of philosophers. For the moralist studies man as a reasonable being whose words and deeds may be observed. In plainer words he studies man as the object of his own experience. Socrates would have everyone to experiment on himself and to study himself. He saw a special meaning in the Delphic inscription : " know thyself : γνῶθι σεαυτόν ".

Socratic induction follows a gradual process, starting from a general and rudimentary idea, and then using further facts of an experimental nature to attain greater precision. The final stage is the effort to reduce particular definitions to the unity of a higher and more universal concept [2].

b) **Deduction.** Socrates uses it much more sparingly. As initiator he had chiefly to furnish good definitions for the foundations of the scientific edifice. Sometimes, however, he

---

[1] *Theætetus,* I, VI, 202; VII, 204.
[2] See, e. g., the three phases in the formation of the concept of *justice*, in XENOPHON'S *Memorabilia,* Book IV, Ch. I. Cf. PIAT, *op. cit.*, p. 109 and foll.; PALHORIES, *Vie et doctrine des grands phil.*, I, p. 49.

does, by means of his questioning, lead the disciple from accepted principles to particular cases or to necessary conclusions [1].

Value of this method. 30. It denotes first of all an acute insight into the nature of intellectual activity, that vital and personal operation in which the master is merely an instrument and the disciple the main cause [2]. The unceasing pursuit of definitions that Socrates leads is one of the most fertile principles of human knowledge. It reveals the true object of our intellect : the essential nature of things perceptible to the senses. No one will henceforth contest the dictum : " Non est scientia singularium sed universalium ".

No doubt these two basic truths remain undeveloped in the Socratic dialogues. Plato on the contrary pushed them too far and it was left to Aristotle to furnish precise formulas [3]. But the very fact that such considerations were introduced into the philosophical syllabus marked a notable advance on the old Physicist theories. As Maritain writes : " It was no longer a question of reducing everything to Water, or to Fire, or to Numbers, or to Being, not of discovering a concept of indefinite connotation in which all things might be enveloped as in a shapeless cloak. A reasoned knowledge of each thing, expressed in a concept which would state its nature precisely and definitely, and which would apply to that thing alone : such was the philosopher's new aim " [4]. Though wrongly restricted to the ethical domain, Socratic induction was therefore, as a means of acquiring knowledge, essentially adapted to the abstractive processes of the human mind. For the two great disciples, Plato and Aristotle, it was the gateway to philosophy, the universal science.

III. ETHICS.

31. Socrates' work was directed, not to the elaboration of a ready made system of philosophy, but to the enlivening of man's zeal for knowledge. Thus the truths contained in the dialogues were solely *analytical*.

---

[1] For instance, starting from the principle that ingratitude is an injustice, he leads his son Lamprocles to conclude that he must respect his mother. See XENOPHON, *Memorabilia*, I, Ch. II, coll. HATIER p. 47; PIAT, *Socrates*, p. 122.
[2] Cf. *St. Thomas*, Pt. I, q. 117, art. I.
[3] Socrates himself failed to elucidate these principles.
[4] *Introd. générale à la phil.*, p. 42.

However, the various converging lines lead to a general conspectus which embodies a leading principle and four main consequences [1].

A) **The leading principle.** *Of necessity all men desire their happiness, which consists in the possession of what is truly good, that is, of what the intelligence perceives as truly good.*

No such clearly formulated principle will be found in Socrates. Like most minor premises in inductive reasoning, it is only implied. In reality this principle is the basis of all that the dialogues contain in the way of interpretation and discussion. It is stated at times almost explicitly and it may be said that Socrates established it on the grounds of personal experience supported by the admissions of his disciples [2].

First consequence. Good synonymous with useful. *Human things are good in so far as they are useful in assuring our happiness.*

It is a direct application of the preceding principle to the concerns of everyday life. Socrates never dwelt explicitly on happiness in its absolute form, that which is supremely good in itself, but rather on what is good with reference to man. And since the function of this relative good is to guide us towards happiness, anything may be declared good for man which is a means to happiness, anything which is *useful* to him.

Hence this important corollary : there are four degrees in the *hierarchy* of the multiple elements which go to make up human good and human happiness :

1. In the lowest place are certain **external advantages,** such as health, beauty, wealth and honor. Their value is real but accidental, since we can live without them, and conditional, since it depends on the use we make of them.

2. **Bodily and emotional pleasures** come next. Their worth is relative because unless regulated, they easily lead to excesses.

3. **Self-control** liberates man from the tyranny of his passions and of his instincts by maintaining the authority of reason. The value of this good, though negative and dispositive by its

---

[1] BRÉHIER, in his *Hist. de la phil.*, p. 42, shows how Socrates endeavored not so much to theorize about morality as to lead men to study themselves and to reform their lives. But he proceeded in no haphazard way : without falsifying his aim, it is possible to group together the guiding principles on which he acted, and to underline their coherence. This is merely to *unfold* his thought.

[2] Cf. PLATO, the *Meno*, init. and XENOPHON, *Memor.* II, Ch. I.

action, is real since it is a necessary means of regulating the
emotions and preparing the soul for the possession of the
supreme good.

4. **Wisdom or virtue** is the absolute and supreme good.
The sage can be happy in the sole knowledge that he is good and
able to make others good. Without this knowledge all other
advantages are powerless to make him happy.

Two further conclusions develop and elucidate the notion of
virtue and happiness.

32. As these fundamental notions show, the ethical doctrine
of Socrates embodies several valuable truths. To begin with, his
general principle implies the notion of *finality* as applied to human
things. Further evolved by metaphysical thought, adapted by
deduction to the nature of the human will, and made to agree with
the idea of the possession of God as the supreme good, this same
principle will serve as basis for the Scholastic system of ethics.
These developments are still remote no doubt, but the precious germ
is already visible.

Utilitarianism as expounded by Socrates is notably different from
the teachings of Stuart Mill and of the other nineteenth century
Positivists. It contained *in germ* two other root elements of natural
morality:

a) **The notion of self-denial.** Convinced of the complexity of
human nature, Socrates asserts the necessity of strife, of privation
and of suffering. This mortification, though not good in itself,
ensures a fuller enjoyment of the other advantages whether bodily,
or, more especially, intellectual. This doctrine was the source of
the current of moral purification which runs through the whole of
Plato's method and which was in itself, thought Socrates, sufficient
to guarantee the success of his dialogues.

b) **The notion of " bonum honestum ".** Socrates, aware of what
was essential and specific in the nature of man, held that the
supremely useful, the ultimate good, was that which satisfied reason.
He called it wisdom. This was equivalent to asserting the primacy
of the " bonum honestum ", known to the Thomists as *that which
reason perceives as good*. Utilitarianism, in the accepted sense of
the term, implies no such exalted conception [1].

Second consequence. Virtue synonymous with knowledge.

33. *The virtuous man is he who has a perfect knowledge of
moral goodness* : *the* MAN OF WISDOM.

Socrates first eliminates quite definitely the notion that virtue
might consist either in a chance agreement of human conduct

---

[1] As will be seen later (nn. 431 and 449), this theory has no aim beyond the
bounds of sense experience.

with the ideal concept of order, or in an instinctive disposition of nature. Since virtue is the highest human perfection, the possession of it should be within our control. It must have the stability, the independence, and the power that reason gives. In a word, virtue is the supremacy of Reason. Socrates holds that in this *knowledge* of moral goodness is to be found, not only a primary condition of rational supremacy, but a sufficient and adequate cause ensuring such supremacy. This again was implied in the fundamental principle : since a man necessarily desires what is good for him, he cannot but accept what he sees to be a true advantage. To reject it would be the act of a madman. No one does evil willingly: " οὐδείς ἐκών ἁμαρ-τάνει ". Vice is ignorance.

It follows that virtue is essentially the science of well-doing. It is one and the same with Wisdom, the philosopher's aim. Virtue is fundamentally one; its name varies according as it is applied to different objects. We call it courage or temperance when it controls the will or the emotions; justice and piety when it regulates our dealings with other men or with the gods.

The Socratic paradox. 34. This bold theory has been termed the SOCRATIC PARADOX. It will be fully understood only if it be remembered that knowledge as identified with virtue is no common knowledge of moral goodness, but a knowledge that rational reflection has converted into a science. It must also attain the force of a conviction that conformity with reason is for us a real good. As a basis for this conviction a proportionate intellectual culture is necessary. Reason must be strengthened by constant exercise in order to be equal to the task of directing our lives. Hence Socrates' amazing persistence in conversing with his fellow-citizens, and his efforts to instruct them in virtue by ceaselessly training them to think. Undoubtedly in this sense, " nothing is stronger than reason " as a moral guide for man.

It is no less justifiable to proclaim the scientific stability and the independence of virtue. Both virtue and science are counted by St. Thomas among the *habits*, which he defines : " *Dispositio difficile mobilis secundum quam bene, prompte et delectabiliter agens operatur* " [1]. But between these two forms of virtue, the intellectual and the moral, there exist irreducible differences.

---

[1] Cf. Iᵃ-IIæ, q. 49-55 and 57, art. I.

Light can be thrown on the Socratic paradox by St. Thomas's searching analysis of the subtle connection between intellectual knowledge and free will. " Whoever has a true knowledge of his own good seeks it necessarily ", says Socrates. A distinction is needed, replies St. Thomas. If one considers good in a general way, perceived as the ultimate and universal aim, or embodied in some form which is a necessary condition of human happiness, such as existence, life, and so on, then the principle is true. If one considers some particular good, a further distinction is needed. There are two ways of knowing this good : first there is the abstract knowledge of the scholar, or the theoretico-practical knowledge of the moralist. This will not of itself insure good conduct. Then there is the knowledge of prudence, that of the practical intellect. This latter is inevitably followed by a good action, because it implies that the good object in question has already been freely chosen. Thus the reason may find its supremacy hampered by that mysterious thing, freedom, with its possible lapses that original sin has rendered more frequent. It is true that Socrates upholds the freedom of the will, although his paradox leads to determinism. Such freedom is a condition of self-control and of the acquisition of knowledge. Here as always Socrates moves in the dawning, if hazy, light of truth rather than in the darkness of error.

Third consequence. Happiness synonymous with virtue.

35. *Man is happy even in this world in proportion as he is virtuous.*

If virtue is the supreme and sole-sufficing good, its possession will infallibly bring true happiness. It should be noted that, as a moralist, Socrates was like all pagans concerned with the *present life.* So highly did he prize the dignity of reason and the excellence of spiritual delights, that he deemed virtue a sufficient reward for the good man and vice a suitable punishment for the evildoer.

A noble ideal, it must be admitted, containing much that is true [1] but, without grace, unattainable for man in his fallen state. The select few could hardly hope to realize it; it was totally beyond the crowd.

Fourth consequence. The obligatory *is in a sense equivalent to the useful.*

The obligation to practice virtue is imposed by *the law:* the written law regulates the organization of the State; the unwritten

---

[1] Even from the purely ethical point of view man's ultimate good is to be ascribed to the *life to come.* (Cf. parag. 90). It is none the less true that the partial happiness resulting in this life from the practice of virtue satisfies noble souls, and amply so in the supernatural order of grace where holiness abounds.

law prescribes natural duties. Socrates sought a rational explanation of this.

Following the normal line of Socrates' thought, one would regard obligatory things as of themselves necessary, destined for our good and happiness. If this be so then the obligatory is equivalent to the useful and to the irresistible attraction of what is good [1].

Socrates is vague on this point. He admits the generally accepted teaching that duty has its last explanation in the will of the gods from whom legislators draw their inspiration and who fashion human nature. This idea is also correct, but it is superficially explored and has no very logical link with the general teaching of the Dialogues.

Note. It should be understood that a synthesis of the Socratic doctrine such as we have attempted in this chapter was neither realized nor even outlined by the Master himself. The author hopes in proposing it to stress the full value of the broad conceptions embodied in the Dialogues, pointing out in the process their actual limitations and their potential resources.

IV. PSYCHOLOGY AND NATURAL THEOLOGY.

36. Socrates kept consistently in the sphere of human interest. But human happiness may be considered with reference either to the nature of our soul and its destiny, or to the existence of God and his Providence. Hence the necessity of studying the ethical aspect of psychology and of theodicy.

A) **Socratic Psychology.** I. Induction leads us to view the soul as an existing reality, distinct from, and superior to, the body. It is a *spiritual* reality which by its intellectual and volitive action controls the physical faculties.

2. **Immortality of the soul.** Since Socrates with true Greek optimism sees in virtue and vice adequate reward (or punishment) for good and evil, his ethical theory does not necessarily imply that the soul is immortal. He holds however that immortality may be reasonably postulated as the natural

---

[1] It would be false to infer this from the Socratic paradox; the Master himself drew no such conclusion.

complement of life and the prolongation of philosophic happiness.   Three reasons suggest this:

a) The soul is a vivifying agent which does not die when it ceases to animate the body.

b) The soul, through the control of the will over man's other faculties, resembles the gods: like them it is immortal.

c) The mind judges with increased vigor in proportion as it becomes independent of matter.

It is not easy however to discern in these reasons what belongs to Socrates and what is due to the fertile brain of his disciple, Plato, who formulated and no doubt developed them. What is certain is that Socrates was the first to have a clear vision of the soul as the principal element in man, of the intelligence as residing in the soul, and of the eternal idea with which the intelligence is penetrated.   That alone singles him out as the founder of rational psychology.

B) **Theodicy.   37.**   Previous philosophers had revealed the play in the universe of powerful natural forces and thereby had undermined mythology without offering a substitute to the religious-minded.   Socrates in turn rejects the coarse features of mythology, the quarrels of the deities, their passions and the like; but he remains faithful to the traditional form of religion. Yet, a penetrating view of the theory expounded by Anaxagoras brought Socrates very near to monotheism.

ɪ.   **Proposition:** *There exists a God whose supreme intelligence ordains all things.*

a) Socrates proved this as usual by induction, but in this case his observations covered a larger field.   He considered the perfectly ordered universe where nothing is left to chance. An immanent finality ordains each being with all its parts to an immediate end, and this end is its perfection as is seen in the wonderful organism of the human body.   Moreover there is interdependence among the different beings and all tend towards a common aim: man's happiness.

Only a supreme intelligence can account for this universal order.   Therefore, the fact of the cosmos presupposes a demiurge.

Here is a fertile principle which Socrates only half unfolds. Without revealing its metaphysical basis, he merely shows it working in human affairs, where the mechanicalist theory is manifestly inadequate. But this general notion of finality is enough to lead him to the conception of God, supreme Law-giver, responsible for the laws that govern things in the natural order.

b) Socrates finds another argument in the imperfect and dependent nature of our intelligence which can only be a derivative of the universal intelligence. It would be absurd to suppose that a non-intelligent cause could have produced intelligent beings. In the same way, then, as the human body borrows its substance from the vast body of the universe, so the human soul is a participation of the universal Soul.

This notion is hardly consistent with the idea of a transcendent God since it leads one to think of Him as the immanent soul of the world. The influence of Anaxagoras is evident and these ancient theological conceptions are, to say the least, indistinct.

2. **Consequences :** *The divine attributes.*

a) In Himself, God is *One,* as is proved by the perfectly ordered unity of the universe. As intelligence He is *invisible* to the senses; He has His own life and is in Himself inscrutable. He is *immeasurable* since He animates the whole universe.

b) In relation to the cosmos God is not creator but merely organizer. He is *Providence,* too, since He is the governing intelligence. Source of all order and beauty, He knows every-thing, sees and hears everything. He watches over each being as well as over the whole world, and in particular He ensures the welfare of the just since He makes all things contribute to that end. In certain difficult circumstances God in His goodness may even reveal to the just man secrets that divine knowledge alone can fathom.

Socrates was thus able to justify divination and pagan oracles. He also admitted a multitude of gods whom he considered as the unseen attendants of the one God, subject to His Providence and sent as messengers to make known His will to men. Socrates himself, we have seen, declared that he enjoyed familiar intercourse with one of these good spirits [1] who spoke to him interiorly and told him particularly what he must not do.

c) To God then we owe the most profound veneration together with a boundless and heartfelt gratitude. We should pray to

---

[1] He called it his *daimon.* See n. 28.

Him to ask His good favors and honor Him by public rites;
our piety should show itself above all in the love of order and the
practice of virtue.

CONCLUSION. **38.** I. Socrates had great **personal influence.**
The Athenian youth loved him for his witty moods, his winning
grace and his subtle appeal. Without calling themselves his
disciples, they came to him in crowds. Nevertheless the longstand-
ing customs of a pagan and democratic city resisted successfully his
mission of moral regeneration. He was regarded as a Sophist, and
much in his outward attitude was calculated to mislead. He was
accused of spreading new ideas opposed to the traditions of family,
state and religion.

1. **Family traditions.** The most refined among the young men of
Athens sought his company and seemed to esteem him more than
their own parents, especially when the latter were ignorant or
lacking in virtue.

2. **Political traditions.** Socrates criticized the direction of public
affairs and the choosing of the magistrates by lot. Himself a member
of an intellectual *élite*, he declared that the government was rightfully the business of the most enlightened. He was an avowed
enemy of conservatism and of democracy.

3. **Even religious traditions.** Was he not seeking to substitute
inward inspiration for the oracles and individual judgment for
regular authority? His monotheism appealed no doubt to the
intellectuals but to the common people it was nothing less than the
destruction of the traditional religion.

Thus in the public eye he was a revolutionary and a free-thinker.
Accordingly, on the accusations of Anitus, a politician, Melitus, a
poet, and Lycon, an orator, he was brought before the court of the
Dicasts. The ironic and haughty tone of his defense helped him to
lose favor and he was condemned to death. With perfect calm he
drank the poison (May or June, 399). He was seventy years of age.

II. **His doctrine.** Socrates produced no coherent and
complete synthesis, even in the domain of ethics. His work
was a philosophical initiation, pregnant with profound truths
which were yet in germ.

He attained a precise and penetrating insight into the conditions of human knowledge which deals with universals. He
discovered the true scientific method in its twofold phase,
induction and deduction; but he arbitrarily restricted its
application to the field of ethics.

His whole morality is directed by the principle of finality, of
which he dimly realizes the sovereign value; — but he fails to
show that the ultimate end and supreme good is outside man, in
God alone. Nor does he see clearly that sanctions, immortality

and obligations are founded in God. Hence it is that Socrates' theory of conduct, centered in man, aiming at human happiness and based on the current opinions of men has a taint of naturalism and lacks breadth. It is none the less far superior to that of the Sophists, who aimed only at success.

Finally, while revealing the power of reason in the search for goodness and happiness, Socrates overlooks the part played by free will. His famous paradox, even if it does not deny liberty, lessens considerably its significance.

Socrates' chief role was, as he wished it, that of *physician to he Hellenist intellect*. Through him Greek thought was cured of its scepticism and put on the road that led to truth. From this point of view his life was a providential favor for humanity and marked an age in the history of thought, for he succeeded in passing on his love of reason to his disciples. The greatest of them, Socrates' most brilliant product, was Plato.

CHAPTER TWO.

PLATO (429-348).

BIBLIOGRAPHY.

1⁰ **Works :** BURNET, J., (ed.), *Platonis Opera*, 5 vols., Oxford, 1899-1907. — JOWETT, B., (Transl.), *The dialogues of Plato*, 5 vols., 3rd ed., 1892.

2⁰ **Studies :** BRÉMOND, A., *De l'Ame et de Dieu dans la philosophie de Platon*, Paris, 1924. — BURNETT, J., *Platonism*, London, 1928. — CORNFORD, F. M., *Plato's theory of knowledge*, London, 1935. *Plato's cosmology*, London, 1937. *Plato and Parmenides*, London, 1939. — DIÈS, A., *Platon*, Paris, 1930. — DEMOS, R., *The philosophy of Plato*, New York, 1939. — FIELD, G. C., *Plato and his contemporaries*, London, 1930. — FOUILLÉE, A., *La philosophie de Platon*, 4 vols., 3ᵉ éd., 1904-9. — GROTE, G., *Plato and the other companions of Socrates*, 3 vols., 3rd ed., London, 1875. — MORE, P. E., *Platonism*, New York, 1919. — PATER, W., *Plato and Platonism*, London, 1909. — PIAT, C., *Platon*, Paris, 1930. — ROBIN, L., *Platon*, Paris, 1935. — SHOREY, P., *The unity of Plato's thought*, Chicago, 1903. *What Plato said*, Chicago, 1933. *Platonism ancient and modern*, Chicago, 1938. — SOULIHE, J., *La notion platonicienne d'intermédiaire dans la philosophie des dialogues*, Paris, 1919. — TAYLOR, A. E., *Plato the man and his work*, London, 1926. *Platonism and its influence*, New York, 1924. — WILLAMOWITZ-MOELLENDORFF, U. VON., *Platon*, 2 vols., Berlin, 1919. — ZELLER, E., *Plato and the older academy*, London, 1876.

39. Aristocles, called Plato (because of his broad forehead), was born on the island of Aegina, in the year 429 B. C. [1]. Through his father he traced his descent to Cadmus, the last king of Athens, and through his mother to Solon. His brilliant education was completed under the philosopher Cratylus, a disciple of Heraclitus. A poet by nature, he wrote plays in his youth, but at the age of twenty, after hearing Socrates, he burnt his poetry and gave himself up wholly to philosophy. He spent eight years in the companionship of Socrates, and when the latter died he set off to supplement his studies by travelling. At Megara he practised dialectic under Euclid and studied astronomy in Egypt. In Italy and Sicily he became acquainted with, and admired, the teachings of Pythagoras and the Eleatics. Finally he visited Syracuse upon the invitation of Dion to whom he expounded his political views. His frankness lost him Dion's patronage and he was sold as a slave.

He regained his freedom through the generosity of the Cyrenaic philosopher Aniceris, and was able to return to Athens. About 387 Plato opened a school of philosophy in the gardens of his friend, Academus, whence the name *Academy* [2]. Subsequently he made two visits to Sicily, the first for the purpose of urging Dionysius the younger to apply his political principles and the second in 361 to defend his patron, Dion [3]. The rest of his life, nearly twenty years, was spent in studying and teaching philosophy. Plato died at the age of 81 in the first days of the war which was to bring Athens and Greece under the domination of Philip of Macedonia.

The Works of Plato. Plato's doctrine is contained in his DIALOGUES, admirable literary works, praised both for the purity and the varied simplicity of the style and, above all, for the true-to-life manner in which the characters speak and act. In the conversations, Socrates is usually Plato's mouthpiece, but sometimes, as in the *Timaeus*, the exposition is put into the plainer form of a long monologue.

---

[1] Or 427; See BRÉHIER, *Hist. de la phil.*, I, p. 96.

[2] The school and garden became the collective property of Plato's disciples who formed a religious society; it persisted until the year 529 A. D.

[3] Dion was the nephew of Dionysius I and cousin to Dionysius the younger, for whom he acted as minister. His admiration for Plato's political ideas was partly the cause of his disgrace.

Each dialogue has more or less the unity of a dramatic composition; in none of them is the subject matter strictly defined; they move with the easy pace and the loose structure of a poem. Here are the most important among them:

1. **Protagoras,** on the Sophists. 2. **Gorgias,** on rhetoric. 3. **Meno,** on virtue. 4. **The Symposium,** on love. 5. **Phaedrus,** on beauty. 6. **Phaedo,** on the immortality of the soul. 7. **Parmenides,** on Ideas. 8. **Theaetetus,** on knowledge. 9. **Sophistes,** on Being. 10. **Timaeus,** on nature. Lastly the ten books of the *Republic,* and the twelve books of the *Laws,* in which is found a detailed account of Plato's views on politics.

Bréhier [1] gives the complete list in chronological order :

1. Dialogues composed before or just after the death of Socrates : *Protagoras, Ion, Apology, Crito, Euthrypho, Charmides, Laches, Lysis, Republic,* book I, *(Thrasymachus), Hippias,* I and II.

2. Dialogues written before the foundation of the Academy: *Gorgias.*

3. Programme-dialogues, following immediately on the establishment of the School: *Meno, Menexenus, Euthydemus, Republic,* books II to X.

4. Dialogues containing an ideal portrait of Socrates : *Phaedo, The Symposium, Phaedrus.*

5. Dialogues which inaugurate a new conception of knowledge and of dialectic : *Cratylus, Theaetetus, Parmenides, Sophistes, Politicus.* (The two last named were to be completed by the *Philosopher* which was planned but never composed.)

6. The last Dialogues : *Timaeus, Critias,* (which remained unfinished and was to be followed by the *Hermocrates*), the *Laws* (also incomplete, published after the death of Plato, largely in the form of collected notes), *Epinomis.*

There remain several dialogues of which the authenticity is denied by modern critics : *Alcibiades* I and II, The *Rivals, Theages, Clitophon, Minos.*

Finally, thirteen Letters, most of which are generally held as authentic. The most notable is the lengthy 7th letter addressed to Dion's friends, which contains many details concerning Plato's relations with Dionysius.

Fundamental principle. 40. Plato's philosophy is centered round, and dominated by, the theory of IDEAS, which may be summed up in the following principle : *The specific object of*

---

[1] *Hist. de la phil.,* I, p. 98-99.

*human knowledge is the real world of Ideas, of which the world
of the senses is but the shadow or the copy.*

His system embodies two clearly distinct parts : the first
deals with the domain of the intelligible, that is the object
of *dialectic* or of true knowledge. The second treats of the world
of the senses where opinion holds sway. Heraclitus and
chiefly Parmenides had already stressed this division; Plato
sets out to explain it by showing that everything in the visible
universe is made intelligible through the directive and
communicative influence of the Forms.

Two sections will cover this double field:

Section I.   Dialectic: the science of Forms.

Section II.   The world of the senses, object of opinion.

ARTICLE I.

DIALECTIC : THEORY OF FORMS.

Plato's first concern is to prove the *existence* of the Ideal
world as the object of knowledge. This object is a new one and
cannot be attained without a suitable *method*. The application
of the method furnishes an analysis of the intimate *relations*
of Forms one with another.

I.   Existence of the World of Ideas.

II.   Plato's Method.

III.   Inter-relations of Ideas.

I.   EXISTENCE OF THE WORLD OF IDEAS.

A) **Proofs.**

41.   The several reasons on which Plato establishes the
basic theory of this whole system may be reduced to two proofs,
the first logical and the second ontological.

I.   **Proof by logic.**   Unlike modern thinkers, Plato accepts
unquestioningly the fact of knowledge. Its existence is for
him an uncontested and necessary reality. The same reality
must therefore be attributed to the conditions on which
knowledge depends.

Now the first condition of knowledge is a permanent and unvarying object, susceptible of being fixed definitely in our minds, sufficiently defined to be intelligible, to retain its identity, and to be handed down intact to successive generations.

No object of this nature can be found in the visible world which is for Plato, as for Heraclitus, " an unlimited and unceasing interflow of movement ", where " everything passes like running water ", and nothing remains.

The conclusion is that there is another world, above that of the senses, where lies the true object of knowledge : the *intelligible world* of Forms.

2. **Proof by ontology.** The visible world proves the existence of the ideal world as the shadow intimates the reality. The senses no doubt perceive admirable perfections in their domain, but these are participated in a greater or lesser degree and are never fully realized. Two facts prove it: earthly things are beautiful, good, great and so on, in varying degrees; or else we find opposite qualities in the same being : a thing is beautiful in one respect and ugly in another, great from one point of view and small from another.

Quite clearly, concludes Plato, these participations and degenerations lead to the conception of some *source* where such qualities are to be found in a pure and perfect state. Somewhere there exists a sovereign Beauty and a sovereign Goodness, a pure and absolute Greatness as well as a pure and absolute Smallness. These exist in themselves and by themselves, and constitute the universe of the intelligible, the true object of knowledge.

B) Plurality of Forms.

42. The preceding arguments, especially the second, brought Plato very near to Absolute Monism. The various perfections are in reality various degrees or modalities of being. The mingling of the perfect with the imperfect, of ugliness with beauty and so on, is merely a participated form of being limited by non-being.

But rather than admit the Eleatic notion of a being solitary and motionless, Plato was ready, as he said " to act like a parricide and raise his hand against the revered Parmenides ". As the Atomists had reduced to particles the Being they held

to be material, so Plato disintegrates this Being conceived
as intelligible and spiritual, making of it a plurality of Forms
which are as so many intelligible atoms.

Two proofs justify this conclusion:

1. **Direct proof.** Rational experience points to ideal
plurality. The common process of human thought is that
of abstracting from sense-phenomena qualities which are
permanent, since they admit of definition, and at the same
time *distinct* and *numerable*, such as humanity, prudence,
strength, etc. Such is the immediate inference of Socratic
induction, to which Plato adheres faithfully and which, though
not expressly formulated by him, is at the very root of his
system.

Now this process of accurate knowledge is possible only if
there exists a real object. And as the visible world offers no
such object, it must be sought in an ideal universe peopled
with many Forms.

2. **Indirect proof.** Unless this plurality is admitted, no
knowledge is conceivable. If being is one and indivisible, then
its own existence is its sole attribute. Nothing is susceptible
of definition, no such thing as a *judgment* may be formed, and
human knowledge, which is a coordinated system of judgments,
is impossible.

Plurality of Ideas is, then, a fact.

To sum up : Knowledge implies : 1. an object, intelligible and
definable and therefore permanent and simple; 2. a number
of Forms on which to found a set of mental statements.

Now, *a*) one must admit with Heraclitus that the things
perceived by the senses are constantly changing and contain
opposite qualities;

b) Being as conceived by Parmenides implies the necessary
permanence, but its absolute unity is opposed to thought;

c) Finally, it is clear that by Socratic induction the mind
abstracts from sense-phenomena qualities that are multiple and
yet permanent, since they are definable.

Therefore the object of knowledge is neither the world of
the senses nor Being in the Eleatic sense, but the genera and
species as defined by Socrates. They include not only substan-

tial genera, such as animal, plant, stone, etc., but also qualities and even relations, such as cold and heat, equality and inequality, etc. They constitute the world of Forms.

C) Nature of Forms [1].

43. The Platonic Form has four properties inasmuch as it is an intelligible object:

1.   SPIRITUALITY: it is imperceptible to the senses and is apprehended by the intellect immediately.

2.   REALITY: it is not merely an abstract notion of the mind nor even a thought conceived by the Divinity; it is something real, having its own *subsistence* [2] and its own individuality. It is, moreover, endowed with life and thought since it is of the intelligible order. Together the Forms constitute a world apart, the sole world that is real. Thus they may be attained directly by the glance of true knowledge and are the fountain-head whence spring the diminished realities of the nether world.

Plato's Idea possesses *reality* as its essential attribute, and possesses it in all fulness, by right and in fact, since it exists " in itself " and " of itself ", and has in itself the whole reason of its existence. The Forms are independent of any cause and are themselves true primary causes each in its own order. There result two other properties.

3.   IMMUTABILITY. The Forms are not affected by change, whether in the nature of birth, variation, progress, decline or death. They are *eternal*.

4.   SIMPLICITY. Each is a perfectly self-contained essence, unadulterated, and in its kind perfect. They are in reality *infinite*, though Plato avoided that term as implying a certain want of definiteness. The Forms are fully determinate and leave no indistinctness in the mind. Each is unmistakably discernible from the others [3].

---

[1] The word Form is written with a capital letter each time it represents the Platonic εἶδος.

[2] The Thomist would call it a *pure form.* Subsistence is clearly attributed to the Forms in the *Phaedrus*, where Plato represents the soul as seeing " into a place beyond heaven " where exist these realities " colorless and shapeless " called Forms. (See BRÉHIER, *Hist. de la phil.*, I, p. 117.) Other passages are less clear; certain texts in the *Parmenides* and in the *Timaeus* have led the neo-Platonists to a different interpretation. (See parag. 129.)

[3] This doctrine will be more easily grasped when the method has been explained.

II. THE PLATONIC METHOD.

44. In Plato's writings there is no precise distinction, such as Aristotle will make, between the three points of reference, viz. 1. the *logical* standpoint, or method; 2. the *metaphysical* standpoint, or the study of things taken in themselves; 3. the *psychological* standpoint, or the functional aspect of the cognitive faculties.

Plato applies the term " dialectic " in general to the efforts of the mind in the order of knowledge, and to the fruits of those efforts. Thus his method includes a logical and a psychological aspect, while the doctrine of participated Forms constitutes the metaphysical aspect.

A) Logical Aspect.

Here we have simply a more skilled application of the method used by Socrates. It is an amplified form of Socratic " irony " with insistence on the function of purification. The dialectic of the Ἔρως gives an impulse to reason in " the pursuit of essences ". It finally becomes a scientific directive, leading the mind by successive degrees to an intuitive view of the world of Forms.

1. The *method by purification* is peculiar to Platonism. Its aim is to free the intellectual soul little by little from the material mass in which it is embedded. It implies the practice of *self-control*, dear to Socrates; the restraining of unruly passions; and an increasing effort to regulate the life of the soul. In order to achieve this the lower inclinations of nature are to be checked by reason, and temporal interests must be abandoned in favor of the eternal realities, of which material things are but the shadows. As a result of this purgation the soul becomes entirely independent of the body and is raised up to the world of Ideas. Thus, according to Plato, the philosopher's true study is to learn to die [1]. He must seek the truth with his whole soul.

2. This elevation receives a secret impulse from the irresistible attraction that the Ideal Good has for the intellectual mind. From this point of view, " purgation " is equivalent to " dia-

---

[1] *Phaedo.* 32. (LIVINGSTONE's trans. p. 132.)

lectic of love ". Discovering in material things a reflected gleam of Good, the soul is fired with an active desire to attain it. Thus is born an impulse which is to be cherished, but which is to be more and more directed towards spiritual things, until, high up in the world of Forms, it reaches the absolute and immutable essence of the Beautiful and the Good.

3. However, this gradual ascension has also a didactic aspect and is in the nature of a scientific discipline. The process is from ignorance, through successive approaches to complete truth. It includes two phases each made up of two steps.

The First Phase concerns the world of the senses.

The first step consists of mere transient impressions of sense phenomena, or of fleeting imaginations, e. g., the noting or the recollection of beautiful music in an effort to pick out the most harmonious passages. The result is simple *conjecture*.

The second step initiates the work of stabilization and of generalization, with a preliminary attempt at definition. This is necessarily inadequate and provisional because based on popular opinion or on notions handed down by poets or priests (such traditions are known as *Myths*), or again on comparisons and probabilities, e. g., the nature of the soul described by comparison with a chariot drawn by two very different horses [1].

It is easily seen that this process is a form of Socratic induction, which, according to Plato, leads to FAITH. Conjectures and beliefs taken together form *opinion*, an acquisition by no means negligible, since it is with reference to opinion that Plato formulates his philosophy of the material universe.

The Second Phase is, however, more important. Its object is the world of things intelligible.

The first step is the study of the exact sciences, mathematics and geometry, which accustom the mind to look for a permanent and essential object, but which are founded on a hypothetical and unreliable basis. These sciences depend on sense data : but the ultimate foundation of scientific axioms and of mathematical or geometrical definitions does not pertain to the senses. To admit them without further explanation is to remain in

---

[1] The *Phaedrus* contains this allegory: the *white* horse represents the heart, and the *black* horse, concupiscence.

the order of hypothesis, to fall short of the absolute [1]. This degree leads to *reasoned knowledge*, scientific but imperfect.

The second step attains the final cause of things, by means of an intuitive view of the Forms and the consideration either of their individual nature or of their inter-relations. Its method is by analysis or deduction. This degree alone reaches the plenitude of the real and begets *wisdom*, or knowledge in its perfect state.

Elsewhere Plato combines the two steps of the second phase under the term *intelligence* or science in general [2].

B) Psychological Aspect.

45. Stress must be laid at the outset on the *intuitive* nature of Platonic mental processes. For if the lower degrees appeal to the senses and prepare the way for induction, it is only in a *psychological* or subjective sense that they initiate the higher degrees. Their necessity is that of preliminary conditions; but once the summit is reached, the intellect seizes its object (the world of Forms) immediately and *intuitively*, and that object is self-dependent and needs no other basis than itself.

This mark of intuition in the Platonic method is further defined in the explanation given of the manner in which man's intelligence attains the Ideal world. It will be found in the theory of RECOLLECTION, which may be thus formulated:

I. **Proposition.** *Sense experience is the incentive or occasion that gives rise to knowledge; it is in no way the source or the subject matter of knowledge.*

It is supposed that the soul came on earth after a previous life in the Ideal world, where it gained true knowledge in the direct contemplation of the Forms. Its union with a body

---

[1] Cf. Dies, *Platon*, p. 145.—Bréhier, *Hist. de la Phil.*, I, p. 111-115 and 121, basing his view on the historical evolution of Plato's philosophy, has a different explanation of the part played by hypothesis. He sees in it an application of the method by mathematical analysis, in which conclusions are drawn from a supposed solution of the problem. Thus Plato, to solve the problem of knowledge, takes the Forms as hypothetical basis of his study; from that assumption he draws conclusions (recollection, eternity of the soul, etc.); after testing these conclusions, he apparently abandons his hypothesis (in the *Theaetetus*); but resumes it in the light of the theory of participated Forms (in the *Parmenides*). Bréhier gives the sequence in Plato's career of the four steps here enumerated.

[2] See the *Republic*, Book VII, mainly in chap. XIV, where a clear summary of the four steps will be found.

induced temporary oblivion. But since the material world is a participation of the Ideal universe, even though a diminished participation, it can help the soul to regain its lost knowledge. Once the mind has been prepared by self-control and the mastering of the passions and by the practice of the earlier steps of the method, the senses lead it by way of suggestion or of irresistible impressions to discover anew the invigorating intuition of the world of Forms.

2.   **Proofs.** a) Frequently Plato presents this doctrine as a simple corollary of the theory of Forms. If the only true object of knowledge is not directly attainable in the world of the senses, the soul must needs have brought with it into the world the notions of reality that it possesses : hence the theory of INNATE IDEAS [1].

b) But the same conclusion, says Plato, can be reached by a *direct induction*. An ignorant man when adroitly questioned discovers new intelligible concepts. For instance, Meno's slave is able to establish by figures certain relations of surface areas. No one taught him those relations, nor are they within the scope of sense experience. The knowledge was therefore previously in his mind; observation revived his memory.

The argument confirms the fact of the existence of the Forms and justifies the method.

C) **Realism and Innate Ideas in Plato.**

46. I. The method consists *essentially* in proceeding either by truncated syllogisms (enthymemes), or by induction, the word being taken in a broad sense allowing for a free treatment of the facts observed and aiming only at the more general notions. And, indeed, these quick movements of thought appear rather as a connected sequence of intellectual glimpses than as a systematic application of the whole mechanism of reasoning. Such a process is particularly well adapted to one class of thinkers : the *intuitives,* or *mystics* [2], as opposed to deductive or positive minds.

2.   Plato's method has its *dangers*. Its interpretations and conclusions accepted as probable are easily incomplete or even false, either because the observer omitted certain facts or

---

[1] An alternative would be the theory that at birth God creates both the mind and the ideas that people it. For Plato, who had no idea of creation, the only explanation was that of the preexistence of the soul. See parag. 58.

[2] For the meaning of this word, cf. parag. 120.

because he failed to grasp the more subtle differences in an idea. The Master himself who worked with the poet's ardor rather than with the philosopher's prudence, did not escape this danger. His basic theory of Forms is vitiated by two errors : an exaggerated realism and the notion of innate ideas.

a) EXAGGERATED REALISM : the term is applicable to the doctrine which attributes identical properties to the objects of intellectual knowledge and to the abstract ideas that represent those objects. The epistemological problem of which this thesis is a proposed solution is that of the *universals* or of the objective value of thought.

For Plato the issue is psychological and metaphysical. The early thinkers, following in that the common sense view, were essentially *realists* and not at all critically minded. They held without exception that knowable objects are distinct from thought itself. If a few minor philosophers hesitated to admit the possibility of any true knowledge of reality, it was only to fall into scepticism; thus some of the Sophists and the followers of Pyrrho. The idealist in the strict sense is a modern product. He claims that what we know is not reality but a subjective phenomenon called an idea or a thought.

How does this realist principle apply in Plato's philosophy? The following syllogism may elucidate his idea and stress its want of balance :

Human knowledge has four characteristics : it is spiritual, eternal, immutable and fully intelligible.

Now reality can be justly regarded as an object of knowledge only if it has the same properties as knowledge itself; any lack of uniformity between knowledge and its object would render truth impossible.

Reality is therefore to be found in the world of Ideas.

The error is in the minor premiss. A thing which is at once knowable and real may be considered in two ways. *In itself*, as *objective equivalent* of an idea, it has the same characteristics in the order of knowledge as in that of reality. Thus, all that the psychologist predicates of human nature taken in itself (freedom, life, immortality, etc.) has its exact counterpart in Peter and Paul.

But the same thing may be viewed with reference to its *mode of existence*, and then its properties in the order of the real are quite different from, and even opposed to, those that it possesses as an object of knowledge. Thus in Peter and Paul, human nature has a physical or concrete existence which necessitates an individual substance and the consequent accidentals of time, place and so on. Seen in its psychological aspect, this same humanity has an ideal (intentional) and abstract existence, independent of all material features, marked with the ideal qualities of permanence, eternity, self-existence, and perfect intelligibility.

Plato's mistake was to transfer into the domain of reality the attributes proper to a concept when stripped of its concrete accompaniments. The true and perfectly adjusted solution is the *moderate realism* of Aristotle and St. Thomas.

b) INNATE IDEAS. According to this theory, ideas or concepts are present in the human soul from the first moment of its existence. In other words our thoughts are born with us. They are a *natural* product and depend in no way on sense experience or on the process of abstraction. By means of this psychological proposition, Plato attempted to account for the *origin of ideas*.

Here again a formal argument may help to make the doctrine clear.

What is spiritual cannot proceed from that which is material and perceptible to the senses.

Our ideas are spiritual. Therefore they cannot proceed from sense data.

The major premiss is faulty. The material obviously cannot be the principle and total cause of the spiritual. But it can play the rôle of instrumental or partial cause; and such is the conclusion that the facts impose. Plato failed to note the true relation of dependence between the content of an idea (at least in so far as it represents the object directly) and sense observation. The latter phenomenon is clearly much more than an incentive to knowledge: it has all the features of an efficient cause.

There remains the problem of harmonizing this doctrine with the evident fact that ideas are indeed spiritual and that some are transcendent and suprasensible in their meaning. The solution is furnished by a new and original application of the Aristotelian and Thomistic theory of *actus* and *potentia* (theory of the *active intellect*) [1]. Thus Plato again passes over some of the facts. Without the notion of abstraction he could not fully comprehend the *object proper* of human thought, which is the essential element abstracted from the sensible object. For him the essence has the properties of being in its absolute form, in itself perfect and infinite, which is the *adequate object* of thought in general. Eager to exalt the nobility of the human mind which is related by its nature to the angels and to God, he forgets that by its union with the body it is also of the world of sense.

3. The *advantage* of Plato's method is its metaphysical tendency. At its root is an effort towards the unification of

---

[1] The theory will be explained in the chapter on Aristotle; see n. 84.

things, a desire to reduce the imperfect to the perfect, the
variable to the immutable, plurality to unity. It contains
implicitly a most suggestive formula of the principle of causality.
Its most valuable application will be studied in connection
with Plato's doctrine on God, the supreme cause of the material
world, and we shall then give a final appreciation of it.

III. INTER-RELATION OF FORMS.

A) The Doctrine of Participation.

47. Plato was satisfied that the application of the intuitive
method to the contemplation of the intelligible world could
furnish an explanation of the entire scope of human knowledge.
Now knowledge is not a mere juxtaposition of concepts, but
a series of predications, taking the form of absolute assertions
or negations, which correspond to the necessary and permanent
agreements or opposition that exist between the Forms.
So Plato was led to formulate the principle of the PARTICI-
PATION of Forms which may read thus :

" *Each Form is essentially compatible or incompatible with
certain other Forms.* " For instance the Form of snow is by its
essence compatible with the Form of whiteness, and incompatible with the Form of heat.

Consequently one must admit a *hierarchy* in the ideal world.
Forms are not to be conceived as homogeneous atoms. The
simplest among them are compatible with the greatest number
of others; they appear as summits whence the light of
truth is shed on a more extensive group of inferior Ideas.
Complexity, on the other hand, induces restriction. The
various Forms, it is seen, are unified in a compact pyramidal
construction built up of genera and species.

These related participations are revealed to us by the simple
application of the intuitive method in an analysis of the
content of each Form, with constant reference to the natural
modalities of its essence, and following a gradual process which
at each step adds a specific difference to the genus previously
discovered [1].

---

[1] This is *division*, the final phase of the Platonic method, in which Aristotle
saw a prefigure of the syllogism. (Prior Analyt., I, 31.)

Plato naturally made no attempt to determine the participations affecting each Form : that would have meant covering in detail every branch of knowledge. He gave a solid foundation to the principle involved, judging that a well conducted analysis of one single Form would lead to the discovery of all the others. He moreover set out to define the nature of " participation " — no easy task for the realist that he was. He had to maintain the essential and clear distinction of one Form from another, and at the same time, explain the close relationship between them as asserted in scientific propositions. It was this necessity that produced the theory of higher genera.

B) The Problem Solved by the Theory of the Five Genera.

48. To show how in the world of forms there can be unification without confusion Plato observes that they all share in being and in non-being.

1. **All Forms are participations of being.** Every reality is either in motion or at rest : MOVEMENT and STILLNESS are two of the higher Forms of which all the others participate. But higher still is the Form of BEING, distinct from the two previously mentioned, since reality is neutral with regard to both of them, and at the same time source of what is real in them. Thus through the medium of MOVEMENT and STILLNESS all Forms participate of Being.

2. **All Forms participate of non-being.** Among the highest genera are also the Forms of SAMENESS and DIFFERENCE, and in these too all the others participate. Plato proves this by the same process. Movement is of necessity the *same* as itself and *different* from non-movement; Stillness also is the *same* as itself and *different* from non-stillness. Both movement and stillness, and through their medium all other Forms, participate, therefore, in the Ideas of Sameness and Difference.

Now the Form of Difference is equivalent to that of non-being, (taken not in an absolute, but in a relative sense) which is in Plato's mind a positive reality, namely that which is not included in the definite quantity of being contained in each Form.

Every Form, then, is a participation of Being (with regard to what agrees with it) and of non-Being (with regard to what is different from it.) And this double current, positive and negative, which runs through the whole Form-peopled universe explains how the Forms themselves can inter-participate without losing their unity or their distinction. Participation is a necessary and essential bond, linking together in the manner of the letters of the alphabet certain Forms which are affected by mutual attraction or by repulsion. It is more than that; it might be defined as : " *an immanent tendency, a kind of vital urge towards sameness* (distinction being safeguarded) *in such a way that Forms are susceptible of unification in plurality* ".

At this point Plato places an important *corollary :* the reality of non-being accounts for the possibility of error, by virtue of which one Form is said to include another (non-being) when in fact it excludes it. If non-being had no existence, false statements would be impossible because they would be without an object; it would no longer be possible to define the Sophist, who applies his skill to the presentation of error in the form of truth [1].

C) The Idea of the Good, Ultimate Explanation of Things.

49. What explains this tendency towards sameness? Plato finds the answer in the influence of the supremely transcendent, all dominating Form of *Good*.

" The Form of Good ", says Plato, " is the source of the existence and of the essence of all the other Forms ". The meaning is apparently as follows : if Being exists, and if all other Forms become developments of it by unfolding the content of its non-being, the reason is that in this way the fulness of the Good is manifested.

It follows that the Good is in the ideal world the supreme source of knowability, the ultimate *raison d'être* and the primary cause of the other Forms. In a well-known comparison it is called the " *Light of the intelligible universe* ", the only light in which each ideal essence is clearly seen.

The Form of Good, writes Plato, is " something much superior in power and dignity to the common Form ". Since Good is the universal intelligible, source of all individual intelligibles, it is itself transcendent of all intelligibility. As ultimate principle of explanation it cannot be itself completely

---

[1] The *Sophistes* develops this theme. This effort to explain error by attributing reality to non-being is another consequence of Plato's exaggerated realism; it has no place in the theory of abstraction.

explained; it is not easily discovered and is almost as much the term of an assumption as an object of knowledge [1].

In its deeper significance, Plato's idea seems to be that the Form of Good is in an order of its own and that it alone excludes all non-being and all limitation. He is here the faithful disciple of Socrates for whom the main problem was to discover *what good leads to true happiness*. Having found the Ideal world Plato has the solution: it is the *absolute Good*, which is self-contained and distinct from all the rest, but which is also the source of all reality, of all virtue and of all happiness. It is identified in us, as Socrates taught, with wisdom or perfect knowledge.

50. The whole of Plato's metaphysical doctrine is vitiated by his realism which brings him, against reason, to explain the purely logical properties of our concepts by the properties of real things. The mistake is patent in the case of the predication in which concepts are identified while remaining distinct, because they connote the same object (materially) under two different aspects (formally). Such an identification is impossible if one admits in the Platonic sense the individuality of Forms. Moreover, one is never justified in deducing real relations between things from the simple analysis of logical relations that exist between ideas.

On the other hand this conception of an ideal universe hierarchically ordered and unified in the Form of the Good is not without majesty and opens the way for Augustinian Exemplarism. Its metaphysical value will be seen better in connection with Plato's theodicy.

It seems that here we have a rudimentary outline of the two most important doctrines of the Peripatetics:

1. The notion of a *relative non-being* which is real and which affects even pure essences, prepares the way for the idea of *potentiality* as principle of limitation and of plurality. Its first application in Thomism is the real distinction in created things between essence and existence, in order to explain the contingency and the specific plurality of those same things.

2. The supremacy given to the idea of Good is a step towards the notion of pure perfection expressed in a *analogous concept*. For Plato, it should be observed, all other Forms, including being, involve non-being and retain their univocal character.

But the ideal world is not only the object of knowledge: it is also the ultimate explanation of the material world and of human life.

---

[1] *Repub.* Book VI, towards the end, and Book VII, Ch. IV.

ARTICLE II. — THE WORLD OF THE SENSES.
DOMAIN OF OPINION.

51. We may first note what Plato asserts of the value of his theories about the world of the senses. " That which is fixed and immutable ", he says, " can suppose only fixed and immutable reasoning... As to that which is the copy of the immutable reality, it behooves us to speak of it in terms of probability and analogy... Provided that my words have at least the probability to be found in those of others, we shall to be satisfied with them... in such matters we can but restrict ourselves to the language of probability " or to considerations of a mythical nature [1].

The knowledge we can obtain of sensible phenomena is, then, inferior to science, but superior to mere conjecture; we call it *true opinion*. It has a double origin:

1) First of all, in *tradition* we hear echoes of what was known by men nearer than we are to the world of Ideas. They come to us in the myths, fabled histories compiled by poets and priests.

2) Then there is *science*, which sheds on the material world the luminous rays that fall from the world of Forms.

Although the function of science is not always clearly defined, its consistent aim is purification and unification. The scientist borrows from tradition those doctrines alone which have some elucidatory value and which lend themselves to incorporation into a systematic whole.

It would be wrong to neglect this second aspect of Platonism. The Master deemed it an essential complement of the first, since it solves the problem which, for a disciple of Socrates, is fundamental : the moral problem. Historically, it foreshadows the main divisions of Aristotle's philosophy. It offers a tentative explanation of the universality of things, first of all of the world in general, with reference to its various causes (general physics) and particularly to the primary cause,

---

[1] See the beginning of Timaeus's speech, in the Dialogue of the same name, where Plato treats of physics and physiology.

God (theodicy); secondly, of the human soul, the highest reality in the world, considered in itself, its nature and its faculties (psychology), or in the organization of the individual and social life (ethics).

Hence four parts in this second section :

I.   General Physics.   III. Psychology.

II. Theodicy.   IV.   Ethics.

I. GENERAL PHYSICS.

General physics has to deal with the nature of corporal substances. Material things, subject as they are to constant change, presuppose a twofold principle : an *infinite*, that is to say, an *indeterminate principle;* and a *finite principle*, to explain determination. The order in the world is produced by the union of these two.

A) The Principle of Indetermination: Matter.

52. The matter or receptacle τόπος, is a primary element, completely indeterminate, and in that sense *infinite*. Of itself therefore, it is empty of all good, of all order, of perfection and of stability. It is a principle " extremely hard to understand ".

Plato's *proof* of its existence is the classical one. The substance of his argument in the *Timaeus* is as follows : all bodies, it is observed, are the centers of radical and continuous changes and they possess no stability of nature or of quality. Now change is only possible if we suppose a substratum denuded of the transitory states which affect it and which are manifested by it. So it is necessary to admit the existence of a universal subject, having no particular form but capable of receiving all forms.

This is already the almost non-existent, but still real, element known by Aristotle as *pure potentiality;* Plato's conception of it implies already its twofold and essential function : it is the principle of corruption in material bodies, and effects an infinite plurality of those perfections which are realized fully in the immutable unity of the Forms.

Plato, however, fails to reach total precision in the metaphysical concept of pure potentiality and his description of matter is in terms of poetry. He sees it as the universal container of Forms, the mirror of Ideas, the mother and the nurse of all that is born and dies. As the inexhaustible source of movement, it has life and animation, but its soul acts aimlessly and without discretion. When uncontrolled, its progress is blind and its end, chaos.

B) The Principle of Determination: the Participated Form.

53. A fact of experience no less striking than that of mutation is the *order* and beauty of the cosmos. This, too, must have its explanation. There must exist some force capable of controlling movement, in order to bring about the conditions favorable to the well-being of each reality (immanent finality) and to the well-being of the universe (extrinsic finality). As opposed to matter, source of aimless movement, this *finite* principle is the origin of determination and of harmony; it consists in a *participated modality of the Forms*.

The nature of this participation is to be explained with reference to the *exemplary cause*. The Forms, although they transcend sensible phenomena, are in a way inherent in them, as the exemplary cause is inherent in the production of which it was the model.

On this point, however, Plato is not very deep. He describes in imaginative terms the infusion of order and goodness into the material world by means of a reflected gleam from the world of Forms. Inspired by this double influence, nature in its entirety vibrates like a living lyre in an endless hymn of praise to the magnificence of the supreme Good. Or again he compares the student of the material world to a prisoner chained up in a cave. On the wall of the cave he sees the moving shadows of living beings who pass behind him in the open sunlight [1]. The metaphors are striking, but they are not equivalent to an explanation.

C) Order in the World.

54. The world manifests at the same time unity and diversity.

1. *Its Unity*. Its author wished to make it as perfect as possible and chose therefore a single prototype. This was the

---

[1] The famous Cave simile will be found in *Repub*. Ch. I-III.

Form of the Living, since in its generality the world is animated by a soul. Its *shape* is that of the *sphere*, considered the most beautiful by the ancients, and the most suitably adapted to this great living thing which has to include in its universal activity the lives of all individual beings. Consequently the world is *limited;* nor can it move from place to place since there is no place outside itself; it moves only to rotate on its own axis.

2. *Its diversity.* This unity is compatible with the most harmonious diversity, and to stress this, Plato describes the world in terms borrowed from the astronomers and scientists of his time. His universe is composed of eight concentric spheres. The outermost one carries the stationary stars, while the planets are distributed over the intermediary spheres. The central sphere is the world itself " turning on the axis of the world ". It alone is motionless. The variety found among earthly bodies is assured by combinations of the four elements, water, earth, air and fire. These in turn are constituted by triangles forming in the midst of matter various geometrical figures. In the heavenly bodies the fiery element is almost the sole constituent; hence that beauty which makes of them " as it were a luminous coronal for our earth ".

II. THEODICY.

A) Proofs of the Existence of God.

55. Plato's conception of the Divinity, mostly given in the form of myths, is never very clear, and has been diversely interpreted. We shall consider first the two main arguments taken one from the *Timaeus*, and the other from the *Laws*. From these we shall gather the true meaning of Plato's theory.

1. **Proof taken from the order in the world: God is the Demiurge.** With Anaxagoras and Socrates, Plato realizes that the order everywhere visible must be attributed to a supreme Intelligence, responsible for the cosmic organism. A partial explanation has already been found in the existence of matter and of the world of Forms. Both these are eternal according to Plato's view; there can be no question of creation. But the very fact that matter participates of the beauty of the Form supposes the agency of a third principle. A block of marble cannot take the form of an ideal model without the action of a sculptor; nor will every sculptor produce the desired result: he must be intelligent, and he must know his art. In the same way, we must admit the existence of a supremely intelligent and eminently artistic mind who, having contemplated the Forms, may communicate their impression to earthly matter. Such is the Demiurge.

To describe this divine action, Plato has again recourse to the Myths. He pictures for us the Demiurge proceeding from the contemplation of the Ideal world to the task of modelling the universe upon it. First of all, from a perfectly harmonious combination of the Forms of Sameness and Difference God fashions a Soul for the world. " A kingly soul, ruled by a kingly mind who organized, and who governs all things ", as it was said before. The interpretation of this allegory will perhaps be made clear by the second proof which reads more didactically.

2. **Proof by movement: God is the royal Soul.** Plato leads off from the evidence of regulated movement in the world, an example of which he finds in the circular motion of the heavenly bodies. The progress of the spheres is by its uniformity and its stability a very image of the intelligence.

Now all movement postulates a cause; it must be generated by a preexisting agent. Both earthly and heavenly bodies can act as agents for one another. But there obviously cannot be an endless series of similar agents. There must exist a primary motor, source of all movement.

Plato distinguishes between the *bodily* agent and the *soul*. The former " is of itself motionless and its movement must come from another source "; the soul " has in itself the principle of its own movement and can therefore communicate it without previously receiving it ". The soul is then anterior, and superior, to the body it animates.

Plato concludes that the first motor, source of all movement, is a universal soul, animating the whole world. But if an ordinary movement is accounted for by an ordinary soul, the splendid and all embracing order of the Cosmos supposes a wise soul, gifted with a supreme and truly royal intelligence.

3. **Conlusion: The Platonic God.** Some historians, following Zeller, identify the Platonic God with the Form of Good, the highest and the most worthy to represent Him. Others see him in the Form of Thought (Logos) as the function of Demiurge seems to require it. Others find God in the intelligible universe taken as a whole, to which the term " divine " is often applied in the Dialogues. But " intelligible " implies " immutable ", and Plato asserts that there is in God a self-produced psychological movement. Moreover, the Demiurge appears to be clearly distinct from his work and his model,

from the Forms and from the world. Finally, the proof by movement leads to the identification of God with the Demiurge and the Soul of the world. Such was, it seems, Plato's own view.

God is thus supreme in our world; but He is inferior to the world of Forms on which He depends as on his model. With regard to material perfections his position is that of intermediary, of a directly efficient cause; He might even be called the formal cause. This notion, which shocks the Christian mind accustomed to regard God as the *Supreme Being*, was quite acceptable to the pagan in whose mind Jupiter, the sovereign deity, was subject to Destiny. The blind power of Fate is " rationalized " in Plato's substitute : the unchanging world of Forms. He could conveniently identify God with a royal Soul since he admitted only an accidental union between the soul and the body [1].

This theory, let us add, like all those in this section, has only the partial clarity of opinion and contains more of implied truth than of explicit precision. The Forms of Good, of Thought and of Soul are, according to Plato, various aspects of supreme perfection. The Ideas of which Good is the form, are all contained in Thought; the soul, in turn, is Thought's activity, modelling the world to the likeness of the Good and subjecting it to the law of the more perfect [2].

It remains true that of the things that Plato calls " divine ", the Demiurge or royal Soul is that which fulfills the best our notion of God.

B) God's Attributes.

56. They all spring from the function of the Demiurge in virtue of which God is related both to the ideal, and to the material world.

I. *In relation to the world of Forms* God's chief attribute is the fulness of WISDOM or PERFECT KNOWLEDGE. Since the Forms are the model of his work, He contemplates them unfailingly and thus participates especially in the Idea of Thought (Logos). He is, above all, Intelligence.

---

[1] See parag. 58, and DIES, *Autour de Platon*, II, p. 522-574.
[2] These three Forms, Good, Thought and Soul have been called the " Platonic Trinity " : its importance will be considerable among the Neo-Platonists. Cf. parag. 132.

However, the main object of his contemplation is the Form of Good, the highest of all Forms, unifying principle of reality and intelligibility in all the rest. It is, therefore, in the Form of Good that God participates the most fully. This explains his plenitude of PERFECTION and GOODNESS, together with his absolute and invulnerable BEATITUDE.

2. *In relation to the material world*, God's essential attribute is his PROVIDENCE in its twofold aspect of intelligence and will.

God's *knowledge* embraces not only the whole of the world of Forms but also the world of the senses in all its details, since it is He who builds it up from within and who untiringly organizes its parts.

Again, He looks on his work with a *benevolent* eye as upon the chief manifestation of that identity between science and virtue which for Socrates was the special mark of the sage. God, with His plenitude of knowledge proceeds infallibly according to the law of the more perfect and watches over small things and minute facts with a care that only neglect, laziness or ignorance could diminish; and those defects are totally incompatible with His sovereign perfection. Thus the Good, as the final cause of God's activity, unifies the changing diversity of the material world after having coordinated the unvarying multiplicity of the Forms. Good is, as Plato says, " the finest part of being, the cause of all that is good and beautiful; the cause of truth and of intelligence in the unseen world, of light and of its source, the planet, in the visible universe " [1]. Through its agency not only does being shed its fulness on other Forms, but the Forms themselves join with matter in order to manifest their perfection in an almost infinite multiplicity of participations, and to impart some measure of happiness to the chaotic realm of the purely durational. The losses incurred through evil or imperfection are the result of resistance on the part of matter. The latter element, however, accounts for the many ways in which the Forms are expressed; this pertains to the more perfect and gives the final victory to the Good.

It is through the same influence that God shows forth His OMNIPOTENCE in the many activities of His providence, and His IMMUTABLE JUSTICE and ABSOLUTE SANCTITY in the impossibility in which He finds himself of acting otherwise

---

[1] *Repub.* Book VII, Ch. IV.

than for the best. Thus neither sacrifices nor prayers nor offerings can alter His decrees.

3. Finally, God is ONE, since He is the royal Soul of a world which, as we have seen, is also one. Plato, however, accepts the old axiom that " the whole world is full of gods ", and while openly rejecting the immorality and the absurdities of mythology, he sees no reason to deny that divine influences in the world are due to certain powers, or secondary gods, who faithfully execute the will of the supreme God. Their nature is left undefined, and they appear as emanations of the universal Soul, or as the wise souls of the various spheres of the world. On this point Plato refers generally to tradition and the ancient revelations.

C) Appreciation of the Platonic Theodicy.

57. Plato's theology leads to a metaphysical estimate of the theory of Forms. His inquiry into the external cause of the universe has the breadth of a metaphysical problem : over and above the efficient cause (the Demiurge), he discovers an exemplary cause (the Ideal world) and a final cause (the Form of Good). Here again, as in the proof of the existence of the Forms, he glimpses the truly metaphysical formula of the principle of causality, strongly impressed as he was by the necessity of always accounting for the imperfection of plurality by the perfection of unity. This gives to his theodicy a comprehensiveness which rendered it susceptible of an exceptionally facile adaptation to the rational solution of Catholic doctrine.

Here again, it must be said, Plato's genius achieves rather a fertile suggestion than a definite thesis. His teaching is incomplete on three essential points :

i. **On the connections between cause and effect.** Plato fails to distinguish clearly the *efficient* cause, which perfects and disposes from without, from the *formal* cause, which perfects and disposes by animating from within. Finding that there is always contact between the efficient cause and its effect, he is chiefly impressed by the vision of a point to point touch and by the notion of formal contact such as we experience between our body and the soul that animates it [1]. The true conception would be that of a causal contact, purely intelligible, implying no relation of mutual dependence, but merely a true dependence on the side of the effect only,

---

[1] On this point Plato's thought is still obscure.

the cause giving of its fulness without suffering any loss. Thus the perfect being, without undergoing any change, explains by the fact of its own perfection the appearance and the persistence of another being, limited and variable, which shares its perfection.

This profound theory of St. Augustine and St. Thomas is in reality that of *creative causality*, of which the pagans had no inkling [1]. (Plato, for instance, conceives matter as anterior to God's action which merely organizes it.) One might see a foreshadowing of this creative causality in the theory of the material world as a participation of the world of Forms. This would suppose that the Forms were not only prototypes but sources of reality and veritable efficient causes. In fact, there is here another deficiency in Plato's thought.

2. **On the nature of the perfect type of efficient cause :** Plato sees quite clearly the great principle that " every perfection received in a restricted form (in various degrees or allied to its contrary) supposes the existence of the same perfection in a pure and unlimited state which will be the origin and model of the limited participations "; but he applies it indiscriminately to every perfection found in material beings : not merely to their beauty, their unity, their life, etc., but even to their whiteness, their smallness, to geometrical figures, and to essences like humanity, animality, etc.

Now there are two kinds of perfections :

a) *pure perfections*, expressed by *analogous* concepts which of themselves, as regards their essential connotation, imply no restriction. *Life* is of this class.

b) *non-pure perfections*, expressed by *univocal* concepts which by their very nature imply restrictions. Such is *humanity*. Those of the second class obviously cannot without contradiction be realized *ad infinitum ;* hence in Plato's Ideal world there can be no univocal Forms. Moreover, the only pure subsistent perfections remaining have in themselves everything perfect already contained in limited perfections, and are therefore adequately efficient causes of everything.

There remains a third weakness in Plato's doctrine :

3. **On the supereminent simplicity of divine or infinite perfection.** Plato's synthesis of the Ideal world in the Form of Good allows for a real distinction between the Forms of pure perfections. If one Form or perfection excludes the others because it is in itself intelligible, then, thinks Plato, it must be distinct from them. Every pure perfection, having its own intelligibility, has also its own reality and individual existence.

Here again we are faced with exaggerated realism in an erroneous application to things of what pertains only to concepts. The properties of a perfection (those, for instance, of life and being)

---

[1] Plotinus, however, will come near to it. See n. 124.

considered as an intelligible object must be distinguished from those of the same perfection considered as a reality. In the abstract realm of thought every pure perfection does indeed imply a definition which differentiates it from others; the knowledge of life is one thing, that of goodness is another. But in reality each perfection realized in itself *ad infinitum* contains, and must contain, the perfection of all the others. Thus Life *in se* is necessarily identified with Goodness *in se*, and so on. In this way all pure subsistent perfections are naturally absorbed in the simplicity of the *Ipsum esse subsistens* of which they are the various attributes. Only in thought are they distinct one from another [1].

Thus purged of its imperfections, the teaching of him whom tradition has named the *Divine Plato* leads up directly to the true God, and infers a perfect Cause, distinct from the world : an Intelligence, *one* in its simplicity, comprising in its perfection the whole intelligible world, but in a transcendent manner and without real distinction; and, according to this exemplar, manifesting its infinite goodness by the creation of the material world.

This view of Platonism is possible only with reference to the interpretation *secundum rei veritatem* proposed by St Augustine and St. Thomas.

III. Psychology.

58. Man is body and soul. The body is made up of the four elements, bound so strongly together that the separate principles are fused into a consistent synthesis.

The human soul is of two parts. The mortal element is the work of the secondary gods; the other emanates from the universal soul and is spiritual. Through the spiritual element, called *Nous,* a sort of basic identity is established between God and man. But Plato is somewhat obscure on this point, and when speaking of the human faculties appears at times to admit three distinct souls. These, however, are probably to be taken not as three substances but as different operations of the same principle.

---

[1] Such a distinction, being based on the eminent wealth of divine perfection which, in its simplicity, is equivalent to all our perfections, is called *virtual* and because this distinction is less complete between the divine attributes than between the metaphysical degrees of the various natures (e. g. between man's animality and his rationality) it is also termed *minor.*

A) The Nature of the Soul.

Plato's teaching may be summed up thus:

The soul is a complete spiritual substance, not merely immortal, but eternal, whose union with the body is accidental.

Plato reaches this conclusion from a study of the intimate relations that link the soul to the world of the Forms. From this point of view he considers the soul before, during, and after its union with the body and formulates three conclusions: pre-existence, accidental union, immortality.

1. **Pre-existence of the soul.** The theory of reminiscence, typically Platonic, proves it, and the transcendent nature of the Forms demands it. The Forms are present in us at birth, and since the possibility of a creative agency is not contemplated, the soul must have acquired them in an anterior life.

The nature of this former life is explained in mythical terms. Plato describes the multitude of souls, at the heels of the gods, seeking like them to look upon the Ideal world; as a penalty for certain evil deeds, they are hurled down on earth and imprisoned in bodies.

2. **Accidental union of the soul to the body.** This is a simple corollary of the previous conclusion. By itself the soul has the appearance of a complete substance destined to live independently of the body; there can be no question of a single nature constituted by an *essential union* of matter and form. What we have here is rather an *accidental union* of two individual natures [1], essentially distinct, and united only by secondary qualities.

The mutual influence resulting from this union is on the whole harmful. The body may be the source of many evils for the soul : its despotic claims and corrupting allurements hinder the soul in the pursuit of wisdom. The soul, in turn, is a potential cause of trouble for the body : " much study is a weariness to the flesh ". Moreover — and this is again in favor of a merely accidental union — the body is of no use to the soul in its own sphere of activity, that is, in the acquisition of knowledge, since the purely intuitive method is the only one

---

[1] Plato says nothing of the body's aptitude for a separate existence. From his theory of matter the body would appear to be merely a period in the flow of matter, a compound stabilized for a moment by the influence of the soul.

adapted to transcendent Ideas.   For this reason the sage finds in death his deliverance.

3.   **Immortality of the soul.**   The idea is complementary to that of pre-existence.   Plato however observes that there is no certain connection between the two; he gives three main arguments to prove the soul's immortality : [1]

First argument : Participation, in a general way, in Ideal reality.   Among the attributes of the Forms are, first of all, invisibility with regard to the senses, and pure intelligibility. Then come simplicity and immutability which are opposed to corruption and postulate *immortality ;* and finally superiority and domination over material things by which the latter are directed towards order and well-being.

Now it is a fact that our soul has some similarity with the Forms and that it possesses most of their properties.   Through contemplation, it enters into direct contact with them and shares their intelligibility.   The soul is also invisible to the senses and is mistress over the body.

Since the properties of the Ideal world form an indissoluble unity, we must conclude that the soul also has in participated form the simplicity and the immortality of the Ideal world.

Second argument : Participation, in a special way, in the Form of life.   It has been seen [2] that there are definite relations between the Forms : each " immutable essence " excludes its opposite; each one also includes certain other " essences ", and consequently excludes their opposites.   Thus the Form of *Three,* (the *Triad,* as Plato calls it) including the Form of *Oddness,* must exclude that of *Evenness.*   Again, the Form of Snow includes the Form of Cold, and must therefore exclude that of Heat.

Now the soul participates essentially and intimately in the Form of Life; the one, as it were, defines the other.   A living being is defined as " that which moves itself " : and it is of the nature of our soul to move ceaselessly, not, as in the case of

---

[1] In the *Phaedo* he begins with a few probable arguments such as that founded on the *theory of contrary states :* all things change according to the law of alternating opposites; death follows life; therefore the life of the soul follows the death of the body. See *Phaedo,* Ch. XVI, in LIVINGSTONE's *Portrait of Socrates,* p. 110.

[2] Cf. n. 47.

the body, by changing its form, but with a psychological motion which is compatible with permanence in being.

If, then, death is opposed to life, the soul must necessarily and completely exclude all participation in death. The soul is eternally incorruptible, as is the Form of Life itself.

Third argument : Moral necessity. The present life does not offer sufficient scope either for the retribution of each one according to his merit or his guilt, or above all for satisfying the deeply-rooted aspirations of the soul towards happiness, that is towards the contemplation of pure Form in which happiness has its source. The soul must, therefore, survive in order that the demands of justice and the aspirations of nature be satisfied.

59. Taken as they are, these proofs have the same value as the theory on which they are based. But, with an eye to the substantial unity of man, they may be adapted to a more inductive scheme of psychology. Then, with their appeal to the spiritual nature of our higher operations, they are essentially sufficient as scientific proofs of the subsistence and the immortality of the soul. In this respect Plato was correct in attributing a spiritual character especially to the *Nous*. For the rest, in his view, all these arguments, founded as they are on opinion, engender not knowledge, but merely faith. Immortality, particularly for what concerns the circumstances of the future life remains " a glorious venture " [1].

B) The Faculties of the Soul.

60. Plato sees in the soul three parts, or three functional groups, each having *a*) a knowledge, and *b*) a corresponding appetence.

I.   **The lower group** comprises first of all *sensation* ($A''\sigma\theta\eta\sigma\iota\varsigma$). Granted that the union of the soul with the body is accidental, sensation is necessarily the act of the soul alone : the body is, in its freer elements (organs), the seat of purely mechanical phenomena : additions, subtractions, pressures, frictions, etc.; each impression received is transmitted to the soul, the seat of the distinctive representation that follows. The inter-dependence of these phenomena is not clearly defined by Plato;

---

[1] The *Phaedo*, Ch. LXIII. These doubts are chiefly apparent in the long mythical description of the dwelling-place of souls in ch. LVII-LXII. Plato remains none the less convinced of the soul's immortality as far as conviction appears to him possible in this matter.

his exaggeratedly spiritual view made it impossible for him to understand the link between the physical and the psychical orders.

Sensation gives birth to *desire* (ἐπιθυμία) which calls for the satisfaction of the senses: these satisfactions are as varied in their objects and in their intensity as formless matter, and elude classification.

2. **The middle group** or intermediary region is guided by *opinion* (δόξα) which, though not immune from error, can in practice take the place of knowledge in the realization of virtue or of good government.

To opinion, in the appetitive order, corresponds *spirit* (θυμός) a spontaneous love of everything beautiful and good, and an instinctive horror of what is ugly and evil in the material world.   This sense of honor is the natural ally of reason in the pursuit of good and the conquering of obstacles.   It is, however, prone to error and must be controlled by the superior soul.

3. **The immortal group** (Νοῦς) is the seat of truly scientific knowledge acquired by the last two degrees of the method, and above all by *wisdom* (σοφία).

The corresponding appetitive faculty is the *will* (βουλή). Plato asserts that the will is necessarily consistent with knowledge, and since *knowledge* or *wisdom* can be concerned only with being and good, it is impossible that the will as such should tend to evil.   In this sense, " No one sins willingly " : Οὐδεὶς ἑκὼν ἁμαρτάνει.

Plato admits the existence of freedom but attempts no rational explanation of it such as we shall find in Aristotle. Indeed, the whole of this classification, based as it is on experience, anticipates the Peripatetic psychology; but, like the rest of Plato's theories on opinion, it has need of adjustment.

IV. ETHICS.

61. In Plato's view, moral science is the most important part, the ultimate aim of his whole system.   Following the line traced by Socrates, he seeks in philosophy the secret of man's happiness.   With the undeviating logic of a mind that knows no inconsistency and shirks no conclusion, he bases his morality on his metaphysics and by a strictly *a priori* process infers the principles of right conduct from the theory of Forms. The way to ensure man's happiness, he thinks, is to enable the Form of Good to pour out on our human nature the fullest possible share of its riches. Hence the theories 1) of happiness; 2) of the virtues; 3) of obligation; 4) of the State; 5) of future sanctions.

A) Happiness.

Happiness is the supreme aim of life; as that which is desired for itself and in function of which everything else is desired, it serves as motive power for all activity.

1. Plato refuses to *identify happiness with pleasure* or the satisfaction of the senses. The Sophists had tried to justify the popular view that man should yield to nature; that natural justice is in favor of the domination of the strongest; that happiness lies in success and that, therefore, man should aim at an ever greater satisfaction of ever increasing desires.

Plato shows on the contrary that happiness cannot come from pleasure, which is unstable, impure and incomplete. Always restricted to the present, pleasure is merely the cessation of a need; the pain which is revealed in the yearning is constantly renewed with greater intensity. Moreover, pleasure disturbs the reason and thus, far from giving us freedom and rest, it puts us at the mercy of things and of events. Finally, the inevitable accompaniments of pleasure are illness and death.

2. Nor is happiness to be found in knowledge alone without pleasure. Had feeling no part in it, its lack of interest would leave us indifferent.

3. Happiness is, then, the result of the *development of all the pleasures* that attend on the three degrees of knowledge, realized in *harmonious subordination according to their relative dignity*. The lower pleasures are acceptable in so far as they are necessary for the maintenance of life and the conservation of the species, as are in like manner the pleasures of the heart, less imperfect and less despotic; both, however, should be controlled by the *Nous*. But the chief element of happiness consists of the pleasures to be found in the arts, in opinion or in the intelligence, and above all in the sovereign science of the Forms. Here is no danger of excess or of adulteration; these may be allowed to flow freely from their divine source.

In this way does the Form of the Good perfect all the elements of our nature and manifest more completely its fulness. For Plato, then, as for Socrates, the essential constituent of happiness is wisdom, the necessary regulator of the other pleasures and a possible substitute for them all. Wisdom unites us to the immutable Forms, and in particular to that of the Good, the compound of all the Forms. Thus are satisfied all our desires in this life and in the next. *True happiness is in the unending enjoyment of Good.*

B) **Virtue.**

62. In general terms, virtue is a disposition which induces man to act in conformity with his nature and with the universal order of things. Plato distinguishes two kinds of virtue:

1. **Perfect virtue,** which is the mark of the spiritual soul. This is nothing else but wisdom, or the science of regulated pleasures in which true happiness dwells. It is in this higher order that we find the full expression of the Socratic dictum : " Knowledge is one with virtue ". Perfect virtue, therefore, is the term of dialectic after the previous degrees of the method have been mastered; a whole sequence of persistent efforts are necessary before the soul becomes independent of matter and is able to rise to the contemplation of the ultimate Good. But virtue establishes between the soul of the man of wisdom and the Form of Good a connate quality which notably sharpens the former's keenness for discerning as by instinct what is in practice good from what is evil.

2. **Common virtue** also aims at a rational ordering of conduct, but is based on *true opinion* (ὀρθὴ δόξα) instead of on knowledge. Its realm of action is the inferior soul and is made up of three elements:

a) The heart is guided by *fortitude* which teaches man to suffer or to face danger when there is necessity.

b) Concupiscence is moderated by *temperance* which regulates the necessary use of bodily pleasures.

c) Finally, there is *justice,* of which the unifying action ensures functional agreement and safeguards the respective rights of the several parts of the soul.

This common virtue is found in the numerous class of men who fail to raise themselves to the contemplation of the Forms.

Here there is no longer identity between knowledge and virtue; instruction is no longer a sufficient guide: such a virtue must be acquired by practice, by education and by the repetition of virtuous acts. This is an important amendment of the Socratic paradox.

There still remains to explain the diversity of results. Plato appeals to the notion of a *divine germ*. A man, he says, has at birth certain predispositions, and all have not the same aptitude for the acquisition of virtue. Some are content with temperance; others cultivate fortitude, while a very small number aim at perfect virtue. Socrates had the noble but impossible ambition of converting all his fellow citizens: Plato opens an Academy for the chosen souls who have in them the divine germ of wisdom.

C) **Obligation.**

63. The human ideal as presented by Plato is no doubt a most desirable one. But it is more than a question of choice for men; it is in the nature of a veritable *imperative*.

 1. To begin with, the moral obligation has an immediate reason in the connection between man's actions and his, or his neighbor's, happiness. Each one has the right to seek his own happiness, and to use for that what help the community can give: correlatively, others have the *duty*, the obligation, to respect each man's rights and to obey the laws which protect them.

 2. There exists, besides, another more remote but equally effective reason for being good: this is God's will, which, under the influence of Good, desires that the greatest possible happiness be diffused in the world. It is, therefore, impious to violate the moral law which is a condition of happiness.

Plato's teaching on this point is doubly defective. First of all he has no notion of a Creator whose will is the source of moral rectitude. The Demiurge is swayed by the Form of Good, and what ultimately explains all obligation is the attraction of the Good, expressed in the all important axiom: " Like draws like ". Sin, for Plato, is against the law of nature more than against the law of God [1]. Moreover, when the application is made to the sage in the Platonic sense (the perfectly virtuous man), we come up against the unacceptable theory of a will infallibly and necessarily influenced for good by knowledge: this would jeopardize liberty and undermine the very notion of obligation.

---

[1] On this point, see E. GILSON, *The Spirit of Mediaeval Philosophy*, N. Y., 1936, p. 333.

D) **The State.**

64. The State, or Republic [1], is an organized society of men. Society exists by right of nature, according to Plato, since it is necessary if man is to reach his aim, which is happiness. Left to himself, man would be incapable of satisfying his most elementary needs; and, furthermore, an authority is required to ensure that all submit to the demands of order and observe the proper hierarchy of pleasures.

In the *Republic,* Plato discusses deductively the social conditions best calculated to safeguard the supremacy of Good with a maximum of order and justice. The system he adopts might be called *rational communism,* based as it is, not on the number and equality of citizens, but on the varied capacities of each one. Thus, although Plato sometimes reaches the same conclusions as the Marxist or the Bolshevist, the principle of this theory is totally different from theirs.

1. **Social classes.** The theory of the *germ* is at the root of Platonic class distinction. The citizens are placed in three divisions according to their capacities, which correspond to the three chief needs of society; each class has its peculiar and independent function to fulfill :

a) The *laborers* or *artisans* provide for the community's subsistence, have no political rights, and aim at no higher virtue than temperance.

b) The *soldiers* protect the State and need the virtue of fortitude : they constitute a permanent army, always on active service. They live on their pay and can claim neither wealth, property, nor right of government.

c) The *leaders* or *archontes,* who govern the State, must attain wisdom. The whole and absolute power of legislation and administration is in their hands.

Justice intervenes, finally, to guarantee the general harmony of things by urging each one to busy himself exclusively with his own occupation. A *proportional equality* is established among the members of the State — it is the only rational one — and each one is given rights in proportion to his worth, and privileges according to his merits, his virtue and his education.

d) The *slaves* are not counted as a regular class. From a natural point of view, their position is a *false* one. They are not all morally

---

[1] The modern State with its millions of men living under the same political regime had no place in Plato's conceptions. He considered only the *cities* which he saw flourishing around him in Greece, where each town with its dependent territories constituted an independent state. He could even hope that some revolutionary movement would provide an opportunity for his *Republic* or his *Laws* to be adopted by one or other of these cities. He tried, but in vain, to have his constitutional ideas accepted by Dionysius, ruler of Syracuse (Sicily).

and intellectually inferior; and those who are have too often been reduced to their low standard as a result of the work and ill treatment which is their lot. Plato sees in slavery a constant menace and a necessary evil towards the diminution of which reason and justice will contribute. Freedmen, however, cannot be considered as citizens and must be submitted to a strict discipline, since long years of subjection have rendered them incapable of proper behavior when they have complete liberty.

2. **Education: the family.** To the State and to the philosophical *élite* who rule it, Plato attributes an exorbitant power over the citizens. A child belongs to the City much more than to its parents. According to his capacities, his *germ*, each individual is placed, by the State, in this or that social class. His whole education is directed by the State, whose aim is to realize the maximum of beauty and perfection in body and soul.

Instruction is obligatory and is to be given in public schools according to a curriculum laid down by the State. The cycle of learning is twofold : during the primary cycle the child studies music (oratory, poetry) gymnastic, (dancing, wrestling, military training) mathematics, astronomy, with an additional course on the existence of God, the eternity of the soul, and virtue. In the secondary or superior cycle, is taught dialectic, which leads to the science of Forms [1]. All, male and female alike, according to their capacities, must undertake these studies.

Moreover, in order to achieve the greatest possible unity among citizens, Plato rejects the family basis, proclaims a communal marriage system and demands that the State should regulate births. Thus the State is a veritable brotherhood [2]. Finally, a process of selection will be necessary for the greater good of the State : non-social elements will be eliminated by exile or death; the incurably infirm will be left to their fate; deformed infants will be secretly disposed of at birth.

3. **Government.** Plato condemns democracy as a form of government; he prefers an aristocracy, but does not reject the monarchy, provided the king be a philosopher and his power be controlled by the laws. Up to the age of fifty, the sage should practice the inferior virtues and steep himself in the science of Forms. After that he may take up the direction of affairs, for then he will be able to work with efficacy at making our world and our society as consimilar as possible to his ideal world.

The law is a rational guidance imposed by the State authority; its object is what is best for all, not merely for a few. It will be respected not so much for the penalties attached to it as for its reasonableness, upon which the legislator will insist when he promulgates it.

---

[1] Plato would have no poets in his State; their fictions are nothing more than the shadow of a shadow, since the material world is but the shadow of reality.

[2] It was chiefly the two higher classes, the soldiers and the leaders, who were affected by this communistic principle. See Dies, *Platon*, p. 164.

Such is the plan proposed in the Republic. It is a Utopian conception, the term of an intuitive process in the course of which Plato disregards several of the conditions to be taken into account in an estimate of what is truly good for human nature. Later experience brought Plato himself to consider it a divine ideal out of human reach. In the *Laws*, he foresees a State with the common virtue — corresponding to *opinion* — as the ruling factor. Marriage is restored, together with the family, as a society existing by right of nature.

E) Sanctions.

65. 1. Plato admits that *in this life* sanctions must be used to enforce the observance of the laws; he vindicates the beauty of punishment as a means of upholding justice. But the law is based primarily on *religion*. Sometimes the author considers piety towards the gods as a special virtue; in other passages it is included in justice. But he never separates ethics from religion; the former, he declares, has no meaning apart from the latter.

Plato puts a distinction between popular religion, that is, traditional polytheism with its whole ritual but purged of its dross, and the more refined religion of the sage. The philosopher understands the futility of offering God gifts and sacrifices. He knows that God's will infallibly aims at what is best according to the law of his nature, and that consequently impetratory prayer has no meaning. Obedience to, and contemplation of, the divinity: in this consists the whole religion of the enlightened. Hence their serene acceptance of pain and poverty, factors of the universal order of things. The sage lives with God in spirit as with a friend, shares thus in his perfection, and is made more and more like to him.

The ideal, like Socrates', is a magnificent one, but only to be realized with the grace of Jesus Christ.

2. It is in the sanctions of the *life to come*, punishment and reward, that the triumph of Good is achieved. Since " Like draws like ", the true philosopher leaves this life only to regain the world of the gods and of the Forms, where perfect happiness reigns. The rest are borne to the realm of the guilty and the imperfect whom they resemble. Later, when the Good permits it (that is, according to a myth, after a thousand years), they resume their process of evolution in the body of

a human being or of an animal, according to their own choice *(metempsychosis)*. The activity of the universe, thus made up of unceasing rebirths, is a great and constant effort towards the more perfect, towards happiness.

CONCLUSION. **66.** Plato manifests all the characteristics of the *metaphysician*, interested solely in pure perfections as such in their remotest causes, and of the *mystic* [1], seeking truth in a direct contact with the spiritual world of the beyond. This explains both his strength and his weakness:

HIS STRENGTH: He discovers or glimpses the most exalted truths concerning the supreme cause, *God-Providence*, the spirituality and immortality of the soul, the value of knowledge, and the connection between virtue and happiness.

HIS WEAKNESS also: He is inclined to ignore the limits of human reason and to neglect the study of the material world without which no organized knowledge is possible and which alone can lead, through analogy, to the evidence of God-Himself. His synthesis is, therefore, defective; in spite of all his efforts, Plato finds his doctrine constantly weakened by a *dualism* which affects the whole system: dualism of the material and the ideal worlds; of knowledge and opinion; of the Form of Good and the Demiurge; of the body and the soul; of the perfect and the democratic forms of virtue; of individual and social rights.

There remains to acknowledge the magnificence of Plato's work. Gifted with an admirable breadth of mind and an untiring solicitude for the greater good of mankind, he raised philosophical thought to hitherto unsuspected summits. His researches covered the whole field of human culture, practical as well as theoretical. And on this all-embracing philosophy a definite unity is stamped by the fundamental doctrine of the Forms on which everything is based.

Plato's influence could not fail to be considerable. Through the medium of Neo-Platonism, his inspiration reached St. Augustine and the great Augustinian current of medieval times. But before this he paved the way for Aristotle.

In Aristotle we shall find a knowledge of universal range, more human and more reliable, but less inspiring. St. Thomas, in a synthesis of what is best in these two glories of Hellenism, will replace on the Aristotelian edifice the crowning ornament of Plato's divine conceptions.

---

[1] The word is here taken in a general sense. See n. 120.

CHAPTER THREE.

ARISTOTLE (384-322).

BIBLIOGRAPHY.

1º **Works:** BEKKER, I., (ed.), *Aristotelis opera*, 2 vols., Berlin, 1835-70. — SMITH, J. A., and Ross, W. D., (eds.), *The works of Aristotle*, 12 vols., Oxford, 1928-52.

2º **Studies:** CHEVALIER, J., *La notion de nécessaire chez Aristote et ses prédécesseurs*, Paris, 1915. — CRESSON, A., *Aristote*, Paris, 1943. — DE CORTE, M., *La doctrine de l'intelligence chez Aristote*, Paris, 1934. — HAMELIN, O., *Le système d'Aristote*, Paris, 1920. — JAEGER, W., *Aristotle*, Oxford, 1934. — JOLIVET, R., *Essai sur les rapports entre la pensée grecque et la pensée chrétienne*, Paris, 1931. — MANSION, A., *Introduction à la physique aristotélicienne*, 2e éd., Paris, 1945. — MANSION, S., *Le jugement d'existence chez Aristote*, Paris, 1946. — MURE, G. R. G., *Aristotle*, London, 1932. — NUYENS, Fr., *L'évolution de la psychologie d'Aristote*, La Haye, 1948 — PIAT, C., *Aristote*, 2e ed., Paris, 1912. — RAVAISSON, F., *Essai sur la métaphysique d'Aristote*, 2 vols., Paris, 1913. — ROBIN, L., *Aristote*, Paris, 1944. — ROLLAND-GOSSELIN, M. D., *Aristote*, Paris, 1923. — Ross, W. D., *Aristotle*, 2nd ed., London, 1930. *Aristotle's physics*, Oxford, 1936. *Aristotle's metaphysics*, 2 vols., Oxford, 1924. — SENTROUL, C., *Kant et Aristote*, Paris, 1913. — TAYLOR, A. E., 2nd ed., London, 1943. — WERNER, C., *Aristote et l'idéalisme platonicien*, Paris, 1910. — ZELLER, E., *Aristotle and the peripatetics*, 2 vols., London, 1897. — ZÜCHER, J., *Aristoteles' werk und Geist*, Paderborn, 1952.

67. " If it is true ", wrote Boutroux, " that the genius of a nation is sometimes embodied in one man, whose strong and comprehensive mind is, as it were, the *actus* and the perfection wherein a whole world of potentialities finds its completion and its term, Aristotle above all others was such a man. The philosophical genius of the Greeks found in him its total and perfect expression. The subject that we approach now is, therefore, not so much an individual philosophy — however great it may be under that aspect — as the Hellenist spirit itself, in the supreme phase of its intellectual development " [1].

Aristotle was born in 384 B. C. at Stagira, in the peninsula of Chalcidice. His family, the Asclepiadæ, claimed descent from Esculapius, and were, by tradition, of the medical profession.

---

[1] *Etudes d'Histoire de la Philosophie*, p. 95.

His father was privy councillor and physician to Amyntas II, king of Macedonia and father of Philip. It was at the Macedonian court that Aristotle received his first education; one may trace his interest in physical science to the influence of his father.

In 367, at the age of seventeen, he found himself an orphan with a considerable fortune at his disposal. He entered the school of Plato at Athens, and there he remained for twenty years, until Plato's death in 348. The Master sensed his keenness and his mental acuity, and used to call him " the Reader " or " the Mind ". Aristotle respected Plato, of whom he wrote a *Eulogy;* but he maintained a distinct independence of thought and to him is attributed the dictum: " Amicus Plato, magis amica veritas ".

After the death of Plato in the year 348, he settled at Assos in Mysia, an outpost of the Macedonian rule in Asia Minor, where his friend Hermias was governor. The latter was killed by the Persians in 345 and Aristotle fled to Mitylene, capital of Lesbos. He married Pythias, the niece of Hermias, who had accompanied him, but Nicomachus, to whom he later dedicated his *Ethics,* was his son by a second marriage. In 342 he was invited to the Macedonian court to undertake the education of Alexander. We have few details on this period of his life and on the influence he had on his distinguished pupil.

Alexander acceded in 336, and the following year saw Aristotle at Athens, founding the LYCEUM. His school drew its name from the nearby temple of Apollo Lyceius. There during twelve years he followed out a vast program of philosophical and scientific studies. His teachings were of a double order : the *acroamatic* discourses attracted a select audience, treating as they did of the more abstruse problems of philosophy; the *exoteric* lessons were for the public. At the same time he was working on various treatises. The Lyceum soon eclipsed the Academy and the other schools of the time [1].

On the death of Alexander in 323, Aristotle was in danger from the anti-Macedonian outbreak at Athens; a charge of impiety was brought against him. Lest the Athenians should " sin twice against philosophy ", he left his school in the care of his pupil, Theophrastus, and retired to Chalcis where he died soon after (322), at the age of sixty-two.

Works. His writings were of two kinds: the first, in dialogue form, were destined to make known his philosophy to the public, and were composed with an eye to literary effect. To these chiefly one may apply the appreciation of the ancients who spoke of " the golden stream of Aristotle's eloquence ", and of " the sweeping force, and the fascinating grace of his style ". These works are no longer extant.

---

[1] Aristotle often walked up and down with his pupils while teaching; hence the name Peripatetics. (From περιπατεῖν to walk.)

The second group of writings, which have been preserved, were for use in the Lyceum. They are in the nature of didactic treatises aiming at strict demonstration and composed with help of memoranda and of the pupils' note books. Here the style is perfectly adapted to the aim. The thought is abundant, and the expression at times eloquent; terms are used with the utmost precision, and shades of meaning delicately distinguished. In places, however, there is lack of polish, and some formulas are concise to the point of rendering the text difficult to understand.

The following is a list of the more important of the authentic works :

A) **Logical treatises.**

1. *Categoriæ seu prædicamenta:* the last five chapters, " *Post-prædicamenta* " are not certainly authentic.

2. *Periheremnaias* or, *De interpretatione*, (analysis of the judgment).

3. *Analytica priora:* rules governing the syllogism.

4. *Analytica posteriora:* laws of demonstration.

5. *Topica:* of the probable syllogism (8 books). The ninth book *(Elenchi)* deals with sophisms.

B) **Natural philosophy.**

1. Eight *physical* treatises, on the world in general.

2. *De generatione et corruptione* (2 books): of the four elements.

3. *Meteorologia* (4 books): physics (in the modern sense).

4. *De cælo* (4 books): astronomy.

5. *De anima*, (3 books): study of the living being in general and of its triple species.

6. About animals : *De historia animalium* (10 books); *De animalium incessu* (1 book); *De animalium partibus* (4 books); *De generatione animalium* (1 book): other books on natural history and physiology.

7. The group of writings known to the Scholastics as the *Parva Naturalia*, dealing with human psychology of both the mind and the senses: *De sensu et sensato; De memoria et reminiscentia; De somno et vigilia; De longitudine et brevitate vitæ; De juventute et senectute.*

C) **Practical philosophy.**

1.   *Nicomachean Ethics* (10 books), certainly authentic; to these are added the *Magna Moralia* (2 books), and the *Eudemian Ethics* (7 books) both of which are probably the work of pupils.

2.   *The Politics* (8 books).

3.   *The Rhetoric ad Theodoctem* (3 books).

4.   *The Poetics*, of which only a few fragments on *tragedy* remain.

D) **Metaphysics and Theodicy.**

The twelve books of the *Metaphysics* [1].

General characteristics.   68.   An ancient historian said of Aristotle that he was " *by temperament, moderate to excess* ". In his personality, as in his doctrine, is embodied the Greek ideal of measure, of a harmonious balance of forces.   Impervious to violent emotions, he was not however deficient in feeling.

It was his habitual serenity that made possible his extensive and uninterrupted studies.   We know, moreover, that he was filled with a veritable passion for knowledge, and that he spent his nights studying.   Thus, while Aristotle is without the poetical imagination and the daring intuitions that we find in Plato, he reaches none the less the highest summits of specu-lation.   He climbs up step by step, each elevation being based on the solid ground of experience.   For this reason, in Aristotelian philosophy, metaphysics is not the sum total of science : it appears rather as the peak of knowledge, domin-ating the vast network of special sciences which lead up to it.

All these sciences are intimately connected, proceeding one from another like the branches of a tree, and springing from one main trunk as from a single basic principle.   In order to stress this character of *unity in universality*, the study will be divided into ten paragraphs the first of which will deal with Aristotle's fundamental theory, and the others will concern its application either in the logical order, or in the domain of reality; the latter allows for a system of subdivision the consistency of which will be pointed out at each new ramification.

---

[1] This is not one single treatise.   Books vi-viii are clearly concerned with the study of substance; book xii is a theological treatise.   Cf. BRÉHIER, *Hist. de la Phil.*, i, p. 170.

I. THE FUNDAMENTAL THEORY.

A) Historical Foundation.

69. With respect to each of his theories Aristotle examines the conclusions of his predecessors; he is the first historian of philosophy. Not that he studies these opinions for themselves — he even uses his own phraseology to express them — but that he knows the collaboration of centuries to be necessary for the building up of the philosophical edifice. He knows that the gropings, the partial truths, even the errors of the past can contribute towards the finding of the true solution. Among previous thinkers, he seeks his forerunners. Thus his fundamental theory may be considered as the conclusion of the whole history of philosophy up to his own time.

The early philosophers were concerned above all with the notion of *being*. One and all were eager to discover, amid the multiple and changing realities that experience reveals, the one immutable element postulated by the intelligence, namely, " *what is* ", or, " that which explains being ".

The early Ionians claim to find the solution in the material elements of water, air, fire [1]. Heraclitus, it is true, attempted to reject being in favor of change; but he merely attributed to movement the unifying and stabilizing force that belongs by

---

[1] They cannot for that be called *empiricists*. They never faced the issue between sense and reason; they thought, so to speak, with all their being. An instinctive animism penetrates their whole doctrine, the fruit of a very primitive psychology. Thales sees in water what Anaximenes sees in air : a reality that develops like a living being.

right to the *ratio entis*. Parmenides, in turn, vindicated the supremacy of being, but his theory left movement unexplained.

The Atomist conciliation was superficial, that of the Sophists
destructive, and it was left to Socrates to suggest a satisfactory
solution.   Socrates drew attention to the soul and to its method
of gaining knowledge; he established, as immutable object of
knowledge, the universal definition, which gives, with reference
to any object, a definitive answer to the question: *What is it?*
Plato's too rigorous insistence on these principles led, through
exaggerated realism, to a kind of ideal Atomism, and neither the
Atomic theory of Democritus nor the Platonic doctrine of Forms
could shed light on the problem of unity in diversity.

On the one hand, by virtue of the principle of identity, so strongly
asserted by Parmenides, all Forms pertain to Being and participate
in the same properties.   Each of them is simple, indivisible,
unchanging, distinct from the others, and, therefore, fully intelligible
and fully comprehended by a direct and rational intuition.   Here,
it seemed, was the principle of stability, the intelligible being,
the true object of knowledge, with movement (and diversity)
relegated to the material world, object of opinion and of sense
experience.

But, on the other hand, Plato still had to account for the multiplicity of the Forms themselves.   Moreover, the material universe
could only be explained by the world of the intelligence, its exemplary cause.   Hence the necessity of attributing reality to the
Form of Other-ness or non-being in order to explain the inter-
participation of the Forms.   This confusing solution ran counter
to the basic lines of Plato's philosophy : since each Form, like
each material thing, is a compound of being and non-being, there
can be no logical distinction between the domain of knowledge
and that of opinion.

To sum up, all the early philosophers had endeavored
to see things from the point of view of the absolute, the one,
and the immutable.   What they sought was, at least implicitly,
the aspect of being, though insuperable difficulties prevented
them from defining the intelligible factor.   In this convergence
of thought, Aristotle saw an unmistakable indication of truth;
but he saw, too, the rocks on which his predecessors had
foundered.   What enabled him to avoid the same dangers
was his theory of ABSTRACTION.

Being is for Aristotle the true object of knowledge; but this
being is neither a universal reality grasped by intuition —
since the material compound alone exists — nor the individual,
concrete being as such — since it has no stability.   The
Aristotelian " knowable " is *the element of stability and unity,
drawn from the material reality by abstraction*.   By means
of this latter ability, reason is enabled to pass over the changing,

multiple aspect of things, and to consider only the essential aspect which links the concrete to the absolute.

Thus, Aristotle reinstates in the material world the Forms which Plato had wrongly " substantialized ". In material things, these *forms* exist with the characteristics of individual entities, but the mind frees them from the individuating conditions of matter, and conceives them as pure ideas. Then reflection reveals their aptitude to exist in many individuals: they are universal. In all knowledge [1], therefore, our thought consists of universal and necessary concepts abstracted from objects which are in reality concrete, individual and contingent; and of simple, immutable concepts of objects which are in reality multiple and changeable.

In confirmation of his thesis, Aristotle brings three objections against Plato's idealism: 1. The universal cannot exist in the form of an individual substance; 2. If the multiple is to be unified, it must be by some principle which is in contact with the multiple, and not outside it; 3. Plato's archetypes are useless and instead of making knowledge easier, they merely double the number of things to be known.

We may now formulate the principle of *moderate realism*, which is the basis of Aristotelianism : *" The specific object adapted to our intelligence is the essence of material realities, while its general object is being "*.

B) **Two Difficulties Eliminated.**

70. In their search for a definition of being, the early sages were faced with a double antinomy : variable multiplicity had to be harmonized with unchanging unity in the *object*, and sense experience with intellectual knowledge in the *subject*. New emphasis is given to this same problem in the mind of Aristotle.

a) First, the study of *being as such*, which is the object of his General Metaphysics, shows clearly that the transcendentals are convertible [2]. *Being* taken as such, without restriction, must necessarily be identified with the perfect *unity* of a reality

---

[1] Except in that part of Metaphysics that deals with God, as the following paragraph will show.

[2] See the view on this question in J. Owens, *The Doctrine of Being in the Aristotelian Metaphysics*, Toronto, 1951.

that is one in its simplicity; with the *truth* of perfect intelligibility; with the *goodness* of absolute perfection. We may, therefore, infer the unvarying stability and positive infinity of being which excludes all non-being and is consequently free from error, from change, from multiplicity, from limit and from every imperfection. Aristotle transposes to this essential order of abstract ideas, where the function of the intelligence is unhampered, all Parmenides' conclusions, and these in the process are enriched with new contributions, particularly with regard to the infinite [1].

b) On the other hand, he leaves to sense-data their full value, and declares that reality, the immediate object of the different sciences, does not consist of immaterial, subsistent forms, but of concrete things. Thus he is led to admit that being is changeable, multiple, imperfect and limited.

How can these two apparently contradictory conclusions be made to agree? The complete solution of the difficulty is contained in two theories: that of analogy, and that of actuality and potentiality.

1. **Analogous nature of the notion of Being.** Our idea of being is not, as Parmenides and Plato thought, a well defined concept, denoting an absolute essence and expressing its entire connotation; its scope, on the contrary, is merely general and *inadequate*. That is why it can be realized, without altering its definition, in many objects and in very different ways, while at the same time, it covers, in a single conspectus, the *whole of reality* without exception.

This precision on the side of the subject or of the idea, demands an exactly correlative precision on the side of the object or the thing, and this is where the two theories are explanatory one of the other.

2. **Actuality and Potentiality.** For if every existing thing were a *perfect* realization of being, and consequently of the transcendentals, which are inseparable from being in its perfect state, there would be no place for plurality, diversity of perfection, and change. Therefore material objects (this man, this tree, etc.) are what they are, that is multiple, varied and

---

[1] Aristotle distinguishes clearly between the *negative* or imperfect infinite (the indefinite), which Plato attributed to matter, and the *positive*, or perfect infinite, which belongs to the purely actual.

variable, only because they do not realize being perfectly and fully, but are composed of two principles:

a) A principle of perfection, called ACTUALITY (*actus*) by which these objects participate in being and in the perfections in which Being finds its expression. This principle, then, gives to things their definite nature, and makes them *what they are.*

b) A principle of imperfection, called POTENTIALITY (*potentia*) by which these same objects are limited and are ranged in divers degrees of perfection distinct one from another. Hence plurality and change, and the acquisition of new perfections.

In order to demonstrate the reality of potentiality, Aristotle appeals especially to the argument from change. If, for example, a marble statue has been made, the block of marble was, initially, a relative *non-being* of the statue, as Parmenides says, " ex nihilo, nihil fit "; one cannot make a statue out of absolute non-statue, nor, on the other hand, from a statue already made which no longer changes, for " ex ente non fit ens, quia jam est ens ". — But Aristotle adds that the marble together with the statue possess a relation which they do not have with other objects, as with a body of water or of sand; this relationship is the *capacity* of being sculptured. This capacity is an evident reality, it is *potentiality.*

In these two principles, our analogous concept of being is realized adequately, but very differently in either case: in actuality, Being is found to be absolute and perfect; pure actuality is nothing else than a synthesis of the transcendentals. In potentiality, Being is relative and imperfect; pure potentiality is a kind of real non-being, of itself insubsistent. Finally, in material objects, which are compounds of actuality and potentiality, Being is realized diversely in an harmonious gradation of genera and species.

It is now possible to formulate more precisely the principle which unifies the whole of the philosophy of Aristotle: " *The formal object of man's intelligence is being, an analogous concept realized in actuality and potentiality* ".

A whole system of ontology is held implicitly in this formula which indicates the true value of the notion of being and of the transcendental properties which it directly includes. Moreover, the comparison of these primary notions provides the primary judgments, or *first principles*, in the light of which all subsequent speculation will proceed : the principles of identity and of contradiction, and the principle of *ratio sufficiens*. This root formula is not the term of a rational proof; it imposes itself on the mind; it is the part that intuition contributes to our rational processes; and this, far from weakening the foundation of our knowledge, is the soundest guarantee of its truth.

It is evident also that such a formula covers every single branch of human knowledge, since it serves as a key to the intelligibility of *everything that is*. It puts a clear distinction between the two orders confused by Plato: the *logical order*, or the role of the intellect in the elaboration of knowledge; and the *real order* or the role of the object and of experience. Before attempting an explanation of the universe it is, then, possible to study scientifically the rules of rational method in the pursuit of truth. Hence the two major applications of the fundamental principle:

1. to the logical order;—2. to the ontological order.

II. THE LOGICAL ORDER.

71. A moderate conceptualism influences the whole of Aristotle's logic. Plato's dialectic was above all a formation for ascetism and mysticism; its aim was to raise man above matter to the intuition of the pure Forms. Aristotle attributes this purifying function to reason, the instrument of abstraction; logic will henceforth be a purely and specifically intellectual method. Logic is *the science or the art of directing reason in its several operations*, so that, avoiding error, it may attain the knowledge of truth, that knowledge which is the aim of the life of the intelligence.

With this aim in view, the logician should study rational activity under its twofold aspect: *a*) the *formal aspect*, i. e. the conditions of its satisfactory progress; *b*) the *material aspect*, i. e. the truth or falsehood of its object. The former, termed *formal* or *minor logic*, is dealt with in the Prior Analytics. The latter, called *material* or *major logic*, because it is concerned with more difficulty and more important questions, is studied in the Posterior Analytics.

A) **Formal Logic.**

72. The main part of the science of logic has to do with *reasoning*, the act proper to the *reason:* but reasoning presupposes the *judgment*, which, in turn, uses *concepts*. Formal logic has, therefore, three chapters in the course of which Aristotle analyzes not only the three acts of the intelligence, but also the three outward signs corresponding to them : the *syllogism*, the *proposition*, and the *term*.

1. **Concepts and terms.** The first treatise of Aristotle's ORGANON is about the concept, the result of simple apprehension, and its manifestation which is the term. The object in view is to instruct the mind in the classification of concepts, and much importance is given to the distribution of ideas into *categories*. But first one must study " the different ways in which an abstract notion may be attributed to a subject " : there are five modes, called *predicables :* (genus, species, specific difference, property and accident).

A second classification groups concepts under the headings of the ten higher genera, known as predicaments (or categories [1]). These are the ten most general modes of being, which are not susceptible of inter-participation. They include every aspect of physical reality, the immediate object of our knowledge. While natural philosophy considers only their specific content (ontological aspect), logic groups, under each supreme genus, series of related predicates according to genus, differentia and species. Thus, logical categories are the rational copies of reality in its different modalities.

If a distinction is made between a material and a formal element, however, then the sciences of the real constitute the *material* element, for they have direct concepts corresponding to modes of reality. The *formal* element belongs to logic, which classifies these very concepts into series of genera and of subordinate differences, so that the progress of both types of sciences are parallel.

Finally, Aristotle expounds under the title " *postprædicamenta* ", certain general notions which find an application in all the predicaments, or in several : opposition, priority and posteriority, simultaneity, possession and movement. Above the categories of univocal concepts, he places the *transcendentals* or analogous concepts.

2. **Judgments and propositions.** The judgment is the identification of two objective concepts, or, in other words, the intellectual view of one and the same object as identical with itself, although seen under two different aspects in the subject and the predicate. The judgment, and not the concept, is true or false, since, writes Aristotle, " a falsehood consists in saying (or affirming) of being that it is not, and of non-being that it is; truth consists in saying (or affirming) of being that it is, and of non-being that it is not " [2].

Aristotle studies the proposition in regard to *a*) quality (affirmations and negations); *b*) quantity (the proposition is universal, particular, or singular); *c*) modality (it is necessary, possible, or

---

[1] From χατηγορία, which means *predicate*.
[2] *Metaphysics*, IV, 7. Cf. SENTROUL, *Kant et Aristote*, p. 62.

contingent); opposition (propositions are contrary, contradictory, subcontrary, or subalternate); and he fixes the rules for the conversion of propositions.

3. **Reasoning and syllogisms.** Aristotle begins by showing that not every truth can be proved by rational demonstration; at the beginning of all knowledge there is a minimum of data acquired by *intuition :* such are the immediate conclusions of external or internal experience; and the first principles, universal truths which are immediately evident. But since these primary truths are very few in number, the principal means of intellectual progress is *reasoning* which is, in a general way : " the movement of the mind passing from something that is known to something hitherto unknown ". The process is either inductive or deductive.

a) INDUCTION is a process by which the mind passes from the concrete to the abstract; from things and facts under observation to concepts and judgments that are universal. The elements involved are less clearly determined than in the syllogism, and Aristotle's treatment of the subject is, in proportion, less complete. The general procedure and the essential characteristics are, however, well defined on the sound basis of his theory of abstraction.

As material for induction he takes all facts of experience, which he classifies in two groups : there is the experience of past ages, summed up in popular sayings, in commonly accepted opinions, and, above all, in the teachings of the philosophers; and there is personal experience, and even personal experiment, the study of facts in their details. This second group, on which Aristotle dwells with insistence, offers satisfactory scope for scientific precision, and is notably superior to the methods of Socrates and Plato.

The effort of the mind in the passage from these concrete facts to the domain of the universal is one of *interpretation.* Different branches of science and different instances demand different approaches. Moreover, if appeal is made to a guiding idea, a directing principle, the latter remains usually understood, and normally the Aristotelian induction has neither mean term nor minor explicitly formulated.

There are, however, certain rules for the proper interpretation of facts. When dealing with a collection of data acquired by personal experience, where the aim is to eliminate accidental properties and thus reveal the universal nature of a thing with its essential characteristics, Aristotle recommends the *comparison* of numerous instances in order to determine the common and essential element.

He also lays down rules for the interpretation of opinions passed on by others. Here, no doubt, it is a matter of historical criticism rather than of induction. The moderns will have the merit of realizing a decisive progress on this point by defining more rigorously the laws of scientific induction. It is nonetheless true that Aristotle conceived and expounded more clearly than the scientists or the *positivist* philosophers the underlying nature and value of this form of reasoning.

He divided induction into two kinds:

1. **Metaphysical or mathematical induction,** which is a passage from very simple facts of experience to either the metaphysical notions which lead to the first principles, or to the concepts of quantity, space, number, and other elements of mathematical definitions. This process is so spontaneous and so obvious that no particular rules are needed : it is equivalent to simple abstraction.

2. **Scientific induction,** or induction properly so-called, which is based on multiple data and which varies in procedure according to the different sciences. Its special aim, in Aristotle's mind, is to determine by systematic research the definitions and principles [1] which make the syllogism possible.

b) DEDUCTION or SYLLOGISTIC REASONING is the passage of the mind from a universal truth to a new judgment, by the comparison of two concepts with a third in an effort to ascertain the identity or non-identity of the same object seen under these three aspects. The syllogism shows that the predicate is contained in the comprehension of the middle term, which also includes the subject in its extension. This can be seen in the following type-syllogism:

M is P.   Omne vivens est substantia.

S is M.   Atqui omnis homo est vivens.

S is P.   Ergo omnis homo est substantia.

Thus the medium by which the mind passes from the known to the unknown is here a concept expressed by a term. The introduction of this MIDDLE TERM is the essential distinguishing mark of the syllogism as opposed to the inductive process. It explains also the rules to be observed. The scientific and definitive theory of the syllogism is due to Aristotle, who prides himself on being its discoverer.

The fundamental rule is that the middle term must be truly the source of the conclusion by its comparison with the two remaining concepts, worked out in the premisses. Hence it is necessary that:

1. The middle term be excluded from the conclusion, since the cause must be distinct from its effect.

2. There be a single middle term to make the comparison possible; that at least once it be taken with universal application, and therefore that the two premisses be neither both particular nor both negative.

3. That the major and minor terms be never given in the conclusion a wider application than in the premisses, since the cause should be proportionate to the effect: hence the principle: " Pejorem semper sequitur conclusio partem ".

---

[1] E.g., the study of the soul should be founded on a definition based on induction.

The position of the middle term in the premisses gives rise to the different *figures* indicated in the mnemonic formula:

" Sub-præ, prima; altera bis-præ; tertia bis-sub ".

The fourth figure (præ-sub) is considered by Aristotle but he declares it negligible as being unnatural. It may be shown that special rules govern the operation of the middle term in the different figures:

For the first figure: " Sit minor affirmans, major vero generalis ".
For the second: " Una negans esto, nec major sit specialis ".
For the third: " Sit minor affirmans, conclusio particularis ".

The author selects from among all the possible forms of the syllogism those modes that are *" legitimate "* according to the quantity and the quality of the premisses and with due observance of the rules. He shows how they may be all reduced to the four legitimate modes of the first figure, by converting and transposing the propositions. Finally, certain complex and less regular forms (especially the modal syllogisms) are explained, with a demonstration of their reduction to the more simple forms.

B) **Material Logic.**

73. From a material point of view, that is, with regard to the value of the premisses and of the conclusion that follows from them, Aristotle distinguishes the *demonstrative* syllogism which begets science; the *dialectic* syllogism, which engenders opinion; and the *sophistic* syllogism, productive of error.

1) **Science and demonstration.** True science is, the *certain and evident knowledge of things by their causes*. Since it is a perfect knowledge, it can be attained only on condition that we know, not merely that the object is (ὅτι), but also *why* it is this object (διότι). We must be able to delve into its nature and discover its *rationes entis*, that is, its ontological causes, both intrinsic and extrinsic. The Scholastics translated this Aristotelian concept into the following formula : " Scire est cognoscere rem per causam, propter quam res est, et quod ejus est causa, et quod non contingit eam aliter se habere ".

True science is the fruit of *strict demonstration*, which term is taken to mean, in general, any proof based on evident and certain premisses, and leading to an infallibly true conclusion. For Aristotle, however, the only demonstration that can be strictly so called (the demonstration *propter quid*), the only one productive of knowledge, is that contained in the syllogisms of the first figure whose first middle term (the starting point of a series of deductions) is the very definition of the object of science, whence are inferred the properties of that object. The first figure alone gives full evidence; and only the definition offers an adequately explanatory reason of things. Thus Aristotle defines demonstration: " syllogismus faciens scire ".

True knowledge therefore cannot be attained by simple experiments which deal with contingent data without determining either their cause or their essential truth. " Non est scientia de singularibus ", said Aristotle. " Knowledge concerns only universals ". Even induction, which aims at universal truth, cannot of itself lead to true knowledge, since it falls short of the universal reason of things and is merely a demonstration *quia*. The precise object of the inductive process is to establish, sometimes by means of long and complicated efforts, the primary definition in which is expressed the essence or form of the object through the medium of its genus and specific difference.

2) **Opinion and dialectic.** *Opinion* as here understood is present in the mind when *adhesion given to a proposition is mingled with some fear of error*. Its domain is that of the probable, that is the conditionally true, the likely, which is realized " *ut in pluribus* " and which justifies a prudent assent but not a necessary acceptance. For knowledge in the scientific sense there must be no fear of error. Opinion also differs clearly from ignorance and doubt, states of mind in which there can be no question of assent.

The sphere of knowledge in the strict sense must needs be very limited, but its prolongation in that of opinion is proportionately greater. Among the objects of opinion are to be included those special branches of learning in which absolute certainty is not obtainable, such as history and pedagogy; and even sciences in their *pre-scientific* and *post-scientific* stages. Much of our knowledge consists of probings (comparative study of phenomena, progress by analogy and induction) which precede essential discoveries. Here the mind possesses no guarantee of absolute truth; its conclusions are merely probable and constitute a " *via ad scientiam* ".

On the other hand, in a series of scientific inferences, in proportion as the principles become more remote, the link between them and the successive conclusions is weakened until certitude is no longer obtainable. No doubt, as long as the mind perceives any reflection of intelligible truth it will give its assent to those conclusions; but it will do so with some fear of error. Thus the luminous rays emanating from the center of knowledge lose themselves in the half-light of the probable.

Besides induction, which attains no essential definition, opinion has another *instrument* in the *dialectic syllogism* [1]. This process differs from demonstration not in form (although the dialectician makes a more common use of the enthymeme) but in the material handled. It is based not on necessary truths but on *probable principles*, so general in their nature as to belong to no science in particular. But inasmuch as they are commonly accepted by men, it is justifiable to advance them in a discussion. In some cases they will even have the value of scientific propositions, but their allegation by the dialectician will always be subject to general

---

[1] *Dialectic* in the Platonic sense is applied to true knowledge, whereas Aristotle uses it only in connection with the *probable*, and as opposed to demonstration.

approval. At other times they have only the value of probabilities, as in the case of the unverified hypotheses of scientists.

Aristotle groups these principles, according to the four dialectic problems, under four headings which he calls *topica* (from τόπος). The questions, *an sit? quid sit?* and *propter quid?* have no place in the dialectician's consideration. He answers only the question *quale sit?* or in other words: " *Utrum tale prædicatum insit subjecto?* " Now a quality may be attributed to a subject in four ways : as genus, as definition, as property, and as accident.

For the accident Aristotle counts 42 topics. For instance, " quod est bonum est eligibile; quod a sapientioribus eligitur est eligibilius " [1]. For the genus he enumerates 75 topics. For example : " If what is given as a genus cannot be attributed to a species, or to an individual of that species, it is not a genus at all ". For the property, 38 topics are mentioned, e. g. " A property must be found in its subject not only sometimes, but always ". Of the 89 topics put forward for the definition, the following is an instance : " Contrary things have contrary definitions ".

3) **Errors and sophisms.** These are dealt with in the last book of the Topics. Aristotle distinguishes between *verbal* and *mental* sophisms.

CONCLUSION. It is easily understood that this theory of method implies that by nature our mind is abstractive and recognizes the value of our universal ideas. In this way logic is truly an application of the fundamental principle.

Opposed to the *logical* order is the domain of *reality* to which the same application must now be made. But the universal character of philosophical knowledge necessitates a subdivision of the subject. According to the several aspects under which reality may be considered (formal objects), Aristotle enumerates the different branches of science specifically distinct one from another. The leading distinction is between 1. physics, which is concerned directly with sense-perceptible reality as such; and 2. metaphysics, which deals with *a*) the suprasensible; *b*) that element in sense-data which pertains to Being, or to such perfections as may be also realized independently of matter. Metaphysics is rightly held to be the keystone of the whole philosophy of Aristotle.

In physics there is a general section dealing with the common properties of all corporal substances, and a special branch in which the specifically distinct nature of each body is studied.

---

[1] Cf. LORENZELLI, *Cursus Philosophiæ*, I, p. 167.

III. GENERAL PHYSICS.

74. The object of general physics is *variable reality*, changing elements as such, *being* under *the formal aspect of mutation*. In order of discovery it is first among true scientific efforts. The first conscious phase of intellectual life is that of ignorance of things scientific. Progress in science is the result of an interpretation of facts in the light of elementary principles formulated by common sense. Now the primary fact, the most generally observed phenomenon, is that of alteration.

At first this phenomenon would appear to be in opposition with the principle of identity. Change implies that a reality ceases to be what it is. That which is *becoming* is not yet what it *will be*, and is no longer what it *was*. Change as such is apparently *something by which a thing is not what it is*. No philosophy based on sensualist principles can solve this antinomy. But a satisfactory solution is offered to the intellect in the division of being into *actuality* (*actus*) and *potentiality* (*potentia*), which make it possible to conceive the fluid reality that we call change. Movement, says Aristotle, is " the actuality or perfection of that which is not yet perfect, but potential considered as such: *actus existentis in potentia prouti est in potentia* " [1]. Thus learning, which is already more perfect than ignorance, is not yet perfect knowledge. The learner is a man of knowledge *in potentia*.

In this definition Aristotle established a strong connection between his basic metaphysical principles and those problems of the physical order which were of primary interest to him. As a working theory it is used by him more frequently than the principle of analogy. The numerous applications, at once pliable and precise, which he makes of it in every approach to reality point to it as to the unifying bond of his whole system. General physics embodies its two earliest applications in the fourfold theory of causality, and of that of substance and accidents.

---

[1] This formula is an attempt to define motion (all transition from one state to another) under the very aspect of mobility, and, if rightly understood, it attains its aim, in spite of Bergson's criticism. It is not, however, an easy definition to grasp, and it is pointed out by Pascal that it is rather in the nature of a thesis to be proved: " It is not a definition, but a proposition ". Cf. Opusc. Philosophiques, *De l'esprit géométrique;* 1st Frag., coll. Hatier, p. 31.

A) **The Four Causes.**

75. A searching analysis of the concept of change reveals that it cannot be fully understood without reference to four reasons, all of which manifest in some way actuality and potentiality. All four are essential to the explanation of each instance of mutation. Hence the theory of the four causes.

1.   Total change, in which an entity would be altered in every part of its being and in its entirety, is impossible. It would imply identical contradictories, an absurdity which was disposed of in our criticism of Heraclitus. No real change is conceivable without a *permanent subject*, an unvarying element capable of being actuated: Aristotle calls it the *material cause*.

2.   Perfect stability is no less contrary to the idea of change. Some principle is needed whereby the changing reality acquires gradually a *perfection*, an actuality which, when the change is complete, will constitute its new quality, its definite form and nature. This is the *formal cause*.

3.   The appearance of the new actuating perfection is made possible by the influence of a *similar perfection pre-existent* in an agent who can transmit it to the variable factor : such is the *efficient cause*.

4.   Finally, some reason must be given for the orderly sequence always and everywhere manifest in causal relations, which ensures individual and general welfare. Regulated variation postulates a *directing principle* in virtue of which the agent shall act in view of a definite aim. This ruling principle is called the *final cause*.

This fourth cause is in reality the same as the formal element in the agent : either the natural form which constitutes what is essential in agents " per naturam "; or the ideal form of agents " per intellectum ". However the final cause is an altogether special aspect of what is formal in the agent : it has reference to the agent as *tending to some good aim*.

By such clarifications Aristotle develops notably the theory of causality, and leads immediately to a scientific explanation of the universe. His solution, however, falls short of perfection under several aspects:

a) In mental revolt against the Ideas with separate existence as conceived by Plato, Aristotle lays insufficient stress on the *exemplary cause*. This he identifies with the intrinsic formal element which constitutes the essence of things, and which is the basis of our universal concepts, individual and numerical distinctions being, on the contrary, explained by the material element. Thus he makes the ideal world an integral part of the sense-universe. His views on divine providence [1] are, moreover, opposed to Plato's exemplarism.

b) To explain the *becoming* of things, Aristotle appeals almost exclusively to the efficient cause, which he defines : " Id quod primum principium est motus "; thus the highest cause is primarily the *primum movens*. Plato's thought on this point is less realist, but more surely metaphysical.

c) Finally, he passes lightly over the connection between the final cause and the essential reason for a thing's existence and on the influence of this final cause on the agent itself, an influence which explains the passage from " actus primus " to " actus secundus " [2]. Aristotle develops this point by comparison with human activity, deriving its inspiration from intelligence and art : finality is art immanent in nature.

B) **Substance and Accidents.**

76. From the evidence of a real distinction between the two elements, potential and actual, in one and the same being, it follows that everything which is subject to change or contingency will be a *compound* of several distinct principles, unity being ensured by the interrelation of act and potentiality.

There is, first, the real distinction between *essence and existence*, a postulate of change. A changing reality can never be in its essence pure actuality. Aristotle saw this distinction but did not dwell on its metaphysical value as a characteristic of creatures as opposed to the Creator.

Of primary importance in the study of variable reality is the distinction between the two fundamental modalities of being :

a) *Substance :* that which exists in itself and by itself, without the need of a substratum other than itself : " ens simpliciter ".

b) *Accident :* that which has no existence except in a subject other than itself, and of which the essential function is to modify the substance : " ens entis ".

It is clear that most variable things change only in part and possess an unvarying element which is merely modified by the addition (or loss) of secondary modalities : these are the accidents, while the stable element is the substance.

---

[1] Cf. n° 93, 3°.
[2] St. Thomas will make his own this metaphysical point of view.

The close interdependence of these two principles, which Aristotle defines, enables us to determine with reliable certainty the nature of substances from the diversity of their accidents : " Agere sequitur esse ".

In so far as these accidental properties enter into the scientific definition of the things they make known, they form the domain of the particular sciences. Moreover, since sensible reality comprises specifically distinct substances, Aristotle is led to the conception of a whole series of special sciences to deal with them. Four main branches of knowledge are concerned with four groups of beings : mineral bodies, plant life, the animal world, and man.

IV. PHYSICS : PHILOSOPHY OF NATURAL BODIES.

77. Aristotle was a great scientist as well as a profound philosopher. By storing up a mass of experience about all kinds of things, he was able to lay the foundations of most of the special sciences. Unlike modern thinkers, he saw the philosophical explanation [1] of the world as one with its scientific study. At least he saw the two views as harmoniously complementary. At the basis of all knowledge of the physical world he places two philosophical conceptions which are applications of the thesis of actual and potential being. These are the theories of *matter and form*, and the theory of the *ten categories*.

A) **Matter and Form.**

The most obvious features of the sense-perceived world are *generation and corruption*. These are radical changes, as opposed to superficial variations of what is merely " accident ". Here the substantial factor itself is affected : the new body is essentially different from the old. This is possible and intelligible only if one admits a further division of actuality and potentiality dividing the body in its very essence. Prime matter, as ultimate substratum, is bare of determining constituents and is very nearly the nothingness of *pure potentiality*. It is non-being, not absolute but relative, that is, non-actuality [2]. On the other hand there is the *substantial form*, the primary

---

[1] With Wolf and Kant came the term *cosmology* to express this. See n. 82.

[2] Aristotle explains it by its negative definition : " neque quid, neque quale, neque quantum, neque aliquid aliud per quod ens determinatur ".

actus of the natural body, root of all its perfections, explanatory of its nature and its place in a given species.

Matter and form are essentially incomplete principles, mutually necessary as immediate constituents of individual bodies. Matter will also serve to distinguish individuals from one another in a given species (principle of individuation). But its principal function is that of substratum in processes of generation and corruption.

With these general truths before him Aristotle sets out to explain all the under-surface changes observed in mineral bodies and achieves a systematic chemical treatise. Faithful to his method, he keeps close to facts, using common experience, and coordinating experiments made by his predecessors. He holds that everything evolves from simple substances : earth, water, air and fire (theory of the four elements). Of the several properties that distinguish essentially these elements, the most important is their natural claim to a definite *locus* (theory of natural places).

To make this last point clear we must remember that according to the astronomic theory accepted by Aristotle, the earth, a spherical mass, is poised motionless in the centre of the universe. Around it is a concentric series of moving spheres, carrying in their rotation the different heavenly bodies. The first sphere, most distant from the earth, is that of the fixed stars. Now the " earth " element is by nature *heavy* and is borne by natural movement towards the centre of the universe, where it comes to rest. *Fire* on the contrary is essentially light and is naturally carried upwards towards the highest sphere called " *empyrean* ", resting place of the element " fire ". Between the two, *water* is placed nearer *earth*, and *air* nearer *fire*.

Other contrary properties are conceived as characterizing the four elements : dry and fluid; solid and fluid; cold and hot. The action of the elements one upon another, as favored by these contrary dispositions, determined all the deeper changes in bodies and " gave birth " to all compounds.

This chemical theory of Aristotle was an attempt to synthesize common experience. To a point it succeeded, but it lacked scientific proof and could be no more than probability. It thus remains inferior to modern chemistry which it could not equal in precise observation of facts.

B) The Ten Categories.

78. The broad division of reality into substance and accident does not solve all problems. A more detailed analysis of the surface movements of things leads to the distinction of the accident into nine separate species which, together with substance, make up the ten supreme genera. To these may be related every distinct modality of corporal existence.

The principal species are :

a) Action and *passion*, whose nature, according to Aristotle, is that of movement (or change) itself considered under two opposite aspects : as caused by the agent and as affecting the passive element.

b) Qualities, quantity and *place*, which determine the three possible kinds of change in the strict sense, or successive movement.

c) Time, which measures this movement.

d) Relation, which exists only as referring to something (πρός τι) and which, by explaining the order of the universe, reveals the finality of change [1].

Here again (particularly in the *Meteorologia*) the author supplements his general thesis with a tentative explanation in scientific terms of the different accidental phenomena observed in the world. He discusses comets, clouds, fogs, rain, thunder, winds (due to variations of temperature in the air), the rainbow (caused by the reflection of sun-rays on water particles in the clouds), the formation of the oceans, earthquakes, etc.

He points out too that quantity and its species (continuous and numerical) is the basis of mathematics [2]; but he left no special treatise on the subject. His astronomy cannot be accepted as it is.

C) **Eternity of the World.**

79. I. Struck by the beauty and the regularity of the firmament, and not altogether uninfluenced, it is probable by mythology, Aristotle sees the heavenly bodies as vastly more perfect than earthly things. The four elements are foreign to their composition : they are formed by a fifth, called *ether*. In them the prime matter is entirely and decisively dominated by the form, which makes them incorruptible and inalterable. Impervious to both substantial and qualitative changes, they are affected only by locomotion which leaves intact their eminent perfection. Since experiments are not

---

[1] Thomism embodies this profound theory without modifying it. Note, however, that the two final categories, *situs* and *habitus* (posture and habiliment) are of little importance and need no lengthy consideration. Cf. GREDT. *Elementa Philosophiæ*, n. 716; II, p. 120.

[2] See, however, these two studies : H. G. APOSTLE, *Aristotle's Philosophy of Mathematics*, Chicago, 1952, and T. L. HEATH, *Mathematics in Aristotle*, Oxford, 1949.

available, Aristotle proves by a priori demonstration that circular movement, being the most perfect, is the only kind suited to the stars and planets [1]. Such hypotheses, as long as they were not disproved by further scientific observation (with the help of the telescope and spectral analysis) could well be admitted as probable by the Christian philosopher. St. Thomas, in fact, taught them as such.

2. So much cannot be said for the theory of the eternity of the world, which is contrary to faith. For Aristotle it followed naturally from the perfect nature of the movement of heavenly bodies. The unchanging order of the firmament is a fact of which the existence must be explained, but not the origin since it had no beginning [2]. Aristotle shows, indeed, that it could not be otherwise, and we shall immediately examine the two principal proofs which he gives.

a) **Direct proof.** It is inconceivable that this movement should have begun in any absolute way. For there is no movement without a moving object, and the *primum mobile* either must have begun to exist or must exist from all eternity, motionless first of all and then set in movement.

In the first case, the appearance of the *primum mobile* is itself a movement which precedes what was by hypothesis the first movement.

In the second case, the transition from rest to motion cannot be its own cause; it postulates some other agent in which must be admitted a movement anterior to the hypothetical first movement. The reason for this is that no cause can actually operate without being in a relation of proximity or at least of influence with regard to its effect, and in the moment of acting every cause must acquire this relationship. But two terms cannot become related in this new way without there being a change in one of them [3].

---

[1] We have here an example of the dialectic syllogism.

[2] The same applied to earthly events. "Aristotle (*Météor.*, 1, 3) adopts the theory of eternal recurrence and asserts that philosophical thought repeats itself identically, not once nor twice, nor several times, but *ad infinitum*". Elsewhere, however, he rejects the idea of the recurrence of individual facts (*De gen. et cor.*, 338, b, 11-19 and *IV Phys.*, 12, 220, b, 14). Cf. JOLIVET, *Rev. thom.*, July, 1938, p. 497.

[3] Grant that this change be the first, and you need another cause, itself affected by change, and so *ad infinitum.*

It is, then, impossible to conceive a change as "initial" without the absurdity of asserting that, while it is first by hypothesis, it supposes necessarily some previous movement. The conclusion is that movement is eternal.

Solution. What escaped Aristotle, as it escaped all pagan thinkers, was the idea of *creation.* If the *mobile* is created, that is, produced in its entire being and not from any pre-existing reality, then there is no longer question of a strictly so-called change, since there is no point of departure *(terminus a quo)* and so the first alternative is disposed of.

Likewise if the cause is truly a creator, perfect, therefore, and independent, only the effect is something new; the cause acquires merely a *relatio rationis.* And as the effect undergoes no real change, the second horn of the dilemma is avoided.

There were those who defended the Aristotelian position. St. Thomas answers them with a deeper analysis of the activity of the perfect cause and proves that, even in the Creator's intention, it is not necessary to conceive a movement anterior to the action of the creative agent. But such a line of argument was foreign to Aristotle's own thought.

b) **Indirect proof.** Since *time,* which is the measure of movement, is eternal, there can be no beginning to movement itself.

The whole reality of time consists in the present moment.

Now every " present instant " is by nature a mean which terminates the past and inaugurates the future, so that, however far removed the existence of a moment that has gone, it inevitably supposes something *past* in relation to itself. Therefore, time is necessarily eternal.

Considered superficially, notes St. Thomas [1], this would appear to be a *petitio principii.* To say that the present moment (real as movement is real) demands a moment anterior to itself, is surely to take for granted that movement is without beginning. But Aristotle's thought goes deeper than that. The term " before ", he reminds us, can only be used in relation to time, which is a succession of *before* and *after* taken a given number of times. If, then, it is admitted that the present moment is the principle of time, it follows that there exists a " before " ; otherwise the very admission would imply its destruction. In other words one cannot conceive the " present moment " as real without implying the

---

[1] *In VIII Phys., Lect.* 2.

reality of " past time " from which the present issues forth, and of a " future time " towards which it moves. Time is nothing unless each moment has its " before " ; and since, without creation, " ex nihilo nihil fit ", we should be experiencing time which did not yet exist.

Solution. Even with its implications thus brought out, the argument still leaves unproved the eternity of movement. Given the notion of creation, this presupposed " *before* " may be simply conceived as negative, as an element of an imaginary time; or else it belongs to God's eternity which excludes all movement, and is not time at all. Just as it is possible to conceive rationally the creation of a *primum mobile* and of its first motion, so we may conceive the creation of a beginning of time before which there was no reality in the temporal order.

This does not prove that there was in fact a beginning to time, movement, or earthly reality, but merely that a beginning is not an impossibility. In St. Thomas' view [1], only by faith can we know that the universe had a beginning; discounting what we know by revelation, Aristotle's teaching remains a possible hypothesis and, perhaps, a more probable one.

V. Plant Life : Biological sciences.

80. The study of the two intermediary degrees between minerals and man is less developed by Aristotle. For each one, however, he proposes a philosophical theory and applies it in a number of particular sciences.

1. **The theory** is that of the Soul as *principle of life.* Its definition is : " Actus primus corporis physici organici, potentia vitam habentis ". The characteristic feature of the living being is the power of self-movement (immanent movement), which reveals a greater measure of independence and of perfection and demands, in consequence, a form or substantial " *actus* " freer of potentiality. For plants and animals this independence is very relative, since their vital activity remains *organic*, subject to a multiplicity of material conditions. The soul is precisely the substantial *form.*

In applying this theory to the different degrees of life, Aristotle refutes the errors of his predecessors concerning

---

[1] Cf. Iᵃ P., q. 46, art. 1 and 2; II *Contra Gent.*, Ch. xxxvi-vii.

the nature of the soul, particularly the doctrine of accidental union and of metempsychosis (Plato); the conception of the soul as a simple harmonizing element (Pythagoras); and its reduction to the status of a less materialized atom (Democritus).

Essentially actual, the soul is manifested by new forms of activity of which the immediate principles are the *faculties*, or operative powers of the order of qualities. Every living body necessarily possesses three of these powers : the faculties of nutrition, of growth and of reproduction.

We may note here the importance of the *quality* in Aristotle's philosophy. His theory is far removed from that of the mechanists whether ancient or modern, for whom everything is reducible to the one element, quantity, endowed with the property of loco-motion. He realizes on the contrary, that the complexities of nature can be scientifically explained only by asserting the reality of multiple qualities corresponding to the many aspects of the perfection of things. The diversity of these qualities or operations forms a basis for the classification of living beings in distinct species. Here is a further application of his leading theory, poten-tiality being the origin of quantity, and actuality, that of qualities.

2. Scientific applications. These concern above all the phenomena of vegetable life in animal species. In treatises where the con-clusions of previous philosophers enrich his own observations and experiments, he deals with such vital functions as respiration, digestion and with the principal organs, like the heart. Thus he lays the scientific foundations of anatomy and physiology. His embryology reaches notable conclusions. His study of plant life has not come down to us [1] but it opened the way for his disciples to the science of *botany*.

VI. ANIMAL LIFE : ZOOLOGICAL SCIENCES.

81. 1. The basic philosophical theory is that of KNOWLEDGE of which the hidden workings are explained by an original application of the theories of causality and of act and potentiality.

Sense knowledge, common, it is clear, to man and beast, is immediately perceived as an operation of a higher order than any vegetable function. It postulates, therefore, a radically specific distinction between plant life and animal life. There is no knowledge of the nature of the animal soul without a study of the phenomenon of sensation.

---

[1] The one attributed to him is not authentic.

Sensation comprises a double phase in the course of which one and the same faculty is seen, first, *in potentia*, dependent on its object; secondly, *in actu*, dominating its object.

a) Passive phase. Aristotle begins with a fact of experience: the object must act upon the faculty before there can be perception. From this point of view the faculty is in passive potentiality and as such is transformed in the likeness of its cause; " Omne agens agit simile sibi ". The result of this first phase is, then, that the knowable object enters, so to speak, into the faculty, not in the manner of a material image (εἴδωλον) as conceived by Democritus [1], but as the impression, in the senses, of its own likeness (*species*, hence " species impressa ") [2].

b) Active phase. The senses are not, like prime matter, pure potentiality; they are, on the contrary, vital and operative functions. So, according to the principle " Quidquid recipitur, ad modum recipientis recipitur ", the passive phase is followed by a reaction : the faculty seizes its object, dominates and assimilates it in an immaterial way (intentionaliter) and thus, while the object remains physically intact, and the faculty is essentially unchanged, there is a psychological identity between the two : " Cognoscens in actu et cognitum in actu sunt idem "; or, more precisely, " Sensibile in actu et sensatio in actu sunt idem ". This dictum, often found in Aristotle, is for him the best expression of the nature of knowledge and of its explanation in the light of his basic principle.

The objective value of sense knowledge is fully vindicated in this theory which shows it as a directly *intuitive* perception of corporal reality. And this is important in a system in which all truth is ultimately founded on sensible experience (Experientia mater philosophiæ). At this point, however, some particularization is needed, since sensations are valuable only in so far as the senses are functioning normally. Aristotle, therefore, studies in separate treatises the different senses and sense-organs. He enumerates five external senses, analyzing in each case the action of their respective objects, whether it be by direct contact (as in the case of touch), or through some intermediary (as in the radiation of sound through the air and of light through the ether).

---

[1] See above, n. 20.

[2] There was no confusion in Aristotle's mind between the images received in the senses and the physical images imprinted, for instance, by a visible object on the retina. This latter was probably unknown to him, and all sensation was dependent on the *species impressa*. Here he is concerned with a *psychological* image of which the existence is proved by the study of one's own consciousness and by reason.

He notes also four internal senses which collect, preserve, unify and sometimes organize and supplement the external senses. These are : *sensus communis* (or sense-consciousness), imagination, memory and *vis æstimativa* (instinct in the animal, and, in man, the sense of what makes for well-being). The work of modern experimental psychologists is foreshadowed in Aristotle's study of the laws of sense functioning both in the state of waking and in that of sleep.

2. **Scientific applications** are duly made. Aristotle distinguishes and classifies nearly five hundred animal species, on the bases of anatomical characteristics and of diversity of instinct and habit. Thus are laid the foundations of natural history.

Consistent with his conception of the substantial form, he considers the species as immutable; they are even eternal like the universe : there have always been men, animals and plants; the individual alone appears and disappears. But since, in virtue of the principle of finality, the inferior is subservient to the superior, all this multitude of species moves harmoniously towards higher perfection, and thus we have a conception of life as perfectly consistent as the theory of evolution.

Branches of Science : Aristotle and the Moderns Compared.

82. With little more than *common experience* at his disposal, Aristotle founded all these special sciences (astronomy, physics, meteorology, chemistry, biology, botany, anatomy, embryology, natural history, experimental psychology). True, he attempted experimental work; but he was without the highly perfected instruments which centuries of progress have placed in the hands of modern scientists. All the more notable is the impetus he gave to what we know as " experimental science ", particularly in the realm of nature. " In the view of modern historians of science ", states Rolland-Gosselin, " before the great Swedish naturalist, Linné, (1707-1778) no new progress was realized in natural history comparable to, and in continuity with, that which we owe to Aristotle " [1].

It should be noted, however, in estimating the scientific value of Aristotle's natural science, that his point of view differs widely from that of the moderns. What he seeks unceasingly to grasp and to explain is the very *nature* of things, both in their general features (in metaphysics and in natural philosophy) [2]; and in their genera and particular species (in the different branches of science). This is why his interpretation of experience is constantly guided by his fundamental theses, above all by that of finality and that of act and potentiality.

---

[1] *Aristote*, p. 45.
[2] The terms used today are *cosmology* and *rational psychology*.

The general conclusions of this form of induction are fully evident, and form the foundations of a true scientific edifice. The method, however, attains in most cases only the probability of pre-scientific inference, when there is question of such particularized conclusions as, for instance, the theory of the four elements. Aristotle makes the best of it and supports it with dialectic reasoning to give scientific value to his opinions [1].

Modern scientists have forged ahead in the exact observation of facts and many of Aristotle's opinions have been rejected in the process. More important still, their approach has been from a different angle. Disregarding the *inner nature* of things, they have sought merely to discover and to formulate in terms of mathematics the laws which measure related phenomena. Thus physics in the modern sense is as distinct from Aristotelian physics as is the mathematician's " vision " from that of the physicist or the student of metaphysics. It follows also that in those conclusions which are certain there is no contradiction, but rather harmonious agreement between the ancient philosopher and the scientist of today. The latter covers a field unoccupied by the former : that of the second degree of abstraction. Each method has its own value. For the utilization of the riches of nature, the modern approach is practically superior, but in view of an intimate and speculative knowledge of physical reality, Aristotle leads the way.

The fertility of the Aristotelian method is above all manifest when applied to the primary object of philosophical study : man himself. For we have in the human consciousness the perfect instrument for the providing of such facts of experience as the scientist needs. This particular branch of physics is, therefore, divided into three parts dealing, respectively, with the spirituality of the soul as postulated by the life of the intelligence (psychology); and the laws governing the soul's activity under its double aspect : subjective aspect, productive of happiness (ethics), and objective aspect, productive of beauty (art).

VII. The subsistent soul : Psychology.

83. Aristotle applies the method derived from his fundamental principle of moderate realism to the science of the human soul : the natures of things are known only by observing their activities and by studying their operative faculties. Man's intellectual life is first considered in this way, and is explained through a dual faculty as a further realization

---

[1] St. Thomas, who accepts without alteration the whole scientific system of Aristotle, discerns clearly this element of hypothesis and of probability.

of the principle of actuality and potentiality. The intellect is either passive (νοῦς παθητικός) or active (νοῦς ποιητικός). Finally, he concludes with scientific proof of the spirituality and immortality of the human soul.

A) Passive Intellect.

Here Aristotle treats the psychological aspect of the theory of abstraction, though abstraction is also treated in logic and in epistemology. His view can be summarized in the following proposition : the intellect by which we grasp abstract essences and construct universal knowledge is 1) *a faculty distinct from the senses;* 2) *pure potentiality,* in the order of knowledge, at birth; 3) *an immaterial quality* in the physical order.

1° **The passive intellect is distinct from the senses.** The most perfect animals, except man, possess all the sensible faculties but are incapable of intellection of any sort. This can be established by noting the absence of opinions or of progressive scientific systems in the animal realm — items which would manifest the work of reason. It must be granted that man has a special and a superior faculty to produce such actions.

2° **The passive intellect is, of itself, pure potentiality to knowledge.** At birth, it can be likened to a bare tablet on which nothing is inscribed. The mind, as well as the senses, depends for its action on the influence of its proper object (sensible reality); this influence is so strong that one of the difficulties of sensation — in breaking this influence — is that it may impede the normal activity of the mind. There are no innate ideas for Aristotle, nor any Platonic reminiscence; all our ideas are received, in docile fashion, from the overpowering contact of experience.

3° Moreover, **the intelligence is also immaterial.** The passive phase is followed by an active phase in which mind shows itself to be dominating and independent. Through knowledge, the mind is capable of becoming all things without exception : " Fit quodammodo omnia ". This capacity distinguishes mind from the senses which are restricted to particular things. Moreover, if a potentiality already has a body in actuality, it is prevented from becoming other bodies without exception inasmuch as a thing does not become that which it already is : " Ex ente non fit ens ". It follows that the passive intellect is of an incorporeal nature, as Aristotle says : " Necesse est itaque, quoniam omnia intelligit, immixtum esse, ut dicit Anaxagoras, ut imperet, hoc autem est, ut cognoscat : Intus enim apparens prohibebit extraneum et obstruet " [1].

4° From the above arguments it follows that the passive intellect is both **separated and impassible.** For it is not joined to a corporeal organ as are the senses, and, consequently, it is less passible than the senses. It is true that both the intellect and the senses are passive in receiving the impressed species. In this process, neither of them loses their perfection and both become enriched by the perfections of the object. But the sense could occasionally and indirectly *(per accidens)* — due to its organic dependence — be hurt and destroyed if the action of the object is too strong and corrupts the sense organ. The mind, on the contrary, is exempted from this accidental corruption; a greater and clearer intelligible object will only make its action more powerful.

B) **Active Intellect.**

84. The active phase of the intellective process is concerned with ideas and with universal sciences, thus showing the existence of a spiritual faculty. Moreover, this phase requires a complementary explanation which Aristotle furnishes by matching the passive intellect, which becomes intelligible things, with an active intellect, which *makes* intelligible things.

The cause must actually possess the perfection of its effect. The passive intellect is not in actuality and cannot, of itself, move itself to the actuality of intellection. The sensible object, on the other hand, whose influence is undeniable, is, without doubt, an insufficient cause; because of its materiality, the sensible object is only potentially intelligible. For, though it contains the ideational object, the universal and absolute essence, it does so only as an unformed lump contains a statue — an artist is needed to evolve the statue. Similarly, color must be actuated by light in order to be visible. In like manner, in order that the sensible object can play its role, it must be actuated or illuminated by a mind essentially in actuality. From this point of view, mind is classifiable under essentially

---

[1] ARISTOTLE, *De Anima*, III, lect. 7. William of Moerbeke's translation, which St. Thomas used in his commentaries, is quoted above; though it lacks literary polish, it is faithful to the Greek. See below, n. 232.

active qualities, termed *habitus :* " Et est intellectus, his quidem talis in omnia fieri; ille vero in omnia facere, sicut habitus quidam et sicut lumen " [1].

Evidently the active intellect is, like the passive, immaterial, separated from any corporeal organ and impassible. Due to the fact that the doer is greater than the receiver, the active intellect has an even greater actuality than the passive : " Et hic intellectus separabilis et impassibilis et immixtus, substantia actu ens : Semper enim honorabilius est agens patiente, et principium materia " [2].

The function of the active intellect, accordingly, is to abstract the intelligible concept from sense experience which is recapitulated in the *phantasms* of the imagination. Following the action of the active intellect, the passive intellect is placed into second actuality, and actual knowledge *necessarily* results according to the axiom : " Intellectus in actu et intelligible in actu sunt idem ". The action of intellection is synthetic and unifies a triple influence : that of the object, which specifies intellection, that of the active intellect, which spiritualizes the object, and that of the passive intellect, which grasps the spiritualized object.

This latter interpretation of Aristotle's view is also that of St. Thomas Aquinas, and is plainly conformable to Aristotle's doctrine. It even appears preferable, historically [3], to an interpretation which attributes to the active intellect alone the contemplation of abstract essences in second actuality [4].

C) The Spiritual Soul.

85. Aristotle states in the first books of the *De Anima* that the inferior souls (vegetal and animal), by reason of their dependence on the body, are corruptible and mortal. The case is different with the human soul. After an analysis of intellection, Aristotle concludes that only the intelligible soul is subsistent, capable of a separate life, and, consequently, is immortal. After the death of man, intellect remains what it is, and it alone is immortal and eternal : " Separatum autem

---

[1] *Ibid.*, lect. 10. See M. DE CORTE, *La doctrine de l'intelligence chez Aristote,* p. 55.

[2] ARISTOTLE, *De Anima*, lect. 10.

[3] Cf. M. DE CORTE, *op. cit.*, p. 57, *ff.*

[4] For this view, see F. PALHORIES, *Vies et doctrines des grands philosophes à travers les âges,* Vol. I, p. 136, and C. PIAT, *Aristote*, pp. 484-5.

est solum hoc quod vere est : et hoc solum immortale et perpetuum est " [1]. Only a being possessing operations which are independent of matter can exist separated from matter through the principle, " Agere sequitur esse ".

Aristotle is content to make but a negative remark about the life of the separated soul, but it is a remark which follows logically from his theory of knowledge. Absented as it is from sensible life, the separated soul can no longer use abstract concepts to remember or to reason. " Non reminiscitur autem, quia hoc [2] quidem impassibile est : passivus vero intellectus est corruptibilis, et sine hoc nihil intelligit anima " [3].

This text causes great difficulties to a Thomistic interpretation. If the passive intellect is corruptible, only the active intellect is immortal, from which it seems that the latter is not a faculty, but a separated substance. This meaning is, in fact, preferred by many scholars [4].

Previously, Aristotle demonstrated that the passive intellect is immaterial and impassible; his remarks here formally contradict his earlier proposals. Such an interpretation is unlikely, and does not seem to be necessary. In order to avoid it, it is sufficient to distinguish two meanings for the expression, passive intellect. Occasionally it designates the spiritual faculty which knows science; at times it is applied to the ensemble of the means of knowing which are superior to external sense experience and which constitute the proximate material for abstractions. Inasmuch as this latter material contains the intelligible in potentiality, Aristotle calls it " passive intellect " and it is evidently corruptible [5]. St. Thomas gives a similar explanation : " The passive intellect is corruptible; this is the part of soul which does not lack the aforementioned passions (love, hatred, reminiscence, etc.,)... for they pertain to the sensitive part. Nevertheless it is called intellect... inasmuch as it somehow partakes of reason, obeying reason and following its movement, as is said in the first book of the Ethics " [6].

Another important doctrine is stated in *De Generationes Animalium* [7]. Inasmuch as the human soul is spiritual and subsistent, it cannot be drawn out of the potentiality of matter, as can other substantial forms. It is not engendered by the parents, but comes into matter from without and as " through

---

[1] ARISTOTLE, *De Anima*, III, lect. 10.
[2] The word, *hoc*, designates the immortal soul, which is impassible, that is, without sensible image.
[3] *Ibid.*
[4] For example, see E BRÉHIER, *op. cit.*, I, p. 238.
[5] See J. FARGES, *Le Cerveau, l'Ame et ses Facultés*, App., p. 490.
[6] St. Thomas Aquinas, In III, *De Anima*, lect. 10.
[7] Book II, Ch. III.

the gate " (Θύραθεν). But this mysterious origin of " that which is divine in us " [1] is not explained by Aristotle.

Finally, Aristotle clearly teaches the *unity of form*. Man has but one soul which is his substantial form, the principle of unity and the common source of its diverse operations.

86. It is evident that this theory is obscure and incomplete on several essential points. The creation of the intellectual soul by God, its individuation through natural union with matter, its personal immortality, and its unique mode of acting in a separated state — these three propositions are Thomistic; they require clarification on Aristotle's part, but he says very little about them.

In a strictly historical view, one can easily suspect that Aristotle tended towards the theory of eternity of souls as did his master, Plato, or towards an impersonal immortality similar to the view adopted by many of his commentators, especially Averroes [2]. But, to support this view, one would have to propose that the agent intellect alone is immortal and that it is to be viewed as a separated form not multiplied in matter. It would, then, have to be united to the passive intellect of each man for the process of intellection. But if the text of the *De Anima* allows such an interpretation, the totality of the Peripatetic doctrine is opposed to it.

Rather, according to the truth of the matter, it must be held with St. Thomas that the intellectual soul is the form of matter, and that all erroneous interpretations are contrary to the Aristotelian principles. This, in fact, is the remarkable value of Aristotle's psychology : it does not affirm anything that is unsupportable with scientific demonstration. Using Aristotle's principles, and penetrating their depth, the Angelic Doctor was able to complete that which Aristotle missed. On these difficult questions, it seems that Aristotle preferred ignorance to error.

VIII. Human activity : Ethics.

87. While preserving its character of practical science, Aristotle's ethics is closely allied to metaphysics and to the speculative study of man [3]. It is dominated by the principle

---

[1] Aristotle, *Nichomachean Ethics*, Book x. — [2] See below, n. 190.
[3] On the other hand, Aristotle's ethics is independent of God and, for this reason, is treated before theodicy.

of finality and has, for its point of departure, the theory of appetite applied to the human will. Both an individual and a social ethics flow from this principle.

A) Theory of Appetite.

" An active tendency of every being towards its proper good " is the general definition of appetite. This good is nothing other than end or purpose. Experience helps make known to us as immediately evident the principle which governs all activity, " every being acts for a purpose ".

In all material beings from minerals to man, appetite is explicable through a new application of actuality and potentiality. Inasmuch as these beings are limited and imperfect through their blend of *potentiality*, their appetite is a desire for that which they lack. They tend towards full *self-actualization* in attaining their good, which is, equivalently, their fulness of being.

Appetite is, of course, diversified according to the degree of perfection of the agents. In addition to the blind tendency of beings without knowledge (called natural appetite), there is a double appetite in beings which possess knowledge. In man it is as follows :

a) **The appetite of sensibility,** source of the passions (emotions). This desire is completely subject to sensible perception if left to its own nature, as is always the case in the animal.

b) **The will,** which tends toward good presented as such by reason. If there is question of the absolute good which is adequate to its aspirations, the will chooses necessarily; but if there is question of some particular good, its choice remains essentially *free*. Aristotle thus proposes a firm and precise view of man's psychological liberty.

The will dominates the sensible appetite in a manner which is somewhat imperfect but still adequate. This is done by imposing the order of reason on the appetite, as well as on the other faculties. The proper role of the will is to conduct man from his imperfect state of potentiality, in which he is born, towards his perfection, in which he will be fully in actuality. Free and voluntary activity is a specifically human trait and constitutes the proper object of ethics.

B) **Individual Ethics.**

88. Perfect happiness, or beatitude, which is constituted by the definitive possession of man's true good, is man's final goal. This aim determines all human activity and all laws. Following Socrates and Plato, Aristotle founds his morality on this principle of finality. Inasmuch as he knew little of the future life, he writes solely from the viewpoint of the *present life*. Within these limits, though, he determined the truly supreme good and the means of achieving it better than any of his predecessors.

1° **Man's final goal.** A critique of hedonism prefaces Aristotle's treatment of man's supreme good. Pleasure, he proposes, is not an activity or a special good which is self-opposed to other goods. In beings possessing knowledge, pleasure is the final flowering of activity made perfect. As a flower is the coronal of the plant and as beauty is the grace of youth, pleasure is the perfection and the achievement of the activity of intellectual beings. There are, however, different pleasures and different activities; one must judge the value of the pleasures by the value of the activities which cause them. The main task is to find the activity which gives man his supreme good and thus procures for him his supreme pleasure, his happiness.

Since he identifies actuality, perfection, and the good, Aristotle asserts at the outset that the achievement of life is the perfect actuation of man's noblest faculty in relation to its highest object. The specific nobility of man, however, is totally due to his intelligence, whose highest object is the First Cause, source of all truths. Man's happiness, consequently, will lie in the intellectual contemplation of God.

It is true that this supreme happiness, viewed as concomitant with the full evolving of intellectual activity, is an almost superhuman ideal, rarely attained and rarely exercised. True happiness, however, should be perpetual. Aristotle resolves this difficulty by simply noting the imperfection of human nature and then moralizing for the present life. He does not relinquish this noble ideal; but he maintains, with a tinge of pessimism, that many men are content with seeking only a relative happiness [1].

---

[1] ARISTOTLE, *Nichomachean Ethics*, Book I, Ch. XI. (See also St. Thomas' commentary, lect. 16.)

2⁰ **Virtue, the means to happiness.** Aristotle does not forget that the intelligence, our participation in the divine, is the substantial formality of man. For this reason, he requires a more perfect actualization of all man's faculties in order that man might progressively and habitually achieve the happiness of contemplation. This is not an absolute goal for each man, but each attains it within the range of his ability, and in a harmoniously dependent hierarchy.

a) The perfection of the vegetative functions is a first requisite for happiness, for their perfect functioning would indirectly assist mental activity. But this is primarily the work of nature, and one must be content to favor the vegetative functions by acquiring a certain bodily well-being, moderated by sufficient rest and avoiding, as much as possible, the needs of both the miserable and the wealthy.

b) What is more needful is the perfect functioning of our conscious life, which is the work of the *moral virtues*. These are stable dispositions or habits (ἕξις). Aristotle considers them as an abundance of active energy or actualization acquired by our free faculties through repeated exercise. With their help, man can follow the measure of reason in his actions, although it is not a matter of drawing out as many actions as possible from each faculty but principally those actions which favor intellectual contemplation. The purpose of the moral virtues, then, is to measure everything according to a *just medium* with the final end, constantly pursued, as the rule.

The moral virtues embrace all the activities of human life : intellectual and voluntary activity, movements of the passions, the use of external goods and social relations — in the measure that these are dependent on the direction of the free or deliberate will. Each of these modes of regulating an activity with a view to contemplation constitutes a special virtue. Aristotle artfully analyzes this rich and complex organism of virtues, insisting strongly on the virtue of friendship. All these minor virtues are referred to the four cardinal virtues as species to genus [1].

3⁰ **Responsibility : evil and duty.** According to Aristotle, man finds himself, at the beginning of his moral life, in an

---

[1] In his *Summa Theologica*, St Thomas utilizes Aristotle's treatment of the moral virtues as the basis for his supernatural morality.

indeterminate state, in *potentiality*. He has, through his
freedom, the power to *actualize* himself, to lift himself to the
happy state of the perfect and the virtuous where his good
habits permit his intellectual life to be fully employed.
Friendship would then be the final achievement of his
prosperity.

Man has the power to refuse true beatitude and to choose vice.
Aristotle seems embarrassed for an explanation of this fact.
His precise formulation of liberty prevents him from following
Socrates and Plato, who denied all voluntary fault. He proposes,
as explanation, a diminution of liberty under the dominion
of the inferior habits, as the vices, which bind the soul to the
fatal conditions of matter [1]. At the same time, he does not deny
responsibility, even though he fails to explain evil.

A similar situation holds for the notion of duty. Does man
have the *obligation* to pursue happiness? His habitual mode
of speaking supposes or affirms the fact of obligation — and
a philosophy of good sense could not reject a truth proclaimed
by the unanimous consent of mankind, even of the pagan mind.
But he is silent on its nature, precise limits and its final
foundation in God. The imperfection of his theodicy, it will
be shown, helps explain this latter point [2].

Aristotle frequently brings together obligation with the
necessity which flows from the natural law. Man is commanded
to practice virtue by the goodness and the beauty with which a
good moral life attracts his free will. But this is also the duty
imposed on every being to realize its own nature according
to the principle of order and universal finality. Granted
the fact of human freedom, is it not still an obligation or moral
necessity for man to pursue virtue, as other beings are
necessitated to realize their natures? Here, again, Aristotle
remains more *incomplete* than erroneous.

C) **Social Ethics.**

89. Society is a natural organization because it is morally
necessary to man in order that he may attain happiness.
Similar to Plato, Aristotle also assigns to society the aim

---

[1] It is only in this sense that Aristotle preserved the Socratic principle that
" every sinner is ignorant ".

[2] St. Thomas clarifies these various points; he distinguishes counsel from
duty, explaining the latter by law. He shows how duty ultimately rests on
the eternal law of God.

of procuring man's happiness, the full actualization of the human person. This principle permits him to deduce both the conditions and the laws of the family and of the city-state. Because he takes experience into consideration, Aristotle succeeds in correcting the Platonic utopia. He does not, however, avoid all error, for he assumes, as basis for his inductions, not only the individual nature of man, but also a blemished, pagan society.

1º THE FAMILY. The family is the first and the most natural of communities, for it is the primordial social unity for propagating the human species.

a) The *father* is the master of rights in the family. He has an obligation of justice to his children only while they are minors. Children are, in a fashion, a simple extension of his own person. He owes them a tender and vigilant love until they are able to care for the normal development of their body and of their soul.

b) The *wife*, though endowed with a less perfect intelligence than the male [1], has rights well defined by her nature. She plays a consultative and deliberative part in family matters, but it is not in her power to decide, and her functions deal solely with the interior domestic order, the needs of her children and of the house. The virtues on which conjugal relations are based are friendship and, more primarily, justice.

c) The *child* owes obedience, affection and respect (τιμή) to his parents, as he does to the gods. The primary education is familial, but is carried out under the active surveillance of the state.

2º THE STATE. It should be mentioned that Aristotle, as well as Plato, had no notion of our modern states, which are constituted by a politically organized nation. For them, the state is a simple conglomerate of families, united solely through community of race, language and civilization, as the Greeks. The state is rather the *city-state*, the perfect and supreme political organization; for example, a city or village with its surroundings, not exceeding 100,000 inhabitants and capable of being governed. Only an offensive or defensive union was considered possible between city-states, a union which was still respectful of the rights of each member state.

Conceived in this wise, the city-state is the natural development of the family. It is an *organized grouping of families* which is not destined for conquest, for war, or for commercial or industrial prosperity; its aim is to make practically possible the acquiring of happiness. The complexity of life requires such mutual assistance as is found in the city-state.

---

[1] As a general rule, Aristotle holds that the masculine temperament is more favorable to the exercise of intelligence; he does, however, allow for exceptions to this rule.

Aristotle considered virtue and happiness somewhat inaccessible to the common man, a view which was pagan in its realism and pessimism. There are two groups in the city-state, the citizens and the servants.

a) The *Citizens* are free men whom birth, education and disposition favor with the worthiness to aspire to the fulness of the intellectual life. The city-state must organize everything so that they can attain this end. This is done through social laws which acquaint each man with his duty in a precise and strong manner, imposing respect and the practice of justice, and permitting friendship to expand in its various forms. To maintain union and social stability, the city-state is bound, especially, to regulate the entire education of children, requiring a uniform method and instruction for each child, so that he may be awakened to love the institutions of the city-state.

An *authority*, enjoying the powers of law-making, of governing and of sanctioning laws, helps the city-state fulfill its task. Aristotle recognized three forms of government, which, dependent on circumstances, could be corrupt and bad, or good and useful : the government of one man (monarchy), that of the better men or the elite (aristocracy), or that of the ensemble of citizens (democracy).

The most perfect government is that which is best adapted to the city-state concerned. A monarchy might work with this combination : a people habituated to slavery as the barbarians and the presence of a supereminent citizen, capable of himself, and better than all others, of understanding and realizing the task of seeking happiness. Except for this rather ideal case, the better government for a free people is that in which the citizens share in the power, not according to a strict equality of rights, as in a democracy, but in a moderated aristocracy. The important positions are reserved to the superior class which is most interested in the common good due to its riches, most worthy and most capable of governing through its heredity, aptitudes and its education. A right of control, however, is given to the assemblies of the people. On the other hand, the free people who govern themselves are always in a minority; the greater portion of the city-state inhabitants is made up of servants.

b) The *servants*. One can speak of those men who live in the city-state but are excluded from the range of citizenship as servants. Their condition makes them incapable of aspiring towards happiness. Among free men, they are such men as the farmers (who do not own the land), the artisans, and the merchants, who take care of mercenary matters. There is a double deprivation in their labors. Their work deprives them of the leisure necessary to acquire science, and it evokes gross habits in them which, in the long run, make them incapable of elevating themselves to virtue.

Among the servants, there is the class of *slaves*. Aristotle justifies this pagan condition as a response to a human necessity.

There are jobs that are inferior and degrading which demand inferior workers; nature furnishes men for these tasks through slavery. By birth, the slave is a man almost deprived of intelligence. He is recognizable by certain physical traits, as his wholly animal vigor, his body being bent towards the earth, and so forth. His call is obligatory and it is most conformable to his interests simply to obey. He is recruited principally from the barbarian prisoners of war, for it would be unjust to reduce a man born free to slavery.

The slave-master has no obligation of justice or friendship to his slaves. Aristotle recommends mildness and moderation to the master, and permits him to love his slaves inasmuch as they are men; but the management of slaves, he remarks, demands a great prudence.

90. Despite its evident merits, these views demand correction on two counts.

1º **From the supernatural point of view.** The determination of the rights of the state in such matters as education, instruction and religion cannot fail to take into account the Church and its imprescriptible rights in these matters. Man has a supernatural destiny. His moral and religious life are henceforth resolved in the society founded by Christ in order to bring him to heaven. The Savior has taken the sovereign authority and the right of legislation away from the state in this domain, which, in the eyes of reason alone, the state could legitimately claim [1]. The state retains its sovereignty, but solely in the order of temporal good.

Furthermore, basing his theory of slavery on the customs of his time, Aristotle ignored that such a decadent state was the consequence of original sin. What he wished to justify was not an institution of right reason, but a degradation of human nature.

2º Finally, **from a natural viewpoint,** his ethics bears the burden of his own ignorance of the future life. Even reason can demonstrate that happiness is not attainable in this life, but only for the separated soul which has finished its time of probation [2]. There the earthly injustices will be balanced off. God has reserved to Himself in the future life the task of dealing with each according to his merits and demerits. These judgments of Divine Providence are ignored by Aristotle.

Aristotle succeeded in achieving only a partial ethics, oriented towards an earthly ideal, and serving a humanity harmed by original sin. It led him to construe his city-state as a place where the minority lived in happiness served by a crowd of servants, as animated instruments, who were necessary and useful for the progression of free men towards the fulness of human life in the contemplation of truth.

---

[1] Aristotle's views safeguard the rights of the family; in this regard, he is less absolute and more defensible than Plato, who made the state too absolute.

[2] See, for examples of discussions on this point, J. E. O' MAHONY, *The Desire of God*, Dublin, 1929 and J. BUCKLEY, *Man's Last End*, Herder, 1949.

This pessimism in so judicious a philosopher proves the great convenience and moral necessity of the dogmas of the Catholic faith, which perfectly re-establish equilibrium. This faith elevates the dignity of the human person, even among the most disinherited, through the promises of the future life and through the Redemption of Christ, offering to all, without distinction, the means of acquiring celestial happiness.

IX. Man's achievement : Art.

91. In order to grasp human nature both in itself and in its properties with fair completeness, it is necessary to deal with a third group of human operations. The first type of operations were the intellectual, regulated by logic; the second type were the subjective operations tending towards happiness, regulated by ethics. The third type of operations are objective, and tend towards placing beauty into exterior things, regulated by the artistic treatises. Aristotle thus founded the study of esthetics, which is divided into two special sections, one on poetry and a second on rhetoric.

1) **Esthetics.** Aristotle did not study beauty in itself, but its expression in art. Art is an essentially practical virtue of the mind whose main role is the imitation of what is real in physical nature or in the moral world. Artistic imitation, however, is not pure copy; it must be taken as expressive and significative, for it attempts to synthesize the disparate and fulfill the incompletion in things. For this reason Aristotle looked to the human word as the maximum of imitation, and as the expression of the real with all its nuances.

The aim of art is to afford esthetic pleasure which, though primarily intellectual, is also sensible. This obtains especially in the " catharsis " in which the soul, admiring its own experiences and emotions in a work of art, finds itself freed and soothed.

2) **Rhetoric.** Connected closely with logic, rhetoric is the art of persuading through discourse. It makes use, above all, of probable principles accepted by all. It makes use of enthymeme as opinion, and even of induction in the wide sense, proceeding by examples. It governs the use of dialectical sources, while taking care of the conditions proper to discourse.

3) **Poetry.** Aristotle composed a general treatise on poetry. All that is available to us, though, is a fragment on tragedy which contains excellent rules on literary compositions concerning the importance of action and its unity, the value of the characters, notes on style, and so forth.

With his artistic treatises, Aristotle closes the cycle of the special sciences whose aim was to have us know sensible nature fully, including man and his affairs. But these multiple and changing riches cannot be clearly explained by themselves. There is a remaining effort for the philosopher, if he wishes to make all intelligible. He must lift himself above nature (a meaning of the word, *metaphysics*) [1] unto the first cause, the explanation of all that is real.

X. Metaphysics : Theodicy.

92. Aristotle herein demonstrates the existence of God and then scientifically deduces His attributes.

A) **Existence of God.**

i. The first proof presented by Aristotle is a popular one, based on the order of the world and on final causality. He has a vivid sense of the hierarchy of essences arranged as an army according to their degree of perfection [2]. Prime matter, as the total negation of actuality, lies at the lowest degree of the scale. At the top, the order is completed by the summation of perfection with total denial of potentiality in God, pure actuality. This admirable order is the result of finality, the constant tendency towards the better and the more perfect. This tendency would be inachievable and incomprehensible, were there not a supreme perfection, a pure actuality to account for it.

2. **The scientific proof** is the famous way of motion demonstrating the existence of a first immobile mover. The argument is developed at length in the eighth book of the *Physics,* and includes three stages :

The first stage : **general necessity of a mover.** Undeniably, motion exists throughout the universe, and, in a special way, in the heavenly revolutions which constitute the unity of the universe. Now that which is being moved is being moved by another called the mover; for movement is a reception of actuality, and the movable in potentiality could not, without absurdity, give itself the actuality it does not possess.

---

[1] The name of this treatise is due to Andronicus of Rhodes, who catalogued it *after* (μετά) the *Physics;* μετά , however, also means beyond or above and thus the word *Metaphysics* is a good designation for the treatise which Aristotle called " first philosophy " or theology. This treatise also considers being and substance; see above, nn. 69-70.

[2] Aristotle, *Metaphysics,* Book xiii, Ch. x.

The second stage: **Necessity of a first mover.** If the mover who explains the movement of the world is, himself, also moved, he must evidently be moved by another, and so forth. But in a series of movers, it is necessary to arrive at a first who possesses in actuality the perfection which is communicated. To recede back, infinitely, is to suppress the source and to declare that all movements are only in potentiality, inasmuch as all are received. One must come to an end (ἀνάγκη στῆναι), says Aristotle. Consequently, there is a first mover who does not receive motion from another : the Immobile Mover.

The third stage: **Necessity of pure actuality.** Of what sort is this first mover? Plato already demonstrated his necessity, but thought of him as the soul of the world, immobile only in the higher aspect of his mind with which he indefectibly contemplates eternal ideas. But by his lower aspect, his royal soul, he would be the principle of his own movement, and through this movement, command the harmonious mechanism of the multiple movements of the universe. Aristotle critizes and rejects this notion. But, though Aristotle does not admit the ideal world whose absolute reality would be the foundation of sciences, he maintains the conviction that the final reason of being for all things must possess this plenitude of perfection, and he attributes it to the only true God. The previous popular proof concluded with the existence of pure actuality, but Aristotle wished to demonstrate this important proposition scientifically. He believed he could do so successfully through his proof from motion, without taking the Platonic way but with the help of the eternity of celestial movements. Having given proof of this eternity [1], he reasons as follows :

An infinite energy must be totally disengaged from all matter, from all quantity or from all potentiality which could limit it.

Now the first mover possesses an infinite energy, for he produces an eternal movement which, not having any limits neither in its origin nor in its term, is infinite; and the cause must be proportionate to its effect.

Thus the first mover is a complete actuality disengaged from all potentiality. It is pure actuality, subsisting as perfection itself.

---

[1] See above, n. 79.

B) **Attributes of God.**

93. After having established the existence of this sublime reality, Aristotle, in order to construct a true theological science, explains, by deduction, the properties which are native to it. He thus finds a double series of attributes. The first are negative, flowing from the lack of potentiality, while the second are positive, pertaining to pure actuality and manifesting its role.

1º **Negative attributes :** *a*) God is IMMATERIAL and consequently inaccessible to the senses; this is evident, for matter is potentiality.

b) He is IMMUTABLE, that is, impassible and immobile, for all movement supposes a passage from potentiality to actuality.

c) He is SIMPLE; or, as Aristotle says, without magnitude, without quantity and thus indivisible. He possesses in himself the perfect unity of simplicity which excludes the unity of composition proper to material beings.

d) He is UNIQUE and very clearly distinct from all others, especially from the world by means of His supreme and solitary perfection. For this, Aristotle gives two reasons. The first is taken from the order of the world; God is necessarily unique if one considers the theory of natural places. For, suppose a system other than our universe : all the heavy elements would meet in a one, common center and all the light elements would reach the extremity and we would thus rediscover our own, unique universe. Furthermore, the unity of the effect establishes the unity of the cause.

A second reason for God's being unique is given. Pure actuality is necessarily unique, for it is plainly exempt from the principle of multiplicity which is potentiality. Although this reason is more decisive and direct, Aristotle does not insist much on it. This may be due to his explanation of polytheism.

2º **Positive attributes :** *a*) God is ETERNAL, principally because his role is that of mover, eternally. Further, because to explain his birth, there would have to be a superior cause which would then be the supreme cause.

b) He is PERFECTION and GOODNESS absolutely. Actuality is a synonym for perfection, and God is pure actuality.

Further, the good is perfection in its role of goal or purpose, capable of fulfilling all desire and every appetite. God, who through his perfection is the final goal of the universe, is thus also the supreme Good.

c) He is SPIRIT and INTELLIGENCE, principally because He is the supreme orderer of the universe; and, according to the principle of Anaxagoras and Socrates, intelligence alone is the source of order. Further, one can attribute to pure actuality the fulness of that which is most perfect here below; but man is the most perfect of these beings, whose nobility lies principally in his spiritual component, and primarily in intelligence.

God, however, must possess supreme intelligence, without any of the imperfections found in man, for there is no mixture of potentiality in his actuality. With a remarkable depth, Aristotle lends precision to the conditions of divine intelligence with regard to its object and with regard to its exercise. The sole object, he maintains, which is capable of specifying the supreme intelligence and of being proportioned to the plenitude of its actuality is the supreme being himself; the proper object of the thought of God is God himself. With regard to the exercise of this divine thought, all passage from potentiality to actuality must be excluded, as well as all composition and real distinction which demands a potential element. Thus it is necessary to exclude from God any distinction between substance and intellectual faculty; he knows through his essence; no distinction between faculty and operation, no ignorance precedes knowledge in him; no distinction between habitual knowledge and actual contemplation, for, without interruption or fatigue, he is Thought in the plenitude of exercise.

God, then, can be defined as: the pure actuality of subsistent intellection, contemplating himself. (Νόησις νοησεως νόησις) [1].

d) He is perfect LIFE, for intellection is life and, as a matter of fact, the most noble form of life.

e) Finally, he is HAPPINESS supreme; for, in contemplating himself, he finds absolute repose in the eternal and unchangeable possession of the supreme Good, for he is this good.

---

[1] ARISTOTLE, *Metaphysics*, Book XI, Ch. IX.

3° **Relations with the world.** Aristotle's view can be stated as follows : *without creating or knowing the world, God is its providence (but in an improper sense), for he is its first mover and its final goal.*

a) For Aristotle, as for his predecessors, the universe is something *given.* One does not seek to explain its existence or its duration. God is interposed solely as the reason of its order and motion.

b) Not only has God not created the world, but, according to Aristotle, he does not know it. In effect, all knowledge is an actuality through which the knower identifies himself (in the ideal order) with the known object and measures his perfection according to the perfection of the object; for it is the object which specifies. Now the world is an essentially imperfect and changing being. If the divine knowledge were to have the universe as its object, it would also become imperfect and variable, which would be contrary to God's supreme perfection.

It is necessary, then, to conclude that God is not providence in the proper sense of that word, because this attribute demands perfect knowledge of all creatures, and deliberate benevolence which procures their good.

Another conclusion follows, namely, that God does not move the world in a conscious and free fashion, which would, again, suppose that he knew it. Nevertheless, he remains in contact with it, for, according to the proof from motion, he is its first mover.

Aristotle's thought on this matter seems to be that God, through his perfection — as other necessary natural causes (as fire heats water) — is the efficient cause of the eternal and immutable movement of the first heaven whose regularity and excellence agree with the eminence of pure actuality. Thus one could also justify the common view that God is localized in the first heaven, even though it is not place in the proper sense.

God immediately moves only the first, outermost sphere; through its mediation, however, he determines all other movements, whether celestial or terrestrial, accidental or substantial, as, for example, the generation of living things. This universal causality is not subject to chance, but operates according to the natural law of finality through which each being, in all the details of its evolution, tends towards pure actuality as towards its ideal and final purpose. Thus God remains the final explanation of all the good of the universe, and, in this improper meaning, is Providence.

4° **Religion of Aristotle.** A man's notion of God determines his conception of his relations with God, or his religion. Aristotle did not absolutely reject pagan polytheism, for he considered every ancient tradition as a depository of a fund of truth. However, more sturdily than did Plato, Aristotle gives polytheism a rationalist interpretation. There are, then, among the multiple gods, some separated intelligences charged with moving each of the spheres of the heavens, according to Aristotle's astronomical system. Spiritual and invisible beings, these intelligences are presented as having pure forms; they are finite and subordinated. Nevertheless, in accomplishing their task, they regulate themselves according to the contemplation of pure actuality in which they find their inalterable happiness. Aristotle did not, however, use the real distinction between essence and existence by which God is reserved an absolutely unique position, and these star-movers appear as multiple pure actualities [1]. There are 47 of them, according to the number of spheres established by the astronomers [2].

God's excellence and supreme perfection demand adoration and the most profound respect ($\tau\iota\mu\dot{\eta}$) from man, which naturally extends towards the other gods. The religion of a wise man is in need of no other virtues, for the immutability and the providence of God, as Aristotle views them, remove all basis for prayer and thanksgiving. These latter devotions are permitted to the people; at the same time, all should conform to the traditional rites practiced in the city-state.

94. The *eminent validity* of Aristotle's theodicy is due to two facts. The propositions which are explicitly demonstrated are completely true (as those on the attributes of God), or they are without positive error even though quite incomplete (as the views on God and his relation to the world).

With regard to divine knowledge, for example, Aristotle surely establishes one of its essential marks : its independence of any external influence. His view, though, must be completed.

---

[1] See M. D. ROLAND-GOSSELIN, *Aristote*, p. 91.
[2] ARISTOTLE, *Metaphysics*, Book XII, Ch. VIII.

Knowledge, he maintains, measures its perfection from that of the object. This is true if one is considering the proper specifying object; and, in the Divine Intelligence, this is God Himself. If one considers secondary objects, moreover, this view is also true for a *passive* intelligence, which knows the object in itself and while receiving this concept, as in human knowledge. However, if one is concerned with an *active* intelligence, which knows in its principle (that is, in itself), the exterior object which it creates, Aristotle's position must be modified; for it is in this way that God knows the smallest details of the universe, whether past, present or future. Summarily, it can be said that Aristotle maintains that God does not know the world as man does; this is true but does not go far enough, for God knows the world *better* than man does.

Some historians [1] think that Aristotle's God is only the final cause of the universe. God does not know the world and, further, He cannot be its efficient cause. The latter would require some sort of contact, a condition which would be at odds with the immutability of God, Who is the final cause which moves without being moved. St. Thomas and most of his disciples, however, hold with good reason that in presenting God as the final end of the universe, Aristotle did not destroy, but merely completed his preceding demonstration of God as motor or efficient cause [2].

There are, of course, grave imperfections in Aristotle's theodicy; the source of these errors lies partly in his highly restrained point of departure. In reacting against Plato, Aristotle became too attached to the solely physical aspect of the problem of God. He searched too earnestly for the supreme cause of the becoming in the universe, and too strongly for the first mover of local movement. Furthermore, outside of the eternal revolutions of the first heaven, everthing else is broken loose from God and is only attached to Him as to a final cause, and almost as an abstract ideal [3]. From this same source arise the serious defects in his conception of the divine knowledge and providence, as well as the divine action on the world. The latter seems to be a natural and necessary causality more than a free and voluntary directive.

Aristotle did not succeed in rising to that fully metaphysical view where Plato, through his doctrine of participation, invited him. He could, there, have conceived of God as the One and the Perfect, as the final reason for the multiple and the imperfect, as the cause not only of the becoming, but of

[1] See, for example, M. DE WULF, *Histoire de la philosophie médiévale*, 4th éd., p. 39. — E. BOUTROUX, *Études d'histoire de philosophie*, p. 140 and 149. — E. BRÉHIER, *Histoire de la philosophie*, p. 223.

[2] See R. JOLIVET, *Essai sur les rapports entre la pensée grecque et la pensée chrétienne*, 1re partie, Aristote et saint Thomas ou l'idée de création.

the *being* of things, as not only the moving cause, but the *creative* cause [1]. At this juncture one can mention the assimilation of Peripateticism by the Christian philosophers, who enriched Aristotle's theodicy with treatises on God as Creator and Mover, on the Science, Liberty, Exemplarism and Providence of God, and on His function as Supreme Rewarder and as the source of the natural law. This was not foreseen by Aristotle, of course; and it might be said that in this regard the Platonic current was closer to the full truth.

CONCLUSION. — **95.** — Of all the Hellenistic efforts concerning wisdom, Peripateticism is certainly the most complete system. If it does not appear as the most brilliant, it is the most balanced, responding best to an ideal shaped according to the humble measure of our pure reason. Aristotle also has presented a synthesis in which all the sciences are fully unified, for he found the unique center point at which two fundamental tendencies of the human mind meet : the *positivist* tendency, insisting on the riches of sensible intuition and the *idealistic* tendency, insisting on the potentiality of the intelligence to attain the absolute. Aristotle clearly saw that the abstractive nature of our reason did not permit him to achieve all truth as scientific without keeping continual contact, directly or indirectly, with experience.

Basically, he gave an exact account of the strength and the weakness of his own mind. His weakness is shown by the fact that he subjected himself to a rigorous method, slow and traditionalistic, which criticized each detail, leaning upon the efforts of his predecessors and proving each new affirmation. His strength is shown in his ambition to resolve all the problems of the universe; he applied his reflection to the most humble realities of the universe as well as to the most sublime perfections of God.

Despite all this, Aristotle nevertheless tends towards positivism. For, despite his reaction against Plato and despite the weakness of reason left to its own devices, Aristotle did not resolve, except in a very imperfect manner, the three essential problems of metaphysics : God, the soul, and the good.

---

[1] In the second book of the *Metaphysics*, Aristotle states, though merely in passing, the formula of creative causality, " The first being is the cause of all being, as the first truth is the cause of all truth ". St. Thomas frequently cites this text to correct Aristotle with his own doctrine.

He was, above all, a physicist, concerning himself with exploring all the riches of nature, creating many sciences in order to interpret them and completing them by a vast web of probable opinions.

His immediate disciples, for about two or three centuries, were little more than physicists. His logic, though, scored a great success.   It was highly esteemed by the Stoics [1], adopted by the Neo-Platonist, Porphyry [2], and is found among the manuals of the Schools of Rhetoric at the time of St. Augustine [3]. The Latin translation of Boethius [4], transmitted his logic to the first Scholastics, who had no other work of Aristotle than this one from the eighth to the twelfth century.

The metaphysical heritage of Peripateticism was collected by the Syrians [5], who transmitted it to the Arabs; through the latter channel Aristotle made his entrance, at the close of the twelfth century and at the beginning of the thirteenth, into the Western schools.   There Aristotle awakened an intense intellectual fermentation, and strongly marked his imprint on the Christian philosophy of Scholasticism. Perhaps one can be permitted to see a providential design in the extraordinary role of pagan wisdom, elaborated through long centuries before Christ, and becoming, during the Middle Ages and even unto our times [6], an instrument perfectly adapted for the theologians of the Catholic Church.

---

[1] See n. 101.
[2] See n. 122.
[3] See n. 144.
[4] See n. 198.
[5] See n. 180.
[6] See F. CAYRÉ, *Manual of Patrology*, Vol. II, pp. 570-574.

THIRD ERA.

Decline and Transition.

FROM 322 : DEATH OF ARISTOTLE (3rd cent., B.C.)

TO 270 : DEATH OF PLOTINUS (3rd cent., A.D.)

(529, A.D. : Close of the School at Athens.)

96. The progress of pagan thought was not sustained after the death of Plato and of Aristotle. Their students, who continued to teach at the Lyceum and at the Academy, did not know how to deepen, nor even to comprehend the great metaphysical doctrine left by their masters. Six centuries of *decadence* ensue, rich in secondary authors, disciples and commentators, all in great numbers but all quite unimportant.

This period, however, is not entirely deprived of philosophical worth, for it also serves as a period of *transition*. It may be viewed as a providential development between Aristotle — the pure rationalist, only admitting reason as the source of truth — and St. Augustine the mystic — who, with the help of the Spirit of Wisdom, realized the new ideal of a Christian philosophy at the service of faith. Scholasticism and Thomism, later, are the full flowering of Augustine's ideal.

The distance between Aristotle and Augustine is covered in two phases : 1) there is a transition from metaphysics to ethics, the latter keeping human nature as an ideal; 2) there is a transition from ethics to mysticism [1], the latter submitting man to religion. Each of these phases is due to a certain number of thinkers who have some originality and some

---

[1] For the meaning of this word, see n. 120.

influence on the development of human thought. Two chapters
will cover this period :

Chapter I.   Ethical Transition.

Chapter II.   Mystical Transition.

The succession of these two stages is not strictly chronological,
the end of the first stage being contemporary to the beginning
of the second. The moral transition begins with the death
of Aristotle (322, B.C.), and continues to the time of Marcus
Aurelius (121-180), the emperor-philosopher. On the other
hand, the mystical transition extends from Philo (40, B.C. —
40, A.D.), a contemporary of Christ, until Proclus (died, 487),
the last important disciple of Plotinus.

BIBLIOGRAPHY (for the third period).

COPLESTON, F., *A history of philosophy, Volume I, Part V*,
" Post-Aristotelian Philosophy", Westminster, Md., 1946. —
SARTON, G., *A history of science, Ancient science through the golden
age of Greece*, Chapters XXII-XXIV, Cambridge, 1952.

CHAPTER ONE.

MORAL TRANSITION.

From Aristotle to Marcus Aurelius.

97. The return to strictly ethical considerations — which
had so strongly marked the work of Socrates — can be explained
by the general social situation in Greece at the end of the
fourth century. It seems that the great force of the
philosophical spirit as well as the ethical nobility of the ancient
Greeks was their patriotism; they loved liberty and were
devoted to the prosperity of their country, at least as found
in the city-state though not to the nation as such. Thus arose
valiant generals to defend the fatherland, powerful orators
to govern her, renowned writers to decorate her celebrations,
and great philosophers to fashion her intelligence and to form
the best social laws.

However, from the third century on, the Greek city-states
were conquered by Alexander and lost their independence.

They were governed by kings from Macedonia and from Pergamos, from Syria or from Egypt; and, in this process, they changed only their state of subjection until they received definitive subjection from Rome. Patriotism was no longer able to support the pagan soul, so that it retired within itself and abandoned itself to decadence. It did not dream of turning itself to religion, for its force had collapsed with that of the city-state, of which it was an integral part. The sole aim of the philosophers was to assure individuals of peace and contentment in such unhappy surroundings. From these social facts arose their disinterestedness for metaphysical and even physical speculations, as well as their predilection for ethical problems. This further accounts for an absence of superior minds among them, and seals this period with three marks of decadence :

1) **Materialism.** Unable to grasp the metaphysical propositions of Plato and Aristotle, the more advanced minds of this period obstinately regarded bodies and bodily goods as the sole reality, and sense knowledge alone as of value.

2) **Egoism.** The principal fault of all these systems of thought, despite their radical differences, is their egoistic trait; they were addressed solely to the individual and aimed only to bring him into an untroubled state. These systems sought for peace of soul and absence of stress, allowing each to find personal contentment without any political or social ideal.

3) **Naturalism.** Deprived of any religious assistance, people sought for happiness through the resources afforded by human reason and liberty alone. They were not concerned with God except to deny Him, to lower Him to the realm of corporeal beings, or to identify Him with man.

This very naturalism became an occasion for some progress in thought. Considering man in this fashion, philosophy became international and cosmopolitan; it could speak indifferently to all men as well as to those in Alexandria or in Rome. Doubtlessly, this is why this view was adopted by the early Roman thinkers who were smitten with universalism. Moreover, the Latin genius, more practical than speculative, easily collected these ethical directions and prolonged them even to the second century after Christ.

But these three traits did not prevent a multiplicity and a diversity of systems. Out of all these systems, three strains of doctrine ensue : Stoicism, Epicureanism, and Scepticism. The views sponsored by the Academicians, by the Eclectics and by the decadent Peripatetics will be considered under Scepticism.

It is remarkable that the source of these three theories goes back beyond Aristotle and Plato to Socrates. The Socratic dialogues nourished not only his two great disciples, but also many secondary schools of thought which remained attached only to the ethical view (the minor Socratics). The three principal schools are :

1º *The Cynics.* This school was founded by Antisthenes, and made illustrious by Diogenes; their stress of independence as an ideal inspired Stoicism.

2º *The Cyrenaics.* This group was founded by Aristippus at Cyrene; their original hedonism turned into Epicureanism.

3º *The School of Megara.* Euclid of Megara founded this school [1], whose dialectical or disputational emphasis led to Scepticism.

This chapter, therefore, has three articles :

Article I.   Stoicism.

Article II.   Epicureanism.

Article III. Scepticism.

ARTICLE ONE. — STOICISM.

SPECIAL BIBLIOGRAPHY.

1º **Texts :** OATES, W. J., (ed.), *The Stoic and Epicurean philosophers : the complete extant writings of Epicurus, Epictetus, Lucretius, Marcus Aurelius,* New York, 1940.

2º **Studies :** ARNOLD, E. V., *Roman stoicism,* Cambridge, 1911. — EVAN, E. E., *Stoics and sceptics,* Oxford, 1913. — CHOLLET, J., *La morale stoïcienne en face de la morale chrétienne,* Paris, 1898. — HICKS, R. D., *Stoic and epicurean,* New York, 1910. — JAGU, A., *Zenon de Cittium,* Paris, 1946; — *Epictète et Platon,* Paris, 1946.

98. Stoicism was founded by Zeno of Citium (336-264) in Cyprus. Ar first he followed his father's commercial trade;

---

[1] Euclid of Megara was a contemporary of Plato, and is not to be confused with the mathematician of the same name.

a shipwreck ruined their fortune, and Zeno turned to philosophy.
He came to Athens and there became a disciple of Crates,
the Cynic. He became a disciple of other renowned teachers
and finally founded his own school at the Painters' Porch,
a beautiful sight in Athens; this is the origin of the term,
Stoicism (Στοα ποικίλη). He reached an advanced age and,
conforming to his principles, committed suicide.

Stoicism succeeded in attracting a great number of superior
minds, and achieved a bright career in the Roman world,
where the haughty nobility seemed to be Stoics by birth.
The more famous Stoics include the following : *Cleanthes*
(300-232), the successor of Zeno at the school of Athens;
Chrysippus (282-204), a powerful dialectician, often called
the second founder of Stoicism; *Poseidonius* (135-51), a man
of vast erudition; *Seneca* (4, B. C. — 65, A.D.) whose *Letters*
show him to be an ingenious casuist, and who was the teacher
of Nero, as well as a close friend of Cato and Thrasea; *Epictetus*
(died 117, A.D.), a freed slave [1] who, like Socrates, lived his
philosophy before it was written up in the *Discourses;* Marcus
Aurelius, (121-180), the emperor, who mitigated Epictetus'
doctrine in his *Meditations*.

Definition. STOICISM *is the ethical view of the effort or intense
preoccupation of mind which is necessary to attain supreme
happiness (untroubledness) and which resides solely in a
reasonable life according to nature* [2].

This definition makes it clear that the ethical viewpoint
unifies all Stoical speculation. More than some of their
contemporaries, the Stoics strived to base their rules of conduct
on a general theory of human nature and of the universe.
The source of their conception of happiness is found in their
pantheistic conception of the life lived according to reason.
Their pantheism is but an effect of their materialism, powerless,
at best, to explain the world. Thus the primordial principle
of Stoicism derives from their view of the physical world and

---

[1] He was at first a slave of Epaphroditus, a freedman of Nero's. Once he
was freed, he wished to stay poor, conformable to his doctrine. He wrote
nothing; his disciple, Arrian, compiled the *Discourses*, the *Life*, and the *Manual*
of Epictetus.

[2] In contrast to the Epicureans, one could say that Stoicism looked for happiness
in a specifically human good, since it is reason which distinguishes us from
animals. See n. 106.

is applied to the intellectual and to the moral domains —
which will be considered in the following three paragraphs :

I.   Source of the Stoic principle : the pantheistic and
      materialistic view of the life lived according to
      reason; Physics.

II.   Speculative corollary : Logic and science.

III. Practical corollary : Ethics.

I. SOURCE OF THE STOIC PRINCIPLE.

Pantheistic and materialistic view of the life lived
according to reason. Physics.

99. " Follow nature " is the essential precept through
which Stoicism pretends to lead man to the independence
of happiness. The meaning of this adage can be grasped if the
Stoic view of the entire universe — of which man is but a part —
be understood. The universe is presented as animated by the
divine Logos who unifies the diverse beings into an harmonious
hierarchy.

A) The Divine Logos.

The physics of the Stoics is replete with a number of profound
views taught by their predecessors, especially by Plato and
Aristotle. For the most part, however, while retaining the same
vocabulary, they lower the doctrine to the level of their own
decadence through a *materialist* interpretation.

1) In the first place, they recognize the celebrated principle
of Anaxagoras, that the order of the universe demands the action
of intelligence; with the help of this excellent notion, they
prove God's existence. Similar to Plato, they conceive of God
as the universal soul, who is one, intelligent and wise and who
organizes the universe while endowing it with formality.
For this reason, they gave him the title of " Seed-bearing
Reason " [1], or of reason as generating the order, beauty and
goodness in the universe.

----

[1] From the Greek, Λόγος, meaning reason, and σπερματικός from σπέρμα,
or seed; for St. Augustine's view, see n. 171.

2) Providence is God's main attribute. He unceasingly works out the progressive organization of the universe, a fact which supposes that He possesses the perfect science of all the events which He conducts, and the efficacious action with which He can distribute goodness and perfection everywhere. But this bountiful action occurs according to immutable and necessary laws, similar to the intellectual unfolding of conclusions from a principle. For this reason, likewise, God is conceived as the *Logos*. One can say, nevertheless, that God is free, for this necessity comes from the very depths of His nature and is not due to any constraint from beings exterior to Him, for none such exist. Against the Epicurean view, the Stoics vigorously defended Providence, but in such a fatalistic sense that they destroyed its true meaning.

3) At the same time, God is also corporeal; only in this way can He function in the role of organizer, since it is inconceivable that pure spirit could act upon matter. This conclusion the Stoics derived from the physical theories of Aristotle on efficient causality, especially from the two axioms : " Agens non agit in sibi simile ", and, " Omne agens agit simile sibi ". Efficient causality not only requires that the receiver of the effect lack the perfection he receives, and thus be different from the cause, but also that he have some similarity of nature to the cause in order to be acted upon by contact. From this notion the Stoics deduced their great principle of *universal analogy*. Inasmuch as all the beings of the universe act on all other beings, as their harmonious order shows, they all enjoy an identity of nature despite their individual differences; without exception, all of them are corporeal and material. For this reason, also, God is fire, the most subtle body; and, synthesizing contradictory attributes, the *Logos* is *Intelligent Fire* as Heraclitus proposed.

4) To make God's action on the world more precise, the Stoics proposed the theory of pantheism and of palingenesis [1].

a) **Pantheism.** Even though God is a body, He is not juxtaposed to the world, but is united to it through compenetration. He infilters Himself within it in such a way that the result is less a composite than a unique being endowed with two aspects : one is a formal and divine aspect manifested

---

[1] From the Greek, πάλιν, anew, and γένεσις, birth.

in perfection, activity and life; the other is a material aspect, manifested in imperfection, variety and change. Only a distinction of reason holds between these two aspects. This is the view of a *complete commingling* (κράσις δι' ὅλων) which the Stoics applied to all bodies. If one would object that experience clearly testifies that incompenetrability is a natural property of bodies, they would invoke facts seemingly in favor of their view, as the mixture of liquids, and the filtering of liquids through thin sheets [1]. But the Stoics were not very insistent on the speculative validity of their theories, and were not prepared to consider their many contradictions. But they certainly did teach the absolute identity of God, conceived as the universal soul, with each being of nature viewed as a part or particular member of the divine body.

b) **Periodic palingenesis.** The activity proper to each perfect being and especially to God becomes, in this materialistic system, a *tension* or an indefatigable effort. Further, when the Divine Fire arrives at the extreme point of tension at which the entire universe is but an immense mass of flame, it is bound to relax and unbend itself in order to be in repose. Thus is born the multiplicity of the real order, for the densest portions are reassembled in a central point (the earth), while the most subtle arrange themselves in a series of spheres, according to ancient astronomy. However, as soon as this evolution has used up all possible combinations, an inverse motion of tension arises, whose goal is a new conflagration of the universe. In this process, a new series of changes occurs, rigorously similar to those which previously occurred; this is the notion of periodic palingenesis.

B) **The Hierarchy of Beings.**

100. Stoic materialism caused their view of Aristotle's hylomorphism to be a deformed copy. They recognized a dual element in bodies; the one was *quality*, which compenetrated the other, *matter*, in order to grace matter with cohesion, differentiation and activity. In brute matter this quality was called an " *habitual state* " (Ἕξις) [2], the principle of unity and of resistance. In plants

---

[1] If these materials are passed through without being destroyed, there has been a total mixture; see PLOTINUS, *II Ennead*, VII, who discusses these matters. One could also point to the fact that the soul, in entering the body, does not augment its volume.

[2] Ἕξις, which the Scholastics translated as " *habitus* ", implies more than the English " habit ". According to Aristotle and St. Thomas, it is a stable though accidental state of being.

it is a " *nature* " (φύσις), conferring capability of nourishment and growth; in animals it is a " *soul* " (ψυχή), as the source of emotions and instinctive movements; finally, in man, the soul is endowed with " *reason* " or a unique " *seed-bearing* " reason.

The human soul is doubtlessly material in the Stoic view, but it is of a matter much more subtle than other bodies. It sits at the peak of the hierarchy of beings, for it is most immediately considered as a spark of the divine fire; or, as Epictetus calls it, " a breath of God ". Further, the soul is not inferior to the many gods who also are corporeal intelligences emanating from the universal soul. But there is no personal immortality for any of these gods, nor for the soul, at least in any definitive sense. At man's death, the soul, in so far as it is material, may perhaps dissolve its elements as those of the body, to be swallowed up in the universal circulation. Or, being of a more subtle and durable element, and being more free in its proper operations without the hindrance of the body [1], it may survive for a time; but its personal self will be completely destroyed on the day of universal conflagration.

Pantheism, accordingly, as applied to the human soul, makes the fundamental principle of Stoicism clear. Happiness lies in the life lived according to reason, for only such a life allows us to dominate the universe in each event and thus to attain an untroubled state in identifying ourselves with the universal *Logos*. We are thus made rich with all the goods of God; happiness consists in possessing these goods with a clear and sure conscience, and, accordingly, in knowing them and willing them. The other two sections of Stoicism point out the double means necessary to realize this goal, one of which is speculative (logic), the other, practical (ethics).

II. SPECULATIVE CONSEQUENCES.

Logic and science.

101. Science, inasmuch as it makes us know the *Logos* and his nature perfectly, is the first means of identification with him. Although the general character of man's knowledge makes this a rather easy task, one must conquer oneself by a triple effort.

---

[1] This seems to be Seneca's teaching; see CHOLLET, *La Morale stoïcienne*, p. 130.

A) **General Character of human knowledge.**

Quite logically, the Stoic view of knowledge is one of sensual empiricism. All reality being corporeal, sensation is the only knowledge possible; there is no spiritual intelligence capable of Platonic intuition or Aristotelian abstraction. The Stoics, however, retained Aristotle's formal logic with its rich classifications. Instead of interpreting the concept as an expression of a universal nature (moderate conceptualism), they viewed it as a simple, common name which summarized a group of sensations or took the place of a group of individuals more or less similar (nominalism). Thus the scientific reason itself was but the highest evidence of sensation.

Deprived of his specific difference, man is still distinct from animal. What is common to both is a pure passive impression received through the sense organs under the influence of objects; true knowledge, however, demands a reaction, a psychological " tension " of which man alone is capable.

B) **The triple effort.**

While suppressing the work of abstraction, the Stoic sensualism did not facilitate the task of science. True to their philosophy of effort, they conceived of perfect knowledge as a bundle of sensations closely knit through three successive efforts :

1.   **The effort of assent** is first required in order to refer back to the object the image received through sensation. This is effected through the judgment which alone possesses truth or falsity and constitutes the beginning of true knowledge.

2.   **The effort of memory** begins the work of scientific unification. The seat of memory is in the brain. Memory retains and associates most sensations, forming much larger natural groups than the individual facts from which they arise. These groups retain merely general traits; they are capable of evoking a large number of objects or past events whose traces they retain, and of opening future perspectives on these realities or on analogous facts. The Stoics called the latter " anticipations ".

3.   **The effort of reason,** finally, synthesizes a great number of previously associated facts under one law, expressing their necessary order of coexistence and succession. In this way we attain the very principle of universal order, the divine *Logos* whose unique role is to realize the fatal development of events. Here, at last, one need not direct one's life through simple guesses or hazardous anticipations, but one can infallibly foresee the direction of his own life.

Zeno summarized his theory as follows : " He showed his open hand, fingers extended, and said, ' This is the representation.' Then, quickly, folding his fingers, he said, ' This is the assent.' Firmly closing his fist, he said that this was perception. Finally, clasping his right fist in his left hand, he said, ' Here is science, which is proper to the wise man ' " [1].

102. In their theory of science, the Stoics seem to be *precursors of the modern positivists*. Both replace the study of essences by that of facts and relations between these facts, which is properly the work of sense knowledge [2]. Both maintain the superiority of man by attributing reason to him; implicitly they even admit the influence of a spiritual faculty, necessary to arrive at the third stage of establishing laws. Further, they both reject any metaphysics from their system, and are content with an appeal to the postulate of universal determinism, to which they submit nature, as well as individual and social human life. On these fundamental points these two views are in full accord, although positivism has profited from the progress of the sciences; and, more reservedly, calls itself agnostic and not materialistic [3].

III.   PRACTICAL COROLLARY.

Ethics.

103. It is not sufficient for man to know his identity with the *Logos* in order to be happy. Man must want happiness; he must voluntarily and consciously accept it. A special theory of virtue and some important consequences follow from this view.

A) **Virtue.**

Stoic virtue is the *disposition through which man* (seeing clearly that he himself together with the universe is necessarily involved in the inexorable evolution of the *Logos*) *freely and spontaneously acquiesces to all the events of his life as to his veritable good.* It is a full realization of the command, " follow nature ", interpreted in a pantheistic sense. Universality and individualism, two apparently contradictory traits, follow from this position.

Man must consider himself, first, as a citizen of the universe, for he is but a member of a vast world; this effects a *cosmopolitan* attitude in him, and teaches him to acquit himself conscientiously of his measure of being man : " Hominem agere ", said Seneca. At the same time, man does not arise to a social or international

---

[1] CICERO, *Academica Priora*, II.
[2] They erred concerning the formal object of human intelligence which is not merely corporeal being but rather the essence abstracted from sensible things.
[3] See nn. 471-3, below.

ethics; his universalism is theoretical, and the second trait, more important because of its practicality, is *individualism*. Every effort devoted to the progress of the universe or of society has a twofold uselessness : universal determinism makes such efforts ineffectual, and, secondly, everything arrives at its best, anyway, in the immense body ordered by the wisdom of the *Logos*. Evil does not exist even for those who fail to subordinate all details for the good of the ensemble; for everything is really good in things themselves. The wise man, accordingly, does not need to operate on external things, but solely on his own personal life, so that it may conform to the rhythm of universal life.

Further, by limiting the domain of virtue only to the interior life of the wise man, another restriction arises. For all the events of our own existence, as well as those of the universe, are, in themselves or objectively, the best for us; hence there is no need to change anything. At the same time, a thing is in our power, and vice is still distinct from virtue, or such is the proper under-standing of events. Epictetus' slave, for example, cannot prevent his master from breaking his leg, but the slave can refuse to admit the sorrow thus caused is real [1]. This autonomy of judgment is a fine thing, according to the Stoics; for, from an ethical view, the value of things depends on the estimate we make of them. This attitude constitutes virtue, vice being nothing but a revolt against the decrees of the *Logos-Providence*.

One can accuse this view of following the Socratic and Platonic identification of virtue with wisdom. At root, every moral reform is intellectual. Asceticism thus has for its purpose the enlightening of the disciple's mind so that he can discern the true from the false goods. But the Stoics also insisted on the notion of " tension "; it represents the effort required that this judgment could always be pronounced and fully accepted. If virtue is but a judgment, it is an act of the free will.

B) Corollaries.

104. A triple corollary devolves from this view.

I. **Condemnation of the passions.** Their materialistic system led the Stoics to divide the movements of sensibility into two groups :

a) The *life of reason*, constituted by the sensible tendencies conformable to the *Logos* or to the universal order.

b) The *passions*, comprising all movements contrary to the *Logos*. Thus every passion is essentially evil; it is always a sin or a vice, a passing disorder or an incurable malady of the soul. The wise man, whose virtuous judgment dominates life, aims constantly to extirpate his passions.

---

[1] See ORIGEN, *Contra Celsum*, VII, 53.

One might admit that passion in this sense is worthy of some condemnation[1], but the Stoics exaggerated this view in practical applications. Beguiled by a false ideal of peace, they contended that any sensible manifestation, especially that of fear or sorrow, was bad in principle. The true wise man, identified with the *Logos*, must enjoy an *absolute impassibility* of such a type, that if the universe were to fall to pieces, he would rest calm among its ruins.

2. **The unity of virtue.** Stoic virtue, accordingly, consists entirely in a general attitude of deliberate will with regard to the goods of life, in making up one's mind for all cases, and in never sacrificing the domain of reason to that of passion. For this reason it is not susceptible of degrees and is necessarily present or absent in such a way that men fall rigorously into two categories, the wise and the foolish.

3. **The possibility of happiness.** The aforementioned virtue, completing our conscious identification with the *Logos*, gives us the fulness of all goods and, thus, perfect happiness; peace and independence follow along with an absolute indifference towards everything else, whether pleasures or sorrows.

In practice, however, the Stoics had to mitigate the rigor of these principles. Aside of the absolute good of virtue, a superhuman ideal and usually unattainable, they admitted some suitable goods to which an honest man had a right to attach himself. For example, they allowed one to enjoy the pleasures which life affords, as long as one regarded them rightly and was not duped by pleasure. " If you love a piece of earthenware ", Epictetus counsels, " say to yourself, I love a piece of earthenware; but if it breaks, you will not be troubled with it further ". They also tolerated the joys of family life, the pleasure of friends, and so forth. These ancient Jansenists knew how to be indulgent directors of conscience and quite supple and human casuists, as is shown in the " *Letters* " of Seneca to Lucilius.

CONCLUSION. **105.** The main vice of Stoicism is its pantheistic materialism, an outgrowth of the decadence of speculation. Inasmuch as God is the organizing intelligence of matter, and because the cause must resemble the effect,

---

[1] One can find a pejorative meaning attached to the word " passion " in Christian asceticism without the errors or exaggerations of the Stoics.

these philosophers concluded that God is a corporeal intelligence, identical with the world. They showed themselves unequal to metaphysical notions by their inability to conceive being as such to be realizable in the infinite, distinct from corporeal being which is experienced. Had they done so, they could have comprehended the perfect cause, a spiritual reality, similar to its effect with regard to its perfection, but plainly distinct from it through the exclusion of all material limits.

It is true that in their formulas the Stoics profited by the progress achieved through the greater Socratics; but their language, so eloquent in speaking of God, intelligence and virtue, suffers from a *constant equivocation*. Though they could be interpreted in a spiritualist and orthodox sense, their meaning was materialist and pantheist. This is especially seen in their theory of virtue. For their perfect submission to the *Logos* becomes, as the peak of Christian virtue, an abandonment to the Will of God. But pantheism prevents this interpretation, for it suppresses personality, and herewith denies true liberty, all obligation, responsibility and merit worthy of the name. Through its attractive appearance, Stoicism beguiled the last great spirits of paganism. The Stoic sage, however, has little in common with the notion of a saint. Sanctity is formed of humility and charity, but the Stoic, without love, submits to an inexorable law governing all things; further, the saint lovingly fulfills, with a wealth of devoted liberty, the will of the Father Who is in heaven.

It is easily seen, however, that among the pagan systems, the Stoic ethics was one of the highest. It had particular merit in reacting against the communizing tendencies of the former moralists who seemed bent on absorbing the individual into the state; in contrast, Stoicism resorted to the value of the human person who enjoys, through reason, some inalienable rights.

ARTICLE TWO. EPICUREANISM.

SPECIAL BIBLIOGRAPHY.

1º **Texts :** (See listing before number 98).

2º **Studies :** BAILEY, C., *The Greek atomists and Epicurus : A study*, Oxford, 1928. — BROCHARD, A., La morale d'Epicure, dans *Etudes de philosophie ancienne et moderne*, Paris, 1912. — JOYAU, E., *Épicure*, Paris, 1910. — LANGE, A., *Histoire du matérialisme*, Paris, 1910. — MARTHA, J., *Le poème de Lucrèce, morale, religion, science*, Paris, 1909. — ZELLER, E., *The Stoics, Epicureans and Sceptics*, London, 1870.

106. EPICURUS (341-270), an Athenian by birth, spent his youth at Samos and at Colophon; at the latter place, his father was a teacher of grammar and his mother, a magician, initiated him into superstitious practices. He was familiar with the writings of most of the former philosophers; but his superficial and restless spirit did not stop until it encountered the system of Democritus which was being taught at Colophon by Nausiphanes. In 306 he opened his own school at Athens where he bought a house and garden for 80 minae; it was there, often in the open, that he gave his lectures, more like a friend than a master. His benevolence and affability together with his attractive doctrine brought him quite a few faithful disciples. He instructed them to live in bourgeois fashion amidst the political difficulties, and wrote voluminously (about 300 works) in which he was careless of literary art, and sought only clarity and practical utility.

The school of Epicurus counts fewer celebrated names than does stoicism, but it exercised a strong influence in Greece, Asia Minor and Italy. At Rome, during Cicero's time, Epicureanism inspired the passionate enthusiasm of the poet LUCRETIUS (99-55), supplying the foundation of his six books, entitled *De Rerum Natura*.

Definition. EPICUREANISM *is the ethics of cessation or of effortless equilibrium which places supreme happiness or untroubledness in sense pleasure* [1].

---

[1] In contrast with Stoicism (n. 98), which located happiness in man's specific difference, reason, Epicureanism places it in the *generically* human good, for sense pleasure is common to animals and man.

This definition appears to set Epicureanism in absolute opposition to Stoicism. However, Epicurus himself wished that the wise man draw happiness out of himself; this is why he was constrained to " rationalize " sense pleasure to such an extent that his full development follows the view of Zeno. These two doctrines are like two travellers leaving from opposite points, one from the top and the other from the bottom of a mountain; they finally meet, for the first wished to ascend by the same route that the other descends. Stoicism begins with the sovereign domain of reason, insisting on the experience of tension as a synthesis of the perfection of intelligence, but it lowered itself through the pantheistic conception of divine fire. Epicureanism, on the other hand, begins with the sensible domain, insisting on the experience of cessation or arrest, as seen in the imperfection and dispersion of matter; but it spiritualized this notion as much as possible in order to achieve independence, and concludes with a genuine asceticism closely related to the Stoic renunciation.

Logic, physics and psychology are even more subordinated to ethics in Epicurus than they were in Zeno. Thus, again, the treatment of Epicureanism will be done in three sections.

I. Source of the Epicurean principle : the rational conception of sense pleasure.

II. Speculative Corollaries : Logic and Physics.

III. Practical Corollary : Ethics.

I. SOURCE OF THE EPICUREAN PRINCIPLE.

The rational conception of sense pleasure.

107. Epicurus begins with an absolute and crude formula of that which is considered the sovereign good. But thereupon a difficulty arises whose solution leads him to a definitive, most precise and refined formula.

I) **The Crude Formula.** *Pleasure* is man's supreme good. To clarify this notion, Epicurus states in his unliterary style : " Pleasure of the stomach is the principle and root of all good ". He means to say, rather, that pleasure whose source is the good state of the vegetative functions. Since he was logically materialist, he recognized sense pleasure only under its various forms as the sole pleasure, as pleasures of taste, of sight, of the ear, " all those agreeable sensations which come to us through the bodily organs " [1].

To demonstrate this principle, Epicurus appealed to the voice of nature which one finds in a pure and free state in animals and children. Spontaneously and constantly, they flee all bodily pain and search only for sense pleasure; this was an infallible sign, thought Epicurus, that there is no other goal we ourselves might aim for and which could make us happy.

2) **The Difficulty.** This supreme good, however, was to exempt the sage from all sorrow and to give him perfect independence by freeing him from any submission to what is exterior and especially to the variations of fortune. " Et mihi res, non me rebus subjungere conor ", said Horace. For Epicurus, as for the Stoics, happiness lies in " untroubledness " or that fulness of peace in which each can, according to his wish and by himself, be always happy.

Further, Epicurus realized that all corporeal and sense pleasures make us slaves to external goods, and a great number of them are rich in sorrows, as experience testifies. In fact, the cares, regrets and even sicknesses which one finds among those who become debauched in the desire of pleasure seem to make it difficult to grant that these would constitute happiness.

3) **The Solution.** The difficulty is solved by Epicurus through " rationalizing " the notion of sense pleasure, which permits him to stabilize it through transferring it from body to soul.

At first a double pleasure is distinguishable :

a) *The pleasure of motion.* This pleasure accompanies the very act which satisfies a need of the organism and reestablishes its broken equilibrium; for example, the pleasure of satisfying a burning thirst through drinking.

b) *The pleasure of repose.* This pleasure is found in the state of perfect equilibrium in which the organism has no need demanding satisfaction.

The first type of pleasure is always imperfect, transitory and mixed with sorrow, for it supposes a desire and a need which must be satisfied; only the second possesses the fulness required for supreme happiness.

---

[1] CICERO, *Tuscul.*, III, 18.

One can clarify this view by comparing it with that of Aristotle [1]. Pleasure, for the latter, is the fruit of action arrived at its goal at which point it is fully spread out in the repose of action; motion, however, or the simple tendency to act, merely awakes an incomplete and mixed pleasure. The joy of knowing does not lie in studying as much as it does in contemplation. Thus, for Epicurus, true pleasure resides in the goal, in the calm equilibrium of the body.

But Aristotle recognized many specifically distinct operations in man, particularly those of intellectual and those of sense life. From them he deduced the specific distinction between various "pleasures" which complete operations, and extolled the pleasure arising from intellectual operation in which there is realized an *active repose* of movement fully disengaged from matter. Epicurus, on the contrary, being a materialist, admitted but one delectable operation, the material motion of corporeal or sense life. He placed supreme pleasure not in motion but in its termination, describing the latter as a physiological and psychological state of equilibrium. In his thought, the sovereign good is not a purely negative state, a simple cessation from sorrow, but a *positive state of well being*, the fruition of the regular course of life unarrested by any obstacle.

The infallible sign of this supreme pleasure is the absence of all sorrow; and whatever be the means of procuring this absence, happiness will ensue. There is a way, according to Epicurus, of arriving at this state not only with a minimum of exterior goods by reducing our demands and our needs, but more often through the *soul itself*, in full independence.

He distinguishes the pleasures of the body from those of the soul; the latter are not of a new species, for he held to the specific unity of pleasures, but simply those of the body which are not subjected to the flight of time through remembrance or anticipation. The soul of the sage must always be capable of taking the sting of present sorrow, and regain equilibrium and happiness; he may do this by recalling some past pleasure which life does not refuse to a man, or by living through desire and hope for some future pleasure. Epicurus adds that extreme sorrows last but a short time, and that those which last are tolerable. He himself, living his own doctrine, said he was happy, despite affliction with sickness, due to the remembrance of his friends.

4) **Definitive formula.** From this attempt to "rationalize" sense pleasure, a more refined expression of the Epicurean

[1] See n. 88.

principle can be derived : *the happiness of the wise man lies
in the life of equilibrium and of moderation which is the source
of supreme happiness, almost always obtained through the free
choice of the soul.*

Thus philosophy has no other purpose than to rid us of all
sorrow, whether physical or moral; it does this by presenting
to us a theory resting on the nature of things, and by indicating
the practice of truly useful virtues.   Thus the speculative
and the practical corollaries arise.

II. SPECULATIVE COROLLARIES.

The Canonic and the Physics.

A) **The Canonic.**

108.   Epicurus' Canonic [1], or logic, is not merely totally empiricist, as that of the Stoics, but hardly worthy of the name of logic.
He is merely interested in knowing that the soul can receive,
retain and faithfully reproduce the impression of corporeal beings
which are the source of our pleasure.   Epicurus admits these
experiences as a fact.   To explain them, he adopts a view of *simple
realism* according to which exterior objects impress themselves
on the soul, similar to an impression on soft wax [2].

He gives more thought to the question of the criterion or canon
of truth as the means of discerning the object-value of these various
representations.   *Sensible evidence* is the criterion he adopts and
distinguishes into four types : those of passion, as pleasure or
sorrow; those of sensation, as sight, touch or taste; those of
conjecture, as the image of objects at first seen, retained and
reproduced; finally, those of reflection, as rational theories whose
truth is measured by their utility, if they are not opposed to sense
evidence.

B) **Physics.**

109.   The physics of Epicurus is plainly destined to deliver
the wise man from three most common errors which are one
of the greatest obstacles to happiness : the fear of destiny, of
death, and of superstitions.   A right idea of the universe, of our
soul, and of the gods, is sufficient to eradicate these fears.

1⁰ **The Universe : Fear of Destiny.**   Epicurus, recalling that
he had studied atomism in his youth, judged that this view

---

[1] From the word κανών, a rule or criterion.
[2] This is Epicurus' version of Aristotle's view; see n. 83.

was capable, if slightly retouched, of procuring the peace of soul required by his ethics. Further, it was well adapted to his materialism. He admits, then, with Democritus, that the entire universe has its origin in a mass of atoms infinite in number, varied in form, unchangeable and falling within the void. But in order to explain their order and combination and avoid the notion of blind necessity, he completed atomism through his personal theory of deviation.

Epicurus maintained that there is a slight deviation or declination in the straight line descent of atoms; this declination is spontaneous, without a cause or fixed law[1]. It sufficed, in the beginning of things, to acount for the collisions of the atoms from which arose the present order of the world; but inasmuch as it is quite weak, its actual effects are not perceptible and lack significance.

As a result, it is not necessary for the wise man to fear the implacable law of destiny, even if a cataclysm ensues. He knows that the world itself is an effect of chance; and, at the same time, he can enjoy an order which is at least practically stable for the duration of a human life.

2⁰ **The human soul : Fear of death.** The above view, somewhat expanded, also resolves the question of our destiny. Like the rest of reality, our soul is an aggregate of atoms which are, however, most subtle and resistant for they are to dominate and direct the body. The declination in movement with which atoms are endowed by nature, allows for freedom of will which is a necessary requisite for ethics. Freedom, in Epicurus' view, is the power to initiate at will an absolute beginning in one's movement; in this way, the soul can orient itself towards happiness.

But the condition of every atomic composite is to dissolve itself in order to serve other combinations. Thus our soul will end, and its ruin takes with it all sentiment and personal life. This doctrine delivers the wise man from all vain fears of death by showing him that death may not be a good, but it is the absence of all evil. " Death, which appears to be the most fearful of evils, is nought but a chimera; for death is nothing while one lives and when it arrives, the soul no longer exists. Death, then, has no dominion over the living nor over

---

[1] See F. COPLESTON, *op. cit.*, p. 405.

the dead; the living need no longer fear its attack, while the dead, being non-existent, are beyond the range of its blows " [1].

3° **The gods : superstitious fears.** The existence of the gods is a fact established by the unanimous consent of mankind and through apparitions. From this double source of information Epicurus concludes that the gods have human form, inasmuch as they show themselves to men. They are corporeal, formed, as our own soul, of subtle atoms which are more ethereal. Their happiness is a complete Epicurean untroubledness and cannot be squared with any notions of providence or of a demiurge. Epicurus insists on this latter point; the construction and governance of a world as vast and complicated as ours would cause the gods labors and cares which would disturb their peace. Further, since the gods are good, they would banish all evil from the universe if they were to interfere. Finally, the decisive proof, is that everything is perfectly explained through atomism without their intervention; at the same time, ethics shows us how to find happiness without their help. The sage, accordingly, is fully exempt from the terrors and the cares which the gods bring to the ordinary populace.

This view seems to lead to atheism; are not useless gods equivalent to non-existent gods? Epicurus, however, maintained the cult of the gods, and he himself practiced great piety towards them. Perhaps this was due to prudence, or to respect for the common view and to prevent any disquietude. It could also have been through personal inclination; conceiving the gods as perfect Epicureans, he was possibly enchanted in contemplating them in order to imitate them; thus he might have viewed them with a disinterested veneration similar to the sentiment of friendship, in which his sense nature could find a delicate pleasure.

110. Epicurus was hailed by his numerous disciples as a *liberator*. This enthusiasm is better understood by considering the deficiencies of the pagan religion. On the one hand, the latter did not promise anything similar to the heaven of the Christians; for the wicked, frightful torments were to ensue; and merely a state of ennui and sadness for the good. Further, paganism imposed heavy duties on the living; they were to appease the impassioned and often hostile gods every moment, so that superstition continued to multiply their vain fears and absurd practices.

Many criticisms of Epicurus were effective against these exaggerations, which, in fact, most philosophers condemned with him.

---

[1] Epicurus, *Letter to Menecee.*

But they were unable to efface the natural aspiration of the soul to God, its spontaneous trust in His goodness, nor its desire for eternal life which leaps from the source of its spiritual being.

III. PRACTICAL COROLLARY.

Ethics.

111. For Epicurus, as for all philosophers, ethics is the science which teaches us the means of attaining happiness through the practice of virtue. But his fundamental view throws Epicurean virtue into a type of calculated egoism. It can be described as the art of organizing one's life with moderation in such a way as to most often achieve perfect equilibrium of body and soul from which supreme pleasure follows. Prudence, accordingly, is the principal virtue; it is completed by temperance, justice and friendship.

1º **Prudence.** The aim of the wise man is not to look for actions which are most often and most strongly pleasurable. On the one hand, one is not to be fascinated by the passing action of the moment, but must aim to organize his entire life so that happiness may reign throughout. On the other hand, the wise man knows that the supreme good is not the pleasure of motion itself, but the stable joy which accompanies final equilibrium; he therefore exercises his ingenuity to foresee what the results of his actions will be. He may temporarily accept a sorrow as a condition for a quite stable pleasure, and he will also avoid vehement pleasures which are inevitably followed by considerable sorrows. This calculated egoism is called prudence by Epicurus.

This " virtue " teaches the sage to avoid anything which could be the occasion of trouble to himself; it inspires his peaceful and free speculations; it teaches him to flee the tumult of public life and the excitement of honors and to dispense himself from the cares of conjugal life. It thus procures for him an honest private life, well moderated through temperance and justice; a life in which happiness lives with the peaceful and sure joys of meditation, of science and of friendship.

2º **Temperance.** The first area in which prudence is exercised is that of the sense pleasures which accompany the satisfaction of corporeal needs. Some of these, as nourishing oneself, are natural and necessary; others, as the thirst for riches, for honors, for luxury and for refined foods, are artificial and useless.

Moreover, if there was question of sensory voluptuousness attached to superfluous needs, the Epicureans accentuated its vanity, its sad and miserable character; a Christian sermon, for example, could not scoff at the love of such things with the harshness of Lucretius. Thus the sage must deliver himself from these goods and retain only the *natural* and *necessary* whose pleasures consist in freeing oneself from the imperious demands of the flesh, of thirst and of hunger. Further, he ought to reduce these bodily demands to a minimum. For frugality [1], with which he should be habitually content, has a triple advantage : it makes the sage independent, it helps him place happiness within the reach of all men, even the most poor, and allows him to relish extraordinary pleasures all the more, if they present themselves.

Temperance, finally, leads the wise man to courage. For if it eventuates that he even lacks necessities, as in poverty or sickness, he contents himself with pleasures of the soul and maintains, calmly, true happiness.

3° **Justice.** Here, also, Epicurus keeps the word and destroys its meaning. He is just who makes himself useful to society; the foundation of right and of equity is a simple agreement that we should not harm each other. The wise man gives to each his due and is obedient to law with the view of maintaining peace and avoiding the confusion of a law suit, and the inevitable embarrassments of all insurbordination. For, even if one avoids actual chastisement, the very fear of being caught troubles the soul and destroys happiness.

4° **Friendship.** Even historians testify that friendship is the most noble virtue practiced by Epicurus and his disciples. Cicero says that they habitually were faithful in friendship [1]. This is rather surprising at first, for friendship is essentially disinterested; however, among the Epicureans, it was viewed as a mutual and stable love, due to which all was common among friends, whether pleasures or pains. It was the unitive principle of their society; for each Epicurean, it was at once both strength and protection in life.

---

[1] Epicurus contented himself with water and brown bread.
[2] CICERO, *De Finibus*, II, 25.

Nevertheless, the irremediable egoism of the system degraded this notion likewise. Friendship is recommended mainly as a means of finding the most useful and faithful help in need, and as the procurement of the most delicate pleasure in the joy of being loved by a friend. The wise man loves himself in friendship and does not love the friend for himself.

This egoist and bourgeois notion is well portrayed in the following " *Portrait of an Epicurean* " : Who has not met, even today, a practical sage, unknowingly epicurean, moderated in his tastes, virtuous without great moral ambition, anxious to live well? He aims to keep body, spirit and soul healthy; he only indulges in pleasures which leave no regrets, in opinions which are undisturbing; he watches his own passions and flees those of others. If he does not allow himself to be tempted by positions and honors, it is due to fear of taking a risk or of being beaten in a contest. Of good humor, polished, more or less a friend of science, he is content with current information. Without being disturbed by metaphysical problems, he has long ago placed God so high and distant that he has nothing to hope for, and nothing to fear. With regard to the future life, he has, so to speak, effaced it from his soul and does not consider death except to decently resign himself to it some day. In the meantime, he disposes his life with a timid prudence, and does not go abroad among men except within the circle of his friends where he can enjoy the sentiments which he inspires and those which he approves. His egoism is noble and delicate and has seen that benevolence is the charm of life whether one is its object or whether one is benevolent to others [1].

CONCLUSION. **112.** More clearly than Stoicism, Epicureanism shows the materialistic decadence which consciously subordinates reason to the inferior functions of the body. Despite a serious effort to elevate itself to a universal and philosophical conception of human life, all is vitiated and lowered in the Epicurean doctrine by their point of departure. If there is talk of friendship and justice, it is but for utilitarian motive; if virtue is commended, it is but as a source of more certain pleasures; if asceticism is being promoted, it is but an asceticism of pleasure which cannot support any general enthusiasm, for in destroying the spirituality of the soul and of God, it lacks any trace of an ideal. The individual is constantly thrust back upon himself, and is moved by a calculating egoism which urges him to seek his own profit. Thus it affords a philosophy that is *sterile* both for a society which it would

---

[1] MARTHA, *Le Poème de Lucrèce, morale, religion, science*, p. 7.

hope to make disinterested, as well as for the individual to whom it offers an interior energy without which his life would fall into the " golden mediocrity " acclaimed by the Epicurean Horace.

At the same time, since there is a great number of men whose character has nothing of the austere or heroic, and who find it convenient to easily abandon themselves to the impulses of nature, there has always been a goodly number of Epicureans. The school of Athens counted many and faithful disciples, perpetuated itself even to the fourth century, and expanded into Asia and Italy. Its aspect of moderation drew more cultivated minds, while its allurement of sense pleasure and of happiness attracted the crowd. The mediocrity of Epicureanism makes it seem tailor-made for an epoch of decadence. If it does not justify debauchery, as it is sometimes accused of doing, it has not grasped man's true nobility and has seen in him only the " animal man whose god is his belly " [1], of which St. Paul speaks. The formula of wisdom which Epicurus gave is powerless to complete the aspirations of human nature as it really is.

ARTICLE THREE. — SCEPTICISM.

SPECIAL BIBLIOGRAPHY.

Studies : BROCHARD, J., *Les sceptiques grecs*, 2e éd., Paris, 1923. — DUDLEY, D. R., *A history of Cynicism, From Diogenes to the Sixth Century*, A.D., London, 1937. — GODECKE-MAYER, *Die Geschichte des griechischen Skeptizismus*, Leipzig, 1905. — MacCOLL, N., *The Greek Sceptics from Pyrrho to Sextus*, London, 1869. — ROBIN, L., *Pyrrho et le scepticisme grec*, Paris, 1944.

113. Scepticism is an even greater sign of decadence than is materialism. It is indicative of the weariness of the mind confronted with abstract speculations and incessant controversies. It flourished in a special way in this era.

One can consider as belonging to Scepticism all the philosophers of this era except the stoics and the Epicureans. One group, renouncing all speculation, inaugurated *universal* or *philosophical scepticism*. The other group, though not denying truth but

---

[1] *Philippians*, 3, 19.

incapable of achieving it, were content to choose the best propositions among the different doctrines about them; these latter are the *eclectics*.

I. PHILOSOPHICAL SCEPTICISM.

The founder of this system was Pyrrho (362-275), citizen of Elea, where, upon Alexander's death (323), he founded his school. His objections renew and aggravate the discussions earlier proposed by the Sophists, and from them he erects a new school of philosophical thought. He even left his name attached to his views, for universal scepticism is sometimes called *Pyrrhonism*.

Pyrrhonism had a variegated success. It threw itself violently against the dogmatism of the Stoics and Epicureans who firmly held to the value of their science; it directed the Aristotelians towards eclecticism, and was especially successful in seducing the Platonists. The latter were already predisposed towards scepticism through the radical distinction they made between the world of the senses as the domain of probable opinions, and the world of ideas as the sole realm of certitude. Further, they were incapable of grasping the metaphysical subtleties of their master Plato, and retained such views as uncertain opinion. Without affirming anything, they contented themselves with contradicting the rival schools, conceding only that there are most probable opinions concerning the practical order with which it is wise to agree; thus arises *probabilism*. This view was personified in two philosophers. The first was Arcesilaus (315-241), founder of the Middle Academy, which he directed from 268 to 241, and who was a personal opponent of Zeno; the other was Carneades (215-126), founder of the New or Third Academy, which he directed from 160 to about 120, and who was an opponent of the Stoic Chrysippus.

Probabilism had its representatives in Rome. Cicero was its most remarkable representative, though he can better be placed among the eclectics.

Philosophical scepticism, though, was perpetuated especially through two men whose writings contain a definitive codification of the system. The first is Aenesidemus of Knossos, who lived sometime during the period from 80, B.C., to 130, A.D., taught

at Alexandria, and wrote eight books on Pyrrhonism; the other
is Sextus Empiricus (second half of the second century, A.D.)
who, following the former's views, collected all the objections
of his predecessors in his *Pyrrhonenses Hypotyposes*. Mention
can here be made of Agrippa, who listed five motives for absolute
doubt, and Favorinus of Arelate, the first Gallic philosopher.

A) **Definition.**

114. As a philosophical theory, Scepticism can be defined
as follows :

*The doctrine that admits the existence of certitudes as a subjective
fact, but maintains that the objective validity of all speculative
judgment is indemonstrable, and thus teaches that it is impossible,
in any proper sense, to obtain a certitude infallibly true.*

" Our Scepticism ", writes Sextus, " consists essentially
in opposing phenomena with essences; the latter are in no way
knowable; but to say that our Scepticism destroys phenomena,
is not our meaning " [1].

This distinction between essence which is objective and
phenomenon which is subjective, and the more general
distinction between speculation and action, permitted the
Sceptics also to consider the problem of happiness. Similar
to the other moralists of this period, they looked for it in a state
of tranquillity of soul. The wise Sceptic, wholly aware of his
total ignorance in speculative matters, had for a universal
rule the complete abstention from, or suspension of judgment.
In practical matters he abandoned himself to custom with a sort
of passive tranquillity; this abstention and abandonment
combined to give him peace and tranquillity of soul. The main
source of man's troubles lies in the absolute judgment which
he makes on the goodness or badness of things. To destroy
this judgment by abstention or suspension of assent and,
at the same time, to acquire the art of utilizing the appearances
of things is to attain happiness.

This same distinction permits Scepticism to develop without
immediately contradicting itself; this would occur by affirming
as a " certain and true judgment " that there is " no certain
and infallibly true judgment ". It was sufficient for the sceptic,
to show the weakness of his adversary's position, merely

---

[1] By phenomenon is meant an internal or subjective impression.

to conclude that what one believes certain (subjectively) remains doubtful (objectively). In speculative matters, they fortified themselves with criticism, and reserved any consent or adherence for the domain of action.

B) The Arguments.

115. The objections gathered in the *Hypotyposes* are of two types; the first are concerned with certitude in general, while the second deal with the different certitudes of the special sciences.

1º **Concerning certitude in general.** Pyrrho gave ten arguments showing that all knowledge is *relative;* Aenesidemus, with eight arguments, overthrew the principle of *causality*, which is the basis of science; Favorinus renewed the ten arguments of Pyrrho, and Agrippa reduced them to five. A resume of them follows : " If a dogmatist affirms, one can always deny (contradiction); if he wishes to establish his affirmation by appeal to another principle, one can deny that one, and so forth (infinitely often); if he declares that one of his principles is evident, one can say that it *appears* true, but lacks proof (relativity); if he makes no attempt to prove it, the principle becomes a contestable supposition (hypothesis); if he risks an attempt at demonstration, then apply the criterion of going about in a circle (vicious circle) " [1].

2º **Concerning special types of certitude.** Sextus shows that in the three types of current philosophy, logic, physics and ethics, there are only contradictions and impossibilities; this was largely true for the materialistic systems which he examined. The most wise attitude, he concluded, is to suspend judgment.

C) Weakness of Scepticism.

116. That the first duty of a critic is to reply to criticism is a well known requisite which is not lacking in value. But to judge the true value of Scepticism, it is sufficient to represent it under the form of simple arguments.

1. Philosophers are in constant contradiction among themselves and each with himself on all the fundamental principles of philosophy, on the causes and natures of beings, on God, on the soul and on ethics; this is the contention of the Sceptic.

---

[1] See D. Barbadette, *Histoire de la philosophie*, p. 90.

Contradictory opinions, however, cannot be true at the same time.

Consequently, it is prudent not to accept any of them.

One can reply that this is so unless one has a criterion for distinguishing the true from the false.

2. The Sceptic objects, however. Such a criterion does not exist, for :

a) Either one admits the criterion without proving its value, and everything still remains uncertain;

b) Or else one proves its validity, and a new criterion is needed to judge the validity of this demonstration; one thus continues on towards infinity, and thus everything is still uncertain.

In answer to the above, a distinction must be made between demonstration in the *strict sense*, which, in effect, is impossible, and a demonstration in a *wide sense* (verification or critical induction) [1] which one can thereupon furnish.

Despite its prudence, such universal Scepticism is self-destructive. For in exempting the practical domain from doubt, it necessarily falls into contradiction; for every voluntary decision is impossible without at least a minimum of speculative certitude, and would not be made without the firm acceptance of the principle, " To will is good ".

Moreover, if Scepticism restricts itself to the practical and subjective order, it makes any intellectual life impossible. Thus, it suppresses all philosophy, and with this suppression, goes sceptical philosophy itself.

II. THE ECLECTICS.

117. In a certain sense, eclecticism resulted from Scepticism. No one of the multiple philosophical hypotheses can definitively impose itself for acceptance; it seems preferable, then, not to look for entirely new explanations. Instead, one can revise former opinions by choosing and collecting especially that which one finds good, and reconciling that which one can.

There was a further cause of eclecticism, at least in Rome. The Romans, men of action, little bent towards speculation, demanded rules of conduct from philosophy; they did not scruple to borrow from various systems whatever they judged capable of favoring their political aims. Two groups of eclectics can be considered, the Romans and the commentators.

---

[1] That which Kant will later call *transcendental analysis*; see n. 394.

A) The Romans.

Cicero (106-44) is the principal representative. Though more of an orator and statesman than philosopher, he wrote a good number of philosophical works, among which are : *Hortensius* (a general exhortation to wisdom); *Libri academici* (logic); *De natura deorum; De divinatione* (theodicy and psychology); *De officiis* (ethics); finally, like Plato, he wrote *De Republica* and *De Legibus*.

Eclecticism is the chief mark of these works. Choosing those doctrines most in conformity with common sense, he adopts the theory of resemblance in the *Libri academici*. " We are forced to admit many probable matters ", he writes, " easy to follow in practice, but which we might fear to defend in theory "; this is his logical stance. He agrees with Plato's speculations on the soul and on God (proof of God's existence through order; spirituality, freedom and immortality of the soul), which is his metaphysical view. He agrees with the Stoics, with strong reservations, on their ethical formulas, which is his basic ethical proposal.

Finally, he derived his theories on law and politics from the Peripatetics; but here he is quite personal and shows some depth. While he hesitates on some fundamental speculative matters — as refusing God the foreknowledge of future free events and the governance of inferior beings, and as considering the soul as an emanation from God — he is very firm in proposing that the natural law, eternal, unchanging and universal, is the foundation of rights and duties, and the source of the validity of all positive law, whether individual or social.

In conclusion, it can be said that pagan Rome had no genuine philosophers but only literary writers who compiled their thoughts, remembrances or impressions (the Stoics), their philosophical poems (the Epicureans), or who were eminent jurists and based their views on common sense (the eclectics).

B) The Commentators.

118. This term applies especially to those disciples of Aristotle who were content with explaining and interpreting the many works of their master. They can be classed as eclectics, however, because of their tendency to borrow complementary views from other systems, especially from Plato and the Stoics.

Three of these commentators are worthy of mention :

1) THEOPHRASTUS (372-288), the immediate successor of Aristotle as head of the Lyceum, a remarkable logician and a keen observer as his well known work, *The Characters*, testifies.

2) ANDRONICUS of Rhodes who, aided by the grammarian Tyrannion, compiled the first complete edition of the works of

Aristotle, which had recently been brought from Greece to Rome by Sylla. He arranged them in order, reassembled the connected fragments, titled the works, and accompanied this whole task with a commentary.

3) ALEXANDER OF APHRODISIAS (close of the second century), who is often spoken of as a " second Aristotle " because of the clearness of his commentary. But in adding precision to Aristotle's thought on obscure points, he proposed some contestable views which corrupted the Peripateticism of the Arabs in the Middle Ages. He seemed to hold to the identity of the active intellect with pure actuality; he denied Providence and the immortality of the human soul.

CONCLUSION. **119.** If the philosophers of this period lacked breadth, they are, none the less, numerous and most influential. During the first two centuries of the Roman empire, they had a deep influence on society; they occupied the professorships instituted in the cities (Rome, Athens, Alexandria) either by the State or by the cities, and attracted to themselves the more cultivated youth. They acted as the familiars of great personages by being intimate counsellors and directors of conscience, and gave similar advice, orally or in writing, to a large number of disquieted people. They became itinerant preachers of a sort, and went from town to town scattering their message either to chosen listeners, or to the people gathered in the stadiums, theaters and other public places [1].

Ethics was the dominating note in this philosophy. However, with a wide, inclusive sweep, the eclectics embraced many elements of various schools, and assimilated whatever was conciliatory with their notions from the national religions. As time went on, their views became enriched with a mystical tinge, and thus they came closer to the Platonic tradition. Finally this view concluded with a renaissance of Platonism; the moral transition slowly became a mystic transition and gave birth to Neo-Platonism.

---

[1] See E. BRÉHIER, *Histoire de la philosophie*, I, p. 367.

CHAPTER TWO

MYSTICAL TRANSITION

From Philo to Proclus.

SPECIAL BIBLIOGRAPHY.

MORE, P. E., *Hellenistic philosophy*, Princeton, 1923. — SIMON, T., *Histoire de l'Ecole d'Alexandrie*, 2 vol., 1843-5. — VACHEROT, L., *Histoire critique de l'Ecole d'Alexandrie*, 3 vol., 1846-51. — WHITTAKER, T., *The Neoplatonists*, 2nd ed., Cambridge, 1918.

120. About the time of the Christian era, while the three strains of naturalistic ethics were prolonging themselves and had come to die in Rome, Greek philosophy rejuvenated itself and produced its last great system by becoming impregnated with *mysticism*.

The term, MYSTICISM, is not taken here in its strict sense of mystical theology [1], but in a broad sense as designating the " belief in the possibility of intimate and direct union of the human spirit with the fundamental principle of being, a union which constitutes a manner of existence and of knowing which is both estranged from, and superior to normal knowledge " [2]. Both doctrine and practice are oriented towards the culminating point of ecstasy, viewed as the achievement of human destiny in the full attainment of truth and of happiness.

Taken in this broad sense, mysticism points to a reality in the history of purely rational doctrines. Plato's philosophy was shown to have a mystic tinge, and traces of it were found in Stoicism in their preoccupation of attaining identity with the *Logos*. But it especially characterizes the last revival of the pagan spirit. Through this revival, the decadence of thought was arrested and transformed into a transition; it oriented thinkers towards a spiritualist and religious philosophy which greatly surpassed that of ancient naturalism.

---

[1] Mystical theology is " that branch of theology which deals with the eminent graces which God accords to virtuous souls so that they may enter into the unitive or perfect way and be capable of accomplishing its acts ". Cf. F. CAYRÉ, *Manual of Patrology*, Vol. I, p. 20.

[2] This definition can be found in Lalande's *Vocabulaire technique et critique de la philosophie*.

Precision is added to this general notion of mysticism by pointing out three of its distinctive traits.

1) The predominance of the RELIGIOUS ASPECT. Philosophy is primarily a theology, treating of the universe and man only by relation to God, viewing them as creatures manifestative of His perfection and as searching the way to return to Him.

2) The assertion of DIVINE TRANSCENDENCE. God is always viewed as spirit, eminently superior to the world; this view is thus clearly opposed to the pantheism and the materialistic negations of the preceding group of thinkers.

3) The recourse to multiple INTERMEDIARIES. These latter permit God to lower Himself to the least of creatures, and allow man to arise, despite the materiality in which he lives, to the transcendent God where he shall find supreme happiness.

There is a double reason for this new orientation in philosophical thought.

a) It is due, primarily, to the *direct influence of the oriental religions*. From Athens, the intellectual primacy passed to Alexandria; the latter was not merely the great seaport open to the commerce of the ancient world, but it was also a place for exchange of ideas. In this cosmopolitan town there could be found a commingling of all races and religions, all superstitions and philosophies. Here Greek wisdom came in contact with oriental religions, with Judaism and, later, with Christianity. Now these religions, in contrast with the paganism stemming from Greece, imposed on the mind a doctrine of God and His relations with men considered as immediately revealed and as the object of faith. They were also suitable for waking philosophical interest and conferring a vigorous impulse of mysticism.

b) It is also due to the *natural aspiration* of the many who were crushed by the collapse of their country and found themselves unable to accept the haughty solution of the Stoic, nor the Epicurean or Sceptic resignation. Caught in spiritual distress, they looked to the supernatural for hope and new comfort; they became attached to the mysteries and revelations which opened prospectives of the future life; they believed in new gods and intermediaries between earth and heaven; they gave themselves avidly to initiations, expiations and purifications in order to be shed of their inquietude of soul and to enter into communion with the divinity. These ideas were typical of the intellectual atmosphere in which the people lived at the beginning of the Christian era. If a man of genius presented himself and condensed these notions into a philosophical system, everything would become penetrated by a religious spirit; this man was Plotinus with his system of Neo-Platonism.

Historical sketch.

121. Before achieving its peak, mystical philosophy went through three centuries of preparation.

A) **Preparation.**

At the beginning of the Christian era, we find a number of attempts at rational interpretation of the dogmas of the various religions, and at elaborating a distinctly religious philosophy with a mystical tendency. Philo was the most outstanding of these harmonizers for Judaism; Plutarch, for paganism, and the Gnostics for Christianity.

1º Philo [1] (40, B.C. — 40, A.D.).

Philo, an Alexandrian Jew, is the principal proponent of the Greco-Jewish school which was founded in Alexandria about 150, B.C. by Aristóbulus. The latter aimed to unify the teaching of the Bible with that of the pagan sages.

Among pagan authors, Philo was especially enamored of Plato; and, in order to discover Plato's views on revelation, he used and misused the method of *allegorical interpretation*. By this method he showed that the divergences were but apparent and produced a profound harmony, the same God being the inspirer of all wisdom.

His efforts had the following sort of result :

a) As the teacher of the Jewish faith, God is unique and the Creator, sovereignly elevated above the universe. His very transcendence makes him unknowable to ordinary minds as yet not exercised by the purifications of philosophy.

b) But there is a number of intermediaries between the ineffable God and man, who reveal God to man, called *Powers;* these are to be identified with the angels of the Bible so often sent to speak in God's name. They are instruments of the creative action, and exemplary causes of the world. The main one among them is entitled the *Logos,* the Divine Word, in which is found the ideal world of Plato.

---

[1] An English translation of Philo's works can be found in the Loeb Classical Library; studies on Philo include the following : GOODENOUGH, E. R., *An Introduction to Philo Judaeus*, New Haven, 1940. — LOUIS, A., *Philon le juif*, Paris, 1911. — MARTIN, H., *Philon*, Paris, 1913.

c) At first these intermediaries appear to be distinct from God. However, after the intelligence has been thoroughly prepared by efforts at reasoning and ascetic practices, it elevates itself into ecstasy wherein it sees their grand identity with the ineffable Divinity. In this high type of contemplation, the soul also finds its supreme happiness.

This is at least a plausible interpretation of the reconciliation attempted between Plato and the Bible. Philonism, far from being a unifying and explanatory theory is, if not contradictory, at least quite obscure. It is thus some adumbration of Neo-Platonism.

2⁰ PLUTARCH [1] (50-120, A.D.).

Born at Chaeronea, Plutarch is the author of the " Lives of Illustrious men of Greece and Rome ". He is the principal representative of the effort made by the mystic philosophy to give a rationalist interpretation to the pagan religion. In this attempt, he achieved a sort of religious syncretism of elements borrowed from national Greek and Egyptian cults, and of Oriental dualism. He admitted a principle of good (God transcendent) and a principle of evil (matter); between these two lie the intermediaries, of which some are the pagan gods and others are wicked spirits.

3⁰ GNOSTICISM [2] (1st and 2nd centuries, A.D.).

This complex movement from which were born the first heresies combatted by St. Paul and St. John the Evangelist, was an ambitious effort aiming to give a rational explanation of all of the Christian Revelation including the Old and the New Testament. It resulted in a group of systems which were half religious and half philosophical; a detailed study of these systems is more properly treated in patrology. Mention should be made of the fact that here, also, we find the three marks mentioned above as belonging to mystical philosophy, added to which is a super-abundance of intermediaries called *aeons* whose ensemble forms the *Fulness*.

B) Neo-Platonism, the Apogee of Mystic Philosophy.

122. Neoplatonism was founded in Alexandria by Ammonius Saccas, a renegade Christian, it seems. He wrote nothing, but was the teacher of Plotinus. He died about 245.

PLOTINUS [3] was born about 205 at Lycopolis in Egypt; he attended the lectures of Ammonius from 232 to 243.

---

[1] An English translation of Plutarch's works can be found in the Loeb Classical Library.

[2] See F. CAYRÉ, *op. cit.*, pp. 100-5.

[3] A bibliography on Plotinus is given below.

He accompanied the Emperor Gordian on an unfortunate expedition against the Persians and then came to Rome where he opened his own school, teaching there eloquently and successfully for twenty-five years (244-270), until his death. He did not begin to write until about the age of fifty when fully matured, and he left a considerable number of writings in which mystic philosophy achieves its peak. In him, it appears, the Greek genius reassembled all its forces in order to coordinate them in a broad eclecticism; he synthesized what was best from the preceeding centuries and adapted this to new needs in response to the religious aspirations current during his time. This religious aspect of Neo-Platonism was so strong that Julian the Apostate (361-363) used it against Christianity.

Porphyry [1] (232-305) was the beloved disciple of Plotinus whom he succeeded as head of the school in Rome. He edited the works of the master, and arranged them into fifty-four sections, or six books of nine chapters apiece, from which the name, *Enneads* of Plotinus. A clear and methodical thinker, he adopted Aristotle's *Organon*, which he edited with an introduction or *Isagoge* (εἰσαγωγή), which was famous in the Middle Ages.

In connection with this latter point, mention can be made here of a certain group of Neo-Platonic commentators on Aristotle. *Themistius* (second half of the fourth century), founded a school at Constantinople and commented on Aristotle; *Simplicius* (5th century), who wrote some informative commentaries on Aristotle's *Categories*, *Physics* and *On the Heavens;* *Ammonius* (close of 5th century), who wrote an essay harmonizing Plato and Aristotle; finally, in the sixth century, the first Christian commentators on Aristotle, Joannes Philoponus and David the Armenian.

Nevertheless, the Neo-Platonic philosophy was not of too long duration. *Iamblichus* (died about 330), the successor of Porphyry, transported the school to Pergamos, then to Alexandria, and complicated the doctrine by multiplying the intermediaries and by increasing the practices of magic and theurgy. *Proclus* [2] (411-485) opened the school at Athens and was the last great disciple. Gifted with an encyclopedic spirit, he attempted to harmonize Iamblichus with Plotinus and produced a large treatise, clear and orderly, but hardly original. Mention should also be made, in addition to some commentaries on Plato, of his two *Theologies* and a treatise *On Evil*.

---

[1] Porphyry wrote a number of other works, among which are : *Life of Plotinus*, *Life of Pythagoras*, *A History of Philosophers ;* he also wrote a violent pamphlet attacking the Christians, parts of which are preserved by Eusebius of Caesarea. On this latter point, see F. COPLESTON, *op. cit.*, p. 474.

[2] For a list of his works and views, see F. COPLESTON, *op. cit.*, pp. 478-481, and L. J. RASAN, *The Philosophy of Proclus*, New York, 1949.

In 529, a decree of Justinian closed the school at Athens, and thus terminated the spread of Neo-Platonism and of pagan philosophy.

From the point of view of a history of philosophy which insists on the movement of thought, Plotinus is of special interest. The richness of his metaphysics and the durable influence of his work entitle him to a detailed study.

PLOTINUS (205-270).

SPECIAL BIBLIOGRAPHY.

1° **Texts :** McKenna, S., *The treatises of Plotinus*, 2 vols., Boston, n. d.

2° **Studies :** Armstrong, A. P., *The architecture of the intelligible universe in the philosophy of Plotinus*, Cambridge, 1940. — Arnou, R., *Le désir de Dieu dans la philosophie de Plotin*, Paris, 1921. — Bréhier, E., *La philosophie de Plotin*, Paris, 1928. — Fuller, B. A. G., *The problem of evil in Plotinus*, Cambridge, Mass., 1912. — Heineman, F., *Plotin*, Paris, 1921. — Henry, P., *Etudes plotiniennes*, Brussels, 1938. — Inge, W. R., *The philosophy of Plotinus*, 2 vols., 3rd ed., Longmans, 1928. — Switalski, B., Krakowski, E., *Plotin et le paganisme religieux*, Paris, 1933. — *Plotinus and the ethics of St. Augustine*, New York, 1946. — Turnbull, G. H., *The essence of Plotinus*, London, 1935.

123. At first Plotinus aimed to collect the heritage of all the great Greek philosophers; he wanted to reassemble and unify all their theories, especially those of Plato and Aristotle, of the Stoics and of Philo. But the man he admired most and to whom he is most indebted is Plato. From him he borrowed his fundamental view of the basic distinction between the real world which is *Idea* and the sense world which is a simple *Image* of the idea. He believed strongly in spirit and in an intelligible world, a belief that is easily recognized in the energy of his affirmations and in the evident mark of his sincerity.

He also adopted the intuitive and a priori method from Plato. Reasoning, for him, was understanding; understanding was the seizure of the real which is spirit, in the full evidence of its ideal clarity; then one puts each thing in its place among the hierarchy of beings, following, so to speak, the natural articulation of essences.

Like Plato, he searched for truth with his whole soul. He did not merely aim to reach being as a summit, but he aimed at the higher region of the Good and the Beautiful which one attains as much by love as by intelligence. It is for such reasons that his philosophy is justly called NEO-PLATONISM.

He was not content merely to reedit Plato or to juxtapose doctrines borrowed from various philosophers. His work is more than an eclecticism; it is a *synthesis* which he animated and unified by a truly original principle, one of such depth within the Platonic metaphysics, that he merits to be ranked among the great philosophers.

At the same time, Neo-Platonism can be viewed as the complete incarnation of *mystic philosophy*. It has the latter's triple mark : its God is transcendent, not merely as the Good or pure actuality, but as the One, almost incomprehensible in simplicity; the One inclines towards us and we reach the One through a series of intermediaries. Finally, with reservations for Plotinian piety, his philosophy is nourished by a *great religious inspiration* whether in its aim at some sort of beatific vision, in its metaphysics which is a theology, or in its ethics, which is an asceticism.

The system of Plotinus, accordingly, is easily divided into two parts, the first describing, in succession, the descent of beings coming from God, the second concerning the mounting of the soul to God through dialectical stages. Two articles present the view of Plotinus :

Art. I. Metaphysics : The Descent of beings coming from God.

Art. II. Ethics : The Ascent of the soul towards God.

ARTICLE ONE. — METAPHYSICS.

The descent of beings coming from God.

124. Every metaphysics is an explanation of the real considered in its totality; it is a determination of the supreme and universal reasons for the being of things, the science of being as such. It is for this reason that although a metaphysics might not explicitly contain the Aristotelian theory of causes, it is always distinguished by its manner of assigning ultimate causes.

Moreover, Plotinus was not content to seek for a primary *exemplary* and *final* cause for beings, as Plato, nor merely a primary *motor* cause, as Aristotle, or a *formal* cause, as did the Stoics; but he determined THE CAUSE OF THEIR BEING. In fact, he speaks of this cause with reference to each degree of being, and it is easy to disengage the fundamental principle which unifies his theory.

Fundamental Principle.

Every perfect being is a perfect efficient cause; that is, it necessarily manifests its perfection in producing a being to its own image of such a kind that its causality enjoys a triple mark :

1. **The agent acts without loss;** as a container which is too full overflows without ceasing to be full, or as the sun produces luminous rays without diminishing in light, so its causal action is " the silent contemplation of its perfection which it exteriorizes outside of itself in an image " [1].

2. The **effect** is necessarily **similar to the cause,** participating in its perfection. From this view, the effect could not be a separated being, but remains intimately joined to the cause as immanent to it.

3. From another point of view, the perfection of the **effect can never equal** *that of the cause;* accordingly, every principle is really distinct from its effects. This is clearly affirmed by Plotinus, and is quite logical with the foregoing; for it would be absurd to identify that which is immutably perfect with the imperfect image which derives from it.

As a summary : *Every perfect image produces, without loss, an image so related to its model that the image is endowed with both similitude and degradation, immanence and real distinction.*

Plotinus does not, properly speaking, demonstrate this principle; but he gives evidence for it through examples. We grant that all those beings which arrive at their perfection, far from reposing sterilely in this state, spread their superabundance outside of themselves : fire illuminates and heats, snow spreads its coldness, and odoriferous objects add pleasure to their surroundings [2]. That which is supremely perfect cannot be jealous of its perfection, nor powerless to let it overflow, but it necessarily communicates it, as does each being, perfect in itself, according to the measure of its perfection. However, the profound origin and justification of this principle

---

[1] *III, Ennead,* VIII, Ch. I-IX.
[2] See below, n. 134, 3°.

lies in the intuition of perfect being conceived by Plotinus as superabundant and active good : " Goodness is self-diffusive " is the Platonic axiom. A better understanding of this theory will, therefore, be seen in its applications.

With the help of this principle, the universe is seen to be constituted by a hierarchy of beings which proceed or emanate one from the other following a descending and continuous diminution. Plotinus reduced these intermediaries of the ideal world to a minimum and proves that there can be no more than three.

1º At the peak is the necessary being, completely perfect, whose proper appellation is the ONE. There is no demonstration of his existence, for he imposes himself as the supreme source of all reality; denying that he exists is tantamount to denying any reasonable explanation for the universe.

2º Immediately after The One comes the essential duality in INTELLIGENCE.

3º Then follows a unified plurality, The SOUL.

4º Nothing more can be found, now, than pure multiplicity, or non-being; this is MATTER.

The One, Intelligence, Soul and Matter are the four applications of the fundamental principle of Plotinus.

I. THE ONE.

125. The One, according to Plotinus, is the proper name of God; or, more exactly, of Him whom one of his disciples [1] called the " Hypertheos " (ὑπέρθεος) the supreme God. Plotinus also speaks of him as Father of the Gods, King of Kings, The First, The Source, The Principle and, in a word, " more than God ". Among all these names, The One was chosen to express the distinctive characteristic of God, His *transcendence*, in virtue of which His ineffable simplicity possesses infinitely more than all the determined and multiple perfections in creatures. In order to explain the nature of God, Plotinus, with the former notion in mind, employs a double procedure, positive and negative.

---

[1] Dionysius the Areopagite, *On the Divine Names*, II, 3 and 4; London, 1930.

A) **Positive Theology.**

Being the principle and source of all perfections, God must possess them in Himself supereminently.

1º The One is first of all, *perfection itself*, inasmuch as He is the realization of the highest immanence in his operation which is most active and totally immutable. It is fully independent from any other activity; it is totally of itself and by itself; it is totally self-sufficient in its solitude; it is the realization of the most absolute *identity*, eternally the same as itself. But this stability is not inactivity; the One is also the supreme power, not passive as is matter, but operative and the first actuality always in a state of alertness. " He is ", says Plotinus, " the power of all things and if he does not exist, nothing exists " [1]. Furthermore the One mainly regards himself and his own proper profundity.

2º One can also attribute to Him in detail each of our perfections if they are at first purified of any element incompatible with His absolute simplicity and supereminent transcendence; as a result :

a) **God is Thought,** but thought as substantial and purely intuitive, without any distinction of subject and object and without any multiplicity of operations. He is also *consciousness*, for He is not ignorant of anything of Himself. But due to the absolute simplicity of His object, His act of thought is, rather, a simple, ineffable contact.

b) **God is Will and Desire,** though purely immanent. He is pleased in himself, He wills himself, since He is beautiful and good through and in himself; his orientation in this regard is totally interior, without any tendency towards a goal or a good that is either exterior or better.

c) **God is Freedom;** or, better, God is **Free, subsistent actuality.** He does not have a servile essence, since He is the first, dependent on none, and holds, in a unique way, all his reality and activity of himself.

d) **God is Happiness of Life,** finally, though absolutely simple and immutable.

---

[1] *III Ennead*, VIII, Ch. **x**.

B) **Negative Theology.**

126. According to Plotinus, it is more true to deny of God not only every imperfection, but also all positive perfections expressed by our concepts. The latter determine and limit these perfections, they introduce some composition or duality into them, and make them unworthy of the simplicity and the transcendence of The One. Consequently :

a) **God has neither thought nor consciousness,** inasmuch as every act of intelligence supposes an essential duality of knowing subject and object known. " If a being has consciousness, " writes Plotinus, " it is so that he can unite himself to himself by this act; if he attempts to know himself, it is because he finds himself ignorant of himself " [1].

b) **God has no will or desire,** for these acts suppose an exterior good towards which one tends, and a succession of actions in order to choose this good.

c) **God is not life,** for life necessitates movement. But although God is not in movement, He is no more properly said to be in repose; this would suppose in Him a distinct subject receiving the formality of stability, which would nullify His full simplicity.

d) **God is not even being** in its most grand indetermination. For Plotinus, being essentially implies a plurality; it designates an essence already specified, one of the ideas of the Platonic world, distinct from others, and in this way it encompasses something of non-being. " The name of the One ", Plotinus writes, " expresses nothing more than the negation of plurality " [2].

This negative theology is but a corollary of the fundamental principle. Inasmuch as God is both The First and The Source of all reality and the cause is so much better than its effect, God distinguishes Himself from all others through possession of the most high perfection. To attribute a perfection to Him which He would have in common with other beings would be to lower Him. " The One refuses to be counted with other things; He is the measure and not measured; one can but say that He is beyond. We speak that which He is not, but not

---

[1] *III Ennead*, IX, Ch. IX.
[2] *V Ennead*, V, Ch. VI.

that which He is " [1]. Briefly, God is *The Ineffable, The Inde-*
termined and *The Transcendent.*

127.   These conceptions do not seem to be far removed from
the Thomistic view, which proposes that we do not know God
naturally except through our analogous ideas expressing pure
perfections, in which there is a dual aspect.   On the one hand,
our ideas give us a genuine knowledge of the divine substance
which they signify in a proper sense, so that the different attributes
of God are not pure synonyms; on the other hand, however, this
knowledge is so imperfect and inadequate that these attributes
have but a purely negative validity in signifying the essence or
the mode of being proper to God.   " We can only know what God
is not, though not what He is " [2], writes St. Thomas.

But Plotinus pushed his negative method so far that he can
be accused, with some justification, of *agnosticism*, for he held
to the basic impossibility of our concepts to express anything
positively of the being of God. But this criticism is based on the
principle that our sole natural means of attaining God is through
abstractive reason; Plotinus, however, places above the knowledge
of concepts not only intuition, but also the knowledge proportioned
to the vision of God, *ecstasy*. In this latter state, God is no longer
unknowable, but He remains inexpressible in words and in concepts.
Accordingly, the Plotinian and Thomistic theologies cannot be
harmonized.

C) **Emanation.**

128.   According to Plotinus' view, God, being supreme
perfection, is also the most fruitful principle.   He produces
a reality distinct from Himself, The Intelligence, which emanates
from His substance both freely and necessarily.

a) **Freely,** for The One, being plenitude, has no need of this
new being.   He produces this being without being impoverished
Himself, without losing or gaining anything; thus He is
absolutely independent and free in this action.   On the other
hand, He acts with knowledge, consciousness and will in the
measure that positive theology grants Him these perfections.

b) **Necessarily,** for since THE ONE is immutable, Plotinus
writes : " if there be a second termination after Him,
it is necessary that it exist without the One being moved,
without the One being inclined, without the One wishing it —
in a word, without any movement.   In what manner, then?
And what should be conceived outside of Him, of Him who rests

---

[1] *V Ennead*, **v**, Ch. IV.
[2] St. Thomas Aquinas, *Summa Theologica*, I, q. III, prologue; see also q. XIII.

as immobile as the resplendent light which is around the sun and comes from it, but is always immobile " [1]. Consequently, this mode of action is natural and necessary.

It is, moreover, essential that every perfect being manifest its fulness in producing an effect in its own image. This emanation is nothing but an aspect of the perfection of The One, and, accordingly, as necessary as He [2].

II. The Intelligence.

129. Plotinus calls The Intelligence *The Nous* and, much less frequently than the Stoics and Philo, the *Logos* [3]. Necessarily emanating from God from all eternity, it exists necessarily from all eternity. At the same time, it is truly an *effect*, and its nature can be made more precise by applying the two aspects of the fundamental principle.

A) Degraded Existence.

This characteristic is manifested from the view of unity, of truth and of beauty.

1º The Intelligence does not possess the absolute simplicity of The One, inasmuch as it implies an essential *duality*, that of subject and of object. It is not uniquely intuition, but primarily contemplation of an other who is God : " It is in considering the Good that it considers itself " [4].

2º Due to this inferiority, it cannot exhaust, in one glance, the transcendental fulness of its object, The One. In The Intelligence, truth is fragmented into a multitude of *Ideas*. Here Plotinus adopts the well-known doctrine of Plato's ideal world, including its ideas of genera, of species, and even of *individuals* [5], harmoniously hierarchical and proceeding from this barely perceptible supreme idea which Plato called *The Good*, and Plotinus calls *The One*.

3º A lesser unity results in a lesser *goodness*. The plurality of ideas demands a sort of receiving and multiplying subject

---

[1] *V Ennead*, I, Ch. VI.
[2] See below, n. 134.
[3] *V Ennead*, I, Ch. VI.
[4] *V Ennead*, VI, Ch. V.
[5] See below, n. 136.

which, though remaining in an immaterial, divine and infinite order, does not have the fulness of perfection of the first actuality.

B) **Resemblance.**

Inasmuch as The Intelligence is the first effect, it has but a minimum of degraded existence and a maximum of resemblance with the unity, the truth and the goodness of The One.

1º It partakes of *unity*, at first, because The One is the unique object of its contemplation. Furthermore, the Ideas (while remaining truly multiple), are not subsisting individualities, as they were for Plato; they identify themselves completely with the unique essence of The Intelligence which reassembles them as a group of specifically distinct forces and which constitute a sole principle of activity. The " ideal world " thus becomes a unique, personal intelligence, an *hypostasis*.

2º The Intelligence also participates in the immutable *truth*. Inasmuch as the ideas constitute its essence, it has all its thoughts by itself; it need not form representative images nor need it reason to acquire the full truth. It is sufficient that it contemplate what it is, the perfect image of The One of such a sort that it never meets an occasion of error. From this flows its brilliant beauty which is the splendor of truth : " First Beauty, entirely Beauty, it itself has no portion in which its beauty could default " [1].

3º This indefectible contemplation of truth in The One brings to The Intelligence a participation in the supreme *goodness* along with perfection and definitive happiness. Plotinus calls it a god who immutably possesses each thing : " Why should it seek to change if it is good? Why should it seek to enlarge itself if it is perfect "? It also possesses " true eternity, of which time, which encloses the soul... is an imitation " [2].

130. These two notions, that the ideas are really distinct and that they are identical with the unique essence of The Intelligence, must be harmonized. Plotinus is often content with juxtaposing two conclusions which reflect the double aspect of his fundamental

[1] *V Ennead*, VIII, Ch. VIII.
[2] *Ibid.*, I, Ch. IV.

principle : " The being which thinks must be both one and two...
It must be both simple and not simple " [1].

Brehier explains this notion as follows : " The Intelligence is
vision of The One, and through this action is knowledge of itself
and of the intelligible world... The most profound conception
one can have of the intelligible world is that of a society of
intelligences or of spirits, each of which, in thinking on itself,
knows all the others and all of which form but one intelligence
or unique spirit " [2].

But it is especially concerning the Soul, where a strong difficulty
is encountered, that Plotinus examines and solves some of these
notions.

III. The Soul.

131. The Intelligence, as well as The One, according to the
measure of its perfection and following the same procedure
of fatal or natural emanation, must produce a third effect
which Plotinus entitles *The Soul of the world*. This soul is thus
necessarily eternal; though inferior to The Intelligence, it also
resembles it.

A) Degraded Existence.

1º Its *unity* is, at first, less strong, for it not only implies
duality, but an almost indefinite multiplicity of elements
really distinct. With the Stoics, Plotinus calls these " seed-
bearing reasons ". They are principles through which The Soul
is immediately disposed to enter into contact with our sense-
perceptible world. More particularly, these principles are
the *particular souls* which constitute the substantial perfection
of all the beings of the sense-perceptible universe, or what
Aristotle called *substantial forms*. Moreover, since The Soul
is the principle of activity and order throughout, every corporeal
being is animated, even the minerals. All these particular
souls dwell within The Soul of the world as the multiple ideas
dwell within The Intelligence.

2º This dispersion of elements involves an inferior possession
of the *truth* for The Soul. It is true that The Soul can attain
the ideal world in The Intelligence, but only by means of
reasoning and not by intuition; it must form notions or concepts
which are imperfect images of the Ideas.

---

[1] *Ibid.*, vi, Ch. i.

[2] E. Bréhier, *op. cit.*, i, p. 457.

3º Consequently, it has less *goodness;* it is of a hybrid nature and lies on the frontier of spirit and matter, so that Plotinus distinguished, at times, two souls : one as divine, turned towards the intelligible world, the other inferior, totally concerned with the care of bodies.

It does not enjoy much of eternity; for, in producing the sense-perceptible world it *engenders time,* to which it submits itself and which is but a mobile image of eternity. Time is but a progressive elongation of the life of The Soul [1].

Among these multiple souls, Plotinus found a place for the pagan divinities, and arranged them hierarchically : the demons, which are corporeal, inhabit the sense-perceptible world, while above them are the stars; the superior gods are in the divine aspect of The Soul, and the most high gods are in the *Logos with the Ideas.*

B) **Resemblance.**

In addition to the consequences which accrue to The Soul because of the fact that every cause is superior to its effect, it has other traits which it possesses because every effect partakes of and resembles its cause.

1º It partakes positively of *unity,* for its essential property is an actual undividedness which unifies these multiple souls under one principle, similar to the group of ideas in The Intelligence. " The Soul of the world gives itself to each according to its extent... It does not break itself up to animate each of the parts of the body through each part, but all the parts live through The Soul completely; it is totally present throughout, similar, with regard to unity and omnipresence, to an engendering father " [2]. Like The Intelligence, it possesses its personal unity : it is an *hypostasis.*

In order to harmonize this prerogative of unity with the distinction of particular souls, Plotinus adduces the example of the oneness of science which flows out into multiple conclusions. Each theorem, though possessing *potentially* all the others, has its own individuality without prejudice to the unity of the science. So each soul through its identity with the Soul of the world, contains the seminal principles

---

[1] *III Ennead,* VII, Ch. XI-XII.
[2] *V Ennead,* I, Ch. II.

of all the others, but it distinguishes itself likewise by manifesting one of these many in a special way [1].

2⁰ The Soul of the world is also of the intellectual order, and is capable of attaining the complete truth. " It is united to The Intelligence, it is filled with and enjoys The Intelligence, and knows itself " [2]. It is beautiful, intelligent and simple; it is similar to The Intelligence.

3⁰ Finally, The Soul of the world is the principle of the *goodness* in the world. In bringing an element of unity and intelligibility to the world, it fills the world with order and beauty; and, with perfection, it brings goodness and happiness. In a word, The Soul of the world is the " Immanent Providence " made famous by the Stoics. It orders everything without effort and without reasoning and only through the natural influence of its perfect being which overflows. From this broad point of view, not only is no substance bad, but that which we judge bad from a more restrained point of view, is really a good necessary to the world, as is the hangman in a well-regulated city [3].

C) The Trinity of Plotinus.

132. The One, The Intelligence, and The Soul are three personal beings or three *hypostases* which constitute the *Divine World* for Plotinus. In all three there are the following : eternity, immutability of a sort inasmuch as the emanation is produced without troubling the tranquillity of the cause, immensity, and even infinity for all three are immaterial and spiritual. This Trinity is clearly opposed to the world where changefulness and limitation, birth and death, time, quantity and place reside. There are some external resemblances to the mystery of the Holy Trinity in this doctrine. Even the *Nous* is called " Son of God " and " Light of Light " as in the Credo [4].

But the very basis of the doctrine is radically opposed to that of the Catholic faith. Instead of three consubstantial Persons, Plotinus has three *hypostases* proceeding through successive degradation. Further, he represents the ensemble of things as gravitating around a luminous nucleus which is The One; outside of this central focus, a first zone is outlined, also totally illuminated and incandescent, The Intelligence; then there is a less brilliant second zone, much involved in darkness because of its closeness

---

[1] *IV Ennead*, IX, Ch. V.
[2] *V Ennead*, I, Ch. III.
[3] *III Ennead*, II and III.
[4] *III Ennead*, VIII, Ch. II; *V Ennead*, III, Ch. IX and VIII, Ch. XII.

to the sense-perceptible world, this is The Soul. Finally, contiguous to the latter, but completely darkened and yet with traces of the influence of the central fire through action of the Soul, is the realm of bodies. Below this, there is nothing more than the dark night of matter.

Furthermore, in this view, The One alone is the true God; The Soul and The Intelligence are but effects or *creatures*. Their role of divine intermediaries is to fill up the abyss made by Plato between matter and the idea; Plotinus fills the gap by a final application of his fundamental principle in order to explain matter.

IV. MATTER.

133. Inasmuch as The Soul enjoys real perfection, it must exteriorize itself by an effect which has to obey the law of *degradation;* this is *matter.*

A) **Degradation.**

The unity of The Soul is so weak that if one were to stop with this notion, matter could not be realized as *pure multiplicity.* Just as being and its perfection are proportional to the degree of unity, so matter becomes pure non-being stripped of every determination and of every perfection.

As a result,

1º Matter has no stability but is *pure becoming* incapable of existing outside of time.

2º Matter has no solidity but is a *pure void,* identical with space. It in no wise has the property of grandeur; quantity makes it appear to be such, but matter is merely a receptacle deprived of all determined grandeur.

3º Matter has no truth, no intelligibility and no beauty, but it is the *principle of all error and pain.* " One considers matter only to the extent that one can consider the most unsightly of realities... it is pure potentiality, mostly non-being, essential falsity " [1].

4º Matter possesses no order or goodness, but it is *original evil,* the source of all moral and physical disorder. " When the

---

[1] *II Ennead,* IV, Ch. X.

defect of goodness is total, as it is in matter, we then have evil itself... the latter alters and corrupts the form by juxtaposing its own nature with form " [1].

B) Resemblance.

Despite all this, matter resembles its cause and attempts to participate in its perfection at least to the extent that it is *reality*. Matter is an inseparable reflection of The Soul, as a shadow is the inseparable wake of a luminous body. This bond endows matter with some consistence, though the smallest imaginable. " It shares in being without sharing in it; it manages to draw something from its immediate neighborhood with it, but its nature makes any intimate union impossible " [2]. It at least has the tenuous reality which Aristotle attributed to a potentiality deprived of all actuality. Plotinus, explaining Plato, gives to matter a certain proper activity and a sort of aspiration; but these latter are quite confused, without order, aimless in direction, unstable, constantly in motion towards form [3].

It seems that this view of matter is best understood under its double aspect of dependence and eternity:

1⁰ **Dependence.** Matter is wholly a function of The Soul, and one could speak of its essential *relatedness*. If matter is evil, it is but as a privation of good, as a lack of order. If matter is pain, it " necessarily shows itself ensnared within the bonds of beauty as a captive covered with chains of gold " [4]. It is similar to a mirror, in which bodies form, transform and reflect as a series of images. This is how it is explained that The Soul, while remaining indivisible and impassible in itself, takes on the aspect of multiplicity and of change in these inferior manifestations. It is the composite which changes, Plotinus proposes; but (the cause producing without suffering any loss) he maintains quite strongly that The Soul really suffers nothing from them.

2⁰ **Eternity.** The Soul produces matter blindly and fatally. It would not be better that The Soul abstain from this action, for to be a cause, even of non-being, is essentially a perfection. Eternity, in this view, is thus necessary to the universe of the senses as it is to the divine universe. Plotinus even defends the *incorruptibility* of matter; it remains unalterably what it is, the peripheral ring necessary to order; and time, which is its characteristic, is the mobile image of immobile eternity.

---

[1] *I Ennead*, viii, Ch. v and Ch. viii.
[2] *III Ennead*, vi, Ch. xiv.
[3] R. Arnou, *Le Désir de Dieu dans la philosophie de Plotin*, pp. 64-5.
[4] *I Ennead*, viii, Ch. xv; See below, n. 160.

At the same time, this property does not exclude the dependence of the effect on its cause. In this connection, the remarks of St. Augustine apply : " The Platonists state that there is not a beginning of time, but a beginning of the cause. They say it is similar to a foot which, from all eternity, is poised over the dust; the imprint will always exist from below, and yet it is made by the foot in such a way that the foot does not exist without the imprint, and yet produces it " [1].

C) The Universe and God : Is Plotinus Pantheist?

134. The *eternity of the world*, and, in general, of all real being is admitted by Plotinus as a simple corollary to the fertile existence of a perfect being. Though this is not demonstrated as is done by Aristotle, it is wrongly considered as a divine right, and it must be similarly appreciated. In philosophy, it is a possible but not a necessary hypothesis, and through faith it is seen as erroneous [2].

This error at least has the advantage of searching back for the metaphysical point of view, legitimate and profound, to which Plotinus constantly returns. He is not concerned to explain the motion or the temporal origin of the world, but rather its nature or its very being; for Plotinus, the sensible realities, variable and multiple though they be, are not fully intelligible of themselves. Plotinus' answer to this question can be summarized as follows : that which is fully explicative of the imperfect is the perfect efficient cause, intelligible in itself as a disinterested source. This reply is not too greatly distant from the Augustinian and Thomistic answer which appeal to a perfect cause of being, the creative cause.

But the solution of Plotinus retains a deficiency both from the point of view of the effect and also of the cause.

a) On the part of the effect. The effect which is to be explained by the perfect cause is not solely the imperfect part of being, as Plotinus maintains, but the subsisting total composite, which is limited and imperfect by one of its principles (potentiality), and through the other principle (actuality) shares in the perfection of God. Consequently, in the total effect there must be granted a formal intrinsic cause, and it is insufficient to explain the total effect even by a perfect efficient cause.

1. It is true that Plotinus saw quite clearly that one consequence of perfect causality producing the very being itself would be the

---

[1] St. Augustine, *The City of God*, Book **x**, Ch. **xxxi**.
[2] See above, n. 79.

very close union of the principle with its effect; but he explained this by the notion of *interior presence* or *immanence*. Justifiably, then, he placed the foundation for this presence in the real dependence which affects the effect in relation to the cause; he affirmed that this dependence is not really one on the part of the source but is wholly and entirely on the part of the imperfect being, in such a way that, properly speaking, the effect is in the cause but the cause is not in the effect. " The Soul is not in the world, it is the world which is in The Soul... The Soul is in The Intelligence, bodies are in The Soul and The Intelligence is in one who is not in any other... All things are in Him, but He is not in all, without being completely distant from them " [1].

Presence of this sort safeguards well the real distinction and the transcendence of the perfect cause; it is especially attributable to The One who is in all things precisely because He is not in each in a manner of belonging to them or of being limited by them, and yet is the perpetual overflowing source of all things while remaining inactive in Himself. From The One all things receive being and life either directly, or through The Intelligence and The Soul. In a somewhat similar fashion, St. Thomas teaches that the creative and conserving causality is explainable by a non-mutual relation, real and transcendental in the effect, but merely a relation of reason in the cause.

2. But Plotinus seems fascinated by the splendor of this grand truth, and seeks within it an explanation of all problems, especially that of the union of soul with body. He explicitly refuses to agree with Aristotle's view, and proposes nine arguments against hylomorphism [2].

In other words, Plotinus never conceived of a relation of mutual dependence between the perfect and the imperfect through which incomplete beings are in transcendental relation, but always had in mind a non-mutual relation of dependence between the effect — an imperfect though completely subsisting being — and the cause — a perfect, inalterable subsisting being. Moreover, experience asserts the substantial unity of the composite as in man, and thus demonstrates the falsity of the Plotinian explanation.

From the above confusion follows the obscurity of his notion of prime matter which, being an effect, pretends to be a complete being, but which is incompatible with the notion of pure potentiality. It likewise follows that it is impossible to render a complete account of *becoming*, which Plotinus explains by a metaphor as the discovery of a hidden perfection or the flowering of a pre-existing seed. It is in this sense that he speaks of the passage from potentiality to actuality, especially in ethics [3].

b) On the part of the cause. The perfect or creative cause of being is neither multiple nor necessary, as Plotinus believes.

---

[1] *V Ennead*, v.
[2] *IV Ennead*, Ch. VIII.
[3] See below, n. 136, 3°; R. ARNOU, *op. cit.*, pp. 215-217.

On the contrary, it is at once absolutely unique because infinite in perfection, and also fully free inasmuch as the whole basis for its activity is the decision of its will in the light of its knowledge, and without any exterior influence.

1.   Plotinus recognizes three superimposed imperfections in reality : pure multiplicity in matter, unified multiplicity in life, and the duality of thought.   From these he concludes to the existence of three perfect or creative causes, inasmuch as above each sphere there must be realized a being possessing by itself the perfection of its effects — that is, of the inferior degree and without its characteristic imperfections.

But experience corrects this conception, as we have said above, in establishing that *prime matter alone* cannot be an effect in a proper sense.   Further, in looking for the cause of *being* or *of substance*, every reality, no matter how weak, participates in pure perfections (being, unity, goodness, and so forth).   These perfections, capable of being realized infinitely, do not have the reason for their perfect being except in the " subsisting being itself ", who realizes them all infinitely.

Plotinus placed the problem of creation, or, more exactly, of conservation in the being of each imperfect creature.   But God alone, or The One, is the creator, as St. Thomas demonstrates [1]. There cannot be several creators as principal causes for there is but one infinite being, nor even as instrumental causes for no creature can be useful to one which draws all being from nothingness; an instrumentality, without any matter which it might dispose, can have no truly causal action.

It is true that one can conceive, without absurdity, a participation in the divine creative action of substances [2]; But the a priori conception of Plotinus must be, in such a case, submitted to the test of experience where no resemblance is discoverable to the existence of The Soul of the world, nor for the intelligible world, nor for the *Nous* distinct from God [3].   Creative causality, as a consequence, admits of no intermediary between God and the least of beings.

2.   Plotinus remarks that it is proper, by the definition of perfect being, that it produce or that it explain the imperfect; it is essential that it be a cause.   Moreover, that which is essential and natural is necessary.   The world is, then, necessarily eternal and God is not free to create or not to create it.

In answer, one can say that the essence of perfect being can be looked upon in two ways.   In the first way, in an *absolute* fashion, in that which constitutes it in itself; in this sense it is not essential to that which is perfect that it create, since it is wholly of and in itself.   Plotinus concedes this point, and he himself asserts

---

[1] St. Thomas Aquinas, *op. cit.*, I, q. XLV, art. 5.

[2] *Ibid.*, q. CIV, art. 2.

[3] See the *a pari* criticisms of Plato's ideal world above, n. 46 and n. 57.

God's liberty under this aspect. One can also consider the essence of the perfect cause in a *relative* fashion, inasmuch as it is defined, with the help of analogy, by its best known effects. In this sense, if it is true that to be a cause in second actuality it is necessary to posit an effect, it is false to assert that to be a cause in first actuality, the existence of an effect is indispensable. Consequently, the Platonic adage, " Good is self-diffusive ", must be understood as a necessary dependence on the part of the creature, and as a free communication on the part of God, the supreme Good.

3. Plotinus' teaching of the necessity of emanation brings up the problem of his *pantheism*. The latter is definable as "A doctrine proposing that everything is God; God and the world make up one entity which can have two fundamental meanings : 1) God is the only reality and the world is but a collection of manifestations having no permanent reality nor distinct substance; 2) The world is the sole reality, God is but the acme of all that exists " [1].

If Plotinus is a pantheist, it is in the first sense. His fundamental principle, as understood even by himself, can lead to two opposed conclusions. If insistence is made on the truth which is affirmed, he absolutely excludes all pantheism, for he recognizes a real distinction between the perfect cause of being and its effect [2]. But if emphasis is laid on the necessity of emanation, one would have to conclude that the being of the effects is part of the being of the cause, for it is their *essential* manifestation; or, that the collection of beings emanating from The One must be considered as an absolutely necessary totality, and they thus constitute the Divinity which defines itself as the necessary being [3].

Historically speaking, Plotinus did not accept the pantheist consequence; he refused to call matter divine, and maintained the distinction between The One and its effects : " Being perfect, The One superabounds, and this superabundance produces a thing *different* from it... Things are not The First, for the latter reside in The One while giving existence to things " [4]. " The cause cannot be identified with its effect " [5].

Nevertheless, it does not seem repugnant from another point of view to conceive of the identification of the many

[1] LALANDE, *op. cit.*, pantheism.
[2] For various views on this matter, see R. ARNOU, *op. cit.*, pp. 151-187.
[3] R. Jolivet, *Essai sur les rapports de la pensée grecque et de la pensée chrétienne*, pp. 123-5.
[4] *V Ennead*, II. — [5] *VI Ennead*, IX, Ch. VI.

individual souls with the unique *hypostasis*, whether it be The Soul of the world, or The Intelligence, for the distinction proposed between them is quite weak. We can conclude that the Plotinian notion of emanation, while explicitly safeguarding the real distinction between the true God and creation, contains a dangerous germ of pantheism.

ARTICLE TWO. — ETHICS.

Ascent of the soul towards God.

135. Every ethics is based on psychological premisses; Plotinus' psychology is but a consequence of his metaphysics. We shall find here, as unifying principle, another application of his fundamental principle, but from another viewpoint. Instead of considering the perfect being who gives himself, one considers the imperfect being which returns to its source through desire, and, by degrees, ascends to the first principle.

These matters will be considered in the following three sections :

  I.   Psychological conclusions.
  II.   Desire : the principle of return.
  III.   The Degrees of purification.

I. Psychological conclusions.

A) **Definition of man.**

136. Man is a complex being formed from a sensible, corruptible material, the body, and from a spiritual and eternal part which is unfolded into two distinct parts, the *reasoning soul* (ψυχή), and intuitive intelligence or *spirit* (Νοῦς which St. Augustine translates as mind). These three elements are not separable, for one proceeds from the other; spirit is the efficient cause of soul, and soul, that of body; from this follows the consequence of their intimate presence to each other, or mutual immanence. They are not, however, substantially united, for there is no relation between them of matter to form.

This definition is but a particular application of Plotinus' metaphysics. Each man is a *creature of The One*, so to speak, one of the multiple rays emanating from his perfection and reunited in a double bundle before The Intelligence and The Soul of the world, before losing himself within matter. Through our spiritual part, which properly constitutes our human dignity, each of us realizes one of the multiple forces unified in The Soul (a λόγος σπερματικός), and one of the multiple Ideas unified in The Intelligence.

B) Corollaries.

A triple corollary flows from this conception of man :

1º **Immortality of the soul.** Our soul, or the immaterial part, is evidently immortal and even eternal, as is God. Before our birth, which, through union with matter, scattered these spiritual elements in various places, we were " Ones " as part of The Intelligence contemplating The One, in the royal part of The Soul governing the universe. We were all together though distinct, sharing in the mode of perfect and happy being which is proper to the superior, divine world.

2º **Faculties of the soul.** After our birth, the soul and the spirit appear as intermediaries, destined to rebind a special part of matter to the first principle, the source of all being, The Ineffable One. To act this part, Plotinus gives the soul and the spirit several faculties which can be classed into two groups. The spirit (νοῦς) possesses a power of superior contemplation in order to achieve The One in *ecstasy*, and a power turned towards the ideal world in order to know it and to make its reflections shine forth in *intuition*. The reasoning soul (ψυχή), possesses a superior faculty of *reasoning* in order to make itself distant from bodies and to elevate itself towards The Intelligence; and it has inferior faculties, *sensible* and *vegetative*, in order to know and organize matter.

Plotinus does not explicitly propose this classification [1]. With regard to sensation, he merely mentions in passing that its essential function is to create matter, and he hesitates much on certain problems of experimental psychology which were being warmly debated in the schools of his time, as on the medium required between vision and its object [2]. As for the other, inferior, beings, sensation is missing in the plants and minerals, in whom The Soul of the world is, as it were, asleep, and creates matter solely through the vegetative functions.

---

[1] *V Ennead*, III, Ch. IX — [2] *IV Ennead*, V.

Nevertheless, there seems to be nothing contradictory for Plotinus himself to propose that a faculty of knowing is at the same time creative. According to his fundamental principle, contemplation is in itself productive, just as a center of perfection illumines its proper richness in a distinct image, without losing anything and without changing in any way at all. It can be said that " For Plotinus, the soul senses because it seizes itself while creating the object of sense " [1], just as The Intelligence creates The Soul in being aware of the ideal world of which it is constituted. The classification of four faculties in two groups seems to be a basic tenet of the system.

3° **Progress of the soul.** If every perfect being manifests itself necessarily through operations, man is not in reality or in actuality except through the part according to which he acts. The other powers are in potentiality; they are latent and asleep, and they become pure non-being in man. " The Intelligence is ours without being ours; it is ours when we use it " [2].

Inasmuch as ethics is destined to lead us to perfect happiness, all its motivation must be to allow us to pass, in this sense, from potentiality to actuality. Ethics must make us return to the state of perfection where only the spiritual parts in us shall be acting; this is the idea of the return through various degrees of purification.

II. Desire : the Principle of Return.

137. From the viewpoint of the effect, Plotinus' fundamental principle can be stated as follows :

" *Every effect returns to its perfect cause through inner desire and there it finds its proper perfection and its happiness* ".

A further explanation of this principle will clarify its nature and its laws of operation.

A) **The Notion of Desire.**

Since desire is the origin of the movement towards perfection, it cannot belong to The One, who possesses the fulness of all perfection, but it is the constitutive activity of all other beings. It can be defined as " *the tendency of every imperfect being to*

---

[1] C. Boyer, *L'Idée de Vérité dans saint Augustin*, p. 171.
[2] *V Ennead*, iii, Ch. iii.

develop in itself that part which resembles its cause ", and thus to develop its positive richness. Desire is the sign of absent or non-existent perfection which is in potentiality tending towards actually acquired being. It is likewise modeled on the degree of imperfection of beings.

In matter, desire is disordered and sterile. It has *pure desire*, for it has nothing in actuality, and also *non-desire*, for it lacks, precise orientation towards a determined object.

In the soul and, more especially, in the spirit (νοῦς), desire is channeled and ordered. Inasmuch as it traces back the course of participated perfections of the first being, desire becomes the principle of the ascension towards God.

In man, who possesses the three elements — matter, soul and spirit — desire is to be conceived as a synthetic activity which forcefully reunites these diverse and opposed strains. Desire can be materialistic and then it is disordered and evil, or it can be spiritual and then it is well-ordered and good. Desire, in a word, is an *intermediary;* it is the force destined to allow a perfection to develop from potentiality into actuality in the sense that it suppresses all inferior operation, in order that the highest part alone can act.

B) **Laws of Desire.**

True desire is oriented towards God by passing through The Soul and The Intelligence; its mode of action, consequently, follows the mode of being of spirits. Spiritual beings are intimately united by their nature; those which are similar compenetrate each other and tend to become identified as far as their distinction permits this to occur. They are not, as a matter of fact, separated in place for they lack quantity, but they are distinct solely through the degree of diminution which affects an inferior being following its emanation. Plotinus, even before St. Augustine, already speaks of the soul as plunged into materiality, as occupied with its own needs, and as living in a " realm of dissemblance " [1].

A triple law of desire follows from the above notions : the law of return, the law of recollection, and the law of purification.

---

[1] *I Ennead*, VIII, Ch. XIII.

1° **Law of return.** Every being basically and explicitly desires its proximate cause, but the final object of its basic aspiration is its union with The One. The motion of desire does not terminate until it has found the supreme good. " All beings ", writes Plotinus, " to the extent that they do not possess the good, wish to change, and to the extent that they possess this good they wish to remain what they are " [1]. For this reason, " any ascension, above all, seeks for The One " [2], for " nothing is desirable except through the good which colors it " [3].

2° **Law of recollection.** The object sought after is not scattered about in things of the senses, but is most intimately present in the soul; desire, then, above all is but an effort of recollection towards the interiority of the soul. The cause remains immanent to its effect as the source of its being, as its root, its center and its goal; accordingly, he who seeks to know himself seeks also to know from whence he came. The more one enters into oneself, the more one elevates oneself towards God. " There is an affinity between intimate and sublime things... Height and depth embrace in a kiss of peace " [4].

3° **Law of purification.** Concentration on oneself is effected through purification which is a radical separation from inferior and especially from material elements. What has actually happened is that the souls and the spirits, at one time united in the intelligible world, have become multiple and dispersed in time and space through the necessary emanation which concludes in matter. They thus contracted various differences which make them mutually self-opposed and prevent them from recovering the stability and luminous perfection once possessed in the intelligible world. By suppressing the differences which are appended to beings on their periphery, — much as a sculptor makes chips fly with his chisel and disengages an ideal form from his material — the soul has a real awakening and takes flight towards God; such is the work of purification.

---

[1] *VI Ennead*, ix, Ch. ix.

[2] *III Ennead*, viii, Ch. ix.

[3] *VI Ennead*, vii, Ch. xxii.

[4] This thought of E. Hello, taken from the grand mystic Ruysbroeck, is also that of Plotinus.

Plotinian asceticism.

138. Plotinus conceived of the union of matter and form as being a union not of information but one of juxtaposition. His purifying asceticism thereby resembles that of the Stoics : a suppression of the sensible aspect of the body, a detachment by a simple and total separation, and a serene abnegation of all which is not The One. For him, matter is an unpleasant neighbor like mud with which the soul has been covered and soiled, or like the unpleasant breath of a strange thing from which one must stay at a distance [1].

Furthermore, this asceticism is not, properly speaking, an ethics. It is not a matter of acquiring virtue and becoming better, but of purifying the eye of the spirit in order to realize contemplation in the vision of The One. Sin is a simple juncture of inferior elements, or of materials which impede this happy speculation. However, there is no blemish of any kind in the soul, which lost none of its proper perfection in following the law of emanation and in being united to matter. A spiritual sin, or a voluntary evil, is inexistent for Plotinus.

In Catholic asceticism, on the contrary, the conflict is not between the spirit and the body, but between two wills, two " egos " which fight for preeminence. It is not a matter of being rid of one's body, but of submitting it to faith and reason. Even in the encounter of which Plotinus speaks, sin is essentially in the deliberate will and is a moral disorder which affects the free faculties; it is the soul which soils itself and must be transformed through penance.

III. The degrees of purification.

139. The purification which consists in the progressive actualization of the superior faculties and the reduction of the inferior operations to a state of pure potentiality, lifts man to The One in three stages. This follows logically, for there are three faculties that need purification : sensibility, reasoning and intuition.

First degree. *The effort of* ABSTRACTION *in order to become soul.*

It is according to the natural law of emanation that our soul, once happy above, has *descended* into a body. The soul has thus become the efficient cause of this portion of matter

---

[1] *I Ennead*, II, Ch. IV, and VI, Ch. V.

which is its body; it has engendered it and organized it through
the instrumentality of its inferior powers, both vegetile and
sensible.

In his treatise, " Of the descent of the soul into the body " [1],
Plotinus sometimes speaks of the *sin* of the soul.   This sin
consists in the soul becoming absorbed in its inferior functions
wherein it plays the role of independent principle; though
completely extrinsic, this sin has the formidable effect of
separating us from happiness not only in this life, but also
in the future.   The punishment of such a sinful soul is to
return, after death, and to reanimate the inferior bodies
according to its vicious dispositions, as Plato had already
taught; *metempsychosis* here functions as a moral sanction [2].

The first degree towards reascension to celestial happiness
is *total abstraction* from matter.   It consists in developing
reason at the expense of sensations in order to rediscover
the proper nature of the soul, which tends to sleep under the
mass of impressions from experience and imagination.
" To purify the passive part of the soul is to cease to be so
strongly inclined towards inferior things and to cease
imagining them " [3].   The Stoic virtues, indifference to the
sensible, and scientific work according to the Aristotelian
method — all contribute towards this result.

Second degree.   *The effort of* INTUITION *in order to become
spirit.*

The second stage must aim to actuate the intuitive intelligence
in man; this is to be done by abandoning the practice
of reasoning for the dialectical method of Plato.   In the superior
part of our soul, which is a partaking of the divine intelligence,
we bear the whole and entire ideal world; but it lies buried,
as it were, under the cover of the reasoning processes of the soul.
If one destroys this cover, this difference leads to pure intuition
by suppressing from our thought every division and succession.
We then see the truth in one glance, and we shall return fully
similar to The Intelligence by having regained our proper
mode of operation.

Then we shall possess, in an eminent fashion, all the virtues.
" In the Intelligence, science or wisdom is thought; temperance

---

[1] *IV Ennead*, viii.
[2] *III Ennead*, iii, Ch. iv.
[3] *Ibid.*, vi, Ch. v.

is its relation with itself; justice is the realization of its proper activity; the analogue of courage is its identity with itself and the persistence of its state of purity " [1]. We shall then know ourselves " as a being who is no longer man but something totally different, who has elevated himself to a higher order, taking with him only the superior part of the soul " [2].

Third degree. *The effort of* ECSTASY *in order to become The One.*

Inasmuch as our spirit is an effect of The One, it possesses a trace or an image which will be actuated by suppression of intuition in favor of ecstasy. Thus, conforming to the law of desire, our spirit will be so intimately joined to The One, that it will there become identified with him, *to the extent that this is possible.*

This sublime unity is produced only when the soul has found absolute silence of the senses, of reasoning processes, or even of intuitions in which the soul is still opposed to the object of contemplation. Such unity is found when the soul has totally freed the fine point of the spirit with which it can, finally, touch the infinite. At such a moment, The One shines within us with an unforeseeable and unexpected enlightening, invading and possessing the soul as inspiration ravished the spirit of the initiated and of the prophets.

Plotinus attempted to characterize this ecstasy. It is a vision, a contemplation, but of an ineffable type in which the subject is not distinguished any more from the object. In ecstasy there is no longer self-consciousness, for this would imply distinction between knower and known, and the union would be imperfect. It is a vision comparable to that of the eye before a pure luminous body. " It sees without seeing anything, and this is, above all, what it wishes. Thus intelligence, in recollecting itself within its interiority, sees a light which appears to it suddenly, alone, pure, and existing in its very self " [3].

But it is impossible to express in words this departure of the self through which the spirit is elevated above itself, and in which man abandons himself to someone infinitely great. It is a stable and unchangeable state, and an activity which is superior to the faculty of knowing; it can be compared to the condition of one who is so absorbed in reading that he loses awareness of his action and identifies himself with the object of his attention [4]. It is

---

[1] *I Ennead*, ii, Ch. vii.
[2] *V Ennead*, iii, Ch. iv.
[3] *Ibid.*, v, Ch. vii.
[4] *I Ennead*, iv, Ch. x.

a transport and an intoxication. It is a lack of consciousness, if one considers the inability of fixating this sublime operation in concepts, and yet it is a superior consciousness of a soul transparent to its own self.

In brief, ecstasy is a supra-rational action of which one can speak only as one does of The One himself.

a) Positively : it is an act of both intelligence and will. It is the perfect possession of all truth, for it is the final realization of the great principle : like is only known by like. Immediate participation in The One, ecstasy is a knowledge connaturally perfect, inasmuch as it is a type of touch or ineffable contact without concept or idea as intermediary. At the same time, it is the fulness of all being and of all happiness, for there is no fatigue nor surfeit in contemplation which would force one to rest [1]; it is such happiness that no misfortune could shake it.

b) Negatively : it is a state of unawareness and impersonality, for its very transcendence replaces and removes all other knowledge and suppresses all sense of duality.

At the same time, the real distinction between man and God seems to be maintained, either because The One remains immutable in his transcendence, or because our spirit remains what it is even during ecstasy, its new condition being but a simple flowering of all its capabilities.

Rationalist Piety.

140. The mysticism and the piety proposed by Plotinus are essentially natural. His notion of ecstasy is but that of philosophical contemplation lifted to its highest degree of keenness. While it is subordinated to the necessary action of God in order that there can be a passage from potentiality to actuality, this fact merely explains its suddenness and rarity, so that even Plotinus himself enjoyed it but rarely [2]. But this action of The One is natural and is necessarily produced so that purification can be achieved. God offers himself to all, as the action of light, without distinction or preference, to such an extent that all depends on ourselves and a methodic

---

[1] *V Ennead*, VIII, Ch. IV.
[2] In his life of Plotinus, Porphyry mentions that while he was with him, (from 263 to 268), Plotinus achieved this state four times; Porphyry himself achieved it only once.

effort will infallibly lead us to him. Furthermore, the spirit of love and of prayer, of humility and of thanksgiving are strangers to Plotinus' theory.

This rationalist trait of piety stands out especially in his conception of the gods and of religion. He could not conceive of an action of Providence which would be independent of the forces of nature; he would not be in sympathy with the redemptive mission of Christ or with the idea of a miracle. At the same time, he had no difficulty in accepting magic, and he explained it as the sympathetic action which binds diverse parts of The Soul of the world. According to Plotinus, it is a natural law that similar parts act on each other without taking account of spatial separation; since The Soul is the guardian of universal order, the results of this inter-activity are always good. Furthermore, our inferior soul is subject to these influences; the sage escapes them and dominates them through contemplation. With regard to the gods to whom incantations and sacrifices are offered, they but aid us unconsciously, spreading their influence as the sun does its light; the efficacy of prayer is merely the utilization of the laws of nature [1].

There is hardly a view which is more opposed to Catholic piety than the latter; Catholic piety perfectly harmonizes the immutability of God with the efficacy of prayer. Furthermore, orthodox mysticism is totally supernatural; ecstasy in the saints is a participation of the beatific vision which is supreme ecstasy; there is in man's nature a great suitability to experience ecstasy, but no demand [2]. Its attainment, not excluding freedom and merit, depends, above all, on grace freely granted by God. Furthermore, if there is question of a mystical union realized here below with the Blessed Trinity, it is the privilege of a few chosen souls, a gratuitous gift of Providence, and there is no certain method to achieve it [3].

Finally, in Plotinus' view, ecstasy is the supreme goal which, if once attained, allows one to neglect all else; there is no notion of a social morality in him. For the Catholic mystics, perfection in this life is conformity with the will of God. The ecstatic union is reserved for the future life; if it is granted occasionally here below, it never dispenses one from the other virtues and gives no authorization to form a transcendent egoism in oneself. On the contrary, ecstasy is a fruitful source of activity and of social works to such an extent, that the apostolic ardor of contemplative souls for the glory of God is one of the signs of true mysticism.

If there is any resemblance between Plotinianism and Christian mysticism, it is, rather, similar to the heterodox form of *quietism*. In both of these there is the same exaggeration of the excellence

---

[1] See *IV Ennead*, IV, Ch. XXXV-XLV, and *II Ennead*, III, Ch. VII-VIII.

[2] See St. Thomas Aquinas, *Summa Theologica*, I, q. XII, art. 1 and art. 4.

[3] Here arises the real equivocation in using the term, " mystic "; see F. CAYRÉ, *Manual of Patrology*, pp. 361-5.

and of the superiority of this extraordinary state, of the possibility given to all of arriving at it, of dislike for action and of a desired and ardently sought state of passivity which abolishes all movement, deadens the will and suppresses the exercise of virtue.

The above criticism, however, does not at all deaden the flame of spirituality which captivated Plotinus; later on, it will interest St. Augustine, in whom it finds its full completion and some significant corrections.

GENERAL CONCLUSION.

141. As a philosophical system, Neo-Platonism is inferior to the synthesis of Aristotle. Furthermore, in adopting the metaphysical and mystical view of Plato, Plotinus shared in his *weakness*. Completely neglecting experience, he gratuitously affirmed the existence of intermediaries between God and man, and his explanation of material reality and its changes remains obscure.

However, Plotinus also shared Plato's *power*. Without attaining a precise idea of creation, he gained remarkable insight into the relations between God as the perfect cause of being and the world which was explainable by the continuing influence of the goodness, life and duration of God. This principle of perfect causality on which the whole Plotinian system rests, is too narrow to explain all the aspects of reality and must be completed by the notions of formal and material cause. However, taken in itself, it is one of the first consequences of the principle of universal intelligibility [1], and it is one of the most profound attempts of reason to explain the universe. Viewed in this light, Plotinus' formula marks some progress over the views of his predecessors and aptly concludes, as a radiant summit, the whole of pagan philosophy.

If one looks at the totality of this rational effort which is called HELLENISM, one cannot deny the vigor of its thought, the grandeur of its results nor the nobility of soul of most of these pagan philosophers. However, they did not say everything that reason can say about the universe and human life; often they remained doubtful on the personal make-up of God, and this fact prevented them from a clear notion of the relations of the creator with the world, as well as of the nature and destiny of man.

[1] See below, n. 258.

Consequently, it can be said that Hellenism is not so much a rational as a *rationalistic* and *naturalistic* view. It inclined to present nature as the manifestation of a principle interior to the world, *The Soul of the world,* who becomes more and more conscious of himself as we go towards more and more perfect beings. And here there is also an ethical compromise, at least under its imperative form; it is but a series of counsels destined to draw out the best possible part of man in a situation. But an unsanctioned and non-obligatory ethics, at least if there be no sanction in this life, is calm and attractive when it conforms to the order of things, but distasteful and troubling through remorse, when it revolts against this order. In this view, man is his own goal; life is experienced for its own sake with the unique aim of assuring complete fulfillment from it, of drawing all beauty out of it, of grasping all the happiness it can give us — this is the logic of pagan morality.

The great and mortal weakness of Hellenism was the absence of a firm notion of a personal God, the Creator, the Legislator and Rewarder; without this notion, neither the logical, moral or social order have any explicative sense. And although these important teachings are not, in themselves, beyond the reach of human reason, the failure of these great geniuses shows the moral necessity of a revelation to instruct mankind " efficiently, with firm certainty and without error " — according to the expression of the Council of the Vatican. Furthermore, the need of a divine authority to guard the divine revelation in its integrity stands out clearly through this history of systems which are merely successive and never succeed in gaining recognition.

Nevertheless, from another point of view, pagan philosophy, in the measure according to which it advanced, approached more and more to the full truth and stirred a love of research in the souls of the elite. It succeeded in constructing some definitive, rational outlines capable of receiving the formulas of faith. It gave to the great natural conceptions of metaphysics such precision and clarity that they permitted a profounder insight into the richness of dogma, out of which there was finally constituted the sublime divine and human science of *theology*. It is in this way that Hellenism can be viewed as a providential preparation for the revelation of the full truth brought to this world by

OUR SAVIOR, JESUS CHRIST.

PART TWO.

PATRISTIC
AND MEDIEVAL PERIODS.

CHRISTIAN PHILOSOPHY.

(2nd-16th century).

BIBLIOGRAPHY (on Christian philosophy in general).

BURCH, G. B., *Early Medieval Philosophy*, New York, 1951. — COCHRANE, C. N., *Christianity and Classical Culture*, New York, 1944. — DE LABRIOLLE, P., *History and Literature of Christianity*, 1924. — RITTER, H., *Histoire de la Philosophie chrétienne*, 2 vols., Paris, 1843. — ROMEYER, J., *La Philosophie chrétienne jusqu'à Descartes*, 2 vols., Paris, 1936. — RUGGIERO, G. DE., *La filosofia del crestianesimo*, 3 vols., Bari, 1929. — SASSEN, F., *Geschiedenis der patristische en middeleeuwsche wijsbegeerte*, Nimeguen and Brussels, 1928. — SERTILLANGES, A. D., *Le Christianisme et les Philosophes*, Paris, 1941.

142. Christianity is not a philosophy, but a religious way of life based on a revelation and conferring on man, in the name of divine authority, a group of truths to believe and of precepts to observe. Furthermore, history shows the importance of the DOCTRINAL IMPACT of faith on reason, especially in the early era of Christianity. The problems on which pagan wisdom became stranded — the existence and nature of God and His relations with the world, the spirituality and immortality of the soul, the notion of obligation and of moral sanction — are given a clear response in Christian revelation. However, these truths were uttered through authority, and reason still desired to comprehend them and to establish their legitimacy.

Quite often, philosophy offered a parallel solution to some of these revealed truths, and the problem of reconciling these two sources of truth arose. The human mind wants unity, and in order to satisfy this need, an intellectual effort developed which would unify these new doctrines with those already acquired by reason; somewhat in this fashion, the science of THEOLOGY arose. The theologian is a believer who uses philosophy in order to translate revelation into scientific formulas capable of clarifying their profundity and their beauty, in order to manifest their credibility, to defend them against objections, to deduce virtually revealed truths from them and to organize them into a unified body of doctrine.

Philosophy did not cease to be itself through such utilization, but was rather renewed and enriched; this historical event is rightfully expressed by the phrase, CHRISTIAN PHILOSOPHY [1]. All the Christian philosophers were simultaneously theologians; the relationship between theology and philosophy, however, did not have the same characteristics for all of these men. Accordingly, three periods can be distinguished:

1) The first pagan philosophers, while remaining in the domain of reason alone, were, above all, theologians and mystics. Similarly, the first Christian philosophers did not clearly distinguish philosophy from *supernatural* theology; the resultant science is the fruit of their effort to clarify dogmatic truths through reason, and to illuminate philosophical truths through faith. This type of attitude characterizes the *first period*, that of the FATHERS OF THE CHURCH.

2) Slowly, however, the truths knowable by reason alone on the one hand, and the revealed mysteries on the other, became separated, each having its own validation. This resulted in a resurrection of pure philosophy, a natural science, complete and independent in its own right, having its own methods and doctrines; at the same time, and advantageously so, philosophy was the willing servant of faith. This is the period of the MIDDLE AGES. Thus arose the SCHOLASTIC SYNTHESIS whose apogee, in the thirteenth century, flourished with great doctors who are philosophers as well as theologians: St. Thomas Aquinas, St. Bonaventure and Duns Scotus.

---

[1] The term is used here in a purely historical sense as designating the salient feature of this whole period; there are, of course, thinkers in this period who lie beyond the margin of Christian philosophy. On the problem of *Christian Philosophy*, see n. 244.

3) While the precision gained in the previous period is not entirely lost, it became obscured in the third period through the subtleties of the various philosophico-theological schools which multiplied themselves and were symptomatic of the decadence which continues until the seventeenth century, when Descartes inaugurates the modern period.

These three periods will deal with Christian philosophy :

FIRST PERIOD : Preparation, Fathers of the Church : 2nd-7th centuries.

SECOND PERIOD : Scholastic Synthesis : 8th-13th centuries.

THIRD PERIOD : Decadence : 14th-17th centuries.

FIRST PERIOD.

Preparation, Fathers of the Church.

(2nd-7th century).

143. The period of the Fathers of the Church is contemporary with that of mystic philosophy. Many eminent Christian thinkers of this era, in order to fulfill their function as theologians, appeal to the doctrines of Plato and, more especially, to those of NEO-PLATONISM. They did so inasmuch as the latter was the ruling philosophy and because this system seemed to them most in harmony with Christianity; the system was quite spiritual, and its ethical aim in detaching men from the world of the senses to lead them to a better life seemed especially appealing.

However, from a strictly philosophical view, their work was not more than one of remote and indirect PREPARATION. Their works were studied and classified; and, in this way, their writings led to the great theological synthesis of the Scholastics. They helped prepare the way for the full flowering of rational wisdom whose progress was intimately connected with the exposition of dogmatic truth.

From this dual point of view — that of assimilating Neo-Platonism and of influencing Scholastic philosophy — St. Augustine ranks most eminently. He synthesized most of the thinkers of this period. Further, while it is difficult to isolate the philosophical system of most of the other Church Fathers, due to their manner of fusing the domain of faith with that of reason, the immense work of St. Augustine contains a truly rational explanation of things. Even though it is impregnated with the doctrines of faith, one can objectively distinguish his philosophy from his theology, so that he is the first Christian philosopher in a complete and proper sense. Accordingly, leaving the study of the other Church Fathers to Patrology [1], we shall see how St. Augustine recapitulates this preparatory period.

---

[1] F. CAYRÉ, *op. cit.*, Vol. I.

SAINT AUGUSTINE (354-430).

Special bibliography.

1º **Texts :** *Ancient Christian Writers : the Works of the Fathers in Translation*, (Quasten, J., and Plumpe, J. C., editors), New York, 1946 ff. — *Corpus scriptorum ecclesiasticorum Latinorum*, Vienna, 1866 ff. — *Fathers of the Church : A New Translation*, (Founded by Ludwig Schopp), New York, 1947 ff. — Migne, J., *Patrologia Latina*, Paris, 1844-55. — Przywara, E., *An Augustine Synthesis*, London, 1936.

2º **Works on St. Augustine :** Alfaric, J., *L'évolution intellectuelle de saint Augustin*, Paris, 1918. — *A Monument to St. Augustine*, London, 1930. — Bardy, G., *Saint Augustin*, 6ᵉ éd., Paris, 1946. — Bourke, V. J., *Augustine's Quest of Wisdom*, Milwaukee, 1945. — Boyer, C., *Christianisme et néo-platonisme dans la formation de saint Augustin*, Paris, 1920. *Essais sur la doctrine de saint Augustin*, Paris, 1932. *L'idée de vérité dans la philosophie de saint Augustin*, Paris, 1920. — Burger, J. D., *Saint Augustin*, Neuchâtel, 1947. — Cayré, F., *Initiation à la philosophie de saint Augustin*, Paris, 1947. — Figgis, J. N., *The Political Aspects of St. Augustine's City of God*, London, 1921. — Gilson, E., *Introduction à l'étude de saint Augustin*, 2ᵉ éd., Paris, 1943. — Grabmann, M., *Der göttliche Grund menschlicher Wahrheitserkenntnis nach Augustinus und Thomas von Aquin*, Cologne, 1924. *Die Grundgedanken des heiligen Augustinus über Seele und Gott*, Cologne, 1929. — Henry, P., *L'extase d'Ostie*, Paris, 1938. — Hessen, J., *Augustins Metaphysik der Erkenntnis*, Berlin, 1931. — Jolivet, R., *Dieu, Soleil des esprits*, Paris, 1932. *Saint Augustin et le néoplatonisme chrétien*, Paris, 1932. — Kälin, B., *Die Erkenntnislehre des hl. Augustinus*, Fribourg, 1920. — *Mélanges augustiniens*, Paris, 1931. — *Miscellanea Agostiniana*, 2 vols., Rome, 1930-31. — Pope, H., *St. Augustine of Hippo*, Westminster, Md., 1949. — Switalski, B., *Neoplatonism and the Ethics of St. Augustine*, New York, 1946. — Zigliara, J., *Della luce intellettuale e dell'ontologismo, secondo la dottrina dei SS. Agostino, Bonaventura e Tommaso*, 2 vols., Rome, 1874.

144. The life of St. Augustine can be divided into two periods : 1) the time before his conversion, during which he fluctuated in various doctrines and underwent intellectual formation [1]; 2) the time after his conversion, in which he finds the truth and writes his important works. These two periods, though distinct, are not in opposition; the moral and intellectual life of St. Augustine, from infancy to death, was but a constant effort and a continuous progress towards the conquest of truth.

---

[1] Only the first period of Augustine's life will be developed here, for it concluded in his conversion and in the discovery of the fundamental principle of his philosophy.

1º Formation. St. Augustine was born at Tagaste in Numidia, November, 13, 354. Providence endowed him with a nature rich in sensitivity and intellectual gifts. His father was a pagan; his mother, St. Monica, a fervent Christian, inscribed St. Augustine as a catechumen and, through her educative efforts, waked in his soul a tendency which nothing was able to destroy and which dominated his whole evolvement : *salvation was in Christ.*

1. Augustine's first personal orientation, however, estranged him from Catholicism. Two reasons help explain this fact, the first of which is his early, official education. After having had his early studies in grammar in his native city, he continued them at Madaura from 365 to 369. Here, the pagan tone of the teaching, the indifference of his teachers to Christianity, the absence of his mother and the fickleness of his youth contributed towards weakening his faith. Secondly, he was dominated by his lower appetites. During his sixteenth year, which he passed in idleness at Tagaste, his disorderly conduct was such that it took him far away from the influence of his mother and from the atmosphere of Catholicism.

Finally, in 370, when his father sent him to Carthage to study rhetoric, these two factors united to separate him completely from Catholicism. He became involved with a disreputable woman and had a child of her, Adeodatus, who was born in 372. His Christianity was expelled from his spirit by pagan ideas and from his heart by the attraction of sensual love; it only remained in him as a remembrance of the name of Christ. He still retained, throughout this time, an unshakable conviction of God's existence, of the existence of Providence and of a future life.

2. When he was nineteen years of age, his reading of Cicero's *Hortensius* marked the beginning of his conversion. This dialogue contains an exhortation to seek for immortal wisdom, which is superior to passing goods and which can be loved for itself. Augustine understood therefrom that true happiness was possession of the truth; the life of the spirit was revealed to him, and he figured that it merited every sacrifice. From this time on he was concerned with the problem for which he sought a solution for thirty-three years : How achieve possession of this beatific truth towards which his whole passionate soul was directed?

3. *Manicheism* was a first, provisory solution. Not for an instant did Augustine think of asking truth from philosophers who could not speak to him of Christ. However, the simplicity and the coarseness of the style in Sacred Scripture failed to satisfy his rhetorical aspirations, and he was vexed by misunderstanding of many passages in the Old Testament. The Manicheans, moreover, excellent speakers, flattered his profane tastes. They promised him what he sought, for they had the word " truth " constantly on their lips. They also allowed him to remain Christian, for Manes himself was spoken of as the " Apostle of Jesus Christ through the Providence of God the Father ".

The time spent with the Manicheans corresponds to the period when he taught rhetoric first at Tagaste (373), and then at Carthage (374-383). He held a position of listener or auditor with the Manicheans, a position which was a type of catechumenate. He admitted the three basic principles of Manes : there is no reality superior to body; the human soul is a part of divinity; evil is a separated substance which does not come from God. Further than this, he was involved in doubts and confusion, but he counted on the renowned Faustus of Mileve to resolve them. He did some proselytizing, and converted his friend Alipius and his benefactor, Romanianus, to Manicheism.

4. At the end of nine years, two factors separated him from Manicheism. The visit of Faustus failed to resolve his difficulties; Faustus was content to cover the poverty of his doctrine with the charms of his eloquence. Then, in the autumn of 383, when he began to teach rhetoric at Rome, the scandals which the " elect " of the sect gave caused whatever prestige their sanctity had in Augustine's eyes to vanish, as their science had previously done. As a result, Augustine inclined — as towards a second, provisory solution — towards the probabilism of the New Academy, as propounded by Cicero.

He remained in Rome until 384, when he sought for and obtained a chair of rhetoric at Milan. Here, the sermons of St. Ambrose succeeded in enlightening him by showing him how a sound exegesis, using allegory reasonably, could give good sense to the passages of the Old Testament indicted by the Manicheans. At the same time, recognizing the weakness of their physical views, he began to prefer the explanations of the philosophers. The arguments of the Sceptics, however, prevented him from accepting any new doctrine, for he feared that he might be duped. Slowly he began to believe that truth was unattainable and that true wisdom lay in prudent speculative scepticism, tempered by practical probabilism as taught by the New Academy.

5. However, he refused to adhere to a purely philosophical explanation, for he was convinced that salvation could not be found outside of Christ. In such a frame of mind, there was no other course open to him but to return to Catholicism; he took the first step in this direction by inscribing himself among the catechumens, and he decided to remain with them while seeking full illumination.

Finally, his reflections led him to a solution of the PRINCIPLE through which *he accepted, in a global manner, the truth divinely revealed* as the writings of the Catholic Church present it. He determined to take this decisive step through a movement of thought which can be summarized in a double syllogism :

a) The *first syllogism* disposed him to see the truth. One would have to deny God and His providence, if it were impossible to attain salvation and, accordingly, attain truth. To admit that the mind, so keen in things concerned with the pleasures of life, is not able to achieve the truth of things which it is most important to know, is to deny the order of the universe and to deny divine Providence.

Moreover, man is incapable of finding the way of salvation if he is left to the power of reason alone; in this latter state, he cannot grasp truth in such a way that his whole soul would be beatified and established in the perfection of its being. Man could not, more exactly, fully know God, Who is the beatific Truth. This is not exactly an essential incapacity, but a moral inability of fact of which Augustine became convinced by the evidence of history, by his personal experience and by the view of Plotinus, who established for him the painful necessity with which man must detach himself from the sensible in order to achieve the idea.

Accordingly, reason can have only a preparatory and secondary role in order to conquer truth (for example, in demonstrating the existence of God and of Providence). There is a light to which man can have recourse, an exterior revelation which shows us the way of salvation.

b) Augustine realized that this help was not directly addressed to each individual conscience; a public evil demands a public remedy. A *second syllogism* enabled him to find the answer in the Church.

One would have to deny God and Providence if a society, though wrongly claiming to possess this revelation, still had conquered the whole human race. However, the Catholic Church had made this conquest under most remarkable circumstances and thereby shown evidence of its divine characteristic. One could not expect a strictly unanimous adherence. But if one could establish the agreement of a great number of people dispersed in various places and of different views on a doctrine of salvation, one would possess a moral unanimity which nothing could limit and which would represent humanity. Consequently, the Catholic Church, which alone achieves this universality, securely possesses the revelation of salvation and the fulness of truth.

But these reasons, which permitted Augustine to regain the faith of St. Monica, are totally extrinsic and did not give him the science of this faith; they left him with his materialistic errors on the soul and on God, and his difficulties on the problem of evil. Hence he was harassed by disconcerting thoughts; his incomplete instruction was picked up by chance during Sunday sermons. Augustine actually received little light : St. Ambrose was absorbed in his own duties, and the Bible seemed insufficient for him. He had little time of his own to go more deeply into these arduous problems, and that which he already knew did not rest harmoniously in his spirit. He believed, and he wished to see, according to the adage, " Faith seeking understanding ".

6. At the moment of his formation when, already converted, he sought to penetrate, order and synthesize his new belief, Augustine read " some Platonic books " [1], and there found the

---

[1] *Confessionum*, Book VII, Ch. IX, 13. In *Christianisme et néoplatonisme dans la formation de saint Augustin*, C. Boyer establishes this evolution of St. Augustine's thought; see p. 60, ff.

FULL SPECULATIVE SOLUTION which he wished. These works were Neo-Platonic treatises : some of the Enneads of Plotinus, and probably some extracts from Porphyry, Iamblichus and Apuleius; all of this he read in a translation of the rhetorician Victorinus, who tended to paraphrase and to accentuate the resemblances between Neo-Platonism and Christianity.

To the Neo-Platonists St. Augustine owes the following :

a) **Doctrinal elements.** He is indebted to them for his conception of the intelligible world of spiritual, invisible realities which are of greater value than the objects dispersed in space-time; in this way, he was freed from Manicheist materialism and from the doubt of the Academicians. This intelligible world is identified with the *Logos* of St. John the Evangelist; the *Logos* is the Word of God and is God Himself : " Et Deus erat Verbum ". This God of Truth is also Creator : " omnia per ipsum facta sunt ". Source of the being and of the ontological truth of creatures, He is also the Illuminator, the source of the logical truth in all intelligences : " Erat lux vera quæ illuminat omnem hominem ". Inasmuch as God is the happiness of souls, philosophy has its true value in making us attain the only reality which has value, the intelligible God. Finally, the problem of evil is solved; if everything comes from God, the Supreme Good, it is absurd to think of evil as an independent substance. From now on, Augustine would look upon it as a *privation;* yet, considered in the totality, the particular privations concur in a universal harmony.

b) **A dialectical method.** There are a number of ways in which Augustine adopted the PLATONIC METHOD, which concurred with the most profound inclinations of his inmost self : by taking, as his point of departure, the intuition of the intelligible world; by the lack of didactic form in his works; by his theory of purification necessary to arrive at the truth; by his custom of progressively elevating himself from an imperfect form towards the idea of Perfection in itself [1]. If he in any way knew or practiced the dialectic of Aristotle [2], he " Platonized " it through his predilection for a metaphysical point of view and by the mystical touch with which he often animated it.

c) But he ruthlessly brushed aside any theory opposed to revelation, as polytheism, the naturalism of Platonic " mysticism ", and the pantheism latent in the notion of necessary emanation. With regard to the distinction and the inequality of *Hypostases,* he did not view them as Plotinus; on the contrary, he was certain that he had discovered in Plotinus the various ways in which the " Son is in the form of the Father ". In other words, Neo-Platonism, though it had the unique function of making him understand his faith, was TRANSFIGURED by Augustine, so that it basically remained the Augustinian philosophy.

---

[1] See below, n. 159, 4°.

[2] *Confessionum,* Book IV, Ch. XXI, 1; when twenty years old, he had but read and understood the *Categories* of Aristotle.

It can be added that the enthusiasm which Augustine had for these pagan scholars somewhat diminished the degree in which he could better comprehend the riches of revelation through meditating on the Scriptures. In his retractations, he writes, " The very praise with which I extolled Plato, the Platonists or the Academicians... rightly displeased me " [1].

7. Despite this full speculative enlightenment, Augustine's moral life underwent no change. The FULL PRACTICAL SOLUTION remained to be found. He achieved it, aided by the Christian influence and counsels of St. Ambrose and Simplicius, the examples and conversion stories of the Saints, and, above all, through the action of grace given as the fruit of his prayers and those of his mother. When, in the garden of Milan, he heard the call of God, " Tolle, lege ", he resolved to abandon all ambitions and desires for marriage in order to give himself uniquely to the study of truth. In other words, he decided to renounce the world in order to consecrate himself to God in religious life (May, 386).

In autumn of the same year, he retired from his professorship and took retreat at Cassiciacum; there, with a few friends, whose conversations furnished him with material for his first philosophical dialogues, he maintained a sort of novitiate or studious retreat. At the beginning of 387, he returned to Milan officially to prepare himself for baptism, which he received from St. Ambrose at Easter time.

2º **Works. 145.** From the time of his conversion, it was clear to St. Augustine that his mission was to be of service to truth; and, until his death, he did not cease to write in order to defend and to make the truth manifest. A few months after his baptism, he prepared to depart for Africa; but, since his mother had died at Ostia, he returned to Rome and did not reach Tagaste until the following year (388). He sold his inheritance and opened a monastery in one of his alienated properties. In this silent retreat, he polished up his writings; and, while finishing his philosophical dialogues, he composed his first commentaries and his first polemic writings against the Manicheans. In 391, he was ordained priest; and, in 395, Bishop of Hippo. From this point on, his activity redoubled : he preached almost daily; he fought with the Manicheans, the Donatists, the pagans, and, later, against the Pelagians; he wrote new commentaries; he wrote lengthy works, as the *De Trinitate* and the *De civitate Dei;* he wrote much correspondence, some of which amounts to treatises. In this way, he enlightened the whole Church from his small diocese.

---

[1] *Retractationes*, I, Ch. I, 4.

The following works are chosen from Augustine's voluminous writings because of their philosophical import [1] :

I. *Before his episcopacy :*

1. ContraAcademicos,BookIII, (386).
2. De beata vita, (386).
3. De ordine, Book II, (386).
4. Soliloquiorum, Book II, (387).
5. De immortalitate animæ, (387).
6. De quantitate animæ, (388).
7. De magistro, (389).
8. De musica, Book VI, (387-391).
9. De libero arbitrio, Book III, (388-396) [2].
10. De vera religione, (389-391).
11. De duabus animabus, (391).

De diversis quæstionibus 83 : collection made in 396.

II. *After his episcopacy :*

Confessionum, Book XIII, (400).
De natura boni, (405).
De Trinitate Dei, Book XV, (400-416).

De anima et ejus origine, Book IV, (419).
De civitate Dei, Book XXII, (413-426).
Retractationum, Book II (427).

Mention should also be made of the most important of his letters : on philosophy (n. 118), and one concerning the presence and the vision of God, (n. 187 and n. 147).

St. Augustine died on the 28th of August, 430, at the age of 76, during the siege of Hippo by the Vandals.

3º **Fundamental Position. 146.** At the completion of his formation, St. Augustine was in possession of the fundamental principle of his philosophy. His unique aim was the conquest of truth; truth was the great question to which he sought an answer. He found the answer to this problem with the help of Plotinus. As his fundamental position, then, he accepts that of Plotinus, though he substitutes the point of view of Truth instead of the transcendent and simple One, and corrects all the pagan errors of Neo-Platonism.

---

[1] An analysis of all the works of St. Augustine can be found in F. CAYRÉ, *Manual of Patrology*, Vol. 1, pp. 614-660.

[2] These nine dialogues have a special importance in establishing the existence of philosophy in its proper sense for St. Augustine; their subject and method move in a purely rational frame of reference.

Augustine's fundamental principle can be formulated as follows :

The Divine Truth is the unique and perfect cause which is immediately explicative of all being in its different modalities of nature and of action.

As in Plotinus, we find philosophy divided into two main parts. The first is *metaphysics*, descriptive of the creative work of Truth, or the descent of beings from God. The second is *ethics*, treating the beatifying possession of the Truth, or the ascent of the purified soul towards God. But, while Plotinus accepted the ideal world as something evident and given, St. Augustine, requiring more of reason than its fluctuating notions, establishes the existence of God, the source of all truth, through philosophical proofs.

Augustine will thus be treated in the following three articles :

Article I.   The Existence of Truth.   (The Source).

Article II.   The Work of Truth.   (Descent of Beings).

Article III. The Possession of Truth.   (Ascent of the Soul).

ARTICLE ONE.—EXISTENCE OF TRUTH.

147. In the demonstration which concludes with the existence of the subsistent Truth, three stages are to be distinguished. In the first, St. Augustine, aiming to disengage himself from Scepticism, establishes that there exists an *intelligible world*, the foundation of certitude and of philosophy. Then, in the second stage, he identifies this intelligible world, to the extent that it has dominion over our reason, with God Himself. Finally, he finds in the Truth the fundamental attribute from which all others flow. Three sections will explain these notions :

1º The Intelligible World.

2º The Existence of God.

3º The Nature of God.

I. THE INTELLIGIBLE WORLD.

148. Augustine's proposition can be stated as follows :

Every philosophy begins with a clear and certain intuition of the intelligible world, that is, of a truth or of an object of knowledge *which reveals itself directly and in full evidence to the spirit independently of the senses, and, consequently, is free from all error*.

This proposition is established by an indirect and a direct proof [1].

A) **Indirect Proof.**

For the affiliates of the New Academy, true wisdom lay in maintaining universal doubt in the speculative order, and in regulating action through probability in the practical order. St. Augustine refutes this position by showing that its very affirmation is self-destructive.

1) These philosophers, Augustine argues, assert the impossibility of acquiring truth through their scepticism; yet, in presenting themselves as a school of wisdom, they affirm that they possess the truth. One cannot separate *wisdom* and *truth*, for a man is not wise if he be ignorant of wisdom. Further, these philosophers aim to show men how to find happiness; but one cannot tend to happiness without tending towards truth, whose possession fills the most fundamental of our desires. It is thus contradictory to pretend to be both wise and sceptical.

2) The New Academicians contradict themselves from another point of view. They propose that to maintain what is but probable is the true means of living well; yet they permit a man to act with a doubtful conscience [2], which is permitting him to act without being certain if he does good. Such a position destroys morality and affirms the impossibility of living well. This critique is enlarged by St. Augustine; he shows that all action presupposes a general but certain knowledge of an end to be attained and that to deny this certitude by accepting universal doubt is to destroy human activity itself.

3) Finally, the Academicians' doctrine is contradictory in its very formulas. One cannot speak of doubt, of errors, of the probable, except as a function of the truth. How can

---

[1] The three books, " Against the Academicians ", composed at Cassiciacum, treat these matters.

[2] This sceptic probabilism is not to be confounded with the probabilism of Catholic casuistry, for the latter shows one how to solve one's doubt in order to do good with moral certitude.

one recognize that which is opposed to, or that which is similar to truth if one is ignorant of that which is opposed or is similar? The basic position that there is no criterion of truth must itself be declared uncertain so that scepticism is self-destructive by its very affirmation.

B) **Direct Proof.**

149. Universal doubt is not merely impossible, it is *illegitimate.* This proposition St. Augustine proves by appealing to the testimony of consciousness which attests to the existence within ourselves of an intelligible object under such conditions that error is impossible. A simple reflection on the content of our thoughts will acquaint us with the unchangeable existence of a great number of truths.

1. In this way the *rules of wisdom* appear which aid us to live well through ethics, or to reason well through dialectics. They address themselves directly to the intelligence, independently of the concrete realities to which they apply, since they are found before action at the very source of activity of which they are the main directors. For example, before desiring to be happy and to act in this fashion, one must know this truth, that " happiness lies in the possession of the good ".

2. The basic notions and the laws of numbers reveal themselves with the same independence of sensible reality, for they also have properties completely different from reality. They do not, for example, have color, sound or odor. *Unity*, especially, which is the principle of numbers, possesses *simplicity* in itself so that it is never realized in a body which necessarily possesses the distinction and, consequently, the plurality of parts. The mind grasps these laws independently of the senses.

3. The intellectual intuition of our thoughts and of our own existence, being most immediate and even discoverable in doubt itself, have a particular importance. " If I doubt ", writes St. Augustine, " if I dream, I am alive. *If I deceive myself*, I am alive; how, then, can I deceive myself in saying that I am if it is certain that I am, if I deceive myself " [1]. Inasmuch as something is true only through the Truth, the soul absolutely discovers the necessary reality of truth through doubt itself.

[1] *De Trinitate*, Book XV, Ch. XII, 21.

This intuition of our own thinking self was not, for St. Augustine, the unique truth from which all others follow, as it was for Descartes [1]. It is merely a particularly striking example, refractory to all objections, of our intellectual aptitude to grasp truth independently of the senses and in its fullest sense. We achieve, in this way, an object of the existing intelligible order, a substantial reality which lives within our spirit and communicates with the spiritual world of eternal truths.

CONCLUSION. An *Intelligible World* exists which, though not demonstrable, establishes its own existence. The truth of this reveals itself infallibly through an immediate evidence which is superior to the senses, and imposes itself on all men.

Items of sensation, if interpreted and controlled by the intelligence, can also be a source of sure knowledge. The senses are, in themselves, faithful messengers; they tell us how they are affected and reason, contemplating within itself the rule of truth, is capable of appreciating their message exactly [2].

II. EXISTENCE OF GOD.

150. St. Augustine never doubted the existence or the Providence of God. This belief, which he received from St. Monica — and which he was to see confirmed by the unanimous consent of mankind and of philosophers, as well as by the miracles of the Gospel — helped him to recover the Catholic faith which gave him definitive possession of this truth.

He was not satisfied with possessing this truth through faith, and sought a demonstration of it that was properly *scientific* [3]. The mystical accent and the impassioned manner of his arguments do not destroy their validity. The Augustinian proof for God's existence is closely allied with his proof for the existence of truth; in fact, it is but a continuation of the latter, showing how the intelligible world not only dominates the sensible, but also dominates our reason and is thereby

---

[1] See n. 319. Though both philosophers accepted this particular truth, the fundamental principle and motivation of their philosophies are different.

[2] " If a man sees a stick as if bent in water, his eye does not deceive him; the message is not bad, but the judge is bad ". *De vera religione*, XXXIII, 62. See below, n. 163.

[3] *De libero arbitrio*, Book II, Ch. II, 5.

divine. It is presented under various forms in which one can recognize most of our cosmological, psychological and moral proofs [1]. Throughout, one finds the same movement of the idea he had in mind, sometimes presented in abridged form, sometimes more developed.

St. Augustine uses the dialectic of Plotinus to mount to the Creative Source from the degrees of participation found in creatures. The complete form of the proof will be given in which — though transformed by Catholic truth — are recognizable the four Plotinian *Hypostases*, matter, soul, intelligence, and The One. The two abridged forms of the proof will be given afterwards.

A) Complete Proof.

151. Augustine, strongly believing in God, wishes to furnish a convincing proof of His existence for any exacting mind. Following the Plotinian method, he aims to *persuade* the soul by leading it through degrees, as through a series of purifications, to the point where it is detached from the sensible so that it may attain the intelligible, and thus reach the supreme intelligible, God. In this ascension of the soul towards God, one can distinguish the point of departure, the lesser stages, and the decisive and superior stage of arrival at eternal truth.

1º **Point of departure.** In order to prove the existence of God, St. Augustine adopts the viewpoint of philosophy itself, which, in his view, is the *quest of God*. There is one incontestable truth which breaks the strongest doubt : *I exist;* I am a living, knowing being, searching for truth and already possessing this first truth of self-existence with untroubled security. With this point of departure, the reasoning soul easily sees itself as *intermediary* between God, Whom it seeks above itself, and the material world, where the senses draw it below itself.

At the beginning of his proof, St. Augustine supposes some matters as well established : the fact of our own existence, and our capability of distinguishing the diverse perfections of beings in hierarchical fashion from the minerals and plants to the animal and to the marvels of our own consciousness. He could rightly assume these truths; except for the sceptic view which he refuted, no one in his age doubted them.

---

[1] D. BARBEDETTE, *Histoire de la Philosophie*, p. 176.

Further, these facts were evident to the senses, and their validity, if controlled by the infallibility of reason, was incontestable [1].

Augustine's proof, then, is based on the existence of the sensible world and its perfections, as well as on the existence of our soul, knowing equally well this external world and the internal world of consciousness.

2º **The lesser stages.** The sensible world reveals many perfections, but the main ones it shows forth are being, life and knowledge. Further, these latter three perfections are discoverable in ourselves as necessary implicates of the primordial truth of our being, for the latter is life and knowledge. These three perfections can be arranged in *ascending order :* it is more perfect to live than merely to be and life supposes being, but being does not suppose life. It is also more perfect to know, for knowledge supposes and includes being and life [2].

Besides our external senses, we are aware of an *internal sense* within ourselves. This sense reassembles and compares the various objects presented by the other senses and it coordinates and directs actions towards that which is useful. It is not the same as reason, for it also manifests itself in animals. In order to show that this internal sense constitutes a superior degree of perfection, Augustine uses a principle which will eventually lead him to the final stage of his argument; it can be termed the PRINCIPLE OF REGULATION [3], and is expressed as follows : " *That which is judged and regulated is inferior to the rule which judges and regulates it* ". Inasmuch as the internal sense directs the external senses and judges concerning matters of utility or opportuneness, it is evidently superior. In a similar way, the external sense is superior to its object for it exercises over it a similar role.

Following this principle, we find in ourselves a perfection superior to all the senses, reason. It *judges* the senses, for it distinguishes them, defines them, arranges them hierarchically, is aware of their demands, directs their activity and uses them for its own ends.

---

[1] See above, n. 149, and below, n. 163.
[2] *De libero arbitrio*, Book II, Ch. III, 7; *De diversis quæst.*, q. LI, n. 2.
[3] This may also be called the *principle of subordination*.

With reason we find ourselves at the summit of human nature. The principle of regulation, however, is applied again. The *eternal truths*, whose existence has been established [1], spontaneously aid us to judge about concrete objects. For example, in judging that a circle is more or less perfect, one is appealing to the ideal perfection of the circle according to which all realizations are regulated; or, in appreciating works of art or just men, one is measuring them according to the absolute idea of Beauty and of Justice.

But these ideas particularly *dominate our reason* as an immutable law dominates that which changes. While our reason passes from ignorance to knowledge and is subject to the variations of time, the truths of the intelligible world — as, for example, the laws of numbers and the rules of wisdom — remain eternal and immutable.

3⁰ **The superior stage of the eternal truths.** Ordinarily, when St. Augustine reaches the summit of these eternal truths, he immediately concludes that *God exists*. Nevertheless, even in his own view, the being of God and the being of these multiple verities within our mind are different beings; from these truths to God another step must be taken [2]. This last step is important, and can be clarified by appeal to another principle of Augustine's.

This principle is the PRINCIPLE OF PARTICIPATION, or of perfect causality, which is the foundation of his whole system. " Every changeable thing must either be perfectible or receive its form... But a thing cannot perfect itself, for it cannot give itself that which it does not have... (Changeable beings) must receive their perfection from a perfection that is immutable and eternally stable " [3]. In other words, nothing can receive " formality " except through Form; nothing is perfectible except through Perfection; *nothing is true except through Truth*. Every sort of participation in the immutable and eternal supposes the existence of a Source possessing, by itself and absolutely, immutability and eternity.

---

[1] See above, n. 149.

[2] St. Augustine's theory of illumination will add clarity to this notion; see below, n. 164.

[3] *De libero arbitrio*, Book II, Ch. XVII, 45. A valid *demonstration* of the principle of participation is given in St. Thomas' fourth proof for God's existence; St. Augustine, however, invokes it only after having proved God's existence and for another reason : to show that every substance is good because it comes from God. This is, rather, an inverse proof of God's existence; see below, n. 158.

Without a doubt, there is something eternal and immutable in the first principles, as in the laws of numbers and in the wisdom according to which we live, for we gather many luminous insights from them. Consequently it is the immutable Truth of God which we attain in them, seeing Him as the unique reason for being and the sole creative source of our intellectual life.

B) **Abridged Forms.**

152. The two abridged forms of proof take their start, respectively, from the eternal truths in our consciousness and from the sensible world.

1º **Consciousness.** St. Augustine enjoyed withdrawing into himself and going over the riches of his consciousness. Therein he discovered many images of God, especially the desire for God as the cure for his own misery and as the fulfillment of his strivings for wisdom and happiness. One could find in these aspirations towards God a proof of God's existence, but a more rigorous form is the one proposed in *De libero arbitrio* [1].

If there be a reality dominating our reason, then God exists. Now, according to common opinion, God is the Supreme Being who dominates the universe. Man's reason, however, is, in a sense, dominative of the universe, for it judges masterfully of the beings and of the natural or living forces in the universe. If there be a reality which dominates our reason, it would, a fortiori, dominate the universe. Now, if this power has no superior, it is God, the Supreme Being; or, it is subject to a superior being and this latter would be supreme; whatever the hypothesis, God exists.

Moreover, the truths or ideal realities of the intelligible world dominate our reason inasmuch as the unchangeable is above the changeable, and the rule above what is measured. Consequently, God exists, for the intelligible world which rules us is ruled by Him and realized in Him.

2º **The Sensible World.** If participation occurs, then the existence of a Source is evident. If one grants the existence of inferior grades of perfection, the supreme degree is necessarily

---

[1] The complete form is given in Book II; an abridged form is given in the conditional syllogism (Ch. VI, 14) which Augustine introduces to reply to the demands of Evodius.

existent.   Nothing is perfect except through Self-perfection and nothing is true except through Truth Itself.

A great number of perfections in the universe are evidently participated, either because of their multiple distribution or because of their variations.   All creatures, for example, have their own beauty, but it is a changing, perishable, mixed and scattered beauty; if questioned, all of them cry out through their very beauty, " We are not God, but it is God Who has made us " [1].

As a result, a source of this beauty exists which is Absolute Beauty and Supreme Perfection; this creative Source is God.

C) Meaning and Value of this Last Proof.

153.   This last, shortened form of proof is very similar to the proof by *efficient cause* presented by most of the Scholastics. St. Augustine, however, did not consider it decisive *alone*, for, every time that he presents a truly rational demonstration, he has to pass through the stage of eternal truths.   Such a strong attitude is striking, especially since he held that God is *immediately* Creator of every thing, whether it be material being, plants, animal or the riches of our soul and the activities of our spirit.   Why did it seem repugnant to him to go directly from sensible reality to God?   The reason seems to be that this way did not seem to him certain.   The order governing sensible things could be adequately explained, as for the Stoics and for Plotinus, by the *Soul of the World;* the latter, however, is but finite and changeable, and was not God Himself.   Knowing by faith that everything was created by The Word of God, St. Augustine looked upon this notion of a world-soul as useless, though he did not think it absurd; in searching for God, he chose to avoid this problem [2].

Moreover, the Platonic method of recollection and purification seemed more efficacious to him.   It permitted him to attain the immutable and eternal God by returning to God through the summation of eternal truths impounded in our innermost self.

This solution had the advantage of preserving the four degrees of Plotinus.   After matter (the sensible world), comes the soul with sensation; then comes the mind with its eternal truths; finally, The One, as the immutable source.   His Catholic belief, however, offered him a double correction : *a*) perfect causality (principle of participation) is reserved to the supreme degree, between God the only Creator and the eternal truths of our mind;

---

[1] *Confessionum*, Book x, Ch. vi, ?

[2] Another explanation is offered by E. Gilson (*Introduction à l'étude de saint Augustin*, p. 26) who holds that the abreviated argument is but a contemplative return of the soul to the sensible world as the image of God; C. Boyer (*Etudes sur saint Augustin*, p. 126), holds that for St. Augustine, the laws of the world are not a truth known by us, as much as a law of our thought.

the other degrees are ordered according to the principle of regulation; *b*) The *Logos*, the Divine Intelligence, is perfectly equal to the Father from Whom He proceeds. This last point solves the theological problem of the Holy Trinity which St. Augustine also considered, but which does not pertain to his philosophy as being considered here.

But this obligatory passage of our mind brings an objection against St. Augustine's demonstration. In relying upon the *character of our ideas*, is there not involved an illegitimate passage from the logical to the real? With the help of the theory of abstraction, we can distinguish two sorts of eternity, or of immutability. 1º Our ideas and our abstract truths are eternal immutable only *negatively*. The nature of the square is called eternal because it can be realized in any time-period, *without one instance of it being required*. For this reason it merely possesses a hypothetical necessity of the ideal order and the existence of an abstractive faculty, as the agent intellect, is sufficient to explain it. One cannot arrive at God through this manner. 2º A *positive* eternity and immutability mark the Divine Ideas. Eternity is a *requirement* of being at all times, and it supposes absolute necessity, or the impossibility of their not existing. This is why St. Thomas, who clarified the abstract character of our knowledge, did not found any of his proofs for the existence of God on the property of our ideas or our truths; his proofs begin with beings existing in nature [1].

There is a profound divergence of method and point of view between these two thinkers [2]; but St. Augustine escapes any objection, for he did not base his proofs on our *abstract* ideas, since he was totally ignorant of abstraction [3]. Eternal truths merely expressed the *facts* of our intellectual life known by the intuition of consciousness in all the richness of their being; in this way they recapitulated and concentrated in themselves the reality of the inferior degrees which they judged and regulated. The illegitimate passage from the logical to the real is thus avoided, and the proof of Augustine, without being perfectly reducible to Thomistic frames of reference, has its full value as a rational demonstration.

III. NATURE OF GOD.

154. God's fundamental attribute, His other attributes, the validity of the knowledge we have concerning Him — all of these follow from Augustine's proof for His existence.

---

[1] See above, n. 137.

[2] St. Thomas Aquinas, *Summa Theologica*, I, q. II, art. 3; see also q. XVI, art. 7, entitled, " Whether created truth is eternal "? The distinction between negative and positive eternity is made in the latter place, and he concludes (ad 2) : " Every sort of universal is said to be everywhere and always inasmuch as universals abstract from the here and now. From this it does not follow that they are eternal, except in an intelligence, if the latter be eternal ".

[3] The coincidence of their doctrines will be shown below; see n. 165.

A) *God is the* Subsisting Truth *wherein all perfections are included and identified.*

The *ideological proof* [1] of God's existence, as developed by St. Augustine, shows God as the supreme Truth, the source of the logical truth of all our knowledge and the ontological truth of the perfections of the world.

Each of the perfections expressed in a Divine Idea necessarily includes all the others and is identified with them. Since they are of supreme degree, each is fully realized; this could not occur if one could attribute a perfection to God which He might lack and from which He would be distinct. If, for instance, one would attribute something to the Supreme Goodness and this would make God better, this would imply that He was not supreme. Every divine perfection, then, necessarily includes all the others. While the Divine Ideas may be objectively multiple in God, they identify themselves subjectively in the unique person of the Word of God; they are the living, personal, subsisting Truth Itself.

B) The *particular attributes* derive from the attribute of truth.

1º **Simplicity.** Inasmuch as all the perfections are identified in the subsisting Truth, God is simplicity itself, excluding all multiplicity and real distinction or all composition. There are no accidents inhering in His substance, but every quality is substantially and essentially His. When we *have* our perfections, as when we have wisdom, we are not wisdom but we possess it, and, even then, not in its entirety. On the contrary, *God is everything which He has;* He is Wisdom, Life, Intelligence, Truth Itself.

2º **Unity**. God has the fulness of unity since He is One in the degree that He *is*. In the supreme degree, the possession becoming perfect identity, God is Being itself in the fulness of His extension and thereby He is perfectly one and unique. Since unity is the principle of *number*, God also realizes number, the source of *harmony* and of *beauty*, but in such a supereminent way that it does not deprive Him of His simplicity.

---

[1] This may also be called the *noölogical* proof, based on the fact of our intellectual life; *cf.* F. Cayré, " Le Point de départ de la philosophie augustinienne. Preuve noologique de l'existence de Dieu ", *Revue de Philosophie*, July, 1936, p. 306.

3° **Immutability.** Inasmuch as the Truth sovereignly Is, it cannot change, for this would imply reception or loss of a certain form of being. Moreover, to receive a new form, one would have to lack it; the Truth, however, not only possesses, but *is* all perfection. There is, consequently, no capacity to receive or obtain new richness in God's absolute simplicity.

For God to *lose* a perfection He would have to destroy Himself, which is absurd. Or He would have to be subject to the action of a nature contrary to His own; such a being does not exist, for God is totally being in such a way that only nothingness is opposed to Him. Creatures act on each other because each has a special mode of being; their changefulness indicates that they are not Being or Truth, but only partake in these perfections.

4° **Eternity.** Divine immutability, considered in *relation to time*, is eternity. Time is the measure of change in creatures; it is the duration of a being which becomes, and cannot be applied to the immutable Being. Furthermore, eternity is not a very long time with infinite extremities, but the simultaneous and immutable possession of every perfection by the Truth. Eternity is the Divine life existing wholly and entirely at a time. Eternity is thus superior or transcendent to time, as the Being of God is transcendent to created being; these two realities are of essentially different orders [1].

5° **Immensity.** Beyond time through His eternity, God is beyond space through His immensity. He is in no wise in place, for, being Truth, He is inextended and incorporeal. " The Eternal Light which He inhabits is not a disk like the sun; the eyes of the flesh cannot know this light " [2]. God is everywhere as He is in Himself because He is simple, and He is present intimately to each being because all share in His Truth, the unique source of being and of life.

C) *Value of our knowledge of God.* **155.** Certain limits are imposed on our knowledge of God because of the supereminent simplicity of His perfection; our knowledge of Him, however, is still valid.

---

[1] *De vera religione*, Ch. XLIX, 97 : " Eternity only is ".
[2] *Sermones*, 4, Ch. IV, 5.

1) " Nothing said of God is said with complete conformity ", writes St. Augustine [1]. The names which we apply to Him must undergo a profound transformation. This applies to those which imply some imperfection among men, as anger, penance, and jealousy. But it also applies to those which express pure perfections, as science, justice and love. From all of these, every element of change, of progress, of time or of limit, must be removed; in addition, they must then be conceived in an eminent degree which still does not express the *mode* according to which they apply to God. Augustine asks that we strive " to think of the illumination of the permanent truth, lighting all things through a unique and eternal contemplation " [2]; such is God. Without doubt, such an illumination is only proportioned to the Divine Intelligence, but is still somewhat accessible to us.

2) There is, nevertheless, a *real value*, albeit imperfect, in our theology. After being purified, our words give us a *positive* and *true* idea of God. Furthermore, we know that God is not the Divine Indetermination, but a personal being with whom we have relationship. We know that He possesses all perfections as their source; and the names of these perfections common to God and creatures have, in being applied to Him, a genuine value [3].

The precision which the theory of analogy later gives to this problem cannot be found in St. Augustine; analogy shows how the names of pure perfections, as those of wisdom and of life, can signify the substance of God without compromising his infinite transcendence [4]. More often, we find Augustine using the double theology of Plotinus, both positive and negative. Plotinus, however, placed the One above the Intelligence, and, consequently, below the intelligible, declaring that The One is attainable solely through ecstasy; instead, St. Augustine identified the Word with God, and with the help of the theory of participation and exemplarism he found a basis for the validity of our purely natural knowledge of God in the mirroring of creatures [5].

---

[1] *De div. quæst. ad Simplicianum*, Book II, q. II, n. 3.

[2] *Ibid.*

[3] Perhaps the best way of expressing this value is to use a double negative; the signification, for instance, of the word " science " as applied to God and man is that of non-ignorance : " the very communication of vocabulary should not conceal in any way ". (*Ibid.*, Book II, Ch. II, 3.)

[4] St. Thomas Aquinas, *op. cit.*, I, q. XIII, arts. 2-5.

[5] See below, n. 159.

Despite all of this, Augustine plainly teaches that the divine perfection is so great that one expresses it only with difficulty and it is grasped more especially in the silence of mystical contemplation : " One conceives of God with more truth than one names Him, and He Is with more truth than He is conceived to be " [1].

ARTICLE TWO.—THE WORK OF TRUTH.

156. " For the invisible things of Him, from the creation of the world, are clearly seen " [2]; this expression of St. Paul's states the ultimate explanation of the created universe that is acceptable to Christian philosophy. Reason can assimilate and develop this directive idea in two different ways. For St. Thomas, it signified the following : after having studied the sensible world in itself and *scientifically*, a world which is the source of our ideas, we can elevate ourselves to a certain philosophical knowledge of God which is also helpful to the theologian in order to sound out the riches of his faith. St. Augustine viewed this directive idea differently : it signified that every sensible reality is but a reflection of the immutable Truth in such a way that by studying the world under this view (as a function of God), we obtain the *true science*.

Furthermore, St. Thomas constructs natural philosophy independently of faith, beginning with experience and using induction; St. Augustine, possessing the truth of faith and seeking to understand it through philosophy, naturally uses the *a priori*, synthetic method, explaining creatures through the influence of the Creator.

In St. Augustine's view, the influence emanating from God first stops at the summits closest to Himself; so emanation in general will be considered first. Then the results of this action in the spiritual world will be treated, especially with regard to man; and, finally, the lower beings of the material world. These matters will be considered in three sections.

I. Emanation in General.

II. The Spiritual World : Man.

III. The Material World.

---

[1] *De Trinitate*, Book VII, Ch. IV, 7; Cf. C. BOYER, *L'idée de Vérité dans saint Augustin*, pp. 107-109.

[2] St. Paul, *Epistle to the Romans*, I, 20.

I. Emanation in General.

157. The basic principle of St. Augustine can now be appreciated in its full strength. God's existence having been established, it can now be shown that it is as the source or principle of emanation that God is the explicative cause of all being. In order to clarify the wealth of this emanative action, we will consider it first on the part of creatures, then on the part of God, and, finally, in their mutual relationship. Each of these points of view implies a master conception : Creation, Exemplarism and Providence.

A) Creation.

158. *Through* Creation, *each of the realities of the universe depends, according to its entire being, on the subsistent Truth.*

1° The *proof* for this proposition is essentially the same as that for the existence of God, but it is presented in a different light and in an *inverse* fashion. It can be stated as follows :

Something is a being, is one, is true, is good or is beautiful only through Being, Unity, Truth, Goodness or Beauty. But these perfections can be realized in only two ways. In the first way, they are realized in the *pure state*, in such a manner that the real exhausts the content of the idea and is identical with it. The second way is by *participation*, so that the degree of realization of the perfection is not equivalent to the idea itself.

Both external and internal experience assure us that all the beings of the universe do not realize these ideas in a pure state by exhausting their content; on the contrary, they possess their perfection in a *limited* fashion. Their hierarchical status; their superior degree of participation, showing the imperfection of the inferior and dominating it; their change-ability and contingence, evident signs of an imperfection which affects even the supreme degree of these creatures, reason — all these are bits of evidence for this limited participation.

All the realities of the universe, as a result, possess their being, unity, truth or goodness only as participatory in the subsisting Truth in which these perfections are realized in the pure state [1].

---

[1] *De libero arbitrio*, Book II, Ch. XVI, 44-6.

2⁰ This participation is a CREATION; that is, it is an emanation of things according to their entire being, or a production " ex nihilo ". For these perfections, which have been shown as flowing from God, exhaust all the aspects of the real and envelop the real completely — even prime matter, as will be shown [1].

This view is CREATION in the STRICT SENSE, a production of the universe at the *first moment*, before which there was nothing but God Himself. This truth was given to St. Augustine through Holy Scripture [2]. In this way, also, he separated himself from Plotinus, who held the eternal necessity of all being [3]; at the same time, it seems, he did not conclude that Plotinus' view was absurd in itself. Augustine showed the possibility of a beginning of some sort, time being for him but a modality which follows upon created being as the measure of its movement. It was thus possible, as for every other finite perfection, for time itself *to be created* with the universe by the eternal Truth, and still the first instant of creation would be upheld.

The basic objection to creation of the Stoics, Manicheans and Neo-Platonists — that a beginning of creation would entail a change in God — is given a double answer. *a*) Augustine first shows that it lacks meaning. God is above the order of time and is not affected by any of its modalities. Asking what God did *before* He created, and what motive He had *before* He decided to create, need no anwer for they signify nothing. *b*) Then he shows that this creation is compatible with the Divine *immutability*. God did not decide to create some day or some hour, but *in eternity* which contains all times and all changes all at one time. If it is necessary that God be present to His effects in order to produce, the eternal Truth could produce all changes of the universe in the first instant of the passage from nothingness.

This latter answer is beyond objection and shows how God, remaining immutable, could be the source of the most varied activities of created beings.

3⁰ The emanation of the world is also a CONSERVATION or *continuous creation* through which things are dependent

---

[1] See below, n. 170.
[2] *Genesis*, I, I; see *Confessionum*, Book XI.
[3] See above, n. 134.

upon God not only at their beginning, but even in their duration and unstable continuation. These beings are not wholly complete, and, at best, they are but reflections of the first Truth. The creative act illuminates these reflections, but they would all become darkened if the subsistent Truth would cease to give them the clarity which constitutes their being. Even the forms and the changes which constitute things are but participations, images, traces and signs of the Truth which maintains them beyond nothingness by an incessant creation.

B) Exemplarism.

159. *God alone, being the unique subsisting Truth, by means of the exemplary Ideas is the immediate explicative source of the hierarchy of beings in all their degrees.*

1º The EXISTENCE of exemplary ideas is a further consequence of the proof of God's existence, resulting in the identification of God with the ideal world. The Divine Word, in Augustine's view, possesses the Ideas of intellectual images of all beings, not merely with regard to their generic and specific perfections, but also with regard to their final, individual determinations.

It is necessary to prove that all the beings, in all their varieties, flow from creation through the subsisting Truth. Now the Truth, because of its very essence, cannot act or create without knowing its work; but this knowledge, or the Divine Idea, is, through its infinite power, creative of that which it represents. Hence the Ideas are " the first forms or the reasons of things, stable and immutable, they have not received their form and remain eternally identical to themselves " [1]. Inasmuch as they are identified with the creative Intelligence, they are not merely static representations, but, as energies of a fruitful infinity, they create by the very fact that they exist.

This radiation of exemplary Ideas is an adaptation of the basic theory of *participation*. In order to grasp its full import, one should see in it not merely an *extrinsic formal* causality, but also an *efficient* causality. With the help of Aristotle's analytic method, the Scholastics distinguished these two aspects. St. Thomas, in speaking of the creative (efficient) causality of God, proposes the theory of ideas as a corollary to the Divine Science [2]. For St Augustine, the Idea synthesized these riches analyzed by the

---

[1] *De div. quæst. ad Simpl.*, 83, q. XLVI, n. 2.
[2] St. Thomas Aquinas, *Summa Theol.* I, q. XV.

Thomistic theory, for the Idea was the means by which God knew His work (science), it was the source of perfection in creatures (exemplary), and the source of their existence and duration (efficient cause). In a word, exemplarism is the same as the theory of creative participation itself, the foundation of Augustinianism.

2⁰ The creative radiation is not to be viewed as natural and necessary, as in Plotinus; God produced the universe in full independence through an act of absolute freedom. Necessity would demand or suppose a real need in Him Who is the fulness of all good. This liberty of God is explained by the proposition that the creative will was not determined by any other reason except that it so willed; to seek for a cause of this divine volition is to suppose, absurdly, that there is a being superior to God.

This does not mean to imply that this will is unreasonable or arbitrary, for it is a realization of the infinite wisdom of the Divine Ideas. One can only find the explicative cause in God Himself; St. Augustine finds it in the free and gratuitous LOVE which God bears towards His creatures. To love is to let one's own goods overflow unto others, and this is what creation is : the effusion of the richness of God even to the least of beings which are participatory in the infinite perfections.

3⁰ Creation is a WORK proper to God alone. Other agents merely modify pre-existing matter from without; God alone immediately creates and conserves all reality. Again, with the help of revelation, Plotinus is corrected, for, in the words of St. John, " All things were made by Him, and without Him was made nothing that was made " [1]. The philosophical reason for this doctrine Augustine finds in his theory of exemplarism. Having shown that all creatures without exception are participations, he concludes that only the subsisting Truth is creative; for, if God possesses in His Word the ideal of all things, why could He not be the Creative Artist of them all? To admit another Creator would be to elevate this other to the supreme rank of Divinity. This explanation will be made more explicit by St. Thomas through the notion of efficient cause; he will show that the sole *proper cause of being* (creative cause) is the Subsisting Being Himself, the unique, true God [2].

---

[1] Saint John's *Gospel*, 1, 3.
[2] St. Thomas Aquinas, *Summa T.* I, q. XLV, art. 5. St. Thomas shows precisely why no creature can create either as principal, or as instrumental cause.

4⁰ Finally, the work of the Creator is arranged in an
HARMONIOUS HIERARCHY.

God is similar to a focus whose radiation extends to great length
and loses, with increase in distance, its intensity and richness [1].
The universe can accordingly be seen as an ordered series whose
superior degree is God Himself; the inferior degrees are arranged
according to their greater or lesser participation. Inasmuch as
Immutability is the best known trait of the Divine Nature, the
beings arranged on the ladder of perfections have their places
and values in proportion to their capacity for change. God, at the
summit, is unchangeable; below, lies the world of spirits who
change only according to time, while at the lowest step is the
world of bodies which change in space and in time.

Thus the idea of a being is first found in God, where it exists
in a simple and immutable manner, identical with the Word; then
it is found in the intelligence of reasoning creatures, where it is not
scattered into space but remains dependent on the Idea which
is in the Word and in which it participates; the realization of the
idea is found, finally, in space, which places the creature in its
proper genus.

This theory is likewise the *ontological basis of the logical process*
through which we are to progressively mount from the universe
to God [2]. The higher we ascend the ladder of beings, the better
these will present to us the image of their Author. As we approach
the focus, we get closer to the brilliance and the heat. Yet, even
after arriving at the highest of created degrees, there is still an
infinite leap before attaining God. But this progressive enrichment
of contemplation has fortified our view, elevated our thoughts,
and strengthened and enlarged the terrain from which we
originally began. Even though each creature is a vestige of God, as
a voice which proclaims Him or as a sign which points Him out,
yet God is best seen in those which mirror Him best. After having
contemplated beauty as it is realized more and more purely —
at first in the brilliance and order of the firmament, then in the
variety and harmony of the plants and flowers, then in the charm
of sensations and the marvels of animal instinct, and finally in the
mobility and fruitfulness of reason — the soul is best prepared
to conceive pure Beauty and the unspeakable wealth which it
contains.

C) **Providence.**

160. *By the very fact that it is creative, the subsisting Truth
is necessarily Providence, the conscious and benevolent Source
of order, of justice and of good.*

---

[1] This is an adaptation of the Neo-Platonic theory of progressive degradation;
see above, n. 132.
[2] An adaptation of the dialectic of Plato (above, n. 44) and of Plotinus
(above, n. 132).

1⁰ Even before his conversion St. Augustine almost instinctively believed in Providence. The Platonic proof of God's existence supplied him with the reason for Providence. Two conditions are required in order that God may fill everything with order and goodness : *a*) He must perfectly *know* the universe and its needs : the theory of exemplarism shows how God possesses supereminent science of all things even in their smallest detail; *b*) He must *efficaciously wish* the goodness of His work. Being the Supreme Goodness, it is not possible that He would fill things with anything but good through communicating Himself by creation. Since everything, without exception, emanates from God, goodness is spread throughout all things.

2⁰ To the active providence of God there corresponds a *passive providence* in the universe. Augustine makes this abundantly clear by celebrating the order and the beauty which reigns throughout, whether it be in each being as in living organisms, or whether it be in the totality of the world, or whether it be in the history of creation or of mankind.

3⁰ **Evil.** The evil which, without doubt, one finds in the work of God is not an insurmountable objection to His Providence [1]. St. Augustine was deeply concerned with this difficulty, but found its solution in the doctrine of emanation.

a) IN PRINCIPLE, since every substance is a participation in the sovereign Good which is God, it is necessarily good. Evil as such, as the contrary of good, cannot be a substance, but is a limit or PRIVATION of being, of substance or of good. For this reason it would be absurd to seek its source in God; it lies wholly and entirely in the deficiency of creatures : " There is no efficient cause of evil, but merely a *deficient* one, for evil is not effected, but a *defection* " [2].

Nevertheless, since each thing depends basically and constantly on God, one can ask in what measure God wishes or permits evil without detriment to His Providence. St. Augustine distinguishes moral and physical evil.

b) PHYSICAL EVIL, or the privation of physical good, has its source in the limitation of creatures; they are not Being

---

[1] St. Augustine develops his solution to this problem in the first three books of the treatise *De libero arbitrio* and also in his works against Manicheism.
[2] *De civitate Dei*, Book XII, Ch. VII.

Itself, but are able to fail and perish, or to oppose and destroy each other. Evidently, God has conceived and planned this order of things without withholding His goodness; every creation supposes a diminishment of being and a consequent possibility of physical evil which is unavoidable unless nothing is to be created. It is better to exist, even with limits, than not to be at all. God could have created only indefectible beings, as the angels. But, in producing inferior beings likewise, He extended to these latter His Benevolence, and this is good.

Furthermore, physical evil, if considered in its totality, is itself the source of order and of good. For *unreasoning* creatures, physical evil permits them to deploy all their riches as much as possible, for the appearance of one demands the disappearance of another according to the law of time — comparable to the manner in which various sounds die in turn in order to constitute a musical phrase. Physical evil, in *reasoning creatures* can be an occasion of merit and of virtue if they are good creatures; for evil creatures, physical evil can be the way which leads to wisdom, being simultaneously a chastisement and a remedy. Finally, since human misery cannot, rationally viewed, always be the result of sin, we know by faith that the full explanation of evil lies in original sin, which also gives it the goodness of just expiation.

c) MORAL EVIL, or sin, is the deliberate refusal to hold fast to the most wise and good order of God. It is more difficult to explain, and its existence is a deep mystery. St. Augustine shows that it is not opposed to Providence by remarking, according to his basic principle, that it is *exclusively the work of the freedom of the creature*. It would be absurd to make God responsible for sin. Each man, when he sins, imputes it to himself. Augustine also holds that God makes moral evil *contribute to the universal harmony*. God has judged it a better and more glorious display of power to draw good out of evil than to suppress evil; evil itself contributes towards the good of the totality and, without justifying sin, this fact justifies God. Sins are not, of course, necessary to the universal harmony, but without them another harmony would exist; but they do not succeed in making the universe a work unworthy of God.

Like the silences and dissonances in a concert or like the licentiousness and daring in a poem, the faults of the moral world beget beauty by making good stand out in relief.

Furthermore, sinners help good people by persecuting them and by correcting and purifying them; the happiness of the wicked shows the insignificance of earthly goods, and their chastisement here below keeps the good in salutary fear. In eternity, the wicked will show forth divine justice.

d) Finally, there is a basic answer to the problem of evil which is especially valid for sin, and which refutes every possible objection. When one says, " This should not be ", he is interpreting the needs of his ideas of beauty, justice and goodness. Being Beauty, Justice and Goodness Itself, God knows the ideas better than we. We are not to judge by our own limited view, as a syllable in a poem or a statue from its niche would attempt to judge the effect of the whole work or edifice. But when God's ways are hidden, let a man believe that they exist, knowing that supreme Goodness cannot grant aught but the good. Then one can say of the total effect of all things : " praise be to God ".

Corollary. Evidently, this theory of emanation supposes the essential distinction between God and the world and excludes all pantheism. Between the imperfect participation which is found in creatures without exception, and their infinitely and immutably perfect source, there can be nothing but a relation of effect to efficient cause, really distinct.

II. The Spiritual World : The Human Soul.

161. Though he does not absolutely exclude experience, St. Augustine prefers, in explaining the nature and activity of creatures, to turn towards the divine Truth as the perfect cause explicative of all things. Thus, again, he uses the Neo-Platonic method [1]. For Plotinus, however, the effect resembled its cause to such an extent that the effect could, in its turn, be a perfect creative cause; St. Augustine, as has been shown, reserved this type of causality to God alone. Each creature, then, according to the measure that it shares in the perfections of God and resembles Him, manifests His richness by an activity that is increasingly extended and powerful. Even though the creature itself is not the source of its activity, there is no restraint or impoverishment in its activity, *dependent upon God*. On the contrary, the creature

---

[1] See above, n. 146.

is enriched by receiving from God not only its substantial reality but all the perfections into which its being expands. It has its own nature, but, under the influence of the creative and conserving Truth, it is *oriented* by universal Providence to produce special effects. St. Augustine's basic principle, viewed from the side of creatures can be stated thus :

The creative Truth, in conferring on beings their substantial perfection, and in conserving them in the evolvement of their duration, is the FOUNDATION *of their proper activities and their final explanation.* " God administers all the things which He created in such wise that He permits them to act and allows their actions to occur " [1].

THE MORE A CREATURE DEPENDS ON GOD, THE MORE PERFECT IT IS.

Occasionalism is a view far estranged from that of St. Augustine. For this reason, though his philosophy of nature is based on a *metaphysical* order because of his basic principle [2], he has a true *psychology* explaining human reality, and a *cosmology*, giving concrete applications to corporeal beings.

The creative influence, however, first clarifies and endows the world of spirits, who are most close to God. St. Augustine studies the ANGELS and analogously applies to them our psychology [3]. This study, however, is mainly based on faith, and is a treatise in theology. It should be noted, though, that he accepts as probable, without absolutely affirming it, the doctrine, which was widely spread in the Middle Ages, of a **spiritual matter** [4].

The human soul in its superior part, along with the angels, constitutes the spiritual world. Without doubt the soul is joined to the body by nature, but St. Augustine, faithful to his Plotinian viewpoint, views the study of man as primarily the study of the soul. For this reason his psychology fits better under the heading of " the spiritual world ".

Applying the basic principle of Augustine to the soul, we find that it is placed at the summit of the sensible universe and is close enough to the divine Truth that it shares abundantly in its power of activity. It has five principle operations :

---

[1] *De civitate Dei*, Book VII, Ch. XXIX.
[2] This is the viewpoint of God; see below, n. 177.
[3] *De civitate Dei*, Book XI and XII; *De lib. arb.*, Book III, Ch. XXV, 75, *etc.*
[4] *De Genesi ad Lit.*, Book VII, Ch. VI, 9; see below, n. 170.

1) It vivifies the body; 2) It produces sensible knowledge in the body; 3) It dominates the concrete through intellection; 4) It dominates its own life by freedom; 5) It cannot cease to exist or to act, and, perhaps, it itself is capable of spiritual propagation.

A) Life.

162. *The human soul is an incorporeal substance whose fundamental activity is that of animation, by which it vivifies and moves its body.*

1) The human soul is *incorporeal*. The body is marked by *quantity*, such that its constitutive parts are mutually exclusive and cannot be in the same place. The soul, however, is absolutely *simple* and exempted from quantity, for it can be totally present in one part of the body without abandoning the other parts. This especially is clear in sensation, in which the soul consciously and totally acts in a sensible function, as in vision, while it also continues to vivify the whole body. This spiritual presence demonstrates its incorporeal characteristic.

This incorporeality is also proved by the intuitive awareness which the soul has of its own existence through its own thought : " When the mind knows itself, it knows its own substance " [1]. In thus knowing itself from within, it is clearly opposed to all corporeal objects which come to it from without.

2) God alone being Creator, the soul has not created its own body, but its *essential function* is to *animate* and to *move* it. When two beings of unequal perfection are reunited into a totality, the nature of the less perfect is such that it is to obey and be moved, while that of the more perfect is to command and to move; this relationship of mover to moved forms a harmonious unity. Moreover, of the two realities which unite to constitute one man (which is a fact of experience), the soul, being endowed with simplicity, is evidently the more perfect; hence its role is to move the body.

This superiority appears more strongly when one realizes that the *same soul* produces the diverse operations in man, whether they be of the vegetative or sensitive life in making use of the body, or of the intellectual life in itself. The soul

---

[1] *De Trinitate*, Book x, Ch. x, 15.

is defined by St. Augustine as " Substance, participating in reason, accommodated to ruling the body " [1].

3) The soul is thus united to the body as to the natural sphere of its activity. It is really distinguishable from the body as the efficient cause is different from the effect on which or in which it acts. Inasmuch as this role is NATURAL to the soul, St. Augustine refuses to consider the soul *alone* as constituting the *whole* essence of man. Man is composed of a soul and a body and is thus defined : " Man is a rational soul using a mortal and terrestrial body " [2].

St. Augustine's personal reflections, aided by revelation, kept him from the principal errors of Platonism [3]. Visibly, he still follows in the wake of the Neo-Platonic explanation, which made the soul the perfect cause of the body, and the intermediary destined to refasten matter to the Divine Ideas [4]. He never speaks of the soul as the form of the body [5], and states that the union of these two substances into one nature is a profound mystery [6]. The notion of *faculty* as accidental quality distinct from substance is nowhere denied by Augustine, but remains foreign to his manner of envisaging and explaining the actions of the soul.

B) Sensation.

163. *Sensation is an activity through which the soul, by means of the impression produced on the outside of the body, becomes aware of the universe while forming a representative image of it within itself.*

Here, too, St. Augustine transfigures Neo-Platonism. " For Plotinus, the soul senses because it perceives itself creating the sensible object, while, for Augustine, the soul senses because

---

[1] *De Quantitate animæ*, n. 22.

[2] *De moribus Eccl. cath.*, Ch. XXVII, 52.

[3] That the union of body and soul is natural is proved by the instinctive fear of death; *De civitate Dei*, Book XIII, Ch. CVI, 1.

[4] See above, n. 136.

[5] Augustine cites the Aristotelian definition, " Man is a rational, mortal animal " (*De ordine*, Book II, Ch. XI, 31, and *De civitate Dei*, Book IX, Ch. XIII, 3), but merely to indicate the intermediary position of man between angel and animal; the theory of actuality and potentiality, of which hylomorphism is but an application, plays no part in his system.

[6] *De civitate Dei*, Book XXI, Ch. X, 1. In *De Mor. Eccles. Cath.*, Ch. IV, 6-8, the question of knowing whether man is constituted by soul alone or by soul united to body is said to be unimportant.

it perceives itself producing an image of the sensible object " [1].
Although God alone is the Creator of the sensible world, the
soul participates in the divine activity by creating within
itself an image of the world.

In a complete view, this activity involves three phases :

1) **Corporeal reception.** The body, being of a passive nature,
plays the part of receiving the innumerable impressions from
other bodies about itself. Most of these impressions are
unconsciously registered; those which modify the sense organs
are, however, of great importance. The sense organs are those
parts of the body which are most supple and most delicate,
and thereby best adapted to act against enemy influences
and easily to receive the proper impressions. The sorrow
or joy which results awakes the attention of the soul and
permits it to produce the second phase which is essential
to sensation.

2) **Conscious reaction.** The soul actively gathers these
impressions, producing within itself an image of the conscious
and spiritual order, perfectly molded on the impression received
by the body, and forms the sensible " world " which is the
actuality of sensation. Its purpose, in creating this image
of the world within itself, is to look after the interests of its
body while maintaining its own equilibrium in the midst
of these exterior reactions, according to its function of animation.
In the latter function, it is purely active and dominating,
for " the soul is in no wise subsumed to the body as matter to
its workman " [2]. Yet its activity in this regard is such that
it is inclined towards the body and is made the servant
of matter.

Through the sensible ' word ' the soul knows the exterior
object. To appreciate this objective value, it should be noted,
however, that if the body always relays the impression which
it has received, it is because it takes into account the active
conditions of the sensible object. It is thus correct that
the eye sees a stick differently outside of water and partially
plunged into water since the conditions have changed.

---

[1] C. BOYER, *L'idée de Vérité dans saint Augustin*, p. 171; also see above, n. 136.
Furthermore, this theory is not very explicit in Plotinus, and St. Augustine's
originality is all the more remarkable.

[2] *De Musica*, Book VI, Ch. v, 8; the whole passage up to VI, 16, develops
the theory summarized above.

St. Augustine concludes that sensation as such always speaks the truth, but may be an *occasion of error* to the judgment which does not interpret it correctly [1].

3) **Psychological organization.** Before being subsumed to the control of reason, external sensations are centralized by an internal sense, permitting man to take these sensations as his own and to compare them to each other. Then they are elaborated in the imagination, and, finally, retained in the treasures of memory. Through these functions, which are of the sensible order, the soul begins the organization of its knowledge. Now, at this stage, it has no need to model itself on the affections of the body, but it acts within itself, " with a remarkable swiftness which is ineffably distant from the slowness of the body " [2].

C) Intellection.

164. Intellectual activity dominates the concrete and frees us from the body, since it is an immediate participation in the LIGHT of the subsisting TRUTH, that is, in the activity of the Divine Intelligence.

The theory of ILLUMINATION has, as its unique aim, the explanation of the basic fact that man *possesses the truth*, as St. Augustine has shown in refuting the Sceptics. This higher type of activity demands a special explanation, for the role of sensation has been shown to be insufficient; to complete the explanation, the necessary intervention of God is required, Who, however, does not suppress the part of the intelligence.

1° **The role of sensation.** In order to clarify the function of sensation, St. Augustine gives capital importance to the Platonic distinction between science and wisdom.

a) Science is knowledge of human matters; it is generalized and reduced to a system principally because of practice.

b) Wisdom is knowledge of divine matters or of realities in so far as they partake of the eternal Reasons and in the immutable Ideas of the Word.

This distinction can be clarified by comparing it with the view of Plato on the difference between true opinion and the science

---

[1] *De vera religione,* Ch. XXXIII, 62; see also above, n. 149.
[2] *De Genesi ad Litt.,* Book XII, Ch. XVI, 33.

of Ideas [1], or even by the modern conception of *experimental science*, sometimes defined as an ensemble of hypotheses designed to unify facts and to favor their usefulness; the latter is often contrasted with *rational science*, whose aim is to search for the reasons of, and to determine the intelligible causes of being [2]. The objects considered by the latter science, being essences and truths which are absolute, immutable and eternal in themselves, are often called " divine things ".

Sensation fully SUPPLIES the *object of science*, but it is INSUFFICIENT to explain the *object of wisdom*. The human matters which are the object of science are wholly material and, as a result, immediately apprehended by sensation, which transmits them to reason. Even the general notions of science can be referred to sensible images as to their sufficient cause, and, thereby, to the concrete object. " From the species of the body which is perceived, there arises the species which is in the sense of the perceiver, and from the latter, the one which is in memory, and from this one, the species which is in the mind of the thinker " [3].

Divine matters, the eternal reasons and immutable ideas which are the object of *wisdom*, are vastly superior to the changing, corporeal object furnished by the sensations, and the latter are not a sufficient origin for them. This disproportion is especially evident in teaching; the words reach the senses but they cannot instruct and attain the intelligence, if the student does not know the intelligible signification; evidently, this is beyond the word itself. If, for instance, one pronounces the word ' head ', either I know the meaning of it and the word teaches me nothing, or I am ignorant of its meaning and the word is but a simple sound which does not reach my mind [4]. Truth must, then, come from another source, from the *interior master*.

St. Augustine does not deny that sensation plays a *necessary role* here below in knowledge [5], but he at first places its insufficiency in relief and then, with the help of his method, seeks the explanation in a special intervention from God.

---

[1] See above, n. 44 and n. 51.

[2] In the view of Aristotle and St. Thomas this alone is science; Augustine calls it *wisdom*.

[3] *De Trinitate*, Book XI, Ch. IX, n. 16.

[4] *De magistro*, Ch. X, 34 and XI, 36. The whole treatise aims to prove the need of an interior master.

[5] This will be explained shortly, see n. 166.

2⁰ **Role of God. 165.** The acquisition of wisdom must be explained by an ILLUMINATION from the divine Truth. This amounts to a *rich creative influence* which makes the soul partake not only in the temporal and spatial perfections (in substantial being, in vegetative life and in animal knowledge) which are subject to change, but also in the immutable perfection of the Truth itself. The proportionate cause for the eternal reasons cannot be found in sensible realities nor even in our soul, whose intellectual perfection is subject to the limitations of ignorance and the variations of doubt; neither of these is the sufficient cause of these immutable perfections. To explain this matter, then, one must not only admit the existence of the subsisting Truth in whom the ideal world is fully realized, as is shown in the proof for God's existence, but one must also assert that our mind, in order to be able to attain and express the truth in itself, must enjoy a most intimate participation in this subsisting Truth. The divine action, as simply creative, is sufficient for all other beings, but it must be *illuminative* for the mind. In this way only can we explain the absolute and universal nature of our judgments.

This illumination is not to be understood as an action accomplished once and for all. It is not as if God created the soul and its faculties as a focus of intelligibility, participated, but capable of further action through its own forces. Rather, it is a *ceaseless participation*, a communication, a contact and an impression from God of such a sort, that, as a constant, actual influence, it immediately explains each human intellection. This is likewise demanded by the doctrine of conservation mentioned earlier [1]. The very action of intelligence itself is a perfection demanding God as its source; the more elevated this action, the greater the requirement for God to support it. Each of our ideas actually is like a ray or gleam emanating from the Divine Focus of Subsistent Truth.

Innate ideas are useless for this theory of divine illumination. After having admitted a type of innatism in his earlier works [2]. St. Augustine explicitly abandons this view and refutes the proof invoked by Plato [3] in the following manner : " It is more

---

[1] See n. 158.

[2] *Soliloquia*, Book, II, Ch. XX, 35. St. Augustine never admitted the pre-existence of souls in Plato's sense (see n. 58), but he did admit a native innatism according to which God endowed each soul, through creation, with a treasury of ideas at least in the virtual state. See R. JOLIVET, *Mélanges augustiniens*, p. 118. — [3] This is the experiential proof of the slave of Meno; see n. 45, above.

credible that a man speaks truths when questioned, as much as he understands, even if he be unfamiliar with the matters under question, because he is present to these matters, and because he sees the light of the eternal reason where these things are immutably true " [1].

This basic and metaphysical view is completed by a statement of the *psychological laws* of our intellectual activity.

3° **Role of Intelligence. 166.** Mention can again be made, here, of the principle which governs the authentic interpretation of Augustine's thought : " Far from destroying or replacing the activities proper to each being, the creative Truth is their foundation and explanation " [2]. With the help of this principle, one can eliminate a number of theories before proposing the positive of St. Augustine himself.

a) There are three inacceptable interpretations :

1. **The theory of total passivity.** This view supposes that the Word of God alone accomplishes intellectual activity in man by using souls as passive instruments and, as it were, as a place of manifestation. This view is inspired by pantheism, and goes counter to the most essential propositions of Augustinianism [3].

2. **The theory of semi-passivity.** In this view, God produces " an image within the soul of those truths which determine our knowledge. In Scholastic language, the role which the Aristotelians give to the *active intellect*, which produces the *impressed species*, is assigned, in this system, to God " [4]. While it is true that there are definite relations between these two views, this explanation deviates from the true Augustinian perspective and contradicts his doctrine. The theory of the active intellect is concerned with the problem of abstraction, which St. Augustine does not consider [5]. Furthermore, the divine influence, in Augustine's view, cannot *replace* or *mutilate* the activities of the soul; on the contrary, it is their foundation and enrichment.

3. **The theory of the vision in God.** This proposal is defended by the *Ontologists* [6]. In St. Augustine's view, evidently, God is the light in which we see all the immutable truths; He is the sun which enlightens all spirits and the sole interior Master of souls. " Where, then, did I find Thee in order to learn about Thee, unless in Thyself above me? " [7] But from these facts one

---

[1] *Retract.*, Book I, Ch. IV, 13.
[2] See n. 161, above.
[3] See n. 160, above.
[4] PORTALIÉ, *Diction. de théol. cath.*, article, " St. Augustine ", col. 2336.
[5] See n. 167, below.
[6] For example, by Malebranche in the 17th century, (see below, n. 341), and by Gioberti and others in the 19th century (see n. 437, below).
[7] *Confessions*, Book, x, Ch. XXVI.

cannot affirm that the immediate object of our intellections is the ideal world as it exists in the Word. When St. Augustine speaks of such a vision of God, he reserves it for heaven or grants it as existing here below only on rare occasions in the mystical life [1], whereas illumination is a gift received by each spirit attaining truth. In addition, St. Augustine has added precision to his thought on this matter by distinguishing the uncreated light of the Word from ANOTHER LIGHT in which the object of wisdom appears to us. Speaking of the latter, he writes " This light is not that light which is God " [2]. We have, then, in ourselves a light which is doubtlessly *incorporeal*, but created and finite so that it is adapted to our soul. It is in this light, as in a participation or image of the divine ideas, that we directly contemplate the intelligible truths [3].

In writing of the " vision of God " St. Augustine simply aims to state the necessary and continual role of God (in conformity with his theory of participation) as the source of each of our intellections. At the same time, this allows him to conclude, through use of the quasi-intuitive Platonic method of reasoning, that the notion of God is so intimately joined to that of the immutable and eternal truths, that one cannot think of the latter without immediately thinking of God. Consequently, the Ontologist interpretation does not appear historically tenable.

In summary, it can be seen that according to the theory of illumination, it is not God Who knows through man; it is not God Who abstracts through man and it is not God who directly shows off His ideas in front of man. Instead, the creative influence of God as Truth permits the highest part of our intellectual life, wherein wisdom reigns, to reproduce in itself a faithful, though imperfect and degraded, image of the world of eternal truths, of which the real world is but a reflection. As a distant focus, we possess the Divine Ideas, which synthesize the multiple and impoverished aspects of our thoughts in their rich unity.

b) In a POSITIVE VIEWPOINT, this *reproductive activity* as the fruit of divine illumination, has five traits :

1.   *It is an act of* MEMORY, or of an activity totally interior (purely immanent) in which the soul distinctly expresses that which it already knows without taking account of itself — as it were, in first actuality. Then, with the help of illumination,

---

[1] He seems to grant it to Moses and to St. Paul (*De gen. ad lit.*, Book XII, Ch. XXVIII, 56, and XXXIV, 67), to explain their ecstasy; sometimes he seems to deny it (*De Trin.*, Book II, Ch. XVI; *In Joan. ev.*, trac. III, 17).

[2] *Cont. Faust.*, Ch. XX, 7. See also E. GILSON, *Intr. à l'étude de saint Augustin*, p. 108.

[3] *De Trin.*, Book, XII, Ch. XV, 24.

it "precontains" the power of grasping every immutable truth. In this sense, one could say that all knowledge is but reminiscence [1].

2. *It is the production of a* MENTAL WORD. In telling itself what it knows, the soul makes explicit the object of its memory. This word is not merely a simple, abstract idea, but the affirmation of an immutable truth; that is, of a judgment or of an equivalent intuition.

3. *It follows the laws of* LOVE. The will, moved by its natural love of the Truth, awakens the attention of the soul and stirs its reflections; in this way, its remembrances and intelligible words are multiplied [2].

4. *It relies constantly on* EXPERIENCE. Illumination, or the contact with the eternal truths, does not directly give content to our thoughts, but is rather a *regulative influence*. From this fact there follows the necessity and eternity of our ideas, which cannot come from our own reason nor from the objects of experience. Human thought obtains its content in the created reflections of the Divine Ideas, either in the sensible vestiges (external experience) or in the most perfect image of the soul (internal experience). This appeal to experience does not solve any problem for St. Augustine. For, according to the Neo-Platonic conception of the hierarchy of beings, the inferior being never acts upon the superior, whereas the superior has, for its essential function, the organization and domination of the inferior beings. Thus our reason, illuminated by God, appears *capable in itself* of decoding the intelligible reflections of God either in the sensible or in oneself.

5. *It is perfected by the* METHOD OF PURIFICATION. The necessary condition for succeeding in our ascension towards God is to be submitted more and more fully to the influence of the subsisting Truth by a progressive detachment from the sensible. *Total purification* is the termination of this effort. This purification is not merely an *intellectual* one destined to disengage us from corporeal images, but also a *moral* one involving the practice of purity and especially of humility. While the wicked can have some knowledge of God, a life

---

[1] See *Confessionum*, Book x, Ch. xi, 18; St. Augustine keeps the word but transforms Plato's meaning (see n. 58, above).

[2] *De Trin.*, Book xi; St. Augustine sees an image of the Trinity in this triple activity.

of sin plunges a man into material preoccupations in such wise that this state is incompatible with the fulness of wisdom.

4° Illumination and Abstraction. 167.

In searching more for the truth than for the historical thought of his predecessors, St. Thomas showed the concordance of this Augustinian doctrine with his own theory of abstraction. God is the light of the soul by being the source in which our intelligence, and, in particular, our *active intellect* participates. The function of the latter is to " illuminate " the sensible object in order to make it intelligible in actuality [1]; this divine action, similar to Augustine's view, is continuous and renewed in each of our actions, for God is wholly and completely the creative, conserving and moving Cause of our intellects [2].

An interpretation of this kind is, assuredly, more acceptable than the theory of semi-passivity. However, it seems insufficient by not taking into complete account the Augustinian perspective. Two points of view can be distinguished :

a) The *metaphysical theories* which this view presupposes — that of participation in St. Augustine, and that of creation and physical premotion in St. Thomas — are totally in accordance.

b) It is difficult, however, to find such concord between the *psychological aspect* of these two thinkers. Being more analytic, St. Thomas often examines the activity of the soul without reference to God; he determines its faculties, and studies the origin of the CONCEPT before dealing with the judgment in which truth is found and with the sciences which are classified as " habits ". Being more synthetic, St. Augustine considers first the problem of our eternal and immutable TRUTHS through participation; when he views our psychological activities in detail, he is generally looking into them for some imagery of God. Furthermore, if one were to insist, in Augustinianism, on the independence of the intelligence — according to the principle that the *superior dominates the inferior without ever being influenced by the inferior* — one would necessarily find some incompatibility with the doctrine of abstraction, for, in the latter view, the intelligence is really *passive* inasmuch as the image illuminated by the active intellect is the *instrumental cause* of the spiritual idea [3]. St. Augustine constantly tended to enlarge the narrow rigor of Neo-Platonism with the help of the teachings of experience, of Sacred Scripture and the aid of his own genius. For this reason, the *negative* point of view which he adopts in all of his writings and which tends to exclude the role of the sensible completely,

---

[1] " Ipsum lumen intellectuale quod est in nobis, nihil aliud est quam quædam participata similitudo luminis increati, in quo continentur rationes æternæ ". St. Thomas Aquinas, *Summa Theologica*, I, q. LXXXIV, art. 5.

[2] This explanation is frequent among Scholastics; see, for instance, ZIGLIARA, *De la lumière intellectuelle*, Chs. XI-XIII, or LÉPIDI, *De ontologismo*, pp. 192-225, or C. BOYER, *L'idée de Vérité*, pp. 174-213.

[3] This seems to be the conclusion of GILSON in his *Introduction à l'étude de saint Augustin*, p. 119.

would be erroneous. However, it plays but a secondary role; it is implicit, unprecise, and overshadowed by the metaphysical viewpoint which always accompanies it. In conclusion, it seems that even in the psychological order the Thomistic theory of abstraction is mainly concerned in making explicit the large part which St. Augustine conceded to the sensible as a means of leading man to wisdom [1].

D) **Liberty.**

168. *Liberty, or the power to cause and to be master of one's own actions (and thus to dominate one's own life) is not only safeguarded, but also given its full perfection through the immediate influence of God.*

St. Augustine made himself the defender, in turn, of human liberty and of divine grace, especially against the Pelagians. While he does not ordinarily distinguish the supernatural from the natural point of view, it is relatively easy to discover an APPLICATION of his PHILOSOPHICAL THEORY. With the latter's help, he has magnificently shown not only the conciliation, but also the harmonious and intimate cooperation of God and of our will in a free, good act.

1° He accepts the notion of liberty furnished by ordinary knowledge. It is a property of the will enlightened by reason, since it is a judgment or sovereign decision. Furthermore, liberty is also the power to act according to our own taste; it is, in a word, the *power of responsibly choosing one's own actions.*

The *existence* of this power is proved by the double testimony of consciousness and of the unanimous consent of mankind. " One cannot be blamed or punished for doing that which it is impossible not to do. Is not this the fact which the shepherds proclaim on the mountains, the poets in the theaters, the ignorant at the crossroads, the wise men in libraries, the masters in the schools, the bishops in the holy places and the whole human race in the entire universe? " [2].

2° This indubitable evidence is easily *reconciled with the foreknowledge of God.*

St. Augustine shows this by appealing to the notion of *eternity*, for since the latter contains, in an immutable instant, all the past and future events of time, it can see all of them with certitude,

---

[1] Perhaps the true meaning of Augustinian illumination can be seen if it be called a " *moderated intuitionism* ".

[2] *De Duabus animabus*, Ch. XI, 15.

though without necessitating them. He also shows that this divine knowledge, far from destroying, *assures* our liberty. If one were to suppose that the divine knowledge necessitates all the objects it attains, then our free will, if known in this fashion, would have to be destroyed; by this very fact, the divine foreknowledge would disappear with its objects. It follows, then, that to assert the latter is to simultaneously assure human liberty [1].

3° The necessary intervention of God in the *actual production* of our free actions is given capital importance; in his approach to this problem, he first establishes a general proposition, and then explains his view.

a) **Proposition :** *Human activity is fully free only through a positive motion of God which is perfective of this activity.*

Using different terminology [2], man's free will (the power to do good or evil), needs GRACE in order actually to enjoy liberty in its fullest sense — an act of that true and perfect liberty which the sinner has lost. As to the intelligence, so to the will there must be applied the fundamental principle : the perfections of creatures are always and actually explainable solely through the influence of the creative Truth. One of these perfections is human liberty, which, however great in itself, is evidently limited, variable, fallible and PARTICIPATED in by mankind. Man's free will, therefore, requires an *actual motion* of God's, just as the process of intellection requires a constant illumination from Him. "Those who are sons of God understand more powerfully that they act through the Spirit of God in doing what should be done... They are ACTED UPON IN ORDER THAT THEY MAY ACT, not in order that they may do nothing " [3].

An important COROLLARY follows from these considerations : *The power to choose between good and evil is not essential to liberty.* It is true that the power to sin is resident in man, as experience testifies. It is also true that the power to sin presupposes responsibility and, as a result, liberty also. But far from being necessary to liberty, the power to sin is a defect and is to be explained completely as a *deficiency* of the human will; for the latter, being drawn towards nothingness, can be the source of *nothingness* or of evil. Inasmuch as liberty is a perfection, the evil of sin necessarily diminishes it in such a manner that full and perfect liberty always lies in a good

---

[1] *De libero arb.*, Book III, Ch. III, 6—IV, II.

[2] That is, in theological terms whose philosophical significance is here set forth.

[3] *De correptione et gratia*, Ch. II, 4.

act which arises entirely from the divine movement (of grace) before being our own proper action.

b) **Explanation :** *This influence, or divine movement, can be explained by the* VICTORIOUS ENJOYMENT *of the good.*

St. Augustine at first grants that all our efficacious acts of will are oriented towards the *better good* (or towards that which we judge as such) so necessarily and infallibly that we are always seeking that object whose enjoyment is the most strong. He does not hesitate to write : " *It is necessary* that we act according to that which is most pleasurable " [1]; or, more mildly, " The more strongly we will anything at all, the more certainly we know how good it is, and the more ardently we take pleasure in it " [2]. Later, he uses the word, " the best " in a *subjective sense;* for it is a certain fact of experience that our will tends towards that which we judge to be best for ourselves at any moment of time.

Liberty consists, however, in dominating the rival pleasures and in deciding the victory to one's own liking. " It is within each man's will to consent to the call from God or to resist it " [3]. If the decision goes counter to the divine law in favor of an evil which we judge to be better for ourselves, it comes from us without being referred back to God; its source is *concupiscence* which furnishes the *victorious pleasure of evil.* However, if the decision is according to law and in favor of the veritable good, it has as its primary and necessary source God, Who is the principle of every good. This divine movement occurs within us as the *victorious pleasure of the good* [4]; and, far from losing our liberty under God's action, it is only in this way that we are fully free, inasmuch as grace, by making us capable of avoiding evil, prevents a deprivation of liberty. " Free will is more free as it is more healthy; it is more healthy the more subject it is to the grace of the divine mercy " [5].

Here, likewise, St. Thomas completely assimilates the thought of St. Augustine, and does not fear that he destroys human liberty by totally submitting man's acts to a divine pre-motion [6].

---

[1] *In Epist. ad Galatas*, n. 49.

[2] *De peccatorum meritis et remissione*, Book II, Ch. XVII, 27.

[3] *De spiritu et littera*, Ch. XXXIV, 60.

[4] Jansenius gave an heretical twist to this formula of St. Augustine's; see E. Gilson, *op. cit.*, p. 205.

[5] *Epistolæ*, CLVII, II, 8. In *De corrept. et grat.*, n. 32, he writes : " What would be more free than free will if it were unable to serve sin? "

[6] *Summa Theol.*, I, q. LXXXIII, art. 1.

He merely adds precision, from the psychological point of view, by a detailed analysis of the acts of the will and of the intellect in their concurrence in a free act [1].

E) **Immortality.**

169. *The soul cannot cease to act and is incapable of dying, for its union with the Immutable Truth is, itself, immutable.*

It has been shown that the process of intellection can be explained only through a special liaison between our intellect and the immutable Truth, which is the perfect cause of its being; this liaison cannot be broken in any way.

a) It cannot be broken by the soul itself, for the necessary tendency of each being is to preserve itself and never to destroy itself. Life being of the essence of the soul, it would be absurd to place within it the source of death. Furthermore, being simple, the soul lacks a principle of composition or corruption.

b) It cannot be broken by creatures. Since the soul partakes in the Divine Ideas, it is spiritual in its manifestation; it dominates the universe and is dependent only on God. Error itself cannot destroy the soul, for it is evident that if the soul deceives itself, it lives. Moreover, being the subject of indestructible truth, it itself is indestructible [2].

c) It cannot be broken by God, whose action does not tend to destroy, but rather to conserve creatures in existence. Moreover, the divine action accommodates itself to the nature of substances, so that in creating the soul as incorruptible in itself, God shows His will to conserve it as immortal.

F) **On the origin of souls,** St. Augustine is less precise than

he is on their destiny. He clearly asserts that the soul of the first man was CREATED by God. On the one side, the soul is not the substance of God and does not proceed from Him by generation; on the other side, it is incorporeal, and cannot be engendered by a corporeal nature [3]. He, of course, rejects the eternity of souls in Plato's sense, because he teaches the creation of the world in time.

On the *origin* of *individual* souls and on the manner in which they come from God, his considerations had not matured

---

[1] *Ibid.*, I-II, q. VI-XVII.

[1] *Solil.*, Book II, Ch. XIX, 33; *De immortalitate animæ*, Ch. I-VI.

[2] *De genesi ad lit.*, Book VII, Ch. III, 4-6 and IX, 12-23.

into certitude. At first he admits as a possible view the *pre-existence* of souls; these were created all at once at the beginning, and were sent by God into bodies at the opportune time or even descended into bodies voluntarily [1]. In his more mature view, however, Augustine hesitates between two views. The first is CREATIONISM according to which God creates each soul at the moment that it comes to animate the body; the second is SPIRITUAL TRADUCIANISM which would make the parents capable, under the movement of God, to produce the souls of their children. This latter would occur without any detriment to the soul's simplicity, for the new soul would proceed from the other by a kind of spiritual emanation, " as a light is lit by another light, so that without detriment to the latter, the former light comes from it " [2].

St. Augustine inclined strongly towards this latter opinion which could rightly be considered a logical effect of his fundamental principle : in propagating itself, the soul would participate anew in the activity of the creative Truth. Furthermore, this solution simplified the explanation of the propagation of original sin, and there was no decisive text in the Bible which would exclude this view. At the same time, he had a constant doubt that an activity so akin to that of creation could be attributable to a mere creature. St. Thomas shows effectively that the spirituality of the soul demands for itself an origin through creation in the strict sense, and, consequently, is reserved to God alone [3].

III. THE CORPOREAL WORLD.

170. The most general and recognizable trait of corporeal beings is their movement or continual transformation. This trait is explained by two principles, one of which is passive, *matter*, while the other is active, the *seminal reasons*. Both of these partake, in their own manner, in the divine Truth, thus yielding another application of the fundamental theory by which St. Augustine has already explained the different activities of the spiritual world.

---

[1] *De lib. arb.*, Book III, Ch. XX, 56.
[2] *Epist.*, 190, ad Opt., n. 15.
[3] St. Thomas Aquinas, *op. cit.*, I, q. XC, art. 2.

A) **Matter.**

*Matter is a reality absolutely deprived of any determination;
it is the last reflection of the subsisting Truth and the source
of movement and of time.*

1º St. Augustine was able to form an exact notion of matter
through the analysis of movement. Existing bodies cease
to be, and others were not able to come into existence. Now
this is not a matter of annihilation or of creation, but " the
passage of one form to another through something which
lacks form ". Matter is thus the receptive substrate of all
forms without itself possessing any of them; as a result,
it is without beauty, without intelligibility, without unity
and, as it were, without being : " nothing whatsoever, a being
not-being " [1].

2º Although matter is necessary for the activity of creatures,
it is not pre-existent to the action of God. It is CREATED
as is every other finite reality, for although it is neither true
nor beautiful, it CAN become such, thus possessing some sort
of affinity with Truth and Beauty. Proceeding from the
latter, it partakes somewhat in them. In other words, to be
solely *capable* of determination without in any way being
determined is to be as weakly as possible. Yet, this is still
being, and thus has come from the first source of being.
Matter is the final reflection of the Truth.

On the other hand, matter was not separately created,
for the determination of existence cannot be attributed properly
to its weak reality. Instead, matter must have been created
at the same time as the first form which determined it.

3º Inasmuch as matter is the internal principle of the
mutability of creatures, it is the source of TIME. Time,
of which St. Augustine made a searching analysis [2], has no
other reality than that of the present instant, " which cannot
be further divided into parts however small and which passes
so quickly from past to future that it does not endure ", and
is thus identified with movement itself [3]. Even the more

---

[1] *Conf.*, Book XII, Ch. VI, 6 and Ch. XII-XIII; in *De gen. ad lit. opus
imp.*, Ch. XV, 48, he writes about matter : " That totality, however, was almost
nothingness because it was wholly lacking in form ".

[2] *Conf.* Book XI, Ch. XIV-XVIII.

[3] St. Augustine is closely allied, here, to the thought of Aristotle and St. Thomas
for whom the whole reality of time was that of movement; see n. 78 and 79,
above.

or less lengthy periods, as days and hours, by which we measure movement, exist in their totality only in the human soul.

4⁰ But because mutability is not proper to bodies alone and is also found in pure spirits and human souls, St. Augustine did not consider it repugnant to admit in the latter a certain *matter* of the spiritual order, *quasi-matter*. " The soul itself, perhaps, before it possesses its proper nature, can have some matter which, in itself, is of a spiritual kind, and which will not again become a soul " [1].

It is for this reason that he sought the decisive criterion for distinguishing the bodies of spirits in QUANTITY, that is, in the dispersion of parts in a place and in space, which results therefrom. Being exempt from quantity, spiritual matter safeguards the simplicity of spirits. With regard to *space*, St. Augustine called it a property of bodies which is nothing beyond the universe. Total space is constituted by the ensemble of all places, place being a part occupied and filled by a quantity.

This theory of *spiritual matter*, celebrated in the Middle Ages, was proposed by St. Augustine with reservations. One should especially see in it an affirmation of a *passive principle* in spirits themselves which is required to explain their contingency. Viewed in this light, one is not too far from the Thomistic doctrine of *essence*, which, through its real distinction from existence, encompasses a true *potentiality* [2]. Adding a *precision* of this sort would quite harmoniously complete Augustinianism by establishing a necessary link between matter and quantity. One could then say, with the help of his fundamental principle, that time is the weakest manner of partaking in the immutable plenitude of God and that space is the weakest manner of partaking in the grandeur of God; for matter, the source of the one and the many, is the last reflection of the subsisting Truth.

B) **Seminal Reasons.**

171. *In order that it might partake in the causality of the subsisting Truth, the world has received, with its being, the active principles of its ordered development; this order is, however, realized under constant dependence upon Divine Providence.*

1. The point of departure of this theory is the fact of the *evolution of the world* which is given in experience and which can especially be found in the story of Genesis. Taking his lead from the words of Scripture, " He that liveth forever

---

[1] *De gen. ad lit.*, Book VII, Ch. VI, 9.

[2] It was the theory of potentiality and actuality which led St. Thomas to look upon *prime* matter as pure potentiality and the source of quantity and to explain the contingence of spirits by the lesser potentiality of essences.

created all things together " [1], St. Augustine believed that creation, properly speaking, was accomplished in an instant. The work of the six days is but the developmental tableau of the richnesses of the universe, shown as an evolution which could dure for long ages and which is continued before our eyes.

This interpretation prevents any recourse to a creation, properly speaking, in order to explain the apparition of new beings, as that of the plants on the fifth, or that of the animals on the sixth day [2]. It is necessary to conclude, Augustine reasons, that at the moment of its creation, the world received, together with its being, a *causal virtue* or a power of evolution in which all future beings were contained, not in a formal sense but *in germ*, as the acorn contains the oak [3]. These active powers are the causal or SEMINAL REASONS. Through the latter, St. Augustine again applied his basic principle : the Divine activity, in creating and conserving substances, *founded* their operations likewise so that the universe could partake in the power of the creative Truth and actively cooperate in the work of Providence. As there is in a child who comes to be born the source of his future maturity and decrepitude even on the first day of his birth, so the world bears within it the causes of its whole and entire evolution. Or, in another comparison used by St. Augustine, " As mothers are heavy with foetuses, so the world is heavy with the causes of things to be born " [4].

2. From the above, the NATURE of these seminal reasons can be grasped. They are, properly speaking, germs, destined to expand into a determined nature, as causes whose effects have not as yet been produced. Thus, on the day of creation, while certain causes were openly realized, others were secreted, enveloped or hidden to become manifest at the proper time.

On the other hand, these principles are immediately and constantly subjected, in their development, to the action of Divine Providence. Providence is the necessary source of all created activity, of the order and of the participated beauty in the universe. Furthermore, God is free not only

---

[1] *Ecclesiasticus*, XVIII, 1.

[2] This was also a reason in favor of traducianism as the origin of individual souls.

[3] St. Augustine also transformed the theory of the Soul of the world of Plotinus; see above, n. 131.

[4] *De Trin.*, Book III, Ch. IX, 16.

to allow the natural course of things to develop itself, but also to intervene in a special manner. For this reason, the seminal reasons can contain their effects either *perfectly* — if the future being is found therein in a determined fashion — or *imperfectly* — if the future being is therein contained with the possibility of its contrary. This latter notion makes a special intervention of God possible, and Augustine requires it each time that there is question of raising oneself to a superior degree of perfection which surpasses that of the causal power; for example, when the body of man appeared, directly formed by God yet not created in the proper sense, for there was pre-existing matter [1]. Thus, also, miracles are to be explained.

3. The MEASURE in which created causality can partake in creative causality can now be made more precise. St. Augustine did not think that this capacity was unlimited, nor did he refuse as did Plato, to appeal to experience. He admits that " the elements of the corporeal world have their forces well defined so that a bean does not spring from a grain of wheat nor wheat from the bean " [2]. Here, also, St. Thomas offers a fine solution. He identifies the seminal powers with the active and *passive* powers which are, in his view, the principles of generations and of natural movements. He also envisions them first, as being in the Divine ideas; secondly, they " ...are in the elements of the world where they were simultaneously produced by a principle as in the universal causes; thirdly, they are in those things which are produced by the universal causes according to the successions of time, as, for instance, in this plant or in this animal, as in particular causes; fourthly, they are in the seeds which are produced from animals and from plants " [3].

But St. Augustine's view is stronger than this, it seems, and is a type of EVOLUTIONISM, though not in the sense of Darwin, who wished to explain the greater by the lesser. Instead, St. Augustine proposed an *immanent force of expansion* which, aided by Divine Providence, could unfold into new riches, even of a superior order. This constant recourse to God has the effect of perfectly safeguarding the principles of sufficient reason, of causality and of finality. As a result, without being fully reducible to the views of Thomism [4], St. Augustine's theory has its own value and its own originality.

---

[1] *De gen. ad litt.*, Book VII, Ch. XXIV, 35; see also E. GILSON, *op. cit.*, p. 265.

[2] *De gen. ad litt.*, Book IX, Ch. XVII, 32; see also C. BOYER, *op. cit.*, pp. 128-130.

[3] St. Thomas Aquinas, *op. cit.*, I, q. XCV, art. 2.

[4] Agreement between the two views can be sought through the theory of *dispositive causes* which act either under efficient (active) causality or material causality; the latter can undergo various, hierarchical perfections.

ARTICLE III.

THE POSSESSION OF THE TRUTH.

172. From what has been said, it follows that St. Augustine's conception of the divine Truth synthesizes all the aspects of our universe in its rich simplicity. Accordingly, after he has resolved the critical problem by dissolving sceptical doubt through evidence, and after he has furnished the matter for theodicy and for natural philosophy, St. Augustine treats of the source of happiness and the rule of morality for man. This latter consideration is, in a sense, the most important, for all of Augustine's speculation is oriented towards the problem of happiness. Finally, even more than it did for Plotinus, the *principle of return* is, for St. Augustine, the commanding principle of his morality and but another aspect of the principle of creative Truth, which unifies all his thought.

A) **Principle of Return.**

Our love is a direct participation in the subsisting Goodness (as our intellection in the Truth) in such a manner that it is God Whom we love in creatures as His reflections; in addition, this voluntary movement cannot rest but in God Himself.

As he previously established the theory of illumination by analysis of the supra-sensible qualities of wisdom, so here, Augustine establishes the above law by analysis of our voluntary activity. As a matter of fact, we can grant that the *urge of our nature* pushes us towards the absolute and the infinite, towards the unmixed Good which our intelligence shows us to be identical with the subsisting Truth, God Himself. Moreover, we cannot conceive of true happiness without the *permanence* which God alone assures it. One of two views must be held : either man is a monster in his nature, being deceived by the very constitutive tendency of his being, or that God is the supreme object and natural goal of our activity, the resting place of our love.

The counter-argument is also decisive. Finite goods bring with them an eternal disenchantment. Since our desire for happiness is but the love of God, if this love be neglected, no created good can capture our heart except as presenting a reflection of the absolute Good and portraying, in some manner, the countenance of God. Likewise, as soon as they show their weakness, finite goods cease to attract. " Thou hast made us for Thyself ", concludes St. Augustine in speaking of God, " and our heart is restless until it rest in Thee " [1]. Through the creative act, our will received a direct participation in the subsisting Goodness; it is for this reason that the movement of love can find repose only in God.

The whole of St. Augustine's morality follows from this principle; from it we get his theory of happiness, towards which we freely ascend through the help of the virtues and with the aid of law and of society.

B) Happiness.

173. *All human activity irresistibly tends towards supreme happiness, which lies in the* LOVING VISION, *immediate, satisfying and definitive, of the subsisting Truth, God.*

It follows from the fundamental principle that only the possession of God gives us happiness. Besides union through identity, the most satisfying mode of possessing God is, in St. Augustine's view, to see God through intelligence. One no longer sees God, in this latter way, through the created reflections of our own ideas, which are but weak, fragmentary and obscure participations in the Truth; but one sees Him in an IMMEDIATE INTUITION, in which God gives Himself wholly and completely. In this way, there arises a transfusion within us of the personal Truth, the substantial and living Goodness which is God within us and which is God Himself.

For these reasons, the intellectual possession of God is necessarily and indissolubly accompanied by a PROPORTIONATE LOVE through which we enjoy God. Knowledge, for its part, permits this love and joy, for it unites us infallibly to the supreme Good. Love, though, is the active principle of this union, for it is the desire of the good; while the good is absent, love is the principle of search, while, in its presence, it spontaneously expands in happiness.

The Augustinian philosophy is, accordingly, an *intellectualism*, for it places at its peak a supreme act of intelligence. This intellectualism, however, is penetrated throughout with a

---

[1] *Conf.*, Book I, Ch. I, I.

current of love, and, in this sense, it can be called a *voluntarism*. If one inquires which of these two aspects, love or vision, is the most essential in happiness, one will find no explicit resolution of this problem in St. Augustine, as can be found in St. Thomas and the Scholastics. St. Augustine places neither at the summit of his view. In his view, happiness is realized in the possession of the subsisting Truth; but this Truth is, at the same time, the personal and subsisting Goodness identical with the Truth, as the Holy Spirit and the Word are, with the Father, an indivisible Trinity. Moreover, the beatifying vision of God is to be explained, Augustine believes, like the ecstasy of Plotinus [1], through a SYNTHETIC ACT which is indivisibly a real possession of the voluntary order (or affective) and an ideal contemplation of the intellectual order. St. Augustine has magnificently synthesized these two aspects in defining happiness as JOY in the TRUTH.

In the meanwhile, this happiness is viewed as being *inaccessible without grace* and it is reserved for the future life of heaven. Never separating faith and reason, St. Augustine knew but one supreme good, that which was promised and merited by Christ; but he showed that this final goal superabundantly responded to all the requirements of moral philosophy.

C) **Virtue.**

174. *Virtue is the perfection of the reasonable life through which one loves that which one ought by conforming oneself to the order of creation.*

To look upon virtue as the reign of reason in human life is common doctrine. St. Augustine defines it as follows: " The perfect reason of man which is called virtue " [2]. Virtue constitutes our progress towards happiness, for reason tells us to conform all our activity to the order of creation. The order of creation is one of a hierarchy in which creatures lift themselves by degrees towards the creator and thus necessarily orientates us towards the loving vision of God in heaven. But, applying the principle of return, the urge of our soul towards God is nothing else but love; accordingly, " virtue

---

[1] See n. 139, above.
[2] *De div. quæst.*, 83, q. xxx.

is the love by which one loves that which should be loved " [1]. Other virtues are but forms of love, and it is sufficient truly to love God in order always to do the good : " Love and do what you please " [2].

One cannot ascend to God without being detached from creatures. For this reason, the activity of virtue has an intellectual and moral *purification* as its general trait, progressively detaching our intellect and our will from every sensible object. The sensible order has the effect of absorbing us into *multiplicity* by spreading us about in space and time; it puts us into *inquietude* by disallowing our hunger for the eternal to be satisfied with terrestrial nourishment; it tricks us into *vanity* by making itself be a substitute for the veritable Being and Beauty. In order to endow us with unity, peace and truth, virtue detaches us from what is sensible, and even from the most noble attractions, as esthetic pleasure, by teaching us not to use that which is but fleeting. In all of this, there is no question of suppressing but of *ordering* love, for every creature becomes a means of leading us towards God, Who alone can be loved for Himself.

The goal of this purification is in the future life; here below, it can but produce loving contemplation [3] of God. In this latter state we have instants of true joy and are privileged with indescribable consolations. Only heavenly contemplation, which is without veil or shadow, must be conquered. There alone does the true love of God hold sway, and there alone are creatures loved in God and for God. In this true love, all virtues find their fulfillment, not in their role of purification, but as the fruit of perfect union with God. Summarily, the love which abides in heaven is the goal of all the virtues in this life.

D) Law.

175. Inasmuch as virtue is the journey towards happiness, to abandon it is folly and supreme unhappiness. It is also a sin and a crime, for it is violation of a LAW. This mark of OBLIGATION in morality is clearly established by St. Augustine.

1º **Definition.** St. Augustine adopts Cicero's formula : " Law is the highest reason which commands those things

---

[1] *Epist. ad Jeron.*, n. 11. Epist. CLXVII, édit. Poujoulat, t. III, p. 424.
[2] *In epist. ad Joan.*, tr. VII, 8.
[3] See F. CAYRÉ, *La contemplation augustinienne*, Paris, 1927, passim.

that are to be done and prohibits their contraries " [1]. This law, he explains, is the Divine Reason itself, united to the will of God, determining and preserving the natural order and preventing it from being disturbed [2]. The relationship between law and virtue is established so that virtue governs all our activity in the order which law obliges us to preserve.

2⁰ **Obligation.** In the supreme Reason, the Word of God, there exists the order of creation under the forms of the ideal world, constituting the supreme ETERNAL LAW; this law is invariable and universal. It governs, so to speak, Divine Providence, and is transmitted through the incessant creative activity of the subsisting Word, whose fulness has been described above. The foundation of moral obligation lies in the complete dependence of every creature on this divine activity. God would be denying Himself if He did not demand the accomplishment of the order which He has conceived and willed. If the sinner is separated from this order, he re-enters it through punishment, while the just man finds the recompense of happiness. At the same time, the Divine Will, as has been shown above [3], imposes itself in order to safeguard and re-enforce human liberty. Thus the full explanation of this type of necessity, which is still respectful of freedom, is found, and is called *moral obligation.*

3⁰ **Promulgation.** Providence, in conducting beings according to the order of the eternal law, impresses upon them a movement which leads them to their destiny. This sharing in the eternal law is called the *natural law.* The natural law imposes itself upon unreasoning beings with a physical necessity; but, in free beings, it presents itself only with the moral necessity of obligation, and, in order to be obligatory, it has to be both known and promulgated.

Moreover, if there is question of the most general duties, either of private or of public life, or even of the international relations between peoples, the voice of conscience accomplishes this promulgation. This entitles the natural law with the basic traits of universality and of preeminence which unwritten laws possess. However, since sin has slowly obscured these general duties for mankind, God has wished to recall and

---

[1] *De Legibus,* I, 6.
[2] *Cont. Faust.,* Ch. XXII, 27.
[3] See n. 168, above.

complete them through an explicit revelation which was first confined to the Jewish people and presented to the universe by the Catholic Church. This is the *divine law* which is contained in Sacred Scripture.

In order that it be applied correctly to the details of life, the natural law is in need of complementary precisions which constitute *human law*. These latter, however, need the notion of society to be correctly understood.

E) Society.

176. The elements of St. Augustine's political doctrine, though offered at various times and under different circumstances, still comprise a homogeneous unit. In conformity with the divine point of view which dominates all his thinking, St. Augustine was not concerned solely with the terrestrial conditions of a particular society; his concern was more global and was such that his theory could be called, " THE POLITICS OF THE CITY OF GOD ". Having made the object of his study precise in this way, St. Augustine then considers *authority*, as an essential condition to it; authority itself establishes the *legislative power*, which it defends through *warfare*, and whose limits are established by an analysis of its *relations with the church*.

1º **Object of politics.** From one point of view, it is true that nature has made men equal so that they can dominate animals and not be like them. At the same time, nature inclines men to be associates of one another, so that men can attain their happiness through peaceful living and defend themselves against common enemies. *Concord*, which is a union of hearts and a spontaneous charity leading to mutual love, is the foundation for this society.

The primary element of this natural society is the *family*, followed by an association of families constituting the *ancient city* of Plato and Aristotle [1]. However, at the time of St. Augustine, Stoicism and the Roman empire had singularly broadened this notion of the city and of the fatherland. The whole universe civilized by Rome was considered to be one fatherland in contrast with the barbarians. St. Augustine favors such an extended notion, though he first purifies patriotism of its exaggerations. He looks with discernment

---

[1] See above, n. 64 and n. 89.

on the pagan past of the empire, refusing to believe in its perenniality and criticizing its unmeasured ambition. True patriotism is to be based on admiration for the virtues of the old Romans, as those of frugality, disinterestedness, courage and loyalty. These "ancient morals" were the grandeur of Rome, and St. Augustine offers them as examples to the Christians, hoping to see them reflected with a new force through the grace of Christ.

Helped by the insights of his faith, St. Augustine enlarged these notions and saw two societies existing here below which embrace all of history and of humanity. One of these is the TERRESTRIAL CITY which is built upon self-love unto the scorn of God; the other is the CITY OF GOD which is built by the love of God unto the contempt of self [1] and which is in exile here below by being confounded with the former city until the day of its eternal fulfillment in heaven. Inasmuch as love is the principle of all societies — for it associates together those who agree on loving the same objects — one can distinguish cities according to that which they love. Every society, it is true, seeks for, and loves peace. Some, however, place this tranquillity in the order of this world in order to *enjoy* earthly goods. Others, wishing to ENJOY God and to USE everything else for His sake as dictated by love, seek for definitive peace in heaven, where, after the earthly combat is over, grace is victorious over concupiscence. This city, which seeks true peace, is the only true city; it is formed by the elect of heaven and by the militant church on earth. And it is Augustine's main concern not only when he spends all his efforts for the church, but even when he outlines the rules for countries and for Christian civil societies, for he considers it as providentially useful, and as a morally necessary means for preparing men for the heavenly kingdom [2].

2° **Authority,** as the nature of things and experience point out, is the first condition essential for every society. Through authority a leader is set up whom others obey in order that the unity of the social body be possible. According to St. Augustine, the leader must be the best of the citizens who imposes himself on others for their acceptance; in justification

---

[1] *De civitate Dei*, Book XIV, Ch. XXVIII.

[2] One should not confuse the "terrestrial city" with the "temporal state"; the latter, as the State itself, pertains to the heavenly city if it pursues its goal in conformity with the love of God.

of this evolution, he cites the adage of Cicero, " Domination is given to whoever is best by nature itself " [1]. There is in this notion a sort of natural law.

But the *real origin* of this dominating power cannot be human nature itself, which is equal in all, nor even the consent or the choice of others. The source of authority must be sought necessarily and directly in God, for " all power is of God " [2]. Now the immediate and constant intervention of God neither destroys nor replaces secondary causes [3]; in fact, it gives them activity according to their nature. God has, accordingly, designated those who are to participate in His authority by means of occurrences freely performed by men (as elections, institutions, customs, and so on). By allowing men to act in this fashion, Divine Providence directs the succession of empires so that it can deal with each people according to its merits and, at the same time, favor the development of the City of God.

With regard to various forms of government, as that of a monarchy, aristocracy or democracy, they are, in St. Augustine's view, indifferent as long as the rulers are faithful mandatories of God. If they are such, they will secure concord and peace so that the virtues leading to beatitude can readily flourish. A triple duty is incumbent upon rulers in this regard : the office of commanding and its accompanying qualities of prudence, decision and force; the office of providing, not to be done for their own, but for the public interest; the office of counselling, so that they are the advisers of all.

3º **Legislative power.** In order to accomplish its social function, authority enjoys the power of making laws. The total obligatory value of these laws, however, stems from their *justice;* for, as Augustine says, " That does not appear to be law to me which is not just " [4]. Through justice, other laws are a legitimate determination of the natural law and the expression of the will of God as favoring the order and peace of the social order. However, inasmuch as man is their immediate source, these laws are *variable*, adapting themselves to the changing circumstances of time, place and custom. As a result, they are always imperfect, and are limited to governing external conduct alone.

---

[1] CICERO, *De Rep.*, II, 19. Similarly, the soul governs the body; see *Contra Jul.*, VI, 61 and *De civitate Dei*, Book IV, Ch. VI; and Book XV, Ch. XVI, 3.
[2] St. Paul, *Epistle to the Romans*, XIII, 1.
[3] See n. 161, above.
[4] *De lib. arb.*, Book I, Ch. V, 12.

A just law is to be obeyed as coming from God even if the authority from which it came is bad. An unjust law is to be resisted as something immoral and impious. However, even though Augustine grants that the *right* of forceful intervention could be legitimate, in order to reestablish the social order as a practical *fact*, the Christian should give but passive resistance by word, by suffering and even by death, as did the martyrs.

The legislative power is, of necessity, complemented by the *coercive power*, for an order without sanction is meaningless. St. Augustine insists strongly on the qualities necessary for judges in order that they can conduct their office with firmness and mercy : honesty, good sense, knowledge, independence and charity. He is against *capital punishment*, believing that God alone has power over human life, and that sanction is best realized by correcting the guilty. He shows the senselessness of *torture* as a means of discovering the guilty. But not being too hopeful about eradicating these inveterate abuses, he proposes that the bishop have the right to intercede in favor of a repentant, condemned man.

4° **War** is never a goal or a normal situation for a people, for the natural state of man is the tranquillity and order of peace. In fact, from one point of view, it is always a detestable scourge because of the physical and moral ravages it leaves in its wake, or because it necessarily presupposes injustice of some sort by one party to a war. Yet, from another point of view, war is a good; Providence uses war as a just chastisement of guilty peoples, and also permits them to regain justice and prosperity through this means. The head of the state is to declare war; it is a permissible and perhaps a dutiful action if done for the welfare of the city. This may occur in cases of legitimate defense, or even to avenge the injustice of a neighboring people which may have neglected to repair its wrongs or to return something unjustly seized.

In his analysis of the causes of war, St. Augustine lists three classes : *political* causes, as annoying overpatriotism, the ambition of leaders, internal dissensions; *economic* causes, as the unbridled desire for riches and for commercial rule; *moral* causes, for as there is in each man a fight between the evil passions and reason, so this may become manifest in the fight between peoples. In addition, St. Augustine has stated the rights of belligerents in this dual principle : right excels force, and peace measures warfare. He required faithfulness to treaties, the renouncement of useless victories, and moderation towards the conquered.

5° **The Church and the State** are two perfect and sovereign societies, the first in the spiritual order of eternal salvation, the second in the temporal order. The state is subordinated to the Church, for terrestrial prosperity is to aid the citizens in their quest for salvation and each society owes to God a public cult. The state, both in its leaders as well as in its members, should be like a child to the Church. At the same time, the state is superior within its domain; in mixed matters, the interest of both societies demands loyal collaboration.

The Church is not to intervene in purely civil affairs. St. Augustine unwillingly accepted two charges which usage had imposed on the episcopacy he was given, that of being the JUDGE and the DEFENDER of the CITY. The tribunal of the Bishop-judge did not replace the civil tribunal; but, because it was less severe and somewhat arbitrary, many submitted their differences to this tribunal even in temporal matters, and the empire, Christian as it had become, recognized the validity of its decrees. The defender of the city was interposed as a mediator between the complaints that arose between the people and the magistrates. This office, instituted by Valerian, had at first been confined to a citizen chosen by the city; Honorius, however, thought it better to impose it on the episcopacy. Augustine himself was not too happy about losing precious time in these matters of temporal interest. He accepted them out of kindness, and only intervened with reserve and hesitation, leaving these duties, as much as possible, to public officials.

Concerning the legitimacy of the civil power's intervention in favor of the Church against heretics [1], St. Augustine stoutly maintains the principle that Catholic truth cannot be imposed by force, but is to be freely accepted according to each man's conscience. In agreement with his stand on this question, St. Augustine at first admitted prayer and persuasion as a means of conversion. If, somewhat later, he allowed the intervention of civil power, it was merely to help repress the crimes of the *Circumcellions* [2] or to aid the group of weak and hesitant souls whose sincere conversion was facilitated by imperial edicts. At all times, though, he refused to admit the death penalty as a punishment for heresy.

CONCLUSION.

177. St. Augustine is, primarily, a FATHER OF THE CHURCH, a theologian who spent all the resources of his genius for the defense and explanation of his faith. Only the history of dogmas can show the total grandeur of his work. But in his attempt to understand revealed truth with his reason, he built up a REAL PHILOSOPHY, or interpretation of the universe, in

---

[1] See F. CAYRÉ, *Manual of Patrology*, Vol. I, pp. 625-629.

[2] They were given this name because they were always seen prowling around the homesteads, *(circum cellas)*.

the light of natural reason. His faith sought understanding, and helped him to stay free of error and to correct and transfigure the pagan systems. From this point of view, his accomplishments are magnificent. He was raised by Divine Providence to collect and to transmit for Christian thought the elaboration of Platonic thought by Neo-Platonism, as St. Thomas would do for Aristotle. His philosophy is openly Platonic, as is evident in its insistence on envisaging all problems from the divine and from the metaphysical point of view, as well as by the mystic urge which is its very soul. The outstanding trait of his philosophy is but a reflection of his own soul — the impassioned love of truth. Like Plato, the Doctor of Hippo is as much poet as philosopher. It is rare that his thoughts are those of reason alone, for he sought truth with his whole soul which was, for him, to seek God. His vivid imagination and his warm heart were always adding color and life to the most cold abstractions : " O Truth, O Truth, the very intimate parts of my soul long for Thee ". At the same time, it was *truth* which he sought, and he did not content himself with some vague sentimentalism; his system, without losing its warmth, is still a powerful intellectualism. It is unified by a most profound and correct principle whose reflections are sufficiently powerful to clarify all the problems which might be brought before pure reason. In a word, Augustinianism can rightfully be entitled a veritable and complete philosophy.

In a comparison of this philosophy with that of St. Thomas, it is readily granted that Thomism follows a more rigorous method and is marked by more complete scientific contours. For St. Thomas, theology had its realm and philosophy had its own, likewise. The different branches of philosophy have their domain neatly delimited by their object and their proper point of view (formal object), and the lower sciences which deal with bodies and even with the soul, develop their propositions without any immediate appeal to God. The universal divine causality is not denied, but is dealt with in another science, metaphysics; the latter is " wisdom ", which crowns and completes the other sciences without being confounded with them. At the same time, metaphysics is the knowledge of " divine things " and is called first philosophy or natural theology.

St. Augustine's philosophy, on the other hand, is completely that of a " wisdom " and can be harmonized with Thomism on the heights of its metaphysical propositions. Yet, instead of placing the study of God at the close, it places it at the beginning of its proposals, as the light and the source of all of its deductions. One could thus call it a SECOND PHILOSOPHY, for it is a manner of re-thinking, from a definite and highly synthetic point of view, all the problems previously resolved from an analytic point of view. Only in this way can the misunderstandings and inexact interpretations be avoided which the system of St. Augustine seems so prone to engender if viewed uniquely as a philosophy. History itself witnesses the number of false disciples who are able to find plausible support for their errors in the texts of St. Augustine. From numerous examples, one can merely refer to the notion of victorious pleasure in its Jansenistic interpretation, or the vision of God as interpreted by Malebranche.

If, finally, one considers this philosophy as conceived by St. Augustine in the fourth century, it is not sufficiently disengaged from speculations which are properly theological, and remains incomplete and obscure on some important points. St. Thomas, with the aid of the progress of science and of the method of Aristotle, adds luminous precision on these same matters. But nothing prevented him from making himself the beneficiary of Augustinianism in order that he might lead it to its proper perfection and fulfillment. In this sense, one can say that St. Thomas is the best interpreter of St. Augustine and the most useful thinker to introduce his doctrine.

Nevertheless, before the appearance of the progress inaugurated by the Thomistic synthesis, it was the synthesis of St. Augustine, rich despite its imperfections, which was to remedy the ills of philosophical thought in the obscure and troubled times which occurred from the fifth to the thirteenth centuries.

SECOND PERIOD.

The Scholastic Synthesis.

(7th-13th century).

GENERAL BIBLIOGRAPHY.

BRÉHIER, E., *La philosophie du Moyen Age*, nouv. éd. corrigée, Paris, 1949. — BURCH, G. B., *Early Medieval Philosophy*, New York, 1951. — COULTON, G. G., *Life in the Middle Ages*, 4 vols., Cambridge, 1928. *Studies on Medieval Thought*, London, 1945. — CROMBIE, A. C., *Augustine to Galileo. The History of Science*, A. D. 400-1650, London, 1952. — CURTIS, S. J., *A Short History of Western Philosophy in the Middle Ages*, Westminster, Md., 1950. — DAMPIER-WHETHAM, *A History of Science and its Relations with Philosophy and Religion*, 3rd ed., New York, 1943. — DE WULF, M., *History of Medieval Philosophy*, 3 vols., 6th ed., New York, 1952-4. *Medieval Philosophy illustrated from the system of St. Thomas Aquinas*, Harvard, 1922. *Philosophy and Civilization in the Middle Ages*, Princeton, 1922. — GEYER, B., *Die patristische und scholastische Philosophie*, Berlin, 1928. — GILSON, E., *La philosophie au Moyen Age*, 2e éd., rev. et augmentée, Paris, 1947. *Reason and Revelation in the Middle Ages*, New York, 1938. *Spirit of Medieval Philosophy*, rev. ed., New York, 1950. — GRABMANN, M., *Die Geschichte der scholastischen Methode*, 2 vol., Fribourg (Br.), 1909-11. *Die Philosophie des Mittelalters*, Berlin, 1921. *Mittelalterliches Geistesleben*, Munich, 1926. — HARPER, T. *The Metaphysics of the Schools*, 3 vols., New York, 1940. HASKINS, C. H., *Studies in the History of Medieval Science*, Cambridge, Mass., 1924. *The Rise of Universities*, New York, 1923. — HAUREAU, B., *Histoire de Philosophie scolastique*, 3 vol., Paris, 1872-1880. — MAYER, F., *History of ancient and medieval Philosophy*, New York, 1950. — MELLONE, S. H., *Western Christian Thought in the Middle Ages*, London, 1935. — PAETOW, L. J., *A Guide to the Study of Medieval History*, rev. ed., New York, 1931. — PICAVET, F., *Esquisse d'une histoire générale et comparée des philosophies médiévales*, 2e éd., Paris, 1907. *Essais sur l'histoire générale et comparée des théologies et des philosophies médiévales*, Paris, 1913. — POOLE, R. L., *Illustrations of the history of medieval thought and learning*, 2nd ed., New York, 1920. — RASHDALL, H., *The Universities of Europe in the Middle Ages*, 3 vols., 2nd ed., Oxford, 1936. — ROMEYER, B., *La philosophie chrétienne jusqu'à Descartes*, 3 vols., Paris, 1935-7. — RUGGIERO, G. de., *La filosofia del Cristianesimo*, 3 vol., Bari. — SHARP, D. E., *Franciscan Philosophy at Oxford in the thirteenth century*, New York, 1930. — SINGER, C., *Studies in the History and Method of Science*, 2 vols., Oxford, 1917-21. — STÖCKL, A.,

Geschichte der Philosophie des Mittelalters, 2 vol., Mainz, 1864-6. — TAYLOR, H. O., *The Mediaeval Mind*, 2 vols., 4th ed., New York, 1949. — THOMAS, E. C., *The History of the Schoolmen*, London, 1949. — THOMPSON, J. W., *The Medieval Library*, Chicago, 1939. — THORNDIKE, L., *A History of Magic and Experimental Science*, 6 vols., New York, 1923-41.— VIGNAUX, P., *La pensée au Moyen Age*, Paris, 1938. — WALSH, G. G., *Medieval Humanism*, New York, 1942.

Texts, studies and periodicals :

Beitrage zur Geschichte der Philosophie und Theologie des Mittelalters : Texte und Untersuchungen, 3 vol., Munster, 1891 *ff.* — *Bibliotheca franciscana scholastica medii ævi*, 7 vol., 1903-32. — *Bibliothèque thomiste*, 17 vol., Paris, 1921-32. — *Etudes de philosophie mediévale*, 16 vol., Paris, 1932. — *Franciscan Studies*, New York, 1924 *ff.* — *Les philosophes belges*, 12 vol., Louvain, 1901-31. — MCKEON, R. *Selections from Medieval Philosophers*, 2 vols., New York, 1930. — *Mediaeval Studies*, New York, 1939 *ff.* — *Progress of Mediaeval Studies in the United States of America*, Boulder, Colorado, 1923 *ff.* — *Speculum : a Journal of Mediaeval Studies*, Cambridge, 1926 *ff.* — *Traditio : Studies in Ancient and Medieval History*, *Thought and Religion*, New York, 1943 *ff.*

178. In the history of thought, the term, SCHOLASTICISM, generally designates the *dominant doctrinal movement in the western or Latin Middle Ages*. While there is both a Scholastic theology and a Scholastic philosophy, it is the latter which will be spoken of throughout this work when the term Scholasticism is employed.

During the long period which goes from the seventh to the thirteenth centuries, the Christian West produced an ensemble of doctrines which interpreted the universe in the light of reason. Although these views were offered by different authors and were marked with numerous and important differences, they have a common kinship permitting them to be called Scholastic. Their unity is guaranteed by a triple bond.

1º **Both method and language are common to all of them.** All the philosophers and all the learned men spoke *Latin;* like the Church, Latin was the international language, enabling all to collaborate in common endeavor despite the differences of race. Moreover, they used a common *method* identifiable by its *intellectual* and *dialectical* marks. This method disclaimed the easy attraction of the oratorical mode which did not demonstrate as much as convince and stir up an audience, and adopted a direct approach to the mind in order to lead it to pure truth itself. Ordinarily, it followed a direct approach; without denying the merit of induction, it showed preference for the syllogism, even presenting experiences themselves in a deductive form. In this way, this method is somewhat opposed to the method of discovery in which minutely described facts play the principal part. The Scholastic method was, above all, aimed at the process of teaching [1].

2⁰ **Assimilation of the past.** In a sense, Scholasticism is but an effort at erecting a system of thought by re-thinking the Greco-Roman philosophy. The effort was alive, original and developed through successive stages, it is true. At the same time, this dependence on the past unifies Scholastic thought. The influence of Aristotle, while not exclusive, is especially dominant.

3⁰ **Submission to faith.** This trait is the most salient unifying factor in Scholasticism. As it was for St. Augustine, so Catholicism was at hand to curtail propositions opposed to the faith, to correct some views, and to suggest a number of truths for consideration which, though revealed, were attainable by unaided reason itself. At the same time, the distinction between the natural and the supernatural orders was gradually given precision; in the thirteenth century, Scholasticism is an independent philosophy and a science perfected in its own order, though remaining subject to faith. In this sense it was given a title which it accepted as an honor, that of being the " handmaiden of theology " or a " Christian philosophy " [2].

In addition to Scholasticism as defined above, two other doctrinal currents of unequal importance are met in the Middle Ages :

a) The first is Byzantine *philosophy* [3] whose most important exponent is *Photius* (about 820-897). He wrote commentaries on the logical writings of Aristotle, and preferred Aristotle

---

[1] On the importance of schools in Scholasticism, see below, n. 199.

[2] These historical characteristics which are historically verifiable, have led M. de Wulf to give a doctrinal import to the term " Scholasticism " : it is a completed system of philosophy taught by the group of thinkers in the Latin, western Middle Ages (see his *History of Medieval Philosophy*, Vol. I, " Introduction "). The main argument against this view is that there is not One, but Several complete and *irreducible* systems. Basically," Scholasticism " merely signifies the Christian philosophy of the Middle Ages; both expressions are given a simple, historical meaning in this book. See n. 244, below.

[3] St. John Damascene, who died in 750, can be considered a precursor of Byzantine philosophy. His work, " The Fountain of Wisdom " was used by Peter Lombard (see n. 227, below); for details of this relationship, see F. Cayré, *Manual of Patrology*, Vol. ii, p. 331.

to Plato. This school of thought, however, the last remains of Greek philosophy, was mainly content with preserving the principal writers of antiquity, thus serving as a channel of thought to the Renaissance.

b) The *Arabic-Jewish philosophy* is of greater importance, but its relations with the western, Christian thinkers were so frequent that their views can be considered as one of the stages in the formation of Scholasticism.

Accordingly, the narrative of the different philosophical doctrines of the Middle Ages naturally arranges itself about the Scholastic synthesis. Following the habitual rhythm of history, this period naturally falls into two parts. The first and longer period is less rich in content, and is one of *formation* (7th to 12th centuries); the second is shorter but productive of the great systems of thought, and is one of *culmination* (13th century). Two chapters narrate the history of this period :

Chapter I. The Formation of Scholasticism (7th-12th century).

Chapter II. The Culmination of Scholasticism (13th century).

CHAPTER I.

THE FORMATION OF SCHOLASTICISM.

(7th-12th century).

179. The barbaric invasions of the fifth and sixth centuries had weakened Roman civilization to such an extent that long centuries were needed to recover the higher type of education which is necessary for any philosophical achievement. Evidently, this preparatory work was especially done by the generations of *Christians* through struggle for continual progress; nevertheless, they were most powerfully aided by contributions and influences outside of Christianity itself. In the order of events, it was the Arabic philosophy, which arose in the eleventh century, which was most influential. It furnished the Scholastics with the first translations of Aristotle and with commentaries on his works; even by its erroneous views, it was helpful in waking minds to profundity of thought. In this sense, the formation of Scholasticism can be indirectly traced to the *infidels* of those times. Consequently, while the work of Scholastic formation had been begun earlier, Arabic-Jewish philosophy will be treated first. Two articles comprise this chapter :

Article I. The Infidels.

Article II. The Christians.

ARTICLE I.—THE INFIDELS.

180. Aristotle's works did not appear in the West except by way of a long detour. The Syrians, especially those of the Nestorian School of Edessa (431-489), were the first to translate a goodly number of philosophical and scientific works from Greek into Syrian. Aristotle's works were the main ones translated, but translations were also made of Galen, and of the following commentators : Alexander [1], Porphyry, Themistius, Ammonius, and John Philoponus [2]. This work was done from the fifth into the eighth century. At this time, the Califs of Bagdad summoned the Syrian savants to their courts. Among these thinkers was Honain Ben Isaac, called *Johannitius* by the Scholastics; he translated the above-mentioned works from Syriac into Arabic. The Arabians, in turn, profited from this doctrinal deposit themselves and transmitted it to the Jews and to the Christians in the eleventh and twelfth centuries.

A summary account of the Arabians and the Jews will be given in two sections :

1º The Arabians : Avicenna. — Algazel. — Averroes.

2º The Jews : Maimonides.

I. The Arabians : Avicenna. Algazel. Averroes.

Special bibliography.

Boer, T. J. De., *The History of Philosophy in Islam*, London, 1903. — Brockelmann, C., *History of the Islamic Peoples*,

---

[1] See n. 118, above.
[2] See n. 122, above.

New York, 1947. — Carra De Vaux, B., *Les penseurs d'Islam*, 5 vols., Paris, 1921-6. — Gauthier, L., *Introduction à l'étude de la philosophie musulmane*, Paris, 1923. — Horten, M., *Die Philosophie des Islams*, München, 1923. — Munk, S., *Mélanges de philosophie juive et arabe*, Paris, 1927. — O'Leary, De Lacy, *Arabic Thought and its Place in History*, London, 1922. — Quadri, G., *La philosophie arabe dans l'Europe médiévale*, Paris, 1947. — *The Legacy of Israel*, Arnold, T., and Guillaume, A., (eds.), Oxford, 1931.

181. The quite remarkable intellectual movement which the introduction of Peripateticism stirred up among the Arabians has a triple characteristic.

1º **Respect for Aristotle.** Aristotle is *the* philosopher; without a peer, he is the sole master capable of teaching both the experimental sciences and the speculations on wisdom.

2º **An unconscious deformation of Peripateticism.** A large number of propositions of Neo-Platonic origin were incorporated into Peripateticism. This was due to two reasons, the first of which was the obscurity endogenous to Aristotle's text on certain points [1], a situation which was further augmented by lack of accuracy in frequent translations. A second reason is due to the direct influence of Neo-Platonic works, some under the form of commentaries, as those of Porphyry and of Alexander of Aphrodisias, and others under the form of apocryphal works attributed to Aristotle. Two of these latter works were quite influential: *The Theology of Aristotle* which is but a résumé of Plotinianism taken from the *Enneads*, and the *Book of Causes*, taken from the *Elements of Theology* of Proclus [2].

3º **The effort to harmonize philosophy with the Koran.** Most of the Peripatetic propositions are opposed to the revelation of Mohammed. The latter held to the creation of the world in time and to the notion of Providence, and to a predestination to hell leading to fatalism; Aristotle, however, held to human freedom and to the eternity of a world not known to God. The problem of harmonizing reason and faith, which had already appeared earlier [3], was thus placed in strong relief,

---

[1] For example, the conclusion of Aristotle's treatise *On the Soul*, and his psychology of the spiritual soul; see n. 84-6.

[2] St. Thomas wrote a commentary on this book, and attributed it to Proclus; see n. 255, below.

[3] Many sects arose which discussed the attributes of God and such subjects as fatalism; these were insinuated, though not directly taught by the Koran. The most powerful of these were the Motazelites, rationalists and defenders of liberty.

and its solution was one of the main sources of divergence among the Arabian philosophers.

The first of the Arabian philosophers seemed quite eager to gather together all the new ideas that were being noised about; they were *encyclopedists*. ALKINDI († 873) and ALFARABI († 950), both of whom had a rationalist tendency, are the most important of this group. They aimed to purify their religious faith of the errors which it contained with the corrective influence of philosophy. In the eleventh and twelfth centuries, when Arabic philosophy was at its height, two different and opposed views arose, one preferring reason as the measure of truth, the other, faith. One finds these tendencies first appearing in the Orient with Avicenna, the philosopher, and Algazel, the theologian; later they appear in Spain with Averroes, the enthusiastic follower and commentator on Aristotle.

1º AVICENNA [1] (980-1036).

182. Avicenna or Ibn Sina (from the Hebrew, Aven Sina), was born at Bokhara in Oriental Persia. A precocious genius, he easily mastered experimental science, especially medicine, and assimilated all the works of Aristotle. At the age of 21, when he began to write, his learning was complete and merely needed deepening. His adventurous life included service under various Sultans or local Emirs, especially at Djordjan, Hamadan and Hispalian in Persia. His numerous works were frequently written at night. His principal works are the following : his *Canon*, a treatise on medicine; the *Chifa* (that is, the Recovery), a philosophical summary; the *Nadjat* (that is, Salvation), a summary of the preceding; the *Icharat*, or a book containing his theorems and reflections on the main philosophical questions.

General principle. Along with the other Arabic philosophers, Avicenna adopts the principle that since truth is ONE, *philosophical science* is marked by *unity*. He especially aimed, in this connection, to harmonize Plato and Aristotle. Moreover, the revelation of the Koran could not be in opposition to philosophy, and the latter must agree with the faith. In order

---

[1] *Avicennæ Metaphysices Compendium*, Rome, 1926. — CARRA DE VAUX, B., *Avicenne*, Paris, 1900. — GOICHON, A. M., *La Philosophie d'Avicenne*, Paris, 1944. — KLEINE, W., *Die Substanzlehre Avicennas bei Thomas von Aquin*, Fribourg, 1933. — SALIBA, D., *Etude sur la métaphysique d'Avicenne*, Paris, 1927.

to functionalize this principle, he proposed the theory of a HIERARCHY of BEINGS and of CAUSES.

The universe is constituted of three orders: the terrestrial world, whose summit is achieved in the human soul; the celestial world, whose summit is the first cause; God, as the highest summit.

A) The Terrestrial World; the Human Soul.

183. Avicenna's philosophy is essentially the same as that of Aristotle's. He explains the universe through the metaphysical and physical theories of actuality and potentiality, of matter and form, of the four causes and the ten predicaments [1]. Further, he accepts all of Aristotle's logic. He has some original views, however, on the intellect, and on the nature of the soul.

1º **The human intellect,** in Avicenna's view, establishes union between the material and the celestial world by means of its five degrees :

1. The *material* intellect is the intellect before it is in operation, and is called " material " by analogy with prime matter. In this sense the intellect is *pure potentiality* in the intentional order.

2. The *possible* intellect is the intellect as endowed with the first intellectual principles (or, perhaps, to the extent that it possesses the origin of these first intellectual habits).

3. The intellect *in actuality* is the intellect in first actuality, or as immediately disposed for action; in this state intellect possesses the idea (impressed *species*) and knowledge in actuality.

4. The intellect in a state of *acquisition* is the intellect knowing in second actuality.

5. Lastly, an *intuitive* faculty of the mystical order which Avicenna calls *a holy spirit* for it unites the soul with God.

Now each of these intellects, being in potentiality, requires the influence of an *Active Intellect* to be in a state of actuality. Avicenna held that this active intellect is separated and is part of the celestial world. Its nature is such that it possesses all ideas [2] and its function is to make man participate in them. Human intelligence, accordingly, detaches itself by degrees from the body to which it is attached and rejoins incorporeal beings.

---

[1] See above, n. 74-8.
[2] This is a possible interpretation of Aristotle; see n. 85, above.

2⁰ With regard to the human soul, Avicenna held that it was separated from the active intellect and was, of itself, spiritual and personally immortal. He offers two good proofs for his views : the capacity of the human mind to receive immaterial ideas, and the soul's power of perfect reflection on its own activity.

Plato and Aristotle can be harmonized by considering the soul from two points of view. In itself, the soul is a simple, indivisible and spiritual substance, as proposed by Platonism. In relation to body, " the first and most fundamental of the functions it there fulfills is to be its *form* " [1]. It can be concluded, as in Peripateticism, that the soul is unique in each living thing, maintaining its individuality after death, and preventing any admission of metempsychosis.

B) The Celestial World : the First Cause.

184. Avicenna gives Aristotle's astronomical views [2] a great philosophical importance in his view of the celestial world. This was partly due to the Platonic infiltrations into Aristotle, which transformed his astronomy into a metaphysics. Avicenna viewed the heavens as a system of concentric spheres which are living and animated, and to which the stars are affixed. Each of these spheres is moved by a separated intelligence. These spheres flow from God through creative participation similar to the *hypostases* of Plotinus.

However, the effect must resemble its cause. God, ineffably simple and immutable, can produce only a very perfect Intelligence who is uniquely occupied in contemplating God without defection. This Intelligence is the FIRST CAUSE, the summit of the celestial hierarchy.

But this Intelligence is endowed with multiplicity, so that its effect can be multiple. It exercises a triple activity : it knows and contemplates God, it knows itself as possible, and it sees itself as having been created. As a result, it produces three things : the first sphere, which it animates; then the soul of this sphere; finally, a second, separated Intelligence. This latter, in its turn, has the same functions with regard to the second celestial sphere and creates a third, separated Intelligence. Thus there is a gradual descent to the Active Intellect, which is the last separated Intelligence and which moves the last celestial sphere. This final sphere immediately surrounds the immovable earth and is the sphere in which the moon is fixed. The last separated Intelligence is creative, and produces human souls and terrestrial bodies.

---

[1] E. GILSON, *The Spirit of Medieval Philosophy*, p. 179.
[2] See above, n. 79 and n. 93, 4⁰.

C) God.

185. As in Aristotle, God is viewed as pure actuality and the first mover; in addition, He is the NECESSARY BEING, as being the only one in Whom essence is identical with existence, for these latter principles are really distinct even in separated intelligences. Avicenna reaches this notion of God through his proof for God's existence.

Possible beings which are actually realized, Avicenna argues, demand a cause for their existence. This cause cannot be a series of contingent beings going back to infinity, nor a series or a circle of such beings in which all of them are contingent and mutually responsible for the other. Consequently NECESSARY BEING exists as the source of all the possible beings.

From necessity, the foundational attribute of God, flow His uniqueness, His ineffable simplicity, and His supereminent perfection containing all goodness and truth. God has perfect knowledge of Himself and, as the first universal Cause, He knows all things in Himself. Nevertheless, He does not know inferior beings in their aspect of material and changing individuality, for this would suppose that He had sensation. He has only a generic knowledge of them, expressive of their necessary and unchangeable aspect, seeing them only in the measure that they are reflected by the First Cause which is His own proper, unchangeable and eternal effect.

186. This latter explanation is Avicenna's remarkable attempt to harmonize his faith in Providence with the philosophical views of Aristotle's notion of God. The solution lacks completion because there is lacking a clear notion of creative causality; instead, Avicenna uses the Platonic notion of participation, which is not lacking in value [1] but is likewise imperfect. The situation is aggravated by the fact that Avicenna adopted the Ptolemeian astronomy which Aristotle himself had accepted; these views were popular at the time, but were not demonstrated, and were subject to revision and even to disappearance with the progress of astronomical knowledge.

Finally, Avicenna asserted the existence of a necessary bond between God and creatures, as if the world completed the divine nature. In this way, he tended towards pantheism, though he was saved from teaching it by viewing God as separated and really distinct through His supereminent perfection.

The remainder of Avicenna's views were, in a general way, sympathetic to those of the Scholastics.

---

[1] See above, n. 134.

2⁰ ALGAZALI [1] (1058-1111).

187. Algazel was born at Tus, a city of oriental Persia, during the time when the Seljuk Turks were establishing their dominion. He had his education at Tus and at Nisabour, becoming acquainted with law and with philosophy under the influence of very good masters. He himself was of a religious and mystic temperament. After four years of brilliant teaching at Bagdad, the capital of the Turkish empire from 1091 to 1095, he sought for solitude in order to achieve contemplation. He then offered himself to the service of various mosques, first at Damas, then at Jerusalem, and also at Hebron, from which latter place he made his pilgrimage to Mecca. Towards the close of his life, he returned to teach at the Academy of Nisabour, and died in his native town in 1111.

Algazel's principal work is called *Ihya*, or the *Revivification of the Religious Sciences*, which " still remains the summation of orthodox Mohammedanism " [2]. His main philosophical work is entitled *Destruction of Philosophers* and is directed against the school of Avicenna. Two other short treatises should be mentioned : *The Tendencies of Philosophers*, a short summary of their opinions, and *Freedom from Error*, which establishes his mystical scepticism.

Algazel was a theological defender of the orthodoxy of the Koran. He sought to harmonize faith and reason on the basis of the principle that reason alone is incapable of attaining truth and recourse must be sought in mystic illumination. His position in establishing the Mussulman doctrine was primary, but in the realm of philosophy he is to be accounted as a SECONDARY PHILOSOPHER. His system does not possess the strong unity of that of Avicenna, nor is his philosophy the " free servant " of faith as it is among the Scholastics and especially in St. Thomas; it has more the aspect of a *subjugated slave*. Algazel's views are marked by two distinct traits, that of scepticism and that of voluntarism.

A) **Scepticism.**

188. Algazel rejects the rational proofs of the immortality of the soul and considers them to be valueless. Further, in his discussion on the significance of the " modes ", or divine attributes,

---

[1] Cf. CARRA DE VAUX, B., *Gazali*, Paris, 1902. — SMITH, M., *Al-Ghazali, The Mystic*, London, 1944.
[2] CARRA DE VAUX, B., *Gazali*, p. 40.

of God, he upholds the agnostic solution. His sceptical outlook seems to stem from his theory on the nature of universals; though he holds that our concepts signify external things, he also proposes that concepts lack fulness of reality and are almost nothing — he thought such weakening necessary in order to explain the universality of concepts.

On the other hand, Algazel fully accepted authority as a proof, and, above all, the authority of the Koran. This outright acceptance of the Koran led him to attack the haughty reason of the philosophers and to strengthen the function of God; this led to his voluntarism.

B) **Voluntarism.**

189. The function of God had been lessened by the views of Avicenna on the eternity and necessity of creation; Algazel defended the opposite views.

a) He endeavors to prove that the eternity of the world involves a contradiction; consequently, it is necessary to admit creation in time. Furthermore, in deciding to create, God was not determined to choose the best possible world of all; he decided Himself which would be the best.

b) God's influence on creation is expressed in the notion of " *absorptive causality* ". At each instant, God Himself creates both the being and the activity of creatures, in such a way that there is left for the creature only an inefficacious decision; God reserves for Himself to do what we wish. This is a type of OCCASIONALISM. If one adds to these notions the contention that God acts with absolute liberty and almost arbitrarily, without considering created causes and human merits, one has a type of fatalism and predestinationism which is often found among the Mohammedans.

Finally, it should be mentioned that Algazel completed his philosophical views by some studies on ethics and on mysticism, both of which have Christian tendencies.

3° AVERROES [1] (1126-1198).

190. There was a dearth of philosophical speculation among the Eastern Arabs after the death of Algazel. With Ibn Roschd, or Averroes, Arabian speculation was born in the West. Born at Cordoba, Averroes enjoyed the favor of the Spanish caliphs; one of them, however, Olmansor, offended

---

[1] ALONSO, M., *Teologia de Averroes*, Madrid-Granada, 1947. — GAUTHIER, L., *Ibn Roschd (Averroes)*, Paris, 1948. — HORTEN, M., *Die Metaphysik des Averroes*, Halle, 1912. — RENAN, E., *Averroes et l'averroïsme*, 3e éd., Paris, 1869. The Scholastics were also acquainted with *Avempace* (Ibn Badja, died in 1118), and *Abubacer*. (Ibn Tufail, 1100-1185), who popularized the theory of the separated active intellect.

by his disrespectful views of the Koran, sent him into exile, where he died.

As Avicenna before him, so Averroes also was a physician. His philosophical views also are similar to those of Avicenna. One of his philosophical works is entitled, *The Destruction of the Destruction,* which aims to refute Algazel's views. Among the Scholastics, Averroes' principal fame rests on his COMMENTARIES on Aristotle which were of three types : brief paraphrases, the " middle commentaries " and the " large commentaries ". The system of Averroes, consequently, is nothing but Aristotelianism mingled with the Platonic infiltrations habitual among the Arabs. Two views, however, are peculiar to the system of Averroes : he offers some distinctions on obscure doctrines whose error he often exaggerates, and he offers a new view on the conciliation of philosophy with faith.

A) Philosophical System.

Averroes follows the principal lines of the lovely but fragile system of Avicenna with its fusion of metaphysics and astronomy; in a more hardy fashion, however, he strongly argues for a threefold error.

a) **The necessary eternity of creation.** Averroes not only adopts the demonstrations of Aristotle on the eternity of movement [1], but he extends these considerations to prime matter, the universal cause of change. Even the concentric spheres with their indwelling intelligences have no originative source, neither by creation nor by emanation from God. The spheres are *coeternal* with God, and are moved by Him only in the order of final causality; their plurality is explained by their inequality in perfection and in simplicity.

b) **The denial of Providence.** God has perfect knowledge of Himself, and this contemplation is sufficient for Him. He knows nothing of the world, and is even ignorant of the primary sphere, inasmuch as He is not its source but merely its final cause. In addition, the entire evolution of beings, including that of human life itself, is subjected to the physical necessity of natural laws.

c) **The Unity of the Human Intellect.** Besides the active intellect, the passive intellect is also said to be separated —

---

[1] See n. 79, above.

at least in its superior portion — to be spiritual and without matter, and to be necessarily unique for all men. Only the inferior soul, the source of vegetative and sensitive life, is numerically multiple and corruptible in its union with matter. There is but one Unique Intelligence, the mover of the lunary sphere, who attains truth by making use of the images furnished by the various sensible souls; in this way, man possesses an *acquired* intelligence which can be defined as : " the impersonal reason participated by the personal being " [1].

B) **Theory of the Three Orders.**

191. In order to harmonize these views with the manifestly different teachings of Mohammed, Averroes maintained the existence of many truths, separated by impervious partitions and separated into three superimposed orders. Although the Koran is addressed to all men, it is capable of three interpretations :

1. *For the people;* here, one can be content with the obvious sense. This is the domain of pure faith, in which proof is lacking and the material is presented in the form of oratory.

2. *For the theologian;* in this case, one looks for the mystical interpretation, and uses probable forms of reasoning.

3. *For the philosopher;* only in this case is the true meaning achieved with the help of scientific demonstration. If there be conflict between the text and the proofs, the latter prevail, and the text is to be interpreted allegorically.

In Avicenna's view, these three meanings are not always harmonizable; instead, each type of mind should be content with that meaning which is proportioned to it, and which is true for its talent [2]. Thus all heresies are avoided and all difficulties are resolved.

Inasmuch as the first translations of Aristotle were accompanied by the commentaries of Averroes and even occasionally mingled with the text itself, we find, in the thirteenth century, a new systematization of these theories. This was done by Siger of Brabant, one of the main opponents of Thomistic Scholasticism [3].

---

[1] M. DE WULF, *History of Medieval Philosophy*, Vol. I, p. 302.
[2] This view became famous under the caption of " the theory of two truths "; see below, n. 249.
[3] See below, n. 247-249.

II. The Jews [1] : Maimonides.

192. Aristotle's work not only awakened a strong intellectual movement among the Arabs, but had a similar effect in re-awakening the philosophical spirit among the Jews, dormant since the era of Philonism. The first rational treatises on the Bible were written in the Orient, about the close of the ninth century by adherents to the free interpretation of the text. The latter were opposed in their views by Saadja (892-942), who defended the authority of the rabbis, but also proposed a rational exposition of dogmas and has, accordingly, been named the first Jewish philosopher. This rationalistic movement achieved its peak in Spain in the eleventh century with Avicebron, and, in the twelfth, with Maimonides.

Avicebron [2] (Salomon Ibn Gabirol), flourished about 1021-1070, and was educated at Saragossa. His fame rests mainly on his work, " Fons Vitæ " which advocates a generalized hylomorphism. All things emanate from God, the simple and ineffable being, successively. The universe in general, or the Cosmic Spirit, is the first in this series; it is formed of a *universal* matter and of a *universal* form, factors which explain the contingency and the limitation of each creature. Then the angels and the spiritual souls emanate from God; they are composed of a *spiritual* matter and a *spiritual* form. Finally, bodies themselves are next to emanate; they possess *prime matter* and a corruptible form. All of these views of Avicebron were widely discussed by the Scholastics of the thirteenth century [3].

Maimonides [4] (1135-1204).

193. " Rabbi Moses ", as he was called by St. Thomas, was born at Cordoba in Spain into a family of fervent Israelites. He fled to Fez (Morocco) in order to escape the Mussulman persecutions, and then to Alexandria, where he died. Many Jews had lost their faith in the midst of the rationalistic

---

[1] See I. Husik, *A History of Mediaeval Jewish Philosophy*, Philadelphia, 1940.

[2] Avencebrolis *Fons Vitæ, ex arabico in latinum translatus ab Johanne Hispano et Dominico Gundissalino*, Münster, 1892-5. — J. Guttmann, *Die Philosophie des Salomon Ibn Gabirol*, Göttingen, 1899. — *Die Philosophie des Judentums*, Munich, 1933.

[3] Some of the Augustinians of this period attributed the " Fons Vitæ " to St. Augustine, and adopted some of its views; St. Thomas strongly disagreed with them. See n. 232bis and n. 250.

[4] Maimonides, *The Guide for the Perplexed*, (Tr. by M. Friedlaender), London, 1928. — G. Fock, *Moses ben Maïmon, sein Leben, seine Werke und sein Einfluss*, Leipzig, 1908. — L. Levy, *Maimonide*, Paris, 1912. — J. Munz, *Moses ben Maimon, sein Leben und seine Werken*, Frankfurt am M., 1912. — S. Baron, *Essays on Maïmonides*, New York, 1941.

difficulties with the Bible, and it was to restore this faith that Maimonides dedicated himself with much success. This motive guided him in writing his principal work, " Guide of the Doubting " a veritable summary of Jewish theology which, being addressed to mature theologians, is less didactic than St. Thomas' work. Mention should be made of his " Commentary on the Talmud " and of " The Repetition of the Law "; the latter work synthesizes, clarifies and gives a rational explanation of the revelation of the Old Testament.

The *fundamental principle* of Maimonides can be expressed as follows :

A necessary harmony exists between faith and philosophy, that is, between the revelation transmitted through Moses in the Bible and the system of Aristotle; *conflicts are to be resolved by an allegorical interpretation of the Bible*. While truth is marked by UNITY, reason seems to have the primacy because it has the right to explain, though not to contradict, the Word of God. Maimonides applied this principle to three philosophical domains : to theodicy, to psychology and to morality.

A) Theodicy.

194. In order to give a scientific proof of the *existence of God*, Maimonides borrows his proofs from his predecessors : from Aristotle, that of the prime mover, and from Avicenna, that of the possible being demanding a necessary being.

He is most original, however, in explaining the VALUE of the DIVINE ATTRIBUTES. He fought against the anthropomorphic materialism of his time which interpreted the sacred text *literally*, and thus reestablished the notion of God, Pure Spirit and transcendent Being. But his reaction to the literalist interpretation became extreme, and he fell into a fragmentary view which can be called " *agnostic relativism* ". Maimonides starts from the very evident fact that we do not know nor do we name God except through His created effects, and then distinguishes three meanings in every perfection attributed to God : a relative, a negative and a positive.

a) The relative meaning simply asserts that God is the cause of this effect. For example, in saying, " God is living ", one means that He is the source of all life, that of trees, men and of angels.

b) The negative meaning shows that God does not possess perfection as does the creature; for instance, eternity expresses the *absence of time* in God.

c) The positive meaning should place in God the same perfection which obtains in the creature.

According to Maimonides, only the first two meanings are admissible; there is no attribute which can express anything of the ineffable substance of God. In the positive meaning, every perfection — whether of genus or species in the strict sense, or whether of accident — is necessarily expressive. This requires a limited perfection or a real relation, whereas God is Infinite and can have only relations of reason with the world.

Nevertheless, swayed by Aristotle's influence, Maimonides seems to make an exception for the positive attribute of *Intelligence* [1]. He teaches the beautiful view of God as Pure Thought, perfectly knowing Himself. Beyond this, Maimonides admitted only the *attributes of action* as worthy of God, for they designate, under various aspects, the unknowable Cause of the world. This view enabled him to answer any difficulties on the foreknowledge on God, on His divine freedom, and so forth, by stating that these words are used merely equivocally of God and creatures. The objector is at fault, then, for transposing into the Ineffable that which solely applies to creatures.

This highly elevated conception of God is not without value. In fact, it enabled Maimonides to propose the same solution to the problem of the time of creation as did St. Thomas Aquinas. Maimonides holds that the eternity of the world is not necessary; however, the eternity of the world is not absurd and is possible, just as creation at a first instant is possible. Nevertheless, Maimonides' position on the inapplicability of positive attributes to God is exaggerated, for it is possible to purify certain concepts of perfections in order to apply them to God *without equivocation* and without placing an accident or a limit within God. In refuting this view of Rabbi Moses, St. Thomas will state that to say that God is Life or that God is Wisdom is to know something of God's very substance [2].

---

[1] See n. 93, above.
[2] *Summa Theologica*, I, q. XIII, art. 2.

B) **Psychology.**

195.   Maimonides explains human intelligence by the theory of degrees proposed by Avicenna [1]; he teaches, though, that spirituality is proper to the two higher degrees, the acquired intelligence and the intuitive faculty.   As a result, immortality is the privilege of the philosophers and of the saints, for the former actually attain science, while the latter lift themselves to the contemplative life.   On the other hand, immortality is *impersonal*, for, once an intelligence is separated from the body which it individualizes, it becomes identified with the separated, Active Intellect.   Maimonides also taught the future resurrection of all men, but this was a mystery of faith.

C) **Morality.**

196.   Morality is based on the psychology proposed above. The aim of virtue is to allow the separated, Agent Intellect to fully irradiate itself over our souls, to spiritualize them and to assure their happy everlastingness.   This happiness procured by virtue begins here below on earth, and constitutes the best moral sanction.

Particular precepts are contained in the Bible.   Maimonides' somewhat rationalistic spirit is shown in his effort to classify these laws and to assign a reason for each.   Here, again, there is a marked similarity between his work and that of St. Thomas Aquinas on the Mosaic law [2]; both tried to apply the logic of Aristotle to the great number of prescriptions which were often put forth by Moses through sheer pressure of circumstances.

THE GENERAL CONCLUSION which flows from this brief treatment is that the Jewish philosophy of the Middle Ages, like that of the Arabs, is, above all, a powerful restoration of Peripateticism.   The Neo-Platonic infiltrations allowed their philosophy to be readily aligned to the Christianized Platonism of St. Augustine, but its master theses and didactic character place it inescapably in the Aristotelian lineage. In this way, Jewish philosophy is part of the total formation of Scholasticism which, basically, is Aristotelian.

The origin of Scholasticism is more immediately due to the doctrinal development in the Christian peoples separated from the barbarians; the history of this movement will now be told as it developed through a number of centuries.

---

[1] See n. 183, above.
[2] St. Thomas Aquinas, *op. cit.*, I-II, q. XCVIII-CV.

ARTICLE II. — THE CHRISTIANS.

197.   During the centuries which intervene between the
work of St. Augustine and the first works of the medieval
philosophers, the Roman empire crumbled and a new world
was slowly formed from its ruins and from the barbarian
peoples.   This period is not a time helpful to philosophical
reflection.   Only a few thinkers, hoping to give a rational
turn to their faith, are of any prominence; they are " similar
to milestones planted by God to point out the route that had
to be followed in order to rediscover the roads of light, of life
and of knowledge " [1].   Among these, mention can be made
of the compilers, as St. Isidore of Seville [2] (about 560-636)
and St. Bede the Venerable [3] (675-735), and of the moralists,
as St. Gregory the Great [4] (560-604) and Cassiodorus [5] (477-570).
The two most important philosophical names, though, are
Dionysius the Areopagite in the East, and Boethius in the West.

A) **Dionysius the Areopagite** [6].

In the fifth century, a number of works on mystical theology
appeared, presumably written by an unknown author who spoke
of himself as St. Dionysius, a disciple of St. Paul.   These works
were entitled *De Cælesti Hierarchia* (Celestial Hierarchy), *De
divinis nominibus* (On the Divine Names), *De mystica Theologia*
(On Mystical Theology), and *De ecclesiastica Hierarchia* (On the
Ecclesiastical Hierarchy).   The author, probably a disciple of
Proclus [7], uses the Neo-Platonic philosophy in order to erect a
truly Catholic mystical theology.   The general view which Dionysius
proposes is that of referring everything back to God, either in
Himself, or as the principle or as the end of all things; at the same
time, he avoids the errors of his pagan masters.

   I.   *God in Himself* possesses all the perfections of creatures :
He is Goodness, Beauty, Strength, and Unity.   He possesses
these perfections, however, in a different manner because of His

---

[1] A. GONZALÈS, *Hist. de la Phil.*, II, p. 97.

[2] F. CAYRÉ, *Manual of Patrology*, vol. II, pp. 253-267.

[3] *Ibid.*, pp. 272-276.

[4] *Ibid.*, pp. 234-253.

[5] *Ibid.*, pp. 221-225.

[6] F. CAYRÉ, *Manual of Patrology*, vol. II, pp. 86-101. — ROLT, C. E. (Edit.),
Dionysius the Areopagite on the Divine Names and the Mystical Theology,
London, 1920. — STIGLMAYR, J., *Das Aufkommen der pseudo-Dionysischen
Schriften und ihr Eindringen in die christliche Litteratur bis zum Laterankonzil*,
Feldkirch, 1895.

[7] Dionysius cites a passage from Proclus on the existence of evil; see F. CAYRÉ,
op. cit., p. 92.

transcendence which makes Him ineffable and obscure. It is in prayer that He reveals Himself at the very heart of His super-luminous obscurity in a silence which is introductory to His mysteries [1].

2. *God is the principle of things*, for He is Goodness which is overflowing. Creatures are the effusions of this Goodness in which they participate according to the designs of Providence. There is a real distinction between God and the world. In going from one to the other, one encounters a whole hierarchy of celestial spirits, of which the ecclesiastical hierarchy is the mundane transference.

3. *God is the finality of things*, attracting all things to Himself. Goodness, after having descended into creatures, returns to its point of departure. Deification extends itself to all creatures, and is achieved in man through grace, love and ecstasy.

B) **Boethius** [2] (480-525).

198. Boethius was a Christian with an Hellenistic education. Theodoric, who looked favorably on him, named him consul from 510 to 522. Boethius attempted to set up an intellectual, cultural atmosphere in the court of the barbarian king. He translated the *Isagoge* of Porphyry and certain works of Aristotle — probably the *Organon*, which was lost and only recovered in the twelfth century, and also the *Categoriæ* and the *Perihermeniæ* used by the earlier Scholastics. In addition, he published personal treatises on the syllogism and other logical subjects, besides doing some writing in theology. Having incurred the disfavor of Theodoric, he was thrown into prison where he wrote his famous *De Conso-latione philosophiæ*, whose title is somewhat indicative of its contents. " In misfortune Boethius seeks happiness; philosophy consoles him by showing him where and how he may find it " [3]. Boethius was executed some time between 524 and 526.

The works of Boethius were responsible for circulating a large number of the ideas of St. Augustine and, more especially, of Aristotle. Until the thirteenth century, Aristotle was known only through the works of Boethius. Among the many famous definitions which he supplied for the Scholastics, the following are notable : *happiness* is " a state perfected by the junction of all goods " [4]; *eternity* is " the total, simultaneous and perfect possession of interminable life " [5]; *person* is " an individual substance of rational nature " [6]. Accordingly, the *Consolations of Philosophy*, though a fragmentary work of little originality, was a powerful influence in the formation of Scholasticism.

---

[1] *De Mystica Theologia*, Ch. i, n. i.

[2] Boethius' works are in MIGNE'S *Patrologia Latina*, Vols. LXIII-LXIV. — BARRETT, H. M., *Boethius*, MACMILLAN, 1940. — PATCH., H. R., *The Tradition of Boethius*, New York, 1935. — STEWART, H. F., and RAND, E. K., (eds.), *The Theological Tractates and The Consolation of Philosophy*, London, 1926.

[3] F. CAYRÉ, *op. cit.*, p. 218.

[4] *De consolatione philosophiae*, Book iii, Pr. 2.

[5] *Ibid.*, Book v, Pr. 6.

[6] *Liber de persona et de duabus naturis*, Ch. iii.

Two periods comprise the formation of Scholasticism. The first is the *period of the schools* and of the first Scholastics, during which the teaching of the liberal arts and of philosophy reappear. During the second period, the *period of systems*, the masters of the schools begin to speculate in their own right, but their lack of experience only effects a multiplication of opinions which is dominated by the problem of the universal. Nevertheless, already in the eleventh century, St. Anselm produces some very personal writings, sufficiently complete to merit a study in themselves. The following three paragraphs will follow the formation of Scholasticism :

I.   The Early Scholastics and John Scotus Eriugena.

II.   The Problem of Universals.

III. St. Anselm.

I. THE EARLY SCHOLASTICS.

(7th-10th century)

BIBLIOGRAPHY.

BRUNHES, G., *La foi chrétienne et la philosophie au temps de la renaissance carolingienne*, Paris, 1903. — DUCHETT, E. S., *The Gateway to the Middle Ages*, New York, 1938. — ENDRES, J., *Forschungen zur Geschichte der frühmittelalterlichen Philosophie*, Munster, 1915. — LAISTNER, M. E. W., *Thought and Letters in Western Europe, A. D. 500-900*, London, 1931. — MAITRE, L., *Les écoles épiscopales et monastiques de l'Occident depuis Charlemagne jusqu'à Philippe-Auguste*, Paris, 1866. — RAND, E. K., *Founders of the Middle Ages*, Cambridge (Mass.), 1928. — THOMAS, E. C., *History of the Schoolmen*, London, 1941.

General Characteristics.

199. Just as the work of the first Greek thinkers separated itself from the religious and mythological speculations quite slowly, so the work of the early Scholastics failed to distinguish philosophy from theology. Then, during three centuries (the middle of the 8th to the middle of the 11th) the history of purely rational views is comparable, likewise, to the attempts of the early Greek sages, for both conclude with a golden age. Of course, thinkers of the Middle Ages were more favored than the pagans, being able to learn profitably from so many predecessors and from their Catholic faith. This period can thus be aptly termed a Scholastic and Catholic revival.

1. **Revival.** The barbarian flood which was released over Europe overthrew both the Roman civilization and the intellectual movement that had begun. Except for the ecclesiastical writers and monastic centers, ignorance was widespread even among the clergy. It was Charlemagne (742-814) who created a number of schools by his decrees on education and initiated a period which is termed the " *Carolingian Renaissance* ".

In this revival of learning, philosophy had not yet arrived at its peak of development. The instructional program comprised the seven liberal arts [1] divided into two groups : the *quadrivium*, including arithmetic, geometry, astronomy and music (later, medicine was added to this group), and the *trivium*, including grammar, rhetoric and dialectic. The latter branch, dialectic, was an explanation of the logical works of Aristotle as handed down and commented upon by Boethius; it was an occasion for considering many philosophical questions. But philosophy did not come into its own until the twelfth century when it had its own place on the Scholastic program, along with the liberal arts and with theology.

2. **Scholastic.** The term is here used in an etymological sense, according to which a " Scholastic " of the Middle Ages is any master teaching in a school. In this sense, it has a very apt designation for this period for the following two reasons :

a) At first, the sole means of becoming a master and of instructing oneself was through the oral teaching done in the schools, so that the progress of learning was closely dependent on the multiplication of schools and the value of the teachers. There were two types of schools : the *monastic*, annexed to the Benedictine abbeys, at first opened to the public and later reserved to the monks; the *episcopal* schools, established at the cathedral, later becoming more numerous and powerful, especially in the eleventh and twelfth centuries.

b) The revival of the Middle Ages can be called " Scholastic " because it is not so much a case of discovery, but rather an effort at ASSIMILATION of the ancient writings; the masters of the schools aimed to comment upon, and to explain these writings, so that their work was called a " lesson " or a " delineation ". The latter was one of the most important functions of the instructional program and comprised a triple exposition : the *literal*, or grammatical explanation; the *meaningful*, or explanation of the thought; the *doctrinal*, or deeper grasp of the doctrinal content. Later on, there arises the " disputation " which is carried on by objections and answers between master and pupils or between pupils under direction of the master. The latter was an exercise in logical reasoning, and was considered of great value, though often exaggerated in importance. Finally, while the Middle Ages were well furnished with literary works during this period, for a long

---

[1] Prior to the Middle Ages, this classification was made popular by Boethius, Cassiodorus and Alcuin. See M. DE WULF, *History of Mediaeval Philosophy*, Vol. I, pp. 53-55.

time the philosophical works available and commented upon were but a few works of Aristotle's logic [1].

3. **Catholic.** But it was especially revelation which proved to be a rich source of natural and supernatural truths during this revival. During this period, the lower branches of learning were subject to the study of the faith and ordered towards the study of the Scriptures. An educational system of this sort arose because of the fact that most of the students were destined to be monks, clerics or priests. The social organization that was being formed was such that even the nobles were not interested in the pursuit of learning. Theology, accordingly, was the instructional coronal. It consisted of commentaries on the Bible which gave occasion for examining various questions of psychology, theodicy and ethics. Along with the problems of cosmology and of metaphysics — which arose in logic from the problem of universals — there arose, in the above fashion, a reconstitution of the entire domain of philosophy, culminating in its clear distinction from the realm of theology.

It is in this way that one can understand the meaning of the theological controversies in this revival of learning, as well as the numerous interventions of the Catholic Church in these discussions. For the Church wisely watched these first attempts of reason to explain faith through dialectic.

In the scholastic organization of this period, the fame and value of a school depended totally upon its master. Charlemagne, for this reason, attempted to attract the best cultivated personages from all realms to his schools. In order to give good example, he founded a school in his own palace and followed the instruction together with his family. ALCUIN [2], (about 730-804) originally from England, who was its first master, had a powerful influence in seconding the emperor's attempts to reorganize instruction, and even founded a school at Tours.

Two of Alcuin's most renowned successors at the Palatine school were RHABANUS MAURUS [3] (about 776-856) of German ancestry, who later became abbot of the monastery at Fulda and, later, Archbishop of Mainz, and John Scotus Eriugena, whose philosophical system merits some study.

---

[1] The only philosophical treatises available at this time were some extracts of Plato's *Timaeus*, and some Neo-Platonic commentaries of Porphyry, Themistius and Alexander of Aphrodisias; see M. DE WULF, *op. cit.*, pp. 58-69.

[2] Alcuin's works are in vols. C-CI of MIGNE's, *Patrologia Latina*. — BUXTON, E. M. W., *Alcuin*, London, 1922. — LA FORÊT, A., *Histoire d'Alcuin*, Paris, 1898.

[3] The works of Rhabanus Maurus are in vols. CVII-CXII of MIGNE's, *Patrologia Latina*. Among his works are *De institutione clericorum*, acknowledging the liberal arts, and *De rerum naturis*, a sort of encyclopedia.

The zeal of these first masters was stirred by the *Predestinationist controversy* revived between 840 and 860 by Gottschalk : " This Saxon monk affirmed that there were two absolutely similar predestinations; that of the good to eternal salvation and of the wicked to hell " [1]. As a rule, this discussion arises from the study of Scripture and of the Fathers of the Church. except for the work of Eriugena.

JOHN SCOTUS ERIUGENA [2]. (Between 800 and 870).

200. Originally from Ireland or Scotland, John Scotus Eriugena was called to a prominent position at the Palatine school by Charles the Bald (840-877). At the request of Hincmar, the Bishop of Rheims, and the great adversary of Gottschalk, Eriugena wrote a work entitled *De Predestinatione*. But above all, he found at the court the works of the Pseudo-Dionysius [3] which had been presented to Pepin the Short by the Byzantine ambassadors in 757, but no one at court could understand them. John, who knew Greek, not only translated them, but also took inspiration from them for his principal work, *De Divisione naturæ*, which is descriptive of the role of Providence in the form of a sweeping synthesis, and is an indirect refutation of predestinationism. The fundamental principle which John freely applied both in his metaphysics and in his psychology is readily found in this work, even though he strives to safeguard the authority of faith in its application.

A) **Fundamental Principle.**

201. This principle can be formulated as follows :

Since God alone is TRUE BEING, *He is the principle, the termination and the means of all things.* This can be recognized as the master theory of Neo-Platonism, adapted to Catholic theology. Without ever being studied and demonstrated in itself, this principle is the source of the speculations in *De*

---

[1] F. CAYRÉ, *op. cit.*, Vol. II, p. 381.

[2] Eriugena's works are in vol. CXXII of MIGNE's, *Patrologia Latina*. — BETT, H., *Johannes Scotus, Eriugena, A Study in Mediaeval Philosophy*, Cambridge, 1925. — CAPPUYNS, M., *Jean Scot Erigene*, Paris, 1933. — SCHNEIDER, A., *Die Erkenntnislehre des Johannes Eriugena im Rahmen ihrer metaphysischen und anthropologischen Voraussetzungen*, 2 vols., Berlin, 1921-1923. — SEUL, W., *Die Gotteserkenntnis bei Johannes Skotus Eriugena unter Berucksichtigung ihrer neo-platonischen und augustinischen Elemente*, Bonn, 1932.

[3] See n. 197, above.

Divisione naturæ and fully unifies them. It can be best understood by viewing it in its applications.

B) **Metaphysical Applications.**

Eriugena at first explains the totality of creatures which he calls *Natura,* or *being-in-general.* Following the method common to the Platonists, he begins with an a priori affirmation of God's existence, the invisible and spiritual source of all that exists. Four stages are distinguished in the evolvement of things from God.

1. INCREATE *Nature* CREATING. (*Natura* INCREATA CREANS). This appellation signifies God considered in Himself, absolutely ineffable and transcendent. John admits the notion of two theologies, one negative and the other positive. The positive, however, since it uses abstract concepts, has value solely as a metaphor; only the negative is worthy of God : " In that nature which can neither be spoken of or understood, the (power of the categories) is defective throughout " [1]. One can only know that God is the source of all things, or, *nature creating.* Furthermore, in this first stage, the Divine Nature is unknowable in itself; this is the factor which determines its evolution.

2. CREATED *Nature* CREATING. (*Natura* CREATA CREANS). In order to know Himself, God exteriorizes Himself or *creates* Himself, so to speak, in an ideal world where His perfection is reflected in an intelligible fashion : " The (Divine Nature) is created by itself in its primordial causes, and, in this fashion, creates Itself; this means that It begins to appear in its theophanies, for It wishes to emerge from the most occult reaches of Its nature where It is unknown to itself because It is infinite and supernatural...; descending, however, into the principles of things, and, as it were, creating Itself, it begins to be in another " [2]. This second stage is to be identified with the Word of Catholic theology.

3. CREATED *Nature* NOT CREATING. (*Natura* CREATA NON CREANS). The Divine Ideas, already multiple though still universal, are active forces which tend to manifest themselves, and thus is born the sensible universe whose individual and specific perfections are but a " *theophany* ".

---

[1] *De Divisione naturæ,* I, 15.
[2] *Ibid.,* III, 23.

According to John, God's name is derived from the Greek θεός which comes from θέω to run : " For He runs within all things and is not at rest in any way, but fills all things by running within them " [1]. This *descensive emanation* of beings constitutes creation or the act through which God creates Himself in the world.

These statements tend to a pantheistic interpretation, inasmuch as all these theophanies are considered *necessary* for the Divine Nature. Eriugena explicitly defends himself from this error by holding that the Supreme Being, immutable and infinite, is really distinguished from His changeful and finite images : " The (Divine Nature) contains within Itself all that it created and creates, in such a way, though, that It is one superessential thing Itself, different from that which It creates in Itself " [2]. Similar obscurities and contradictions are found among Platonic thinkers; an attempt is made to resolve them by appealing to a higher, intuitive knowledge, or to conceptual immediacies.

4. *Nature*, NEITHER CREATED NOR CREATING. (*Natura* NEC CREATA NEC CREANS). The process of emanation is completed by the return of what has been created towards its first principle. There it finds, with a fulness of perfection, a type of deification, and its own happiness. The final termination, accordingly, is Nature which is both increate and, since it no longer acts in the proper meaning of that word, it is not creating. In this way Nature attracts only as loving; it is the final, and not the efficient cause : " It is the cause of all things in such a way, that it reduces all things to Itself without any movement, but only by the power of Its beauty " [3]. Here, again, we have the dual affirmation of our basic transformation in God and of our individual permanence.

C) Psychological Applications.

202. Our knowledge is but an image of the divine evolvement, and thus follows four stages :

Understanding, the highest degree, is the first stage and allows us to achieve a valid theology. This power can be considered in two ways : in the first, an *a posteriori* view,

---

[1] *Ibid.*, I, 12.
[2] *Ibid.*, III, 17.
[3] *Ibid.*, I, 75.

it is the sum of all lower knowledge and it attributes the perfections of other creatures to God; in the second, an *a priori* view, it goes directly to God, giving us a very high sort of intuition akin to ecstasy wherein the soul loses consciousness of itself. The second stage of human knowledge is termed *reason;* in order to know itself, the soul exteriorizes itself in the multiple ideas representative of the primordial essences of the *Logos. Reason,* which is also intuitive, makes the ineffable knowledge of *understanding* most distinct.

Beyond the domain of intuition, there is a corporeal manifestation of the Divine Nature which also comprises two degrees. The first is the *interior sense,* which grasps the universal essences however they may be realized in matter, and the *exterior sense,* which attains only the individual, sensible and exterior attributes.

Moreover, it is by reascending this chain through reflection and purification that we rediscover our goal and our happiness according to the order of divine predestination.

D) Faith and Reason.

203. In the view of Eriugena, philosophy is not perfectly distinguishable from revealed truth. The Scriptures are the first source of philosophical truth, while human reason is the secondary source, although reason is to be preferred over authority, even over the authority of the Fathers of the Church. Inasmuch as faith and reason arise from the same source there can be no conflict between them. Reason, here, of course, designates the second degree of knowledge or the higher intuition of abstract ideas. This illumination of ideas is, in his view, a veritable grace, and it is not by natural effort but solely by grace that one is lifted to the ecstasy of understanding.

It is reason understood in the above sense which is declared capable of grasping the true sense of the Scriptures; if, then, one calls this view rationalistic, it is such only in a special sense, for it might also be termed " fideism ". Furthermore, Eriugena did not add precision to the Platonic method, which does not clearly distinguish the domain of philosophy from that of theology [2].

---

[1] The *interior sense* corresponds to the abstractive reason of Aristotle and St. Thomas.

[2] " All of this is metaphysics, or philosophy, and to take away from Scotus the title of philosopher is to take away from his personality ". M. DE WULF, *op. cit.,* p. 131.

CONCLUSION. **204.** The work of Eriugena is a personal reconstruction of the essential views of the Neo-Platonic system insinuated by the Pseudo-Areopagite. In a period that contained little philosophy of its own, his view was a somewhat coherent and general explanation of the universe. He had considerable influence on the philosophers who followed, even on the more important ones, as on Gerbert, Abelard, Alanus of Lille, Hugh of St. Victor and others. Alongside the growing influence of Aristotle, he perpetuated that of Plato.

His work, however, is not without speculative dangers; its absolute formulas, lacking the finer nuances of thought, could lead to pantheism. In fact, a good number of heretics shielded themselves with his patronage. Berengarius of Tours (1009-1088), for example, besides his errors on the Eucharist [1], subordinated reason to faith. "At the end of the twelfth century, Amalric of Bene drew from the *De divisione* his own pantheistic theories; the Albigenses also appealed to it, which explains why on January 25th, 1125, Pope Honorius III condemned the *De divisione naturæ*, which had already been forbidden in a Council at Sens" [2].

This period of formation can be completed by mentioning GERBERT (935 or 938-1003), who later became Pope Silvester II [3].

Gerbert had studied the quadrivium — at that time almost unknown in France — at Spain, under the direction of Atton, Bishop of Vichy, a man well versed in Arabic learning. He journeyed to Rheims, where Archbishop Adalberon placed him at the head of the episcopal school; here Gerbert distinguished himself and the school, and attracted pupils from France and from Germany. Among them was Robert, son of Hugh Capet. In the realm of philosophy, Gerbert did not rise above logic, as his work, *De rationali et ratione uti*, testifies. He was more famous for his knowledge of arithmetic and astronomy, and for the ingenious instruments which he deployed in illustrating his lectures. He was also quite active in politics. His election to the Archiepiscopal see of Rheims in 991 was not ratified by Pope John XV; somewhat later, through the favor of Emperor Otto III, he became Archbishop of Ravenna and, in 999, Pope. During his stay at Rheims, and during his short pontificate, he gave a powerful impulse to the scientific revival which was to arise during the following two centuries.

---

[1] See F. CAYRÉ, *op. cit.*, pp. 387-389. — [2] M. DE WULF, *op. cit.*, Vol. I, p. 135. — [3] Gerbert's works are in vol. CXXXIX of MIGNE'S, *Patrologia latina.* — BRÉMOND, H., *Gerbert*, Paris, 1906. — CONTARDI, E., *Gerberto d'Aurillac meraviglia del suo secolo*, Rome, 1939. — DELZANGLES, F., *Gerbert*, Aurillac, 1932. — ECHENGRÜN, F., *Gerbert als Persönlichkeit*, Leipzig, 1928. — PICAVET, F., *Gerbert ou le pape philosophe*, Paris, 1897.

II. The Problem of Universals.

(11th-12th century).

Bibliography.

Carré, M. H., *Realists and Nominalists*, Oxford, 1946. — De Wulf, M., *Le problème des universaux dans son évolution historique du IXe au XIIIe siècle*, Münster, 1896. — Loewe, K. H., *Der Kampf zwischen Realismus und Nominalismus im Mittelalter*, Prague, 1876. — Robert, G., *Les écoles et l'enseignement de la théologie pendant la première moitié du XIIe siècle*, Paris, 1909.

205. The natural development of the teaching in the schools led to a *literary revival* in the eleventh and twelfth centuries, and the works of St. Bernard, Abelard and John of Salisbury are those of genuine humanists. In the meanwhile, the translation of Aristotle's logic during this period gave a new stimulus to dialectic and became the occasion for raising one of the most absorbing and fundamental problems of philosophy, the problem of universals. With the solution of this problem, the Scholastic movement definitely took steps towards a DOCTRINAL *progress*.

This question was not solved without trials and struggles. In fact, the masters disputed on this question for a long period of time, and the two centuries which this period embraces are truly a golden age of philosophical systems. By outlining the *problem of universals* in its historical development and solution, an idea of the philosophical ferment can be obtained. This question, of course, while it is the main one, is not the sole matter under discussion. In addition to the quite remarkable synthesis of St. Anselm — which will be here considered — other secondary types of progress occurred during this period, and led towards the definitive formation of Scholasticism.

Statement of the Problem. **206.** Porphyry's *Isagoge* [1] or introduction to the categories of Aristotle was, during this period, the manual of the teachers in dialectic. His work concludes by offering the following difficulty : he refuses to state whether genera and species are subsistent entities or whether they consist in concepts alone; if subsisting, whether they are material or immaterial and whether they are separated from the sensible objects or not, this question being a mysterious matter and worthy of more

---

[1] See above, n. 122.

investigation. Boethius, the translator of Porphyry's work, does not offer a more satisfying response. It was with this problem that the first philosophical masters were concerned. It is one of the basic problems of philosophy, a question which dominated Platonism and is to reappear again in Kantianism — What is the validity of our mind and of our knowledge?

It was especially the first part of the latter question which attracted the attention of the early Scholastics in this form : Are the universals real? The universal seems to signify a nature common to many realities, or the idea which makes one know this nature and these realities. Moreover, there at first seems to be an opposition between the characteristics of individual realities and the traits of ideas and of the various branches of learning, for experience witnesses to the fact that individual realities are multiple, changeful and localized. On the other hand, ideas and the various branches of learning deal with an object that is unique, unchanging, necessary and eternal, as, for example, humanity in itself. The masters of the Middle Ages proposed diverse systems in answering this problem; the problem can be better grasped, however, if the possible responses to it are first given.

A) **Theoretically,** four solutions are possible :

1. **Realism.** This view denies the reality of the concrete object (as the object of science) and replaces it by a subsisting idea which possesses all the marks of our abstract concepts; this was Plato's solution. In some fashion, universals have an absolute value or reality; but the solution must be completed in determining where these realities exist — in a separated world, in God, or immanent in material things?

2. **Nominalism.** This view denies the reality of the spiritual idea, and replaces it by a common name which is simply representative of a group of concrete individuals. Furthermore, it holds that there is full correspondence between the universals and the things signified. However, the universality and necessity of the various branches of learning still need explanation.

3. **Conceptualism.** In this view, ideas are considered as given *a priori*, independently of the concrete object. However, between these two extremes, whose existence is admitted, the question of their correspondence is not answered. " The universals have no objectivity other than that fabricated by the mind; a conceptual objectivity, not a real one " [1].

4. **Moderated conceptualism** or **Moderate realism.** This view distinguishes in the universal the nature expressed and its different modes of being. The nature, though remaining the same, can be concretized in matter (theory of individuation), universalized in concepts (theory of abstraction), or realized supereminently

---

[1] M. DE WULF, *op. cit.*, p. 138.

in God as the creative source (theory of exemplarism). This view alone offers the full solution to the problem.

B) **In the Middle Ages,** the philosophers involved in the debate did not at first suspect these nuances of the problem, and merely replied to the question of the reality of universals with a simple affirmation or negation. The earlier Scholastics, as John Scotus Eriugena and Gerbert, generally were inclined to consider the universals as realities, while Rhabanus Maurus calls them pure ideas and Berengarius of Tours reduces them to mere names.

Nevertheless, these first philosophers of being did not run afoul of common sense. Though pure nominalists, they did not deny the existence of ideas in man; or, if pure conceptualists, they did not deny the existence of things outside of man. These are two verities, one of the psychological, and the other of the ontological order, which spontaneously impose themselves on reason. Furthermore, in order to make this presentation conformable to the historical pattern, only two groups of medieval philosophers should be distinguished : 1) the *realists*, who adopt the ontological viewpoint and strongly assert that the universals are in things; 2) the *anti-realists*, who forced the realists to add precision to their view by voicing psychological objections. In this way, slowly and through various systems, speculative thought was directed towards the true answer.

1⁰ — THE REALISTS : METAPHYSICAL ASPECT.

207. Inasmuch as man knows reality, the universals must be among things which exist apart from man; this opinion was viewed as " ancient doctrine " until the twelfth century. ODO of Tournai (or of Cambrai, † 1113) [1] looked into this question in order to explain the transmission of original sin. He concluded that God did not create each of the human souls, but only the accidents which distinguish the individuals of a pre-existing human nature.

A brief historical sketch, in a triple phase, will point out the logical development of this doctrine into pantheism.

---

[1] He wrote a treatise entitled *De peccato originali ;* see M. DE WULF, *op. cit.,* Vol. I, pp. 146-147.

A) **William of Champeaux** [1] (1070-1120).

208. There is little information available concerning William of Champeaux, whose doctrine is known principally through the works of Abelard. He was, for a time, a student of *Anselm of Laon* [2] († 1117) and of the anti-realist, Roscelin [3]. About 1100, he was accoladed a master at the school of Notre Dame in Paris; here he taught the " ancient doctrine " and defended realism quite successfully. The objections of his student, Abelard, had the effect of causing him to modify his position and, finally, to retire to St. Victor in 1108. There he opened a new school which he directed until 1113, when be became Bishop of Châlons-sur-Marne.

William admitted, successively, a theory of identity and one of indifference.

1. **Theory of Identity.** According to this view, one nature — humanity, for example — is numerically one and identical in all individuals in such a way that it is totally realized in each one; the individuals are distinguishable through accidents. From this view, Abelard concluded that Socrates, though actually at Athens, is, at the same time, at Rome, where also is found the human nature which he totally possesses. " The absurdity follows that if Socrates be whipped, then every substance is whipped " [4]. William answered this objection with a distinction.

2. **Theory of Indifference.** It is conceded that only the individuals are real and that the essences are multiplied in them, so that wherever there are many persons, there are also many substances. But in these we must distinguish : *a)* that which is proper and personal to each; and, *b)* that which is common and *indifferent* towards all. This latter element alone constitutes the universal (genus and species) with its own special unity, one of similitude more than of identity : " The humanity of each (i. e., of Peter and of Paul) is not

---

[1] Fragments of William's works can be found in vol. CLXIII of MIGNE's edition of the Latin Fathers. See also G. LEFÈVRE, *Les variations de G. de Champeaux et la question des universaux*, Lille, 1898.

[2] This Anselm was the author of the first theological summary known in the Middle Ages; see M. DE WULF, *op. cit.*, Vol. I, p. 242.

[3] See below, n. 212.

[4] Translated from a quotation in M. DE WULF, *op. cit.*, Vol. I, p. 171, fn. 2.

the same, but similar " [1]. This specific or essential unity [2] is safeguarded by numerical or accidental distinctions.

These latter distinctions tend towards the view of moderated realism, but two important points remain obscure : *a*) in what sense is that which is proper to an individual also *accidental;* as a logical [3] or as a metaphysical [4] accident? *b*) is the unity of the universal purely of an ideal order or does it have a foundation in things? These problems will be taken up and sounded out by the school of Chartres.

B) The School of Chartres [5].

209. Founded in 990 by St. Fulbert (960-1028), the school of Chartres had a special brilliance in the twelfth century, having three successive famous masters. BERNARD OF CHARTRES († 1130), whom a contemporary labelled " the perfectionist of the Platonists of our age, " [6] taught there from 1114 to 1119 and wrote a work entitled *De expositione Porphyrii.* GILBERT DE LA PORRÉE [7] (1076-1154), the disciple and successor of Bernard, taught there twelve years before becoming Master at Paris (1141) and, somewhat later, Bishop of Poitiers. He wrote commentaries on the *De Trinitate* and the *De duabus naturis in Christo* of Boethius. He is more celebrated, however, by his work, *Liber sex principiorum,* in which he completes some of Aristotle's work by treating of the six predicaments, action, passion, time, place, position and *habitus.* This work became a classic in the Middle Ages. His application of realism to the theology of the Trinity, however, was quite rash; and, in 1147, at the request of St. Bernard, a synod of Rheims condemned most of his assertions, which he thereupon retracted. THEODORIC OF

---

[1] G. LEFÈVRE, *op. cit.,* p. 24.

[2] This notion of a " unique nature " is a vague and obscure concept, seemingly possessing contradictory attributes; while it is real, it is also *multiplied* within individuals, and while it is universal, it is *not multiplied.*

[3] That is, not connected with the definition of abstract nature, but capable of pertaining to concrete substance.

[4] That is, not pertaining to every substance, even concrete substance, as a blush in a man.

[5] CLERVAL, A., *Les écoles de Chartres au moyen âge du Ve au XVe siècle,* Paris, 1895. — PARENT, J. M., *La doctrine de la création dans l'Ecole de Chartres,* Paris, 1938.

[6] JOHN OF SALISBURY, *Metalogicus,* IV, 35.

[7] See vols. XLIV and CLXXXVIII of MIGNE's edition of the Latin Fathers. BERTHAUD, A., *Gilbert de la Porrée et sa philosophie,* Poitiers, 1892. — HEYSSE, A., *Liber de sex principiis Gilberto ascriptus,* Munster, 1929.

CHARTRES († 1155), a brother of Bernard, was a savant and philosopher. He wrote a treatise called *De sex dierum operibus*, another called *Eptateuchon*, a manual of the seven liberal arts, and, probably, a commentary on the *De Trinitate* of Boethius [1].

It was with the help of Platonism that these three masters set themselves out towards solving the problem of universals.

1. **Bernard and Theodoric** defended somewhat the same doctrine. In order to resolve the opposition between the concrete and the universal, they appealed to two Platonic theories. At first, they explained *individuality* by means of *matter*, which was drawn out of nothingness by a creative act of God, but which exists apart, as a chaotic and disordered mass. Later, they explained the *universal* and its different characteristics by means of the *exemplary idea*, immutable and eternal, which presents the generic or specific perfection that is to be created within matter to the divine Intelligence; in this way, it is multiplied in individuals.

The manner in which this union of the Divine Idea with matter is realized, is not too clear. Certain texts seem to assert that the union is immediate. Theodoric, for instance, writes : " The Divinity is the form of being for single things, for just as something is luminous from light and warm from heat, so single things are apportioned their being from the Divinity " [2]. This view appears to tend towards pantheism. But other texts clearly distinguish God from His work and speak of " *native forms* " as of intermediaries created in the image of the Divine Ideas in which they participate, and as destined to place order in the chaotic material [3].

These native forms seem to possess two contradictory properties, as did the " apparent nature " of William of Champeaux. For they are at once *a*) unique and immutable, as participatory in the Divine Ideas, and *b*) multiple and changeable by their contact with matter. For Bernard, " they securely possess unity and fixity in contrast with the whole series of changes which correspond to sensible bodies; they alone are the corporeal being, the rest being naught more than a fleeting shadow ". Theodoric writes,

---

[1] See M. DE WULF, *op. cit.*, Vol. I, pp. 175-180.

[2] W. JANSSEN, *Der Kommentar des Clarenbaldus von Arras zu Boethius De Trinitate*, Breslau, 1926, p. 108; this volume includes extracts from Theodoric's *De sex dierum operibus*.

[3] M. DE WULF, (*op. cit*, Vol. I, pp. 187-188) frees the Chartrain philosophers from any vestige of pantheism.

" humanity is numerically one despite the mobile series of individuals in which it exists. *Nature is always one, persons are diverse* "[1].

2. **Gilbert de la Porrée** adds precision to this last point by reviving, in his theory of CONFORMITY, the theory of resemblance of William of Champeaux. At first, he simply affirms that the " native forms " are really distinct from the Divine Ideas of which they are copies, and are multiplied with individuals. But, in comparing these latter among themselves, one finds realized there the same form which reason takes aside *by abstraction;* "somehow, it abstracts "[2]. This *conformable* element, an image of the Divine Idea, constitutes genus or species.

Gilbert, however, is classifiable as an exaggerated realist because he multiplied real distinctions after diverse ideas. For instance, in one individual as Peter, he considered individuality and humanity as perfections really distinct, and even certain attributes, as unity, were viewed in this way. His total view, however, is well oriented towards moderate realism.

3. In addition to its philosophical import, the school of Chartres had a more general influence on the intellectual movement of the twelfth century. The schools of this period often had no other fame than that of the master whose fame made it what it was. Sometimes a school would specialize in a certain realm of learning, as did Tours in poetry, Paris in dialectic and theology, and Montpellier in medicine. The school of Chartres, though, was renowned equally well in all branches of the *Trivium* and the *Quadrivium.*

Two other masters of this period belong to the school of Chartres. WILLIAM OF CONCHES[3] (about 1080-1154) was a humanist and a masterly physician; in philosophy, he defended atomism and the notion of a world soul. JOHN OF SALISBURY[4] (born between 1115 and 1120, died as Bishop of Chartres

---

[1] As quoted in M. DE WULF, *op. cit.*, p. 179.

[2] *In Boet. De Trin.*, (MIGNE, ed., Vol. XLIV), col. 1374.

[3] His *Philosophia* can be found in vol. XC of MIGNE's edition of the Latin Fathers. A recent study on William is H. FLATTEN, *Die Philosophie des Wilhelm von Conches*, Coblenz, 1929.

[4] John's works can be found in vol. CIC of MIGNE's edition of the Latin Fathers. A critical edition of *Metalogicon* was issued by C. C. J. WEBB (Oxford, 1929) as also of his *Policraticus* (2 vols., Oxford, 1909). See also, C. C. J. WEBB's *John of Salisbury*, London, 1932.

in 1180), was the author of *Historia pontificalis* and of a philosophical poem entitled *Entheticus*, or a treatise on the dogmas of philosophers. He is more known for his *Polycraticus* and his *Metalogus* in which he has left a summary history of the different systems of his times. Both of these latter humanists, along with Theodoric of Chartres in his *Heptateucon*, carried on a vigorous and efficacious campaign favoring classical studies; they also defended the usefulness of dialectic, but only by combating the exaggerations of the *sophists*, of whom ADAM *du Petit Pont* was the most famous [1].

C) The Pantheists.

210. The absolute formulas of exaggerated realism tended logically towards pantheism. In the Chartrain school, BERNARD OF TOURS, or Bernardus Silvestris, in his philosophical poem *De mundi universitate*, written between 1145 and 1153, accentuated this tendency by representing the Word of God as the Soul of the World. A little later, at the close of the twelfth century, two philosophers became completely pantheistic, though they did so through two opposed paths.

1. AMALRIC OF BENE [2] († about 1206) is an *idealist*. He adopted the Platonic realism of the school of Chartres as his basic view. In his view, all things are one through participating in God : " All things are one, because whatever is, is God ". God manifests Himself through diverse ideas which are realized perfectly in each being [3]. At the opening of the thirteenth century, a sect of Amalric's followers proposed some heretical consequences in dogma and in morality drawn from Amalric's views. They taught that every man becomes the Holy Spirit (Soul of the World) after five years of age; from this fact it was possible for them to hold that man is beyond sin, and they could justify all moral disorders. The errors of the Cathari

---

[1] Adam was so called, because he taught in a school situated near the little bridge over the Seine river. In his school, they discussed whether a pig led to market is held by a rope or by the one leading it; these and similar discussions, though sometimes identified with Scholasticism, are its counterfeit. See M. DE WULF, *op. cit.*, pp. 209-210.

[2] C. CAPELLE, *Autour du décret de 1210 :* III. *Amaury de Bène. Etude sur son panthéisme formel*, Paris, 1932.

[3] St. Thomas Aquinas writes : " Some maintained that God is the formal principle of all things; this seems to have been the opinion of the Amalricians ". (*Summa Theol.*, I, q. III, art. 8, c.).

and the reveries of *Joachim of Flores* [1] († 1202), during this same period, stemmed from the same source.

2. DAVID OF DINANT in Belgium [2], who is found at the court of Pope Innocent III around 1205, fell into *materialistic* pantheism. In explaining the Aristotelian physics, whose first translations were then appearing, he applied a realistic and sophistic dialectic.

He distinguished *reality*, which is one and unchangeable, from the changing multiplicity of individuals which comprise sheer appearance. There were, then, three realities : primary matter, the common and stable element as the basis for corporeal variety; mind, the common source of thought; God, who plays a similar role for the separated forms. At the same time, these three fundamental and indeterminate realities are to be identified. Their simplicity precludes the possibility of their being different (taking this latter word in the logical sense of a perfection added to a genus to form a species, which would suppose a composition); accordingly, since they cannot be different, they are identical. Both Albert the Great and Thomas Aquinas, speaking of David's view, hold that it makes God's creation of prime matter a senseless affair [3].

Both Amalric of Bene and David of Dinant were condemned in 1210, at the Council held in Paris under Peter of Corbeil, Archbishop of Sens. In 1215, the reading of their works was prohibited by the Cardinal Legate Robert of Courçon, along with those of John Scotus Eriugena [4]. In this way, the vigilance of the Church kept these philosophers from the excesses of their speculations, and favored an anti-realistic reaction.

2⁰ — THE ANTI-REALISTS : PSYCHOLOGICAL ASPECT.

211. To the common sense realist principle that asserts " our ideas are objective, " another common sense principle also proposes, " only the individuals are real ". Already in the eleventh century, Berengarius of Tours had become

---

[1] BETT, H., *Joachim of Flora*, London, 1931. — FOURNIER, P., *Etude sur Joachin de Flore*, Paris, 1909.

[2] G. THERY, *Autour du décret de 1210*. I. *David de Dinant. Etude sur son panthéisme matérialiste*, Paris, 1925.

[3] For discussion on this point, see F. COPLESTON, *op. cit.*, Vol. I, pp. 184-185.

[4] M. DE WULF, *op. cit.*, pp. 239-240.

involved in this latter view, even to the extent of being nominalistic [1]. But in the twelfth century and later, this new view of the universal was sustained with great success; in order to resolve the apparent contradictions which arose, the philosophers were forced to lend precision to the part of the mind in the elaboration of the universal.

A) **Roscelin** [2] (about 1050-1120).

212. Roscelin was a Canon at the Cathedral of Compiegne, and a rather celebrated teacher in this city about 1085. William of Champeaux and Abelard were his pupils; what we know of his doctrine has been preserved through Abelard, and from the accounts of some of his opponents.

Roscelin is known as the first defender of anti-realism. A contemporary writes of him as " the first who, in our times, stabilized the meaning of words " [3]. Roscelin's doctrine, however, was primarily negative and critical. He strongly denied that universals, as general, abstract natures, could be realized in this way. Universals are not things, nor are they concrete individuals. He further held that the object of logic, as Boethius had previously maintained, is primarily the ORAL *universal term ;* in this sense, " the universal is a sound, an utterance of voice " and logic becomes but a superior type of grammar.

But it does not seem that Roscelin pushed his theory any further. Though he denied the proper existence of a " universal in things, " he affirmed the existence of a " universal in speech ". The question then arises : Is there a concept signified by the word and representing things abstractly, a " universal in the mind "? Roscelin is silent on this matter. However, in applying his anti-realism to the explanation of the Holy Trinity, he concluded that the three Divine Persons were really three gods, similar to three angels, and their unity consisted solely in possessing the same power, wisdom and will. This heresy of TRITHEISM was condemned at the Council of Soissons in 1092. His views were refuted by St. Anselm, from the theological, and by Abelard from the philosophical viewpoint.

---

[1] See above, n. 204.
[2] F. PICAVET, *Roscelin, philosophe et théologien d'après la légende et d'après l'histoire*, 2e éd., Paris, 1911. Of Roscelin's writings, we have only a letter addressed to Abelard.
[3] OTTO OF FREISING, *Gesta Frederici imper.*, I, 47.

B) **Peter Abelard** [1] (1079-1142).

213. Born into a military family, Peter Abelard has been called the " Knight of Philosophy ". After brilliant studies under the most celebrated masters, Roscelin, William of Champeaux and Anselm of Laon — during which time he was already proficient in voicing objections — he himself became one of the most famous teachers of the twelfth century. His clarity, fruitfulness, dialectical and critical traits helped to attract thousands of students to the school of St. Genevieve in Paris. But his pride and disorderly life with Heloise brought him numerous disappointments which he tells about in his *Historia calamitatum mearum.* He was forced, principally due to this latter episode, to retire to the abbey of St. Denis and, later, to *Le Paraclet,* where he wrote his principal works. From 1136 to 1140 he returned to teach at Paris, where he had John of Salisbury among his students. Condemned at the Synod of Sens at the insistence of St. Bernard, he was warmly received by Peter the Venerable, the Abbot of Cluny and, later, died penitent at the monastery of St. Marcel lez-Chalons.

Abelard wrote numerous works : expositions of logic under the form of glosses, and a very personal work entitled *Dialectica ;* the *Theologia christiana,* a redaction of an earlier treatise entitled *De unitate et trinitate divina,* and of which another redaction was made called *Introductio ad theologiam;* the *Sic et Non,* a collection of patristic views; the *Scito teipsum,* a treatise on morality which is mindful of the theological frame of reference, but insists on the philosophical notion of conscience, which Abelard places at the center of his doctrine.

1. On the question of universals, Abelard was primarily a demolisher of systems. He proved the exclusive existence of universals against William of Champeaux's realism; against the verbalism of Roscelin, he established the existence

---

[1] Cousin, V., *Ouvrages inédits d'Abélard,* Paris, 1836. — *Petri Abelardi opera,* 2 vols., Paris, 1849-1859. — Geyer, B., *Die philosophischen schriften Peter Abelards,* 4 vols., Munster, 1919-1933. — Gilson, E., *Heloise et Abélard,* Paris, 1938. — McCallum, J. R., (transl.), *Abailard's Ethics,* Oxford, 1935. — Ottaviano, C., *Pietro Abelardo, La vita, le opere, il pensiero,* Rome, 1931. — Remusat, D. De., *Abaelard,* 2 vols., Paris, 1845. — Sickes, J. G., *Peter Abaelard,* Cambridge, 1932. — Waddell, H., *Peter Abaelard,* London, 1939.

of a concept signified by the concrete word[1]. But he also brought together and unified the principal elements of the solution of moderate realism. He proposed that the universal idea (that which he calls "name") expresses a common reality which is nothing other than the *nature* immanent to concrete individuals. This thought content, however, neglects the individual traits due to the *abstractive* action of the mind. Abelard added a *critical* aspect to this psychological view; the universal does not deform the real, for it would then be useless, but, without saying everything, it does speak of that which is. If, for instance, in an individual man, one considers only the nature of substance, "indeed, I understand that which is in him, but do not look towards all that the individual possesses... One thing is understood separately from another thing, but is not considered separated... Through abstraction the mind operates *divisim*, but does not affirm the *divisa*, or else error would occur"[2]. This solution allowed Abelard to insist on the distinction of nature between mind, whose object is the abstract and universal, and sense, whose object is the concrete and singular; it also enabled him to state the significant law of the human mind, that it finds all of the material for its knowledge in sensible experience.

2. Abelard's success as a teacher was even more significant in the application which he made of dialectics and philosophy to theology. Aided by these distinctions, he was able to resolve apparent contradictions in the Fathers of the Church and to explain their teachings. He made popular the method of presentation by precise arguments, arranged in objections and answers to these objections *(sic — non)*, and conceived of a systematic exposition of revelation. In these and other ways, he gave a meaningful impulse to the growing intellectual movement which terminated in the works of the great theologians of the thirteenth century. For Abelard was motivated by a principle which was, in itself, excellent : granted that faith and reason are essentially distinct, it is nonetheless true that theology cannot attain scientific status without the aid of philosophy. As a matter of fact, however, Abelard

---

[1] In other words, Abelard recognized a "name" in addition to the word, or a discourse related to a content which is signified and a reality which is thought about. In this sense, John of Salisbury calls him the founder of the nominalist sect, though this nominalism is, rather, a conceptualism. See M. DE WULF, *op. cit.*, Vol. I, pp. 196-197.

[2] *Dialectica* (Geyer's ed.), p. 26.

applied this principle rashly. For instance, on the pretext
that one must comprehend mysteries to believe them reasonably,
he held that one could demonstrate them. This was his
position with regard to the Holy Trinity and similar mysteries
and led to his condemnation by the Church [1].

C) Moderate Realism.

214. All of these struggles and discussions were not useless.
Abelard's influence, especially, was quite decisive for the
problem of universals and in an anonymous work written
towards the close of the twelfth century, entitled *De intellectibus*
— probably the work of one of his disciples — the perfect
solution of the problem of universals is given. This solution
of MODERATE REALISM is one which concedes that only the
individual exists and yet the universals are expressive of the
real, the word being the symbol for the spiritual idea. These
diverse points are reconciled by the theory of abstraction,
which proposes that the universal is abstracted from individuals.
The mind does not consider the individual traits, but only
the nature that is alike in all. The nature which the universals
truly express is clothed with two distinct modes of being :
concrete and material in the thing, abstract and universal
(spiritual) in the mind. This is the solution which will finally
be accepted unanimously by the Scholastics, and its progressive
elaboration will be pointed out.

However, the common trait of all these philosophers whose
efforts we have outlined is the *lack of systematization;* their
efforts are ineffectual, incomplete and are attempts at settling
some isolated problems. This defect is not found in the work
of St. Anselm, and his work must be given more detailed
attention, as it was of special importance in the whole area
of philosophical speculations.

III. SAINT ANSELM.
(1033-1109).

SPECIAL BIBLIOGRAPHY.

1⁰ **Works :** MIGNE, J., *Patrologia latina*, vols. CLVIII-CLIX. —
SCHMITT, F. S., *S. Anselmi Cantuariensis Archiepiscopi opera
omnia*, 2 vols. completed, Rome, 1938-1940. — DEANE, S. N.,

---

[1] M. DE WULF remarks (*History of Mediaeval Philosophy*, vol. 1, p. 203):
" We will confine ourselves to remarking that in theology, as in philosophy,
the present tendency of historians is rather to rehabilitate Abelard ".

(transl.), *St. Anselm : Proslogium; Monologium; An Appendix in Behalf of the Fool by Gaunilon; and Cur Deus Homo*, Chicago, 1938.

20 **Studies :** BARTH, K., *Fides Quaerens intellectum*, Munich, 1931. — CHURCH, A. W., *St. Anselm*, 3rd ed., London, 1873. — DOMET DE VORGES, S. *Anselme*, Paris, 1901. — FILLIATRE, C., *La philosophie d'Anselme de Cant.*, Paris, 1920. — FISCHER, J., *Die Erkenntnislehre Anselms von Canterbury*, Münster, 1911. — KOYRÉ, A., *L'idée de Dieu dans la philosophie de S. Anselme*, Paris, 1923. — LEVASTI, A., *Sant' Anselmo, Vita e pensiero*, Bari, 1929. — OSTLENDER, H., *Anselm von Cant., der Vater der Scholastik*, Dusseldorf, 1927. — RIGG, J. M., *St. Anselm of Canterbury*, London, 1898. — RULE, M., *The Life and Times of St. Anselm*, 2 vols., London, 1883. — WELCH, A. C., *Anselm and His Work*, Edinburgh, 1901.

215. St. Anselm was born at Aosta in Piedmont. About the age of 20, when his mother died and his father took an unkindly attitude towards him, he left his country and went to Burgundy, then to France, and, finally, to Normandy. Attracted by the fame of his compatriot, Lanfranc, then Abbot of Bec, he went to the abbey to study and entered the religious life there in 1060. He became head of the school, and attracted numerous pupils both by his learning and by his kindness. In 1078, he succeeded Lanfranc as Abbott of Bec, and, in 1093, succeeded him also as Archbishop of Canterbury. In this latter post, he did not abandon his intellectual labors and, at the same time, defended the liberty of the Church against the evils of lay investiture. Anselm nobly resisted the demands of William II Rufus (1087-1100) and was exiled into France and into Italy. Henry Beauclaire (1100-1131) recalled him to England, but further dissensions forced Anselm into exile for three years at Rome. Finally, peace was restored, and Anselm's remaining years were spent in peace with his king.

The main works [1] of Anselm of philosophical interest are : MONOLOGION, a scientific exposition of seventy-nine chapters concerning rational and supernatural theology; to this latter work Anselm added a PROSLOGION, a smaller work containing a decisive proof for the existence of God; *De grammatico* is a work preparatory to a study of the categories; *De veritate* and *De libero arbitrio* are two dialogues written during his abbacy at Bec; the *De fide Trinitatis* is a work refuting Roscelin; other works include treatises on evil, on Redemption, on the

---

[1] See an analysis of these works in F. CAYRÉ, *Manual of Patrology*, Vol. II, pp. 397-404.

fall of the devil, and his *Cur Deus Homo*. His last work, *De concordia*, points out the concord of free will with the divine foreknowledge, predestination and grace.

Anselm adopted St. Augustine as his master and, like him, is principally a theologian. He had the same intense desire of clarifying the truths proposed by revelation with reason as did Augustine, and also had a like notion of the relations between reason and faith which helped to unify his various philosophical views. Anselm, however, is not concerned with the problem of universals, which he treats only incidentally in refuting the tritheism of Roscelin. He was rather concerned with enlarging the field of learning as is shown in his different theological [1] and philosophical researches. While many of the latter are fragmentary, largely due, perhaps, to his many occupations, he can be credited with constituting *theodicy* as a science.

A) **Fundamental Theory.**

216. " Believe in order to understand " [2] : faith is the source of all learning, philosophical and theological, both as the essential foundation producing all truth, and as the moral preparation and guide.

St. Anselm proposed the above proposition as declaratory of the very nature of faith and of knowledge. In his view, faith is an immediate and infallible knowledge of the truth, albeit obscure. Faith comes from outside of man; it is obtained through the teaching of Jesus Christ and His Church and is not the fruit of personal reflection. Faith demands moral conditioning, for it must be accepted by an act of good will as the fruit of grace. At the same time, in thus giving us truth completely fashioned, faith does not open to us its intimate meaning and profound understanding.

This obscurity is to be dissipated by the effort of reason; in this way, faith begets science. Science is thus the clear possession of the truth whose inner content and detail is thus obtained. Man, however, would be incapable of discovering these objects of study if revelation had not presented them to him.

---

[1] In this connection, F. Cayré writes, " The *Cur Deus Homo*... is one of the most penetrating and thoughtful works in the history of Christian speculation ". (*op. cit.*, pp. 402-403).

[2] *Proslogium*, Ch. i.

The respective roles and mutual aid of reason and of faith are thus clarified. Faith is both source and foundation, for its role is to bring the ensemble of truths for philosophical speculation, and to direct reason by orienting its research and preserving it from error. Reason has a double function : it defends the faith and leads unbelievers to its acceptance and it explains what has been revealed by all sorts of arguments, whether merely probable or possible, or necessary and demonstrative.

This collaboration of faith and reason is already constitutive of the Scholastic *method* which grants reason the power to elevate itself to certain truths and to explain revelation. At the same time, Anselm preserves the Augustinian traits of piety and mysticism in his mode of approach; he goes towards the truth as wholeheartedly, and he directs all his investigations towards God, Who is the main concern of faith. It is this high viewpoint which marks his approach to all questions, and is shown, principally, in his theodicy. Thus his principle, " Credo ut intelligam, " serves as a unifying factor in all his philosophy.

217. The domain of faith and of philosophy are not, of course, as scientifically delimited in the above view as they will be in Thomism [1], which will use the notion of formal object. Instead of considering these two sciences in their very nature and the relationships they have as a matter of *right*, St. Anselm views them as actually united in the believer as a *fact*, and applies his reason as much as possible towards comprehension of his faith. If the argument is demonstrative, its domain is that of philosophy, while if it is not, it pertains to theology in the strict sense. This lack of precision is dangerous and could lead to an exaggerated or a minimized function of reason with regard to faith. From one point of view, St. Anselm seems to consider faith in a primary and absolute fashion, without insisting on the necessary preparation of reason, which gives the motives of credibility, thus inclining towards *fideism*. On the contrary, he sometimes seems to credit reason with the power of demonstrating certain mysteries, as that of the Holy Trinity, inclining him towards *rationalism*. Likewise, it seems that the formula, " *Crede ut intelligas* " can be understood as pointing out the moral need of *believing in truth* in order to find it efficaciously [1] or, better, as applying solely to believers without expressing a general law. Nevertheless, St. Anselm, guided by a sure Catholic insight, always recognized the transcendence of mysteries and their inability of being measured by human

---

[1] DOMET DE VORGES, *Saint Anselme*, p. 135. M. De Wulf finds this view exaggerated, and prefers the second; see his *History of Mediaeval Philosophy*, Vol. I, p. 167, n. 4.

reason. It can be concluded that Anselm, similar to every great initiator, expresses the grand truths which he glimpsed in formulas that are not false, but incomplete.

B) Miscellaneous Research.

218. From the apostolic view which he generally adopted, Anselm considered man as the creature most intimately related to God. Obliged to be eternally joined to God by means of his *soul*, man does this by submission to *truth* and by doing the good as an exercise of true *liberty*. There are three important questions of the rational order which arose for St. Anselm from this general position.

1º **Man and the human soul.** Following St. Augustine, Anselm holds that man is composed of two substances, soul and flesh [1], joined in the unity of the person in such a way that the soul is entirely present in each of the parts of the body. He leaves the question of the origin of the soul undecided; for, on the one hand, paternity seems to require that both body and soul come from the parents, and, on the other hand, the soul, being certainly spiritual and capable of knowing God, seems to point to a direct creation of itself by God.

219. The *immortality* of the soul is demonstrated by the following argument. The natural destiny of the soul is to know eternal Truth and to love the absolute Good — to possess God Himself. God, however, exists forever, and it is not possible that He would separate from Himself that which He loves and that whose happiness He has placed in contemplation of Himself. Therefore, the soul must always exist.

The argument is presented in an intuitive mode and in the Augustinian method. While it seems to be valid only for the souls of the just, one can easily show its universal validity by pointing out the two principles which it assumes. The first of these is that the nature of the object determines the nature of the faculties, while the second is that the perfection of the faculties measures the perfection of the substance. Then, inasmuch as the will and the intellect have an immortal object, they require that the soul in which they reside be immortal.

---

[1] *Meditatio*, 19.

2⁰ **Truth and Knowledge. 220.** " The Truth of things is their rectitude " [1] is a general definition of truth given by St. Anselm, by which he understands that each thing realizes the thought of God in such wise that all beings are true through their very essence. This common trait of truth is found in the propositions of logical truth which are called " rectitude of enunciation " and in which the words state that which they should. It is also found in the various uses which Holy Scripture makes of the word " truth " as when it says, for instance, that the devil has lost the truth; the meaning of this use of truth is that the devil keeps his intellect, but has lost the rectitude of the will. When Christ says that he who does the truth will find the light, the expression " does the truth " means " acts with rectitude ". In a strict sense, however, the word truth should be reserved to the intellectual domain, and is then defined as : " Truth is rectitude perceptible by mind alone " [2]. In this latter sense, truth is the rectitude of being as envisaged by reason. The rectitude of the will is most often called justice or moral virtue [3].

St. Anselm's view of truth, similar to that of St. Augustine, is based on the study of God, wherein we search for the LIGHT that will clear our knowledge in the exemplary ideas, and wherein we find the source of our sciences and the explanation of the immutability and of the eternity of our participated truths. Anselm also grants the cooperation of the sensible in the formation of our ideas. Intelligence, in his view, turns towards memory, which conserves outward impressions; in order to explain what things are, mind forms unto itself an image which is similar to that which it sees. In this fashion there arises the mental " word " in memory [4].

From this Augustinian perspective, St. Anselm naturally inclined towards realism in the problem of universals. He does not treat the question except incidentally in his refutation of Roscelin. The latter held to tritheism because he held that only individuals were real. St. Anselm, instead, compared the unity of the Divine Nature existing in three Persons to the unity of space existing in many individuals, as if the reality

---

[1] " Veritatem rerum esse rectitudinem ". *De Veritate*, 7.
[2] " Justitia est rectitudo voluntatis propter se servata ". *De Veritate*, 12.
[3] *Ibid.*, 12.
[4] *Monologium*, 47. This is the Augustinian doctrine of illumination; see above, nn. 165-167.

pertained especially to the universal nature. These realities, however, he located in the exemplary Ideas, in which all creatures partake. The notion of a " *universale ante rem* " he placed in the Creative Word.

3° **Liberty. 221.** In his study of liberty, St. Anselm adopts his customary moral viewpoint. He declines to define liberty as the power of choosing between good and evil, for this definition excludes liberty from God and from angels. Inasmuch as liberty is a great perfection to be found not in sin but in virtue, it is rightly defined as the power of maintaining the rectitude of the will [1].

St. Anselm did not deny the existence of liberty in bad actions, but he aimed to refute the " libertine " who claimed to be necessarily enchained to evil and he wished to show him that in giving man liberty God gave man the power of never yielding, despite himself. Anselm's view of the will, then, is more moral than psychological. Liberty presupposes both will and reason, and can never be attributed to beings inferior to man.

In order to harmonize liberty with the divine foreknowledge, Anselm appeals to the divine Eternity present in an indivisible and simultaneous fashion at all times, and to the principle that knowledge does not change the nature of the object known but merely accepts the object and expresses what it is. In this way, though knowing all our free actions, God does not make them occur necessarily.

In Conclusion, the above views are fragmentary and their point of view remains incomplete. Anselm's view of psychological liberty is but fragmentary, and his theory of illumination is not coordinated with the views on the value of universal ideas which were prevalent in his time. In him, however, there can be found, in a germinal state, some of the great Scholastic views. Finally, Anselm's theodicy, which shall be examined, is also incomplete.

C) The Founding of Theodicy.

222. In the latter part of the *Monologium* Anselm develops this branch of philosophy, and, in using reason to help explain

---

[1] " Libertas arbitrii est potestas servandi rectitudinem voluntatis propter ipsam rectitudinem ". *De libero arbitrio*, 3.

faith, according to his principle " Credo ut intelligam ", founds theodicy as a true science. The rigor of his reasoning, however, does not mar the genuine piety of his treatise, and he aimed to help the monks elevate their hearts to God through an understanding of their faith. He divides theodicy into three branches : the existence of God, God's relations with the world, and God's intimate nature.

1º **The existence of God.** God's existence is first established through the Platonic and the Augustinian proofs : the multiple and varied beings, perfections and degrees of greatness which we behold demand a source which is essentially Being, Perfection and Greatness. Anselm, interested mainly in loving God, insists strongly on the aspect of *goodness*. There are many good things in the universe which are not absolutely good but merely partake in it; reason demands the existence of Goodness Itself, through which all other things are good, and this Goodness is God. This argument is also given in a most personal fashion; from the inequality of perfections and the hierarchy of natures, he concludes to the existence of a supreme, independent degree, the Divine Nature.

223. St. Anselm is well known for his A PRIORI ARGUMENT [1] for God's existence; the argument is found in his *Proslogion*, and is considered as an infallible, short and easy way of silencing the senseless man who says that there is no God[2]. The essential statement of the proof follows : God is a being greater than which none can be thought to exist; the fool himself understands this definition and can be convinced that such a being exists, at least in mind. But that which is so great that nothing greater than it can be conceived, cannot exist only in mind; for, supposing that it existed solely in mind, one could represent to himself some thing which would exist both in mind and in reality — which latter thing would, then, be greater. Therefore, this being, which is such that no greater can be conceived, exists, without any doubt, both in mind and in reality.[3]

---

[1] The argument is also called " *a simultaneo* " by some scholars, inasmuch as it does not argue from effects to causes, but through mere analysis of the concept. Kant calls it ontological, in contrast with cosmological proofs. Various views on this argument are collected in S. N. Deane's translation, *St. Anselm*, cited in bibliography, above.

[2] " The fool hath said in his heart : there is no God ". *Psalm* XIII, 1.

[3] *Proslogium*, 2.

This argument was not acceptable to Gaunilon, a monk of Marmoutier. The latter wrote a short work, *Liber pro insipiente*, in which he maintained that one could never conclude to the existence of a thing through an analysis of its idea. If one conceives of a most beautiful island in the ocean, does it follow that the island exists? Anselm answered this objection in his *Liber apologeticus ad insipientem* [1], that the objection is valid for all other ideas *except that of God;* only the idea of God is expressive of a nature so great that one cannot conceive of a greater, and such a nature comprises existence among its essential perfections, for it is the nature of a necessary and eternal being. Consequently, such a Being necessarily exists.

This argument is famous throughout the history of philosophy. It is defended by some thinkers, though colored to suit their views; among these are St. Bonaventure [2], Duns Scotus [3], Descartes [4], and Leibniz [5]. Some, following the lead of St. Thomas Aquinas, and some moderns, following the view of Kant, reject the argument as being an illegitimate transfer from the logical to the real order. St. Thomas writes : " Granted that anyone will understand the name God to signify ' that greater than which nothing can be conceived ' it does not follow that what he understands as signified by the name is in reality, but solely in the apprehension of the mind. It cannot be argued that it exists in reality, unless there would be something in reality greater than which nothing could be conceived " [6].

2º **Relations with the world. 224.** Here Anselm adopts the Augustinian theodicy [7]. Except for the supreme Goodness of God, everything has a participated goodness and being, so that it necessarily owes its existence to God; He lets His perfection overflow into each being according to the pattern of the exemplary ideas. This participation is a CREATION, or a production of each being with nothing being presupposed. God could not transform a preexisting material, for the latter, being the weakest of realities, has no being of itself and does not preexist to the divine action; nor could God transform non-being, which could furnish nothing to His action. God is the Creator in the proper sense of the word.

Two corollaries capable of nourishing piety towards God flow from this view. First, the world continually depends on God through His conserving power, for He has produced

---

[1] " Omnia possunt cogitari non esse, præter id quod summe est ". *Liber apologeticus,* 4.

[2] See below, n. 271-I.

[3] See below, n. 295.

[4] See below, n. 329.

[5] See below, n. 364.

[6] *Summa Theologica,* I, q. XI, art. I, ad 2.

[7] See above, n. 158-160.

the entirety of its being both as to its duration and as to its appearance; in this way, the mind is naturally lifted towards its Author. Secondly, it can be concluded that God is intimately present to all things and especially to man, who can adore and love Him always.

3° **Nature of God. 225.** Having arrived at the existence of the infinite Goodness Who is Self-existent and at the Necessary Being Who cannot be conceived of as non-existent, Anselm next considers the attributes of God, which he deduces scientifically.

a) God is absolutely SIMPLE and IMMUTABLE. Composition of any sort cannot be His characteristic, since the union of parts demands a superior cause on which it depends. God is a substance without accidents, an essence identified with His existence; from the latter trait follows the impossibility of God ever ceasing to be. His immutability follows from His simplicity, for one can neither change nor destroy a simple being.

b) God is *supereminently* PERFECT. Inasmuch as one can give only that which he himself possesses, God possesses all the perfections with which He has filled the world : life, goodness, liberty, intelligence, and so forth.

St. Anselm distinguished two types of perfections. The first are those *whose negation makes them better*, for they are always mixed with limits and imperfections, as to grow, and to learn; it is much better to possess life or knowledge in an immutable manner. The second are those which are *always better than their negation* [1], for they involve no imperfection at all, as intelligence or goodness. Properly speaking, God possesses only these latter perfections and even these in an unspeakable mode, much more perfectly than creatures; in fact, they are all to be identified with the divine simplicity.

Two other attributes, God's OMNIPRESENCE AND ETERNITY follow from the above. God's excellence is manifested through dominating all places and all times, which He fills with His Power and, accordingly, through His essence, which is indistinguishable from His Power. Furthermore, since He is simple

---

[1] *Monologium*, 15. This is the first time this important distinction is taught; it is later called a MIXED or a PURE perfection, and enables us to be precise in our knowledge of God.

and immutable, He is totally and entirely in every place at every moment.

c) Anselm's theodicy is concluded with a theological study of the Trinity. He shows that the difficulties of Roscelin's tritheism can be avoided if a distinction be made between the *absolute* perfections of God which pertain to His nature, and the *relative* [1] attributes which express the intimate life of God. In his analysis of the Second Person, the Word of God, Anselm shows how God possesses perfect science and Providence.

CONCLUSION. **226.** St. Anselm's system is incomplete, and his work contains the imperfection of the patristic period in its lack of clear distinction between the domain of philosophy and that of theology. At the same time, through applying his powerful mind towards the understanding of faith, he is the precursor of the great theologians of the thirteenth century, even though he uses a less rigorous and more personal form of argumentation. His researches are like a voyage of discovery in the realm of Divine Truth, in which the soul will find its happiness, but it lacks the achievement and classicism of a work like the *Summa Theologica* of St. Thomas Aquinas.

Without making this his explicit intention, St. Anselm worked towards restoring philosophy as a science, distinct from dialectical exercises and from theology. This he did by bringing up the main problems of psychology, theodicy and ethics. In recovering its role and proper domain, philosophy acquires the right of having its own place in the realm of sciences.

227. The intellectual movement inaugurated by St. Anselm was continued in the twelfth century. Slowly philosophy became distinguished from theology. Three groups of theologians were operative in this task :

1⁰ The *dialecticians*, following Abelard [2], aimed to continue the work of Anselm by applying reason to the understanding of faith. Their precipitancy in this regard, however, led some of them into heresy and awakened the reaction of a econd group.

2⁰ The *intransigent theologians* formed a group which either completely or in large part wished to proscribe dialectics from theology, holding that theology is a sacred study into whose pu view

---

[1] Thus, for instance, *Goodness* is common to all three Persons (as are the works *ad extra*, as creation) ; but Paternity is proper to the First Person.

[2] See n. 213, above.

only the commentaries of the Fathers of the Church and the pious meditations of prayer could be admitted. St. PETER DAMIEN [1] (988-1072) was the precursor of this group; he held that profane science is subordinate to sacred science " velut ancilla dominæ ". In the twelfth century, St. BERNARD [2] (1091-1153) is the vigilant defender of the faith and of this view. Others of this group were more extreme, and one of them called dialectics the art of the devil [3].

3° The MIDDLE group comprises those who did not reject the use of dialectics, but limited its usage. They used it less as a means of demonstrating truth and explaining faith and more as a means of coordinating the materials of teaching.

This latter view is found especially in the *Mystical School of St. Victor*, whose two main representatives are HUGH OF ST. VICTOR [4] (master of the school from 1125 to 1142), and RICHARD OF ST. VICTOR [5] († 1173). These men proposed a new classification of the sciences in which a good place was reserved for philosophy; the object of philosophy, in their view, was the study of all human and divine things. They also furthered psychology through their teachings on moderate realism and on the notion of abstraction. Their principal contribution, though, is the study of affective contemplation of divine things which surpasses the forces of nature and is achieved with the help of faith and supernatural grace. This latter aspect is the one which made their influence lasting and effective.

The *eclectics* can also be placed among the theologians of this middle group. They aimed to unify logically all the theological views being taught at this time. They are known as the authors of the " *Summas,* " as ALAN OF LILLE [6] († 1212), and PETER LOMBARD [7] (about 1100-1160), whose *Liber Sententiarum* became a theological classic and was commented upon hundreds of times.

These attempts at synthesis and at classification, which became multiplied at the latter part of the twelfth century,

---

[1] Damien's works can be found in MIGNE, vols. CXLIV-CXLV; see also J. ENDRÈS, *Petrus Damiani und die weltliche Wissenschaft*, Munster, 1910.

[2] St. Bernard's works can be found in MIGNE, vols. CLXXXII-CLXXXV; see also the following : GILSON, E., *The Mystical Theology of St. Bernard*, London, 1940. — MITERRE, P., *La doctrine de saint Bernard*, Bruxelles, 1932. — VACANDARD, E., *Vie de saint Bernard*, 2 vols., Paris, 1910.

[3] This expression comes from Gautier of St. Victor.

[4] Hugh's works can be found in MIGNE, vols. CLXXV-CLXXVII. — BERTAZZI, G., *La filosofia di Hugo da S. Vittore*, Albrighi, 1912. — MIGNON, A., *Les origines de la scolastique et Hughues de Saint-Victor*, 2 vols., Paris, 1895.

[5] Richard's works can be found in MIGNE, vol. CXCVI. — EBNER, J., *Die Erkenntnislehre Richards von Sankt Viktor*, Munster, 1917.

[6] Alan's works can be found in MIGNE, vol. CCX. — BAUMGARDNER, B., *Die Philosophie des Alanus de Insulis*, Munster, 1896. — HUIZINGA, J., *Ueber die Verknüpfung des Poetischen mit dem Theologischen bei Alanus de Insulis*, Amsterdam, 1932.

[7] Lombard's works can be found in MIGNE, vols. CXCI-CXCII. — ESPEN-BERGER, J., *Die Philosophie des Petrus Lombardus und ihre Stellung im XIIen Jahrhunderts*, Munster, 1901. On the authors mentioned above, see F. CAYRÉ, *op. cit.*, Vol. II, pp. 421-469.

are a sign of maturity in the teaching of the schools, whose prosperity in intellectual matters was on the increase. Nor was it possible, during this period, to arrest the development of natural reason or philosophy even in the name of faith; the dialecticians finally carried away the victory. The later appearance of the works of Aristotle makes this force of reason irresistible and leads to the apogee of Scholastic philosophy.

CHAPTER II.

THE CULMINATION.

(13th century).

GENERAL BIBLIOGRAPHY.

CHENU, M.-D., *La théologie comme science au XIIIe siècle*, 2e éd., Paris, 1943. — DENIFLE, H., and CHATELAIN, A., *Chartularium universitatis Parisiensis*, 4 vol., Paris, 1889-1897. — DE WULF, M., *Histoire de la Philosophie médiévale, II, Le XIIIe siècle*, Paris, 1936[1]. — FÉRET, P., *La faculté de théologie de Paris et ses docteurs les plus célèbres*, 7 vols., Paris, 1889-1904. — KREBS, E., *Theologie und Wissenschaft nach der Lehre der Hochscholastik*, Munster, 1912. — LANDRY, B., *L'idée de chrétienté chez les scolastiques du XIIIe siècle*, Paris, 1929. — LITTLE, A. G., and PELSTER, FR., *Oxford Theology and Theologians, A. D.* 1282-1302, Oxford, 1934. — MANDONNET, P., *Siger de Brabant et l'averroïsme latin*, 2e éd., 2 vols., Louvain, 1908-1911.

228. The immense labors of doctrinal formation which had gone on for four centuries blossomed out, in the thirteenth century, into a magnificent revival of both theology and philosophy. As in the golden age of the pagan era, so here, too, we find no schools or fragmentary views, but powerful personalities, each of whom offers a complete philosophical synthesis. The schools rather follow and continue the teachings of the great masters. St. Thomas is incontestably the greatest of these men. He is preceded by important thinkers, of course, and other independent or rival thinkers abound. Three articles will deal with this golden era :

Article I.   The Precursors to St. Thomas Aquinas.

Article II.   St. Thomas Aquinas.

Article III.   The Non-Thomistic Syntheses.

---

[1] Unless otherwise indicated, references are henceforth translated from this edition.

ARTICLE I.

THE PRECURSORS TO ST. THOMAS AQUINAS.

229. The expression *precursors* here refers not only to the masters and especially to St. Albert the Great, whose doctrines St. Thomas knew and utilized, but also to the manifold circumstances from which Thomism arose. This great synthesis was possible only through the convergence of a certain number of causes which explain many of its tenets and its general orientation. Furthermore, these originative causes explain more than the rise of Thomism itself, for they form the general frame of reference in which all the varied systems arise. In this way they point to the common parentage and common doctrinal bases which mark the Scholastic epoch. Three paragraphs will expand upon these notions:

I. The Circumstances.

II. The First Aristotelian Masters.

III. St. Albert the Great.

I. The Circumstances.

230. At the opening of the thirteenth century, a triple circumstance was especially favorable towards furthering the culmination of Scholasticism and the birth of Thomism : the rise of the universities, the founding of the mendicant orders, and the translations of Aristotle.

A) The Rise of the Universities [1].

Towards the close of the twelfth century, the fame of the episcopal schools of Paris attracted masters and students in increasing numbers, causing the latter to unite into associations modelled on the trade guilds of that period. The

---

[1] Bonnerot, J., *La Sorbonne. Sa vie, son rôle, son œuvre à travers les siècles*, Paris, 1927. — Denifle, H., *Les Universités françaises au moyen âge*, Paris, 1892. — Ehrle, F., *I piu antichi statuti della facolta dell' universita di Bologna*, Bologne, 1932. — Feret, P., *La faculté de théologie de Paris et ses docteurs les plus célèbres*, 4 vols., Paris, 1894-1897. — Gibson, S., *Statuta antiqua Universitatis Oxoniensis*, Oxford, 1931. — Leach, A. F., *The Schools of Mediaeval England*, Oxford, 1916. — Luchaire, F., *L'Université de Paris sous Philippe-Auguste*, Paris, 1899. — Rashdall, H., *The Universities of Europe in the Middle Ages*, 3 vols., Oxford, 1934.

body of teachers and students associated with the Cathedral School of Notre Dame and the other schools of Paris acknowledged the jurisdiction of the Chancellor of the Cathedral. In 1200, Philip II Augustus approved this union, and Robert of Courçon sanctioned its statutes in 1215. Thus the first and most famous university of the Middle Ages was born. It served as a model for all the others : Bologna (beginning of thirteenth century, famous for law), Toulouse (1233), Salamanca (1248), Oxford [1] (1258), Montpellier (1289, famous for medicine) and, much later, Louvain (1425). The University of Paris had most of the great Scholastics as teachers, including St. Thomas. A few notions will be given concerning its organization.

Following the traditions of the various cathedral schools of Notre Dame, the University of Paris comprised two faculties, that of theology and that of philosophy. The latter was spoken of as " Master-of-arts " due to the seven liberal arts in which the philosopher was educated; later, law and medicine were added to the faculties.

In a sense [2], the faculty of " arts " was the most important, since it served as a preparation for the others. In addition, the " art-students " formed the majority of students, grouped according to the various nations, French, Picards, Normans, English and Spanish. Since one remained affiliated to his own nation after he terminated his philosophical studies, these national groups represented the whole University. The " art-students " had the right to elect a " Rector " as their head; the latter was in constant conflict with the Chancellor, and, in the fourteenth century, supplanted the chancellorship.

The statutes required an age of twenty for teaching in the arts; the arts course lasted six years. In theology, these requirements were thirty-four years for teaching and eight years of study. The student was required to pass through three stages. The first of these was the Baccalaureate; it required a preliminary examination in the presence of three or four masters, followed by a public defence of his thesis during the season of Lent. This action was called the " determination ", for the candidate did

---

[1] While the beginnings of the University of Oxford date to the early part of the 13th century, its definitive organization was not accomplished until 1258. The University of Cambridge in England was founded about this same time.

[2] " The members of the Faculties of Arts were in the majority and also the most turbulent. After a century and a half of agitation they succeeded in obtaining their own rector. But this numerical and administrative advantage cannot hide the fact that the arts were merely a stage leading to the superior courses and degrees, notably theology, which held first place. Philosophy, which crowns the arts, is but the servant of theology... ". F. CAYRÉ, op. cit., Vol. II, p. 471.

not merely argue in favor of or against the proposed theses, but was to resolve and determine he disputed points [1]. During the next two years, as a bachelor and under the direction of the master, the student explained the manuals in use; then he presented himself to the Chancellor to receive his " license " or permission to teach in his own right. The final step occurred when he gave his first, solemn inaugural lecture, and it was then that he was entitled " Master of Arts " or " Doctor ".

The faculty of theology also had three stages, through that of the Baccalaureate in theology had three subdivisions. During three successive Lenten seasons, the aspirant had to defend his propositions by explaining first the Bible in a literal interpretation, then the Book of Sentences of Peter Lombard, and finally the Bible in a more profound sense; this led to the distinction of a Baccalaureate with regard to the Bible, the Sentences, and a completed Baccalaureate [2]. Following the above, the student had to defend successfully four argumentations before his colleagues, permitting him, thus, to receive his " license " and his " mastership ".

The course of teaching followed that of the schools [3], which included the lesson or commentary, and the disputation, which was of special interest when directed by a celebrated master. The most famous of these disputations were held in theology, but the Scholastic method, especially as practiced by St. Thomas Aquinas, constantly obliged the master of theology to deal with philosophical propositions [4].

LIBERTY AND INTERNATIONALISM were the two principles which dominated the organization of the University of Paris. Whoever had successfully undergone the examinations could establish himself as a master, at the service of the national group which chose him, or even remain a master on his own. The students were free to choose their courses; their sole obligation was to be attached to a master. This freedom was very favorable towards enhancing the influence of the more famous masters and, of course, engendered rivalries. But all did not remain at Paris as entitled professors engaged in actual teaching *(Magistri actu regentes)*, some were merely honorary doctors *(Magistri actu non regentes)* who either gave themselves over to further study or returned, as professors, to their own country.

Paris was, at this time, the great intellectual center; it was also international, for students from all the western world flocked there. The title of Doctor from the University of Paris was of such great renown that in 1292, Pope Nicholas IV granted those holding it the right to teach in other universities without undergoing a new examination. The kings of France protected and endowed

---

[1] M. DE WULF, *op. cit.*, Vol. II, p. 10.

[2] This was the origin of the numberless Scholastic commentaries on the Bible and on the Sentences of Peter Lombard.

[3] See above, n. 199, 2.

[4] Two forms of disputation were distinguished : the *ordinary*, on a subject chosen by the master, and the disputatio *" de quolibet"*, on any subject at all. For further details see below, n. 239-241.

this prosperous and influential university. But it was especially the Church and the Sovereign Pontiffs which determined the direction of the university. At a time when most of the students were destined for the priesthood [1], an intellectual center like the university was, necessarily, either a seed bed of heresies or a source of Catholic truth for the whole of Christianity. In order to assure the latter result, the Popes continually watched what was being taught, condemned heretical books, expelled dangerous teachers and favored the most orthodox teachers. Thus a legitimate control was exercised over the faith, while reason was left at liberty in its pursuit of truth.

B) The Mendicant Orders [2].

231. At the close of the twelfth century, philosophy flourished especially in the Cathedral schools; during the first part of the thirteenth century, only secular professors taught at the University of Paris. Two great religious orders, better adapted to the intellectual needs of their times than were the ancient monks, were founded during this period; the Franciscans, by St. Francis of Assisi in 1214, and the Dominicans, by St. Dominic in 1217. These religious orders soon took over the lead in the theological and philosophical movement, were often attacked by the jealousy of the secular masters, but were strongly defended by papal intervention.

The Dominicans, who inscribed a course of studies into the rule of their society, set up houses in the various intellectual centers, as Paris and Bologna. There they found a great number of recruits among the teachers and the masters. Each of the Dominican houses had its own school; officially, it is true, these schools had " sacred studies " as their principal function, but theology and Scripture were obligatory branches for religious, and open to secular students. Three types of centers were distinguished : the *studium ordinarium*, with a master and a few assistants; the *studium solemne*, for a province, with a master and one or two bachelors who interpreted the Bible and the *Book of Sentences* and held public debates; the *studium generale*, with a master and two

---

[1] Most of the great Scholastic philosophers, with rare exceptions, as Siger of Brabant (see n. 247, below), were theologians.

[2] DE MARTIGNE, S., *La scolastique et les traditions franciscaines*, Paris, 1888. — DE SEESEVALLE, F., *Histoire générale de l'Ordre de Saint François*, Paris, 1935-1937. — DOUAIS, C., *Essai sur l'organisation des études dans l'Ordre des Frères Prêcheurs aux XIIIe et XIVe siècles*, Paris, 1884. — FELDER, H., *Geschichte der wissenschaftlichen Studien im Franziskanerorden bis um die Mitte des 13 Jahrhunderts*, Fribourg (B.), 1904. — GRATIEN, P., *Histoire de la fondation et de l'évolution de l'Ordre de Frères mineurs, au XIIIe siècle*, Gembloux, 1928. — MANDONNET, P., *Saint. Dominique. L'idée, l'homme et l'œuvre*, Gand, 1911. — MORTIER, P., *Histoire des maîtres généraux de l'ordre des Frères Prêcheurs*, 5 vols., Paris, 1903-1911.

bachelors, which performed the same functions as the latter, but recruited its masters and its students from all the provinces.

The most famous *studium generale* was that at the convent of St. James in Paris; it was incorporated into the University of Paris in 1229, and a second chair was conceded to it in 1231. In 1248, four new general centers were established : at Oxford, Cologne, Montpellier and Bologna. At the close of the thirteenth century, most of the eighteen Dominican provinces had their own intellectual centers.

Theology, as it was taught in the best schools of this period, required a philosophical formation. Accordingly, despite the custom which prevented religious from teaching the seven liberal arts, the Dominicans prudently [1] organized purely philosophical studies in their centers; originally reserved to religious, they were opened to the public in the fourteenth century. This action gave the Dominicans a great doctrinal influence in the great age of Scholasticism, and the Papacy found them to be of great help in preserving the Catholic spirit throughout the powerful intellectual movement within the universities, and especially in the University of Paris. Pope Clement V (1305-1314) founded a school in the pontifical palace at Avignon and put it under a Dominican master; he instituted the office of " Master of the Sacred Palace " which has since been filled by a Dominican.

The Franciscans also entered into the movement of studies and were encouraged and favored by the Popes; their school at Paris was incorporated into the university in 1231. The example of both of these great orders led others to open schools in Paris also : the Cistercians in 1256, the Hermits of St. Augustine in 1287, and the Carmelites in 1295. The seculars themselves followed this example, forming *colleges* where the theology students were trained for debate and for preaching. The most famous of these was the Sorbonne, founded by Robert Sorbon, chaplain to Louis IX, in 1253.

C) **Translations of Aristotle** [2].

232. Until the thirteenth century, the Scholastics were not acquainted with Aristotle except for his logical treatises as translated and commented upon by Boethius. But the Crusades and contact with the Arabs in Spain opened to them the doctrinal treasures of antiquity; these writings arrived at a time when everything was ready in the schools to profit most from them. Thus it was through the Arabian intermediary that the thought of Aristotle

---

[1] The constitutions of 1228 allowed them to do this by way of exception; gradually, the exception became the rule. See F. CAYRÉ, *op. cit.*, Vol. II, p. 486.

[2] CALLUS, D. A., *Introduction of Aristotelian Learning to Oxford*, London, 1944. — GRABMANN, M., *Forschungen über die lateinischen Aristotelesübersetzungen des XIII Jahrhunderts*, Munster (W.), 1916. — JOURDAIN, A., *Recherches critiques sur l'âge et l'origine des traductions latines d'Aristote*, 2e éd., Paris, 1843. — LUQUET, J., *Aristote et l'Université de Paris pendant le XIIIe siècle*, Paris, 1904. — TALAMO, S., *L'aristotelismo della scolastica nella storia della filosofia*, 3e ed., Paris, 1876.

was translated into Latin at the close of the twelfth century;
Archbishop Raymond (1126-1151) established a college of such
translators in his diocese. *John of Spain, Gerard of Cremona*
(† 1187) and *Dominicus Gundissalinus* [1] are of special importance;
they translated, besides Aristotle, the principal works of Alkindi,
Alfarabi, Algazel, Avicebron, Avicenna, Maimonides and Averroes,
and other scientific works, as those of Ptolemy and Galen.

At the beginning of the thirteenth century, a new group of
translations of the same type was done in Sicily at the court
of Frederick II (1194-1250) and Manfred (1258-1266), whose more
famous translators were *Michael Scot, Herman the German* and
Bartholomew of Messina; they were especially instrumental in
popularizing the work of Averroes.

The imperfection of these translations from the Arabic was
evident; most of the great Scholastics preferred Latin translations
done directly from the Greek. Two men were distinguished in
this regard : the Englishman *Robert Grosseteste* (1175-1253)
who translated the *Nichomachean Ethics* and the Pseudo-
Dionysius, and especially *William of Moerbeke*, a Dominican
(died as Archbishop of Corinth about 1286). At the request
of St. Thomas Aquinas, the latter gave a new Latin edition of the
principal works of Aristotle directly from the Greek, and also
translated commentaries of Simplicius, Alexander of Aphrodisias,
Themistius, the *Elementatio theologica* of Proclus which included
the *Liber de causis*, the medical works of Hippocrates and Galen,
the treatises of Archimedes and others. These translations were
considered classics both then and even now; they are literal and
faithful even though lacking in elegance of style [2].

The Scholastics found this influx of new ideas a rich mixture
for their own studies, not merely in philosophy but in medicine,
chemistry, astronomy, mathematics and the whole ensemble
of human learning. Thus was accompli hed what can, in a wide
sense, be called the RENAISSANCE, [3] which allowed Latin Europe
to ass milate all the aspects of ancient culture. The thirteenth
century thus discovered the thought of the ancients synthesized
in the work of Aristotle, and, through the influence of the Arabs
and Augustinian followers, the riches of Platonism.

The entrance of the Philosopher [4] into the schools was
an event which gave the thirteenth century its proper tone.

---

[1] Gundissalinus was an eclectic compiler, inclined towards Aristotelianism
and to Arabic Neo-Platonism; five of his works are extant : *De divisione Philosophiæ, De immortalitate animæ, De processione mundi, De unitate* and *De anima.*

[2] See M. DE WULF, *History of Mediaeval Philosophy*, Vol. II, p. 245 (5 th ed.).

[3] Three stages can be distinguished in the *Renaissance*. The first is the *juridic*
Renaissance in which Roman law was adopted as the basis for the new societies
devolving from barbaric invasions in the 11th to 12th centuries. The *doctrinal*
Renaissance is the one referred to above. The *literary* Renaissance in the
16th century, which absorbed the ancient conceptions into various artistic
forms, is the third. This latter is usually called Renaissance without qualification;
see below, n. 311.

[4] This is the Scholastic term for Aristotle, *the Philosopher.*

Pagan wisdom, expressed in a vast, scientific synthesis with its own ideal of life, confronted the wisdom of Christianity, which had, until then, been the sole governess of spirits [1]. Of course, the encounter was one which witnessed many clashes.

Four stages of the progressive conquest of Aristotle over the medieval thinkers can be distinguished, especially at the University of Paris [2]. The first, which extended from about 1200 to 1230, is that of the " first skirmishes " between philosophy and the orthodox view. During this period the attempts of the Latins to use Aristotelianism was not very successful, occasioning the pantheistic doctrines of Amalric of Bene and of David of Dinant [3]. The ecclesiastical authorities had to intervene in this matter. In 1210, a Council of the Province of Sens met at Paris, and prohibited the private or public teaching of the " natural philosophy " of Aristotle [4] and of the Arabic commentaries; it was this same Council which condemned Amalric of Bene and David of Dinant. In 1215, Robert of Courçon, the Papal Legate, sustained this prohibition for the university, and this state of affairs was generally observed even around 1230.

From about 1230 to 1260, there occurred the second stage of " appeasement, " which worked favorably towards Aristotle and secured a triumph in the official teaching. In 1231, at the time of the reorganization of the University of Paris and in the wake of the grave scholarly decline of 1229, a scholarly attempt was made to correct the prohibited works, and Pope Gregory IX (1227-1241) no longer upheld the prohibitions except provisorily. The Pope nominated a commission of three Masters in theology, who were to check over the works of Aristotle. A new spirit arose in favor of Aristotle as a direct result, so that about 1245, Roger Bacon was able to explain

---

[1] Inasmuch as St. Augustine was the main source from which the masters of this period derived their doctrine, there was a strong current of Augustinianism, mainly theological, though bearing with it some elements of Neo-Platonic philosophy. This current remained throughout the 13th century, and formed the main bulwark of resistance against the rising influence of Aristotle. See below, n. 250.

[2] Paris, at this time, was the center of philosophical and theological culture, and the development of doctrine there observable is a faithful reflection of the whole of Latin Christianity. See, in this connection, F. VAN STEENBERGHEN, *Siger de Brabant d'après ses œuvres inédites*, 2 vols., Louvain, 1931-1932.

[3] See n. 210, above.

[4] Aristotle's logic or ethics were never banned.

all the works of Aristotle in Paris, as he had done at Oxford and other places [1] without provoking any prohibitions. This teaching of Aristotle, while optional at first, quickly became general, and the new statutes of the Faculty of Arts of the University of Paris, promulgated on March 19, 1255, officially required studies on all the known works of Aristotle. Thus the previous prohibitions fell into disuse with the tacit approval of the Church [2]. With an acclaim that was almost unanimous, the thinkers of this period assimilated the richness of Greece. The great commentaries of Averroes, which were known in Paris about 1245 [3], were favorable to this movement and yet were preparatory for the dangers native to new teachings.

In the meanwhile, this intense study of pagan philosophy brought about a crisis which constitutes the third period, that of the " great struggles " (1260-1277). During this time, a triple attitude is discernible concerning Aristotle : one of submission, another of defiance, and a third, of assimilation.

One group, comprising especially the younger men of the Faculty of Arts, were enthusiastic about the riches of the vast Peripatetic system which embraced all human sciences in a vast unity; they proclaimed, along with Averroes, that the genius of Aristotle was the last word in human learning [4]. They submitted themselves without reserve to all his positions; and, in a more serious vein, they followed the interpretations of Averroes on obscure points as expressive of pure Aristotelianism.

A second group reacted to this view. It consisted mainly of theologians strongly attached to tradition, and preferring the ancient, Augustinian method. They nurtured a defiant attitude towards Aristotle which eventually led to an actual hostility; they were satisfied to point out his defects and errors, without ever distinguishing Aristotle's thought from that which was added to him by the Arabs. They were quite

---

[1] Actually, the prohibition mainly concerned Paris, so that already in 1229, the masters of Toulouse, in order to attract students, advertised themselves as teaching all of Aristotle.

[2] The Bull of Urban IV (Jan. 19, 1263), confirming the statutes of the University of Paris, and maintaining the prohibitions of Gregory IX, does not seem to have much historical significance. The same expressions are maintained, but the ecclesiastical authorities never urged its application. See F. VAN STEENBERGHEN, *op. cit.*, Vol. II, p. 491.

[3] Averroes was hardly known in Paris before 1230; *ibid.*, Vol. II, pp. 410-412.

[4] See texts on this matter in P. MANDONNET, *Siger de Brabant et l'averroïsme latin,* 2ᵉ éd., Vol. I, pp. 153-154.

aware of the dangers which might mar the purity of their faith, and, in order to combat the Averroistic views successfully, maintained that it was necessary to sacrifice Aristotle himself on many points, and to return to the principles of St. Augustine.

Between these two groups there was a third formation of clear thinkers who were respectful of tradition and yet independent. They realized that the sole way of arresting the harm being done by Peripateticism was to capture its power in favor of the faith; this would be helpful to Catholic doctrine, and also assure the beneficent dominion of theology. These men found their leader in St. Thomas Aquinas who possessed the necessary genius of grasping Aristotelianism in its entirety, of re-thinking it and correcting its errors by his own principles.

The hostility of the Augustinian theologians broke forth with the condemnation of 1277, which included in one prohibition both the heterodox Aristotelianism of the Averroists and the Aristotelianism of St. Thomas. This event led to the fourth period, that of " two philosophies, Thomism and Augustinianism ". As a result of these condemnations, Thomism led a triumphant march both in theology and in philosophy; Augustinianism, as a result, took stock of common views that it shared with Thomism in philosophy, and organized these into a coherent system which might be called Neo-Augustinianism. Scotism is the logical development of this new view, while the heterodox Aristotelianism developed towards the Latin Averroism of the fourteenth century in Padua.

Aristotle was, accordingly, the dominant problem of the thirteenth century. Before considering the definitive work of St. Albert the Great and his disciple, St. Thomas Aquinas, it will be instructive to look at the attempts of the first Aristotelian masters.

II. The first Aristotelian Masters.

232[bis]. During the period of appeasement when Aristotle was being more widely studied, a number of thinkers produced some rather important writings. However, the new theories which they met came to these men along with traditional propositions of Augustinian wisdom and many Neo-Platonic influences. The *Liber de causis*, a summary of Plotinus

attributed to Aristotle, is a stellar example of this situation.
These, and similar influences stemming from the Jewish and
Arabian thinkers, produced a rather grand " eclecticism "
which was founded on Aristotle. The work of St. Albert
the Great and of St. Thomas Aquinas, which occurred during
this same period, was not so much a reaction but a continuation
of this mentality. Their work successfully achieved its purpose
through the help of these other imperfect attempts. These
precursors of Thomism did not have a philosophy [1] that was
systematically defined; they kept their independence and often
held divergent opinions. Nevertheless, their common attempt
to assimilate Aristotle made common among them a certain
number of ideas which can be called a " Neo-Platonizing,
Aristotelian Eclecticism " [2]. Their views will first be presented
synthetically, and then the more important representatives
will be mentioned.

A) Doctrine.

The more generally defended propositions can be grouped
under two headings, the first of which is mystical doctrine,
while the second concerns a theory on matter.

1) *Voluntarist Mysticism.* The Neo-Platonizing eclecticism
of this period followed the logic of Aristotle and adopted his
classification of the faculties of the soul. But inasmuch as
it sought truth in some immediate contact with God, this
view can be called a " mysticism " [3], for it required a special
illumination from God not merely for supernatural contemplation, which supposes revelation, but also for natural truths,
at least with regard to first principles.

It was in this fashion that the tendency arose to fuse
philosophy and theology into one branch equally dependent
upon God in its two parts, the natural and the supernatural.
Both of these were conceived as inseparably destined to lead
us to God. While the difference between them was maintained,
no precision was given to their distinction; they were viewed

---

[1] In theology, they sided with the great current of Augustinianism which
will be dealt with below; see n. 250.

[2] Many historians, following Mandonnet, speak of a " Pre-Thomistic Augustinianism ". But F. Van Steenberghen has shown that as a philosophical system
or plan, Augustinianism is inexistent during the first part of the 13th century
(see his *Siger de Brabant*, Vol. II, p. 442). The term " Augustinianism " will,
accordingly, here refer to the theological current; see below, n. 250.

[3] The term is here used in the philosophical sense indicated above; see n. 120.

as two stages or two different degrees of one and the same knowledge.

It was for these reasons that love was given priority in the acquisition of wisdom or science in the strict sense. Moral goodness seemed to be the essential prerequisite for divine illumination. This led to a mysticism that became *voluntarist;* the will was viewed as surpassing intellect; the notion of the good was prior to truth and helped define truth; happiness was *formally* constituted by an act of the will and an act of will entered *formally* into the act of faith; God is, above all, the supreme Goodness.

For these philosophers, the primacy of will over mind was a means of safeguarding human freedom and the freedom of the creative action of God; they thus tried to correct Aristotle with St. Augustine. At the same time, concerning the much disputed question of the *eternity of the world*, they upheld the necessity of creation in time. They thought it absurd and impossible that the universe could be both created and eternal, and this view became one of the characteristic propositions associated with their eclecticism.

2) *Primary matter as incomplete actuality.* In the twelfth century, matter was regarded, as in St. Augustine, as endowed with *seminal reasons* as the active principles of its development. In the thirteenth century, guided by the terminology of Aristotle, which was becoming more in vogue, this view became that of considering primary matter as incomplete actuality. This replaced the previous understanding of matter as being pure potentiality, but it was still incompletely understood.

Inasmuch as primary matter was actual, it is not essentially bound up with quantity or with body; it could raise itself up to the level of spirits and there one could distinguish a corporeal matter whose correlative form was always localized and corruptible, and a spiritual matter in angels and the human soul, whose form is always outside of place and is incorruptible. This is the view of *generalized hylomorphism*, a heritage of the *Fons Vitæ* of Avicebron [1].

Consequently, the human soul can be individualized independently of body. Soul unites itself to body after it is already endowed with a substantial form, at least with the

---

[1] See above, n. 192.

form of corporeity. This is the manner in which the view of a plurality of substantial forms arose [1], which many of these philosophers defended.

Finally, the above views account for the fact that the view of human faculties or powers, as accidents really distinct from substance, was never really grasped. The plurality of forms seemed sufficient to explain the diversity of operations in man. Slowly, this latter view was replaced by the conception of man's abilities as *functions* [2] emanating from the soul without involving a real distinction.

B) The main representatives.

1º *The Seculars*. In the first beginnings of the University of Paris, some doctors occupied themselves with the purely theological method of Peter Lombard, while others became interested in the recently discovered philosophical works and became oriented towards Aristotelianism. WILLIAM OF AUXERRE († 1231), a master at Paris at the beginning of the century, was so competent an Aristotelian that Pope Gregory IX named him, in 1231, a member of the three-man commission to revise Aristotle; death, however, overtook him before he was able to realize his task. He wrote a rather important work called the *Summa aurea* containing some remarkable attempts at systematization : he identified the soul with its faculties; he proposed the ontological proof of God's existence, although he defended himself from any accusations of personifying abstractions; he proposed that the soul, God's image, sees God Himself and contemplates true justice in Him [3]. —PHILIP OF GREVE (about 1170-1236), a Chancellor of the University of Paris, and a master during the first decade of the thirteenth century, wrote a *Summa de bono*, which is the first synthesis made in the Middle Ages on the different species of the good [4]. — Also worthy of mention are two commentators on Aristotle who flourished during the first half of the century. PETER OF SPAIN, who became Pope John XXI in 1272, wrote a work entitled *Summæ logicales* and a *Compendium* of logic. NICHOLAS OF PARIS, who wrote much, was also interested in logic [5].

But WILLIAM OF AUVERGNE († 1249) is the first great Scholastic of the thirteenth century; he is often called William of Paris, since he became bishop of this city, in 1228. His principal work

---

[1] This view arises in opposition to Thomism in the following period; see below, n. 250.

[2] One group, represented by William of Auvergne, taught that the powers are really identical with the soul, their diversity being explicable merely by the diverse roles which the soul could perform (See A. FOREST, *La structure métaphysique du concret*, p. 260). Others, as Alexander of Hales and St. Bonaventure, taught that they were distinct, and yet were not accidents (see n. 277, below).

[3] See C. HERTZ, *Les rapports entre la philosophie et la foi*, p. 93.

[4] For more detail on this section, see M. DE WULF, *op. cit.*, Vol. II, pp. 10-14.

[5] *Ibid.*, pp. 85-88.

is *Magisterium divinale*, a treatise on God, the human soul, the world and ethics, in which he makes much use of Aristotle, though correcting him with the help of faith. This work is the first attempt at a metaphysical and psychological synthesis. — *a*) In his *metaphysics*, God is the summit of the universe, as the creative source of all being. Creation occurred in time; in order to offset the objections of Aristotle, William holds that this new appearance of being in no way changed the divine perfection, for creation was dependent on the free will of the Creator. He also maintains that only the necessary and infinite being has His essence identical with His existence; contingent beings are marked by the distinction between these two realities. The angels are spiritual beings who have their place in the hierarchy of being; their essence is really distinct from their existence, but there is no composition of matter and form in them; the latter composition characterizes bodies which are subject to quantity, local movement and corruption. At the same time, William is partisan to the view of a plurality of substantial forms; the latter are numbered according to the number of irreducible perfections in each body. — *b*) In *psychology*, William held that the human soul, being spiritual, had no matter, similar to the angels; the soul is, however, fundamentally identifiable with its faculties. His theory of knowledge uses the technical formulas of Aristotle, but his doctrine remains quite Augustinian : the knowledge of the external world is the work of the senses, which are passive with regard to their object, but in order to discover abstract natures, ideal and universal forms, the mind is not subject to the action of the sensible but engenders these ideas in itself with sensation as an *occasion*. Moreover, in order to possess this activity, which makes it capable of grasping the immutable and the eternal, the mind must be passive in regard to God and needs divine *illumination*. The latter is especially required for the knowledge of first principles which are the foundations of all knowledge. Of course, this divine action makes Aristotle's notion of an active intellect a useless one [1].

2⁰ *The Dominicans.* Prior to being subject to the Thomistic influence, the Dominican masters of this time generally defended the view of Neo-Platonist eclecticism. ROLAND OF CREMONA (died after 1244, perhaps after 1258) was the first Dominican aggregated to the University of Paris. He authored a *Summa Theologica* in which there are numerous, though vague, citations of Aristotle and from the Arabians. — HUGH OF ST. CHER († 1264) was a master at Paris about 1230-1244, and later a Cardinal. He showed his sympathy for the new studies by intervening, at the request of St. Albert the Great, in favor of St. Thomas Aquinas, so that the latter would also be allowed to obtain his degrees at Paris though he lacked the proper age requisite. He wrote a commentary on Peter Lombard's Sentences, which was modelled mainly on the theological plan. — THOMAS OF CANTIMPRE is found among the Dominicans at Louvain in 1232, and authored an encyclopedic work, *De natura rerum*. About this same time in England we

---

[1] *Ibid.*, pp. 14-84.

find RICHARD FISHACRE who taught at Oxford from 1240 to 1248. In his commentary on Peter Lombard's Sentences, he often invokes the authority of Aristotle alongside that of St. Augustine, but is more faithful to the latter. He explains human knowledge through d vine illumination, defends the theory of seminal reasons, and admits a spiritual matter within the human soul. A little later we find PETER OF TARENTAISE [1] (1225-1276), a master at Paris from 1258 to 1265, who later became Pope Innocent V. Most of the propositions from his commentary on Peter Lombard's Sentences were explained by St. Thomas. He was the author of four philosophical treatises, *De unitate formæ*, *De materia cæli*, *De æternitate mundi* and *De intellectu et voluntate*, but is generally considered to be in the pre-Thomistic period [2].

3° *The Franciscans*. While they exploited the works of Aristotle along with the other thinkers of this period, the Franciscan masters as a group remained eclectic with a Platonic tendency until the end of the thirteenth century. The most renowned of their group before the time of St. Thomas Aquinas was ALEXANDER OF HALES (1180-1245); he became a Franciscan about 1231 and was the first titulary in the chair of theology granted to his order by the University of Paris. His best known work is the *Summa universæ theologiæ*, a voluminous and well-known writing. Alexander never completed this work, and later attempts were made to finish it by adding sections to it from Philip of Greve (the Chancellor), William of Auxerre, John de la Rochelle, and even from St. Bonaventure. Nevertheless, his work is a good synthesis of Franciscan eclecticism in this period, and it was often called the *Summa minorum*. In this work, Alexander defends the hylomorphic makeup of every creature inclusive of man and angel, but he distinguishes a terrestrial matter as the source of local motion and corruption from a spiritual matter exempted from these two imperfections. In psychology, Alexander unifies Aristotle with St. Augustine; he adopts the theory of abstraction in explaining knowledge of corporeal natures, but adopts a divine illumination of the active intellect in explaining knowledge of spirits and of God. — Mention can also be made of JOHN DE LA ROCHELLE (1200-1245), the titulary successor of Alexander. He authored a *Summa de anima* in which he defends the real distinction between essence and existence in creatures; at the same time, he also attempted to fuse Aristotelian and Augustinian psychology. — ST. BONAVENTURE and his followers will be dealt with later [3].

---

[1] M. DE WULF, *ibid.*, p. 202.

[2] M. H. LAURENT, *Le Bienheureux Innocent V* (Pierre de Tarentaise) *et son temps*, Rome, 1947.

[3] See below, n. 274 ff., and n. 282.

III. Saint Albert the Great.

(1206-1280).

Special bibliography.

Works : *Opera Omnia*, A. Borgnet, A., (ed.), 38 vols., Paris, 1890-1899. — *Alberti Magni opera omnia*, Institutum Albert Magni Coloniense Bernhardo Geyer præside.

Studies : Albert, S. M., *Albert the Great*, Oxford, 1948. — Dörfler, P., *Albert Magnus*, München, 1940. — Garreau, A., *Saint Albert le Grand*, Paris, 1932. — Gorce, M., *L'essor de la pensée au Moyen Age, Albert le Grand, Saint Thomas d'Aquin*, Paris, 1933. — Grabmann, M., *Der heilige Albertus der Grosse, Ein wissenschaftliches Charakterbild*, Munich, 1932. — *Der Einfluss Alberts des Grossen auf das mittelalterliche Geistesleben*, in Vol. II of *Mittelalterliches Geistesleben*, Munich, 1936. — Simone, L., *Introduzione alla vita e al pensiero di Alberto Magno*, Naples, 1942.

233. Albert the Great was born at Lauingen in Swabia of the family of the Counts of Bollstadt. While pursuing studies at Padua, he was moved by the preaching of Jourdain of Saxony to join the Dominican order in 1223. Gifted with a great natural talent for all branches of learning, he gathered all sorts of items of knowledge through study at the Universities of Bologna, Fribourg, Cologne, and through travel. Between 1240 and 1248, he taught at Paris and there obtained his theology degrees. From there he was sent to found a *Studium generale* of his order at Cologne, where he had St. Thomas Aquinas as one of his students. He began to acquire fame, at this time, by his commentaries on Aristotle. Beginning with the year 1254, he became involved in the active life, which distracted him somewhat from his intellectual labors. He acted as intermediary in various disputes, and was Provincial of his order in Germany. In 1256, Pope Alexander IV (1254-1261) ordered him to the court at Anagni where he engaged in a dispute on Averroism, a doctrine he refuted in his work, *De unitate intellectus*. In 1259, he went to Valenciennes, where, together with St. Thomas and Peter of Tarentaise, he drew up a new plan of studies for the Dominican order. In 1260, he became Bishop of Ratisbon, but he resigned this post in 1262. From 1263-1264, he was in Germany, preaching a crusade; in 1274, he attended the Council of Lyons, and then retired to Cologne. Finally, in 1277, at the age of 71 years, he went to Paris to defend the doctrine of St. Thomas. He died in 1280, six years after his great disciple, St. Thomas.

St. Albert wrote a great amount, and it has often been said that he is the most prolific of all writers. Many of his writings are directly concerned with philosophy, as his paraphrases

on the treatises of Aristotle [1], his commentary on the
Neo-Platonic work, *De causis et processu universitatis*, and
such works as *De unitate intellectus contra Averroem*, and *De
quindecim problematibus* [2]. Others of his works are but indirectly
concerned with philosophy, such as the *Summa de creaturis*,
a *Summa theologiæ*, commentaries on Peter Lombard's Book
of Sentences and on the works of Dionysius the Areopagite [3].

There was one aim which St. Albert sought for; it constituted
at once his providential mission and the unifying principle
of his system — to make Aristotle available to the Latins.
" Nostra intentio est omnes dictas partes (physicam, mathe-
maticam, metaphysicam) facere latinis intelligibiles " [4]. From
this aim, his method, doctrine and influence can be ascertained.

A) Method.

234. In its *general* makeup, the method of St. Albert is
somewhat approximative and incomplete. It lies mainly
in reproducing the encyclopedic work of Aristotle, whose vast
proportions have been noted above [5]. This is not done by
following the text, but by reproducing each of the treatises
with its division into books and chapters. Without citing
Aristotle, he reproduces his entire work and completes it with
his own knowledge, drawn from other sources or from his
own personal discoveries.

While this procedure was favorable towards popularizing
Aristotle's work, it led to a lack of clarity. Sometimes, for
example, St. Albert explicitly refutes Aristotle, sometimes
he merely states his opinions without accepting them, while
at other times he explicitly approves of Aristotle's views.
In the absence of formal declarations of his own opinions,
the historical value of Albert's treatises is debatable.

Nevertheless, in its *essential rules*, St. Albert's method
is thoroughly *scientific*. He at first distinguishes the domain
of philosophy from that of theology quite clearly, through
distinguishing the formal objects of each of these, as St. Thomas

---

[1] For various views on the exact time in which these works were written
and published, see M. DE WULF, *op. cit.*, Vol. II. p. 131.

[2] These are 15 propositions of Averroes, 13 of which were condemned in
1272; see n. 250, below.

[3] An extract from this commentary, falsely attributed to St. Thomas, is the
work, *De pulchro*.

[4] *In Phys.*, l, i, tr. i, ch. i.

[5] See n. 67, above.

will also do later [1]. He also inaugurated a new trend of thought, the cultivation of philosophy and of the sciences not solely as simple instruments for theology, but for themselves and for theology [2]. Furthermore, St. Albert made judicious use of deduction and of the syllogism to add order to his treatises, and of induction and experimentation as the basis of all philosophy and as the special instrument of the sciences dealing with nature. This latter point gives him his special claim to fame; he had a marked predilection for the " sciences " in the modern sense of the term. His works contain expositions on zoology, botany, geography, astronomy, mineralogy, alchemy and medicine, and he held that only by repeated observations could the truth be obtained in these matters. Finally, he was able to criticize the opinions of Aristotle, and often corrected them by his own observations [3].

B) Doctrine.

235. 1º In *essentials*, the teaching of Albert the Great is avowedly Peripatetic. He holds and explains the fundamental propositions of philosophy in their true sense : in *metaphysics*, he deals with potentiality and actuality, matter and form, substance and accidents. In psychology, he is concerned with the spirituality of the soul, and the various faculties of knowledge; he is insistent on the importance of sensation, and studies its physiological conditions in the brain and its experimental laws; he refutes the errors of Averroes on the mind, maintaining that each human soul has its own active and passive intellect. In *theodicy*, the notion of pure actuality gave him the means of adding precision to the attribute of infinity in God. In *logic*, he held the view of moderate realism, and distinguished clearly between three aspects of the universal concept as being in the Divine Ideas " ante rem " or as in the multiple, material individuals partaking in the same form, " in re ", and as being in human concepts " post rem ".

2º But in the *application* of these principles, Albert's synthesis lacks unity. He hesitated on some questions, and adopted Augustinian or Platonic solutions incompatible with perfect Peripateticism on other matters.

---

[1] See below, n. 244.
[2] M. de Wulf, *op. cit.*, Vol. ii, p. 132.
[3] F. Copleston, *op. cit.*, Vol. ii, pp. 296-297.

An illustration of this latter point is his application of the theory of matter and form. He admits the notion of seminal reasons in St. Augustine's sense, which compromises the notion of pure potentiality or prime matter in Aristotle's sense. He explains a mixture by holding to the permanence of anterior forms despite substantial change, which is an exception to the Aristotelian theory of the unity of form. In his view, the human soul is the unique principle of the threefold vegetative, sensitive and intellective life in man; at the same time, he holds that the soul does not directly and essentially animate the body, rather that this animation is the most basic function which the soul exercises in the body [1].

His view of *liberty* is another example of indecision. Sometimes he explains it in Aristotle's sense as due to the will or rational appetite, incapable of being necessitated by particular goods. At other times he makes liberty a property of the mind, which can fulfill its final degree of actuality only when it is, in Avicenna's terminology, " intellectus adeptus " [2]. These two points of view are not harmonized.

Finally, in dealing with the *angels*, he considers them to be pure forms. Yet he seems to hold to some sort of numerical multiplication of them, for he attributes a common, generic element to them which he calls " fundamentum " and is unwilling to call this element matter, for it has no relationship with quantity.

C) **Influence.**

236. The immense work of Albert the Great is but a first attempt at synthesis, and lacks internal cohesion. It is not a definitive system, but a *vigorous* ORIENTATION *towards perfect Aristotelianism*, and this is the proper statement of its PHILOSOPHICAL INFLUENCE. Albert not only revived Aristotelianism for his own age, but, through constant vigilance, he purified it from its interpretation in various commentaries and from the evident deformations it suffered from the Arabians; he began its *Christianization* through the reasoned assimilation of its theories, and especially of its scientific tenets. By a direct exposition of Aristotle's thought, Albert showed that the supernatural truth of the Catholic faith has nothing to fear

---

[1] See above, n. 183.
[2] *Ibid.*

from the treasures of natural truths accumulated by pagan wisdom; rather, there is great profit in using these truths, either for the theological explanation of dogmas, for the completion of the array of the sciences of nature, or for the teachings of the Bible.

Albert's SCIENTIFIC INFLUENCE was extremely great. His development of the experimental sciences was particularly tasteful to his contemporaries, and accounts, in large part, for his being called " the Great " even during his own lifetime. Roger Bacon, who quite strongly argues against Albert, is nevertheless obliged to acknowledge and cite him as an authority. Furthermore, despite the universal custom of naming only the ancients whom one quoted and not naming one's contemporaries, exception in this regard was made both for Albert the Great and St. Thomas, whose authority equalled that of an Aristotle or of an Averroës.

The most important work of St. Albert from the philosophical and theological point of view, was the formation of St. Thomas. He discerned his genius, encouraged him, and helped to arrange circumstances most favorable to his development. He considered Thomism as the completion of his own effort, so that the glory of his disciple absorbed and slowly made obsolete that of his master [1]. But one can also say that if the great Scholastic age was essentially Peripatetic, this condition was primarily due to Albert the Great, who performed this function by being both a revealer of the greatness of Aristotle and the master of St. Thomas.

ARTICLE TWO. — SAINT THOMAS AQUINAS.

(1225-1274)

SPECIAL BIBLIOGRAPHY.

Works : *Opera Omnia* (Vatican, or Piana edition), 18 vols., Rome, 1570-1. — *Opera Omnia* (Parma edition), 25 vols., 1872-3; Reprint, New York, 1948. — *Opera Omnia* (Vivès edition), 34 vols., Paris, 1872-80. — *Opera Omnia* (Leonine edition), 15 vols. completed, 1882, *ff.* — *Summa Contra Gentiles* (English transl.), 5 vols., New York, 1928-9. — *Summa Theologica* (English transl.), 2nd rev. ed., 22 vols., London, 1912-36. — *Truth*, (English transl.), 3 vols., Chicago, 1952-4.

---

[1] It was only in the 20th century that Albert the Great was canonized and received the title of a Doctor of the Church by Pope Pius XI (Dec. 16, 1931).

Bibliographies and Indexes : BOURKE, V. J., *Thomistic Bibliography*, 1920-1940, St. Louis, (Mo.), 1945. — GRABMANN, M., *Die echten Schriften des heiligen Thomas von Aquin*, Munster, 1920. — *Die Werke des heiligen Thomas von Aquin*, Munster, 1931. — MANDONNET, P., *Des écrits authentiques de Saint Thomas*, Fribourg (Sw.), 2nd ed., 1910. — MANDONNET, P., and DESTREZ, J., *Bibliographie thomiste*, Paris, 1921. — SCHÜTZ, L., *Thomas-Lexikon*, (Reprint), New York, 1949. — DEFERRARI, R. J., and others, *A Lexicon of St. Thomas Aquinas*, Washington, 1948-53.

Life : CHESTERTON, G. K., *St. Thomas Aquinas*, London, 1933. — DE BRUYNE, E., *St. Thomas Aquinas, Le milieu, l'homme, la vision du monde*, Brussels, 1928. — ENDRES, J. A., *Thomas von Aquin*, Mayence, 1910. — GRABMANN, M., *Das seelenleben des heiligen Thomas von Aquin*, Munich, 1924. — *Thomas Aquinas*, New York, 1929. — MARITAIN, J., *The Angelic Doctor*, London, 1931. — SERTILLANGES, A. D., *St. Thomas Aquinas and his Work*, London, 1933. — THONNARD, F.-J., *Saint Thomas d'Aquin*, Paris, 1933. — WÉBERT, J., *Saint Thomas d'Aquin*, Paris, 1934.

Doctrine (general treatises) : D'ARCY, M. C., *Thomas Aquinas*, Westminster (Md.), 1944. — FOREST, A., *L'esprit de la philosophie thomiste*, Paris, 1933. — *Saint Thomas d'Aquin*, Paris, 1923. — GILSON, E., *The Philosophy of St. Thomas Aquinas*, St. Louis, 1929. — LATTEY, C., (editor), *St. Thomas Aquinas*, London, 1924. — MANSER, G. M., *Das Wesen des Thomismus*, Fribourg (Sw.), 1931. — MEYER, H., *The Philosophy of St. Thomas Aquinas*, St. Louis, 1944. — OLGIATI, F., *A Key to the Study of St. Thomas*, St. Louis, 1925. — PEILLAUBE, E., *Initiation à la philosophie de Saint Thomas*, Paris, 1926. — SERTILLANGES, A. D., *Foundations of Thomistic Philosophy*, London, 1931. — *Saint Thomas d'Aquin*, 2 vols., 4th ed., Paris, 1925.

Metaphysics and Knowledge : BUCKLEY, G. M., *The Nature and Unity of Metaphysics*, Washington, 1946. — DE TONQUÉDEC, J., *Les principes de la philosophie thomiste, La critique de la connaissance*, Paris, 1929. — DE FINANCE, J., *Etre et agir dans la philosophie de Saint Thomas*, Paris, 1945. — FOREST, A., *La structure métaphysique du concret selon Saint Thomas d'Aquin*, Paris, 1931. — GARRIGOU-LAGRANGE, R., *God : His Existence and His Nature*, 2 vols., London, 1934-6. — *Le sens commun*, Paris, 1909. — HABBEL, J., *Die Analogie zwischen Gott und Welt nach Thomas von Aquin*, Ratisbonne, 1928. — HOENEN, P., *Reality and Judgment according to St. Thomas*, Chicago, 1952. — MARC, A., *L'idée de l'être chez Saint Thomas et dans la scolastique postérieure*, Paris, 1931. — MEYER, H., *Die Wissenschaftslehre des Thomas von Aquin*, Fulda, 1934. — NOËL, L., *Notes d'épistémologie thomiste*, Louvain, 1925. — PEGHAIRE, J., *Intellectus et Ratio selon Saint Thomas d'Aquin*, Paris, 1936. — ROLFES, E., *Die Gottesbeweise bei Thomas von Aquin und Aristoteles*, 2nd ed., Limburg-sur-Lahn, 1927. — WÉBERT, J., *Essai de métaphysique thomiste*, Paris, 1926. — WILPERT, P., *Das Problem der Wahrheitssicherung bei Thomas von Aquin*, Munster, 1931.

Cosmology and Psychology : CHOISNARD, P., *Saint Thomas d'Aquin et l'influence des astres*, Paris, 1926. — COCONNIER, *L'âme* *humaine*, Paris, 1890. — CORNOLDI, G. M., *The Physical System of St. Thomas*, London, 1895. — GARDAIR, L., *La nature humaine, Corps et âme, La connaissance*, 3 vols., Paris, 1892. — GARIN, P., *La théorie de l'idée suivant l'école thomiste*, 2 vols., Paris, 1932. — Mc WILLIAMS, J. A., *Physics and Philosophy, A Study of Saint Thomas' Commentary on the Eight Books of Aristotle's Physics*, Washington, 1945. — MONAHAN, W. B., *The Psychology of St. Thomas Aquinas*, London, n. d. — PEGIS, A. C., *St. Thomas and the Problem of the Soul in the Thirteenth Century*, Toronto, 1934. — ROUSSELOT, P., *The Intellectualism of St. Thomas*, London. 1935.

Morality : DE LA BARRE, A., *La morale d'après Saint Thomas et les théologiens scolastiques*, Paris, 1911. — DELLA ROCCA, G., *La politica di S. Tommaso*, Naples, 1934. — DOTRES, F. X., *S. Thomas de Aquino y las leyes, Ensayo de filosofía de derecho*, Madrid, 1932. — GARDAIR, J., *Philosophie de Saint Thomas, Les vertus morales naturelles*, Paris, 1901. — GILSON, E., *Moral Values and the Moral Life*, St. Louis (Mo.), 1931. — GMUR, H., *Thomas von Aquin und der Krieg*, Leipzig, 1934. — KURZ, E., *Individuum und Gemeinschaft beim hl. Thomas von Aquin*, Munich, 1932. — GRABMANN, M., *Die Kulturphilosophie des hl. Thomas von Aquin*, Augsburg, 1925. — LOTTIN, O., *La vertu de religion d'après Saint Thomas d'Aquin*, Louvain, 1920. — *Le droit naturel chez Saint Thomas et ses prédécesseurs*, 2nd ed., Bruges, 1931. — *Loi morale naturelle et loi positive d'après Saint Thomas*, Louvain, 1920. — PIEPER, J., *Die ontische Grundlage des Sittlichen nach Thomas von Aquin*, Munster, 1929. — ROLLAND-GOSSELIN, B., *La doctrine politique selon Saint Thomas*, Paris, 1928. — SERTILLANGES, A. D., *La philosophie morale de Saint Thomas d'Aquin*, 2nd ed., Paris, 1947.

Various works : *Acta hebdomadae thomisticae*, Rome, 1924. — DE WULF, M., *Etudes historiques sur l'esthétique de saint Thomas d'Aquin*, Louvain, 1896. — *Le 6e centenaire de la canonisation de saint Thomas d'Aquin à Avignon*, Vaison, 1924. — LITTLE, A., *The Platonic Heritage of Thomism*, Dublin, 1953. — *Mélanges Thomistes*, Kain, 1923. — RICHARD, T., *Comment étudier et situer saint Thomas*, Paris, 1938. — RIMAUD, J., *Thomisme et méthode*, Paris, 1925.

237. A powerful vitality marks the Thomistic philosophy of our times, for it is a system that is intelligible — at least in its directive principles and vital essence — independently of the period of its origin. It is most useful, however, and conducive to a better understanding of Thomistic philosophy, to study it in its *historical realization*, and to learn the favorable or unfavorable conditions, the evolvement and the struggles which St. Thomas experienced in constructing his synthesis [1].

Furthermore, since the Thomistic school has progressed in the past and is progressing today, historical research can help

---

[1] The exposition of St. Thomas' development will include mention of many secondary authors, both Augustinian and Averroist.

to clarify the thought of its founder. The historical study which follows will not be overly concerned with doctrinal details. It will consider his doctrine as a unit, and then show its *proper characteristic* and determine the *special contribution* of St. Thomas in the evolution of thought. In this way, it will be clear in what way Thomism can be viewed as one of the better realizations of the perennial philosophy and a better manifestation of the rational view of the universe.

Two sections will cover the study of St. Thomas :

Section I : The Historical Realization.

Section II : The Thomistic Synthesis.

SECTION I.
THE HISTORICAL REALIZATION.

238. Thomas Aquinas was born in 1225 [1] at the castle of Roccasecca near Naples, of the family of the Counts of Aquino. Through his paternal ancestry, he was a nephew of Frederick Barbarossa, cousin of Henry VI and of Frederick II; through his maternal ancestry, he was descended from the Norman chiefs made famous by such men as Guiscard, Tancred and Bohemund. As a man, St. Thomas had the Germanic patience and tenacity, the chivalrous ardor of the Northern French and the quickness of the Latin spirit. His temperament was complemented by his education, which was Latin at Monte Cassino, German at Cologne and French at Paris.

Already at the age of five years, he attended school at the celebrated Benedictine monastery of Monte Cassino, where he made quick progress in studies. From the age of ten to eighteen, he attended the University of Naples, where he was initiated into dialectic, metaphysics and ethics. At this latter place he took the habit of the order of Friars Preachers in 1244, and, despite the strong opposition of his parents, who held him prisoner, he persevered in this goal, regaining his freedom in the spring of 1245. At this time he made his profession in the Dominican convent of Paris. Thus, already at the beginning of his formation, he was prepared for his doctrinal and religious role through his zeal for study and his fidelity to his calling.

---

[1] " He was born, therefore, before March 7th, 1225, either at the beginning of that year or at the end of 1224 ". F. CAYRÉ, *op. cit.*, Vol. II, pp. 530-1.

His entrance into the Dominican order offered him a special providential preparation through the teaching of Albert the Great. St. Thomas studied under him from 1245 to 1252, first at Paris, where Albert was obtaining his degrees and beginning his great commentaries on Aristotle [1]; then at Cologne, where both men founded a *Studium generale* in 1248. Thomas was, accordingly, both pupil and collaborator. In this way, Thomas was exposed for a long time to Christian Peripateticism, which, along with his scholarly formation, led him to elaborate a complete philosophical synthesis.

Throughout his entire life he had a double intellectual mission. His first aim was to receive and assimilate, as thoroughly as possible, the riches of Aristotle and thus to propose a regenerated *Peripateticism*, thought through and, so to speak, *baptized* by his Christian and saintly intelligence. His other purpose was to use this latter as a rational foundation for constructing a vast, *theological synthesis* which would be his own original work. Towards accomplishing these aims, Thomas generously sacrificed every external dignity [2], wishing to remain but a simple friar preacher, a professor of theology.

The historical realization of Thomism will be studied in three periods :

I. Period of Foundation : The first sojourn at Paris (1252-1260).

II. Period of Extension : The sojourn at the Roman court (1260-1268).

III. Period of Struggle : The second sojourn at Paris (1268-1272).

Then follow the last two years of his life, which he spent in Italy, which are the conclusion to his life and the completion of his work.

I. PERIOD OF FOUNDATION.
(At Paris : 1252-1260).

A) The Philosopher.

239. In 1252, despite his youth, St. Thomas was appointed to teach at the Convent of St. James in Paris, and to obtain his degrees at the University. This was done at the instance

---

[1] See n. 233, above.

[2] In 1250, Thomas refused the Abbacy of Monte Cassino and the Bishopric of Naples; these the Pope offered him at the request of his parents.

of St. Albert. From the moment that Thomas began his public lectures, he was recognized as a master and drew many disciples to himself. The cause of this immediate influence was the clear, firm, logical and new philosophical position which he proposed. His first biographer, William of Tocco, writes : " He considered new articles in his teaching, a new and clear way of stating his positions, and brought forth new reasons for his determination of questions. No one who heard him teach these new things or settle doubtful matters with new arguments could doubt that God had illumined him with the rays of new light — for he immediately was of such certain judgment that he did not hesitate to teach or to write new opinions which God had newly inspired in him " [1].

Marvelling at the limpidity and precision of his metaphysical propositions, his listeners, doubtlessly, asked him to summarize them; accordingly, St. Thomas wrote his first work, *De ente et essentia* [2]. The traits of the master are already found in this work — brevity, precision, clarity and depth. In this work a great portion of his own doctrines can be found : the complete passivity of prime matter; the identification of individual with specific unity in the angels and the absence of all matter in them; the real distinction between essence and existence in creatures. This work permits one to say that his *philosophical synthesis* was already achieved at this time.

The above remarks on this first work of St. Thomas show that the chronological order of his works is of less importance than it is, for example, in St. Augustine. It can, of course, be revealing by showing a progress in his manner of exposition. In theology, on the other hand, the developmental variations with time are more noticeable.

The *De ente et essentia* begins with a brief preamble. Chapter one is devoted to definitions of such terms as being, essence, and so forth. The rest of the work is divided into two unequal parts : the first part treats of substances (chapters two to six), and the second of accidents (chapter seven); composite substances are dealt with in chapters two to four, simple substances in chapter five; chapter six is a brief summary of the preceding. Throughout the work, both logical and metaphysical considerations are intermingled.

---

[1] William of Tocco, *Vita St. Thomae*, Ch. III.

[2] This work was written about 1252, or, according to some critics, in 1256. It has enjoyed great prestige in the Thomistic School. In 1491, Cajetan wrote a famous commentary on this work, in order to explain it and to defend it against the Scotists. Various editions of this work have been edited; see *On Being and Essence*, (Transl. by A. MAURER), Toronto, 1950.

A second philosophical work of this same period is *De principiis naturæ*, which deals with the four causes.

B) **The Theologian.**

240. During this time, St. Thomas was at Paris teaching theology and aiming to get through the three-year cycle which would obtain for him his baccalaureate in theology[1]. As a result, the purely philosophical point of view was officially secondary in his work. Inasmuch as his teaching consisted mainly in explaining the Book of Sentences of Peter Lombard, he composed his first large work, the commentary on the above work[2] (1255-57). In this work he aimed to interpret and coordinate revealed dogma with the help of philosophy, attempting to erect a theological synthesis. The commentary reveals a certain progress in Thomism, not with regard to the fundamental propositions in which the influence of metaphysics is most immediate, but more with regard to particular conclusions. There are traces of Augustinianism in this work; many of these will be retracted explicitly in his own summary of theology.

In the official catalogue of St. Thomas' works of 1319, there is mention of a second commentary on the first book of the Sentences. It may be that he was dissatisfied with his first commentary and began another; then, cramped by the narrow view of Peter the Lombard, he abandoned this second attempt in order to compose his own summary of theology.

The teaching of the Scholastics also involved various public discussions or disputations[3] at which the students themselves could assist, sometimes including masters of other schools. St. Thomas made these discussions regular, periodic and gave them a connected subject matter; from these discussions arose what were called the " *ordinary disputations* ".

During his first sojourn at Paris, St. Thomas held a considerable number of these sessions in order to answer the need of his pupils. He held them twice a week, along with the sessions of the corresponding " determinations " which occupied four afternoons each week[4]. Accordingly, he had 253 meetings in three years, the

---

[1] See above, n. 230.
[2] See F. Cayré, *op. cit.*, Vol. ii, pp. 532-3.
[3] See above, n. 230.
[4] This frequency was partially caused by the disputes of the secular masters; see below, n. 241. The " ordinary disputations " were later held only every fortnight.

subject matter of which is contained in his work *Questiones disputatæ de Veritate*, a work which is divided into the following 29 questions : on truth in general (I); truth in God, or the Divine Science (II) and related problems; the exemplary ideas in God (III); on the Word of God (IV); Providence (V); Predestination (VI); the Book of Life (VII); the knowledge proper to angels (VIII-IX); the knowledge proper to man (X-XX), which considers natural knowledge, either direct (X) or indirect, through a teacher (XI) and then supernatural knowledge, as prophecy (XII), ecstasy (XIII) and faith (XIV); special functions proper to human intelligence, as superior and inferior reason (XV), *synderesis* (XVI), conscience (XVII), the knowledge of the first man (XVIII), of the separated soul (XIX) and that of Christ as man (XX). Questions 21 to 26 deal with the faculty which accompanies knowledge, treating of the notion of good (XXI), of appetite in general (XXII); the will is then considered as in God (XXIII), then the notion of freedom of will (XXIV), the sensible appetite (XXV) and the passions (XXVI). Finally, concerning the supernatural means of action, grace is treated (XXVII), the idea of justification (XXVIII) and the particular case of the Grace of Christ (XXIX).

" In these disputed questions, St. Thomas gives free rein to his talents. He quotes from the Bible, and the Fathers of the Church; he indulges in historical digressions and syntheses; he uses proofs taken from all the domains of learning; he opens each article with as many as ten or twenty objections which are answered in detail so that truth can be given its final luster and precision. A veritable profusion of doctrine and learning is found in these writings " [1].

C) The Polemicist.

241. The success of St. Thomas as a teacher brought him his first great problem. The students flocked to his courses in crowds, deserting their secular masters, thus arousing the jealousy of the secular masters against the religious. The dispute which thereupon arose over the right of religious to occupy a chair at the University of Paris soon degenerated into a theological quarrel over the excellence of the religious life as contrasted with that of the secular. The turbulent William of St. Amour was the leader of the seculars; beginning with the Lenten season of 1253, William and other secular masters from the faculty of theology began an attack on the Dominicans and Franciscans which was so violent that St. Thomas and St. Bonaventure, who were preparing for their licentiate and mastership, could not graciously swallow their accusations.

---

[1] J. Coconnier, *L'âme humaine*, p. 279; see *passim*.

In 1255, William of St. Amour published his book, *De periculis novissimorum temporum*, which was proposed as the result of collaboration among the secular masters. In it he held that by the study and contemplation of truth alone, without the help of manual labor, the regulars could not reach eternal salvation. He proposed a false interpretation of the Evangelical counsels, especially that of poverty, along with an erroneous notion of the religious state and of the vows.

St. Thomas answered this work with one of his own, *Contra impugnantes Dei cultum*[1] (1257), in which he studies the nature and the perfection of the religious state. In this work he shows the senselessness of William's objections, showing that the religious can teach, enter a college of masters, preach and hear confessions without having direct charge of souls; it is absurd to require that they quit all this work and live as monks. Finally, his work points out the evil involved in the vilification of the religious doctors.

These quarrels caused some disorder in the faculty of theology. Towards the close of 1256, the seculars went on strike, and William of St. Amour returned to the pontifical court. It was as a remedy for this situation that St. Thomas undertook, as was seen above, the regular disputations twice every week. In order to demonstrate the capability of the regulars to teach, he initiated the *ad libitum disputations*. These were quite solemn meetings to which other masters and the students were invited and at which St. Thomas answered questions brought up on any theological or philosophical subject whatsoever[2]. These were held twice a year, at Christmastime and at Eastertime. These St. Thomas edited, ordering them as well as possible, and this is the origin of his work *Questiones quodlibetales*[3].

Pope Alexander IV condemned William of St. Amour's book; in a letter of 1257, he forbade the publication of pamphlets against the regulars, validated their incorporation into the University and made it possible to receive academic degrees from them. The principal supporters of the quarrel, along with William of St. Amour, were expelled from the

---

[1] St. Thomas had a first edition of this work in 1256 when he was called to the meeting at Anagni to defend the position of the regulars before Pope Alexander IV (1254-61); William of St. Amour had put them in a bad light at the Pontifical court. The work itself, however, was issued in 1257. An English edition of this work is J. PROCTOR's (transl.), *An Apology for the Religious Orders*, London, 1902; see also, *The Religious State*, by the same author, London, 1903.

[2] This explains how they got the name " Disputatio *de quolibet* " or, briefly, " *quodlibet* ".

[3] See F. CAYRE, *op. cit.*, Vol. II, pp. 548-9, and p. 549, fn. 1.

University. Thus the first phase of the struggle concluded. Protected by the Pope, St. Thomas was able to give his first inaugural lecture as a Doctor and became a teaching master [1]. At this time he wrote his commentaries on Isaias and St. Matthew (1257-9) in his capacity as master; privately, he added to them his commentary on the *De hebdomadibus* and on the *De Trinitate* of Boethius (1257-8).

II. PERIOD OF EXTENSION.

The Sojourn at the Roman Court; Italy : (1260-1268).

242. In 1260, the Pope named St. Thomas professor of theology at the school attached to the Papal court. Accordingly, his travels took him to Anagni with Alexander IV (1254-61), at Orvieto with Urban IV (1261-4), and at Rome [2] and Viterbo with Clement IV (1265-8). The development of Thomism during this period was done in the realm of philosophy, of theology and in a mixed domain.

A) The Philosophical Domain.

At the Pontifical court, St. Thomas met the Hellenist, William of Moerbeke. Urban IV brought them together after he had lifted the condemnation of Aristotle, in order that they might revise the current understanding of Greek philosophy before it became established in the West. It was at this time that St. Thomas, aided by the new translations of Aristotle, edited his main philosophical commentaries on Aristotle's *Physics* (about 1265), the first twelve books of his *Metaphysics* (1265), the three books of the *De Anima*, the minor works *De sensu et sensato, De memoria* (1266), the *Nichomachean Ethics* (1266), on the first three books and chapters I-VI of the *Politics* (1268), and on the *Prior* and *Posterior Analytics* (about 1268).

The Thomistic commentaries are a great improvement over the paraphrases of St. Albert the Great. They adopt the literal method of Averroes, and begin with a detailed analysis

---

[1] According to Mandonnet (St. Thomas createur du " Quodlibet ", *Rev. sc. phil. et theol.*, 1926, pp. 477-506 and 1927, pp. 5-38), St. Thomas received his doctorate at the beginning of 1256; he taught as *Magister actu regens* from 1256 to 1259; his commentary on the Sentences (1255-7), lasted for two years, the third year of his baccalaureate and the first year of his doctorate.

[2] Clement IV resided at Viterbo; at the request of Charles of Anjou, the king of both Sicilies, he sent Thomas to teach for two years at Rome (1256-7).

of the divisions of the work. Then follows a minute analysis of the text in order to grasp its meaning and argumentative power. Finally, and this is the perfection of the Latin commentary which makes it superior to those of the Arabs, it pauses from time to time to summarize the detail of the preceding arguments and points out its synthetic beauty. In this way, the primary purpose of the commentary — to explain the text clearly — is well fulfilled. Two other purposes were in the mind of St. Thomas in commenting on Aristotle : one of these was to separate the true Aristotle from the erroneous interpretations introduced through the Arabic commentaries, which he accomplished by explaining even the most obscure truths; the other was to refute the positive errors of Aristotle which remained after this expurgation, though these were but small in number. In the latter instance, St. Thomas corrected Aristotle by a profound application of Aristotle's own principles.

St. Thomas was rigorously exact in this task. He did not insist on favorable interpretations as if they came from himself; he brings up objections only rarely, especially if an opinion seems to be contrary to his faith [1]. In conclusion it can be said that these commentaries were a true edition of Aristotle, expurgated and " baptized " as the Pope desired.

B) **Theological Domain.**

243. The great work of St. Thomas was the setting up of *theological science*. During his sojourn in Italy, he worked at this task, at first through some scholarly works. The ordinary disputations which he continued to hold regularly, though from now on only every fortnight, resulted in the valuable *Questiones Disputatæ :* the *De potentia Dei*, divided into ten questions (1259-1263); the *De malo* in sixteen questions (1263-1268); the *De virtutibus, De unione Verbi incarnati, De caritate, De correctione fraterna, De spe, De virtutibus cardinalibus*, all of which have but one question (1268).

The *De potentia Dei* begins with an introduction on the Divine Power in general; then it studies this power in God the Father engendering the Son, in the creation of the world, its general extent and its relation to prime matter (qq. I-VI). Then it shows

---

[1] For instance, in the second lesson of the eighth book of the Physics, St. Thomas refutes the reasons given by Aristotle favoring the eternity of the world (see above, n. 79). In the twelfth book of the Metaphysics, lesson twelve, where Aristotle holds that God knows Himself but not the world, St. Thomas shows that " By knowing Himself, God knows all things ". (See above, n. 93).

the consequences of God's work, which makes Him relative to what He has made without destroying the simplicity of His essence (q. VII). It concludes with distinguishing these latter relations from the real ones which are constitutive of the Divine Persons (qq. VIII-X).

The *De malo* opens with a general treatise on evil and then treats of sin and its causes; it studies original sin, its nature, its chastising effect; it also considers venial sins, the capital sins and, finally, the nature of devils.

Two smaller works can be mentioned here, the *Contra errores Græcorum* (1261-2), which is dedicated to Urban IV, and defends the Catholic doctrine on the Holy Trinity, the Incarnation, and the primacy of the Pope[1]; the other work is the commentary, *In Dionysium de divinis nominibus* (after 1259).

But it is especially through the composition of his TWO SUMMARIES that St. Thomas systematically realized his plan of a sacred science.

a) **The Summa contra Gentiles,** also somewhat improperly called his " philosophical summary ", was begun at Paris at the request of St. Raymond of Pennafort, and completed in Italy (1259-1264). In the four books of this treatise, St. Thomas coordinated the whole of theology, both natural and revealed, with an apologetic aim. The first book treats of God, the second deals with creatures, the third, with happiness as the purpose of creation and with law and grace as the means of arriving at happiness, and the fourth explains the mysteries of the Holy Trinity, the Incarnation, the Sacraments, the future life and their accord with reason.

Entering into the powerful movement of the defence of religion against the attacks of the Jews and the Moors, this work is a rational apology for the Catholic faith considered in both its categories of truths : the natural truths accessible to reason and the supernatural, surpassing reason. The early part of the work contains a short sketch of the fact of revelation by summarizing neatly and vigorously the reasons which clear the Christians of the accusation of believing too easily — such as the Evangelical miracles, the prophecies of the Old Testament, and, especially, the conversion of the world along with the circumstances which make the latter a miracle perpetuating all the others.

Nevertheless, neither St. Thomas nor any other Scholastic of this time considered the science of apologetics[2] as a separate

---

[1] The treatises *De articulis fidei et sacramentis* and the *De rationibus fidei* (against the Greeks, Armenians and Saracens), written in the same period, have the same purpose.

[2] The elements of the science of apologetics are found in both of the *Summas* and in various smaller works. See, for instance, the *Summa Theologica*, I-II, qq. I-XVI, where the relationship between faith and the motives of credibility are studied.

branch, as is done today; the foundations of faith were not as strongly shaken then as they have been by the modern rationalists.

b) **The Summa Theologica** [1]. At the beginning of 1265, St. Thomas began his great work, with which he was occupied until the close of his life, though without completing it. In Italy, he wrote the first part *(Pars Prima)* and the first section of the second part *(Prima Secundæ);* at Paris, he wrote the second section of the second part *(Secunda Secundæ);* at Naples, he wrote the third part *(Pars Tertia)* up to question 90.

In this work, St. Thomas refers everything to God as He is in Himself, and as the finality of all creatures, especially of men. He divides his exposition of Catholic doctrine into three large sections [2]:

The *first* treats of the nature of God and of His works.

The *second* deals with the return of man to God, pointing out the intrinsically necessary means for attaining this end.

The *third* points out the means which are extrinsically necessary, those, namely, which arise from the free will of God.

Prima Pars. Having first determined the nature and the method of theology (Sacred doctrine) and after distinguishing it from philosophy (q. I), this first part deals with the nature of God under the headings *De Deo uno* (qq. II-XXVI) and *De Deo Trino* (qq. XXVII-XLIII); concerning God as the first principle of things, there follow the treatises on *creation* (qq. XLIV-XLIX), on the *Angels* (qq. L-LXV), the creation of the corporeal world (qq. LXVI-LXXIV), the human soul (qq. LXXV-LXXXIX), the first man and the state of innocence (qq. XC-CII), and on the general government of the world (qq. CIII-CXIX).

Secunda Pars. This part is divided into two main sections, inasmuch as practical science requires, for its full perfection; both a general study (I-II) and a special study (II-II).

First section of Part Two *(Prima Secundæ).* Having established that God is the finality or happiness of man (qq. I-V), the means for attaining this end are studied : the essential means are the diverse rational activities, therefore there is a treatise on human actions (qq. VI-XXI), the passions (qq. XXII-XLVIII), on the habits and virtues and vices in a general view (qq. XLIX-XC); then the external principles of uman activity are considered, law (qq. XCI-CVIII) and grace (qq, CIX-CXIV).

Second section of Part Two *(Secunda Secundæ).* A detailed study of the virtues is undertak n : the theological, faith (qq. I-XVI), hope (qq. XVII-XXII) and charity (qq. XXIII-XLVI); the moral,

---

[1] There are a great number of editions of this work in all languages, as well as all sorts of works explaining or summarizing its doctrine.

[2] For a more complete analysis, see, for example, F. CAYRÉ, *op. cit.*, Vol. II, pp. 554-569.

which are grouped under the four cardinal virtues of prudence
(qq. XLVII-LVI), of justice (qq. LVII-CXXIII) — under which the
virtue of religion is considered (qq. LXXXI-CII) — of fortitude
(qq. CXXIII-CXL) and of temperance (qq. CXLI-CLXX); finally, two
treatises deal with prophecy (qq. CLXXI-CLXXVIII) and the
various states of life, especially the states of perfection
(qq. CLXXIX-CLXXXIX).

Tertia Pars. Through revelation, the free will of God has made
other means necessary for man; these are contained in the economy
of the Incarnation and Redemption of Christ. The nature of the
Incarnation is treated (qq. I-XXVI) and its historical realization
(qq. XXVII-LIX). The sacraments are first treated in general
(qq. LX-LXV), followed by a treatise on baptism (qq. LXVI-LXXI),
on confirmation (qq. LXXII), on the Eucharist (qq. LXXIII-LXXXIII)
and on penance (qq. LXXXIV-XC).

In many editions of this work, a supplementary section is added;
it was taken from St. Thomas' commentary on the Book of Sentences
by Reginald of Piperno, the companion of St. Thomas. It continues
the treatise on penance (qq. I-XXVIII), treats Extreme Unction,
Sacred Orders and Marriage (qq. XXIX-LXVIII). This is followed
by the treatise on man's final states in the next life (qq. LXIX-C).

Faith and Reason [1]; Theology and Christian Philosophy.

244. In writing his theological summary, St. Thomas
outlined the relations between reason and faith, pointed out
their respective domains, and showed their mode of collaborating
in the construction of a Christian philosophy and theology.

1° **Respective Domains.** *a*) Both faith and reason have
juridical possession, independently, of their own domains.
Every truth known with intrinsic evidence, either through
experience or through demonstration, belongs to reason alone.
Every truth known without intrinsic evidence but through
the teaching based on the authority of divine revelation
belongs to faith alone. From the above principles it follows
that the same truth cannot be simultaneously an object of
science and of faith, for the latter excludes the type of evidence
which characterizes science. This distinction does not arise
on the part of the object known considered in itself which is
identical, God and His work (the material object), but from
the particular aspect which is considered in this object or

---

[1] GILSON, E., *Christianity and Philosophy*, New York, 1939. — HEITZ, T.,
*Essai historique sur les rapports entre la philosophie et la foi, de Bérenger de Tours
à saint Thomas d'Aquin*, Paris, 1909. — LANG, H., *Die lehre des hl. Thomas
von Aquin von der Gewissheit des Glaubens*, Augsbourg, 1929. — STOLZ, A.,
Glaubensgnade und Glaubenslicht nach Thomas von Aquin, Rome, 1933.

the special light which makes us know — which is either the natural force of reason itself, or the supernatural power of revelation (formal objects).

b) Nevertheless, as a matter of *fact*, the most important natural truths are knowable by mankind *promptly, readily, without error,* through the grace of faith. This fact establishes the moral necessity of revelation to augment reason; it does allow the philosopher, at the same time, to construct his science as a totality and even independently of faith.

2⁰ **Mutual Relations.** *Faith and reason can never contradict each other,* for they derive from the same origin, God, the sole Truth.

This fundamental principle was commonly accepted by all the philosophers of the Middle Ages. St. Thomas, however, knew better than the others how to show the detailed application of this principle, and pointed out the full accord between revealed truths and those of reason. This harmony arises from the good services which faith and reason lend each other.

I. Faith has the following double function with regard to reason :

a) **Medicinal function.** Inasmuch as faith is a supernatural virtue properly residing in the intelligence, it serves as a special light of grace for the mind. Grace does not destroy but rather perfects reason; this is why it re-establishes reason in all its native power, healing the injuries of ignorance and of error due to original sin. It also has an indirect effect; by appeasing troublesome passions and removing the prejudices of pride, it gives the mind the necessary conditioning for finding truth, especially in the practical order. More directly, in doctrines which are closely allied to salvation and which are very basic in philosophy (as God and creation, the human soul and its destiny) [1], faith shows in advance and with infallible certainty the goal which rational demonstration should attain; in this way it frees the mind from the hesitation and the gropings on which error is readily founded.

b) **Elevating function.** The influence of faith on reason is even more profound in the case of a fervent Christian life, for it is accompanied with the gifts of the Holy Spirit, as the

---

[1] It was these very doctrines on which pagan philosophy became stranded; see n. 141, above.

gift of Science, of Intelligence and of Wisdom; these strengthen
the soul for the contemplation of the highest mysteries. For
even though it is true that faith presents man with mysteries
which are not evident in themselves, faith is an eminent light
which does not decrease but increases the power of reason and
stretches its view towards the infinite. Thus, in studying the
Incarnation and the Trinity, Christian philosophers discovered
excellent precisions on the value of human knowledge, the
nature of mind and its actions, and on such notions as
personality, relation and nature.

Corollary. The above discussion shows that Thomism is a
philosophy in the strict sense, and also makes clear in what sense
one can speak, as a Thomist, of a CHRISTIAN PHILOSOPHY [1].

If one views philosophy as a natural wisdom taken in itself,
there is no Christian philosophy for St. Thomas as there is no
Christian astronomy or chemistry; these subjects have their own,
independent domain and their proper, specifying object. But
because of the powerful help which faith gives to rational wisdom,
philosophy, more than any other branch, can be said to be *Christian*,
as long as it makes use of the supernatural aid of grace and to the
extent that it looks for inspiration into the field of revealed truths [2].
This is evidently the case for the great Christian thinkers, Augustine
and Anselm, as it is for St. Thomas; many of their philosophical
doctrines were occasioned by their theological works [3].

On the other hand, it seems that Thomism, through its neat
separation of the natural and supernatural, merits the title of
" Christian philosophy " much more than the Augustinian system.

One could consider the studies which reason makes on the
content of revelation from the outside, so to speak, also as
" Christian philosophy ". In this view we would have a form of
apologetics, which would link up with the other aspect of the
relations between faith and reason.

---

[1] The followings works deal with the problem of " Christian philosophy ".
BLONDEL, M., *Le problème de la Philosophie catholique*, Paris, 1932. — GILSON, E.,
The Spirit of Mediaeval Philosophy, New York, 1940. — JOLIVET, R.,
La philosophie chrétienne et la pensée contemporaine, Paris, 1932. — *La philosophie
chrétienne*, (Journée d'études de la Société thomiste, Sep. 11, 1953). —
MARITAIN, J., *De la philosophie chrétienne*, Paris, 1933.

[2] The phrase " Christian philosophy " expresses a *double connection* between
faith and reason : 1) *subjective*, in the mind of the Christian philosopher which
has been illuminated by supernatural truths and thus could better understand
natural truths; 2) *objective*, in the propositions which are proper to Christian
philosophy, for it prefers those doctrines of metaphysics, of theodicy, of psychology and of morality which are contained in Revelation.

[3] Whatever the exact *speculative notions* involved in the expression " Christian
philosophy " may be, the existence of " Christian philosophies " in the sense
indicated above is an incontestable fact, and the history of philosophy must
take them into account. See, in this connection, E. GILSON, *Christianity and
Philosophy*, New York, 1939.

II. Reason has the following triple function with regard to faith :

a) **Apologetic Role.** Philosophy " demonstrates those things which are preambulatory to faith " [1]. Reason can lead the mind towards the threshold of faith, by demonstrating such fundamental truths as the existence of God and the possibility of the fact of revelation. This constitutes the " credibility " of revelation, and the proofs of these truths are coordinated in the science of apologetics.

b) **Theological Role.** Philosophy is helpful " in making known by means of some similitudes, those items which are matters of faith ". Reason is explanatory of faith; it does not explain, of course, through demonstrative proofs; by their very definition the mysteries of faith are incapable of rational demonstration. Mysteries are established through the authority of the Scriptures, wherein they are divinely sanctioned by miracles, and through the official teaching of the Fathers and of the Church herself. Rather, reason proposes arguments for the suitability of these mysteries; reason arranges the various revealed truths in logical order and explains their meaning through comparing them with the various propositions of philosophy. The science of theology is constituted of the conclusions which are thus deduced by reason and integrated logically with the revealed dogmas themselves.

c) **Polemic Role.** Philosophy is helpful " in resisting those things which are said against faith, either by showing them to be false or showing them to be unnecessary ". Reason defends faith by refuting all the objections which are opposed to it, pointing out their falsity or lack of efficacy; as a result, while the mystery still remains " incomprehensible " and below the measure of reason, it is shown as *not being opposed to reason* and as not being contradictory to it.

It was in fulfilling this triple function that St. Thomas deployed the resources of his powerful mind in writing his two theological summaries [2], as well as his numerous theological treatises.

---

[1] This text and the two quoted in the two following paragraphs are taken from St. Thomas' commentary on the *De Trinitate* of Boethius, q. II, art. 3.

[2] The *Summa Contra Gentes* especially realizes the third function mentioned, and also the first. The *Summa Theologica* perfectly realizes the second and third functions through its 3113 articles, each of which answers countless objections.

C) **Mixed Domain.**

245. The relations of St. Thomas with the more important noble families of his time spread his influence into the political and social realm. His recommendations and views in these realms arise both from philosophy and from theology. Two works contain some of his views in this area :

1º *De regimine Principum,* or *De Regno* (1265-9), was written for the education of Hugh II, King of Cyprus [1]. It is principally a detailed code of the duties of rulers. It opens with an exposition on the nature of political society, showing the reasons for power and includes a critical sketch of various constitutions of states. This work contains the most complete systematization of the Thomistic doctrines on society.

2º *De regimine Judæorum* (1269-72) is addressed to the Duchess of Brabant, who consulted St. Thomas on the manner of regarding her Jewish subjects. The doctrine contained here is repeated or completed in various sections of the *Summa Theologica.*

The Thomistic position in this mixed domain has a triple characteristic :

a) A firmness of principles which proclaim rights in an absolute fashion;

b) Moderation in applying these principles, by which opposed rights are mutually tempered.

I. — *In Politics.* St. Thomas based the necessity for authority on the social nature of man; for this reason, all political power comes from God as the Author of nature. But this power resides, in first instance, in the " people " as the community seeking to organize for the common good. While a ruler is indispensable, his mode of designation (through election, heredity, and so forth) is undetermined and depends upon circumstances. The form of government which seemed most preferable to him was a *limited monarchy :* one ruler, whose authority is controlled and assisted through a social organization.

II. — *The Jewish question.* St. Thomas established the *right* of the Christian group to defend itself against the Jews. He allowed this from the religious point of view, so that Christians could defend themselves against the propagandizing effects of the errors of the Jews; he liberated them from the injunctions the

---

[1] This work is certainly authentic, at least until the middle part of book two; the rest seems to have been edited from similar materials in other works of St. Thomas by Bartholomew (or Ptolemy) of Lucca (1245-1327).

Jews laid upon them, for the Jews wished to hold the Christians in servitude. From the social point of view, St. Thomas accepts this principle, " the Jews are servants ".

In practice, this right of the Christians must be harmonized with the natural law under its various forms. For instance, parents have rights over their children, and, accordingly, the children cannot be baptized without the consent of their parents; " for, by natural law, children are under parental care as long as they are unable to provide for themselves ". This right must be harmonized with the freedom of conscience; one cannot do violence to the Jews in order to Christianize them, " for belief is proper to the will, which cannot be forced ". The right of all men to life and to charity must also be respected; therefore, while it is true that the " Jews are talliable and liable to forced labor at pleasure ", they must have the necessities of life and their habitual mode of life should not be thrown into convolution — and here St. Thomas counsels the Duchess to be content with the taxes fixed by her predecessors. Finally, Judaism has rights inasmuch as it was the nation which announced the coming of Christ; the Jews, accordingly, should be authorized to practice their religion. This is not liberty, but tolerance for the Jews.

From the economic viewpoint, which is here of great importance, the Jews were the great *usurers* of this period. St. Thomas condemned the interest on loans as an injustice [1]. He required, as a consequence, that the Jews be obliged to restitute their gains and to return the product of legal confiscations to their legitimate owners; or, if this were impossible, to employ these goods in good works. He thought, though, that it would be better to prevent usury by forcing the Jews to procure some useful and remunerative work.

Other important works were written during the sojourn in Italy, among which are his commentaries on the Canticle of Canticles, on the Lamentations and on Jeremias, on St. Paul [2], and the Office of the Blessed Sacrament composed in 1264 at the request of Urban IV. At the suggestion of the same Pope, he undertook the compilation of the lovely *Catena Aurea* which aims to explain the four Gospels by enchaining in a continuous text the best commentaries of the Fathers of the Church [3].

---

[1] See also his *Summa Theologica*, II-II, q. LXXVIII; if money brings no profit to the borrower, he need not return anything more than the loan to its owner, for mutual assistance of this sort is an essential condition of social affairs. One can apply this view only to the actual economic conditions of the Middle Ages, vastly different from those now prevalent.

[2] For a short analysis of all these commentaries, see F. CAYRÉ, *op. cit.*, Vol. II, pp. 551-554.

[3] The commentary on St. Matthew dates from 1261-2; the three others from 1265-7.

III. PERIOD OF STRUGGLE. The Second Sojourn at Paris.

(1269-1272).

246. In January of 1269, St. Thomas returned to Paris to occupy a chair of theology as a teaching master. This return was somewhat exceptional [1], for the Dominican order recognized only masters who had been degreed from the University of Paris and kept such masters in Paris only a short time, in order to multiply their number, and never returned them; there is but one other exception in the whole of the thirteenth century. This move was, no doubt, due to the great authority that St. Thomas had acquired in the intellectual world both through his writings and his doctrinal struggles; and there were grave interests of truth in stake at this time in the university. In fact, St. Thomas there encountered a triple type of opposition : from the seculars, the Averroists and from the Augustinians.

A) The Seculars.

William of St. Amour, though in exile, managed to stir up the animosity of the Parisian masters; when Clement IV became Pope (1265), a man of French nationality, William hoped to win back the favor of the pontifical court and addressed a work to the Pope entitled *Liber de Antichristo et ejus ministris* which, however, was not favorably received by the Pope. In 1268, Gerard of Abbeville, a secular master and friend of William's who was still at Paris, published his *Contra adversariorum perfectionis christianæ*, which again stirred up the old attacks on the regulars. The latter responded vigorously : St. Bonaventure wrote his *Apologia pauperum*, John Peckham, the regent of the Franciscan school at Paris, wrote a work called *Tractatus pauperis contra insipientem* and St. Thomas wrote a work entitled *De perfectione vitæ spiritualis* (1269).

In his work St. Thomas shows that the essence of perfection consists in charity whose various degrees can be found in God Himself, in the Blessed and in the souls of the just on this earth. (Chs. 1-6). He then shows that poverty, chastity, love of one's neighbor and obedience are the means for acquiring this perfection (Chs. 7-14). Finally, he treats of the state of perfection itself : what it is in general, the state of the episcopacy and that of religious, and a comparison of diocesan with religious clergy (Chs. 15-25). He mentions the works that are proper to religious clergy, which

---

[1] It was in order to replace an ailing teacher that St. Thomas received the order, in November, 1268, to go to Paris, where he arrived in January, 1269. His superiors kept him there because of the gravity of the circumstances then existent at the university.

are the same as those mentioned in his earlier work, *Contra impugnantes Dei cultum.*

In 1270, Nicholas of Lisieux, another influential secular master, wrote a short work in reply to St. Thomas dealing with the perfection and excellence of the clerical state. St. Thomas answered this with another work, *Contra pestiferam doctrinam retrahentium homines a religionis ingressu.*

This work is avowedly polemical. After mentioning various instances from the Gospel when Christ called certain persons to the life of perfection, St. Thomas recalls the effort of Jovinian and of Vigilance to lead men away from perfection. He compares the present situation to these latter attempts, for they also refuse entrance into religious life to persons unless they are already exercised in the commandments, as also to young men and to new converts. In their view, long consideration and time should be spent before the state is entered, one should not take a vow to enter religion, and poverty should be toned down. All these difficulties are exposed and refuted and similar objections are resolved.

The struggle on this point was carried on in public disputations, as can be seen in many *Quodlibeta.* In the meantime, the secular masters, although unchanged and obstinate in their view, became less numerous and influential; the death of two of them put an end to the agitation at Paris [1].

B) **Averroism.**

247. Averroism is a term coined by St. Thomas to describe a current of radical Aristotelianism that arose at Paris between 1260 and 1265; it was called by this name because it adopted the explanation of Arabic philosophy on the obscure answer which Aristotle gave on the nature of the human mind [2]. Until St. Thomas' return, no great personality had taught at Paris, and the enthusiasm of the young masters of arts for their new manuals of Aristotle could easily have evolved into quite heterodox views.

SIGER OF BRABANT was the head of this Averroistic view. Born in 1253, he was a canon at St. Martin in Liege, a master of arts of the national group of Picards and, for about ten years, the center of the various agitations which occurred at

---

[1] These two men were Gerard of Abbeville († 1271) and William of St. Amour († 1272).

[2] This problem had vexed the Christian thinkers of this period for some time. About 1256, Urban IV had asked St. Albert the Great to clarify this question in the presence of the cardinals of the Pontifical court. Albert's work, *De unitate intellectus contra Averroem,* the fruit of this conference, makes no allusion to an error that was actually being taught in the universities; the problem of Averroism, as explained above, only arose about 10 years later.

the University [1]. About 1266, he appears to have been audacious and intransigent in his views, and in conflict with the papal legate, Simon of Brie. In 1270, it seems that about a sixth of the philosophers, especially from the Picard and Norman groups, followed his views, along with several masters including Boethius of Dacia and Bernier of Nivelles [2].

Siger had a clear, penetrating and supple mind; he wrote many works which were lost for some time but are now known to be his. Some are original treatises while others are reports on his lectures; the latter were revised and edited either by himself or are simple copies of his students' notes. They can be distributed into three groups [3]. A number of these were written before St. Thomas returned to Paris; among them are the following : *Quæstiones logicales*, a series of commentaries on Aristotle's *Physics* (Books I-IV), on his *De Generatione*, and especially on the third book of the *De Anima*, which defends his view of the soul. Other works were written contemporaneously with the controversies with St. Thomas : the six *Impossibilia* or exercises on logic; *De æternitate mundi ; De necessitate et contingentia causarum ;* the famous *De anima intellectiva ;* a second series of commentaries on Aristotle's Physics (Books I-IV). After the death of St. Thomas, he wrote a commentary on the eighth book of Aristotle's Physics, a new commentary on the third book of the *De Anima*, and some short treatises on psychology.

These works show a rather important doctrinal evolution. Siger had a systematic philosophy similar to that of the Arabs, and kept faithful to it until he died. The first form of Averroism will be given below, which is its most radical position; the variations in this view which resulted from the struggle with St. Thomas will also be pointed out.

I. Doctrinal Synthesis of Siger of Brabant.

248. *a*) **General Traits.** As all the masters of the Middle Ages, Siger looked at the comprehension and objective explanation of Aristotle as his first duty. He was not, however, a pure historian. He made Aristotle's synthesis his own,

---

[1] On this whole question of Averroism, see F. COPLESTON, *op. cit.*, Vol. II, pp. 435-441; see also his bibliography on this question, p. 583.

[2] These two men were included with Siger in the condemnation of 1277.

[3] See F. VAN STEENBERGHEN, *Siger de Brabant d'après ses œuvres inédites*, Louvain, 1931, Vol. II, pp. 551-564.

seeing in it an ideal of life and of happiness on the human and philosophical plane, to which theology could be content to add a crowning unity. He succeeded in erecting a remarkable synthesis of authentic Aristotelianism by adopting his fundamental views on actuality and potentiality, matter and form, substance and accident, and so forth, totally cleansed of eclectic confusion. In this regard, he is wholly in accord with St. Thomas. But if one looks into the works now actually known to be his, and distinguishes in them that which is his own as distinct from pagan philosophy and from Thomism, one finds two series of propositions : in physics and metaphysics, and in psychology.

b) **Physics and Metaphysics.** The universe is formed of a hierarchy of species, which are immutable, necessary and eternal. Below, there are corporeal beings, composed of matter and of form, whose representative individuals are destined for birth and corruption. Above, there are the celestial spheres, subject to accidental change and local motion only, and moved by intelligences which are pure forms, eternal in their own right. At the summit, Pure Actuality is the coronal of all.

The existence of God is demonstrated by the proof from the first mover (Aristotle [1]) and the proof of the necessary being (Avicenna [2]), and the attributes of God are given profound treatment. Being Pure Actuality, God is necessarily *unique* and the unique efficient cause of all being. Having no principle of limit or of change, He is infinite, immutable and eternal. Every other being, composed of actuality and potentiality, is really distinct from Him. In order to clarify the relations of causality holding between God and the universe, Siger appeals to what can be called the " principle of symmetry ", according to which a passive potentiality corresponds to every actuality : matter to form, accident to substance, and so forth. To Pure Actuality there corresponds, in all other beings, the fundamental potentiality for existence. This *potentia ad esse* — which is comparable to the Thomistic notion of essence as distinct from existence — is a logical potentiality for Siger; it is the basic characteristic of each finite thing to be *participatory*, not to have the reason for its existence in itself, and to have been derived from Pure Actuality.

---

[1] See above, n. 92.
[2] See above, n. 185.

It follows that God is truly *Creator*, the very cause of being as such. His action, producing everything without a pre-existing subject, is universal and continuous; it is a conservation. Since He created it, God knows the world not only in a general way, but even with regard to its individual modalities; God is Providence in the proper sense. Siger did not arrive at an understanding of the freedom of the creative act. In his view, this act was necessary, for it flowed from the very essence of Pure Actuality. This necessity is also found on the part of the effect in the sense that both the spiritual beings as well as the essences as such, even corporeal essences, partake *immutably* in the being of God. Following Avicenna and Averroes, Siger maintained that the immediate effect of God is necessary, eternal and unique; this effect is the First Intelligence, " from whom the other intelligences, the heavenly spheres and all the movements of the heavens derive by the same law of necessity. The heavenly bodies, in their turn, exercise a profound and permanent influence on the sublunary world and various aspects of this causality can be distinguished. Finally, the particular causes from whom the sublunary world is formed, act upon each other, some producing certain effects *necessarily and per se*, others only *in most cases and per se*, while others only, *per accidens* " [1].

In this well-coordinated view, Siger includes the notion of *contingence*. Because of the successive complications of the celestial spheres, their physical causality allows for the existence of effects on earth which are unforeseeable, inasmuch as the ordinary cause could be prevented from always producing the same effect. This causality, then, has only a relative necessity, and this is what Siger means by contingence. The human will is a cause fully similar to all other physical causes. There is no independent and dominating activity in it, but its activity must be explained also by the laws of nature. The variety of effects which the will causes is but a case of interference of laws, and the uncertainty of its future action is explained as an effect of chance.

Higher above, in the world of *essences* and of *spirits*, the reign of immutable necessity holds : this universe is something " given " and necessarily existent from all eternity. Furthermore, the sidereal and terrestrial movement which constitutes the actual order of the world is necessarily eternal. Here the

[1] F. Van Steenberghen, *op. cit.*, Vol. ii, p. 600.

Averroists use Aristotle's proofs [1] and from the *eternity* of the immediate effect of God they deduce the proposition that from the latter effect " flows the eternity of the separated substances, including the intellective soul, the eternity of material species, of matter, of motion, of time and of generation " [2]. The evolvement of our universe is thus conceived as an immense unrolling of logically connected events, each of which is necessarily the fruit of celestial influences at every moment, so that after a period of 30,000 years, when the stars would assume the same position as today, the same events would be reproduced in all their details.

Briefly, the universe is created, conserved and governed by God, but *necessarily*, as is proper to an effect of an immutable and eternal cause.

c) **Psychology.** Siger's characteristic proposition here is that of the *unity of intelligence.* Inasmuch as intellection, a spiritual action, is accomplished without a physical organ, the intellectual soul cannot be the form of body. It is only matter which gives numerical multiplication; the human soul is necessarily unique and is to be identified with the last celestial Intelligence, who moves the sphere closest to the earth, the moon.

Men are, nevertheless, multiple and numerically distinct through the sensible portion of their being. Since the law of human intelligence is to know through abstraction, that is, by uniting with a sensible phantasm, the multiple variety of human acts of intelligence can be explained. Only in this sense can intellection be attributed to an individual man : he furnishes the material for the operation of abstraction which occurs within him.

A conception of this sort destroys personal immortality. Only the human race, concentrated in this unique intelligence, is immortal and eternal as the universe. Since it is spiritual, the human race avoids all the vicissitudes incumbent on corporeal substances; it is unbegotten and incorruptible. It has necessarily existed from all time and is, at one and the same time, always substantially separated and always united for action to the successive generations of men here below.

Through abstraction, the mind goes beyond the phantasm by ridding it of individuating traits and thus arriving at the notion of a nature in itself which is universal, eternal and

---

[1] See above, n. 79.
[2] F. Van Steenberghen, *op. cit.*, Vol. II, p. 610.

necessary. In this latter point Siger rejoins the moderated realism of Aristotle and of St. Thomas. But when one looks for the metaphysical foundation of these essences, he does not find them in the exemplary Ideas of God, in the system of Siger, but rather in the immutable order of the universe eternally unrolling from God.

II. The Struggle. The Doctrinal Evolvement of Siger of Brabant.

249. This vast synthetic and connected view is directly contrary to Catholic teaching on more than one point; it could not fail to stir a reaction among theologians. In 1267, St. Bonaventure, adopting the viewpoint of faith, eloquently denounced the new heresy in a series of sermons given at Paris. During the year 1270, the ecclesiastical authorities edited and circulated an official catalogue of the principal errors proposed for condemnation; it contained fifteen propositions which had been examined and discussed in the schools. St. Albert the Great, then at Cologne, had received a notification of these through a friend, and had refuted them in his work, *De quindecim problematibus*. But it was especially St. Thomas who vigorously interposed. In a sermon preached to the students of St. James on July 20, 1270, he condemned those philosophers who placed themselves in contradiction with the faith, as if there could exist such opposed truths. To combat their view, he showed, through the example of personal immortality, the incertitudes and the errors of pure reason in the presence of the clarity and certitude of faith [1].

Of all the Averroistic errors, the most dangerous was that of the *unity of the intelligence*, especially due to its practical consequences. In 1270, St. Thomas published his work, *De unitate intellectus contra averroistas*. In this work he did not examine an original treatise of Siger's, for none had as yet been published, but rather criticized his oral teaching, which had been so sensational and had circulated among the lecture notes of the students. Siger took this work of Aquinas as merely a reply to his thoughts on Aristotle and to the demonstrations of pure reason. St. Thomas declared himself willing to meet Siger also on the philosophical terrain in order to refute him.

---

[1] " Today ", said St. Thomas, " an old Christian woman knows more of God and of the soul than all the pagan philosophers but together ".

a) In this work, St. Thomas first *adopts the authority of philosophers and especially that of Aristotle.* He justifies his interpretation of the *De Anima* by basing it on the definition of the soul there given : the first actuality of a physically organized body. The human operations are those of vegetation, sensation, comprehension and self-movement; these four abilities are in the same subject, the soul, and the intelligence is a power not using a corporeal organ.

Siger objects that if the intellectual soul is the form of the body, the intelligence is nothing more than the faculty of a material composite, and would have to be a form joined to a corporeal organ — which Aristotle denies.

St. Thomas answers that by its position in the hierarchy of forms, the human soul partakes in the nature of spiritual and of corporeal beings in such a manner that it is at once both joined and separated, according to its diverse faculties. In this way he resolved the essential objection against the Thomistic interpretation of Aristotle.

St. Thomas referred to other authors, and showed that he was in agreement with three other commentators, Algazel, Avicenna and Themistius; the latter he knew through a recent translation made by William of Moerbeke [1], which had been ignored by Siger.

b) St. Thomas also *resolved the problem on its own merits*, showing that only his view is demonstrable by reason. The fundamental proof is the argument taken from consciousness; in order that the testimony of experience " that each man comprehends " be really intelligible, it is necessary that each possesses his own intelligence. Other a priori reasons, based on the definition of man, on the nature of his essential unity, and similar arguments are added [2]. St. Thomas also remarks that the unity of intelligence involves the unity of the will in all men, a conclusion which would involve the destruction of independence and of personal responsibility, both of which notions are affirmed by consciousness. Finally, the existence of science in some individuals and its exclusion from others, and the fact of contrasting errors in various men demand that each has his own mind. On the other hand, he concedes that these reasons have full validity only for the passive intellect, and that the unity of the active intellect could strictly be admitted [3].

St. Thomas finally answers the objections which Siger made and points out the odd position of a Catholic philosopher who would defend, as demonstrable by reason, propositions formally opposed to the teaching of faith. Such a man is logically forced to hold to the existence of *two realms of truths*, the one natural and the other supernatural, and that these truths could be contradictory [4]. But such a view is absurd and rejected by all Catholics.

---

[1] See n. 232, above.

[2] These proofs are also found in the *Summa Theologica*, I, q. LXXVI, art. 2.

[3] In the first part of the *Summa Theologica* (q. LXXIX, art. 5), which was written in Italy, St. Thomas showed that each man possesses his own *active intellect;* he does not retract this position here, but treats it sparingly because some Augustinians, as Roger Bacon, identified the active intellect with God.

[4] This theory was defended by Averroes, who held to the existence of three independent realms of truth; see above, n. 191.

He concludes by defying Siger to answer : " let him dare to write against this work, and let him not speak in the corners or in the presence of young men who cannot judge of difficult matters ". This defiance shows how dangerous he judges the Averroistic views to be.

Siger was vividly impressed by this vigorous attack which struck him in his own domain; he answered the challenge by his treatise, *De anima intellectiva.*

This work is divided into ten chapters [1] and treats of the most difficult and uncertain doctrines of Aristotle concerning the soul. The first two chapters give a nominal and a real definition of the soul as the form of body and are in accord with Thomism. Chapter three, however, states more precisely the mode in which the soul is the form of body; then, having treated of the eternity and of the separated life of the soul, it brings up the multiplication of intelligences according to bodies. Here, Siger names Albert the Great and Thomas of Aquin, whom he calls two significant men in philosophy, as his opponents. In order to answer St. Thomas' opuscule, which named Averroes as the " corrupter " rather than a commentator on Aristotle, he openly abandons the Arabic view and concentrates on the Aristotelian texts of the *De Anima.* He then presents a personal exegesis which is opposed to that of St. Thomas, and claims it is more faithful to Aristotle's meaning. In order to answer the basic objection brought by St. Thomas of how " this man understands ", Siger proposes that the unique intellectual soul unites itself to each individual human being not through the simple abstraction of the phantasm (Averroes), nor as a true, substantial form (St. Thomas), but as a " form intrinsically operating ". By acting, he holds, the intelligence is united to each body through its very nature [2]. But this modification still leaves unchanged the major views of his system, even in psychology, as that of the unity and of the eternity of intelligence, and the notion of necessary creation from eternity.

At the same time, Siger agrees with St. Thomas that many propositions defended as authentically Aristotelian are opposed to the faith; in this case, he adds, the *faith is to be held.* Similar declarations are found in the second and in the third group of his writings, and it is difficult to doubt his sincerity [3]. A man of the Church as well as a philosopher, Siger was vividly touched by the vehement reproaches of St. Thomas. From this time on, the problem of relating his philosophy to his faith,

---

[1] The tenth of these chapters is either lost or was never written.

[2] *De anima intellective,* Ch. III.

[3] A better knowledge of the works of Siger has allowed us to correct the view of P. MANDONNET (*Siger de Brabant,* Vol. I, p. 179), who considered these statements of Siger's to be valueless.

which Siger had previously neglected as being a question of pure theology, forced itself upon him as a matter of conscience.

Logically, he should have given up the theory of the two truths; but his principles prevented him from doing so. In his view, " there cannot exist a contradiction between revealed truth and truth discoverable by reason, for truth is that which is, and God Himself cannot reconcile contradictories " [1]. At the same time, it seemed to him that " revealed truth is superior in excellence and in certitude to the truth seen by human reason " [2]. From this it follows that in case of conflict, faith is to be preferred to philosophy. In explaining these conflicts he states that reason is limited and fallible, and that God can intervene in a miraculous or supernatural fashion so that a proposition rigorously demonstrated by Aristotle, as the eternity of the world, could be corrected by faith if God decided " miraculously " to create the world in time.

Influenced by the demands of faith and by the explanations of St. Thomas, Siger continued his study of the unity of the intelligence. In the third group of his writings he approached the Thomistic solution. The intellectual soul, he held, is the *substantial form* of the body, and is independent of the body in its higher operations; in this way, it can also be multiplied numerically with each man. It is not eternal, but created by God as the conclusion of human generation; moreover, it is subsistent and immortal [3]. Finally, Siger corrected his doctrine of human liberty and explains it, as did St. Thomas, through the lack of proportion between the particular good freely chosen and the absolute good which is the formal object of the will.

Nevertheless, despite these important modifications, Siger held pretty much to his own views until the close of his life, and especially to his notion of a system of celestial spheres necessarily and eternally devolving from Pure Actuality.

C) The Augustinians.

250. The heterodox Aristotelianism mentioned above waked vivid opposition from the theologians. There was another group, strongly traditionalist, who held to some Neo-Platonic

---

[1] F. Van Steenberghen, *op. cit.*, ii, p. 693.
[2] *Ibid.*, ii, p. 695.
[3] *Ibid.*, ii, pp. 657-661.

propositions, mainly borrowed from St. Augustine. They
were inclined to condemn Aristotelianism en bloc as tainted
with heresy. This is why they were opposed to Averroes,
to Siger of Brabant, and to Thomism.

In order to make clear the position of St. Thomas with
regard to this *Augustinianism* of the Middle Ages, it is necessary
to distinguish two aspects in the latter view, one theological,
and the other, philosophical. About the close of the twelfth
century, under the influence of St. Augustine's works, a body
of theological doctrine was formed which constituted more
of a spirit or attitude than a system[1]; this view was part of
the traditional teaching in the thirteenth century. Thus,
a strong current of " *Augustinianism* " is found in this period,
and no one is as faithful to it as St. Thomas himself. In this
connection it can be noted that there was unanimous opposition
to Averroism, finally leading to the December 10, 1270, condemnation of thirteen propositions [2] by Bishop Stephen Tempier
of Paris.

The Augustinian theology implicitly contained a true *philosophical* doctrine. It was, however, amalgamated with Aristotelianism and resulted in the Neo-Platonic eclectism mentioned
above [3]. St. Bonaventure, the most eminent of the traditionalist theologians, got his main inspiration from St. Augustine
and, without neglecting the new riches of Peripateticism,
created an authentic Augustinian philosophy [4]. Most of the
other theologians were much more eclectic; and the rise of
Averroism led them away from Aristotle and towards organizing
Augustinianism in philosophy.

The following masters who flourished during this third period
of doctrinal struggles should be mentioned. *a*) The *seculars.*

---

[1] " Although there does not exist an Augustinianism in the strict sense either
as a complete general system or as a body of philosophical learning, there is
a wider Augustinianism consisting in the theological spirit of St. Augustine and
disciples... The spirit in question is based on the GREAT THESES dear to
St. Augustine, whether they derived from Platonism or a Christian source :
1) the fundamental importance of the *idea of God* in all philosophical and
theological speculation; 2) the *doctrine of exemplarism* that teaches the way
to God through his creatures, for whom He is the eternal archetype; 3) the
rights of God always affirmed in His providential government of His creatures;
4) *mysticism*, or the stressing of man's power of achieving in this world an
affective union that entails the vision of God in some measure; 5) a definite
moral doctrine, teaching that man must act in conformity with grace to the
extent of letting it rule his whole life ". F. CAYRÉ, *op. cit.*, II, p. 357.
[2] The last two propositions were not condemned, though it is unknown through
whose influence.
[3] See above, n. 232bis. — [4] See below, n. 274 ff.

Among this group, Henry of Ghent († 1293) authored a *Summa theologica* and fifteen *Quodlibeta;* he was enthusiastic about St. Thomas, but defended his own views, as that of the existence of a *form of corporeity* in man, in addition to the spiritual soul [1]. Godfrey of Fontaines († 1303), whose *Quodlibeta* (sixteen of which are known) show him as opposed to Henry of Ghent and to St. Thomas, for he denied the real distinction between essence and existence and denied individuation through matter [2]. Stephen Tempier, the Bishop of Paris and Peter of Auvergne († 1304) are worthy of mention; the latter left some *Quodlibeta* which he disputed between 1296 and 1302. Henry Bate of Malines (1246-1310) wrote the *Speculum divinorum et quorumdam naturalium* [3] in which he tried to reconcile Aristotle with Plato and St. Augustine, and in which he accuses St. Thomas of an exaggerated attachment to Peripateticism.

b) The *religious*. Giles of Rome, a hermit of St. Augustine [4], and the English Dominican Robert of Kilwardby († 1279) are important names. The latter taught at Paris and at Oxford before becoming Archbishop of Canterbury (1272-8) and cardinal. He commented on the Book of Sentences of Peter the Lombard, and on various works of Aristotle. In his *De ortu et divisione philosophiæ,* he adopts the Aristotelian outlines; however, in his *De unitate formarum* and in a letter to Peter of Conflans, he resolutely holds to the notion of seminal reasons and to the plurality of forms. Robert used all his influence to rid the University of Oxford of Thomism. The Franciscans were disciples of St. Bonaventure [5]. The main representative among them during the second sojourn of St. Thomas at Paris was John Peckham (about 1240-1292), who succeeded Robert of Kilwardby to the see of Canterbury in 1278. He wrote commentaries on the Book of Sentences, various disputed questions and *Quodlibeta*, and some letters which vividly reveal the doctrinal struggle of the age.

In the eyes of this group of thinkers, St. Thomas naturally takes on the figure of an innovator and an imprudent ally of Averroism, since he defended the fundamental propositions supported by Siger and which were opposed to some special theories dear to the Augustinians.

For instance, far from fusing philosophy with theology [6], St. Thomas maintained the autonomy of reason within its own domain. He rejected the theory of seminal reasons and defended

---

[1] M. DE WULF, *op. cit.*, II, p.

[2] *Ibid.*,

[3] This is a vast work, divided into 23 parts; it was originally written for the education of Prince Guy of Hainault.

[4] See below, n. 282, II.

[5] See below, n. 282, I.

[6] Many Augustinians distinguished these two sciences, but insisted on the servile role of philosophy. They were inclined to deny the title of perfect science to it which St. Thomas adopted.

the absolute potentiality of prime matter. He excluded all matter from the angels and the human soul, teaching that the latter directly informs the body. The Augustinians were inclined to conclude that a direct union of soul with matter would make the soul lose its immortality. They did not deny that the soul was the form of body[1], but that it was directly the form of prime matter. St. Thomas develops this doctrine of " pure forms " in his opuscule, *De substantiis separatis* written during this period of struggle; in this work he takes special exception to the *Fons Vitæ* of Avicebron.

Discussion on these various points ordinarily occurred during the scholarly exercises, but especially at the public meetings on disputed questions or at the " adlibetal " sessions of Christmas and Easter. At these meetings, St. Thomas was calm and impassioned; he answered every difficulty possible in as short and precise a manner as possible. At the same time, he was always respectful of Church authority, humbly submitting his teaching to the judgment of the Church. On one occasion, John Peckham tried to turn to his own advantage St. Thomas' reply to a question Peckham asked on the unity of form; this meeting was held in the presence of Bishop Stephen Tempier. Peckham, however, did not succeed in confounding St. Thomas. In fact, a close study of the various places in which St. Thomas answers the many objections offered him show that he held his position on this matter faultlessly.

It seems that, stimulated by these struggles, St. Thomas undertook an explanation of the doctrine on the soul as one of his ordinary sessions of dispute; these meetings were held every five days. This work, *De anima*, is not a complete tract on psychology, but a selection of questions that are perennially important, as the relations between soul and body, knowledge and its objectivity, the soul and its faculties, the unity of intelligence, the spirituality of the soul and personal immortality.

With the same goal in mind, St. Thomas took up the question which resulted in his work, *De spiritualibus creaturis*. This work rejects the composition of matter and form in angels (art. 1), treats the union of body and soul (2-4), studies the angels (5-8), the unity of the passive intellect (9) and the unity of the active intellect (10), and the distinction of the powers of the soul from its essence (11).

These same problems reappear, though in less orderly fashion, in the seven *Quodlibeta* which he held during his second session of teaching at Paris; according to Mandonnet, they are: *Quodlibeta I-III* (1268-70); *Quodlibetum XII* (Christmas, 1270); *Quodlibeta IV-V* (1271-2).

---

[1] The Augustinians accepted, without difficulty, the rule of the Council of Vienna in 1311 on this matter; see F. COPLESTON, *op. cit.*, II, pp. 451-2.

The work, *De æternitate mundi contra murmurantes* belongs to this same period. In it, St. Thomas shows against the Augustinians, who wished to demonstrate the necessity of creation *in time*, that the eternity of the world is not self-contradictory, though without conceding to the Averroists that it is necessary. In St. Thomas' view, only faith can make us certain of the fact that the world had a beginning.

Following the condemnation of 1270, Averroism was no longer officially taught at Paris, but it still had partisans. At Christmas of 1271, upon the occasion of Alberic's election as Rector, an extremist group from the faculty of arts separated itself and elected Siger of Brabant as their choice. At the same time, difficulties arose with Bishop Stephen Tempier and the University, so that a strike was declared. It was in the midst of these troubles that St. Thomas quitted Paris at Easter, 1272 and, at the demand of Charles of Anjou, the brother of St. Louis, was sent to Naples to found a general house of studies.

The faculty of philosophy was strongly opposed to this move, and many masters wrote to the General Chapter of the Dominicans (June 1272), in order to have him recalled; this effort, however, failed.

Before he left, St. Thomas found time to address three small works to John of Verceil, the Master General. The first, *De Articulis XLII*, was concerned with points disputed among the Dominican students; in it, St. Thomas, always moderated, shows that most of these articles, being questions of pure philosophy [1], can neither be affirmed as revealed dogmas, nor rejected as contrary to faith — " and thus one can prevent wise men from misunderstanding Catholic doctrine ". In the second, *De forma absolutionis*, he shows that the form of absolution is not merely imprecatory but indicative, as a judiciary sentence. The third work is entitled *De articulis CVIII sumptis ex opere Petri de Tarentasia*.

---

[1] These questions are mainly concerned with the astronomical theory of the celestial spheres, of which the Averroists, following the lead of the Arabs, had made much (see above, nn. 77, 93, 184, 249). Aristotle taught that the spheres were moved by Intelligences or separated forms, whom the Christian interpreters identified with the *angels*. Article III asks the question as to whether angels are the movers of celestial bodies. The same questions reappear in a small work of the same period (1271), *Responsio ad lectorem Venetum de articulis XXXVI*. In this work, St. Thomas says : " It seems to me that it could be demonstratively established that celestial bodies are moved by some intelligence, either immediately by God, or through the angels as intermediary; it would seem more congruous with the order of things that they be moved through the intermediary of angels ". This answer shows that he did not seem to evaluate these theories too greatly.

St. Thomas also commented on the *Liber de causis*, a work falsely attributed to Aristotle. He knew of its Neo-Platonic origin due to the complete translation of the work of Proclus, *Elementatio theologiæ*, recently done in Italy by William of Moerbeke, and of which the *Liber de causis* is but an extract.

Last years and **DEATH** of St. **THOMAS.**

251. At Naples, St. Thomas' life took on the aspect of a conclusion : he remained, until death, a simple professor of theology, continuing his doctrinal, philosophical and theological work, and pursuing the composition of numerous works. He wrote the third portion of the *Summa theologica* at this time; he finished his commentaries on St. Paul (the Epistle to the Romans, and the first Epistle to the Corinthians); for his faithful companion, Reginald, he wrote the *Compendium theologiæ*, a fine summary of the theological summa, but did not complete the work [1]. He continued, as he had done throughout his life, to preach sermons, especially to the students; some of these have been preserved.

In philosophy, he was engaged in the scientific part (in the modern sense of science) of the Commentaries on Aristotle. He commented on the *Meteorologica*, on *De coelo et mundo* (incomplete) and on *De generatione et corruptione* (which contains Aristotle's rudimentary chemistry). He had promised to send some Parisian artisans all of these works, and to compose, at their request, a treatise, *De aquæductu*, and another treatise on machines. Thus, faithful to his program, he wished to follow his exposition of the metaphysical doctrine of Aristotle with an explanation of the scientific riches of the Ancients.

But Providence halted him in the midst of this full activity. In 1274, as he was returning from the Council of Lyons, to which Gregory X (1271-1276) had called him, he became ill near the Cistercian monastery of Fossa Nuova, where he died on March 7, while commenting on the Biblical work, the *Canticle of Canticles*.

After his death, the Averroist agitation continued at Paris. The masters of arts, believing in the autonomy of their teaching, would not accept the doctrinal directives imposed by the authorities; many of them continued to maintain propositions contradictory to faith. In 1277, Pope John XXI required an

---

[1] St. Thomas here assembles his doctrine under the three theological virtues; however, he completed only faith and hope.

investigation into their orthodoxy, and Bishop Stephen Tempier had the faculty of theology make up a list of two-hundred and nineteen condemnable propositions. This syllabus, arising from the traditionalist viewpoint, included in the same disapproval the notoriously heretical theories of Averroism and the Peripatetic innovations judged dangerous to faith. Most of the latter propositions were defended both by St. Thomas and by Siger of Brabant, and Bishop Tempier, somewhat overshooting the mark, laid a decree of censure against the doctrine and of excommunication against the persons involved. Nevertheless, due to the brilliant defense of St. Thomas, he did not dare to condemn the theory of the unity of form. At the same time, however, Robert Kilwardby, then Archbishop of Canterbury, condemned thirty propositions, most of them dealing with the unity of form; this was done at Oxford. Tempier, who was preparing further condemnations, was halted by the death of John XXI and the intervention of the Cardinals of the papal curia who were favorable to St. Thomas.

This condemnation of 1277 marks an important date in the history of Scholastic philosophy. At first, it put a stop to the teaching of Siger of Brabant at Paris, and prevented the formation of a " Latin Averroism " in the thirteenth century. Cited before the Grand Inquisitor of France, Simon Duval, Siger appealed to the Roman court and took refuge in Italy. He died at Orvieto, between 1281 and 1284, assassinated by his cleric, who had gone mad.

But the condemnation especially encouraged the resistance of the traditionalists against the influence of Aristotelianism. The eclectic group, especially the Franciscans, took stock of their common philosophical propositions and gave birth to a current of *Neo-Augustinian Philosophy*, which we will find in the disciples of St. Bonaventure, in Raymond Lull and in Duns Scotus.

But even these events did not stop the rise of Thomism. The Dominican order, which had adopted it as its official philosophy, vividly protested, and considered the condemnation — to the extent that it affected their own St. Thomas — as not having occurred. In 1319, when St. Thomas was canonized by Pope John XXII, the condemnation was officially recalled.

LIST OF THE AUTHENTIC WORKS
OF S. THOMAS [1].

252. — I. PHILOSOPHY.

A) Commentaries on Aristotle.

1. In Perihermeniam.
2. In Posteriores Analyticorum.
3. In VIII Libros Physicorum.
4. In III primos libros de coelo et mundo.
5. In III libros de generatione et corruptione.
6. In IV libros Meteorum.
7. In librum De Anima.
8. In II et III De Anima.
9. In librum De Sensu et Sensato.
10. In librum De Memoria et Reminiscentia.
11. In XII libros Metaphysicorum.
12. In X libros Ethicorum ad Nicomachum.
13. In IV libros primos Politicorum.

B) Various works.

14. De occultis operationibus naturæ.
15. De principiis naturæ.
16. De mixtione elementorum.
17. De æternitate mundi.
18. De motu cordis.
19. De unitate intellectus.
20. De substantiis separatis.
21. De ente et essentia.
22. In librum Boethii de Hebdomadibus.
23. In librum de Causis.
24. De Rege et Regno.
25. De Regimine Judæorum.

II. SACRED SCRIPTURE.

a) Old Testament.

26. On the Book of Job.
27. On IV first nocturns of the Psalter.

---

[1] The listing follows P. MANDONNET; see his article in *Revue augustiniene,* (XVII), November, 1910, pp. 610-623.

28. On the Canticle of Canticles.
29. On the Book of Isaias.
30. On the Book of Jeremias.
31. On the Book Threni.

b) New Testament.

32. On Matthew.
33. On Mark. } Called *Catena Aurea* or
34. On Luke. } Golden Chain (gloss).
35. On John.
36. Exposition on Matthew.
37. Exposition on Mark. } not edited.
38. Exposition on Luke. }
39. Exposition on John.
40. Lecture on Matthew. } not edited.
41. Lecture on John. }
42. On all the Epistles of St. Paul.

    a) To the Romans.

    b) First Epistle to the Corinthians.

    c) Second Epistle to the Corinthians.

    d) Epistle to the Hebrews.

III. THEOLOGY.

43. In IV Libros Sententiarum.
44. In I librum Sententiarum (lost).
45. Summa Theologica.
46. Compendium Theologiæ (incomplete).
47. De articulis fidei et sacramentis.
48. In Dionysium de divinis nominibus.
49. In Boethium de Trinitate.
50. De fide et spe.
51. De judiciis astrorum.
52. De sortibus.
53. De forma absolutionis.
54. De emptione et venditione.

IV. PHILOSOPHICO-THEOLOGICAL WORKS.

55. Quæstiones Disputatæ (II quæst.).
56. Quodlibeta.
57. Responsio de articulis XXXVI.
58. Responsio de articulis XLII.

59. Responsio de articulis CVI.
60. Articuli iterum remissi.
61. Responsio ad articulis VI.
62. Responsio ad Bernardum Abbatem.

V. APOLOGETIC WORKS.

63. Summa contra Gentiles.
64. De rationibus fidei.
65. Contra errores Graecorum.
66. Contra impugnantes Dei cultum.
67. De perfectione vitæ spiritualis.
68. Contra retrahentes a religionis ingressu.

VI. CANON LAW.

69. In 1^{am} Decretalem.
70. In 2^{am} Decretalem.

VII. HOMILETICS.

71. Collationes dominicales.
72. Collationes de Pater Noster.
73. Collationes de Credo.
74. Collationes de decem præceptis.

VIII. LITURGY.

75. Officium Corporis Christi.

SECTION TWO.
THE THOMISTIC SYNTHESIS.

253. St. Thomas' originality was such that he was able to profit from his predecessors and, at the same time, to construct his own philosophy from a viewpoint independent of every historical contingency. Based on experience and on common sense, Thomism is simply *the philosophy of being*. After outlining the proper character of the work of St. Thomas, the fundamental principle of Thomism will be pointed out and explained; from the latter flows its universal amplitude, by which it is rightfully termed common doctrine. Its unity will then be shown as well as the way in which it is, nevertheless, original doctrine. These matters are covered in the following four sections :

I. The Creation of Thomism.

II. The Foundational Principle of Thomism.

III. The Universality of Thomism.

IV. The Unity of Thomism.

I. THE CREATION OF THOMISM.

254. The apparition of Thomism in the doctrinal movement of philosophy can aptly be characterized by stating that it was a " FRUITFUL REVOLUTION " in the thirteenth century. It was " a profound change, not by way of subversion or radical destruction, but by a positive development and a vital perfectioning "[1].

The appearance of Thomism had the outward marks of a revolution; it was rapid, and important in its consequences. In twenty years, from 1253 to 1273, St. Thomas wrote an extensive number of works; it has been estimated that during his last sojourn at Paris, he wrote the equivalent of four thousand pages in 4to yearly. The subjects treated are quite varied, even though they are concentrated in the realms of theology and philosophy. Nevertheless, this work, whose value equals its extensiveness, is prodigious, and the influence of its author has spread out boundlessly.

It is true that this work was achieved with the help of providential circumstances. Placed within an intellectual milieu of the Universities and of the Dominican order, St. Thomas had an *excellent teacher* in St. Albert the Great and an excellent originator in Aristotle. His holiness, no doubt, gave him supernatural assistance, and he was trained more in the school of the Crucifix than in that of books. These exterior aids allowed his genius full expansion. But, according to the law of Providence, he was not dispensed from action, so that it was only through incessant labor that he created Thomism, by reassembling materials and organizing them under a directive principle through a powerful intellectual effort. His work, as a result, has a triple characteristic : conservation, originality and progress.

---

[1] J. MARITAIN, *Théonas*, p. 138.

A) The Characteristic of Conservation : the Materials.

255. Far from searching for novelty at any price, St. Thomas, contrarily, seems to be most occupied in citing his predecessors. He does this to such an extent, in fact, that his function might sometimes appear to be reduced to that of collector or organizer of the doctrines of the Fathers and of other Doctors.

It was actually his constant aim to conserve all the truths acquired by mankind until his time, and his information in this regard was quite vast. He was aided in this task by numerous Patristic collections then in circulation, arranged according to their contents. He completed these efforts, doing special research into the translations of Greek authors. But he is not a simple compiler [1], and even in this preliminary work he set himself to the task of discernment, interpretation and organization of materials with much prudence and wisdom.

1) *Discernment.* With a quite remarkable critical spirit, he set aside a whole apocryphal literature attributed to Aristotle and to St. Augustine, and sometimes imputed these works to their true authors. Evidently, he did not correctly resolve all cases of mistaken authorship, but his results were remarkable for the Middle Ages. For instance, due to the translation of a work of Proclus, *Elementatio theologiæ*, he discovered the true author of the *Liber de causis* [2]. Its authenticity being better known, he was more able to interpret the texts exactly, sometimes even taking exception to an author cited against him. But above all, he looked for the choicest materials; this led him to be attached to some writers by preference : in philosophy, to Aristotle, complemented by Dionysius the Areopagite; in theology, to the Bible and to St. Augustine.

2) *Interpretation.* Ordinarily, St. Thomas does not adopt the historical point of view, except, as has been seen, when discussing the true doctrine of Aristotle with the Averroists.

---

[1] In *Le système du monde*, Vol. v, p. 589, Pierre Duhem writes : " The vast composition... looks like a patchwork in which there lie juxtaposed, neatly recognizable and distinct from each other, a multitude of pieces borrowed from Hellenistic paganism, Christian patristics, Islamism and Judaism ". A. D'ALÈS remarks about this view of Duhem's (*Dictionnaire apologétique*, article " *Thomisme* ", col. 1694) : " This judgment is somewhat precipitate. The truth of the matter looks different if, in place of making an inventory of sources, one takes the trouble to grasp the texture of development. One then grants that St. Thomas transforms whatever he has absorbed ".

[2] See above, n. 232 and n. 250.

In his major works, as for example in the two summaries, he pursued a uniquely doctrinal motivation. In citing and explaining his predecessors, he was not attempting to determine what a writer thought, but rather to establish the truth. This is why, and especially when dealing with Aristotle and St. Augustine, he never put himself in direct opposition with them. In difficult and obscure passages, he indicates the acceptable meaning of their writings *according to truth*, and thus places them in their proper philosophical positions. He himself called this method " reverential exposition " and offered, as part justification for this method in theology, the notion of a dogmatic progress which obliges a theologian to use most precise formulas after the appearance and condemnation of heresies [1].

His procedure is also explainable by the theological customs of his age which prevented anyone from finding error in the ancient Fathers of the Church. With " intellectual charity ", St. Thomas was always full of respect for these great geniuses of the past. In fact, St. Thomas strove to show the profound harmony of his doctrine with tradition, even avoiding, as far as possible, any violent conflict with the opinions of his contemporaries. On the other hand, he knew how to refute or even to reject inadmissible parts of the authors whom he cited or to whose opinions he objected, as one can see especially with regard to Averroes and Plato.

3) *Organization.* Among the great number of opinions which he met, St. Thomas chose first those propositions which were fully evident and were uniquely based on common sense and common experience. These seemed to have the mark of infallible truth, and so he laid them down as the bedrock of his philosophy. He recognized that Aristotle had made the same effort as much as possible, remarking, " It is a mark of his philosophy that it does not depart from what is manifest ". When he met explanations that were properly *scientific* (in the modern sense), he practiced a great reserve, always anxious to disengage fundamental doctrines from problematic data. Thus, he did not follow the Averroists in incorporating the theory of the celestial spheres into his metaphysics, and he declared, on the contrary, that " if we grant these suppositions, then appearances are accounted for; it does not mean that these suppositions are true, for possibly according to some

---

[1] See above, n. 232 and n. 250.

other method as yet not known to men, we can account for
that which has been observed about the stars " [1].   He also
classifies among probabilities the theory of the animation of
the stars, and declares it a matter of indifference whether
they are said to be moved by the separated Intelligences or
directly by God [2].   Due to this organization and hierachy
of opinions, the Thomistic philosophy and theology even retain
their validity today.

B) Originality : Intellectual work.

256.   All of the materials he uses become, for St. Thomas,
part of a living and autonomous system, not only because
he revived Aristotelianism and led it to its metaphysical
perfection, but especially because he created a completed
theology.   This was not done without a large amount of work,
and some of his contemporaries mention his concentration
on speculative subjects was so intense that he often lost contact
with the external world.

The spirit of Thomism is marked by a *metaphysical sense
which is at once profound and moderated.*   It was in the
metaphysical domain that he most frequently moved and it
was there that he searched for the special points from which
to get his " vision of the world ".   His vision enabled him to
look at things habitually from the point of view of God and
of pure perfections; he looked for the deepest reasons in things
which he regarded from the metaphysical view.   At the same
time, he gave an experiental foundation to the highest speculations.   His rigorously critical and progressive method made
him a Peripatetic; the metaphysical questions which he
discussed made him also a Platonist.   He harmonized in
himself the idealist and the positivist spirit which are so often
found opposed in a given thinker.   And he was both analytic
and synthetic.

a) **Analytic.**   St. Thomas distinguished multiple aspects in
real being; he based his division of sciences on the proper
experiential facts and assigned a proper method to each :
definition and a priori deduction in metaphysics; introspection
and the facts of consciousness in psychology; a priori principles
governing duties in morality, with concrete circumstances

---

[1] 1 *Contra errores graecorum*, prologue.

[2] *In II cœlo et mundo*, lect. 17; a similar remark is found in *Summa Theologica*, I,
q. XXXII, art. I, ad 2.

surrounding their application; a preponderance of external experience in the study of nature. These exactitudes on the object of the sciences is based on a thorough analysis of the diverse nuances of reality; they complete each other in the effort followed in each science for arriving at special conclusions.

b) **Synthetic.** Each detail which is analyzed is referred to a few invariable principles which make up the essence of his metaphysics. This trait of synthetic unity is forced upon one when he compares Thomism to other attempts at organization; lacking such unification, his two summaries on theology would be incoherent. St. Thomas put order into this chaos; no trifling or useless materials, no irrelevant notions and no repetitions. Instead, he introduced new problems which were useful and necessary, reduced quotations and processes of reasoning to the demands of the problem, gave each part its proportionate development and perfectly harmonized the parts within the whole. His style itself has the quality of depth; it is clear, precise, sober, and adequate to the thought. Out of most authors of his time, St. Thomas is easily the most readable.

Considered in itself, the synthetic property of Thomism emphasizes its worth. It is not presented, as is done in some philosophies, in the straight line of mathematical deduction from one first principle or one primary idea [1]. Instead, spread out like a fan with its multiple rays joined in the same center, it safeguards and fully interprets the complexity of reality. Sometimes, it is true, the direct accord between remote conclusions is not always visible, but most of the truths are strongly attached to the central core.

Thus, Thomism is a synthesis resembling the totality of knowledge with perfect cohesion between its simple and clear framework and possessing a relentless originality which made it appear a true *revolution* to the Augustinians.

C) **Progress : Directive Principle.**

257. In order to utilize his sources so throughly, St. Thomas was guided by the *principle* of progress, a theory which he proposed and which can be formulated as follows :

Inasmuch as human knowledge is the common good of reason, it should progress through the collaboration of thinkers of all times, without being limited except to evidence and (if He deigns to speak to man through revelation) to God.

---

[1] Such was the method of Descartes; see below, n. 323.

The slowness of progress in scientific matters and the possibility of always accomplishing something new therein follows from this principle. " Human genius ", he writes, " seems to have proceeded quite slowly in the investigation of the origin of things ". What one man can produce by his genius, he states again, is but little by comparison to the total ensemble of knowledge; if it is something great that has been discovered, it is through the labor of many men [1]. St. Thomas himself did not look upon Aristotle as an ideal who would never be superseded.

This principle explains his respect and recognition for past thinkers. All of them can be helpful in the realm of thought, and even their errors help by allowing others to see better what they might have missed. At the same time, this principle explains his full independence of all *human* authority which, in philosophy, is placed at the lowest rung : " Authority which is founded on human reason is, as a source, most weak " [2]; accordingly, the judgment of a philosopher is no greater than the evidence or the force of the reasons supporting his views.

From this same principle derives his confidence in thinking through and in explaining his faith through philosophy. He knew that through contact with the highest truth, human reason would find approval of its clear evidence : the conception of God as Pure Actuality; the preservation from grave errors, as that of pantheism; the clarification of its doubts and ignorance, as in the question of creation or the survival of the soul; the confirmation of its probabilities, as the hypothesis of pure forms in Aristotle, identifiable with the angels of Sacred Scripture.

Through its effort at incorporating the doctrinal riches of the schools of the Middle Ages, and through its success at assimilating ancient thought under the light and safety of the Catholic faith, Thomism is more than an exceptionally great personal work testifying to the power of St. Thomas' philosophical genius. It is the most perfect synthesis of the Scholastic epoch, and has a triple attribute : it is a renewal and development more than an invention; it is destined above all for the schools; it is totally illumined by faith. It is in this sense that St. Thomas' work merits the name of a " fruitful revolution ".

---

[1] *In I Metaphysicorum*, Lect. 1.
[2] *Summa Theologica*, 1, q. 1, art. 8, ad 2.

II. The foundational Principle of Thomism.

258. St. Thomas is openly Peripatetic; in philosophy, especially, he aimed to revive Aristotle, and not to invent a philosophical view. One could adopt the foundational principle explained above [1] and would not find a different formulation in St. Thomas. But what is new and stands out in relief here is his impersonal quality and his pure objectivity. For other philosophers, their basic principle is explained in large part by historical circumstances, such as their education, a striking event in the life of the author, opposition or dependence on current systems of thought. Aristotle himself was no exception. Aristotle was dependent on the systems of ancient Greece, of which he is the most metaphysical expression, while remaining, as the Greeks, essentially a *naturalist*. Even in his fundamental principle, it is actuality and potentiality which he brings out in strong relief.

St. Thomas, on the other hand, put himself uniquely at the viewpoint of the truth which he wished to grasp and to explain as fully as possible. He searched for the principle which would found his philosophy *in itself* and in an absolute fashion, before finding the unshakable basis for Catholic theology. Having found it in Aristotle, he appropriated it [2], though he just as frequently explains it independently of historical consideration as being merely the natural truth. This principle will be made most clear by showing, briefly, its formulation and its place in philosophy.

A) **Formulation.**

The principle of " universal intelligibility " can be stated as follows :

Everything IS INTELLIGIBLE THROUGH BEING; " *Whatever can be, can be understood* " [3]. All knowledge, in effect, is a mental

---

[1] See nn. 69-70, above.

[2] In adopting this principle, St. Thomas thought it through and transformed its import. His " vision of the world " or fundamental intuition is no longer physical but metaphysical (which enabled him to correct and complete the Aristotelian system). By placing himself in the purely objective view of truth he was led to this metaphysical aspect in which the real is fully intelligible, because the real is either God or some participation of God. This root position of Thomism thus synthesizes the notion of Platonic participation and the moderated realism of Aristotle. See, in this connection, A. Forest, *La structure métaphysique du concret*, p. 321 and pp. 324-328).

[3] *Summa Contra Gentiles*, II, Ch. XCVIII.

engagement with an object about which it is known *that it is* (the question, Does it exist?) in order to know more fully *its mode of being* (the question, What is it?).

To this general formula, common sense immediately requires four important precisions, whose necessity can be readily ascertained.

1. Before all else, being expresses a *real nature*, independent of and, as a consequence, exterior to our thought, while also being in our most intimate possession due to the " assimilative seizure " of our mind (what psychology calls " intentional identification " of the object known and the knower in actuality). This *reality* of being is admitted by St. Thomas unhesitatingly, for it reveals itself as primary evidence and thus as a fact of common sense. Thus, precision is given to " that which is " intelligible; *the object of philosophy is the real*.

2. Being is, of itself, a perfection not requiring any limitation and is thus fully realizable in the infinite; that is, being is *of itself actuality*. St. Thomas devotes some deep analysis to this notion of the *infinite*, neatly distinguishing it from the material infinite, and the " infinite " of indetermination in the Platonic sense, by opposition to which the finite becomes perfection. The expression, " of itself ", is used to indicate the negation of limit and to indicate that limit is but a negation of being. The infinite, then, is seen as the fulness of the realization of being. Thus, the order of being is manifested as a privileged order, the unfailing source of actuality from which all reality draws its perfection; " esse est actualitas omnium rerum " [1].

3. Likewise, being is a " nature " (a " *ratio* ") so universal that it contains all realities, despite their multitude and their absolute diversity; it contains these implicitly, it is true, but in such a way that no difference is added from without to explain or to enrich being. In other words, *being is expressed by an analogous concept*. St. Thomas often states this precision when showing that being is not a genus; for being exceeds all the essential, absolute and defined modes of being, so that it belongs to a " transcendental order ". It can, accordingly, have inferior members endowed with natures that are simply diverse without knowledge becoming afflicted with the sophistry of equivocation.

---

[1] *Summa Theologica*, I, q. IV, art. 2, ad 3.

4. At the same time, being is also an abstract " nature " which we find realized first, though in a limited way, in the concrete, changeable and multiple objects (even though being of itself does not implicate limitation). In other words, *being is also a composite of potentiality and actuality.*

This last point adds distinction to the sense in which being is, in his view, the first thing known to mind, the light which renders everything else intelligible. It is not a notion taken separately and purely before the immaterial glance of the soul. On the contrary, this perfection, which is of itself infinite, is at first known as encountered in the concrete object of sensible experience! The necessity of abstracting, proper to the human intelligence as human, prevents the mind from ever seeing an absolute perfection if it is not among the relative participations whereupon it only partially reflects. The formal, adequate object of the human mind which encompasses the mind's amplitude is being as such; its formal, proper object, to which it is proportioned, which it first attains, and as a function of which it sees everything else is being as the " essence of sensible things ".

The fundamental principle which unifies Thomism as well as Aristotelianism can now be restated : EVERYTHING IS INTELLIGIBLE THROUGH BEING, *an analogous concept, realizing itself in actuality and in potentiality.*

B) The Place of this " Principle " in Philosophy.

259. Thomism might appear as a closed system in which all the parts are so strongly intertwined that one cannot, at first, discover its entrance. This entrance is, doubtlessly, the principle of universal intelligibility just outlined. The question might be asked, however, is it a proposition of criteriology, of logic, of psychology, of natural philosophy or of metaphysics? It seems to hold, in turn, for each of these sciences.

1. It begins, as a matter of fact, by an affirmation of criteriology. Thomism is a REALIST philosophy, which holds as possible the concordance or the perfect " adequation " of a true judgment, especially a scientific, universal and necessary judgment, with the exterior object truly known to be such as it is. Nor is this a naive, exaggerated or even a dogmatic realism. Following Aristotle, St. Thomas recognized that the initial attitude of

---

[1] *De ente et essentia*, Ch. II; Cajetan's expression is " ens concretum quidditati sensibili "; see his commentary on this chapter.

philosophical thought is " doubt "; moreover, if it be a question of first philosophy, which is to examine the absolutely first bases of speculation, this will be a sort of universal, critical doubt, and a refutation of universal scepticism through showing the latter's absurdity [1].

The Thomistic position is none other than that of moderated realism or mitigated conceptualism. This position was already defended by Aristotle, rediscovered by Scholasticism in the preceding centuries and, finally, it is one of the citadels of Thomism.

It should be acknowledged, though, that the critical point of view is secondary in St. Thomas. Most often he is content merely to affirm his realism as a truth of common sense. To justify the restrictions which he admits on this view, and to resolve the difficulties which were opposed to it, he methodically constructed his philosophy while showing it to be in constant accord with conclusions gleaned from the facts of experience.

2. The *psychological* aspect of abstraction, closely connected with the critical solution of the problem of universals, is of great importance. It involves the function of the intelligence, its primacy over the will, and its double object, one characterizing the mind as such (being), while the other specifies mind as human (abstract essence of sensible things). Thomism, under this consideration, is an INTELLECTUALISM whose essence is quite distinctive among other systems. One can, with much reason, choose this center of perspective in order to characterize most of the propositions of St. Thomas [2].

It must be acknowledged that St. Thomas consumed much energy in defending the validity of the human intelligence; in maintaining its independence from faith in philosophy; in explaining its complete natural functioning; in specifying its role in voluntary activity; in pointing out its progressive ascension, pushed by a sort of natural " desire " for God as the first being. All these multiple aspects of his intellectualism have a large place in his system.

Nevertheless, the above is but a part of the whole and a special application of a more universal principle. For, at the moment when St. Thomas looks for this dominating principle which unifies everything without exception, he leaves the subjective view of mind as " grasping " being, in order to consider the very nature of being itself from a purely objective point of view.

3. This latter viewpoint is not often attained directly, and St. Thomas proceeds through the *logical aspect* of his principle. He hoped, in this way, to make himself understood to his contemporaries, who were quite desirous of logical precision, no matter how subtle. In this realm, he quite remarkably completed the position of Aristotle in clarifying the analogical validity of

---

[1] *In III Metaphysicorum*, lect. 1. See, in this connection, J. MARÉCHAL, *Le point de départ de la métaphysique*, Vol. IV, " Le thomisme en face de la philosophie critique ", Paris, 1926.

[2] See, for example, P. ROUSSELOT, *The Intellectualism of St. Thomas*, New York, 1935.

the idea of being; one can justly call his whole doctrine the "philosophy of ANALOGY". He often recalls the intermediary position which analogy implies, for it excludes univocal attribution which would make being an absolute essence, well delimited, and thus destroy the *transcendence* of being; it also excludes equivocal attribution which would make of being solely a common name, without common signification in the proper sense. His view on this matter is called the *analogy of proper proportionality* [1] a detailed exposition of which is one of the most original portions of Thomism.

260. 4. But the whole bearing of this theory is seen when it is realized that it applies to every pure perfection and, especially, to God. This fact indicates the true position of the foundational principle of Thomism in philosophy : it is, above all, a *metaphysical* proposition. In effect, Thomism is properly the PHILOSOPHY OF BEING [2].

If being is the first intelligible, containing in itself all the other "natures" *(rationes intelligibiles)*, there are a certain number of explicit modes of being which equal it in amplitude. For this reason, they arise by themselves, as it were, from simple experience. These notions and perfections are also *transcendental;* they are unity, truth, goodness. They are really identifiable with "that which is", although they enrich for us the explicit knowledge of being. They enjoy the same privileges of analogy and of spontaneous intelligibility or immediate evidence. Furthermore, comparing them with each other, other formulas flow from them which give us the principle of universal intelligibility from another aspect. The principle of sufficient reason is one of these; it states that whatever exists through itself or another being, is endowed with truth and is explicable, for *everything has reason for being.* Another of these is the principle of finality governing activity; it affirms that every active tendency is explicable by the good which is its goal, or, *every agent acts for an end.*

It is at this point that St. Thomas, interpreting the changefulness and multiplicity of the beings of our experience with the help of the above first principles, discovers the key to the archway of Aristotelianism, *actuality and potentiality.* It has a most important application in natural philosophy as the

---

[1] This terminology comes from the disciples of St. Thomas, though the doctrine is clearly his; see, for example, *Summa Theologica*, I, q. XIII. A good work on this question is M. T. L. PENIDO, *Le rôle de l'analogie en théologie dogmatique*, Paris, 1931.

[2] See the fine synthesis of A. D. SERTILLANGES, *Saint Thomas d'Aquin*, 2 vols., Paris, 1925.

theory of fourfold causality. Both Aristotle's and St. Thomas'
philosophy of nature are but a detailed application of these
derived and directly useful formulas. Pagan philosophy,
however, emphasized the *physical* aspect, wherein being is
especially a composite of actuality and potentiality; it hardly
mentioned God as Pure Actuality and as First Mover of the
sensible universe. Christian philosophy emphasizes the *metaphysical* aspect, wherein being is, above all, a " pure perfection ";
it hardly considers sensible things in themselves (except for
man) and only in a sort of transcendental light. The Christians
were preoccupied with looking into creatures for a means of
knowing God and of explaining divine mysteries. This led
them to seek pure perfections, as life, knowledge, freedom and
love, and to show in each of these a further realization of the
properties of analogous being.

The above sketch of his rich ontology somewhat explains
how everything is intelligible through being and how the
multiple sciences which aim to explain multiple realities are
but a more explicit statement of the reasons for being. It also
shows how St. Thomas, though adopting the Aristotelian
principle, incontestably supersedes it through his metaphysical
insight, as will be shown better in its applications below.

III. The Universality of Thomism.

261. The principle of universal intelligibility is all-inclusive
in scope. From the subjective viewpoint, it includes all the
possible knowledge of man, and, from the objective viewpoint,
it seems capable of clarifying all realities.

As a matter of fact, however, and, as one could conclude
from the above observations, the applications of Thomism
could not practically reach out to an absolute universality.
Though Thomism tends to be a " universal science ", there is
but a central core that is properly " scientific " (in the Scholastic
sense); the extension of this science is such that it is always
capable of progress and is provisorily completed through
probable knowledge. Accordingly, there are, in the view of
St. Thomas, four stages along which human knowledge proceeds.

First stage : **Intuition.**

262. Taking man's intellectual life as a point of departure,
there is a triple source of immediate knowledge, whose truth

is not proved but is self-evident. In this latter sense, there is a triple intuition.

a) **Sensible intuition** [1] yields concrete objects which are rich in details, but poor in extension. Sensible intuition furnishes the facts of experience, and has the distinction of being an intuition in the *strict sense :* it is immediate attainment of the exterior object as really existing outside of our knowledge [2]. However, sensible intuition is under the control of intelligence, for it does not as yet have truth, which demands judgment. In the restricted domain of its proper, formal object it is infallible if everything is in a normal state, in the sense that it expresses the concrete object such as it is.

b) **Intellectual intuition** yields being, a notion quite poor in details, but unlimited in extension. This evidence of being can be called an " intuition " (in the broad sense) as signifying not only that being is immediately evident but also, in St. Thomas' view, that being is spontaneously concretized in the same object as that of sensible intuition, and that such an identification is accepted as valid. Accordingly, the mind is not directed towards its own thinking self in its first reflections and only then passes to its awareness of the exteriority about it. Rather, it is directly placed within the bosom of the exterior world and then returns upon itself through a reflex act of consciousness.

This very reflection itself, for St. Thomas, constitutes a true *intellectual intuition* of the thinking self, not in order to know its *essence* [3], but only its existence, if there is question of the soul united to body [4]. It is true that the soul must always go through the senses for its intellectual activities; at the same time, in an indirect fashion, it can immediately know itself in its act of thought as an actual and living reality.

c) **Intuition of common sense.** This intuition yields the first principles which, by unfolding the transcendental richness of being (as has been shown) [5], furnishes the necessary

---

[1] External senses and external experience are being referred to here.

[2] Intuition in the strict sense requires that knowledge be immediate and that it attain a real object as actually existing; if one or the other of these two conditions is lacking, there remains intuition only in the broad sense. See below, n. 540.

[3] This is Descartes' view; see below, nn. 325-327.

[4] In the soul separated from the body, this *intuition of self,* (even with regard to essence), becomes the proper and fundamental object of intellectual activity; see *Summa Theologica*, I, q. LXXXVII and q. LXXXIX.

[5] See nn. 259-260.

intellectual light for a scientific interpretation of the facts of experience. St. Thomas outlines the nature of this intuition with much care. Partly intuitive and innate, partly abstractive and acquired, these principles are the active principles or intellectual virtues which reside germinally in the natural dispositions of reason, and open up equally in each man at first contact with experience. Reason is said to act, in this primary domain, more as " intelligence ", because with a direct glance it grasps the immediate evidence of these principles, and holds them with such a certitude that no demonstration could increase their validity or stability. It is to signify this special mode of intellection that one can here speak of intuition.

A double manifestation of this intuition is distinguished by St. Thomas. One of these could be called *speculative common sense* (the habit of first principles) which is the point of departure of the branches of learning; the other is *practical common sense (synderesis)*, the point of departure of morality.

Second stage : **Induction.**

263. The mind progresses towards truth through *reasoning*, which is the natural movement of " reason " or discursive intelligence. It consists of a passage from the known to the unknown, by the mind comparing truths previously acquired among themselves.

Because of the analogy of being, the universal principles that make everything to be known without exception, though implicitly, at first become more explicit through contact with concrete objects. This intellectual interpretation of sensible experience is called *induction*. Its aim is to make precise the degree of being or the nature (essence) of concrete beings, and its ideal is to establish a definition in the strict sense by stating the proximate genus and specific difference.

The important function of induction in Thomism is easily seen. Its literary presentation, especially in the *Summa theologica* should not deceive one as to its importance. In keeping with the spirit of the times and with the synthetic purpose of its author, doctrine is ordinarily set forth in syllogistic form. Quite often, though, as in the treatise on the human passions, on human acts and on the particular moral virtues, there is no a priori reasoning at all, and a real induction has taken place.

Following Aristotle, St. Thomas distinguishes a double type of induction [1]. The first is induction in the *broad sense*, when there is question of establishing the general notions of metaphysics or universal definitions as those of pure perfections. In this case there is need of a very precise abstraction, and of few and simple facts. Induction in the *strict sense* occurs when it is needful to establish the definition of more detailed natures, as those of stone, or horse. This type of induction is reasoning of a special sort, with particular rules; it requires detailed and numerous facts of experience, and would not very easily be proposed in syllogistic form.

St. Thomas knew of this latter form and appreciated it; he employed it, though, only in commenting on Aristotle's works on nature; the modern thinkers have completed Peripateticism on this point. In his effort to enlarge the metaphysical basis of his philosophy (as has been shown), he frequently uses the first form of induction. This is to his advantage, of course, because the universal view and the simplicity of indubitable facts make full evidence possible and allow for the conquest of infallible truths.

Such a mode of procedure is quite in agreement with his fundamental principle. Beginning with a very general point of departure, one can establish only generic definitions at first (as those of substance and accident, body, animality). In order to go towards the definition of more minute species, whose perfect knowledge is rightfully [2] among the diverse parts of natural philosophy, it is necessary to proceed slowly through detailed experiences.

Third stage : **Deduction.**

264. St. Thomas always understands science in the strict sense as not capable of being constituted by pure induction, for science is the perfect intellectual knowledge of a determined essence; such knowledge includes all properties of the thing known and their complete explanation through proper and intrinsic reasons. It is the fruit of the demonstrative syllogism. It is thus made up of series of deductions, whose first middle term (as Aristotle also teaches [3]), is, by necessity, the definition of the nature or special essence which is the object of science,

---

[1] See above, n. 72.
[2] As the *fourth stage* just below shows, one rarely arrives at this state of affairs.
[3] See above, n. 73.

and which was previously established by an evident induction. This definition clarifies and unifies all the following definitions; it is the formal object of the science which specifies it and distinguishes it from all others.

It should be mentioned that the second and third stages outlined above, are but an application of the logic of Aristotle, which St. Thomas adopted and estimated sufficiently perfect that he changed nothing in it.

Fourth stage : **Systematization.**

265. The total knowledge of reality, then, is to be sought through a multitude of sciences hierarchically ordered, aiming at encompassing all the essential details of experience. This ideal is unrealizable for man on two counts : in the realizations of being, the two extremes, God and the individual, remain impenetrable to reason.

a) **God.** Because of the greatness of His perfection, and due to the fact that God is known only as mirrored through creatures, human reason can never attain Him in His intimate essence. His degree of absolute being cannot be " defined " but only characterized through a cumulation of negations; " We are able to know what God is not but not what He is " [1]. A *scientific* remedy is found for this first lacuna — in addition to its being filled in so greatly by faith — in the analogical speculations of theodicy. Though not a special science, the latter is an essential, the most noble and best deductive part of the true science of metaphysics.

b) **The individual,** at the opposite extreme, is impenetrable to reason by its excess of imperfections and lack of completion. The individual is constituted in its character of proper individuality in the strict sense (that is, in the sensible natures which are numerically multipliable), through a principle of pure potentiality, prime matter. The human intelligence, obligated to receive impressions of objects in order to know them, abstracts necessarily from every aspect of individuality. There cannot be a science of the singular, material thing ; science can only be had of universals. To this radical impotence of the mind, there can be added the additional fact that a large amount of the degrees of being, scientifically knowable in themselves, remain unexplored by human reason; as a result,

---

[1] *Summa Theologica*, i, q. ii, prologue.

in the domain of natural philosophy, the luminous core of strict science is reducible to some basic propositions of cosmology.

There are remedies for this latter gap. First of all, sensible intuition compensates for this intellectual helplessness and admirably completes abstract science by attaining the individual as such. But its sphere of activity, even as enlarged by memory and study, remains quite restrained. In order to remedy this narrowness of sensible experience, and to take the place of sciences not as yet constructed, reason forms an ensemble of probable opinions called a " system ". Opinion, for St. Thomas, is not the equivalent of ignorance nor of doubt. It is a positive affirmation, endowed with verisimilitude, or with approximative truth. Such knowledge has its own richness, for it is based on inductions which are harmonious though lacking in full evidence, and is confirmed by a priori reasons and by analogies.

This effort at systematizing and at completing scientific deductions results in a broad idea of the ensemble of reality, consisting of a definitive part in the evident conclusions of science and an approximative and provisory part in the probable conclusions of opinion. This continuity of explanation, similar to the impression of unity and harmony which flow from it, further increases the probability of the systematic propositions.

St. Thomas incorporated into his philosophy a great number of theories of this sort, especially in astronomical, chemical and physical matters (in the modern sense). Sometimes he prefaces such views with the expressions that " it is manifest " or, " it appears ". At other times, he will mention that they are purely probable conclusions [1]. Most often, he will cite them as examples of views commonly admitted, and will use them as illustrative, and as helpful for understanding more profound and certain truths. This entire systematic portion, which is not wholly the proper work of St. Thomas but of Aristotle, is evidently subject to correction and has become quite obsolete. It should be replaced by the progress made in the modern views on these matters.

In a developmental conception of philosophy as the one of St. Thomas, every intellectual effort has a legitimate place, so that every true branch of learning could become a ramification of Thomism. For this reason, St. Thomas merits the title of " Common Doctor ".

---

[1] See, for instance, *Summa theologica*, I, q. LXVI, art. 3, where he recounts various opinions on the heavens, stating that they are not very cogent.

IV. The Unity of Thomism.

266. The rigor with St. Thomas kept his universal vantage point and which he firmly pursued in applications to both scientific and probable conclusions, gives a perfect unity to Thomism. His whole doctrine is developed by projecting the selfsame principles of general metaphysics into the various objects of speculation.

This unity further accounts for *his originality*, which distinguishes him from other philosophers. While the latter are often in accord with St. Thomas in their foundational evidence, they unify their materials under a more restrained viewpoint; then, as they develop, they elongate themselves farther from Thomism, and their opposition falls apart in their systematization. The foundational and metaphysical portion needs emphasis in any philosophy; for if one adopts the viewpoint of doctrine most faithfully, he has more chance to go farther with deductions on demonstrative evidence.

Of course, the perfect construction of philosophy as a universal science, as outlined in the paragraph above, cannot be achieved by one thinker, and demands the collaboration of centuries. St. Thomas himself merely desired to bring his foundation stone to the edifice already begun by Aristotle; his merit was to be able to discern the properly scientific solidity of the system, and to establish its full validity. Moreover, the most significant developments for which philosophy is indebted to St. Thomas are in the metaphysical order (the study of God and the Angels) and the psychological and moral orders (the study of nature and human action).

Concentration on these areas was quite in conformity with St. Thomas' aim, which was essentially theological. He left us no direct synthesis of his philosophy as he did of theology. Thus it is possible to reconstitute his philosophical synthesis from various viewpoints. While keeping the fundamental principle as the metaphysical foundation, in the sense given it above, a principle certainly expressive of the spirit of Thomism, one can conduct the applications of this principle in two ways. In the first way, insistence is made on the role of induction and the method of discovery. The progressive birth of various propositions through sense experience is shown, following the manner of experimental science. This procedure is more in keeping with modern Thomism, anxious to adapt itself to the mentality of the age. In the second way, deduction is emphasized, and the mode of Scholastic exposition is followed, as in showing the logical sequence of conclusions which follow from applying the metaphysical principles to God. It was this latter method that St. Thomas followed, for he had an eminent and synthetic view of the principles and the conclusions and was in accord with the general tendency of his times. At the same time, he was not wholly neglectful of the first way, especially in determining the degrees in the scale of beings studied in natural philosophy.

Adopting this latter point of view, the essential framework of Thomism will now be outlined in the three areas of metaphysics, natural philosophy and morality; for it was in these areas that the historical influence of St. Thomas was especially remarkable.

A) **Metaphysics.**

267. God. Following a synthetic order, after the fundamental principle has been established, then God is the first reality to be explained, for He is the full realization of being, the realizing and explicative force of all other beings.

On the human mode of knowing the existence and nature of God, St. Thomas holds a position intermediary between the excessive mysticism of the Augustinians — who exaggerate the role of intuition — and the physical and agnostic view of the Averroists and Maimonides — who placed God in the order of purely motory and unknowable causes.

a) The light of being is given to man primarily to know " sensible essences ". As a result, God is knowable only a posteriori, in the natural order, in the mirror of His creatures.

b) The principle of sufficient reason requires that the participated perfections of the universe have a perfect cause, intelligible in itself. As a result, God is knowable through ideas which retain their own significance and yet signify His substance. At the same time, the diversity of proportions according to which perfections are realized in God and in creatures implies that man's knowledge of God is analogous (proper proportionality).

These ideas are those of the transcendentals and of pure perfections which are constitutive of the Divine attributes and are perfectly synthesized in God *(Ipsum Esse subsistens)*. The latter name, " Self-Subsisting Being " is the name most properly applied to God[1]. This " quasi-definition " of God is thus the luminous summit of the philosophy of being.

In relationship to creatures, God is " defined " as pure Existence, and is thus the *Proper and perfect Cause of being as such.* This is the Platonic view of *participation* which St. Thomas here assimilates to the scientific rigor of Aristotle[2]. The various aspects of this universal causality are deduced : creation *from nothingness;* the conservation or stable production of the duration of being; transcendent motion, which is not like that of Averroes' first mover, but inclines to the metaphysical view of St. Augustine of a creative impulse assisting the activity of each, though specially safeguarding human freedom[3].

Finally, the notion of God as the Cause of being allows Him to be conceived not only as knowing and loving Himself. Through His creative omniscience (theory of diverse sciences and multiple ideas in God) and through his dominating Love, He can be known as creating and governing all things for His glory (theory of Divine Liberty, Providence and Predestination).

The Creature. The definition of contingent being, or creature, follows that of God. This definition, following the synthetic order, is the most generic. St. Thomas formulates it as follows : *Every creature is a substance composed of essence and existence, as of two really distinct elements,* which are, however, inseparable, and ordered to each other as actuality to potentiality.

The *limitation* disclosed by multiplicity, which is essential to every creature besides Pure Actuality, demands, on the one hand, that actuality be blended with potentiality in each creature. At the same time, there is a demand that these essences be *actuality* and not pure potentiality or matter. This is needed to explain the perfection of natures (in the diverse sensible essences, each endowed with a special and positive degree of being, but especially in pure spirits, exempted from the imperfections of extension and localization).

In order to understand and conciliate these two aspects of experience, it is necessary to conceive of essence as playing

---

[1] *Summa Theologica,* I, q. XIII, art. II.

[2] For a recent view on this Platonic influence, see A. LITTLE, *The Platonic Heritage of Thomism,* Dublin, 1953.

[3] Much later, this notion is called theory of *physical premotion,* a name given it to help distinguish it from the theory of *simultaneous concurrence* associated with Molinism. See above, n. 168.

the role of actuality, giving a specific nature to being, and to function as potentiality, conferring limitation in a given order. As a result, while receiving the unlimited and unique perfection of existence, it can contract it to its own measure and make possible its multiplication [1].

From this definition of contingent being, there flows the necessary property of a *real distinction between substance and accidents*. Only God, since He is Infinite Being, can act through His own essence. Every finite being must make use of active principles, really distinct from its substance; these principles are called faculties or powers. These powers are, for the creature, manifestative of its perfection. The relationship between substance and accident is envisioned by St. Thomas, with the help of the principle of sufficient reason, as one of actuality to potentiality, and as one of cause to effect. This permits him to utilize a principle in determining the various degrees of being in natural philosophy, namely, that action flows from and is a clue to being *(agere sequitur esse)*.

B) **Natural Philosophy (Physics).**

268. The third, general definition found in Thomism is " that of body, the object of natural philosophy or the ancient Physics ". *Body is a substantial composite of prime matter and substantial form.* These two elements are also really distinct and related as potentiality to actuality.

A twofold series of accidental properties manifests corporeal essence. The first are *quantitative* properties, as extension, number, and the accidents which flow therefrom, as place, time, position and habiliment. The second are *qualitative* properties, as the operative powers, forms, sensible qualities, color, heat, and so forth. To this latter class also belong the changes corresponding to these accidental properties, but which are such that they sometimes involve the transformation of substances themselves (generation and corruption). All of these properties and changes can be intelligible only by a principle of the substantial order which is purely potential, lacks determination, and is incapable of existing without

---

[1] St. Thomas was not the first thinker to defend the real distinction between essence and existence. He did, however, give it an exceptional place in his philosophy, using it to explain the relation between God and the universe. One could justly entitle it " the fundamental truth of Christian philosophy ". — See N. DEL PRADO, *La vérité fondamentale de la philosophie chrétienne.*

form : the principle of *prime matter*. This principle is proper to bodies alone. It is indissolubly united to quantity and is absent from pure spirits.

On the other hand, the variety of operations manifest the hierarchy of physical species. Immanent motion characterizes life and the vegetative soul. The activity of knowledge, in which a living thing begins to immaterialize itself in assimilating " another thing as other ", requires a more perfect soul in the animal. Abstractive activity seizes the object under the universal aspect and must be intrinsically free from all matter, requiring a spiritual nature in man. It is within this framework of the " Physics " that St. Thomas studies man as a corporeal composite, defining him as a substantial composite of prime matter and of a reasoning, spiritual and subsistent soul.

The most fundamental position of Thomism in natural philosophy, a daring but simple one, is that of the *unity of substantial forms and of their individuation through matter*. Every corporeal being, man included, is constituted by but *one sole* substantial form naturally and directly united to prime matter. The fundamental proof of this truth is that the reason for the substantial unity of bodies as given in experience lies in the unity of the actualizing element of substance (form).

This theory was so new in his age that St. Thomas had to defend it in various ways. The proof is developed by proposing a triple series of considerations.

a) **Metaphysical considerations.** The unity of form is placed in relationship to the transcendental unity of being; a thing is one through the one form by which the thing has being. Moreover, inasmuch as substantial form completes the primordial imperfection of matter, so that the union of these two constitutes the essence, every other form is necessarily accidental, for it actuates a being which already possesses its own substantial unity.

b) **Physical considerations.** The theory of a plurality of forms would make substantial change impossible; for the very basis of a being constituted by the form, say, of corporeity, would not be modified by the corruption of other forms.

c) **Psychological considerations.** Only a unity of form can explain the solidarity of the vital functions in man, for independent forms do not generate themselves in these functional activities. Furthermore, the unity of form alone explains the identity of a living and a resurrected man.

The mode of this unity is explained by St. Thomas in two ways :

a) The notion of the *hierarchy of forms*, through which a more perfect principle contains in itself the active virtues of the less perfect. At the same time, St. Thomas grants that the immediate and proportionate explanation of the diversity of operations is due to the various " powers " or faculties, conceived as proper accidents flowing from the unique soul.

b) The notion of *succession of forms*, according to which matter is first actuated by an interior, transitory form; then, as soon as the ultimate dispositions of matter are readied, this transitory form cedes its place to a higher form which virtually contains the former. In man, the intellectual soul, immediately created by God, is this final form; immediate creation by God is required for it due to the spirituality of the soul.

This proposition is completed by the *principle of individuation*. Potentiality alone is the source of limitation and multiplicity; hence, the reason for numerical multiplicity of forms within the same species is due to prime matter, which is the source of quantity. From this line of reasoning, it can be concluded that each of the pure forms (angels) is a subsisting individuality which exhausts its species and is necessarily unique. The problem of individuation is not met with here.

The theory applies to the human soul itself, even though it be subsistent. Since soul is not produced " from matter ", it is created " in matter ", which signifies that it is created in direct relation to this portion of prime matter which it individualizes. Inasmuch as this relationship is inscribed in their essence, souls (even when separated) remain numerically distinct; they retain their natural aptitude to form a substantial unity with body.

Thus, we have the same explanation. The composition of pure potentiality and essential actuality (matter and form) explains most complicated situations without undue involvements, and neatly distinguishes man from the angelic world. Finally, this same composition of actuality and potentiality, in the higher order of essence and existence, distinguishes the angelic world from God.

C) **Morality.**

269. St. Thomas is the first philosopher of the thirteenth century who built a Scholastic moral synthesis on an Aristotelian basis. His work in this regard can be outlined as an example of scientific deduction which gives full meaning to human life.   Rooted in psychology and in metaphysics, morality leads man to his purpose through appropriate means by determining his individual and social obligation.

1.   **Psychological and Metaphysical Foundation.**   Thomistic morality is rooted in the theory of *appetition*, whose reason and explanation lies in the metaphysical notions of the good, and of final and efficient cause.   Appetite is an active principle by which each being seeks for full actuation or perfection; it is the inclination of a thing towards its proper good.   There is a diversity of appetites corresponding to the diversity of the degrees of being.

The purely physical forms are endowed with a simple, natural appetite.   Knowing beings, due to the " intentional " form superadded to their physical being, enjoy a spontaneous (elicited) appetite which is the source of movements and is as varied as the passions.   Finally, because reason is capable of grasping the universal aspect of good, man possesses a voluntary appetite, necessarily drawn to desire absolute good and happiness as such, though remaining *free* in choosing the particular means which lead it thereto; every concrete good is unequal to man's capacity.   This theory of freedom, covering the relations of freedom to reason, wherein freedom finds its source and specification, and including the influence of the passions, is one of the most perfected parts of Thomism and one of the most secure bases of morality.

2.   **The Final Goal.**   Because of the fact that the object of the intellectual appetite in man is the good as such, man's true happiness can lie only in the possession of God.   God is the only happiness without mixture of evil.   He alone is capable of equalling fully and definitively all desires of the will.

But the human faculty which essentially realizes this possession is intelligence.   The action proper to intelligence is to know " another as other ", and this action identifies man, in some fashion, with the object of knowledge.   The will, on the other hand, is the principle of movement, which precedes, and of delectable repose, which follows this possession.   Will is indissolubly united to intelligence.

Happiness, as a result, is formally constituted by the " contemplation " of God.   In philosophy, this notion of contemplation must be reduced to an analogical, abstractive and discursive " wisdom ", proportionated to man.   But as a theologian, St. Thomas spoke of a natural desire which inclined human reason to have no rest until it attained the vision of the primary, Divine Essence, and reason finds this answer to its desire only in that human happiness which is truly definite, the beatific vision of heaven. Through a bad use of liberty, man can doubtlessly choose some other beatitude, but this would make him unhappy and *culpable*, as long as he was not oriented towards God.

3. **The Means.** Man's material condition necessitates a progressive march towards happiness. The means which lead there are the many human actions which man performs. These actions must be good; that is, they must fully realize their being as human acts, according to the adage, " Good arises from an integral cause " [1].

By repetition, human actions progressively actualize the indetermination of freedom and of the human powers which liberty commands. Actions engender new principles of action, permitting man to act with perfection and pleasure; these new principles are called habits, or, in the order of the good, virtues. St. Thomas analyzed the complex organism of the virtues. In doing so, he used the principle that as long as there is a special reason for activity to be in conformity with right reason, there is a formal object specifying a virtue. In his analysis, all virtues are naturally unified in prudence, and supernaturally, in charity.

4. **Obligation.** All good actions are capable of leading to happiness. There are, however, a certain number of them having an essential relationship to happiness, so that one could not omit them without renouncing his final goal. Obligation, then, is the necessity proper to liberty, and presupposes the complete dependence of our liberty on the Creator.

The supreme rule of morality and the final explanation of obligation is not the Will of God, as the Augustinians proposed. Every act of will follows intellection, which is its true explanation and which specifies will acts. The true foundation is an act of practical reason declaring that this means or this action is necessary to obtain an end. This declaration constitutes *law;* pronounced by Divine Reason, it is *eternal law,* which is but the order between essences conceived by God; reflected in created essences, it is the *natural law,* as physical

---

[1] " Bonum ex integra causa ".

in unreasoning creatures, and moral in human nature, where it is declared by reason with the help of practical sense *(synderesis)*. It follows from the above, that if the Divine Reason is the supreme rule of morality, human reason, through moral conscience, is the immediate and proximate rule of morality.

The study of the various virtues adds precision to the goodness or badness, the obligatoriness, or the supererogatory character of human actions. The formation of conscience through acquiring prudence governs the application of law to particular actions.

5. **Society.** By nature, man is a social animal, for society is necessary that man may overcome the material and moral insufficiencies of the individual. Due to this fact, the natural law not only formulates the obligations of individuals, but also contains the rules of social life. Authority, which is necessary to coordinate the thoughts, volitions and will acts towards a common end, is necessary for society, and comes immediately from God [1], the Author of society and of the essential conditions of its existence. The function of authority is to add precision to applications of the natural law by conformity with distributive justice; this is achieved through the construction of a code of positive laws.

The directive activity of reason, which has its source in the Eternal law, and which is similar to God's reason, can be heard through the intermediary of conscience and of authority even down to the minor details of human life. All of the activity is directed entirely towards the acquisition of happiness, which is nothing other than the complete flowering of the intellectual life.

CONCLUSION. **270.** The Thomistic philosophy has the privilege of being the sole official philosophy of the Catholic Church [2]. The brief sketch of this philosophy outlined above, aimed to show how this choice is fully justified by the intrinsic pedagogic and scientific value of this doctrine. Thomism is, fundamentally, the philosophy of good sense; it is both universal and Catholic.

This does not mean that Thomism has found every truth and achieved every intellectual progress. Lacordaire stated

[1] On the origin of political power according to St. Thomas, see above, n. 245.
[2] *Codex Juris Canonici*, 1366.

that St. Thomas was a lighthouse and not a milestone. For instance, by his own principles, St. Thomas lets the field open to discovery by the studies of nature; he but prepared the rational frames for them in order that they might be coordinated with philosophical knowledge [1]. If the Thomism of the thirteenth century knew how to welcome and to enliven ancient science as found in Aristotle, Thomism of the twentieth century should know how to justify and validate the new branches of learning brought forth by a Newton or by a Descartes. Furthermore, as every human work, that of St. Thomas contains a systematic portion that can be ameliorated : his students analyze his fundamental propositions, and, with their help, find new problems to resolve, as those of idealism or the modern critical spirit, or those of the economic and social orders.

But if one looks at the central core — at that body of doctrines demonstrated and constituted as " science " (in the Scholastic sense), Thomism is the system of most equilibrium. It is, furthermore, most solidly founded on that portion of common sense which is least subjective and which fully responds to the idea of an eternal or perennial philosophy. In addition, in relation to other doctrines, it is comprehensive, being pitiless with regard to certain errors yet clarifying the truth proper to each doctrine. It thus shows its marvelous aptitude of receiving all other partial truths brought out by other systems within its own embrace.

It is, consequently, with good reason that St. Thomas has received the title of the Common Doctor and has been named the guide for students [2]. In him there is not found the thought of one man alone, but the voice of the truth common to all men, and the most beautiful reflection of the Increated Light of the Word of God, Who enlightens every man coming into this world.

ARTICLE THREE.
THE NON-THOMISTIC SYNTHESES.

271. The struggles which St. Thomas was forced to meet show that his synthesis was not unanimously accepted in the thirteenth century. In addition to the Averroistic synthesis and the Augustinian tendencies, whose principal exponents

---

[1] See n. 265.
[2] Pius XI, " *Studiorum Ducem* ", June 29, 1923.

have been mentioned [1], the work of two contemporary Franciscan thinkers is of special importance. These two men are Roger Bacon and St. Bonaventure, both of whom presented an original adaptation of Augustinianism.

St. Augustine's doctrine was kept alive in the *Franciscan order*, and it gained new life through contact with Aristotle and through its interpretation by these two thinkers. Bacon is a more analytic thinker, and enriched his thought with scientific doctrines. St. Bonaventure, like St. Thomas, is more synthetic, and impregnated his work with a mysticism worthy of a St. Francis. Towards the close of the century, the synthesis of Duns Scotus appears; his view is one of the most remarkable of Scholasticism, and, at the same time, the least reducible to Thomism. Three sections will cover these men :

    I.   Roger Bacon.

    II. St. Bonaventure.

    III. Duns Scotus.

I. ROGER BACON.

(about 1210-1292).

SPECIAL BIBLIOGRAPHY.

1° **Works :** BREWER, J. S., *Fratris Rogeri Baconi opera quædam hactenus inedita*, London, 1859. — BRIDGES, J. H., *The Opus Maius of Roger Bacon*, 2 vols., Oxford, 1897. — *Supplementary volume*, Oxford, 1900. — BURKE, R. B., *The Opus Maius of Roger Bacon*, 2 vols., (English) Philadelphia, 1928. — RASHDALL, H., *Fratris Rogeri Baconi Compendium studii theologiæ*, Aberdeen, 1911. — STEELE, R., *Opera hactenus inedita Rogeri Baconi*, 16 fasc. to date, Oxford, 1905-40.

2° **Studies :** BRIDGES, J. H., *The Life and Work of Roger Bacon*, London, 1914. — CARTON, R., *La synthèse doctrinale de Roger Bacon*, Paris, 1929. — *L'expérience mystique de l'illumination intérieure chez Roger Bacon*, Paris, 1924. — *L'expérience physique chez Roger Bacon*, Paris, 1924. — CHARLES, E., *Roger Bacon, sa vie, ses ouvrages, ses doctrines*, Paris, 1861. — CROWLEY, T., *Roger Bacon : the problem of the soul in his philosophical commentaries*, new ed., London, 1950. — EASTON, S. C., *Roger Bacon and his search for a universal science*, New York, 1952. — LITTLE, A. G., *Roger Bacon, Essays contributed by various writers*, London, 1914. — NEWBOLD, W. R., *The Cipher of Roger Bacon*, Oxford, 1929. —

---

[1] See above, nn. 247-250.

WALZ, R., *Das Verhaltnis vom Glaube und Wissen bei R. Bacon*, Fribourg (Sw.) 1928. — WOODRUFF, F. W., *Roger Bacon : A Biography*, London, 1938.

272. Roger Bacon was born at Ilchester in England, about 1210-14. He was attracted towards the observation and experience of nature already from his youth. He studied at Oxford under Robert Grosseteste who seems to have been the first chancellor (about 1221) of this famous English university and to have given it a vigorous orientation towards the study of languages and of the sciences of nature [1]. The university, at any rate, was the most favorable atmosphere for the full flowering of Roger's genius.

At the same time, the University of Paris was the model of the University of Oxford [2], and the English masters were wont to go there for courses and lectures. Roger Bacon is found there about 1245-6, though shortly after he is again at Oxford, where he remains. It was at this time that he decided to enter the Franciscan order. There, with unflagging ardor, he continued his studies in language and in such experimental sciences as astronomy, physics, and geography. He also taught theology, but, around 1258, poor health forced him to abandon this work, and he reserved his strength for the studies he liked best.

Although Roger wished to publish the results of his studies, his superiors judged them too advanced and did not grant him permission. One of his friends became Pope under the name of Clement IV (1265-8), and requested Roger to send him his projected works. Aided by this protection, Roger prepared his *Opus Majus*. The work consists of seven parts : the causes of human error, the relationship of philosophy and of science to theology, linguistics, mathematics, perspective, experimental science and moral philosophy. This work was followed by an *Opus Minus* and an *Opus Tertium*, which resumed and clarified the teachings of his first work. Quite a number of smaller works are extant; they deal with some aspects of theology, philosophy and science (as the work, *De multiplicitate specierum*), which appear to be fragments of a large work, *Scriptum principale*, which Bacon had planned to write [3].

---

[1] In addition to the translations mentioned above (n. 232), ROBERT GROSSE-TESTE authored a rather large number of works treating on physical, psychological and metaphysical questions. Robert had a high esteem for mathematics, and " His cosmological and astronomical teaching concerning the formation of the universe and the movements of the planets and comets, and his project for the reform of the calendar, together with his investigations on perspective, colors, the rainbow, tides, heat, sound, etc., constitute Robert Grossetete one of the most prominent men of science of his time ". (M. DE WULF, *History of Medieval Philosophy*, Vol. 1, p. 89). In all of these ways, Bacon got inspiration from his master, Robert.

[2] For example, about 1240, Robert Grosseteste invited the theologians of Oxford to follow the order adopted at Paris in their teaching; M. DE WULF, *op. cit.*, p. 18.

[3] A number of youthful works are still extant, including commentaries on Aristotle's Physics and Metaphysics, and on the *Liber de causis;* they are the results of his teaching as a Master of Arts.

Tempier's [1] condemnations of 1277 affected certain doctrines of Bacon and moved him to write his *Speculum astronomiæ*. Bacon's opposition, together with his incessant criticisms of the Scholastics, brought upon him the condemnation of his superior general, Jerome of Ascoli; this action definitively terminated his doctrinal career [2].

General Characteristics. Roger Bacon is a complex personality and a mixture of striking contrasts. Though an impassioned critic of the Scholastics, he accepts their essential doctrines; while extolling the experimental method, he held strongly to Augustinian illumination; he delighted in scrutinizing nature, though he proclaimed the supremacy of mysticism. The synthesis of these tendencies is found in his theory of the unity of science.

At first, Bacon appeared to the Middle Ages as a pitiless judge of Scholasticism. He was greatly busied with this criticism, dealing with it in a number of special works [3], and in long chapters of his larger works. For instance, the *Opus Minus* analyzes seven capital sins which vitiate current theological studies : the custom of theologians to treat purely theological questions *ex professo ;* the ignorance of theologians concerning positive experimental sciences and of language; the countless errors in their commentaries; the preference given to the Book of Sentences of Peter the Lombard, a human book, over the Bible, a divine book; the corruption into which the Bible has fallen through the theologians; the abusive use of the spiritual meaning of the Bible and the misunderstanding of its literal meaning; the madness of preachers to deal with purely philosophical questions. The philosophers were severely criticized also; they neglected the sciences and the methods of observation and indulged in a priori reasonings which led them to ruin. These defects were not concocted by Bacon, for they were common among the crowd of less talented masters, and became one of the principal causes of intellectual decadence. But it is to be regretted that Bacon allowed himself to be blind to the merit of the great doctrinal systems that were being erected, for the most part, in his very times. His criticisms of Alexander of Hales and of Albert the Great are manifestly exaggerated, and even the importance of the nascent Thomism affected him little. This view is partially explicable by the esteem in which he held the positive sciences, in contrast to the less favorable view of most of his contemporaries [4].

In effect, Roger Bacon was especially interested in the concrete aspect of problems. For example, he underscored the defect

---

[1] See above, n. 251.

[2] It has been said that Bacon was incarcerated (see, for example, M. De Wulf, *op. cit.*, p. 270) for his errors. Delorme, however, writes : " The four-year imprisonment which some say that Bacon was given is but a pure fable, and rests on no evidence ". (" Bacon ", article in *Dictionnaire théologique catholique*, col. 10).

[3] One of these is entitled *Metaphysica de vitiis contractis in studio theologiæ*.

[4] It seems that Roger should have been in accord on this question with Albert the Great; but it seems that Roger never quite understood Aristotle.

of the Julian calendar and of the Vulgate edition of the Bible, requesting the Pope to remedy them. He showed the usefulness of geography and mapped out a chart of the known world [1]. He exposed the illusions of optics in astronomy; he looked for more certain means than direct observation for determining the real magnitude and distance of the stars; after mature consideration, he rejected the Ptolemaic system. He insisted on the study of languages, especially of Hebrew, Arabic and Greek, inasmuch as they were necessary for understanding ancient documents, and he applied himself vigorously to their study. Above all, he held that the true explanation of the phenomena of nature must be *quantitative*, and that the sciences of nature need the application of geometry and mathematics for their progress, which he envisioned as follows : " His work, *De secretis operibus artis et naturæ*, is filled with visions of the future : steamships, trains, balloons, diving suits, telescopes, microscopes, and the awesome effects of powder are there indicated literally " [2].

One should not think of Roger Bacon, however, as one would of a modern savant who might be totally estranged from the Catholic faith or even ready to fight against it [3]; he was a Scholastic, and was profoundly attached to the spirit of the ancient, Augustinian school [4]. As he never sought to separate himself from religious obedience, so he never believed that philosophy or the sciences would separate him from his faith. He considered God the source of each truth, whether human or supernatural; truth is transmitted from one generation to another by tradition, a fact which points up the importance of languages in collecting the items of tradition. Even the pagan philosophers drew their truths from this universal source : " It was impossible that man should arrive at the wonders of the sciences and of the arts of himself, but it was proper that he have revelation " [5]. Roger, like most of the Fathers of the Church, believed that the sages of Greece knew the revelations made to Abraham and to Moses.

From all that has been said above, one can conclude to the principle of the unity of science for Bacon : inasmuch as each truth comes from God, the truths of all knowledge of the particular sciences, of philosophy and of theology are to be subordinated and completed in order to constitute a unique science, possessive of the full truth. This is the fundamental position of the philosophy of Roger Bacon.

Philosophical Doctrines. 273. The philosophy of Roger Bacon is not lacking in originality. His conception of *natures* is fully harmonized with his propositions on *knowledge*, and his principle of the unity of science includes his theory of experience.

---

[1] The map is lost, but Bacon's explanations of it are found in his *Opus majus*.

[2] *Dictionnaire théologique catholique*, article " Bacon ", col. 17.

[3] This is the trait of modern philosophy, especially in its opposition to Scholasticism; see below, n. 313.

[4] See above, n. 232bis and n. 250. Perhaps this is one of the reasons for Roger's opposition to the school of Albert and Aquinas.

[5] *Opus majus* (Brewer edition), Part two, III, p. 53.

1. **The natures.** Faithful to his Augustinian ancestry, Bacon views each created nature as a composite of matter and form, for matter is the principle of limit and of multiplicity. The existence of corporeal natures, and, consequently, of a plurality of substances is an evident fact. Every sort of pantheism, as that of Amalric of Bene and of David of Dinant [1], is a pure absurdity.

But his strong proclivity for the concrete, caused Bacon to hold that only the individual is real. Though our universal ideas express reality, the internal organization of corporeal substances is to be conceived as requiring " superimposed stages " [2]; each metaphysical degree (corporeity, vegetative, sensitive and intellectual life) comprises a matter and a form which, joined together, play the role of potentiality to the higher pair. Each of the " stages " has its own individuality which is knowable through a universal idea; only the superior degree, however, by its dominating force, constitutes the perfect individual.

Bacon adopted another Augustinian proposition : though at the lowest degree of reality, prime matter has its own proper existence and contains the seminal reasons actively directive of the evolvement of bodies. Bacon adds to this view by defending not only the plurality of forms but also the *plurality of prime matters;* each species has its own, so that specification as well as individuation is given through the union of matter and form. " Accordingly, the donkey does not differ from the horse through form alone, but through another specific matter " [3].

2. **Knowledge.** This conception of individual natures involves, for Bacon, an *intuitionistic theory* of both sensible and intellectual knowledge. External sense experience grasps the concrete fact only in a global fashion; intellectual ideas, however, seize therein the generic and specific natures which are found there with their individuality and can thus reveal themselves to us directly. This doctrine makes the work of abstraction and the existence of an active intellect useless, at least in the sense proposed by Aristotle and St. Thomas. Bacon even taught that the active intellect is God Himself, the source of all knowledge; His illumination is needed by every created intellect in order that it might grasp the reflections of eternal truths hidden in the world. This is the Augustinian doctrine of illumination, which is presented by Bacon rather strangely and in the technical terminology of Aristotle's philosophy.

This illumination, in Bacon's view, is required for every act of the intelligence without exception. It seems that Roger conceived of the general concourse of God in a fashion similar to that of Augustine. In this connection, De Wulf writes that " Bacon merely means that God is the light of our intellects, and that the general concourse which He gives to every creature in order that it may be able to act, is called in the case of knowledge an illumi-

---

[1] See above, n. 210.
[2] See M. DE WULF, *op. cit.*, Vol. II, p. 274.
[3] *Opus tertium* (Brewer edition), p. 126.

nation of truth " [1]. In order to obtain true science, and especially in order to get the perfect wisdom of theology, a *special illumination* is needed which is a gratuitous aid like that of inspiration. At the first degree, in order to attain true philosophy, " purely sciential illuminations " are needed; these are on the boundary of the natural and the supernatural [2], and the pagan sages were favored with them. Finally, there is a series of other, supernatural favors attached to the gifts of the Holy Spirit, leading the mind beyond faith and theology into mystical intuitions. In this wise, the unity of science and the explanation of knowledge are clarified and mutually corroborative.

3. **Theory of experience.** Bacon's view of experience has a special meaning and is basic in his system of thought. There are three sources of knowledge : authority, reason and experience. True science cannot be gained by authority alone, nor by reason itself; the latter must admit conclusions on the basis of argumentation and does not yield perfect certitude. Experience alone can constitute science : " An argument does not certify nor remove doubt so that the soul can rest in the intuition of truth unless it be found by way of experience " [3].

Two types of experience are distinguished, internal and external. External experience is constituted by the exercise of the external senses; in order that it have scientific value, its observation must be made precise and subject to the aid of instruments; finally, these results must be interpreted in the light of mathematics. These precepts already constitute a rather remarkable outline of the method to be followed in positive sciences. It is true that Bacon adds that one must take into account the occult influences of nature; but he carefully distinguished scientific conclusions from the reveries of occultism, categorically rejecting, for example, the theory of transmutation of metals [4]. He applied his method in numerous cases, and " even attempted to constitute a general science whose general aim would be to reduce all the reciprocal actions of bodies and natural agents to mathematical principles. This new science, which cost him ten years of effort, is outlined in the *De multiplicatione specierum* " [5].

External experience, however, is but a first stage. The march towards truth is especially realized through *internal experience*,

---

[1] M. De Wulf, *op. cit.*, Vol. ii, p. 277. R. Carton (*L'expérience mystique chez Roger Bacon*, p. 69), believes that there is question here of a special illumination.

[2] R. Carton believes that these illuminations are supernatural (*op. cit.*, pp. 35-39), while M. De Wulf (*op. cit.*, p. 219, fn. 10) holds them to be natural.

[3] *Opus majus* (Brewer edition), i, c. vi, p. 168.

[4] " He exercised a scrupulous care so that his physics would not be mixed up with divination, nor his chemistry with alchemy, nor his astronomy with astrology ". A. Delorme, article " Bacon ", *Dictionnaire théologique catholique*, col. 18.

[5] *Ibid.*, col. 17. As for Grosseteste, the " species " are, in Bacon's view, the reciprocal influences of bodies and especially the luminous influences. Bacon did not admit that the propagation of light occurs instantaneously...

which is the intuition of truth obtained by the various special illuminations mentioned above. Understood in this sense, the view that only experience gives science is but another form of the principle of the unity of science and is inspired by the Augustinian tradition.

Conclusion. Roger Bacon can be viewed as the precursor and the first founder of the contemporary English philosophical school, which is totally penetrated with the positivist spirit and with an esteem for experimental science. He is a creature of his times through his central doctrine of the unity of science and through his admission of the dominating role of theology and mysticism over philosophy and the sciences of nature. He is not at all a rationalist, and freely unifies enthusiastic love for the Catholic faith with a love of experimental method. This union, though, seems unintelligible to the modern spirit; " it is an inexplainable union ", Brehier writes, " if there is question of the experimental method as it is understood today. As a matter of fact, it is not this method which is being considered here " [1]. On the contrary, it has been shown that Bacon is concerned with the same scientific method which has permitted the magnificent modern inventions. Bacon integrates a general conception of the science in the Augustinian spirit which is fully in accord with " Christian philosophy "; this notion of science loses none of its value by being hierarchically placed on the ladder of knowledge.

There are, of course, many ways of conceiving of a hierarchy of knowledge. The Thomistic mode safeguards the legitimate independence of the positive sciences much better. But Bacon's merit was to have insisted, more than others, on the use of experience and to have vigorously protested against the errors of his times in this regard. True, he can be reproached with exaggeration in his criticisms, and of showing himself " impulsive, vain and self-sufficient " [2]. One could just as well see in his violent diatribes a vivid grasp of the very real defects in many Scholastics, whose future decadence was to show their real harm.

But the views of Roger Bacon were too much in advance of his time, so that they were unable to determine a stream of succeeding ideas, as did Thomism and Scotism. " He was a brilliant meteor, and left no traces in philosophy. Perhaps some data of experimental science and philosophy were borrowed from him in the fourteenth century. The Scholastics of the sixteenth and seventeenth centuries ignored him, and his name reappeared only with Jebb's edition of the *Opus majus* in 1733 " [3]. Bacon's light has the merit of shining in our days in order to show the possibility of harmonizing the Christian faith and even the mystic spirit with a true predilection for the positive sciences.

---

[1] E. Bréhier, *Histoire de la philosophie*, Vol. I, p. 697.
[2] M. De Wulf, *op. cit.*, Vol. II, p. 272.
[3] *Ibid.*, p. 281.

II. Saint Bonaventure.

(1221-1274).

Spécial bibliography.

1⁰ **Works** : *Opera Omnia*, 10 vols., Quaracchi, 1882-1902.

2⁰ **Studies** : Bissen, J.-M., *L'exemplarisme divin selon Saint Bona-venture*, Paris, 1929. — Gilson, E., *The Philosophy of St. Bona-venture*, New York, 1938. — Luyckx, B.-A., *Die Erkenntnislehre Bonaventuras*, Münster (W.), 1923. — Sestili, G., *La filosofia di San Bonaventura*, Turin, 1928.

274. Born in Tuscany, St. Bonaventure entered the Fran-ciscan order at the age of seventeen. During his years of study at Paris, he was able to know and even to hear the celebrated Alexander of Hales, a fervent Augustinian [1], whom he called " our father and master ".

Bonaventure's teaching as a bachelor at Paris coincided with the first sojourn of St. Thomas in that city. Together they combated the seculars and suffered their hostility; they pronounced their inaugural lectures as Doctors on the same day [2], under order of the Pope. Despite their divergent opinions, they were always joined in closest friendship. But while St. Thomas was able to remain in his purely doctrinal labors until death, St. Bonaventure, after teaching for thirty-six years, was elected Minister General of the Franciscan order, charged to write a life of St. Francis and also to draft the Constitutions of the order. After he had refused the Arch-bishopric of York, he was forced to accept the cardinalate in 1273. He died in 1274 at the Council of Lyons, whither he had gone to contribute his talents towards the reconciliation of the Greeks and the Latins.

From the philosophical viewpoint, Bonaventure's principal works are the following : *Commentarii in IV libros Sententiarum* (about 1248-1255); *Quæstiones Disputatæ; Itinerarium mentis in Deum* (1259); *Breviloquium; De reductione artium ad theo-*

---

[1] See above, n. 232bis, and see F. Cayré, *Manual of Patrology*, Vol. ii, p. 499.
[2] Bonaventure received his doctorate in 1253 and occupied the Franciscan chair at the University of Paris from 1253 to 1257; in this latter year, however, after the persecution by the seculars had subsided, he was again received as Doctor, and at this time, St. Thomas also was received. See M. De Wulf, *op. cit.*, Vol. ii, p. 113.

logiam. He also wrote treatises on Aristotle's *Topics, Meteo-rologica* and the *De generatione* [1].

General Characteristic. 275. St. Bonaventure's philosophical work is an original and profound synthesis of Augustinianism, whose principal doctrines have been mentioned previously. Augustinianism is recognizable by four traits : a conservative tendency; a Peripatetic frame of reference; a central, Augustinian view; a particular and proper principle.

1° **General tendency.** St. Bonaventure is a conservative and moderated thinker who aimed to reconcile the new Peripateticism with traditional Augustinianism by allowing *mysticism* to dominate and to be the coronal and the goal of all science, philosophy and theology. The unity of his philosophy is first constituted by this *constant tendency* to gather the evident truths discovered by Aristotle (in the Catholic interpretation as defended also by St. Thomas) and, at the same time, to respect other ancient opinions as much as possible.

2° **Frame of reference.** The major propositions of Aristotelian metaphysics form the frame of reference for Bonaventure's thinking : actuality and potentiality are applied to creatures through the constitutive principles of essence and existence, of matter and form, of substance and accident. The four causes are recognized, and their assistance in helping man mount to God through creatures. The value of all these propositions is recognized by Bonaventure and by Aquinas, but there are important nuances of difference in their understanding of them. While St. Thomas' inflexible logic allowed him to go counter to current opinions, St. Bonaventure was respectful of tradition; while St. Thomas was busily engaged in the new Peripatetic directions, St. Bonaventure immersed himself deeply in the sources of Augustinianism.

3° **Central viewpoint.** *Exemplarism* [2] is the unifying view in Bonaventure's system. In accepting the widely different view of traditional Augustinianism along with the new doctrines of Aristotle, Bonaventure was not content with a slightly

---

[1] For an analysis of all of St. Bonaventure's works, see F. CAYRÉ, *op. cit.* Vol. II., pp. 501-505.

[2] See above, n. 159. St. Thomas also received the notion of exemplary ideas favorably, but did not give them as great an importance as does St. Bonaventure or St. Augustine. He distinguishes their causal power from the efficient cause. Bonaventure and Augustine unite under the *Idea* both formal extrinsic causality (exemplary) and efficient causality (participatory).

homogeneous eclecticism. He aimed to refer everything to the same central view; being a true disciple of Augustine, he placed himself at the viewpoint of God Himself. Instead of explaining the divine perfections through those of creatures, he aimed to understand the universe through the Goodness and the Wisdom of the Creator, Who gives each being, according to its degree of perfection, a participation in the richness of being which the Word of God bears in His exemplary Ideas. This leads to the following formulation of Bonaventure's fundamental theory :

All things are intelligible through the exemplary Ideas of God.

4° **The principle of incomplete beings.** The various doctrines that he wished to organize were, in their totality, so complex and so restricted to the physical order that they could not be immediately explained by the metaphysical theory of exemplarism. St. Bonaventure found a principle which was less ample in spread but more directly applicable; with its aid he could harmonize most of the theories he adopted. Though not stated explicitly, it is easily disengaged from its many applications; it is the principle of " incomplete beings ", and can be formulated as follows :

Every property of a distinct degree of perfection requires, as its reason for being, an actual principle or a special form; these forms, in the same individual, being hierarchized as incomplete beings, maintain the substantial unity of beings.

This new principle does not introduce duality into his system; it is but an application of exemplarism. Following the habitual tendency of Platonists towards total realism, St. Bonaventure aimed to discover the distinctions corresponding to our *ideas* in real *natures;* both ideas and natures were but attenuated and multiplied reflectoins of the exemplary Ideas synthesized in the unique, Divine Nature. The hierarchy of forms is but an expression of the plan of Divine Wisdom rediscovered by human reason as it contemplates creation in the light of the divine illumination.

This principle, with its Peripatetic twist, is not demonstrated or deduced from the fundamental theory of exemplarism. It did permit Bonaventure, however, to give an acceptable meaning to traditional theories and to enrich the metaphysical doctrine of Augustinian wisdom with the more scientific precision of Aristotelian proposals.

This dual viewpoint is an inevitable source of complexity
in any system. Inasmuch as St. Bonaventure left us no philosophical synthesis, it is possible to reconstruct his system
according to different plans. In order to stay faithful to the
spirit of St. Augustine, exemplarism, showing God as the
explicative source of things in philosophy and in theology,
will be treated here first. Then it will be shown how the
Franciscan Doctor, applying his principle of *incomplete beings*
to the domain of natures and of operations, attempted to
reconcile Augustine and Aristotle. Throughout, it will be seen
how the Divine Ideas are reflected in the simple vestiges of
nature as well as in the more perfect operations of the soul.

   I. EXEMPLARISM : God as the explicative source of
       everything.

   II. NATURES : God in His vestiges.

   III. OPERATIONS : God in His image.

I. Exemplarism.

It is Bonaventure's conception of the existence of God
which leads him to his basic view of exemplarism. From this
summit within divinity itself, he gives us a broad view of
creation as a radiation from the Divine Ideas.

A) Existence of God.

275. I. It is totally in conformity with the spirit of the
Seraphic Doctor to place God at the initial stage of speculation.
God is the light capable of explaining all things, for His existence
is an established fact not needing demonstration in a strict
sense [1]. At the same time, there are certain " ways " in which
reason, aided by reflections or arguments, lifts itself to the
contemplation of God. Bonaventure signalizes three of these.

   I. The first way is the *way of causality*, founded on the
most distant vestiges of God; these are the perfections of
sensible things, such as their beauty and their order mingled
with their deficiencies [2]. A methodical classification of these
sensible phenomena is not given, but Bonaventure shows that

---

[1] See below, n. 279, for an explanation of how man has an intuition
or " contuition " of God.

[2] This first way, in comparison with the other two, is considered by
Bonaventure as of little value. St. Thomas considers it the proper method,
for his five ways of proving God's existence (See *Summa Theologica*, I, q. II,
art. 3) are based on the *vestiges* of God.

all things join in chorus to proclaim the existence of the Creator; " As the cause shines forth in the effect, and as the wisdom of the artist is manifested in his work, so God, the artist and the cause of the creature, is known through the creature " [1].

2. The *way of the spirit* [2] shows us a resplendent image of the Divinity which animates us with Its presence in our very selves. Human aspirations spontaneously tend towards the fulness of truth and towards eternal happiness; they suppose that man knows the object of these aspirations, the immutable Truth and the absolute Good Who is God. Each of our infallible truths shows us the luminous source on which it depends.

3. Finally, the *way of Saint Anselm* directly leads man to God through the very idea which we make within ourselves, for it is of the very essence of perfect Being to exist. In other words, He Whom we adopt as the source of the beauty of the world and as the source of the activities of our spirit, appears to us as realizing existence through essence necessarily; consequently, He appears as incapable of not existing [3]. " For God, or the highest Truth, is Being itself, than which nothing better can be thought of; hence, He cannot not-exist, nor be thought of as not-existing " [4].

God, accordingly, is the first object of the mind as it seeks to explain the universe. To the eyes of the believer as well as of the philosopher, He is the supreme and perfect Being, the first uncaused Cause possessing all perfections without stint or limit. " He does not change in place, for He is everywhere; not in time, because eternity is simultaneous; not in form, because He is pure Actuality. Change in form would remove simplicity; in time, eternity; in place, immensity. Accordingly, the highest stability lies in the Godhead " [5]. Finally, for Bonaventure as for Augustine, God is, above all, the subsisting Truth explaining all things by His Ideas; this view is exemplarism.

B) Nature of Exemplary Ideas.

275. II. Exemplarism is the doctrine of Platonic inspiration which explains the changing and multiple perfections of this world as being participations in an ideal source which realizes

---

[1] *In I Sententiarum*, dist. 3, I, q. 11, concl.
[2] Augustine called this " *mens* " and Plotinus " νοῦς ".
[3] See above, n. 223.
[4] *In I Sententiarum*, dist. 8, I, art. 1, q. 11, concl.
[5] *Ibid.*, art. 2, q. 1, concl.

them in a supreme degree and in all their fulness and purity. For Christian philosophers, these models, or exemplars, are always viewed as Divine Ideas.

Bonaventure defines the exemplary Idea as " The similitude of the things through which it is known and is produced " [1]. The idea first pertains to knowledge, which is a certain " assimilation " or similitude between knowing subject and object known. But this similitude is not of a static order; it is the fruit of a living activity, leading Bonaventure to designate knowledge ordinarily by the word " expression ". " This similitude is the *expressive* reason for knowledge " [2]. He does not consider the idea in the termination achieved, in which the object is contemplated, but mostly in the action in which the spirit engenders in itself, or " conceives ", a resemblance of the object which it knows [3]. Truth, which is none other than perfect knowledge, is, consequently, defined as " the light [4] expressive in intellectual knowledge "; that is, truth is the vital action of the intellect which expresses in itself the perfect similitude with the thing as thought.

Besides this expression of the ideal order, there is a *causal* expression through which perfection seems to leave itself and communicate itself beyond its own confines by creating beings which partake in its perfection. It is this fecundity *ad extra* which best characterizes exemplarism; " The exemplar bespeaks the reason for production " [5].

As long as we are concerned with the exemplary Ideas of God, there is, evidently, no real distinction between them; all are identifiable with the unique, simple and infinite essence. This raises a double problem. How can their *multiplicity* be explained? This is required so that they could express all the distinct essences. The other problem is: How can the Infinite be conceived as similar to created essences which, so to speak, have nothing in common with the Infinite?

---

[1] *In 1 Sententiarum*, dist. 35, q. 1, fund. 2.

[2] *Ibid.*, art. 1, q. IV, concl.

[3] This attitude seems to be due to the influence of the dogma of the Holy Trinity, in which the Word of God, subsisting Truth and the perfect similitude of the Father, is the fruit of the generative act of the Father. As a theologian, St. Bonaventure places the doctrine of exemplarism in the Second Person of the Trinity. (See J.-M. BISSEN, *L'exemplarisme divin selon saint Bonaventure*, sect. B, pp. 101, ff.).

[4] Though Bonaventure is fond of this metaphor of " light " in explaining knowledge, it does not seem to have further significance than a figure of speech.

[5] *In I Sententiarum*, dist. 31, II, art. 1, q. 1, ad 3.

Bonaventure answers these problems by distinguishing a double similitude. The first is *in the genus*, and supposes a common, univocal perfection, as that of the father and of the son in human nature. The other, proper to God alone, is *beyond genus* [1]. " Since the divine exemplar is most simple and perfect, it is pure actuality; since it is infinite and unlimited, it is beyond every type of genus. For this reason, though being one, it can be the expressive similitude of a great number of things " [2]. Understood in this fashion, similitude is not univocal, but is founded on a simple *analogy*, though the doctrine of exemplarism insists especially on the community of perfections without, at the same time, denying the degradation and distance of participations.

It is through His Ideas that God knows all His works; He is their cause, not by nature, but as an artist carries within himself the plan of a work which he will carry out through deliberate will. " The creature comes out of the Creator, though not by nature, since it is of another nature; hence, it comes about through art, for there is no other noble way of emanating than through nature, or through art or will " [3]. It is also through His Ideas that God creates each thing by radiating His perfection.

C) The Radiation of the Exemplary Ideas.

275. III. By their definition, the exemplary Ideas strictly express only present or future realities; thus, they are not merely representative lights, but also sources of radiation. However, having chosen exemplarism as a center of perspective, Bonaventure enlarges its meaning, and teaches that there are an infinite number of Ideas in God expressing all possibles. For, if exemplarism implies a relation to production, this could be an habitual relation, and a relation in potentiality. " The

---

[1] *Ibid.*, dist. 35, art. un., q. II, ad 2.

[2] *Breviloquium*, I, c. 8. This notion of a " similitude beyond genus " is clarified in Thomism by the distinction between *pure* perfections, which God possesses eminently and *formally*, because of their analogy, and *mixed* or univocal perfections, which God possesses eminently but *virtually*. The difficulty is created by the fact that the similitude demanded by the *idea is formal* in such wise that the Divine Ideas must univocally express each created perfection. If God formally possesses these mixed perfections, it is only and uniquely in the order of knowledge, with His own essence as intermediary. St. Thomas explains this by the notion of imitation, while St. Bonaventure, by a similitude beyond genus.

[3] *Collationes in Hexaemeron*, col. 12, n. 3.

exemplar bespeaks a similar relation habitually or in potentiality, for God knows and is capable of many things which He does not make " [1]. Through His Ideas God knows all the possibles inasmuch as He is capable of producing all of them [2].

In a fuller sense, the exemplar is He Who radiates Himself in creation. A principle of Bonaventure's here embraces all these conclusions : the Divine Ideas, through their creative efficacy, fully establish the truth of things; they establish ontological truth, by setting up each thing according to its degree of perfection according to their greater or lesser participation in the divine perfection. The Divine Ideas also establish logical truth for God, for they are the means by which God knows His work; they also establish logical truth for man because, in comprehending creatures, we merely grasp in their essence the reflection of their infinite source. Since, then, things have more of truth in God as their source than in themselves, man knows them better in their eternal Ideas than in themselves.

Although the Divine Ideas establish the reality of things, they are not content with expressing merely their specific perfection. Plato held this view, for he eliminated matter, which was presupposed and viewed as coeternal with God. The divine art rather produces things in their concrete reality, as existent individuals; the Divine Idea, due to its similitude beyond any genus, is capable of expressing the singular thing as well as the universal. " This similitude is the expressive reason for knowing not merely the universal, but also the singular, although it itself is not universal, nor singular, as God Himself is not " [3]. In this way, St. Bonaventure efficaciously refuted the error of Aristotle and of the Arabians, who refused to grant God a perfect knowledge of the world. He concluded that God possesses a proper idea of prime matter, for, in his view, matter has a reality in its own right, independently of form [4].

---

[1] *In I Sententiarum*, dist. 27, II, art. un., concl.

[2] In the *De Veritate* (q. III, art. 3, ad 3), St. Thomas writes : " A thing can be called an exemplar if something could be made in its imitation, even though it would never be made ". But in the *Summa Theologica* (I, q. XV, art. 3), he reserves the term exemplar to signify idea as directrix of action, and as referable to all those things which are made by God in some period of time.

[3] *In I Sententiarum*, dist. 35, art. un., q. IV, concl.

[4] St. Thomas described prime matter as a pure potentiality, incapable of existing without form; he would, accordingly, say that God has no special idea of matter alone, but of the composite. See *De Veritate*, q. III, art. 5, ad 7.

But if things receive their being and their intelligibility from divine, eternal Ideas, is not the order of the world also eternal, or, at least could it not be such? Bonaventure would concede that the Ideas could inform an eternal matter, if such could exist. " If matter is coeternal to its author as something opaque — as it is reasonable to hold that the Son, the Splendor of the Father, is eternal — it would seem to be reasonable that creatures, or the world itself, which is a shadow of the highest light, is eternal " [1].

But the Divine Ideas are not content merely with informing things; they explain every being even in its minutest parts, both in matter and in form. They are creative in the strict sense, that is, they have drawn the universe out of nothingness. Moreover, it seemed to Bonaventure that there would be a contradiction in supposing things to be drawn out of nothingness, without ever having been in nothingness but in having been from all eternity. For this view he adduces several arguments. " If the universe would continue to exist after an infinite time had already elapsed, it would have to be admitted that the infinite could be augmented, as new days are added to old ones... or that the world had no initial beginning and, as a result, was not able to arrive at an actual termination, for the duration it had to traverse was infinite... and if the world were eternal, it would have an infinity of men, and it would have, again, an actual infinity of immortal souls, which would be contradictory " [2]. From these arguments, it is necessary to conclude that the world was created necessarily in time [3].

Finally, exemplarism is the foundation of Divine Providence. In producing the world as a work of art, God had no other goal but His own glory which He manifested in pouring out His Goodness, and in leading each thing towards happiness. Bonaventure resolves the problem of evil as did Augustine [4],

---

[1] *In II Sententiarum*, dist. I, I, q. II, concl.

[2] E. GILSON, *La philosophie au Moyen Age*, 2e éd., rev. et augmentée, p. 448.

[3] In this proposition, St. Bonaventure takes the extreme opposite of Averroism, which defended the *necessity* of an eternal *world;* St. Thomas, adopting a middle view, established that the eternity of the world is neither necessary nor impossible (see above, nn. 249-250). St. Thomas was not ignorant of the reasons adduced by St. Bonaventure; he examined them explicitly and solved them; see *Summa Theologica*, I, q. XXXXVI, art. I and 2; *Summa Contra Gentiles*, Book. II, ch. 34 and 37; and see A. SERTILLANGES, *Saint Thomas d'Aquin*, I, pp. 279-292.

[4] See above, n. 160.

showing that evil in the physical order is but a condition of
beauty and universal order, and evil in the moral order is only
permitted for a much greater good.

II. Natures.

276. Bonaventure chose Aristotle's physical theory of
matter and form in order to explain the various created
natures and to conserve ancient views as much as possible.
He enlarged this view, however, and gave it a metaphysical
sense. The distinction of matter and form reveals the real,
fundamental composition which constitutes each contingent
being. It applies by right to each creature, distinguishing
creatures from God, Who alone is pure actuality, the sole
being exempted from matter.

This manner of interpreting hylomorphism allowed Bonaventure to retain four important Augustinian propositions.

Proposition I : *prime matter is incomplete actuality.* In
Aristotle's view, prime matter is conceived as pure potentiality
and as absolutely deprived of any determination. Due to
this indetermination, concludes St. Bonaventure, one can find
it in all creatures without exception, though he adds that this
" common matter " so considered is but a purely ideal being
and cannot be realized in nature. Every real matter must,
then, be privileged with a *beginning* of actuality and demands,
by its essence, a determined form as complement.

This conception can be compared to the Thomistic distinction
between essence and existence. In both causes, there is question
of an actuality [1] which remains in a relation limited of itself,
potential and incomplete, requiring the complementation of a final
form or of a supreme actuality. In this way, from the view of
metaphysical importance, it is the distinction of matter-form
which, for Bonaventure, replaces the essence-existence distinction.
The reality of the latter distinction is not clarified by Bonaventure
it seems that he considered it a simple logical distinction, the
fruit of intellectual abstraction.

Proposition II : *spiritual matter.* If the real distinction of
matter and form characterizes contingent beings, it is evident
that the human, separated soul and the pure spirits are also

[1] That is to say, for St. Thomas, the actuality of *essence*, which, in relation
to *existence*, plays the role of potentiality and of material cause; for
St. Bonaventure, the incomplete actuality of *matter*, which, in relation to *form*
plays the same role of potentiality and of material cause.

material beings, since they are creatures. Thus the angels, like corporeal beings, could be numerically multiplied, having matter as their principle of individuation. Matter, on the other hand, in order to be individuated, acts in conjunction with form.

The essential difference between corporeal and spiritual matter should be noted. The first is the source of quantity and of the consequent divisibility and spatial localization; spiritual matter is fully exempted from these imperfections. The first is the source of continual and profound changes which lead to corruption and to death, for it is never fully actuated by the form which it possesses. Spiritual matter, on the contrary, does not prevent incorruptibility or immortality, for it is fully dominated by its actuating form.

This domination and incorruptibility of the spiritual form is based, in St. Bonaventure's view, on intellectual operations. The spirit could not have a contrary to whose corruptive action it would be subject, for it possesses and assimilates the most opposed realities by the same idea. Thus, by the idea of color, it grasps both black and white. Accordingly, despite their matter, angels and the human soul are naturally incorruptible [1].

If the spiritual form is incorruptible, it cannot be produced through generation, but must be directly created by God; traducianism must be repudiated.

On the other hand, inasmuch as each soul henceforth bears with it its portion of matter, if it had drawn it from the pre-existent matter of the universe, the disposable quantity would diminish without stopping. So, in order not to trouble the order of the world, God created with each human being the spiritual matter which it was to inform.

Proposition III : *the seminal reasons.* Since corporeal matter is passive, it cannot alone explain the transformations of nature; the influence of efficient causes must be granted. This influence is subjected to laws whose explanation can be found in primary matter. The latter, because of its incomplete actuality, which orients it towards a certain category of forms, is endowed with diverse *virtualities*, allowing it to be successively completed by diverse forms directive of substantial change. This virtual pre-existence in seminal reasons is understood in

---

[1] St. Thomas recognized the value of this proof and appropriated it (*Summa Theologica*, I, q. LXXV, art. 6).

a broad sense by St. Bonaventure, so that the seminal reasons contain opposed forms, and, as a result, always need the determining activity of an efficient cause.

Proposition IV : *plurality of forms.* In order to determine matter, there is a certain number of hierarchical forms in each creature; these range from the most general, which is being, down to the specific form. Many of these are secondary and accidental, but others are of the substantial order. In St. Bonaventure's view, the unity of substance is compatible with a plurality of substantial forms on condition that the latter are as *incomplete beings* which mutually complete each other, and that the final, specific form fully dominates the others and imposes its unity on them.

There are two main substantial forms in man, each having its corresponding matter, the form of corporeity and of the spiritual soul. The latter is not only the intellective soul, but it is constituted by the reunion of three principles of life (vegetative, sensible and reasoning life), which are as three incomplete beings naturally destined to form a unit. Thus, soul and body are two substances, each complete in its own genus; but, since they are destined for each other, the one functions as potentiality and the other as actuality, and they unite to constitute the unique substance of man.

This notion of incomplete beings is far from absurd, and really upholds substantial unity, as long as one supposes that the diverse and really distinct parts are ordered by their very nature to form a unit[1]. Of course, if a theory is not absurd it is not thereby *true* or expressive of reality as it is. If our mind draws its knowledge from things by abstraction, as St. Thomas proves, one cannot legitimately conclude to the composition of elements really distinct in the manner of matter and of form, but only if the properties that need explanation reveal themselves to experience as irreducible and opposed, excluding each other as perfection and imperfection[2]

Now the various degrees of being which these diverse forms are destined to explain are not opposed in a proper sense; they complete each other in the order of actuality. Thus, sensitive life does not deny but rather completes vegetative life; intelligence does not deny but completes sensible knowledge. Accordingly reality is fully explainable by one unique form in each substance.

This is a purely objective solution, in which the problem is resolved in itself and independently of the solutions furnished

---

[1] In Thomism, this is done by the relations between potentiality and actuality though more sober in applying this principle, St. Thomas grants its validity.

[2] Thus, in corporeal beings, passivity and corruptibility, on the one hand, an activity on the other, require matter and form.

by tradition. St. Bonaventure's position was too greatly engrossed in historical contingencies, though it at least had the merit of introducing unity into the variety of Augustinian propositions.

III. Operations.

277. St. Bonaventure considered the principles of action, or faculties, as " *consubstantial with the soul* " and not as super-added accidents. Finding in the multiplicity of forms a sufficient explanation of the various operations, he was led to attenuate the distinction between substance and accident. At the same time, he did not hold to a radical identification of the soul and its faculties. The latter are distinguished from the soul " to the extent that they are faculties, but they identify themselves with soul by the total positive content of their being " [1]; they can be looked upon as the " immediate issue of substance " [2], for one cannot think of the soul without its triple power of remembering, knowing and loving [3], so well analyzed by Augustine [4].

At the same time, Bonaventure adopts the Aristotelian classification of vegetative, sensible and spiritual faculties; this forced him to integrate the Augustinian doctrine of illumination with the Peripatetic aspect through the unifying force of his theory of exemplarism. His integration will be shown especially with regard to knowledge, in which faith and reason intimately collaborate, and for the will, whose moral life is governed by the divine law.

A) **Knowledge : Faith and Reason.**

278. St. Bonaventure's theory of knowledge has a particular importance, since it forms the basis of his view of mysticism. It harmonizes the doctrine of Aristotle with that of St. Augustine by showing how knowledge leads us to the knowledge of God, the source of all true science. His view can be summarized as follows :

The various aspects of our intellectual knowledge are to be explained by two orders of complementary operations : the

---

[1] This is a sort of distinction intermediary between the real and mental distinctions, a sort of foreshadowing of the formal *(a parte rei)* distinction of Duns Scotus.

[2] E. GILSON, *The Philosophy of St. Bonaventure*, p. 347.

[3] See F. CAYRÉ, *op. cit.*, Vol. II, pp. 512-513.

[4] Bonaventure took his inspiration here from St. Augustine's work, *De Trinitate.*

*first is abstractive and inferior, and the second is intuitive
and superior.*

a) **The order of abstraction.** In order to acquire the science
of contingent beings, man has a passive intellect which is
complemented by an active intellect; the latter disengages
the intelligible species from the sensible image and thus permits
the passive intellect to appropriate the intelligible species and
to know the nature and the laws of sensible things.   This is
Aristotle's theory, proved by experiential facts, which show the
dependence of our reason on images and on the good functioning
of our senses.   The two intellects, at the same time, are not
two faculties, but two complementary functions of the same
intellective soul.

This first order of operations explains the imperfect aspect
of our reason.   Its judgment follows temporal principles and
objects; it is " inferior reason " and corresponds to Augustine's
notion of " science " [1].

b) **The order of vision.** As a completion to his inferior reason,
man enjoys *illumination from God;* this participation of divine
truth makes him see truths through intuition and in their
" eternal reasons ", though without giving him the discovery
of God's essence.   This is Augustine's [2] view with its accompanying proof : the traits of necessity, immutability and eternity
which belong to truth, dominate the sensible world and the
spiritual soul as well.   These traits cannot be explained by
the activity of the soul, nor even by the agency of the active
intellect.   They demand God's immediate intervention in the
form of a certain union of human with divine reason, allowing
us to participate in the Truth.

The nature of this illuminating vision is not absolutely clear.
It is not the simple, universal influence nor the creative influence
of God, for illumination is needed to attain God in addition to
the latter influence.   Nor is this illumination supernatural revelation
reserved to grace, nor the vision of the Divine Essence reserved
to heaven.   It is an " immediate contact " which makes God
present as the Truth regulating our judgments and as the Intelligence giving impulse to our acts of intellections, that is, " regulating
and moving ".   While in this view we do not see every truth in
God, nevertheless, each truth does not acquire its full certitude
except through a sort of intuition [3] of God which He gives us

---

[1] See above, n. 164. — [2] See above, nn. 165-166.
[3] St. Bonaventure calls this the " contuition " of God; see n. 279, below.

indirectly. The latter, at first of the natural order, then tends to become supernatural and mystical, as the collaboration of our various complementary faculties demands.

c) **Considered in their mutual relations,** these two orders of knowledge seem made for each other. The abstractive order is more precise, but lacks firmness; the order of vision, which deals with most general truths, is made precise by contact with particular sciences, and is the necessary complement of science so that we can attain full certitude [1].

Here again, the principle of incomplete beings, under the form of " complementary functions ", is applied in order to reconcile Aristotle with St. Augustine.

Object of illumination : Intuition of the soul ; Co-intuition of God.

279. For Augustine and for Bonaventure, the essential problem is not the origin of concepts or abstract ideas, but the eternal value of our truths. As a result, the proper object of illumination is the gift of *first principles.* They are *innate,* but only in a broad sense. They are not deposited in the mind from the time of creation, for it is continuously, in each act of intellection, that the divine illumination is exercised [2]. The mind " forms them with so spontaneous an ease — at its first contact with things — that we find it difficult not to image them as virtually preformed in the thought which bespeaks them " [3].

These principles furnish us principally with general rules which direct us in the speculative order for acquiring wisdom, and in the practical order for living the good life. But they likewise give us, in Bonaventure's view, the knowledge of two concrete objects, the soul and God.

a) **The soul,** being present to itself, directly knows itself through intuition. There is no need to have recourse to abstraction, for soul is not a sensible object. Of course, there is not question of knowing the abstract nature of the soul, but rather the living reality by which we are personally constituted; we have a proper " intuition of the *self* ".

---

[1] Even the light of faith, which philosophical reason asserts, is itself attained by mystical contemplation.

[2] See n. 165, above; illumination excludes *innatism.*

[3] E. Gilson, *op. cit.,* p. 373.

b) **God** is a totally spiritual being; the knowledge we have of Him has no need of being abstracted from the sensible. It is *innate*, as are first principles, by the fact that the Creator of our soul and the Illuminator of our intelligence is intimately present within us : " The Light close to the soul, even more close than the soul is to itself ".

Of course, one does not know God in His essence. But it is sufficient to reflect on oneself in order to have an idea of Him, for the intelligence grasps His presence indirectly though infallibly in every eternal truth which it affirms. This indirect and quasi-intuitive knowledge is called CONTUITION *of God*, which Gilson defines as " The indirect apprehension by thought of an object which itself eludes us, the presence of which is in some way implied in that of the effects which follow from it... " [1]. Here again we have come to the position of Augustine, who, at the summit of eternal truths, also affirms God's existence and grasps at the very Source of truth more through intuition than through a process of reasoning [2].

What makes this hardy flight towards God more likely is that the intelligence of the Christian is wholly bathed in the supernatural. In a word, for the Seraphic Doctor, the philosopher cedes his place to the theologian, and the imperfect science demands of revelation that it be affirmed. The respective domains of reason and faith are not determined by means of their formal objects, but by opposing them as two diverse but complementary sources of knowledge. Reason is always subjected to ignorance and to error; revelation is infallible and can give us all truth. He shows that their union is indispensable by pointing out the imperfection and dangers of pure philosophy, declaring philosophy incomplete in itself and wholly ordered as a means towards theology.

At the same time, they are of mutual service to each other. Reason aids faith in refuting objections, in showing weak souls the suitability of mysteries, and in explaining dogmas to strong minds. Faith, however, being of a superior and

---

[1] *Ibid.*, p. 400.

[2] See above, n. 151. A favorable comparison can be made between *contuition* and the indirect knowledge of the self of St. Thomas. In the latter's view, God is present in each act of intellection *per contactum virtutis*, through His action and *physical premotion*, which is always required, and which is similar to Augustinian *illumination*. This " contact ", for Bonaventure, would permit knowledge of God in one's soul, in the same way that the soul knows itself through consciousness by a " simple reflection " of an intuitive kind.

divine order, crowns reason by giving it full and entire certitude
on divine matters.

B) **Will and Morality.**

280. Exemplarism is not only the explanation of man's
intellectual life, but also the source of his moral life. In this
area, God directs man's will indirectly by illuminating it,
directly by informing it.

A *moral illumination* in man must be admitted. Just as
we have speculative first principles in the mind as the source
of all our knowledge, so there are first principles of the moral
life[1]. The immutability and eternity with which these rules
dominate man cannot be explained except through God's
influence. As we attain the Immutable Truth in every truth,
so in every good action we achieve the Supreme Goodness.
" It is impossible that our affection would directly tend towards
good without, in some way, attaining the highest good "[2].

These inborn rules in our souls constitute the natural law,
a reflection of the divine law expressed in the wise plan of
the Ideas of the Word of God. St. Bonaventure shows how
the Decalogue, as the external manifestation of this law, is
founded on the very nature of God, one in three Persons[3].

By directing our will towards the good, these rules bring
forth within us the various moral virtues which Bonaventure
treats of abundantly, especially in their practical applications[4].
But he especially delights in referring them to their divine
exemplar; in particular, he shows how " four illuminations
from the exemplary light impress themselves on the soul and
give birth to the four cardinal virtues : God's supreme purity
inscribes temperance on the soul, the Beauty of His Splendor
gives prudence, the force of His Power brings fortitude, and
the rectitude of His diffusiveness lends justice to the soul "[5].

The divine influence is not content with clarifying our action,
but it also communicates a sort of " *information* " to the will.
The latter is an inborn predisposition towards virtue, corresponding to the innate principles through which intelligence

---

[1] Bonaventure calls the group of these principles " *synderesis* ", as do Aristotle
and Aquinas.
[2] *De scientia Christi*, q. IV, fund. 29.
[3] See J.-M. BISSEN, *L'exemplarisme divin selon saint Bonaventure*, p. 284.
[4] *Collationes in Hexaemeron*, col. 5 and col. 6.
[5] *Ibid.*, col. 5, n. 10.

contemplates truth. These dispositions are like " seeds of virtue, planted within the very nature of our spirit " [1]. It is up to us to develop them in following freely the exercise of virtues with the aid of divine grace.

LIBERTY, for St. Bonaventure, is an habitual state *(habitus)* common to intelligence and to will, for these two powers intimately collaborate in the production of the free act. On the one side, the good must be known in order that action can occur, and the choice always follows practical judgment; on the other side, the impulse stems from the will, which, in final analysis, depends only on itself to determine itself.

It follows from these remarks that, following the Augustinian strain, the will enters into the definition of faith. For, being free, faith is a synthesis of actions which are equally intellectual and voluntary.

This important position given to the will, as also the preponderant role of faith and of intuition in knowledge, marks Bonaventure's philosophy with a certain *voluntarism*. He holds that moral purification is necessary to achieve the fulness of science or " wisdom "; and, without explicitly demonstrating his view, he prefers will to intelligence, for will has a greater part to play in the movement towards God.

CONCLUSION. **281.** St. Bonaventure is one of the greatest disciples of St. Augustine, and, like his master, is principally a *theologian*. He was well able to rediscover, through the maze of theories reputedly Augustinian, the metaphysical spirit of the Doctor of Hippo, and it is from the divine point of view that he focuses his " vision of the world ". God seemed to appear in so transparent a fashion throughout creation, and especially in the soul, that His existence was presupposed in every speculation.

Among these speculations, there is found in Bonaventure, as in Augustine, an ensemble of rational doctrines organizable into a *true philosophy*. The narrow relations which he affirmed between reason and faith were no obstacle to the existence of this rational wisdom. He invites us to consider it only as a " second philosophy ", [2] in which all problems are resolvable from the viewpoint of God and in the light of His creative influence and His well-ordering wisdom. Understood in this

---

[1] *In III Sententiarum*, dist. 23, art. 2, q. v, ad 6.
[2] See above, n. 177.

fashion, the work of St. Bonaventure is a quite remarkable essay in authentic Augustinian Scholastic philosophy.

At the same time, this essay was rather premature. The theories of traditional Augustinianism which he supported needed to be purified before they could be fused with a triumphant Aristotelianism in a truly coherent doctrine [1]. The Seraphic Doctor saw clearly the work that had to be done, and he entered into it with a truly philosophical spirit, animating all of his views with a powerful unifying principle. But the imperfection of the materials which be brought to this work and the later orientation of his life towards the practical order of things, prevented him from achieving a perfect synthesis, at least in the rational order of things.

His true title to glory does not lie in the humble, human science of philosophy — for which he expressed a rather parsimonious esteem — but of being an incomparable master of Catholic mysticism.

282. Following the death of St. Thomas and of St. Bonaventure, the double doctrinal current initiated by each of these two great Doctors developed through a series of disciples.

I.   In the Franciscan order, the religious and mystical stamp perpetuated itself as a tradition. St. Bonaventure had a number of disciples [2], among whom was JOHN PECKHAM, who was his student at Paris, before becoming a master at Oxford, and then Archbishop of Canterbury; he has been mentioned earlier [3]. — MATTHEW OF AQUASPARTA [4] (about 1240-1302), another disciple, was a man of such equable temperament that even his defence of Augustinianism is marked by a calm exposition (wrote a *Commentary on the Sentences, Disputed Questions*, etc.). — WILLIAM DE LA MARE († 1298), a friend of Roger Bacon, is well known for his polemical treatises against Thomism; in his *Correctorium* he brings up 118 (or 123) rectifications to be made in St. Thomas' *Summa Theologica*, his *Questiones Disputatæ*, his *Quodlibetales* and the first book of his *Commentary on the Sentences*. — RICHARD OF MIDDLETON [5] (died at close of 13th or opening of 14th century) is one of the judges who was concerned in the condemnation of Olivi, though he was a faithful Augustinian and a defender of the theory of plurality of forms. — ROGER MARSTON was a disciple

---

[1] This is precisely the work which was accomplished by Thomism.

[2] On all of these authors, see, for example, F. COPLESTON, *A History of Philosophy*, Vol. II, Ch. 43.

[3] See above, nn. 248-251.

[4] See M. DE WULF, *op. cit.*, Vol. I, pp. 219-251.

[5] HOCEDEZ, E., *Richard de Middleton. Sa vie, ses œuvres, sa doctrine*, Louvain, 1925. — RUCKER, P., *Der Ursprung unserer Begriffe nach Richard von Mediavilla*, Münster, 1934.

of John Peckham. — PETER JOHN OLIVI [1], often called simply Olivi (1248-1298), pushed the mystical tendency to the extreme, and became head of the spirituals, a group of adversaries of any profane studies. He deviated from the plurality of forms theory by holding that the intellective part does not directly inform the human body, but only through the intermediary of the sensitive part — though at the same time remaining *substantially* united to it. Otherwise, he held, the spiritual soul would make the body immortal. This doctrine was declared " heretical " by the Council of Vienna (1311) [2].

II. St. Thomas, even more quickly than St. Bonaventure, had a group of disciples and followers. Among the early Thomists [3], mention should be made of REGINALD OF PIPERNO, who completed St. Thomas' *Summa Theologica.* — GILES OF LESSINES was a friend of Albert the Great, and a defender of Thomism in his work, *De unitate formæ.* — JOHN QUIDORT (about 1269-1306) refuted William de la Mare and composed a commentary on the Book of Sentences in the form of questions. — BERNARD OF AUVERGNE († 1307) wrote his *Improbationes* and his *Impugnationes* against the Augustinians, Godfrey of Fontaines and Henry of Ghent. — GILES OF ROME [4] (1247-1316) introduced Thomism into the newly founded order (1260) of the Hermits of St. Augustine. He was a pupil of St. Thomas at Paris (about 1270); he at first defended the unity of form, but had to retract this view in order to get his license to teach (about 1285). He upheld the real distinction between essence and existence in creatures, but in an exaggerated form.

Towards the close of the thirteenth century, Thomism became preponderant in the schools. In 1282, it is true, the Franciscan chapter ordered that the *Summa Theologica* should not be circulated without having with it the *Correctorium* of William de la Mare. But this latter work, which some began to call " *Corruptorium* ", was answered by many writers *(Correctorium Corruptorii),* which is testimony to the Thomistic influence.

From the University of Paris, Thomism spread rapidly throughout Europe. — RICHARD KLAPWELL, a master at Oxford around 1284-6, and THOMAS SUTTON, also a master at Oxford, were Thomists; the latter defended Thomism against Duns Scotus. — In Spain, RAYMOND MARTIN was a leading Thomist, whose treatise *Pugio fidei adversus Mauros et Judæos* was inspired by St. Thomas' *Summa Contra Gentiles.* — In Italy, we find PTOLEMY OF LUCCA (1236-1326), who wrote a continuation of St. Thomas' *De regimine principum.* — In Germany, JOHN and GERARD OF STERNGASSEN solidly implanted Thomism at Cologne. Finally, DANTE ALIGHIERI (1265-1321) got his doctrinal inspiration for his poetry from Thomism.

---

[1] See F. COPLESTON, *op. cit.,* Vol. II, pp. 451-3.

[2] See above, n. 250, and see F. COPLESTON, *op. cit.,* Vol. II, pp. 451-453.

[3] On these early Thomists see M. DE WULF, *op. cit.,* Vol. II, pp. 202-218.

[4] See F. COPLESTON, *op. cit.,* Vol. II, pp. 460-465, for a more complete treatment.

The struggles of Thomism were, however, far from completed. At the close of the thirteenth century and after the condemnations of 1277, we find the work of Raymond Lull and of the most redoubtable adversary of Thomism, Duns Scotus.

RAYMOND LULL [1] (1232 or 35-1316).

Born at Majorca, Raymond Lull spent several years at the court of James II. He then renounced the world and became a hermit; then he became a Franciscan tertiary and consecrated his life towards combating Averroism, especially by converting the Mussulmans. At the beginning of his attempt to convince them, he studied Arabic, and invented a new logical method which he called the GREAT ART *(Ars Magna)*, a sort of algebra of concepts destined to demonstrate even the most profound truths. Then he travelled all over the world, fighting against Averroism. He went to Africa to convert the Moors and there, in 1316, he found martyrdom.

" Lully was a philosopher, a mystic, an artist, a linguist, and the most brilliant Catalonian writer in the Middle Ages " [2]. About 123 works are attributed to him. The main ones of philosophical import are the *Ars Magna*, the *Liber principiorum philosophiæ*, and numerous works written in refutation of Averroism.

Raymond Lull strongly opposed the Averroist theory of the two truths and what he considered an exaggerated reverence for pagan philosophy. He attempted to answer these with his double principle : reason can and should demonstrate everything [3], even the truths of faith; faith is a preliminary disposition necessary for all knowledge, whether natural or supernatural. Philosophy then became a pure apologetics [4], destined to defend the faith and to demonstrate its truth.

The fecundity of his genius and his originality made Lull a strong influence, and gave him many disciples as well as adversaries.

---

[1] **Works :** *Opera Omnia* (ed., I. SALZINGER), 8 vols., Mainz, 1741-1742. — *Obras de Ramon Lull*, 17 vols., Parma, 1906-35.
Studies : BLANES, F. S., *El beato Ramon Lull, su epoca, su vida, sus obras, sus empresas*, Madrid, 1934. — KEICHER, O., *Raymundus Lullus und seine Stellung zur arabischen Philosophie*, Münster, 1909. — MARTINEZ, T. A., *Raimundo Lulio*, 2nd ed., Barcelona, 1941. — OTTAVIANO, C., *L'ars compendiosa de Raymond Lulle*, Paris, 1930. — PEERS, E. A., *Fool of Love : the life of Raymond Lulle* London, 1946. — PROBST, J. H., *Caractère et origine des idées du bienheureux Raymond Lulle*, Toulouse, 1912. — *La mystique de Raymond Lulle et l'Art de Contemplation*, Münster, 1914.
[2] M. DE WULF, *op. cit.*, Vol. II, p. 310.
[3] At least in this sense, that " reason shows those who contradict the faith that they are wrong for rejecting it "; *ibid.*, p. 313.
[4] " Augustinianism, at the service of apologetics, is the basis of Lull's philosophy ". *Ibid.*

III. John duns Scotus.

1266 (or 1274) — 1308.

Special bibliography.

1⁰ **Works :** (A critical edition of Scotus' works is being prepared by the Franciscans of Quaracchi; in this connection, see the following : BETTONI, E., *Vent'anni di Studi Scotisti* (1920-1940), Milan, 1943, and *Ratio criticæ editionis operum omnium J. Duns Scoti*, 2 vols., Rome, 1939-40. — *Opera omnia* (ed. by L. WADDING), 12 vols., Lyons, 1639; 2nd ed., 26 vols., Paris, 1891-5. — *B. J. D. Scoti Commentaria Oxoniensia*, 2 vols., Quaracchi, 1912-14. — *Tractatus de Primo Principio*, Quaracchi, 1910. — MUELLER, P. M., *Tractatus de Primo Principio*, editionem curavit Marianius, Freiburg (Br.), 1941.

2⁰ **Studies :** AUER, J., *Die menschliche Willensfreiheit im Lehresystem des Thomas von Aquin und Johannes Duns Scotus*, Munich, 1938. — BARTH, T., *De fundamento univocationis apud Joannem Duns Scotum*, Rome, 1939. — BELMOND, S., *Essai de synthèse philosophique du Scotisme*, Paris, 1933. — BERTONI, A., *Le Bx. Jean Duns Scot. Sa vie, sa doctrine, ses disciples*, Levanto, 1917. — BETTONI, E., *L'ascesa a Dio in Duns Scoto*, Milan, 1943. — DE BASLY, D., *Scotus Docens ou Duns Scot enseignant la philosophie, la théologie, la mystique*, Paris, 1934. — GILSON, E., *Jean Duns Scot, Introduction à ses positions fondamentales*, Paris, 1952. — HARRIS, C. R. S., *Duns Scotus*, 2 vols., Oxford, 1927. — HEIDEGGER, M., *Die Kategorien — und Bedeutungslehre Des Duns Scotus*, Rubingen, 1916. — LANDRY, B., *La philosophie de Duns Scot*, Paris, 1922. — LONGPRÉ, E., *La philosophie du Bx Duns Scot*, Paris, 1924. — Mc GREGOR, M. B., *Sources and Literature of Scot*, Glasgow, 1934. — MESSNER, R., *Schauendes und begriffliches Erkennen nach Duns Skotus*, Freiburg (Br.), 1942. — MINGES, P., *Der angeblich exzessive Realismus des Duns Skotus*, Vienna, 1908. — *Der Gottesbegriff des Duns Skotus*, Vienna, 1906. — *J. Duns Scoti Doctrina Philophica et Theologica quoad res præcipuas proposita et exposita*, Quaracchi, 1930. — PELSTER, F., *Handschriftliches zu Skotus mit neuen Angaben über sein Leben*, Munich, 1923. — PLUZANSKI, J., *Essai sur la philosophie de Duns Scot*, Paris, 1887. — VACANT, A., *La philosophie de Duns Scot comparée à celle de Saint Thomas*, Paris, 1891.

283. Little is known of the life of Duns Scotus. Born in Scotland (in England, or in Ireland, according to some scholars), he entered the Franciscan order in 1290. He took his studies and began his teaching at Oxford (1290-1302), where he was doubtlessly subjected to the anti-Thomistic influence then prevalent at the university. During this period, he composed his main works : the *Quæstiones in libros IV Sententiarum*, which is called *Opus Oxoniense;* the *De Primo Principio*, dealing with metaphysical questions on God, on the angels, on the soul and on knowledge; the *Theoremata*[1], a collection of general principles used in the sciences.

In 1302, Scotus went to Paris (where he had already been around 1293), in order to get his doctorate, and he taught there until 1307. The works he wrote during this period have been joined under the title of *Reportata parisiensia* or *Opus parisiense;* in them he reviews and completes his commentaries done at Oxford. It was here at Paris that he defended the doctrine of the Immaculate Conception. His last work is entitled *Quæstiones Quodlibetales*, which were written at Paris. In 1308 he was sent to Cologne, where he died the same year, when about forty-two or forty-three years of age.

General Characteristics. 284. The quite complex genius of Scotus can be characterized by three traits : a critical spirit; a preoccupation in defending faith through reason; a powerful and subtle logical mind.

1. **Critical and analytic spirit.** At the end of the thirteenth century, Scotus found already completed the works of the great Scholastics. His aim was to test their validity, which he fulfilled by examining their various opinions on each question; he looked into St. Thomas Aquinas, Alexander of Hales, Saint Bonaventure, Henry of Ghent and others. What struck him and what he underscored in his writings was not that part of the truth which confirmed his views, as did St. Thomas, but principally the *divergence* of views. He examined these and then concluded indirectly in what way one should seek for truth [2]. This places analysis as an important part in his works.

2. **A preoccupation with Apologetics.** Scotus' criticisms were not haphazardly made, and were unified by his hope of destroying two major heresies which had been brought to the attention of the Catholic Doctors of the time. In the first place, the doctrinal censures of 1277 had again condemned Averroism and its system of the world which denied creation and which insinuated that St. Thomas had made too great a concession to Aristotle. Secondly, in the Franciscan order itself, the Chapter of Avignon (1283) had condemned Peter

---

[1] On the question of the authenticity of Scotus' works, see F. COPLESTON, *op. cit.*, Vol. II, pp. 476-481.

[2] His criticisms were not meant to be destructive alone; he aimed at constructing a new synthesis. See F. CAYRÉ, *op. cit.*, Vol. II, pp. 645-646.

John Olivi and his work with the "spirituals"; this group had a false mysticism, and were enemies of science as well as of obedience. For these and other reasons, Scotus aimed to defend the free action of God with regard to the world, and to correct Augustinian mysticism by a science which would be basically Aristotelian.

3. **Powerful and subtle Logic.** Scotus aimed to achieve his purposes with a remarkably powerful and deadly logic. He has a centralized position wherein all his solutions meet, and, despite the multiplicity of his analyses, his work has the traits of an organized synthesis governed by a fundamental principle. Three applications of his principle will be made : to individual substance, to the human soul and to God.

It should be noted that Scotus' aim is not vastly different from that of St. Thomas; both aimed to defend the faith. Furthermore, their conclusions are often the same, or similar. But the spirit which coordinates and governs each system is frankly different and opposed, a fact which will be shown now in analyzing their fundamental theories.

I. Fundamental Theory.

285. Scotus' fundamental view can be expressed as follows :

1) *Reality is formed of absolute individuals, uniquely dependent on the Divine Liberty;*

2) *and wholly intelligible (through the sciences), due to the univocal idea of being which is diversely realized by means of formal distinctions.*

The first statement constitutes his *voluntarism*, while the second, his *formalism*.

Part One : Voluntarism.

In order to prove the first part of his fundamental position, Scotus follows his critical method of showing the insufficiency of previous solutions; in this way he aims to prove the truth of faith that God created the world, and that He continues to conserve and to direct it *with full liberty*. Inasmuch as it was St. Thomas and the Averroists whom he opposed in this regard, a good way to understand Scotus' principle is to oppose it to St. Thomas' view.

I. **For St. Thomas,** every potentiality is a transcendental relation defined by the actuality which it delimits; only the composite is absolute and subsistent, and the parts of the composite — as essence and existence, matter and form — are incomplete beings, often inseparable. It follows, therefore, that :

a) Prime matter, conceived as pure potentiality, is unintelligible *of itself*. All truth concerning it, as well as its whole nature, is relative to form. For man, prime matter remains inaccessible with the individual which it helps constitute, and escapes our knowledge and science [1].

b) Individuals are not independent in their evolvement, but matter, through its dispositive causality, *requires* certain forms.

The Averroists must conclude from the above (and, according to Scotus, a Thomist must logically accept these conclusions likewise) :

a) That the events of the world are so rigorously intertwined that God Himself must submit to this necessity of things;

b) That God Himself could not know the material individual, and consequently could not produce or govern it.

II. **For Duns Scotus,** aiming to uphold the fully free influence of God, the following statements hold :

a) Each reality, not merely that of the composite, but each *really distinct* element, is an absolute and separable individual. It follows that if there is to be a potentiality in creatures distinct from actuality in order to make contact and interaction of beings possible, then it must also be maintained that one element does not ever require the other.

b) Moreover, the assemblages which constitute the beings of the universe, as experience testifies, do not obey necessary laws and are upheld only by the free will of God. In this way, each of the parts, even individual matter, being an *absolute reality*, is fully knowable and manageable by God, and, in the same fashion, can be included in human knowledge and science.

---

[1] See above, n. 265.

Part Two : Formalism.

286. This second aspect of Duns Scotus' thought arises in answer to the general problem of knowledge : How can an abstract knowledge, unified by the idea of being, deal with concrete and multiple objects?   This question is a most fundamental one in philosophy, and St. Thomas answered it in all its amplitude by his fundamental principle of universal intelligibility [1].   In a sense, Scotus also bases all his philosophy on the same principle, but the interpretation which he gives to this principle is less objective.   It is hemmed in by his care of avoiding the mysticism of the Augustinians, and especially by his voluntarism, which is the true source of his formalism.

a) The Augustinians looked for the solution in the eternal reasons or Divine Ideas by means of which all the diversified natures of the sensible order were synthesized and identified in the Being of God.   The properties of our ideas and the reality of individuals of whom God is Creator is explained in the same fashion; furthermore, knowledge is based on divine illumination.

Scotus agrees with St. Thomas that all our knowledge comes to us from the senses through abstraction; he wished to replace this mystic Augustinian illumination by that of the natural light of being.   This would help achieve his aim of combating the false mysticism of the " *fratricelli* ".

b) St. Thomas based his solution on the *analogy* of being, which is the very basis of all our judgments attributing concepts to things.   Many distinct things can correspond to but one concept, as if one attributes the same humanity to Peter, to Paul, to John and so forth, or the same " life ", in a sense, to a tree, to spirit and to God.   Moreover, to one thing there can correspond many concepts without real distinction, as if one says of Peter that he is living, a man, good, and so forth.   This is so because when one speaks about " that which is " one is implicitly expressing the totality of reality.

From this it follows, *a*) that one and the same reality, taken as subject and known solely as a " being " and whose existence is experientially evident, can receive many diverse explicit predicates without a real distinction being demanded.   For instance, if one says of Peter, " this being whom I see is the same thing who is man, living and good ", then " that which is " takes the individual in his totality and as containing in himself (implicitly, without a doubt, but actually and intrinsically) all the modes of being which one makes explicit.

---

[1] See n. 259, above.

For the same reason, *b*) the same mode of explicit being, taken as an attribute, can be identifiable in several individuals, without suppressing their real distinction. For example, " that which is *man* " is identifiable with Peter, then with Paul, and so forth. In this case " that which is " also signifies the ensemble of realities, though they are distinct, and maintains in itself (implicitly, but actually) all the modes of distinct beings, as in fact are the individualities of Peter or of Paul.

Accordingly, in this Thomistic conception, one cannot conclude, through considering the distinction or the identity of our concepts, to these selfsame properties in reality. Each objective distinction " *a parte rei* " must be established inductively by demonstrating its necessity in making evident facts intelligible. For instance, the facts of change and of multiplicity require the distinction of substance from accidents, of matter from form, of essence from existence, and similar ones.

In Scotus' view, on the contrary, every reality being an absolute (as his voluntarism requires), every objective idea is necessarily univocal. This is so because the objective nature which an idea expresses must be comprehended in itself because of its absolute quality; consequently, it must enjoy a mode of determined being which realizes itself identically throughout. This makes the notion of Thomistic analogy inconceivable, and it is to be rejected as pure equivocation [1].

Scotus proposes that in saying " that which is " one is not taking the totality but a part of reality (a branch of being) distinct from every other " *a parte rei* " and independently of our consideration. Furthermore, every distinct idea requires a distinct portion in reality, with the idea of individuality (which will be explained below), through which being has its final independence and distinction.

It is in this way that Scotus tries to assure the full intelligibility of reality; there is perfect correspondence between each of our concepts and the objects which they express. This requires acceptance of a certain realism or of some sort of existence of the " universal natures " as we conceive them.

This realism, though, cannot be absolute. If this were the case, the nature of being, whose amplitude is such that it leaves nothing outside of itself and thus unifies all our judgments and knowledge, would also be a unique reality, similar to a

---

[1] The following equations can be helpful in illustrating these consequences :
Absolute = comprehensible in itself = to one mode of determined and fixed being = **univocal.**
Relative = comprehensible through another = to one mode of variable and functional being = **analogical.**

substantial foundation really common to all being. The
multiplicity of substances, evident to experience, must be
safeguarded, as also the distinction of God from the world
pointed out by faith. For these reasons, and after having
declared that all our concepts are univocal, Scotus distinguishes
two very different instances of their realization : in one case,
the absolute natures expressed by our ideas can exist separately,
as the body and the soul; in another case, the natures appear
to be inseparable, as in the case of being and the other transcendental perfections. Furthermore, only in the first case is there
a real distinction in the proper sense; in the second, the
distinction is neither real nor purely logical but intermediary
and is called a *formal distinction on the part of the thing
(a parte rei).*

Accordingly, there are three types of distinctions according
to Scotus :

1) The *real* distinction, which holds between two beings or
absolute elements *capable of existing separately;*

2) The distinction *of reason*, which hold between two manners
of expressing the same essence, formally identical;

3) The *formal, a parte rei* distinction, which holds between
two *formally distinct* essences *incapable of existing separately.*

These distinctions explain the two main types of scientific
judgment :

a) One and the same being, known through its individuality
as being such as it is — Peter, for example — due to its various
" formalities " can be declared living, man or good without
a real distinction being involved at all.

b) At the same time, a universal formality — that of being,
for example — can be attributed to many diverse things,
and even to all things univocally, without concluding to their
pantheistic identification. This can be held because this
formality, being in fact inseparable from several irreducible
individualities, still safeguards the real multiplicity of things.

CONCLUSION. **287.** FORMALISM makes Scotism a coherent,
scientific system [1]. With its help, the univocal idea of being

---

[1] The theory of " formalities " is not new; traces of it are found in Henry
of Ghent and in St. Bonaventure. Scotus, however, is original for having made
this notion one of the pivotal points of his system. See M. DE WULF, *op. cit.*,
Vol. II, pp. 318-9.

clarifies and unifies everything, and can be looked upon as the universal inspiration of all our judgments while being diversely realized through the formal distinctions *a parte rei.* But this view itself is based on VOLUNTARISM. The latter is a doctrine teaching the primacy of free activity in such a way as to make it the final, explicative principle of all things; even truth and intelligence are conceived as dependent upon it.

This, then, is the position of Scotus. He begins with an affirmation of the absolute liberty of God; he sets up his system of the world as a function of this affirmation; he uses it to interpret the activity of our mind and the value of our concepts. The principle of voluntarism is not demonstrated, for it is a first principle; its validity should be established in philosophy. It seems, however, that this principle imposed itself upon Scotus as a requirement of faith, pointed up by the condemnations of Averroism.

The intellectualism of Thomism, which has been set forth above, can safeguard the full liberty of God just as well, if it is fully understood.

Formalism, as a theory, has the following difficulties :

a) If one attempts to explain fully the meaning of the Scotistic formal distinction, one is led to think of the distinct but inseparable " forms " as ordered, by their very essence, to exist together in order to complete each other. In this way, they no longer are " absolute " elements, as the theory requires, but transcendental relations. This involves either a contradiction or an irremediable obscurity in Scotism.

A double interpretation of Scotism, then, appears possible according to the actual state of things. If one makes of Scotus' " formal distinction " a pure virtual distinction of reason, one is completely in Thomism. In this case, the *univocity* of being signifies that the idea of being is said of all reality in a *proper sense* and not only by way of metaphor. If, however, one makes of Scotus' " formal distinction " a real distinction, one falls logically into pantheism, for the special formality of being (beyond which there is nothing) tends, by its proper or univocal mode, to be infinite and unique, and to overrun everything while suppressing everything for its own gain. However, while these two points of view are reconcilable only with difficulty, Scotus, " according to history ", tried to synthesize them, and gave all problems a moderated solution, always susceptible of a Catholic interpretation [1].

The manner in which Scotus used his principle on the various parts of philosophy will now be shown, and his originality in this regard, made clear.

II. The Individual Substance.

288. Three propositions allow Scotus to conceive of the individual as a reality fully subjected to God and wholly intelligible.

Proposition I. *Every creature is composed of matter and of form.* Inasmuch as essence and existence are evidently inseparable in creatures, they cannot be considered to be really distinct. It is, then, matter which is the principle necessary to explain the passivity and the progress inherent in every contingent being.

From this aspect, the notion of " pure form " implies a double absurdity in Scotus' view. Having no material limitation, pure form would enjoy the absolute infinity of God and thus cannot be a creature; furthermore, all its activity would be reduced to a purely transitive operation necessarily flowing " by nature " from its being, as is true in the case of minerals. For, deprived of a material subject, which alone makes substance capable of progress, a pure form could not receive a lesser enrichment from God nor could it, as a living thing, progress by its own action. It would be isolated and dead, a conclusion opposed to the very nature of spirits.

Proposition II.   289. *A real distinction obtains between matter and form.* Independence and separability are required for these two principles because of the opposed role which they are required to perform. Form is the principle of perfection and of activity, while matter is the principle of passivity and of limitation. Three consequences follow from this proposition :

a) Matter and form are each an absolute reality, fully intelligible in themselves. One could not, in fact, conceive of the one by means of the other, unless their very essence were related. In Scotus' view, no real being can be conceived in this fashion, for its essence, corresponding to the univocal idea of being, is necessarily absolute. Accordingly, *every relation* is but an accident, and matter and form, being of the substantial order, are in no way relative.

---

[1] Gilson maintains that the Scotist understanding of univocity is a radical negation of pantheism; see his *The Spirit of Mediaeval Philosophy*, p. 266.

b) Since matter is an absolute reality, it is not a pure potentiality. It is, doubtlessly, the minimum of actuality, for it is the principle of passivity; but matter is actual. Thus, it can exist alone, just as form. To deny this possibility, would be to limit the free, Almighty Power of God.

c) However, matter does not contain seminal reasons, capable of predetermining the direction of the changes in creatures, for its actuality is self-constituted without any necessary bond with form. If there are any physical, necessary laws governing the evolvement of the mineral world, these laws do not flow from their nature but depend on the free will of God.

Proposition III. 290. *Neither matter, nor form, but haecceitas is the principle of individuation.*

The general reason why matter and form must be so well separated is that both are common to all the individuals of the species, while individuality is proper to each. St. Thomas resolved this question by means of the notion of transcendental relation : prime matter has a basic relation towards this quantity and is thus determined for this individual; the human, subsisting form keeps an essential relation towards matter and thus remains individuated though separated from body [1]. Such relationships do not make sense in Scotus' view, for they are but accidents which suppose substance already individuated and which cannot themselves be the source of individuation. For Scotus, the Thomistic solution is but Averroistic, and logically leads to the unity of the separated intelligence.

Moreover, Scotus considers the individual as the most positive and the most perfect element of being; this is a special reason for refusing matter the power of individuating. Applying his formalism, he concludes that individuality is constituted by an actual, special element which determines universal substance to be this or that one, and which is well named " thisness " *(haecceitas* — by which substance becomes *this).*

There is no real distinction between nature and *haecceitas,* for the latter is not realizable outside of the substance which it individualizes. However, independently of the mind, there is a formal distinction between them, for the perfection express- ed by each idea is fully independent. In analyzing humanity, for example, one cannot find therein the individual perfection of Peter or of Paul.

Haecceitas, being conceived as the final, actual achievement of the individual, must belong to every portion capable of existing

---

[1] See n. 268, above.

separately as well as to the totality. This fact yields three types of *haecceitas* in bodies : that of matter, that of form, and that of the composite [1]. Moreover, since the individual is actual, it is by right fully intelligible and can enter in as an item of knowledge and of science. Finally, having given the individual the perfect aspect which St. Thomas reserves to the notion of person, Scotus is led to characterize personality as a pure negation of dependence [2].

III. The Human Soul.

291. The fundamental theory is applied to the human soul in two ways : first, inasmuch as man is himself an individual reality and the most noble of the sensible world; second, inasmuch as man is able, by will and intellect, to conquer the ensemble of individualities which constitute the universe.

Proposition I. *Even though substance ordinarily has but one form, man is constituted by two substantial forms, that of corporeity and that of the reasoning soul.*

It is evident that Scotus holds that the various metaphysical degrees, as corporeity, vegetality and animality are, as other perfections, separated by a formal distinction *a parte rei*. In this sense, Scotus admits the plurality of forms as did St. Bonaventure. However, like St. Thomas, he denies that there is a real distinction between these perfections, since the form, being the principle of perfection, must explain substantial unity through its own unity.

However, influenced by the condemnations of 1277, Scotus made an exception for man, being moved to do so especially for a theological reason. If the intellectual soul is the unique form of body, the latter changes its species at death. Then one would have to hold that during the three days during which the body of Christ was in the tomb, the Word of God was united to " another thing " than to a human body; to hold this Scotus would deem impious and heretical.

This doctrine had confirmation in experience. It is evident that after a man's death, his body seems to remain, for some time, with a proper form distinct from other mineral forms, but lacking life. This proves the unity of the soul for the three degrees of life, and it also proves the existence of a special form of corporeity. The latter, moreover, by its quick dissolution, shows its dependence

---

[1] This third *haecceitas* seems to be a union of the two preceding.

[2] As the other Scholastics, Scotus developed this view in connection with the mystery of the Hypostatic Union : the only difference between the human nature possessing its own created personality and that of Christ is that the union to the Word of God removed the " absence of dependence " from this individual nature.

on the soul, which maintains the substantial unity of man, despite these two forms.

There is no real distinction, in the human soul, between its three modes of life, nor between substance and the faculties which necessarily flow from it. This view holds since these elements cannot exist separately. There is, however, a formal distinction *a parte rei* between them, since they are known through distinct concepts.

Proposition II. 292. *The will, man's master faculty, is an autonomous or essentially free power which best realizes for man the possession of reality.*

Just as the affirmation of divine liberty is the fundamental view commanding Scotus' entire system, so human liberty is the prerogative which must, at all costs, be defended in man. This liberty would disappear, Scotus thought, if one would hold, with St. Thomas, that the will is to be looked upon as a " rational appetite " whose nature is to follow intelligence. In such a view it would appear that when several goods are placed before it, the judgment would have to declare one of these as better and the will would necessarily choose that one; or, it would have to declare them equal, and the will would rest in equilibrium without acting. In both cases, liberty perishes, and the judgment cannot be looked upon as a cause of willing. One can readily grant that judgment ordinarily precedes and clarifies the procedure, for human will is not merely arbitrary or capricious. But, basically, human will is fully autonomous and independent, and is not explicable by intelligence, but by itself.

In contrast with Thomism, then, liberty is not a property of a group of actions in the order of execution, but belongs essentially to every act of will, whether concerned with means, with end, or even with the good in general, its final goal. And even if one must concede that one cannot will evil, it does not follow, Scotus holds, that one necessarily wills good, because it is proper to will to be spontaneous and not necessary.

Accordingly, the possession of God in happiness does not occur through intellectual vision, but through an act of will which formally assures possession of the Supreme Good; " Will is formally adductive of the possession of the highest good ". Finally, will exercises its domination over man's entire intellectual life, as will be shown.

Proposition III.   293.   *Since it has real and individual being for its proper object, the intelligence permits man to conquer all of reality, but only under the efficacious motion of will.*

1.   Following his custom, Scotus establishes this proposition at first by criticizing St. Thomas.   The Thomistic notion of the abstract concept as bespeaking nothing of the individual and expressing only the universal nature is inadmissible. For, if the intelligence is ignorant of the individual, it could never draw out a " nature " from the individual as the theory of abstraction proposes [1].   Furthermore, a particular judgment, or the induction by which mind reasons about concrete facts, becomes impossible [2].   Scotus proposes that the capacity of our intelligence to know the individual is directly proved, since it is known by faith that man will, some day, know God and the angels in their individuality.   Psychological experience assures us, furthermore, that we know our own spiritual self. The proper object of the intelligence, therefore, is not the abstract essence, but the veritable reality which is individual being.

This view, of course, reduces itself radically to the funda- mental principle of Scotism.   If being is univocal, the three intelligences, divine, angelic and human, which are defined as faculties concerned with being, must have the same formal object, real or individual being.

2.   With regard to the *role of intelligence*, Scotus conceives it, one can say, in the likeness of voluntary activity.   Being a perfection, the intelligence is not purely passive, but its activity, instead of being fully autonomous, is conditioned by the presence of its object.   The active intellect, which is but another aspect of the same faculty, does not have the abstraction of a universal nature as its function; a universal nature is not the termination of the intellective process.   It merely *adapts* the force of intelligence, so to speak, to a special object presented through an image.   The force of intelligence is similar to an activity under pressure but indeterminate, needing such precise orientation in order to function.

---

[1] See above, n. 263.

[2] These criticisms of abstraction arise from Scotus' notion of *haecceitas;* they are inefficacious against Thomism, according to which the intelligence *truly* knows the individual, but indirectly " through a certain reflection ". See St. Thomas Aquinas, *Summa Theologica*, I, q. LXXXVI, art. I.

This intellectual activity grasps, before all else, the distinct and, in some way, universal " formalities " *a parte rei* in the real individuals. Does intellect also form a special concept to express the individual, or is this intuition reserved for the senses? After long hesitation, Scotus admitted, and logically so, that since *haecceitas* is a formality fully intelligible, the mind has a special concept for each individual. But this special idea of the individual does not add anything to sensible intuition but is somewhat like its intellectual double; which view, of course, is difficult to establish.

It follows that the need of recurring to phantasms (which experience upholds) is an " accidental " matter for reason. It does not follow from the nature of mind, but is due to original sin.

3. Finally, it is the *efficacious influence of free will* which makes the development of intelligence possible. For, if the intelligence were fully passive in regard to its object, it would receive the first, strongest influence from its strongest object, which is being, and would stay rooted in the contemplation of the principle of identity. But the free action of the will can moderate the influence of the object and allow the intelligence to enumerate the various aspects of reality.

This last bit of reasoning supposes that being is a unique formality, distinct *a parte rei*. It is different in the theory of analogy: since the principle of identity does not contain each thing implicitly, intelligence spontaneously tends to be concerned with most precise judgments. Scotus replaces the dynamism proper to human reason by a dynamism of the will.

294. In a general way, Scotus' tendency to think only of the absolute, leads him to " substantialize " these various faculties and to exaggerate their independence; it is an abuse of analysis. More synthetic, St. Thomas insists on the complementary aspect of man's faculties. Thus, for Scotus, the intelligence is fully separated from sense and must itself directly attain the concrete; for St. Thomas, it is *man* who seizes the object under a concrete aspect directly through his senses, and only " *per accidens* " as substance; at the same time that he grasps the same object by his intelligence directly and under a universal aspect, he does so indirectly as an individual.

Again, for Scotus, the will is fully separated from intelligence and is itself the explicative source of liberty. In St. Thomas' view it is *man* who, through his intelligence, judges an object better in the *here and now*, because at the same time, by his will, he chooses it in preference to others. To pursue the explanation of the real to this depth, Scotus needed the notion of transcendental relation.

Scotus is quite reserved on the question of the immortality of the soul, and it seems that, in his view, faith alone assures us of this property. The value of the main proof of immortality becomes enervated if one makes intellectual knowledge like sensation. On the other hand, following his voluntarism, " the spiritual nature of the soul does not establish the absolute necessity of its immortality, or one would have to deny that God, Who can do whatever is possible, could allow it to fall into nothingness "[1].

IV. God and Morality.

295. It has been shown that full divine liberty is the first foundation of Scotism. In addition to holding this as a dogma of faith, however, Scotus looked into philosophy to see how reason could demonstrate or explain this truth.

Proposition I. *The existence of God is a truth that* 1) *should be demonstrated, and* 2) *can be demonstrated, but only with the help of the univocal concept of being.*

1. The notion of God commonly admitted and the notion furnished by faith is that of an *infinite* being. However, it is not at all evident that the idea of the Infinite necessarily contains the attribute of real existence. Infinity is a negative concept, the fruit of the work of intelligence, and there is nothing to assure us that it expresses more than a pure possibility. Hence, God's existence needs demonstration.

2. Thomistic analogy, however, cannot give any true knowledge of God. For, every concept, Scotus maintains, in being applied to another proportion, loses its definition and every precise meaning. If, then, after a purification and an elevation, one can have the same positive sense in a concept, one supposes implicitly that one knows God through some univocal idea, seeing that one compares Him to the creature. This reason is sufficient for Scotus, who wants every idea to express an absolute : to change the degree of the realization of a concept is to destroy the concept and to be guilty of equivocation. Analogy is not possible if the concept of a pure perfection is a *relative* perfection, having various kinds of realization [2].

---

[1] M. De Wulf, *op. cit.*, Vol. II, p. 346.
[2] See n. 286, above, footnote.

Thus, Scotus concludes, the univocal idea of being is required if theodicy is to be a true science. Its existence and its role are attested to by experience and by all peoples who have attained through it the knowledge of God.

An important corollary follows from the above : " *between the divine attributes there is but a formal distinction a parte rei* ". For, in being applied to God, our ideas keep their proper meaning and their well determined content, so that they mutually exclude each other. For example, the Divine Intelligence knows, but it does not will.

3. Among the proofs for God's existence, no validity is granted by Scotus to the argument concluding with a First Mover. The principle, " whatever is moved, is moved by another ", does not rise above the order of bodily being in Scotus' view. The most perfect beings, endowed with liberty, escape this principle by the autonomy of their operation. Moreover, Scotus granted only probability to the proof from the degrees of perfection or from the desire of the Infinite, for he maintained that the analysis of the finite (whether of finite perfection or finite desire) can in no wise be evidence for the Infinite.

Scotus prefers the proof from contingence : being does not have the reason for its existence in itself, and requires another, and, finally, a necessary being Who exists by His essence. He also attempted to rehabilitate the argument of St. Anselm [1]; " This supreme intelligible cannot be only in the intelligence, for then it would be possible inasmuch as it is thinkable, and it would not be possible, since it could not exist through another " [2].

Proposition II. 296. *The attribute of Infinity flows from liberty and constitutes the specific difference or metaphysical essence of GOD.*

1. St. Thomas concluded to the divine infinity from the fundamental attribute of God, His " subsisting being ".

Scotus begins his analysis by rejecting this opinion, believing that being or actuality is, as every perfection, *an absolute* which cannot be limited by its relation to a potentiality; it must at first be either finite or infinite, before being united

---

[1] " His reasoning can be colored ", Scotus writes of Anselm (*In I Sent.*, i, d. 2, q. ii).

[2] *De primo principio*, ch. iv, 24; see also DOMET DE VORGES, *Saint Anselme*, p. 296.

to the matter in changeable beings or realized without matter in immutable being.

But what is proper to God is full liberty, and from this, one can conclude to INFINITY as also proper to Him. A full liberty, as God's, requires a power which is not arrested by anything, and which is, consequently, capable of producing, beyond real things, an infinity of other creatures; this latter power evidently supposes God's Infinity.

2. With the help of his distinction, " formal *a parte rei* ", this perfection of Infinity can play the role of a specific difference. In uniting itself to other perfections which are common to God and creatures, the perfection of Infinity makes their divine mode of realization precise. In this sense, Infinity is the *metaphysical essence* of God. It is God's *distinctive* attribute, His *haecceitas*, while Liberty is His fundamental essence.

3. From the Divine Liberty, one also concludes to the attribute of Intelligence, for knowledge is a condition of willing.

Proposition III. 297. *Created essences have their necessary foundation in the Divine Intelligence, but in dependence on Divine Liberty so as to maintain God's full dominion over creatures and especially on the limits of good and of evil.*

1. In order to explain the foundation of essences or of possibles, Scotus distinguishes three phases of reason in the eternal and simple actuality of God. At first, the Divine Intelligence knows Itself; then, being thus become fully in actuality, it can create, as an ideal world, an infinity of realizable essences; finally, It compares these possibles to the Divine Essence and verifies that they are participations of It. This is a natural and necessary operation in God, which helps explain the necessity of first principles, which affirm that every essence is that which it is; in this way the immutable validity of our knowledge is maintained and explained.

2. Each of these possible essences is an independent absolute, having no necessary bond with the others. Moreover, if there is a question of choosing from these possibles which are realizable those which in fact shall be realized, the Divine Liberty can fully intervene. It is Divine Liberty which imposes stable combinations on certain essences, as a man who establishes the relations between the notions of side, angles, and figure so as necessarily to conceive of a triangle with three sides and three angles. It is Divine Liberty which establishes the dependence between agents and what is acted upon, and

which founds physical and moral laws. In fact, Liberty could determine them otherwise than they are.

Scotus made two remarkable applications of this doctrine :

a) *The limit separating the natural from the supernatural* depends on the free determination of God. Thus, God could make an act meritorious of heaven without grace; He could justify a sinner and give grace to him without removing the sin, for there is no *essential* relation between nature and grace.

b) *In morality*, the duties of creatures to God (the first three commandments) alone are of absolute natural right. Other duties, regulating the relations of men among themselves and to other creatures, are of the natural law as consecutive upon the free will of God. Thus, by His will God could make a delusion out of a good act or declare hatred of one's neighbor a virtue, and so forth.

CONCLUSION. **298.** By insisting on the weakness of the opinions which he refutes, Scotus sometimes seems to lose confidence in the value of natural reason. He gives examples of this tendency in his criticism of the Averroistic system. In the latter view, God, being only the *motor cause* of the first heaven, is not present in all places; nor is God provident, for after He produced all beings He let them evolve according to their own laws [1]. Scotus shows in detail that the Thomistic refutations of these views are inefficacious in his own judgment. He says that one cannot deduce ubiquity from the divine causality since, on the contrary, presence precedes causality; one cannot admit the Thomistic explanation of Providence with the aid of the theory of " premotion ", in which God alone is the *proper cause of being*, for if the creature is not the " cause of being " it cannot have any other activity, and so on.

But, having demolished, he did not always feel capable of reconstructing, at least in the philosophical order. He returns to the Augustinian tradition which appeals to the supernatural light to supply for the darkness of reason. He declares that the conservative activity of God and the Divine Providence are dogmas of faith. Thus, though Scotism may be far from scepticism, it is certainly marked by an *exaggerated distrust of reason*.

---

[1] See above, nn. 190 and 248.

However, once one admits the double foundation of the primacy of the free will and the validity of the formal distinction, the rest of the philosophy of Scotus follows logically and the amplitude of its construction must be given credit. His theories, owing to their subtlety, are not always very clear, and the numberless detours of proofs, encumbered with criticisms written in a style often involved, do not facilitate their understanding. But, understood in Scotus' sense, they are Catholic and organized into a complete philosophical and theological " science ". As a result of this, the Franciscans, who had been divided into various schools until then, grouped themselves around their Subtle Doctor and chose him as the Master of their Order, as the Dominicans have done with St. Thomas Aquinas.

In brief, the Blessed [1] Duns Scotus set up a true synthesis of vast proportions in which all solutions are inspired by the same principle. Despite the boldness of many of his views, he was respectful of the demands of his Catholic faith and brought to a worthy close the period of the apogee of Christian and Scholastic philosophy [2].

The Catholic Church has preferred, and with good reason, the luminous synthesis of the Angelic Doctor, St. Thomas, for one must admit, despite everything, certain signs of decadence in Scotism. The considerable place given to criticism in which abuse is easy, and more especially, the subtlety of his fundamental position, in which distinct formalities become multiplied, helped much towards awaking a nominalistic reaction.

_____

[1] " His name is honored with a public and immemorial cult at Nola, in Hungary, at Cologne, in Spain, and the times do not seem too distant when the Roman Curia may sanction this cult with its own authority ". P. RAYMOND, article " Duns Scot " in *Dictionnaire théologique catholique*, col. 1866.

[2] It should be added, in order to have a complete appreciation of Scotus, that he is, primarily, a *theologian*. " ... His philosophy was wholly in function of his theology; and this is particularly noteworthy not only because of the special synthesis it provides, but also, and mainly, on account of the historical part played by its defenders in their final elaboration of a number of important doctrines ". F. CAYRÉ, *Manual of Patrology*, Vol. II, p. 652.

THIRD PERIOD.

Decadence.

(14th-17th centuries).

BIBLIOGRAPHY (for the third period).

DE WULF, M., *A History of Mediaeval Philosophy*, Vol. II, London, 1926. — JACOB, E. F., *Essays in the Conciliar Period*, Manchester, 1944. — SALEMBIER, J., *Le grand schisme d'Occident*, 5e éd., Paris, 1921. — THORNDIKE, L., *A History of Magic and Experimental Science*. Vols. III and IV. The fourteenth and fifteenth centuries, New York, 1934. — VIGNAUX, P., *Justification et prédestination au XIVe siècle*, Paris, 1934. — WERNER, A., *Die Scholastik des späteren Mittelalters*, 4 vols., Vienna, 1881-7. — WOLF, A., *A History of Science, Technology and Philosophy in the 16th and 17th centuries*, London, 1935.

299. A marked decline in Western philosophical thought occurs between the fourteenth and the seventeenth centuries. Scholasticism tried to live on its past laurels and thus, little by little, it lost control over the scholars who moved into rival philosophical camps.

There is a double reason for this decadence :

1° **The decline of studies in a larger number of universities.** In the fourteenth century, a large number of universities obtained or usurped the right of creating Doctors; in order to be successful in this aim, the requirements for admission were lowered. Mention should be made also of the large number of degrees secured through patronage. The period of study was curtailed in many places, which promoted ignorance of the great Scholastic doctrines in many students.

2° **The inadequacy of the Scholastic masters.** In this period there are no great personalities; it is the period of a Thomistic, Scotistic, or Ockhamistic school. It is a time of compendiums summarizing the masters, rather than one of original work. While keeping the common patrimony of the faith and of the fundamental doctrines of Scholasticism, more attention and emphasis was placed on minute and detailed points of opposition. The period flourishes with subtleties and arguments of verbiage, sometimes to the neglect of the fundamental theses of the great masters. Even language reflected this confusion of thought; Scholastic Latin became encumbered with neologisms and barbarisms, and fell into full decadence.

These direct causes of decline were furthered by the indirect influences of political and religious troubles occurring during this period. The Great Western Schism (1378-1417), the Hundred Years War, the Great Plague of the fourteenth century and the struggles between Papacy and Empire, tended to disorganize society and to deprive the thinker of the tranquillity which is helpful towards deep study.

These three centuries of decadence are divided into two parts, each dominated by a rather remarkable thinker. **William of Ockham** is a definitive factor in furthering the decadence of the period by his terminism. **Suarez**, at the close of the sixteenth century, partially arrests the movement, at least in Spain, by his original eclecticism.

Two articles will cover this period :

Article I : William of Ockham and Terminism.

Article II : Suarez and Eclecticism.

ARTICLE ONE.

WILLIAM OF OCKHAM AND TERMINISM.

(1280-1349 or 1350).

SPECIAL BIBLIOGRAPHY.

1° **Works :** *Quodlibeta septem*, Paris, 1487. — *Super quattuor libros sententiarum subtilissimæ quæstiones*, Lyons, 1495. — *Summa totius logicæ*, Paris, 1948. — *Ockham : Selected Philosophical Writings*, Ph. Boehner (edit.), London, 1952. — *The Tractatus de successivis, attributed to William Ockham*, Ph. Boehner (edit.), New York, 1944. — *The Tractatus de prædestinatione et de præscientia Dei et de futuris contingentibus of William Ockham*, New York, 1945.

2° **Studies :** BAUDRY, L., *Guillaume d'Occam. Sa vie, ses œuvres, ses idées sociales et politiques. I.*, *L'homme et ses œuvres*, Paris, 1949. — GUELLUY, R., *Philosophie et théologie chez Guillaume d'Ockham*, Louvain, 1947. — HOCHSTETTER, E., *Studien zur Metaphysik und Erkenntnislehre des Wilhelms von Ockham*, Berlin, 1937. — LAGARDE, G. DE, *Naissance de l'esprit laïque au déclin du moyen âge. Cahier IV : Ockham et son temps ; Cahier V : Ockham ; Bases de départ ; Cahier VI : Ockham. La morale et le droit*, Paris, 1942-6. — MOODY, E. A., *The Logic of William of Ockham*, London, 1935. — TORNAY, S. C., *Ockham : Studies and Selections*, Chicago, 1938.

300. Born at Ockham in England, William entered the Franciscan order and was sent to take his studies and to teach at Oxford. He followed the lectures of Scotus at Paris, and taught there himself about 1320.

It was during this first period that he composed his great works, among which are *Super Libros IV Sententiarum, Quodlibeta, Expositio aurea super totam artem veterem* and *Summa totius logicæ*. From about 1323 onwards, William became involved in political and religious quarrels, siding with the " spirituals " against superiors, with the emperor against the Pope; he especially fought against Pope John XXII. Called to Avignon to defend himself, he sojourned there about four years. Then he took refuge with Emperor Ludwig of Bavaria, where he died in 1349 or 1350.

1º **Foundational principle. 301.** William of Ockham adopts the synthesis of Duns Scotus, though he instills into it an original note of *simplicity*, according to the principle :

" *Beings are not to be multiplied without necessity* ".

It must be admitted that the Scotistic tendency, which was exaggerated by his disciples, was to multiply real distinctions needlessly. At the same time, one could not state that every creature was simple, for this purity was proper to God alone. What principle gives one a clue as to the number of real distinctions? St. Thomas, following his fundamental principle, would say that one must admit all real distinctions, but only those which are demonstrably necessary through clear induction as demanded by facts. In this sense, Ockham's principle of simplification has validity.

But William, a disciple of Scotus, demanded *separability* as a criterion for a real distinction. Hence he merely kept the distinction of matter and form which, in Scotism, constitutes contingent being. All other formal distinctions *a parte rei* become purely logical distinctions. The distinction between essence and existence, between substance and accident, between soul and its faculties and between the various faculties are no longer real; they are but various aspects of the one same reality. Moreover, there is no formal distinction, in the Scotistic sense, between the divine attributes, nor a virtual distinction in the Thomistic sense; all attributes are synonymous and theodicy becomes a game of mental logic. The most remarkable of his simplifications, however, is that concerning the intelligence, which led to terminism.

2⁰ **Terminism.** **302.** Following Scotus, William viewed intelligence as an active power whose function is to form universal ideas with the help of the senses; these ideas are to be coordinated into sciences. He also concludes to the uselessness of intelligible species abstracted from the sensible, for intelligence is capable of producing the image of the object through its own, immanent activity. William sees no need for impressed species, nor for the active intellect; all he requires is an *efflorescence of universal ideas*. The latter are one of the manifestations of the soul's perfection, and they are grouped under the heading " from the intelligence ".

What is the validity of human knowledge? With regard to sensible intuition, or with respect to the concept expressing the individual, no difficulty arises, for both immediately attain reality. Ockham, like Scotus, admits this point of departure. But universal ideas can no longer be explained by the objective existence of formalities, distinct *a parte rei;* the validity of the latter, however, is safeguarded by the logical theory of *supposition.* Just as the word, or oral term, takes the place of (supposes) the idea when used in judgments and processes of reasoning, so also the idea, the universal concept or *mental term* takes the place of real individuals in scientific speculations. However, while the word signifies but *one idea,* the mental term signifies *a whole group* of individuals. Inasmuch as the ideas are thus reduced to pure " supposital terms ", this solution has been called " terminism ".

Thus, the view of moderate realism, which was so strong in the great Scholastics of the thirteenth century, was slowly forgotten. It is here replaced by a mixed solution, one fashioned from nominalism and from conceptualism, and which serves as a presage of the extreme solutions of positivism and of Kantianism [1]. An erroneous view of the proper nature of human reason is the source of these deviations, for reason was made in order that it might grasp the real object (materially the same as the sensible object) under the most profound aspect of abstract essence or intelligible being.

Without a doubt, William is like Scotus, remaining moderated in his conclusions, as will be shown. But his principles contain the germ of errors which grow into modern philosophical systems.

3⁰ **Corollaries and Influence.** **303.** Ockhamism is a form of simplified Scotism in which the formalities become pure

---

[1] " Fourteenth century philosophy was evidently a stage towards so-called modern philosophy for which it paved the way ". F. CAYRÉ, *op. cit.*, Vol. II, p. 663, fn. 2.

beings of reason; formalism becomes terminism. As a result, a great part of metaphysics is carried into logic, and William's influence is first found in the aftermath of popularity given to him in the schools on logical matters. This fact points up clearly one of the main defects of decadent Scholasticism, the abuse of the syllogism and of distinctions.

Furthermore, the terminist solution does not assert confidence in the value of human reason. Agreeing with Scotus, William affirms the powerlessness of reason to demonstrate the spirituality and the immortality of the human soul, as also God's existence; these are truths of faith. Thus Ockhamism tended towards *scepticism*.

Inheriting the voluntarism of Scotus, Ockham declares that it is impossible to determine, rationally, the limits of good and of evil. God alone has fixed these limits through His free will. In this way, he prepared the way towards *utilitarian morality* and, by his struggles with the Holy See, he presaged the *Protestant revolt*. One can thus find in Ockhamism the source of a large number of errors and of modern tendencies.

In Ockham himself, however, these consequences remained veiled by his desire of conforming with faith in his teachings. From the strictly intellectual viewpoint, he kept the same validity in his synthesis as did Scotus. He held the fundamental view of the domination of free will and of the univocity of being in science, and but added to Scotism the attractive trait of simplicity. This latter addition explains his prodigious success : in the fourteenth and fifteenth centuries, he conquered most of the universities, so that Ockhamism was a rival of Thomism and of Scotism.

Among his more celebrated disciples is Cardinal PETER D'AILLY (1350-1420), who played an important part in the Council of Constance (1414-18), which resolved the Great Western Schism. — JOHN BURIDAN († around 1358), rector of the University of Paris from 1328 to 1350, devoted his best research to the problem of liberty, and defended psychological determinism [1]. — MARSILIUS OF INGHEN († about 1395) was also rector of the University of Paris from 1367 to 1371 and, about 1379, founded the University

---

[1] The story of the donkey dying between two bales of hay equal in quantity and quality is not in Buridan's writings. Perhaps he made use of it in his lectures to show the difference between a free act of man and the necessary act of the brute, or it might have been invented by his contemporaries to ridicule the theory.

of Heidelberg. — GERSON[1] (1364-1429), a disciple of Peter d'Ailly, was especially a moralist and a mystic.

304. During this time, there were defenders of the Thomistic position. The Dominican masters[2] began, in the fourteenth century, to comment on the Thomistic works in their lessons, through a Chapter decree of 1314. Finally, in the fifteenth century, the Dominican Order adopted the *Summa Theologica* as a manual of theology, to replace the Sentences of Peter the Lombard.

Among the Thomists of the fourteenth century, mention can be made of HERVÉ NÉDELLEC (HERVÆUS NATALIS) († 1323), the author of a commentary on the Lombard's Sentences, and of *Defensa doctrinæ divi Thomæ*. — DURANDUS OF AURILLAC († 1380) or DURANDELLUS, who was the strong adversary of DURANDUS OF SAINT-POURCAIN. — HERVÆUS OF CAUDA (about 1350-60) was the author of the first alphabetical table of the doctrine of St. Thomas.

In the fifteenth century, despite the general decline in doctrinal studies, the Dominican order had some Thomists of renown. JOHN CAPREOLUS (1380-1444) wrote a work called *Libri defensionum*, earning for him the title of the *Prince of Thomists;* it defends St. Thomas against such men as Scotus, Durandus, and Henry of Ghent. — SAINT ANTONINUS, Bishop of Florence in 1446, authored a *Summa theologiæ moralis.* The work of the mystic, DIONYSIUS THE CARTHUSIAN († 1471), was also inspired by an authentic Thomism.

The vitality of Thomism leads to the Spanish renaissance, in the sixteenth century, through Francis Suarez.

ARTICLE TWO. — SUAREZ AND ECLECTICISM.
(1548-1617).

SPECIAL BIBLIOGRAPHY.

1⁰ **Works :** *Opera Omnia*, 28 vols., Paris, 1856-1878. — *Selections from Three Works of Francisco Suarez, S. J., De legibus, Defensio fidei catholicæ, De triplici virtute theologica*, 2 vols., (text and translation), Oxford, 1944.

2⁰ **Studies :** ALEJANDRO, J. M., *La gnoseologia del Doctor Eximio y la acusacion nominalista*, Comillas (Santander), 1948. — BOURRET, E., *De l'origine du pouvoir d'après saint Thomas et Suarez*,

---

[1] CONNOLY, J. L., *John Gerson, Reformer and Mystic*, Louvain, 1928. — CAYRÉ, F., *Manual of Patrology*, Vol. II, pp. 687-688 and pp. 709-711.

[2] Some Dominicans did not accept Thomism, as DURANDUS OF SAINT-POURÇAIN († 1334), who was a nominalist, and denied an active intellect. The decrees of the chapter were aimed at encompassing those who were against Thomism.

Paris, 1875. — DE SCORAILLE, R., *François Suarez, l'Etudiant, le Maître, le Docteur, le Religieux*, 2 vols., Paris, 1911. — GOMEZ ARBOLEYA, E., Francisco Suarez, Granada, 1947. — KONZE, E., *Der Begriff der Metaphysik bei F. Suarez*, Leipzig, 1928. — LILLEY, A. L., *Francisco Suarez. Social and Political Ideas of some Great Thinkers of the XVIth and XVIIth centuries*, London, 1926. — MAHIEU, L., *François Suarez, Sa philosophie et les rapports qu'elle a avec la théologie*, Paris, 1921. — WERNER, C., *Franz Suarez und die Scholastik der letzten Jahrhunderte*, Ratisbon, 1861.

305. The Scholastic revival which occurs in the sixteenth century is primarily in the realm of theology; it is one aspect of the Catholic Counter-Reformation begun with the Council of Trent (1545-1563). The close union which obtained between faith and reason in Scholasticism effected a renewal of Christian philosophy likewise. Already at this time, it showed two traits which Leo XIII will impress so profoundly on Scholasticism : *a*) it is a complete return to the great syntheses of the thirteenth century, and especially to the Thomistic synthesis; *b*) it showed a laudable attempt to adapt itself to *modern* problems which, at that time, were those of the Renaissance.

Sadly enough, this double orientation was not pushed far enough. The " modernization " principally bettered the form of Scholasticism, and credit is due to these men for " the reinstatement of " the pure and clear language, the sober and precise method of Thomism... " [1]. In doctrinal questions, these men were concerned with the new political and social problems; in other areas, they retained the habitual program, as determined by commentaries on the books of Aristotle.

The Thomistic revival was marked by the adoption of the *Summa Theologica* of St. Thomas as the replacement for the Lombard's Sentences. The doctrines of the Angelic Doctor were not restored in their original purity; they were interpreted and contrasted with the positions of other schools; this critical work led to eclecticism.

This renaissance was centered in the Universities of Spain and of Portugal, especially at the Universities of Salamanca, Alcala and Coimbra; the latter had chairs of Thomistic, of Scotistic and of Ockhamistic philosophy.

The revival first began among the Dominicans. FRANCIS OF VITORIA (1480-1546) was a master at the University of Salamanca from 1526 to 1544. Besides several theological works, as a commentary on St. Thomas' *Summa Theologica* and on the Lombard's Sentences, he concerned himself with current problems on the

[1] M. DE WULF, *op. cit.*, Vol. II, p. 594.

relations between Church and State and the problems of colonization. These matters are treated in his *Relectiones*, which are entitled *De potestate Ecclesiæ, De potestate civili* and *De Indis* [1].

Vitoria gives precision to the relations between Church and State in terminology that is later found in the Encyclicals of Leo XIII. Church and State are two equally sovereign societies, each in its own order, the latter in temporal matters, while the former in religious and supernatural concerns, with regard to all those things connected with eternal life. Accordingly, the affairs of civil society can *indirectly* belong to the Church and to the Pope, who have the mission of directing and of judging every human activity, even social action, in relation to God.

Vitoria was especially interested in the **problem of colonization.** He proposed that the natural law would guarantee that those indigenous to a country, the *barbarians* [2], are truly masters of the country they occupy, both politically and economically. The various titles which the sovereign colonizers present as justification of their conquests are then examined, and a goodly number rejected. For example, Vitoria does not admit that the Emperor is master of the world, as some theologians of the royal court proposed, nor that the Pope had the power to concede Spain the right of conquering the Americas. It is true that arbitration by Alexander VI had wisely delimited the zones of influence of Spain and of Portugal [3], but this action gave him no right of possession over the lands and the men of those countries. Moreover, Vitoria would not grant the title of discovery: " We have no more right to take their lands than they would have to take ours if they had first discovered our continent ". One is not allowed to make warfare against these people in order to punish their crimes, nor to impose Christianity on them by force; the diffusion of the Gospel is to be done by pacific means, and no one has established the Spaniards as judges of the Indian peoples [4].

Vitoria then gives some solid bases for colonization. All men have the right to travel about the world and to be received kindly; they can exploit the goods left open. Christians have the right to preach the Gospel; if they are unjustly opposed by violence, they can, by natural right and by supernatural right, undertake a just war to defend these rights. One could hold that the colonizing people do an act of charity if they aid the backward people to rise to a higher type of civilization [5]. At all costs, colonization

---

[1] Vitoria did not edit these while living; after his death, his disciples edited some of his courses; these are called *Relectiones theologicæ.*

[2] This expression, " barbarians ", is not used in a pejorative sense by Vitoria; it is synonymous with " indigenous " or " native ".

[3] The Constitution, " *Inter cetera* ", May, 1493. See A. FOLIET, *Le droit de colonisation*, Paris, 1930.

[4] Vitoria here but echoes his great contemporary, LAS CASAS (1474-1565). The latter was a man of action (a Dominican in 1523, then Bishop of Chiapa, Mexico), who fought constantly to free the Indians from the yoke of the Spanish colonials, and merited the title, " Father of the Indians ".

[5] Vitoria admitted this with hesitation, though today this notion is highly esteemed.

is not legitimate if it is solely in favor of the colonizing people. Morality absolutely forbids the exploitation of man by man.

Among the adversaries of Vitoria, mention should be made of JOHN SEPULVEDA (1490-1573), a theologian and the historiographer of Charles V. A disciple of Aristotle, Sepulveda defended free will against the Protestants [1]. In his work on social morality, *De Regno et Regis officio*, he admitted the pagan view of slavery [2]. There are three categories of men : the first are *naturally* slaves [3], for they unify a great physical vigor with an arrested mentality, as Aristotle says; there is a second group which are neither slaves nor masters by nature; a third group are naturally masters. It is in this way that he justifies the wars of conquest undertaken by the colonizers [4].

Vitoria had some disciples, among whom the best known are his own religious brethren. DOMINIC SOTO (1492-1560), whose principal work, entitled *De justitia et jure*, is a complete treatise on individual, social and international rights and morality, in which the author harmoniously unifies rational exposition with theological proof. — MELCHIOR CANO (1509-1560) is well known for his *De locis theologicis*, in which he contributes to the Scholastic reform by fighting against the abusive appeal to human authority and against indulgence in useless questions.

305[bis]. The principal figures in this sixteenth century Spanish renaissance are from the Society of Jesus. St. Thomas was chosen the official doctor of the Order by Ignatius Loyola (1491-1556). A general meeting of 1593 imposed the obligation on the Jesuits of following St. Thomas on all theological questions, though leaving freedom on purely philosophical doctrines. The Jesuits of this period are to be counted as defenders of Thomism, though their support is marked by a remarkable independence. Among the best known is MOLINA (1536-1600), whose famous *Concordia* caused a great stir among theologians. — GABRIEL VASQUEZ († 1606), wrote a commentary on the *Summa Theologica* of St. Thomas, and a work *Disputationes metaphysicæ*, wherein he abandons the real distinction between essence and existence. — RODRIGUEZ ARRIAGI (1592-1667), was author of an unfinished and voluminous course of theology, and of a *Cursus philosophicus*, which is quite eclectic.

But the most celebrated and most influential of these mitigated Thomists was FRANCIS SUAREZ, who was born at Granada in 1548. He finished his studies at Salamanca, and, at the age of twenty-two, began his professorial career, which he exercised in various Spanish universities, Segovia, Valladolid,

---

[1] This is done in his work, *De fato et libero arbitrio contra Lutherum.*

[2] See above, n. 89.

[3] " He is a natural slave who is strong in body but dull in intelligence and slow in initiative ".

[4] Sepulveda held, though, that this doctrine could not be known with certainty; see A. GONZALÈS, *Histoire de la philosophie*, Vol. III, p. 25.

Alcala, Coimbre; he taught five years at the Roman college (1580-5), and thus spent his whole life in teaching until he died in Lisbon in 1617.

Suarez composed a great number of works, mainly theological. His principal philosophical works are : *De Deo Uno, De Anima,* the famous *De Legibus,* and especially his *Disputationes metaphysicæ,* which has been spoken of as one of the most finished, complete and clear works of Scholastic metaphysics [1].

1º **General Characteristics. 306.** Suarez' work is unified by a methodological principle which can be stated as follows :

To report, orderly and faithfully, the opinions of his predecessors on the various theological and philosophical questions, in order to discover or to choose the truth, by taking from all of these men whatever is good — that is, by finding a middle road between St. Thomas, Scotus and William of Ockham.

This respect for tradition is, on the whole, quite Scholastic. St. Thomas himself followed it, for he wished to retain, in his system, all truths discovered prior to his time. But there are two ways of viewing tradition : one can consider various opinions as a means of more deeply penetrating a proposition established by other means and of seeing its applications better; or one can use tradition as a means of forming a system, by gathering the partial truths which are to be coordinated. The first view of tradition is that of St. Thomas, and it culminated in a doctrine whose parts were powerfully unified by a logical connection which attached them to the same fundamental principle. The second view is that of Suarez. It led him to a collection of theories which have no necessary link between them; instead, each view appears as the most likely reconciliation between diverse opinions. This accounts for Suarez' eclecticism.

In the presence of three great schools of thought, Thomism, Scotism and Ockhamism, then in vogue in the sixteenth century schools, Suarez did not intend to found a new system. He presents himself as a commentator on St. Thomas, and believes himself to be essentially faithful to Thomas. But his understanding of Thomas is not stringent and exact; he occasionally succumbs to the simplifying tendencies of Ockham, but more often he leans to the dissociative tendency of Duns Scotus, though correcting Scotus by an effort at unification which

---

[1] M. De Wulf, *op. cit.,* Vol. II, p. 598.

approaches the Thomistic view. In order to understand Suarez, it is sufficient to note his divergences from St. Thomas.

2⁰ **Anti-Thomistic Positions. 307.** Following Scotus, Suarez views the constitutive elements of a composite as *absolute*, essentially and easily separable. This separability is the criterion for real distinctions, and can be called the *tendency towards dissociation*, which accounts for the origin of most of his anti-Thomistic views. He moderated this tendency, however, recognizing a sort of mixed or diminished separability in addition to one which is perfect; in mixed separability, only one of two distinct elements disappears, as when wood loses its form in order to acquire another. This yields the *modal distinction*, or that between a substance and its mode; without being purely logical, the modal distinction is less than the real, and approaches the formal distinction *a parte rei* of Scotus. But, in order to establish the existence of this distinction, Suarez was not content merely to make a simple distinction of concepts. An objective necessity was needed for the modal distinction, and the main role of the *mode* is to formally constitute the union of the parts of a composite into a unity of the whole. Thus he attenuated, though without suppressing them, his divergences from St. Thomas. His metaphysics and psychology show even stronger differences from St. Thomas.

I. METAPHYSICS.

A) **Propositions. 308.** Suarez conceived of pure potentiality as a simple *possible*. In order to be real (each reality being an absolute), it had to possess, necessarily, a proper actuality and a proper existence. Two anti-Thomistic propositions ensue.

a) There is no real distinction between essence and existence in creatures.

In fact, there is not even a modal distinction between these two elements, for they can in no wise be separately realized. If one objects that existence identical with essence becomes necessary and infinite, the reply is that such a being would remain contingent because it is created by God and dependent on His conserving power. Suarez granted, however, a certain validity to the Thomistic position, but judged his own much more probable and much more simple. The simplifying tendency comes in here to appease his eclecticism.

b) Prime matter is a commencement of actuality. Prime matter also has its proper existence and can subsist without form; here, there is a real distinction in the strict sense. However, in order to safeguard the unity of the composite, there must be added *a mode of union* between matter and form, which essentially orders these two principles, viewed as absolutes, towards each other.

B) **Corollaries.** The proposition identifying essence and existence implicates answers on the problem of personality, that of prime matter as incomplete actuality, and that of quantity.

The solutions of Suarez on these points are directed by Catholic dogma, as those of the Incarnation and of the Holy Eucharist. While St. Thomas found a basis for new theological conclusions in the philosophical propositions which he fully established beforehand through natural reason, Suarez allowed the truths of faith to function as premises for various philosophical conclusions. As for the rest, he was content with applying his methodological principle.

a) **Personality** must be constituted by a separable element, for there is in Christ an individual humanity with human personality. It must, further, be superadded to existence, for the latter is not distinct from essence. This will then be a *positive mode*, which, in completing existence, gives to the individual his full incommunicability.

b) **Quantity** cannot have the conferral of integral parts as its essential role, for prime matter, through its actuality, has already conferred these on substance. The role of quantity is to apply the parts to place, or at least *an aptitude* for place, for the actual application can be avoided by a miracle. Furthermore, perfect separability, learned from the mystery of the Holy Eucharist, makes one conclude to a real distinction between substance and accidents, in the strict sense, and then to the existence of a mode of union in order to maintain the real, physical whole. This mode of union in the accident is *its inherence*, modally distinct from its essence.

c) Finally, being unable to conceive of a pure relation, Suarez denied the distinction between this accident and its foundation. In his view, every relation is, by necessity, a perfection [1], conceived as " bearing towards another ". In this way, the notion is simplified. But when it is applied in theology to the mystery of the Holy Trinity, Suarez found himself obliged, in order to resolve his difficulties, to assert that the principle of identity did not, perhaps, apply to the divine mysteries.

---

[1] That is, a reality already classed in one of the predicaments, as a *quality*.

II. Psychology.

309. The same tendency to simplify led Suarez to deny any real distinction between the passive and active intellect, which are but two aspects of the one, same faculty. They can never exist, one without the other, alone. But here also, his tendency towards dissociation became manifest :

A) At first, concerning the *formal object of human intelligence*, Suarez separated himself from St. Thomas in two ways :

a) This object of intelligence is *analogous being*, and not fully univocal being, as Scotus wished, for there is a difference of degree between the divine and the created nature. But Suarez meant the analogy *of intrinsic attribution* and not the Thomistic analogy of proportionality. He argued that the *unity of the concept of being* must be maintained, at all costs, and especially in order to prevent equivocation. For Suarez, a mere resemblance of relations established a great diversity in the multiple significations of the idea.

This position of Suarez is readily conformed to his proposition on the non-distinction between essence and existence. For, if the criterion for distinguishing the Infinite being of finite essences is that they are *created* or *participated*, it is then a *causal bond* which permits one to attribute the same perfections to God and to creatures; this is analogy of attribution.

Thomism resolves this difficulty by the notion of a perfection essentially relative [1], but Suarez, incapable of understanding this notion, would accuse St. Thomas of the proportionality of equivocation. But if intrinsic attribution maintains the diversity of degrees, it could not explain itself except through this notion of a relative perfection diversely realized. But this statement is the thought of St. Thomas in different language.

b) The proper object of human intelligence is no longer and uniquely that of abstract essence, but there is a *proper concept of the individual* as such. With Scotus, Suarez did not grasp the complementary functioning of sense and reason. Since, he held, in reflecting on the phantasm, reason grasps the

---

[1] See above, n. 286. The difficulty does not lie in the notion of a *causal bond* between infinite perfection and finite participated perfections. St. Thomas knew of this, and admits, in this sense, an analogy of attribution between God and creatures. But the delicate point is to maintain a *sufficient unity* in the concept (for instance, in the concept of life), so that it can designate, in turn, and in a proper sense, two realities as different as the finite and the infinite.

singular, it is able to grasp the singular in itself and to make from it an idea.

B) Moreover, concerning the *will*, Suarez conceives of it as a fully independent faculty, so that the free act is clarified, though not " caused " by practical judgment.   There is a question of concomitance but not of subordination.   For this reason, in explaining the influence of God on human actions, Suarez rejects the notion of physical premotion.   The will merely receives a simple concourse from God, allowing it the initiative to refuse or to accept.

III.   SOCIAL MORALITY.

309[bis].   It is here, in *social morality*, that Suarez is most original.   He is no longer opposed to St. Thomas, but adds precision and completion to his thought.   Suarez was faced with the Protestant theory of the *divine right of kings*, which was especially defended, along with other errors, by James I (1603-1625) of England in his work, *Triplex cuneus* [1].

Suarez opposed his view with the proposition of the *natural sovereignty of peoples*.   It is of natural right, he argued, that men unify in society.   It is an obligation for man to do so, so that he can attain his purpose — which is to elevate himself to a degree of civilization conformable to right reason and more apt to procure God's glory.   From this obligation flows the existence of sovereign power, one flowing from the other through natural necessity, so that God, being the immediate cause of human nature, is also the immediate cause of this power.   But there is nothing in right reason to indicate that this divine power resides in but one man, as a monarchy; or in one group, as an aristocracy; or even in the people taken as a whole, as in democracy.   Moreover, this latter form, being the most fundamental and the most closely knitted to the nature of things, is, in a certain way, of *natural right* [2];

---

[1] In this work, the King-theologian denies the indirect power of the Pope on temporal matters, and claimed, in his work, to expose " all the schismatic errors and all the anti-pontifical prejudices which formed the essence of Anglicanism " (L. MAHIEUX, *Suarez*, p. 70).   It was to refute James' work that Suarez wrote his *Defensio fidei*: the origin of power is treated in Book IV, Chs. II and III; on the question of *indirect power*, he defends the same doctrine as Vitoria (see above, n. 305); he admits, though only in certain cases and with many restrictions, the legitimacy of *tyrannicide*.

[2] " This can be held by the negative, but not by the positive law of nature; or, rather, by the natural law as conceding, though not as simply commanding ". *Defensio fidei*, I, III, Ch. II, n. 8.

the latter proposition obtains if, positing a perfect society, one must of necessity place in the people the power of directing the members of the society towards the common good.

Accordingly, kings in a monarchy and senators in an aristocracy do not receive their sovereignty immediately from God. Sovereignty always comes through the people as intermediary, who, by a sort of contract in view of more efficaciously attaining the common good, cede to the rulers the rights of sovereignty. In short, authority, which comes from God [1], resides primarily in the people and then passes on to its representatives and to its princes and kings.

One can conclude from this view that if the prince shows himself unworthy of his mandate, the people can retire him. But it does not follow, as James I held, that this view constitutes a stimulus towards revolts and revolutions; for, once the contract exists, the people no longer have the right to refuse it at their own pleasure. One must resist the tyrant, but also has the duty of being submissive to his prince, to the extent that the latter wills what is for the common good [2].

CONCLUSION. **310.** The incontestable merit of Suarez lies especially in his erudition, in the clearness of his methodical and historical exposition, and in his loyal efforts at conciliation. In this latter task he was mindful of the number and of the value of theological works, especially of positive theology, which helps explain the great influence which he had on the Scholastics of the seventeenth century, and even on our times. He stands as proof of the vitality of Catholic thought at this close of the Middle Ages, when the center of Christianity is found in Portugal, the land of great discoveries, and in Spain, the land of the Empire of Charles V.

Suarez, however, did not have the philosophical breadth of the great creators of systems in the Scholastic apogee. The coherence of his doctrines does not stem from an interior, unifying principle from which all his consequences flow, but rather from an effort at conciliation between opposed theories under the shadow of the great rule of unity, the Catholic faith.

---

[1] In acknowledging God as the final source of power, Suarez' theory is radically distinguished from that of Jean Jacques Rousseau; see below, n. 453.

[2] Suarez sagaciously answers the argument James 1 brought from the Bible; for example, James held that Saul and David received their power *directly* from God, but Suarez answers that they were directly *designated* by God, but the people *created* them kings. See *Defensio fidei*, I, III, Ch. III, n. 6-7, and *De legibus*, I, III, Ch. III and IV.

His view is an interpretation of Thomism, but is inspired in many ways by Scotism. His thought was too personal to be that of a disciple, and insufficiently synthetic to be that of a master. Despite his power and his originality, Suarez remains an eclectic.

In addition to Suarez, other schools had their partisans. The *Ockhamists* perpetuated themselves through GABRIEL BIEL (about 1425-1495), whose *Collectorium* is a clear exposition of terminism. — The *Scotists* were numerous among the Franciscans : PETRUS TARTARETUS (close of 15th cent.), a commentator on Aristotle, and ANTONIUS TROMBETA († 1518), who wrote against Cajetan [1].

The Thomistic school counted two brilliant representatives :

1) SILVESTER OF FERRARA (1474-1526) is a noted commentator on the *Summa contra gentiles*.

2) CAJETAN [2] (1469-1534), Thomas de Vio, was born at Gaeta and became bishop of that city. He wrote a noted commentary on the *Summa Theologica*. He sounded out many points of metaphysics, and also deserves fame as an exegete.

In the seventeenth century, two other Thomists are of marked importance. JOHN OF SAINT THOMAS (1589-1644) wrote a *Cursus philosophicus*, which is a quite clear and faithful synthesis of Thomism; GOUDIN (1639-1695) helped further the influence of a profound and authentic metaphysics, though its thought was too closely associated with ancient physics.

311. These worthwhile philosophers are, however, rather the exception, and the Scholasticism which then reigned officially in the schools, no longer lived in men's spirits [3]. The RENAISSANCE movement of the fifteenth and the sixteenth centuries, stirred Italy and all of Europe with a great enthusiasm for the pagan thinkers. This movement, whose makeup is quite complex [4],

---

[1] This he did especially in his commentary on St. Thomas' *De ente et essentia*, written at the age of 22 years.

[2] See the article by MANDONNET in *Dict. theol. cath.*, " Cajetan ", col. 1311-1329. The activity of the Thomistic school during the Renaissance was especially *theological*. Mention should be made especially of the Dominican, DOMINIC BANEZ (1528-1604), who put a powerful metaphysical spirit at the service of a rigid Thomism, defending efficacious grace *ab intrinseco* and *physical premotion*. — Banez' main adversary was the Jesuit, MOLINA (1536-1600), who, in his celebrated *Concordia* (1588), proposed the system of *simultaneous concourse* and of a *middle science* in order to explain how God foresees man's free actions and gives man graces without destroying liberty. This doctrine, examined at Rome at the *Congregatio de Auxiliis* (1598-1607), was not condemned. See F. CAYRÉ, *op. cit.*, Vol. II, pp. 748-751 and pp. 771-777.

[3] One could summarize the causes of this persistent lack of success, and indicate the part that Scholasticism played in the development of thought; this is done in the following paragraphs by clarifying, in contrast, the origin and the traits of modern philosophy.

[4] See the analysis in F. CAYRÉ, *op. cit.*, Vol. II, pp. 712-717.

was primarily an assimilation of the past in the realm of beauty more than that of truth, and a concomitant return to *nature* as exalted by pagan Hellenism. It led, rapidly, to the abandonment of the austere morality of Catholicism. Scholastic philosophy was bitterly criticized, accused of being enslaved by theology and of speaking a barbarous tongue. Moreover, as the artists adopted anew the ancient art forms, the philosophers revived most of the ancient thought-systems. Despite the widespread confusion which characterized this profusion of thought, several main currents are distinguishable [1].

1. **Platonism.** The main adherent of this view is CARDINAL NICHOLAS OF CUSA [2] (1401-1464), who was created a Cardinal in 1448. Neo-Platonism was his main inspiration. In his *De docta ignorantia*, he maintains that truth cannot be attained by reason but only by intuition, so that true science is found by confessing our ignorance. The world appears to him as recapitulated in the Being of God, and as flowing from Him by emanation; the distinction between God and the world, however, is always safeguarded.

The Platonic Academy, founded at Florence during the reign of Cosimo and Laurence de' Medici, was made famous by the Byzantine GEORGE GEMISTUS PLETHON († 1450) and by its more famous adherent, MARSILIUS FICINUS († 1409); the latter translated Plato and Plotinus from Greek into Latin and summarized their doctrines in his writings. — JOHN PICO DELLA MIRANDOLA (1463-1494), who was strongly influenced by Marsilius, wrote an allegorical interpretation of Genesis which was condemned; he died a Dominican. — The German philosophy of JAKOB BÖHME is of some importance; his Platonism becomes pantheism.

The movement developed in Italy until the seventeenth century, at which time we find BERNARDINO TELESIO (1509-1588). He developed a universal animism out of Platonism; in his own studies of nature, he explained its changes by the force of expansion (of heat) and of contraction (of cold). — GIORDANO BRUNO (1548-1600) was condemned to the prisons of the Holy Office for eight years before being burned at the stake as a heretic. He was an enemy of Aristotle, but sympathetic to all other philosophers. He was an atomist, a partisan of Copernicus, and a Neo-Platonist turned *pantheist*. In his view, God, Intelligence, the Soul of the World and Matter are reducible to one thing, the one and multiple life of the universe — the " holy, sacred and venerable animal " [3]. — TOMMASO CAMPANELLA (1568-1639) wrote a work *De sensu rerum et magia*, defending animistic pantheism.

---

[1] All the aspects of the Renaissance, including adequate bibliographies, can be found in F. COPLESTON, *A History of Philosophy. Volume III, Ockham to Suarez*, Part II and Part III.

[2] Cusa's works are being edited : *Nicolai de Cusa, Opera Omnia*, Leipzig, 1932 ff. See also, BETT, H., *Nicholas of Cusa*, London, 1932. — DE GANDILLAC, M., *La philosophie de Nicolas de Cuse*, Paris, 1942. — VAN STEENBERGHE, E.' *Le Cardinal Nicolas de Cuse, l'action, la pensée*, Paris, 1920.

[3] E. BRÉHIER, *Histoire de la philosophie*, I, Ch. VI, p. 780.

2. **Averroism.** The system of Siger of Brabant had its followers in the fifteenth and in the sixteenth centuries at the University of Padua, where the Senate of Venice protected the philosophers from the Inquisition. PIETRO POMPONAZZI (1462-1525) was the most famous of the Averroists. He defended the doctrine of providence in a fatalistic sense [1], denying freedom and the possibility of miracles, on which points he was in accord with all the Averroists. On the question of human intelligence, he held that the soul perishes entirely along with the body, for intelligence cannot think without images; this notion he developed from Alexander of Aphrodisias. The pure *Averroists*, as ALEXANDER ACHILLINI († 1518) and MARCUS ANTONIUS ZIMARA († 1532), defended the view of a separated intelligence and of an impersonal immortality.

3. **Scientism and Scepticism.** The effort to establish the discoveries of science within philosophy began with the Renaissance, especially through the work of LEONARDO DA VINCI (1452-1519), who was one of the initiators of mechanics and of modern physics [2].

But the scientific discoveries, in overthrowing the secular foundations of Aristotle's experimental physics, provoked a sceptical reaction. MICHEL DE MONTAIGNE (1533-1592) is the main proponent of this reaction. His *Essais* proposes that truth varies according as things are considered by different men in different times, and in varying fashions.

4. **Moralists and Political Writers.** The reappearance of *Stoicism* comes into the Renaissance, especially through JUSTUS LIPSIUS (1547-1606), who tried to make Stoical doctrines known by adapting them to the Christian mentality. The same view was proposed by PIERRE CHARRON (1541-1603), whose work, *Sagesse*, is replete with the maxims of Epictetus. These humanists were not openly opposed to Catholicism, but stayed on the plane of pure nature through deliberate choice, avoiding notions and questions of faith and of grace.

A most independent group are the theorists of law. HUGO GROTIUS (1583-1645) is well known for his *De jure belli et pacis;* he founded the nature of the state on a sort of social contract theory, a prelude to Rousseau's views on this matter. — NICHOLAS MACHIAVELLI (1469-1527) is well known for his work *Le prince*, in which he teaches that the interests of the people are identified with that of the prince, who is thus the embodiment of supreme law, so that " end justifies means " in political matters.

Of such a variegated sort is the non-Scholastic philosophy of the Renaissance, arising from multiple directions, some of which are contradictory and confused. It is " an incoherent philosophy, resembling a crowd escaped from confinement, indulging in a series of sterile enterprises, only united by the

---

[1] See above, n. 249.
[2] M. DE WULF, *op. cit.*, Vol. II, p. 576.

struggle against Scholasticism and by a desire for independence from the Church " [1]. All the ancient systems, Platonism, Aristotelianism, Stoicism, Epicureanism, Atomism and Scepticism were taken up with an equal lack of success. The Renaissance brought to light a " new " science and also renewed interest in letters and in the arts, but the bankruptcy of philosophical systems was complete. In the seventeenth century, the philosophical field is free, for it is lacking in philosophers, and this fact helps explain the rapid advance of the ideas of Francis Bacon and of Descartes, the initiators of modern philosophy.

---

[1] M. De Wulf, *op. cit.*, Vol. II, p. 564.

PART THREE.

MODERN ERA.

MODERN AND NEO-THOMIST PHILOSOPHY.

(17th-20th centuries).

---

312. With regard to its philosophical spirit, the modern period is readily distinguished from the Christian period by being its direct antithesis. It can be characterized by the expression, " Anti-Scholastic Revolution ", which is expressive of its origin.

The Middle Ages, as has been seen, were witness to a *Doctrinal Renaissance* in which Europe assimilated to itself the thought of the East, and especially of ancient Greece. This assimilation was fecundated and controlled by the light of Christian faith which, by the *supernatural* aid it offered human intelligence, began to restore it to its native power.

Moreover, even in philosophical matters [1], the apogee of Scholasticism was greatly prepared for by the work of the Fathers of the Church. St. Augustine was especially influential in this work, for his influence caused the Platonic current of thought to rejoin and complete the Peripatetic current in the Middle Ages. St. Thomas fully reconciled and purified both currents, guided by the helpful light of faith.

At the same time, and under the influence of Aristotle and his completion by the Arabian thinkers, a great group of particular sciences [2], offering a general explanation of nature, became incorporated in the teaching of the schools. This helped Thomism, an incontestable summary of Scholastic thought, appear as a powerful synthesis which had its own valid philosophy and, by its central " scientific " [3] core, enjoyed

---

[1] In the *theological* realm, the Fathers of the Church had an even greater influence on Scholastic thought.

[2] The expression refers to the physical, chemical, biological and astronomical sciences, as well as to mathematics; in a word, whatever constitutes " sciences " in the modern sense.

[3] *Science* here is taken in the Thomistic sense; see above, n. 264.

the validity of eternal truth. At the same time, Thomism was a synthesis of its own period on two accounts : first, for being a Christian philosophy [1] and the servant of the Catholic faith; second, by its conception of the particular sciences (sciences in the modern sense), as being in full continuity with philosophy. Thomism, accordingly, is a doctrine sufficiently powerful and true that it can perfectly synthesize all the partial truths of the human sciences, and all the truths of the Catholic faith.

But, in opposition to this Doctrinal Renaissance, there arose the *Literary Renaissance*, having its origin in Italy around 1453. It took on the appearance, *in its totality*, of a movement of revolt of humanity itself against the beauty and the super-human and divine thoughts of the Middle Ages; and, consequently, against the Catholic Church. It is for this reason that, though it did not engender any philosophical system of value, it logically developed into the *Protestant Reformation*.

In the meantime, this movement was arrested in France by a vigorous Catholic reaction in the religious, literary and political realms. However, the philosophical realm witnessed no effort towards restoring Thomism and of pointing out a metaphysical doctrine capable of being the foundation for the new sciences. Accordingly, modern philosophy became the manifestation in the speculative order of a revolutionary spirit through which society set itself up as greater than, and rejectful of Faith, the Church, and God.

There are two main causes which help explain this deficiency of Scholasticism, and especially of Thomism, in the seventeenth century.

1⁰ *The lack of a metaphysical spirit* among most of the Scholastics of this period. Ockhamism was the favored system, for it simplified and facilitated philosophical thought. It led, however, to nominalism by its exaggerated development of logic, leaving a profuse wake of formulas, and of subtle and useless questions. The university doctors did not defend their views through powerful metaphysical arguments, as St. Thomas had done, but through royal decrees which proscribed or imposed one system or another [2].

---

[1] In the sense explained above; see n. 244, above.

[2] In 1264, the theological faculty of Paris asked Parliament to condemn the philosophy of Jean Bitaud. In 1671, the King himself asked Parliament for a decree in favor of Aristotle. See M. DE WULF, *op. cit.*, Vol. III, p. 615.

2⁰ *The misunderstanding between Thomistic science and modern science.* This situation arose as a consequence of the dearth of metaphysics among the Scholastics. In pointing the attention of the savants to the material world, the Literary Renaissance led to remarkable progress in the particular studies of nature. Helped by the invention of numerous observational instruments and especially by the idea of a measure methodically applied to all phenomena, allowing them to be submitted to mathematical analysis, the savants began the erection of a modern science, most of whose laws seemingly contradicted Aristotle's conceptions.

This new science is true and legitimate, in the Thomistic view, if it is properly placed. It is formally mathematical but materially physical, and in no wise metaphysical[1]. It does not seek the knowledge of being and of phenomena through their deepest causes; it merely aims to establish a network of quantitative (or algebraic) relations between observed facts, because of their usefulness or industrialization.

The Thomists of the sixteenth century had the means at hand of showing this proper validity of the new science, and of assimilating and completing it; they should have analyzed the metaphysical meaning of their *science* and arranged its conclusions hierarchically. They should have sacrificed the probabilities known to be false, though preserving intact their patrimony of properly philosophical truths. For instance, neither the theory of the incorruptibility of the heavens, nor that of the immobility of the earth are embodied with the true Thomistic " philosophy "; Galileo's discoveries should have persuaded them to sacrifice these views without damage.

Instead, the Scholastics of the decadent period defended Aristotelianism en bloc, believing that their living metaphysics was inseparable from their decadent astronomy and physics. The few great metaphysicians of the period[2], isolated and too disdainful of the new orientation of thought, had no influence on the movement of new ideas.

---

[1] In other words, it is a mathematics applied to physical phenomena which one does not seek to explain, but merely to view in their measurable aspect. See, for example, J. MARITAIN, *The Degrees of Knowledge*, New York, 1938, *passim*, or the same author's *Réflexions sur l'intelligence et sur sa vie propre*, 3ᵉ éd., Paris, 1930.

[2] Such men as Cajetan, John of St. Thomas, and Goudin, mentioned above, n. 310.

In the face of this insufficiency of philosophy, one must admit at the same time, the presumption of the new savants, joining their *mathematically* demonstrated laws to false and anti-Scholastic hypotheses, naively considering them as an explanation of the nature of things. It is, rather, a need of our intelligence to explain being in itself. These thinkers, however, thought that their discoveries overthrew all ancient metaphysics. It is in this way that, properly speaking, *modern philosophy* was born.

313. This origin of modern philosophy explains how its spirit is marked by two errors which are still widespread in our days, liberalism and laicism. These two principles, applied in the speculative order of things, constitute the dual aspect of the basic attitude called rationalism.

1. **Liberalism.** In this erroneous view, human liberty is a power of absolute independence, without any limit of good or of evil, of man or of God; accordingly, the liberty of the philosopher consists in drawing out all science from his own spirit. In a view of this sort, " Liberty and interiority consist essentially in an opposition to the non-self and in the recovery of independence within by relation to what is without. Truth and life must be sought for uniquely within the human subject; every action, every help, every rule, every teacher who provides from what is *other* (from the object, from human authority, from divine authority) being but an outrage against the spirit ".

2. **Laicism or Naturalism.** In this error, human nature is considered as good itself, without any divine influence; as a result, the modern philosopher tends to replace God with man, while he is still searching for the necessary Being, the center of his system. "By this very fact, and reciprocally, there is nothing *granted* as a measure and a rule of man, but man's innermost depths transcend and command whatever is given : natures and laws, definitions, dogmas and duties have no objects which impose themselves as through *another*, but are pure expressions from within and from the creative activity of the spirit within man " [1].

Accordingly, the modern spirit is *laicized* in philosophy. It spontaneously repels, as interference, any intervention from

---

[1] J. MARITAIN, *Antimoderne*, Paris, 1922. Maritain calls these two matrix-ideas of the moderns the *immanentist* principle (independence from within as related to what is without), and the *transcendentalist* principle (one's own inner depths transcend all that is given).

faith. It is *naturalistic;* in order to find the final explanation of the universe, it turns itself towards the forces of nature, and to the resources of the thinking self. While it is deploying itself in this liberty, it falls invariably into pantheism or into atheism [1].

In a word, the modern spirit is wholly *rationalistic;* that is, it not only " has faith in reason, in the evidence of demonstration and belief in the efficacy of the natural light of reason ", but it also proclaims that " one need rely only on reason (in natural knowledge to the extent that it is opposed to revealed knowledge), and admit only those religious dogmas which it sees as logical and satisfactory by the natural power of reason " [2]. A spirit of this sort is the direct negation of Christian philosophy and of Scholasticism. Between faith and reason, it places the mutual aid of collaboration through mutual ignorance, blind rivalry and often open conflict. It is *anti-Catholic* in essence.

On the other hand, the modern philosophers taken individually are not necessarily atheist or irreligious. In fact, they can bring to light an aspect of the truth which will help us to understand philosophy better and to make it more explicit on certain points.

The role of Scholasticism, in the meantime, was not terminated. In the nineteenth and in the twentieth centuries, we are witness to a renaissance of this strong doctrine, especially of Thomism. It even appears that Neo-Thomism has taken for its main task, in the realm of human truths, the curing of the modern spirit from the double error which ruins it, and of reducing the secular misunderstanding expressed as opposition between science and philosophy. It is for this reason that this third period is entitled *modern* and *Neo-Thomistic.*

DIVISION. The exposition which follows is forced, by the nature of the case, to be that of modern thought. The origin and the developments of the various strains will be shown, and it will be pointed out how they generally lead to one or another form of pantheism. As a conclusion, the fact of the Thomistic Renaissance, and its speculative hopes will be noted.

Two men dominate the crowd of modern philosophers. The first is Descartes, who is an initiator, and the second is Kant,

---

[1] This will be shown to be the case with Spinoza, Hegel, A. Comte, Taine, the modernists and even Bergson.

[2] The above description of rationalism is taken from A. Lalande, *Vocabulaire technique de Philosophie,* " Rationalism ", sections " D " and " E ".

who marks the apogee of modern thought. This leads to the division of modern philosophy into two periods :

The First Period : The Cartesian Spirit (XVII-XVIII th centuries).

The Second Period : The Kantian Spirit (XIX-XX th centuries).

BIBLIOGRAPHY (on the modern period in general).

1º **Texts :** RAND, B., (ed.), *Modern Classical Philosophers*, 2nd ed., Boston, 1936. — ROBINSON, D. S., (ed.), *An Anthology of Recent Philosophy*, New York, 1929. — RUNES, D. D., (ed.), *Twentieth Century Philosophy. Living Schools of Thought*, New York, 1943. — SMITH, T. V., and GRENE, M., (eds.), *From Descartes to Kant*, Chicago, 1940.

2º **Studies :** CALVET, J., and LAMY, R., *Les philosophes du XVIIIᵉ siècle*, Paris, 1937. — COLLINS, J., *A History of Modern European Philosophy*, Milwaukee, 1954. — ETCHEVERRY, A., *L'idéalisme français contemporain*, Paris, 1934. — FALCKENBURG, R., *Geschichte der neueren Philosophie von Nikolaus von Cues bis zur Gegenwart*, 9th., rev., ed., Berlin, 1927. — FULLER, B. A. G., *A History of Modern Philosophy*, New York, 1938. — GILSON, E., *The Unity of Philosophical Experience*, New York, 1937. — HABERT, O., *Le Primat de l'Intelligence dans l'Histoire de la Pensée*, Paris, 1926. — HIRSCHBERGER, J., *Geschichte der Philosophie, II., Neuzeit und Gegenwart*, Freiburg (Br.), 1952. — HOFFDING, H., *A Brief History of Modern Philosophy*, New York, 1912. — *A History of Modern Philosophy*, New York, 1924. — HOENIGSWOLD, R., *Geschichte der Philosophie von der Renaissance bis Kant*, Berlin, 1923. — JOAD, C. E. M., *Introduction to Modern Philosophy*, Oxford, 1924. — JONES, W. T., *A History of Western Philosophy*, 2 vols., New York, 1952. — MARÉCHAL, J., *Précis d'Histoire de la Philosophie moderne, I, De la Renaissance à Kant*, rev. ed., Paris, 1951. — MARITAIN, J., *Antimoderne*, Paris, 1922. — *Theonas : Conversations of a Sage*, New York, 1933. — MAYER, F., *A History of Modern Philosophy*, Cincinnati, 1951. — MERCIER, D. J., *The Origins of Contemporary Psychology*, London, 1918. — MERZ, J. T., *A History of European Thought in the 19th Century*, 3 vols., London, 1896-1913. — MILLER, H., *An Historical Introduction to Modern Philosophy*, New York, 1947. — PALHORIES, J., *Vie et doctrine des grands philosophes*, vols. II and III, Paris, 1919. — PERRY, R. B., *Philosophy of the Recent Past*, New York, 1926. — RANDALL, J. H., *The Making of the Modern Mind*, rev. ed., Boston, 1940. — ROYCE, J., *The Spirit of Modern Philosophy*, Boston, 1892. — SASSEN, F., *Geschiedenis van de nieuwere Wijsbegeerte tot Kant.* — *Geschiedenis van de Wijsbegeerte der Negentiende Eeuw.*, 2 vols., Anvers-Nimègue, 1934. — SEROUYA, H., *Initiation à la philosophie contemporaine*, Paris, 1934. — SORTAIS, G., *La philosophie moderne depuis Bacon jusqu'à Leibnitz*, 3 vols., Paris, 1920-1929. — SOULIHE, J., *La philosophie chrétienne de Descartes à nos jours,*

2 vols., Paris, 1934. — STALLKNECHT, N. P. and BRUMBAUGH, R. S., *The Spirit of Western Philosophy*, New York, 1950. — THILLY, F., *A History of Philosophy*, rev. ed., New York, 1951. — UEBERWEG, J., *A History of Philosophy*, 2 vols., New York, 1903. — VERNEAU, R., *Les sources cartésiennes et kantiennes de l'idéalisme français*, Paris, 1936. — WAHL, J., *Tableau de la philosophie française*, Paris, 1946. — WALSHE, T. J., *The Quest of Reality*, London, 1933. — WILLEY, B. *The Seventeenth Century Background*, London, 1949. — *The Eighteenth Century Background*, London, 1949. — *Nineteenth Century Studies*, New York, 1949. — WRIGHT, W. K., *A History of Modern Philosophy*, New York, 1941. — WOLF, A., *A History of Science, Technology and Philosophy in the Sixteenth and Seventeenth Centuries*, New York, 1935. — *A History of Science, Technology and Philosophy in the Eighteenth Century*, New York, 1939.

THE FIRST PERIOD.

The Cartesian Spirit.

(17th-18th Centuries).

314. Modern thought rightfully acknowledges as its masters two men of unequal value : Francis Bacon, who restored to them the taste for experience; René Descartes, who renewed the metaphysical spirit, though impregnating it with mathematics. Descartes, especially, was the *initiator* of modern philosophy; with his bold method he initiated the era of critical philosophy; the newness of his doctrines swept away the traditional teaching of Scholasticism. All the philosophers of the seventeenth and of the eighteenth centuries were subject, in various ways, to his influence. Though not always faithful disciples of his and even posing as adversaries, they lived from his spirit [1]; their various systems, although quite diverse, are but the development of the Cartesian innovations.

At first, following the logic of the rationalist principle, Cartesianism evolved towards *pantheism;* after becoming the doctrine of Occasionalism with Malebranche, Cartesianism concluded with the pantheism of Spinoza (at the close of the seventeenth century).

It is true that other thinkers (towards the close of the seventeenth, and especially in the eighteenth century) openly contradicted more than one fundamental principle of Descartes. In Germany, Leibniz abandons the mechanist explanation for dynamism. In England, the honorable position accorded to empiricism wins out victoriously over the theory of innate ideas. But the depth of inspiration and especially the method of these doctrines remain Cartesian. Thus the urge initiated by Descartes, travelling into the eighteenth century, enters into *reaction* with these other influences and systems which it has engendered; it climaxes in the nineteenth century, with the great critical effort of Kant, whose figure dominates the whole modern epoch.

---

[1] There is no exception but for Jean-Jacques Rousseau; Locke himself, the master of the seventeenth century, places his own effort in the Cartesian lineage; see below, n. 372-3.

[2] See above, n. 313.

Three chapters will cover this period :

Chapter I. The Masters : Francis Bacon and René Descartes.

Chapter II. Towards Pantheism : Spinoza.

Chapter III. Reaction and Transition (xviiith century).

CHAPTER ONE.

THE MASTERS OF MODERN THOUGHT.

I. Francis Bacon (1561-1626).

SPECIAL BIBLIOGRAPHY.

1º **Works :** Spedding, Ellis and Heath (eds.), *The Works of Francis Bacon*, 15 vols., Boston, 1864.

2º **Studies :** ANDERSON, F. H., *The Philosophy of Francis Bacon*, Chicago, 1948. — BROAD, C. D., *The Philosophy of Francis Bacon*, Cambridge, 1926. — BROCHARD, J., *La Philosophie de Bacon*, Paris, 1926. — DE MAISTRE, J., *Examen de la philosophie de Bacon*, Paris, 1836. — FARRINGTON, B., *Francis Bacon : Philosopher of Industrial Science*, London, 1951. — FISCHER, K. F., *Bacon von Verulam*, Leipzig, 1856. — FONSEGRIVE, G., *F. Bacon*, Paris, 1893. — FROST, W., *Bacon und die Naturphilosophie*, Munich, 1927. — GIBSON, R. W., *Francis Bacon*, Oxford, 1950. — GREEN, A. W., *Sir Francis Bacon, His Life and Works*, Denver (Colo.), 1952. — LEVI, A., *Il pensiero di F. Bacone*, Turin, 1925. — NICHOL, J., *F. Bacon, his life and philosophy*, 2 vols., London, 1888-1889. — SPEDDING, J., *Account of life and times of F. Bacon*, 2 vols., London, 1879.

315. Born in London on the 22nd of January, 1561, Francis Bacon made his studies at the University of Cambridge, where he became initiated into Scholasticism, becoming sorely perplexed by its defects. He soon conceived of a radical renewal of all the sciences, as his first work, *Temporis partus maximus* [1], indicates; he reports that this work was written about 1585. His ambition did not remain purely scientific. He studied law, was admitted to the bar in 1587 and canvassed for political honors. During the reign of Elizabeth he was named to her Learned Counsel, but could rise no higher, despite his election as a member of Parliament

---

[1] This work is not possessed in its original form, but seems identical with the posthumous work entitled *Temporis partus masculus sive de interpretatione naturæ*.

in 1593 and the protection of the Earl of Essex [1]. But under the reign of James I (1603-25) he obtained great honors. He was named Solicitor General in 1607, Attorney General in 1613, Lord Keeper of the Great Seal in 1617 and Lord Chancellor in 1618. He was made Baron of Verlaum and Viscount of St. Albans in 1621. He was a zealous defender of the interests of the Crown, without forgetting his own interest. Accused of misappropriation of funds by Parliament, he admitted his guilt and was sentenced to pay a fine of 40,000 pounds and was declared disqualified from holding any political office at all (May, 1621). The rest of his days were spent in his intellectual interests.

Throughout the vicissitudes of his political life, Bacon never forgot his great project of a scientific renewal. He conceived a plan for a great work which he called *Instauratio Magna*. It was to consist of six parts : " Beginning with the actual status of science, with all its omissions (i), Bacon aimed, first, to study the new organon to take the place of Aristotle's (ii); to describe the investigation of facts (iii); to go one to the study of laws (iv); and to descend to the actions which these items of knowledge permit us to utilize on nature (v-vi) " [2]. After having undertaken his task, he admitted that he was unable, alone, to complete this immense project; he completed only the first two parts. In 1605, he published the work, *Of the Proficience and Advancement of Learning*, which was translated into Latin and later developed, becoming *De dignitate et augmentis scientiarum*, in nine books (1623). Then he wrote his *Novum Organum, sive indicia vera de interpretatione naturæ* (1620), in which he proposed inductive logic as replacement for the logic of Aristotle and the Scholastics. He gathered materials for the other parts, and wrote some smaller works, as *De sapientia veterum*, *Historia naturalis et experimentalis ad condendam philosophiam* (1622), *Historia ventorum* (1622); *Historia vitæ et mortis* (1623); *Topica inquisitionis de luce et lumine* (1653); *Historia densi et rari* (1658); *Inquisitio de magnete* (1658), and others. Mention should be made of the *New Atlantis*, published in 1627, in which he decribes the ideal city in which each man could work towards the restoration of the sciences. Finally, he wrote a number of *Essays*, on moral and political matters (1597), and other works on history and on law.

Bacon was an *initiator*, or, as he called himself, the " trumpeteer " of the new science which he saw germinating from the ruins of Scholasticism and whose excellence he could not stop praising. " For an initiator, he has the fire and the strong imagination which underscores his statements with unforgettable traits; but he also has the spirit of organization, the almost meddlesome prudence and the desire of an administrator, in his work, of distributing to each (the observer,

---

[1] When the Earl of Essex was disgraced, Bacon felt himself obliged, in order to curry the favor of the court, to be the main accuser of his benefactor.

[2] E. Bréhier, *Histoire de la philosophie*, ii, p. 21.

the experimenter, the discoverer of laws) a limited and precise task " [1]. It is for these reasons that the center of Bacon's thought is constituted by the new logic which modern philosophy was to use in order to attain the true science. This is his most original contribution, the only part of his thought explicitly developed; from it there flow, as corollaries, his other doctrines concerning psychology, nature and God. These matters will be treated in two paragraphs :

I. The New Logic.

II. Doctrinal Corollaries.

I. The New Logic.

315[bis]. Logic implies science; the *Novum Organum* was written as a function of the modern, positive science which Bacon envisioned. It is in the light of this notion of logic that he estimates the ancient philosophers, and proposes a general classification of knowledge [2].

A) Positive Science.

The great, modern idea of physico-mathematical science, with majestic theories built up in full independence of philosophy, did not unfold itself at the beginning in perfect clarity. As all intellectual accomplishments, it was the fruit of long collaboration, and was actually constructed before the philosophers had a definitive notion of its contours. Bacon himself did not define it, but in announcing and prophesying its triumphs, he indicated a few of its essential traits.

At first, the new science was to be a *science of the concrete*. Every Scholastic, faithful to the Socratic adage so well explained by Aristotle, had held that there is no science of concrete and singular things [3]. The first condition for establishing a demonstration was to elevate oneself to universal and abstract notions; the sciences of nature, as the Peripatetic of the Middle Ages looked upon them, were no exception to this rule. Bacon raised his voice vehemently against this conception. He looked upon these views as a vast accumulation of sophisms and hollow verbiage. He reproached Aristotle ceaselessly with having put the force of real things into ten categories which were but empty abstractions and of having reduced the riches of nature to the two inert limits of matter and form [4]. He opposed the Socratic adage with his own, " There is no true science but of the concrete ". That which is

---

[1] E. BRÉHIER, *ibid.*, p. 23.

[2] Bacon opens his *Instauratio Magna* with a vast classification of learning; the meaning and value of this classification will be more clear after his method has been explained.

[3] See above, n. 30; *Non est scientia de singularibus*.

[4] *De augmentis scientiarum*, Book III, Ch. V, and Book IV, Ch. III.

to be studied is reality, by which he meant experiential facts, and observable phenomena. Accordingly, the first part of learning was to be constituted by *history*.

The new science which has come down " not from heaven, but from the clouds above the earth " [1] loses the trait of meaningless wordiness which the ancient science had. It is to be a *science of inventions*, not of speculation. Bacon is the avowed enemy of contemplation and of disinterested study. He reproaches the ancients with having founded parties through which they imprisoned and sterilized truth. The new science was not to be a sect of this sort; its unique aim was " to enrich human life with new inventions and new riches " [2]. The savant most certainly does not pursue his egoistic goal to be personally enriched; he is concerned with mankind at large, and wishes to find the means of living the longest time possible on earth, and of finding the maximum of pleasure with the minimum of pain.

This ideal was truly new [3], but a bit vague and general. When Bacon added precision to his plan, he turned resolutely towards nature and its immense resources, which he wished to appropriate. Thus arises the third trait of the new science : it is the *science of the laws of nature*. Some of the ancients, the first inventors and the alchemists, had suspected this richness and had begun to exploit it. Bacon approves and admires them; but instead of proceeding by chance, as they did, he looked for a universal art of making discoveries [4]. The infallible method of finding this art is to penetrate methodically into the laws of nature in order to apply them to human profit. " One does not triumph over nature except by obeying it " [5].

This, then, is Bacon's conception : an experimental science, capable of fruitful applications, which makes the laws of nature better known. It was a truly penetrating and prophetic view of what is called " positive science ". But this description lacks the final, important trait of recourse to mathematics in order to establish and coordinate the laws of nature. Bacon completely misunderstood this point, and protested against the haughtiness of the mathematicians who wanted their science to command physics to play the role of a servant [6]. Despite his desire of escaping from the yoke of Aristotle, he was faithful to the current conception which considered natural phenomena as *corporeal qualities*.

B) Inductive Logic.

Aristotle's *Organon* [7], containing his logical treatises, was useless for this new science. Bacon reproached the logic of the syllogism

---

[1] J. BROCHARD, *Études de philosophie ancienne et médiévale*, " La Philosophie de Bacon ", p. 306.

[2] *Novum organum*, I, 82.

[3] Bacon was enamored of this originality of his; see the dedicatory letter of *Novum organum*.

[4] *De augmentis scientiarum*, V, Ch. II.

[5] *Novum organum*, I, 129.

[6] *De augmentis scientiarum*, III, Ch. VI.

[7] See above, nn. 71-3.

for its powerlessness in discovering true principles of things and in holding back the advance of the sciences. " Those who make use of it are content with common, insufficient experiences. Thus the fundamental notions are confused and extracted from things by chance... There is no hope in true induction " [1]. This explains the title of his work, the " new instrument ".

Before laying down positive rules, Bacon enumerates the causes of error which must be avoided; he calls them *idols*, or imaginary representations and phantoms, which deceive man. There are the illusions based on human nature and the makeup of the human spirit *(idols of the tribe)* : thus, man's spirit, being endowed with a homogeneous nature, always looks for the simplest answer, as Kepler imagined that the stars wrote perfect geometrical figures [2], forgetting the complexity of nature. — The second class are those which are proper to each individual, and are comparable to Plato's cave *(idols of the cave)* : Aristotle, for example, reduced all of philosophy to logic, and Gilbert tried to reduce it to magnetic attractions [3]. — The third type are those which are proper to current language *(idols of the market place)* : these seduce us, for instance, by making us believe in that which does not exist, as the ancients believed in the celestial spheres. — Finally, there are the systems of philosophers, which, in their turn, recite their doctrines as a theatrical play *(idols of the theater)* : the exaggerated respect of the masters and of the schools prevents us from seeing the facts.

Faced with all these causes of error, Bacon maintains that one must adopt an attitude of methodic doubt at the beginning of each problem before interrogating nature and awaiting its response. This is the positive aspect of the experimental method, in which several phases are distinguishable.

The first phase is constituted by " literate experience "; this is written experience, so called because one must mistrust one's memory and note in writing the facts and the circumstances which are observed. There is question here of *observation* as cumulating a large number of facts as materials for future induction. Bacon is not aiming to give the conditions of good observation, but is merely interested in avoiding the " idols ", which will guarantee freedom from error. What he asks for is that one explore nature in every way, lifting oneself to the " pursuit of Pan ", guided by a sort of scientific flair [4].

To remedy the weakness of the senses and to collect as many facts as possible, he included, under the term " experimentation ", eight sorts of means or observational procedures. Experience must be varied *(variation)*, for example, in grafting forest trees as one does fruit trees, or observing how the attraction of rubbed amber varies if heated, or by varying the amount of substance involved in an experiment. Experiences must be renewed

---

[1] *Novum organum*, I, 12, 13, 14.

[2] *Novum organum*, I, 45.

[3] *Ibid.*, I, 54. It is useless to answer the injustice of his reproaches against Aristotle. Gilbert was a celebrated chemist, a contemporary of Bacon.

[4] " Experience, which is more powerful than wisdom, and a sort of hunting odor "; *De dignitate scientiarum*, v, Ch. II.

(repetition), as re-distilling wine-spirits after a first distillation. Experience must be extended *(extension)* ; as one can, with certain precautions, keep water separated from wine in the same container, and see if one can also separate the heavy from the light particles of wine. To transfer from nature to art *(transference)*, as one can artificially produce a rainbow in falling water. One should inverse experience *(inversion)* ; for instance, having determined that heat is propagated in a rising motion, see if cold is propagated in a falling motion. Experiences should be suppressed *(compulsion)* ; one can determine if certain types of bodies will suppress the attraction between a magnet and iron if they are put between the latter. Experiences should be used to discover some useful property *(application)*, for instance, the salubrity of air in various places or in various seasons can be determined by the speed of putrefaction. Finally, many experiences should be unified *(copulation)*, as Drebbel, in 1620, lowered the freezing point of water by mixing it with glass and with saltpeter. There remain but the hazards of experience *(chance)*, which consist in a slight change of conditions; for example, by producing combustion in a closed vessel, though it ordinarily takes place in the free air [1].

By the above method, one can set up a veritable " forest " of facts, as Bacon's work, *Sylva Sylvarum* exemplifies. In order to interpret and discover the laws of nature, one applies the *method of the three tables*. This consists in choosing a particular phenomenon, for example, that of heat. In the first table, one writes all the observed facts in which the phenomenon has taken place, taking the most diverse subjects possible : this is the *table of presence*. In the second, or *table of absence*, one notes all the facts most similar to the preceding, but in which the phenomenon has not occurred. In the third, the *table of differences*, one writes all facts equally similar in which the phenomenon has varied. Induction properly called, from which the discovery of laws arises, results from the simple inspection of these tables.

The originality of Bacon does not lie in taking account of favorable facts alone, but in attaching great importance to the exceptions in the tables of absence; this method allows one to retrace the field in which the phenomenon occurred and to grasp its essential conditions. " Take for example the determination of the definition of heat. Bacon notes fifty-seven cases in which heat is produced; thirty-two, analogous to the first, in which heat is not produced (for example, to the case of the sun heating the earth as an instance of presence, he opposes the sun not melting the eternal snows, as an instance of absence), and forty-one cases in which it varies. After elimination, the residue which remains is the movement of vibration whose effect can be seen in the flame or in boiling water; it is defined by Bacon as an expansive movement, directed from below on high, not affecting the whole body but its smallest parts and then repelled in a way so that it becomes alternative and expansive " [2].

---

[1] *De Augmentis*, v, Ch. ii, 8-14; see also E. Bréhier, *op. cit.*, ii, p. 35.
[2] E. Bréhier, *ibid.*, p. 37.

Nevertheless, despite the number of cases envisaged, we are but at the beginning of induction. The definition obtained is but a first vintage or provisory notion which must be made precise by further experiences. When does one know whether he has eliminated all the unfavorable cases in order to attain a definitive result? This occurs when one makes use of the most powerful aids, which are nine in number : the prerogatives of instances, the support of induction, the rectification of induction, the variety of researches, the examples taken in nature, the direction of research, regular deduction, the models of research, and the ascending and descending scale of axioms. But the English philosopher realized that such a vast program was impossible for one man. In his *New Atlantis* he portrays as an ideal a utopian city of savants; he himself was content with developing the prerogatives of instances. He did this with his customary sumptuosity, enumerating twenty-seven classes of instances or privileged facts. For instance, the " solitary instances " in which the nature sought for manifests itself outside of habitual circumstances, as the production of colors by light traversing a prism; or the " migrant instances ", in which nature is suddenly manifest, as the whiteness in water which foams; or the " ostensive and clandestine instances ", in which nature is at a maximum or minimum; or the " instances of divorcement, " in which two ordinarily united facts are separated; or the celebrated *crucial facts*, in which the spirit finds itself like a voyager at the crossroads, obliged to admit or reject an hypothesis. If, for example, one asks if the tides are caused by transferring the whole liquid mass from one shore to another, crucial experience will be the observed fact that tides occur at the same time on both sides of the ocean.

The day when all thinkers, through mutual aid, will put these multiple procedures into practice by applying them to nature as a whole, will constitute the day on which the only true human science is born; all others are but parts or dependencies of this science.

C) Classification of Sciences.

The *De augmentis scientiarum* contains a general classification of these sciences. Three great groups, based on the three principal faculties in man, are distinguished. HISTORY, which is related to memory; POETRY, related to imagination; SCIENCE, to reason. In Bacon's view, according to which science has concrete reality for its object, history naturally has a choice place. It is subdivided into natural history, showing forth the order of events of nature [1], and into civil history, doing the same job for human life. One is surprised, though, to find *poetry* classed so highly. But by it Bacon understands the ancient fables, which he examines in his *De sapientia veterum* [2], in which he finds scientific truths under

---

[1] Bacon has left several models of this notion of history : the *Historia ventorum*, the *Historia vitæ et mortis*, and so on.

[2] These studies were highly favored in the " Literary Renaissance ", to which Bacon was greatly attached by his own encyclopedic, literary and anti-Scholastic taste.

the form of enigmas [1]. " Basically, these three sciences, history, poetry and philosophy, are but three successive stages of the spirit in the formation of the sciences : history is concerned with accumulating materials; poetry is to write them down at first chimerically, as a sort of dream of science, in which stage the ancients remained; finally, philosophy is the solid construction of reason " [2].

This latter stage, philosophy, is the most important. Bacon subdivided it into the ancient categories, but by transforming their meaning. He at first distinguishes three large sections : the science of God, or theology; the science of nature, or physics; the science of man. The first is not further subdivided. Physics is divided into theoretical and into operative. Theoretical physics aims to discover the four causes indicated by Aristotle, the material and efficient causes being the objects of special physics, the final and formal causes being the object of metaphysics [3]. Operative physics contains the mechanical arts and natural magic; the latter, abandoning the complicated results of empirical magic, will realize even more wonderful transformations through the use of scientific laws. Mathematics is but an appendix to physics [4], its role being to furnish an instrument for making experience precise through its measures and calculations.

The science of man has two main branches : a) the science of the individual man, or the " philosophy of humanity ", which considers man in his body, as in medicine; or it considers man in his soul, speculatively treating the laws of the spirit (logic) and the rules of the will (ethics); or it considers man as a composite, in the study of the passions, physiology, and interpretation of dreams; b) the science of human society, or " civil philosophy ", which teaches the art of social relations, of business and of government.

Bacon himself did not realize this encyclopedic task. He specialized in logic and in the study of the methods necessary for obtaining the new science, of which he was the herald. His other doctrines are but corollaries of the above view.

II. Doctrinal Corollaries.

316. It should be mentioned that Bacon did not consider the perennial problems of philosophy as the great founders of systems had done. His doctrines on God, on man and on the world are but sketches or fragmentary treatises. But the great vision of the positive sciences which enchanted him impressed on his ideas a tendency towards the very theories which will be developed in the nineteenth century, especially in England. In psychology, he tends to empiricism; in natural philosophy, towards positivism; in theodicy, towards agnosticism; in ethics, towards utilitarianism.

---

[1] For example, the fable of Cupid signifies the action of atoms on each other.

[2] E. BRÉHIER, op. cit., II, p. 31.

[3] This metaphysics is vastly different from that of Aristotle; see below, the theory of forms, with which metaphysics is concerned in Bacon's view.

[4] " It should be placed in the appendices rather than among the substantial sciences "; De Dignitate scientiarum, explanation of table at beginning.

A) **Knowledge. Tendency towards Empiricism** [1].

Aristotle's logic of the syllogism was but a consequence of his fundamental theory of abstraction [2]. The *Novum Organum* of Bacon could not be inclined towards anything but empiricism or sensualism. Properly speaking, Bacon does not consider the problem of knowledge. The doctrine current at his time, which he learned at Cambridge, admitted a spiritual intelligence, distinct from sense, the faculty of an immortal soul created by God. He did not dream of doubting this teaching. He even insists on numerous errors due to sense, and is far from thinking with Condillac [3] that our ideas are but transformed sensation. Bacon wished that reason and sense be allies and control each other mutually for the conquest of truth.

But it is true that in Bacon's view the concrete fact of experience alone is the sole object of science. It is seizable in reality only by sensation and not directly by our abstractive reason. " Summarily, it seems that the function of reason in Bacon's conception is to compare, under the supreme rule of the principle of contradiction, the various data of sense and to correct them until they are in accord with experience. The senses are judges of experience; that is, observation is the court of final appeal " [4]. This betrays a marked tendency towards *empiricism*, in which view sensation and experience are the unique source of human knowledge.

It should be noted that this empiricism has nothing idealistic about it, as does that of Locke and the English philosophers of the eighteenth century [5]; it is openly *realist*. Bacon, like Aristotle and the Scholastic masters, admits that the senses, once separated from the fallacious " idols ", grasp reality as it is, and he considers physics as the most excellent science.

B) **The Forms. Tendency towards Positivism.**

Bacon's view on nature serves as a transition from the Scholastic to the modern attitude. He assigned the discovery of *forms* as the object of physics, and thus leaned towards the Aristotelian theory of substantial forms. He believed that each body has its own makeup (specific form) joined to a certain number of observable and useful qualities. But nature possesses a multitude of these, mingled in an inextricable complexity. The scientific problem consists in isolating these forms, in order to learn the law of their composition. The application of this law would permit the introduction of the properties of any body into any other; one could, as the alchemists wished, transform everything into gold; or, if judged more useful, into some other material.

---

[1] On the import of these terms, see below, n. 356, 2.
[2] See above, n. 71.
[3] See below, n. 379.
[4] J. BROCHARD, *op. cit.*, p. 310.
[5] This idealism is due to the Cartesian theory of the " clear idea "; see below, n. 356.

Bacon's attitude to hylomorphism is thus superficial, and contains irreducible divergences. *Form* does not designate for him a profound, substantial reality, capable of being known by an abstract concept and as the necessary source of properties deducible from the definition through the demonstrative syllogism. It is rather the thing itself; and this real thing is the concrete, observable, sensible phenomenon. This real form arises as the residue of inductions, somewhat as a chemical body rests at the bottom of a retort after multiple filtering.

Moreover, this residuous phenomenon which is the *form* of things is identified, by Bacon, with a certain organization of matter, which he calls " latent schematism " [1]. Only when it has been discovered, can a true definition be given which is no longer descriptive, but essential, indicating its true specific differences. One then has the constitutive *law* enabling him to use the form at will. Bacon, calling nature in its entirety, as Aristotle called God, " pure actuality ", defines the form as " the law of pure actuality " [2].

But it is difficult to wrest these secrets from nature. Its multiple combinations are realized before our very eyes, but through *latent processes*, which screen reality in a partial way. These processes are the *efficient causes*, with which we must be content, provisorily, and which are the object of operative or special physics. In the meantime, as inductions increase, one can hope to attain the schematisms themselves; to the very *forms* which are the objects themselves. This is the object of metaphysics.

Certainly a doctrine of this type is not pure positivism, according to which doctrine everything is relative and which, by defining law as a constant relation between two phenomena, assigns for the object of science the research into efficient causes alone. Bacon gives credence to absolute natures and wished to find them by his method; by staying in the study of pure observable phenomena, however, he made himself incapable of discovering them and shut himself up within the confines of positivism. One is struck, here, in Bacon's spirit, with the presentiment of a science of pure phenomena as contrasted with the ancient ideal of a science penetrating the very nature of things themselves. Bacon looked for a solution by conceiving of the form as a scheme, a law accessible to induction. The positivists, made docile by the progress of the sciences, resolve the same difficulty by excluding absolute natures from the realm of reason, and Bacon himself tends in this direction.

It should be added that the constitutive law to which induction points is a *mechanical state* of the elements of nature. This is evident in all the examples he has given; thus, heat is defined by a movement of expansion upwards; the form of whiteness consists in " a mixture of two transparent bodies with a certain simple and uniform disposition of their optical parts " [3]. These laws seem to be susceptible of precise measurement and of being stated

---

[1] " Latens schematismus ", *Novum Organum*, ii, Ch. vii.
[2] *Novum Organum*, ii, aphorism 17.
[3] *De augmentis scientiarum*, iii, Ch. iv, § 11; see E. Bréhier, *op. cit.*, p. 38.

in mathematical formulas, as is done in modern science. Bacon, quite precisely, calls them axioms; and, having assigned meta-physics the task of finding " middle " axioms close to the facts, he speaks of a " first philosophy " which works on these first formulas. From them, and aided by induction, one draws out other more general axioms, until one arrives at an ascending and descending ladder of axioms, the summation of knowledge. This vision of the world, especially in the case of mathematical laws, is analogous to the positivist construction of Taine [1], in which everything flows from an eternal axiom.

Bacon did not see this possible outcome of his doctrine. He held to the qualitative conception of natural phenomena, and even enriched nature with a certain " appetite " as the source of its activities, similar to Aristotle's view. If the constitutive laws are of the mechanical order, it is an unforeseen result of his inductions. His mechanism is not, like that of Descartes and of Hobbes, a reflected system, based on basic principles. There is, however, a remarkable coincidence which accentuates the tendency towards positivism.

C) God. Agnostic Tendency.

Bacon assigned to metaphysics the task of seeking *final causes* as well as formal causes, because, in his view, nature was made for man [2]. At the same time, he absolutely proscribed, due to their anthropomorphic character, or to their sterility [3], the use of final causes in induction and in seeking for laws. The role of final causes is to lead us to God; the coincidence between the deployment of efficient causes in nature and the usefulness of final causes cannot be explained except through a supreme, coordinating Intelligence, God [4].

Bacon is not an agnostic. He proves the existence of God, and holds that God's principal attributes, as His Power, Wisdom, Goodness and Providence can be established by a consideration of His works [5]. He does not, however, give the same validity to this proof as he does to scientific inductions. Theology is more a spark of science than a science properly called [6]. This obtains because God appears to Bacon as an hypothesis explicative of the unity and order of the world; an hypothesis is not fully certain unless it can be translated into facts and be experienced repeatedly which is not possible for God. The spirit, Bacon says, " glides '

---

[1] See below, n. 492. It should be noted that Taine, as all positivists, grant a role to deduction, while Bacon holds only to induction.

[2] *De sapientia veterum*, Ch. xxvi.

[3] *De augmentis scientiarum*, iii, Ch. v. Bacon here compares final causes to virgins consecrated to God but not bearing fruit.

[4] *Ibid.*, iii, Ch. iv. If Bacon commends Democritus and Epicurus for their mechanism, he also adds that their atheism has aroused a cry of universal derision.

[5] *De augmentis scientiarum*, iii, Ch. ii. Bacon outlines a plan for theology, but did not carry it out.

[6] *Ibid*; see G. FONSEGRIVE, *François Bacon*, p. 238.

into the affirmation of God, more than demonstrating it [1]. This is a strong tendency towards agnosticism.

Bacon turned to revelation in order to resolve the problem of God more fully, as he did on the problem of the spirituality and immortality of the soul. In this way, he but continued the view of decadent Scholasticism, which was imbued with nominalism; he likewise reserved to supernatural theology a great portion of metaphysics.

D) Ethics. Tendency towards Utilitarianism.

In the ancient view, ethics was concerned with indicating man's supreme good and with pointing out the means of attaining it. Bacon keeps this basic notion. The first part, in which reason determines the goal of life, is called the *doctrine of the model;* the second, which shows how man should submit his passions and will to reason, is called the *georgic of the soul.* These ancient conceptions are animated by a new spirit in Bacon's work, however, and we find here again a transition from the Scholastic view, considering the glory of God as the supreme rule of the good, to a modern empiricist view, considering human utility as the norm of virtue.

In order to discover the goal of life, one must use the natural light of reason, which " shines in the soul as a natural instinct and as a reflection of God " [2]. At the same time, revelation must be asked for a complete idea of human destiny. In the meantime, it is possible to use the resources of induction and of psychology towards establishing a corps of precepts forming a philosophical ethics.

It is easy to admit that the good, the goal of man's life, is twofold, being either the happiness of the individual or the happiness of all. Natural instinct does not make precise which should be chosen, but induction teaches us that a more general law is always preferable to special laws. In stepping up the ladder of axioms, the most universal are also the most fruitful in inventiveness and in good things for all. Thus, *the good of humanity* [3] is the end of human life. As a consequence, Bacon explicitly disavows any individual utilitarianism [4]. However, it is no longer God who governs moral life, but social and human utility. Virtue has the same goal as the new science : to procure for man the most happiness possible by aiding him to conquer the empire of nature. If, as a believer, he admits eternal life as the final goal, he reverts to the pagan ideal as a philosopher. He analyzes an ethics for this life, in which he announces as possible and proximate, a golden age, made possible by the progress of the sciences.

The means for attaining this goal are found in the resources of our psychological life, which is to be submitted to the direction

---

[1] *De augmentis scientiarum*, IV, Ch. III.

[2] *Ibid.*, IX, Ch. I.

[3] By aid of these principles, Bacon rejects the ethics of the Stoics, as that of Epicurus, as too concerned with the individual. He also condemns the contemplative life, for only the active life is useful for society.

[4] *De augmentis scientiarum*, VII, Ch. VII.

of reason. There are two principal sources of action in man : *character*, which is innate, natural and relatively stable, and *passion*, which is variable and changeful. When, through the inductive method, one has constituted the double science of character and of passions, one has the means of perfecting oneself and of working for the good of others.

Until such a time, however, our moral weakness is to be remedied by the acquisition of the habits [1] directed towards the common good. These habits are the virtues, which elevate us to practice the highest virtue, *charity*, envisioned not as the love of God, but as the love of mankind, for whose happiness we should devote our lives. This aim is the one goal necessary, and Bacon gives many means for attaining it. He recommends, for example, the pursuit of office and of honors, even by employing ruse and trickery, for one can do more good to men if one has authority [2]. Briefly, " that is good which is useful to humanity "; thus his ethics, while reprobating personal egoism, tends towards utilitarianism.

CONCLUSION. **316**[bis]. Francis Bacon left no complete system; his doctrines on God, on the soul, and on the world do not stand out in relief sufficiently to impose themselves for consideration. Nor did their unfortunate tendencies strike his contemporaries, in whose eyes the philosopher-Chancellor remained an open, spiritualistic thinker. If these tendencies have been underlined and made somewhat explicit here, it was but to show in this herald of modern science the origin and semination of a philosophy which will later proclaim itself as the " servant of science ". But this *positivism* was not perceived in the seventeenth century.

It is not so much as a savant that Bacon has an important place in history. The examples of induction which he left " do not always do honor to him, and each case was outdated in his own age, which witnessed the inductive-deductive method of Galileo that was more sober, more exact and more fruitful. The English Chancellor did not suspect, perhaps, the wisdom of his own appreciation of his role in science : ' I am but a herald, and do not enter the fight ' " [3]. Though he made no discoveries, he knew how to encourage them. His own work caused a great stir, and made the atmosphere favorable to discovery by pointing out the right scientific method.

This is the true glory of Bacon. He was the first *theorist* of the inductive method of the positive sciences. His merit

---

[1] Bacon insists on the influence of " habits " and gives useful counsel for acquiring them.

[2] *De augmentis scientiarum*, VIII, Ch. II.

[3] J. MARÉCHAL, *Précis d'histoire de philosophie moderne*, p. 227.

was to grasp and to synthesize one of the aspects of the modern
spirit in his work : the love of experience, or the desire to study
nature for itself and for usefulness, rather than for discovering
metaphysical truths. He proclaimed the legitimacy of such
a goal, and was the first to present the rules of scientific induction
with precision and a luxury of remarkable details. John Stuart
Mill, in his famous *Logic* [1], while imposing a more measured
outlook and more clarity on Bacon's exuberance, keeps the
same spirit, and shows its value and efficacy for discovering
scientific laws.

It would be an exaggeration, however, to think, as some
say, that Bacon was the *inventor* of induction. Others employed
it, as Galileo, and quite successfully, before the composition
of the *Novum Organum*. Furthermore, his originality in this
regard concerned but one form of induction, the form which
has here been termed scientific induction properly so called,
and which is the basis of experimental science. If one takes
induction in a general sense as " reasoning destined to establish
a universal truth [2] through the interpretation of the facts of
experience ", the theory of this induction, as was shown above,
was given by Aristotle and adopted by the school of St. Albert
and St. Thomas [3]. These philosophers not only based their
" science " on the constant use of induction, but, aided by
their doctrine of abstraction, they justified its validity much
better than Bacon, who merely gave a detailed exposition of
its method.

A more profound view of Thomism permits one to complete
the inductive method by the legitimate use of the syllogism.
The criticism of the latter, given by Bacon, holds perhaps for
the nominalistic Scholastics of the decadent period. For the
latter, logic was often but a dispute of words. Bacon's criticism
does not touch the usage which Aristotle and his great disciples
made of the syllogism, which remains indispensable for arriving
at the perfection of a scientific system [4].

While Bacon was the first theorist of scientific induction, his
contemporary, Galileo, applied it with such success that his name
deserves mention here.

---

[1] See below, n. 486.
[2] Bacon calls this an " axiom ".
[3] See above, n. 72, n. 234 and n. 263.
[4] See above, n. 264. In modern science, the Aristotelian syllogism is replaced
by mathematical deduction; but the latter completes Bacon's view of induction
in the same way.

GALILEO GALILEI [1] (1564-1642) was prepared for his rejection of Aristotle's physical theories by his humanistic education. He defended the Copernican system of astronomy. His main works are : *Il Saggiatore* (1623); *Dialogo sopra i due massimi sistemi del mondo* (1632), which was followed much later by *Discorsi e dimostrazioni matematichi* (1638), and occasioned the famous trial in which he was condemned by the Holy Office (1633) [2].

From the philosophical point of view, Galileo prepared for the universal mechanism which Descartes later defended. He did not teach it, " but was led there by creating a physico-mathematical science of nature, capable of predicting phenomena. He does not state what things are, but he shows, by proof, that the triangles, circles and other geometrical figures of mathematics are the only language capable of reading the book of nature " [3]. With a master genius, he applied the inductive method as it will be defined later by John Stuart Mill.

Bacon and Galileo, the first as a theorist, the second as practitioner, inaugurated the triumphal march of modern science which rose to attack Aristotelianism in order to replace its explanation of the physical world. At the same time, Descartes personified another aspect of the modern spirit, more profound and philosophical : he esteemed mathematics so highly that he wished it to replace metaphysics in the scientific interpretation of the world. This is what makes Descartes the principal initiator of modern philosophy.

II. RENÉ DESCARTES (1596-1650).

SPECIAL BIBLIOGRAPHY.

1° **Works :** *Œuvres de Descartes*, ADAM and TANNERY (eds.), 12 vols., Paris, 1897-1910 and Supplement, vol. 13, Paris, 1913. — *Correspondance de Descartes*, ADAM and MILHAUD (eds.), 5 vols. completed, 1936 ff. — *The Philosophical Works of Descartes*, HALDANE and ROSS, 2 vols., Cambridge, 1931.

2° **Studies :** ADAM, C., *Descartes, sa vie et son œuvre*, Paris, 1937. — BALZ, A. G., *Cartesian Studies*, New York, 1951. — *Descartes and the Modern Mind*, New Haven (Conn.) 1952. — BECK, L. J., *The Method of Descartes*, Oxford, 1952. — BOUILLIER, F., *Histoire de la Philosophie cartésienne*, 2 vols., 3rd ed., Paris, 1868. — BRUNSCHWICG, L., *Descartes et Pascal*, Newchatel, 1945. — CASSIRER, E., *Descartes*, New York, 1941. — CHEVALIER, J., *Descartes*, 17th ed., Paris, 1937. — ESPINAS, A., *Descartes et la*

---

[1] *Le Opere di Galileo Galilei*, 20 vols., Florence, 1890-1909. — ALIOTTA, A., and Carbonara, C., *Galilei*, Milan, 1949. — CARRA DE VAUX, *Galilée*, Paris, 1908. — FAVARO, A., *Galileo Galilei*, Modena, 1910. — *Nel terzo centenario della morte di Galileo Galilei*, Milan, 1942. — TAYLOR, F. S., *Galileo and the Freedom of Thought*, London, 1938.

[2] This episode is more properly treated in the history of science and in apologetics, rather than in philosophy. See F. S. TAYLOR, *Galileo and the Freedom of Thought, passim.*

[3] E. BRÉHIER, *op. cit.*, II, p. 11.

morale, 2 vols., Paris, 1925. — GARIN, P., *Thèses cartésiennes et thèses thomistes*, Paris, 1933. — GIBSON, A. B., *The Philosophy of Descartes*, New York, 1932. — GILSON, E., *Index scolastico-cartesien*, Paris, 1913. — *La doctrine cartésienne de la liberté et la théologie*, Paris, 1913. — *Le rôle de la pensée médiévale dans la formation du système cartésien*, Paris, 1930. — HAMELIN, O., *Le système de Descartes*, 2nd ed., Paris, 1921. — JASPERS, K., *Descartes et la philosophie*, Paris, 1938. — LABERTHONNIÈRE, N., *Etudes sur Descartes*, 2 vols., Paris, 1935. — LAPORTE, J., *Le rationalisme de Descartes*, Paris, 1945. — LEROY, M., *Descartes, le philosophe au masque*, 2 vols., Paris, 1929. — MAHONY, M. J., *Cartesianism*, 2nd ed., New York, 1934. — MARITAIN, J., *The Dream of Descartes*, New York, 1944. — *Three Reformers : Luther, Descartes, Rousseau*, New York, 1928. — MATTEI, A., *L'homme de Descartes*, Paris, 1945. — MESNARD, P., *Essai sur la morale de Descartes*, Paris, 1936. — RIDEAU, E., *Descartes, Pascal, Bergson*, Paris, 1937. — ROTH, L., *Descartes' Discourse on Method*, Oxford, 1937. — *Spinoza, Descartes and Maimonides*, Oxford, 1924. — SCOTT, J. F., *The Scientific Work of Descartes*, London, 1952. — SERRURIER, C., *Descartes, l'homme et le penseur*, Paris, 1951. — SERRUS, C., *La méthode de Descartes et son application à la métaphysique*, Paris, 1933. — SMITH, N. K., *Studies in the Cartesian Philosophy*, London, 1902. — *New Studies in the Philosophy of Descartes*, New York, 1953. — VERSE-FELD, M., *An Essay on the Metaphysics of Descartes*, London, 1940.

317. René Descartes was born at La Haye in Touraine. He was educated at the Jesuit College at La Flêche, where he became a close friend of Mersenne, who later joined the Franciscans. In order to complete his education, he served in the armies of various German princes. Then he travelled over Europe as a spectator and observer. He retired to Holland, where he sojourned for twenty-three years and composed his principal works. Here he wrote *Discours de la méthode*, which aimed to give the rules of the conduct of reason in searching truth in the sciences; three specimens applying this method followed, the *Dioptrique*, the *Meteores* and the *Geometrie* (1637) [1]. This was followed by *Meditationes de prima philosophia*, in which the existence of God and the immortality of the soul were demonstrated (1641); then he wrote *Principia philosophiæ* (1644), *Des passions de l'âme* (1649); the *Traité du Monde* [2],

---

[1] Already the first edition contained six series of objections and answers; they had been received from various theologians and philosophers (Caterus, Hobbes, Arnauld, Gassendi, and others), through the help of his friend, Father Marin Mersenne. The approbation sought from the Sorbonne was not obtained. A second edition, in 1642, added objections from Bourdin with Descartes' replies. See E. BRÉHIER, *op. cit.*, II, p. 49.

[2] This treatise was written at the time of Galileo's condemnation (1633); since Descartes taught the movement of the earth in it, he did not dare publish it at the time.

De l'homme, and *Regulæ ad directionem ingenii* were published after his death.

Called to Sweden by Queen Christina (1632-54), who desired philosophical instruction, he died at Stockholm in 1650.

Descartes was, primarily, a *mathematical genius.* His aim was " to acquire a certain and clear knowledge of all those things which could be of some use to men for life " [1]. He hoped to discover the secrets of nature with a clarity and a precision equal to those of a geometrical theorem. The thought of setting up a *universal mathematics* decided his philosophical vocation for him in 1619, while he was a soldier, and rested for the winter near the Danube at the town of Ulm, where " he had all the leisure he wished to indulge in his thoughts " [2].

Descartes' directive idea was wholly modern : instead of referring back the new science to philosophy, he aimed to construct his system as a function of this formally mathematical science. He applied himself to metaphysics only in the measure that he thought it necessary to found the " science " that was to take up the better part of his time; this explains the incomplete aspect of his philosophy. Furthermore, he fully accepted the principle of modern rationalism [3], aiming to draw out all truth by meditation on the self without recourse to any external aid, whether that of authority, of tradition, or of the objects of experience. This is the foundation of the method of clear ideas and of the universal doubt, with which he studied the nature of the soul and the corporeal world. Cartesianism is logically presentable in three steps :

Article I : The Method of Universal Doubt and of Clear Ideas.

Article II : The Spiritual World.

Article III : The Corporeal World.

----

[1] *Discourse on Method,* Part I.
[2] *Ibid.,* Part II.
[3] See above, n. 313.

ARTICLE ONE.

THE METHOD OF UNIVERSAL DOUBT AND OF CLEAR IDEAS.

318. One can distinguish four stages in the logical progression of Descartes' thoughts until he established his new method : 1) he adopted universal doubt; 2) he found, in this very doubt, the first principle of all certitude; 3) the examination of this principle; 4) finally, he established some rules transforming this principle into a universal method.

First stage : **Universal Doubt.**

Descartes was struck by the fact that in philosophy " there is not a single matter within its sphere which is not still in dispute, and nothing, therefore, which is above doubt " [1]. In order to arrive at a science which would be wholly free from doubt, he thought it necessary " to reject as absolutely false anything about which there could be imagined even the least doubt " [2]. Inasmuch as philosophy is the foundation of all other sciences, " I was constrained to admit that, among all the opinions which I had at one time received and held as true, there was not now one which I could not doubt, not through any inconsideration or levity, but by strong and naturely considered reasons ".

Applying this in detail, he rejected not only commonly accepted opinions, but also the testimony of the senses, for they occasionally deceive us; he rejected the information from consciousness, as the belief that one is sitting at a table, because one sometimes dreams the same thing; even the demonstrated and most evident truths, as that two and three are five or that the square has four sides, were doubted, " for God, permitting me to be sometimes deceived, might perhaps permit me to be always deceived ". Finally, this universal doubt is a law for the budding philosopher, inasmuch as the faculties of knowledge themselves are suspect. " Perhaps the idea of a good God is but a fable and we depend on some evil genius who takes pleasure in the fact that we err in each of our actions ". And

---

[1] *Discourse on Method*, Part I.
[2] This text and the following are taken from *Meditations on First Philosophy*, I

this last reason, the most radical of all, suffices to impose an absolutely universal doubt.

Adopting this point of departure, Descartes poses the *critical problem* in all its amplitude. In general, the critical problem is concerned with knowing whether we possess truth and by what means we are assured of its possession. Furthermore, the problem is taken up with *good intent;* that is, its unique goal is to look for a solid foundation for knowledge as such. At no point in his critical efforts did Descartes fear being accused of absolute scepticism. If one defines *methodic doubt* as " that which is deliberately willed and freely chosen as a means of attaining the truth ", the first stage of the Cartesian method is *universal methodic doubt* [1].

Second stage : **The Foundational Truth.**

319. " But immediately upon this I observed that, whilst I thus wished to think that all was false, it was absolutely necessary that I, who thus thought, should be somewhat; and as I observed that this truth, *I think, hence I am,* was so certain and of such evidence that no ground of doubt, however extravagant, could be alleged by the sceptics capable of shaking it, I concluded that I might, without scruple, accept it as the first principle of the philosophy of which I was in search " [2].

This principle, Descartes remarks, is not a process of reasoning that would suppose a truth already known; it is an immediate intuition of fact. Since " to think " is " to be thinking ", in having consciousness of thought, of doubt, and so on, I have consciousness of being and of existing. It is the weakness of language which demands the two verbal expressions, " I think " and " I am ", in order to express this one simple fact.

Third stage : **The Clear Idea as the Supreme Criterion.**

320. " And as I observed that in the words *I think, hence I am,* there is nothing at all which gives me assurance of their truth beyond this, that I see very clearly that in order to think it is necessary to exist, I concluded that I might take, as a general rule, the principle that all the things which we very clearly and distinctly conceive are true " [3]. In another place,

---

[1] Descartes accepted, meanwhile, the rules of a provisory morality and the truths of faith; see below, n. 335. Concerning the question of the legitimacy of his doubt, see below, n. 321.

[2] *Discourse on Method,* Part iv.

[3] *Ibid.*

Descartes says that a *clear idea* is one which is present and
manifest to an attentive spirit [1]; a *distinct idea* is " one which
is so precise and different from all other objects as to comprehend
in itself only what appears manifestly to him who consider
it as he ought " [2]. Every distinct idea is necessarily clear
but not vice versa : the idea of an object clearly perceived can
remain confused because of the prejudices about its nature
The first step in attaining truth is to make precise the content
of our clear ideas, in order to make them distinct.

The clear and distinct idea, thus disengaged, is the center
not only of the method [3], but also of the whole of Cartesianism
In order to form a right notion of it, its four traits should be
studied : it is indubitable, intuitive, infallible and innate.

a) **Indubitability.** It is impossible to doubt a truth once
known. The mind can turn away from it or ignore it, but
once it has received an idea, it cannot be prevented from
holding it as true. It is thus dominated, and is, as it were
passive in front of the clarity of the object. This property
is most apparent and is eminently evident in the principle
" cogito, ergo sum ", for the very doubting of his principle
fortifies certitude. However, indubitability is but a subjective
sign which should not be separated from the remaining
properties.

b) **Intuitive.** Descartes defines intuition as " the firm con
ception which is born in a healthy and attentive spirit by the
light of reason alone, being more certain by deduction because
it is more simple " [4]. The object of intuition is *simple* natures
or " those whose knowledge is so precise and so distinct that the
intelligence cannot divide them into several others known
more distinctly; of this sort are figure, extension and move
ment " [5], as also the action of knowing, of willing, of doubting
of existence and duration, of unity, and so forth.

Descartes thus established a perfect correspondence between
the object of knowledge, called a *clear and distinct idea*, and
the action of knowing, called *intuition*. There is no difference
between the case of an *abstract* object, in which the spirit does

---

[1] Similarly, in the sensible order, one sees an object clearly as long as it act
strongly enough on our eyes, and does not leave the neighborhood of vision.

[2] *Principia philosophiæ*, n. 45.

[3] For this reason the method of Descartes can be called the *method of the
clear idea*.

[4] *Regulæ ad directionem ingenii*, III. — [5] *Ibid.*, XII.

not consider real existence (for example, the notion of figure), and the case of the *concrete* object seized by the spirit as factually existing (for example, my real self) [1]. Of the two traits of intuition, knowledge without intermediary and the seizure of an object as existing, he retains especially the first, and opposes it with knowledge by reasoning. Briefly, Cartesian intuition is well definable as " knowledge of an evident truth, of whatever nature it be, which serves as a principle and a foundation for discursive reasoning " [2].

In the meanwhile, if one stays faithful to Descartes' thought, one finds the second condition of intuition in the above definition. For truth, as common sense requires, supposes a real object, existing outside of the knower. From this notion follow the two other properties of the clear idea.

c) **Infallibility.** The main consequence of the intuitive character of the clear idea is to make it infallibly true. As a matter of fact, error is not possible unless we mingle with the object known a foreign element, drawn out from our own depths. But this is absolutely impossible in the intuitive vision in which a simple object, distinctly grasped, reveals itself clearly. There must be a complex operation uniting two ideas in order for error to occur : " Whence it is concluded that we can deceive ourselves only when we in some way compose the things which we believe are from ourselves " [3].

Composition of this sort is the work of *judgment,* which is no longer an act of the intelligence alone, but always demands the active intervention of the will. Judgment is not always infallible. Only intuition, a simple and purely intellectual act, necessarily and always states " that which is ". Intuition performs this task perfectly and without awaking any fear of error, so that we can conclude from the properties of the clear idea to those of reality existing outside ourselves.

d) **Innatism.** If one asks Descartes on what basis this exceptional validity of the clear idea rests, he would not appeal to the object revealing itself as it is, for his universal doubt interdicted such an answer. He most often refers to the Vera-

---

[1] Descartes was faithful to his times in this regard; the philosophers commonly admitted that our concepts attain the individual. This was particularly the opinion of Suarez; see above, n. 309.

[2] A. LALANDE, *Vocabulaire technique de la philosophie,* " Intuition ", division " A ".

[3] *Regulæ ad directionem ingenii,* XII.

city of God, Who, in creating our soul, enriched it with its clear and distinct ideas, so that they are with us when we are born. They are *innate* within us.

The importance of God in Cartesianism is thus evident. He is the foundation of our certitudes [1]. Descartes went so far as to say, " But if we did not know that all which we possess of real and true proceeds from a Perfect and Infinite Being, however clear and distinct our ideas might be, we should have no ground on that account for the assurance that they possessed the perfection of being true " [2].

Here we meet a difficulty of interpretation. In order to establish the existence of God, which has been doubted with everything else, Descartes had to rely on the principle, " cogito, ergo sum ". If the divine truth, in turn, is the basis of this truth, there is certainly evidence of a vicious circle; even while Descartes was alive, his adversaries reproached him with this fact. In reply, Descartes distinguished two sorts of infallible truths. The first, of which the " cogito, ergo sum " is the primary one, are endowed with actual intuitive evidence and are self-validated; the second, " in which memory can recall, since we no longer attend to the reasons from which they were deduced " [3], must be referred to the divine Veracity in order to remain indubitable.

But this answer diminishes the strength of his first proposals. Descartes, it seems, impressed by the motives of doubt accumulated in the first stage, and especially by the objection of the evil genius, thought it necessary to found all certitudes on God. This motivated another definition of intuitive knowledge; it is " an illustration of the spirit through which one sees, in the light of God, the things which it wishes to discover, through a direct impression from the divine clarity on our understanding; in this situation, the intelligence is not considered as an agent, but only as receiving the rays of light from the Divinity " [4].

It seems that one could avoid the vicious circle by following the logic of the system, that is, by insisting on the *intuitive* trait as a point of departure. If the clear and distinct idea of the thinking self manifested to us all at once its object (the self) and its origin (God the Creator), there would be no subordination of these two fundamental ideas, but they would be more two aspects of one and the same primitive intuition [5]. If this be the foundation of his thought, Descartes has said nothing about it.

Value of the Cartesian Method. 321. In raising the critical problem, Descartes announced the aurora of a new science

---

[1] See below, n. 331.
[2] *Discourse on Method*, Part IV.
[3] *Meditatio de prima philosophia*, 2nd response to objections.
[4] *Lettre au Marquis de Newcastle* (1648).
[5] At this point one is close to the *vision in God* of Malebranche.

whose legitimacy is unquestionable and which marks a real progress in the evolvement of philosophy. But this initial essay has a triple imperfection, on the position of the problem, the meaning of the question and the criterion proposed to resolve it.

1) **Statement of the Problem.** One can hardly heap reproach on Descartes for having instituted a *universal methodic doubt* [1]. It is normal, at the beginning of a science, to consider as doubtful that which one wishes to demonstrate. Since epistemology aims to establish the truth of the ensemble of our certitudes, it seems that it should at first consider them as doubtful. But to be truly *methodical*, that is to say, reasonable, and to conform to the demands of the science and to find use in the solution of the problem, the universal, critical doubt should have two qualities which Descartes did not know :

a) The doubt must be purely *negative*, the fruit of a simple absence of reasons and not founded on positive, or very strong reasons. Being universal, such a positive doubt accepts no principle — a condition indispensable for resolving difficulties efficaciously — and if none of them would be valid, it would lead to absolute scepticism. The error of the method is manifest especially in the hypothesis of the wicked genius. If this notion be taken but once into consideration, every truth, even that of the " cogito " could not resist it at all [2]. Furthermore, since we do not have the simultaneous intuition of our self and of the existence of God [3], the vicious circle becomes inevitable in order to free oneself from an awkward hypothesis.

b) The doubt must stop before *all* those certitudes which one can call *necessary*, for they impose themselves by their immediate evidence. The " cogito, ergo sum " is but one of these, but not the only one, as Descartes wished. At least the principle of identity and of contradiction impose themselves with the same force. Moreover, in refusing such affirmations as *three and seven are ten*, Descartes seems to have gone beyond his first principles; this extension is arbitrary [4].

2) **Meaning of the Question.** To determine which of our certitudes are infallibly true, is the main aim of epistemology. Given the abstract character of our sciences, two problems must be resolved to attain the goal of criteriology : the first is of the *ideal order*

---

[1] Some, it is true, reject this method, as J. Tonquédec, *La critique de la connaissance;* E. Gilson, *Le réalisme méthodique;* J. Gredt, *Elementa philosophiæ.* — Others, for good reason, accept it : D. Mercier, *Critériologie générale;* J. Maritain, *Les degrés du savoir;* J. Noel, *Notes d'épistémologie thomiste.*

[2] Descartes argued that the " cogito, ergo sum " does resist this error; a happy correction, but inconsequential.

[3] See below, n. 329, on the necessity of proving God's existence; see also n. 533.

[4] Descartes corrected himself in applying this criterion of truth; he also found other principles to be immediately infallible, as that of sufficient reason; see n. 327 and n. 329.

and lies at the interior of consciousness, dealing with the conditions under which the intelligence possesses the truth; the second is of the *real order* and outside of consciousness, inquiring whether exterior things exist outside of us and in what measure our sciences allow us to know them. Descartes did not distinguish these two problems at all. The truth of which he speaks designates, indifferently, abstract theorems and concrete realities. This marks his solution with a great lack of precision.

This defect is explainable by the very particular meaning which he gives to his clear idea; a meaning which is easily contestable.

3) **The Criterion of the Clear and Distinct Idea.** At first blush, this criterion seems close to the notion of *evidence*, in which St. Thomas sees the sign of truth. The criterion is not purely subjective, as some have said; it does not signify that everything which *seems to us* clear and distinct is true. In Descartes' view, these ideas are not fabricated at will; they are in us without our will.

Nevertheless, the Cartesian criterion has no purely objective value, and is different from that of evidence in two ways :

a) In Thomism, the passivity of our knowledge [1] is a fact granted as incontestable. *Evidence* is the constraining influence from the object itself which manifests itself as it is and thus produces perfect adequation between what is known and the knower. This evidence resolves clearly the double problem of epistemology. For one meets it, either in the abstract natures of intelligence or in the concrete objects of sensible intuition; one meets it even in the collaboration of these two faculties, inasmuch as the same object (*this man*, for example) seized by the sense evidently appears as identical with the content of an abstract idea (for example, the idea of *substance* or of *humanity*). Thus the immediate support of the truth of external reality to our consciousness is the sensible world [2], from which we mount towards God by means of analogy.

The *clear idea*, on the contrary, does not have its clarity from the object, but of itself; or, better, from God, Who has deposited it within us. This explains Descartes' tendency to express univocally the divine thoughts and God Himself, for it is through their intermediary that we arrive at knowledge of the sensible world. This also explains the Cartesian tendency to conclude from rational evidence to the real existence of the object considered, and its failure to distinguish the two problems of ideal truth and extra-mental reality; our thought, so to speak, measures the truth of things. For it is the property of the Divine Ideas to be creative of their objects, and the clear idea of Descartes becomes a participation in the Divine Ideas. The initial doubt, which cuts off all connections with the external world, demands this solution, except, perhaps, for the idea of the self. But even for this latter idea,

---

[1] This passivity does not, for that matter, exclude activity, as that of the judgment, the reasoning process and abstraction.

[2] The Thomistic view also recognizes the value of the intuition of the self (see below, n. 327), but its realism has a much wider basis.

Descartes prefers the guarantee of the divine influence to that of the object.

b) In Thomism, evidence does not justify the idea but rather the *judgment*, which alone is the depository of full truth; the judgment is, moreover, a purely intellectual action, admitting the influence of the will only in its imperfect forms (as faith and opinion). This shows proper respect for discursive reasoning, which is a purely immanent activity, wholly subject to the influence of the evident object.

Cartesian evidence is not concerned with justifying the judgment, which is never infallible, but only with the *idea*. The latter, by its intuitive character, has the value of judgment or of principle, but is conceived as a simple act, a pure, *static*, intellectual reflection of an object which has come from God. This is a misunderstanding of the proper nature of our abstractive intelligence. Kant will rediscover the notion of the activity of intelligence, and the importance of judgment in epistemology, though he will confuse immanent activity with production, which is a transitive action [1].

For Descartes, the spirit *reflects* purely on the real world which it bears within itself. For Kant, the spirit *fabricates* the real world, which it objectivizes outside of itself. For St. Thomas, the spirit *assimilates* the real world which comes from without into itself.

Fourth Stage : **The Rules of Universal Method.**

322. After the criterion of the clear idea is understood, it is applicable, in detail, to all our truths. Moreover, in order to construct a universal science comparable in evidence to mathematics, it is sufficient, Descartes observes, to follow four rules :

1) " Never to accept anything for true which I did not clearly know to be such; that is to say, carefully to avoid precipitancy and prejudice, and to comprise nothing more in my judgment than what was presented to my mind so clearly and distinctly as to exclude all ground of doubt " [2]. This foundational rule not only condemns the method of authority which was so abused by decadent Scholasticism, but it especially proclaims the exclusive value of *intuition* in attaining infallible truth, as Descartes will soon remark.

2) " To divide each of the difficulties under examination into as many parts as possible, and as might be necessary for its adequate solution ". It is *analysis* which is destined to

---

[1] See below, nn. 403-5, where it will be shown in what sense Kant has intelligence *fabricate* the exterior world.

[2] These four rules quoted above are found in *Discourse on Method*, Part II.

recover, in what is complexly given, the simple elements and the clear ideas which express them.

3) " To conduct my thoughts in such order that, by commencing with objects the simplest and easiest to know, I might ascend little by little, and, as it were, step by step, to the knowledge of the more complex; assigning in thought a certain order even to those objects which in their own nature do not stand in a relation of antecedence and sequence. " This step is *synthesis* or *deduction*, which is not, however, a sequence of syllogisms, but a series of uninterrupted intuitions; the latter grasp the order which holds between the simple natures to form a whole, as one grasps the unity of a chain by verifying the union of each link with its neighbor. Deduction is thus distinguished from intuition by the fact that the latter is stable and is based on actual evidence, while deduction implicates movement and is based on the memory of the preceding intuitive evidences. But these differences are accidental, and, little by little, the spirit tends to proceed from one trait to a whole deductive chain, as if done in one, long and intuitive glance.

4) " In every case to make enumerations so complete, and reviews so general, that I might be assured that nothing was omitted ". This is *enumeration* or *induction* which does not consist in drawing out a nature or a universal definition from the concrete, for ideas are innate. Experience plays but a minimum role; it intervenes when a series of consequences, equally possible, flows from one and the same simple nature; experience then helps to reveal which the Creator has chosen. Experience also directs reasoning, without, however, being the source of its truth. It also seems that experience does not furnish certain intermediary notions, necessary for a series of deductions; they must be supplied by inventing appropriate hypotheses.

The role of induction, then, is to gather all the simple natures without exception. In the process of reasoning, it is to assure the presence of all the real or hypothetical steps with no omission; induction, consequently, is but the fulfillment of intuition.

Cartesian Science. 323. The Cartesian ideal of science is quite different from the Thomistic notion.

For St. Thomas, science is a synthesis of ideas or of abstract concepts which are, by means of judgments, *hierarchized under the idea of being*, whose various aspects they make explicit [1]. Being is a privileged idea, since it is the very light of intelligence and its formal object. The effort of the scientist is to reduce his knowledge to being through demonstrations and strict processes of reasoning; he explains things by the principle of their reason for being, even at the price of some obscurity in the idea [2], or of some meanderings and complications in the deductions. Human intelligence, passive and limited, must submit to the real, which enters into it through objective evidence.

For Descartes, on the contrary, the world presents itself with many elements, simple in themselves, and intuitively knowable through clear ideas. The latter are irreducible among themselves, and are not hierarchized into genera and species. From each of these there flows a series of applications, themselves knowable intuitively and always proceeding in a straight line as a series of geometric theorems. The effort of the scientist is to make for himself a *tableau of the ensemble* of the world by an uninterrupted and coordinated continuation of clear ideas, all fully intelligible. Human intelligence, because of innatism, dominates and measures reality in some way.

The Cartesian method, or the method of the *clear idea* is, by definition, an *intuitive* method. One could also call it the *mathematical method*, because it is wholly a priori. The mathematician reasons only on abstract magnitudes, without being overly concerned if bodies fully realize his conceptions. Furthermore, the Cartesian method is *simplificatory*, dispensing with the rules of Aristotle, which Descartes thought too complicated, just as the mathematician proceeds only by simple comparisons between magnitudes. Thus Descartes was led to his important mathematical discoveries [3]. The method is also proper to modern physics, which seeks to reduce phenomena to mathematical equations; the method furnishes its hypotheses (atomism, theory of vibrations, and so forth), a veritable tableau destined to support the imagination in the calculation of laws. From this method Cartesianism got its success.

But this method is insufficient in philosophy in order to explain reality. The grave defect of the scientific ideal which this method looks for, is to by-pass the powers of our abstractive reason and to adopt the method proper to a spirit or an angel [4]. It is proper to angels to have, for their usage, innate and intuitive ideas, formally endowed with truth; these ideas are similar to human judgments and constitute a science independent of experience.

---

[1] Thus, all sciences are not conceived as being of the same type, but are subordinated according to the various degrees of abstraction.

[2] Thus the idea of *pure potentiality* (prime matter) is far from being clear and distinct; without it, however, bodies and their changes would remain unintelligible.

[3] After having made the method of algebra precise, Descartes applied it to the study of space and founded *analytic geometry* (1637).

[4] Maritain calls this the *angelism* of Descartes (see his *Three Reformers*, New York, 1929, p. 82). Descartes' view of the human soul follows from the above; he looks upon it as pure spirit. See below, n. 326.

In order to make us angels, Descartes deprived us of our natural source of truth, sensible experience. Since, as a matter of fact, man has no angelic source of intuition, the logical bent of Cartesianism is to the idealist scepticism of Hume [1].

In Summary : *Having doubted everything, Descartes found this one indubitable truth: " I think, hence I am ", since in the very fact of his doubting, consciousness asserted this fact to him clearly and distinctly. He makes this notion the foundation of his philosophy, which is constructed by the intuitive and mathematical method of the clear idea.*

ARTICLE TWO. — THE SPIRITUAL WORLD.

324. By applying his method of the clear idea, Descartes made the spiritual world rise totally from the analysis of his own thought, for " cogito, ergo sum " is his unique certitude. He at first considers his thought from the *subjective* viewpoint; that is, he takes it in itself, as a phenomenon affecting the subject, and draws out *psychology* from it. Then he considers his thought from the *objective* viewpoint, that is, in its content, to the extent that it makes this or that reality known, and thus draws out *theodicy* from it.

I. THE SUBJECTIVE VIEWPOINT : PSYCHOLOGY.

Beginning with his principle of the *cogito*, Descartes assigns thought alone as the object of psychology. He considers, however, the relations of this thought with the soul from which it has come.

A) The Object of Psychology.

Descartes sought to make a clear and distinct and fully veridical idea of this fact, " I exist ". The latter is not equivalent to " I am a reasonable animal ", which is a complex idea and not very clear. Nor is it equivalent to " A being having a figure, arms and body ", for the hypothesis of the evil genius makes me doubt the reality of my own body. Nor is it equivalent to " A being that is moving, eating, sensing ", which would suppose the reality of the body. What, then, am I? — A thinking thing, it has been said. But what is a thinking thing? It is a thing that doubts, understands,

---

[1] See below, Ch. II, and nn. 380-5.

affirms, denies, wills, refuses, that imagines also, and perceives " [1].

Thus, *thought*, the object of psychology, encompasses the following : 1) the properly intellectual ideas; 2) voluntary activity; 3) the sensible phenomena, knowledge and passions. In brief, the object of psychology is THOUGHT, which designates " every fact of consciousness " [2].

In thus classifying sensible knowledge among thoughts, Descartes broke resolutely with the theory, commonly held until his time, according to which sensation was defined as an act common to soul and to body : *actus conjuncti*. Sensation, instead, is now broken into two heterogeneous elements : on one side, there are the organic phenomena which are explained by mechanism [3], but which remain, for the moment, in the penumbra of the methodic doubt; on the other side, sensible knowledge, being a fact of consciousness immediately expressed by the clear idea of the self, is endowed with infallible truth. It evidently follows that, for Descartes, sensible perception is an operation exclusively proper to the soul, and that it enjoys the same properties of simplicity and of spirituality granted to intellectual activity [4] and to other " thoughts ", as will be shown.

B) **Relations between Thought and Soul.**

325. In sounding out the depths of the clear idea of the " thinking self ", Descartes considered that he had brought out two important and precise points : the self is both substantial and incorporeal.

Proposition 1. *Thought is constitutive of the substance and of the essence of the personal self, because thought is its foundational attribute.*

In order to establish this proposition, Descartes based his view on the notions of substance, of attribute, and of mode.

Substance is defined as " a thing which so exists that it needs no other thing for existing ". In the strict sense, Descartes

---

[1] *Meditations on First Philosophy*, II. See also D. MERCIER, *The Origins of Contemporary Psychology*, pp. 5-9.

[2] *The Passions of the Soul*, Pt. I, IV.

[3] See below, n. 333.

[4] See below, n. 335. The positivist psychologists, faithful to the Cartesian view though applying it in reverse, consider each fact of consciousness, even intellectual and volitional, as an organic activity. Hume, Stuart Mill and Taine are examples.

notes, God alone realizes this definition. But the created natures themselves " may be conceived under this common concept; for these are things which, in order to be existent, stand in need of nothing but the concourse of God " [1]. Substance is the reality which completely corresponds to the clear and distinct idea, for it exists in itself, well separated from any other. It follows that between two substances, the objects of two clear ideas, there is, necessarily, a *real distinction*.

However, substance does not reveal itself to our idea through its nude existence, but through its attributes and its modes.

The Attribute is a quality inseparable from substance. It is not possible to have a clear and distinct idea of substance without thinking of its attributes. Here, then, there is but a *distinction of reason*. One of the attributes stands out as the most important, for it is the source of all others; it constitutes the *essence* of being.

Modes are variable qualities, not necessary for the clear and distinct idea. Descartes, without further precision, sets up a *modal distinction* between substance and its mode, or between two modes of the same substance [2].

In applying these notions, one sees at first that the self is known by a clear and distinct idea, since it is grasped by the foundational intuition, " cogito, ergo sum ". It manifests itself as capable of existing independently of every other subject, needing only the concourse of God. The self, then, is a substance.

On the other hand, thought is a quality absolutely inseparable from self; it is so identified in its existence with self, that " perhaps it would even happen, if I should wholly cease to think, that I should at the same time altogether cease to be " [3]. Thought, thus, is an attribute which identifies itself with the substance of the soul.

Finally, thought is the foundational attribute from which all other facts of consciousness, as volitions, desires, and so forth, are but consequences or forms. Thought is the very essence of the personal self.

As to the rest, there is not always question, it seems, of an actual thought, but it may betimes remain virtual and implicit.

---

[1] *The Principles of Philosophy*, Pt. I, 51.

[2] These distinctions appear to be a souvenir of Suarez (see above, n. 307) whom Descartes most likely studied with the Jesuits at La Flèche.

[3] *Meditations on First Philosophy*, II.

In this sense, the child possesses a thinking self from the beginning, for " it has the ideas of God, of itself, and of all those truths which are known by themselves, just as adult persons have them when they are not thinking of them ".

Proposition 2. 326. *Our soul is a complete substance, absolutely simple, and, consequently, spiritual and immortal.*

This proposition, which harks back to the absolute dualism of Plato [1], also follows from the theory of the clear idea.

At first, the idea of the thinking self appears " very evident " to Descartes, as that of a complete thing; that is, of one thing, " which can be conceived completely alone by denying to it all other things of which it has ideas " [2]. From which it follows (by supposing that the divine veracity guarantees the objectivity of the clear idea), that this thing exists completely alone, and is fully distinguished from everything else, and, particularly, from the body.

Moreover, it is easy to see that all the properties of thought are opposed to the body. Thought is not extended and it is not divisible, but absolutely simple. Thought is not at all inert or subject to movement impressed from without, but it is the very source of activity, especially under the form of free will. Descartes insists on this power of the will, which, he says, has a sort of infinity about it. Our soul, as a result, is fully incorporeal or *spiritual*.

It should be noted that this Cartesian proof is drawn not only out of the activity of the intelligence and of the will, but from every *fact of consciousness*, even that of sensible facts; this makes the simplicity of the soul stand out in relief, from which it can be concluded that it is a manifestation of the soul to the exclusion of the body.

Finally, the soul must be said to be *immortal* of itself, for, on the one hand, its simplicity places it beyond dissolution, and, on the other hand, it is not believable that the material change accompanying death [3] affects a substance fully independent of the body in any way at all. " But if it be asked whether by God's absolute power he has perchance decreed that human souls cease to be at the same instant that the

---

[1] See above, n. 58.

[2] *Reply to Fourth Objections.*

[3] This sort of change, in Descartes' mechanistic theory, is merely a simple variation of figure; see below, n. 333.

bodies to which they are joined are destroyed, it is only God's business to reply " [1].

Value of the Cartesian Psychology. 327. One can say that the Cartesian psychology is opposed, in every aspect, to that of the great Scholastics and especially to that of St. Thomas. The latter, resting, above all, on the fact of experience, aimed to interpret these facts through the proposition that the soul is at once subsistent and the form of body. Descartes neglects these facts for his a priori deductions. He does not deny the dependence and the union of soul and body, and, in fact, writes : " You should profess that you believe man to be a true being *per se* and not *per accidens*, and that the mind is really and substantially united to body " [2]. But these clear affirmations empty the Scholastic formulas of all their meaning, and Descartes admits that the problem is insoluble for philosophy [3].

The source of these grave deviations is in the exaggerated view which he gives to the intuition of the self. We do not have, as he proposed, a direct vision of the soul as being a complete and spiritual substance. On the other hand, to be motivated by the demands of rigorous criticism, and thus to hold that we attain the soul only through internal experience as a fact of consciousness and as a pure phenomenon separated from the subject, is to adopt the exaggerated view of Kant and the Phenomenalists.

The truth resides in a just mean. By a sort of intuition we know both the facts of consciousness and the existence of a thinking, substantial subject, for it is immediately evident that not even one thought can exist without an acting substance which produces it [4]. But this evidence is not valid alone, left as some residue of methodic doubt, and adoptable as the foundation of all certitude. There are other affirmations equally evident and consequently known as infallibly true at the beginning of epistemology, whether in the order of external facts by sensible intuition, or in the order of first, abstract principles.

One can, in the meanwhile, concede a double advantage to the " cogito, ergo sum ". Its object is most easily present, and this object is, in some way, spiritual. In this sense, Descartes could legitimately choose it as the privileged point of departure. But in order that this intuition be infallibly true, it must rest upon immediate evidence, and even then it does not reveal to us anything explicit about the nature of the thinking self. Is the thinking self a complete or incomplete substance, a material or spiritual one? This must be established by reasoning, by showing, for example, that certain facts of consciousness cannot be explained except through a spiritual principle; by conforming to the rules of critical evidence in this way, we also attain infallible truth. But the intuition of our sensible consciousness, which also has full value, assures us that our complete self is a mixed being and not a pure spirit.

---

[1] *Reply to Second Objections.*
[2] *Letter* to Princess Elizabeth, June 28, 1643; see CHEVALIER, *Descartes*, p. 231.
[3] See below, n. 334. — [4] See above, n. 262.

Descartes has magnificently placed two great metaphysical truths in the limelight : the supereminence of thought over body, and the subsistence of the human soul. He presented these truths in the new critical background which made them stand out in strong relief. In minimizing the value of experience, however, he revived the old Platonic error of exaggerated spiritualism. He was led to this position by following the steps of his own method. While the more moderated view of abstraction has the proposition of the spiritual soul being the form of body as a corollary, the principle of the purely intuitive clear idea leads irresistibly to the proposition of the soul as a complete, spiritual substance.

One can thus reproach Descartes with not following his method. After he had placed all truths in a state of doubt but the one of the thinking self, he uses a great number of principles and of definitions which he has not deduced from the self. In order to demonstrate the existence of God, he uses the principle of sufficient reason without scruple. In his defense it can be said that critical philosophy, in order to advance and to resolve its problems, must use all its *evident* bits of knowledge; Descartes, thus, does always appeal to the natural light, that is, to his intuition of the clear idea [1]. Nevertheless, the rigor of his initial doubt seems to defend him somewhat, and we have unmasked an implicit view and a correction of that which he exaggerated.

II. The objective viewpoint : Theodicy.

328. From the subjective point of view, all our thoughts are identical; they are facts of consciousness, simple and spiritual acts. But from the objective point of view, they do not all have the same value in revealing reality. Descartes begins by classifying them. Then, by analyzing one of them, he concludes to the existence of God. Finally, God's existence is the objective foundation for all other ideas.

A) Classification of Thoughts.

Three groups of thoughts or facts of consciousness are distinguishable :

a) **Purely Representative Facts :** these have reserved for themselves the title of *ideas*, or of images expressing an object, " as when I think a man, a chimera, the sky, an angel, or God Himself " [2].

---

[1] The Cartesian method thus gives to science too large a foundation; not only the simple *cogito*, but every object of intuition or of a clear idea. The third and fourth stages of the method would permit this interpretation, though the second seems to exclude it.

[2] *Meditations on First Philosophy*, III.

b) **Purely Active Facts,** which are subdivided into two groups : 1) Volitions, including all those acts in which the soul is efficient cause, as to love God, to desire a reward; 2) the affections or sentiments, including pleasures and sorrows, as the joy in a friend, the suffering from a wound [1].

c) **Representative and Active Facts,** which are judgments that consist in the attribution of one idea to another, accomplished by free will [2].

Of these three groups, only the ideas can validly express external reality. The active facts suppose reality to be known, and judgments are never infallible. But three sorts of ideas can be further distinguished :

1) The *adventitious ideas*, which seem actually to come from without, as " if I see the sun or if I feel heat ".

2) The *factitious ideas*, which we ourselves fabricate by means of others, as " sirens, hippogryphs, and the like, are inventions of my own mind " [3].

3) The *innate ideas*, which we possess by our very nature and which are, precisely, the clear ideas, as that of the soul, of God and of extension.

In order to determine which among these ideas are representative of reality, one cannot evidently trust himself to the subject, for *factitious* ideas have no objective value. One cannot, either, refer them back to the influence of the external object, because only the clear idea is the source of infallible truth. *Adventitious* ideas, similarly, have no objective value. For these reasons, appeal is made to the *natural light*, through which " it is manifest that there must be at least as much reality in the efficient and total cause as in its effect " [4]. This general principle, then, is Descartes' solution :

The objective content of an idea must have, for sufficient reason, a real being which possesses this perfection either formally or eminently; otherwise, one would have to hold that there is in the idea something of reality which comes from nothing.

---

[1] One recognizes here the classification current in experimental psychology, of three main faculties : the intelligence, sensibility and volition. No distinction is made between the sensible and the spiritual orders.

[2] See above, n. 320.

[3] *Meditations on First Philosophy*, III.

[4] The quotations in the remainder of this section on God, unless otherwise indicated, are taken from *Meditations on First Philosophy*, III.

Moreover, armed with the objective reality of the ideas of God and of the self, one can explain all others. The idea of the self contains the elements of those of other men, of animals, and even of extension (at least eminently). The idea of God explains that of angels. The self has already given us psychology; the idea of God will now be examined to draw out a theodicy from it.

B) The Existence of God.

329. We have the idea of an Infinite Being, Who is perfect, the Creator and the Uncaused Cause. Through it, we can demonstrate the existence of God in two ways :

a) **Way of Sufficient Reason.** " I should not, however, have the idea of an infinite substance, seeing I am a finite being, unless it were given me by some substance in reality infinite ". This proof is an application of the principle mentioned above : the content of the idea of the infinite demands, for sufficient reason, the existence of God. One cannot object that this idea is obtained by *denying* the limits in finite perfections, for " I clearly perceive that there is more reality in the infinite substance than in the finite ". The idea, then, is a positive one and I am incapable of producing it myself. This perfection of the idea of God shows, besides, that it is *innate*, as is the idea of the self.

I who have this idea, Descartes adds, cannot explain my own existence by myself. I began to exist, and then will cease to exist. I do not have the chance to give myself being, as I cannot alone pass into nothingness. It is useless to appeal to parents, " seeing that the question raised respects not so much the cause which once produced me, as that by which I am at this present moment conserved ". It follows, then, that God, the Necessary Being, exists as the creative and conservative source of my contingent being; and since I am intelligent, free and possessive of the idea of the infinite, God is also Intelligent, Free and Infinite.

b) **Way of the Clear Idea.** " There is nothing in itself more clear and more manifest than to think that there is a God, that is to say, a Sovereign and Perfect Being in the idea of Whom alone necessary and eternal existence is understood and Who, as a consequence, exists ". If a triangle is considered, there is found in its essence three angles equal to two right angles, but not the real existence of such a figure. On the

contrary, if the idea of God is considered, one grants, among
his essential properties, that of real existence, because His
perfection demands that He be the necessarily existing Being.
" And consequently, it is at least as certain that God, who
is this Perfect Being, is, or exists, as any demonstration of
geometry can be " [1].

C) **Value of these Proofs.**

330. With this latter proof, Descartes revives the ontological
argument of St. Anselm, whose value and weakness has been
explained above [2]. The theory of the clear idea and of Cartesian
intuition is but an open application of the same view.

In itself, the proof from contingency attains its goal, if one
admits that despite universal doubt at the beginning, the truth
of the principle of causality still holds. But in Descartes' view,
this proof does not constitute a special argument; for, in order
to conclude to the existence of the True God Who is Infinite Being,
one must consider that we possess the idea of the infinite without
ourselves being its source.

With regard to the proof from the idea of the infinite, its merit
is questionable. It confuses the *perfect idea* which knows God
as He is and requires intuition of His essence, and the *imperfect
idea* which makes God known by analogy with His creatures.
The latter is the only one which man has here below, and it can
be produced through abstraction, generalization, and reasoning.
From another point of view, the principle of sufficient reason,
which is the foundation of this proof, rules the real world in such
a way that from a real effect, as heat, one legitimately concludes
to a source of heat. But Descartes applied it to the ideal world :
from a perfection which is *thought*, he concludes to the *real* existence
of this perfection; here, again, he is arguing from the fundamental
principle of the clear idea.

D) **The Objectivity of the External World.**

331. Descartes has not left us a complete theodicy. Later,
he speaks of God again in order to explain motion. Now,
however, having rediscovered this second [3] infallible truth of
God's existence, he makes it the basis of all other certitudes.
" Since God is not subject to any defect, it is quite evident that
He could not be a deceiver, for the natural light teaches us
that deceit depends necessarily on some defect " [4]. God,
accordingly, does not deceive us in creating and conserving
our ideas, and the objection of the evil genius is resolved.

---

[1] *Discourse on Method*, Part IV; see also, *Principles of Philosophy*, n. xiv.
[2] See above, n. 223.
[3] The first was the existence of the self.
[4] *Meditations on First Philosophy*, *ad finem*.

It follows that all the ideas which we naturally hold as objective, actually are such. The only condition for not being deceived is to hold on to those ideas which are clear and distinct. We find, in this statement, the solid foundation for the objectivity of the world in Descartes' view : if the world did not exist, God would be deceiving us while He is actually placing the innate idea of the body within us [1].

Descartes concluded from this also that all truths depend on the divine pleasure. God, being essentially free, could have endowed us with a different reason and with wholly different ideas from those we possess; so that two and three are four could become evident and certain [2]. This voluntarism is nothing else but the reverse of rationalism. In Descartes' view, God is not the source of our truths as the ultimate foundation of essences, but He is only their *guarantee* through His creative power. Beginning with the clear idea, our science is self-sufficient and has full, rational clarity.

E) Cartesian Idealism.

Having looked at God's function, Descartes has completed his solution of the critical problem. It is a *realistic* solution, though it arises by way of detour after having begun with an openly idealistic solution. His beginning point is an ensemble of ideas which is conceived, not as a means of knowing the object, but is the object of knowledge itself and fixes the glance of the spirit upon itself [3]. Strengthened by this consciousness, the critical philosopher also represented these ideas as wholly subjective images, given independently of reality, and then asks " if the ideas which I find in myself are similar or conformable to things which are outside of myself " [4]. It is clear that at this moment, if one states the problem, *we know only our own ideas*, the result is idealism [5].

---

[1] Descartes proves the existence of *particular bodies* by the adventitious ideas, which presuppose a cause. " ...I showed in express terms that they often come from bodies, and it was owing to this that the existence of corporeal things was demonstrated " *(Reply to Objections V)*.

[2] See his *Lettre à Mersenne*, May 27, 1630.

[3] Maritain calls this the theory of " tableaux ideas " in contrast to the Thomistic notion of the *objective concept;* the latter is a formal sign, or a means of knowing the object expressed without it itself being first known (see his *Réflexions sur l'intelligence)*. Thus, by the idea of tree, I know the generic nature of all trees (a *reality other* than the self), without knowing, except through a subsequent reflection, that I have the idea of tree.

[4] *Meditations on First Philosophy*, Part III.

[5] See below, n. 356, for the definition of idealism.

Descartes joins himself to reality in throwing the bridge of divine veracity and of the innatism of the clear idea between the self and the non-self. History shows us how weak a bridge this was, for a great number of other idealistic systems arose from these first seedlings.

In Summary : *The analysis of thought permits Descartes to reconstruct :* 1) *psychology, by defining the soul through its attribute, thought ;* 2) *theodicy, since the idea of God can be caused by no other but God Himself. At the same time, he finds in God the objective basis for the corporeal world.*

ARTICLE THREE. — THE CORPOREAL WORLD.

333. The clear idea of thought led Descartes to an exaggerated spiritualism and opened the way to idealism. The clear idea of body led him to mechanism, and opened the way to positivism. A radical dualism arises which makes the problem of the union of soul and body insoluble; this will now be considered and a few notions on morality will conclude his study of man.

A) **Mechanism.**

In this theory, Descartes finds the explanation of bodies in general, even if they are living, including man, and the origin of motion.

1. **Bodies in General.** *Extension* is the essence of bodies in Descartes' view. In order to find the clear and distinct idea of body, one must eliminate all that which one can without destroying body itself; once this is done, there remains but extension or quantity. This is the fundamental attribute of body and its very essence; other attributes of body are its *divisibility*, its *figure* and its *movement*.

Moreover, these properties are totally opposed to those of thought, so that the body, which is extension, cannot act on the soul, which is merely thought. From this follows an important corollary. Our ideas of colors, of sound, and of other sensible qualities, by the same title as our thoughts of the affective order, as sorrows and joys, are in us on the occasion of the presence of a body, but tell us nothing on the nature of this body. They are the exclusive work of the soul. These latter properties are called " secondary qualities " by opposition to quantity, which is called " primary quality " [1]. Descartes thus teaches a definitively idealist solution.

2. **Living Bodies.** The plant, the animal and the human body are evidently bodies; consequently, their total reality is extension endowed with movement. Thus, the whole portion of psychology which treats not only vegetal powers but also the sensible powers (external and internal senses, to the extent that they reveal bodies), becomes a chapter in mechanics. All of " These functions naturally follow in this machine by the very disposition of its organs, no more nor less than do the movements of a clock or other automaton with its balance weights and wheels " [2]. For there " does not exist in the whole universe anything but one sole and same matter ", known through the clear idea of extension. Thus, the laws of mechanics explain all the phenomena of nature, " as we shall see ", says Descartes with assurance; there is no need to look for other principles, such as the vegetal or sensitive soul. Animals, not having a thinking soul, are pure automatons.

Thus, outside of psychology, Descartes admits but one true knowledge of reality, *mechanism*, which can be defined as follows : " The philosophical theory explaining all substances and all properties and transformations of the corporeal world solely by two principles, a homogeneous matter and local movement " [3].

But matter, being inert, can receive movement only from without; this brings up the need of searching for the causes of movement.

3. **Causes of Movement.** One must at first proscribe *final causes*, for we should not be so pretentious as to think of penetrating the secret designs of God. It is sufficient, then, to determine efficient causes or the laws of movements [4], whose variety constitutes all the modifications of matter. This research is the very program followed by modern science, so that Cartesianism seemed to be made expressly in order to justify this program philosophically.

---

[1] These are Locke's formulas; see below, n. 375; see also *Principles of Philosophy*, nn. 69-70.

[2] *Traité de l'homme.*

[3] A. LALANDE, *op. cit.*, " Mechanism ", meaning " C "; Lalande notes that the term has many different meanings.

[4] There is question here of local movements, measurable in the strict sense, as the various kinds of vibrations.

The *general cause* of all the movements of the world can be none other than God Himself, for the universe, being an inert mass, must have its movement created by drawing it from nothingness [1], which requires infinite power.   Since God is unchangeable, He conserves immutably that which He produces : *the quantity of the movement of the universe is unchangeable*.   This law, in the most general form of the principle of conservation of energy [2], is one of the bases of modern science.   Descartes gave an a priori reason for it, while the modern savants, on the other hand, have shown its value as being conformable with experiential facts.

B) **Dualism.**

334.   The *particular causes* of the various movements are studied in his scientific works [3].   Only one case is of interest here, a particularly embarrassing one for Descartes :

The human soul is the particular cause of the movements of its body.

The soul acts and experiences with body, it suffers and desires, following bodily dispositions.   Descartes admits this evident fact : " Nature likewise teaches me by these sensations of pain, hunger, thirst, etc., that I am not only lodged in my body as a pilot in a vessel, but that I am besides so intimately conjoined, and as it were intermixed with it, that my mind and body compose a certain unity " [4].

But body and soul remain two complete substances, whose attributes are irreducibly opposed; body, it appears, cannot act on the soul, nor can soul directly move the body.   In order to resolve this difficulty, Descartes teaches that the soul resides, especially, in the pineal gland, where it is in contact with the

---

[1] Descartes did not understand the definition of motion (or change) of Aristotle and St. Thomas (see above, n. 74).   He conceives it as a series of states communicated from without, so that the inertia of the body consists not only in resting by itself in a state of repose, but also in remaining by itself in movement which it possesses; this explains the necessity of a " creation " of movement at the beginning of the universe.

[2] In modern science, movement is one of the forms of energy; in Cartesian mechanism, it is the only form admitted, so that in Descartes' view, " conservation of movement " is equivalent to " conservation of energy ".

[3] Descartes wished to write a work *Le Monde*, which would contain his scientific studies; but he completed only fragments of it : *Dioptrics*, *Mechanics*, and *Geometry*.   In order to explain physical phenomena, he developed the famous *vortex* theory; the latter view displaced Aristotle's, and then was itself dethroned by the views of Newton; see below, n. 369, A.

[4] *Meditations on First Philosophy*, VI.

" animal spirits " [1], and in this way directs the movements of body and receives counter influences from it. But what sort of union is this? He tried to make its nature more precise by help of the *idea of force*, a primitive notion which we find in ourselves, and which we attribute wrongly to physical phenomena, as to gravity; this idea of force is given us by nature in order to understand this very union of body and soul " as the force with which soul acts on body ". But he concludes with a note of powerlessness: " It does not seem that the human spirit is capable of conceiving, distinctly and at the same time, the distinction between the soul and the body and their union, because one would have to conceive of them as one thing, and at the same time conceive of them as two, which is contrary " [2].

C) Morality.

335. When he entered into his universal doubt, Descartes established three rules of a provisory morality, destined to let him live a tranquil life, despite his theoretical doubt. They can be summarized in three expressions: *a) Social conformity*, ordering him to follow the laws of religion and his country; *b) constancy of will*, permitting him to retain equableness of soul; *c) moderation in desire*, or " to endeavor always to conquer myself rather than fortune, and change my desires rather than the order of the world " [3]. Now, having established the nature of God, of the soul and of the world, he rediscovers these rules as conclusions scientifically deduced, and, so to speak, mathematically evolving from the preceding certitudes.

From these philosophical truths previously established, come the general principles of conduct, as well as the particular applications. Descartes presupposes that ethics teaches us to conduct our thoughts and to regulate our actions so that they will combine to make us happy [4].

1) *A dual, general principle* flows from the nature of God and of the soul. The first is the All-Powerfulness and Infinite Goodness of God; " everything that comes to us is inevitable, but comes to us for our good ". For this reason, metaphysics " teaches us to accept confidently all events, founded as they are on the love of God Who has sent them ".

---

[1] The " animal spirits " are " like a very subtle wind, or rather a very pure and vivid flame "; produced by the heart, they are transmitted through the nerves into the muscles in order to give movement to the bodily members (*Discourse on Method*, Part V).

[2] *Letter to Princess Palatine*.

[3] *Discourse on Method*, Part III.

[4] *Discourse on Method*, Part III (the two quotations which follow are taken from this section).

Finally, the soul, being spiritual and radically distinct from the body, should banish the fear of death and despise the goods of the world. The latter, being an immense extension, conceals energies which escape us and which it would be unreasonable to become occupied with. We should respect other men with whom we live, and the society which gathers us together. It is an evident duty of justice and of gratitude. *Social conformity* is thus justified.

2) In order to *apply* these two general rules in detail both in our actions and in our judgments, *irresolution* is the principle obstacle. " The irresolute person is a man who does not decide, since he does not see clearly what he should do, and concludes, as a general rule, in deciding by chance "; this leads to disastrous errors, troubles and regrets. The source of irresolution, " which, habitually masks the way that decisions should take ", are the *passions.* The best remedy is knowledge, reflecting on our passions.

According to the principles of his dualism, Descartes distinguished two types of passion : a) *the conscious portion,* which has the properties of thought, and which are the six customary ones of admiration, love, hate, desire, joy and sadness; and, in this domain, free will has the power to make passions subject to reason; b) *the corporeal portion,* which is constituted by certain movements of the *animal spirits,* and follows the laws of mechanism and here the precepts of medicine come to aid morality, by calming organic troubles and more easily mastering these passions.

This latter mastery permits us to live according to right reason and thus to attain wisdom and true happiness by practicing *moderation of desires* and *constancy of the will,* which thus find their justification.

In Summary : *Since the clear idea of the body comprises only extension with figure and movement, the only true science of the body is mechanistic. The ideas of other properties are not objectively valid (idealism). The opposition created between soul and body makes insoluble the problem of their union and of their reciprocal action. Applied in practice, these principles orient us towards a morality of stoic tendencies.*

CONCLUSION. **336.** The tremendous influence of Cartesianism on modern thought comes both from its intrinsic value and from the opportuneness of its appearance. " Reuniting in himself most of the aspirations of his age, Descartes knew how to give a response that would be satisfactory to the many thinkers who were disenchanted from the official philosophies. He had the merit of restoring the metaphysical sense which had been lost. As a mathematician, he reintroduced into philosophy the need for rigor and systematic unity; as a physicist, he grasped and dominated the most basic scientific tendencies of his age. Thus, he quite satisfactorily answered three great and inevitable demands of human thought : the eternal demand for a metaphysics, the demand for rational unity in speculation, and the demand for harmony between philosophical doctrine and the theoretical and practical interests of his times " [1].

But in accomplishing this great task at which a decadent Scholasticism had failed, Descartes was not content with merely showing respect for the new truths of a nascent mathematics, he plainly espoused the *rationalist spirit* [2]. His doctrine is a resolute affirmation of total independence and of the self-sufficiency of our reason to attain the full, natural truth.

At first he refused all aid of the supernatural order. " He never allows the least dogma, specifically Christian or Catholic, to arise or interfere with his philosophy " [3]. He deliberately avoids looking for inspirations from revealed dogmas, or of clarifying his own thinking with the help of faith.

He freed himself even more from tradition : " That which the ancients taught is so little a thing and for the most part so little credible, that I could not in any way hope to approach the truth except by elongating my path from the one which they followed ". For this reason he decided to found his own system by rejecting, once and for all, all the opinions which he had received in his formation [4].

Finally, experience itself had but a secondary role in discovering the truth for Descartes. He does not appeal to the influence of the object, but only to the lights of the clear idea. He does this so often, that in a most profound sense these ideas tend to measure reality as the divine, creative Idea of which it is but a participation. This he does instead of having them dependent, as our abstract ideas actually are.

Until his death, Descartes remained a convinced Catholic. He is, furthermore, a great philosopher, but his doctrine is no longer Christian philosophy. He inaugurates, instead, the wholly new orientation of modern philosophy, in which reason is jealous of its independence, and so rashly confident in its own proper resources that it finally comes to divinize itself by accepting pantheism [5].

---

[1] J. MARÉCHAL, *Le point de départ de la Métaphysique*, II, pp. 25-26.
[2] See above, n. 313.
[3] E. BRÉHIER, *Histoire de la philosophie*, II, p. 65.
[4] *Discourse on Method*, Part II.
[5] For these reasons, since 1663, the Church has kept Descartes' works on the Roman index.

CHAPTER TWO.

TOWARDS PANTHEISM.

337. Descartes left his influence on most of the writers of his century; he became the " fashion for philosophical thought " [1]. All thinkers occupied themselves with his thought, though they separated into two groups; some greeted him with reserve, or even opposed his views [2], while others fully assimilated his spirit and developed the consequences of his principles. Pascal holds a place apart from both groups.

a) Among the first group, mention can be made of FÉNELON (1651-1715), who wrote *Réfutation du système de P. Malebranche*, and *Traité de l'existence de Dieu*. Fénelon gives a clear statement of the universal doubt; he acknowledges as a source of truth, the intuition of ideas through the interior light of God, " the sun of spirits " [3]; he defines body by extension and soul by the thinking self. Briefly, he adopts Cartesianism on many points. — BOSSUET (1627-1704) wrote several philosophical [4] works for the education of the Dauphin : *Logique, Traité de la connaissance de Dieu et de soi-même, Traité des causes* and *Traité du libre arbitre*. These works are essentially faithful to Scholastic philosophy, and Bossuet declares " it is a strange metaphysics which declares that the substance of the soul is solely thought and will " [5]. His psychology is that of Thomistic Peripateticism, but he shows himself somewhat favorable to Cartesian notions by attenuating the distinction between substance and accident, and by founding on the eternal truths, independently of experience, a proof for the existence of God.

But neither Bossuet, nor Fénelon are professional philosophers. Orators, polemicists, educators, and especially Catholic theologians, they were preserved from Cartesian rationalism by their faith.

---

[1] Descartes' physics especially stirred the minds of the time; see E. BRÉHIER, *Histoire de la philosophie*, II, p. 113. La Fontaine, however, vigorously protested against mechanism and defended the notion of an animal soul; see His *Fables*, Book x, i.

[2] There is no question here of thinkers who were opposed to Descartes a priori, and who appealed to political power to defend their Aristotelianism; see above, n. 312.

[3] *Traité de l'existence de Dieu*, Part I, Ch. II.

[4] An edition of Bossuet's works has been put out as *Œuvres philosophiques* by Bonne Presse of Paris. See also, W. J. SIMPSON, *A Study of Bossuet*, London, 1937.

[5] *Traité de la connaissance de Dieu*, Ch. I.

D. Huet [1] (1630-1721), Bishop of Avranches, took a position quite openly against Descartes, publishing a work *Censure de la philosophie cartésienne*. However, he still came under Descartes' influence; in resolving the critical problem in his *Traité philosophique de la faiblesse de l'esprit humain* (published in 1723), he defends *fideism*. Reason, he proposes, is so weak that it cannot attain certitude either of divine or of human matters, except through the light of supernatural faith, which thus becomes the supreme criterion of truth.

Pierre Gassendi (1592-1655) revived the atomism of Epicurus and his explanation of sensible knowledge; he superimposed on this, however, the belief in a spiritual soul in man, and belief in God the Creator, Who explains the order of the world. While a partisan of mechanism, as was Descartes, he strongly opposed the latter's explanation of phenomena. He fought against the notions of the *plenum* and the vortex theory, and defended the idea of a void and juncture of atoms.

At the close of the seventeenth century, there arose the school of the *Cambridge Platonists* [2]; these men are of the Cartesian lineage by their esteem for intuition, but they opposed Descartes on other points. The principal adherents were clergymen. John Smith (1616-1652), inspired by Plotinus, compared men who use reason coldly to the enthusiast and the intuitionist; he believed that the latter were much closer to truth. One can know of the immortality of the soul with full certainty by seeing it in a superior light, even though it may not be a logically demonstrable truth. — Henry More (1614-1687), carried on correspondence with Descartes from 1648-49, in which he proposed his theory of the divine extension. " Everything existing should be extended, and even God is an extended being; God must be such so that He can be omnipotent and the universal mover " [3]. In his *Enchiridion metaphysicum, in quo agitur de existentia et natura rerum incorporearum*, he elongated himself further from Cartesian mechanism and defended a pan-animistic cosmology. — Ralph Cudworth (1617-1688) admitted also that all bodies possess life in varying degrees [4]. " His main work, *The true intellectual System of the Universe* (1678), defends final causes in Physics; entelechies, as organoplastic principles in Biology; innate ideas in Psychology; the absolute, a priori nature of moral principles " [5].

b) But the group of *fervent disciples* was equally large. Arnold Geulincx [6] (1625-1669) taught for six years at the

---

[1] C. Bartholmes, *Huet, évêque d'Avranches ou le scepticisme théologique*, Paris, 1850.

[2] Compagnac, E. T., *Cambridge Platonists*, London, 1902. — De Pauley, W. C., *Candle of the Lord*, New York, 1937. — Pawson, G. P. H., *Cambridge Platonists and their Place in Religious Thought*, New York, 1930. — Powicke, F. J., *Cambridge Platonists*, Harvard, 1926.

[3] J. Maréchal, *Histoire de la philosophie moderne*, p. 109 and p. 238.

[4] *Ibid.*, p. 237.

[5] J. Maréchal, *Précis d'Histoire de Philosophie moderne*, p. 237.

[6] De Wulf., M., *Les philosophes belges*, Louvain, 1910. — Van der Haeghen, V., *Geulincx, Étude sur sa vie, sa philosophie et ses ouvrages*, Gand, 1886.

University of Louvain, and introduced Cartesianism there [1]. An acerb critic of Peripateticism, he denied that the body can act on the soul. He deprived bodies of all efficient causality, for he believed that all activity demands consciousness; bodies act only as *instruments of God*, which is already an expression of Occasionalism [2].

LOUIS DE LA FORGE should also be mentioned here; in his view God is the sole motive force whose influence can explain the union of soul and body. — CLAUBERT (1622-1665) introduced Descartes into Germany, and K. DIGBY (1603-1665) introduced him to England [3].

338. BLAISE PASCAL [4] (1623-1662) has his own proper traits. Worthy of being numbered among the *great philosophers*, and also among the Cartesians, it has correctly been said of him, Pascal " is not a philosopher; he is a savant, and an apologete for the Catholic religion " [5].

a) As a savant, Pascal reveals himself a master of the experimental method and as a man impassioned with scientific truth. In various *Opuscules*, he sets down a number of rules which form an abridged logic. His master idea is to find, for each domain explored, the demonstration and the principles perfectly adaptable to the subject. Thus he nicely distinguishes [6] the domain of history and of theology, in which proofs are drawn from authority, and the domain of reason, especially of the physical sciences, in which he proclaims the need for progress founded on reasoning with little value for argument from authority.

Then, wishing to react against the abuses of the syllogism, he reduces [7] the whole of logic to eight rules; three of these concern definitions, two deal with axioms, and three refer to demonstrations.

---

[1] Geulincx died in the Protestant faith.

[2] Two works of Geulincx, *Metaphysica vera* and *Metaphysica ad mentem peripateticam*, did not appear until 1691-98, after the works of Malebranche.

[3] On these authors, see E. BRÉHIER, *Histoire de la philosophie*, II, pp. 116-128.

[4] **Works :** CAILLIET, E., and BLANKENAGEL, J. C. (eds.), *Great Shorter Works of Paschal*, Phila., 1948. — STEWART, H. F., (transl. and ed.), *Pensées*, London, 1950.
Studies : BOUDIN, E., *Etudes historiques et critiques sur la philosophie de Pascal*, 3 vols., Neuchâtel, 1945-47. — BISHOP, M., *Pascal: The Life of Genius*, New York, 1936. — BOUTROUX, E., *Pascal*, Paris, 1900. — CHEVALIER, J., *Pascal*, Paris, 1922. — CRESSON, A., *Pascal*, Paris, 1938. — EASTWOOD, D. M., *The Revival of Paschal, A Study of His Relations to Modern French Thought*, Oxford, 1936. — GIRAUD, V., *Pascal, l'homme, l'œuvre, l'influence*, Fribourg, 1898. — *Pascal, étude d'histoire morale*, Paris, 1910. — *Vie heroïque de Blaise Pascal*, Paris, 1923. — JOVY, E., *Etudes pascaliennes*, 5 vols., Paris, 1927-28. — MESNARD, J., *Pascal, His Life and Works*, New York, 1953. — SOREAU, E., *Pascal*, Paris, 1935. — STEWART, H. F., *The Secret of Pascal*, New York, 1941. — STROWSKI, F., *Pascal et son temps*, 3 vols., Paris, 1907-9.

[5] E. BRÉHIER, *Histoire de la philosophie*, II, p. 127.

[6] See the *Fragment d'un Traité du vide*, " De l'autorité en matière de philosophie ".

[7] See his *Fragments sur l'Esprit géométrique*.

The ideal of science is to demonstrate everything, but the weakness of the human spirit obliges us to admit the definitions and axioms proper to each problem at the beginning of its study, without proving them.

b) As an apologete, Pascal left to the world his famous *Pensées*, profound and eloquent appeals to convert the incredulous, based on a philosophical doctrine which is difficult to disengage from its setting. The following reconstruction of his philosophical thought can be proposed.

Of the ideas circulated by Descartes, Pascal develops that of *infinity*. The world is infinite both in the large and in the small; depending on one's point of view, each thing is infinite. Infinity involves incomprehensibility. The universe which Descartes thought comprehensible by his principles, escapes, for the most part, our systems of knowledge. " What, then, is left to him but a glimpse of the mean of things, in eternal despair of ever knowing either principle or end... The author of these wonders comprehends them — none other can " [1].

Man, infinitely small by reason of his body, is infinitely great by thought. " Man is little more than a reed, the most feeble thing in nature, but he is a thinking reed " [2]. Man's thought, however, in itself is but small and miserable by dint of the limits and the contradictions he meets within himself. Pascal accumulates all the arguments of *scepticism* against reason; these arguments, though powerless against *dogmatism*, cannot be refuted by the latter view. " Nature confuses the Pyrrhonians, and reason confuses the dogmatists ". Of itself, reason is powerless to attain certitude; nor can reason rest on God, as Descartes thought, for " nature shows God the while she hides Him; we see too much of it to doubt it, and too little to believe ". Of God, Pascal writes, " we cannot know either what He is or if He is " [3].

Nevertheless, between dogmatism and scepticism, mere *abstention* is an impossible solution, for there is no question here of pure speculation, but of moral conduct. We are already embarked on the voyage, and practicality requires that we choose. The latter cannot be rational, for reason is powerless. Often a decision involves self-interest. Hence we have the notion, now famous, of the *wager :* an unbeliever, having considered the situation, grants that in betting on the faith,

---

[1] *Pensées*, art. I, I.
[2] *Ibid.*, art. I, VI.
[3] *Ibid.*, art. 10, I.

he has all to gain and nothing to lose; in betting against the faith, he has all to lose and nothing to gain.

If Pascal taught the use of this method in order to achieve truth in general, he would be classifiable as a *fideist*. " The solution of the foundational problem of certitude would be for him a mere game, throw of the dice, or a wager " [1], for supernatural faith would be the supreme criterion of truth.

But below reason, Pascal mentions another faculty which he calls the HEART. The *heart* grasps intuitively the truths which escape rational demonstration. It sees the justice of the affirmations of good sense and it causes the value of a spirit of finesse in ordinary lives. It is also the faculty of first principles, for it grasps the definitions and the axioms of geometry . [2] It is, hence, certainly distinct from reason : " The heart itself has reasons of which reason knows nothing " [3]. Even though it does not attain science in the proper sense, the heart, in its own order, attains infallible truth.

Having distinguished the order of bodies, constituted by extension, from that of spirits, in which thought is ruler, Pascal speaks of an order infinitely elevated above these. This is the order of *charity*, the proper domain in which the heart and faith dwell. " God is sensible to the heart " [4]. In this realm, the supernatural truths resolve all the antinomies of reason. Pascal's system, accordingly, is a type of *mysticism*.

This quite personal doctrine is opposed to that of Descartes on more than one point. At the same time, one can still trace the Cartesian influence in the radical separation of body and spirit, and in the high esteem Pascal places on the mathematical idea of science.

One dislikes to denature this rich and powerful thought, however, by trying to propose it as an abstract and definitive system; it is rather a living apology addressed to real men in order to convert them. Viewed from this angle, even the most profound paradoxes become profound truths, though not of the philosophical, but rather of the apologetic and theological orders [5].

---

[1] D. J. MERCIER, *Critériologie Générale*, p. 134.

[2] *Pensées*, art. 8, VI. — [3] *Ibid.*, art. 24, V.

[4] *Ibid.* " It is the heart which senses God, and not reason. Behold, this is what faith is : God is sensible to the heart, and not to reason ".

[5] H. BRÉMOND, in his *Histoire littéraire du sentiment religieux en France*, IV, " La conquête mystique : l'école du Port-Royal " (Paris, 1920), pp. 318-417, studies the accusations made against Pascal of having Jansenistic strains in his thought.

In Pascal, as in Fénelon and Bossuet, the rationalistic seeds planted by Descartes were unable to develop but were quenched, not so much by an adverse philosophical attack as by the efficacious control of the Catholic faith. These seeds expand into full bloom, however, with Malebranche and with Spinoza; in two quick leaps, they reach pantheism. Two articles will outline this development.

ARTICLE I : Malebranche.

ARTICLE II : Spinoza.

ARTICLE ONE. — MALEBRANCHE.

(1638-1715).

SPECIAL BIBLIOGRAPHY.

1º **Works :** *Œuvres complètes*, 11 vols., Paris, 1712. — GINSBERG, M. (transl.), *Dialogues on Metaphysics and on Religion*, New York, 1923.

2º **Studies :** BLAMPIGNON, J., *Etudes sur Malebranche*, Paris, 1862. — CHURCH, R. W., *A Study in the Philosophy of Malebranche*, London, 1931. — DOLBRES, V., *Etude sur la philosophie de Malebranche*, Paris, 1925. — GAONACH, J. M., *La théorie des idées dans la philosophie de Malebranche*, Rennes, 1909. — GOUHIER, H., *La philosophie de Malebranche et son expérience religieuse ; — La vocation de Malebranche*, 2 vols., Paris, 1926. — JOLY H., *Malebranche*, Paris, 1930. — LE MOINE, A., *Des vérités éternelles selon Malebranche*, Paris, 1936. — LUCE, A. A., *Berkeley and Malebranche*, Oxford, 1934. — OLLÉ-LAPRUNE, L., *La philosophie de Malebranche*, Paris, 1870-72.

339. Born at Paris, Nicolas Malebranche entered the Congregation of the Oratory in 1660, where he was able to satisfy his desire to study. His modesty and his love for solitary meditations were well known. During the years he spent studying philosophy and theology at the Sorbonne, he was disheartened by the subtle discussions which encumbered the Scholasticism of his times.

Having read Descartes' *Traité de l'homme* (1664), he was somewhat seduced by the simplicity of mechanism there outlined, and took Descartes as his philosopher by preference.

Malebranche's principal works are : *De la recherche de la Vérité* (1674-1675) and *De la nature de la grâce* (1680), in which he applied his new philosophy for explaining his faith; these works precipitated prolonged controversies with Arnauld and

Bossuet. In order to defend himself from the attacks of these men, he wrote : *Le traité de morale* (1683), *Les méditations chrétiennes* (1683) and *Les entretiens sur la Métaphysique et la Religion* (1688).

General Characteristics and Directive Principles. By accepting Cartesianism in his master principles, Malebranche wished to retain full liberty in correcting and in completing them. His theological formation and especially his love for St. Augustine, the preferred master of the Oratorians, helped him sound out and criticize one of the weak points of Cartesianism, namely, the innatism of clear ideas and their relation to God, the source of their truth. At the same time, his unshakable fidelity to the Catholic faith prevented him from continuing on towards the full unification of his thought. As a result, there are two foundational principles in his philosophy.

a) **The Principle of the Clear Idea.** This principle is wholly absorbed from Descartes. Malebranche states that *one must accept as truth only that which is contained in the clear idea, as long as one sees it with evidence.* This leads him to misunderstand experience, learning and the deductive, a priori trait of his own propositions.

b) **The Principle of Infinity.** This principle is quite original, but it is less absolute and announced more as a tendency : *the infinite is the supremely clear idea.* The infinite is so manifestly sovereign that it can unify and explain everything; but since the open adoption of this principle leads to pantheism, Malebranche preferred to complicate his system somewhat, and admit some deficiency in the value of our clear ideas.

The application of this double principle clarifies three principal objects : *God*, through ontologism; the *world*, through occasionalism; *man and morality*, through both occasionalism and ontologism.

I. GOD AND ONTOLOGISM.

340. Malebranche's point of departure in philosophy is the double evidence furnished by the clear idea of the infinite : God exists, and man sees everything in God.

A) **Existence of God.**

It is not necessary to give a proof, in the proper sense, for God's existence, since the simple examination of our intellectual life furnishes us with its intuition. It is not possible to think without affirming *being*, and being is the infinite, not only in a negative sense as the absence of limit, but in the positive sense, as Descartes viewed it, as excluding all limitation through the affirmation of its riches. Evidently, the idea of such fulness of being necessarily contains existence. Thus, man is not by himself his own natural light, but God exists, the Infinite Being in Whose intelligible clarity all our truths are steeped.

B) **Vision in God.**

341. From the existence and the function of the Infinite, this proposition follows :

It is in God, uniquely and immediately, that man contemplates the object of all his intellectual ideas.

If, as a matter of fact, each of these ideas involves the affirmation of the infinite, as follows from the properties of necessity, immutability and eternity of ideas, and especially from their universality, which permits the same nature to be realized an infinity of times — then it is impossible that any created object could furnish a perfection so great, and that our finite soul could contain it. God alone can contain the infinite; in fact, the Word of God, as in Augustine's view, contains within Himself the ideal world of Plato, wherein are the eternal and infinite Archetypes of all things. All human knowledge has no other object than these Divine Ideas and their essential relations. This especially justifies the value of mathematical sciences, whose object, extension, is a clear idea best proportioned to our reason, and consequently most perfectly contemplated in God from here below on earth.

This theory is the most frank expression of ONTOLOGISM; it will be taken up again by Gioberti and others in the nineteenth century [1]. Ontologism can be defined as " the doctrine explaining the spiritual trait of our intellections by proposing as the unique object of human reason the Divine Being Itself, immediately known through intuition, and in Whom reflection discovers all other truths ".

Pressed by the demands of his faith and by the objections of theologians, especially those of Arnauld and Bossuet, Malebranche gave some important nuances to his view. At first, he admitted as beyond the Divine Ideas themselves, some created ideas which are the finite modifications of human reason. Only the object

---

[1] See below, n. 437.

expressed by them is an infinite, and cannot be perceived but in God alone.

Furthermore, by his notion of the *vision in God*, Malebranche does not mean a perfect intuition of the Divine Essence in its ineffable simplicity. It is but a view limited to one particular aspect. God manifests Himself in a determined mode, as that of extension, so that there must be distinguished two things, the object of our idea and the divine attribute. Accordingly, intelligible extension, the source of geometry and mathematics in general, is the Divine Essence seen as participable by all possible bodies; however, the divine immensity, as the attribute to which this latter extension corresponds, is an extension from which all imperfection must be removed, as well as divisibility and localization through parts. Extension is in God wholly, entirely and throughout at once. This perfection makes God actually inaccessible to human reason. If one asks Malebranche how an *intuitive* view can see *but a part* of an *absolutely simple essence*, he would answer that this is an impenetrable mystery; if one denies it, he would fall into the horrible error of pantheism.

This powerlessness of our reason is well explained, in St. Thomas' view, by the necessity, incumbent on man in the natural order, of knowing God *analogically* by the help of abstract concepts of the created perfections in which an aspect of the Divine Essence is reflected. Malebranche misunderstood abstraction, and these restrictions, while good in themselves, seemed philosophically arbitrary. However, his theory of vision in God helped him at least to correct the voluntarism of Descartes. For Malebranche, the necessary relations between essences, as expressed by our ideas and our knowledge, are at first the object of the Divine Intelligence; hence they are immutable, and do not depend uniquely on the Liberty of God.

II. THE WORLD AND OCCASIONALISM.

342. The principle of the clear idea requires that, if the world exists, it not only be a created world, but that it be directed by the unique causality of God, Whose supreme law is simplicity.

A) Existence and Creation of the World.

Evidently, it is not possible for Malebranche to get any reliable certitude on the reality of the corporeal world through sensible knowledge. The unique source of truth is the clear and distinct idea of extension. But does it not suffice, in order to admit the world's objectivity, to admit its existence in God, wherein we see it by intuition, so that the real existence of a corporeal world would be useless? Philosophically, Malebranche admits the value of this hypothesis. But many dogmas, as that of the Incarnation and Redemption, seemed to require a real world. He admits its reality through faith, and explains it, on the other hand, through pure Cartesian mechanism.

With regard to the origin of the world, the clear idea of the infinite requires that it be created by God. The fulness of the Divine Being, and especially the intelligible extension which is but an aspect of the infinite essence, is a source from which all bodies, as finite and participated extensions, evolve.

B) Occasionalism.

343. If the world exists as created and conserved by God, its role must be delimited. No body can act in any way at all; God alone is the unique, efficient and efficacious cause, immediately productive of all the actions in the universe. Creatures, by their presence, merely furnish Him an *occasion* of manifesting their activity according to the laws of His wisdom. This proposition is deduced from the clear idea of the infinite, and from the idea of extension.

a) *The infinite* evidently involves absolute domination over all the finite. On the one hand, in creating and conserving bodies, the infinite produces all their determinations, and thus their state of repose or their movement. On the other hand, this sovereign, efficacious production, which nothing can resist, makes all other production of movement utterly useless[1]. Thus God alone is the cause of the interaction of bodies.

b) The clear idea of *extension* provides the same view. Extension expresses a wholly passive essence, an inert being, receptive of movement but not conferring it on itself, nor on others. Furthermore, in order to move, the body would have to conceive an end and voluntarily direct its mobility thither, which is absurd.

C) Law of Simplicity.

While it is true that God does everything in the universe, this fact does not make scientific research useless, because He acts according to laws.

God does everything through the most simple ways and for His greater glory; this is the foundational law of Divine Providence demanded by the perfection of the idea of the infinite. From

---

[1] For Malebranche, as for Descartes, there is a certain immutable quantity of movement in the universe; it was created by God at the beginning of things (see n. 333). With this presupposition, the argument becomes more clear.

this it follows that God contents Himself in formulating, though efficaciously, some *general volitions*, not very numerous, but quite rich in their applications; they are furnished by the diversity of occasional causes. The object of science is to make these particular laws precise and to coordinate them into the general volitions.

From this principle it again follows that the actual world is the *best possible*, if not absolutely at least to the extent that it involves the best possible good obtained by the most simple methods.

Occasionalism thus understood is a sort of poor transposition of secondary causality, such as the Scholastic doctrine grants to creatures; in this view, though creatures receive even the very being of their action from the divine premotion, they have their own proper power which guarantees the reality of their causality. For Malebranche, this proper power becomes a simple, inefficacious sign which, however, infallibly involves the efficacious action of God alone through the law of infinite wisdom.

This hypothesis, though not a priori impossible, is certainly contrary to experimental evidence; it is an *error* arising from the excessive application of the procedure of the clear idea. Furthermore, created activity, far from being opposed to the divine perfection, is rather a new manifestation of it, for the creature participates in God not only in its being, but also in its activity. Finally, since the ultimate reason of the being of things lies in their operation, in proclaiming God as the sole agent, one is inextricably involved in saying that He is the only substance existing; Malebranche seems to lead to Spinoza.

III.   MAN AND MORALITY.

344. In applying these two theories to man, Malebranche establishes some propositions of psychology from which he then deduces a morality.

I) **Psychology.** The nature of the human soul was less clear to Malebranche than it was to Descartes. Without doubt, we have the intuition of its existence by the fact of thought, but it is not possible, here below, to contemplate within God the idea of the thinking self with the same perfection that one sees the idea of extension. If such an intuition were given man, it would distract him too much from the Divine Glory, which is man's sole purpose. Hence it is reserved to heaven, where it subordinates itself to the more captivating and perfect vision of God's essence.

Here again, Malebranche seems hesitant, fearing pantheism. For if the spiritual nature of the thinking self gives it the eternity, necessity and infinity of the other abstract ideas, its individual character could no longer be seen in God except through identity. One can avoid this conclusion, again, by affirming this to be a mystery.

The theory of occasionalism did supply Malebranche, however, with an explanation of the union of soul and body, which had been an insoluble problem for Descartes.

Soul and body having opposed attributes, they can in no way act upon each other. Their union is a *law* freely established by God according to which one portion of extension, the body, is the occasion for parallel movements in the soul; both movements are directly produced by God. On the other hand, the inefficacious wishes of our soul are infallibly followed by parallel movements in the body, and through the body in other bodies, these actions also stemming from God alone.

A law of this sort, without doubt, cannot be explained naturally[1], but it must be considered as a *proof;* and, since original sin, as a chastisement which permits the soul to merit heaven.

Thus, the human soul is immediately joined to God; and, through the intermediary of the divine causality, united to the body. The soul sees the idea of extension in God through the intermediary by which it knows the body. And, as the sensible qualities are absent from the clear idea of the body, the testimony of the senses has no value, at least in the speculative order wherein it is essentially deceived; its true and unique role is in the practical realm. It teaches us to be resigned to bodily needs; moreover, before sin, the exercise of the senses depended so much on the will that one could not be deceived with regard to their purpose.

2) **Morality. 345.** Occasionalism, by depriving man of his free activity, is destructive of morality. But Malebranche distinguished the physical reality of an act of will, as the act of studying, from speaking, which is produced by God alone. *Consent* is a purely immanent action which remains in the power of free will, so that by refusal, we suppress the occasional cause and the effect of the divine act which is joined to it. Thus responsibility, the basis of morality, is somewhat safeguarded. Furthermore, since God acts directly only through His general volitions, He allows free play to our liberty; yet, there is nothing in human action which escapes His causality.

---

[1] One can say that according to the natural law, sensation is always *auxiliary* to the soul, as it was before original sin. If it is now a source of trouble and of error, this holds because in applying the same law, sensation aids a soul depraved by sin. For this interpretation, see E. BRÉHIER, *op. cit.*, II, p. 208.

The " vision in God ", by discovering this law of simplicity, directive of the conduct of Providence, opens up to us a *universal rule of morality*. Sin consists in following its egoistic inspirations and in judging that to be good which is personally agreeable, in opposition to the good of the totality willed by God. Perfection consists in judging nothing to be good except by eternal relations seen in the Divine Ideas, so that man's consent is always conformed to the laws of the Divine Will. From this view, Malebranche deduces a group of rules for Catholic morality. It is a rather excellent morality, because, even though the notion of the vision of God on which it is founded is contestable, it is true that conformity of man's will to the divine will is the supreme law of morality.

In Summary : *The Augustinian doctrine of the explicative influence of God, whether on our ideas as the source of eternal truths, or on the universe as the source of all perfection — interpreted in the Cartesian view of the clear and distinct idea — led Malebranche to two extreme positions. In the first, that of the vision in God, he suppresses all activity from objective evidence to the benefit of the Divine, exemplary Idea. In the second, that of occasionalism, he suppressed every transitive activity of creatures to the benefit of the creative influence of God. But his Catholic faith kept him from pantheism.*

CONCLUSION. **346.** Malebranche is a profound and original thinker, and the clearness of his style assured him a powerful influence. He is deeply attached to the Christian doctrine of revealed mysteries, but his rational system in no wise merits the title of a Christian philosophy [1]. If one considers its foundational principle in its very essence, it is but Cartesian, and, as a result, rationalistic. Faith cannot come in here any more as a light or stimulant, but mainly as a restraint and a hindrance to the full flowering of a philosophical system. The mutual aid of faith and reason becomes a fight.

The conflict is manifested mainly in the capital problem of the relations between God and the world. Often, in the course of this exposition of his thought, it was seen that his thought was arrested from the tendency to pantheism by the requirements of the Catholic faith. This seems to be experimental proof that the logic of the Cartesian system leads there

---

[1] In the historical sense explained above; see n. 244.

infallibly. A more independent mind, free from the happy restraints of dogma, could bring this error into the full light of day; this was Spinoza.

ARTICLE TWO. — SPINOZA.
(1632-1677).

SPECIAL BIBLIOGRAPHY.

1º **Works :** *Benedicti de Spinoza Opera,* J. VAN VLOTEN and J. LAND (eds.), 2 vols., 1895, and 4 vols., 1914. — ELWES, P. (transl.), *The Chief Works of B. Spinoza,* 2 vols., New York, 1951. — WHITE, W., (transl.), *Ethics,* New York, 1949.

2º **Studies :** BIDNEY, D., *The Psychology and Ethics of Spinoza,* New Haven, 1940. — BRUNSWICG, L., *Spinoza,* 3rd ed., Paris, 1923, — *Le platonisme de Spinoza,* Paris, 1923. — DARBON, A., *Etudes Spinozistes,* Paris, 1946. — DELBOS, V., *Le problème moral dans la philosophie de Spinoza,* Paris, 1893. — *Le Spinozisme,* Paris, 1916. — DUFF, R. A., *Spinoza's Ethical and Political Philosophy.* Glasgow, 1903. — FISCHER, K., *Spinoza, Leben, Werke und Lehre,* 5th ed., Heidelberg, 1909. — FRIEDMANN, G., *Leibniz et Spinoza,* Paris, 1946. — GILSON, E., *Spinoza interprète de Descartes,* La Haye, 1923. — HAMPSHIRE, S., *Spinoza,* Baltimore, 1952. — HUAN, G., *Le Dieu de Spinoza,* Arras, 1913. — JOACHIM, H. H., *Spinozas' Tratactus de Intellectus Emendatione : A Commentary,* Oxford, 1940. — KALLET, H. L., *Æternitas, A Spinozistic Study,* Oxford, 1930. — LACHIEZE-REY, P., *Les origines cartésiennes du Dieu de Spinoza,* Paris, 1932. — MC KEON, R., *The Philosophy of Spinoza,* New York, 1928. — RATNER, J., *Spinoza on God,* New York, 1930. — RIVAUD, A., *Les notions d'essence et d'existence dans la philosophie de Spinoza,* Paris, 1906. — ROTH, L., *Spinoza,* London, 1929. — *Spinoza, Descartes and Maimonides,* Oxford, 1924. — SAW, R. L., *The Vindication of Metaphysics : A Study in the Philosophy of Spinoza,* London, 1951. — SEROUYA, H., *Spinoza, Sa vie. Sa philosophie,* Paris, 1947. — SIWEK, P., *Spinoza et le panthéisme religieux,* new ed., Paris, 1950. — *Au cœur du Spinozisme,* Bruges, 1952. — RUNES, D. D., *Spinoza Dictionary,* New York, 1951. — VON DUNIN-BORKOWSKI, *Der junge de Spinoza,* Munster, 1910. — *Aus den Tagen Spinozas,* 4 vols., Munster, 1933-36. — WOLF, A., (ed. and transl.), *Life of Spinoza, or the Oldest Biography of Spinoza,* London, 1927. — WOLFSON, H., *The Philosophy of Spinoza,* Harvard, 1948. — ZWEIG, A., *Spinoza,* Paris, 1940.

347. Baruch (or Benedict) Spinoza was born in Amsterdam of Jewish parents who were originally from Spain. His early thoughts were molded by a rabbi enamored of the rationalist exegesis of Maimonides. Spinoza soon showed himself to be of gifted intelligence, and independent and daring in thought. He had a basic desire for unity in thought; this factor, along with influences from the Jewish traditions of the Cabala and, in particular, of the Zohar [1], oriented his thought towards pantheism. Having learned Latin, he was able to read the modern philosophers of the Renaissance, as Giordano Bruno [2], which moved his thoughts in the same direction. Descartes, beginning with 1654, was the decisive influence in his life; he found in Cartesianism the doctrinal frame which, he believed, enabled him to give a rigorous demonstration of the monistic view of things by which he was so fascinated [3].

His pantheism was directly opposed to orthodox Judaism on many points, and for this reason, in 1646, he was solemnly excommunicated by the Synagogue. At this same time, he began to feel the first attacks of tuberculosis, to which he would later succumb. Oppressed by these miseries, he retired to a frugal and austere life, refusing a professorship at the University of Heidelberg, and earning his own living by polishing lenses.

All of his works were written in Latin; the main ones are *Tractatus Theologico-politicus* (edited in 1670), *Principia philosophiæ Cartesianæ;* after his death, there appeared his *Tractatus de intellectus emendatione,* and his master work, *Ethica Ordine Geometrico Demonstrata.* The last work is presented, even by title, as being done " in the geometrical mode ", with definitions, axioms, theorems and corollaries. It is the triumph of the mathematical method of the clear idea.

General Characteristics. Not only did Spinoza adopt the method of the clear idea, but he also gave it its full meaning and applied it with a rigorous logic. At first, he defended, with complete freedom, the total independence of *reason* with regard to *revelation* in the pursuit of truth. He held there was no communication between faith or theology and philosophy and thus no conflict to resolve. Theology is not at the service of philosophy, nor philosophy at the service of theology [4].

---

[1] The Zohar, or " Book of Splendor ", " studied with zeal in the Jewish milieu of Amsterdam around 1647 ", taught that there is but one substance and that all things are one in God (see J. MARÉCHAL, *op. cit.,* p. 108).

[2] " The dependence of Spinoza on Bruno is generally affirmed because of striking analogies between them. The argument is not decisive, for they could both have drawn, independently, from the same Neo-Platonic source " (J. MARÉCHAL, *ibid.,* p. 111).

[3] Some historians of philosophy try to attenuate the Cartesian influence on Spinoza, and emphasize the fact that Spinoza had an intuition of pantheism before knowing Descartes' thought. It is, nevertheless, true that Spinoza's thought is the logical development of Descartes' position.

[4] L. BRUNSCHWICG, *Spinoza,* p. 24.

The Bible merely requires the believer to accept the unique dogma of God's existence, and to obey the precepts of justice and of charity. The domain of speculative and of practical truth is reserved to reason.

In the philosophical domain, Spinoza distinguished confused ideas, which are subject to error, from clear ideas, which are infallibly true. The latter must have a simple object according to the rules of Cartesian deduction, but *of such a sort that each element has its own place in the unique system, making the universality of the real intelligible.* For this reason, his procedure is to adopt a few definitions which impose themselves by their own evidence, and from them to deduce the explanation of all things, from God, the summit of the universe, down to the human soul; he concludes with a treatise on the manner of living which is most capable of making man happy. The criterion of infallible truth of each of his conclusions is its aptitude in taking its own place within the total edifice of science, and in forming one of the rings of the unique chain of intuitive deductions which make the whole of reality intelligible.

This requirement of absolute unity or of universal intelligibility is not illegitimate, for it is natural to reason. Descartes had arbitrarily admitted but a number of independent, clear ideas. But in a methodology admitting only deduction as a process of reasoning, and in which the whole explicative cause is intrinsic and constitutive of the effect, it was inevitable that its rigorous application would lead to absolute monism or to pantheism.

As a matter of record, Spinoza fashioned the first form of *pantheism* in modern philosophy. His view of it can be called " intellectualist "; that is, objective or realist, for it pretends that it can be proved through a rigorous demonstration of reason. This demonstration is developed in three stages : the first establishes that God is the unique substance, known through His attributes; the second explains how the infinite God and the finite world can coexist; the third deduces a morality from the above, though with a new and original twist. Three paragraphs will present this material :

    I : God known through His Attributes.

    II : The Coexistence of the World and God.

    III : Morality.

I. God known through his attributes.

348. A) Spinoza first establishes the **reality of God.** Beginning with the clear idea of substance, he deduces three propositions from it.

1° **Substance exists necessarily.** For Spinoza, as for Descartes, the clear idea of substance is that of a being which has no need of another in order to subsist [1]; this is the idea of a perfect being who subsists by Himself. From this definition of substance, one moves on to the affirmation of its *real existence*, for the denial of its existence destroys its definition; to stipulate its definition is to stipulate its real existence. Besides, since we have an intuition of this definition through the clear idea, which is infallible, we thus know that substance exists necessarily in reality.

2° **This substance is infinite.** It would be repugnant to hold that substance, whose total definition implies existence through itself, could, in some way, be any sort of " non-being ". But *finite being* can be understood only as a sort of " non-being ", and as a limitation which is a non-perfection. It is thus impossible that substance be finite; it is infinite by definition.

3° **This substance is unique.** As a matter of fact, a second substance, which would be distinguishable from the first, is impossible. For to hold this, the first would have to possess a perfection which the second one would not; in that case, the second substance would involve some " non-being " and be *finite*, a situation which would be impossible, since it has been demonstrated that every substance is infinite.

This substance, Spinoza concludes, is God, the necessary being, infinite and unique, simple, immutable, eternal and sovereignly independent.

This proof for God's existence has the same value as the Cartesian method of the clear idea, but no more than that. It will fall, as will that of Descartes and of Leibniz, under the blows of Kantian criticism [2], which, in this regard, is in agreement with St. Thomas.

It is, however, quite right to deduce God's infinity and uniqueness from that which fully realizes the notion of substance; but the latter has *several manners* in which it can be realized. Besides

---

[1] This is the definition of Descartes (see above, n. 325). Descartes corrected it in order to avoid pantheism and Spinoza knew of this correction, as can be seen in his *Principia philosophiæ Cartesianæ*, Vol. IV, p. 143). His pantheism, accordingly, has much deeper roots than merely that of a false definition.

[2] See below, n. 408, III.

the infinite and absolute manner in God, there is a finite and participated manner in creatures [1]. In order to demonstrate this view of pluralism, the *value of experience* [2] must be accepted as the source of infallible truth; but this acceptance involves a whole methodology which is opposed to that of the clear idea.

349. B) Spinoza next takes up the question of **what sort of knowledge can be acquired of God.** We seek to conceive of God as a determined nature, in order to form for ourselves a clear idea. With this end in view, we look for the attribute which constitutes the Divine Essence (following the Cartesian doctrine) [3]. But, in a proper sense, *God does not have essence;* one cannot determine a fundamental property which would define Him, as one defines the soul through thought; every attribute, being determined, implies a *limit*, but God is *infinite* being. From this it follows that a triple condition is required in order that a proper idea of God be obtained :

1º We must identify His essence with His existence, while these two elements are really distinct in creatures [4].

2º We must conceive each of the attributes (extension, for example), as infinite in its own order, although, by definition, it is finite as essence [5].

3º Finally, in order to correct this necessary limitation, we must conceive of an infinity of attributes in God. God can be defined, then, as the perfect being constituted by an infinity of attributes, each of which is infinite in its own order.

But of all these attributes, we know but two, thought and extension [6]; for, as Descartes has shown, only these two are constitutive of our world.

---

[1] In other words, the idea of substance or of being existing of itself, is *not univocal* but analogous; see above, n. 259, 3.

[2] Experience here is either internal or external and sensible with its intuitively given materials; see above, n. 262.

[3] The *essence* of a being, for Descartes, is knowable only through its attributes; see above, n. 325.

[4] The essence or nature of " creatures " is constituted by the modes; see below, n. 350.

[5] The attribute is the object of the *clear and distinct idea;* following the Cartesian logic, this object should really be distinguished from others. Spinoza clearly affirms the identity of all attributes with the unique, divine substance; but he does not examine the possible reconciliation of these two points of view.

[6] Extension, as a divine attribute, and as known through the same clear idea as body is known, logically would introduce into God an element incompatible with His perfection, namely that of *matter*. This is one of the most debatable points about Spinoza's view. One would at least have to hold that God does not possess this property of extension " formally "; Spinoza did not make this distinction, however.

In Summary : *God, Substance or necessary Being, infinite and unique, knowable by right through an infinity of attributes or clear ideas, is known to man, as a matter of fact, through two attributes, that of thought and that of extension.*

II. COEXISTENCE OF THE WORLD AND GOD.

350. If God is the unique substance, it is evidently impossible to find any other substance outside of Him. Nevertheless, Spinoza held that the world is distinguished from God by its *nature;* this permits him to speak of its emanation, or even of its creation. It also makes it possible for him to construct a psychology of man.

A) Distinction of the World from God.

It is not only evident that substance is unique, but it is just as evident that the world exists [1] and is composed of multiple beings, which are mobile, finite, and contingent. These two certitudes Spinoza attempts to reconcile by admitting but one Being or only one *subsistent* being, but *two really distinct natures.* 1) The Divine Nature *(natura naturans)* is one of these ; it is constituted by the *attributes* and is absolutely simple and immutable. 2) The created nature *(natura naturata)* is constituted by the *modes*, which are realities incapable of existing in themselves, but solely in God and through God. These modes, at least in their inferior degrees, are finite, multiple and changing, and constitute the particular things of our experience.

In order to connect these contingent realities to the Divine Essence, Spinoza conceives of a series of intermediaries in the fashion of Plotinus. Two *finite* modes are distinguished, and two *infinite* ones. The infinite modes are of two types : the first and most perfect emanate directly and immediately from each divine attribute; the second come forth only mediately and through the first, and from these second infinite modes there springs forth the mobile series of finite modes. Thus, the attribute Thought directly produces the infinite intelligence as its immediate mode; from the latter, it seems [2], as mediate modes, there comes forth the whole ensemble of immortal and eternal souls, which, in turn, give rise to the multiple human souls on earth. In parallel and similar

---

[1] The incontestable facts of experience, as the existence of thought and of the world, are presented by Spinoza as " axioms ". See V. DELBOS, *Le problème moral dans la philosophie de Spinoza*, Paris, 1893, p. 79.

[2] This is Delbos' conjecture; see his *Le Spinozisme*, p. 61.

fashion, the attribute Extension directly produces movement in general as its infinite mode; from the latter emanates that which Spinoza calls "the visage of the entire universe "[1]. The latter expression seems to signify nature considered as a sort of individual totality, permanent and stable through the law of conservation of energy. And this infinite, mediate mode is, at last, the source of all the finite modifications of extension which make up the corporeal world.

These intermediaries seemed necessary to Spinoza in order to make intelligible the passage from the absolutely infinite to the finite. But the infinite modes are readily distinguished from their attributes by their nature as dependent and subordinated effects. Hence, in Spinoza's view, God is the unique being, subsisting in two distinct natures.

B) **Emanation or Creation of the World.**

When does this distinction of nature arise? It is not the work of the free will of God, as, according to Catholic teaching, the Word of God freely became incarnate, nor in the way that Descartes held essences to be dependent on the Divine Will. Here Spinoza explicitly abandons the Cartesian voluntarism, even by following the methodology of the clear idea; that is, by following the demands of the divine, infinite perfection expressed by the clear idea of God. God is, without doubt, perfectly free and independent in the sense that, being the unique being, He can have no constraint upon His person. But He is not free in the sense that He could be other than He is or could produce something other than He actually has *in fact;* for the latter situations to occur, He would have to change and to cease from being absolutely perfect being, which would be impossible.

In this way, God is made to be a principle infinitely fruitful in its simplicity, and, just as from one truth there follows necessarily an infinity of conclusions, so from each divine attribute there follows an infinity of corresponding *modes.* Accordingly, besides our world, which is constructed of the two modes of thought and extension as manifesting these two divine attributes, there is an infinity of other worlds to manifest the other divine attributes. The unrolling of this modal series is as necessarily eternal as the unique divine substance in which they subsist. THE ETERNITY OF THE WORLD is an inevitable corollary of pantheism.

---

[1] *Letter to Schuller,* (Van Vloten and Land ed.), Epist. LXIV, p. 219; see V. DELBOS, *op. cit.,* p. 58.

It follows from the above that contingency and liberty do not really exist in reality. They are but illusions, for man knows but a minimum part of the infinite series of modes. If man had intuition of the Divine Essence, he would see in each attribute, as in its explicative source, an infinite series of modes not only generally, but in every detail; all temporal occurrences without exception come forth from the attribute with the same inflexible logic.

351. This fatalistic evolvement of the modes is called **creation.** It seemed to Spinoza that he had thus resolved the problem of *efficient causality* by suppressing it, and no other Cartesian had been able to form a clear idea of this type of causality. Spinoza's solution does not require any production or *action* from God, but merely *formal participation*[1] in the divine being.

Nevertheless, by establishing a real distinction between the divine and the created natures, Spinoza pushed the problem back farther. Since *natura naturans* is immutable, it cannot constitute *natura naturata*. What follows, then, is that the latter is really produced, even though it partakes of the divine substance (as the Humanity of Christ was created, although participating in the existence of the Word of God). Here again, the only reasonable explanation requires the application of the principle of efficient causality and the notion of *participated being*, which notions break the limited confines of the clear idea.

C) **Psychological Consequences.**

352. Evidently, body and soul are no longer two complete and distinct substances, but solely two modes of the unique, divine substance. The series of our thoughts, as that of corporeal movements, falls under the common rule; both are subjected to a rigorous determinism, and no room is left for liberty.

From another point of view, the two modes of body and of soul are adequately distinct as modes, for they correspond to the two clear ideas of thought and extension. They manifest two attributes which *identify themselves* in the divine simplicity. They do this by an equal number of corresponding " manifestations " : to each body there corresponds a soul, and to each movement of the body, there corresponds an idea or a thought, and vice versa. *The parallelism of the modes,* founded on their substantial identity in the divine being,

---

[1] One could say, in Scholastic terminology, that the created modes are *formal effects* of the unique, divine subtance, as the properties necessarily joined to a nature are the formal effects of this nature.

explains, without any difficulty, the union of body and soul and their apparent interaction.

Moreover, this mutual dependence becomes, for human thought, a necessity of taking as the proper and immediately proportionate object of thought the very body to which it is united; this explains the limitation and inequality of intellectual knowledge. As a matter of fact, adequate knowledge should express, *at the same time* as the object of the idea, the cause or reason for this object. Now this situation is realized neither in the idea which the soul forms of itself, nor in the idea which it acquires of the body. If it considers itself " as a finite mode of thought, it has its cause in another finite mode "; if it considers its body, " the existence and the makeup of this body depend on the influence of the exterior bodies which escape it " [1]; finally, it knows other bodies only through the intermediary of movements or variable " affections " upon its own body, where they are manifested quite imperfectly. The soul can form only *confused and inadequate ideas* of others, which are, as a consequence, subject to error [2]. Thus the source of error no longer is free will, but the inferior situation, so limited and incomplete with relation to everything divine, in which this " special mode " of thought exists which constitutes our spiritual soul. For this reason, Spinoza entitles this part of his ethics, " Concerning Human Slavery ".

Meanwhile, there is a remedy for this slavery. There lies a third source of knowledge beyond the realm of common experience, which is always fallible, and the scientific generalization, which is so imperfect [3]; this source is the intuition of clear ideas infallibly true. The modes possess, at their deepest source, the reality of the infinite substance of God, whose richness they explain with rigorous necessity. In them one can find, beyond the multiplicity of corporeal movements and of the soul's thoughts, the simple, immutable and infinite perfection which is the divine attribute, and one can see, more and more, the fully explicative reason for all human vicissitudes.

---

[1] E. Bréhier, *Histoire de la philosophie*, II, p. 176.

[2] Spinoza says they are " like consequences separated from their premisses " (*Ethica*, II, prop. 28).

[3] Spinoza grants a real value to the truth of knowledge of the second type, that is, to reasoning. It leads us to grasp the infinite modes and we begin to see things under the aspect of eternity. It also functions, as the infinite modes, in the role of intermediary between sensible and imaginative knowledge, which are always subject to error, and the intuition of the divine attributes, always infallible, and the source of human salvation.

This intuition knows how to consider each thing from the divine point of view, " under the likeness of eternity ". This ascension, which culminates in perfect wisdom, also constitutes, under its affective aspect, the whole of morality.

In Summary : *There is but one being, one sole subsistent thing, but the nature of the world, constituted by the modes, is really distinct from the nature of God, constituted by the attributes. The modes explain the attributes, at least in their development, which is as necessary as a logical process, and, in a sense, parallel. This helps explain the union of soul and body and the inadequate character of our ideas.*

III. MORALITY.

A) Indicative Morality.

353. In the ordinary sense of the word, morality is a *practical and imperative science* and not merely a speculative one. It not only expresses that which is and that which one does, but *that which should be done*. Basing itself on the nature of man as endowed with liberty and as subject to the laws of the Creator, morality deduces the rules of action which make human life good, perfect, and tendential towards happiness as a merited recompense, while infraction of these rules involves chastisement.

Spinoza's morality is founded on the negation of human liberty and on the affirmation of an absolute determinism. It cannot be *imperative*, and none of its rules can be obligatory. It is purely *indicative* and simply states that which occurs. From this point of view, evil, and even moral evil, has no meaning; all the events are necessary manifestations of the Providence of God, Who is Good, essentially. Hence, all is good; crimes as well as virtues are justified by their very existence [1].

However, not everything has the same degree of goodness. Among men, some are " determined " to know the true goods

---

[1] Spinoza keeps the vocabulary of " good " and of " evil ", though defining them in his own way. " By the good I understand that which we certainly know to be a means of drawing us closer and closer to that model of human nature we have set up for ourselves; by evil, on the other hand, what we certainly know to prevent us from reproducing this model " (*Ethica*, IV, Preface). This " model " does not designate an ideal which must be realized and which we can freely thrust away, but it shows us what we are as a mode emanating from the divine substance. See V. DELBOS, *op. cit.*, pp. 141-2.

by the eyes of reason and to achieve this good. These are the best men; they are the virtuous, and thereby determined to be fully *happy*.

The others, the vicious men, are " determined " also, but by other influences than that of reason; they are not, therefore, blamable, but rather to be held in low esteem. They are reprimanded legitimately, however, for the good men are determined to dominate the evil by establishing justice and public peace.

With these new notions, Spinoza set about to construct a complete morality, both individual and social. He begins with the principle that *every idea of itself implicates a tendency*. Descartes had considered the judgment as the common work of two faculties, will and intelligence. Spinoza, remarking that the activity of judgment, which is assent affirming or denying, is truly a knowledge, concludes that these two functions are always inseparable, and, as a consequence [1], really identical. Will and idea are but two aspects of the same mode of " thought ", which constitutes the " nature " of the soul. In expanding his view of morality, Spinoza considers the affective aspect, or the will, in a special way.

B) **Morality of Joy.**

354. In its development, the foundational desire or tendency of the soul is necessarily and uniquely divided into two affections, sadness and joy. If an obstacle is encountered which limits or diminishes the tendency, sadness results. Spinoza calls sadness " the least action " and defines it as " the passion through which the soul passes to a lesser perfection ". If circumstances are favorable, desire expands into joy, which is " the passion through which the soul passes to a much greater perfection ". All the other sentiments are but combinations of these two primary states, so that the whole problem of morality becomes conquering the greatest and the *true* joy.

The nature of this true joy and the means of acquiring it evidently follow from the theory of ideas. In fact, Spinoza's whole view of morality can be summarized in the following proposition :

The supreme happiness both for individuals and for peoples consists in elevating the self above the passions through the intellectual love of God.

1. To confused and inadequate ideas, which are always susceptible to error, there correspond imperfect and incompleted tendencies which one properly calls the *passions*. To give in to one's passions is to condemn oneself to live in the narrow limit of the

---

[1] In the theory of the clear idea, the notion of inseparability involves identity; see above, n. 325.

finite modes, in which desires knock against and interfere with each other and multiply sadness. The only remedy possible is to oppose the passions among themselves in order to harmonize their disordered movements.

2. As a matter of fact, this condition holds for most men. For this reason, *politics*, which is destined to guide people as they are, should be founded in the first instance on the play of the passions, opposing men among themselves with the aim of realizing an equilibrium most favorable for peace among the citizens. The government most apt for obtaining this result is not, in Spinoza's view, a monarchy, but a republic in which each has the most liberty possible. On the other hand, whatever laws or decrees there may be — if the political chiefs unify in order to impose them — are morally good to the degree that they are efficacious, since all the activities which they command are but various manifestations of the divine modes. Thus, the doctrine of Spinoza justifies both the political liberalism of the people and the despotism of the rulers.

3. But if the tumultuous world of the passions brings forth confused ideas, intellectual intuition, which goes beyond the changing modes to seize immutable divine substance and sees all *sub specie æternitatis*, becomes, in its affective aspect, an *adequate* desire which expands without constraint towards the infinite. This is the *intellectual love* of God, so called because it is identical at root with the supreme wisdom, the contemplative and intuitive science of the divine substance, the " stuff " of the universe.

The life of the sage, while wholly intellectual, is at the same time a continual exercise of very pure love of God. The re-descending look from these eternal heights towards the double series of finite modes (extension and thought), which are constitutive of the human person, make fully clear the reason which attaches man to God; consequently, it always and joyfully accepts the necessary evolvement of things. Then, grasping in the same light the life of other men, it encircles them in its love and benevolence, so that a society of sages would be an ideal state, resembling one grand familial group.

Finally, this disinterested and dominating love of God assures the sage of immortality. Doubtlessly, it is but an impersonal immortality, but it is real, for whatever is best in one's terrestrial life is preserved and realized in the eternity of God. With the help of the intermediary modes, Spinoza makes his thoughts more precise on this matter. He teaches the eternal permanence of the individual modes which make up each of our souls, at least with regard to their intellectual part. Our souls are finite and variable modes by reason of their union with body. But to the extent that the intuition of clear ideas is effective in them, they partake in the eternal substance of God and become eternal. All of them together, forming an infinite series, " constitute the eternal and infinite understanding of God ". Spinoza attributes this to the infinite, mediate mode, which functions as the second intermediary between the infinite nature and our changing world [1].

In Summary : *Since pantheism denies liberty, Spinoza's morality merely states the facts which occur, denying the idea of evil, and replacing it by that of a man being of little repute. But, since the idea spreads itself out into tendency, inadequate ideas beget passions as the source of sadness, while intuition of eternal truths engender the intellectual love of God, the source of veritable joy which is the goal of the sage's life.*

CONCLUSION. **355.** Spinoza's view avoids the immediate contradiction which would identify the divine, immutable and unique nature with the changing and multiple universe. But its development leads it to antinomies which are but contradictory propositions. Thus, he affirms an infinite multitude of adequately distinct attributes in God, and, at the same time, states that the divine substance is one and simple. Among these attributes, he places extension, formally identical with the extension of bodies, which are essentially limited, divisible, imperfect and requiring potentiality and matter; at the same time, he states that the divine infinity is purely actual and perfect. He looks upon the evolvement of the modes as necessarily flowing from the Divine Essence; this essence is the perfect cause which lacks nothing, and remains free and dominative of its effects. So many flagrant contradictions appeared that Spinoza, carried by logic from his point of beginning, affirmed them without resolving their difficulties and even without examining them. Their presence is a mortal defect in his system.

Perhaps it is not impossible to resolve them if one insists on the distinction between the personal unity and the multiplicity of two natures, one of which is infinite, while the other is finite. Somewhat in this way, Catholic theology explains the Incarnation without falling into contradiction; if this great mystery is possible once, as Catholics believe, it is possible millions of times; this would be similar to Spinozism [2].

---

[1] *Ethics*, Part V, Prop. XL, Schol. I. This doctrine reintroduces a certain personal immortality into Spinoza's system; but while it may sweeten the rigor of his monism, it does not destroy his essential error.

[2] This solution is developed in an article entitled " Pantheism " by Valensin (*Dictionnaire apologétique de la foi catholique*).

But in this favorable interpretation, it is easy to show the falsity of pantheism, for it cannot be in accord with the fact of human responsibility. Evidence shows that each man is *personally responsible* for his actions; for example, a man can say to himself, "I am not responsible for the actions of that assassin or of that hero, but I am for those actions which I consciously perform".

Now, every personal responsibility requires a subsistent being, really distinct, as subsistent, from all other beings.

Then, it is impossible that all men be but one subsisting thing, as pantheism proposes; pantheism is an *evident error*.

The minor of the above argument is easily demonstrable. He who is the independent and free cause of his actions acts through himself.

Now, one does not act except in the measure that one exists.

Then, in order to be responsible for actions, one must exist by himself and be a subsisting thing distinct from all others.

But this interpretation, which requires the belief in supernatural faith, will always remain estranged from pantheistic philosophers who uniquely confide in their own reason.

This rash confidence in pure reason is one of the most clear manifestations of the rationalist spirit, which marks, as has been said [1], modern philosophy. If Spinoza has given us a more palpable proof of this, it is because he fully and freely accepts all the conclusions logically contained in the principle of a very modern philosophy, that of Descartes. It is to Spinoza's glory and to his shame that he brought the Cartesian principle to its termination by an inflexible logic; with it he fashioned a vast synthesis. At the same time, he never retreated from the horrible error of pantheism which he saw himself constrained to adopt.

CHAPTER THREE.

REACTION AND TRANSITION.

(18th century).

356. During the eighteenth century, the philosophical current issuing from Descartes developed along three main lines. The first group, following Leibniz, exaggerates Cartesian spiritualism and tends toward absolute idealism. La Mettrie and the *philosophes* of the eighteenth century are in the second group, which becomes attached to mechanism and tends toward

---

[1] See above, n. 313.

materialism. The English school is the third and intermediary group, which tries to fuse *idealism* and *positivism*.

It will be helpful, at this point, to define these two views of reality, whose appearance in modern philosophy has continued to our day.

1. **Idealism,** in general, designates " the philosophical tendency which consists in referring everything existing to thought in the broad sense of the word; that is, in the Cartesian sense, to the facts of consciousness. Two forms can be distinguished : *a*) that which tends to refer existence to the thought of the individual; *b*) that which tends to reduce existence to thought in general " [1].

Idealism defined in this fashion was not actually taught by Descartes, but it arose as an answer to the critical problem which Descartes raised. This problem supposes, as has been shown [2], that the *unique object known* at the beginning of philosophy is *thought*, or the totality of subjective modifications, among which our ideas are similar to representative images. But the objects thus represented by ideas are, precisely, *real things* [3], which man seeks to know and to explain through his sciences. Descartes, a realist philosopher, admits that " existence " or the real object is distinct from thought. Idealism, judging the proof of this assertion as decadent, affirms that the object of science, or the real existent things, are identified with thought. Two formulas, exactly equivalent, express idealism :

Man knows only his thoughts.
Only thought is real.

This thought in which reality is centered also makes up the thinking subject. This fact has given rise to the term *subjectivism*, defined as " the tendency to refer all existence, either to the existence of the subject, or to the existence of thought in general, to the exclusion of things themselves " [4]. The things existing outside of the knowing subject, or " trans-subjective " [5] things, are declared unknowable. From the viewpoint of realism, which shows the value of our sciences as explicative of the real, idealism is a *partial scepticism*.

2. **Positivism** is the system which admits but one valid mode of thought for attaining truth, the mode in which the object does not go beyond experience, and, ordinarily, not beyond sense experience. " This name is given to doctrines which have as common statements that only the knowledge of facts is fruitful and that the archetype of certitude is that furnished by the expe-

---

[1] A. LALANDE, *op. cit.*, " Idealism ". Various other historical meanings are explained here.

[2] See n. 332.

[3] Or *existence*, as used in the definition of idealism.

[4] A. LALANDE, *op. cit.*, " Subjectivism "; this term has other, different implications, which make it less precise than *idealism*.

[5] This expression is taken from J. GREDT, *Elementa philosophiæ*, II, n. 686 ff. Kant uses the expression, " thing-in-itself ".

rimental sciences; that the human spirit, in philosophy as well
as in science, cannot avoid verbalism or error except by constantly
keeping in contact with experience and by renouncing every a
priori element; finally, that the domain of things-in-themselves
is inaccessible to thought, which can only attain to relations and
to laws " [1].

Through this denial of the value of human knowledge in the
order of substances, positivism also is, from a realist point of view,
a *partial scepticism*. It is, though, distinguishable from *materialism*,
according to which there exists no other substance but matter [2],
or an ensemble of bodies without substance being real [3]. Positivism,
however, often leads to materialism, since it grants only that
sensible experience is of value.

Quite often one can distinguish positivism from sensualism and
from empiricism.

Sensualism is "the ideological theory which sees sensation as
the unique source of all knowledge " [4]. Thus defined, sensualism
can designate even a spiritualist doctrine as that of Aristotle and
St. Thomas, who used the adage that there is nothing in the intellect
without its first having been in the senses [5]. But this latter adage
is commonly given a restrictive meaning, so that sensualism, in
contrast, admits no knowledge as valuable beyond sensible experience. It is, accordingly, but a *positivist psychology*.

Empiricism is the doctrine which grants value only to experience,
whether in psychology, as the unique source of knowledge (it thus
denies all innatism), or in epistemology, "by making knowledge
of truth rest solely on experience, beyond which it admits only
definitions or arbitrary hypotheses " [6]. It is easily seen that
sensualism is a designation for psychological empiricism [7].

Compared to positivism, empiricism designates primarily a
method, while positivism is a *doctrine;* the first view, however,
leads to the second, and in reality they are but one system of
thought.

Idealism and positivism have no logical bond between them.
History, however, shows that they are compatible views, and

---

[1] A. LALANDE, *op. cit.*, " Positivism ", meaning " B ". In the first sense
above, positivism is equivalent to the view of A. Comte (see below, n. 457 ff.),
who coined the word. The origins of positivism, though, stem from Descartes;
see J. MERCIER, *The Origins of Contemporary Psychology*, Ch. II.

[2] A. LALANDE, *op. cit.*, " Materialism ", Meaning " A ".

[3] See below, nn. 471-473.

[4] J. MERCIER, *op. cit.*, p. 51. Lalande (*op. cit.*, " Sensualism ") states that
it is the " Doctrine proposing that all knowledge comes from sensations and
only from them "; he adds that " the term is badly chosen and has a pejorative
ring since it awakes the meaning of *sensual*... its normal form would be
sensationism ".

[5] In this case, however, the soul, by means of its spiritual faculties, lawfully
outreaches the limited purview of sensations through abstraction.

[6] A. LALANDE, *op. cit.*, " Empiricism ", Meanings " A " and " B ".

[7] For simplicity, we will be content to use the more clear expression, *empiricism*.

it will be seen in the amalgamated view below how they are proportionately mixed until they issue in the phenomenalism of Hume.

Phenomenalism can be defined as " the doctrine according to which only phenomena exist " (meaning objects of experience which are, at the least, possible) [1]. Using this definition, it is sufficient to join idealism and positivism by declaring that the only facts of experience knowable are the facts of consciousness.

This wholly unexpected [2] union of these two lines of thought can be explained by their common historical origin in Cartesianism, the psychology of which engenders idealism, and the mechanism of which leads to positivism.

While the Cartesian influence is always recognizable and dominant in the eighteenth century, it is modified by many other secondary influences with which it enters into reaction. This explains the fragmentary and transitional nature of these various systems. The termination of this total movement, in idealistic phenomenalism, is a scepticism that is no longer merely partial, but absolute and total. This position then serves as a transition to the mighty critical effort of Kant.

This chapter, treating of the *Reaction and Transition,* will have the following three articles :

Article I : Idealistic Current : Leibniz.

Article II : Positivist Current.

Article III : Mixed Current.

ARTICLE ONE.
IDEALISTIC CURRENT. LEIBNIZ.
(1646-1716).

SPECIAL BIBLIOGRAPHY.

1º **Works :** *Die philosophischen Schriften von G. W. Leibniz,* C. I. Gerhardt (ed.), 7 vols., Berlin, 1873-1890. — COUTURAT, L., *Opuscules et fragments inédits de Leibniz,* Paris, 1903. — GRUA, G., G. W. Leibniz, *Textes inédits,* 2 vols., Paris, 1948. — HUGGARD, E. M. (transl.), *Theodicy,* New York, 1952. — LANGLEY, A. G. (transl.),

---

[1] A. LALANDE, *op. cit.,* " Phenomenalism "; in this view, the " thing-in-itself " is but a word.
[2] See below, n. 371.

New Essays Concerning Human Understanding, 3rd ed., La Salle (Ill.), 1949. — LATTA, R. (transl.), *The Monadology and other Philosophical Writings*, Oxford, 1948. — MONTGOMERY, G. R. (transl.), *Leibniz's Discourse on Metaphysics, Correspondence with Arnauld, and Monadology*, Chicago, 1902. — WIENER, P. (transl.), *Leibniz Selections*, New York, 1951.

2° **Studies** : BLONDEL, M., *De vinculo substantiali et de substantia composite apud Leibnizium*, Paris, 1893. — CARR, H. W., *Leibniz*, London, 1929. — CARRA DE VAUX, *Leibniz*, Paris, 1909. — COUTURAT, L., *La logique de Leibniz*, Paris, 1901. — FISCHER, K., *Geschichte der neueren Philosophie*, Volume III, 5th ed., Munster, 1920. — FRIEDMAN, G., *Leibniz et Spinoza*, 4th ed., Paris, 1946. — GUEROLT, M., *Dynamique et métaphysique leibnizienne*, Paris, 1934. — HILDEBRANDT, K., *Leibniz und das Reich der Gnade*, The Hague, 1953. — HOLBWACHS, M., *Leibniz*, 2nd ed., Paris, 1929. — HUBER, K., *Leibniz*, Oldenbourg, 1951. — IWANICKI, J., *Leibniz et les démonstrations mathématiques de l'existence de Dieu*, Paris, 1934. — JALABERT, J., *La théorie leibnizienne de la substance*, Paris, 1947. — JOSEPH, H. W. B., *Lectures on the Philosophy of Leibniz*, Oxford, 1949. — KABITZ, W., *Die Philosophie des jungen Leibniz*, Heidelberg, 1909. — MACKIE, J. M., *Life of Godfrey William von Leibnitz*, Boston, 1845. — MEYER, R. W., *Leibnitz and the Seventeenth Century Revolution*, Chicago, 1952. — PIAT, C., *Leibniz*, Paris, 1915. — ROLLAND, E., *Le déterminisme monadique et le problème de Dieu dans la philosophie de Leibniz*, Paris, 1934. — RUSSELL, B., *A Critical Exposition of the Philosophy of Leibniz*, 3rd ed., London, 1951. — STAMMLER, G., *Leibniz*, Munich, 1930.

357. Born at Leipzig, where his father was a professor at the university, Gottfried William Leibniz got his first intellectual formation by reading books from his father's library. He read the ancient thinkers avidly, as Plato and Aristotle, following these with the Scholastics; at the age of fifteen, he began to read the moderns, Bacon, Kepler, Hobbes, Galileo, and Descartes. From 1672 to 1676, he sojourned in Paris as the ambassador of the German emperor, in order to convince Louis XIV to join a crusade against the Turks. His mission was unsuccessful, but he learned to speak French and began to perfect himself in the sciences and in philosophy by his dealings with Huygens, Arnauld, Malebranche and others. The last forty years of his life were spent at Hanover as librarian and secretary to the Prince Elect.

A universal genius, Leibniz was not only an original thinker in philosophy, but also a famous mathematician. He discovered the differential and integral calculus. He led a very active political life through his letters and personal activity, pleading with Peter the Great of Russia to turn against the Turks. From 1681 to 1693, he worked arduously for the reunion of

Catholics and Protestants, and carried on an important correspondence with Bossuet on these matters. Finally, he set up an algebra of logic (logistics), in order to simplify and to make infallible the work of the mind. In all these various domains, Leibniz had a strong influence.

The great number of his occupations, however, prevented him from fully deepening his philosophical system. While it is a complete and unified system, it is more brilliant than stable. Three works, written in French, give the main outline of his system : *Les nouveaux Essais sur l'entendement humain* (1704), in which he answers and discusses Locke's *Essays;* *Theodicée* (1707), in which, to justify [1] Divine Providence, he outlines his view more fully; the *Monadologie* (1714), a short work which summarizes his system for Prince Eugene of Savoy, and which was published after his death. Finally, various letters develop particular points.

General Characteristics. 358. The work of Leibniz is as complex as its author. It seems to arrest the modern spirit, and, again, to push it forwards. It looks like a strong reaction, in the name of traditional doctrine, against the individualism and the destructive criticism of Descartes. Leibniz has great respect for the ancients and uses them largely; he wished to rediscover what he called " perennial philosophy ", which was to be made up of the true elements of all systems. His general spirit seems anti-Cartesian, and one can even find various Thomistic [2] ideas in his writings.

As a matter of fact, however, the principle which is the soul of his philosophy is in no wise Thomistic, but *Cartesian.* His system is an effort to reconstruct the world, without recourse to experience, by determining its simple, primordial elements and by combining them according to the rigorous method of mathematics. It is a new attempt at applying the methodology of the clear idea. To avoid pantheism, however, Leibniz set himself about making his *fundamental theory* precise; then he developed it in the *logical* order, and

---

[1] The term " theodicy ", which Leibniz originated, means " to give God justice " (from θεός, God, and δικαία, give justice); Leibniz' work is a complete treatise on God. The word, today, commonly designates rational or philosophical theology in contrast with the study of God based on revelation and often called, simply, *theology.*

[2] In his history of philosophy, Barbadette (*Histoire de la philosophie,*pp.403-407), collects a series of Leibniz' statements on logic, God, the world, man and morality which are reminiscent of doctrines of Aristotle and St. Thomas.

then in the *real* order as an explanation of the universe. These three notions will outline the presentation of his thought.

I. FUNDAMENTAL THEORY.

359. The metaphysical doctrine, of which the monadology is but a synthesis, is only a portion of a vast system which haunted Leibniz' imagination. In order to form a proper estimate of his ambition, his unified outlook will first be given from the *logical* or methodological point of view, and then only from the *metaphysical* aspect.

A) **Logical Synthesis.** The directive idea of Leibniz can be expressed in the following proposition :

There exists a universal science of a mathematical type, capable of giving reasons, a priori, for each thing which exists.

Through this proposition, Leibniz is the continuator of the method of the clear idea, even though he contradicted and criticized Descartes on many important points [1]. His aim was to resolve all the problems proposed by man with the same clarity with which the mathematical proof excludes controversy. He wished to replace reasoning by a calculus, in the similarity of algebra. To accomplish this, he long sought to construct a " universal characteristic " in which all ideas of the various disciplines would be replaced by signs (as letters in algebra), so that it might become possible to resolve any sort of difficulty by a type of logical calculus.

He had at his command for this task, not only the ordinary calculus, but the resources of the infinitesimal and integral calculus which he invented. Thus, while he admitted Spinoza's principle that every substance is infinite, he avoided pantheism by holding that there are *several infinites*. For example, in the series of numbers which lie between the numbers 1 and 2, there is an infinite series, $1 + \frac{1}{2} + \frac{1}{4} + \frac{1}{8} + \frac{1}{16} \ldots$, whether there is question of length, of feet, of surface, and so forth. In a like manner, each of the created substances contains in itself the infinite series of world events [2], but each from its own point of view. They are " infinities " from a certain point of view. The universe, in turn, could thus be constituted of

---

[1] For example, he condemns the method of universal doubt, and begins philosophy by the affirmation of first principles; he rejects the identification of corporeal substance with extension, and so on.

[2] See below, n. 362.

an infinite series of substances, comparable to the infinite series of numbers lying between the numbers 1 and 2. God is conceived as the *limit* of the series; He is the supreme perfection in which the total series has its reason for being. Thus is constituted a science of the mathematical type.

This ideal supposes that every true affirmation is reducible to an identity between two terms, as in mathematics; Leibniz' view, then, would be that every true proposition is analytic. By analyzing the subject, it is always possible to find the a priori reason of the predicate, not only in universal and necessary propositions, from which the properties of an essence are deducible, as " every triangle has its three angles equal to two right angles ", but even in affirmations of fact, as " Caesar conquered Pompey at Pharsalia ".

It is in this sense that Leibniz adopts two great principles as the basis of all his speculations : that of *identity*, every being is that which it is, and that of *sufficient reason*, nothing exists without a sufficient reason [1]. As the principle of identity rules in the mathematical sciences, wherein proof is developed by *perfect substitution*, the principle of sufficient reason is destined to extend this mathematical evidence to all other materials, whether historical, moral and religious, or physical and metaphysical. Throughout, by use of sufficient reason, demonstration becomes as rigorous as a calculus, whether it be the ordinary, or the integral and infinitesimal calculus.

Does not this conception of a universal science efface the distinction between necessary and contingent propositions, and does it not involve an absolute determinism, as does Spinoza's pantheism? Leibniz does not think so, for the two types of propositions do not correspond to the same attribute in God. The necessary propositions depend uniquely on the Divine Intelligence, and they constitute the world of possibles; the contingent propositions depend on the Divine Will, and they express the facts of the real world which God has freely chosen to create out of all possible worlds [2]. While this creation is free, it was *determined* by a sufficient reason which is, for him who penetrates to it, the a priori explanation.

---

[1] In his *Histoire de la philosophie* (II, p. 241), Brehier has collected some of Leibniz' formulas; e. g., " There is a reason why each thing is as it is rather than being otherwise ", and " Every true proposition which is not known of itself, receives its proof a priori ".

[2] It is evident that the principle of sufficient reason is especially regulative of the real world, while the principle of identity is sufficient for the world of possibles.

This causes another distinction between these two types of propositions in relation to man. If man is able to discover, by analysis, the evidence for necessary propositions, he is incapable of forming a concept sufficiently adequate to real or contingent things so that he could discover therein the explanation of the properties or circumstances which would occur to the thing. God alone can do this, since He created things. Man can only approach this goal, by seeking the a priori explanations which are the most probable. The universal science is an inaccessible ideal in fact, but it is one towards which man can tend through a sort of calculus of probabilities.

For Leibniz, the principle of sufficient reason is but an extension of the theory of the clear idea to contingent beings. He asserts that whatever as a *matter of fact* occurs is a priori intelligible to him who fully knows the definition of the concrete subject. Thus understood, his view is far from being evident; it is more a postulate, the fruit of rationalism. Leibniz is much closer to Spinoza than he would wish to be.

In contrast, it must be held that the principle of sufficient reason is immediately evident, all the while maintaining the divine liberty, the world's contingency and its basic distinction from God. " Everything has its reason for being " is the same as " Everything is intelligible ", but in two ways. In the first, this can mean that every being has *in itself* the reason for that which is essentially proper to it or through itself (this is the *intrinsic* sufficient reason, another form of the principle of identity). In the second, this can mean that the reason for what is proper to a thing *lies in another*, and that a being does not have this reason through itself (this is the *extrinsic* sufficient reason, the general form of the principle of causality). Thus, a square has within itself the reason why it has four sides; but if it be white or red, it owes this peculiarity to another. Only God has the reason for His existence in Himself, for He alone is the necessary being. Other contingent beings and historical events have some reason for being, but not a priori in their definition or very essence; they depend, in final analysis, on the free will of the Creator or of man, and are accessible to human knowledge only a posteriori. Only the domain of essences is strictly scientific.

Leibniz attempted to realize his ideal in every domain. In *religion*, he concluded to the possibility of all confessions of faith being based on common evidence, and he addressed himself to Bossuet with this goal in mind. But the rationalistic virus which vitiated his attempt made him give it up [1]. In

---

[1] Bossuet asked Leibniz if he granted the dogmatic authority of the Church as a rule of faith, but Leibniz replied that he would accept " dogmas " demonstrable to all men by reason.

applying his ambition to the metaphysical domain, he constructed an original and quite unified system.

B) **Metaphysical Synthesis. 360.** The directive idea of Leibniz can be expressed as follows :

Everything in the universe is explainable by the monad, a simple and active substance.

The monad is an energy or a force which constitutes the primordial element of all being, giving it perfect and substantial unity [1], making it simple in itself and distinct from all others. It seems that Leibniz was led to hold to a simple element as the first principle of everything by the indefinite divisibility of matter and of extension. It seemed evident to him that " the composite is merely a mass or *aggregate* of simple elements " [2]. In his view, a multiplicity of parts is incomprehensible except through the simple elements which compose it, as it is customary to refer the line to an infinite series of unities in order to make the line intelligible in its treatment by calculus.

On the other hand, these elements, " truly atoms of nature " [3], are essentially *active*, and endowed with at least virtual energy. This is evident for living beings, and especially for those which have self-consciousness, as the human soul. But even among bodies themselves, one never finds any that are absolutely inert. Leibniz proves this by the fact that it is more difficult to move a large mass than a small one, a sign of active resistance. Moreover, if a block of stone were fully inert, a ball thrown against it would move it along without difficulty, instead of rebounding. Thus, the primordial element of all being is a substance at once *simple* and *active;* this is the monad (Theory of DYNAMIC ATOMISM).

Aided by this principle, Leibniz explains the universe by first considering the world of monads in a *possible order*, then as God has made it come to pass in the *real order*.

II. THE ORDER OF POSSIBLES.

361. In Leibniz' view, the possible is everything which does not imply a contradiction. From this viewpoint, even before its existence, the world of monads must satisfy the

---

[1] " By the monad, I understand a substance truly one, that is, one which is not an aggregate of substances " (*Correspondance avec Bernoulli*, II, p. 398).

[2] *Monadologie*, n. 2. — [3] *Ibid.*, n. 3.

principle of identity and of sufficient reason with regard to their number, their nature and their mutual relations.

A) **Number of Monads.**

Leibniz is a resolute *pluralist*[1] and is horrified at Spinoza's monism, which he rejects. But, to justify his own position (which he doubtlessly held from common sense and from his education), his system required that he make appeal to the direct evidence of experience. He contented himself with an indirect proof, inspired by the method of the clear ideas; it is a proof which generally remains *implicit*. The proof can be stated as follows : pluralism is true, for it can enter into a system that is scientifically coherent, if reality be interpreted by the double principle of identity and of sufficient reason.

In admitting as an initial postulate the possibility of really distinct substances, it seems to follow that their number will be, of necessity, *infinite*. This can be proved a priori, for there is no sufficient reason for stopping at one sum rather another; it can be established a posteriori, for extension shows itself divisible to infinity, and thus must be composed of an *infinite number* of simple elements.

Furthermore, *a)* the monads are totally different in perfection *(the principle of indiscernibles)*, otherwise they would be indistinguishable, and would identify themselves so that the postulate of their plurality would become absurd; *b)* the monads range from less to more perfect through insensible degrees, without any void between them *(the principle of the continuity of nature)*, for if their succession were irregular, one could not assign a sufficient reason for them.

B) **Nature of the Monads.**

362. Since each monad is simple it cannot have extension or figure, nor be divisible. It can be realized only through creation and is, of itself, incorruptible. But " the monads have no windows through which anything could come in or go out "[2], for, in a simple being, there are no parts susceptible of being moved or displaced by an external influence. At the same

---

[1] *Pluralism* is " the doctrine according to which the beings which compose the world are multiple, individual, independent, and cannot be considered as simple modes or phenomena of a unique and absolute reality ". A. LALANDE, *op. cit.*, " Pluralism ".

[2] *Monadologie*, n. 7.

time, finite modes can move themselves and even continually; Leibniz, by asserting this, agrees with common sense, and doubtlessly sees this as following from his initial pluralism [1]. As a consequence, if each monad could have only immanent movements, it has them necessarily : it is a living thing and it conducts its proper life as if it were absolutely alone.

Now one can account for these operations by analogy with the human soul, which is a monad of the most perfect type. Three groups of activities are thus distinguishable.

a) **Dull Perceptions,** or minimal perceptions, are those through which each monad is like a mirror in which all the events of the universe are reflected; in this way each monad becomes an immense reservoir in which the universal science is virtually contained. These perceptions are, for the most part, *unconscious,* but one can prove their existence by such facts as remembrances without previous experience. Their existence can be proved also by the principle of sufficient reason, for the absence of this unconscious life would make the development of conscious life unintelligible.

b) **Clear Perceptions,** or " apperceptions ", are those through which we are distinctly conscious of certain objects, and primarily of the nearest monads. They are the result of a work of reflection and analysis on the complex and confused items given in dull perceptions.

c) **Appetition (or Desire)** is that by which we pass from one perception to another. It is a force of expansion which lies in the very essence of the monad. It tends towards perfection and leads us to enlarge, more and more, upon the realm of clear perceptions.

By the aid of these operations, one can distinguish three principal orders in the series of monads :

1) *The Inferior Order,* comprising the vegetal and even the mineral realm; these beings enjoy life and have dull perceptions, but lack any form of consciousness.

2) *The Intermediary Order of Animals,* who enjoy distinct perceptions, and who can imitate reason with the help of the laws of association of images.

3) *The Superior Order of Reasonable Beings,* who alone attain necessary truths. Only this group of beings, through applying the principles of identity and of sufficient reason, arrive at a clear consciousness of the self, of others, and especially of God. And, while all monads basically have the same nature, the privilege of knowing God seems to require for the reasonable monad a superior perfection, which Leibniz, however, never clearly explained [2].

---

[1] An active, *immutable* substance would be *pure actuality*, infinite and unique.

[2] For Leibniz, each monad is eternal and immortal, but he thought it a " Scholastic prejudice " to hold to the existence of souls entirely separated from their bodies; *Monadologie*, n. 14.

Leibniz summarizes his theory with the adage of Aristotle, though with a correction : " Nothing is in the intellect which was not first in the senses, *except the intellect itself* ". In other words, our sciences are but the explanation of the unconscious world which each monad bears within its nature under the form of dull perceptions. But this explanation further requires in reason the virtual preexistence of first principles, as sources of universal and necessary ideas. The sense of the Aristotelian formula is transformed; from realism, it becomes idealism.

C) Mutual Relations of the Monads.

363. A consequence of this theory is that corporeal substance is not constituted by extension, as in Descartes' view. It can only be an aggregate of inextended principles, endowed with life and latent consciousness, whose assemblage is intelligible only by a psychological bond or correspondence of perceptions. It is in order to explain this " aggregate of monads " and to make the order of the universe possible, that each monad must be an abridgement of all the others coupled with a tendency to know its closest neighbors.

The human body is but a particular case of a general law. Living things are constituted by the presence of a superior monad in the center of the composite; this is the soul, which dominates the other monads through its more clear perceptions. The first object of the soul-monad is its own body. Accordingly, each variation in the body is reflected in the variations of the psychological life of the soul. Body and soul are like two well-regulated clocks, always striking the hour at the same time [1]. This correspondence, flowing from the nature of monads, also explains their apparent interaction, and especially the union of soul and body (theory of *pre-established harmony*).

This whole possible world lived in the Divine Intelligence before it existed in itself. It must now be determined how this reality came about.

III. THE ORDER OF REALITY.

364. Under this heading, we have a special application of the principle of sufficient reason in order to demonstrate God's existence, and to explain creation and human liberty.

---

[1] There is no mutual influence, nor assistance of God to place these clocks in perfect accord at every moment; Leibniz did not understand the profound notion of divine premotion.

A) **Existence of God.**

The principle of sufficient reason affords a double proof for God's existence.

1) *A posteriori.* Besides necessary truths, intelligible in themselves, there exist contingent truths, or truths of fact (for example, the action of writing), which require an exterior cause. But, in the created order, the series of causes is infinite; that is, it is always incomplete. Hence this series cannot be the perfect and complete sufficient reason satisfying rational demands. This reason must be sought outside of the series in a unique, universal and necessary substance, who contains in Himself the sufficient reason for His existence.

2) *A priori.* The idea of God can be used to demonstrate His existence a priori, if a small change is made in the Cartesian proof [1]. God exists, if that is possible, for the possibility of God, being that of one who " exists of necessity ", evidently involves necessary existence [2]. This result will appear more palatable if one notes that every possible is a " tendency towards being " and towards realizing that which it signifies, for this tendency is the sole, explicative reason for the existence of some possibles rather than others. Now, in God, possible perfection is *infinite*, and it includes an infinite and irresistible tendency to exist, so that God exists necessarily.

B) **Creation.**

365. Within the Divine Intelligence, which knows everything that does not imply a contradiction, there exists an infinite number of possible universes. Each of these, taken alone, has no need to exist, being a pure possible. For this reason, the Divine Power, taken in itself, is not necessitated and remains free to create one or another world. But if these worlds are compared with each other in the light of the Divine Wisdom, there is certainly one that surpasses all the others in goodness, and, as a result, in a need to exist. Now the divine action, under penalty of being imperfect, must have a sufficient reason for acting, and this reason cannot be other than the greatest good. It must then be held that the actual world is the best possible (theory of *Cosmological Optimism*).

---

[1] See above, n. 329.
[2] *Monadologie*, nn. 44-5; see also R. LATTA, *Leibniz*, " Appendix G, Proof of the Existence of God ", pp. 274-7.

C) **Human Liberty.**

366. Man's reasonable activity, like that of God's, should have a sufficient reason. If liberty were a power to act without reason, it would be absurd and bad. It must then be conceived, on the one hand, as a spontaneous energy whose operation satisfies a natural tendency that is not imposed; in this way, reasonable activity shows its independence. But, on the other hand, its act is infallibly determined to choose the object which, in this particular psychological circumstance, imposes itself as the *best*, and in this way it has a sufficient reason for acting (theory of *Psychological Determinism*).

CONCLUSION. **367.** The initial lack of precision on the meaning of sufficient reason led Leibniz to other lacks of precision. Thus, Leibniz practically denied divine and human liberty, for he could not recognize in a perfect efficient cause (as the free agent), an *extrinsic* sufficient reason fully explicative of action, yet openly distinct from the *intrinsic, essential* reason. The latter is brought back into his system under the guise of a *necessary bond* between every cause and its effect. The *best possible* world tends to become a *formal effect*, indispensable to the divine perfection, which is its *formal cause;* this is more similar to the series of modes constituting Spinoza's world than Leibniz would like to admit [1].

In this regard, the pluralistic system of monads is less coherent and stable than Spinoza's monism; its unity rests on the double meaning of the principle of sufficient reason; that is, on an equivocation.

From another point of view, Leibniz can be said to be more *idealist* than either Descartes or Spinoza. While the view of pre-established harmony, like a " deus ex machina ", safeguards the objective reality of the world and of its order, our monad-soul knows only its subjective modifications and its ideas, which is sheer idealism. Furthermore, the theory of simple monads deprives the ideas of extension and of space of any objective value.

Thus, despite an attempt at reacting in favor of traditional philosophy, Leibniz actually developed the idealistic germs of Cartesianism, favoring the unity of " thought " to the detriment of extension.

---

[1] See above, n. 350.

His disciple, Christian Wolff [1] (1679-1754), retained this idealistic influence and gave it to Kant. Wolff popularized Leibniz' views; he was a professor at Halle, an author of many works, and had considerable influence by his clarity of presentation and by his logical method. He presented himself as a disciple absolutely faithful to Leibniz. " In general, he levelled off the thought of his master and cut off some of its more original portions, as the theory of monads " [2]. But Wolff kept his idealistic rationalism, and even aggravated it by referring the principle of sufficient reason to that of identity, making all philosophy but the study of the *possibles*.

ARTICLE TWO. — POSITIVIST CURRENT.

368. Although the term " positivist philosophy " was not coined until the nineteenth century [3], the current of ideas which it involves originates with the third portion of Cartesianism, the explanation of the corporeal world through pure mechanism. England is the land of election, where it flourished from the seventeenth century onwards in the system of Hobbes, a remarkable synthesis of Baconian empiricism and Cartesian mathematical deduction.

Though steeping himself in the positivist current to the extent of teaching materialism, Hobbes kept a taste for the great constructions which haunted the thinkers of the seventeenth century, Descartes, Spinoza and Leibniz. Beginning with the eighteenth century, however, there is a lassitude in intellectual effort. Powerful syntheses are abandoned; the philosophers, or those who kept this title, are numerous, but treat only of fragmentary problems. The most important problem under consideration is that of the value of human knowledge, placed in this honored position by the *Essay* of John Locke; it will be studied under the mixed current [4], along with the reaction of " sentiment " which it stirred.

The philosophers of France and of England can all be grouped under positivism. Many of them are primarily savants and

---

[1] See E. Bréhier, *op. cit.*, ii, pp. 359-365.
[2] J. Maréchal, *Le point de départ de la métaphysique*, ii, p. 105.
[3] It was Auguste Comte who popularized this expression; see below, n. 459.
[4] See below, Art. iii, n. 371 ff. Locke, by reducing the Cartesian spirit to more limited proportions, exerted great influence on contemporary thought; in philosophy, he was the master of the eighteenth century.

admirers of Isaac Newton, one of the best discoverers of positive science. This admiration, joined to the popularity of Locke, accounts for a good part of the doctrine of the French " philosophes " of the eighteenth century. — There is a second group of thinkers who continue the practical preoccupations of Francis Bacon, studying moral questions and political economy, trying to apply the laws of positive science to these realms. — There is a third group which occupied itself with religious philosophy, proclaiming the rights of reason, and attacking revelation. They placed God so distant from man that they became involved in the darkness of the purely human religion of positivism. It is in this broad and restricted sense that the expression " positivist tendencies " is used of English thought in the eighteenth century, and of French philosophy of the eighteenth century. Three paragraphs will deal with these matters :

> I : The System of Hobbes.
>
> II : Positivist Tendencies in England during the Eighteenth Century.
>
> III : The French " Philosophes " of the Eighteenth Century.

I. THE SYSTEM OF HOBBES (1588-1679).

SPECIAL BIBLIOGRAPHY.

1⁰ **Works :** *Opera philosophica quæ latine scripsit*, W. MOLESWORTH (ed.), 5 vols., London, 1839-1845. — *The English Works of Thomas Hobbes*, W. MOLESWORTH (ed.), 11 vols., London, 1839-1845.

2⁰ **Studies :** BOWLES, J., *Hobbes and his Critics : A Study of Seventeenth Century Constitutionalism*, London, 1951. — BRANDT, F., *Thomas Hobbes' Mechanical Conception of Nature*, London, 1928. — GOUGH, J. W., *The Social Contract : A Critical Study of its Development*, Oxford, 1936. — LAIRD, J., *Hobbes*, London, 1934. — LYON, G., *La philosophie de Hobbes*, Paris, 1893. — POLIN, R., *Politique et philosophie chez Thomas Hobbes*, Paris, 1953. — RICKABY, J., *Free Will and Four English Philosophers*, London, 1906. — ROBERTSON, G., *Hobbes*, Edinburgh, 1886. — STEPHEN, L., *Hobbes*, London, 1904. — STRAUSS, L., *The Political Philosophy of Hobbes*, Chicago, 1952. — TAYLOR, A. E., *Thomas Hobbes*, London, 1908. — TONNIES, F., *Hobbes Leben und Lehre*, 3rd ed., Stuttgart, 1925. — *Hobbes, der Mann und der Denker*, Leipzig, 1912. — VIALATOUX, J., *La cité de Hobbes*, Paris, 1935.

368bis. The son of a Westport clergyman, Thomas Hobbes was educated at the University of Oxford. He studied there for fourteen years, during the period when a decadent Scholasticism had already become nominalistic. In 1608, he became tutor of the son of Lord Devonshire, and made his first tour of the continent. He was in France in 1610 at the time of the assassination of Henry IV, and his written sketch of this event is so vivid and durable that he does not mention the name of Ravaillac without accompanying it with a curse [1]. During this period, he was quite preoccupied with literature and with art, and, upon his return to England, he translated *Thucydides*. He visited with Francis Bacon, who asked him to translate some of his *Essays* into Latin. On a second voyage into France, he discovered Euclid's *Elements*, and became enthusiastic over the mathematical method. Upon his return to England, he again served as tutor in the Devonshire family (1627-31) [2]. He made a third voyage to France and to Italy (1634-37), which determined his philosophical orientation. He visited Galileo in Florence, but spent more time in Paris with Father Marin Mersenne, who introduced Hobbes to the circle of thinkers who gravitated about him. Thinking about the problem of the nature of things and of human life, Hobbes finally thought he saw a way of explaining everything mathematically by basing everything on movement. This was the year in which Descartes, who resided in Holland, edited his famous *Discourse on Method*, which so brilliantly defended the mathematical method and the theory of the clear idea. It can be surmised that Hobbes' conversations with Mersenne, a confidant of Descartes, aided Hobbes in the formation of his own system. But, more involved in political circumstances, he especially turned his reflections towards moral and social life.

Upon returning to England, he joined the defenders of the King, whose position had been menaced by the liberal revolution; during this period he wrote *The Elements of Law, Natural and Politic* [3] (1640). Fearful of the anti-royalists, however, he fled to Paris, where he was well received by his friends; he stayed there eleven years (1640-51). During this time, Mersenne asked him to write up his objections against Descartes' *Meditations*. The correspondence which resulted led to a strong antipathy between the two men; for, although they were in accord on the mathematical method and the mechanistic explanation of the corporeal world [4], Descartes posed as the defender of pure spiritualism, while Hobbes tended towards a radical materialism. In opposition to Descartes [5], Hobbes devoted himself especially to politics. In defense of absolute royalty, then being menaced in his own country, he published his *De Cive* in Paris (1642). This was to be the third part of a philosophical synthesis whose first two portions were

---

[1] G. SORTAIS, *La philosophie moderne*, II, p. 274.

[2] Hobbes left the family at the death of the young earl, his pupil, in 1628; he returned, in 1631, as the tutor of the elder son of the deceased.

[3] This work was first circulated in manuscript form and was only published in 1650, in two parts, *Human Nature* and *On the Body Politic*; it summarizes the work developed in the *De Cive* and *De Homine*.

[4] This agreement is quite remarkable, because Hobbes fits into the positivist current stemming from Descartes.

[5] Descartes wrote little about morality and nothing on politics.

entitled *De corpore* and *De homine*. During this Parisian stay,
he also wrote his principal work in political philosophy, *Leviathan,
or the Matter, form and power of a Commonwealth, Ecclesiastical
and Civil* (1651).

Returning again to England, he completed his system by
publishing *De corpore* (1654) and *De homine* (1658). His doctrines
raised many objections and polemical treatises; the remainder
of his life, about twenty-eight years, was largely spent in defending
his views. Hobbes defended absolute determinism in his fight
with Bishop Bramhall, who argued for freedom as the basis of all
morality. He was attacked by the mathematician, John Wallis,
the astronomer, Ward, John Boyle, the physicist, who was then
at the University of Oxford, and by others; despite his inadequate
replies to their objections, he kept his view and defended it.
Many bishops, and Chancellor Hyde, accused him of atheism; he
protested that he respected the religion of the state, and indulged
in religious practices. But he also had friends; Charles II was kind
to him and paid him a pension, and others befriended him.
The many attacks on his views are illustrative of his wide influence
on the English thought of that time. He died in 1679, on the
vigil of the triumph of liberal ideas, which he had so strongly
opposed throughout his life.

Hobbes defines philosophy as the study of things by the
light of pure reason, and excludes from it anything which
refers to revelation. In his view, reason discovers only measurable bodies in the universe with properties which are explainable by movement. This is the foundational principle from
which the division of his writings stems : bodies form two great
divisions, those produced by nature, which are the object of
physics, and those formed by man's will. The latter are the
social groups, in which are distinguishable the movements of
each individual, which are the concern of ethics, and the
contracts between many individuals, the concern of politics.

A) Foundational Principle : Universal Mechanism.

The central vision of Hobbes can be expressed in this
principle :

*Every being is corporeal and whatever occurs is explainable
by movement.*

This open declaration of universal mechanism is a pretense
at explaining everything not only in the world of extension,
as Descartes wished, but in the entire universe : in man or
outside of him, in the psychological as well as in the physical
order. Two principles are involved in this explanation, homogeneous matter and local movement. Hobbes does not deny

the multiple varieties of change which are realized by bodies endowed with various properties, as minerals and living things. But he imagined that he could make all of this intelligible by simple, local movements which beings communicate by mutual influence, or which take place in the corporeal parts in which change occurs. For these reasons, he also presents his basic principle in this form : " It is necessary to hold that change is nothing else besides the movement of the parts of changing bodies... change is movement of the parts of agent and patient " [1].

This general principle seems to have been looked upon as an object of an intuition [2], rather than as the fruit of a demonstration. It involves two other notions which Hobbes used with unequal emphasis : the first is materialism, which Hobbes tried to conceal; the second he insisted upon greatly, borrowing it from current scientific theory which was becoming quite fashionable, namely, mechanism.

" Every being is corporeal ". While Hobbes did not state this so clearly, he surely thought in this way, and his works give evidence of his acceptance of this statement. In looking for the fundamental notions of his philosophy, he found in *space* a primary notion in which he sees the very condition of existence. " Space is a phantasm of an existing thing to the extent that it exists; that is, no other accident occurring to the thing is considered, except that which appears beyond the person imagining " [3]. It is, thus, impossible to exist without being in space, and, as a result, without being body, for the latter is defined : " Body is everything which, independently of our thought, coincides with a portion of space or is coextended with it " [4].

That his thought was of such a sort appears clearly when one reads his teaching on Christianity and on pure spirits : " We who are Christians admit that angels, good and bad spirits, exist; that the human soul is a spirit and that it is immortal, as are the angelic spirits. But it is impossible for us to know this with natural evidence. For every bit of evidence is a conception, and every conception is but imagination deriving from the senses. Now, it is commonly agreed that spirits are substances which do not act at all on the senses; from this it results that they are in no wise conceivable " [5]. The only philosophical idea we can form of spirit is that of a " figure without color "; and, since a figure has dimensions, to conceive of a spirit is to conceive something which has dimensions or a body, quite subtle indeed, but nevertheless a body " [6]. The supernatural idea of a substance without dimensions appears contradictory.

---

[1] *De corpore*, Ch. IX, § 9.
[2] This is the usual situation with the foundational principle of a philosophy.
[3] *De corpore*, Ch. VII, 3.
[4] *Ibid.*, Ch. VIII, 1.
[5] *Human Nature*, Ch. XI, § 5. — [6] *Ibid.*, § 4.

Hobbes is less explicit on the nature of God, for he was preoccupied in clearing himself from accusations of atheism. To make God a body seemed to be equivalent to denying that He exists. But Hobbes, on the contrary, attempted to demonstrate His existence by the principle of causality. A series of effects must stop at a first cause, a being through itself, and all-powerful. Omnipotence was the foundational attribute of God; Hobbes looked on God as the despot or supreme Master of the universe [1], concluding that man especially owed God honor, cult, and especially fear and obedience. But it seems that this idea of God is presented simply as a *psychological fact*. The men who should be united into society believe in God and are religious; this is a fact which must be taken into account. But it is explained, as everything else, by universal mechanism, and the " All-Powerful " plays no role as the foundation of morality or of the state.

Furthermore, Hobbes nowhere states that his principle involving the inconceivability of a pure spirit does not apply to God. Logically, then, God, being a substance, is also corporeal. Normally, the bodies accessible to rational study are composites, and subjected to various movements; God, however, is simple and unchangeable. For these reasons, Hobbes states that any study of the nature and of the attributes of God is excluded from philosophy [2]. It can be concluded, then, that Hobbes speaks of God and pure spirits only in connection with the believers to whom he is explaining social life. The sole object of philosophy for him is the universe considered as a corporeal mass, in which the variety of things and of events is simply explained by the variety of movements affecting various parts of the body.

To attempt an explanation of everything in terms of mechanism was a bold undertaking. Of course, the fundamental principle that every change is but a local change, is easily contested [3]. Hobbes, declaring it evident, tried to give an a priori demonstration of it which is quite laborious and hardly convincing [4]. The proof rests on the postulate that no other reality but body exists, a postulate which is the fundamental mistake of every form of positivism [5].

Nevertheless, inspired by this principle, Hobbes constructed a system which is quite imperfect, but also has its own grandeur. He deduced from his principle a philosophical methodology which is nominalistic logic; then, to explain the universe and human life, he wrote up a morality and social philosophy.

---

[1] In connection with the *cult* which is due to God, Hobbes speaks of the *goodness* of God, Who is Father (*De Cive*, Ch. xv, 14); but this idea seems more relevant to the Bible than to philosophy.

[2] *De corpore*, Ch. i, § 8.

[3] This is the principle of the early atomists whose philosophical insufficiency has already been shown; see above, n. 21. See, in this section on Hobbes, under *Conclusion*, the general estimate made of the materialism and mechanism of Hobbes.

[4] *De corpore*, Ch. viii and ix.

[5] See below, nn. 471-473. The *fact* which these philosophical idolators of facts neglect is the existence of spiritual thought, and, as a consequence, of soul and of God.

B) Nominalistic Logic.

Struck by the rigorous chain of reasoning in mathematics, Hobbes conceived all reasoning as a calculus. To reason is but to add or subtract [1]. In philosophy, however, one does not manipulate unities and numbers, but *names* designative of bodies through certain properties [2]. " The proposition is constituted by the addition of two names; the syllogism, by that of two propositions; demonstration, by several syllogisms. This manner of procedure leads to science. For, once the names are defined well through the connection of names in propositions and of propositions in syllogisms, one arrives at a conclusion which is the summation of all antecedent propositions. And this is *science*, the knowledge of the consequences of one word as related to another word " [3].

Accordingly, the scientific edifice reposes on names. There are two sorts of these : proper, which designate but one individual, and common, which designate a collection of individuals and make up the total reality of universals. " The concepts which correspond to them are images or phantasms of singular objects in the spirit. Thus, to know the value of the *universal*, no other faculty than imagination is required, which brings back to us how words of this sort have awaked one thing within our spirit, and sometimes another " [4].

In holding forth for this nominalistic interpretation, Hobbes keeps Aristotle's logical classification into categories, propositions and syllogisms. He states that a proposition is true, as long as it joins two names which are proper to the same thing; false, if to different things. Furthermore, he distinguishes two general methods : analysis, which uncovers the notions and fundamental definitions as gotten from experience, and synthesis, which, following a series of deductions and beginning from primary ideas, proves and explains all of these realities. Evidently, he prefers deduction, and he uses it well in his works.

This type of nominalistic logic was taught at Oxford while Hobbes was a student, as in most universities where Ockhamism was in full power. But for people of the latter following, the doctrinal conclusions which might otherwise suffer were corrected by theology, which, in the name of revelation, defended the great inheritance of truths on God, the human soul and its destiny, and similar truths inaccessible to nominalism. For, in the nominalistic view, the unique object of science is but a collection of sensible individuals; there is no room for mind rising above the material world by its own power. In Hobbes, however, nominalism found its proper field of growth. It is the logical doctrine spontaneously adopted with materialism's denial of spiritual thought, and its explanation of psychological life by pure mechanism. Hobbes,

---

[1] " Every bit of reasoning is reducible to two operations of the soul, addition and subtraction "; *De corpore*, Ch. I, § 2.

[2] There is no real distinction, in his view, between accident or properties and substance.

[3] *Leviathan*, Ch. VIII.

[4] *De corpore*, Ch. II, § 9, *ad finem*.

accordingly, simply adopted this position without criticizing it or examining it deeply, as his successors, Hume, John Stuart Mill and Taine, will do.

C) Physics and Mechanistic Psychology.

In applying his philosophical method, Hobbes at first set up some fundamental ideas by analysis; these ideas are closely allied to mechanism. Then he announced the *principle of causality*, which immediately follows, and placed the explanation of all natural phenomena and of the soul in the frame of an absolute determinism.

In his view, every being, since it is corporeal, is constituted by a material mass essentially endowed with extension. This extension escapes generation and corruption, according to the principle of the conservation of matter. In addition, each body possesses a certain number of properties or accidents which are but various manners of looking at a body, and which are constituted by special forms of motion. These accidents mutually modify each other, as can be observed in the profound or in the superficial changes of nature, as a change of color or heat, or of birth and death. Bodies, then, are agents; they act upon others, and are acted upon by others. " Cause " is the ensemble of properties of the one involving change of the other. " Cause consists in the determined accidents of the agent and of what is acted upon; if all are present, the effect is produced; if one of them is lacking, the effect is not produced " [1]. It readily follows that every true cause is necessary and that every event is rigorously determined by its antecedents [2] which explain it. Hobbes fully accepts this consequence; according to him, one attributes an effect either to chance or to liberty, as long as one is ignorant of the causes which, in reality, are the condition *sine qua non* of the effect. Everything, even in the human domain, is ruled by an absolute determinism.

Having established these views, Hobbes then studies the mathematical principles of motion in geometry; then he goes on to mechanics, which treats of the effects of the movement of one body on another; finally, he concludes with physics, which considers the effects of movements upon the particles of bodies [3]. These three tracts, which fill a large portion of the *De corpore*, pertain more to the particular sciences than to philosophy, and they propose positions which men like Wallis and Boyle found difficult to accept. Without insisting on the point, it should still be mentioned that despite his desire to proceed deductively at all times, Hobbes is obliged to return to the study of facts in physics. His method is to observe the phenomena, as light, wind, or ice, and to propose an explanatory hypothesis by demonstrating *a priori* that this supposition makes the fact *possible*. This method

---

[1] *De corpore*, Ch. IX, § 3.

[2] SORTAIS, *La philosophie moderne*, II, p. 402.

[3] In this realm, Hobbes' works left no comparable effects to those of Descartes or Pascal.

may be quite fruitful in the scientific domain [1], but in the philosophical realm it breaks the deductive chain, and can only introduce confusion in the development of an empiricist and mechanist system in which the recourse to facts is always a normal procedure.

Moreover, in considering the moral sciences, and in psychology, ethics and politics, Hobbes made further recourse to experience; he appealed to the facts of introspection, which gave him his fundamental evidence and the starting point of his deductions [2]. Leaving these facts behind, he then constructs his system with an intrepid logic that fears no consequences.

In PSYCHOLOGY, Hobbes explains the soul and its faculties through pure *mechanism*. Since only body exists, the soul is corporeal and occupies space; one calls it " spirit ", however, since it is a body too tenuous and too subtle to be represented. It has two groups of faculties [3], one of knowledge, and the other of action.

1. Knowledge begins with external sensations, which are determined movements produced in the sense organs by external bodies. These movements are transmitted through the nerves to the head, and are there transformed, in a way that Hobbes does not explain, into sensible qualities. Thus, sound, colors, and other similar things are but mere appearances. " The things which really exist outside of us in the world are the movements, the causes of these appearances " [4]. The head is capable of conserving these movements, but under the form of weakened and impoverished traces. It reproduces them through imagination and memory, the only difference between these two faculties being that the first " considers phantasms such as they present themselves ", while the second " such as time has made usage of them " [5].

These images associate themselves in consciousness and form a mental discourse. Hobbes tried to determine the laws of this discourse, which he later termed " association of ideas ". Perhaps, he said, mental discourse develops at random, as in a dream, although quite often a more attentive observation will find in unconsciousness the bond which associates disparate images [6]. Sometimes, " the series of our thoughts is directed by some passion, urging us to attain a determined goal; the desire of this goal remains the regulator of the series " [7]. This is the law of interest which Hobbes speaks about; intellectual interest explains the construction of the sciences.

Reason, proper to man, is nothing more than a most perfect use of imagination. It is first manifest through the imposition of names, " then, following a correct method, it goes from names

---

[1] *Human Nature*, Ch. XI, § 4.

[2] Faculties are accidents; for Hobbes this means that they are the manner through which we envisage a being.

[3] *Human Nature*, Ch. II, 10.

[4] *Ibid.*

[5] *De Corpore*, Ch. XXV, 8.

[6] See the famous example that Hobbes gives in *Leviathan*, Pt. I, Ch. III.

[7] *Ibid.*, Ch. III.

to propositions, from propositions to syllogisms, until it comes to know the consequences of all the names which fit together into science " [1]. Everything in the realm of human knowledge, then, is explained by the exterior movements which enter into the soul through the senses, where they reverberate, associate and organize, finally, into scientific constructions.

2. Knowledge, however, is not pure speculation; the movement received in the soul rebounds into *action;* thus, the imagination is the explicative source of the various actions of human life. When the reaction is complete, external activity results, as words, walking, and so forth; if the reaction is incomplete, in a skeletonal state or a state of internal effort, it constitutes passion. The latter has two basic forms, tendency (love) and aversion (hate). Tendency carries us towards objects capable of being favorable to our lives (and, for this reason, called *good*), whose possession causes joy, and whose absence excites desire. Aversion separates us from an object harmful to our lives (and, for this reason, called *bad*), and whose influence engenders sadness or chagrin.

Since man is involved in a network of influences, some favorable and some hostile, the reactions of our passions constitute a struggle for power in which a man will impose himself on the most weak in order to satisfy his desires, or accommodate himself to the most powerful in order to obtain a better situation. Comparing our life to a race course in which our goal and recompense will be to be placed ahead of those against whom we are running, Hobbes summarizes the diverse movements of passions as follows. " To strive hard is *desire.* To relax is *sensuality.* To consider those who are behind, is *glory.* To consider those who are ahead, is *humility.* To lose ground by looking backward is *vain glory.* To hold oneself back is *hate.* To go back over one's steps is *repentance.* To be in good condition is *hope.* To be tired is *despair.* To strive to attain what is nearest is *emulation.* To supplant or to reverse is *envy.* To resolve to clear a foreseen obstacle is *courage.* To clear an unforeseen obstacle is *cholera.* To clear an obstacle with ease is *grandeur of soul.* To fall back before little obstacles is *smallness of soul.* To fall unexpectedly is the disposition to *mourn.* To see another fall is the disposition to *laugh.* To see someone surpass against our wish is *pity.* To see someone grasp what lies ahead against our wish is *indignation.* To attach ourselves to someone is *love.* To push ahead someone to whom we are attached is *charity.* To hurt oneself by being precipitate is *shame.* To be continually behind is *misery.* Constantly to surpass someone who is ahead, is *happiness.* To abandon one's course is *death* " [2].

Here again, faithful to his positivism, Hobbes admits nothing beyond passion. There is no absolute supreme good, capable of definitively supplying perfect happiness. The only beatitude towards which man should tend is the successive satisfaction of desires which are constantly being reborn. The will, on the other hand, which compares to man's reason, is nothing more than the

---

[1] *Ibid.*, Ch. v.
[2] *Human Nature*, Ch. IX, 21.

group of passions. Deliberation is but a state of soul in which, by relation to the same object, there successively arise the movements of tendency and aversion which counterbalance each other until the moment when the strongest wins. But the psychological activity of man, although quite complex, is ruled, like all the other movements of the universe, by the laws of mechanistic determinism. The only freedom admitted consists " in the absence of all those impediments to action which are not contained in the nature and in the intrinsic quality of the agent " [1]. This is freedom from " coaction ", or the simple absence of constraint; the liberty of " indifference ", or free will, is but an illusion. It is a *word* destined to hide the ignorance which we have of the true causes of our decisions.

These are the psychological foundations on which Hobbes boldly built his morality and his politics.

D) Egoistic Morality and Absolutistic Politics.

Morality cannot be separated from politics in Hobbes' view. It is by passing from the state of nature to the social state that man penetrates into the moral order and discovers himself subject to the natural law. The doctrine of absolutism in politics is merely the full solution of the problem of moral life, stirred up by the complete egoism of the individual life of man.

1⁰ In the **state of nature**, according to the above principles, man can be moved only by his passions, which lead him towards conquering good or pleasure or the commodities of life, or glory, the pleasure of the soul. The essential rule of life is *egoism*. Hobbes denies any altruistic tendency in man or any natural inclination to mutual help or towards association. The proof of this, he believes, lies in experience : men are constantly occupied in fighting amongst themselves, and especially in taking pleasure in speaking evil of those absent [2].

This regime of egoism or of the passions (whose movement is as fatal as that which bears a stone downward) [3], creates for each man the fundamental right not only to conserve his life and his members, but also to procure for himself everything which gives the commodities of life, each being judge of that which he thinks necessary. In the state of nature, " usefulness is the measure of right " [4], so that everything is permitted to each man.

At the same time, men find themselves faced with each other, endowed with equal force from the physical point of view, for the weakest can, in final resort, kill the strongest in order to establish equilibrium; they are also endowed with equal force from the intellectual point of view, because nature gives them aptitudes that are almost equal in order to acquire experience and the prudence useful for success. In this way, their pretensions to possess everything annul each other, and the only way to obtain

---

[1] *Of Liberty and Necessity.*
[2] *De cive*, Ch. I, § 2.
[3] *Ibid.*, § 2.
[4] *Ibid.*, § 10.

a seating in the banquet of life, is to take possession of one. From all of this follows the natural inclination of men to be mutually harmful, and a regime of force in which the fight and the victory indicate who is the strongest. Thus, the natural state is that of warfare of all against all, in which each man is an enemy to man : " Homo homini lupus ", and " Bellum omnium in omnes " [1].

There is nothing more miserable than such a condition, in which no civilization or peace is possible. It is a state in which " man leads a solitary, indigent, unsavory, animal and short life " [2]. But since each man desires happiness and has the right to obtain it, one must conclude that whatever establishes peace is conformable to right reason, and is just and morally good. This is the origin of the natural law.

2° **The natural** law is " the order of right reason indicating what must be done and what omitted for the preservation of life and bodily members as long as is possible " [3]. From this arises the fundamental principle : " One must look for peace where one can hope to obtain it; if this appears impossible, one must look on all sides for the resources of war, and it is licit to use them " [4]. This is the fundamental right; and, if everything human is regulated by egoism, the old formula, " do good and avoid evil ", becomes, " seek for peace, the source of the greatest well-being, and avoid as much as you can the disagreements of war, while looking, in the meantime, for allies ".

From this fundamental right, Hobbes deduced five other natural laws, whose principles deal with contracts and pacts. The contract is " a mutual transfer of right ". A pact occurs when the parties to the contract do not immediately execute the object of contract and promise to do so in the future. There is an obligation for each man to cede " his right to everything", which he holds by nature, to other men disposed to make the same concession, and to be content thereafter with a just part of the common good " by not doing to others what you would not want them to do to you " [5]. A contract of this sort is the sole means of obtaining a durable peace and of establishing oneself in society.

At the same time, each man keeps his right to defend and to develop his life, his members and his well-being by all means possible. If, then, a man with some associates hopes for the greatest advantages by the use of force, he recovers his liberty and returns to the state of initial warfare. As a consequence, in order that the social contract establish a durable peace, two conditions must be met. First, " it is necessary that the multitude of associates be so great that the adversaries of security could not hope by

---

[1] *Ibid.*, § 11.

[2] *Leviathan*, Ch. XIII.

[3] *Ibid.*, Ch. II, § 1 and 2.

[4] If circumstances give man a superiority so that he can impose himself on the weakest men and demand his own profit of them, the use of force is legitimate; " in the state of nature, certain and irresistible power confers the right of ruling those who cannot resist, and of commanding them " (*De cive*, Ch. I, § 14). But the natural law aims to make this state more endurable.

[5] This rule is but a summary of the others, as will be explained below.

a small number of helpers to achieve victory " [1]; the society naturally capable of living is civil society. Furthermore, in order that in a society of such mutual help the natural divergences do not trouble the peace, " each must so submit his will to the other *(man* or *assembly)*, that all the decisions made by this man or this assembly as necessary for safeguarding the common peace are taken as the expression of the will of all and of each one " [2].

In practice, this contract supposes that each " commits himself never to refuse the sovereign the help of his resources and of his forces against anyone at all "; from this it follows that the desires of individual revolt against society will always be efficaciously counterbalanced by the fear of superior and inevitable sanctions [3].

A twofold series of consequences follows from these principles : in morality, and in politics.

3° With regard to **morality,** it is clear that man enters into the moral order by entering into civil life through the social pact. In the state of nature, there is no justice and no natural law. For, in times of war, " force and fraud are the two cardinal virtues " [4]. But with the social pact dictated by reason in order that peace can reign, the dominion of justice [5] and of moral virtue begins. The obligation of conforming in these areas holds for all times in conscience; it cedes only before the primordial right of defending one's life and one's bodily members.

The perfect accomplishment of this law supposes, for Hobbes, that one avoid the ingratitude, the outrages and the arrogance which make concord impossible; that men be accommodating to each other, pardoning the guilty if they furnish guarantee, punishing evil without cruelty by hoping for the correction of evil-doers; that the usage of goods be moderated, observing equity in their distribution and leaving for common usage those that cannot be divided. If argument arises, an impartial and disinterested judge must be sought [6]. Such are the derived natural laws which reason deduces from the fundamental principle. He who does not see this deduction is not held to observe it, but he must always realize the common rule accessible to all men of not doing to others what you would not have them do to you.

4° **In politics,** Hobbes proposed a most dangerous absolutism in which the power of the sovereign is practically unlimited. The constitutive pact is not, as it is for Rousseau [7], between the people and their ruler so that the latter is at the command of his

---

[1] *De cive,* Ch. v, § 3.

[2] *Ibid.,* § 6.

[3] The contract establishing society could be freely consented to by the citizens; it could also be imposed by force, if one victorious nation imposes its domination on the losers. The second case is morally better than the first. The family, for instance, is a case of the second type. Parents impose their force on the weakness of their children; on the other hand, the State rules everything.

[4] *Leviathan,* Ch. xiii.

[5] " Injustice is but a violation of pacts ". *Leviathan,* Ch. xv.

[6] See *De cive,* Ch. iii, nn. 1-14.

[7] See below, n. 453.

mandatories. Hobbes held to a contract between the citizens alone, who agree among themselves to renounce their " right to everything " in order to deliver this to the hands of a sovereign charged with procuring peace. The sovereign, accordingly, need not answer to any one for his administration. He is the source of laws and subject to none. There is no earthly sanction for him; all he must do is follow right reason [1]. His subjects are not freed from the duty of obeying him unless he become powerless in assuring them what they demand of him : durable peace and prosperity.

In order to be assured of this result, the sovereign should concentrate all powers in himself. He has the sword of justice in order to inflict violators of the peace with penalties, " for pacts without the sword are merely words " [2]. He has the right over war and peace, for the citizens must be efficaciously protected against enemies from without, as from discords from within. He has supreme legislative power, and his laws state what is good and bad, honorable or dishonorable [3]. In maintaining peace and in procuring the greatest good, he automatically determines the applications of the natural law, which have no other reason for being. He has the right to solve doctrinal questions in the measure that their discussion is troublesome to the peace.

But the sovereign endowed with this omnipotence can be, indifferently so, either an assembly elected by the citizens, a man elected for life or for a time, or a hereditary king. Hobbes prefers the absolute king, but he admits the legitimacy of other forms of government. He excludes every mixed or temperate form, as that of a constitutional monarch, for, in his view, the presence of several sovereigns necessarily brings about competition and troubles the peace [4].

Hobbes made a bold application of these principles to a domain which is beyond philosophy, that of revealed religion. The Christian church, in his view, is but a civil society formed of Christians. In such a city, it is the civil sovereign, and he alone, who holds supreme authority, even in matters of cult, hierarchy and religious belief. This sovereign would name the bishops, determine the liturgy, and settle doctrinal controversies by authority. This is the only way in which peace could be secured as the final goal of the state : " Salus populi, suprema lex ".

This total subordination of religion to the state shocked even the Protestants, who were anxious about the dignity of Christianity. But it is in open opposition to Catholic doctrine, which holds to the independence of conscience and to the independence of the Church

---

[1] Hobbes declares that he is accountable to God for his administration " under pain of eternal death " (See *On the Body Politic*, Pt. II, Ch. IX, § 1, and *De cive*, Ch. XIII, § 2). One could wonder about this sanction in a materialistic system, of course.

[2] *Leviathan*, Ch. XVII.

[3] *De cive*, Ch. VI, § 9.

[4] Experience has shown Hobbes wrong on this point; the constitutional monarchy established in England shortly after his death constituted an excellent government which knew how to secure peace and prosperity for its people.

of Christ. The latter, in the Catholic view, is a perfect and universal society, possessing sovereign authority in the moral realm, spiritual goods and an eternal destiny, while recognizing in each civil society or state an equally sovereign authority, in the order of temporal goods and earthly civilization.

CONCLUSION. The system of Hobbes, viewed from without, at first looks like a beautiful construction whose propositions are well arranged and bound together by a vigorous logic. By his universal mechanism and his empiricism, which looked towards experience as the sole source of truth, he continued the positivist current so brilliantly inaugurated by Francis Bacon. But while the latter, exuberant and rich with images, incessantly looked for facts and adopted the *inductive stage* in his positivism, Hobbes, inspired by the mathematical ideal, reduces to a minimum the few facts of external or internal experience on which he founded his doctrine, and places the *deductive stage* of positivism in relief [1].

The very basis of his thought is the assertion, without proof, of MATERIALISM. Despite the rational aspect which is shown in his unrolling of consequences, this principle remains the sign of a profound philosophical decadence. It is to the credit of reason, as a spiritual reality established in an immaterial " thinking substance ", to lift itself beyond its own activities and to lift itself from sensible effects to their first, suprasensible cause, the Infinite Intelligence of God Himself. The abandonment of these doctrines can be nothing more than an arbitrary denial and a dismissal of reason. From this point of view, the system of Hobbes is a century ahead of itself. His materialism and moral egoism received refutation and refusal only in the great century of Louis XIV. While his system is a follow-up and an enlarging of Cartesian mechanism, it is quite antithetical to Descartes. His system does, however, find full approval in the French " philosophes " of the eighteenth century [2].

But it is especially Hobbes' views on man which are worthy of attention, and which are among the best portions of his work. His psychological analyses serve as precursors to the experimental psychology of the eighteenth and nineteenth centuries. His effort to submit moral life to mechanical laws

---

[1] G. SORTAIS, *La philosophie moderne*, p. 427.

[2] Helvetius adopted his moral egoism, Voltaire eulogized it, though with some restrictions. Holbach translated his *Human Nature*, of which Diderot stated that it was a book to read and to comment upon throughout life.

is continued by the doctrines of the economists. His politics, though absolutistic, deduced a priori and contradicted by facts, was studied by jurists, and led the sociologists to examine the origin of society much more closely [1].

Among the partisans of Hobbes in the seventeenth century, we find VELTHUYSEN [2] (1622-1685) in Holland. In his *Epistolica dissertatio de principiis justi et decori*, which contains a eulogy for the most clear treatment in Hobbes' *De cive*, he adopts the principle of personal preservation, though he also recognizes the role of God as Creator, as Providence, and as the supreme sanctioner of law. — In Germany, the jurist PUFENDORF [3] (1632-1694) was a professor of law in the Universities of Heidelberg and of Lund. In his two works, *Elements de jurisprudence universelle* and *Du droit de la nature et des gens* (1672), he eulogized Hobbes and borrowed most of his doctrine from him, though correcting him somewhat. Thus, the origin of society is the good love of self. This sentiment of egoism urges men to fight against those who menace their means of existence. It also inclines them towards those who are similar in order to satisfy their mutual needs. The obligation of justice or of law which rules this society has its immediate origin in law, the fruit of the will of the sovereign. But it has the Divine Will for its first principle. The Divine Will founded law by a fully free decree and has no other justification but God's Omnipotence; this view recalls the despotism of Hobbes.

But the spirit of Hobbes is especially found in the positivist current in England and in France throughout the eighteenth century.

II. POSITIVIST TENDENCIES IN ENGLAND
DURING THE EIGHTEENTH CENTURY.

369. One can distinguish three groups among the philosophers who were inspired by the positivist current in England during the eighteenth century. One group, with Newton, insisted on the viewpoint of the positivist sciences; another group, with the deists and the free thinkers, vindicated the rights of a reason which can be called positivist; the third group was especially concerned with morality and with politics.

---

[1] The natural origin of society was fully established by the ancients; see above, nn. 64, 89, 176, 269, 5⁰. These observations are sufficient to refute Hobbes' theory on the state of nature.

[2] See G. SORTAIS, *op. cit.*, III, pp. 456-460.

[3] G. SORTAIS, *op. cit.*, II and III; A. GONZALES, *Histoire de la philosophie*, III, p. 319.

A) The Influence of Newton.

ISAAC NEWTON [1] (1642-1727) was born at Woolsthorpe in Lincoln county, England. He studied at Cambridge, where, since the time of Francis Bacon, the scientific spirit had made great progress. He received his master's degree in 1668, attending the lectures of the geometer, Isaac Barrow (1630-1677), whom he succeeded, in 1609, as holder of the chair of optics. He became a member of the Royal Society of London in 1672, and became president in 1703. King William III made him Warden of the Mint, a post which he held until the end of his life. His two principal works are *Mathematical Principles of Natural Philosophy* (1687, revised editions in 1713 and 1726), and *Opticks* (1704).

Newton's work is principally in the scientific realm. In astronomy [2], his theory of universal gravitation was a powerful synthesis in which a great number of previously discovered facts and laws found unification and explanation. It was a scientific exposition of the phenomena of nature that was wholly new in the eighteenth century and became commonly accepted. It had the effect of dethroning Descartes' views in this regard. Descartes' views can be compared with those of Newton in order to understand Newton's theory and influence.

In Descartes' view, all phenomena of nature are explainable by two principles : a homogeneous corporeal mass and an unchangeable quantity of movement which God gave to it and which He conserves for it. From this it follows that all physical actions are reduced to *shock* by means of which movements are communicated and diversified. Descartes established a priori, seven laws of shock [3]. But how account for the great variety of phenomena in nature? The Cartesian method begins with an arbitrarily chosen hypothesis outside of experience, and then proceeds deductively in order to make the actual facts probable. Now, Descartes believed in the *plenum* and admitted no void in nature; from this comes his famous *vortex* theory. If one body moves, another must take its place, being itself replaced by another, and so on. But in its rectilinear motion, one body meets resistance from neighboring

---

[1] **Works :** *Isaaci Newtoni Opera*, 5 vols., London, 1779-1785. — *Opticks*, New York, 1952. — *The Mathematical Principles of Natural Philosophy*, Berkeley (Cal.), 1934. — Mc LACHLAN, H. (ed.), *Theological Manuscripts*, Boston, 1950.

Studies : BLOCH, L., *La philosophie de Newton*, Paris, 1908. — CARRA DE VAUX, *Newton*, Paris, 1907. — CLARK, G. N., *Science and Social Welfare in the Age of Newton*, 2nd ed., Oxford, 1949. — FAYE, H., *Sur l'origine du monde*, 3rd ed., Paris, 1885. — Mc LACHLAN, H., *The Religious Opinions of Milton, Locke and Newton*, Manchester, 1941. — MORE, L. T., *Isaac Newton*, New York, 1934. — SNOW, A. J., *Matter and Gravity in Newton's Physical Philosophy*, Oxford, 1926.

[2] Newton's discoveries on light are also important, but are rather specialized for the point of view adopted here.

[3] Given that the quantity of movement is invariable, these laws show how this quantity is divided into two bodies after collision and how direction changes (see E. BRÉHIER, *op. cit.*, II, p. 91). The laws, however, do not apply to real bodies which are not perfectly hard; experience is against the Cartesian view.

ones; their pressure pushes it back towards the center so that the resultant of the two forces is a circular, or *vortex* motion. Our solar system is engendered by one of these turbulent movements of which the sun is center.

The history of the universe, in Descartes' view, supposes that at the beginning of time there was an accumulation of bodies almost equal, endowed with opposed forces, and, by the laws of shock, bumping against each other. These collisions are angular and form a power or subtle matter whose movements explain light; from this, rounded bodies arise which are quite mobile, and whose mass makes up the fluid or liquid element. Certain agglomerations of this element, wholly penetrated by fire, constitute the heavenly bodies. The earth and the planets are formed of the solid element, from particles issuing forth from the fluid element; the particles have various forms, so that placed in repose by the laws of collision, they are quiet and constitute solid bodies. Thus Descartes, " with his subtle matter, his heavenly liquids and his matter which was solid in the parts from which it could make the forms it wished, flattered himself that he could construct the mechanisms explaining all terrestrial phenomena, gravity, light, heat, tides, the chemical constitution of bodies, and the magnet " [1].

The Newtonian method is diametrically opposite to the Cartesian. It does not begin from gratuitously imagined hypothesis; as Newton says, " Hypotheses non fingo " [2]. If one tolerates hypotheses, they must be immediately suggested by the facts, for the first step is always observation of the facts as they actually are. Observation must not be cursory, but accompanied with precise measurements. This application of mathematics to the measurement of physical phenomena was a decisive progress made possible by the calculus of fluxions, or the infinitesimal calculus recently invented [3]. " This calculus, the only language adequate to the new mechanics, not only expresses, as does analytic geometry, what the condition of a quantity is at a given instant, but also how it varies at this instant in intensity and in direction " [4]. In this way, having established the mathematical laws of the movement of the stars by induction, one can certainly predict the direction of future events.

However, while Descartes explained all phenomena by his method, even with regard to their very origin, Newton had to admit *conditions of fact* which cannot be explained by laws and are, at the same time, indispensable. For example, in actual conditions, the attraction of the sun on the planets can be calculated by neglecting the influences of all the other bodies situated outside the solar system; some other disposition might multiply and

---

[1] E. BRÉHIER, *ibid.*, p. 94.

[2] *Mathematical Principles of Natural Philosophy*, " General Scholium ".

[3] The calculus was discovered and developed simultaneously by Newton and Leibniz; much argument on their priority in this regard has occurred. For discussion on this matter, see J. M. CHILD, *The Early Mathematical Manuscripts of Leibniz*, Chicago, 1920, pp. 3-10.

[4] E. BRÉHIER, *op. cit.*, p. 313.

perturb matters, making all calculation impossible. These conditions of fact need explanation, but through other causes than the mathematical laws of phenomena. Thus, Newton clearly distinguished the domain of the physico-mathematical sciences from that of philosophy; the first study the so-called " mechanical causes ", or the laws formulated in equations which are mutually deducible; in this sense, universal gravitation is but a simple, mathematical function of mass and distance, based on the supposition of central forces. The second, philosophy, looks for the so-called " efficient causes ", or the real explanation of these laws and these phenomena.

Newton is without an equal in the domain of physico-mathematical science, but he did not set the boundaries upon science. He also dealt with philosophy, but with less genius. He thought it absurd to attribute the marvelous disposition of the stars to chance, seeing that they realized such precise mathematical laws; God alone is their sufficient reason, He is the creative and ordering Intelligence [1]. In order to explain the movements of the heavenly bodies, Newton admitted the notion of *absolute space*. The latter was infinite and eternal, immediately in contact with the Divine Omnipresence; it was an infinite *sensorium* through which God sensed things [2]. He also held to an *absolute time*, equally eternal and limitless; both absolute space and time were anterior to the world created by God in space and in time [3]. Finally, in order to explain gravitation, he appealed, as to an efficient cause, to the elastic milieu of ether, in which bodies are plunged.

But Newton's philosophical ideas had little influence. He was considered to be but a physicist explaining nature by mathematical laws, and it was especially his universal law of gravitation that won him the admiration of all [4]. For this reason, his influence in the eighteenth century appears to be anti-Cartesian; until his time, the system of vortex motion was quite generally adopted, but quickly gave way to the Newtonian system. However, if one considers the truly philosophical source hidden behind Newton's view, one finds the same *mechanistic theory* viewed as the unique explanation of corporeal nature and its properties, just as in Descartes. A homogeneous matter and local motion : these are the two

---

[1] This is the proof for God's existence popularized by Voltaire; see n. 370.

[2] See J. MARÉCHAL, *Précis de l'histoire de la philosophie moderne*, p. 262.

[3] J. MARÉCHAL, *ibid.*, p. 272; see below, n. 383, for Hume's criticism of these ideas.

[4] Most thinkers, as Berkeley, Hume and Kant, admired Newton as an astronomer, but criticized his metaphysical views on space and on time. Some, as Voltaire, admitted God's role but interpreted gravitation as if it were a new corporeal property discovered by Newton. Others, finally, seek the explanation of the sidereal order in a " scientific cosmogony " and offer the hypothesis of a primitive nebula, as in the Kant-La Place system.

elements of the Newtonian mathematical laws as they were for the Cartesian vortices. Newton's influence causes these two elements to appear in the cosmological theories of the eighteenth century, as well as in the evolutionistic systems of the nineteenth. While Newton is the rival of Descartes as physicist, he is the authentic continuation of his philosophical spirit.

SAMUEL CLARKE [1] (1675-1729) followed Newton not only in physics. He admitted an absolute space and an absolute time, which he made into divine attributes, at least in the sense that they are in God as in the subject of inhesion; thus, they are necessarily eternal and infinite [2]. But Clarke is mainly a theologian and an apologist who wished to use reason to defend " the great Christian conceptions of divine transcendence, moral responsibility and freedom, immortality of the soul, the absolute value of ethics, final causes and so forth " [3]. He spent his life in fighting the free thinkers and anti-Christian deists.

B) Deists and Free Thinkers [4].

Towards the close of the seventeenth, and during the eighteenth century, a number of writers in England, and also in France, gave themselves the name of *deists*, by which they wanted to be freed from the charge of atheism, then in general disfavor [5]. Their doctrines, however, are quite diverse; they are in agreement in their admiration for the Newtonian physics and their hostility to revelation, whether Protestant or Catholic. This last trait won for them, during the controversies of that age, the title of free-thinkers.

JOHN TOLAND [6] (1670-1722) is the first representative. Born in Ireland of Catholic parents, he accused Presbyterianism of

---

[1] *The Works of Samuel Clarke*, 4 vols., London, 1738-1742. — LE ROSSIGNOL, J. E., *Ethical Philosophy of Samuel Clarke*, Leipzig, 1892.

[2] Clarke defended this position against Leibniz and corresponded with him on this matter; he also defended the rights of psychological liberty against Leibniz' determinism.

[3] J. MARÉCHAL, *op. cit.*, pp. 252-53.

[4] BROCKDORFF, C., *Die englische Aufklärungsphilosophie*, Munich, 1924. — BURTT, E. A., *The Metaphysical Foundations of Modern Physical Science*, New York, 1932. — CARRAU, L., *La philosophie religieuse en Angleterre depuis Locke jusqu'à nos jours*, Paris, 1888. — LECHLER, V., *Geschichte der englischen Deismus*, Stuttgart, 1841. — FORSYTH, T. M., *English Philosophy*, London, 1910. — SETH, J., *English Philosophers and Schools of Philosophy*, London, 1912. — SORLEY, W. R., *A History of English Philosophy*, New York, 1921. — STEPHEN, L. *A History of English Thought in the Eigthteenth Century*, 2 vols., London, 1876.

[5] Atheism was considered dangerous, as a menace to the state and to legal sanctions. A bill against blasphemy and profanity was voted by the House of Commons in 1667, but vetoed by the House of Lords.

[6] See BERTHOLD, G., *Johann Toland und der Monismus der Gegenwart*, Munich, 1876. — LANTOINE, A., *Un précurseur de la franc-maçonnerie, John Toland*, Paris ,1927.

falling into unbelief. In his work, *Christianity not Mysterious* (1696), and in his *Letters to Serena* [1] (1704) and in his *Pantheisticon* (1720), he developed the usual anticlerical themes : diatribes against the clergy for allying with the civil powers in order to exploit the people, accusation of superstition with regard to religious cult, and a eulogy of primitive Christianity free from the mysteries which were added later. As a philosopher, he defended universal mechanism [2], and interprets it in the materialistic sense, as did Hobbes. In his view, God is but the corporeal universe taken as a totality, in which everything occurs through mechanical laws. Thought itself is but a modification of the brain.

Henry St. John, Viscount BOLINGBROKE (1678-1751), the English Voltaire, is similar to Toland by his materialism in psychology and in morality, and by his irreligious views. He tended strongly towards scepticism, especially in metaphysics. At the same time, he believed the existence of God demonstrable by the proof from the order of the world.

MATTHEW TINDAL (1675-1733), who had an important place in the national clergy, and THOMAS WOOLSTAN (1669-1731), who was one of the great enemies of the Anglican clergy, agree in respect for the Bible, in which they looked for a purely rational religion, without mysteries or miracles. This confusion between the domain of revelation and that of philosophy, or the referral of revelation to philosophy, characterizes many of the thinkers in the deist movement.

ANTHONY COLLINS (1676-1729), in his *Discourse on Freethinking*, shows himself more aggressive, accusing the Bible of extravagances and rejecting miracles as frauds. A disciple and correspondent with Locke, he accentuated empiricism in his *Essay on the Nature and Destiny of the Human Soul*, in which he taught that thought is a property or affection of matter, for thought is but a follow-up of the action of matter on our senses.

DAVID HARTLEY (1705-1757), in his *Observations of man : his frame, his duty and his expectations*, exposes an empirical doctrine inspired by Locke; he remained in the realm of psychological analysis, however, without entering into the critical problem. He attempted to employ the method of analysis and of synthesis followed by Newton, and he explains the association of ideas through the vibrations of an ether contained in the sensorial organs, in the nerves and in the brain.

JOSEPH PRIESTLEY (1733-1804), defends a similar psychology, affirming that thought has its origins in the frontal nerves. At the same time, he disavowed atheism and thought that his materialistic theories could be reconciled with God's existence. He believed Christianity could be expressed in purely rational doctrines, and thus is an authentic representative of deism.

All of these philosophers, though strong positivists, admitted the existence of the corporeal world. Two thinkers, however,

---

[1] This work was dedicated to the Queen of Prussia, and published in London.
[2] He proposed this view in one of his *Letters* which is entitled " Movement as an essential property of matter ".

did not incline towards this view, and should be mentioned as inclining towards the mixed current: JOHN NORRIS (1657-1711) and ARTHUR COLLIER (1680-1732) [1]. In his *Essay towards the theory of the ideal or intelligible world,* Norris took inspiration from Malebranche, and criticizes Locke; he proclaims the need for a vision in God. In his *Clavis universalis or a new inquiry after truth, being a demonstration of the non-existence or impossibility of an external World* (1713), Collier concludes that an external world is impossible, because one can demonstrate contradictory attributes concerning its nature: that the world is finite and infinite in extension, that matter is always divisible and composed of indivisible elements, that movement is necessary and yet inconceivable, and so forth. In his view, " the world consists in the system of perceptions which the divine will makes us feel, and, if the universe seems to be outside of us, it is because that same will requires that it appears to us as exterior " [2].

C) Moralists and Economists.

The English positivist morality of the eighteenth century is characterized by the fact that it does not found its rules of action on God or on authority, but on the scientific [3] observation of human tendencies. From this viewpoint, one can distinguish two groups of moralists: the first agree that man is egoistic, as Hobbes held, and it defends various forms of utilitarianism. The second discover altruistic tendencies [4] in man, and propose a sentimental morality.

BERNARD DE MANDEVILLE (1670-1733), a Holland medical doctor who lived in London, proposed the egoistic theory in his famous work, *The Fable of the Bees, or Private Vices, Public Benefits* (1723). He attempted to show that " far from resting on altruistic inclinations and on virtue, society is basically egoistic, and that its economic, social, and political progress need the indispensable stimulant of the passions and the vices of particular people " [5]. The eighteenth century retained his affirmation of the full accord between egoism and social utilitarianism.

But the great defender of utilitarianism was JEREMY BENTHAM (1748-1832), who founded a school in the nineteenth century and who was the teacher of John Stuart Mill [6].

The morality of sentiment is represented by a group of moralists who gave birth to the Scottish school of Reid and is best understood as a reaction against Hume [7]. Here we need only mention ADAM

---

[1] See R. BENSON, *Memoirs of the Life and Writings of the Rev. A. Collier,* London, 1837.

[2] J. MARECHAL, *op. cit.,* p. 257.

[3] This " scientific " morality is found in the positivism of the nineteenth century, as in the works of Taine and of Durkheim; see below, n. 500 and n. 516.

[4] Comte, in his positivist morality, has synthesized these two aspects; see below, n. 466.

[5] J. MARÉCHAL, *op. cit.,* p. 256.

[6] See below, n. 484.

[7] See below, n. 386.

SMITH (1723-1790) [1], who was a student of Francis Hutcheson at Glasgow; Smith, however, did not hold to a moral " sense ", as did the Scottish school. In 1759, he published his *Theory of moral sentiment*. Smith travelled to Paris in 1765, where he met the economists. On his return to England, he wrote his famous *The Wealth of Nations*, published in 1776.

Smith bases all morality on *sympathy*, which he defines as the communication to our soul of the emotions of another. This is the sole means of distinguishing in practice what is good. " How is it possible to find invariable rules which fix the point at which, in each particular case, the delicate sentiment of justice is nothing more than a frivolous scruple or which would show the precise instant in which reserve and discretion degenerate into deceit? " [2]. One can arrive at this point only through sympathy or repulsion, which he tests and which is finally completed in a judgement of approbation of the good, and disapproval of the evil. But this sympathy has no moral value unless it be fully disinterested; it has value primarily for others. In the question of one's own life, we must adopt the attitude of an impartial and disinterested spectator. From these considerations, the basic rule of this morality can be stated as follows : we always do the good, if we act in such a fashion as to merit the most pure and the most universal sympathy possible.

Through his work, *The Wealth of Nations*, Smith became one of the founders of the new economic science. He teaches, in this work, that there exist natural laws regulating the economic activities of humanity, so that the best means for a government to procure the prosperity of a country is to respect and to favor the free activity of these laws. He explains the industrial rise of England by the law of division of work and the law of supply and demand. He holds that the source of a nation's riches lies in *work*. " Thus, according as there is a greater or smaller proportion among the number of consumers and the product of work or that which one buys with this product, the nation will be better or worse provided for in relation to the needs and to the commodities of life " [3]. This proportion can be influenced by two factors. The first factor is the perfection brought to the work itself, and here the principal progress comes from the *division of work*, which increases the dexterity of the worker, avoids loss of time and benefits the general product. The second factor is the number of useful workers in comparison to the parasitic citizens. " The number of useful and productive labourers... is everywhere in proportion to the quantity of capital stock employed in setting them to work, and to the

---

[1] **Works** : *The Collected Works of Adam Smith*, 5 vols., Edinburgh, 1811-1812. **Studies** : CHEVALIER, M., *Etude sur A. Smith et sur la fondation de la science économique*, Paris, 1874. — GINZBERG, E., *House of Adam Smith*, New York, 1934. — MONTGOMERY, G. S., *Return of Adam Smith*, London, 1949. — MORROW, G. R., *Ethical and Economic Theories of Adam Smith*, Ithaca (N. Y.), 1923. — SCOTT, W. R., *Adam Smith*, Oxford, 1923. — WEULERSSE, G., *Le mouvement physiocratique*, 2 vols., Paris, 1910.

[2] ADAM SMITH, *Théorie des sentiments moraux* (Fr. transl. by de CONDORCET), II, p. 257.

[3] ADAM SMITH, *The Wealth of Nations*, " Introduction and Plan of the Work ".

particular way in which it is so employed " [1]. In other words, it is the *law of supply and demand* which rules the market of work and influences salaries. This led Smith to study the nature of capital and control. He exposed and criticized various economic systems, some favorable to agriculture, others insisting on the advantages of industry and of commerce. Finally, he studied what expenses are indispensable to a well governed state, and what means the state must use to favor the richness of nations; this is the question of taxes and public loans. His work is a remarkable attempt to submit properly human and social activity to experimental or positive science [2].

The French *physiocrats*, disciples of QUESNAY (1694-1774), taught the same doctrine. They are of a different mind in the practical order, seeing the source of riches in agriculture rather than in industry. But their theoretical principle is identical, for they hold to the existence of economic laws which should be followed; in their view, the Medieval Guilds merely prevented economic laws from functioning properly. The effort of the *physiocrats* led to the Revolution of 1789 and to the law (1791), prohibiting every form of economic association.

III. THE FRENCH " PHILOSOPHES "
OF THE EIGHTEENTH CENTURY [3].

370. Descartes' influence on the English positivist moralists was rather weak, and the doctrinal current stemming from Francis Bacon was more powerful in guiding their thought. This situation does not occur in France; La Mettrie, and the thinkers called " philosophes " are the continuation of Cartesianism. They achieve a certain sort of unity, not as Leibniz did, by favoring thought, but by suppressing spiritual thought and adopting mechanism and materialism.

The physician, LA METTRIE [4] (1709-1751) is, chronologically [5], the first of these thinkers. His frank materialism caused him to

---

[1] *Ibid.*

[2] This goal will be realized by A. Comte; see below, n. 464.

[3] BOAS, G., *French Philosophies of the Romantic Period*, Baltimore, 1925. — *French Thought in the 18th Century*, Philadelphia, 1953. — GUNN, J. A., *Modern French Philosophy*, London, 1922. — LEVY-BRUHL, L., *History of Modern Philosophy in France*, Chicago, 1899. — Rousseau, another 18th century philosopher, also belongs to this group, but will be treated below in connection with positivism, n. 448 ff.

[4] *Philosophical Works*, 2 vols., London, 1751. *Studies.* QUEPRAT, N., *La philosophie matérialiste au XVIIIe siècle. Essai sur La Mettrie, sa vie et ses œuvres*, Paris, 1873. — On others in the school : FAGUET, *Etudes littéraires*, XVIIIe s., Paris, 1890. — LANGE, A., *The History of Materialism*, New York, 1925.

[5] Doctrinally, the most important philosopher is Condillac, whom we shall discuss below, n. 379. Among the others, there is no leader; all are secondary thinkers. We place La Mettrie first insofar as he is first in time.

be banished successively from France and from Holland, and he took refuge with Frederick II (1712-1786). His works are entitled *L'Homme-Machine* and *L'Homme-Plante;* in them he teaches that every reality is but matter and movement regulated by the necessary laws of mechanism. Consequently, God and the soul are but chimeras. He did not draw the moral consequences of his views.

D'ALEMBERT [1] (1717-1783) and DIDEROT [2] (1713-1784) were the founders of the famous *L'Encyclopédie* (1751-1752), " the work of a large group of irreligious writers who conducted, in this *Dictionnaire raisonné des sciences et des arts,* a strenuous war against Christianity " [3]. D'Alembert is the author of *Traité de dynamique* and of the *Discours préliminaire* of the Encyclopedia. The latter treatise deals with the origin and the classification of the various sciences, from which metaphysical and religious doctrines are excluded as being useless. — Diderot wrote *Pensées Philosophiques* and *De la suffisance de la religion naturelle,* and various articles in the Encyclopedia, for the completion of the latter work fell to him entirely after the year 1759. In his writings he defends *naturalism,* crediting every material thing with life, and viewing nature as the source of an evolution in which particular beings are reabsorbed.

In a similar vein, we find ROBINET (1735-1820), who, in his *De la Nature,* teaches a similar animism.

HELVETIUS [4] (1715-1771) and CABANIS [5] (1757-1808) apply the positivist methods to the study of conscious life. In his *De l'Esprit* (published during his lifetime) and his *De l'Homme* (printed in 1772), Helvetius, supposing that everything within the spirit comes from physical sensibility, shows that psychological diversities are the effects of the *passions,* and that the latter hark back to the search for pleasure and the flight from pain. Education and society are capable of regulating the passions for the good of the group, and

---

[1] *Œuvres philosophiques* (ed. Bastien), Paris, 1805. — *Studies.* BERTRAND, J., *d'Alembert,* Paris, 1889. — MULIER, M., *Essai sur la philosophie de Jean d'Alembert,* Paris, 1926.

[2] *Œuvres complètes* (ed. Assezat), 20 vols., Paris, 1875-1877. — *Studies.* BARKER, I. E., *Diderot's Treatment of the Christian Religion in the Encyclopedie,* New York, 1941. — COLLIGNON, A., *Diderot,* Paris, 1895. — CROCKER, L. G., *Two Diderot Studies: Ethics and Esthetics,* Baltimore (Md.), 1952. — FELLOWS, O. E., and TORREY, N. L., (eds.), *Diderot Studies,* Syracuse (N. Y.), 1949; — *Diderot Studies, II,* 1953. — HERMAND, P., *Les idées morales de Diderot,* Paris, 1923. — LE GRAS, J., *Diderot et l'Encyclopédie,* Amiens, 1928. — LEPPOL, I. K., *Diderot, Ses idées philosophiques,* Paris, 1936. — MAUVEAUX, J., *Diderot l'encyclopédiste et le penseur,* Montbeliard, 1914. — MORLEY, J., *Diderot and the Encyclopedist,* 2 vols., 1878, London, 1921. — ROSENKRANZ, K., *Diderot's Leben und Werke,* 2 vols., Leipzig, 1886. — VARTANIAN, A., *Diderot and Descartes,* Princeton (N. J.), 1953.

[3] BARBEDETTE, *Histoire de la Philosophie,* p. 430.

[4] *Œuvres,* 5 vols., Paris, 1792. — *Studies.* KEIM, A., *Helvetius, sa vie et son œuvre,* Paris, 1911. — GROSSMAN, M., *Philosophy of Helvetius,* New York, 1926.

[5] See E. BRÉHIER, *Histoire de la Philosophie,* pp. 607-610.

the ideal legislation is to bind the general interest to the particular interest in such a way that each can acquire more of his own interest in observing the law than in violating it. — Towards the close of the century, Cabanis, in his *Mémoires sur les Rapports du physique et du moral* (published in 1802), continued this psychological positivism, referring the facts of consciousness back to physiological phenomena as to their explicative cause [1].

With the work of Cabanis, there can be associated that of CONDORCET [2] (1743-1794), who wrote the famous *Esquisse d'un tableau historique des progrès de l'esprit humain* (1794). This work applies the positivist method to the study of mind, not in each individual, but rather to explain the evolution of sciences in humanity. He distinguishes ten periods of this evolutionary process which show a steady progress by its constant disengagement from religious and dogmatic appeal, and its arrival at the experimental sciences of the sixteenth century and beyond. These sciences have become the field for unlimited action and their progress will never be completed [3].

There remained only an explanation of moral and social life, the tendencies of which had been pointed towards in the work of Helvetius. This work was done by HOLBACH [4] (1723-1789), who was born in the Palatinate, but lived in Paris; he was the friend and the patron of the *philosophes*. He authored *Système de la nature* and a large number of anti-religious writings, in which he accuses the clergy of having invented religion in order to dominate the people. He aimed " to build a new morality, entirely separated from all positive religion " [5]. His work aims to show that the order of nature is not the result of a divine plan but of the laws of physics. Assuming that all human actions aim at pleasure or flee from pain, he proposed that society is founded on mutual aid; universal morality should, then, teach man the way to help others by the recompenses or the penalties which it promises. Thus, " the moral problem is a problem of legislation; a system of sanctions should be set up which will move man to the pleasure of accomplishment by acts that are virtuous or useful to others " [6].

---

[1] DESTUTT DE TRACY (1754-1836), a friend of Cabanis, and author of *Elements d'idéologie*, was the most influential of the *ideologists* at the end of the 19th century; it was he who kept empiricist psychology alive until it was at last replaced by eclecticism. See below, n. 441, and also BRÉHIER, *op. cit.*, II, pp. 600-606.

[2] *Œuvres complètes*, 21 vols., Paris, 1804. — Studies. BURLINGAME, A. E., *Condorcet, the Torch Bearer of the French Revolution*, Stratford, 1930. — CAHEN, L., *Condorcet et la Révolution française*, Paris, 1904. — FRAZER, J. G., *Condorcet on the Progress of the Human Mind*, Oxford, 1933. — SCHAPIRO, J. S., *Condorcet and the Rise of Liberalism*, New York, 1934.

[3] The same notion reappears with A. Comte; see below, n. 457.

[4] CUSHING, P. M., *Baron d'Holbach*, New York, 1914. — PIEKHANOV, G. V., *Essays in the History of Materialism*, New York, 1934. — WICKWAR, W. H., *Baron d'Holbach : A Prelude to the French Revolution*, London, 1935.

[5] E. BRÉHIER, *op. cit.*, p. 441.

[6] *Ibid.*, p. 442.

Though not properly speaking a philosopher, VOLTAIRE [1] (1694-1778) wrote much about it, especially in his *Philosophe ignorant*, *Traité de l'âme*, *Dialogues d'Ephémère* and his articles in the *Dictionnaire philosophique*. He fought against the encyclopedists, but sought, as they did, for the destruction of all religion and especially of Catholicism. Deep speculation and metaphysical thinking were abhorrent to him. Having no proper doctrine of his own, he was a popularizer, especially of Locke's thought, " the wise author of a type useful to mankind " [2]. His master idea was the struggle against intolerance [3], by which he meant dogma. He fought for the full independence of reason with regard to any authority, whether divine or human. In this respect, his work can be associated with that of modern thought.

Common to all these *philosophes* is the abandonment of the spiritualist and metaphysical propositions which gave Cartesianism its grandeur. They are drawn towards *mechanism*, whose attraction became irresistible after the magnificent discoveries of Newton, who was considered one of the masters of the eighteenth century. But the mediocrity of these thinkers is so great that this decadent century of philosophical thought rapidly was led to hold that matter was the only reality.

The thinkers that have been mentioned above were drawn to materialism by a need for unity and a desire for simplicity, for the mode of existence and of operation of a spiritual soul in the pineal gland was hardly sensible. In its turn, modern science encouraged and multiplied the objections against the soul : by acting on the body, it could change the immutable sum of movements in the universe; its existence is useless, for things can be explained without it. At the opening of the nineteenth century, the scientific discoveries encouraged the hope of a " universal mechanistic science " which would be prepared to justify the materialistic hypotheses or at least to explain their success.

---

[1] *Œuvres complètes* (ed. Beuchot), 72 vols., Paris, 1829-1834. — *Studies*. ALDINGTON, R., *Voltaire*, New York, 1934. — BRANDES, G. M. C., *Voltaire*, London, 1930. — CARRÉ, J. R., *Consistance de Voltaire, le Philosophe*, Paris, 1939. — DESNOIRESTERRES, *Voltaire et la société au XVIIIe s.*, 8 vols., 1867-1876. — GRIGGS, E. H., *Voltaire and the heritage of the 18th century*, New York, 1933. — JORDAN, W. G., *Voltaire*, London, 1930. — NOYES, A., *Voltaire*, New York, 1936. — WADE, I. O., *Studies on Voltaire*, Princeton (N. J.), 1947.

[2] E. BRÉHIER, *op. cit.*, p. 458.

[3] As an apostle of tolerance and a sceptical philosopher, Voltaire had a 17th century precursor in the protestant, Pierre BAYLE (1647-1707), who, in his *Dictionnaire historique et critique*, attempted to show that all dogmas are invalid, insofar as they do not have a solid foundation in reason. The latter belongs to his own times by his attachment to the faith of his fathers, but he did want individual freedom of belief. See J. DELVOLVÉ, *Essai sur Bayle*, Paris, 1906.

ARTICLE THREE. — MIXED CURRENT.

GENERAL BIBLIOGRAPHY.

GONZALÈS, A., *Histoire de la Philosophie*, vol. III, Paris, 1891. — LASKI, H., *Political Thought in England from Locke to Bentham*, New York, 1920. — LYON, G., *L'idéalisme en Angleterre*, Paris, 1888. — MARÉCHAL, J., *Le point de départ de la métaphysique*, vol. II, Paris, 1923. — METZ, R. A., *Hundred Years of British Philosophy*, New York, 1938. — SORLEY, W. R., *A History of English Philosophy*, Cambridge, 1937. — STEPHEN, L., *History of English Thought in the Eighteenth Century*, New York, 1902. — WILLEY, B., *The Eighteenth Century Background*, New York, 1941.

371. At first blush it seems that the orientation of idealism and of positivism is contradictory and exclusive. In exalting the idea, the first favors spiritualism; in holding to sensible experience alone, the second gives first place to material facts and seems to sacrifice any notion of spirit. The history of philosophy seems to show that this situation does not necessarily obtain, and that one can hold, in turn, that everything is ideal and that everything is corporeal if one takes idea or thought in the Cartesian sense of " fact of consciousness " and refers all facts of consciousness to the sensible order of reality.

This evolvement was accomplished in the eighteenth century, as if in three stages : 1) *Locke*, respecting the notion of causality, strongly shatters the notion of substance; 2) *Berkeley* sacrifices all corporeal substance and retains spirit; during this same time, *Condillac*, in France, sacrifices spirit by explaining all conscious life through sensation; 3) Finally, *Hume*, delving into the very depths of criticism, rejects every substance and every cause, retaining only the facts of consciousness and their laws.

These philosophers are the continuation of the series of great thinkers, at least in the sense that they take up and deepen the important problem of modern philosophy, that of the value of human knowledge. They look for a solution to this problem by the Cartesian method. Faithful, however, to the concrete approach of English philosophy, they adopt the empiricist outlook, from which they progressively deduce all critical consequences.

I. The first stage. John Locke (1632-1704).

Special bibliography.

1º **Works** : *Works*, (ed. by E. Law, 4 vols.), London, 1823. — *Philosophical Works* (annotated ed. by J. A. St. John), 2 vols., London, 1908. — *An Essay concerning human Understanding*, (ed. C. Frazer), 2 vols., Oxford, 1894. — L. King, *The Life of J. Locke with extracts from his correspondence, journals and common-place books*, London, 1829-1830.

2º **Studies** : Aaron, R. I., *John Locke*, New York, 1937. — Baker, E., *Social Contract : Essays by Locke, Hume and Rousseau*, New York, 1951. — Bourne, H. R. F., *The Life of John Locke*, 2 vols., New York, 1876. — Carlini, A., *La filosofia di Locke*, 2 vols., Florence, 1920. — Didier, J., *J. Locke*, Paris, 1911. — Fechtner, E., *J. Locke*, Stuttgart, 1898. — Fraser, A. C., *Locke*, London, 1890. — *John Locke as a Factor in Modern Thought*, Oxford, n. d. — Gibson, *John Locke*, Oxford, 1933. — *Locke's Theory of Knowledge and Its Historical Relations*, Cambridge, 1917. — Gough, J. W., *Locke's Political Philosophy*, New York, 1950. — Hefelbower, S. G., *The Relation of John Locke to English Deism*, Chicago, 1918. — James, D. G., *Life of Reason : Hobbes, Locke, Bolingbroke*, New York, 1949. — Kiemt, A., *John Locke : Theoretische Philosophie*, Meisenheim, 1952. — Krakowski, E., *Les sources médiévales de la philosophie de Locke*, Paris, 1915. — Lamprecht, S. P., *The Moral and Political Philosophy of John Locke*, New York, 1918. — Marion, H., *J. Locke, sa vie et son œuvre*, Paris, 1876. — Morris, C. R., *Locke, Berkeley, Hume*, New York, 1931. — O'Connor, D. J., *John Locke*, Baltimore, 1952. — Ollion, H., *La Philosophie générale de John Locke*, Paris, 1908. — Pollock, F., *Locke's Theory of a State*, Oxford, n. d. — Smith, N. K., *John Locke*, Manchester, 1933. — Tellkamp, A., *Das Verhältnis John Lockes zur Scholastik*, Munster, 1927.

372. Locke was born at the town of Wrington, near Bristol. Intended for an ecclesiastical career, he studied at Oxford (1652-1658). There he acquired a strong distaste for the formalism of the teaching, and became filled with the nominalism of Ockham. When, towards the close of his studies [1], he read Descartes, he was charmed by the manner in which he envisaged the great problems of thought; without accepting all his doctrines, he became a fervent admirer of his method. Not inclined towards the ecclesiastical career, he began the study of the sciences, especially of medicine under Boyle; in 1666 he entered the household of Lord Ashley as informal physician. Ashley became the first Earl of Shaftesbury, and Locke helped him as secretary in his various political functions. Both men were strongly liberal in their thinking. Somewhat later (1668), Locke was elected to membership in the Royal Society. He was

---

[1] He was then 27 years old.

closely associated with the celebrated physician, Sydenham, and even wrote two short medical tracts, *Anatomica* (1668) and *De arte medica* (1669). He was more concerned with political and religious questions, as two short treatises of the same period show [1]: the *Infallibilis Scripturæ interpres non necessarius*, and his *Essay on Tolerance* (1666) [2]. It was about 1670 that he first conceived of his basic philosophical work, *An Essay concerning Human Understanding*, working on it when his health and other duties permitted him. From 1675 to 1679 he lived in France to help regain his health; he stayed at Montpellier, and then at Paris, where he was interested in the works of Malebranche, Gassendi and De Nicole. Returning to England, he became involved in the intense political activity of Lord Shaftesbury. Shaftesbury was imprisoned in the Tower of London, then freed, headed the Protestant opposition to James II and took refuge in Holland, where he died. Locke, fearing himself suspected by the government, followed his master into Holland, where he met two influential Protestant theologians, Jean Le Clerc and Philip van Limborch. It was to the latter that Locke's *Essay on Tolerance* was addressed, and this essay was the first work of his published (1689). The same year saw the arrival of William of Orange with the constitutional monarchy, and Locke returned to England. There he edited *Two Treatises of Government*, in order to justify the recent turn of political events, and the first complete edition of his *Essay concerning Human Understanding* (1690) [3]. He then turned his thoughts to education, and especially to political and economic questions, writing his, *Some Considerations on the Consequences of the Diminution of interest and the Increase of the Value of Money*. From about 1700 on, Locke retired to an estate at Oates, owned by his friend, Lady Masham, the daughter of Ralph Cudworth. He died in 1704.

Locke is a conciliatory thinker and quite unsystematic. His ideas are dispersed in many and even disparate domains, as science, politics, religion and psychology, and do not, at first view, seem to form a coherent system. His entire work, however, is dominated by three tendencies, the love of tolerance, the attraction for the positive sciences, and his esteem for the Cartesian method. These three tendencies find their equilibrium in Locke's *Essay*. As the other thinkers of this period, he gives speculation a practical aim : " There is no knowledge worthy of the name excepting those which lead to some new

---

[1] Locke habitually noted his reflections and wrote many short treatises; most of these were only published much later.

[2] Various subjects are treated by Locke in his treatises, as error, the priesthood, Sacred Scripture, tradition, and so on.

[3] In 1688, Le Clerc published an abridged version of this work in his literary journal, *Bibliothèque Universelle*. The second edition of the *Essay*, published in 1694, had many additions and changes.

or useful invention " [1]. Faced with the evils let loose through religious and political squabbles, Locke ardently desired to secure peace and social prosperity. To attain this end, he steered clear of all extreme methods. His taste for the sciences led him to reject absolute intellectualism, and especially the appeal to intuition and to enthusiasm, which was advocated by Cudworth and the Cambridge School, and which Locke strongly refuted; he denounced them as the source of fanaticism and of religious dissensions harmful to peace. On the other hand, he disdained with equal vigor the absolute empiricism of Hobbes, considering any materialism atheistic and as loosing the basest instincts of man. He kept respect for the great truths of common sense, as the existence of God and of a natural law, and founded his morality on the reason and on the will of the Creator.

It was through the help of Descartes that he found the way of sage moderation. Locke thought that by using the method of the clear idea to determine the limits of human reason, he would establish solid ground where agreement could be had on essentials, and tolerance on accidental matters. Thus, the unifying principle of his system is less speculative than practical; it can be stated, doctrinally, as follows : *The limited value of our understanding determines the domain of certitudes, which must make human life rest on a common accord, and the vast realm inaccessible to certitude, in which liberty of opinion must be respected.*

Locke's *Essay* forms the center of all his doctrines. Having indicated its aim and method, it will be shown how he resolved two problems : the origin and classification of ideas (the psychological problem), and the value of ideas (the critical problem). From his view on these problems flows his delimitation of the domain of certitudes and that of free opinions.

A) **Aim and Method of Locke's Essay.**

373. If the general and subconscious aim of Locke in all his works is to affirm the spirit of tolerance as the surety of peace, his immediate and explicit aim in his *Essay* is to resolve the problem of the value of human knowledge. " This, therefore, being my purpose, to inquire into the original, certainty and extent of human knowledge, together with the grounds

---

[1] *De arte medica.*

and degrees of belief, opinion and assent "[1]. He takes up the critical problem opened by Descartes, not in order to lay an infallible foundation for the sciences, but because he sees this as an efficacious means of concord. Instead of plunging hazardously into empty disputes, men should carefully examine the capacity of their understanding, in order to discover how far their knowledge extends. If men distinguished that which they can conceive from that which surpasses their intelligence, they would retain the common truths with more assurance and be more reserved towards other truths [2]. Locke's immediate aim, however, is to determine the certitude, evidence and extent of human knowledge — which is the very aim of any critical approach to knowledge.

Without insisting on initial doubt, as did Descartes, and without looking for a method appropriate to a critical philosophy, as did Kant, Locke believed he had found the solution through simple *psychological analysis*. He excluded from his study any research on the nature of the soul and the influence of the body on psychic functions; he merely aimed to examine, step by step, in an historical and clear way, all the faculties of the human spirit [3]. In his view, the problem is to rediscover the simple elements with which, by hypothesis, all the facts of consciousness are formed. Then, he wished to study the formation of complex states by clarifying and evaluating the bonds which tie them together; this would result in a judgment on their value.

This purely psychological method, affirmed at the beginning and followed throughout the work, has merited for Locke the title of " Founder of Experimental Psychology ", at least as the science of introspection [4]. Here also he continues and amplifies the influence of Descartes. Like Descartes, Locke does not distinguish the sensible from the intellectual realms; he considers the facts of consciousness as they present themselves to internal intuition or as facts synthesizing the double activity of spirit and of sense; he considers the facts of consciousness as phenomena of the soul, which he classifies empirically and whose reciprocal influences he describes.

---

[1] *Essay*, Introduction, § 2.

[2] *Ibid.*, § 7.

[3] *Ibid.*, § 2.

[4] " The true founder of empirical psychology, of psychology considered as the science of internal phenomena, is Locke ". Janet and Seailles, *Histoire de la philosophie*, p. 34.

It would be minimizing this method to attribute a purely psychological significance to it; it has a *critical value*, as does the Cartesian theory of the clear idea. Locke's approach has two implications : science is referable to simple ideas, and these primitive elements have infallible truth of themselves. Admitting these two suppositions, Locke's psychological method, which is followed by all critical philosophers until Kant, can attain its goal in determining the value of human knowledge, as long as it is granted that in themselves, psychology and epistemology are quite distinct.

What Locke absolutely refused to accept from Descartes, however, was the interpretation of the clear idea as an object of intuition. By this refusal, he renewed the critical problem and oriented its new solution both towards empiricism and towards idealism.

B) **Origin and Classification of Ideas.**

374. By *idea* Locke means that which is the object of our understanding when we are thinking. " It being that term which, I think, serves best to stand for whatsoever is the object of the understanding when a man thinks, I have used it to express whatever is meant by phantasm, notion, species, or whatever it is which the mind can be employed about in thinking " [1]. This description is not too clear, for it joins several quite diverse aspects : the viewpoint of *sensation*, which represents the concrete, and the viewpoint of *intellection*, which considers the abstract; the *subjective* aspect, according to which an idea is a special internal phenomenon, a fact of representative consciousness; the *objective* aspect, according to which the idea embraces the whole field of human knowledge, both concrete objects and universal natures. The best interpretation seems to be that by " idea " Locke means what Descartes meant by " thought " : *every fact of consciousness*. One item is quite clear; both philosophers adopt the same idealist beginning, holding that we at first know our thoughts or our ideas. This is why Locke states that our ideas constitute the total object of our knowledge.

---

[1] *Essay*, Introd., § 8. Locke uses Scholastic terms, *phantasma* and *species*. In Thomism, the first designates an image of the sensible order, especially the object of the imagination; the second is broader in meaning, and is applied to concepts of the mind, as well as to sensible knowledge. The correct usage of these terms implies some fine nuances of thought which Locke was prepared to bypass completely.

But in contrast with Descartes, Locke holds that *there are no innate ideas,* and that all, without exception, come from experience. This is a quite fundamental view with Locke, and he supports it with many proofs, some of which are negative and aim to refute innatism, others of which are positive, analyzing and classifying our diverse ideas by showing their sensible origin.

Locke at first proves that the mind does not possess innate principles, even in the speculative order [1], as the principle of identity, nor in the practical order [2], as the rule of doing unto others what you would have them do unto you. If these principles were innate in the mind in its natural state, one would have to believe that children and fools understood them, which is contrary to fact. Moreover, the child would have to use these principles in daily life, as when it would admit that an apple is not the fire [3]. But though the child accepts this concrete evidence, he does not understand the abstract formula of identity; this proves that the principle is not innate. The same holds for the rules of morality, and especially for the five truths which Lord Herbert proposed, and which Locke examines in particular [4].

The Cartesians and the Cambridge Platonists defended innatism, not in a formal, but in a virtual sense. But Locke replies that there is no mean between a complete nude faculty and the idea or principle formally known. " For if these words (to be in the understanding) have any propriety, they signify to be understood; so that to be in the understanding and not to be understood, to be in the mind and never to be perceived, is all one as to say anything is and is not in the mind or understanding " [5]. Besides, the principles could not be innate if the ideas of which they are composed are not; in having ideas we do not produce or supply the notion of identity, nor that of the whole and its parts, nor that of identity, of God or of substance [6]. Briefly, there are no innate ideas, and, as a consequence, they all come from experience. On the other hand, by exposing the origin and the classification of ideas, Locke establishes his thesis positively.

He begins by distinguishing, in agreement with the Cartesian method, the *simple ideas,* to which the mind is purely passive,

---

[1] *Essay,* Book. I, Ch. II.

[2] *Ibid.,* Ch. III.

[3] *Ibid.,* Ch. II, § 23.

[4] Locke refers to HERBERT OF CHERBURY, a theologian of the Cambridge Platonist vintage. In his *De veritate* (1628), he wanted to settle religious argument by distinguishing common truths, which are innate, from others in which liberty of opinion holds. The five innate truths are God's existence, God should be given cult, virtue is the best cult, sins are to be repented, and there are sanctions in the future life. See *Essay,* Book I, Ch. III, § 15.

[5] *Ibid.,* Ch. II, § 5.

[6] This demonstration is given in the *Essay,* Book I, Ch. III, § 4-19.

and the *complex or derived ideas*, which the soul actively produces in itself through simple ones.

1° **Simple Ideas.** At the beginning, as a matter of fact, the understanding is truly a " white paper " or a " bare tablet " [1], which is destined to receive the imprint of simple ideas. They come from two sources, sensation and reflection.

a) Sensation is external experience which gives us ideas of objects outside ourselves, such as those of white, yellow, cold, soft, sweet, and bitter [2]. This first activity evidently pre-supposes the exercise of the external senses. Locke, however, considers them synthetically as a perception through which the soul or spirit consciously acquires the idea of the exterior object. In his Cartesian perspective, the problem concerns the *human soul*, which, according to common opinion, is spiritual [3].

The ideas of sensation which represent the qualities of bodies are themselves divided into two groups. The original or *primary qualities* form the first group; they are " those qualities of bodies which cannot be separated, as solidity, extension, figure, number, motion and rest ". The second group includes the *secondary qualities*, or those which, " in the body, are effectively no other thing than the power to produce various sensations within ourselves by means of their primary qualities..., as colors, sounds, tastes, etc. " [4].

This famous distinction, also taught by Descartes, is less justifiable in Locke's empirical system [5]. Experience itself suggests that we place extension, movement, and such qualities in second place. What Locke calls primary qualities, the Scholastics called *common sensibles*, for the senses do not grasp them except through the *proper sensibles*, which Locke calls secondary qualities. Thus, the eye cannot see the figure of a body, unless it sees it *colored* in a certain fashion. — But this distinction was also held by Locke's master, the physician Boyle, and is explainable by the triumph of mechanism in the sciences. The savants submitted to the tendency of referring all sensible phenomena to the various types of motion, as Newton did for light. The philosophers concluded

---

[1] The expression, " bare tablet ", is Aristotle's (see above, n. 83); the white paper is Locke's (*Essay*, Book II, Ch. II, § 2).

[2] Locke gives these examples in the *Essay*, Book II, Ch. I, § 3.

[3] Though Locke did not deny the spirituality of the soul, he did not think it demonstrable.

[4] *Essay*, Book II, Ch. VIII, § 9 and 10.

[5] For Descartes, this distinction arose due to the identity asserted between corporeal substance and extension; Locke does not admit this identity, and refers everything to experience.

that these quantitative and measurable qualities were essential, " original and primary " by relation to the others.

b) Reflection is internal experience which furnishes us the ideas of the psychological operations, as " perception, thinking, doubting, believing, reasoning, knowing, willing, and all the different actings of our own minds " [1]. Reflection, for Locke, is also presented as a synthetic act, including every fact of consciousness, intellectual or sensible. It always supposes the intervention of the spirit in order to account for our interior life and to distinguish its manifestations. But it is concerned with sensible facts, imagination, passion, and so forth, as with the superior aspects of consciousness. Moreover, there are no longer any purely spiritual acts in us, whether of knowledge or affection, and Locke held himself to the observation of concrete facts [2]. Briefly, reflection, as sensation, is an intuition of phenomena. " ...Though it be not sense, as having nothing to do with external objects, yet it is very like it, and might properly enough be called internal sense " [3].

Although the definition of these ideas implies many elements, they are called simple in the sense that they are primitive, for the analysis of their origin can go no further. They are irreducibly *given* and before them the soul is purely receptive [4].

2⁰ **Complex or Derived Ideas.** In this general group, three classes are distinguished. " The acts of the mind, wherein it exerts its power over its simple ideas, are chiefly these three : 1) Combining several simple ideas into one compound one, and thus all complex ideas [5] are made. 2) The second is bringing two ideas, whether simple or complex, together, and setting them by one another so as to take a view of them at once, without uniting them into one, by which way it gets all its ideas of relations. 3) The third is separating them from all

---

[1] *Essay*, Book II, Ch. I, § 4.

[2] The distinction between the sensible and the spiritual operations is legitimate and quite important for defining the human soul; it supposes an analysis of the facts of consciousness in the light of principles of a rational psychology, as found in Thomism.

[3] *Essay*, Book II, Ch. I, § 4.

[4] E. Bréhier (*Histoire de la philosophie*, II, p. 280), notes a third category : simple ideas which are both of sensation and reflection, as those of existence, duration and number.

[5] In order to distinguish this first group of the general category of complex or derived ideas, they will here be called " ideas complex by combination " or " combined ideas ".

other ideas that accompany them in their real existence : this is called abstraction, and thus all its general ideas are made " [1].

a) The first category furnishes us with many important ideas whose formation Locke explains, with the hope of eliminating the controversies to which they have given place. He thus distinguishes among ideas *complex by combination* the following : that of *substance*, or the idea of things which exist by themselves, as a man; that of *mode*, the idea of things which exist in another, as a triangle. The mode is subdivided into a *homogeneous* (simple) mode, formed by the combination of the same idea with itself, and the *mixed* (complex) mode, formed by combination of heterogeneous ideas, as that of beauty or murder.

Locke's reflections on the idea of SUBSTANCE are not too clear. On the one hand, he explicitly declares it to be an *idea complex by combination ;* it is formed by the constancy recognized in a group of properties (simple ideas), to which one gives but one name. On the other hand, substance so defined is not distinguishable from the *mixed mode*, which is also a stable grouping of simple ideas designated by the same name. For these reasons, Locke goes on to another conception : " The mind... takes notice also that a certain number of these simple ideas go constantly together; which being presumed to belong to one thing, and words being suited to common apprehensions and made use of for quick dispatch, are called, so united in one subject, by one name; which, by inadvertency, we are apt afterward to talk of and consider as one simple idea, which indeed is a complication of many ideas together : because, as I have said, not imagining how these simple ideas can subsist by themselves, we accustom ourselves to suppose some substratum wherein they do subsist, and from which they do result; which therefore we call substance " [2]. Locke concedes that we legitimately assert the *existence* of this *substratum* distinct from its properties, for one cannot conceive of modes without a subject which bears them up; we are, however, totally ignorant of its nature or *quiddity* [3], for our ideas, coming from experience, do not allow us to know simple qualities and their diverse combinations in any proper sense. It

---

[1] *Essay*, Book II, Ch. XII, § 1.

[2] *Ibid.*, Ch. XXIII, § 1.

[3] This position will suggest the solution of Kant (see below, n. 406) and the theory of the unknowable of Herbert Spencer (see below, n. 481).

is clear in this theory that substance, in the ordinary sense of the word, designates a vague something of which we have no clear idea and whose essence it is impossible to penetrate.

Among the *modes* there are found the ideas of the infinite, space, time and liberty, all of which were the object of famous controversies equal to that of substance.

The infinite is a homogeneous or simple mode, formed by the repetition of the same unity, whether of number, duration or space. The finite expresses a stoppage of repetition; but, if one continues " by always advancing the same thing without ever coming to an end of the additions " [1], one has the idea of the infinite, the only one conceivable by man. Locke does not deny the existence of a positive infinity, not even that of substance; but this reality is totally unknown to us, because of its inaccessibility to our knowledge, whose elements are always drawn from experience.

Space and *time* are also simple modes, obtained by the repetition of the portions of extension or duration furnished by experience. But the elementary idea on which space is based comes from visual sensation. The idea on which time is based comes from reflection, by which we acknowledge a succession in our ideas; this succession is, for us, " the measure of other successions " [2].

Liberty is also explained by a similar analysis. It is an elaboration of the idea of *power*, which is itself a homogeneous or simple mode, obtained by the repetition of the experiential idea of action. Having been subjected to action from without or having exercised action ourselves, we conceive of the possibility of an indefinite repetition of this influence we exercise or undergo; in this way we obtain the notion of power, both active and passive. This idea is born from experience, whether external or internal; in the latter domain, the active power of our soul on the body constitutes the *will* [3]. One ordinarily asks if the will is free; Locke says this question is badly put. Freedom itself is another active power, that of acting or of not acting conformably to a choice [4] or a judgment of the spirit : " Liberty consists in a power to act or to forbear acting, and in that only " [5]. This is the Scholastic " freedom from coaction ", or the simple absence of constraint, making Locke's view still compatible with the most rigorous determinism, as in Hobbes and in Spinoza. Locke remarks, however, that liberty supposes reason and will; one does not attribute it to a ball, even though it travels without any constraint, but only to man. However, liberty is not proper to

---

[1] *Essay*, Book II, Ch. XVII, § 7, 12.

[2] *Ibid.*, Ch. XIV, § 2, 6, 12. — Kant himself attributes time to internal phenomena and space to exterior facts; see below, n. 398.

[3] *Essay*, Book II, Ch. XXI, § 5.

[4] Locke calls " choice " a judgment of the mind, while for St. Thomas choice *(electio)* is the very act of free will. See St. Thomas' *Summa Theologica*, I-II, q. XIII.

[5] *Essay*, Book II, Ch. XXI, § 24.

will, no more than a square figure to virtue, because a power pertains to the agent and not to another power.

One can ask, however, if the soul, possessing these two powers, can apply its liberty to the exercise of its will; that is, if it has the power to will and not to will according to its choice, which is the problem of the " liberty of indifference ". Here, as in the question of substance, Locke is not clear. On the one hand, following the logic of his empiricism, he teaches that all our volitions have determined motives which are not actions preliminary to the will. One cannot ask " whether a man can will what he wills ", for this " must suppose one will to determine the acts of another, and another to determine that, and so on in infinitum " [1]. The main motive which psychologically determines our wills, is inquietude or the uneasiness which results from the absence of a good. This is shown by countless experiences : the little efficacy of belief in eternal pains or rewards when faced with satisfying an immediate need; the powerlessness of the drunkard to resist, despite resolutions, the uneasiness which results from his habit. Briefly, the greatest good, even when known as such, does not determine the will; for, if it awakes a desire in proportion to its excellence, it awakes a corresponding desire of equal uneasiness [2]. These states of uneasiness are continuously successive, so that if one is satisfied, another is ready to take its place, so that our wills always find their determining causes without leaving any place open for liberty.

On the other hand, Locke admits exceptions to this law that the most pressing uneasiness determines the will to that particular, proximate action. " We are endowed with a power to suspend any particular desire, and keep it from determining the will, and engaging us in action " [3]. This power comes from the ability of our reason to examine the value of the goods and evils of our desires; having made our true happiness precise, liberty consists in giving this idea a true efficaciousness which determines our will. These remarks are quite meaningful and are beyond empiricism; they are on the way towards understanding true liberty, whose root lies in our spiritual reason [4]. What Locke's thought lacks here in coherence, it gains in truth.

The ideas of *good* and of *evil* are connected with the idea of will; Locke interprets them with pure empiricism. They are referred back to the ideas of pleasure and of pain. Psychologically, that is called good which quells the uneasiness of our will, or what is useful towards this goal; evil is this uneasiness itself, or that which causes it. In considering the notion of law, we enter into the moral order. " Moral good and evil, then, is only the conformity or disagreement of our voluntary actions to some law... which good and evil, pleasure or pain, attending our observance or breach of the law by the decree of the law-maker, is what we call reward and punishment " [5].

---

[1] *Ibid.*, § 25. — [2] See JANET and SEAILLES, *Histoire de la philosophie*, p. 340.

[3] *Essay*, Book II, Ch. XXI, § 50.

[4] " The root of freedom is situated in reason ", writes St. Thomas *(De veritate*, q. XXIV, art. 2).

[5] *Essay*, Book II, Ch. XXVIII, § 5.

b) Among the complex ideas of RELATIONS, that of *causality* is the most important. Locke defines cause as " that which makes any other thing, either simple idea, substance, or mode, begin to be ", while effect " is that which had its beginning from some other thing " [1]. The notion of causality comes from internal or external experience, when we grant in some ideas the constant conditions for the production of other ideas. Locke thinks there is little difficulty in distinguishing the various types of causality, as creation, generation and alteration. He declares this idea wholly satisfactory and does not pursue its criticism [2], doubtlessly because he needed it to establish many traditional truths which, in harmony with his purpose, he did not wish to sacrifice.

c) The third activity of the spirit forming new ideas is ABSTRACTION; for Locke, this activity consists in a *separation* exercised on complex ideas. At first we form, through combination, extremely complex ideas of individuals; thus, the infant acquires those of the nurse, of the mother and of the father. But soon, the comparison of these multiple, individual groups makes us aware of the common characters among them. The spirit retains these by separating them from their proper parts, and then to this abstract residue or general scheme it joins the common name of habitual usage; for instance, the word man to that which is found in the nurse, the mother and the father. In pursuing this task methodically, one obtains the hierarchy of genera and of species. Abstraction, then, presupposes some work on the part of understanding [3]; the universals or abstract ideas which result, however, express only a schematized collection of simple ideas in which there are retained common traits designated by a common name. This view is, at one and the same time, conceptualism and nominalism.

Locke's psychological analysis is completely based on the empiricist principle that all our ideas come from sensible experience. For this reason he is led to hold that the mind is powerless to have any positive knowledge of infinity or of substance, and that the mind supersedes nominal essences by its abstract ideas. Locke's proofs for rejecting the theory of innate ideas are valuable; it is also true that the content of all our ideas, at least of those

---

[1] *Ibid.*, Ch. XXVI, § 2.

[2] This critical work will be undertaken by Hume; see below, n. 384.

[3] Locke speaks of spirit or understanding in a general way throughout his works.

which are positively expressive, come from sensible experience; the latter rule applies even to the most metaphysical concepts of man. But the view which Locke adopts is too narrow, and there is a middle road between the Platonic and Cartesian innatism, which he rightfully refutes, and the pure empiricism which he adopts : one could call this view that of virtual innatism of a spiritual faculty through whose help man discovers, in the concrete, an aspect of being or of essence participating in the infinite Being, which serves as the foundation of a truly " scientific " [1] metaphysics. Leibniz, in his *New Essays*, was not far from this solution when he stated, " Nothing is in the intellect without first having been in the sense, except the intellect itself ", but Leibniz gave this axiom an untenable, idealistic twist [2]. The correct doctrine on this point, as held and elaborated by Aristotle and his disciples, and especially by St. Thomas, has been explained above [3]. It explains perfectly how our abstract ideas are *really* expressive of the essences of things, though in a rather modest measure. With regard to substance, one must distinguish the most universal idea of substance, which has analogical value and is quite close to the notion of real being [4], from the idea of this particular, determined substance. The general notion of substance is valuable, as is every abstract idea, but it constitutes only a first exactitude or precision and a first victory over man's native ignorance. The precise definition of this substance is the goal sought for by science; in order to achieve it, the patient work of numerous inductions is needed. These latter inductions, it is true, are concerned with experiential facts, and their immediate object is the realm of properties or phenomena. They lead, however, to the knowledge of substantial being on the basis of this incontestable principle : " As the properties, so the substance, or, action derives from being ". The only sufficient reason for permanent properties is the permanent nature of the being which is manifested through them.

Locke, sadly enough, ignored this perfectly equilibrated solution. Holding out for experience alone, he was forced to resolve the problem of the value of our ideas by means of the Cartesian theory of the clear idea, adapted to his empiricism.

C) **Value of Ideas and of Knowledge.**

375. Unlike Descartes, Locke does not see in man's ideas the intuitive depositaries of truth or of error. In order to determine their value, he considers them from different viewpoints. They can be, he says, " *real* or *fantastical*, according as they do or do not have a foundation in nature " [5], or they

---

[1] The word " science " is taken here in the Thomistic sense; see n. 264, above.
[2] See above, n. 362.
[3] See above, n. 69 and n. 262.
[4] This is the only meaning which Locke seems to have retained.
[5] *Essay*, Book II, Ch. xxx; simple ideas are wholly real, but in different degrees, as will be shown.

can be *complete* or *incomplete*. Simple ideas, of course, are always complete; for other ideas to be complete they must gather in themselves all the elements which custom requires, if they are ideas formed by convention, or they must not omit any elements of the thing, if they are expressive of the real[1]. They can be *true* or *false;* Locke observes, however, that ideas are hardly true or false, for " truth and falsehood belong, in propriety of speech, only to propositions "[2]. The main question, then, is the *truth of judgments.*

1⁰ **The Principle of the Solution.** Though refusing to the idea the quality of truth, Locke does not abandon the Cartesian criterion of the clear and distinct idea which is essentially intuitive. Since the proposition (or judgment) is nothing else but " the perception of agreement or disagreement of two ideas "[3], the only condition requisite and sufficient to have truth is the relation of agreement or disagreement appearing clearly and distinctly to the mind. Locke casts no doubt on the aptitude of the mind to express truth, as long as it is clear with Cartesian evidence. Everything devolves, in his view, on delimiting the bearing of the ideas compared, and in appreciating the clarity of their relationship.

There are four species of judgment established between ideas : **1)** *Identity* or *diversity,* as in definitions; **2)** *Relation,* as in a theory on the equality of triangles; **3)** *Coexistence* or necessary connection, as between substance and its properties; **4)** *Real existence,* as in the affirmation, God exists. All of these relations, though quite diverse, are true as long as they appear clearly so to mind. They do not, for that matter, have the same value. Locke examines their value in a rather abstruse fashion; to present his thought, two problems will here be distinguished. The first is certitude, the subjective state which ordinarily accompanies the possession of truth, and the second is realism, the objective viewpoint which requires that our thoughts correspond to things.

2⁰ **The Three Degrees of Certitude.** Judgments draw their certitude from three sources, intuition, demonstration and sensation.

Intuition is the perfect application of the Cartesian criterion and yields full satisfaction. This is the highest type of certitude and on it " depends all the certainty and evidence of our

---

[1] From this viewpoint, substance is always incomplete, since we are ignorant of the real essence of things.

[2] *Essay,* Book II, Ch. XXXII, § I.

[3] *Essay,* Book IV, Ch. I, § 2.

knowledge... for a man cannot conceive himself capable of a greater certainty than to know that any idea in his mind is such as he perceives it to be; and that two ideas wherein he perceives a difference, are different and not precisely the same "[1].

Demonstration furnishes a second degree of certitude, close to the first, for it is but a succession of intuitive glances, as with Descartes [2]; in order for demonstration to be of value, each of its degrees must be held with intuitive evidence [3]. At the same time, however, demonstration is inferior to intuition, for it has need of memory; one does not formally draw a conclusion except through recalling its premises.

Sensation, having given us an idea of an exterior object as a subjective representation, permits us to affirm the existence of the represented object outside of ourselves. The interior feeling that we have of this evidence seemed, to Locke, a sufficient motive for truth, though of an inferior degree. " But yet here I think we are provided with an evidence that puts us past doubting; for I ask any one, whether he be not invincibly conscious to himself of a different perception when he looks on the sun by day, and thinks on it by night "[4]. This third problem opens the problem of the objective value of our sciences, which involves, for Locke, the problem of the degree of human certitudes. This is the problem of realism.

3° **The Problem of Realism.** In Locke's view, our ideas and, as a result, our judgments have, by definition, a representative function. Does this representation allow us to know objects as really existing outside of our ideas? Locke has no more doubt of this than did Descartes, but he notes degrees in the realism of various ideas.

Only an immediate intuition of existence gives us full certitude of it, and this state is verified uniquely in the intuition of the thinking self. Consciousness, in accompanying each of our interior facts, constitutes our personal identity, which we know without any shadow of a doubt. But the criticism made above of the idea of substance imposes limits on this knowledge. Evidently man has a soul, and a thinking soul, since there exists a substance to support accidents. But the nature of

---

[1] *Ibid.*, Ch. ii, § 1.
[2] See above, n. 322.
[3] *Essay*, Book iv, Ch. ii, § 7.
[4] *Ibid.*, § 14.

this soul is not knowable to us. We can hold nothing about its spirituality or its immortality, and " we will never be capable of knowing if a purely material being thinks or not ", for it is possible that " God gives, if He so wishes, some degrees of thought to a certain amount of matter which He joins together, as He sees fit " [1]. This is a most plausible conclusion to draw, for Locke never distinguishes the sensible from the spiritual aspect in the facts of consciousness; with this perspective, if one can conclude that sensations are spiritual, one can also assert that intellections and volitions are of the sensible order [2].

There is likewise some certitude in demonstration. It is this type of certitude that we have of *God's existence*, which is based on the notion of causality, considered valuable by Locke. " Man has a clear idea of his own being; he knows certainly that he exists, and that he is something "; this is an immediate, internal perception. " In the next place, man knows by an intuitive certainty, that bare nothing can no more produce any real being, than it can be equal to two right angles ". Accordingly, if some thing exists, " it is mathematically evident that something has existed from eternity ", since " everything which had a beginning must have been produced by something ". This " eternal being ", since it is the source and the principle of all other beings, " must be all-powerful " and " all-knowing " and, consequently, must be God [3].

This demonstration is excellent in itself, but only on condition that our idea of a cause expresses something other than a simple fact of experience. In all the great realist philosophers, pagan or Scholastic, the principle of causality is admitted as a law of being [4]; this allows for the possibility of rising from creatures to their Author. Locke wished to remain in this tradition, but attributes to reflection, the second source of our ideas, the power of grasping the value of this notion of causality. But in granting causality this value, he goes beyond the rights which his initial empiricism conceded him, and which he so clamorously set up at the opening of his *Essay*. Causality is more than a mere fact of experience. It has ontological and metaphysical value, which

---

[1] A. GONZALÈS, *Histoire de la philosophie*, p. 338.

[2] Thus, one should be little surprised to see Locke's doctrine evolve into the positivist phenomenalism of Hume.

[3] *Essay*, Book IV, Ch. X, § 1-9; the above quotations are taken from this section; see also J. MARÉCHAL, *Le point de départ de la Métaphysique*, II, p. 140.

[4] Kant will not admit causality as a law of thought; the Thomistic epistemology, however, fully justifies the realistic value of this principle; See below, n. 409.

presupposes a solid doctrine on the spirituality of human reason. By his desire for moderation, Locke loses doctrinal rigor and admits a conclusion which will bring about the criticism of Hume.

Finally, we have but the one certitude of sensation for the existence of the exterior world; this certitude entails certain restrictions, conformable to the preceding analyses. At first, the corporeal qualities which we directly attain by simple ideas do not all have the same value. Only the primary qualities exist formally outside of us as we know them; the secondary qualities are there only causally, in the sense that they " are produced in us by the impressions which are made on our senses by the various movements of bodies which are so small that we are unable to perceive them "[1]. Finally, our complex ideas of substance, as we have said, do not permit us to know the nature of any determined corporeal reality. Thus, our sciences do not ever bear on real essences; they must be content with *nominal* essences, or with stable collections of simple ideas distinguishable only by a common name. The latter, though, are not fashioned arbitrarily. The grouping imposes itself on us, in the physical sciences, by experiences, and in the moral sciences, by usage and universal custom [2].

Locke is thus led to distinguish two classes of science. The first class is that of the fully certain, for it deals only with evident relations between ideas considered as dependent solely on the spirit. In this group he puts mathematics and the moral sciences; the latter are included because their fundamental notions are but nominal essences (mixed modes), having their full value by common agreement. The second class is one whose certitude is somewhat questionable. Here we find the physical sciences; their conclusions, bearing on the grouping of phenomena (real essences) and their laws, are always subject to the control of experience.

D) Applications and Corollaries.

375bis.   Circumstances forced Locke to occupy himself with various problems on religion, on education, on economics and on politics. Without being rigorously deducible from his theory of the human understanding, they can be referred to it by their adoption of the limits imposed on our certitudes. They are also an application of his general tendency towards tolerance which serves to unify his entire system.

---

[1] E. Bréhier, *Histoire de la philosophie*, ii, p. 281.

[2] *Essay*, Book ii, Ch. xxxiii. The stability of the various groups is guaranteed by the law of association of ideas — a forecast of Hume's solution.

1º **Moral and Religious Philosophy.** Although Locke wrote no treatise on ethics, he left a sufficient number of theories which are logically unifiable with his doctrine on knowledge. In his view, the foundational ideas of good and of evil [1], and even those of the particular virtues and vices are elaborated in the fashion of mixed modes by being founded on the customs of a certain country in a certain time. From this viewpoint, they can easily change. But as long as they are formed, our judgments establish between them some fully evident relations which are moral rules; one can thus demonstrate with the same clarity as in mathematics that a murderer should be punished. The two columns of morality, however, the idea of the personal self as creature and of God as Creator, escape all change; in facing them, one discovers evidence for an order of necessary relations which founds a code of duties [2].

Nevertheless, this moral science remains theoretical. It cannot present itself to our will as a duty to be done *freely*, since psychological analysis has shown us that we lack such freedom. In order for a motive to direct our lives it must be transformed into an efficacious motive, such as the lack of satisfaction or the fear of suffering. Hence, the best means of assuring the observance of divine and human laws is to teach them along with insistence on the sanctions attached to their infraction. — On the other hand, our duty towards God does not go beyond natural religion. Locke admitted only a " reasonable Christianity ", and he wished for the greatest tolerance for all positive religious cults, reserving, meanwhile, the rights of the state.

2º **Thoughts on Education.** Locke wrote his " Some Thoughts Concerning Education " for the Earl of Shaftesbury's son; they are motivated by a *liberal* ideal. One is to respect, in the child, the spontaneity of its nature without submitting it to a despotic formation; this would transform the life of school children into that of galley slaves. Hence, private education is preferable to the common formation in colleges. In every case, punishment and excessive constraints are to be banished [3]. Similar ideas are to be found in Emile Zola and in Jean-Jacques Rousseau [4].

3º **Doctrines on Law and on Economics.** In order to know society, one must study the individuals composing it, just as one can appreciate a complex idea only by analyzing it into the simple ones of which it is formed. Man in the state of nature is not an amoral animal, as Hobbes held; he possesses true rights. For Locke, a right is nothing more than the power of doing what is useful for oneself. Upon analysis, it seems to be an alternate name for liberty, in the sense of pertaining to our voluntary activity.

---

[1] See above, n. 374, 2º, where the analysis of these ideas is referred back to those of pleasure and of pain.

[2] *Essay*, Book IV, Ch. III, § 18.

[3] Locke, with good reason, also protested against the almost exclusive use of ancient languages in the schools of his time; St. John Baptist de la Salle, in the same era, worked in France towards introducing the vernacular into the schools.

[4] See n. 451.

First of all, man has a natural right over his person, its conservation and its development. From this flows man's right over his work and the product of his hands; this is the foundation of the right of ownership. If one legitimately appropriates a good belonging to no one, this action is justifiable because occupation is a veritable type of work. One can possess a field only in the measure that one can labor in it and fructify it. Briefly, it is work alone which is the origin of proprietorship, and which remains its rule and its limitation [1]. Finally, parents have a natural right over their children, for the family itself is a natural institution.

It is Locke's belief that these doctrines are solidly demonstrated without admitting any laws or innate moral principles, but by examining the ideas which we form of our nature and of its activities. They are deduced, in particular, from the relations between Creator and creature, so that belief in God is their ultimate basis.

4° **Political System.** For Locke, as for Hobbes and Rousseau, the origin of society lies in a contract consented to by the citizens. But this contract is not, for Locke, the source of all rights, for it presupposes them; nor does he believe they are totally given up into the hands of the governmental representatives, for the contract merely aims to insure their full exercise by allocating the forces of each man for common usage. The social contract, for Locke, merely implies the giving up of the right of correction and of punishment. Each citizen, considered by himself, can defend his right even with violence. But this can better be realized by means of a common organization; by its laws, it establishes the rules for social peace, it executes them by its authority, it resolves doubtful cases and it avoids quarrels and private wars.

On these fundamental notions, Locke builds up a system of liberal politics and of tolerance. In order to attain its goal, society must enjoy the triple power, legislative, executive and judicial. But these three powers cannot legitimately be concentrated in the hands of one person, who could exercise them as if he had received them directly from God or as if he had absolute dominion over his subjects. These powers, on the contrary, come from the people, who always retain the ability to withdraw what they had conceded. They have the right to revolt if the State does not guarantee the exercise of their natural rights. Accordingly, the best form of government is a *tempered monarchy*, in which the three powers are in the hands of different persons, along with a fundamental law establishing their coordination. This is a condemnation of absolute royalty of divine right and of despotism, so dear to Hobbes, and a justification of the constitutional monarchy established in England through the revolution of 1688.

---

[1] Locke adds that the right of ownership is subject to two conditions : 1) that the possessor does not let the thing perish; 2) that, in appropriating certain things, he leaves some of them for others. See his *Treatise on Civil Government*, Ch. VI, and see A. GONZALÈS, *op. cit.*, p. 347. Locke's economic theories, which, in a sense, presage those of Marx, should be considered with caution; see below, n. 482-483.

Both State and Church, in Locke's view, have their proper missions, and should be entirely separated. Each is a law-making body and acts in full independence. On the other hand, the dogmatic truths are inaccessible to man, for they comprise the field of faith and of free opinions, in which the greatest tolerance is the rule. The state retains the right of interdicting and of taking action on anything which would attempt to prevent it from using its full powers; for this reason, the state should not tolerate moral and social atheism, for belief in God is the foundation of all moral and social laws. At the same time, Locke proscribes the Roman Catholic religion for submitting its subjects to an alien power.

Although Locke's theory is different in spirit from that of Hobbes, he falls into the same errors by a similar misunderstanding of the rights of the Church [1]. The same view, essentially, will be found in Rousseau, through whose mediation the later view of democratic politics developed [2].

CONCLUSION. Locke is a thinker who follows the golden mean. His doctrines are unified, though less by a powerful principle from which all aspects of the real are deducible than by the practical and moderated direction of his thoughts, quite habitual with the British mind. He was too respectful of good sense and of tradition to put the great truths on God, the soul and the world in any doubt; he was too fearful of the excess of fanaticism to condemn intuition; he was too preoccupied with positive studies to quit the solid materials of experience; and, finally, he was too great a friend of reason and of the philosophical and scientific renewal of his age to forbid a warm welcome to the spirit of Descartes, leading him to hold a semi-empiricist view, balanced by a semi-rationalist outlook. This very moderation was the source of his success in the eighteenth century; he inspired the *philosophes* of the Encyclopedia in France, just as his rationalism, inimical to everything supernatural, continued the tradition of the modern spirit.

Nevertheless, though Locke is not one of the great philosophical geniuses, he should be credited for bringing up one of the problems whose elaboration is to the credit of modern thought, that of the value of human knowledge. In this way he continues the thought of Descartes, whose thought he adopted with its two postulates, the idealistic position of the critical problem, and the value of human understanding in knowing reality. His work became his own by his denounce-

---

[1] See above, 368, D), 4°.
[2] See below, n. 453.

ment of a grave defect in the Cartesian solution : Descartes' unjustifiable disdain for sensible experience. Locke established anew the great law of abstractive intelligence that all our knowledge comes from the senses [1]. However, going to the other extreme, he resolutely decided for EMPIRICISM. Though he did not develop all the consequences of this latter position, it was by reflecting on the analyses in his *Essay* that Berkeley and Hume worked out the doctrinal development of empiricism.

II. THE SECOND STAGE : 1º BERKELEY (1685-1753).

SPECIAL BIBLIOGRAPHY.

1º **Works :** FRASER, A. C. (ed.), *The Works of George Berkeley*, 4 vols., Oxford, 1901. — LUCE, A. A., and JESSOP, T. (eds.), *The Works of George Berkeley*, 6 vols., London, 1948-1952.

2º **Studies :** BALADI, N., *La pensée religieuse de Berkeley et l'unité de sa philosophie*, Paris, 1945. — BENDER, F., *George Berkeley's Philosophy Re-Examined*, Amsterdam, 1946. — BROAD, C. D., *Berkeley's Argument about Material Substance*, Oxford, 1942. — CASSIRER, E., *Berkeley's System*, Gressen, 1914. — DIDIER, J., *Berkeley*, 1911. — FRASER, A. C., *Berkeley*, London, 1881. — *Life and Letters of George Berkeley*, Oxford, n. d. — HEDENIUS, I., *Sensationalism and Theology in Berkeley's Philosophy*, Uppsala, 1936. — HICKS, G. D., *Berkeley*, New York, 1932. — JOHNSTON, G. A., *The Development of Berkeley's Philosophy*, New York, 1923. — JOSEPH, H. W. B., *Comparison of Kant's Idealism with that of Berkeley*, Oxford, 1929. — JOUSSAIN, A., *Exposé critique de la philosophie de Berkeley*, Paris, 1920. — KAVEESCHWAR, G. W., *Metaphysics of Berkeley Critically Examined in the light of Modern Philosophy*, New York, 1933. — LUCE, A. A., *Berkeley and Malebranche : A Study in the Origins of Berkeley's Thought*, New York, 1934. — *Berkeley's Immaterialism : A Commentary on his " Treatise Concerning the Principles of Human Knowledge "*, London, 1945. — *The Life of George Berkeley, Bishop of Cloyne*, London, 1949. — METZ, R., *George Berkeley*, Stuttgart, 1925. — OLGIATI, F., *L'idealismo di Giorgio Berkeley*, Milan, 1926. — PENJON, A., *Etudes sur la vie et les œuvres philosophiques de Berkeley*, Paris, 1878. — WILD, J., *George Berkeley : A Study of His Life and Philosophy*, Cambridge (Mass.), 1936.

376. George Berkeley was born at Dysert, Kilkenny county, Ireland, of a Protestant family of English ancestry. He studied at Trinity College, Dublin, where Descartes, Newton and Locke were favored authors, and matriculated there in 1707. He was, successively, professor of Greek, Hebrew and Theology. " An original and vibrant personality, he gave the impression of being

---

[1] " Nothing is in the intellect unless first in the senses ", according to the Aristotelian principle; see nn. 69, 83, 262.

a somewhat disconcerted but passionately devoted personality; later, his friends declared him possessed of all virtues " [1].

Berkeley became interested in a problem proposed by the geometer, Molineux [2]: " Can a man born blind but who has recovered sight distinguish a cube from a sphere by sight alone? " He proposed a solution to this in his *An Essay Towards a New Theory of Vision* (1709), in which he is definitely steering towards the theory of immaterialism definitively elaborated in his main work, *A Treatise concerning the Principles of Human Knowledge* (1710). His book of notes, the so-called *Commonplace Book*, written between 1702 and 1710, contains the developmental outline of this doctrine, and his plan and proofs for applying his view to optics, geometry and morality. The work was not as successful as Berkeley hoped for; he himself went to London in order to recruit friends. There he wrote his *Three Dialogues between Hylas and Philonous* which gives his views in a more literary style. About this time, he began his polemical work against the freethinkers, and especially against Collins by a series of articles in the paper, *The Guardian* (1713). Berkeley, a member of the clergy and possessed of a very religious spirit, directed his system of immaterialism against atheism and materialism.

From 1713 to 1720, he toured Italy, Sicily and France; at the latter place he wrote his *On Motion*, which attacks Newton's physics. On his return to London, he was named Dean of Derry (1721); two years later, having inherited the fortune of Esther Vanhomrigh, he wished to employ it towards the conversion of the American peoples recently colonized by England. He wanted to set up an academic and missionary institute in Bermuda to fulfill this aim. Accordingly, he embarked for America in 1728, taking a library with him and a government promise for a subsidy of 20,000 pounds. He got no farther than Rhode Island, waiting there two years for the government subsidy which never came. He occupied himself in the study of Plato, Plotinus and Proclus, and in writing his principal work against the freethinkers, *Alciphron or the Minute Philosopher* (1732). His dreams for a missionary activity being unrealized, he returned to London, where he edited his previous works and answered criticisms through his work, *The Defence and Explanation of the Theory of Vision*, and *The Analyst* [3] (1734).

In 1734, Berkeley was named Anglican Bishop of Cloyne, a diocese peopled with a large number of Roman Catholics [4]. He was greatly concerned about the economic situation of his people, did many charitable works, opened schools, and wrote, on this subject, *The Querist* (1735), and *Letter on the National Bank of*

---

[1] J. MARÉCHAL, *Précis d'histoire de la philosophie moderne*, 1, p. 259.

[2] W. Molineux had offered this problem to Locke, who replied negatively, in accord with Molineux' solution. Molineux' son was a fellow student with Berkeley at Trinity College.

[3] *The Analyst* is a discourse addressed to an unbelieving mathematician.

[4] Berkeley was party to an agreement with Catholics; in 1745, on the occasion of the Scottish revolt in favor of the Stuarts, he aimed to pacify the situation and wrote *Letters to the Roman Catholics of the Diocese of Cloyne;* in the same spirit are his *Word to the Sages* (1749) and his *Maxims of Patriotism* (1751).

Ireland (1737). He continued, in the meantime, his fight against atheism through his *Discourse against the License and Irreligion of the Times* (1737). In 1740, an epidemic ravaged his diocese, and he used a remedy valued dearly by the American Indians, tar water. He applied it with some success, and took it as an occasion for writing his final work, *Siris, A Chain of Philosophical Reflections and Inquiries Concerning the Virtue of Tar-Water* (1735). This work opens with a discussion on the properties of this marvelous remedy, and concludes with mystical considerations on God and His relations with nature, written in a Neo-Platonic fashion. In 1752 he retired to Oxford, where he died on January 14, 1753.

Foundational Principle. Berkeley's system is given the name of IMMATERIALISM, for, in following the logical process of empiricism towards idealism, he denied the reality of any material substance and retained only spirits (the soul and God), as subjects of ideas. This negation of matter, which was quite a scandal in the eighteenth century [1], was found, germinally, in the theory of the clear idea as the unique object of knowledge. Descartes, however, considering ideas as representative, or endowed with objective value, assigned the existence of things as their reason for being. From this it follows that the idea of extension presupposes the existence of matter. The central intuition of Berkeley is to give the subject who produces them as their reason for being, instead of their object. In his view, *our ideas, which are the unique object of our knowledge, are fully explicable by the activity of spirit,* whether it be the human spirit, or the Sovereign Spirit. This is the basic principle of his system.

In order to give this principle its full meaning, it must be replaced in the positivist atmosphere from which it arose. Berkeley's point of departure is completely empiricist, though it concludes with radical idealism. However, in explaining the idea through its subject, his idealism is corrected by a spiritual realism which finds its normal and, possibly, necessary conclusion in the Neo-Platonic speculations of his work, *Siris.*

A) Empirical Point of Departure.

376[bis]. Berkeley, the redoubtable adversary of matter, is in no wise opposed to sense knowledge or even to external experience. On the contrary, he adopts the same beginning as did Locke, and distinguishes three types of ideas : 1) those

---

[1] J. Percival wrote Berkeley that he had spoken to a physician about his views; the physician remarked that Berkeley had gone mad and should immediately take some remedies.

which are actually impressed within the senses; 2) those which arise from the affections of the spirit (reflection); 3) the complex ideas obtained by a combination of the preceding, whose total value lies in simple ideas. He even tried to correct Locke's empiricism by a more rigorous view which would exclude every abstract idea.

It has been shown that Locke kept a type of conceptualism, for the spirit is active in the formation of universals; the latter, for Locke, are complex ideas formed by a schematized collection of simple ideas, grouping together only those common traits found in several individuals and designating them by a common name. Such a notion, Berkeley believes, is neither possible nor useful.

This notion is *impossible* to construct, Berkeley believes, for if one seeks a more precise meaning for this universal, one finds contradictory attributes. That of triangle, for example, can be represented *at one and the same time* by scalene and isosceles triangles, and would have to have three angles and three sides *at once* both equal and unequal; this is an impossible image [1]. One is led to hold such a view by reason of the *common names* which seem to require it, and especially the general demonstrations of a subject as geometry. In most cases, one uses names without associating them with a determined meaning, as one does with algebraic letters, " which always designate particular quantities about which one is not obliged to think in order to reason correctly " [2]. If one really wants to get to the bottom of this situation, one should consider thought before the use of language, " as a solitary man, who is alone in the world and endowed with remarkable capacities, could know without words " [3]; thus, one grants the non-existence of every abstract idea.

On the other hand, Berkeley did not reject the common name nor the general idea. However, he believes that abstraction is *useless* in explaining the latter, and, for purposes of explanation, a determined image is sufficient, if it be taken as the representation of other, similar, images. One could reason, for example, on triangle in general by thinking of a

---

[1] This type of reasoning cannot be refuted if Locke's empiricism is taken as a starting point, since it holds that the total content of our ideas is referred to sensible elements. But this is exactly the point of contention between this view and the doctrine of abstraction; see above, n. 69 and n. 374.

[2] E. Bréhier, *op. cii.*, II, p. 345.

[3] This notion is found in Berkeley's *Commonplace Book*.

triangle which is actually scalene, but without being concerned over the nature of the angles or of the particular relation which exists between its sides. Thus, in Berkeley's view, " thinking is not a seizure of an abstract essence, whether real or nominal, it is but a passage from one idea to another with the aid of the sign assumed by the idea " [1]. Consequently, there are no abstract ideas; the general or universal idea is but a particular idea, taken as a sign of other particular ideas and, in this way, designated by a common name [2].

B) **Radical Idealism.**

377. " Man's ideas constitute the unique object of all his knowledge " : this statement began to take on the aspect of an axiom since Descartes and Locke proposed the problem of knowledge in this way. From it, Berkeley concludes, and with equal evidence in his view, that the whole reality of sensible objects lies in their being perceived. For these objects, *esse est percipi;* this house, this tree, these birds, and all the riches of nature are real when we see them or when we perceive them sensibly, but disappear when we no longer think of them [3], for *there is nothing in reality but our ideas or the facts of consciousness.* By his spiritual realism, Berkeley aimed to insist on the good sense of his view by maintaining a difference between subjective imaginations and the objective perceptions of the external world; at the same time, he constantly argued against any belief in matter.

He begins by erasing every distinction between *primary* and *secondary qualities,* giving both merely an ideal value. This follows as a consequence of denying abstract ideas. If one attempts to form an idea of a primary quality separately, for example, of an extension without color or of a movement without swiftness or visible direction, one immediately falls into the absurdities of abstract ideas. These qualities, as a result, are but common names designating a concrete [4] and determined object; not figure, for instance, but *this* figure or *this* triangle. This authentic idea, whether it be simple or composed, definitively is nothing more than a fact of consciousness, an immediate or elaborated sensation.

---

[1] E. Bréhier, *op. cit.*, ii, p. 345.

[2] This theory will be found again in Hume, where it will be evaluated; see n. 382, below.

[3] If no one thinks of them, they are pure nothingness; but for Berkeley, God is always thinking of them.

[4] This *concrete extension*, the only one admissible, is not divisible infinitely; accordingly, in Berkeley's view, the infinitesimal calculus of Newton and Leibniz is a sterile work based on a crude abstraction.

Moreover, from the viewpoint of introspection, the perception of extension, of movement and of solidity, manifests absolutely the same traits as the other perceptions. One there meets similar illusions; thus, an object which a man " can hardly perceive, appears as an enormous mountain to an extremely small animal " [1]. Furthermore, " that which seems hard to one animal, seems soft to another if the latter is stronger and possessed of vigorous members ". The only difference is that secondary qualities, as " heat and cold, and tastes and odors, affect us with more vividness than an agreeable or disagreeable sentiment " [2]. But every sensation, whether it be affective or even indifferent, remains, equally, a sensation or a fact of consciousness which does not exist but in the soul.

If, in particular, one examines *vision*, we find that it gives us only the sensation of color and not of distance, volume or figure. Distance, for instance, is nothing else but a line directly pointed towards the eye, and " a line placed in this way cannot certainly be perceived by sight ", and hence is not a proper and immediate sensible of sight; it pertains more properly to touch. To explain sight at a distance, which is familiar to all of us, one must appeal to the association of ideas operated spontaneously through practice. We concede that every sensation of color in order to be touched always requires a motion exercised in time, as the extending of the arm, or moving three feet. And, by the " order and constancy of nature ", we then conclude from the first to the second; this is what we know as sight at a distance. The same holds for figure and for volume. A man born blind who had recovered his sight would simply grant the existence " of a new order of sensations actually existing within his spirit "; that is, the sensations of color disengaged from the primary qualities.

These shrewd remarks of Berkeley's are well supported by the research of experimental psychology. They kill any attempt at naive realism, as in the Epicurean view [3], which places an object outside of us for our perceptions just as it is. One must distinguish the initial intuition of the senses, an analytic act of *sensation* which only attains a crude object, and not very precise (as a colored spot, in vision), from *perception*, a synthetic act whose object stands out distinctly (as, for example, to see *one's father*). The latter involves education of the senses and association of ideas. But if colors are not seen at a distance, Berkeley has no right to conclude that they exist only in the spirit. The initial intuition, without being too precise, incontestably grasps colors as coming from *outside* of the spirit, and also as affected with a real extension. Touch, in particular, clearly testifies to the *concrete existence* [4] of

---

[1] GEORGE BERKELEY, *Three Dialogues Between Hylas and Philonous*, Dial. I.

[2] *Ibid.;* (the above quotations are all taken from Dialogue I). — [3] See n. 108..

[4] This evidence of the senses should not be confused with the objective evidence of the intellectual order, which possesses a judgment bearing on the existence or the nature of a corporeal object outside of man. In order to justify the value of this judgment, a more profound " demonstration " and a more critical one is required than that of simple, sensible intuition; the latter is but a point of departure.

a " non-self " or of a resisting object placed outside of consciousness and endowed with extension. The modern psychologists, with William James and Bergson, have rediscovered this truth.

If Berkeley refers primary qualities to the realm of secondary, it is only to conclude that both are simple facts of consciousness; this implies the uselessness of matter. In arguing against the reality of matter, one can also bring forth the impossibility of forming a precise idea of a *substratum* or a support for accidents [1]. Finally, in order to give this hypothesis of real matter a final blow, Berkeley proposes a double reduction to absurdity.

a) There is a contradiction in admitting the objective existence of any corporeal reality whatsoever. For, if this exterior object is perceived, it is but an idea, as is all perception; that is, a subjective, spiritual fact. If it is not perceived, none of our ideas can represent it, because only another idea can be similar to an idea. This reasoning holds, not only against every corporeal substance, but also against every exterior sensible property, without distinguishing between primary and secondary qualities.

b) In a more general way, there is a contradiction, according to Berkeley, in affirming that an exterior reality exists in itself without being actually known. For if we *affirm* that it exists, it is such only as actually known by us. If no one asserts anything about a thing, it is only because it means nothing for the world; that is, because it is pure nothingness. Thus, for the objects of our ideas, to exist is to be perceived.

The idea, the unique object of our knowledge, is at once a fact of consciousness, or subjective phenomenon seizable by introspection [2], and a determined *object*, as a color, a figure, or, in our more complex ideas, a man or a tree. Berkeley never distinguishes this double aspect, triumphantly answering that he has reduced ideas to things! On the contrary, this indissoluble union results in making our knowledge of " things ", understood in this way, infallible; for we have within us the immediate intuition of them, and they *are* totally what we think of them, and yet they are nothing more than our ideas. The criterion of the clear idea is here applied without difficulty.

---

[1] *Three Dialogues between Hylas and Philonous*, Dial. I.

[2] In this sense, Berkeley does not distinguish reflection from sensation; both are equally and uniquely facts of consciousness. In another context, he admits, as does Locke, two sources of ideas : an external source (God), and an internal one (consciousness).

" The more a man knows the connection between ideas ",
Berkeley concludes, " the more he knows the nature of things " [1].

C) Spiritual Realism.

378. In the meantime, our ideas are not fully intelligible
by themselves, for they show themselves to be variable, multiple
and especially passive. A color or a triangle, for instance,
is an image totally objective, incapable of producing anything;
ideas associate among themselves, but do not mutually cause
each other. In order to explain them there must be admitted
a source, which, as intuition informs us, is the *spirit* which
sees and wills them. " I have always had the experience that
I perceive many ideas, and, by an act of will, I can form a
multitude of very different ideas " [2]. This intuition, as that
of Descartes' *cogito, ergo sum* [3], grasps the permanent and
spiritual substance of the *self*, which is naturally incorruptible,
and it grasps this fact beyond the passing phenomenon of the
idea. But, in maintaining this substance, Berkeley defends
his entitlement of it with the role of *substratum*, whose emptiness
he had shown for matter. In his view, a spirit is simply an
active principle, endowed with intelligence and will. Intelligence designates, as with Descartes, knowledge in general,
whether that of sensation, imagination, science or of the speculations on God and morality. The will is the power of acting,
of stirring up or combining ideas, of producing movements
or the series of sensations which are called " movements " [4].
The will is endowed with *liberty*, for we grant that we act by
our own choice. This is the spiritual substance which is the
explicative principle of ideas, because it is capable of receiving
them passively while understanding them by its intelligence [5],
and of actively producing them in forming them by the will.

This view, far from justifying the existence of matter for Berkeley,
furnished him with new arguments against it. He could justify
himself only by use of the productive cause of sensations. There
is no action or production conceivable beyond that which we

---

[1] *Three Dialogues*, Dial. III.

[2] *Ibid.*, Dial. I.

[3] See above, n. 325 and n. 327.

[4] For Berkeley, since the total reality of our body is in being thought,
" to lift an arm ", for example, means to be capable of producing the series
of kinaesthetic or visual sensations which form this object : " an arm which
lifts itself ".

[5] To say " that objects are in the intelligence " is to say " quite simply
that the intelligence comprehends or perceives these objects ". *Ibid.*, Dial. III.

experience in ourselves, that of the soul producing the ideas through the will [1]. Matter, having no will, cannot cause sensations, nor can it receive them, for it lacks intelligence. Briefly, the spirit is at once the necessary and sufficient explanation of the object of all human knowledge.

Nevertheless, the human soul cannot account for everything. For, among our ideas, there are found two opposed series. The first depends totally on ourselves; these are the *imaginations*, which we form and manage with full liberty, and our soul is their sufficient reason. The others, which are called *external sensations*, manifest themselves independently of our " self " and we receive them passively within our intelligence; the order of their succession follows a law which is imposed on them from without. On this point, Berkeley wished to be in agreement with common sense and he succeeds in doing so. For him, as for all, there is an external world irreducible to the ideas of our " fantasy "; if one sees a tree in the garden, it must be said to be outside of ourselves; if a great number of men see it, it is, in a sense, the *same* object which is perceived by all. When one ceases to think about it, it remains outside of us, in a sense, as it was perceived. But his explanation of why this occurs is one with which common sense could not agree.

It has been demonstrated, as a matter of fact, that matter is nothing and that the total reality of sensible things lies in their being perceived. But, since a spirit alone can produce ideas, and since my sensations do not depend on my thought, there must be some other spirit in which they reside. This spirit, " which constantly perceives the sensible world and gives it thereby its exterior reality (by relation to ourselves) and its permanence " [2], is God. We grasp His existence by an immediate inference, and beyond the existence of the sensible world or of our sensations, of which we also have an intuitively certain intuition. In this sense, Berkeley affirms the *reality of bodies;* that is, the existence of rich ideas produced in us by God, and thus distinct from other ideas which we create at will.

In addition, the characters of the sensible world reveal to us the attributes of God, and this is the true God of the Christians,

---

[1] This is why Berkeley criticized the Newtonians, who placed the attractive force of gravitation in bodies; he admitted the laws discovered by Newton, but merely as regulatory of the flow of our sensations.

[2] *Three Dialogues,* Dial. I.

in Whom " we live, move and have our being " [1]. For, inasmuch
as phenomena reveal to us an unlimited power in their cause,
it is God Who is this active and All-Powerful Being; He is the
Sovereign and infinite Spirit. If one cannot sufficiently admire
the order, regularity and proportion of phenomena, it is because
God is infinitely Wise, Foreseeing and Good beyond all power
of expression [2]. If, on the other hand, He is the cause of our
sensations, some of which are imperfect, as sorrow, He is not
affected thereby. " He is a pure spirit, disengaged from all
sorts of natural bonds in which our spirit finds itself engaged.
He knows all, for this is a perfection ". But He knows all
things in an immutable fashion, without Himself undergoing
our sensible variations [3]. One need no longer fear that He is
the author of evil, for He produces every reality of things in
producing our ideas; evil is but the disorder of the free wills
residing in our souls. On the contrary, the doctrine of immaterialism, showing us God as immediately present, should stir
us to piety and the observance of moral laws. In denying
matter, this view resolves, with one blow, all the insoluble
problems brought up on this subject by the philosophers [4],
and in explaining the sensible world through God, it closes the
mouth of all atheists. The physical sciences are thereby
affirmed and ennobled, for the object of study is but the series
of ordered sensations produced by God according to laws He
has determined; nature becomes a language which reveals to
us the secrets of the Divine Wisdom. In sounding out the
advantages of this view of God, Berkeley introduces a new
and novel aspect of his system.

D) Platonic Integration.

378 [bis]. During the last period of his life, Berkeley discovered
a more efficacious means of attaining God, in the study of Platonic
writings. Our ideas, though authentic and derived from sensible
experience, tell us nothing about the Divine Nature. They express
objects in a wholly passive fashion, while God is an essentially
active spirit. On the other hand, an empiricist philosopher cannot

---

[1] Berkeley favors this expression of St. Paul's, and quotes it often; it is taken
from *Acts of the Apostles*, XVII, 28.

[2] *Three Dialogues*, Dial. I and Dial. III.

[3] *Ibid.* : " Properly speaking, God has no sensations ".

[4] Berkeley cites discussions on the extension of matter, in its continuity, its
homogeneity and its divisibility, the transmission of motion, the interaction
between bodies, the nature of substantial forms, substance and accident, the
principle of individuation, the origin of ideas, and so forth. See *Three Dialogues*,
Dial. III.

rely on abstract, intellectual concepts or on reasoning founded on them in order to construct a "scientific" theodicy as did St. Thomas [1]. He must be content with asserting that God is a spirit, analogous to the soul, and confess his inability of forming a truly conformable idea of His nature.

Now, by the help of the Platonic purifications, the Bishop of Cloyne hoped to lift himself to a truly intellectual intuition, superior to that of sensible ideas and even to that of the self. He hoped to grasp the intuition of the *archetypal ideas*, which constitute the Divine Spirit Itself, the creative source of all those marvelous chains of sensations which, in turn, constitute the sensible world and its laws. These ideas, regulative of the universe, have nothing in common with abstract ideas, which Berkeley has definitively condemned. They are true realities, intellectual and uncreated, the principles at one and the same time of the order of things and of our highest forms of knowledge. But " the most refined human intellect, exerted to its utmost reach, can only seize some imperfect glimpses of the Divine Ideas, abstracted from all things corporeal, sensible, and imaginable " [2].

In order to explain the creative influence of the Divine Ideas in the world, Berkeley represents it as an animated being, of which God Himself is the life, not through any pantheistic identification, but in the sense that nature is like an immediate instrument which God uses to manifest His Ideas. There is a sort of theophany in which the Creative Spirit takes a finite form in order to be proportionated to created intelligences. This finite form, as would be demanded by an empiricist doctrine, is a sensible reality although it is an invisible one : it is a very pure and subtle *fire*, quite similar to the Stoic conception of the soul of the world [3]. Being impregnated with the Divine Wisdom, whose instrument it is, this fire penetrates all things, constituting the various qualities or sensible ideas; it binds these ideas in a vast and perfectly ordered network in which each part is coordinated with the totality and is equilibrated with the others for the good of all. Inasmuch as tar water has an abundance of this very pure fire, it is a marvelous remedy, and becomes an instrument of Providence to spread good among men [4].

In analyzing the most profound reasons for being, Berkeley still remains faithful to his immaterialism. This world of nature and the subtle fire have no other reality but that of being perceived by our souls. Since they are an emanation from God, they make Him intimately present to us; while they explain the sensible world, they still remain exterior to us, endowed with their own proper laws which are equally imposed on all things. From this it follows that if our spirit is a first, explicative condition of ideas and of things, the Divine Spirit is their final reason for being through His archetypal Ideas and the subtle fire in which He expresses

---

[1] See above, n. 267.
[2] *Siris*, n. 337.
[3] See above, n. 99.
[4] The eighteenth century was little inclined towards Platonic intuitions; its only interest in Berkeley's *Siris* was its curiosity about tar water.

Himself. This explanation goes way beyond the empiricist horizon, of course; though it does not follow necessarily from his initial principle, it does not contradict it, and is harmoniously integrable with it.

This Platonic integration, however, has less solidity than beauty. Having strongly argued to establish that the whole content of our ideas is of the sensible order, it is quite arbitrary to endow us with an intuitive power capable of penetrating the secrets of divinity [1]. Human reason is abstractive, and the intuition proper to it does not surpass the modest limits assigned to it by St. Thomas [2].

From this viewpoint, Berkeley was right in holding to a real intuition of the self as a thinking substance, as did Descartes [3]. It was also proper that he demanded an exterior cause for our sensations; even their origin, God the Creator, is an incontestably *sufficient* reason. If one adopts the position of the critical problem as given by Descartes and Locke, it is difficult to avoid the persistent dialectic towards immaterialism which supresses bodies as being useless. It is the very position of the critical problem which must be restated. We do not begin by knowing our own thoughts; sensation, as has been said, gives us the object in its concrete and *trans-subjective* reality; that is, as outside of our consciousness. The value of this fully evident intuition cannot be denied without denying the possibility of every true judgment and of all knowledge. Finally, it is sufficient to show, in resolving the problem of universals, that our abstract ideas have the same content [4] as our sensible intuitions in order to fully justify the objective value of all types of human knowledge.

In seeking the reasons for our knowledge outside of matter, Berkeley flattered himself in thinking that he put man in the presence of God with an evidence superior to any other way. It is with good reason that he regards God in this way. His thoughts are but a small reflection of the theories of St. Thomas' realistic metaphysics [5] on the nature of ontological truth. Nothing in reality can exist in itself without being intelligible, and, consequently, without being thought, and even *actually* so, at least by the Creative Intelligence of God. In order to explain this truth, the Cartesian theory of the clear idea fully applies; there is perfect correspondence between idea and reality, so that with regard to the object, to exist is precisely to be thought about. But, following the realists, this creative thought has placed *real things* into being, whose existence we ascertain by sensible intuition and which is truly attained by our abstractive sciences [6]. Immaterialism, as

---

[1] Far less reason do we have for positing the existence of a *subtle fire* which acts as an instrument of God.

[2] See n. 262 and n. 540.

[3] This intuition, moreover, is but a point of departure which does not dispense with much research and work to set up a science of the soul; see n. 327.

[4] See n. 409, below.

[5] See above, n. 260.

[6] Our knowledge does not express individuals as individuals, but the properties and the laws are the same in our sciences and in reality; there are two different modes, one is universal and the other is individual.

every error, does not sin insofar as it affirms, but to the extent that it denies. God is needful as first cause to explain each of our sensations and each of the objects or sensible phenomena which we perceive, and He is definitively the full reason for the stability and the order of nature. But the first cause does not suppress the secondary ones; instead of explaining everything by God [1], our sciences should be directed towards creatures and then, through them, elevate themselves to the Creator

Finally, one can argue about the merit of Berkeley's ascension to God. For, in order to attain it, one must equivocate the principle of causality. On the one hand, if there is question of the sensible world, the phenomena do not act on each other; fire, for example, does not burn, for, in the view of idealistic empiricism, there are but two ideas which follow each other; we can merely discover the laws of succession governing these ideas (or phenomena), as a reflection of the Divine Wisdom, and the notion of cause has no other meaning. — On the other hand, if there is question of God and the soul, the productive cause of ideas is a substance and even the Infinite Spirit which efficaciously creates them; this gives an entirely different twist to the principle of causality. This meaning, of course, can be quite legitimate, as in the view of moderated realism. But it is not at all compatible with the absolute empiricism of Berkeley, which Hume will make abundantly evident.

CONCLUSION. Berkeley has left us with a curious mixture of empiricism and of spiritualism, of positivism and idealism, of a taste for the sensible and an aversion for matter. What he rejects under the title of matter, however, is not bodies, but the unknowable *substratum* of which Locke spoke, as constituting the essence of sensible realities and of which phenomena are but the envelope. " Both you and I are agreed ", says Philonous to Hylas, " that we only perceive sensible forms, but there is disagreement between us, because what you regard as empty appearances, I hold to be real beings. You do not believe in your senses, but I believe in mine " [2]. This is one of the most profound traits of Berkeley : an esteem for the facts of experience. It is quite curious, however, to see this joined with an irresistible pull towards spiritual realities and towards God which colors all his views with immaterialism in some way similar to Augustinianism. This can partially be explained by the deep religious sentiments of a clergyman and Anglican bishop, preoccupied with preserving his people

---

[1] This solution harks back to Malebranche and the vision in God, although in his view our knowledge attains the Divine Ideas in the intelligible order; Berkeley admits only sensible and concrete phenomena. " Looking at things entirely, there are no principles as completely opposed as those of Malebranche and mine ". *Three Dialogues*, Dial. I.

[2] *Ibid.*, Dial. III.

from the dangers of atheism and immorality quite rampant during those days. But one can also see a sort of psychological affinity between the taste for sensible intuition and for that of intellectual intuition; following this bent, Berkeley tried to penetrate the concrete phenomenon, considered as the true reality, and was thus led to penetrate to spiritual substance no less concrete than his own soul, and finally to the wholly spiritual reality of God.

But, above all, it is his empiricism and his taste for the sensible which dominates his system of immaterialism. It is the most solid and best elaborated portion of his thought, and the one that had the most influence on the development of ideas. Balanced by his spiritualism, Berkeley did not destroy one bit of Locke's realism, but his empiricist idealism permitted his successor to complete his critical work. Already in France, Condillac, also a disciple of Locke, holding fast to empiricism, prepared for the destruction of spiritual substance.

2⁰ CONDILLAC[1] (1715-1780).

379. The abbé Etienne Bonnet de Condillac, who never exercised his priestly powers, was a tutor to the young son of Louis XV. He composed a whole course of studies for the lad, including a grammar, an art of writing, an art of reasoning, and an art of thinking. He is, however, especially known for his famous *Traité des sensations*, which is a further development of his *Essai sur l'Origine des connaissances humaines*. He also wrote a *Traité des systèmes* in which he criticizes Descartes, Malebranche, Leibniz and Spinoza. Two other works, *Traité des animaux* and *Logique*, complete his doctrine. A friend of Rousseau, of the Encyclopedists, and especially an avid reader of Locke, he was the most remarkable of the *philosophes* of the eighteenth century.

Condillac's theory is but the empiricism[2] of Locke, simplified by the suppression of the second source of ideas, reflection. All our ideas come uniquely from experience; that is, from *exterior sensation*.

At first, helped by the education of the senses, the spirit exercises itself in *attention*, which is an internal sensation concentrated on the object in order to perceive it perfectly.

---

[1] 1⁰ **Works :** *Œuvres complètes*, 16 vols., Paris, 1882.

2⁰ **Studies :** DE PUCHESNE, BAGUENAULT, *Condillac, sa vie, sa philosophie, son influence*, Paris, 1910. — DIDIER, J., *Condillac*, Paris, 1911. — LENOIR, R., *Condillac*, Paris, 1924. — LE ROY, G., *La psychologie de Condillac*, Paris, 1937. — SCHAUPP, Z., *Naturalism of Condillac*, Lincoln (Nebr.), 1926.

[2] It is also frequently called a *sensualism;* concerning this term, see above, n. 356.

Then, with the help of memory and of imagination, the spirit attentively *compares* several sensations among themselves, and can form new ideas. This comparison is called *reflection*, which is not a special source of ideas, but a first work of elaboration. Through this means, the spirit constructs its *abstract ideas*, which are " partial images "; to these, a common name or *general denomination* is affixed, and this comprises the total reality of our abstractions. Finally, by perceiving the relations between these general sensations through the judgment, and by ordering various judgments through *reasoning*, the spirit constructs its sciences, so that *science is but a well made language* and all the operations of the spirit, as a result, are but transformed sensations.

In order to illustrate the sensible origin of ideas, Condillac gives the example of a statue in his *Traité des sensations.* The statue acquires, one after another, the usage of the senses. He then explains, as Berkeley, that the idea of extension, absent from vision, is obtained through touch, although his view on this point varied.

Despite his absolute empiricism, which should have led him to the negations of positivism, Condillac admitted a spiritual soul, capable of thinking by itself, but actually having no other function than that of organizing sensations [1]. If one takes " idea " in the Cartesian sense as a *fact of consciousness*, indifferently spiritual or sensible, this concept can be understood, though it is not logical, as the pitiless criticism of Hume will easily demonstrate.

III. The third stage. David Hume. (1711-1776).

Special bibliography.

1º **Works :** GREEN, T. H., and GROSE, T. H. (eds.), *Works,* 4 vols., Oxford, 1898. — HENDEL, C. W. (ed.), *Political Essays.* — SELBY-BIGGE, L. A. (ed.), *A Treatise on Human Nature,* Oxford, 1896.

2º **Studies :** BRAHAM, E. G., *Life of David Hume,* London, 1931. — BRUNIUS, T., *David Hume on Criticism,* Uppsala, 1952. — CHURCH, R. W., *Hume's Theory of the Understanding,* Ithaca (N. Y.), 1935. — COMPAYRÉ, G., *La philosophie de D. Hume,* Toulouse, 1873. — CRESSON, A., and DELEUZE, G., *David Hume, sa vie, son œuvre, sa philosophie,* Paris, 1953. — DIDIER, J., *Hume,* Paris, 1913. — GLATHE, A. B., *Hume's Theory of the Passions and of Morals,* Berkeley (Cal.), 1950. — GREEN, T. H., *Introduction to Hume,* London, 1874. — GREIG, J. Y. T., *David Hume,* New York, 1931. — HEINEMANN, F., *David Hume,* Paris, 1940. — HENDEL, C. W., *Studies in the Philosophy of David Hume,* Princeton (N. J.), 1925. — HUXLEY, T. A., *Hume,* London, 1880. — KRUSE, L. F. V.,

---

[1] Condillac held that in the next life our immortal soul will exercise faculties which are superior to sensation

Hume's Philosophy in His Principal Work : A Treatise of Human Nature, and in his Essays, Oxford, 1939. — KUYPERS, M. S., *Studies in the Eighteenth Century Background of Hume's Empiricism*, Minneapolis (Minn.), 1930. — KYDD, R. M., *Reason and Conduct in Hume's Treatise*, New York, 1946. — LAIRD, J., *Hume's Philosophy of Human Nature*, London, 1932. — LANG, B. M., *David Hume*, New York, 1932. — LE ROY, A., *La critique et la religion chez D. Hume*, Paris, 1930. — MAC NABB, D. G., *David Hume : His Theory of Knowledge and Morality*, London, 1951. — MAUND, C., *Hume's Theory of Knowledge*, New York, 1937. — METZ, R., *David Hume, Leben und Philosophie*, Stuttgart, 1929. — MOSSNER, E. C., *The Forgotten Hume*, New York, 1943. — ORR, J., *David Hume and His Influence on Philosophy and Theology*, New York, n. d. — PASSMORE, J. A., *Hume's Intentions*, Cambridge, 1952. — PRICE, H. H., *Hume's Theory of the External World*, Oxford, 1940. — SHARP, F. C., *Hume's Ethical Theory and its Critics*, London, 1921. — SHEARER, E. A., *Hume's Place in Ethics*, Bryn Mawr (Pa.), 1915. — SMITH, N. K., *The Philosophy of David Hume : A Critical Study of Its Origins and Central Doctrines*, New York, 1941. — TAYLOR, A. E., *David Hume and the Miraculous*, New York, 1927.

380. David Hume was born at Edinburgh (Scotland) into a family of comfortable means, so that he was always free from material cares. Having finished his studies in law, he tried to enter commerce, but only for a short while, since he was ambitious to make a name for himself in literature and especially in philosophy. Like Descartes, he believed that none of his predecessors had discovered any certainty. He retired to France, where he composed his first work, *A Treatise on Human Nature* [1]. This work, which exposed his sceptical outlook quite brazenly, had but a moderate success. Accordingly, beginning in 1741, he published a series of *Essays Moral and Political*, in which he moderated his views somewhat and dressed them up in literary style. Through this work he acquired a close friendship with Adam Smith, and also won public favor. He revised his *Treatise* then, publishing it as *Philosophical Essays concerning Human Understanding* (1748) [2]. He wrote *Dialogues concerning Natural Religion* about 1749, though they were not published until 1779, after his death.

Having become librarian for some lawyers at Edinburgh, he occupied himself with history and published his *History of Great Britain* (1754-1759), and his *Natural History of Religion* (1757). Shortly afterwards, he went to Paris as secretary to Lord Hertford, the British ambassador (1764-1766). By this time he had become a celebrity, and was well received in society; his simplicity made him the man of the hour. In Paris he encountered the various thinkers of that period, as Helvetius, Montesquieu, Holbach, Diderot and others. On returning to England, he took Rousseau

---

[1] The first two volumes here published at London in 1739, the third, in 1740.
[2] From 1758 on, the title of this work became *Inquiry concerning Human Understanding*. The work was translated into German in 1756, and had a great influence on Kant's formalism; see below, n. 388.

with him, offering him refuge at his own home, though Rousseau did not stay there long [1]. He became Undersecretary of State for Scotland (1767-1769), and then retired to Edinburgh. " Hume was quite stout, and flattered himself on his knowledge and on his culinary art. Despite a long sickness, he kept his serenity until death, which came on August 25, 1776 " [2].

Hume takes up the double problem which formed the basis of Locke's doctrine : the psychological problem of the origin and classification of ideas, and the critical problem of their value. In resolving these questions, he stayed faithful to the two theories of his predecessors, *empiricism* and the *methodology of the clear idea*. But he has no preoccupations estranged from science in making his reflections : if the practical consequences of his views seem disastrous for life, he is not thereby changed or moved. He counts on instinct to correct them, stating that " when an opinion leads to absurdities, it is certainly false, but it is not certain that an opinion is false because it has dangerous consequences ". His metaphysical views are not to be justified by their usefulness or by their mutual agreement; they are like the playful sport of a vigorous spirit [3]. His one aim was to attain glory among the philosophers as Newton had done among the astronomers by scientifically explaining the life of our consciousness as Newton had explained the movements of the stars. This outlook enabled him to lead radical empiricism to its final consequences through the methodology of the clear idea. The great law of our psychological life is that of *association*, and Hume's directive principle can be stated as follows :

Beginning with our simple ideas, whose object is infallibly true, all intellectual and scientific constructions are explainable by the laws of habit and of psychological association.

In realizing this principle, Hume first classifies knowledge and explains the origin of abstract ideas; then he criticizes the value of knowledge, and, especially, of the principle of causality. He concludes with absolute phenomenalism, which unifies the two currents of idealism and positivism that began with Descartes.

A) Classification.

381. Hume accepts, as given in his reflections, only the interior world of consciousness. He also supposes it as an

---

[1] See below, n. 448. — [2] J. DIDIER, *Hume*, p. 5.
[3] E. BRÉHIER, *op. cit.*, II, p. 404.

evident affair that the object known by us is never the real, external thing, but solely the fact of consciousness, the phenomenon or subjective modification. In general, he calls this *perception*.

Now, " All the perceptions of the human mind resolve themselves into two distinct kinds, which I shall call *impressions* and *ideas*. The difference betwixt these consists in the degrees of force and liveliness with which they strike upon the mind, and make their way into our thought or consciousness. Those perceptions, which enter with most force and violence, we may name *impressions;* and under this name I comprehend all our sensations, passions and emotions, as they make their first appearance in the soul. By *ideas*, I mean the faint images of these in thinking and reasoning " [1].

a) The *impression* is a perception characterized by intensity, force and vividness.

b) The *idea* is a weak perception, pale, and less vivid.

In each of these classes, analysis concludes with *simple* elements, which are used to construct either impressions or especially *complex* ideas. For example, the idea of an apple is obtained by combining this form, color, taste, and hardness. At the same time, one has the complex impression of the apple, if one touches it, looks at it and tastes it.

Not only do complex impressions become resolved into simple ones, but to every simple idea there always corresponds a simple impression of which the idea is but a weakening [2]; consequently, all the content of our mental life has its origin in simple impressions. But the latter are always reducible to the objects of sensible experience. We receive them passively from an external cause whose nature is unknown to us [3], but they are sufficient to explain all subsequent combinations [4].

---

[1] *A Treatise on Human Nature*, Book I, Part I, Section I.

[2] Hume thus escapes Berkeley's criticism that one idea cannot represent anything but another idea; " it is true that every idea is representative, but only of an impression which is of the same nature as itself, and superior only in intensity " (E. BRÉHIER, *op. cit.*, II, p. 406).

[3] " Whatever impressions there may be coming from the senses, their ultimate cause is, in my view, perfectly explainable by human reason "; *Treatise on Human Nature*, Book I, Part III, Section V. See also J. MARÉCHAL, *Le point de départ de la métaphysique*, II, p. 151.

[4] Complex ideas can be construed by the will so that there is no complex, corresponding impression; but they are reducible to simple ideas to which there always respond simple impressions.

Thus Hume establishes the empiricist principle : all our perceptions have no other origin than sensible experience.

This classification is evidently inspired by Locke; in order to conform totally to Locke's views, Hume distinguishes two other types of impressions, some coming from *sensation* and others from *reflection*. " An impression first strikes upon the senses, and makes us perceive heat or cold, thirst or hunger, pleasure or pain of some kind or other. Of this impression there is a copy taken by the mind,... this we call an idea. This idea of pleasure or pain, when it returns upon the soul, produces the new impressions of desire and aversion, hope and fear, which may properly be called *impressions of reflexion*, because derived from it " [1]. Thus, the impressions of reflection are of a subjective and affective order, as the desires or the passions, and they are derived from ideas that are revivified. The impressions of sensation are of the objective and speculative order, and they are primitive and original [2]. All other knowledge is derived from these impressions of sensation : they constitute something given, they are the final residue of analysis and the first principle beyond which there is nothing more to question.

Briefly, that which Descartes called thought, Locke and Berkeley, idea, Hume calls perception. In clear terms a perception is every *fact of consciousness* under its double aspect, as subjective and as representative of an object. From this second point of view, a perception is especially called *idea*. Every clear idea, for Descartes, represents a real substance in a fully scientific way; for Locke, in a purely hypothetical way; for Berkeley, only in the case of spirits; for Hume, the idea represents nothing more than another fact of consciousness, a primitive impression. The critical problem has thus become wholly immanent, and idealism has replaced realism. The whole question, for Hume, is to explain how human knowledge, so rich and so complex, can be referred back to primitive impressions which form the solid basis of knowledge and the source of its truth. He does not answer his problem without leaving pure empiricism and getting involved deeply in psychological mechanism which, in his view, leads through memory and imagination into abstract ideas and into the highest speculations.

As a matter of fact, the combinations of sensations and especially of ideas are not done haphazardly, but according to the great *law of association*. Hume recognizes three main forms of it : *resemblance*, spatial or temporal *contiguity* and *relation* between cause and effect. This is the great principle of explanation for Hume. " Here is a kind of attraction which

---

[1] *Treatise on Human Nature*, Book i, Part I, Section 2.
[2] If the term *innate* means original and not copied from a preceding impression, " one would have to hold that our impressions are innate and that our ideas are not "; see J. DIDIER, *Hume*, p. 7.

in the mental world will be found to have as extraordinary effects as in the natural, and to shew itself in as many and as various forms " [1].

This law aids us, first, in distinguishing *memory* and *imagination*. Impressions, by conserving themselves within the spirit, give birth to two sorts of ideas : the first are completely impoverished and weakened, and, as it were, detached from reality, and these are images properly speaking. The others are intermediaries between sensations and images; less vivid than the first, they are more strong than the second, and consequently most precise, least variable and most solid, and these are memories. Moreover, the law of association can account for these characteristics of memories : memory reproduces groups of ideas similar to complex impressions coming from without, and the association which has cemented the latter, causes a great coherence among the memories. It is proper to imagination, on the contrary, to dissociate these groups by freeing each simple idea which constitutes them; it thus becomes a fine means of analysis. On the other hand, the law of association also rules the movement of ideas, but independently of impressions. It especially explains the formation of abstract ideas.

B) **Abstraction.**

382. The existence of universal ideas in man is an undeniable fact. Hume, with his customary empiricism, reduces all the content of ideas to an incomplete, sensible image, designating but one individual in reality. How, then, does one explain the *universal usage* which we make of this concrete representation by giving it a common name enabling it to designate an indefinite number of similar individuals?

One must have recourse, for an explanation of this fact, to habit, the source of the law of association.

Once we have seen by numerous experiences that a concrete image, properly prepared, as the one which stands for this particular man, can be used to designate another, similar individual, we designate the image by a *word*. We then habitually associate any sort of similar individual with the word.

This habit, once set within us, has a double property. *a*) It becomes an *evocative tendency*, so that the common name is applied to any individual whatsoever, and is ready to pass

---

[1] *Treatise on Human Nature*, Book I, Part I, Section 4.

to all of those associated with the preceding experience; at the same time, it does not always awake in consciousness the whole clear series of individuals already experienced, but, according to the need or desire of each, it is restricted to a group, letting the others be in the potential state. *b*) It includes a *spontaneous force of adaptation*, allowing it to eliminate whatever is contrary and to gather whatever is proper to it. This force first exercises itself with regard to the content of the idea [1]. " Thus should we mention the word, triangle, and form the idea of a particular equilateral one to correspond to it, and should we afterwards assert, that the three angles of a triangle are equal to each other, the other individuals of a scalenum and isoceles, which we overlook'd at first, immediately crowd in upon us, and make us perceive the falshood of this proposition, tho' it be true with relation to that idea, which we had form'd " [2]. This same force permits the idea to embrace all individuals of the group [3], even those whom experience has not as yet attained. Hume remarks that we use the idea often to designate the *totality* of individuals, as in saying, for example, " every man is living ", a statement impossible to verify in all individuals. In this case, he says, we take an abridged route; we choose a certain number of experiences capable of delimiting the field of application of the same name. For example, we take, for the idea of man, individuals of various races and different ages; for the others, we fall back on our psychological habit and its instinctive force of adaptation, " and find but few inconveniences to arise in our reasoning from that abridgment " [4].

This double property, working in the unconscious, is somewhat mysterious, but imposes itself as a fact of experience. With its help, the general idea, termed abstract, can be explained.

The essentials of this theory will again be found in the nineteenth century in the nominalism of Stuart Mill and of Taine [5]. Its merit lies in its quite exact analysis of the *very exercise* of intellectual abstraction; but it is powerless to explain the evident facts of consciousness which come from the sensible realm. It is evident that the abstract nature not only possesses this extraordinary

---

[1] In logical terms, the *comprehension* of an idea.
[2] *Treatise on Human Nature*, Book I, Part I, Section 7; see J. Maréchal, *op. cit.*, II, p. 156.
[3] In logical terms, the *extension* of an idea.
[4] *Treatise on Human Nature, ibid.*
[5] See below, n. 486 and n. 497.

power of being extended to an infinity of cases, future as well as past (which already is inexplicable by a mere psychological habit), but that it acquires this power by one action; for example, in establishing a geometrical definition. Moreover, the abstract nature possesses a demand for full intelligibility which makes it necessarily what it is even independently of experience (principle of identity) and, by combining with the contingent fact of experience in which this nature is evidently [1] realized, it finally obliges one to ascend to the real existence of a Perfect and Infinite Being (principle of causality).

But this is merely pointing out the essential defect of every positivistic empiricism : the neglect of an experience which imposes itself with the same force as all sensible experience — the existence of the spiritual, intellectual idea.   The latter, or the psychological fact of knowing a nature, is seized very clearly under the transcendent aspect of being, and is thus the source of a realistic metaphysics fully justifiable in epistemology.   Thus, there can be found, in the mysterious, evocative habit of Hume, a transposition of the properties of being and of the formal object of human intelligence, forming, so to speak, the very stuff out of which concepts are made.

C) Critique of the Sciences.

383.   General ideas being thus explained by pure empiricism, Hume then establishes their primordial function in the sciences, which they make up by being assembled according to logical rules.   By virtue of the analytic method which owes its inspiration to the Cartesian theory of the clear idea, Hume grants an infallible truth only to simple ideas which are the objects of immediate intuition, and to groups of ideas formed by a chain of intuitions; that is, to those which are perfectly decomposable into simple ideas.

Do the relations between ideas used in man's sciences enjoy this privileged state?   In order to answer this, Hume makes a rescension of them; they are seven in number, forming two groups.   The first group includes resemblance, contrariety, quali- tative degree and quantitative or numerical proportion; the second group includes the relations of space and time, identity or substantial permanence and causality.   There is no difficulty with the first group.   These types of relations are not distinguished from ideas themselves, and are but an aspect of them, so to speak. They are discoverable at first sight and refer properly to the domain of intuition rather than to that of demonstration [2].   For example,

---

[1] This evidence (for example, that this concrete tree which I see *realizes* the nature of a living thing) is the foundation of the moderate realism defended by St. Thomas, and which will be found as a correction in Kant's criticism of Hume; see below, n. 409.

[2] See J. MARÉCHAL, *op. cit.*, p. 156.

visual sensation does not only grasp colors separately, as whiteness, redness and so on, but also their differences or opposition, or even the resemblance between two equally red bodies. These relations, as a result, afford a solid foundation to the sciences.

The relation of *quantitative proportion*, however, requires further precision. In a certain measure, it is the object of intuition; thus, one immediately sees that four balls are two doubled. But, by the aid of repeating unity, does one understand these relations beyond any possible certification in the mathematical sciences? Are the latter valuable? Hume, in answering, distinguishes sciences.

Only the exact sciences, arithmetic and algebra, enjoy absolute evidence, for the notion of unity they employ is invariable and uniform. This permits perfect substitution of quantities having the same value as experimental intuition. These sciences are perfectly analytic.

Geometry approaches this ideal, but spatial unities (lines, surfaces, and so on), which it employs, do not have the same fixity experimentally. The conclusions of geometry are merely very probable.

The relations of this second group are, for that matter, quite important speculatively, since they are used in most of the sciences. An attentive examination will show how all of them are based on the notion of causality.

Consider, for instance, spatial and temporal relations which, together with numerical relations, constitute the object of the physical sciences. The idea of *space* appears, upon analysis, as a derivation of extension which, in turn, is formed from simple visual and tactual sensations. We see a series of colored points and we touch a series of solid points; this series of simple and indivisible impressions [1] can, in no way, constitute the idea of extension, divisible infinitely. One gets this idea, and that of empty space, by pursuing experience. We can certify that the series of our tactual and visual sensations are accompanied by movements of the arm, the hand, the muscles of the eye, and so on. These muscular sensations still remain even if one suppresses their intermediaries, and the passage from the first object to the last requires the same sensations. Now, this is the total content of the idea of space : a determined muscular impression with a possible series of tactual or visual impressions. The idea of time is constructed in a similar manner, by considering a series of instants, or of colored or resistive points, no longer stable but successive and moving. In supposing the origin of these impressions outside of ourselves, and in extending their possible field of action indefinitely with the imagination, we obtain the ideas of absolute time and space, in Newton's sense.

---

[1] For Hume, the objective point and the psychological impression are but the same thing, the unique object of our immediate perceptions.

Briefly, there is nothing of value in this series of visual and tactual impressions arranged orderly and held up by a permanent, muscular impression. Through abstraction, we call space or time the presumptive objective *cause*, capable of explaining the return of similar impressions in ourselves.

This critique would be efficacious against the Newtonian conceptions. In the doctrine of Aristotle and of St. Thomas, space has no other reality but that of *a relation of distance between two bodies*. If one were to suppress every body capable of founding the reality of this relation, there would remain nothing but purely imaginary space, a simple being of reason; this is the empty, absolute space of Newton. In a similar way, absolute time, conceived as an exterior receptacle of movements, is nothing more than a being of reason, for all of its reality lies in movement. Taken as a measure of duration, it supposes the action of memory, which retains before itself a total movement in order to cut it up into a unity (a day, an hour) capable of being indefinitely repeated. Time, Aristotle says, is formally in the soul and only foundationally in things. This foundation of the relation of space or of temporal measure is, as Hume wished, the origin or objective cause of these two notions. It should merely be noted that the Thomistic analysis grants an *intellectual* content to these ideas, and not merely a sensible one; they thus have scientific value, but according to the critical rules of moderate realism.

Finally, as we shall show [1], the idea of substance or the relation of abiding identity, as well as that of exterior existence are also founded on the relation of causality. This makes it necessary to give a thorough criticism to the principle of causality.

D) Criticism of the Principle of Causality.

384. At first, it was by means of the principle of causality that philosophers flattered themselves into thinking that they could attain objects beyond experience. Thus, Locke and Berkeley elevated themselves by its aid to God's existence as the foundation of religion and of morality. Hume, in the name of empiricism, begins by reducing their pretentious thoughts to nothingness. How can the principle that every thing which began has a cause, be justified? It is not evident by intuition or by demonstration. Sensible intuition does not certify a *necessary connection* between two facts, but only their succession; for instance, one perceives the visual impression of a flame, then the tactual impression of a burn. But the causal link totally escapes the senses. Rational demonstration of this principle, by the method of the clear idea, is impossible.

[1] See below, n. 384bis.

For, in looking for all the simple ideas which are constitutive of an effect, one does not find therein that of the cause, or, in the cause, that of the effect. " It will be easy for us to conceive any object to be non-existent this moment, and existent the next, without conjoining to it the distinct idea of a cause or a productive principle " [1]. Consequently, it is impossible to demonstrate, *a priori*, through the simple analysis of ideas, the necessity of a cause to explain that which happens [2]. This relation, Hume concludes, through which one infers to the existence of a distinct cause from the existence of an effect, or through which the presence of the same cause makes us admit the necessary existence of the same effect, has no speculative value, since it is beyond experience, the unique source of infallible truth. One should not, however, proscribe it completely, but delimit its value by explaining its origin.

By psychological analysis we are aware of a triple element in the relationship of causality which we employ. *a*) There are two successive facts of experience intuitively known through an actual impression or at least reproduced by memory; for instance, the movement of a billiard ball, followed, after contact, by the movement of another. *b*) One can then certify that the same experiences repeat themselves and one acquires a habit of association which makes the succession constant and practically necessary, so that the sight or the memory of one of the facts invariably invokes the attention to the other, even in the future. When we see the player hit the first ball, we are sure, that if it meets the second, this one will, in turn, move. *c*) Finally, we consider this second fact so grasped not only as an idea, but as having *real* and independent *existence*, due to a transfer of assent or of belief. It is by this final element that the relation of causality is distinguished clearly from any other association of ideas; as re-enforced by habit, it becomes not only a constant succession, but a necessary bond in virtue of which one real object produces another. There but remains a determination of the value of this belief in order to know the value of causality.

Belief, for Hume, is nothing else but the assent given to the existence of the object of a perception. This assent or judgment

---

[1] *Treatise on Human Nature*, Book I, Part III, Section 3.

[2] In accepting the statement of the problem in the mode of idealistic empiricism, as did Locke and Berkeley, this criticism of Hume's becomes irrefutable. Of course, it is this very position which needs to be rectified. See above, n. 375.

of existence is attached to certain ideas which are thus distinguished from fictions of the imagination; it always accompanies our impressions of sensation. But, according to the principle of empiricism, we have no right to admit anything real but perception itself. We do not have infallible certitude (justified by critical reflection) of the existence of a reality distinct from the fact of consciousness. " The idea of existence, then, is the very same with the idea of what we conceive as existing. To reflect on any thing simply, and to reflect on it as existing, are nothing different from each other " [1]. If, then, we admit by belief to a double existence, one of ideas or impressions, then that of exterior objects, this latter is but an incontrollable hypothesis. But belief has no need of this hypothesis in order to be explained; it is engendered by the especially high degree of *vividness* which a perception enjoys. " The incredulous and the believing have the same ideas in their spirit; but, in the believer the ideas have more force, vividness, solidity, firmness and stability " [2]. For this reason, it is normal that every *impression* is accompanied with belief.

Now the impression has this property of communicating to *ideas* which are in connection with it, something of its own vigor and vividness. From this fact, for example, it follows that the impressions which religious ceremonies give, strengthen the belief of the faithful. But more precisely, causality establishes between the impression and the idea a more narrow connection; thus, aided by this very strong association, the belief which determines the " reality " of one of two facts is spontaneously transported to the other. From this it follows that from a real effect one can conclude to a real cause, and from a real cause one always goes to a real effect.

As a consequence, the total necessity of the principle of causality is referred to the stability of a psychological habit, often strengthened by heredity, but which could, without absurdity, actually change. This habit, for Hume, justifies the usage of the notion of cause in daily life, but not in the sciences. That which remains speculatively indubitable and definitively true is, uniquely, the fact of consciousness, the subjective phenomenon taken either in itself, or as an element of various groups. Every attempt to go beyond this object

---

[1] *Treatise on Human Nature*, Book I, Part II, Section 6.
[2] E. BRÉHIER, *op. cit.*, II, p. 410.

is condemned before critical reflection; there is no further guarantee of truth.

E) **Applications. Scepticism and Phenomenalism.**

384bis. It is easy to see what happens to the ideas so dear to common sense in the face of this pitiless criticism. There is no *substance* any more in external things or in the self; there is no *immortal soul* or *God;* there is no *morality.*

1° **Substance.** This notion is one of the most frequently used in philosophy, but also the most contestable in an empiricist doctrine. Following the criticism of Locke and of Berkeley, Hume concludes with ruins. One cannot define substance, as did the Scholastics, as " that which exists *per se* ", for this definition is proper to every clear and distinct perception, that is, to that which one calls phenomenon or accident. In order to speak of substance, one must have a group of properties sufficiently permanent and stable through time. We actually admit such permanent objects, either outside of ourselves or within us.

What do we know of the external world? In the proper sense, it is impossible to attain any other thing but our actual impressions and their grouping. For example, this color with this form, taste and odor, constitutes an orange. These impressions are passing, but experience makes us aware that these same groups can be easily and often reproduced. Though we do not continually perceive an orange, we will periodically meet one on the table for desert. From this arises the association of ideas strengthened by habit; and, following the natural bent of our spirit, we seek to explain this fact to ourselves by a cause. *Substance* is this *cause;* that is, the reality beyond experience, supposedly permanent and identical through time, and destined to explain the return of the same impressions and the existence of the stable groupings of simple ideas. But no more than space and time does this concept of substance have any objective value. The causal bond is but a subjective, psychological law, and this continued existence of a real object outside of ourselves is nothing but an hypothesis or a fiction due to the work of the imagination.

But if we are ignorant of exterior things, can we not, as Berkeley and Descartes believed, seize our own proper substance, our spiritual self through intuition? The empiricist logic does not allow for this. " ...When I enter most intimately into what I call *myself*, I always stumble on some particular perception or other, ... I never can catch *myself* at any time without a perception... When my perceptions are remov'd for any time, as by sound sleep; so long am I insensible of *myself*, and may truly be said not to exist " [1]. This, then, is the total content of the intuition of a thinking self : " a bundle or collection of different perceptions, which succeed each other with an inconceivable rapidity, and are in a perpetual flux and movement " [2]. Here again, we form the idea of the *substantial self* or of the soul by means of causality. Aided by memory, we certify the return of the same grouping of internal impressions or of ideas, forming the bottom of our consciousness. And then, going beyond the limits of all possible experience, we conclude to the presence in ourselves of a permanent reality, existing even before all thought and capable of indefinitely enduring in the future. But this new conception has no more value than the concept of exterior things.

And thus, after analysis, substance no longer exists for the philosopher seeking infallible truth, except as a pure, *permanent possibility of associated perceptions*. For a group of special impressions or vivid impressions, this would be the external body; for a general group of ideas or facts of consciousness, this would be the self.

2° With regard to **the spirituality and the immortality of the soul**, our ignorance is but a corollary of the preceding doctrine. " One pretends that impressions or ideas, by their nature, cannot be inherent except in a spiritual substance. But one does not know what this inherence is, nor what substance is; how can we know substance when we cannot know the impressions or ideas which are copies of substance, and when the impression, being but a mode, cannot represent one substance? " [3].

In addition, all the facts of consciousness, the unique material of our sciences, are of the sensible order. Experience shows that every conscious perception is necessarily joined to a similar movement in the brain. In applying the principle of causality in the sense indicated above, one must hold that the corporeal movement is a cause of thought. And, as the effect evidently cannot surpass its cause, all our perceptions are corporeal, or of the sensible order. Nothing authorizes one to place a difference between the destiny of our soul and that of other corporeal substances. We know only one thing : " death is the extinction of all particular

---

[1] *Treatise on Human Nature*, Book I, Part IV, Section 6.
[2] *Ibid.*
[3] E. Bréhier, *op. cit.*, II, p. 415.

perceptions " [1]; of what happens after death, philosophy will give us no certitude.

3° **God and Religion.** If the whole value of the principle of causality is due to a psychological law, it loses its efficacy in leading us to God. From this viewpoint, Hume easily overthrew the demonstrations for God's existence proposed during his age. Does anyone, for example, wish to say that God is the Intelligence required by the magnificent order of the world [2]? One is thus comparing the universe to a great machine, of which God is the mechanic. Is it not arbitrary, however, to extend to this case that which experience teaches us for well defined and limited cases? It is but a hypothesis, and nothing more; the procedure of analogy which suggests it could also lead one to conclude that God is an imperfect worker, encountering much resistance, or even that He is corporeal and works with His hands, and this would be no more than a false God.

But does not the changeful and imperfect universe demand a necessary and perfect being as its source [3]? Applying the theory of the clear idea in an empiricist fashion, we find that the idea of a necessary being becomes a valueless abstraction, for all its positive content refers back to a copy of impressions none of which has any necessary tie with existence. Furthermore, there is nothing easier than to make a clear idea of God, even so perfect an idea that one can suppose, though without asserting it, that God exists. The necessary being presupposed at the origin of things is not the fruit of a correct application of the principle of causality, but of a fiction of the imagination which extends the object of our experiences to infinity. One could also work this same notion out for the material universe, exterior to us by hypothesis, and it would become useless to give God as an explicative cause placed outside of the universe itself.

Briefly, the existence of God, of His Providence and His attributes, are irremediably inaccessible to all science. Hence, speculatively, no religion is justifiable. All religions are of equal value, for they all lack any basis. But religious beliefs and their habits of association have an explanation in instinct and in the habits of association which arise from it. This habit, as has been shown, explains the wide usage of causality, and applies in the same way to religion. Adherence to a religion is legitimate, if religion has some role in life as a source of consolations, of mutual aid and of social bonds. One should exclude from it all unreasonable fictions of the imagination, especially all belief in mysteries and in miracles [4]. The only useful religion is natural religion.

---

[1] See Hume's *Essay on the Immortality of the Soul.*

[2] This is Newton's proof, which was popularized by Voltaire; see n. 368 and n. 370, above.

[3] This is the Platonic proof presented by Clarke and the Cambridge School of Platonists.

[4] In Hume's view, no testimony supporting a miraculous fact can break the certitude that every event is produced according to natural laws; this latter conviction, founded on a very strong habit, cannot be broken by any testimony, however exceptional.

4° **Morality and Politics.** By the term, *morality,* one ordinarily understands the science of the rules or of the laws which must be followed in order to attain the true good and resultant true happiness by practicing virtue. Hume does not define it otherwise, but the first result of his criticism is to overthrow its traditional bases. It is impossible to found morality on God and on His Will which governs us; we are ignorant of His existence. It is impossible to appeal to reason as setting forth necessary and universal moral relations, so that virtue would be the manner of acting conformably to these relations [1], for it is one thing to know, and another thing to be obliged. Reason has speculation as its domain and not practicality; reason does not produce duty, but certifies it, and, as a consequence, it presupposes it instead of being its source. " Cold and disinterested reason cannot be a motive of action; it can only direct the impulse received from the appetite and from the inclination " [2].

For this reason, the foundation of morality lies in a *natural instinct*, which, under the form of taste or sentiment, determines the good and the bad. According to the empiricist doctrine, it is normal that the good be that which is useful to sensible life and satisfies its aspirations; evil, that which is harmful and opposed to its inclination. However, according to Hume, there is question not of personal or egotistical utility but of the *general utility;* for instance, if one estimates ability and prudence, one should prefer good will and justice, which procure the utility of many. To justify this rule, Hume merely refers to the sentiment which inclines us to love the good of all men, which he calls *humanity* [3].

There but remains the task of explaining the universality of the judgments determining good and evil and constituting the moral code, which imposes itself as an obligation on individuals and on peoples. Here, again, Hume has recourse to the force of habit issuing from social relations. When an action, which is useful to us, encounters the approbation of others, we find therein a double advantage : the satisfaction of our own desires, and the exercise of benevolence towards humanity. This action is thus catalogued as virtuous, while common disapproval would make it vicious. Experience shows that social reactions are regularly repeated and that our life is subject to customary laws comparable to the laws governing physical phenomena. In this way the universality of judgment is established; for between that which we judge as good or bad and the approbation of others, there is a practically stable accord which determines that which is virtuous or viceful, and constitutes the moral code considered by all as obligatory.

In objection, one can offer the variations of social customs; have not certain peoples approved manifest crimes, as the exposing

---

[1] This was Clarke's method for justifying traditional morality.

[2] *An Inquiry Concerning the Principles of Morals*, Section I.

[3] This doctrine is similar to those of Smith and of Hutcheson; see n. 386. Hume, however, does not admit a moral sense, and sees in sentiment merely an instinct which is good to follow in practice, but which, in theory, is unjustifiable.

of infants or of suicide? Hume answers that in essentials, as in courage, or in freedom, and so on, concord exists, and that these variations on secondary matters are legitimate [1].

This theory presupposes in man a natural inclination to live in society. Hume actually admits this as the fruit of our " sympathy " for others. It is good for us to aid each other in order to best attain what is useful to us. Social life requires organization and a political authority. Faithful to his empiricism, Hume rejects both the theory of the social contract and that of the divine right of kings; the first, because history does not approve of these contracts, but shows the birth of nations as due to the force of ambition; the second, because metaphysical thinking escapes us. One must judge of the legitimacy of government by the common good which it actually procures for the people; if it fails in this task, but then only, can one resist political authority [2].

In Summary. The pitiless, critical reflection of Hume sapped the whole edifice of sciences and of morality at its very base. In the entire domain of the physical and metaphysical world, the last word is *scepticism*. Substance, God, soul — man is ignorant of them all. Hume, it is true, tried to correct this speculative desolation by offering us instinct and nature as a practical guide and for comfort. Men always believe in the existence of an exterior world, and, guided by the principle of causality, continue to exploit it. Society itself will always impose its customs, and all men accept them spontaneously as the rules of honesty and of virtue; even the philosopher himself, when he leaves his speculative reflections, follows them. If nature and speculation suggest inverse conclusions to us, it is always nature which prevails; Hume states that this victory of instinct has, summarily, nothing but good results [3]. Theoretically, however, the philosopher regards all of this as a beautiful, imaginative fiction. One object remains infallibly true for Hume : the ensemble of perceptions and their laws, the phenomena of consciousness which are at once objective and subjective, and whose marvelous mechanism our sciences attempt to grasp. Without these we have no way to escape, either from ourselves or from experience

---

[1] The exposing of infants, for example, was a form of paternal love in a very poor country; a difference of circumstances justifies this action. One sees that Hume's laws are quite fragile.

[2] This principle of the *common good* is not evil; but one should not place the whole of this good, as did Hume, in the sensible order.

[3] This opposition between philosophical reflection and nature is already a presumption against phenomenalism. The following chapter will show how Kant's criticism, if rectified by Thomism, can surmount the redoubtable logic of Hume.

which is entirely of the sensible order. The empiricist criticism concludes with absolute phenomenalism, at once both idealistic and positivistic, which is the modern name for scepticism.

CONCLUSION. Since Descartes, modern philosophy became more and more involved in the solution of the critical problem. If followed two paths which were indistinct at first, but gradually excluded each other.

One group of thinkers fully adopts the *rationalist principle* that *our evident concepts have their full objective value of themselves* (theory of the clear idea), so that the existence of things is measured, in some fashion, by the system of our concepts scientifically constructed, since one can go from one concept to the other. The logic of this view concludes with the monistic pantheism of Spinoza, but remains an objective view. If good sense corrects these startling conclusions for some men, it is only by placing restrictions on the rationalist principles which are not critically justifiable.

Others adopt the principle of *empiricism* that *all the positive content of our concepts is of sensible origin*, thus referring the critical value of the clear idea to sensible intuition alone. Logic leads this view to absolute phenomenalism, or idealistic positivism.

Thus, in order to resolve the critical problem, one group denies that we have a conscious, independent life, and identifies us with the unique, divine substance. The other denies that any substance or exterior reality exists, and identifies the whole universe with a series of facts of consciousness.

At the same time, both groups unanimously accept as a starting point of their critical reflections, the idealistic principle that " man primarily knows only his own ideas or subjective modifications ". This affirmation becomes, for every modern philosopher, a self-evident axiom. Historically, the origin of this viewpoint traces back to Descartes. He took up the false notion of the " impressed species " which a decadent Scholasticism had offered as the object directly known, and then formulated as the essential problem of criticism the question of the resemblance between our ideas and exterior realities [2]. But the persistent domination of the idealistic principle even into our own times is beyond the influence of Descartes, and seems to be due to two causes.

---

[1] On this term, see n. 356, above.
[2] See above, n. 332.

a) The difficulty inherent in a metaphysical and psychological analysis of knowledge, in which the living synthesis of subject and object is in operation; this applies especially to conceptual knowledge in which the object is held in an abstract and universal manner, opposed to the concrete manner of real being. Scholastic philosophy, especially that of St. Thomas, offered a profound analysis which took care of all the facts, acknowledging the part of intuition in knowledge, both intellectual and sensible. In this way, by delimiting its sphere, he justified the affirmations of common sense, so invincibly convinced of the objective value of our knowledge [1]. But his view has a favorable stance, that of psychological and metaphysical examination.

The modern thinkers, on the contrary, choose the reflective view of pure criticism, which is most difficult and the least favorable to certify the direct contact of the spirit with sensible reality [2]. Their method encloses them within the thinking self, where they take the reflections of their own thought as objects, and as separated from all exterior reality. They are thus led to assert that " everything beyond thought is unthinkable ", as Le Roy will say in the nineteenth century. For, an exterior object considered at one time as " known " or as present to consciousness, and considered " in itself " or as outside of consciousness, implies a contradiction. It should be noted, though, that the philosophers of the Cartesian period did not see this absurdity, for most of them even defended the possibility of our ideas to express external reality. In this way, they remained faithful to good sense, while allowing their idealistic principle to develop all its possibilities.

b) There is another cause of idealistic empiricism in the progress of the mathematical sciences of the nineteenth century. The latter, seeming to confirm the mechanist hypothesis of Descartes, encouraged the belief that colors, sounds and other sensible qualities were, in themselves, nothing but local motion. Furthermore, the savants pretended to explain everything in terms of local motion, which leads to the same idealistic view that we know only our own ideas.

The satisfactory and solidly established solution to these difficulties, which was proposed by the realist philosophy of

---

[1] See above, n. 262.

[2] This point of view, on the other hand, is excellent for constituting epistemology as a *science* in a proper sense; we are here merely noting the *difficulties* which give occasion for idealism.

the Scholastics, and especially of St. Thomas, has been mentioned [1]. But since the seventeenth century these doctrines had fallen into quite general oblivion, so that from now on, we will witness the laborious efforts of reason, left to itself, attempting to free itself from the scepticism where idealism had led it, and to join itself to a reality on which it can again found its destiny to possess God.

IV. THE COUNTER-MOVEMENT OF SENTIMENTALISM.
THE SCOTTISH SCHOOL [2].

386. The phenomenalism of Hume, which had destroyed the very foundations of morality and of all knowledge, stirred a double reaction, that of Kant, which will be treated a little later, and that of the Scottish School. The latter, prepared by the defenders of a morality of sentiment, had its apogee in Thomas Reid.

A) The Precursors.

Even before the work of Hume had synthesized the principles devolving from idealism and from positivism, the theories of the freethinkers had stirred up a reaction from a group of moralists; from this reaction there was born the Scottish School, which had an ambitious program to combat the ensemble of phenomenalism.

SHAFTESBURY [3] (1671-1713), or Anthony Ashley Cooper, the third earl of Shaftesbury, is the leader of the group. Enamored of the Neo-Platonic ideas of the School of Cambridge, he wanted to have a profound harmony reign in all things, which issued forth from the effusive good of Divine Providence. He held that we have within us, in order to grasp this order, an *innate moral sense*. " By this he means an esthetic capacity, quasi-mystical, and an ' enthusiasm ' before the harmonies of the universe, along with a blessed need, wholly spontaneous, of creating the harmony there

---

[1] See, in particular, n. 82 for Aristotle's view, and nn. 260, 265 and 332.

[2] LAURIE, A., *Scottish Philosophy in Its National Development*, London, 1902. — METZ, R., *A Hundred Years of British Philosophy*, Ch. I, New York, 1938. — McCOSH, J., *The Scottish Philosophy*, New York, 1890. — SEGERSTEDT, T. T., *Problem of Knowledge in Scottish Philosophy*, Sund University, 1935. — LETH, A., *Scottish Philosophy : A Comparison of the Scottish and German Answers to Hume*, London, 1885.

[3] **Works :** *An Inquiry Concerning Virtue*, London, 1699. — *The Moralists*, London, 1709. — *A Letter concerning Enthusiasm*, London, 1708. — **Studies :** ALDRIDGE, A. O., *Shaftesbury and the Deist Manifesto*, Philadelphia (Pa.,) 1951. — BREADY, J. W., *Lord Shaftesbury and Social-Industrial Progress*, London, 1934. — BRETT, R. L., *Third Earl of Shaftesbury*, London, 1951. — HAMMOND, J. L., and BARBARA, *Lord Shaftesbury*, New York, 1936. — HIGHAM, F. M. G. E., *Lord Shaftesbury*, New York, 1945.

where order no longer reigns " [1]. This instinct guides us securely in the practice of the good. As for the rest, reason controls this moral sense, and determines its needs. It shows it as its goal the union with God by the perfecting of humanity, by going through the mutual aid of society. This is not the fruit of egoism, as Hobbes wished, but of an innate love of order and beauty which translates itself into an instinctive sympathy.

FRANCIS HUTCHESON [2] (1694-1746), of Irish ancestry and a professor at Glasgow, tried to show that this *moral sense* was truly a faculty; thus he is the founder of the Scottish School. The object of this sense is *moral goodness*, a simple quality which is immediately grasped as is color by the eye. This goodness consists in actions which tend towards the good of another, and in the disinterestedness which is as manifest in us as is egoism. The morality of disinterestedness seems to be independent of God and of country; one approves generous acts without thinking of God, and one despises a traitor to his country, unless the latter is useful to our own. Hence, goodness is a separable quality, and one which can be grasped only by a special sense. Since this object is in consciousness, the moral sense is an *internal* sense and is distinguished thereby from the external senses.

Mention should also be made of JOSEPH BUTLER (1692-1742), the Bishop of Durham; — of ADAM FERGUSON (1729-1797), a Scottish moralist and sociologist; — and of two esthetic thinkers, interested in the sense of beauty, HENRY HOME (1696-1782) and EDMUND BURKE [3] (1792-1797), born in Dublin; — in France, at the beginning of the century, the Jesuit CLAUDE BUFFIER, whom Thomas Reid acknowledged as his precursor. In his *Traité des premières vérités* (1717), he denounced as erroneous Descartes' idealistic principle according to which we primarily know only the modifications of our soul; he refutes Descartes by appealing to common sense. Buffier looked upon common sense not so much as a treasury of innate ideas, but " a simple disposition to think in a certain way and with a certain conjecture; for example, to affirm, while we are sensing them, that exterior objects exist " [4]. The value of this inclination he sees in its being an expression of our nature, the work of God. The principal job of the philosopher is to disengage common sense from every source of illusion, familiar habits, the curiosity of the savant, and so on.

---

[1] J. MARÉCHAL, *loc. cit.*, p. 255.

[2] **Works :** *Inquiry into the Original of Beauty and Virtue*, London, 1725. *Philosophiæ moralis institutio compendiaria*, Glasgow, 1742. *A System of Moral Philosophy*, Glasgow, 1755. — **Study :** SCOTT, W. R., *Francis Hutcheson*, New York, n. d.

[3] **Works :** *A Philosophical Inquiry into the Origin of our Ideas on the Sublime and Beautiful*, London, 1756. — **Studies :** COBBAN, A., *Edmund Burke and the Revolt against the Eighteenth Century*, New York, 1929. — MAC CUNN, J., *Political Philosophy of Burke*, New York, n. d. — MORLEY, J. M., *Edmund Burke*, New York, 1924. — MURRAY, R. H., *Edmund Burke*, Oxford, 1931. — YOUNG, G. M., *Burke*, Oxford, 1944.

[4] E. BRÉHIER, *op. cit.*, p. 333.

B) The Apogee.

The most remarkable philosopher of this group was the Scot, THOMAS REID [1] (1710-1796); he is responsible for the title, Scottish School. Faced with the ruins left by the criticism of Hume, Reid set himself to the task of taking up the problem of philosophy in its totality. He stated that everything hinged on the principle of Locke, which is both positivist and idealist : " man primarily knows only his ideas, and these ideas are, primitively, facts of consciousness of the sensible order and the elements of our whole psychological life ". He questions this very principle, but instead of subjecting it to a methodic criticism, he denies it resolutely *in the name of common sense.*

Reid defines common sense as " The degree of intelligence which is sufficient for acting with common prudence in the conduct of life, and sufficient to ascertain the true from the false in evident matters, as long as they are distinctly known " [2]. This common intelligence is exercised in each of our sensations and is the basis of all our knowledge. To explain a sensation, say, of smell, three things are distinguishable : *a)* the action of the one who smells, an act having its own proper traits; *b)* the affirmation that this act pertains to the man; *c)* the affirmation that this odor comes from the outside, as from its cause. These three aspects require a triple exercise of common sense : *a)* it distinguishes one sensation from another; *b)* it certifies the existence of the " self " as the necessary subject for supporting the affections and diverse actions of consciousness; *c)* it affirms the principle of causality, for the sensation of smell requires an odoriferous object. Thus, common sense spontaneously admits the existence of the exterior world, the existence of the " self " as thinking subject, the value of sensible experience and of the first rational principles, as that of causality. Reid thought that this belief was a sufficient refutation of Hume.

With this notion of common sense, Reid was able to restore many propositions of traditional psychology. First, the notion of the *soul* as the subject of thought. " Every act or operation supposes an agent and every quality a subject; we do not give the name of spirit to thought, or to reason, or to desire, but to the being who desires, thinks and reasons " [3]. He distinguishes several faculties in the soul, holding that this notion is not at all obscure, as Hume pretended. " Every operation supposes a *power* of the being who acts; to suppose that a thing acts without the power to act is a manifest absurdity " [4]; this power is the faculty.

The faculties of knowledge are classed according to our various immediate perceptions. Reid enumerates them in the following way. The first is *reason,* the faculty of the sciences and of philosophy, the source of the rules of morality and of esthetics,

---

[1] HAMILTON, W. (ed.), *Works*, Edinburgh, 1864. — *Studies :* DAURIAC, L., *Le realisme de Reid*, Paris, 1889. — JONES, O. M., *Empiricism and Intuitionism in Reid's Common Sense Philosophy*, Princeton (N. J.), 1927.

[2] E. BRÉHIER, *op. cit.*, II, p. 498.

[3] *Essai sur les facultés intellectuelles*, I, Ch. 1.

[4] *Ibid.*, Ch. II.

and whose basic activity is common sense. — *Consciousness* is the second faculty, " which has, for its object, our present pains, pleasures, hopes, fears, desires, doubts, thoughts of all types; in a word, all the passions, all the actions and all the operations of the soul at the moment in which they are produced " [1]. — The *external senses* are the third class; their proper activity is the immediate perception of sensible qualities and of bodies existing outside of us. — *Memory* is the fourth faculty, dealing with the immediate perception of the past; it is a primitive faculty, as inexplicable as the intuitive knowledge of the future. If we have the first, and not the latter ability, it is because " the supreme legislator has thus ordered matters ". Memory is always accompanied by belief in the past existence of the thing recalled, as perception is always accompanied by belief in the actual existence of the thing which we perceive [2].

The ideas conserved in memory combine themselves in consciousness under the influence of the *will*. They have the power to associate themselves, and habit permits the series thus formed to be reproduced with ease. But the will is the first origin of their various groupings, by putting the faculties of intelligence to work. In the affective order, Reid also has done some good analysis. He distinguishes the *appetites*, as hunger, thirst, and the need for rest, which refer to the conservation of the body, from the *desires* which are not like appetites. Desires are periodic and accompanied by disagreeable sensations, and they tend to realize social life; the principal desires are the desire for power, for good esteem and for knowledge. Reid also considers the passions in a way that will be later adopted by experimental psychology : " By the word, *passion*, I do not mean a certain class of principles of action, distinct from affections and from desires, but a certain degree of vehemence to which the affections and the desires can be carried, and which produces definite effects in the spirit and in the body " [3].

Finally, there is a *moral sense*, " the faculty by which we acquire the notions of good and of evil, and by which we recognize the morality of human actions " [4]; it is nothing else but the application of the common sense to the order of our human life.

The views of the Scottish School were continued by JAMES BEATTIE (1735-1803), who taught at the University of Aberdeen, and especially by DUGALD STEWART [5] (1753-1828), a professor of the University of Edinburgh. Stewart wrote *Elements of the Philosophy of the Human Mind*, in which he maintained Reid's position without offering any new doctrines, and " in an era in which almost the whole of England, with Bentham, was utilitarian " [6]. Reid's views reached France with the *Eclectics* [7].

---

[1] *Ibid.*, VI, Ch. V.
[2] *Ibid.*, III, Ch. I and II.
[3] JANET and SEAILLES, *Histoire de la philosophie*, p. 317.
[4] A. GONZALÈS, *Histoire de la philosophie*, III, p. 375.
[5] *Collected Works* (ed. W. Hamilton), 11 vols., Edinburgh, 1854-1858.
[6] E. BRÉHIER, *op. cit.*, II, p. 668.
[7] See below, n. 442.

In Germany, they found favor with JACOBI [1] (1743-1819), who founded truth on faith. " Man possesses a mysterious sense which receives impressions of the truth, of the beautiful, and of the moral good. The object of this spiritual sentiment *(Geistesgefühl)*, is prior to reasoning; we do not perceive the object, but we believe in it " [2], and, in this way, we escape all doubt.

The analyses of the Scottish School have a remarkable psychological finesse; in affirming the rights of common sense, Reid found the incontestable base of all true philosophy, without which there is no science, or any valid morality. St. Thomas also founded his view on the intuition of good sense, be it that of the speculative order (the habit of first principles) or of the practical order *(synderesis)* [3].

But the appeal to common sense was not sufficient to resolve the quite legitimate question of the value of all human knowledge. These timid views were not at all able to neutralize the dissolution that Hume's views had begun. The reaction of Kant's *criticism* was quite powerful, however; through his amplitude of spirit and by his originality, he opened a second period in modern philosophy.

----

[1] *Works. Werke*, 6 vols., Leipzig, 1812-1825. — *Studies.* CRAWFORD, A. W., *The Philosophy of F. H. Jacobi*, Ithaca (N. Y.), 1905. — LÉVY-BRUHL, L., *La philosophie de Jacobi*, Paris, 1894. — VON WEILLER and THIERSCH, *Jacobi's Leben, Lehre und Werken*, Münster, 1918. — WILDE, N., *Friedrich Heinrich Jacobi*, New York, 1894.

[2] D. J. MERCIER, *Critériologie générale*, p. 166.

[3] See above, n. 262.

SECOND PERIOD.

The Kantian Spirit.

(19th-20th centuries).

387. We have seen how the thinkers who followed Descartes had a common orientation in his philosophical outlook. The philosophers of the nineteenth and twentieth centuries are also rooted in Cartesianism, as reinterpreted in the critical philosophy of Kant. But this work of Kant is quite complex. It gives a new twist to the two great currents of idealism and positivism which issued from Descartes. The result is a great multitude of systems, which are quite diverse and often mutually opposed. Among these are generally distinguished the three great branches of idealism, positivism, and twentieth century pragmatism. However, between idealism and positivism, which are at opposed poles in Kantian thought, there is found, in the nineteenth century, a group of philosophers with quite different doctrines; some are Catholics and others are rationalists, but all are joined by a common esteem for tradition. Finally, since Leo XIII, Thomism finds new life, even among Catholic lay philosophers, and gradually begins to win back the place which its inner merit deserves.

This second period will comprise the following six chapters:

Chapter   I. Kant.

Chapter II. Idealism.

Chapter III. Traditionalism.

Chapter IV. Positivism.

Chapter V. Pragmatism.

Chapter VI. Neo-Thomism.

—⁓⁓⁓—

CHAPTER ONE.

KANT (1724-1804).

SPECIAL BIBLIOGRAPHY.

1° **Works :** *Werke*, J. ROZENKRANZ (ed.), 12 vols., Leipzig, 1838-1842; edition of the Academy of Berlin, 19 vols., 1902-1928. — SMITH, N. K. (transl.), *Immanuel Kant's Critique of Pure Reason*, New York, 1934.

2° **Studies :** ADICKES, E., *Kant als Naturforscher*, 2 vols., Berlin, 1924-25. — BORRIES, K., *Kant als Politiker*, Leipzig, 1928. — BOUTROUX, E., *La philosophie de Kant*, Paris, 1926. — CAIRD, E., *The Criticism of Kant*, 2 vols., Glasgow, 1889. — DEHOVE, A., *Les principes généraux de la morale kantienne*, Lille, 1912. — DELBOS, V., *La philosophie pratique de Kant*, Paris, 1905. — FISCHER, K., *Kants Leben und die Grundlage seiner Lehre*, Berlin, 1909. — KRONENBERG, J., *Kant. Sein Leben und seine Lehre*, Munster, 1904. — LINDSAY, A. D., *Kant*, New York, 1934. — MARÉCHAL, J., *Le Point de départ de la métaphysique, vol. III, La critique de Kant*, Paris, 1923. — MESSER, A., *Immanuel Kants Leben und Philosophie*, Stuttgart, 1924. — *Zu Kants ethischen und religionsphilosophischen Hauptschriften*, Leipzig, 1929. — NATORP, P., *Kant über Krieg und Frieden*, Erlangen, 1924. — REINHARD, W., *Ueber das Verhältnis von Sittlichkeit und Religion bei Kant*, Berne, 1927. — RIEHL, J., *Kant und seine Philosophie*, Berlin, 1907. — RUYSSEN, T., *Kant*, Paris, 1907. — SENTROUL, C., *La philosophie religieuse de Kant*, Brussels, 1912. — *Kant et Aristote*, Paris, 1913. — SMITH, A. H., *Kantian Studies*, Oxford, 1947. — VAIHINGER, H., *Zur Kritik der reinen Vernunft*, 2 vols., Stuttgart, 1922. — WARD, J., *A Study of Kant*, Cambridge, 1922. — WATSON, J., *Philosophy of Kant Explained*, New York, n. d. — WENLEY, R. M., *Kant and His Philosophical Revolution*, New York, 1910. — WHITNEY, G. T., and BOWERS, D. F. (eds.), *Heritage of Kant*, Princeton (N. J.), 1939. — WHITNEY, G. T., and FOGEL, P. H., *Introduction to Kant's Critical Philosophy*, New York, 1914. — WILM, E. C. (ed.), *Immanuel Kant; 1724-1924*, New Haven (Conn.), 1925.

Specialized Studies : ARDLEY, G. W., *Aquinas and Kant*, New York, 1950. — BASCH, V., *Essai sur l'esthétique de Kant*, Paris, 1927. — BOHATEC, J., *Die Religionsphilosophie Kants in der " Religion innerhalb den Grenzen der blossen Vernunft "*, Hamburg, 1938. — BOURNE, B. P., *Kant and Spencer*, New York, 1912. — CASSIRER, H. W., *A Commentary on Kant's Critique of Judgment*, London, 1938. — DEHOVE, A., *Essai critique sur le réalisme thomiste comparé à l'idéalisme kantien*, Lille, 1907. — DENCKMANN, G., *Kants Philosophie des Aesthetischen*, Heidelberg, 1950. — DE VLEESCHAUWER, H. J., *La déduction transcendentale dans l'œuvre de Kant*, 3 vols., Paris, 1934-1938. — DUNHAM, B., *Study in Kant's Aesthetics*, New York, 1934. — ENGLAND, F. E., *Kant's Conception of God*, New York, 1930. — EVELLIN F , *La raison pure et les antinomies*, Paris, 1907. — *L'évolution de la pensée* *kantienne*, Paris, 1939. — GARNETT, C. B., *Kantian Philosophy of Space*, New York, 1939. — GARRIGOU-LAGRANGE, R., *God, His Existence and Nature*, 2 vols., St. Louis (Mo.), 1948. — GRACANIN, G., *La personnalité morale d'après Kant*, Paris, 1935. — HERRLIN, O., *Ontological Proof in Thomistic and Kantian Interpretation*, Lundequistska, n. d. — JANSEN, B., *Die Religionsphilosophie Kants*, Berlin, 1929. — JONES, W. T., *Morality and Freedom in the Philosophy of Immanuel Kant*, New York, 1940. — PATON, H. J., *The Categorical Imperative : A Study in Kant's Moral Philosophy*, Chicago, 1948. — SCOTT, J. W., *Kant on the Moral Life*, New York, 1924. — SOURIAU, M., *Le jugement réfléchissant dans la philosophie critique de Kant*, Paris, 1926. — TEALE, A. E., *Kantian Ethics*, New York, 1951. — WEBB, C. C. J., *Kant's Philosophy of Religion*, Oxford, 1926.

388. Immanuel Kant was born at Königsberg in 1724. He was educated by his mother, who was an affiliate of a Protestant sect called Pietism, and greatly influenced by a pastor of the same sect, who was a friend of the family. Both influences combined to place him beyond the pale of any discussion on the existence and value of morality or of religion. At the same time, his attendance at the University of Königsberg exposed him to the modern sciences, and especially to the astronomical system of Newton; the latter impressed him greatly, and furnished him with another stalwart fact, as evident and indisputable as morality : the existence of a positive science which is necessary and universal.

Kant is a typical German thinker : very profound even to the point of obscurity; methodical even to the extreme of meticulosity; as prudent as he is bold, and strongly reliant on his predecessors (at least his immediate ones), but not fearful of bypassing them through his own reflections; defiant of intuition, but assured of conquering truth more certainly and fully by the unceasing labor of reasoning; indifferent to the beauties of style as long as it contained the force of his thought. He had all the good qualities of his race, and some of its defects. Except for a short absence, he never left his native village, and remained a university professor all his life. Living a well-regulated life, he succeeded, despite frail health, in having a long life, filled with intellectual labors and with his reflections, which are at once profound, though come about by slow, patient and persevering effort.

From the viewpoint of philosophy, his life is divisible into two periods. In the first, the " pre-critical " (1745-1772), there is a slow blossoming of the critical view in stages. At the beginning, Kant firmly believed in the objective value of reason, due to the thought of Leibniz and of Wolff [1], but without being able to justify its value; he was a dogmatic rationalist. He was quite occupied, during this time, with the positive sciences, and edited several works in this realm, as his *Thoughts on the True Estimation of Living Forces* (1747), and his *General Natural History and Theory of Heavens;* the latter contains the first hypothesis of a primitive nebula (1755).

Soon, however, his reflections became strongly aided by reading Hume (who had been translated into German in 1756). Hume interrupted his dogmatic slumber, as he himself says [2]. He had already abandoned the radical idealism of Leibniz and accepted the existence of bodies, and Newton's notions of absolute space and time. Now he began to insist on experience as the source of scientific material, as is evident in his work, *Fundamental Principles of Natural Theology and Morals* (1764).

In the meantime, Hume's empiricism had established scepticism, crushing the value of metaphysics in its treatment of supersensible realities as God and the soul, denying any validity to the positive sciences, whose necessary laws became simple habits of association, and reducing all morality to egoism [3]. Kant could not resign himself to these sacrifices.

His reflections broke forth into the " great enlightenment " of 1770, which showed him, in the idealization of space and time, the efficacious means of safeguarding the value of scientific laws. He proposed these views in his *On the Form and on the Principles of the Sensible and Intelligible World* (1770). Finally, as he explains in a letter [4], a more attentive examination made him rediscover, about 1772, the *problem of the object* which is the basis of his great critical works, the first of which appeared only after nine years of patient study.

The main works in which Kant develops his system at great length are the following : *The Critique of Pure Reason* (1781); *Prolegomenon to all Future Metaphysics* (1783); *The Foundations of the Metaphysics of Morals* (1785); *The Critique of Practical Reason* (1788); *The Critique of Judgment* (1790); *Religion within the Limits of Reason Alone* (1793). Finally, he wrote an essay, *Political Peace* (1795), and two works on *The First Metaphysical Principles of Doctrine*, the first on *Law* (1797) and the second on *Virtue* (1797).

---

[1] This was the leading philosophy of the time, and was being taught at the University.

[2] *Prolegomenon to all Future Metaphysics*, III.

[3] See above, n. 384. Between 1760 and 1770, at the same time as Hume, Kant read the British moralists, Hutcheson, Shaftesbury, and especially Rousseau. He was enthusiastic over Rousseau's view on moral conscience as the source of law and of the good. He was overjoyed at the French Revolution, and though he condemned its excesses much later, he always considered it one of the mightiest efforts undertaken by a people to found its political order on rational morality. It was during this period that he changed the course of his daily walk in order to get the latest news from France.

[4] *Letter to Mark Herz*, January 21, 1772; see J. MARÉCHAL, *Le point de départ de la métaphysique*, III, pp. 53-56.

389. The work of Kant is not easily presented. Three aspects of it can be distinguished. 1) His *vocabulary* is his own in great part, containing ordinary words with special meanings, and a great number of new technical terms; these must be understood in order to grasp his new approach to the critical problem. 2) The *conclusions* at which he arrives lead to a partial, speculative scepticism; these are understandable without too much difficulty. 3) The *reasoning process* which, in Kant's eyes, establishes his conclusions. This is the most important and the most difficult aspect of Kant, for his reasoning process constitutes the unity of his system; it measures its value and it explains its great influence. But, inasmuch as it is presented in new terminology and is developed in the abstractness of epistemology, it derails our usual habits of thought. For these reasons it has seemed necessary, in order to present Kant's thought clearly, to transpose his technical language into the corresponding vocabulary of Scholastic philosophy, and to explain his views according to the well known tract, *Critériologie*, of Cardinal Mercier[1].

This last point will not be derogatory towards an objective presentation of the thoughts of Kant. As a matter of fact, Kantianism is, itself, divided into two parts : *Kantian Science*, which examines the value of sensible experience and of concepts, corresponding to the two problems studied in general epistemology, that of the subject of judgment and that of the abstract predicate; *Kantian Metaphysics*, which examines the value of reasoning and of faith, and also resembles the problems resolved in special epistemology. A preliminary part on *the Statement of the Critical Problem* will give a general idea of Kantianism and will habituate one to his special point of view. Three articles, then, will present Kant's position :

Article I. The Statement of the Critical Problem.

Article II. The Kantian Theory of Knowledge.

Article III. The Metaphysics and Morality of Kant.

ARTICLE I.

STATEMENT OF THE CRITICAL PROBLEM.

390. Kantianism is a powerful attempt by critical philosophy to definitively establish the value of *science*, in the modern

---

[1] " Criteriology includes two sections : the first *(General Criteriology)* studies that which is common to all certitude "; this is the problem of the *true judgment* in general which examines the synthesis of judgment, the value of the abstract predicate, and then the subject, who, through sensible experience, rejoins external reality. — " The second part *(Special Criteriology)* studies the various certitudes which the human mind possesses ", obtained by inductive or deductive *reasoning*, and by authority or *faith;* D. J. MERCIER, *Critériologie*, p. 4.

sense, and to delimit the value of metaphysics, through avoiding the rationalism of Leibniz and the phenomenalism of Hume. This definition will be explained by indicating what Kant means by the object and the method of the critical problem, and from this will follow the ensemble of general marks applicable to Kantianism.

I. OBJECT OF THE CRITICAL PROBLEM.

A) Classification of Knowledge.

391. In a general way, the critical problem looks for a means of discerning, among all human certitudes, those which are infallibly true; the object of this critical approach thus embraces all types of knowledge without exception and without preference. But Kant, as most philosophers, did not construct his system in a purely objective fashion as demanded by the very science which he created; rather, he was led there, as we have seen, by his reflections on various contemporary problems. This is why he states the critical problem and delimits its object *by certifying the state of speculation in his own age.*

Kant was struck by a double fact. On the one hand, he found the *sciences* in the modern sense of the word, as mathematics, geometry, and mathematical physics which, along with Newton's astronomy, were henceforth accepted without argument. The value of all of these was consecrated by their success; that is, by the accord they held among thinkers, and the constant progress in their discoveries. On the other hand, there was *metaphysics* in the garb that it had worn since Descartes; it was the study of three principal substances: the world (Cosmology), the human soul (Psychology) and God (Theodicy). Metaphysics, in contrast with science, seemed to be but a perpetual succession of contradictory and self-destructive systems.

This led Kant to the first precision of the critical problem. One must examine, first, if metaphysics be possible before one sees if it is valuable. With regard to the sciences, one need only ask if they are infallibly true, for their success has adequately justified them. The only task remaining is to see *how* they are true, or to find the rules which reason has so well followed in constructing these sciences so gifted with truth. It is easy to see that the determination of these rules is the essential problem. The lack of success in metaphysics should doubtlessly be attributed to a fundamental error in the very functioning of reason. It should suffice to apply to metaphysics, with some modifications, the laws discovered by the sciences in order to confer on both branches of knowledge the same, definitive value.

B) Classification of Judgments.

392. Following this first precision in his thought, Kant added a second, more important one. From the first pages of his work, after having remarked (here in accord with St. Thomas), that the central object of the critical problem is the *judgment*, which is the sole depositary of truth and of error [1], he excludes from his examination judgments which are purely analytic, and synthetic a posteriori judgments (purely synthetic). He retains only *synthetic a priori judgments*, which alone, in his view, are *scientific*. Since there is question of determining the functioning of reason in the sciences, only the laws of synthetic a priori judgments can be studied profitably. Kant's whole system reposes on this classification of judgments and their meaning must be clearly grasped.

1) A judgment is called *analytic*, for Kant, when the predicate repeats and develops the *formal content* of the subject; for example, the judgment that " body is an extended substance ". A statement of this sort is but a tautology; it is sterile and incapable of helping science to progress. Moreover, it has no other value than the concept itself, which does not suffice, in his view, to express a true item of knowledge. For these reasons, the analytic judgment is not scientific. In other words, this judgment is but the application of the *principle of contradiction* to a particular concept. This principle is the most general form of analysis, and plays uniquely but a *negative role* in our judgments in the sense that every judgment implicating a contradiction is necessarily erroneous, while the absence of all contradiction does not suffice that a judgment be called true or scientific. For the concept, even upon analysis, contains no truth at all [2].

2) A judgment is called *synthetic* when the predicate is foreign to the *formal content* of the subject, and is attributed to it for another reason than merely the analysis of its content. In this sense, every judgment, except total or partial

---

[1] See St. Thomas Aquinas, *Summa Theologica*, I, q. XVI, art. 2.

[2] This affirmation is proved below, n. 401.

definitions [1], is synthetic. Thus, not only in affirming that "every man is a musician" but also in stating that "every being is intelligible", one pronounces a synthetic judgment: in the latter example the notion of intelligibility is derived from the special factor of intelligence which is not necessarily required by the notion of being. From this it follows that the synthetic judgment has the advantage over pure analysis by being *extensive*. It can enrich and advance science; for, instead of remaining in the purely ideal order of the concept, it always appeals, in some fashion or another, to the *real order* of intuition or of experience.

Kant distinguishes two types of Synthetic Judgments :

a) **Purely Synthetic Judgments** *(Synthetic, a priori judgments)* are those in which the reason for attributing a foreign predicate to a subject, is *solely the actual experience;* for example, "my teeth are hurting me", or, "this water is cold", or, "this stone is falling" (in the sense that the fact is simply and actually certified). These judgments are in no wise scientific, for they are purely *subjective*, valuable only for him who utters them. Such judgments are content with presenting a simple, sensible intuition in the form of a judgment, just as the purely analytic judgment expresses a simple concept. They lack the universality and the necessity required for the judgments of science.

b) **Synthetic, a priori Judgments** are those in which the reason for attributing a foreign predicate to a subject, is more than sensible intuition; it is rather a presupposed condition, independent of experience, added to reason in order to clothe it with necessity and universality. For example, take the judgment, "every contingent being has a cause". The notion of contingency, or of *indifference to exist or not to exist*, does not imply the notion of a cause or of a perfect and really distinct being on whom another depends for existence; nor does the reverse situation hold, if one holds to the purely *formal signification* of concepts. In order to assert and to certify that these two notions agree, one must refer to experimental reality, or to the intuition which, in Kant's view, is always of the *sensible* order.

---

[1] That is, if the definition is taken in the *strict sense*, in which the notes constituting the idea of the subject are simply made explicit by the predicate without adding any. Thus, man is definable as a reasonable animal, but not as a *sociable* animal.

At the same time, even if a sensible experience is repeated throughout the centuries and becomes rooted in us by an hereditary habit, it cannot explain and justify the necessity and the universality which belong to the principle of causality and which make it scientific. With good reason, Kant believed that Hume's empiricism destroyed all true science. This double trait of universality and necessity must, then, be explainable by an *a priori* condition which is presupposed within the spirit and thus dominates experience. Of such a sort are the synthetic a priori judgments which are scientific; for, in being synthetic, they enrich and further science, and, in being a priori, they are necessary and universal.

Not only metaphysics, but especially the modern sciences are, in Kant's view, constituted by a connected system of synthetic a priori judgments. Besides the principle of causality, he gives examples : physical theories, as the principle of conservation of energy; geometrical definitions, as that the straight line is the shortest distance from one point to another, and mathematical affirmations, as that $5 + 7 = 12$. These last judgments are evidently " a priori " (in the Kantian sense), but it is difficult to show that they are synthetic. Kant remarks that it is not needful to have an actual experience, but it is sufficient that the experience be imaginary or possible. In this sense it is true that these universal truths are not, on the one hand, pure tautologies; and, on the other, that they can always be concretized in experiential facts, and thus can be called " synthetic a priori ".

Beyond these universal judgments which are eminently scientific, we form particular or singular judgments about the real and objective order. For instance, we say, " the earth turns over on itself every 24 hours ". Since these judgments are instructive and independent of the subject, they also are, in Kant's view, scientific and synthetic a priori. They are universal and necessary in the sense that all men, in validating them, experience the same impression; consequently, they also require the intervention of necessary, a priori laws which rule the activity of our spirit [1].

Accordingly, in making the object of critical philosophy more precise by the question, In what way are synthetic

---

[1] C. SENTROUL, *Kant et Aristote*, p. 200 : " That I say, *I am warm*, is a purely subjective judgment, and quite meaningless, for Kant. But if I say, *it is getting warm*, or, *there is heat*, I must refer my impression to a proportionate cause, in which an objective judgment mediates a general notion ".

a priori judgments possible?   Kant examined all of man's
judgments in the proper sense — or all those which possessed
truth or error.

C) Value of the Kantian Classifications.

393. If one adopts the purely critical and, in itself,
legitimate view of Kant, the existence of synthetic a priori
judgments can be admitted as a new classification; in fact, it
is a defensible one.   The definitions of Kant are not contradictory, and respond to three authentic aspects of man's
intellectual life.   At the same time, this application, when
given to a group of the most important judgments man has,
is better understood if one presupposes Kant's *idealistic solution*,
in which analysis of the subject would never yield, in any
fashion, the content of the predicate except through a tautology.
If, as a matter of fact, the concept never expresses the external
reality or the thing in itself, one can no longer examine it except
in itself, independently of its object — or to the extent that
it makes us formally and actually know, and here nothing
new can be found.

In contrast, the *realistic solution* of St. Thomas permits one to
consider all necessary judgments, even those that Kant believes
scientific, as *analytic*.   In Thomism, that which is analyzed is not
the pure formal signification of the idea, but its content, the real
object as known under this formal aspect.   For instance, it is
not humanity, but a real being known as possessing humanity,
namely, *that which is man*.   From this it follows that analysis
can uncover two things : *a*) that this " note " is contained in this
subject; for example, man is animal; *b*) that in such a property
there is contained or necessarily implied the definition of the
being, even though this definition can be understood separately.
For instance, human liberty implies rationality, and the following
judgment, " man is free " is analytic, even though human nature
can be defined without thinking of liberty [1].
One could also, in other formulations, distinguish a double
comprehension in the concept.   The first is the *logical*, or formal
and subjective, aspect, which makes the concept *distinct*, but not
complete, including only the notes of the definition (or of the

---

[1] In other words, analysis disengages *whatever is per se proper to a thing*.
Several cases can be distinguished.   " Primus modus dicendi per se est, quando
id quod attribuitur alicui pertinet ad formam ejus ", and this description fits
the tautological analysis defined by Kant.   " Secundus modus dicendi per se
est, quando subjectum ponitur in definitione prædicati quod est proprium
accidentis ejus ", and this is the analysis which enriches knowledge, but which
Kant rejects.   See St. Thomas Aquinas, *In I Analyticorum*, Lesson X; see
also J. Mercier, *Criteriologie*, p. 235.

quasi-definition, of analogical terms). The other is the *ontological*, or the real and objective, aspect, which makes the concept *complete*, and *adequate* for us, including all the properties which necessarily flow from the definition; this concept is equivalent to the perfect knowledge of the real object which it expresses. Thus, liberty is not contained in the *logical* comprehension of the concept of man, but in its *ontological* comprehension. Similarly, the property of having a cause does not lie in the formula, but in the real comprehension of contingence.

Since he was an idealist, Kant admitted only the first comprehension, and ignored any analytic bond affirmed by the extensive judgment between a property and its essence. St. Thomas, being a realist, admits the two types of comprehension and the double analysis which comprises all scientific judgments, even extensive ones. This basic opposition explains the repugnance of most Scholastics to admit the existence of synthetic a priori judgments [1], and one could hardly accept Kant's classification as any speculative progress. Nevertheless, according to the rules of historical method which oblige one to know and appreciate the proper value of the various points of view adopted by philosophers, it must be said that Kant's error does not lie in this first, preliminary classification, and that the latter can be legitimately used in delimiting the object of the critical problem.

Similarly, science in the Thomistic sense is restricted solely to judgments that are formally universal, and is thus distinguishable from Kantianism, which comprises all synthetic a priori judgments. Both critical views, however, have the same object; Thomism examines *all* judgments, scientific or not, while Kant calls scientific *all* judgments properly so called.

II. THE CRITICAL METHOD.

394. In order to answer the new question which he had formulated — How are synthetic a priori judgments possible? — Kant used a new, double method which he adapts to his own purposes, and which is much better than the psychological analysis of the English thinkers. The method is that of *critical reflection*, or the examination of knowledge from the viewpoint of its functioning and of the value of its affirmations. This reflection has two aspects.

1) **Critical analysis,** whose aim is to determine the elements and the laws which intervene, when a true judgment is produced. It is readily distinguished from the psychological analysis of Locke and Hume, who used the theory of the clear idea and the hypothesis that complex ideas are merely compounded

---

[1] For example, BARBEDETTE (*Histoire de la philosophie*, p. 469), having noted that every system rests on this classification, declares that synthetic, a priori judgments do not exist. This criticism seems a bit superficial.

of simple ideas. Kant justly looked upon their method as arbitrary and inadequate, for it neglects the fact that truth pertains to the judgment alone, and that judgment is not a static construction similar to a composite in which each atom retains its own nature, but is rather a living and complex action, whose elements can become modified in being mutually related. Critical analysis, then, is the examination of this living action of judgment in order to determine the conditions under which it is true; for instance, it asks if sensible material is required, or a universal concept, and so on.

This analysis is thus distinguished from the objective or logical analysis, which divides the potential totality into its subjective parts, as that of a universal genus and its various species. It can be compared to demonstration in a broad sense, or to a sort of critical induction in which we determine, by simple, reflective certification, both the material and the laws of our intellectual activity. Briefly, one can say that *critical analysis* (or, *transcendental analysis*, as Kant will call it) is an effort at an intuitive sort of reflection, bearing on the scientific [1] judgment, in order to determine its constitutive elements and the laws of its union.

2) **Critical Deduction** is that through which one demonstrates the absolute necessity of admitting one or another condition on the judgment, under penalty of destroying the objective judgment itself, and of making all truth, all thought and all intellectual and human life impossible. This procedure is similar to the demonstration by absurdity used in the Thomistic criticism of the judgment. Kant, however, gave it a new importance and a quite special development; for, being deprived of basing it on external reality, he viewed it as the sole permanent foundation of thought. On it he founded the objective value of universal and necessary science, independently of any purely psychological habit or of any purely subjective intervention.

Kant called his method *transcendental reflection*, since it examines the judgment in the preliminary conditions required even before the judgment has any content. These conditions are, accordingly, called *a priori;* that is, they actually make judgment possible, no matter what the object to which it applies. In more simple terms, we can say that this reflection is not developed in a spontaneous fashion (as, for example,

---

[1] This judgment, according to Kant, is the a priori, synthetic judgment.

in psychology), but in a critical order, which, leaving in the penumbra of methodic doubt all the particular objects of judgments, *goes beyond them* to look upon the manner of judging in general (and, in this sense, is transcendental).

More precisely, this reflection examines the faculties of knowledge *in action* [1], by abstracting at once from the diversity and from the substantial reality of the objects known, as well as from the ontological reality of these faculties [2]. This reflection, then, looks upon the faculties as laws, regulating the actions which flow from them.

Kant also uses the qualitative term, *pure* (for instance, *pure* reason, *pure* concept or *pure* science) to name these faculties, concepts or sciences. By this term he aims to show that they are considered in the laws of their activity, or in that part of their object which depends uniquely on these subjectively necessary and universalizing laws; and that abstraction is made from all else (in particular, from any application to external reality and to the facts of detailed experience).

For these reasons, at the beginning of his criticism, and in order to give himself an object for incontestable study which would in no wise prejudice his solution (on the objective or subjective value of our judgments), Kant distinguishes a double object of the synthetic a priori judgment.

a) The object without which the judgment could not be understood as a fact of consciousness for examination; Kant calls this the *phenomenal object*. It is the objective content of the judgment taken in itself, abstraction being made of its inherence in a faculty and in a soul as its subject, and abstraction being made of its representative value of an objective reality, distinct from every fact of consciousness.

b) The real object, which he calls the *noumenal object;* this brings up a problem whose solution is reserved to the second portion of Kant's work, metaphysics.

395. In Kant's view, the critical problem supposes three things as given, each of which is indispensable. 1) The existence of spontaneous certitudes; these are the synthetic a priori judgments to be examined. 2) The power of critical or transcendental

---

[1] Criticism studies the judgment; but the latter, for Kant, is a work of several faculties acting together : sensation, imagination and understanding *(Verstand)* ; see below, n. 401.

[2] Kant does not ask whether these faculties are accidents, nor if there is a substantial soul to support them.

reflection.   3) The fact of necessary certitudes concerning which no doubt can be had : this means the acceptance of scientific judgments as valid, in which one looks for the reasons of validity. These same three items can be used to set up the basis for an epistemology of Thomistic inspiration [1]. Moreover, Kant's position is less rigorously critical, since he admits, without restriction, all scientific laws, while, on the other hand, special epistemology would even study in what measure they are valid.

The very notion of the phenomenal object, taken as the unqualified beginning of criticism, is very similar to the effort of any universal doubt, negative and methodic though partially fictional, which one can require, with strict, scientific method, at the beginning of epistemology [2].   Both Kant and Thomism are concerned with not presupposing any doctrine before justifying others, and also of avoiding an arbitrary dogmatism.   If this exact restriction is placed on Kant's notion, so that the phenomenal object is but a pure abstraction which neither affirms subjectivism nor realism, one can accept it as quite legitimate, in the same sense that his synthetic a priori judgments were accepted above.

But here also, a profound divergence quickly reveals itself. Kant, fascinated by the idealistic prejudice (to which his solution is consecrated), perseveres in his viewpoint of the phenomenal object, and concludes with a justification of the value of all modern sciences without making any appeal to the reality of the things of nature (except as a vague postulate). Thomism, on the contrary, even in its first critical reflections, aims to find the motive of infallible truth in objective evidence.   It validates the evident possession of objective reality through scientific judgments; since it is free from prejudice, it sees this fact as among those objectively given with the critical problem, and thus completely abandons the purely subjective view at the beginning.

For this reason, while realizing that Kant's error does not lie in his conception of the phenomenal object, this notion cannot be accepted as any sign of progress, for its usage has meaning only in terms of the idealistic hypothesis.

III.   COMPREHENSIVE VIEW OF THE CRITICAL PROBLEM.

396. The presentation of Kant's views has shown how he faced the critical problem.   One can readily disengage four distinctive characteristics of his quite complex system.   It is at once a conservative and a pitiless criticism; it is idealist and tries to unify the resulting dualism by the idea of law.

---

[1] See D. J. MERCIER, *op. cit.*, p. 38, where he writes : " The problem can be formulated in these terms. When the intellect reflects on its spontaneous adherence, can it in any way discern which are legitimate from those which are not? ".   Much later (p. 122), Mercier states that the mind is in possession of certitudes at the beginning of its critical search, making doubt impossible.

[2] This is the view of the school of Mercier; see above, n. 321.

1) **Conservative.** This first trait of Kantianism results especially from his attitude towards the modern sciences; he accepts them without distinctions. One could remark that *physics* went through as many fluctuations as metaphysics; but Kant was subjected to the rise of the great discoveries of Newton and Galileo, and was especially fascinated by the immemorial stability of mathematics. Thus, far from posing as a sceptic or a revolutionary, Kant proposed to justify the validity of all human knowledge; first, of the sciences, and then of metaphysics, which he wished to establish as solidly as were the sciences.

2) **Critical.** Nevertheless, despite his intentions, he fell into disastrous results, at least with regard to the " science " [1] of metaphysics, and all through the demands of his criticism. This trait, which is of the very essence of Kantianism, ordinarily makes his view resolve into a *scepticism*. This is true if partial or relative scepticism is meant in regard to things in themselves; this scepticism arose from his idealism, and it is only partial because Kant concludes by admitting a *belief* in reality founded on morality.

3) **Idealistic.** This is the most profound mark of Kantian thought. In its negative form — " the thing-in-itself is evidently unknowable " — it often appears in his thought, and then with the value of a conclusion demonstrated by his whole critical system. But before being demonstrated in any way, it is already admitted as a latent presupposition, or as a self-evident axiom.

Idealism seems to have imposed itself on Kant for two reasons, which are but two forms of the opposition between subject and object. *a*) The opposition between *thing-in-itself* and *thing-within-us* seems to make the seizure of an object by consciousness, which is not a fact of consciousness, contradictory. *b*) The opposition between *the concrete and the abstract* also plays a role, for even if reality comes into us somehow by sensations, which Kant admits, it has the marks of contingency and of particularity which are absolutely opposed to the universality and the necessity of science. Kant thereupon concludes that reason must add these traits from its own inner depths, so that science cannot express, for the most part, anything but our ideas.

---

[1] *Science* here is used in the Thomistic sense; or, better, wisdom. See above, **n.** 266-7.

The consequence of this idealism is an irreducible duality, between that which appears (or the *phenomenon*) and that which is (or the *noumenon*). As a result, to these two objects there correspond two faculties, and two special parts of knowledge. 1) It is the understanding *(Verstand)* which applies its concepts to sensible phenomena in order to constitute objective science. 2) It is reason *(Vernunft)* [1] which thinks in a vacuum on the unknowable noumenon, by means of ideas which make up the science of metaphysics. " All human knowledge begins with *intuitions*, then goes to *concepts*, and is completed in *ideas* " [2].

Accordingly, there are two large divisions, " The Kantian Theory of Knowledge " and the " Moral Metaphysics ", which will be studied just below.

4) **Normal.** Faithful to the demands of unity, Kant tried to remedy this dualism by the idea of *normality* or of *law*, which is thus the unifying and foundational idea of his thought. In order that science have objective value and be true, it suffices that it be built on the necessary *laws* of understanding. In order that metaphysics (the work of the speculative reason) also find its objectivity and truth, it is sufficient to consider reason under another aspect, that of practical reason subject to moral *law;* the latter is law in the highest sense, and it brings forth the highest type of truth.

Thus the idea of law dominates and unifies the whole system. It permits Kant to look upon himself as the savior of all human knowledge, so viciously menaced by Hume. At the same time, he can disengage himself from the rationalism of Leibniz, whose affirmations and arbitrary theories could not hold up under the criticisms of Hume.

ARTICLE TWO.
THE KANTIAN THEORY OF KNOWLEDGE.

397. For Kant, as for the moderns, the *sciences* (in the modern sense) have, as their unique object, the *phenomena* which are to be reduced to mathematical laws. Thus, in his

---

[1] The German word *Verstand* is translated by the English, understanding, implying the ensemble of discursive operations of the spirit, to conceive, to judge and to reason (A. LALANDE, *Vocabulaire technique de la philosophie*, " Entendement ", Maaning, " C "). *Vernunft* is translated by the English word, reason; it is rather badly chosen, but is common practice. See below, n. 406. — [2] *Critique of Pure Reason*, Part I, Conclusion.

endeavor to justify the value of these sciences, by showing that their method is conformable to the natural laws of the human spirit, Kant sees nothing inconvenient in holding strictly to the critical view of the phenomenal object. Through this method he aimed to mount above the two currents of rationalism and positivism to that synthetic point in which these two were joined. In so doing, he comes to re-establish a Thomistic proposition, that every true judgment of the human mind (that is, every *perfectly objective* knowledge in which the knowing subject is opposed to the object known, in knowing itself or in affirming the object evidently conformable to itself) necessarily requires two elements : sensation, and an abstract concept, joined by the intermediary of the imagination, and synthesized in the very activity of judgment [1].

But the quite abstract point of view in which Kant moved prevented him from finding the whole doctrine of St. Thomas, and he succeeds in seeing but a part of it, colored by his own nuances and restrictions, some of them erroneous, as shall be shown. The object of critical philosophy thus corresponds to two points in a Thomistic view : the examination of sensible experience, and of the universal concept [2].

With regard to the proposition of objective evidence as the supreme motive of infallible truth [3], Kant seems to admit it implicitly when he considers scientific judgments as infallibly true, for these judgments necessarily involve a knowing subject faced with a known object and asserting itself to be in evident conformity with it.

But this viewpoint is completely implicit and wholly unexplored in Kantianism, whose total effort is to discover the *how* of the process; that is, the laws of the functioning of true judgments, before delimiting its legitimate applications.

---

[1] The two theories are identical only in a very broad sense; their divergences will be noted below, see n. 403. Here are some Thomistic axioms which are similar to Kant's views : nothing is in the intellect without first having been in the sense; there is no intellection without conversion to phantasms; the subject of every judgment, at least in the ultimate sense, is the concrete individual; the predicate is always an abstract concept; the intelligible species arises from the phantasm as from an instrumental cause and from the active intellect as from a principal cause.

[2] D. J. MERCIER, *op. cit.*, Book IV, " The solution of the objective value of our judgments ". This can be shown by *a*) showing the objective value of sensible experience, and *b*) showing that the universal concept has the same validity (p. 352).

[3] This proposition is a solution to the first problem : Do we possess a criterion of truth? D. J. MERCIER, *loc. cit.*, p. 244.

Without a doubt, to do this is indirectly to delimit even the application of objective evidence. But Kant did not sound out this latter point, not even with regard to the law of intellectual activity which is presupposed by evidence and whose consideration would reverse all his idealistic conclusions. There are, then, only two points to examine in order to justify science in Kant's theory.

    I. The Objective Value of Sensible Experience.

    II. The Objective Value of Universals.

I. THE OBJECTIVE VALUE OF SENSIBLE EXPERIENCE.

398. Kant entitles this part of his criticism, *Transcendental Esthetic* [1], taking the latter word in its etymological meaning of a *critical examination of sensibility* or of sensible experience. Without becoming involved in the quite complicated and technical details of his view, one can present his solution in three steps, and complete it with two corollaries.

A) **Solution.**

1) **Passivity of the Senses.** By critical analysis, Kant first certified that in all our judgments (synthetic a priori) there remains, after having eliminated that which comes from our own activity, a primitive, " given " element, which has a double trait. First, it imposes itself on us from without so that we are plainly *passive* in its regard. Second, it is contingent, multiple and variable, so that it furnishes the variety of facts required by special, scientific experiences.

In order to fixate these notions, Kant, following his habitual custom, introduces here some technical terms with a new meaning. In order to receive this impact from without, or that which is " given " and imposed, there must be a *passive faculty*, or, in the critical sense, a function of this receptivity. Kant calls this *sensibility*. That which is thus given constitutes the materials of experience, or the material object which we know under a certain aspect; Kant calls this *sensation* (in the sense of *sensatum* and not of *sensatio*). Finally, the act of sensible knowledge itself is called *sensible intuition;* but in order to be produced, it requires something else besides " sensation ".

---

[1] From αἴσθησις, sensibility. There is no question or reference here to the beautiful.

2) **The A Priori Forms of Sensibility.** A second reflection shows that every act of sensibility is necessarily ruled by two previous conditions : *space* (for the external senses) and *time* (for the internal senses) [1]. These two conditions play the role of necessity and universality. They are *necessary*, for to suppress them is to destroy by that act every sensible action, whereas the suppression of every particular experience leaves them immutable in themselves. They are *universal*, for they are required for all the acts of sensibility whatever they may be, and without exception.

They are thus opposed to what is contingently " given ", which functions as matter; they are thus *a priori* and play the determining role of form. This is why Kant called them the two *a priori forms* of sensibility; they do not in any way pertain to reason, as will now be shown.

3) **The Imperfection of the Pure Phenomenon.** The total action of sensible intuition is thus composed of a matter and a form — of the " sensation " unified by the " a priori forms " of space and time — and the sensible object thus elaborated is called the *phenomenon* [2]. Now, critical analysis makes it evident that these forms, universal and necessary in themselves, lose these two traits by uniting themselves immediately to the contingently " given " material. As a matter of fact, they concretize themselves, so that the pure, sensible phenomenon is fully identified with the passing and individual act of our consciousness, and as a consequence, it is incapable alone of being an object endowed with truth. In itself, the knowing subject is not sufficiently opposed to its object in order to know whether or not it is conformable to the object. The " phenomenon " can furnish an element for a true judgment, but standing alone it is but the object of an imperfect and partial knowledge. Thus, sensible intuition, even expressed in the judgment form, remains a purely synthetic judgment, without any scientific value. Kant calls it the " judgment of perception ", distinct from apperception [3] or the judgment

---

[1] The happenings of events of consciousness have no extension in the proper sense; the only a priori condition which governs them is temporal succession; but when the internal senses, as memory and imagination, also grasp the facts of external experience, the latter are regulated at once by both a priori forms of space and of time.

[2] The bare, sensible fact as it exists in nature is also called a *phenomenon*.

[3] This terminology goes back to Leibniz, who distinguished mute perceptions from *apperceptions* (clear perceptions); see above, n. 362.

of experience, which is a synthetic a priori one. Thus, in order to attain truth, *a*) something sensibly " given " is always necessary (as against the rationalists), and *b*) it alone is insufficient (against the empiricists).

This last conclusion, to the extent of its positive affirmation, rediscovers a precise truth. The Thomistic epistemology also considers sensation as a simple element of judgment, necessary but incapable alone of conferring truth. In addition, since our sensations are not fully disengaged from matter, they necessarily have a concrete object, always placed in space and in time. One can say, from the purely subjective view which is that of Kant, that the organic character of our sensible faculties is a preliminary condition (a priori form) which determines them to seize their object as always and necessarily in space and in time. It should be noted, though, that this viewpoint is quite incomplete, and if it alone were used to explain whatever occurs in passing from the reality of the sensible object, it would also lead to the idealistic error.

B) Corollaries : Geometry and the Exterior World.

399. 1) Kant requires that space be a priori, universal and necessary in order to make geometry possible as a pure science; that is, geometry considered in itself as a connected succession of necessary and universal judgments, bearing on possible objects, independently of the concrete realizations of these objects. If geometric notions draw all their value from experience, they could not signify that which need be absolutely; for example, that every triangle should have three angles equal to two right angles, but they would only state that which had been certified. The geometric notions would be only a resume of past experiences with possible future exceptions. One could not, then, explain their value, Kant concludes, by the necessity of the a priori forms of sensibility; this is a new proof of the a priori character of these notions, since it is an incontestable fact that geometry is a science.

One can certainly concede that the necessity of geometric theorems is based neither on pure induction (as the laws of experimental physics) nor on a purely metaphysical necessity : they express the laws governing the constructions of our imagination. But geometry does not have these subjective laws as its unique foundation; it is also based on the laws of real quantity. Here, again, the affirmations of Kant, taken in their direct and positive sense, are admissible; but, in the exclusive sense they have within the " Critique ", they lead to the idealistic error.

2) The passivity of sensation evidently supposes *the existence of the exterior world*. Kant admits this consequence, stating that he never doubted it. In order to answer the accusation of scepticism [1], he introduced, in the second edition of his

---

[1] A review of Kant's *Critique of Pure Reason* accused Kant of absolute idealism; Hamann called him the " Prussian Hume ". — Many commentators,

Critique of Pure Reason, a refutation of idealism founded on the testimony of consciousness [1]. It should be mentioned, however, that this proof has only the value of an argument *ad hominem,* for the principle of causality in Kantianism is inefficacious if one begins from the self. As for the rest, in the *Transcendental Esthetic,* the existence of the exterior world cannot be a truth fully justified, since only a portion of the scientific judgment which it affirms has been examined. It is thus admitted as a *postulate,* and, to that extent, is legitimate. The rest of his criticism will show in what measure we can know the things of nature either by the sciences, by metaphysical ideas, or by the belief founded on morality.

II. Objective value of universals.

400. This second portion of Kant's *Critique* is called *Transcendental Analytic* (or transcendental logic), just as Aristotle called his logic the first and second analytics, because he studied the judgment, or reasoning, not so much as a "complex totality" but in its first, simple elements, *the concepts.* It should not be forgotten that Kant always speaks from the critical (transcendental) viewpoint; there is no question here of objective concepts, as in Aristotle's predicaments, but only of the laws of the functioning of judgments. It is this which will now be explained by first looking at Kant's notion of demonstration, then at the value of science thus justified.

A) **Demonstration.**

401. There is question here, not merely of certifying, by analysis, the presence of the concept in the true judgment, but of demonstrating the necessity, through reduction to absurdity, of what Kant calls the *transcendental deduction of concepts.* To this proof, he adds two complementary theories to explain fully how the synthetic a priori judgment is formed.

ı) **Necessity of Concepts.** Critical reflection, Kant believes, demonstrates that to have a true judgment it is necessary

---

as K. Fischer, B. Erdmann, believe that Kant changed his doctrine in demonstrating the existence of a "thing-in-itself", since the latter had, at first, no role in knowledge. Other historians, as Boutroux and Maréchal, believe that they can show that this point is well unified in Kant's system.

[1] *Transcendental Analytic,* Book ıı, Ch. ıı, Sect. 3, n. 4. Kant wanted to prove that the "consciousness of my existence as determined in time" is not possible except through the existence of real things which I perceive outside of myself.

to add to sensible knowledge a function of an active, superior faculty called understanding *(Verstand)*. Understanding is the spirit whose role is to clothe what is sensibly given with universality and necessity, and thus to constitute the sensibly given as an object of thought.

What follows is a summary of this " deduction " in Scholastic terminology.

Every truth [1] in the proper sense, supposes three things. 1) That the thinking subject knows himself at least implicitly *(in actu exercito)*. 2) That the thinking subject distinguishes itself from the true object about which it thinks. 3) That it refers the object to itself by declaring that it is conformable or identical with the object. For example, the true judgment, " man is free ", signifies " I have consciousness that my judgment (which is myself-judging) expresses well that which stands opposed to me, this object of thought, " man ". In other words, every judgment demands opposition between the knowing subject and the object known, reduced to unity by consciousness. This unity Kant calls the *unity of pure apperception*, not expressing a substantial self in Descartes' sense, but only a logical condition which permits the production of a true judgment (an apperception). But what should especially be noted is that this unity is synthetic; that is, it embraces the opposition of subject-object.

Now, Kant muses, this opposition is impossible, on the one hand, if one takes the pure sensible phenomenon separately; for sensibility, which has an intuition of the phenomenon, is wholly passive and incapable of returning to itself by reflection in order to oppose itself to that which it knows. On the other hand, this opposition would be possible, even as a relation to a contingent and concrete object, for an *intuitive intelligence which would*, while knowing, *create* the very concrete content itself of its idea. There would then be a distinction of cause and effect. But this is surely not the case in our scientific knowledge, which is purely speculative [2].

---

[1] We are speaking here of *logical* truth as a property of the judgment, according to Kant and St. Thomas.

[2] In other words, the subject-object opposition is impossible in a purely analytic judgment (in understanding alone), for the concept, being *abstract*, has no *content*, and is not an object in the proper sense. It is an *empty form* which can be filled only by a *phenomenon*, the object of sensible intuition. On this point, Thomism corrects the transcendental deduction, by recognizing in the abstract concept an intuitive validity in the broad sense; see below, n. 409.

The possibility remains that this opposition is not possible for our scientific judgments except through apprehension of what is sensibly given, under a universal and necessary aspect. From this, in fact, comes the sensible content which, as has been shown, coming from without, makes itself to be the object. At the same time, the universal and necessary point of view which surpasses this sensibly contingent " given " allows the thinking subject (in the understanding) to distinguish itself from its object and to seize it by opposing itself to it [1].

Thus, the second condition so that the scientific (synthetic a priori) judgment can be possible is that there be, beyond the sensibly given, a function capable of making the object universal and necessary. This function has an active and determining role as form in relation to the sensible phenomenon which is its matter. It is a requisite and preliminary condition, not of a temporal or psychological priority, but of a critical one. Without it, every true judgment becomes impossible. It is, then, an *a priori form* of the understanding. Kant calls it the *concept* or the *category*. Inasmuch as there are several species of judgment, affirmative and negative, universal and particular, and others, there are several sorts of universalizing and necessitating functions. Kant numbers twelve of them; they are the twelve concepts or categories (a priori forms of understanding) [2] which have nothing in common with the name or with the ten predicaments or categories of Aristotle.

---

[1] Sense, on the contrary, in seizing a concrete object under its concrete aspect, cannot, itself, be distinguished from the object.

[2] Below is a table of Kant's twelve categories, the details of which are unimportant, and were not even retained by his disciples. See J. COLLINS, *A History of Modern European Philosophy*, pp. 483-490, and p. 488, table.

Logical Table of Judgments.		Table of Categories.
a. According to Quantity.	General. Particular. Singular.	*a*) Unity. *b*) Plurality. *c*) Totality.
b. According to Quality.	Affirmative. Negative. Indeterminate. (when the predicate is negative).	*a*) Reality. *b*) Negation. *c*) Limitation.
c. According to Relation.	Categorical. Hypothetical. Disjunctive.	*a*) Substance. *b*) Causality. *c*) Mutual Action.
d. According to Modality.	Problematic. Assertoric. Apodictic.	*a*) Possibility — Impossibility. *b*) Existence — Non-existence. *c*) Necessity — Contingency.

These concepts are not innate ideas, though similar to them by being a priori. They are not known in themselves, but are merely elements made known by critical reflection as necessary to perfect or true knowledge, which pertains only to the judgment.

2) **Complementary Theories.** Wishing to explain, basically, *how* the synthetic a priori judgment is produced, Kant remarks that the sensible phenomenon and the concept are too absolutely opposed to be unified without an intermediary. If the phenomenon would be lacking, the concept would have to concretize itself as the a priori forms of space and time, and it would lose its reason for being. Kant found this intermediary in a general frame of reference, pertaining at one and the same time to the sensible by its concrete elements and to the intelligence by its indetermination; these are the so-called *schematisms of the imagination*. The schematism is not a static image, but rather a method of constructing the image in time; for instance, the method of representing a causal influence [1]. There are twelve schematisms which prolong, so to speak, each concept towards the sensible in order to permit the changeful multiplicity of phenomena to be synthesized in an essence which will be the object of universal and necessary science; or, as Kant says, of " being *subsumed* by the a priori unity of the concept ".

This synthesis is not produced haphazardly. For each concept the synthesis follows special laws which Kant determined, calling them *principles of pure understanding*, or fundamental principles of all true knowledge [2].

3) **Conclusion and Examples.** As a result of these critical reflections, every synthetic a priori judgment is a complex whole, necessarily formed of three elements. 1) Sensible intuition is the first element as the matter of judgment; it comprises the experientially given which is passively received, and the a priori sensible form. 2) The concept, or a priori intellectual form, is the second element. 3) The schematism,

---

[1] This can be explained by a comparison : the spatial image of a triangle will necessarily be equilateral, isosceles or scalene; the schematism would be the imaginative method of construction, common to the three species of triangles.

[2] Kant classed them into various categories, as " axioms of intuition ", " anticipations of perception ", " analogies of experience " and " postulates of empirical thought in general ".

or intermediary of the imagination [1] is the third element. For example, in order to pronounce this a priori synthetic judgment, " The rising of liquids in a void has a cause ", the understanding, in Kant's view, formulates a hypothetical judgment, as " If one posits the rising of a liquid, one necessarily posits its cause ". This judgment is such that there is between the two terms a bond of non-reciprocal dependence, that of effect upon cause. The raising of the liquid depends on the weight of the atmosphere, and not vice versa. Thus, when a savant perceives the concrete fact of a liquid raising itself in a void, the *a priori form of causality* is released in his spirit; and, beyond the frame of *temporal succession* (schematism of the concept of causality) and in virtue of the principle or general law that " all changes occur in following the liaison of effects and causes ", he pronounces the scientific judgment, " the raising of liquids in a void is produced by atmospheric pressure ".

Taking another example, in affirming that " each man loves the good ", the understanding pronounces a categorical judgment; that is, it asserts the static inherence of this love in humanity, in the fashion of an accident inhering in a substance. Then, as soon as a psychologist perceives a good, concrete act of man, the *a priori form of substance* is let loose in his spirit, and, beyond the frame of temporal simultaneity (the schematism of the concept, substance), and in virtue of the general law that " substance persists throughout phenomenal changes and its quantity is neither augmented nor diminished in nature " [2], he judges that the " love of the good " immutably pertains to man, remaining the same in itself despite the number of good actions. In other words, he pronounces that " each man loves the good ".

B) Various Points of View : Critical; — Psychological.

402. In order to grasp the deep meaning of these views, one must adopt the same critical stance that Kant had. Now, the Thomistic criticism demonstrates the objective value of universals by certifying, through critical induction, the identification of the object (the abstract nature taken absolutely) with the content of sensible intuition. Kant arrives at a similar conclusion through

---

[1] The object of this judgment is the *phenomenon*, so that this term designates these three different things : a) *the brute phenomenon*, which is simply the experientially given; 2) *the sensible phenomenon*, which is this " given " material unified by space and time; 3) *the scientific phenomenon*, which is the fact under the form of a universal and necessary law.

[2] See J. MARÉCHAL, *op. cit.*, pp. 142-3.

a quite different process of critical reasoning which can be formulated as follows : if one does not admit the value of universals, one makes every true judgment impossible. But the very abstract view of the " phenomenal object " in which he reasons, narrows down the scope of his thesis. He considers pure knowledge, whether sensible or intellectual, abstracting from the reality of its object; he thus shows the necessity of uniting the receptive, sensible functions, which are passive, with active intellectual [1] abstraction through the mediation of the imagination, in order to get a true judgment. But here, again, he is silent as to whether this true judgment bears on the thing-in-itself, or whether it has merely subjective value. — The Thomistic attitude, in contrast, by examining the senses and universals, fully justifies the objective value (aptitude for expressing the real) of every judgment whether it be of the ideal or of the experimental order, if it is immediately evident. Briefly, holding to the positive aspect of the Kantian position thus far proposed, a Thomist could accept this much of Kant as a portion of his own larger and more inclusive view.

However, it is quite difficult to maintain this strictly critical point of view. No Kantian interpreter has succeeded at this, and even Kant himself occasionally departed from it, despite himself, to enter into the psychological and ontological domain which is clearly that of St. Thomas. One can set up comparisons here, however, which will show the great divergence between these two views.

a) **The Psychological Point of View. 403.** The *a priori forms* of understanding can be compared to the active intellect, which is somewhat like a preliminary condition, and, in this sense, a priori required to explain the universality and necessity of scientific judgments. The schematisms correspond to the instrumental role of the phantasm, so that the intelligible species, while going beyond the concrete through its aptitude at expressing an infinite number of subjects, retains several traits borrowed from the concrete by virtue of the specification imposed on it by the phantasm.

But an essential difference separates the two theories. On the one hand, the agent intellect does not make the object expressed by the universal concept or the judgment *out of nothing*. This content is totally drawn out from concrete reality and the agent intellect is content to *leave aside* the individual characteristics in order to reveal the absolute nature or abstract essence; for instance, humanity in Paul. — In contrast, the *a priori form constitutes the content* of the object, independently of reality. That which is known by the synthetic a priori judgment is the phenomenon which is a scientific fact but for the most part subjective; then the exterior world, from which it has drawn its origin with

---

[1] It is true that Kant did not explain the psychological theory of *abstraction*, but one can say that the active role of concepts in making the phenomenon universal and necessary is but another way of expressing the *abstractive role* of our intelligence, disengaging the universal and necessary essence from the concrete.

the aid of sensation, is but a postulate and is never known as substance.

When Kant states in technical language that " the concept is a necessary, a priori condition to make the constitution of the object as such possible ", there are two possible ways in which he can be taken. The concept is but a pure function of necessary universalization alone, and nothing can be concluded as to the content of the object known (a legitimate, critical meaning); the concept constitutes the content of the object of judgment, and Kant did not escape this second (psychological) and erroneous meaning.

Kant did not complete his critical viewpoint by the psychological study of abstraction in order to rediscover the only true theory of moderate realism. Ignorant of this solution, he knew only the two opposed errors of Plato's exaggerated realism and the nominalism of the empiricists (Hume). He resolved the problem of universals by conceptualism [1], believing this to be the only possible conciliation.

In addition, in order to explain the judgments bearing on the real order, St. Thomas maintains the close collaboration of senses and intellect, along with their perfect distinction. Two complementary theories enabled him to do so : the first being that " the universal nature [2] is the *per accidens* object of sensation ", and the second that " the concrete, singular thing is, *indirectly*, the *object known* by intellect ". The content expressed by both knowledges, *sensible and intellectual*, is perfectly identical; it is that which is real (the material object), but the manner of knowing (formal object), is irreducible. The senses know through the *concrete* aspect an individual reality intuitively seized; the mind knows under the aspect of essence, as a participation in being, and consequently as a nature indifferent to individuality and actual existence, but clothed with a demand for full intelligibility which infinitely surpasses the concrete. — Kant, however, having no sort of union with objective reality, conceived the synthesis of sensation and of intellection in the judgment of experience by the *compenetration* of formal objects. Two complementary adages can state his views : " intuition without a concept is blind ", and " the concept without sensible intuition is empty ". Taken separately, each of these lacks truth and, as a result, has no independent formal objects. They are but two incomplete elements (matter and form), necessary for the only true type of knowledge, the synthetic a priori judgment.

b) **From the Ontological Viewpoint.** It is easy to see what one can deduce concerning the value of science for Kant; that will be done in the conclusion to this article, below.

---

[1] Kant's conceptualism, however, is so unique that it should not be confused with other forms.

[2] The universal nature is the *per accidens* object of sense; not the whole universal nature, but that which is quite easy to comprehend and which the mind immediately grasps on the occasion of a sensation. Thus, one *sees* a substance, that is, a man.

C) Value of the Kantian Science.

404. Having demonstrated the critical necessity of concepts, Kant concludes that their usage is always legitimate and susceptible of truth, if the subject of judgment is something sensibly given. He adds, as a consequence which he believes evident, that this legitimate usage is *limited* in application to the sensible; the concept, without intuition, is empty. He thus falls into a positivism and an idealism of a special type, so that he was able to conserve, in a new way, the truth and the objectivity of sciences in their modern acceptation.

I. **Intellectual Positivism.** Only positive or experimental science is valid, or that whose object does not extend beyond the phenomena perceived by the senses, for it alone is constituted of synthetic a priori judgments. All scientific knowledge surpassing the sensible, as metaphysics and the Scholastic sciences, are doomed to the speculative point of view as making an abusive use of concepts. On the other hand, absolute phenomenalism, admitting but sensations, is equally condemned; for the scientific phenomenon is *necessary* and *universal* through the concept which formalizes it. In this way, Kant canonizes the *modern sciences;* physics and astronomy, with their laws and hypotheses, are sciences of the same title as is geometry.

It can be remarked that the Thomistic notion of science is at once more broad and more narrow than Kant's. It rejects the particular judgments gathered by Kant, and imposes restrictions on the value of modern scientific laws. But it accepts more portions of science wherein an object of the purely spiritual order is encountered, as in theodicy.

II. **Transcendental Idealism.** It is in this terminology that Kant himself looks upon his theory. He recognizes that the phenomenon, after the elaborations which it undergoes, only retains a value which is mainly subjective. The nature which science achieves is not a faithfully reflected copy. It is but an ensemble of forms which properly pertains to our understanding and which is clothed in the vague sort of reality of a thing-in-itself, unknown but postulated at the beginning of sensation. Through this theory, Kant thought he had, to his glory, introduced the same sort of revolution in philosophy that Copernicus had done in astronomy. Before his time,

---

[1] Kant develops this position in speaking of metaphysics; see below, n. 408.

it is true, all the moderns, empiricists as well as idealists, had admitted the principle of correspondence of the two orders (the real and our knowledge), explaining *all the characteristics* of our knowledge by the exterior object. Kant explained the laws of nature by the laws of the spirit; not, it is true, in their details and particularities, which come from experience, but in their necessity and universality, which derive from the a priori forms. Our sciences gravitate beyond things; in final analysis, it is nature which gravitates about our spirit.

Kants idealism is *transcendental*, for this elaboration is ruled by transcendental laws. These laws dominate scientific work. They are imposed by nature before any activity of the spirit, and are not acquired by habit, as in Hume's view. Thus the necessity, universality and the truth of science are maintained.

III. **Normative Truth.** In order to conserve truth, Kant had to modify its definition. Truth becomes a property of synthetic a priori judgments alone, if they are normalized; that is, pronounced according to the laws which rule the synthesis of the concept and the sensible intuition. These laws are not those of reality itself, as they are in Thomism, but psychological laws. At the same time, they are not proper to the individual as such, but to humanity, or the human species; from thence comes their necessity and universality. Accordingly, universal consent is a secondary criterion of the truth. The laws of sensibility, however, are individual, and error arises when the understanding follows these laws without sufficient consideration.

Kant, however, also states that truth is the " conformity of judgment with thing or object ". 1) A fundamental law of understanding is, precisely, to objectivize, en bloc, the phenomenon unconsciously elaborated. 2) This phenomenon has a basis in real objectivity, due to the postulate of the world as the source of sensation. This second definition of truth, then, can be harmonized with the first. For our judgment to be conformed with its object is for it to be conformed with its own laws.

This conception of truth puts emphasis on the *immanentist principle* and on the *radical rationalism* [1] of modern thought. For Kant, our sciences are truly drawn out of ourselves; reason is autonomous and imposes its laws on reality, though with

---

[1] See above, n. 313.

this well marked difference that these laws also dominate individuals; it is more humanity itself, or impersonal reason, which becomes the center of everything.

In Summary : *In order to justify the value of scientific judgments by holding himself to the strictly critical view of the phenomenal object, Kant conceives truth not as a conformity of judgment with the thing in itself (grasped through the idea and sensation), but as conformity of judgment with the laws (subjectively inevitable) which govern the elaboration of phenomena.*

This conception gives rise to a science that is I) *positivist, for its object is restrained to sensible experience;* 2) *idealist, for the better portion is given a priori by the subject;* 3) *intellectualist, for the essential function is due to abstract, or universal and necessary concepts.*

ARTICLE THREE.
THE MORAL NATURE OF METAPHYSICS.

405. In developing his critical justification of the sciences from the viewpoint of the pure *phenomenon*, Kant is led (in the final part of his *Critique of Pure Reason*) to raise the problem of the thing-in-itself. As opposed to the sciences, metaphysics has the thing-in-itself as its object. Does this external reality, the thing-in-itself, exist, and in what measure do our true judgments permit us to know it? Kant's solution to this question has two parts. The first, in the speculative order, denies any theoretical value to metaphysics, and reduces it to a mere unification of the sciences by means of *reasoning*. The second, in the moral order (the *Critique of Practical Reason*), rediscovers a real truth-value for metaphysical notions, though not as science, but as *faith*. Kant's critique, in thus terminating with a " moral metaphysics ", has sufficient correspondence with questions treated in special epistemology[1], though he defends many propositions opposed to Thomistic realism. Two paragraphs will present his views on these matters.

    I. The Value of the Reasoning Process : Speculative Metaphysics.

    II. The Value of Faith : Moral Metaphysics.

---

[1] See above, n. 389, fn. to that section.

I. THE VALUE OF REASONING : SPECULATIVE METAPHYSICS.

406. Kant calls the last part of the *Critique of Pure Reason* by the name, *Transcendental Dialectics;* this is because dialectics treats merely of " probable " matters, and because this section studies the functioning of reasoning processes. In his general solution to this section, Kant concludes with a problematic thing-in-itself; then, by analyzing the reasoning processes which are proposed to determine each of the things-in-themselves, he indicates both the legitimate and illegitimate role of these reasonings.

A) General Solution.

One must at first assert the real existence of a thing-in-itself taken in a general way; that is, of a substantial reality as exterior or distinct from the self (considered as the critical subject). Kant always regarded this existence as a truth of primary evidence. He never gave an explicit reason for it, but it is certainly not due to the principle of causality, which is valid only for the phenomenal order and is thus incapable of attaining to substance. The reason for its existence seems to be more profound, and most likely it is one of the items given with the critical problem in his system. In taking the notion of phenomenon or of the purely phenomenal object as his starting point, one has to admit as correlative, the existence of an absolute or of the thing-in-itself in general; only in this way could this " given " element of exterior, existent reality be made intelligible and acceptable in philosophy. A pure appearance, by definition, is completely relative; it would be unthinkable and imply a contradiction with an absolute of which it is the appearance.

On the nature of this absolute only a negative knowledge can be had, in opposition to the phenomenon of which it is the necessary support. The phenomenon is but a passing property, the proper object of sensation; it needs something else for its existence. What is opposed to the phenomenon is a stable reality which exists in itself as substance, and would be the proper object of intelligence. Phenomenon is that which appears, the substance is that which is. Kant calls the latter the thing-in-itself, the absolute or the NOUMENON; it is that which is intelligible, an object capable of being signified by concepts taken apart and detached from their sensible content.

As a matter of fact, we are naturally borne towards the use of concepts in order to add precision to our notion of substances; all philosophers prior to Kant constructed their metaphysics in this way. Now, to the *scientific usage* of concepts, whose legitimacy has been demonstrated above, Kant adds the notion of a *metaphysical usage* (Kant calls this, transcendental) before making more precise the nature of the noumena. What, then, is the value of this second usage? Kant has a definite reply to this question, which is deduced as a simple corollary from the analysis of synthetic a priori judgments. In order that the aptitude of concepts to signify the noumena be established, one would have to show that this is necessary under penalty of making *every true judgment impossible*. Then we would have a " transcendental deduction " similar to the one which justified the value of the sciences, and metaphysics would also be a speculative science in the strict sense, as the modern sciences. But this is not the case, for the formation of synthetic a priori judgments (of scientific judgments known to be infallibly true) has already been explained without recourse of any sort to the thing-in-itself (except as an initial postulate, corresponding to the indeterminate existence of the noumena).

Consequently, the detailed science of the nature of noumena can never be infallibly true in the *speculative order*, even though it remains in itself a possible feat. Through its reasoning processes, metaphysics falls into *hypotheses* but never into demonstrated *propositions*. It lacks a fact of experience drawn from the noumenon, as we have a sensible experience which attains the phenomenon. The pretension of philosophers to explain substances is but an *illusion*. It is, however, an expected or natural illusion, inevitable and even necessary for those who omitted to forearm themselves by the *Critique*. Kant calls it a transcendental illusion. This now makes clear, in Kant's view, the explanation for the persistence of metaphysics as well as for its constant bankruptcy.

Kant thus distinguishes, in human intelligence, two irreducible faculties. The first is understanding *(Verstand)*, which scientifically explains phenomena by means of concepts. The other is reason *(Vernunft)* [1], which thinks about the

---

[1] **Vernunft** properly designates an *intuitive* faculty, immediately attaining substantial reality beyond sensible experience, similar to the etymology of the word *intellectus (intus legere)*, so often referred to by St. Thomas. It is thus opposed to the discursive activity proper to the faculty which St. Thomas

hypothetical noumenon by means of ideas, and as in a void. Kant's general solution can thus be summarized in this formula : *In itself, speculative metaphysics is but a transcendental illusion.*

However, in qualifying this illusion as transcendental, which is to call it natural because it follows the very laws of our intelligence, Kant has to find its sufficient reason. He takes up the question, then, of the utility and legitimate role of ideas.

B) The Legitimate Use of Ideas.

407. Kant recognized and placed in strong relief the *law of unity*, which commands our total psychological activity. Now, the precise role of reason is to assure the full application of this law, and this explains its legitimacy and its necessity. As a matter of fact, the multiplicity of phenomena, after a first unification under the action of the a priori forms of sensibility, is definitively fixed in the universal and necessary unity of concepts through the synthesizing action of the scientific judgment. But the science itself is made up of a multiplicity of judgments which it attempts to reduce to unity by a system of *reasonings*.

Here, Kant distinguishes two sorts of reasonings which correspond to the notions of induction and deduction of Aristotle. Induction belongs to understanding, and cannot make unification progress; the second, which is reasoning in the strict sense, consists in *subsuming* under a more universal principle a more particular judgment. This is the syllogism which tends of itself towards more and more general and unifying principles, and such is the proper work of *Vernunft*.

In this latter class, Kant distinguishes anew three species of reasonings, whose demands for unity require three fundamental noumena of metaphysics, the soul, the world, and God. The first form of reasoning has an absolute major premise (A is B), in which the regression towards unity is made by taking the predicate as the subject of a new principle (B is C; C is D, etc.); this form thus tends towards a first major premise in which *the subject is only the subject*. This unconditioned subject, the support of all attributes, is the *substantial self*.

The second form of reasoning has a hypothetical major premise (If A, then B), in which the regression is made by taking the effect as a new cause, the condition of a new effect (If B, then C; if C, then D, etc.). This form thus tends to a cause *which is only cause* in the order of sensible experiences. This unconditioned cause, the source of all experiential facts, is *the world*.

---

calls *ratio*, and would be better translated by *intellectus* rather than *ratio* in Kant's system. The νοῦς of Plato and the *intellectus* of St. Thomas is what Kant and his successors wanted to restore under the name of *Vernunft* (A. LALANDE, *op. cit.*, art., " Raison ", p. 671).

The third form of reasoning has a disjunctive major premise (A is B or C or D), in which the regression is made by taking the " subjective part " (expressed by the attribute), as a new *potential total*[1] (D is E or H; H is I or K or L, etc.). This form thus tends towards a supreme Being Who cannot be part of a *potential total*. This supreme absolute, in which all other realities participate, is God, Who is thus the achievement of the perfect unity of all judgments and of all sciences.

This manner of concluding (through the concepts of substance, of causality and of totality)[2] to the existence of noumena as the perfect sources of unity, evidently surpasses experience, and by-passes the normal construction of the synthetic a priori judgments of understanding *(Verstand)*. For example, it is not possible to synthesize all the facts of consciousness, past, present and future, under the concept of substance, in order to affirm, scientifically, that there is a substantial or noumenal self. This work belongs to reason, whose role is to think in full independence of experience, in order that it can synthesize the multitude of facts by conceiving of a unique condition for all of them. This statement, not guaranteed by an intuition, is but a pure hypothesis; but because it resembles scientific judgments, we give it the same value. It is a natural illusion, comparable to the optical illusions of a table in perspective. Critical philosophy, in unmasking the illusion, has re-established the true limits of science.

In order to distinguish the objects thought about by *Vernunft* from the objects of science, Kant calls the latter *ideas*, by allusion to the Platonic Ideas[3], which, being in a supra-sensible world, also unified and stabilized the changeful multiplicity of the material world[4].

One readily sees that the ideas are fully capable of fulfilling their role of unification. Since they are of another order of things, they orient and direct the scientific experiences without ever impeding them. In respecting the progress of science, always incomplete, they are like the ideal and definitive fate of science. Despite the radical distinction between the sciences and metaphysics, unity is still maintained, because metaphysics is but a continuation of the sciences; the sciences awake, in *Vernunft*, the desire to think its unificatory hypotheses, and they are a necessary achievement for the sciences. In summary, *the pure ideas are but legitimate and necessary hypotheses to unify the sciences*.

---

[1] These are expressions taken from logic; the genus animal is a *potential total*, of which humanity is but a subjective part.

[2] See the table of categories, p. 673, fn. 2.

[3] *Critique of Pure Reason*, " Transcendental Dialectics ", Book I, Sect. I; Kant here speaks of the meaning which Plato gave to " idea ".

[4] See above, n. 41.

Finally, the idea of God manifests itself to reflection as an *Ideal*, or as an Idea of a Being Who is at once Infinite and determined, uniquely subsistent and the Creator of everything; in a word, as the Necessary Being and the *Ens realissimum*, possessing all the attributes of the true God, *if He exists*. This preparatory work of speculative reason will have utility, since morality will always require the existence of God as one of its postulates.

The source of this law of absolute unity proclaimed by Kant can be found in the formal object of our intelligence, in the idea of *being*, which is the soul of all our scientific and metaphysical judgments. The idea of being, not implicating any sort of imperfection, limit, or multiplicity, rightly identifies itself with perfect unity. Thus, to interpret everything as a function of being [1], is necessarily to unify everything. Kant, it is true, by accepting idealism, has denied that the intelligence can know or interpret the world of substances by being. But in his attempt to unify the sciences and metaphysics, he somewhat corrected his dualism for his own good, and approached the Thomistic unity.

One can even compare the Kantian ideas to ideas analogous by the analogy of proper proportionality, which, in Thomism, have a value that is greatly *negative*, being incapable of designating the degree of being or of the essence of things, especially of God [2]. Theodicy, as a matter of fact, by completing the sciences whose final cause it discovers, also is respectful of their indefinite progress. But the radical difference is that, for St. Thomas, corporeal substances are known by univocal ideas; and even analogous ideas, when applied to spirits and to God, keep their truth-value by being able to produce science in the proper sense. The Kantian ideas, on the other hand, excluded from the domain of scientific certitude, embrace *all substances*, spiritual and corporeal.

C) The Illegitimate Use of Ideas.

408. Philosophers, however, have never been resigned to the modest role of unification assigned to their metaphysical reasons; they have tried to uncover the nature of the three substances, God, the soul and the world. This explains the origin of the three parts of metaphysics, theodicy, psychology and cosmology. In order to convince them of their illusion, Kant proposes to show, in detail, their powerlessness in applying the laws and the categories of understanding to the study of noumena. In this way, he also finds an indirect confirmation of his positive critique.

---

[1] See the Thomistic principle explained above, n. 258 : " Everything is intelligible through being ".

[2] " We do not know what God is, but what He is not "; St. Thomas Aquinas, *Summa Theologica*, I, q. II, *Prol.*

I. **In Psychology.** All reasonings are vitiated here, by a fundamental *paralogism*. One has to make use of the idea of the *self*, which can signify two things. 1) *The phenomenal self*, or the ensemble of psychological facts which legitimately enter as matter in the synthetic a priori judgments; this self is the object of psychological science, in which the rule of necessary laws holds, as in every science. 2) *The noumenal self*, a free, spiritual substance, which escapes all experience and remains inaccessible to science in the proper sense. To attain science here, one would have to make use of the principle of causality, whose scientific value is restrained to the order of experience, or to the phenomena [1].

II. **In Cosmology.** The application of abstract concepts leads to four unresolvable antinomies, which can be stated as follows.

1) The World *a*) *is eternal;* otherwise, the first instant could be localized at a precise date, as every temporal event, and one would have to have a prior time, or an instant before the first instant, which is impossible [2]; *b*) *has a beginning;* otherwise in order to arrive at the present time, an infinite series of events would have to be traversed, which is impossible.

2) Every corporeal composite must be formed *a*) *of simple elements;* otherwise, in separating the composing parts, one would be led to the pure absence of unity, or to nothingness, which is absurd. *b*) *of elements divisible* to infinity, for with a simple element one cannot make a divisible one [3].

3) A free cause *a*) must necessarily be admitted as the final explanation of the world, which requires a first cause, fully independent; *b*) is *impossible*, because it would have to determine itself without there being any sufficient reason for its determination, if it be given that nothing exists before it that could influence it [4].

4) Necessary being *a*) must exist in order to make possible the series of contingent beings which compose the world; *b*) *cannot exist* at all, neither in the series of contingent beings, for then it is necessary, nor even outside of this series, for, by creating the series, it must necessarily enter into contact with the series and it thus becomes the first rung [5].

III. **In Theodicy,** Kant reduces proofs for God's existence to three.

1) *The ontological argument* of St. Anselm, as taken up by Descartes and Leibniz. He accuses St. Anselm, as St. Thomas had done, of passing improperly from the logical to the real order, and of drawing from an abstract concept, by pure analysis, an extra-conceptual existence to which only intuition and experience can lead us.

---

[1] See above, n. 327, for a solution of this paralogism.
[2] See above, n. 79, for Aristotle's analogous reasoning and his solution.
[3] See above, n. 16, Zeno's arguments and their solutions.
[4] See above, n. 158, for St. Augustine's solution of this difficulty.
[5] See above, n. 134, for the true notion of the creative cause, which corrects Kant's views as well as those of Plotinus.

2) *The cosmological argument,* based on the existence of imperfect and contingent beings, avoids this illegitimate reasoning of the above argument. However, to conclude with God's existence, one must make use of the principle of causality, which, as has been seen, has no efficacy in the order of phenomena. If one then concludes to a necessary being, it is only as to an abstract ideal whose real existence cannot be affirmed except through an unconscious return to the ontological argument.

3) *The teleological argument,* or through the order of the universe. This argument Kant believes to be most efficacious, the easiest and the most impressive for all. However, in itself, it merely concludes to an Intelligence superior to the world, who must, in all rigor, be finite and contingent. In order to complete the argument, one would have to revert back to the cosmological proof, which itself rests on the sophism of St. Anselm [1].

D) Kantian Agnosticism and Moderate Realism.

409. Kant's conclusion on the subject of speculative metaphysics is definitively an attitude of *agnosticism;* man can never attain the scientific knowledge of substances. An epistemology of Thomistic inspiration can correct this agnosticism by demonstrating the value of abstract knowledge, and especially of the concepts of substance and of causality as expressive of the " trans-subjective " reality (that of the substantial self and of other, exterior beings), in their special determinations.

The foundational propositions of a critical realism can be demonstrated in two ways.

1. The first is by direct certification, or critical induction, which insists on the collaboration of the senses and intelligence explained above [2]. Two conclusions impose themselves equally. On the one hand, since the object of the senses is not accident as opposed to substance, but the real object under a concrete aspect, it can also be seized *itself* by the intelligence under another aspect (what can be termed abstractive intuition). Thus (the value of induction based on the various degrees of abstraction having been established), the physical sciences can legitimately search not only for the mathematical laws of phenomena, but also for the real nature of substance. Moreover, the case of man is particularly favorable, because of his internal experience, for establishing a definition which is not only generic and descriptive for other beings, but also strictly specific and essential. — On

---

[1] For a complete statement and Thomistic solution of these difficulties, see R. GARRIGOU-LAGRANGE, *God, His Existence and Nature,* Vol. II. His presentation shows that without losing its moderate realism, Thomism can solve the Kantian difficulties.

[2] See above, n. 403.

the other hand, the aspect of being under which our mind seizes the same object as the senses, being transcendent, furnishes a basis for strictly speculative truth of the principles of metaphysics, and especially that of causality; consequently, it gives a value to science even in the propositions of theodicy [1].

2. One could also adopt the viewpoint of Kant by a provisory acceptance of the problem of the phenomenal object. One would then demonstrate, by reduction to absurdity, that to deny the existence of particular noumena corresponding to phenomena known experientially as irreducible (to deny the existence of natures substantially determined, and especially that of God), is to make the production of the true and scientific judgment impossible.

This latter approach to Kant has been attempted by Maréchal [2]. The essential point of this " transcendental deduction ", which is very efficacious though long and laborious, is to certify that the affirmation of judgment refers the concrete object implicitly to absolute being, which is a form of judgment. In judging, one always states, in final analysis, how an individual reality participates in being, so that in every true judgment reason affirms its natural tendency to possess absolute being.

Now, this latter tendency would be absurd : 1) without the real existence of God, as the source and final goal of reason; and 2) consequently, without the real existence of particular essences as intermediary goals, affirmed as leading to the final goal or as limited natures, viewed as participation in absolute being. To deny the knowledge of particular substances is thus to make *every* true judgment impossible, even those of Kantian science. Both methods are an efficacious refutation of Kantian agnosticism.

II. THE VALUE OF FAITH : MORAL METAPHYSICS.

410. The three metaphysical ideas remain, in the speculative order, pure hypotheses. They lack an intellectual intuition which would give them some " matter ", as sensible intuition gives its " matter " to concepts. They remain purely a priori, and only synthetic a priori knowledge is endowed with scientific truth. But *Vernunft*, which thinks these ideas, is also the Practical Reason which commands duty under a rather novel aspect. Could not reason enter into immediate contact with the " noumenal real " and thus furnish an absolute beginning for metaphysics which would be capable of definitively establishing its value, just as the impact of experience has founded the objective value of the sciences? Kant believed it could, on condition that one would find, not a totally personal activity

---

[1] This is the method adopted by D. J. MERCIER and most Thomists.
[2] J. MARÉCHAL, *Le point de départ de la métaphysique*, Vol. v, *Le Thomisme devant la Philosophie critique*, Paris, 1926; see p. 477 and *passim*.

which would have merely subjective and relative value, but an action which imposes itself on humanity in a universal and necessary fashion. This action exists, and is the **moral fact,** as indubitable and as universally admitted as the existence of science.

After he has made the condition of its existence more exact, Kant shows that this fact implies three postulates, personal liberty, the immortality of the soul and the existence of God. These three have a real, noumenal value and correspond to the three metaphysical ideas, God, soul and the world. This explains the value attributable to metaphysics by Kant. It can be summarized as follows : *due to the moral fact, the hypotheses of reason, without being able to become the object of science, are, nevertheless, transformable into propositions which are definitively legitimate but are the object of belief or of faith.*

A) **The Moral Fact : The Categorical Imperative.**

411. Alongside of the fact of science with its universal and necessary laws, there stands the equally undeniable fact of morality with its laws and duties, which are just as universal and necessary, for they reach all men without exception and impose on each a strict obligation. Kant asks himself, here also, what are the conditions required in man in order to explain this fact or make it possible.

I.   Until this time, metaphysicians have explained this fact and the characteristics of morality by appealing to the *object* of human action, or the seeking of the good (what Kant calls the *matter* of the law) [1]. Some, as Hume and the empiricists and as Epicurus, founded morality on *interest* and on *pleasure,* or on a rule of action essentially individual and unstable, often contradictory to duty; this evidently destroys all true morality.

Others, as the rationalists, the Scholastics and the ancient Stoics, looked for a foundation in the existence of an *absolute good* which is God; they made this the final goal, as presupposed and dominating, and towards which all men have the obligation to tend. But from the *Critique of Pure Reason* we know that such a foundation merely begets ruin; the objective existence of God and of the supreme good is but an hypothesis, scienti-

---

[1] This is why Kant speaks of moral *material*, to which he opposes his notion of moral *formality.*

fically indemonstrable; instead of being the basis of a necessary and universal morality, it is merely the fact of an independent morality, valuable of itself, which should be rather the basis for the existence of God. If, then, one follows Kant's view and recognizes the illusion of a presupposed existence of a supreme God imposing Himself as the final goal and the supreme rule of morality, one can in reality conclude that even while pretending to seek an exterior good, one seeks only his own interest or personal enjoyment in such a morality. Even though this latter morality is quite refined, it is always of the subjective and individual type, and consequently refers to sensibility and not to reason [1]. Thus, theological morality, just as much as the morality of utility or of pleasure, destroys the universality and necessity of human morals by placing the determining principle of the will in sensibility.

2. In order to safeguard true morality, only one way is possible. One must explain its value without appealing to its object; one must not look for the *matter*, but for the *form* of law. The form which is characteristic of moral laws is *pure obligation*, demanding for each morally good act absolute disinterestedness; duty done purely for the sake of duty. Everything can then be explained by seeking in practical reason an *a priori form* which is parallel to the forms of understanding *(Verstand)*. Just as the latter imposes its twelve categories on nature in order to set up a universal and necessary science, so practical reason possesses a kind of category or a priori form. The functioning of this latter form is dependent on the basic structure of human nature, and thus can be imposed on all human acts and on all men in order to build a universal and necessary morality. This category is the CATEGORICAL IMPERATIVE, the a priori form of all moral laws which it distinguishes from maxims or rules of sensibility by giving them the value of absolute obligation, just as concepts give phenomena their scientific value.

3. In a further meaning, which flows from the above, the *categorical* imperative is opposed to the *hypothetical* imperative. Sometimes obligation pertains to the means, when, for instance, it imposes a condition of willing a goal as in the proverb, " he who wills the end wills the means ". This is but an *hypothetical* imperative," imperative of success or of prudence ",

---

[1] In this sense, the Kantians and the moralists inspired by him accused the Christians of *egoism*, because they are working for *heaven*.

which cannot found morality, inasmuch as the end from which
it derives is always a personal good (as will be shown) and
thus is basically but a caprice of sensibility.

But obligation can become the final and unique goal of
action, as in the proverb, " come what may, do what should
be done ". Then we have an absolute or categorical imperative,
which alone founds morality. Kant insists on the need for
acting uniquely for duty's sake, if one wishes to perform a
morally good action. Even if an action performed is conformable to law, it is legal, but not moral, and merits the name
of hypocrisy if done for a motive of interest. This obtains
even if a spiritual good is sought, as the heaven of the Christians.
He judged it even dangerous to allow such a motive to subsist
aside of a pure motive of duty; it is more perfect to be virtuous
with difficulty than with pleasure. Briefly, then, every action
truly directed by reason should be done purely for duty's
sake, and not vice versa; only the motive of duty is a reasonable
one, every other comes from sensibility. For these reasons,
Kant calls practical reason *The Good Will*, the source of every
virtuous act.

4. By means of the categorical imperative, practical reason
formulates a fundamental, synthetic a priori judgment which
is the supreme principle conferring a moral value on all
particular laws. Kant has given three famous formulations
of this principle : 1) Act in such a way that the maxim
of your will could always be valid, at the same time, as
a principle of universal legislation "; or, briefly, " act in such
a way that your action could serve as a universal law ";
2) " Act always so that you treat humanity, whether in your
own person or in that of another, always as an end and never
as a simple means "; 3) " Act in such a way that your will
could consider itself as making universal laws by its maxims ".

These are but three ways of expressing the same thought.
Our will, or practical reason, because of the nobility which
its a priori form confers on it and through which we identify
ourselves with absolute humanity, should dominate our sensibility, which makes up our own individuality. At the same
time, practical reason is not dominated by anything other,
and finds in itself the unique source of obligation, in full
independence of any objective influence [1].

---

[1] See J. COLLINS, *A History of Modern European Philosophy*, pp. 515-534,
on Kant's ethical doctrine, and pp. 523-531 on the place of these maxims in
Kant's view.

B) **The Postulates of Practical Reason.**

412. Thus interpreted, the moral fact permits us to attain the noumenal world directly by reason of the liberty which it implies and because it requires the immortality of the soul and God's existence. Liberty, immortality of the soul and God are the three postulates of practical reason which correspond to the three ideas of speculative reason.

1. **Liberty.** For Kant, as for common sense, liberty (or autonomy) is the quality of an act which is accomplished without any foreign influence. Thus, to say that in order for an action to be morally good, it must be done for the motive of duty alone and in full independence of any objective influence, is evidently to say that it enjoys perfect autonomy or liberty. Accordingly, in Kant's view, liberty and duty, the autonomy of will and the moral law, are absolute synonyms; " formal " morality, based on the pure categorical imperative is also independent morality.

But this liberty, as real as the undeniable fact of morality itself, has no place in the world of phenomena, wherein universal determinism is imposed by the concept of *causality*. All the events of conscious life follow the necessary laws of psychological science just as the phenomena of nature follow the laws of physics. Liberty is possible, however, in the noumenal world, as is shown by the speculations of reason elevating itself to the idea of a first, unconditioned cause. Accordingly, what was a pure hypothesis in metaphysics here becomes a certified fact : the existence of noumenal liberty, or of the free substance which is our own moral personality.

From this it follows that our free person is the ontological source (the *ratio essendi*) of the moral law. But the moral fact is the logical source (the *ratio cognoscendi*) of our personal liberty. For, on the one hand, liberty, pertaining to the world of substances, escapes our experience, which grasps only phenomena; however, on the other hand, we have immediate consciousness of the pure obligation of duty, which thus entrains the affirmation of liberty, as Schelling says, " You should, therefore you can ".

This theory also conciliates, for Kant, the autonomy of duty and the sentiment of obligation. It is man's superior part, his moral being or citizenship in the intelligible world which is autonomous. We make commands to ourselves, so that we live in the phenomenal world through our interior and sensible portion. Thus, every moral evil originates in the predominance given to sensibility, which, instead of obeying, subsumes reason to its own interests; at the same time, the natural subordination of sensibility to practical reason explains the sentiment [1] of obligation.

413. A serious difficulty remains, however. How can our free person insert its influence in our phenomenal life, which, as we have seen, is entirely governed by the necessary laws of psychology? In order to resolve this problem, Kant supposes that man pre-exists as noumenon, and, at the moment of birth into phenomenal life, he places a basic act of freedom which becomes reflected on all his existence and determines its orientation towards moral good or moral evil.

It is useless to insist on the inadequacy of this theory, which involves such inhuman consequences. In the case of sin, for instance, there are no attenuating circumstances possible, as ignorance, passions, habit or the like; the latter come from the world of phenomena and have no influence on the free determination of the noumenal order.

One can even say that free reason, in Kant's sense, is by right incapable of sinning, since there is no superior to disobey, and all that is necessary is spontaneously to follow the laws of duty. How, then, does one explain that free reason is so often dominated by the very sensibility whose influence should not touch it at all? Through the radical separation of the thing-in-itself from the phenomenon, the noumenal self takes on the guise of a spirit or of an angel; St. Thomas would even grant the natural impossibility of sinning to an angel. But the Thomistic thesis on the spiritual soul as the form of the body permits of a better explanation of the interaction between the two parts, one spiritual and the other sensible, both in the free will and in the passions [2].

Another difficulty arises from the identification of liberty and duty, and from making practical reason autonomous and the unique source of obligation and of moral law. By so doing, Kant has made these fundamental notions of morality, as *obligation*, *law* and *duty*, difficult to comprehend. The only possible definition of obligation is that of *necessity respectful of our liberty;* this requires the influence of a superior will, capable of imposing itself efficaciously without doing violence to our liberty. And this action is proper to the unique, creative influence of God.

Kant himself implicitly recognized this notion of common sense in speaking of the subordination of the sensible life to reason. But, on the one hand, if sensibility can be subjected, it does not

[1] This sentiment imposed on sensibility by law is, in Kant's view, RESPECT. It is not an inclination nor an aversion, for it does not seek recompense nor chastisements which could come from the thing or from the person respected. It is a submission accompanied by the conviction that one aggrandizes himself through obeying. It is an intermediary between the two parts of man, and it slowly engenders a harmony between the sensible dispositions and the demands of the moral law. See E. BOUTROUX, *La philosophie de Kant*, p. 300.

[2] See above, n. 269; see also, A. D. SERTILLANGES, *Saint Thomas d'Aquin*, Vol. II, pp. 284-286.

have the liberty essential to moral obligation; moreover, reason, which enjoys liberty, has nothing superior to itself obliging it. There is, for the independent morality which Kant proposed, an incurable vice : in refusing our intelligence the right of attaining God, he destroys the unique foundation capable of giving sense to a true moral obligation.

It should be granted, however, that Kantian morality is opposed, rightfully, to any idea of obligation whose total source is an exterior commandment or the good pleasure of a master, even that of God. It is true that obligation arises, in some way, from our liberty and our reason to the extent that our conscience, participatory in the eternal law of God, is the proximate rule of action. But to keep some meaning in obligation, St. Thomas, without destroying our free initiative, submits it, as a created thing, to the transcendent influence of the Creator.

2) Immortality of the Soul and the Existence of God. 414.

In analyzing moral duty more deeply, Kant concludes with two other postulates, the immortality of the soul and God. Actually, the essential object commanded by the moral law is the attainment of the *sovereign good*. In this good, our reason sees the necessary union of virtue or absolute moral perfection (*sanctity*, says Kant) with the supreme and definitive good. Here, a double difficulty arises.

a) If sanctity is man's duty, it seems impossible in this sensible world in which there always remains some egoistic inclination towards domination. Kant immediately concludes that this moral perfection must consist in an *indefinite progress*, always approached and never achieved, towards the perfect conformity of man's will with law. This progress is equivalent to the sovereign good in the sense that this infinite series of acts appears to the divine intuition, "for whom time is nothing", as the perfect accomplishment of duty. Thus, progress not only fills up the present life, but demands the endless permanence of our moral person; that is, the *immortality of the soul*.

b) Now, daily experience shows that the union of happiness and virtue is not always a necessary effect of the practice of the good life. Happiness is due, though in a lesser way, to the influence of the good that follows upon our progress toward sanctity, since each fully disinterested action is morally good; by virtue, Kant holds, we are able to make ourselves worthy of the supreme happiness, but never to take it as our end. Accordingly, since the moral law exists and commands the harmony of happiness and sanctity, the existence of a Being sufficiently powerful and good to realize this harmony must be admitted. He is the author at once of the moral and of the physical order, and He is God.

Liberty, the soul and God are the three *things-in-themselves* which Kant calls *the three postulates of practical reason.* Their proper value is to be intermediary between the object of pure science, whose reality is speculatively guaranteed, and an object of pure practice, as a duty. We do not have the duty to admit these three truths, but it is necessary to admit them so as to make the moral fact possible and to answer the demands of reason. Without being the object of science, nor being but purely hypothetical ideas, these three are objects of belief, postulated by the existence of duty.

3) **Correspondence of the Three Postulates with the Three Ideas. 415.** The moral fact guarantees and requires the existence of three noumenal realities, our liberty, our immortality and God. Speculative reason, as has been shown, concluded with three hypothetical noumena, God, the self and the world, as the unification of the sciences. In order to terminate his metaphysics and give some objective value to the speculations of *Vernunft,* Kant has nothing left but to show the correspondence of the three postulates of pure practical reason with the three ideas of pure speculative reason. Now it is easy to see that the God of morality well fulfills the attributes of the metaphysical Ideal, and that the self, the final subject of the conscious life, is identified with the soul endowed with liberty and immortality. With regard to the idea of the world, it corresponds indirectly to the double postulate of God and of liberty. The world is conceived as a contingent being, and hence created by God; it is also the source of all the facts of sensible nature, and hence necessary to the soul so that the soul may deploy the free activity of its moral life.

This correspondence of postulates with ideas unifies all of metaphysics, and suffices, in Kant's view, to form a unity which is the true, objective science. It is not that the ideas ever become a speculative knowledge of the *thing-in-itself;* reason always thinks of them in a void, in the absence of intellectual intuition which would fill up its speculations. Their closeness to moral certitude, however, confers an extrinsic certitude on them which suffices to transform mere hypotheses into propositions.

In Summary : *Due to the categorical imperative, an a priori form of necessary and universal moral laws, reason becomes connected by three postulates to the three metaphysical ideas and confers on them an extrinsic certitude; in this way the hypotheses of God, the soul and the world, become transformed into propositions.*

C) Corollaries.

416. 1) **Religion.** The idea of God, in Kantianism, though founded on the moral fact, a secondary foundation, becomes sovereign and dominating from another viewpoint. For God is both the Ideal which unifies all science, and the Creator Who assures the perfect accomplishment of the moral order by harmonizing *duty* and *happiness.* Every moral action, done to accomplish duty, becomes thereby the fulfillment of the Divine Will. This makes " religion with the limits of reason " the only admissible one; it is identified with moral metaphysics and has the same content, the same certitude and the same immunity from any speculative objection, for criticism has shown the full incompetence of speculation in attaining the noumena. As a consequence, Christian dogmas have no speculative, but only a practical value. Christ is an historical man but not God; He was presented to the faithful as the Son of God in order to make them gradually aware that they had an immortal, noumenal soul within them capable of uniting them to God and of making them " sons of God ".

417. 2) **The Criticism of Judgment** [1]. Kantian science offers no explanation of nature, except some general framework. It gives a *quantitative vision* of the world by justifying mathematics, but in no way inclines towards a *qualitative vision* which would account for the hierarchy of genera and species, and no explanation of the necessity of their distinctness or their interaction [2].

Now, having completed the *Critique of Practical Reason,* Kant sees that he can furnish this explanation by the law of finality, which joins the order of scientific phenomena to the order of moral action. In order to realize the sovereign good, as an imposed duty, man must use, as means, real beings, as plants, animals and so on. Since the utility of all of them depends on their specific nature, the necessary distinction of genera and species has been guaranteed by God, Who guarantees the final union of accomplished duty with the possession of

---

[1] See J. COLLINS, *op. cit.*, pp. 534-540.
[2] This qualitative vision, for instance, is given in Aristotle's natural philosophy; see nn. 77-80, above.

the sovereign good.   Kant remarks that this mode of applying finality to nature is *to judge* it in some fashion, though this judgment is different from the synthetic a priori judgments. Kant justifies this new type in his *Critique of Judgment.*

Thus, he remarks that the judgment of finality, as opposed to the scientific judgment, brings us a certain satisfaction, inasmuch as its object is fully adapted to the needs of our faculties.   This gives Kant an occasion to institute a critique of taste.

When there is a harmony between our sensible and intellectual faculties, we have something *agreeable*, or an interested and wholly subjective sentiment.   But if there is a harmony with our intellectual being, with the absolute finality commanded by the categorical imperative, one has a disinterested sentiment, which is universal and absolute (the esthetic sentiment), whose object is the *beautiful*.   The beautiful is thus defined as " *that which universally pleases without concepts* " ; that is, being known not by the reasoning of *Verstand* (understanding), but by a sort of intuition of practical reason.   There is some concordance here between Kant's and St. Thomas' definition of transcendental beauty as *id quod visum placet.*

418. 3) **Law and Special Morality.** Having established the basic principles of a moral metaphysics through his three critiques, Kant applied them in deducing the various duties of special morality, including individual, political and international rules. It should be mentioned that, faithful to his view of the autonomy of reason, he states the general principle of law as, " that action is just or lawful whose maxim permits liberty to each by being in accord with the liberty of all ". His fundamental rule is, " act exteriorly in such a way that the usage of your liberty could be in accord with the liberty of each following a general rule ". From these statements and others, it follows that the only just law in a nation is that which is elaborated by the collective will of the members of the society; such a law is always just and obligatory. It also follows that a citizen is outside of his legality if he questions his obligation, and that social authority, the sovereign interpreter of law, must always be obeyed.

In international morality, Kant considered each nation a moral person, autonomous and sovereign in itself, but subsumed to the absolute directives of law. The actual situation in which war is, as a last resort, ruling the relations between peoples, is properly a state of barbarianism.   One should tend towards setting up a " society of nations " into which each nation enters freely in order to rule the remaining nations with the principles of international justice.   As a consequence, Kant wrote his project on *Perpetual Peace*, in which he establishes and explains a priori, in ten articles, the necessary conditions for realizing this ideal.

These practical applications of his criticism stand out more in relief in Kant's successors, and were not foreign to the success of his system.

D) Value of the Kantian Metaphysics.

419. Kant attempted to unify all human knowledge by giving the primacy to practical reason. This notion clearly points up his dominating idea of the autonomy of reason. However, he thus fell into a dualism which logically tends to scepticism.

1) **Primacy of Practical Reason.** All the truth possessed by metaphysics has its origin in the ability of the moral fact to place us into immediate contact with noumenal reality. This absolute beginning of practical reason, which corresponds to sensible intuition, the absolute beginning of the " science " of phenomena, has a double superiority.

a) It is not a postulate, as that of understanding, but a sort of immediate intuition, not requiring any further justification. Without doubt, it is not properly knowledge or a science, but it is more a matter of will. It is a practical judgment which has its own full truth and directly reveals the noumenal world to man.

b) This truth or immediately objective and practical certitude reflects back on the speculative ideas, and, through them, on the whole of science. The latter, as a matter of fact, is constructed by understanding between the postulated " world " which supports science and the three ideas which surround and complete it.

This wholly ideal speculation of pure reason is but a type of union permitting practical reason to affix to reality (which it immediately attains) the whole edifice of " science ", which is, thus, founded on a simple postulate. For this reason, metaphysics and morality pertain to the same faculty of *Vernunft*, which is double faced : speculative in order to think the ideas, and practical in order to formulate the moral imperative. This sort of compenetration makes the throwback of moral certitude on the ideas and on science more acceptable. Of course, the idealism of science is not thus completely corrected, for it remains an elaboration through a priori forms. But this influence sets up a *pragmatism* [1], in which the predominating truth is defined by relation to moral value rather than by its conformity with intelligence.

---

[1] On the meaning of this theory, see below, n. 524.

2) **The Transcendental Autonomy of Reason.** This prag-matism is a direct result of the master-idea of Kantianism, which aims to explain human knowledge by a priori laws; morality, possessing the most excellent laws, must possess supreme truth. In this sense, Kantianism is summed up in the expression, *the autonomy of reason.* Speculative reason, independently of noumena, fabricates science; practical reason, independently of any exterior mobility, proscribes duty of itself.

But this autonomy is *transcendental.* Each individual is not permitted to construct his own science and duty. Rather, he finds in himself absolute and universal laws which dominate his intellectual and moral life, which Kant calls transcendental. In conforming to these laws, the individual attains both truth and virtue. This conception permits Kant to give a broad enough definition of truth so that it can include both science and metaphysics, despite their radical differences. Truth is always a " conformity. of judgment with the laws of intelli-gence "; the laws of understanding give a true knowledge or science, the laws of reason, a simple belief.

It is here that the deification of man stands out as the logical endpoint of modern philosophy; God is but the sovereign measure of the true and the good. Kant has made this absurdity more palatable by deifying humanity, which dominates all the member individuals. But inasmuch as humanity is not real except within each of us, each man must then become the source and the center of all truth and of all morality. This, as we shall see, will make *pantheism* spring forth from Kant's principles.

3) **Dualism and Scepticism.** It must be acknowledged that Kantianism is a powerful attempt at synthesis. But its basic idealism opposes the self and the non-self so strongly that no unity can be achieved. Kant's idea of law proposes a dualism which logically leads to absolute scepticism. Human truth, as well as the certitude accompanying it, is homogeneous of itself, and cannot be given two contradictory definitions. If objective truth is found in conformity to practical laws as the primary of practical reason implies, it is thereby banished from conformity to speculative laws. Logically, this gives absolute scepticism in metaphysics and in science. We could never know, in any way, whether or not our knowledge reunites with the noumena.

But the very pragmatism in which truth here takes refuge is untenable, if the idealistic principle is admitted. The moral law, and the categorical imperative itself, are but abstract and universal pronouncements, wholly similar to synthetic a priori judgments. For instance, the moral imperative is similar to the principle of causality; yet the latter has no value in the world of phenomena. How distinguish understanding from reason when, as a matter of fact, they judge and reason in absolutely the same way? And if there is but one faculty, practical certitude is involved in the ruin of speculative certitude, far from having the power to establish it. This result is inevitable, for truth, by definition, pertains to the speculative, and not to the practical order. The successors of Kant have set this in relief by overthrowing logic and giving their master a reputation of being a *sceptic*, which his doctrine, but not his intentions, fully merit.

In Summary : *Kantianism is characterized* 1) *by the transcendental autonomy of reason, such that every truth is obtained by conformity to a priori laws (laws of the spirit for speculative truth, moral laws for metaphysical truth) and the complete independence of man is thus upheld;* 2) *by the primacy of practical reason; for moral certitude, which is drawn from law par excellence, must give a definitive value to the ensemble of objective knowledge. In fact, practical truth, being of a wholly different order, can only make speculative truth lead to absolute scepticism, and it follows speculative truth into ruin, for every truth is essentially speculative.*

CONCLUSION. **420.** Kant's work can be compared to a building composed of three quite distinct parts. The main part of the structure is formed of the sciences, temporarily constructed in the air, for they repose on a postulate. They are completed by a roof which rises quite high above them and which is not in contact with the walls which are not as yet built (for the sciences are essentially progressive) : metaphysics unifies speculation through its three hypothetical ideas. Finally, in order to make this theoretical structure rest on a solid base of reality, morality brings in its categorical imperative (which plunges the foundations into the noumenal world) and offers its postulates as three pillars.

In this wise, Kant synthesizes all the tendencies of the modern age, in an imposing structure. The idealistic principle is untouchable; the experimental sciences monopolize perfect knowledge, for they alone merit the high title of " science "; a free hand is given to liberty as a result of the critical philosophy, which points out a new direction to truth by the moral view of the autonomous self. In a word, Kant took the rather lowly structure which Descartes had built, and constructed a palatial structure to which all modern philosophers have come for shelter, considering it as definitive and unbreakable.

What is durable in Kant, however, is not the detailed arrangement of this construction, but rather its general style, as being a motley assortment of idealism, of scientism and of pragmatism.

a) **Idealism.** Metaphysics, in the ancient sense, is judged incapable of giving truth, for it is a world of empty abstractions in which systems are built like epic poems. The less audacious philosophers have replaced it by a " modern metaphysics ", in which there is no longer question of attaining being, but of criticizing reason in order to delimit its functions.

b) **Scientism.** The mathematical and the physical sciences are queens over men's minds, and their object is reduced to sensible phenomena. Thinkers are not interested in substance and in its causes; they are content with commodious hypotheses which prolong and unify experience. Their whole effort is bent towards discovering laws governing the relations between phenomena and their expression in more simple, general and fruitful mathematical equations.

c) **Pragmatism.** Finally, religion and morality are definitively separated from the realm of speculation. No doctrine or truth, even that of God's existence, is deemed necessary to found morality, for duty imposes itself on all in its autonomous fashion. All of morality rests on this extraordinary efficaciousness which has been falsely attributed to morality, but whose basis in the new philosophy derives from defining truth as " the property of that which is favorable to action, to life or to happiness ".

The idea of dominating laws in morality, as in science, which give cohesion to the three parts of Kant's thought, did not hold up with the passage of time. His three foundational elements became dissociated, giving rise to three distinct philosophical currents : 1) the metaphysicians, or pure idealists in Germany; 2) the positivists, especially in France and in England; 3) pragmatism or contemporary immanentism. Thus, history sets up Kant's weakness in relief : his failure to justify knowledge of the *thing-in-itself*. He failed to understand how reason was able, by the analogy of being as its formal object, to attain the noumena, or the sensible natures of experience, and through these, in some fashion, attain the suprasensible substances of God and the self. With the help of this fundamental truth, Thomism, while respecting the legitimate demands of modern criticism, can also correct modern errors.

CHAPTER TWO.
IDEALISM.

SPECIAL BIBLIOGRAPHY.

(This bibliography refers to the chapter; for various authors, see footnotes).

BOWEN, F., *Modern Philosophy*, New York, 1906. — DELBOS, V., *De Kant aux postkantiens*, Paris, 1940. — JONES, W. T., *Contemporary German Thought*, 2 vols., New York, 1931. — PERRY, R. B., *Philosophy of the Recent Past*, New York, 1926. — ROYCE, J., *Lectures on Modern Idealism*, New Haven, 1919. — SPENLE, J. E., *La pensée allemande de Luther* à *Nietzche*, Paris, 1934.

421. If Kant was a true founder of a school of thought, it was not his disciples who merely commented upon and taught his work who were of the greatest importance. Of greater doctrinal impact were the independent thinkers who imported some of his fundamental views and from them deduced a series of consequences. As Cartesianism expanded into Spinoza's views, so Kantianism, in its metaphysical and idealistic aspect, likewise developed quickly towards pantheism. It was in Germany itself that Kant found some bold disciples, unafraid of pushing the logic of his thought farther than the master himself. Fichte, Schelling and Hegel are the three main representatives of this trend.

The three names are naturally associated. Despite important differences, all three men were contemporaries, and passed their whole lives in being professors at universities. In 1800, they were together, with GOETHE and SCHILLER at Jena, where Fichte and Schelling collaborated, and Hegel was their confidant. Speculatively, also, they are quite in accord by interpreting Kantianism as *idealistic pantheism*.

At the same time, their diversity of character was too great as not to be reflected in their systems of thought; while they can be harmonized, they also continue and complete each other's views.

JOHN GOTTLIEB FICHTE [1] (1762-1814) was a strong-willed man who lifted himself, by his tremendous energy, from being a shepherd to that of a professor of philosophy. He emphasized the *self*, making it the source of the scientific universe in his *Basis of the Entire Theory of Science* (1805). The moral and political consequences of this work are developed in his *Human Destiny, Instruction for the Happy Life* and his *Addresses to the German Nation*, delivered to uphold German patriotism against Napoleon.

FREDERICK WILLIAM JOSEPH SCHELLING [2] (1775-1854), a poetic and changeful spirit, was especially fraught with the wealth of nature and chose it as the starting point of his deductions, as Fichte had chosen the self. He wrote the following : *Ideas towards a Philosophy of Nature* (1797), *The Soul of the World* (1798), *First Sketch of a System of Philosophy of Nature* (1799), and *The System of Transcendental Idealism* (1800).

After this period, Schelling began to look outside in the absolute of the non-self for a synthesis of the other and the self on which the whole scientific universe could hinge. His notions on this are expressed in *Exposition of My System of Philosophy* (1801), and *Philosophy and Art* (1805). Then he turned his thoughts to the religious question, writing *Philosophy and Religion* (1804), *Inquiries on Human Liberty* (1908), *The Ages of the World* (1815). In these latter works, he substitutes the idea of a divine spirit for that of absolute nature; his system, however, remained unfinished.

---

[1] **Works :** *Sämtliche Werke*, 8 vols., Berlin, 1845-46. — JONES, R. F., and TURNBULL, G. H. (transls.), *Addresses to the German Nation*, Chicago, 1923. — SMITH, W., (tr.), *Vocation of Man*, Chicago, 1931. — **Studies :** ADAMSON, R., *Fichte*, London, 1893. — ENGELBRECHT, H. C., *Johann Gottlieb Fichte*, New York, 1933. — EVERETT, C. C., *Fichte's Science of Knowledge*, London, 1884. — GUÉROULT, M., *La doctrine de la science chez Fichte*, 2 vols., Strasbourg, 1930. — LÉON, X., *Fichte et son temps*, 3 vols., Paris, 1922-27. — MÉDICUS, F., *Fichte's Leben*, Munster, 1922. — STEINER, R., *Spirit of Fichte Present in our Midst*, London, 1934. — TALBOT, E. B., *Fundamental Principle of Fichte's Philosophy*, Ithaca (N. Y.), 1906. — THOMPSON, A. B., *Unity of Fichte's Doctrine of Knowledge*, Cambridge (Mass.), n. d.

[2] **Works :** *Sämtliche Werke*, 14 vols., Berlin, 1856-61. — BOLMAN, F. W. (transl.), *Of Human Freedom*, London, 1936. — GUTMAN, J. (transl.), *The Ages of the World*, New York, 1942. — **Studies :** BRÉHIER, E., *Schelling*, Paris, 1912. — DE FERRI, E., *La filosofia dell'identita di Schelling*, Turin, 1925. — GRAY-SMITH, R., *God in the Philosophy of Schelling*, Philadelphia (Pa.), 1933. — VON HARTMANN, E., *Schellings philosophischen System*, Leipzig, 1897. — WATSON, J., *Schelling's Transcendental Idealism*, London, 1882. — WÉBER, A., *Examen critique de la philosophie religieuse de Schelling*, Strasbourg, 1860.

George William Frederick Hegel [1] (1770-1831) was a systematic and finished personality. He wrote nothing until he had achieved the elaboration of his system through long reflection and thus presents his views orderly and systematically.

Hegel's main work is his *Logic*, a large treatise (1812-1836), originally published in three volumes. Mention can be made of his *Phenomenology of the Spirit* (1817), his *Philosophical Encyclopedia* (1817) and *Elements of the Philosophy of Law*.

A general introduction on the pantheistic idealism common to these three men will be given first, and then their various systems and followers will be mentioned; this will be done in two sections :

I. Idealistic Pantheism.

II. The Various Systems.

I. Idealistic Pantheism.

Pantheism, a rather absurd view, is not openly and bluntly taught by these men. What makes pantheism acceptable to idealists is the manner in which they approach the philosophical problem, using it as a principle of solution.

---

[1] **Works :** *Werke*, 18 vols., Berlin, 1832-45; *Sämtliche Werke*, 20 vols., Stuttgart, 1827 ff. — Baillie, J. B., (tr.), *Phenomenology of Mind*, New York, 1931. — Johnston, W. H., and Struthers, L. G., (transls.), *Science of Logic*, 2 vols., New York, 1952. — Knox, T. M., (transl.), *Philosophy of Right*, Oxford, 1942. — *Early Theological Writings*, Chicago, 1948. — Sibree, J., (transl.), *Philosophy of History*, London, 1949.

Studies : Adams, G. P., *Mystical Element in Hegel's Early Theology Writings*, Berkeley (Cal.), 1910. — Caird, E., *Hegel*, London, 1883. — Chang, W. S., *Hegel's Ethical Teaching*, New York, 1925. — Cooper, R., *Logical Influence of Hegel on Marx*, Seattle (Wash.), 1925. — Cross, G. J., *Prologue and Epilogue to Hegel*, Oxford, 1935. — Fischer, K., *Hegels Leben, Werke und Lehre*, 2 vols., Heidelberg, 1901. — Foster, M. B., *Political Philosophy of Plato and Hegel*, Oxford, 1935. — Grégoire, F., *Aux sources de la pensée de Marx; Hegel, Feuerbach*, Paris, 1947. — Hibben, J. G., *Hegel's Logic*, New York, 1902. — Hook, S., *From Hegel to Marx*, New York, 1950. — Hyppolite, J., *Genèse et structure de la Phénoménologie de l'esprit de Hegel*, Paris, 1946. — Lion, A., *Idealistic Conception of Religion*, Oxford, 1932. — Mac Intosh, R., *Hegel and Hegelianism*, New York, n. d. — Mac Vannel, J. A., *Hegel's Doctrine of the Will*, New York, 1896. — Marceuse, H., *Reason and Revolution; Hegel and the Rise of Social Theory*, Oxford, 1941. — Mc Taggart, J. M., *A Commentary on Hegel's Logic*, Cambridge, 1910. — *Studies in the Hegelian Dialectic*, Cambridge, 1922. — Mure, G. R., *A Study of Hegel's Logic*, Clarendon, 1950. — *Introduction to Hegel*, Oxford, 1940. — Noel, J., *La logique de Hegel*, Paris, 1933. — Reyburn, H. A., *The Ethical Theory of Hegel; A Study of the Philosophy of Right*, Clarendon, 1921. — Stace, W. T., *The Philosophy of Hegel*, New York, 1924. — Wahl, J., *Le malheur de la conscience dans la philosophie de Hegel*, 1929. — Wallace, W., *Prolegomena to the Study of Hegel's Philosophy and Especially of his Logic*, Clarendon, 1894.

A) **Statement of the Problem.**

422. These philosophers affirm *transcendental and absolute idealism*, which can be described as the view that " our knowledge, in all its elements, is adequately explained by a priori laws ". In this way they show themselves to be more logical than Kant. Why suppose the existence of a noumenon independent of the self which acts through sensible intuition and which one attains through morality? This supposition has no meaning if one does not admit that the principle of causality can take us beyond ourselves. If this principle has only ideal value, one must affirm that our intellectual activity creates both phenomena and noumena, both concepts and sensible intuition.

There is a double advantage to this solution. It fully unifies Kantianism, and it makes reality fully intelligible. Hegel's axiom is that " all the real is rational and all the rational is real "; while Fichte's is that " there can be no fact imposing itself on philosophy ", for a contingent fact does not have its reason for being fully in itself and thus cannot be intelligible or rational.

These axioms are not an explicit denial of the principle of contradiction, as if they affirmed that " the imperfect identifies itself with the perfect ". They are rather an expression of a subtle conception, difficult to grasp; in it, to avoid contradiction, one affirms that there is nothing beyond our idea and our knowledge, so that one is forced to explain everything by our intellectual activity alone.

This is, then, the way in which the *philosophical problem* is raised for absolute idealism. On the one side, we have clear consciousness of being passive in knowledge, especially with regard to sensible representations; the idealists recognize this, as did Kant. On the other side, it must be asserted that the human spirit actively constructs every object of science, and thus creates the universe [1]. Immediate contradiction is avoided by stating that this construction is *unconscious* [2], and does not prevent consciousness from giving testimony of its passivity. It should now be explained, however,

---

[1] Not, indeed, a material universe, but an *ideal* universe, which is the only one which exists for the idealistic hypothesis.

[2] To prove this unconsciousness, Schelling involves the notion of *artistic creation;* a man of genius, while wholly realizing the aim (beauty to be realized), is not ordinarily aware of the means which he uses.

why this duality of subject and object is adopted and how
the objective development of the spirit is brought about.

B) Principle of the Solution.

423. Everything is clarified by the *foundational postulate :*
the unconscious Creator of the world (an ideal world, that is)
is Absolute Spirit, a common source with whom we are
identified and who needs to exteriorize himself in the external
world (that is, in the ideal object of our sciences) in order to
be conscious of himself in us. This is Spinoza's pantheism
transferred to an ideal order. The unique being becomes
spirit or idea, and the sole reality; consciousnesses take their
position as multiple modes. All men are thus identical under
the aspect of the unconscious spirit, but they are distinguished
among themselves and from the absolute being by their
individual consciousnesses.

This postulate makes intelligible how we construct things
in understanding them. The absolute spirit, or God, evidently
possesses consciousness which is the supreme intellectual
perfection. Consciousness essentially implies an object opposed
to the subject. This object cannot be God Himself; being
infinite, He is unknowable in Himself, for He would be limiting
Himself in being opposed to Himself. God, accordingly,
cannot be conceived without an infinite series of objects which
constitute the world [1]. Thus it is God Who, in each of us,
partially is conscious of Himself by exteriorizing Himself in
the object of our sciences.

How can this postulate be demonstrated? No direct proof
is possible, but idealistic philosophy is an indirect proof of it.
In fact, we know *a posteriori*, through the scientific experience,
the result of the creation of the exterior world [2] by the spirit.
Moreover, if the postulate is true, we can discover in our
conscious intellection the laws of the unconscious activity
which presided at this creation, since they can be supposed
to be identical with the Creator-Spirit. These laws can be
made exact, as Kant had already done with regard to the
laws of science; then, beginning with something " given "
that is well chosen, one can reconstruct the universe *a priori*

---

[1] These objects are analogous to the *modes* of Spinoza; here, however, the
world is *ideal*.

[2] In the idealistic sense, the *exterior world* is the object to the extent that
it is opposed to the conscious subject; but this world is of an ideal order, just
as the facts of consciousness.

through logical deduction. This process will involve no histor-ical or ontological pretensions, but will simply show how " God being posited, the world follows ". If this deduction is in accord with the real world [1], or the object of our sciences, it will show the truth of the pantheistic postulate. This is the origin of the great a priori systems which mark these idealists.

424. Pantheistic idealism is a type of pantheism that concludes with absurdity. It conceives of a perfect, infinite, free Cause, absolutely immutable and independent in its fulness of perfection, as *dependent* in some way on finite realities which are changeful and imperfect, and the objects of our experience. Its central view of *divine* and *infinite* consciousness is conceived according to the mode of *human* and *finite* consciousness; and even, in a sense, according to the mode of *sensible* consciousness. It is proper to sensible consciousness to require an object opposed to it strictly with a *real* distinction. In purely intellectual reflection, on the other hand, thought can become transparent to itself, so to speak, by the wholly immanent opposition of subject and object or of first and second actuality, without a real distinction being needed. This distinction makes the difficulty derived from the infinite trait of divine consciousness fall of itself. It is true that the infinite in quantity or in extension cannot be grasped in one glance by sensible knowledge. In opposing itself to its object, sensible consciousness must limit itself. But there is no impossibility for something infinite in perfection being seized and emptied by one act of intellection, itself infinite, and this conception is true if one understands the analogical validity of our ideas of intelligence and of consciousness as applied to God. In God's perfect intel-lection, the notion of consciousness is eminently upheld by excluding all imperfection and every real duality.

The solution to this question, of course, is based on the realist doctrine which clearly distinguishes beings in the *physical* order (where real distinctions obtain), and in the *psychological* order of consciousness (where distinctions of reason hold). By proclaim-ing that all of reality is ideal, idealism removes any significance from these distinctions without which the problem of knowledge becomes insoluble. In idealism, since every consciousness requires the duality of an object opposing itself to the subject, a limitation is immediately involved.

II. The various Systems.

A) Fichte (1762-1814) [2].

425. Wanting to remain a disciple of Kant, Fichte constantly used the terminology of the critical philosophy. His pantheism

---

[1] *Real world*, it should not be forgotten, has the same meaning as *exterior world* for idealism, as in the preceding footnote.

[2] For a recent and complete view of Fichte, see J. Collins, *op. cit.*, pp. 544-569.

is but a rearrangement of Kantianism. For his starting point he takes the primitive fact of the critical view, that " every judgment implies an affirmation of the self "; this is not, however, the substantial, but the critical self [1], or the consciousness of judging. For example, to judge that a triangle is a figure, one thinks as follows : " *For me*, the essence of the triangle realizes that of this figure; *I have consciousness* of this truth ". In this sense, Fichte holds, " the self posits itself by affirmation ".

Now, he adds, if this affirmation is taken in itself, abstracting from the special object of the judgment, it implies no limit. It merely states in general " that which is " and, since being is without limit, the source of the pure affirmation will also be without limit. This is the explanation of Fichte's principle that " everything begins by the absolute and infinite self which posits itself ".

The infinite self, in order to become conscious, must develop in a series of judgments of science, as we can certify. The passivity which characterizes these judgments posits negation as opposed to affirmation, and the non-self as opposed to the self.

Finally, this opposition of thesis and antithesis, is conciliated by supposing that the infinite self cannot be manifest to itself or know itself without limiting itself. *Limitation* is thus the synthesis of affirmation and negation; the self and the non-self unite within consciousness. By means of this essential law of evolution, Fichte attempted to explain the various sciences as diverse manifestations of the infinite self, seeking to know itself better.

From these principles, it evidently follows that God, in order to be infinite, must be impersonal, and that each man, having his personality constituted by a partial consciousness (the phenomenal self), is but one of the multiple aspects of God Who is total consciousness (the universal noumenal self). The fundamental law of moral life, then, is that our lives be a development and an exteriorization of God.

This continuation of Kant's critical philosophy is called TRANSCENDENTAL EGOISM by Fichte himself.

B) **Schelling** (1775-1854)[2].

426. An independent disciple of Fichte's, Schelling substitutes *nature* for the transcendental self. Thus, in his view, the universal

---

[1] Kant calls this self, *the unity of pure apperception ;* see above, n. 401.
[2] See J. COLLINS, *op. cit.,* pp. 569-597.

activity of nature which tends towards a fluid homogeneity,
infinitely expanded, opposes itself with a limit or an attractive
force which produces various degrees of cohesion in this fluid;
activity and cohesion are synthesized in the organism, which is
at once activity and thing, or a thing penetrated with activity [1].
Then, using the scientific theories of his time from chemistry,
physics, biology, and so on, Schelling ordered the phenomena
of nature into a chain of deductions, parallel to the phenomena
of the self, and deduced according to Fichte's philosophy.

Much later, in order to unify his system, he placed an Absolute
at the summit of things, whose nature and whose spirit can be
deduced in all the richness of their determinations. We have, in
Schelling's view, an intuition of this absolute and of the fundamental law according to which it progresses by analysis and by
synthesis. " Thus nature, under its real and objective aspect,
is disorder and cohesion; under its ideal aspect, it is light, and,
being identity, it is disorder penetrated with light or organism.
For its part, the spirit in its real aspect is Savior, and, in its ideal
and subjective aspect, Action, and, in the identity of both, Art " [2].

But this dialectic became too abstract for Schelling himself.
Under the influence of the pantheistic philosophy of Böhme,
he sought to apply the law of evolution to society and to religion.
Following these notions, he shows the reaction of Christianity
to polytheism, which should, in his view, make place for a fully
spiritual religion, inspired by philosophy.

C) **Hegel** (1770-1831).

427. That which Schelling attempted to do in conciliating
the self and the non-self in Nature and in the Absolute, Hegel
fully accomplished. While remaining fully idealist, and also
subjectivist, he constructed a quite objective system in which
the consciousness of the self has its place not at the center,
but at a moment of universal evolution. This new attempt
to justify the pantheistic solution of the philosophical problem,
is demonstrated by developing its thought [3]. The import of the
foundational principle must be clearly obtained; it is the very
soul of all the deductions and knits them into a profound
unity. After analyzing the principle, its application to logic
and ontology, to physics, to morality and religion will be shown.

I) **Foundational Principle.**

*Everything is intelligible through being, which, identical at base
with spirit or infinite idea, manifests itself in the concrete universe
by a dialectical movement of thesis, antithesis and synthesis.*

---

[1] E. Bréhier, *op. cit.*, ii, p. 716.
[2] *Ibid.*, ii, p. 721.
[3] See above, n. 423.

The basic intuition of Hegel is faithful to pantheistic idealism, and proposes that all the riches of phenomena and of concrete individuals, with humanity and all its history, are necessary manifestations in the universe, intelligible a priori, and devolving from a *unique* reality. This reality is infinite spirit, which, being of the ideal order, can contain no irrational or inexplicable element : " all of reality is rational ". Hegel's whole philosophy is but an effort to make explicit, in minute detail, this central viewpoint.

In order to fulfill this aim, Hegel judiciously chooses BEING as his starting point; it is the most simple and the most abstract notion, and the intelligible light which clarifies all other ideas. Following the pantheistic postulate, he tried to show that the fundamental law of this being, or unique reality, necessarily involves its manifestation in the multiple objects and concrete phenomena as certified in experience and in our positivistic sciences.

On the other hand, Hegel does not give to this deduction the import of a theogony or a real emanation, as if he held that the greater came from the less or that the abstract engenders the concrete. He only wanted to separate the ideal law, which makes the concrete universe of experience intelligible, by showing how each of its details inevitably flows from the reality lying beneath its multiple appearances — the spirit of the idea which is absolute being [1]. The general notions which make up the first part of this deduction find their origin in most rich and real facts, as the abstract idea is drawn from the concrete. There are two series of these, the one ideal, written up in philosophy, the other is real and is certified to by the positive sciences.

Idealism, of course, makes this distinction a precarious one, for it asserts the coincidence of idea and reality. " Whatever is rational is real ", Hegel maintains. But, in his view, it suffices that the perfect correspondence between the a priori system and experience be verified at the conclusion of the deduction, without demanding an entire parallelism between ideas and facts at every stage.

Now, the law of necessary evolvement of the universe is that of *dialectics*, following which every abstract idea, beginning with that of being, if considered in its state of abstraction,

---

[1] Thomism itself is no different when it also states its principle that everything is intelligible through being; but because it distinguishes the real from the ideal world, it avoids the equivocations and the difficulties of Hegelianism.

necessarily affirms its negation or its antithesis. This contradiction, in order to be resolved, requires the affirmation of
a more comprehensive synthesis which constitutes a new idea,
rich with the content of the two others. This forward march
is not arbitrary; it is found, upon analysis, in the very
essence of the abstract idea. To the extent that the synthetic
idea thus obtained has an abstract side to it, it manifests to
reflection a new identity with its contrary, a new demand
for progress until the final synthesis expresses the concrete
fact of experience which alone really exists. The philosopher's
task, then, is to include in one view the great amount of concrete
realities forming the universe by means of more and more
abstract stages unto their common origin in being or absolute
spirit. Once this preliminary analysis is done, the system
consists in showing us the a priori unravelling of these cascades
of notions falling upon each other in trilogies, and following
a logical necessity as rigorous as the deduction of Spinoza's
modes. Hegel had the audacity to attempt the construction
of this synthesis, after he had made himself familiar with
the state of positive science in his time, for its experimental
content was to be incorporated into his system. His system,
due to the dialectical method, was to be an evolutionistic one.

This "dialectic", if well understood, does not seem to be
the denial of the principle of contradiction, as some have said.
It is rather an effort to avoid contradiction by passing to
a synthetic notion which reconciles the thesis and the antithesis.
But, in his preliminary attempts, Hegel was of the view that
our spirit *truly thinks* contradictions. If one interprets every
abstract idea in the absolute, idealistic sense, this may well
turn out to be the case.

Let us illustrate the above with the first trilogy, of which
all others are but an application; it is the trilogy of being,
non-being and becoming. Purely abstract being, which is
merely being without any precision, quality, or relation, is
but an empty form of affirmation. It is " that by which "
whatever has reality is real. At the same time, it is not mere
nothingness, since it *identifies itself* with the realities which
exclude themselves. The circle is of being and the square
also; white and black are of being; the living tree and the
inert stone are equally of being. Being is that which thus
constitutes the reality of each of these. As prime matter is
not actuality but pure potentiality, since it can become all
corporeal things, so being is no being, since it can become all

beings. To think of it, is to think of absolute nothingness at the same time, a contradiction in itself.

In Thomism, one escapes this contradiction by noting that the nature thought about, while remaining the same of itself, is found in two different and opposed states. It is found in the *concrete nature* of the real individual, as animal nature in the dog; it is also found in the *abstract nature* of the universal idea, as in the concept of animality. Thus the nature of being, while remaining that which is (and noting that here the content of the idea is an *imperfectly abstract* nature which realizes itself in an analogous fashion only in its inferiors, and not univocally as the animal nature), can *identify itself* with the most divers and most exclusive modes of being, and that at the same time and without contradiction, for *in itself,* being is *indifferent.* It is indifferent to the infinite or the finite, to life and to death. In order to be, it is not necessary to have life or to exclude it; one can require it (as the tree does) or exclude it (as does the stone). The ideal or abstract state of this nature of being, or that which is proper to it to the extent that it is thought by us, permits this indifference, even though this cannot occur in the state of reality, or of actually existing being.

But these distinctions, which define the theory of moderate realism so conformable to common sense, lose all their value in idealism, in which the real and the ideal are but one. If, in idealism, one attempts to think of abstract being, one must necessarily conceive of it as really identical to the objects which exclude it, and this is contradictory. At the same time, thought cannot remain in the contradiction, for this is psychologically impossible. Moreover, to think of being, identical throughout, is not to think of nothing, but it entails the antithesis, and being changes into non-being. Hegel concluded from this that what is *really being* is the synthesis of these two contradictories. Now that which already is, without being fully, is *that which becomes.* The basis of the universe is not a static, but a dynamic reality. It is not being, but becoming which puts order in the swarming of contradictory modes of being, all of which are identical with abstract being. Becoming makes them all intelligible by indicating their place in the inflexible evolvement of the virtuality of being.

It is the analysis of this evolvement that Hegel calls the " deduction of the categories [1] of being ". Each of these three stages of this basic trilogy is the source of countless applications,

---

[1] This is an allusion to the transcendental deduction of Kant's categories. Kant, however, performed his deduction only for the positive sciences, while Hegel wished to do it for all human knowledge. He substitutes absolute, for the more moderated (transcendental) idealism of Kant.

in which we rediscover all the human sciences interpreted by absolute idealism and distributed into three domains : that of *logic*, including *ontology;* that of *nature;* that of *morality* and of *religion.*

2) The Domain of Logic and of Ontology.

428. The first deductions of being were forced to stay in the abstract; this explains why one finds there the principal problems studied by Greek philosophy, for they had only a science of the universal. The categories of which Hegel speaks are the supreme genera of Plato [1], and the main predicaments or transcendentals are those of Aristotle's ontology [2]. Hegel attempted to assign to both types of categories their natural place in the evolvement of the spirit.

Being, which is merely being and the starting point of all deduction, following its first opposition to nothing, must primarily be conceived as determined. This is the being of *quality*, which, opposing itself to non-being, becomes a *something (aliquid).* The latter is the first concrete being, the subject endowed with quality. Being itself, it opposes itself to that which it denies, or to the *other*, and thus shows itself to be *relative.* Through this other-relationship, being shows its *limitation;* but its abstract limit is contradictory, as the point which both affirms and denies the line, for it is both its constitutive element and its limit; thus the finite passes into its contrary, the *infinite.* The latter, when it is fully realized due to the internal becoming by which being absolutely uses all its qualities, is " being absolutely determined in itself ", or the *one.*

To the quality-being thus concentrated in the " one ", there is opposed being as dispersed in the multiple, *quantity.* Besides, in Hegel's view, the multiple brings forth the one, for the multiple, being distinct from all other, is exclusively of the totality which is outside of itself; but that which it excludes is not the other, a preliminary category already gone over. It excludes itself, thus affirming multiplicity. A plurality, in its ensemble, is *one*, being a synthesis affirming and denying unity in its turn. This synthesis especially appears in the continuum, the actuality of it, but which virtually contains the multiple since it is always divisible. In this way, it engenders its contrary, the discontinuous. The same phenomenon is produced in number, which is a group of unities specifically determined by the final unity. Taken abstractly, however, number requires no special limit. It goes over to its contrary, the infinite, and, as every quantity can be increased or diminished, one finds the infinite in two opposed directions, that of the infinitely small and the infinitely large. Here Hegel incorporates the mathematical doctrines on the infinitesimal calculus, as he had appropriated the theories of the ancient atomists, seeking to conciliate stable being with becoming.

---

[1] See above, n. 48.
[2] See above, n. 70 and n. **72.**

Abstract quantity, without assignable limits, cannot realize itself without self-determination of some sort; this determination, which is properly the quality of quantity, is *measure*, the true synthesis of quality and quantity. Everything in reality is a measure, for the plant and the animal can vary in quantity by oscillating between a maximum and a minimum which is their measure.

These various categories consider being from the positive view-point of existence (this is the thesis). Considering being as the real subject identifying itself to a degree with opposed aspects, it appears to be contradictory in itself. In order to understand being in this way, thought goes beyond what is immediately given and considers the elements necessary for explaining it, that is, *essence*. The essence is thus the negation of existence and the antithesis of being; it develops itself in numerous trilogies. Without going into these quite abstract deductions, it can be stated that one meets the notions of species and of specific difference of Scholasticism, and then the theory of matter and form. Essence, considered in itself, is *identity* with itself. But since identity supposes that the essence is compared with itself as an object opposed to another, and in denying that it is other than itself, Hegel states that identity contains its contrary, though in a suppressed fashion. On the other hand, essence in its abstraction is identified with any determined natures; if its identity is that of absolute indetermination, we have *matter;* each of the deter-minations, which also are of the essence, constitutes *form*.

If essence is now taken in its totality, as a thesis, it entrains phenomenon as its antithesis. For essence must appear, and it becomes intelligible only through the properties which determine it and reveal it to us. But if essence is the veritable being, the phenomenon is but an appearance, a non-being. These appear-ances, in the meantime, receive consistency from the idea of law which binds them together; thus, the philosophers who have argued for this stage of deduction have reduced all science to the study of phenomena and their laws; these are the phenomenalists. But this new concept again involves a contradiction. Law, as a universal and necessary principle, must precede the phenomenon which it explains. As a matter of fact, it follows it and is drawn from it by induction. This yields the new dialectical stage, for essence and phenomenon are synthesized in *reality*. Concrete reality is that which manifests itself directly, so that its whole essence lies exactly in manifesting itself. By thus suppressing every relationship with another, the real becomes the *Absolute*. This absolute, whose essence is to exist, necessarily manifests itself through properties which are called *modes*. This is Spinoza's view, which has a partial truth for Hegel, as being an authentic step in the deduction of ideas; Spinoza's fault was to have stopped where he did, when dialectics really commanded him to continue his deduction.

The totality of essence, with its proper trilogies, when faced with being, is but an antithesis, a non-being. The synthesis of both is realized in the *notion*, to which one arrives with several dialectical steps. Essence produces causality. The latter, through generalization, becomes reciprocal action, through which, in turn, the whole universe can be conceived under the form of *unity*, no longer inert and subsumed to necessity, but living and free. This is Hegel's *notion;* it is the definition of a nature, dominating its particular realizations, as an ideal in the light of which one appreciates them and sees them as the source from which they have sprung.

The notion, by developing itself, engenders as antithesis the *judgment,* and, as synthesis, *reasoning.* Here we find the various aspects of Aristotle's formal logic conceived, not as laws of thought, but as successive steps in the deduction of the idea [1].

3) The Domain of Nature.

428. I. Compared to the idea, nature is an exterior object which opposes itself to it and is its negation; nature is non-being, and the antithesis of being. But it likewise is a manifestation of the idea, and develops according to the ternary rhythm of dialectics. Hegel here assimilates all the positive science of his age; his aim is to show that by beginning with most general notions, all others are necessarily deducible. He chooses *mechanics* as a point of departure, for its law of inertia defines abstract corporeity, and develops itself into its contrary, the law of gravitation ruling the planetary world.

Mechanics represents the quantitative aspect of bodies. *Physics* is its antithesis, as the study of qualities. Light, whose opposite is heat, is resolved into magnetism, from which comes chemistry with its opposed elements, synthesized in mixed bodies.

In their turn, mechanics and physics are synthesized into *life*. The latter, for Hegel, animates the whole earth and makes of it a large organism, whose vegetal elements, by their tendency to dispersion, become the antithetical negation; the synthesis is realized in the animal, whose more perfect organism unifies the two preceding stages [2].

In this whole portion of philosophy, Hegel adopts the viewpoint of *objective realism*, which, in his view, possesses truth as a stage in the development of the idea. The problem which it attempts to resolve is that of *creation*. If the Creator is absolute being, outside of which nothing exists (this being from which logic has evolved such rich manifestations), how can one conceive of a creature really distinct from Him? If the universe is distinct from God, He limits it by placing Himself against it, and then God is not the absolute being which makes everything intelligible. And, if God is identical with the Absolute, how can He appear to us as limited and imperfect? Hegel responds that the world distinguishes itself in a sense from the idea of the absolute; that is, as a stage in its evolution, radically denying the preceding.

---

[1] The final portion of Hegel's logic writes up the abstract order of deducing the categories which we find in the philosophy of nature.

[2] In cosmology, with regard to plants and animals, Hegel holds to their fixity; man alone has evolved and historically progressed.

But it is a necessary and provisory stage. Without it, the idea could not be what it is, since, by positing itself, it denies itself. But this inevitable contradiction is resolved in the doctrine of the spirit, who conciliates in his conscious life the opposition of subject and object, of Creator and creature. Thus, the universe, despite its imperfections, remains fully intelligible a priori, due to the rigorous chain of all its manifestations bound together by dialectics.

This solution is quite pantheistic, although somewhat less radical than Spinoza's. But its total value depends on the worth of the dialectical method [1]. In the meantime, the philosophy of common sense easily escapes the Hegelian dilemma. Instead of beginning with being and its a priori demands, it certifies the existence of the finite, multiple and changeful, though real and substantial being, and from it concludes to the existence of the Infinite; the latter is no less real, since it causes reality, but is immutable and unique in the fulness of perfection. The coexistence of the infinite and of the finite remains intelligible due to the purely analogical value of the abstract concept of being which can be realized in essentially different modes. In place of copying the real from concepts, the proper manner is to fashion concepts based on reality; if the coexistence of God and the world remains mysterious, it is not absurd.

4) The Moral and Religious Domain. Philosophy of the Spirit.

428. II. Hegel here treats matters that are more accessible to all, as history, morality, politics, art, and religion. The views which he defends had such success that they added merit to his whole system. For Hegel, however, this deduction of the most concrete realities was but a logical and necessarily a priori follow-up of the dialectics of being. This " being ", which is also Idea and Spirit, having opposed itself to the objective or exterior non-being of nature, irresistibly tends to surmount this contradiction by returning upon itself in order to possess and know itself. Every thought naturally tends to know itself, for this is the fundamental law of its becoming. This law, having been the hidden resort of all the preceding syntheses, now leads to the idea as taking consciousness of itself in Spirit. The latter, taken subjectively, gives birth to the facts of the elementary psychology of the soul. Taken objectively, it gives birth to the manifestations of duty and of morality, in order to fulfill itself in religion, of which philosophy is the highest summit.

The first effort of nature to take consciousness of itself constitutes the elementary phenomena of sensations, the

---

[1] See below, n. 428 III, for an estimate of this dialectical method.

sentiments and the habits which Hegel calls the " corporeity of the spirit ", and which psychology actually calls the " subconscious ". Below this *soul*, again immersed in matter, there is clear *consciousness*, with the sensible intuition of the fact and the perception of the object of experience — two opposed activities which are reconciled by understanding *(Verstand)*, whose role, pointed out by Kant, is to subsume the fact in its a priori laws. Finally, dominating and synthesizing the soul and consciences, we find reason *(Vernunft)*, in which the determinations of consciousness appear at the same time as the determination of things. In other words, it is the spirit which is at once theoretical, penetrating to the depths of the object, and practical, placing conscience as the rule of universal life. The theoretical and practical synthesize within the free Spirit, which wills itself as object.

In contrast with these *subjective* displays of consciousness, objective manifestations arise as antitheses. The rules of law, the duties of morality and the social institutions in which spirit finds its full liberty are among them; the main purpose of all of these is to give full liberty to the spirit. This liberty, however, does not involve indifference of choice; it is rather the fulness of positive perfection possessed by the spirit when it has reabsorbed in itself its own negation; it is, Hegel says, " truth of necessity " [1]. But the spirit will not attain it fully except in the final stage of its evolution; in this preliminary stage, it conquers it little by little through law, morality and society.

Law at first appears as a thesis in *ownership*, through which one exercises his liberty in making himself master of an exterior object through an act of will. But this domination will be limited and then denied in this way to others. From this arises the *contract*, in which law results from an exchange of wills with regard to possessing an object. As there often occurs conflict between rival rights, synthesis is realized by the *penal law*, whose aim is less the correction of the guilty than the re-establishment of justice. The latter quite legitimately, in Hegel's view, can demand the death penalty.

This liberty guaranteed by law with regard to exterior things is but an incomplete abstraction which goes over to

---

[1] " The free being is one which can support the negation of its own immediacy, the infinite sorrow; that is, to keep itself affirmative in this negativity " (as cited by E. BRÉHIER, *op. cit.*, II, p. 764).

the contrary of *interior liberty* of the subject as faced with duty; this is *morality*. As for Kant, morality consists in duty for duty's sake, or in the " good will ", which, obeying only its own law of the categorical imperative, remains fully free by docilely realizing obligations. As Kant, Hegel holds that this moral ideal is so elevated that it is inaccessible to the individual, carried away, as he is, towards egoism and towards evil. In order to free himself, the individual must be aided by *society;* first, the family, in which monogamy assures the good education of children; then, the social organization of the professions and of economic life; finally, in order to assure harmony between these two forms of mutual help, the STATE.

The *state,* in Hegel's view, is not created by individuals or by families so that the governments need give account of their administration to the citizens. The state is rather the fruit of nature, which means the fruit of the Spirit in its evolution. The state is the realization of " objective liberty ". Being the highest point in which Spirit is realized, it has no one above it on whom it might depend. It is sovereign, its authority has no limits and it is the infallible expression of justice, since it is the absolute spirit incarnate. It thus imposes itself on all without exception. At the same time, it assures each citizen of his rights and true liberty; it absorbs his rights and particular liberties, limited and defective as they are, into the fulness of law and the universal liberty of the common good.

Hegel takes up the problem of the multiplicity of sovereign states, whose rivalry often brings about disorder and war. In order to remedy this situation, Hegel did not appeal, as did Kant, to a society of nations. In his view, philosophy should not impose its laws on reality, but merely grasp the law which makes reality intelligible [1]. Now there was as yet no historical reality of a society of nations; the state always appeared as the supreme stage of the objective evolution of the idea. But the solution can be found in this very evolution. There is always, in every historical period, a state predestined to be at the head of others and impose the unity of its more advanced civilization; as a result, conquest is a duty, and all wars are justifiable by their success. In this perspective, history is transformed; it is but the explanation

---

[1] This is the meaning of the adage, " all the real is rational, and all the rational is real ".

of this evolution of the Spirit whose acts necessarily realize the a priori law, and throughout it, one finds the rhythmic trilogies. The despotism of the great Asiatic empires was opposed by the domination of Athens, a free and democratic state. These two tendencies conciliated themselves into the Christian civilization, of which the Germanic development, its most perfect expression, was destined to the final triumph in history.

It should be noted that, for Hegel, the omnipotence of the state is not anonymous or dispersed in the people. It is incarnate in the ruler, whose will is necessarily oriented towards the common good, like a *Fuhrer* in whom is concentrated the spirit of his people. In order to clarify this point, Hegel proposed a legislative council formed by the best representatives of the national forces; these were the intellectuals, who were to have a consultative voice, while the ruler kept absolute power and remained totally sovereign. In order that such a power would not degenerate into despotism, and become egotistic and unjust, Hegel harks back to the wisdom of the divine spirit, of which the ruler is one of the highest manifestations.

A final stage remains to be traversed, the opposition between the subjective liberty of the spirit and the objective institutions concentrated in the state. These two synthesize in the highest unity, that of *religious life*, in which there is finally realized the absolute spirit of God. Religion, for Hegel, is not an attitude of the creature towards a God supposedly existent. It is rather the supreme principle of unity in which the spiritual life of man conciliates in itself all the opposed riches of the previous stages. God is less the object than its result. For God is this total consciousness which the Spirit takes of itself in us, and which becomes realized in the two antithetical stages of art and of religion, in which there occurs the speculative domination of the idealistic philosophy.

Art, for Hegel, is a first manifestation of the religious life, for it attempts to give finite expression to the infinite itself. Its various forms are arranged in three stages of increasing spirituality : sculpture, the type of classical art, architecture, the type of symbolic art [1], and romantic art, which expresses the divine beauty in the most spiritual forms of sounds, of color, and especially of poetry.

---

[1] Hegel analyzes here, in particular, Gothic art, which expresses so well the elevation of the soul towards heaven; see BRÉHIER, *Histoire de la Philosophie*, II, p, 780.

As opposed to *art*, in which God *exteriorizes Himself*, there is *religion*, properly so called, in which God *interiorizes Himself* by taking consciousness of Himself within mankind. In the meantime, this perfect consciousness is not realized except at the summit of the evolution in Christianity, which was prepared for through a cascading of inferior forms arranging themselves triadically. The lowest form was the naturalistic religion of the Orient with its three phases : magic, revering unconscious forces of nature; Buddhism, adoring a more spiritual God, but without subjective fixity; finally, the religion of Zoroaster, in which light, as divine substance, wished to affirm itself as against darkness. The latter is the religion of " abstract subjectivity ".

To this first form, in which God revealed himself as a universal reality, infinite and impersonal, there is opposed the religion of spiritual individuality, in which God tends to manifest Himself personally and as living. This stage is represented by the religion of Judaism with its transcendent and sublime God, dominating the universe by His absolute power. Its antithesis arose in Greek religion, in which God took an esthetic form among the habitants of Olympia, divinizing bodies themselves. The synthesis of these was in the religion of the Romans, which " again made spirit the center of divine life; a utilitarian religion, it considered human consciousness and its interests as the goal to which the divine beings are but the means " [1].

From these two opposed forms, the one naturalistic and the other personalistic, Christianity made the synthesis. In it, the Infinite God personally joins Himself to finite humanity in the dogma of the Incarnation. In Christ, says Hegel, " the universal substance, leaving its abstraction, realized itself in a consciousness which was individual, and made the son of its eternity enter into the course of time. In him it showed evil as suppressed in himself. But beyond this, the immediate and sensible existence of the concrete absolute grew dim in the sorrow of negativity, in which, as an infinite subject, he became identical with himself. This absolute became for itself, since it is the absolute return, the universal unity of the universal and of the individual, the idea of spirit as eternal, and especially as living and as present in the world " [2]. To

---

[1] E. Bréhier, *op. cit.*, ii, p. 782.
[2] *Encyclopedia*, § 569; see E. Bréhier, *op. cit.*, ii, p. 780.

the thesis of the Incarnation there is opposed the antithesis of the Passion, which synthesizes the history of the Church as Christ's mystical body. Thus the mysteries of faith are referred to a simple moment of rational evolvement of the idea, and therein find their full explanation by the same title as any other historical fact. The Holy Trinity is interpreted as follows : God the Father corresponds to the pure idea; God the Son, to the philosophy of nature and the Holy Spirit to the consciousness in which all is harmonized. It is in this way that Hegel is the master of the liberal Protestants and of the rationalistic school of Scriptural exegesis (The Tübingen school).

The Christian religion, though, is not the summit of the revelation of the Spirit. Art and religion finally synthesize in philosophy and only there is God fully realized, for human culture and the life of our consciousness there achieve full expansion. The succession of philosophical systems throughout history is the ascending march towards this final triumph. The Being of Parmenides and the Becoming of Heraclitus are synthesized in the comprehensive doctrine of Aristotle. The Greek philosophy, as the study of matter, is opposed to the Middle Ages' study of spirit, while modern philosophy synthesizes them in a higher unity whose most perfect stage, evidently, is Hegelian idealism. It is therein that the divine spirit finally takes full consciousness of itself, reconciling, in a supreme synthesis, all the contradictions which being as identical with non-being has undergone in the course of its evolution. In this stage, everything is rationally explained, since all the contraries are absorbed into unity. This stage is the TOTAL in which each part remains distinct, as a moment of the evolution (and, from this point of view, our world with its events, its substances and its free persons remains really distinct from God); but in which all the parts disappear by identifying themselves with the infinite Spirit, who surmounts them while absorbing them (and from this viewpoint, we have the triumph of pantheistic idealism in which all of reality finds its a priori reason for being). The cycle is thus closed, and everything, without exception, whether abstract essence or concrete fact, becomes intelligible by being or absolute spirit.

CONCLUSION. The Hegelian vision of the world is one of incontestable grandeur. It encompasses in a powerful and simple unity a vaster domain than any other system. It gathers the concrete and the abstract, absorbs all the branches of knowledge whether that of positive science, or history and art. Throughout, Hegel's erudition, without being free of errors, is quite remarkably rich for his age. It is this grandiose unity derived from a basic intuition along with the clever detail of his deductions which has seduced many a mind and has assured Hegel of a considerable influence in the history of thought.

His whole system rests on the dialectical method, which is not easy to grasp or to appreciate. William James tried to clarify it by concrete examples. " Peace we secure by armaments; liberty by laws and constitutions; simplicity and naturalness are the consummate result of artificial breeding and training; health, strength and wealth are increased only by lavish use, expense, and wear. Our mistrust of mistrust engenders our commercial system of credit; our tolerance of anarchistic and revolutionary utterances is the only way of lessening their danger; our charity has to say no to beggars in order not to defeat its own desires; the true epicurean has to observe great sobriety; the way to certainty lies through radical doubt; virtue signifies not innocence but the knowledge of sin and its overcoming; by obeying nature we command her, etc. The ethical and religious life are full of such contradictions held in solution " [1]. But Hegel's main genius lay in transporting this concrete law into the domain of the abstract concept; for, in his view, every concrete reality had an ideal essence. Why is not the result gathered by the efforts of many, so legitimate in daily life, not also efficacious in the life of the intelligence? As a matter of fact, if one penetrates to the very spirit of the Hegelian dialectic, it has a great source of truth. The concept, conceived analogically as an aspect of the divine spirit (this is Hegel's central position), has not more than an abstract content. It is not an immutable and well defined nature, a simple, static reflection of reality; it expresses a *reality* which identifies itself basically with the very essence of God. Consequently, its richness implicitly contains that of all others, although it presents itself under one aspect. In order to express God, all other ideas are complementary, and one inevitably entrains all the others.

---

[1] WILLIAM JAMES, *Radical Empiricism and A Pluralistic Universe* (two volumes in one), " Hegel and his Method ", p. 99; see also, pp. 99-100.

But Hegel went too far in his view. Since the created universe is but a participation, a reflection of the Divine Ideas, he believed it was subsumed to logical necessities. In place of leaving God His transcendence, Hegel imposed on Him the law of concepts drawn from the finite. He hoped to explain the creature by God; it is God, on the contrary, Whom he conceived in the imperfect image of the creature.

" All the real is rational "; this is true, for God but not for man. God has a power and a wisdom great enough to be the " reason for being " which is fully explicative of everything without suppressing either liberty or contingence. For this reason, our sciences, which must be fed on effects and not on the divine source, inevitably run into this double barrier. Aristotle's synthesis, as that of St. Thomas, respects this view; while their system may be less comprehensive, it alone is conceived in the measure of human intelligence.

The method of these latter men is based on common sense, going to truth by induction, and using the riches of science by a deduction which is not sterile, but finding in the conclusion only that which is virtually contained in the premises. This method is natural to man and is spontaneously adopted by our reason. One encounters an almost insurmountable repression in attempting to become familiar with the Hegelian method. The succession of abstractions — as in a continuous stream — which Hegel employs, and the frequent formulas in which contradictory terms are violently thrown against each other, stop the careful reader at each moment, and keep him from advancing until he has grasped the connection of the succeeding affirmations. One admires the power of a mind capable of creating a system of this sort, and of writing it up so easily, but one hesitates to accept or to follow it. Most of his disciples adopted his vision of the world and the principle of his method, but they looked for a simplification of its applications. But it is this very method which remains a matter of argument, for it treats concepts as if, in contradicting themselves, they were not thereby self-exclusive.

The central *error* of Hegel is his *absolute idealism*, followed all the way into pantheism. It is always greatly absurd to divinize man, even if this be only at his source, for this action often, in turn, debases God to human proportions. Every true wisdom must begin by asserting the fact of the world and of the finite self which imposes itself with irresistible evidence. The means of making these facts intelligible is not to dissolve them by identifying them with the infinite. Instead, one should make precise the analogical value of metaphysical ideas as pointing out the finite and variable participation of the universe in an immutable and infinite source, which unconfusedly affirms and inseparably joins the two terms indispensable for any rational explanation of things : God and the universe, the Creator and his work.

D) The Continuators.

429. 1) Among the Hegelians of the Tübingen school, DAVID STRAUSS [1] (1808-1874) is important; he published his *Life of Jesus* (1835) and developed Hegelianism towards materialism. F. E. D. SCHLEIERMACHER [2] (1768-1834) is more of a preacher than a philosopher; he explained the Gospels through Hegelian methods. — L. FEUERBACH [3], in his *The Essence of Christianity* (1841), made Christianity the product of human consciousness through the use of the dialectical method.

2) K. C. F. KRAUSE [4] (1781-1832); while keeping the Hegelian ideal of a total and unique science deducible from but one unique object, as the logical and real source of all things, Krause tried to attenuate the pantheistic and subjectivistic formulas. He defended PANENTHEISM. He established his system through two stages.

a) **The analytic stage** is preparatory to science. Using Descartes' intuition of the self as his starting point, but of a universal and general self (from Fichte), Krause analyzed its subjective and objective content. He concluded that reality is constituted of three elements, spirit, nature and humanity. From them he lifted himself to the supreme reality, the common foundation of the three essences, God.

b) **The synthetic stage** constitutes science. In making the relations between God and the realities of the universe precise, it is possible to explain their properties, their laws and their developments in order to constitute a universal science. Krause formulated his basic thesis as follows : " The world is through God and *in God*, not alongside of God, but IN HIM and under His dependence, as the part is in the whole, as the effect is in the cause, as the creature is under the Creator ". As a consequence, God is transcendent to man and to nature, but in the manner

---

[1] LEVY, A., *Strauss, sa vie et son œuvre*, Paris, 1910. — ZELIER, E., *D. F. Strauss, in seinem Leben und seinen Schriften*, Bonn, 1894. — ZIEGLER, T., *D. F. Strauss*, 2 vols., Strasbourg, 1908.

[2] BRANDT, R. B., *Philosophy of Schleiermacher*, New York, 1941. — CHAPMAN, J. A., *Introduction to Schleiermacher*, London, 1932.

[3] F. ENGELS, *Feuerbach*, Chicago, 1903. — *Ludwig Feuerbach and the Outcome of Classical German Philosophy*, New York, 1934.

[4] LEONHARDI, *Krause's Leben und Lehre*, Leipzig, 1902. — *Krause als philosophischen Denker gewürdigt*, Leipzig, 1905. — MARTIN, B., *Krause's Leben, Lehre und Bedeutung*, Leipzig, 1881.

that an indetermined infinity distinguishes itself from its finite determinations. Briefly, *panentheism* freely uses formulas susceptible of a true sense, but uses them equivocally or obscurely. Basically, Krause is but a pantheist, as the sequence of his deductions readily shows.

Divine nature is a life and a liberty whose essential law is one of incessant evolution. This explains why the human soul, contained in God, participates in this life and, by its finite liberty, manifests that of God. Thus is justified the categorical imperative, " One must will and do the good, because it is the good " [1]; that is, because it is but a part of the divine essence realized within time.

It then follows that humanity is not limited to our planet nor to our life. Being in God, it is as eternal as God Himself, and our souls pre-existed before they had terrestrial birth. Humanity is thus expanded throughout the universe as is God [2]; all the stars are inhabited, in such a way, though, that all the parts of humanity are in communion with the totality. These conclusions savor of spiritualist theories on the " astral bodies ", of the influence of souls after death, and of successive reincarnations.

3) Arthur SCHOPENHAUER [3] (1788-1860). **430.** The founder of *pessimism*, Schopenhauer oriented himself towards pragmatism by replacing Idea with Will as the principle of everything. In his view, the unique thing-in-itself, the very " stuff " of the universe, is Will, which appears as an irresistible power of life and of growth. At first lacking consciousness in the stars, the minerals and the inferior living things, Will engenders *consciousness* in man, which is of the intellectual order. But consciousness is not a new reality, it is rather an illusory growth projected in the unreal world of ideas which Will realizes.

Moreover, this universal and eternal Will (of which each human person, constituted by a distinct consciousness, is but a fugitive moment), having progress as its essence, finds in consciousness an always new desire for happiness never satisfied; that is, of pain. Each degree of perfection, in multiplying desires, increases pain; each satisfaction, by making desire greater, is the source of the greatest sorrows. Thus, pain is a natural state of mankind,

---

[1] See above, n. 411.

[2] These conclusions have a strong pantheistic flavor.

[3] **Works :** *Sämtliche Werke; herausgegeben von Julius Frauenstaedt*, 6 vols., Caspar, 1922. — DURANT, W. (ed.), *Works of Schopenhauer*, New York, 1928. — HALDANE, R. B., and KEMP, J., (transls.), *World as Will and Idea*, 3 vols., New York, n. d. — SAUNDERS, T. B., (sel. and transl.), *Studies in Pessimism*, London, 1937.

Studies : BEER, M., *Schopenhauer*, Dodge City (Kans.), 1914. — CALDWELL, W., *Schopenhauer's System and its Philosophical Significance*, London, 1896. — CARO, E., *Le pessimisme au XIXᵉ siècle*, Paris, 1880. — COPLESTON, F., *Arthur Schopenhauer*, London, 1946. — FISCHER, K., *Schopenhauers Leben, Werke, und Lehre*, Heidelberg, 1893. — MEDITCH, P., *La théorie de l'intelligence chez Schopenhauer*, Paris, 1923. — RIBOT, T., *La philosophie de Schopenhauer*, Paris, 1874. — RUYSSEN, T., *Schopenhauer*, Paris, 1911. — WALLACE, W., *Life of Arthur Schopenhauer*, New York, 1890. — ZIMMERN, H., *Schopenhauer*, New York, 1932.

and the goal to which nature tends. Our world is bad in itself (pessimism).

All the precepts of a reasonable morality, accordingly, can be summarized in but one : " To destroy in ourselves, by all means, the Will to live ". But violent or physical means are inefficacious for this goal. Schopenhauer teaches that one must resort to the double recourse of art and of Buddhistic contemplation. *Art* rediscovers, in the evolution of things wherein the will-to-live is expanded, the unique, stable and impersonal idea whose expression causes beauty; in this way, it gives one an escape from life and its sorrowful desires. In order to attain the supreme happiness, there is nothing left but to destroy whatever remains of personal consciousness through vanishing into the *Nirvana* of the Buddhists.

4) Edward HARTMANN [1] (1842-1906) **431.** Hartmann is especially known for his work, *The Philosophy of the Unconscious*. He accepts pessimism, but completes Schopenhauer with Hegel. Hartmann believes that Will constitutes but an aspect of reality. In order to explain the specific distinction of the beings which impose themselves on our experience, one must add an ideal element to principles of action. To unify these two aspects, one must consider them as a manifestation of a more profound reality, *the unconscious*. This is the universal and unique basis of all things, which diversifies itself by developing according to the law of pessimism.

Pushing the morality of pessimism to its extreme, Hartmann assigns as the finality of each thing, an ideal goal towards the evolution of absolute nihilism. For the world, the apogee will be annihilation, and the goal sought for by morality is the destruction of *the unconscious itself*. However, this goal demands that each man devote himself patiently and disinterestedly to collaborate in the universal evolution aimed at universal destruction. Hartmann is thus openly opposed to Catholic morality, especially condemning its search for happiness and its metaphysical bases of God and soul.

CHAPTER THREE.

TRADITIONALISM.

SPECIAL BIBLIOGRAPHY.

DEDIEU, J., *Les philosophes du XVIIIe siècle*, Paris, 1936. — PALMER, R. C., *Catholics and Unbelievers in Eighteenth Century France*, Princeton, 1939. — TERRAZ, M., *Histoire de la philosophie en France au XIXe siècle*, Paris, 1880.

---

[1] See COUPLAND, W. C. (transl.), *Philosophy of the Unconscious*, New York, 1931. This is Hartmann's fundamental work, serving as the basis for a number of others on morality, the philosophy of religion, political and social questions, and, finally, on the theory of knowledge.

432. Between the idealistic and the positivistic viewpoints, history presents us with a group of secondary philosophers whose systems are an attempt at union. Although many of them are Catholic, they are not Scholastics; all of them, whether by the problems they examine (the value and origin of knowledge, the criteria of truth), or through the influences which color their thought (Kant, Hegel and so on), pertain to modern philosophy. At the same time, they are seen as fighting against the excesses, and are united by the common will to safeguard or to rediscover the great traditional truths of human society about God, the soul, and the objectivity of knowledge. In this sense, they can all be treated under the title of *traditionalism*.

There are two main groups of these thinkers. The first, openly Catholic in their initial doctrines, tend to humiliate the pride of modern reason by submitting it to faith; this is traditionalism proper. The others, whose starting point is rationalism, try to gather the common, traditional truths from the various philosophies; this is *eclecticism*.

To these two groups there can be joined, as precursors or continuators, some quite personal thinkers who deserve special mention.

    I. Catholic Traditionalism.

    II. Rationalistic Eclecticism.

I. Catholic Traditionalism.

433. Having its origin in France after the ruins of the French Revolution, the traditionalist school was dominated by Descartes' problem : What method will lead us to infallible truth? They aimed to construct an epistemology. However, the social question was also important to them, and they reacted, as a result, against Cartesian individualism. Their unifying master-idea became the following : *human reason is incapable of attaining truth by its own forces.*

All along, however, these philosophers are ignorant of ancient doctrines and the reasonable solution which the ancients offer to their problem. They did not succeed in rediscovering these ancient truths. In place of objective evidence, the criterion of truth, they sought for an external criterion in revelation, tradition, or universal consent. They are traditionalist by their negligence of the philosophical tradition.

Joseph de Maistre [1] (1754-1821) was a great polemicist and the precursor of traditionalism. The main representatives of this view are De Bonald and De Lamennais, each of whom develops an argument to demonstrate the same proposition : " Every true philosophy must begin by an act of faith in certain foundational truths, coming from without ".

A) **Louis De Bonald** [2] (1754-1840).

434. The Viscount Louis de Bonald, a peer of France under the Restoration, worked hard to repair the social ruins of the Revolution, especially through his numerous works favoring the principle of authority. His main works are : *Essais sur les lois naturelles de l'ordre social; La législation primitive; L'origine du pouvoir; Les recherches philosophiques sur les premiers objects des connaissances morales.*

In order to demonstrate the truth of traditionalism, De Bonald gives *the argument from language.* Human language, as we possess it, is inexplicable through the work of man alone. Without doubt, sensible images are sufficient for the ideas of inferior objects, serving the needs of the body. But elevated ideas, as those of virtue, or of justice, which are the basis of all society and of all morality, as well as those which express actions and its shades of difference, as I think, and I walk, are impossible without the word which expresses them. Hence, this aphorism holds : *man thinks his word before speaking his thought.* The material word is not the cause of the spiritual thought; the latter is found in the intelligence in a latent state. But the word, as the body, is absolutely necessary for us to have knowledge of the idea. For instance, it is impossible mentally to express this idea, " I think ", without pronouncing the word which, in all languages, signifies this action.

Now the word could not be invented by man, for invention requires research and profound thought — but this is impossible without the word itself. Hence, it is given us by education; without the latter, I would not even have consciousness of my own existence, no more than does an animal. It follows, then, that God revealed language and its signification to the

---

[1] GOYAU, G., *La pensée religieuse de Joseph de Maistre*, Paris, 1921. — PAULHAN, T., *Joseph de Maistre et sa philosophie*, Paris, 1893.

[2] **Works :** *Œuvres complètes*, Paris, 1817-30; MIGNE, J. (ed.), 3 vols., 1859. — **Study :** DE BONALD, V., *De la vie et des écrits de M. le vicomte de Bonald*, Paris, 1853.

first man. This is the primitive revelation transmitted by education or by tradition, in which the foundation of all truth as well as the basis of all philosophy is to be found.

Experience confirms this proof : all truths, even those of mathematics, need to be known and taught in order to be meaningful to man. But this is especially true of moral and social truths; each man should accept them by faith in teaching, under penalty of making all social and even individual life impossible. For all the philosophers who confided in their own reason have erred; to suppose that one particular man discovered these truths would be to forget that no one man has sufficient authority to impose them, as the social order requires.

B) De Lamennais [1] (1782-1854).

435. Félicité de Lamennais was born at St. Malo. His education was under the care of a Voltairean uncle. He read Rousseau quite avidly, and became estranged from his faith. Converted again, and ordained a priest, he composed, in collaboration with his brother, John, his great work : *Essai sur l'indifférence en matière de religion* (1817-1823). In order to combat the excesses of individual reason more effectively, for he saw in the latter the cause of the general abandonment of God, he proposed his system of common sense. It is not " private sense " or individual reason which can attain truth but " common sense ", or the universal consent of men as the general reason of humanity. In order to establish this view, one can bring forth arguments of private reason which lack value; to be convinced of this view, it is sufficient to certify three facts.

1) Individual reason, left to itself, can only conclude in absolute scepticism. It discovers strong reasons to doubt the testimony of the senses, or of reasoning, which demonstrates the *pro* and the *contra*, or of evidence itself, which is a subjective variable among individuals with regard to the same proposition. One is thus invincibly entrained even in doubting such an evident fact as his own existence.

2) Every man believes, quite invincibly, in a great number of truths (for instance, that bodies having nutritive properties, exist). One must live, and these truths are indispensable to all social, moral and even physical life. Nature hinders one from acquiescing to the conclusions of his own weak reason.

---

[1] **Works:** *Œuvres complètes*, Paris, 1836-37; *Œuvres inédites et correspondance*, Paris, 1866. — **Study :** JANET, R., *La philosophie de Lamennais*, Paris, 1890.

3) Finally, one can certify that each man, in order to distinguish true from false certitudes, naturally adopts universal consent as the rule. One calls him a " fool " who thinks and speaks contrary to common sense; a reflective and prudent spirit, seeing himself only in his own regard, begins to doubt that which appears evident to him. In a case of disagreement, one must have an arbiter outside and above the antagonists. This cannot lie in the individual reasons in litigation, each of whom would decide in his own favor, but it must lie in general reason or common sense expressed and concretized by authority.

Beginning with these certifications, one demonstrates God's existence by the unanimous consent of peoples. This proof has such force that to renounce it is to renounce reason and all human life.

Now this truth, God exists, clarifies and admirably explains the three arguments above, so that God becomes the speculative basis of all philosophy.

1) Individual reason cannot find truth in itself (as Descartes wished, through his *cogito, ergo sum*), for truth is nothing but the " reason for the being of that which is ". Now man does not possess his own reason for being, but this lies in God the Creator. Isolated reason cannot, thus, have any movements but against nature; it thus tends to scepticism as to its own destruction.

2) Nevertheless, reason, being spiritual, cannot destroy itself. The essence of intelligence is to possess truth (a reason without knowledge is inexistent). Thus God, in creating man, gave him an ensemble of primordial truths with words destined to express them and to transmit them to others. This is why each man naturally adheres to truth with an invincible belief.

3) Finally, one understands universal consent to be the supreme rule of infallible certitude, for God created all men alike. To rediscover this primordial element of truth, one must take that which is common in reason, and discard that which the private reason has added [1].

Thus De Lamennais proves his view that philosophy should commence by an act of faith in primitive truths, received from tradition by language or the consent of all men. He also proposed that the infallible authority of the Pope, the

---

[1] *Essai sur l'indifférence en matière de religion*, ii, Ch. xiv-xvi.

depositary of this tradition, should be accepted. After his condemnation in 1832 by Gregory XVI (in the encyclical, *Mirari vos*), he appealed to common sense in his *Paroles d'un croyant* [1] (1834).

Much later, in constructing an otherwise remarkable system, in his *Esquisse d'une philosophie*, he fell into pantheism. But he recognized that his private reason needed confirmation by universal reason, and that his views were merely hypotheses.

Placing the origin of things in the Trinity, but excluding original sin and the Redemption [2], he tried to explain the universe as a reflection of God. " One finds in each being an image of the Trinity, more and more clear as one goes from the most simple body which supposes a force or a power which places it and a form which determines its contours and properties, unto man who is an active, intelligent, and loving being " [3]. But this creation does not come about from God's free choice; it is rather a necessary evolving from the Trinity; a view which touches on pantheism.

436. The foundational error of the traditionalists is to place *an act of pure faith* as the basis for philosophy, and as preceding all science. This act is impossible, for to understand is, essentially, to see the truth. Since faith is an intellectual act endowed with legitimate certitude, it requires the vision (or extrinsic evidence) of the motives of credibility; otherwise, it would be an act of unreasoning reason. Hence, the starting point of philosophy cannot be an act of faith, but it must be an intuitive vision of being. The supreme criterion of truth must be intrinsic to our intellection; this is evidence, or the property of our intellective process of expressing simply that which it sees or that which is.

This system, however, has a great number of truths in it.

1º The first acts of intelligence are spontaneous certitudes resembling acts of faith, since one does not clearly see the criterion or the reason determining this certitude; critical reason, however, must control and justify these certitudes.

2º Divine revelation is *morally necessary* to the ensemble of men in order to give them truths of the natural order which are indispensable for moral life; this holds because of the many accidental hindrances which are opposed to their acquisition. This is a thesis of apologetics.

3º The universal consent of mankind is a *secondary criterion* of truth, for it is a sign of evidence. If there are no circumstances favoring error, the accord of all men on the same proposition is explained by the fact that the thing imposes itself as evident to all.

---

[1] " The monarchs conspire against the people, the wickedness and the cupidity of owners prevent men from partaking, fraternally, of the goods of the earth; the announcement of a decisive battle between the good and the evil — these are the themes of this ardent and somber book " (E. Bréhier, *op. cit.*, II, p. 595). It was condemned in the encyclical, *Singulari vos* (1834).

[2] De Lamennais thus returns to the Christianity of Rousseau.

[3] E. Bréhier, *loc. cit.*, p. 596.

In Summary : *Traditionalism declares as an essential incapacity the accidental difficulties which individual reason meets in attaining truth. It looks for an exterior basis for truth in tradition which, by means of language and of common sense, transmits the primitive revelation of God, to which one must assent before philosophizing.*

C) Secondary Schools.

437. 1º **The Semi-Traditionalists** [1]**.** Among these are Louis BAUTAIN (1796-1867), BONNETTY (1790-1879), VENTURA (1792-1861) and UBAGHS. These men require revelation in order to *discover* truth, but grant reason the power of demonstrating it later; this distinction is illogical and their view was condemned.

2º **The Ontologists** [2]**.** GIOBERTI [3] (1801-1852), LA FORÊT (1823-1872) and UBAGHS (1800-1855) believed that our ideas and our true judgments, being universal (thus infinite and necessary), can have no other source but the natural and immediate vision of God [4]. These thinkers belong to traditionalism, since they all looked for a more immediate contact with God as the basis for truth, allowing them to escape idealism and positivism.

438. 3º ANTOINE ROSMINI [5] (1797-1855), an Italian priest and the founder of the Society of Charity, had a great influence, especially in Italy, both through his holiness and through his works; the boldness of his ideas also played a part in his influence. His principal works are : *Nouvel essai sur l'origine des idées; Psychologie; Théodicée; Logique;* His *Les cinq plaies de l'Eglise* was condemned by Rome while he was still alive. His *Exposition critique de la philosophie d'Aristote* and *Théosophie* (a five-volume work), are posthumous works; forty propositions were taken from them and condemned by the Holy Office in 1889.

The philosophy of Rosmini is a remarkable effort to Christianize the idealism of Hegel. His basic principle can be formulated as follows :

Every man possesses the innate intuition of the idea of being, an intuition which, by constituting the spiritual part of the soul, explains its proper mode of acting and of being.

In order to give some idea of his system, it will suffice to show how Rosmini proves this principle, and to point out the main consequences he deduces from it.

a) Proof of the principle. Man has two faculties of knowledge : the senses, which seize the real, concrete existent, and the intelligence, whose object is the abstract or possible nature. Now,

---

[1] See A. GONZALÈS, *Histoire de la philosophie*, vol. IV, pp. 438-448.

[2] See J. ZIGLIARA, *De la lumière intellectuelle*, 3 vols., Paris, 1878.

[3] See F. PALHORIÈS, *Gioberti*, Paris, 1908.

[4] This is a return to the vision in God proposed by Malebranche; see above, n. 341.

[5] BRUNO, J. F., *Rosmini's Contribution to Ethical Philosophy*, New York, 1916. — PALHORIÈS, F., *Rosmini*, Paris, 1929.

the analysis of diverse ideas shows two things : 1) their traits of universality, infinity, necessity and eternity prevent them from finding their origin in sensation; the latter is required, but merely as a simple condition *sine qua non*.

2) The supreme idea, the most pure and the most universal, is that of *being*, for it is constrained by no other, and constitutes the basis of all others. As a consequence, the character of our ideas must be explained by the illumination of the idea of being, which is, in his view, like an " appurtenance of God " (one could interpret this as an impression of the divine light on our souls); consequently, it is not abstract, but *innate*, created with our soul by God. In other words without being, man would not possess intelligence; it is an element of the mind's nature and constitutes the spiritual part of its being.

b) *Consequences*. From the above view there derive six stages in human knowledge. 1) Knowledge begins by the intuition of the idea of being as absolutely undetermined. 2) Sensation, as an antithesis, brings in a precise element of determination. 3) There then follows a spontaneous " information " of the sensible object by the idea of being. One certifies that there is something precise, and has the general notion of a " limitation in being ". 4) Universalizing abstraction makes this result precise by constituting a universal and necessary type, an idea or a determined nature, as humanity. 5) Knowledge by affirmation or judgment restores this universal type to the sensible object. 6) Finally, by considering this universal nature separately, in its aspect of perfection, intuition lifts us to God

One can note that this analysis states, in a somewhat similar way, the principal steps of science as indicated by St. Thomas, going from induction to the analogous study of God [1].

Rosmini was less accurate in his conclusions concerning the *origin of the soul*. Since its spirituality is constituted by the intuition of the idea of being, one can say that the parents engender the soul of the child; the child, then, on receiving this intuition from God, becomes spiritual and subsistent. This is a very weak point in his system.

Finally, it should be mentioned that Rosmini accepts a sixth sense, the *fundamental sense* which gives us consciousness of our corporeal existence and also explains the union of soul and body.

439. 4° Two Catholic priests with rationalistic tendencies should be mentioned here : HERMÈS (1775-1831) in Germany, and GÜNTHER (1785-1861) in Austria. Both were strongly influenced by German idealism.

Hermès, considering that faith should be reasonable, taught that before accepting faith one should subject it to universal methodic doubt; then its truth could be demonstrated by reason. His error was to confound the demonstration of the value of the motives of credibility (in Catholic apologetics) with that of the truth contained in the faith (Kantian rationalism).

---

[1] See above, nn. 261-5.

Gunther asserted that the content of faith, being eminently rational, can be transformed into a veritable science through help of reflection and theological demonstration. He was strongly influenced by Hegel and taught that creation is a *necessary* manifestation of the divine life; and also by Kant, through his proposal that one can distinguish two souls in man besides his body. The first is natural, the seat of imagination and understanding *(Verstand)*, and is the faculty of phenomena and of science; the second is spiritual, endowed with metaphysical reason *(Vernunft)*.

II. RATIONALISTIC ECLECTICISM.

440. The desire to rediscover a corps of truths harmonizable with the Catholic faith in the modern systems of thought, led Rosmini, Hermès, Gunther and others to set up a view of Catholic eclecticism. This same preoccupation marks a group of thinkers who are estranged from the Catholic faith. The undoubted leader of the latter group is V. Cousin in France; the precursor to the movement is Maine de Biran.

A) **Maine de Biran** [1] (1766-1824).

441. The philosophy of Maine de Biran is, above all, an expression of his own interior life. It is found less in some works which he published, as *Mémoires sur la décomposition de la pensée, Sur la perception immédiate,* and *Sur les rapports du physique et du moral,* than in his *Journal* and his *Pensées inédites,* published after his death. Having begun with the sensualism of Cabanis and of Destutt de Tracy [2], his friends, De Biran lifted himself through psychological reflections to spiritualism and to God. By these two traits he initiated eclecticism, which defended his spiritualism and adopted his psychological method in opposition to positivism. Guizot, Royer-Collard and Cousin were among his close friends.

Maine's basic proposition can be stated in the following way :

Human personality cannot properly be grasped except by a psychological intuition of VOLUNTARY EFFORT *which opposes*

---

[1] **Works :** Cousin, V. (ed.), *Œuvres posthumes,* Paris, 1841. — Tisserand, P. (ed.), *Œuvres,* 12 vols., Paris, 1920 ff. — **Studies :** COUAILLHAC, M., *Maine de Biran,* Paris, 1905. — LE ROY, G., *L'expérience de l'effort et de la grâce chez Maine de Biran,* Paris, 1937. — MONETTE, A., *La théorie des premiers principes selon Maine de Biran,* Ottawa, 1945. — TRUMAN, N. E., *Maine de Biran's Philosophy of Will,* Ithaca (N. Y.), n. d. — VANCOURT, R., *La théorie de la connaissance chez Maine de Biran,* Paris, 1947.

[2] See above, n. 370.

itself, at first, to sensible passivity and to the unconscious in which it is rooted; personality then can expand itself into a participation of the divine life through prayer.

1) This philosophy is, above all, one of *effort,* which De Biran considers as a primitive fact, capable of giving an object to psychology by revealing the self, and even an object to metaphysics by furnishing its first principles. By effort he does not mean a pure act of the will nor a simple physical push, but the specifically human and mixed activity in which, in order to move the body, all the power of a free decision of the will may be involved.

This *voluntary effort* is marked by its opposition to sensation. The latter is passive, necessarily undergoing exterior influence, and is multiple and variable. Effort, on the contrary, is a living activity, fully free, such that its opposition to what is without reveals its independence. It is permanent, always keeping the same nature, and thus constitutes the unity of the self in which sensations, passions and other conscious facts are synthesized.

In this primitive intuition of effort, the intelligence can directly grasp the first principles of science, though not as ideas fully innate or perfectly abstracted, but as a direct insight of the concrete — as of ideas already engaged in facts. The first notion thus seen is that of *cause,* which explains this effort or force; then that of *substance* follows, as the result of the permanent identity of the self keeping its substance active when faced with the outward impacts; finally the two complementary notions of *freedom,* in relation to ourselves, and of *necessity,* in relation to what is without.

2) Before lifting himself above the self, De Biran recognized a most profound reality which he calls " simple affection " (the unconscious); it is a pure desire of living underlying all sensation. It perseveres even in the absence of conscious perception and reveals its existence in dreams and in certain illnesses, wherein it alone is the directive principle of our actions. This fundamental appetite, a degraded form of effort [1], has a strong influence on orienting our life towards a determined goal. It explains the natural sentiments of antipathy or of sympathy and the hypnotic facts in which

---

[1] One can compare this notion to the *natural appetite* of Thomism, where the latter is the least perfect form of tendency towards action. See *Summa Theologica,* I, q. LXXX, art. I.

the will of another transmits itself to ours by means of the unconscious. Joined to the bodily dispositions, it is the source of the violent impacts of the passions, and gives meaning to the " *homo duplex* " of Buffon.

3) But this movement can also be prolonged *upward and above.* By the aid of first principles, and especially that of causality, we conceive the existence of a supreme cause, the idea of which is so perfect that it must be in us as known with a sort of direct vision and as a reflection of God's very presence within us. Even from the psychological point of view alone, one can be aware of this presence by the recollective effects it introduces within us at certain times. Now, while these effects do not depend on ourselves and are gratuitous, we can prepare for them especially through *prayer.* Thus, though respecting the liberty of our " voluntary effort ", God comes into us at first through thought and, in this way, attracts our will and enriches us with a deep and peaceful life in which true happiness resides. Faithful to his conclusions, Maine de Biran became a convert and died a Catholic.

B) **Victor Cousin** [1] (1792-1867).

442. Cousin was official head of education in France from 1830 until his death, and thus had some sort of protection by the state. The weakness of his system was compensated by the eloquence of his teaching. His official spiritualism was vividly combatted by the triumphant positivism of Auguste Comte, by Taine, and even the Catholics attacked his rationalism. His two main works are *Du vrai, du bien, du beau* and *Histoire générale de la philosophie.*

His philosophy is quite weak, but what is permanent in it is the methodological theory of eclecticism of which he himself attempted an application. He became acquainted with Hegelianism by a voyage to Germany, and based his method on Hegel's views.

1) **Theory of Eclecticism.** According to Cousin, the history of the human spirit, displaying its natural tendency, is summarized in its production of four great systems. *Idealism,* which seeks the explanation of everything in the spiritual, logical

---

[1] **Works:** *Cours de l'histoire de la philosophie moderne,* 8 vols., Paris, 1815-1830.
— **Studies :** BERZOT, E., *V. Cousin et la philosophie de son temps,* Paris, 1880.
— SAINT-HILAIRE, B., *V. Cousin, sa vie, sa correspondance,* 3 vols., Paris, 1885.
— SIMON, J., *V. Cousin,* Paris, 1877.

order, is the first. The second is *materialism,* which looks for explanations in the corporeal and sensible order of reality. From these contradictory views arises the third system, *scepticism,* which concludes that truth is inaccessible. The fourth, *mysticism,* unresigned to the defects of scepticism, looks for truth outside of man. Now, none of these systems is absolutely true or false; perfect philosophy must reunite them into one body, so that their elements have a common base and, by mutual reaction, eliminate erroneous parts; this is *eclecticism.*

This method is based on a belief that results from an impartial history of these doctrines, for pure error is impossible [1]. One can also doubt that the means of disengaging the truth is that of a simple facing or fusion of contradictory opinions. The powerful help of a directive principle is more efficacious for this task, if it is sufficiently profound and rich enough to refute errors. Progress is then made not by simple mixture or juxtaposition, but by a *living assimilation* in which thought, transforming other theories into its own substance, so to speak, perfectly eliminates every erroneous germ [2].

443. 2) **Attempts at Application.** As the basis of his system, Cousin teaches the Scottish philosophy of common sense [3]. But on his return from Germany (1824), he adopted Schelling's and Hegel's ideas. This second phase of his development is most original. He was strongly dominated by the *rationalistic principle,* " Philosophy, as the highest development of human reason, aims to know the finite and the infinite and their mutual relations; it is thus, by right, the rule and the source of all truth, and supernatural revelation is an illusion and an impossibility ".

Following Hegel's views, Cousin attempted to explain creation better than had the Catholics. In his view, substance is infinite of itself, and is the unique being, the creative source of the universe. But the conception of a production *ex nihilo* is absurd. In order to understand creation, one must compare it to the action by which a man draws from himself a voluntary act; in a similar way, God draws the universe out of His substance through a natural evolution which is voluntary and yet necessarily derivative from His absolute perfection. Thus, the life of the universe as well as that of man and of all people is but a manifestation of the divine life, so that the rationalistic principle is justified, that " It suffices for man to follow his pure reason in conquering truth and perfect moral goodness ". Cousin also accepted the social consequences of the Hegelian evolution. Success was, for Cousin, the sanction of divine evolution and the justification of fortunate wars.

---

[1] See above, n⁰ 2 : The eclectics were logically led to cultivate the history of philosophy, and their efforts in this field were quite useless.

[2] Such is the method of the great philosophies, especially of Thomism. On this principle of assimilation, see J. MARITAIN, *Antimoderne,* Paris, 1922.

[3] See above, n. 386.

From about 1833 onwards, Cousin disavowed his pantheistic doctrines, correcting them in a Cartesian sense. But he remained faithful to the rationalistic principle throughout.

C) Eclecticism had other notable representatives in **Royer-Collard** (1763-1845), a predecessor of Cousin's and disciple of Reid's, and **Théodore Jouffroy** [1] (1796-1842). The latter was Cousin's main disciple, and placed the supreme criterion of truth in a blind instinct of reason.

However, while the Catholic reaction was halted in its errors by condemnations from the Church, the rationalistic eclecticism, despite official favor, did not have much influence beyond the universities, and no lasting influence on modern thought. The situation is quite different for the positivistic current, which continues the science of Kant, as idealism continued his speculative metaphysics.

CHAPTER FOUR.

POSITIVISM.

SPECIAL BIBLIOGRAPHY.

BRUNETIÈRE, F., *Sur les chemins de la croyance*, Paris, 1905. — DE BROGLIE, L., *Le Positivisme et la science expérimentale*, 2 vols., Paris, 1881. — DUCASSE, P., *Essai sur les origines intuitives du positivisme*, Paris, 1939. — FAGUET, E., *Le XVIIIe siècle : Politiques et Moralistes du XIXe siècle* (2e séries), Paris, 1898. — FOUILLÉE, A., *Le Mouvement positiviste et la conception sociologique du monde*, Paris, 1896. — GRUBER, H., *Der Positivismus seit Comte bis auf unsere Zeit*, Berlin, 1891. — HAWKINS, R. L., *Positivism in the United States* (1853-1861), Harward, 1938. — JOAD, C. E. M., *A Critique of Logical Positivism*, Chicago, 1950. — JÖRGENSEN, J., *Development of Logical Empiricism*, Chicago, 1951. — KRAFT, V., *Vienna Circle*, New York, 1953. — MORRIS, C. W., *Logical Positivism, Pragmatism and Scientific Empiricism*, Paris, 1937. — STEBBING, L. S., *Logical Positivism and Analysis*, Oxford, 1933. — VON MISES, R., *Positivism, A Study in Human Understanding*, Cambridge (Mass.), 1951. — WEINBERG, J. R., *Examination of Logical Positivism*, New York, 1936.

444. Along with idealism, positivism is the most characteristic mark of the modern spirit, and especially of philosophical thought in the nineteenth century.

---

[1] **Works :** *Cours de Droit naturel*, 1834-35. — *Mélanges philosophiques*, 1833. — *Cours d'Esthétique*, 1843. — *Nouveaux mélanges philosophiques*, 1842.
  Studies : OLLÉ-LAPRUNE, L., *Th. Jouffroy*, Paris, 1899. — POMMIER, J., *Deux études sur Jouffroy et son temps*, Paris, 1930. — SALOMON, M., *Th. Jouffroy*, Paris, 1907.

Considering it from a general point of view, positivism has two distinctive properties.

a) At first blush, its doctrinal makeup seems quite different from that of the critical philosophy. More realistic and more objective, it holds exclusively to the value of the facts studied by the sciences, of the very items of knowledge which the Kantian criticism had fully justified. It is in this way that it arises in German philosophy; it is the heir of Kantian science. But, throwing together under the heading of " metaphysics " all idealistic and critical speculations, positivism proclaims itself " anti-metaphysical ".

b) Moreover, positivism gives an important place to *sociology*, as being the sole, positive manner of studying man in his qualities and specifically human prerogatives. This study is also viewed as the only one capable of remedying the evils brought about by the French Revolution. This aspect of positivism has its origins in the republican ideas sewn in France in the eighteenth century by Rousseau. Accordingly, before presenting the synthesis of Auguste Comte, the true founder of positivism, and before sketching the ramifications of positivism in the nineteenth century, its pre-Kantian origins in the eighteenth century will first be presented.

Three articles will comprise this chapter :

Article   I : The Pre-Kantian Origins.
Article II : The Synthesis of Auguste Comte.
Article III : Derived Forms of Positivism.

ARTICLE I.
THE PRE-KANTIAN ORIGINS.

445. Alongside of the critical problem which Descartes brought up, whose depths Kant sounded out, and which dominates modern speculative philosophy, the eighteenth century gave birth to the *social question* in the practical domain. The origin of both problems lies in the same spirit of individualistic revolt against all authority. This spirit claims absolute independence for each man, and the right of submitting only to his own commands (liberalism). A special feature of this spirit is independence of the Church (laicism) [1].

---

[1] On the traits of the modern spirit see above, n. 313.

This violent reaction against the tutelage of the Church is a trait common to all the writers of the eighteenth century. All of them [1] seem to follow the same goal : the destruction of supernatural influence in order to establish the reign of pure reason. But they are mainly united only in these negative attitudes; the positive means for determining these goals divides them into two broad groups.

The first group is *rationalistic;* believing in the efficacy of reason and of the rising sciences, it looks to them for the rules of life. This is the group of " intellectuals " of the *Encyclopedie* [2].

The second group is *sentimentalist.* Defiant of individual reason and of all speculation, it looks for independence in love of the good. It is thus led to develop morality. But inasmuch as it never places the cause of evil in man, it looks for the cause in political and social institutions. One can thus partially explain how the social question was raised by this second group, the moralists of the eighteenth century.

The views of this second group found their precursor in Montesquieu, and their chief exponent in Rousseau. Their teachings did not remain pure speculation, but the Revolution of 1789 was an attempt at practically realizing Rousseau's notion of the republic. The ruins which resulted had the effect of orienting the efforts of philosophers to rehabilitate the situation; this they did by inaugurating social studies. In addition to the Catholic reaction already mentioned above [3], the most characteristic reaction is found in the positivism of Auguste Comte and his school.

This article will comprise two paragraphs :

    I. The Precursor : Montesquieu.

    II. The Theorist of the Revolution : Rousseau.

I. THE PRECURSOR : MONTESQUIEU (1689-1755).

SPECIAL BIBLIOGRAPHY.

1⁰ **Works :** LABOULAYE, J. (edit.), *Œuvres complètes,* 7 vols., Paris, 1875-79. — *Persian Letters* (tr. J. Davidson), New York, 1929. — NEUMANN, F., (ed.), *Spirit of the Laws* (tr. T. Nugent), 2 vols., New York, 1949.

2⁰ **Studies :** BARCKHAUSEN, J., *Montesquieu, ses idées et ses œuvres,* Paris, 1913. — DEDIEU, J., *Montesquieu,* Paris, 1913. —

---

[1] At least, all those to be discussed.
[2] Treated above; see n. 370.
[3] See nn. 433-438.

FLETCHER, F. T., *Montesquieu and English Politics* (1750-1800), New York, 1940. — ILBERT, C. P., *Montesquieu*, Oxford, n. d. — LEVIN, L. M., *Political Doctrine of Montesquieu's Esprit des Lois*, New York, 1936. — MORGAN, C., *Liberty of Thought and the Separation of Powers*, Oxford, 1948.

446. Though having a well balanced nature and an essentially moderated spirit, Montesquieu hated every form of despotism and esteemed every form of individual liberty. He believed man to be naturally good; as not needing any supernatural helps from revelation and, perhaps, not even from Providence.

His main works are; *Lettres persanes, Considérations sur les causes de la grandeur et de la décadence des Romains,* and *Esprit des lois.* From these works one can draw out a political doctrine, despite the fact that they contain more of a critical history of laws, and especially of ancient laws. His judgments and criticism show how he looked upon law and politics, at least in a general purview.

A) Foundational Principle.

The best government is that which guarantees individual liberty most certainly. It is obtained by a mixed form of governing in which there is established the equilibrium of powers that are independent enough to prevent each other from becoming despotic.

B) Application.

447. Three powers make up the essential machinery of government : the legislative, the executive or governing power, and the coercive or judiciary power.

1º In order to maintain true liberty, it is evidently necessary that the life of the state be dominated by a code of just laws. In order to put laws into execution (for decision demands rapidity, precision and discretion), the government should be confided to one independent and responsible person; his function is to give orders conformable to law. This person is the king.

This sovereign power must be modified by the influence of the clergy and of a hereditary aristocracy. Their function is always negative; they have the right of veto against arbitrary orders of the king.

The people, incapable of governing themselves, can be associated in political life in two ways : *a*) through the assembly of representatives, they have the right to propose their views; *b*) through the jury chosen from their membership, they share in the application of laws. The government which results is thus a royal aristocracy mixed with democracy.

2º The making of laws, requiring mature and prudent reflection, is confided to two assemblies, whose members are to have diverse tendencies [1], and thus are mutually corrective.

---

[1] As an example, Montesquieu gives the two English sections, the House of Deputies and the House of Lords. The Chamber of Deputies and the Senate, in France and in Belgium, are realizations of the same notion.

3° The deposit of law and punishment of its infractors are confided to a body of magistrates which is not named by law nor by the chambers, but constitutes a separate body with its own privileges of independence, autonomy and irremovability. The best recruitment seems to require that they be hired for life, which would give them a permanent stability.

This is the basic constitution of Montesquieu's government. The legislative body is composed of two parts, one of which enchains the other by their power of mutual prevention, while both are joined by the executive power. The legislative power has the same effect of control over the executive [1].

In order that such a complex machinery might operate, one has to take into account the needs of interior and exterior political life; this can be done by foreseeing moderative principles.

Montesquieu realized that this perfect government would be a rare thing; people are human and, considering their defects, they always tend towards despotism. There are, of course, fortunate despotisms, and the best government in fact seems to Montesquieu to be that one which is best adapted to the current situation of a given people.

C) **Moral and Religious Foundation of the State.**

Montesquieu at first proposed that the first condition of prosperity was the practice of virtue, and especially that of justice for peoples and for governments; he proclaimed the good influence of religion in this regard. He founded positive law on the natural law written in the essence of things, to which all men must submit. But he placed in human nature, which he considered naturally good, the unique source of this " virtue ". He was silent on the question of subordination of civil society, in some aspects, to religious society, and especially with regard to supernatural revelation.

It was through his liberal rationalism that Montesquieu prepared the way for Rousseau.

II. THE THEORIST OF THE REVOLUTION :

JEAN-JACQUES ROUSSEAU (1712-1778).

SPECIAL BIBLIOGRAPHY.

1° **Works :** MUSSET-PATHEY (eds.), *Œuvres complètes*, Paris, 1818-1820. — GAUSS, C. (ed.), *Selections from Works*, Princeton (N. J.), 1914. — SCHINZ, A., *Vie et œuvres*, New York, 1921. — VAUGHAN, C. E. (ed.), *Political Writings*, 2 vols., New York, n. d.

2° **Studies :** AMIEL, H. F., *Jean-Jacques Rousseau*, New York, 1922. — CASSIRER, E., *Rousseau, Kant, Goethe*, Princeton (N. J.), 1945. — COBBAN, A., *Rousseau and the Modern State*, London, 1934. — FAGUET, E., *Rousseau penseur*, Paris, 1912. —

---

[1] *Esprit des Lois*, Book XI, Ch. VI.

GRAHAM, H. G., *Rousseau*, Philadelphia, 1883. — HENDEL, C. W., *Jean-Jacques Rousseau, Moralist*, Oxford, 1934. — HÖFFDING, H., *Jean-Jacques Rousseau and his Philosophy*, New Haven (Conn.), 1930. — HUDSON, W. H., *Rousseau and Naturalism in Life and Thought*, New York, n. d. — JOSEPHSON, M., *Jean-Jacques Rousseau*, New York, 1931. — LEMAÎTRE, J., *J.-J. Rousseau*, Paris, 1907. — MOREAU, J., *J.-J. Rousseau et le siècle philosophique*, Paris, 1870. — MORLEY, J. M., *Rousseau and His Era*, New York, 1923. — MOWAT, R. B., *Jean-Jacques Rousseau*, London, 1938. — OSBORN, A. M., *Rousseau and Burke*, Oxford, 1940. — SCHINZ, A., *La pensée de Jean-Jacques Rousseau*, Northampton (Mass.), 1929. — TEXTE, J., *Jean-Jacques Rousseau*, New York, 1929. — VULLIAMY, C. E., *Rousseau*, London, 1931. — WRIGHT, E. H., *Meaning of Rousseau*, Oxford, 1929. — WYMKEN, F. A., *Rousseaus Einfluss auf Klinger*, Berkeley (Cal.), 1912.

448. Born at Geneva of Calvinist parentage, Rousseau spent the first forty years of his life far from society as a vagrant and vagabond. His formation was one of being completely self-taught, his only masters being contact with nature herself, which he savored romantically in poetry, and his avid but disordered lectures. The high point of this period is his conversion to Catholicism and his relationship with Madame De Warens, which resulted therefrom. He was a weak convert, lacking firmness in dogmatic and moral matters, and De Warens was his sole master in religious matters. At the end of 26 years, he returned to Protestantism.

When 40 years old (1752), he presented himself in Paris, where he was favorably received. But his great pride soon cooled these friendly relationships, and he considered the social setting, into which he had gone without preparation, as corruptive of humanity's natural goodness. This idea, developed with a lyrical and sentimental oratory, quite tasteful to the mentality of this period, accounts for the success of his works. Sadly enough, his views were condemned both by civil and religious authority. In 1762, menaced by imprisonment, he fled to Switzerland and then to England, where David Hume received him cordially. Harrassed by the belief that he was being persecuted, he persuaded himself that he was the victim of a plot, accused Hume of treason, and fled to France; there, because of the state of his mind, he was permitted to live out his life.

Rousseau's works are a logical development of his doctrine in accordance with the order of their appearance; all of them reflect his personality quite purely. He wrote the following : *Discours sur les sciences et les arts* (in reply to a question from the Academy of Dijon, 1750); *Discours sur l'origine et le fondement de l'inégalité parmi les hommes* (1754); *Lettre à Voltaire sur la Providence* (in which he defends optimism); *Lettre à d'Alembert sur les spectacles* (he proscribes them as immoral, 1759); *La nouvelle Heloise* (a somewhat immoral novel, 1761); *Emile* (on the reform of the individual, 1762); *Contrat social*

(social reform, 1762); *Les Confessions et les Rêveries d'un Promeneur solitaire.*

Doctrine. All of Rousseau's works, partly written in the style of a novel, deal with the statement and the resolution of the social question. Having no solid speculative basis and founding everything on sentiment, he is filled with sophisms and contradictions. There is a dominant idea in his work which can give it an aspect of unity and add some meaning to his views on education and on politics, whether it be in his attempt to reform the individual or society. Three divisions will treat Rousseau's thoughts :

1º The Foundational Theory.

2º Education, or the Plan for Reforming the Individual.

3º Politics, or the Plan for Reforming Society.

A) The Foundational Theory.

449. Rousseau's basic theory can be stated as follows : *man's natural state, if considered alone in society, is to be good, that is, perfect and happy, since :*

a) he has but few needs, and these are quickly and fully satisfied ;

b) he is completely free, not dependent on any person and having no limits to his action but that which comes from his own power ;

c) and this natural state of goodness is equal in all men.

As proof for his basic theory, Rousseau offered the following.

1. **The Affirmative Proof.** Rousseau wrote the history of man as he imagined it to be, without any care for documentary evidence. He first describes the state of nature in which each human being lived a solitary life, without knowing his parents, nor his own children. This man was without language, industry, desire, but was fully free and happy. The multiplication of men led them to make contracts between themselves, to invent language and to indulge in various rivalries.

Thus, one man began to see that by appropriating land, he could gain profits for himself and for others, and in this way dominate his equals. As a matter of fact, the association of men in this fashion saw its need of defending itself against similar groups. The proprietor saw that in persuading others to be joined with him, they would be seeking their own

interest. Thus there arose both proprietorship and the magistrature, two inequalities.

In order to protect themselves better, men saw that a supreme
and absolute authority, vested in a chief, was necessary.
This explains the rise of despotism, the third inequality.

2. **The Veritable Proof** of his fundamental theory, for
Rousseau, seemed to lie in establishing that society, or civilization, depraves mankind and is the source of all its ills.
Granting Rousseau's ideal of the absolute independence and
of the natural perfection of mankind, the evils of civilization
are threefold.

a) Perfectibility, which is the creation of new and artificial
needs, which then become the source of privations.

b) Inequality; at first this is an inequality of rich and
poor, deriving from the theory of private property; then it
is one of chiefs and subjects, flowing from the magistrature
which was necessary to defend one's riches; finally, it is one
of masters and slaves, flowing from the despotism of the chiefs.

c) Slavery, whether in the strict sense, or in the sense of
being subject to an absolute king.

Of course, there is no question here of logical demonstration.
These evils follow from Rousseau's supposedly true principle
of man's natural goodness, and from other factors which,
for him, show forth its absolute truth.

450. Rousseau's theory is often presented as a triple dogma
or a triple sophistic axiom, mingled with truths and errors which
should be clearly distinguished.

I. *Man is Naturally Good.*

In order to understand this statement it is necessary to
distinguish two orders of goodness :

a) **The order of being.** Human nature, in fact, is metaphysically
good by that which constitutes the very essence of man. But
man is not such in an historical sense, in which "natural" designates
the primary state without any perfection of reason. Man, at the
beginning, is not good *simpliciter* but *secundum quid*, writes
St. Thomas. Rousseau confused these two meanings, defining
nature as the " state of primitive and pure simplicity of every
civilization, which the Creator granted to the first man as a demand
of his being, and which is the source of his happiness, and a state
towards which man must return ".

b) **The order of activity,** or of acquired perfection. Is it true
that every natural movement or that every first movement is
good? In the psychological order (each acting according to his

nature), this is true in the sense that every activity and every tendency is directed toward the good as towards its proper goal. But in the moral order, a precise distinction must be made. The higher faculties, as reason and will, have a morally good natural tendency, being conformable to reason by definition; the inferior faculties, however, sometimes tend, even in their first movement, to oppose the order of reason.

Furthermore, it is false that man has attained goodness or moral perfection through education alone, and does not need grace for this task.

Rousseau's dogma is an outright perversion of the Catholic dogma that the state of original justice [1] is not the fruit of grace and of preternatural gifts; it was conferred on human nature. Instead of original sin, Rousseau holds that it was society which made mankind lose this state of goodness.

II. *Man is Born Free.*

Here, again, there are distinctions that hold on man's freedom.

If one is speaking of the *faculty* or of the basic power itself, it is true that liberty is natural to man, for it flows from reason. If there be question of the *actual exercise* of this faculty, man, by his very nature, enjoys a partial but not a total independence of action. His corporeal and sensible properties, which also belong to his nature, and the very bearing of his spiritual faculties are natural principles leading him to submit to society. The domain of his full liberty is restrained to formally human and personal activity of actions which are from deliberate will.

For Rousseau, liberty is like a pure perfection of a pure act of humanity : the state of the savage in the woods, who fulfills the abstractive notion of the independent man.

III. *All Men are Equal* (by nature).

One can distinguish a triple domain of equality.

a) The first concerns the constitutive elements of man's specific nature, taken abstractly; in this way, with regard to the basic rights pertaining to this nature as well as to its duties, all men are equal.

b) With regard to the individual nature, considering the more or less favorable circumstances of their appearance on earth as well as their corporeal dispositions and intellectual aptitudes, men are not equal, neither in fact, nor as a matter of right. The variety of talents which each receives (and this holds even more for the order of grace), depends on the free Providence of God; here, human nature cannot require equality.

c) With regard to personal merit or demerit, all men are equal if one is speaking of an equality of proportion required by justice,

---

[1] This phrase, state of original justice, is used to designate the state of our first parents in terrestrial paradise before their sin. This *justice* gave them, along with God's friendship, several privileges. In particular, they were exempt from sorrow and from death. See St. Thomas Aquinas, *Summa Theologica*, I, q. xciv-cii.

but not with regard to a mathematical equality. It is neither the ideal nor a right that each receive the same reward or punishment, but that each receive according to the proportion of his works. There is a new element of inequality in the free activity of each man.

For Rousseau, however, " nature " demands the most strict equality realizable among all men, so that in every political setup which is respectful of nature and its author, an absolute social equality must compensate exactly for natural inequalities. Rousseau confuses the various meanings which the notion of equality can have.

B) Education : The Plan for Reforming the Individual.

451. The *supreme goal* of education is to lead man back to the state of nature in which he can find perfection and happiness. Since progress achieved is irreversible, this goal cannot be realized; however, it should be approached as much as possible.

The *program* suggested by this aim includes four periods in which there are to be formed, in succession, four different aspects of life : the life of nature, the intellectual life, the moral life and the religious life.

1) **Infancy : the life of nature.** Until the age of twelve, the total educational effort must be aimed at forming the body and at leaving the soul completely inactive. This is so because one must respect and re-establish the rights of nature, whose primary movements are good. One must watch that he does not pervert this aim by correcting children or by completing their education with good habits. " The only habit which the child should contract is of having little, and one will do the most good by leaving them content with nothing ".

2) **Adolescence : the intellectual life.** From the age of twelve to fifteen, the child will be formed in natural knowledge; one should avoid teaching by books and moral lessons, in which the child grasps only words. The child will mainly instruct itself by direct contact with things, and will discover by its own inventiveness and personal observation of nature what is needful of science and of art.

3) **Youth : the moral life.** After the age of fifteen, the young person is to be initiated into moral life, in which he should especially learn charity towards his neighbor. Then also he can grasp the idea that he has a soul and that God exists.

His marriage, for which he prepares from the age of twenty-two onwards, should be delayed by travel which is destined to instruct him on society, its uses, its vices and dangers, its trades and useful professions.

4) **Mature Age : the religious life.** In order to complete education, *Emile* adopts religion and the *profession of faith of the Vicar of Savoy*, encountered and consulted on his travels. This faith has two aspects :

a) From the *positive* viewpoint, it contains the essential dogmas of God's existence as supreme being, His Providence, Goodness and Wisdom, though one does not bother whether He is creator or if He possesses eternity. The spirituality and immortality of the human soul is accepted as most probable (but not for an eternal chastisement, unworthy of God). To these two types of dogma which Rousseau *believes* and *feels* (or requires as a source of consolation), though he does not justify them, one must add a third, that of the holiness of the social contract [1].

b) From the *negative* viewpoint, it is easily seen that a religion of this sort is purely natural, excluding revelation as useless, accepting the Gospels as beautiful but purely human works, and denying every miracle and prophecy. The main reason for these exclusions is that revelation violates the rights of man's personality. If God wished to reveal, He would do so directly to each soul. If the miracle would have value, each man would have to be able to see it and control it. The prophecy would have value only if each man could understand and establish its realization.

452. This educational program is but a retracing of Rousseau's own life. One can call it the " sanctity of nature " [2]. Its aim is not to reform oneself in order to act more fully with supernaturalized reason, but to follow all the tendencies of one's nature with an absolute sincerity, even if they are morally bad, for Rousseau declares all of them good. This view is founded on the absolute domination of sentiment, in which reason plays a dual role. Reason legitimizes all sentimental needs by furnishing defensive sophisms (and Rousseau was expert at these). Reason also contemplates and approves virtue, living dreamily according to the good while devoting oneself to evil, and adding the approval of innocence to the pleasure of sin.

This dream Rousseau himself realized towards the close of his life, and it was nothing more than the fulfillment of his own egoism pushed to extremes. His holiness consisted in loving himself as being self-sufficient and as making him independent of all others; in this way he realized a sort of *pure act of humanity*. However, he did this only by taking the self not as a reasonable being, but as individuality : with its qualities and its defects, naturally good, affectionate, sensible, and leading towards sensuality.

Rousseau thus returned to filling himself completely with the self so that he had nothing to be virtuous toward, and hence was good; he thus had no complaint towards other men, he pardoned them and was self-sufficient; he had nothing to hope for from God, he was his own happiness, and God could only approve of his sincerity.

C) Politics : the Plan of Reform for Society.

453. The application of the basic principle to society brings up an arduous problem, whose solution results in Rousseau's theories on politics.

---

[1] As indicated above, n. 453. — [2] See J. MARITAIN, *Three Reformers*, pp. 93-164.

1) **The Principle.** The unique, legitimate form of association is the social contract.

In fact, since each man is by essence free and sovereignly independent, the renouncing of this liberty is forbidden to him as a criminal act. A double conclusion follows from this notion.

a) The conception and the makeup of a state by means of natural and hierarchically arranged associations, as the family, the city, and corporations, is an absurdity and a crime. The elements constitutive of society, or its members, can be none other than the independent individuals.

b) Since this society no longer is the normal flowering of natural tendencies but rather a corruption of this nature, it will be legitimate only if it has the free consent of the individual wills as its origin; that is, the social contract.

Besides this direct proof, Rousseau confirms his thesis by the following argument. Society cannot be the development of the family, for the latter dissolves when the infant grows up, nor can it be imposed by force, since force cannot be the foundation of right and of social justice. Hence, society must be constituted by free consent, or the social contract.

2) **The Problem.** Here one finds the essential problem of true society : to find a form of association such that the common forces efficaciously protect life and the goods of each associate, so that everyone is obedient to himself alone and remains free though in a weaker sense.

3) **The Solution.** Rousseau discovered it in his " *Republic, one and indivisible* ", or that which is set up through the unanimous accord of all citizens who totally abandon their rights in favor of the *general will*. Thus, the people alone remain sovereign, always free and good, the source of their own laws, and are guided only by the Lawmaker. Each of these elements of Rousseau's society merits some explanation.

a) *The general will.* This notion must be carefully distinguished from a mere ensemble of individual wills, for the latter merely tend towards their own *particular goods*, which may thus remain opposed. The general will tends towards the *common good* alone, for it is the natural and, hence, always good movement of a new being, the state. This sort of God-State is created by the social contract.

The general will is made known by absolute majority of the assemblies. Number does not create it, but determines where the general will lies. The minority must conclude that they have been deceived; in submitting, they follow the general will. Each man, through the social contract, identifies himself with the general will in the sense that each equally gives over his proper will and sacrifices all his individual liberty. There is no particular interest left, and all inequality disappears; there is no longer chief or subject, and each is obeying himself. One thus goes from individualism to state absolutism, and liberty, in Rousseau's view, still remains intact.

b) The sovereign people. The people, an amorphous mass of independent citizens absorbed into the state by their identification with the general will, remain the sole depositary of sovereignty, the source and the agent of power. The law which they obey is the expression of their own will; at the same time, the chief, or the government which is needed by him for the execution of law, is but the people's mandatory; he simply executes orders which remain revocable and always subject to the people.

A faithful image of the man of nature, the people are not only free and sovereign, they are also good and incorruptible. They always want the general good and only need guidance and clarification.

c) The law. When the general will becomes codified, it is the sole rule of justice and of injustice for the state, and the sole measure of good and evil. Religion itself, with its dogmas and cult, is regulated by this law (the independence of religion is one of the causes of trouble and conflict, as in Catholicism). No one is left free so that he could not conform to the law; those who are refractory are to be exiled from the state, not as culpable, but as unsociable. Whoever, having promised to obey law, rejects it, has committed the greatest of crimes and is worthy of death.

d) The Lawmaker. In order to constitute law, the authentic interpreter of the general will, the people need an eminent guide, a veritable " superman " [1]. There is question here of surpassing human nature, of " corrupting " it in order to perfect it, since society is an anti-natural condition. This

---

[1] Rousseau considered himself this " superman ", counselling the peoples by his doctrine.

transformation will be progressive, because the social contract will make the goodness and happiness unconsciously possessed by man in the state of nature a conscious matter, and one freely consented to.

454. The central thesis of Rousseau's politics, the general will, is not a utopia, for it does not exist except in particular wills. What remains of his view, even today, is the exaggerated respect for the " majority ", as if number alone could be the legitimate source of government, of law and of justice. His view leads to an insoluble problem, however : one cannot keep the full liberty required by Rousseau when entering into social life; the latter supposes a natural dependence of man which manifests the limits of liberty even though it does not deny its existence.

In Summary : *Basing his view on sentiment and not on reason, and expressing in his theory his own proper life and self, Rousseau declares that human nature is good by itself, and legitimately desirous of liberty and equality; civilization, or society, however, has deprived man of these rights. The program of individual reform calls for a completely naturalistic education ; the program of social reform leads to the social contract, by means of which each citizen of the republic, having freely given all his rights to the general will (expressed by the majority of wholly equal voices), keeps his liberty by obeying none but himself.*

CONCLUSION. **455.** The widespread influence of Rousseau is explained by his literary value, which comes from a sincere and vital style, handled by a romantic artist, poet and orator. His perfect adaptation to his contemporaries also explains his influence; many of them were frightened by a libertine atheism, and Rousseau's sincere eulogies on virtue, and his religiosity, made him admired and esteemed. In this way he prepared men's souls for the convolutions of the Revolution of 1789 [1], and directly inspired the work of Robespierre.

As a philosopher, he figures more as a precursor, not so much to the scientific nineteenth century as to contemporary thought; he plays this role through his anti-intellectualism, his pragmatism and his desire for being a reformer. In order to find a basis for faith, he declares all speculative thought valueless, but his need for belief is so decisive that he was attached to it irrevocably, as to a peaceful dream. A pragmatist and an immanentist by tendency, he looked for usefulness in dogmas before accepting them, saying of others, " What do

---

[1] The revolutionaries recognized this paternity and voted a statue to Rousseau.

they mean to me? " He claimed to have direct contact with God, and saw in his own " good " nature, the source of all justice and happiness. Finally, despite all his faults, he did not even fear to teach seminarians. He believed himself a reformer, a professor of morality and even of religion. But his religion is totally corrupted by his naturalism, and he made heresies out of Catholic dogmas. It is in his whole spirit that he is the father of Modernism.

Rousseau's views are also, in part, the origins of positivism. First, he helped to raise the social question through his disastrous experience with the Revolution; secondly, the work of Auguste Comte was an express reaction directed against Rousseau.

ARTICLE TWO.
THE SYNTHESIS OF AUGUSTE COMTE.

(1798-1857).

SPECIAL BIBLIOGRAPHY.

1º **Works :** *Cours de Philosophie positive*, 6 vols., 2e éd., avec préface de Littré, Paris, 1864. — *Système de politique positive*, 4 vols., 3e éd., Paris, 1890-95. — *General View of Positivism* (tr. J. H. Bridges), Stanford, (Calif.), 1953. — *A Discourse on the Positive Spirit* (tr. E. S. Beasly), London, 1903. — *System of Positive Polity* (tr. Bridges, J. H., et al.), 4 vols., London, 1875-1877. — *The Catechism of Positive Religion* (tr. R. Congreve), London, 1858. — *General View of Positivism* (tr. J. H. Bridges), Stanford (Calif.), 1953.

2º **Studies :** CAIRD, E., *The Social Philosophy and Religion of Comte*, New York, 1885. — CRESSON, A., *Auguste Comte*, Paris, 1941. — DEFOURNEY, M., *La sociologie positiviste. A. Comte*, Paris, 1902. — DUCASSÉ, P., *Méthode et intuition chez A. Comte*, Paris, 1939. — GOULD, F. J., *Auguste Comte*, London, 1920. — GOUHIER, H., *La vie d'Auguste Comte*, Paris, 1931. — *La jeunesse d'A. Comte et la formation du positivisme*, 3 vols., Paris, 1933-41. — GRUBER, H., *A. Comte, der Begrunder des Positivismus. Sein Leben und Seine Lehre*, Fribourg, 1889. — HARRIS, M. S., *Positive Philosophy of Auguste Comte*, Ithaca (N. Y.), 1923. — LEVY-BRUHL, L., *The Philosophy of Auguste Comte*, New York, 1903. — MARVIN, F. S., *Comte : the Founder of Sociology*, New York, 1937. — MAURRAS, C. A., *Comte et son œuvre*, Paris, 1909. — WHITTAKER, T., *Comte and Mill*, New York, 1908.

456. Auguste Comte was born of Catholic parents at Montpellier, but lost his faith at the age of fourteen, while attending the Lyceum. A brilliant mathematics student, he was admitted to the Polytechnic school at Paris, where he completed his education by reading numerous philosophical works, especially those of Hume, Condorcet, De Maistre, De Bonald, Bichat and Gall.

From 1818 to 1824, he was a disciple and secretary to SAINT-SIMON (1760-1825), the famous socialist reformer, from whom he inherited a strong impulse towards social philosophy, and some of his guiding ideas. Three points should be noted especially.

a) Saint-Simon [1] clearly distinguished the spiritual power devolving on the learned men from the temporal power possessed by the manufacturers.

b) He aimed to reform Catholicism by developing the precept of fraternal charity and sketching the dream of a " universal altruism ".

c) In the new society which he hoped to organize, he took as the rule of justice the principle : " to each according to his capacity, and to each capacity according to its works ".

The school of Saint-Simon wanted to realize social reform immediately. Comte, on the contrary, was persuaded by reading Joseph de Maistre, that the first condition for reawakening was to establish at first the unity of faith and thought among men, as was enjoyed in the Middle Ages through the influence of Catholicism. For this and other reasons, Comte separated himself from Saint-Simon at the age of twenty-six, in order to carry on in his own name.

Comte read *Esquisse d'un tableau historique des progrès de l'esprit humain*, a work of Condorcet [2] (1743-1794), and was persuaded that a pure and simple return to the Middle Ages was not possible. The progress of humanity required that " modern science " be the successor to Catholic dogma. Hence Comte decided to found a new philosophy, capable of rallying men to his views by replacing their old beliefs with new thoughts.

The realization of his work comprises two periods, that of his *Cours* and that of the *Politique*. During his first, or *scientific*, period (1824-1842), Comte, unable to get an official position as professor, opened a course in positive philosophy on his own. This work was interrupted after the first three lessons by a mental breakdown which came partly from his nervous temperament and partly was occasioned by domestic troubles. The lessons were resumed in January, 1829. From

---

[1] See below, n. 482, II.
[2] See above, n. 370.

1830 until 1842, Comte edited and published his *Cours de philosophie positive*. He strictly followed his " mental hygiene ", according to which he abstained from reading anything concerning the materials that the course treated, in order to remain original.

During the second, or *mystical*, period, he completed the scientific work of the course, by seeking for a unification of thought and of the whole of human life through the " positive religion " which is explained in his work, *La Politique positive*. From 1845 onwards, his evolvement towards moral and mystical preoccupations was favored by his intimate relationships with Clothilde de Vaux, in whom he saw the ideal of womanhood; after her premature death (1846), she was venerated as the first saint of the positive religion. Comte considered himself as the great high priest of the new religion, and received annual subsidies from his followers. He died on September 5, 1857.

Comte's two main works are the *Cours de Philosophie Positive* (1830-1842), and the *Système de politique positive* (1851-1854). Before 1830, he wrote some rather important smaller works which contain a summary of his ideas : *Plan de travaux scientifiques nécessaires pour réorganiser la société* (1822); *Considérations philosophiques sur les sciences et les savants* (1829); *Considérations sur le pouvoir spirituel* (1826). Between the two periods of his life, he wrote some transitional works : *Discours sur l'esprit positif* (1844); *Discours sur l'ensemble du Positivisme* (1848). Finally, he wrote some complementary works of a practical bent, after his political work : *Catéchisme positiviste* (1852); *Appel aux conservateurs* (1855); *Synthèse subjective* (1856). In this latter group he points out the future condition of society.

Division. During his first formative period, Comte was convinced of humanity's progress and expressed this notion in the law of the three stages. This law became his *directive theory*, from which there followed the *positive character* of philosophy, and the conception of *sociology* as a science unifying all others. These three points will be presented below, along with a conclusion on the extent of his influence, and a summary of the essential doctrines of positivism.

I. Directive Theory.   III. Sociology.

II. The Positive Philosophy.   IV. Conclusion : The Essence
                                       of Positivism.

I. Directive theory.

A) The Law of the Three Stages.

457. This law can be formulated as follows:

The first stage, the theological, was succeeded by the metaphysical, and the positive stage is now to supplant the latter.

1) **The theological stage** is the first condition of the human spirit. Faced with the phenomena of nature, man at first aimed to know them in themselves, or in their nature and causes (*absolute* object). But the fact remained mysterious in this early stage, and man sought for a *transcendental* explanation in supernatural beings, as the gods. In so doing, man did not use reason as much as *imagination*.

Three traits qualify this stage of experience: an absolute object, a transcendental explanation, and the predominance of imagination over reason. This stage reached its peak in Catholicism, which admirably synthesized all its supernatural explanations by the concept of a unique God, directing all things by his decrees.

2) **The metaphysical stage** adds only an accidental perfection to the preceding. It replaces the mythological divinities and the divine decrees by *metaphysical entities*, as causes, substances, faculties, and so on. Here again one finds an absolute object as the point of study, and the predominance of imagination over reason; the explanation, however, is no longer transcendent, but *immanent*. The apogee of metaphysical reasoning lies in pantheism, in which nature uniquely synthesizes all metaphysical entities.

3) **The positive stage** is opposed to the two preceding in three ways. It abandons any absolute in order to be content with the relative, or an object proportioned to reason: the facts of experience and their relations or laws. Moreover, there is no longer an immanent, nor a transcendent explanation, for reason, achieving its majority, knows now to consider, positively, in a nature, that which is attainable. This explains the increasing preponderance of *observation* over imagination.

Now, these three stages are incompatible and tend to supplant each other. This incompatibility, for that matter, does not exclude their coexistence in time; the same man, can, for some objects, accept theological as well as metaphysical explanations, and attend to positive science in others. Men living in the same epoch may remain in the backwardness of the theological and metaphysical explanations, while the more advanced peoples will be in the stage of positive explanations.

However, the general law cited above remains true if one takes the predominant stage of a people in a given age : theology is first-born, it is opposed by metaphysics, and followed by positive science. The latter is the only stage capable of definitive existence, since the preceding stages, based on imagination, always lead to new conjectures and discussions. The positive spirit, appealing to facts, gathers all men to itself and forms a unified doctrine. The positive stage does not replace the others by combatting them, but by letting them corrupt of themselves as old hypotheses which one abandons because they have fallen into desuetude, and the best explanations have been found.

B) Proofs.

458. Comte gives three proofs for this fundamental theory.

1) **Proof by induction,** which he uses by an historical exposition of the progress of humanity [1]. This is the most direct and reliable proof, but is most complicated and often remains contestable.

2) **Proof by analogy.** One can certify in a normal man three stages of development. The child is content with transcendent explanations, the young man looks for immanent causes, while mature age most prudently holds to the observation of laws. Now the ensemble of humanity follows the same development that each man does in his own life.

3) **Proof by reason.** Starting from the fact that the positive stage, as inaugurated, is the definitive and most perfect development, one can demonstrate that it necessarily had to be preceded by the other two. Primitive man, pushed by his natural desire to think, wished to observe nature, but was deceived by the various hypotheses furnished by scientific observation, the first vicious circle. Besides, because of their natural instinct to live in society, men felt the need of a common doctrine which would unify their wills. This doctrine would normally be the fruit of social civilization : a second

---

[1] This proof constitutes " dynamic sociology " explained below; see n. 467.

vicious circle. There was but one means of escaping these vicious modes of reasoning; that was an appeal to a supernatural being. This appeal brought in extraneous hypotheses for the mind, and imposed an authoritative unity of faith and of thought. This solution was almost irresistible under the influence of the spontaneous tendency which leads us to explain the intimate nature of phenomena by making them similar to acts produced by our will.

This constructive solution is but provisory, and the distance separating it from the positive solution is quite considerable. Accordingly, there is required a stage of transition of a purely negative nature whose role would be to destroy the theological absolute, by opposing its own, metaphysical absolute, leaving the field clear for positive construction which remains totally within the relative. The science of the relative, in fact, can replace the theological absolute but it cannot destroy it, for the two are so estranged that there is nothing common between them.

In this way one can also explain the coexistence in time of the three stages; it is not only possible, but also required by their mutual relations from the moment that the definitive and exclusive reign of positivism begins.

Despite these proofs, this law of the three stages is not accepted without reservations, even by contemporary positivists. Its whole value rests on the positivist postulate which will be examined below [1].

In fact, in Comte's thought, the conviction that humanity progresses in perfection in proportion to its duration, arose from the magnificient rise of the sciences of nature; this evidence led him to his theory.

Descartes and Kant, as has been seen, were also fascinated by the new sciences. Comte's originality was to conceive of a philosophy which not only respected, but *identified* itself with them, being content to universalize their results and unify them through sociology.

II. THE POSITIVE PHILOSOPHY.

A) Definition.

459. The expression, " positive philosophy " was invented by Comte to name a *system of universal and scientific knowledge*.

---

[1] See n. 473, below.

a) Universal. This knowledge was destined to answer all questions which men could *legitimately* ask on their actual existence and destiny.

b) Scientific. This knowledge was not merely to be valuable because its answers were based on facts, but it was to be demonstrable and controllable by experience according to the methods of modern science.

Until his time, Comte held, all sciences were but special studies; only theology had a general synthesis, which accounted for its success and provisional usefulness. Metaphysics had the power to destroy this synthesis, but could not replace it, because of its heavy reliance on imagination. Positive science, then, has the function of constructing a truly universal science, or philosophy, by the use of reason.

Such a philosophy is not only independent of faith (which is a normal relationship), but it is *specified* by its dual role of replacing the faith and of keeping to experience alone as the sole source of truth. In the modern sense, positive science is to observe *measurable* realities, and thus to be concerned with material and corporeal facts expressible in mathematical formulas, as is done in chemistry, astronomy and so on. This last point is the *fundamental postulate* of positivism, and is but an immediate consequence of the law of the three stages.

Philosophy will acquire this positive character through its method and in its content.

B) The Positive Method.

460. 1) For Comte, the unique and legitimate source of science is external, sensible experience. Two special sciences are thereby suppressed: ontology, whose object is the purely intellectual " being-as-such ", studying spirit as well as body; and psychology, as the special science based on internal experience.

Comte did not deny the existence of conscious facts, but he denied their value as testimony to the validity of consciousness as a source of scientific observation. In this way, he strongly opposed any eclectic psychology. As a matter of fact, he held, one can classify the facts of consciousness into two groups: cognitive and affective facts. With regard to the first, he held that observation of consciousness by itself was an absurdity, for in positivism every power of knowledge, even intellectual, is but *organic*, having as object the sensible and measurable fact. Now, an organic faculty cannot act at the same time that it regards itself.

Affective facts can be observed by consciousness, since they belong to another organic power. But the testimony so reaped is negligible for science. Affections are fully known only through their effects, which are exterior, and the troubles of the passions prevent any serious, internal observation [1].

The study of man is not suppressed, but divided between two other sciences. *Physiology* studies the various organs, as the brain, and their functions. *Sociology* deals with the external observation of social customs, in order to find the laws which govern specifically human activity.

2) In order to apply this method, the *division of labor* is a condition for success, as experience readily shows. But to avoid a breakdown and to assure the progress of this universal science, the division of labor is to be complemented by creating a new class of savants, that of the philosophers, who will be occupied with no particular domains but with the unification of them all.

C) The Content of Positive Philosophy.

461. *The positive philosophy* is comprised by the ensemble of positive sciences arranged in order between mathematics, which is their broadest basis, and sociology, which is their summit and regulator. The function of positive philosophy is not to resolve new problems strange to the sciences, but rather to organize in a solid totality the multiple scientific solutions whose ensemble can fully satisfy human reason. There is, from this point of view, a lacuna which must be bridged. Comte closed it by creating *sociology*, by which he suborned to *science* not only man's body, but also the specifically human side of his intellectual and moral life, whose exterior manifestations form society.

In positivism, *a) science* can be defined as *an ensemble of laws regulating the relations of one precise object with others*. Biology, for instance, exposes the relations of the living realm with all other beings.

b) Law, for positivism, is *a general fact*, or a fact whose *constancy* can be measured or made precise, despite the variety of its applications; for instance, the fact of universal gravitation.

---

[1] Many positivists, on the other hand, do not adopt this suppression; see below, *The Psychological Current*, nn. 483, ff.

This law becomes, for all men, a *mental power* or a logical principle for classifying facts, and a *material power* or a means of directing and utilizing the forces of nature[1]. Comte synthesized these definitions in the phrase, " To know in order to predict, and thus to be able to provide "[2].

This notion of science assumes the basic postulate of *determinism in nature's laws.* They are viewed as immutably necessary so that the relation once certified between two phenomena, or even the conditions which determine the existence of a fact, will invariably reproduce the same effects in the same circumstances. The success of the mathematical sciences applied to all these domains will suffice, no doubt, to impose this new postulate on all of them[3].

This determinism does not prevent man from modifying natural laws, in a sense, by turning them to his profit, for there is question of dominating them by submitting to them, and of respecting them while utilizing them. Thus, by applying the laws of electricity, a lightning rod prevents fire which would occur by these very same laws.

The principle of classifying sciences can be formulated as follows : *the multiplicity of sciences does not imply the independence of each, but sciences are naturally coordinated as superimposed stages, based on the degree of the simplicity of their object and the corresponding generality of their laws.* It is easy to admit that the more simple the object of science, the more universal or the least changeable are its laws; in this way, the six degrees of science are coordinated.

In the first place are the *mathematical sciences,* whose object is the most simple possible, or *bodies as such.* In positivism, being in general, the object of our reason, and corporeal being, or being observable through sensible experience, are completely identified. Mathematical laws are totally immutable, and they apply to all objects without distinction.

Astronomy, whose object embraces all the astral bodies, is in the second place.

Physics, which studies our earthly planet in general, is the third science.

---

[1] A. Littré, *Auguste Comte et la Philosophie positive,* p. 42; Littré coined these expressions. See also D. J. Mercier, *The Origins of Contemporary Psychology,* p. 62. — [2] *Savoir pour prévoir, afin de pourvoir.*

[3] Only with considerable reservation can one apply this postulate, as did Comte, *to the intellectual and moral life of man.* The same applies to the positivist definitions of science and laws. See below, n. 469 and n. 473.

Chemistry, whose domain among terrestrial bodies is the mineral realm, is the fourth type of science.

In fifth place, Comte places *physiology,* which is restricted to organized or living beings.

Finally, *sociology* is in the sixth place; it is reserved to the study of specifically human facts, and is called social physics. Its object is thus the most complex, and its proper laws are least universal of all studies. It should, however, use all other laws with a practical goal; for instance, if one changes the climate with the help of physical laws, man's intellectual and moral situation will profit from this action [1].

The nature of sociology, as dealing with the complex, requires that it be in last place, as does the fact that it presupposes the other sciences already constituted. Now that sociology has been created, Comte estimates that the positive spirit has become universal, and the dependency which it dicovers among the sciences will permit it to unify them in a vast synthesis.

D) The Unifying Science.

462. In order to synthesize the ensemble of sciences, the ideal is to find a unique law to which one can always refer the facts of experience. This law would thus confer objective or speculative unity. *Mathematics* and its laws fulfill this unifying function, for its object is the most universal. Comte had hoped to constitute a synthesis based on a mathematical law (perhaps on the law of universal gravitation), but he judged it an impossibility for some time, though not for always; it had to be postponed until a sufficient number of facts had been gathered, especially with regard to man.

Instead, Comte chose to set up a subjective synthesis, geared for the usefulness of humanity. Accordingly, *sociology* would be the unifying science, because its object is most complex and most mutable.

Since humanity's progress is partially dependent on biological, chemical, astronomical and similar conditions studied in the

---

[1] Comte's synthesis is remarkable for its simplicity and its moderation. His principle of classifying sciences perfectly unifies them. It recalls, in a broad way, the *formal objects* of Aristotle and St. Thomas, though a positivist definition is given to these notions. As to the details of his synthesis, the constant progress of research, creating new special sciences, requires that his listing be added to, even though these new sciences are not opposed to his thought. See below, with regard to morality, n. 466.

various sciences, sociology must first make precise the meaning and the laws of this progress. Once this has been done, it can effectively direct all the other sciences by determining lines of research useful to humanity, by distinguishing useful from imaginary speculations, and in making each branch of science profit from the progress realized in other branches. Thus there can be established a true unification of all scientific works by this method and with the goal of working, each in its sphere, for the progress of humanity and the remedying of social crises. This is what Comte calls his " subjective synthesis ".

The importance of sociology to positivism is quite evident from what has been said. Comte himself dedicated three volumes of his work on positive philosophy to this branch.

III. SOCIOLOGY.

463. Sociology can be defined as follows :

The special science whose object is the observation of intellectual and moral facts, through which human societies are constituted and by which they are progressive.

Three conditions are required for the existence of a special science : an object, a method, and laws.

a) The object is the group of facts which one encounters only in men; it includes those facts proper to human society, as organized families, industries and artistic life.

b) The method can be indirect or direct.

1. *Indirectly,* sociology uses the methods of all other sciences, by adapting them to its own object. Historical observation is especially prominent, but experimentation on the social maladies and the success of past remedies is also found as taking the place of facts intentionally undergone in order to demonstrate a law. The deductive and comparative method can supply for the silence of documents on man's origins. The method consists in deducing man's primitive life by help of the physiology of our organs and natural faculties, or by comparison with the more advanced animal species or the groups of less civilized peoples.

2. But the *direct method* of sociology is history, which discovers and demonstrates the laws governing past or present society, and thus permits us to foresee its future evolution.

c) The existence of sociological *laws* is, for Comte, a corollary of his basic postulate. In his view, determinism governs society as it does other natural phenomena, so that he spoke of sociology as " social physics ". He admitted, however, that the complexity of human facts keeps their interpretation from being too evident, and that one must frequently be content with probable laws or conclusions. He completes his scientific method by adding poetry, or the imagination, which adds concrete facts to abstract laws, permitting one to outline the future development of society in a living tableau, immediately practicable and usable by the rulers.

Sociology, then, has a practical aim [1]. While humanity develops according to necessary laws, we can act efficaciously by procuring the circumstances favorable to accelerating progress or avoiding inevitable crises. Three means present themselves in securing this practical aim : the *biological* reactions modify the conditions of physical life, as nutrition; the *social* reactions, as contracts between various civilizations; *political* action is the third means. The latter is most in our power, and yet the least efficacious, for government is primarily a general expression of the actual status of society. It can, however, react upon the social conditioning of mankind, and direct mankind towards true progress.

Before it can progress, a society must exist, and thus it must realize certain conditions; this gives a division into static and dynamic sociology.

A) Static Sociology.

464. This science studies mediate conditions which are necessary that social life, in any time or place and independently of its evolution, be possible in itself. There are two groups of these conditions : the institutions and their functions.

I. *Institutions.*

The *institutions* are the conditions of social existence taken objectively as means which man needs in order to establish himself in society. Before explaining their nature and number, one must study, first, the origin of society.

This origin is not at all due to the experience of social benefits, which suppose a society already established; it must

---

[1] This practical aim allows Comte to unify the sciences in a *subjective synthesis;* see above, n. 462.

be sought for in man's natural instinct. Now there are two
natural tendencies in man : *egoism*, which leads him to seek
his own interests, and *altruism*, which leads him to love others
and to do good to them. These tendencies constitute moral
life, which, along with intellectual life, is the very material
of sociology : the ensemble of specifically human or social
facts.

The basic sentiment, and the only one capable at the
beginning of leading to actions, is egoism. Its role is to regulate
intellectual life, halting its speculative or imaginary researches
by proposing to man the real and practical goal of organizing
his terrestrial life. But, in its turn, the intellectual life, by
showing the nobility of being disinterested, orients activity
towards altruism. These two tendencies thus complete and
mutually direct each other through the assistance of intellectual
life.

Now, society is evidently impossible unless the altruistic
instinct is dominant. Three institutions, accordingly, are
necessary to insure this dominance.

1. **In the material order : property.** Man is not condemned
to spend his life in the satisfaction of egoistic needs, whose
principal one is nourishment; he must produce beyond his
own needs, and store his provisions. These then constitute
a " capital " which others can use for their own profit.
Appropriation is the fundamental condition that makes this
first step towards altruism possible.

2. **In the moral order : the family.** A natural institution,
the family is based on a double subordination of the sexes
(male and female) and of ages (parents and children). The
family is necessary as a transition between the individual and
society in two ways : it harmonizes the opposition of characteristics which arise from the different aptitudes of its members,
for, if society needed this diversity, it would be destroyed
by family intimacy. In the family, each naturally has a role
to play which is in accord with his capacities. Secondly,
the family is also the school in which the social sentiments
are born and progress. *Solidarity* is there, in the cooperation
of parents in educating their children; *submission* to the past
is found, in the child, who sees his own egoism repressed by
the obligation to obey; *foresight* is also there, especially in
the parents, who have to take care of the family patrimony
for the future.

3. **In the intellectual order : language.** Language is the means for men to enter into communication with each other, allowing them to pool their thoughts and affections; from this there also arises the efficacy of prayers[1]. Language is also the means of amassing an intellectual capital, and this is its main social function.

2. *The Functions.*

465. *Functions* are those conditions of social existence taken *subjectively* in man or the special forms of human activity required by social life.

The essential trait of every society, from this point of view, is the specialization of the activities or functions (division of labor) and their cooperation in the same goal. Now this characteristic has its basis in the three great social forces; authority directs it and religion unifies it.

1) **Social Forces.** A social force is the result of the activity of several contemporary or successive men, synthesized in one and the same individual. Three are distinguishable : *a*) *the material force,* based on number and on riches, pertaining especially to warriors and manufacturers; *b*) *the intellectual force,* proper to savants and to the clergy, is the most universal for it extends to the universe just as the laws studied in the sciences; *c*) *the moral force,* based on the development of altruistic sentiments, is the special gift of womankind. The latter is the most noble, for it crowns the others; but woman, because of her native weakness, exercises this force only in the family.

Material force is the most fundamental, for the other two forces depend on it in their exercise; material force itself depends on the *earth* for its development, for man is affixed to the earth. The nature of the soil begets a common characteristic of occupations among the inhabitants and, as a result, in their material forces. Thus, it is the source of cooperation between families which make up the city or the state. Soil is, then, the proper domain in which material force is to be exercised, and it constitutes the framework in which society truly begins.

---

[1] Comte is thinking here of *vocal* prayer, which is not, for him, an elevation of the soul towards God, but the mutual communication of our thoughts and sentiments.

In comparing society to a living organism, one can say that the social forces are like its tissues, that the family is like its cell, while the states, cities or communities constitute its diverse organs.

2) **Authority.** Authority is the social function destined to curb the dispersion of ideas, sentiments and interests in order to coordinate various separated occupations. As for the other functions, so the title to authority lies in the capacity of exercising it. Authority is an especially perfect synthesis of the three social forces; in order to be efficacious, it must rely on the riches and on the number of partisans, but it must impose itself especially through moral and intellectual superiority.

Even though one man (and especially at the beginning) can fulfill all the conditions of a chief, the perfect government supposes two quite distinct powers : the temporal power, belonging to manufacturers and to the military, corresponding to material forces; the spiritual power, belonging to the savants, and corresponding to the intellectual forces. Woman, for her part, as the depositary of moral forces, is naturally subject, and only indirectly is she concerned with authority. Spiritual power objectively depends on temporal power with regard to the material conditions of life; but subjectively, with regard to the principles of action which it furnishes, spiritual power is superior, and its role is to assure that every government is good.

3) **Religion.** Religion, a characteristic of the human species, is not defined as that which binds man to God, but as the great unifying principle of all the faculties of a man and of all the individuals among themselves, for it gives all of them the same goal for their actions. It is constituted by three elements : *faith* in an exterior power; *cult*, a sentiment of respect and honor for this power; a *regime* of exterior moral conduct, liturgy or politics, imposed by this respect.

The role of religion is to regulate and consecrate the exercise of authority, and in this way, favorably to support all social functions.

B) **Dynamic Sociology.**

466. Dynamic sociology is the study of immediate conditions which determine social life at any moment of its evolvement; it establishes, in this way, the laws of society's progress.

Comte's thoughts on this matter can be summarized as four laws.

1) **The general law of evolution.** Human nature, different from other animal species, is endowed with faculties outfitting man for a continuous development called *progress*. Humanity progresses not by advancing towards an absolute goal, which would be inexistent for positivism, but in the sense that its life is constituted by a series of states; these manners of being and of acting are enchained as causes and effects, just as the embryo is developed in passing through a series of stages until it becomes a perfect animal. The progress of humanity is thus as necessary and irreversible as any physical law. It is also indefinite; everything being relative in life, man can never attain the plenitude of his perfection, which would be an absolute.

The direction of progress is indicated by the three special laws which concern man's three faculties : the intellectual, the active and the affective.

2) **The law of intellectual progress.** This is the law of the three stages explained above [1]. By this law, intellectual progress is accomplished by the increasing predominance of reason or of positive observation over theological and metaphysical imagination.

3) **The law of progress in activity.** The need to act is essential to man, and expresses itself through wars of conquest, followed by defensive wars, then by economic ones, accompanied with a constant predominance of pacific and industrial occupations which are, finally, to supplant the others. Comte established a close correlation between the stages of these two last laws; it is clear that the industrial era must accompany the positive stage and its scientific discoveries.

4) **The law of affective progress.** The twofold natural sentiment in man of egoism and altruism develops in such wise that the altruistic sentiments, though weak at first, become stronger until they fully dominate egoism.

Here again, affective progress is in close correlation with the other laws. Thus, the union of individuals in the family, the union of families for warfare, and the cooperation of all for industry serve to underscore the stages that are more and more favorable to altruism. Moreover, since positive science is universal, it well corresponds to world-wide altruism.

This fourth law constitutes the essential of Comte's **morality** [2], and from it there follows the necessity for positivism to suppress the idea of *right*, a theological notion supposing a superhuman or divine authority which dominates mankind. His whole notion of morality can be synthesized in the notion of *duty*, definable as : " The natural tendency to subordinate the satisfaction of personal appetites to the good of the entire

---

[1] See above, n. 457.

[2] Morality is the final chapter of sociology; however, considering its importance, Comte decided to make it into a *special science*.

species, according to the law of the predominance of altruistic sentiments ". The axiom of Comte's morality could, then, be expressed as, " to live for others ".

467. In order to demonstrate these four laws, Comte bases his conclusions on history, not on the history of all humanity, however, but on that of the most advanced peoples of every age. Beginning with the Egyptians, he continues with the Greeks and the Romans, and concludes with the Europeans and the French. This historical sketch is looked upon as sufficient to point out all the stages which people must necessarily traverse in their progress. Inasmuch as progress has for its foundation the physiological constitution of our nature, which is sensibly the same throughout, it must necessarily go through the same stages more or less rapidly.

These laws of evolution apply to various institutions and functions studied in static sociology. Since the clearest law is that of the three stages, one could summarize Comte's remarks under three headings.

The first would trace the situation with regard to social elements in the theological age, as subdivided into three eras. The first is that of fetishism, or of origins; the second is that of polytheism or of progress; the third is that of Catholicism, the apogee, the latter giving everything to the positive spirit that is possible, except for sacrificing dogmas.

The second heading would trace the destructions of the metaphysical age which began towards the close of the Middle Ages by systematically opposing Catholic theology with its positive theses (as one would see in the Protestant theory of free interpretation destructive of the dogma and of the authority of Revelation, and in the revolutionary legalists destroying the idea of a king in favor of the people, or pantheism destroying Catholic morality, and so on). This stage, however, created nothing positive for the reconstruction of society.

The third stage is that of positivism, which alone profits from the metaphysical destructions by taking into account the framework of progress elaborated by Catholicism, but which realizes how empty it is of theological significance. Positivism transports this progress into a *purely relative* plan along with the motivation of positive science.

a) Activity, already become a peaceful portion of civilization through the Church's influence, becomes industrial and rural by suppressing the causes of war.

b) Altruism, already extended into Europe through Christianity, becomes universal or planetary, due to science.

c) Authority keeps the same precise distinction of a twofold power, the one temporal and the other spiritual. Similar to the Pope, the spiritual chief of Europe was fully distinguished from the temporal heads of each nation. In a similar way, the sociologists, at the head of other savants, are the spiritual chiefs of the universe, and are distinguishable from the bankers and manufacturers and other industrial leaders, who are temporal heads of many little states [1], and who are to constitute the mundane, federative republic of the positive age.

d) Property, which Catholicism made socially prominent by making the rich man a mandatory of God, keeps its true nature not only for oneself, but also for others. The rich must assure the material living conditions for the savants, and pay workers a family wage sufficient for seven persons.

e) The family keeps the double law of monogamy and of indissolubility of marriage, adding that of perpetual widowhood (as most conformable to its goal).

f) Finally, the arts, much favored by the Catholic peace, are freely deployed in order to outline a living and attractive tableau of future society, and to depict the grandeur of humanity and of matter. They thus collaborate towards progress.

C) **Positive Religion.**

468. Beyond this help afforded by the arts, Comte added, as a conclusion to scientific laws, a complementation of the imagination which he thought essential : *positive religion.* Religion should evolve, in his view, just as the other functions of society, and in the same sense, for religion is necessary for the full flowering of man's affective tendencies and for the perfect unification of man's life. Its purely subjective role permits it to use hypotheses and imaginary constructions which will be legitimate as long as they do not contradict any scientific law.

In this religion, God is replaced by a concrete, relative, changeful and imperfect master, who is still greater than any man. This god is *humanity*, constituted by the ensemble of men, and especially of the geniuses whose lives are useful to progress. This being, of which each man is but a part, dominates us and merits our adoration. Poetry allows one to associate earth and air with humanity (the positive trinity is : humanity, the great being, earth, the great fetish, air, the great medium), and to make of them benevolent beings worthy of our homage.

As any other, so this religion has its priests, who are the sociologists, and its rites, whose detailed ceremonial Comte outlined. The basis of it is the cult given to deceased savants, for the recompense of positivist good is subjective immortality in the memory of humanity.

---

[1] Comte is a republican; he thought that, for good government, a state should not be larger than Belgium.

If this is not atheism, it can at least be called *materialistic pantheism*. It is true that the positivists do not accept the qualification of " pantheism " when applied to their doctrine, for that is an error of the metaphysical age. Nor do they accept the label of " atheism ", for that supposes an affirmation in the metaphysical domain. They call themselves *agnostic*, for they are content to consider such problems, especially that of God, as beyond the legitimate range of our scientific reason. In practice, this avowal of ignorance is no different from the negation of God. It is a grave mutilation of human destiny. Finally, we see here again the termination towards which the rationalistic spirit is irresistibly drawn : the divinization of man and replacing God with man [1].

D) **Value of the Comteian Sociology.**

469. The elements offered in Comte's static sociology are mainly acceptable, but the laws of dynamic sociology are quite contestable. Even modern positivists do not hold that sociology, as a positive science, has as yet emerged from its gropings towards full development and maturation.

There is a triple reason for this weakness :

a) First of all, Comte's wholly *arbitrary recasting of historical events*, especially on human origins and on the origin of religion. For instance, he attributes the foundation of Catholicism to St. Paul. Also, the existence of the Hebrew people and of the patriarchs is an historical refutation of the order of necessary progress. Polytheism, instead of being the primitive state, seems a degradation of monotheism, which was finally re-established. The return to spiritual values in our days shows that the scientist ideal is not as yet definitive [2].

b) Moreover, Comte completely neglects an important factor, *human liberty*. This element of variation does not allow one to think of sociology as a simple " social physics ", having laws as rigorous as those of the physical sciences. It should rather be classed among the *moral* sciences, in which the notion of determinism has a much larger meaning.

c) Finally, if one wishes, as did Comte, to make of sociology the unique science of the activities proper to man, *agnosticism* will always result. For this view refuses to base the study of human activities on man's nature and on the absolute goal of God, towards which man tends. Thus the project conceived by Comte of creating a *positive morality*, is destined to failure [3]. Without

---

[1] " The great notion of Humanity... will eventually and irrevocably eliminate that of God ". A. Comte, *Système de politique positive*, i.

[2] See H. BERGSON, *The Two Sources of Morality and of Religion*, where the contemporary return to spiritualism is well stated.

[3] E. Durkheim undertook this same task but without much success; see below, nn. 516-519.

the double basis of a Creator and Provident God, and of a law inscribed in human nature as the source and rule of positive laws, duty as well as right remain unintelligible. The morality of pure altruism, and all morality become impossible.

Nevertheless, in the broad framework of St. Thomas' classification of the sciences [1], it does not seem impossible to assign a proper place to sociology, as constituting a special science, under the same title as experimental psychology. In sociology, as in experimental psychology, one finds the three conditions requisite for a special science : an object, a method and laws. In both, one finds a sort of *determinism* as the necessary foundation for any inductive law, although not having the same rigor as in the physical sciences. But, all human activities, even the highest, are normally [2] subjected to material conditions in which determinism is quite powerful. It seems possible, accordingly, to study human societies from the *viewpoint of external experience alone*, in order to establish the conditions of their existence (static sociology) and of their evolution (dynamic sociology) [3].

In order to set up such a *particular science*, however, there is no obligation systematically to *ignore* the existence of God and of man's true destiny, nor the other doctrines of morality and of metaphysics. This agnosticism of Comte's is a final weakness that needs correction. It is, as a matter of fact, impossible to judge whether a future state, germinally contained in a present or a past one, will be a progress or a retrogression. There must be an absolute rule : a good or a final purpose to which one compares the life of humanity, according to which one dictates the rules which man is to follow in order to arrive at his destiny. This, of course, pertains to morality as a practical and imperative science, and not to sociology.

There is, of course, such a close bond between these two sciences even today, that no one as yet has been able to treat them separately. Comte had the merit of suggesting their distinction and of pointing the way towards this new science, sociology. But his positivist prejudice did not permit him to appreciate its true value or to determine its true position in the hierarchy of knowledge [4].

In Summary : *Founded on the hypothesis of a constant progress of the human spirit, of which positivism would be the apogee, the philosophy of Comte has, as its unique source, a multiplication of experiences through the division of labor ; the content of this*

---

[1] See above, n. 261 ff.

[2] The miracle remains a possibility in human events as in the realm of nature; for example, the miraculous propagation of Catholicism is a fact, socially miraculous.

[3] See P. BUREAU, *Introduction à la méthode sociologique* (Paris, 1923), where this view is defended.

[4] Comte places sociology at the summit and considers it as essential and as replacing morality and religion. As a matter of fact, sociology is more of an auxiliary to morality, constituted as a science with its own methods for a long time previous to Comte.

philosophy is the ensemble of positive sciences, arranged according to the degree of their complexity and of their object, and unified by sociology, or from the viewpoint of human utility. In order to found the latter science, Comte analyzed the static elements, whether they are institutions (property, family, language) or functions (social forces, authority, religion), which are essential to every society. But he vainly attempted to make the laws of social evolution precise, and he crowned his work by a religion of pure imagination.

IV. Conclusion: the essence of Positivism.

A) The Influence and the Disciples of Comte.

470. Auguste Comte is the perfect incarnation of the positivist spirit, for with it he built up a system that was coherent, universal (as much as possible) and exclusive. This spirit dominates him, and projects beyond him, for it is but an emanation and a prolongation of the great movement towards the sciences of nature, which characterize modern times with their remarkable success. As Scholasticism was the servant of faith in the Middle Ages, so positivism, in the nineteenth century, became the philosophy serving science.

From this latter viewpoint, positivism is but the logical development of *Cartesian mechanism*, which had already confined the philosophy of nature to the limits of modern science. Mechanism attempted to refer all physical phenomena to simple local movements of matter, and to explain these facts by only those laws which govern their stable succession, excluding final causality and substance. This is precisely the domain of modern science.

In the seventeenth century, this mechanism brought about the materialism of the *philosophes* and the phenomenalism of Hume. Finding it impossible to explain the interaction of soul and body, one materializes the spirit and submits mental phenomena to the ordinary laws of physics. But even these systems, established by a process of reasoning, have some metaphysical import about them. Pure positivism, basing all knowledge, philosophical as well as scientific, on sense experience alone, was the work of the nineteenth century, mainly as done by Comte. It is, thus, the logical result of the movement begun by Descartes.

At the same time, as has been noted [1], Kant's criticism, by conferring a privileged position on the sciences of experience and by giving them the monopoly on objective knowledge, prepared minds for the restrictions of positivism. The social upheavals provoked by the utopia of Rousseau helped give Comte's system its sociological twist.

[1] See above, n. 404.

In so identifying himself with positivism, Comte became the chief of one of the most powerful philosophical schools of the nineteenth century. But just as the positive spirit extended beyond him, so those who are called his *disciples* often depend on him only partially or indirectly. Some of these, however, definitely continue his thought, and form two distinct groups, the orthodox and the dissident.

a) **The orthodox positivists** admit all of Comte's work, including his religion. They form a sect which is not very numerous, and which continues today in some countries. In France, Pierre Laffitte became the highpriest after Kant, and was succeeded in 1903 by Charles Jannole. The English group was directed by Richard Congreve, and then by Francis Harrison. Nyström was head of the Swedish group. The most prosperous sect arose in Brazil, where it was founded by Benjamin Constant, and had an active part in the revolution which made Brazil independent. The temple to humanity is at Rio de Janeiro. The sect exists today under the direction of Michael Lemos, and extended into Chile with George Lagarrigue [1].

b) **The dissident positivists** accepted only the first part of Comte's view, or the purely scientific part of his course, and rejected his religion.

Emile LITTRÉ (1801-1881) is the main representative. A clear and methodical thinker, he wrote in a lighter style than the master, and did much towards popularizing scientific positivism. In his work, *Auguste Comte et la philosophie positive*, he defends the pure Comteian conception of philosophy and declares the realm of substance, soul and God as wholly inaccessible: "It is like an ocean which comes to hit against our stream, and for which we have neither a boat nor a sail" [2]. He rejected the religion of humanity as an antiquated mysticism. He also wrote *Conservation; Révolution et Positivisme* (1852); *La science au point de vue philosophique* (1873); *Fragment de philosophie positive et de sociologie contemporaine* (1876).

Comte's disciples added nothing significant to his doctrine. Those whom he influenced indirectly, however (who will be considered in Article III, just below), completed various aspects of positivism and constructed their own synthesis, and are thus referable at least to the positivist spirit of Comte.

B) Foundational Principles of Positivism.

471. The essence of positivism derives from two principles, one of which is quite radical, while the other is corrective.

---

[1] See L. CANTECOR, *Le Positivisme*, pp. 132-135.
[2] E. LITTRÉ, *A. Comte et la philosophie positive*, (3rd ed., 1877), p. 505.

I. *Radical Principle.*

We can know only sensible phenomena and their laws. This is equivalent to Comte's statement that " everything is relative, and this is the only absolute principle ".

Thus, in positivism, *being* and *corporeal being* are one and the same idea for human reason. There is no spiritual faculty in man capable of knowing a spiritual object; all metaphysical speculation is the work of imagination. The only object proper to and proportionate to reason is not the absolute but the relative of observable and measurable facts, of sensible facts and their relations and laws. With regard to other objects, as substances, causes, the human soul and God, there is but pure and simple *agnosticism,* an avowal of ignorance so complete and radical that its whole defense is but denying the existence of these other objects. Positivism refuses the epithets of atheism or of materialism, for they call these metaphysical theories which pretend to attain the inaccessible domain of the absolute by their negations [1].

This radical principle, supposed throughout, is never directly demonstrated. It is a principle admitted without challenge in the face of Kantian criticism and the success of modern science as contrasted with the contradictory fluctuations of metaphysics.

2. *Corrective Principles.*

472. The savant can make legitimate use of a principle in order to discover laws, and to coordinate, conciliate and unify these laws in an organic whole.

For positivism, an *hypothesis* is every speculative construction which surpasses the strict observation of facts, and, by that fact, is a work of the imagination. The hypothesis is still held to be both necessary and legitimate.

a) **Necessity.** Positivism does not deny the existence of *reason* in man; that is, it does not deny a faculty superior to the sensible knowledge that is common to men and to animals; but it assigns as its exclusive domain the *organization of the material world.* This task does not require a spiritual faculty,

---

[1] See above, n. 469. There is but a slender speculative difference between materialism and agnosticism; in practice, their consequences are the same, the denial of morality and of religion.

but simply that one surpass the simple enumeration of facts for the following reasons. One may do so in order to determine the causes of the facts in the positivist sense, which is to determine their exclusive, stable and *necessary antecedents*. One may do so in order to generalize the observations and interpretations of facts, in order to establish useful laws. Or one may do so in order to unify the various laws in a scientific treatise. These possibilities cover the role assigned to the hypothesis [1].

b) **Legitimate role,** positivism adds, on condition that the hypothesis be fully submitted to sensible experience which suggests it, proves it, demonstrates or changes it, and that the hypothesis be useful and fruitful for discovering and systematizing laws.

473. This notion of useful and provisory hypotheses hides a rudimentary metaphysics and a mingling of imagination; but it is real metaphysics, for it is impossible to think in any other way except through the light of the formal object of the human intelligence, that of being. This is why the positivists, attempting to unify and to explain facts, seek for the reasons of things; their hypotheses take the place of the first rational verities and suppose them admitted. Thus, the second principle of positivism not only corrects the first, but actually destroys it.

The influence of metaphysics is especially manifest when the experimental proof establishes the existence of necessary laws, fruitful in applications, following the thesis of " determinism ". The notion of law, in fact, under penalty of remaining an arbitrary postulate without value, supposes the application of the principle of causality to corporeal substances. In addition, the metaphysical analysis of causality adds a fine precision to the value of scientific laws, and defends it more efficaciously than does positivism. Of course, the notion of *cause* is first distinguished from a *condition sine qua non*, which is not done through the positivist notion of a necessary antecedent joined to its consequent by determinism [2]. Moreover, metaphysics shows spirituality as the source of liberty, and thus distinguishes *necessary* causes of the material order, the proper domain of determinism, and *free* causes of the spiritual order, which escape absolute determinism.

---

[1] In a strict sense, the savants speak of *hypotheses* at the beginning of their researches, before any experimental justification. To the extent that facts verify it, the hypothesis becomes a *theory* (See P. DUHEM, *The Aim and Structure of Physical Theory*). In positivism, both hypothesis and theory can have only an extra-scientific value. In chemistry, for instance, the hypothesis of atoms as substantial realities (the hypothesis of the atomic theory), can never have undeniable truth. This is the result of the agnosticism of positivism.

[2] The true cause supposes, even more than a necessary bond, the communication of a perfection.

Somewhat in this way the legitimacy of the modern sciences is recognized, and their position in the tableau of sciences arranged according to St. Thomas [1].

It is true that material phenomena occur according to stable laws, and that they are always accompanied with local movements, as vibrations of light, sound and heat, which allow them to be measured mathematically and thus to establish their laws in mathematical formulas. It is also true that experience is the sole means of discovering them. This mode of envisaging the world, which Comte called the *positive spirit*, has a legitimate interpretation and is even more fruitful for material progress than the search for deeper causes.

Understood in this sense, modern science is no longer an enemy of faith and of traditional philosophy, nor even destined to rule instead of the latter views. It is, on the contrary, a subalternated science, founded on the first principles of metaphysics, and giving a more exact, though partial and restrained, view of the universe from the mathematical viewpoint. The philosophical viewpoint, seeking for the final reasons of things, also remains legitimate and necessary to respond to the moral and social needs of man, and to show his true dignity.

ARTICLE THREE.

DERIVATIVE FORMS OF POSITIVISM.

474. The positivist spirit, especially as summarized in Comte's work, went through various manifestations throughout the nineteenth century. Some thinkers are quite independent of him, while others directly or indirectly receive their essential theses from him. All, however, accept the two basic principles of his system. Since the various derived theories complete and develop certain aspects of Comte and logically proceed from him, they can be called " derived forms of positivism ".

Adopting this viewpoint in classifying the systems more according to doctrine than according to time, one finds three quite distinct currents in the positivism of the nineteenth century. The first group, faithful to the master-thought of Comte, look upon philosophy as an effort at unification of science; this is the *scientific current*. Others are unwilling to sacrifice psychology as a special science, and attempt to reconstruct it according to the method of positivism; this is the *psychological current*. Others, finally, attach themselves to the social aspect of positivism, and seek to draw out a complete moral theory; this is the *sociological current*.

---

[1] See above, n. 82 and n. 265.

The first two currents are contemporary and traverse the whole of the nineteenth century; the third is only born at the end of the same century. Three sections, subdivided into various paragraphs, will present these forms of positivism :

Section   I. The Scientific Current.

Section II. The Psychological Current.

Section III. The Sociological Current.

SECTION ONE.
THE SCIENTIFIC CURRENT.

475.   While Auguste Comte thought it premature to set up an objective unification of the sciences, others clung to this hope and attempted to realize it through the theory of evolution. Charles Darwin was the initiator of this theory, but it was Herbert Spencer who used it in setting up a complete synthesis of thought.

Alongside of this effort towards an all-inclusive view of the sciences, which embraces psychology, and which still remains open to metaphysics, one finds another vision of the world also founded on the theory of evolution. This other view, however, tends to be materialistic and to encompass life in the narrower limits of the economic sciences — this is the effort of socialism, and especially of Marxism. Three paragraphs will develop these notions :

I. Darwinism.

II. The Synthesis of Herbert Spencer.

III. Socialism.

I. Darwinism.

Special bibliography.

1⁰ **Works** : *Autobiography* (ed. by Sir Francis Darwin), New York, 1950. — *Descent of Man*, New York, n. d. — *Journal of Researches into the Geology and Natural History of Various Countries Visited by H. M. S. Beagle*, New York, 1952. — *Life and Letters* (ed. by Sir Francis Darwin), New York, 1911. — *Origin of Species by Means of Natural Selection*, 6th ed. reprint, Oxford, 1951. — *Variation of Animals and Plants under Domestication*, 2 vols., New York, n. d.

2⁰ **Studies** : Cuenot, Dalbiez, et al., *Le Transformisme*, Paris, 1927. — De Dorlodot, H., *Le Darwinisme*, Paris, 1921. — Duilhe de Saint-Projet, *Apologie Scientifique de la foi catholique*, refondue par Senderens, Paris, 1903. — Dorsey, G. A., *Evolution of Charles Darwin*, New York, 1929. — Duggan, G. H., *Evolution*

and Philosophy, Wellington (New Zealand), 1949. — GRASSET, C.,
Le dogme transformiste et la philosophie, Paris, 1918. — MESSEN-
GER, E. C., *Evolution and Theology*, New York, 1931. — *Theology
and Evolution*, Westminster (Md.), 1949. — MIGNON, A., *Pour
et contre le transformisme*, Darwin et Vialleton, Paris, 1934. —
POULTON, E. B., *History of Evolution*, London, n. d. —
ROMANÈS, G. J., *Darwin and After Darwin*, 3 vols., Chicago, n. d.
— ROSTAND, J., *Charles Darwin*, Paris, 1948. — SIMPSON, G. G.,
The Meaning of Evolution, New Haven (Conn.), 1949. —
THOMPSON, J. A., *Darwinism and Human Life*, London, 1946.
— THOUVEREZ, E., *Charles Darwin*, 2nd ed., Paris, 1907. —
WEST, G., *Charles Darwin. A Portrait*, New Haven (Conn.), 1938.

A) Origin.

The idea of explaining the diversity of beings, especially
of living beings, through evolution is foreign to the positivism
of the eighteenth century. In fact, BUFFON [1] (1707-1788),
the famous naturalist, taught the fixity of species and placed
the harmonious hierarchy of things in the plan of the Creator;
the succession which this hierarchy realizes is a purely ideal
one [2]. Even Comte held to the impossibility of explaining
the higher degree of being by the lower, and admitted to
progress only in the same species, especially in human society.

One finds this notion, however, in the French naturalist,
Jean LAMARCK [3] (1744-1829). In his *Philosophie zoologique*,
he attempted to explain the origin of animal species by making
them derive from a primitive organism under the influence
of three factors : adaptation to environment (external causes),
custom (internal reaction of the subject) and heredity (charged
with fixing and transmitting the variations obtained [4].

---

[1] **Works** : *Histoire Naturelle*, 24 vols., Paris, 1750-1788. — *Epoques de la
Nature*, Paris, 1778.

Study : H. DAUDIN, *Les méthodes de classification et l'idée de série en botanique
et en zoologie, de Linné à Lamarck* (1740-1790), Paris, 1905.

[2] In order to express the complexity of the facts, he compared this order
to a spider's web; nature, he believed, did not take a step without it being a step
in all directions. Another naturalist, *Pallas*, compared this order to a branched-
out tree, a figure which Bergson adopted.

[3] **Works** : *Philosophie zoologique*, Paris, 1809. — *Zoological Philosophy*
(tr. H. Elliot), New York, 1914.

Studies : LE DANTEC, F., *Lamarkiens et Darwiniens*, Paris, 1889. —
TSCHULOK, S., *Lamarck : Eine kritischhistorische Studie*, Zurich (Sw.), 1937.

[4] " The spirit of Darwin is quite different from that of Lamarck. Darwin
looks on the variations as brute facts which are unexplainable, while Lamarck
refers them to the exercise of an internal need, whose results are fixed by habit.
For Darwin, they occur in any way, while Lamarck views them as tending
towards a better adaptation. Darwinism, accordingly, is essentially mechanistic, considering only the results of chance which occur in animal life, and
excluding all finality ". See E. BRÉHIER, *op. cit.*, Vol. II, p. 923.

The chief of the evolutionism of the nineteenth century was the English naturalist, Charles DARWIN (1809-1882). He got the first idea of his system while on a voyage around the world which was taken by a number of English savants with an aim to study conditions in other lands (1830-36). Struck by the profound resemblances of the diverse living species, especially animal species, and by their varieties so perfectly adapted to their proper environments, he looked for an explanation of these two facts. In 1838, he found the solution with the help of the works of Thomas MALTHUS (1766-1834). Malthus had tried to prove scientifically, or by facts, that the law of every living thing is that it multiply itself in a proportion that is much greater than the quantity of nourishment at its disposal; he concluded that it is necessary to delimit birth. Darwin himself, however, concluded that the only means of self-perpetuation for a living thing was the *struggle for life*, which factor gave him the solution he desired.

This notion is developed in his main work, *The Origin of Species* (1859), in which he restrains his conclusions to the animal realm. He finally concluded by extending transformism to the whole realm of living things from plants to men in his *The Descent of Man* and in his *The Expression of Emotions in men and animals*.

B) The Laws.

476. According to Darwin, the multiple, actual species of living things can be explained by one or at most a few primitive types which developed and multiplied themselves according to the fundamental law of *natural selection*.

Just as breeders, by a methodical choice of reproductive stock, create quite diverse varieties, so the development of life appears as a choice of a *selection* spontaneously operated by nature under the pressure of the *struggle for life*. Natural selection, working on a great number of subjects and for a very long time, can create the most important differences. For, granting the considerably greater number of seeds in relation to the number of living individuals, it appears that only the *strongest* survive to conquer existence; these are the best endowed, the fittest, and the most apt to profit from circumstances. These factors make up the choice of nature.

This work of elimination is intensified in the higher realms through *sexual selection*, according to which instinct, also acting in the manner of a breeder, leads the animals to exclude the weakest in order to keep the functions of reproduction in the strongest.

This fundamental law can be called the *law of preservation of the most apt beings*. Two other, secondary laws can be added to this basic law; they help explain the rich variety of species existing.

a) The *law of adaptation* is the first, and *b*) the law of *usage and non-usage* is the second. These two laws are complementary. They state that the diverse organs and functions of a living thing are susceptible of transforming themselves, either under the influence of an exterior environment (law of adaptation), or under the influence of an interior need (law of usage and non-usage, evidently conditioned by environment). The existing organs either develop or become atrophied, or even entirely new organs are created by needs.

c) The *law of heredity* states that acquired variations are fixed in the organism and transmitted through descendants. The existence of this law, taken in general, is the postulate of *artificial selection*, which is just as good as natural selection. " No breeder doubts... the tendency to inheritance; that like produces like is his fundamental belief " [1]. Many variations can doubtlessly be explained by constant, external influences which act on the descendants as on the parents. In certain cases, however, heredity plays an indisputable role; for instance, the transmission of very special traits acquired by an individual with the help of an extraordinary confluence of circumstances, and which is preserved in the family. Heredity also intervenes, probably, in other cases. " Perhaps the correct way of viewing the whole subject would be to look at the inheritance of every character whatever as the rule, and non-inheritance as the anomaly " [2]. On the other hand, if the general law is certain, the rules of its special applications are, for the most part, unknown to us. Darwin singled out this rule, that a particularity transmitted tends to reappear in the children at the same age in which it appeared in the parents.

C) **The proofs.**

476 [bis]. Darwin's view was that transformism is an hypothesis not as yet fully demonstrated, but legitimate and

[1] CHARLES DARWIN, *The Origin of Species*, Ch. I.
[2] *Ibid.*

scientific, for it interprets a great number of *facts* left unexplained by other theories. There are three main groups of facts which it helps explain.

1. **Facts of variation.** This group includes the most numerous and most important facts, for the plasticity of living things cannot be disputed.

It is certain that there are *individual differences* transmitted by heredity. Often they are of little value, but they often affect important internal organs. Thus, " the branching of the main nerves close to the great central ganglion of an insect [the Coccus]... may almost be compared to the irregular branching of the stem of a tree " [1].

Noticing these differences, man has realized profound changes in nature through methodical breeding. Darwin made a special study of domestic pigeons and found a striking diversity of breeds. " Altogether at least a score of pigeons might be chosen, which, if shown to an ornithologist, and he were told that they were wild birds, would certainly be ranked by him as well-defined species. Moreover, I do not believe that any ornithologist would in this case place the English carrier, the short-faced tumbler, the runt, the barb, pouter and fantail in the same genus; more especially, as in each of these breeds several truly inherited sub-breeds, or species, as he would call them, could be shown him " [2]. Nevertheless, despite these profound differences and the actual impossibility of certifying the inter-fecundity of these breeds, it must be held for several decisive reasons that they are all descendents of the same wild species, the rock-pigeon *(columba livia)*. The case of pigeons is but an instance of other animals and plants useful to mankind. The transformations are most often obtained not by increasing the diverse varieties, but by choosing the individuals endowed with preferred qualities in order to establish them as reproducers. This very choice, by becoming perpetuated, leads to new changes.

Now the multiple forms of living things in nature are diversified in a manner quite similar. This explains the rules which the naturalists adopt in order to arrange their classifications and to discover what they call the plan of nature or the plan of the Creator. They are unknowingly searching for the descent of various branches issuing from one common ancestor and of the gradual separation of these branches through the destruction of intermediary species. Numerous facts point this out. In the animal realm, we have the great differences which obtain between males and females, which are classed as individuals of the same species because of their genealogy. The same holds for plants : " As soon as the three Orchidean forms, Monacanthus, Myanthus and Catasetum, which had previously been ranked as three distinct genera, were known to be sometimes produced on the same plant, they were immediately considered as varieties; and now I have

---

[1] *Ibid.*, Ch. II.

[2] *Ibid.*, Ch. I.

been able to show that they are the male, female, and hermaphrodite forms of the same species " [1]. When one studies a group of living things in detail, one finds numerous *doubtful species* which join the forms with an eye to differentiation. Among the same branches, the struggle for life has suppressed these intermediaries by establishing clear lines of difference; but at the interior of each branch, the classification often follows a chain of affinities and seems to restore the main lines of evolution. In this way one can place under the same category the descendants of one and the same ancestry, so that often the two extremities of the series, as in the case of the shell-fish, have hardly a common trait. Thus, in order to establish these groups, one does not rely on the most important, but on the most stable organs. For instance, one classes, in a group of shell-fish, the *Cypridina*, which have a heart, and the two allied genera of *Cypris* and *Cythera*, in whom this organ is deficient [2]. All the rules of the method testify, it seems, in favor of transformism.

Another evident fact is the adaptation of plants and animals to the various countries in which they live. Thus, the furs of animals grow in the measure that they reside in more frigid zones. At the same time, a difficulty arises against the hypothesis of a common descendant, insofar as the same fauna or flora are found in environments absolutely separated, as the summits of mountain chains of various continents, unless one admits the possibility of migration from one point to another. Thus, " the plants on the White Mountains, in the United States of America, are all the same with those of Labrador, and nearly all the same, as we hear from Asa Gray, with those on the loftiest mountains of Europe " [3]. Darwin explains this fact by the great transformations of the glacial periods in which living things from the cold countries spread all over the globe, even to the center of Africa; when the glacial materials receded, the species living in the plains mounted towards the mountain summits, where the climate was convenient to them and where they have remained until today.

There are also variations in the organs brought about by non-usage, as the loss of wings, of horns and of eyes. " It is well known that several animals, belonging to the most different classes, which inhabit the caves of Carniola and of Kentucky, are blind. In some of the crabs the footstalk for the eye remains, though the eye is gone " [4].

One of the facts most favorable to transformism should be mentioned in connection with the non-usage of organs; it is the *rudimentary organ.* " It would be impossible to name one of the higher animals in which some part or other is not in a rudimentary condition. In the mammalia, for instance, the males possess rudimentary mammae; in snakes, one lobe of the lungs is

---

[1] *Ibid.,* Ch. xiv.
[2] *Ibid.,* Ch. xii.
[3] *Ibid.,* Ch. v.
[4] *Ibid.,* Ch. xiv.

rudimentary; in birds, the ' bastard-wing ' may safely be considered as a rudimentary digit, and in some species the whole wing is so far rudimentary that it cannot be used for flight. What can be more curious than the presence of teeth in fetal whales, which when grown up have not a tooth in their heads; or the teeth, which never cut through the gums, in the upper jaws of unborn calves? " Even in plants, in the most differentiated species, the female flower alone has the pistil developed, while the male flowers have it only in a rudimentary state. Sometimes these organs, becoming useless, disappear, so that in certain plants and animals we note the complete absence of parts which, by the laws of analogy, we would expect to find in them, and which are occasionally manifest in monstrous specimens. All of these facts are easily explainable by the hypothesis of transformism. These rudiments are like the remainders of perfect organs possessed by the ancestors of existing species. One can compare them " with the letters in a word, still retained in the spelling, but become useless in the pronunciation, but which serve as a clue for its derivation ". The partisans of Creationism ordinarily state that God created them " ' for the sake of symmetry ' or in order ' to complete the scheme of nature '. But this is not an explanation, merely a re-statement of the fact. Nor is it consistent with itself : thus the boa-constrictor has the rudiments of hind-limbs and of a pelvis, and if it be said that these bones have been retained ' to complete the scheme of nature ', why... have they not been retained by other snakes, which do not possess even a vestige of these same bones? " [1].

2. **Facts of morphological resemblance.** The unity of the plan of nature is another fact favorable to evolution. " What can be more curious than that the hand of man, formed for grasping, that of a mole for digging, the leg of a horse, the paddle of the porpoise, and the wing of the bat, should all be constructed on the same pattern, and should include similar bones, in the same relative positions " [2]. Another example is the mouth of insects : " ...What can be more different than the immensely long spiral proboscis of a sphinx-moth, the curious folded one of a bee or bug, and the great jaws of a beetle? — yet all these organs, serving for such widely different purposes, are formed by infinitely numerous modifications of an upper lip, mandibles, and two pairs of maxillae " [3]. In the plant also, " the sepals, petals, stamens, and pistils... though fitted for such distinct purposes ", are " all constructed on the same pattern ". All these facts suggest the hypothesis of a common origin : " If we suppose that an early progenitor — the archetype as it may be called — of all mammals, birds, and reptiles, had its limbs constructed on the existing general pattern, for whatever purpose they served, we can at once perceive the plain signification of the homologous construction

---

[1] The above quotations are taken from Ch. XIV.
[2] *Ibid.*
[3] *Ibid.*

of the limbs throughout the class " [1]. The same may be said with regard to the mouth of insects or to plants.

Darwin was not afraid to apply his theory to the most difficult cases, such as that of the complex function of the eyes, showing their progressive development according to the same plan. " ...When we bear in mind how small the number of all living forms must be in comparison with those which have become extinct, the difficulty ceases to be very great in believing that natural selection may have converted the simple apparatus of an optic nerve, coated with pigment and invested by transparent membrane, into an optical instrument as perfect as is possessed by any member of the Articulate Class " [2]. He approaches the question of instincts in a similar fashion to answer the overworked objection of sterile insects, as the worker bee, which are unable to transmit their instinct : heredity in this case should be applied to the family, not to the individual [3].

3. **Facts of embryogeny.** Embryos provide an especially striking analogy of the scheme of nature, for if heredity causes differences to reappear at the age in which they were acquired by the progenitors, it is to be expected that the earliest stages should be most alike. " The embryos of mammalia ", writes Von Baer [4], " of birds, lizards, and snakes, probably also of chelonia, are in their earliest states exceedingly like one another, both as a whole and in the mode of development of their parts : so much so, in fact, that we can often distinguish the embryos only by their size. In my possession are two little embryos in spirit, whose names I have omitted to attach, and at present I am quite unable to say to what class they belong. They may be lizards or small birds, or very young mammalia, so complete is the similarity in the mode of formation of the head and trunk in these animals ". This remarkable similarity is easily explained if one grants to all living beings, whatever be their differences in the adult state, a common ancestor; their diversity is explained by the struggle for existence. The same idea governs our classifications; thus " ...cirripides, though externally so like shell-fish, are at once known by their larvae to belong to the great class of crustaceans " [5].

Sometimes an embryo possesses organs which no longer need to be operative. " ...Thus the tadpole of the common Salamander or Water-newt, as Mr. G. H. Lewes remarks, ' has gills, and passes its existence in the water; but the Salamander atra, which lives high up among the mountains, brings forth its young full-formed. This animal never lives in the water. Yet if we open up a gravid female, we find tadpoles inside her with exquisitely feathered

---

[1] *Ibid.* Of course, one can say that God has willed it so in order to have beauty in His work; but recourse to the First Cause does not do away with the search for secondary causes.

[2] *Ibid.*, Ch. VI.

[3] *Ibid.*, Ch. VIII.

[4] As cited by Darwin, *ibid.*, Ch. XIV.

[5] *Ibid.*, Ch. XIV.

gills; and when placed in water they swim about like the tadpoles of the water-newt. Obviously this aquatic organization has no reference to the future life of the animal, nor has it any adaptation to its embryonic condition; it has solely reference to ancestral adaptations, it repeats a phase in the development of its progenitors ' " [1]. These facts suggest the law that the higher being, in its life as an embryo, passes through the same stages as the species passed through in the actual evolution by which it reached its present state.

Finally, the well known metamorphoses of insects bear witness to the great plasticity of the living organism, as is proposed by evolution.

D) Conclusion and Influence.

477. Inasmuch as Darwin's transformism is presented as a scientific hypothesis explicative of facts, it cannot be a priori rejected, but its value must be submitted to the control of induction based on experience.

One must distinguish the following points of view :

1) **Evolutionism**, which enlarges the theory by commencing with a primitive nebula and concludes with man through a continuous progress. The absurdity of this view is easily shown, for it aims to explain the greater by the less, life by matter and spirit by body. It can be called monism to the extent that it excludes God and creation, and refers all reality to matter [2].

2) **Transformism** limits evolution only to living things, and, in its strict sense, excludes man by reason of his immortal soul. It can be *universal*, if it teaches the passage from one primitive cell to man's body, or *mitigated*, if it restrains itself to living things of one kingdom alone.

Now, *a)* no form of transformism can dispense with the admission of creation; for, if transformism be true, it still explains only the historical origin of living beings. But it is always necessary to explain the actual existence of these beings (contingent and imperfectly alive) through God, the perfect source of life.

b) Mitigated transformism is a priori not opposed to faith nor to Scholastic or Thomistic philosophy, which can adopt it without denying its own concept of species [3]. Even universal transformism is acceptable on condition that it safeguard the requirements of the principle of sufficient reason by having recourse, for example, to the laws of Divine Providence, as did St. Augustine [4].

c) Nevertheless, the Darwinian hypothesis is far from being demonstrated, for many of the facts adduced are contestable.

---

[1] *Ibid.*, Ch. xiv.
[2] See below, n. 480, under the monism of Spencer.
[3] A. D. SERTILLANGES, *Saint Thomas*, ii, pp. 23-29.
[4] See above, n. 171, for Augustine's theory of seminal reasons.

Even the experts, as Vialleton [1] and Driesch [2], have shown the falsity of the law of embryogeny. Other facts (as the infecundity of hybrids) are opposed to it, and the facts most favorable to it can be interpreted in the light of other theories.

478. In fact, Darwinism shared the success of positivism in the nineteenth century, for it also presented itself as a direct consequence of the science of observation. It appeared to allow for a positive interpretation of life according to the principles of mechanism, without recourse to any " supernatural " explanation — without final causes and without the act of the Creator. Darwin admitted creation, but only at the origin, and not for the human soul, whose reason is looked upon as a more perfect animal instinct.

Many of his disciples went to the extreme of monism. The principal theoretician was the German, Ernst HAECKEL [3] (1834-1919), especially in his work, *The Riddle of the Universe.* In his view, eternal matter is the only necessary being; the origin of every living thing, including man, lies in the spontaneous composite of nitrogen, hydrogen, oxygen and carbon. This material, after a first condensation, becomes the *nucleus,* and, by successive transformations, pithecanthropus and, finally, man himself. Haeckel counted twenty-two intermediaries, which he described as fossils, though he modified the forms of several and covered the gaps by means of imaginary types, supposedly real.

The materialists, as L. BÜCHNER (1824-1899), and VOGT (1817-1895) in Germany; — Félix Le DANTEC (1869-1917) in France; — MOLESCHOTT (1822-1893) in Holland — all prolonged Darwinism even to our times.

But it was especially in England that Darwinism took root; its principle followers will be indicated [4], after it has been shown how SPENCER integrated Darwin's views in a much broader synthesis.

---

[1] See his work, *Membres et ceintures des vertèbres,* 1828; see also the article, " Transformism ", in *Dictionnaire apologétique,* col. 1814.

[2] See H. DRIESCH, *The Philosophy of the Organism, passim.*

[3] **Works :** *The Evolution of Man,* Transl. from the 5th enl. ed. by Joseph McCabe, 2 vols., New York, 1910. — *The History of Creation,* E. R. Lankester (transl.), rev. ed., 2 vols., New York, n. d. — *The Riddle of the Universe,* Joseph McCabe (transl.), London, 1929.

Studies : LAMINNE, J., *L'univers d'après Haeckel,* Paris, 1910. — WASMANN, E., *La probité scientifique de Haeckel,* Paris, 1911.

[4] See below, n. 482.

II. THE SYNTHESIS OF HERBERT SPENCER.

(1820-1903).

SPECIAL BIBLIOGRAPHY.

1º **Works :** *First Principles*, London, 1937. — *Principles of Psychology*, 2 vols., New York, 1902-03. — *Principles of Sociology (Synthetic Philosophy)*, 3 vols., New York, 1900-1901.

2º **Studies :** ASIRVATHAM, E., *Herbert Spencer's Theory of Social Justice*, New York, 1936. — BOURNE, G. C., *Spencer and Animal Evolution*, Oxford, 1910. — BOWNE, B. P., *Kant and Spencer*, New York, 1912. — COMPAYRÉ, G., *Herbert Spencer et l'éducation scientifique*, Paris, n. d. — DUNCAN, D., *Life and Letters of Herbert Spencer*, 2 vols., New York, 1908. — LACY, W., *An Examination of the Philosophy of the Unknowable*, Philadelphia, 1883. — MORGAN, C. L., *Spencer's Philosophy of Science*, Oxford, 1913. — RIBOT, Th., *La psychologie anglaise contemporaine*, Paris, 1870. — RUMNEY, J., *Herbert Spencer's Sociology*, London, 1934. — SHEPPERSON, M. F., *Comparative Study of St. Thomas Aquinas and Herbert Spencer*, Philadelphia, 1925. — TAYLOR, A. E., *Herbert Spencer*, New York, n. d. — THOUVEREZ, E., *Herbert Spencer*, Paris, 1920.

479. The son of an English schoolmaster, Herbert Spencer was intended, at first, for an engineering career, and his first studies were in the realm of economics and politics. But his tastes led him irresistibly towards philosophical generalizations. From 1852 to 1857, he published several *Essays* and a first edition of his *Principles of Psychology,* wherein he is already impressed by the great idea of evolution [1]. But it was in 1860 that he conceived and made known by a prospectus his plan for a vast, synthetic work whose task would be to assemble in one coherent system all the scientific productions of his times; it would be in harmony with all the philosophical and religious views then prevalent, at least in the measure that he judged them legitimate. Overcoming the obstacles of precarious health, he began to realize this goal by publishing the series of his *Principles*, from the *First Principles of a New System of Philosophy*, which appeared in 1862, to the *Principles of Morality*, of 1892, with the principles of biology, psychology and sociology in between. He added several essays on the *Classification of the Sciences* (1864), *On Education* (1861), and an *Autobiography*.

---

[1] It should be noted that Darwin's *Origin of Species* was not published until 1859.

Despite the complexity of such a work, and even though a number of details were varied in the course of his exposition, there is a remarkable stability in his fundamental principles of interpretation. An essentially synthetic thinker, endowed with a great power of assimilation, Spencer stated that " it was always impossible for him to read a book which began from a point of view estranged from his own ". He believed that all the new details discovered could be arranged in a unique system. The central idea of this system was EVOLUTION, which can be stated as the following fundamental principle.

All the knowable is explainable by evolution; the latter, in being applied to metaphysics and to religion, permits us to prove the existence of the Unknowable.

It should be noted immediately that Spencer fully accepts the fundamental principles of positivism [1]. The knowable, for him, is the relative, the ensemble of phenomena, or the facts of experience whose laws are to be established. But, more boldly than Comte, he constructed an *objective* synthesis, unified by a physical law to which he subjected all scientific phenomena, including those of consciousness [2]. Moreover, he believed that the ensemble of positive knowledge leads us irresistibly from the relative to the affirmation of an absolute. Even though the essence of this absolute remains inaccessible, this notion of the Unknowable is the true coronal of Spencer's synthesis. His views will be presented under the following five headings :

A) The Universal Law of Evolution.

B) Physical and Biological Evolution.

C) Psychological Evolution.

D) Moral and Social Evolution.

E) Metaphysical and Religious Evolution : THE UN-KNOWABLE.

A) **The Universal Law of Evolution.**

480. Appealing to the general opinion among thinkers, Spencer at first establishes that philosophy is not characterized

---

[1] See above, n. 471.

[2] In this way, Spencer belongs to the current of positivist psychology. He is placed in the scientific current, because his central theory is of a mechanistic inspiration.

by its object; for, like all knowledge, whether common or scientific, it bears on the facts of observation and their laws, but in a most general and synthetic fashion it wishes to attain this object. " Knowledge of the lowest kind is non-unified knowledge; Science is partially-unified knowledge; Philosophy is completely-unified knowledge " [1].

It seems difficult, on first consideration, to refer the immense complexity of facts to one unity by indicating a unique law of which each is but a manifestation. In order to make this conclusion, Spencer begins by determining the fundamental elements of this synthesis; and, faithful to mechanism, whose dominance has become wider since Descartes and Newton, he wished to reconstruct everything with two elements, *matter* and *movement*. Matter is a resistant mass endowed with extension; movement is manifested by traversing a certain space during a certain time [2], and thus these two basic notions synthesize the sciences.

The existence of these elements is governed by quite general laws which apply to all domains and thus enhance philosophy. The main ones follow. The first is the law of the *indestructibility* or the conservation *of matter*, certified in all facts since Lavoisier introduced the balance in the observation of corporeal changes. Another is the law of the *continuity of movement*, an aspect of the inertia of matter, since it supposes movement always equal to itself. Many secondary laws flow from these, one of which is that of the transformation of energy into equivalent energy, each of which (electricity, heat, sound, light) are but a transformed movement. The *law of rhythm* is another secondary law; it states that a movement moves itself periodically into an opposed, antagonistic movement. All of these laws, however, are deducible from one law which is the supreme principle of the synthesis; it is the *law of the conservation of energy*, which Spencer calls the law of the *persistence of force* [3]. Force [4] manifests itself in a static manner in resistant matter, and in a dynamic manner in movement and in all the various energies into which it is transformed. The indestructibility of matter then follows, as does the continuity of movements; all laws are but various aspects of the law of persistence of force. The latter is a fundamental postulate, absolutely indemonstrable, for it is presupposed in all other scientific demonstrations.

However, with this supreme law, we now have the unifying idea which we seek, for " to have ascertained the laws of the factors is not to have ascertained the laws of their cooperation. The thing to do is not to know how one or another factor, as matter, movement or force, behaves... The thing to be expressed is the

---

[1] *First Principles*, § 37.

[2] See below, n. 480 II, for Spencer's conception of space and of time.

[3] Spencer prefers the word *persistence* to *conservation* since it better applies to the energies which transform themselves; he speaks of *force* more than of *energy*, since the latter word is poorly applied to the static resistance of matter.

[4] See below, n. 480 II, for Spencer's notion of force; see *First Principles*, § 60.

joint product of the factors under all its various aspects " [1]. In other words, it is a law explaining the synthesis of all events without exception. This great law is that of *evolution*, together with the antagonistic movement which necessarily follows by the law of rhythm, *dissolution*.

In a general way it can be said that evolution supposes a movement of *synthesis*, an integration of matter, going from the simple to the composed, as long as dissolution implies the inverse movement of *analysis*. Numerous facts show that concentration is accompanied by the loss of external or internal movement, while every dissolution entrains an accumulation of movement under any form at all. Hence, the general definition follows : " We shall by *dissolution* everywhere mean... the absorption of motion and disintegration of matter; we shall everywhere mean by *evolution*, the process which is always an integration of matter and dissipation of motion " [2].

But while dissolution always follows a quite simple pattern, the same situation does not hold for evolution. Besides *simple evolution*, formed from but two elements alone, there is *complex evolution*, in which the redistribution of matter, which forms the composite, is accompanied by several secondary characteristics having the value of laws. Facts oblige us, Spencer maintains, to distinguish three meanings of evolution. *a*) It operates by *consolidation*, going from a less to a more coherent state; for instance, the stars, coming out of the inconsistent environment of the nebula, acquire cohesion, or the living organs, by formation, solidify themselves. *b*) It operates by *differentiation*, going from the homogeneous to the heterogeneous; this increasing multiformity accompanies progress throughout, but especially in living things : " The history of a planet and that of an animal, by showing us how their volume increased, tells us how their parts became, at the same time, most different " [3], in passing from a primitive cell to an organism. *c*) It operates by *determination*, going from the indefinite to the definite; it progresses from confusion towards order, from an indetermined to a determined arrangement [4]. Dissolution could also increase heterogeneity; a morbid germ introduces great variety into organic activity, but by disorganization. Evolution is distinguished from dissolution, since

---

[1] *Ibid.*, § 90. — [2] *Ibid.*, § 97.
[3] *Ibid.*, § 118. — [4] *Ibid.*, § 129.

it tends towards greater order and unity. One can establish this (as for the other two characteristics) in every series of facts, in the formation of worlds, in living organisms, and in the psychological and social orders. Thus, the first men " had tools made of flint which completely lacked precision " in comparison with the machines of modern industry [1].

Finally, in complex evolution, change does not dissipate itself wholly, and the part conserved also tends to become most firm, most heterogeneous and most ordered; this gives a general formula :

" *Evolution is an integration of matter accompanied by a dissipation of movement, during which matter passes from an indefinite homogeneity which is incoherent, to a definite heterogeneity which is coherent, and during which even the return movement undergoes an analogous transformation* " [2].

Such is Spencer's law, which synthesizes all knowable phenomena from those of the primitive nebula to the social facts of the most civilized state of man.

But the summit of organization is not the last stage. Dissolution, which constantly accompanies progress, will one day be on top, for the movement and the diverse forms of energy, by always dissipating themselves, will finish by setting up a state of universal equilibrium equivalent to universal death. Must this return to primitive unsubstantiality be definitive? Spencer admits that this question is scientifically insoluble. The affirmative is a plausible hypothesis; one can also hold that below the world accessible to our sciences, there are infinite reserves of energy [3], so to speak; under their influence, the universe would return to the nebulous state and again take up its trend towards organization. We thus arrive at a great rhythm of evolutions and of dissolutions whose duration defies every calculation and whose succession has neither beginning nor end. This is the vision of the world already possessed by the Stoics [4]; every synthesis founded on mechanism instinctively goes back to their view.

There is one effort left in order to complete this synthesis. The law of evolution with its various aspects, is a quite complex, inductive formula. Spencer has listed all of its elements by *deduction* from an absolutely primary law, that of the conservation of energy. If one admits an invariable quantity of force [5] in the

---

[1] *Ibid.*, § 137.

[2] *Ibid.*, § 145.

[3] This latter explanation depends on the existence of the Unknowable, who, being absolute, would be the source of the infinite energy of the universe; see below, n. 481.

[4] See above, n. 99, and see also Herbert Spencer, *First Principles*, § 183.

[5] In the sense explained above, including the static force of matter and the dynamic force of various energies.

universe, it is necessary that complex evolution, as Spencer described it, follow. The parts of the homogeneous mass, being variously exposed to the same force, react differently, so that one cause alone would produce a multitude of effects (the same shock would produce movement, heat, light, electricity, and so on), and would thus entrain increasing heterogeneity. At the same time, under the action of these forces, the similar parts *should* gather together; from this would arise a better defined order. On the other hand, final dissolution follows with the same necessity from the same law, for these forces produce evolution only by colliding in order to equilibrate themselves, the strongest partially giving way to the weakest. Since their quantity is invariable, one can obtain only a universal levelling which is also the dispersion of the nebula. Everything is thus explained by " persistence of force ", flowering out into the great law of evolution.

This view has all the beauty of a truly unified synthesis, and, at the same time, all the frailty of pure mechanism, whose philosophical weakness has already been shown [1]. From the sole viewpoint of physical energies, the principle of the equivalence of forces is, doubtlessly, a truth of experience for modern science, which considers only the quantitative and measurable aspect of phenomena in an abstract fashion. But in philosophy, this view cannot be defended. From the *qualitative* viewpoint, such realities as movement, heat, light and electricity are in no wise equivalent. This qualitative point of view, that of Aristotle and St. Thomas, is the only one admissible in a total interpretation of reality, and is conformable to right reason. But before giving an appreciation of Spencer's system, the applications he made of his principles should be presented.

B) Physical and Biological Evolution.

480. I. Spencer made no special application of his fundamental principle to inorganic nature. " I have judged it proper not to treat this great subject, for even with omitting it, my plan is too vast; furthermore, the explanation of organic nature by the method proposed is even more important " [2]. He did, however, take many of his examples from this realm, showing how he viewed the genesis of worlds in Laplace's hypothesis, and how the facts of the geological, physical and chemical orders could be organized under the law of evolution.

In biology, Spencer assimilated and integrated in a vast unification, the transformist views of Darwin. He used the impressive mass of facts which Darwin had collected, showing without difficulty how the facts of embryogeny, of morphological similitude, and so forth, realize the threefold aspect of the law of evolution : the passage from homogeneous to heterogeneous, the consolidation of the ensemble and the determination of a better order. He is, however, faithful to the mechanistic spirit of the modern sciences. More explicit than Darwin, he refers the progress of biological

---

[1] See above, n. 21.
[2] *First Principles*, Author's preface.

organization and the differentiation of species to a transformation of mechanical forces. For instance, the fundamental Darwinian law of the *persistence of the fittest*, through natural selection and the struggle for life, becomes an illustration of the mechanical law of the segregation of similar parts in a mass subjected to any sort of force. If one throws a mixture of varied corpuscles to the wind, the largest fall together and the lightest are dispersed. It is similar for the individuals of a species subjected to the forces of the struggle for life : the similar or the strongest gather together and are best resistive to dispersion; they then persist, and the weakest disappear. Moreover, Spencer considered life as a synthesis of most fertile forces, better ordered, but of the same kind as chemical forces. " Life is definable as the continuous adjustment of internal relations to external relations " [1]. There are but two systems of forces, that of the environment and that of the living operations which influence one another and preserve themselves in mobile equilibrium.

C) **Psychological Evolution.**

480. II. It is, thus, by imperceptible stages that progress arises even to the world of consciousness; so well is this done that it is practically impossible to indicate the line of demarcation between physiology and psychology. Everything leads one to look upon psychology as a transformation of physiology. " Impossible as it is to get immediate proof that feeling and nervous action are the inner and outer faces of the same change, yet the hypothesis that they are so, harmonizes with all the observed facts; and... no other verification is possible for us than that which results from the establishment of complete congruity among our experiences " [2].

At the same time, the differentiation produced by evolution allows one to characterize the group of phenomena of the soul. Spencer here resolves a double series of problems, some of experimental psychology, and others of critical philosophy, on the origin of the first notions of thought and the value of our sciences.

I. **Problems of Experimental Psychology.** In order to classify our psychological activities, Spencer explains their origin. " This is the first truly scientific attempt at a history of the various phases which the evolution of mental life undergoes ", writes Ribot [3]. Applying the general definition of life, Spencer shows a continuous adjustment of internal with external relations. At the lowest degree, the environment is simple, as that in which

---

[1] *First Principles*, § 25.
[2] *The Principles of Psychology*, § 51. This is the theory of psycho-physical parallelism, which will be dealt with below; see n. 506, 2.
[3] T. RIBOT, *Psychologie anglaise*, p. 215.

the *gregarina*, a monocellular animal, lives; it inhabits the intestines of certain insects and is washed by the nutritive fluid it assimilates [1]. The correspondence of the living thing with such an environment is direct and homogeneous. But to the degree that external influences become complicated, the adaptation becomes diversified (heterogeneous). It extends itself into space by means of the external sense, and, in man, through the intellectual life [2]. It prolongs itself in time with the aid of the faculty of foresight, weak in savages, but quite developed in civilized peoples. At the same time, it gains in precision and in richness by concentrating mainly in well ordered organisms, finally constituting scientific and social systems. It is, then, a successive and imperceptible enrichment which permits him to refer all the highest forms of intellectual life to the definition of all life : an equilibrium of internal and external forces which, in final analysis, are of the mechanical order. Our current classifications, which distinguish instinct, reason, memory, and so on, are but superficial and conceal a complete identity.

Nevertheless, the progress of organization goes through several stages which themselves suggest a classification. At first, the vital phenomena of the physical or conscious order form two classes, " neatly distinguished by this : one of the classes includes the changes which are at once simultaneous and successive; the other, only the successive changes. As long as the phenomena which are the object of physiology are produced under the form of an immense number of different series joined together, the phenomena which are the object of psychology, contrarily, are only produced under the form of a simple series " [3].

The facts of consciousness are, without a doubt, simultaneous throughout but only in a general way, for their proper nature is to be successive only in time, while the physiological life also spreads out into space. The fundamental law of this succession is that of *association* formulated as follows : " The force of the tendency such that to an antecedent of a psychical change there should follow its consequent is proportionate to the persistence of the union between the external objects which it represents " [4].

Instinct is the first manifestation of psychological life; its roots lie in physiology, for Spencer defines it as a *composite reflex action*. To an elementary excitation, the nervous system responds by adapting itself through a simple reflex. In going upwards in the organization of living things, the environment becomes more complex, and vital adaptation becomes the " series of instinctive acts " formed, according to the law of evolution, by a coordinated and complex integration of simple reflexes.

---

[1] *Ibid.*, p. 181.

[2] For example : " A vessel guided by a compass, stars and a chronometer bring to man, from the other side of the Atlantic, information which permits him to adapt his purchases to prices from over there "; *Principles of Psychology*, " General Synthesis ", Ch. VIII.

[3] T. RIBOT, *op. cit.*, p. 187.

[4] *Ibid.*, p. 190. This law of association, already exploited by Hume, characterizes English psychology in the nineteenth century; see below, n. 484.

By becoming enriched with experience, instinct engenders *memory*, for the remembrance is, for Spencer, but a *beginning of nervous excitation*. For instance, to recall the color red, is to be, in a feeble degree, in that psychical state which the presentation of the color red produces. To recall a movement made with the arms, is to feel, in a feeble way, the repetition of those internal states which accompany movement; it is a beginning of excitation of all those nerves whose strongest stimulation has been established during movement " [1]. Inasmuch as superior instinct has organized a great number of movements, many of them cannot exteriorize themselves and remain in the state of tendency; they transform themselves into remembrances, ready to reappear when adaptation requires them. Briefly, memory is an accumulation of experiences which, increased by heredity, become a source of constant progress by permitting a larger, richer and more precise adaptation with exteriority.

Thus, from memory, reason is slowly born. Thought, as all life, is but an *adaptation;* to know is always to compare a new object with an object already known [2], by grasping at one and the same time the differences and the likenesses between them. If, for instance, one is passing near a field and hears an unknown noise and then, turning one's head, sees a flight of partridges, the noise is also " explained " in our reason, since we can give its " cause " — that is, we can easily *classify* this particular case among the phenomena called " flight of birds " [3]. This operation of classifying is, for Spencer, the fruit of experiences accumulated by memory. Animals and infants are content to go from one fact to another. But, along with the progress of the human race and of social life, classification has produced some great scientific systems, as meaningful as they are well ordered, and which are the proper work of reason.

Parallel to the progress of knowledge there is developed the affective aspect which completes the vital work of adaptation begun by thought. The most simple sentiment is *desire*, which accompanies instinct as a tendency to lay hold of the external object. In order to respond to a most complex situation, the simple sentiments form groups; the groups associate together and engender the many nuances of emotional life [4]. When the complexity becomes so great that adaptation is no longer automatic but, in the crowd of movements which arise as stimulation, many antagonistic groups counterbalance themselves, this state of soul is called *deliberation*. When the strongest stimulus

---

[1] T. Ribot, *op. cit.*, p. 192.

[2] " To know is to recognize "; if one objects that in this view, the first act of knowledge is impossible, Spencer replies that " knowledge properly called is formed only little by little... it slowly disengages itself from the confusion of consciousness with a view to development to the extent that the experiences are arranged in groups " *First Principles*, § 26.

[3] *Ibid.*, § 23.

[4] For instance, Spencer shows the complexity of *love* in which affection, admiration, approval of the person loved, self esteem and sympathy are involved. See T. Ribot, *op. cit.*, pp. 196-7.

occurs, one has a state of voluntary decision. This interpretation evidently excludes *liberty*, which, for Spencer, is an *illusion* arising from the fact that we consider our " self " as distinct from the group of phenomena which constitute the " self " at each moment [1].

From another aspect, in considering the most perfect knowledge, Spencer indicates its principal degrees. At the summit, he places *composite quantitative reasoning*, as one finds in the generalizations of mathematics and their application to industry. For example, the act of an inventor who, having determined the elements of an iron bridge, establishes by the calculus those of a bridge of double strength. Next in order we find the same type of reasoning in a simple state. This is succeeded by *qualitative* reasoning, in which the identity of measures is replaced by the similitude of perfections; this latter, in its imperfect state, becomes an *induction* founded on pure analogies. In all these processes of reasoning, the spirit makes a classification of *relations;* later, a classification of *attributes* is called *perception*, for it supposes many simple sensations bearing on the simple or secondary qualities of bodies and it synthesizes them by classifying them through association about a central property [2]. At the lowest point are the most simple *perceptions*, which refer to that of resistance. The latter lead us to the second series of problems.

2. **Critical problems : the value of fundamental notions and of the sciences.** All the knowable phenomena, according to Spencer, are explained by only two elements, matter and movement, which are deployed in a marvelous diversity according to the law of evolution. Even these two elements are referable to but one, *force*, which, under its dual static (matter) and dynamic (energy) form, persists indefectibly throughout. But of what value is our perception of this fundamental element?

Spencer believes that our knowledge cannot seize the exterior reality as it is in itself; he rejects the " naive realism ", as he calls it, of the ancients. Not only does the thing-in-itself escape us [3], but the phenomena whose laws are established by science are not necessarily, in themselves, such as they are seen in our knowledge. Spencer proclaims the " relativity of knowledge ". On this point he adopts the conclusions of Hamilton and of Mansel, corroborating them with his own reflections. If the aim of knowledge is to adapt our internal influences to external influences, it is sufficient that knowledge teach us that to a given external relation there corresponds, of necessity, an internal relation. For example, in order to preserve ourselves from being burned, it is sufficient to know that to the perception of a fire followed by contact, there necessarily corresponds in us a sensation of sadness which accompanies the destruction of tissue. It is useless

---

[1] See below, n. 501, the similar view of Taine on this matter; there is no other position possible for positivism, but it cannot be defended.

[2] Perception grasps the simple relations between the various attributes and makes a first synthesis of them; reasoning grasps the complex relations of phenomena and makes larger syntheses of them.

[3] See the positivist principle, n. 471, above.

for us to be adapted to the environment, if the flame is as we see it. Thus, the fundamental perception of force or resistance has our own *muscular effect* as its intimate experience. This can be certified readily, for, by lifting an arm, we dispense a certain muscular energy, and thus conclude that there is outside of us an equal force which equilibrates it, and we suppose that it is of the same nature as our internal energy. Nothing guarantees the truth of this hypothesis. On the contrary, reflection condemns this view, for it implicitly supposes that all the bodies are endowed with consciousness, a position which is hardly intelligible. Thus, all our knowledge is relative, which is to say that its unique object is *relations :* those which bind our conscious life to the exterior, unknown in itself; those which bind together the unknown things themselves. These relations are always limited and precise, for they suppose measurable elements. They are the inseparable " condition " [1], indispensable for all scientific knowledge, since " to think " is but to *relate* a new object to a class already known.

This complete relativism of our sciences does not imply idealism. Spencer prefers it to realism for two reasons. The first is negative, which he calls the " argument of priority ". " Suppose that realism was not sufficiently established, one would still have to prefer it to idealism, for it is impossible to formulate the latter, and a fortiori to prove it without presupposing realism at each step and taking one's bearing from it " [2]. The presumed chances of error in realism are thus found, doubled in fact, in the idealistic view. Then, in positive fashion, he shows that the object of the sciences, by its very relativity, requires an absolute reality of which it is the manifestation [3].

Finally, his theory of evolution allows him to complete the relativity and the realism of our knowledge by interpreting the Kantian doctrine of a priori forms so as to safeguard the rights of empiricism, of which English thought is so fond. Spencer first shows that space and time are not, as Kant wished, innate and primitive forms, but the fruit of abstraction working on experience. Thus, when our primitive conception of resistance shows us several simultaneous points, we form an idea of extension. It is sufficient, for abstraction, to consider this extension as empty but capable of containing resistant points, in order to obtain the idea of space. If the resistant points are successive, they engender the idea of movement and the same effort of abstraction gives the notion of time. Space and time are thus derivatives of experience.

Nevertheless, our perception is endowed with two a priori forms that are most profound; they are *resemblance* and *difference*.

---

[1] See the principle of Hamilton, below, " to think is to condition " (n. 484, A).

[2] *Principles of Psychology*, § 404. If an idealist, Spencer remarks, wished to explain to a non-philosopher that sound is a subjective fact, he would speak to him of *vibrations* of a clock which are transmitted to his ear; this presupposes the reality of these objects.

[3] Through this proof, psychology is joined to the metaphysics of the Unknowable; see below, n. 481.

The act of thinking consists in relating a new object to an object already known; this would be impossible if one did not admit a difference between the two objects which distinguishes them and a resemblance which allows them to be classified together. These two conditions are thus presupposed, necessarily, before all thought; they are a priori, deposited in us by nature. Besides, these conditions, which are a priori needed for our *actual* thought, are also the resultant of experience. According to the law of evolution, they have been formed and impressed little by little in the human brain by the patient efforts of past generations. They are thus the fruit of accumulated experience, which consists, at the beginning, in a direct response of consciousness to its environment and which is progressively organized in reasonings and scientific systems as the most fertile and efficacious response to a larger and more complex environment.

Here we fall into a *transfigured realism*, as Spencer calls it. Our perceptions and our sciences have a real relationship to the organized phenomena outside of us, since they come from them and are an adaptation to them. But this relation is comparable to that of possessing a figure in perspective with its model. One does not express the other as it is, but each of its elements corresponds to various elements in the other. Truth, then, is defined as " the accurate correspondence of subjective to objective relations " [1].

Within these limits, Spencer effectively defends the infallible truth of our sciences, giving *inconceivability* of the contradictory as the supreme criterion. When a judgment joins a subject to an attribute, we speak of certitude, if the union is indissoluble and resists all our efforts at breaking it. For instance, in thinking that " the bird is brown ", it is easy to think that it is black; this proposition can only be *doubtful*. If we say that " the ice is cold ", it is more difficult to make the substitution, " the ice is warm ". Nevertheless, if I imagine a freezing point of water which would be higher than the temperature of the blood in the organism, I could arrive at breaking the association of these states of consciousness expressed by the words, ice, cold, and replace them by the association, ice, warm [2]. The powerlessness to think " the ice is warm " is but relative. If, however, I state that " every triangle has three angles ", it is impossible to break this association; all our efforts fail. We thus have a certitude which is complete truth. Now this inconceivability is not only a *subjective* powerlessness for Spencer, because its cause is in the lack of accord with all our personal observations and with the uniform and permanent results deposited by past experiences in our cerebral organization [3]. In thus being based on experience, Spencer's criterion returns to that of " objective evidence " and thus seems to justify infallible truth quite completely.

---

[1] *First Principles*, § 25.
[2] D. J. MERCIER, *The Origins of Contemporary Psychology*, pp. 88-9.
[3] *Ibid.*, p. 91.

D) **Moral and Social Evolution.**

480. III. In the absence of free will, traditional morality loses its significance. It is not a practical science presenting human liberty with a code of *obligatory* laws, so that their observance *merits* recompense and their violation, chastisement [1]. It is true that Spencer uses customary language and speaks of a " rule which can well direct our conduct " [2], but this rule is nothing but the necessary flowering of the law of evolution. Morality can, then, be defined as " the deduction of the more and more perfect forms which human action, whether individual or social, necessarily adopts, subject to the fundamental law of evolution ".

By adapting itself to its environment, as does all life, human life pursues its good, or that which is *useful*. Moreover, as experience shows, we find our happiness first in sensible pleasure before it becomes the higher happiness of the thinker or the citizen. In this sense, Spencer's morality can be called *utilitarian* or even *hedonistic*. But just as Comte, Spencer recognized in man a disposition to altruism, in addition to his egoistic tendencies, as the foundation of social life. Conformable with his evolutionary outlook, he also affirmed that the altruistic tendencies are destined to predominate more and more. By progress, humanity passes " from a confused uniformity and promiscuity of beginnings to the harmonious variety of individualities. Just as the innumerable distinct stars have come from the primitive nebula, so from the unformed mass of savage tribes there has emerged the individuals of civilized societies " [3]. Each man thus acquires an increasingly rich and full personality. But at the same time that it specializes on a part, the personality is better harmonized to the social " totality "; this adaptation, the source of its perfection, also gives it happiness and morality. At the conclusion of progress, right conduct will be the only natural one remaining. " The actions to which men are today subject with repugnance because they are presented as obligatory will be accomplished without effort and with pleasure; in addition, those which man now avoids by a feeling of duty, he will then avoid, because they are disagreeable to him " [4]. Each will find his joy in devotion to others, and this is happiness on earth, the necessary fruit of the progress of the law of evolution.

Actual humanity, then, is but on the march towards the ideal; this explains the deficiencies of its morality. Heredity incorporates, little by little, general sentiments and altruistic tendencies into our organic structure, thus concretizing moral goodness.

---

[1] See the same remark concerning Spinoza, n. 353, above.
[2] *First Principles*, § 32.
[3] G. COMPAYRÉ, *H. Spencer et l'éducation scientifique*, p. 88.
[4] *Ibid.*, p. 89.

The first human generalizations have aided this progress by imagining religious systems in which the gods, by their authoritative laws and redoubtable sanctions, have repressed a powerful egoism. The education of parents and public morality have slowly succeeded in transforming this sort of life into an agreeable habit. For those adept in the evolutionistic doctrine, these helps have become needless and have been replaced by social influences and sanctions. They have also been replaced by what Spencer calls "moral institutions"; these are philosophical reflections which habituate us to seize the true meaning of our destiny by persuading us that our true happiness is in the accomplishment of the good, the fullest flowering of our nature.

In this theory, social progress is parallel to moral progress. Spencer has shown, in detail, how humanity has slowly egressed from the animal world according to Darwinian laws, and has progressively lifted itself towards civilization to the very peak of the English society of his age. In this latter state, there is a rich heterogeneity in all domains (language, sciences, arts, politics, industry, and so on), joined to a nice delimitation of functions, veritably a perfect harmony and a real stability of the social order. The best government, in his view, is the liberal system in which each individual can fully deploy his personality and freely join with others in order to get the particular aims of life, as economic, moral, religious and artistic progress. The state and authority are more and more restrained to the role of *protecting* these rights which each man possesses, and of preventing disorders and injustices by efficacious sanctions.

In order to show that the same evolutionary law governs social life as it rules the inferior stages of corporeal life, Spencer developed the comparison between society and the living organism. He mentions four principal resemblances. 1º Both commence by being but small aggregates; their mass increases, and they can even become a hundred times what they were at their origin. — 2º Their structure is at first so simple that one can say they possess none; but during the course of their development, the complexity of structure generally increases. — 3º At their origin, the mutual dependence of the parts hardly exists at all; finally this dependence becomes so great that the activity of life in each part is not possible except through the activity and the life of the others. — 4º The life of the body is much longer than that of the elements which constitute it; the total organism survives the disappearance of the individuals which compose it and it can even grow in mass, structure and activity, despite these successive losses [1].

Spencer was well aware that these are more analogies than identities, and he was acquainted with striking divergencies. 1º Societies do not have exterior forms as well defined as plants and animals. — 2º The social organism does not form a continuous mass as the living body. — 3º While the last living elements of the individual body are most often fixed in their relative position,

---

[1] T. Ribot, *Psychologie anglaise*, pp. 162-3.

those of the social organism can change places, for the citizens can come and go at will in order to conduct their affairs. — 4° The most important difference lies in the fact that in the animal body, there is but one tissue endowed with sentiment (nervous tissue), while all the members are so endowed in society [1]. However, if one adopts Spencer's viewpoint, in which there is nothing in the universe but a deployment of phenomena equal in essence, since all are manifestations of the same force, and even though one does not know if they are diverse manifestations of the same force, one can understand that the divergences between social states and physiological organisms tend to lose their importance; at the same time, the similitudes become exaggerated and become various applications of one identical law.

But it is especially this positivist postulate which makes Spencer's beautiful system so frail in its various parts. This frailty especially stands out in sociology as in psychology. The " members " of society are comparable neither to pure phenomena, nor even to their *members* without independence, and integrated in the living body. Society is made up of autonomous *persons*, free substances endowed with proper activities and enjoying an immortal destiny. Besides, by explaining all the manifestations of consciousness by the transformations of simple reflex movements, Spencer unduly refers the superior to the inferior reality. The order of conscious facts is as real as that of physiological facts, but it is of a most immaterial nature, manifesting a degree of superior perfection. In consciousness, the activities of intelligence and of free will are of a still higher order, having a fully spiritual nature and requiring immortality of the principle in which they are rooted, the human soul. These great truths necessarily escape every mechanistic system, but they are based on incontestable facts which one cannot neglect without error.

There is nothing astonishing in the fact that the moral destiny proposed by Spencer is incapable of satisfying the aspirations of an immortal soul. It is quite evident that this state of moral and social perfection, in which the ideal human life is to expand, cannot be definitive. Dissolution must always follow evolution, and thus the supreme happiness is but provisory. Humanity, like all things, plunges back into chaos, and is condemned to an eternal recommencement of an evolutionary cycle from barbarity to civilization.

Among this universal process of change, one thing remains as an ultimate point of reference, and the proof of its existence is the coronal of Spencer's synthesis : this is the UNKNOWABLE.

E) **Metaphysical and Religious Evolution : The Unknowable.**

481.   The habit of considering questions from their most universal aspect led Spencer to the conception of an element

---

[1] *Ibid.*

that is most profound and more real than the ensemble of
phenomena. Thus he surpasses pure positivism by proving
the existence of the absolute and of the infinite. The two
proofs which he presents, inspired by his evolutionistic theory,
show that this supreme being is what he calls the Unknowable.

1. **Proof by the Object of the Sciences.** This object, as we
have seen, is the *phenomenon*, or that which appears; it is
also the *relative* expressed by our precise, quantitative laws,
and thus finite. But it is impossible to think an appearance,
if there is nothing which appears. A relation is totally
inconceivable if there is no relative subject, related to another.
There is, accordingly, at the bottom of our thoughts, like an
indestructible residue, a reality distinct from thought and
independent of ourselves — it is an ABSOLUTE without which
no true knowledge of the relative is possible. Since this Absolute
is not related to any other which could limit it, it is also the
Infinite. All the phenomena explained by our scientific laws
are but a manifestation of this final Reality.

But if we attempt to form a clear idea of it in ourselves,
we fall into all sorts of contradictions. Take exterior facts,
for example : the fundamental notions in the mechanistic
conceptions of Spencer are space and time, matter and force.
Now, " ...space and time are wholly incomprehensible. The
immediate knowledge which we seem to have of them proves,
when examined, to be total ignorance " [1]. This is so for many
reasons, among which is the fact that their reality requires
that they be *infinite entities*, while all the *scientifically* knowable
entities must be determined, measurable and finite in order
to be expressed in laws. Matter, in turn, is absolutely
incomprehensible. " Whatever supposition we frame leaves
us nothing but a choice between opposite absurdities " [2].
Spencer examines the hypothesis that matter is totally solid,
or, as in Newton's view, formed of separated atoms joined
by force, and even the view of Boscovich that matter is
constituted by centers of inextended forces. He finds these
views filled with impossibilities. *Force*, a wholly primary
notion, is known to us only by analogy with the energy of
which we are aware; a fallacious analogy, since it supposes
all beings endowed with consciousness, " So that it is absurd
to think of force as in itself like our sensation of it, and yet

---

[1] *First Principles*, § 15.
[2] *Ibid.*, § 16.

necessary so to think of it if we represent it in consciousness at all " [1]. If we go on to interior facts, the absolute reality which is manifested to us there is the *thinking self*, and we spontaneously believe we attain an intuition of its existence. But no knowledge is possible, if there is no distinction between subject and object. " If, then, the object perceived is self, what is the subject that perceives? Or if it is the true self which thinks, what other self can it be that is thought of? " [2].

This double movement of the human spirit, which cannot surpass itself to affirm a thing of which it is incapable of forming a conception, clearly demonstrates the thesis that the Absolute exists, but it is the Unknowable.

2. **Proof by Religion.** Religion supposes the existence of a supreme being, transcendent and infinite, who is to be adored as the creator of the universe, and recognized as the supreme ruler and goal of human life. This being is the Absolute by which all is explainable. This thought of a supreme being is essential to humanity; evolution shows us, along with the birth of human societies, the formation of primitive religions which progress from primitive fetishism to the cult and the theologies of the civilized world.

Yet if one takes up a criticism of the basic ideas of religions, one finds them as untenable as those of the sciences. For example, they pretend to explain the origin of the universe, but this is an insoluble mystery. One cannot conceive that the world exists by itself, nor that it is created by itself, nor that it is created by God. For the second hypothesis is but a form of the first, and the third supposes that God exists by Himself. Now, it is precisely this notion of " existence through Himself " which is, for Spencer, unrealizable. Such a notion surpasses the facts, for the latter are explained by causes all having a beginning themselves, and one goes towards an existence without cause and, hence, without beginning. Now, by no mental effort can we do this. To conceive existence through infinite past-time, implies the concept of infinite past-time, which is an impossibility " [3]. And, continuing his analysis, Spencer declares, with Mansel, " The conception

---

[1] *Ibid.*, § 18.

[2] *Ibid.*, § 20. Also see above, n. 424, for the same difficulty and its solution. All these supposedly unresolvable antinomies can be resolved in Thomism. See above, n. 267.

[3] *First Principles*, § 11. All of Spencer's reasoning is founded on the positivist prejudice that only the *fact* is knowable.

of the absolute and of the infinite, from whatever side it is considered, seems involved in contradiction ".

Religion gives us the same picture as have the sciences. There is a universal persuasion of an Absolute, and yet a total powerlessness in expressing it; this is evident proof that it exists, and is the Unknowable.

The doctrine of evolution, applied to metaphysics as to religion, further confirms this conclusion. The progress of science, in fact, shows more and more the insufficiency of metaphysics and the breakdown of its theories. In finally declaring that all knowledge is "relative and conditioned" or encamped in finite phenomena, science makes the object of metaphysics appear as the Unknowable. — The same holds for religions : the essence of the religious spirit, found in all its forms, is the adoration of a mysterious, transcendent and inaccessible being. At the inferior stage of civilization, following the natural movement of thought, man represented this being in the image of that which surrounded him; this explains fetishism and polytheism. With the progress of science, which explained more and more of reality in a rational way, the gross imagery of God was pushed back, and the purified conceptions of theology were born. In advancing onwards, science concludes by becoming universal, throwing back one or another dogma, and leaving to religion its veritable object, the Mystery and the Unknowable. This, Spencer holds, is real progress, for it constantly reconciles religion and science by always granting to religion in all its purity that which is its very soul, the sense of mystery.

3. **Nature of our Knowledge of the Absolute.** Spencer concedes that we are incapable of knowing any divine attribute : we do not know whether the Absolute is a person or an unconscious being, whether it is one substance or fragmented into finite substances deriving from an infinite source; we do not know whether it is Creator, or Providence. In fact, we are totally ignorant of it [1]. He holds, however, that we do attain the Absolute, and he made a remarkable attempt to indicate in what fashion this occurs.

At first, this knowledge proceeds by *negation*. " Aside of definite consciousness, there is also an indefinite consciousness which cannot be formulated. Aside of complete thought and of thoughts which, though incomplete, can still be

---

[1] *First Principles*, § 31.

completed, there are thoughts which are impossible to complete " [1]. The knowledge of the Absolute is of this latter type; it remains incurably negative.

In the meanwhile, it is not to be regarded as a pure absence of thought. There is at the base of every phenomenon a " residue ", signified by our " conception of the non-relative or absolute. Although it is impossible to give this conception any qualitative or quantitative expression, it is none the less true that it imposes itself on us as a positive and indestructible element of thought " [2]. Without doubt, in order to form an idea of the Infinite, we only arrange finite, determined and relative elements, but we do represent " something " which is beyond. How, then, Spencer asks, can we conceive of this something? Evidently by combining successive concepts deprived of their limits and of their conditions. We form this indefinite idea as we form several of our definite ideas, by fusing a series of ideas. More exactly, we fuse *all* our ideas without exception, in order to throw together that which they have in common. That which is common to all ideas and which we are not able to reject is what we designate by the common name of existence. Separated from each of these modes which are in perpetual change, this existence remains as an indefinite conception of something which is constant under all modalities; it is an indefinite conception of existence isolated from its appearances.

Conclusion.

482. In Summary, the doctrine of Spencer centers about two superimposed and intimately united propositions. The first is the *theory of evolution : all the knowable is made intelligible by the unique law of evolution, which explains the variety of things by their diverse aspects, and their decadence by the dissolution which follows, which derives from the supreme mechanistic principle : the persistence of force.* Then, the *theory of the Unknowable : there exists an Absolute, the foundation of our sciences and the object of religions, but he is, for mankind, the Unknowable.*

A contemporary of Comte, Spencer took pains to distinguish his doctrinal position from that of the French thinker. But

---

[1] *Ibid.*, § 36.
[2] *Ibid.*, § 38.

his thought is plainly positivist: he has the same notion of philosophy, proclaims the same ignorance of anything beyond experiential facts, and the same esteem for the positive sciences. In a certain sense, Spencer, being more systematic than Comte, is more positivist. His system is better unified, more complete by its inclusion of psychology, but also less stable, because it does not sufficiently account for the various degrees of phenomena. The hierarchy of perfections is dissolved into a levelling evolutionism in which unity is from below. The higher activities are referred to the most elementary manifestations, those of mechanism. For its part, this synthesis properly belongs to the scientific current, but it also has affinity with the more radical materialism of Karl Marx and the socialists. Spencer defends himself, stating that he is not materialistic, although he refers the ensemble of phenomena to the manifestations of matter and of material force. "The interpretation of all phenomena in terms of Matter, Motion and Force, is nothing more than the reduction of our complex symbols of thought, to the simplest symbols; and when the equation has been brought to its lowest terms the symbols remain symbols still"[1]. The reality symbolized, for Spencer, is neither material nor spiritual; it is the Unknowable. Good sense, on the other hand, requires a man to judge things manifested by facts through the facts which manifest them; if all of them are material, one falls inevitably into materialism.

From another side, however, Spencer is less agnostic than the rigid positivists, and one can say that he rediscovered, in part, the way of doctrine followed by the great Christian philosophers, especially of St. Thomas. His formulation of doctrine, of course, is quite incomplete. But there is no contradiction in speaking of the existence of an Unknowable, if one does not thereby deny all *positive* knowledge of God's *essence*, and if one asserts that the existence of the supreme cause is required by the facts of experience exempted from the imperfections of their effects (a relative and negative knowledge)[2].

In conclusion, Spencer's solution is deficient. Our knowledge of God, by the aid of analogy, can have a true *positive value*, though it is inadequate. Without resorting to naive

[1] *First Principles*, § 194.
[2] This position was already proposed by Maimonides; see n. 194, above.

realism, a sound critical view allows us to attain more than one infallible truth concerning the domain of created substances [1]. Despite everything, Spencer remains imprisoned in the Kantian and positivist negations.

Following the master works of Darwin and Spencer, the scientific current of English positivism continued with a series of thinkers, each having his own nuances of thought. Among them is THOMAS HUXLEY (1825-1895), the author of *Man's Place in Nature* (1863), and of some *Essays* (1894). Huxley was faithful to Spencer's metaphysical agnosticism. The fundamental axiom of positive philosophy, in his view, is that materialism and spiritualism are two opposed poles of the same absurdity, that of imagining that we know something of spirit or of matter. He was quite favorable to Haeckel's theory on the origin of life, for a time believing that he had found a rare specimen called *bathybius* which was to account for the origin of life, but he recalled this error. He was quite insistent on the relations between physiology and conscious facts, and inclined towards epiphenomenalism [2]. — WILLIAM K. CLIFFORD († 1879) tended to refer physical facts to psychological experience, but by materializing thought more than by spiritualizing matter. In his view, the primordial element of things is *mind-stuff*, parts of which, by unifying, constitute consciousness or the spirit. Some spirits can partially coincide through the common portion of *mind-stuff* which unites them. This explains why we have a partial knowledge of the consciousness of others. Each spirit is also in communion with the *mind-stuff* that is not unified, and thus there is a " cosmic emotion ", the basis of religious sentiment and of a social consciousness, which dominates mankind. — LESLIE STEPHEN, the author of *Science of Ethics*, believed that evolution does not result in individual happiness, as Spencer held, but in the constitution of a perfect social body. The health, vitality and power of this social body is the true goal, and not its happiness. The calculation of pleasure, which depends on a momentary impression, does not necessarily coincide with this goal [3].

Other evolutionists, less attached to mechanism than Spencer, approached some form of spiritualism. Among them is G. ROMANÈS († 1894), who wrote *The Mental Evolution of Man, Intelligence and the Animal, Mental Evolution in the Animal,* and *A Candid Examination of Theism*. He holds that our reason is a developed instinct, and considers the concept as the fruit of experience. He adduces curious facts as proof that the animals possess the notion of *cause* and that their lack of power to speak is uniquely due to the formation of their organs. But he also holds that one cannot explain vital adaptation without recurring to the influence of an intelligent finality, and his later writings are favorably inclined towards God. — JOHN FISKE, the author

---

[1] See above, n. 409, for the remarks made on Kant in a similar connection.

[2] For the meaning of this view, see below, n. 494.

[3] See E. BRÉHIER, *Histoire de la Philosophie*, II, p. 931.

of *Darwinism* (1879) and of *The Destiny of Man* (1884), also acknowledged an immanent finality in evolution, which he looked upon as an immanent God Who is the soul of the world.—LE COMTE, the author of *Evolution and its Relation to Religious Thought* (1888), also saw the life of God in nature and a parcel of the divine energy in the human spirit.

Finally, B. KIDD, the author of *Social Evolution* (1894), made a special study of evolution in humanity. He shows the influence of a calculating intelligence, always at the service of individual interests, and the action of Darwin's natural selection, which often sacrifices individual interest to the profit of the race. Progress, he concludes, operates by the intervention of a powerful irrational factor, religion.

III. — SOCIALISM.

SPECIAL BIBLIOGRAPHY.

ARENDT, L., *Le mouvement ouvrier*, Brussels, 1928. — BEER, M., *Social Struggles and Socialist Forerunners*, New York, 1929. — CASTELEIN, J., *Le socialisme et le droit de propriété*, Brussels, 1876. — COLE, G. D. H., *Socialist Thought : The Forerunners*, 1789-1850, New York, 1953. — DAWSON, C. H., *Religion and the Modern State*, New York, 1935. — DELAYE, J., *Pour connaître le communisme*, Paris, 1936. — HANSFORD, C., *Fallacies of Socialism*, New York, 1932. — HEARNHAW, F. J. C., (ed.), *Social and Political Ideas of Some Representative Thinkers of the Age of Reaction and Reconstruction*, 1815-65, New York, 1932. — *Survey of Socialism, Analytical, Historical, and Critical*, New York, 1935. — KOTHEN, R., *Le socialisme*, Louvain, 1946. — LAIDLER, H. W., *History of Socialist Thought*, New York, 1933. — LASKINE, A., *Le socialisme suivant les peuples*, Paris, 1920. — LEO XIII, Encycl. *Rerum Novarum*, May 15, 1891. — LOUIS, P., *Histoire du socialisme en France*, 1789-1945, Paris, 1946.—MACKENZIE, N. I., *Socialism : A Short History*, New York, 1950. — MARKHAM, S. F., *History of Socialism*, New York, 1931. —- PIUS XI, Encycl. *Quadragesimo Anno*, May 15, 1931. — *Divini Redemptoris*, March 19, 1937. — TAFT, P., *Movements for Economic Reform*, New York, 1950. — VON MISES, L., *Socialism : An Economic and Sociological Analysis*, New Haven (Conn.), 1951. — WEILL, A., *Histoire du mouvement social en France* (1852-1924), Paris, 1924. — WINTERER, J., *Le socialisme contemporain*, Paris, 1894.

The socialist movement, which had a great developmental phase in the second half of the nineteenth and in the twentieth century, is primarily an economic theory. It is a continuation of the work of Adam Smith and the physiocrats [1], but with a marked tendency towards practical realization. Many of its leaders are fighters who lead the army of workers to the

---

[1] See above, n. 369.

assault on capital, as Karl Marx, or give themselves to political action even to the fomenting of violent revolutions, as Lenin. There are, however, some directive ideas which allow socialism to be treated under the scientific current of positivism, and which have expanded, into our times, into a full-blown, materialistic synthesis. The *philosophical principles* of socialism will be treated first; this will be followed by some special doctrines of the main theorists, and especially the view of Marxism and contemporary Communism.

A) Directive Principles of Socialism.

482. I. Despite the diversity of socialist doctrines, one can find a common fund of thought throughout; it may be inspired by Rousseau, or, more often, by the positivist mentality. The economic theories take on the value of a positivist morality, founded on an equalitarian notion of justice, evolving according to the law of progress.

1. **Positive Morality.** For socialism, the supreme good which orients man's moral activity lies in the good organization of man's material and sensible life so that each finds the full satisfaction of his needs as recompense for work performed without pain. For every sincere socialist, " the adoption of this doctrine is a sort of quasi-religious conversion, and the apparition of a new conception of life and of social relations " [1]. This view is a clear statement of positivist agnosticism [2], declaring that the only legitimate study is that of the facts of sensible experience. Moreover, the problems of the immortality of the soul, of the existence of God and of our duties to Him are totally passed over in silence, and one irresistibly glides towards materialism and atheism.

2. **Equalitarian Justice.** The necessary and sufficient means for obtaining happiness is the partition of all earthly goods between all men according to a strict equality. This distribution makes up the exercise of *justice*, the basic virtue of human life. This principle, as has been seen, is that of Rousseau — all men are equal [3].

There is some divergence of views as to the concrete application of this equality. In general, it is understood

---

[1] A. Lalande, *Vocabulaire technique de philosophie*, " Socialism ", p. 777.
[2] See above, n. 471.
[3] See above, n. 450, III.

as a proportional equality, as a function of the needs and of the work furnished by each man. But all are in accord that the main obstacle to justice is the right of *private property*, especially in the form of riches accumulated by the capitalists. One can thus characterize socialism by its opposition to the right of private property, for it wishes to suppress, or at least to restrict this right, for it is viewed as altogether alien to the natural law.

The remedy generally proposed is the intervention of society, which, inasmuch as it possesses all goods in common, can distribute them equally to each. Following the logic of this exorbitant function attributed to the state, and just as Rousseau's individualism founded equalitarian justice, so socialism ordinarily is against the family, against the indissolubility of marriage, and reserves the total education of children to society.

3. **The Law of Progress.** Every socialist is persuaded that by realizing his ideal, he will procure the good of the working class. This persuasion, among the theorists, is based on the law of progress by which human society is on the march towards more happiness and more justice. When justice is established throughout, it will favor solidarity and mutual aid, so that we are faced with an ideal, like that of Comte, of a future state in which universal altruism will be the basis of the moral life [1].

These common traits allow one to group the theorists who are *properly called socialists* today, by stating that *socialism is every doctrine which, placing the ideal of human life on this earth in economic prosperity, attempts to procure this status by a new organization of society in which the right of private property will be suppressed completely or in part* [2].

---

[1] See above, n. 466.

[2] According to Lalande's view, socialism is " every doctrine which prevents one from free activity in individual initiative or interest in economic matters in order to assure a satisfactory social order; it judges as possible and desirable, a substitution for the present social organization, one which concertedly aims to get results which are not only most equitable but also most favorable for the full development of the human person " (*Vocabulaire technique de la philosophie*, " Socialism "). This broad definition can apply to social Catholic doctrines, as to those of De Mun (see below, n. 521). But official documents, particularly the *Rerum Novarum* and the *Quadragesimo Anno*, have condemned socialism as anti-Catholic. This explains why the definition in the text characterizes socialism by its underlying philosophical views and especially by its opposition to private property. See, in this connection, the article " Socialisme " in *Dictionnaire Apologétique*, col. 1396.

B) The First Theorists.

482. II. The working class suffered many disastrous consequences beginning with the close of the eighteenth century. The industrial revolution helped to replace the small, familial workshop by great industrial enterprises [1]. At the same time, towards the middle of the nineteenth century, the liberal doctrine of Adam Smith [2] became triumphantly accepted and influential [3]. Many writers protested against this situation, and proposed remedies inspired by socialism. Besides those which flourished before or during the French Revolution of 1789 [4], mention should be made of the special effort of Saint-Simon and of Fourrier, and then of Proudhon and Louis Blanc.

1. Count HENRY OF SAINT-SIMON (1760-1825), mentioned above [5], took over many of Comte's ideas in his works, *La société européenne* (1814) and *Système industriel* (1821). He stressed the needful preponderance of industrial over other occupations in order to obtain peace and constitute social progress. In his work, *Nouveau christianisme*, he presents himself as the new Messias with the task of taking up anew the mission confided by Christ to the Church, for the latter had not acquitted its job properly. Christ's whole mission can be summarized in this law, " love one another ", and both Protestants and Catholics have lost the true meaning of this universal charity. In order to realize his task, he did not rely on the workers but appealed to the heads of the state and to a group of philanthropic spirits whom he hoped to count among his disciples.

After his death, *Saint-Simonism* was organized under the direction of ENFANTIN [6] (1796-1864) and others, who attempted

---

[1] The beginning of the transformation dates from 1759, when Watt's steam engine was introduced into the English mills.

[2] See above, n. 369.

[3] The English school of Manchester, whose chiefs were Cobden and Bright, contributed much towards this triumph. It was assured in 1860 by the commerce treaty between France and England, based on the principle of free exchange; other countries imitated this treaty.

[4] The first French socialists before the Revolution were Meslier, Morelly, Mably and Brissot de Warville, who considered private property as the cause of pride and egoism. During the Revolution, Babeuf and Maréchal founded the *Secte des égaux*, getting four thousand adherents, but they were discovered and beheaded. In England, between 1790 and 1805, Spence, Goodwin and Hall were active socialists.

[5] See above, n. 456. — **Works :** Œuvres de Saint-Simon et d'Enfantin, 46 vols., 1865-1877. — *Œuvres choisies*, 3 vols., Brussels, 1859. — MARKHAM, F. M. H., (ed. and tr.), *Selected Writings*, New York, 1953. — **Studies :** CHARLETY, S., *Essai sur l'histoire du saint-simonisme*, Paris, 1930. — LEROY, M., *La vie véritable du comte H. de Saint-Simon*, Paris, 1927. — SHINE, H., *Carlyle and the Saint-Simonians*, Baltimore (Md.), 1941.

[6] See F. ROTHWELL (tr.), *Life Eternal; past, present, future*, Chicago, 1920.

to put this theory into practice. As Brehier puts it, the movement appeared " as a bizarre mixture of noisy advertising, naturalistic morality, socialist doctrine and practical enterprises " [1]. The doctrine had socialistic inspiration, seeking for a new social and economic order in which the individual would sacrifice his egoism for the good of all, and, in line with this aim, proposed the *limitation* of the right of private property [2]. Property is but the refuge of laziness and riches are forces which should be put to work.

2. CHARLES FOURRIER [3] (1772-1837) belongs under socialism by his aim to reform the working organizations. He hoped to set up " appealing work " which would be able to bring economic prosperity without imposing any laborious burdens on the workers. This ideal seemed possible since Providence had established a marvelous harmony in the world of bodies and of living things, in which opposed forces and diverse aptitudes spontaneously tend to mutual aid for the good of the group. It is impossible to think that this same law does not govern the moral and economic activities of men; if society is disorganized, it is because this providential law has been ignored and violated. According to Fourrier, the natural law of man is to follow the impulse of one's passions, multiple and varied, but oriented towards activity and towards work, which are its spontaneous fruits.

However, in the actual organization of economic life, the industrial worker furnishes a work of whose destiny he is ignorant; nothing favors his tastes, and everything encourages the indulgence of his passions. Fourrier aims to cure this situation by proposing a more restrained association of workers whose natural inclinations would be respected, and whose personnel would include all the trades. Thus, through cooperation and according to the providential law of mutual aid, the good of all would be realized. This organization would be like a *phalanx* of workers, counting about sixteen hundred and twenty associations in order to take care of all possible combinations of workers.

Fourrier attempted to organize such a group, believing that it would serve as an example and conclude with the transformation of society into a number of such groups; he failed, however, due to a lack of funds. One could have foreseen the effect of such an association of egoisms, however. In order to maintain unity among them, Fourrier was hoping for a profound transformation of humanity, so that the most diverse passions would harmonize among themselves. This was a rather wild hope, for only reason, subject to legitimate social authority, has been providentially entrusted with the mission of imposing order on the passions.

Fourrier had disciples who continued to diffuse his ideas. V. CONSIDÉRANT (1808-1893) was the main one. He edited the

---

[1] E. BRÉHIER, *op. cit.*, p. 856.

[2] For example, they wanted the State to be " the principal heir in all successions in the collateral line " (*ibid.*, p. 859).

[3] **Studies** : BOURGIN, H., *Fourrier*, Paris, 1905. — FRIEDBERG, M., *L'influence de C. Fourrier sur le mouvement social contemporain en France*, Paris, 1926. — PELLARIN, C., Vie de Fourrier, Paris, 1871.

journal at first called *Le Phalanstère* and then *La Phalange*. He defended a mitigated socialism, for he believed that the concurrence and the struggle between the classes was due only to accidental circumstances, and that the future lay in an association of capital, talent and work [1]. Fourrier's views contributed somewhat to the Revolution of 1848, but he had little lasting influence on the working class.

3. JOSEPH PROUDHON [2] (1809-1865) had a much greater influence. He wanted the working class to direct its own progress, and he inspired syndicalism and mutual insurance aids. He wrote numerous works, among which are : *Qu'est-ce que la propriété ?* [3] (1840); *De la création de l'ordre dans l'humanité* (1843); *Système des contradictions économiques* (1846); *De la justice dans la Révolution et dans l'Eglise* (1858); *La guerre et la paix* (1861). He voices strong criticism on the errors and harshness of liberalism and of the Marxian utopia; his own views lack clarity, and his ideas are wanting in precision. What is similar to socialism in his thought and seems most important is the idea he has of *justice*. The latter is " a universal reality which manifests itself in nature by the law of equilibrium, and in society by a reciprocity founded on the equality of persons " [4].

From this notion, Proudhon deduces an ideal of economic organization which he calls *mutualism*. In this setup, the workers become masters by universal suffrage; they direct enterprises, banks and other social institutions. For each service received, they give one of equal value in return.

The clearest position of mutualism is its total suppression of interest. In Proudhon's view, money is unproductive and the lender cannot in justice ask for more than he has loaned [5]. Capitalism fails in its duty by enriching itself from the fruits of money alone. Capitalists should be forced to work in order to live.

Aside of equality, Proudhon made room for *liberty*. In order to safeguard it, he maintained private property, especially among

---

[1] See E. Bréhier, *op. cit.*, ii, p. 845.

[2] **Works :** *Œuvres complètes*, 26 vols., 1867-1870; — Bouglé and Moysset (eds.), 9 vols. completed, 1923-1930. — *Solution of the Social Problem* (ed. H. Cohen), New York, 1927. — *General Idea of the Revolution in the Nineteenth Century*, London, 1923.
Studies : Brogan, D. W., *Proudhon*, London, 1934. — Bouglé, A., *La sociologie de Proudhon*, Paris, 1911. — De Lubac, H., *Un-Marxian Socialist : A Study of Proudhon*, New York, 1948.

[3] In this work, Proudhon states his famous definition : " Property is thievery! " To this he adds : " Possession is lawful, property is against the law ". He means to say that work is the only valuable title which serves as a basis for what he calls " possession "; all other wealth is " thievery ".

[4] E. Bréhier, *op. cit.*, p. 896. It is in the name of this justice stemming from the Revolution that Proudhon violently attacks the Catholic Church, accusing it of sacrificing the lower classes to the privileged. Due to this anticlericalism, the work of Proudhon is on the Index.

[5] See above, n. 245, where the same condemnation of interest is given by St. Thomas Aquinas. Nevertheless, under certain circumstances, Catholic moralists consider a *moderate* interest to be legitimate.

the peasants, and left a certain margin for individual initiative in his system of mutualism.

4. LOUIS BLANC [1] (1811-1886) is especially known for his role in the Revolution of 1848 and his unfortunate essay on the national working class; its failure led to the bloody days of June. This essay is but an application of the social doctrine contained in his two brochures, *De l'organisation du travail* (1846) and *Du droit au travail* (1849).

Every man, Blanc believes, has a *natural right to life*, which, in order to be secured, supposes the right of private property or, for those who have no private goods, the *right to work*, for work is the sole means of achieving livelihood. In capitalistic society, the right of private property is constantly exploited by a few rich men, and has so concentrated goods in their hands that a great number of the proletariat are practically despoiled of their right to life. Having no other means by which to live than work, the proletariat are constantly menaced by unemployment or by fear of being insufficiently recompensed.

The only way to remedy these abuses is to have recourse to the state, whose rigorous duty it is to furnish to each man the means of existence and, to workers, the means of earning their livelihood. In order that this may be done, the state must own the instruments of labor, as the goods of production, enterprises, and so on. Only then can it realize an equitable distribution among all the citizens. This expropriation of capitalists will restore money to its true role, which is to be of service to all and permit to each member of the proletariat the exercise of his " right to work ".

Karl Marx [2] (1818-1883) and Communism.

482. III. Karl Marx was born at Trèves of Jewish parents who had converted to Protestantism in 1814. He studied Hegel's system, whose dialectics inspired his theory of class-struggle, and, for a while, he held a chair in philosophy at Bonn. From 1841 onwards, he threw himself into social action and politics. He became a journalist and a revolutionary. With his friend, FREDERICK ENGELS, he published, at Brussels, the famous *Com-*

---

[1] See J. CASTELEIN, *Le socialisme et le droit de propriété*, Brussels, 1876, pp. 167-304.

[2] **Works :** DUTT, C. P. (ed. of English edition), *Selected Works*, 2 vols., New York, 1939. — LEE, A. (ed.), *Essentials of Marx*, New York, 1946.

Studies : BERDIAEV, N., *Les sources et le sens du communisme russe*, Paris, 1938. — BÖBER, M. M., *Karl Marx's Interpretation of History*, Cambridge (Mass.), 1948. — BOUSCAREN, A. T., *Imperial Communism*, Washington (DC), 1953. — CORNU, A., *Karl Marx. L'homme et l'œuvre*, Paris, 1934. — COOPER, R., *Logical Influence of Hegel on Marx*, Seattle (Wash.), 1925. — GARANDY, R., *Le communisme et la morale*, Paris, 1945. — GRAZIADEI, A., *Le capital et la valeur*, Paris, 1937. — JOSEPH, H. W. B., *Labour Theory of Value in Karl Marx*, Oxford, 1923. — LENIN, L., *Theoretical Principles of Marxism*, New York, 1939. — MC FADDEN, C. J., *Philosophy of Communism*, New York, 1939. — ROSENBERG, A., *History of Bolshevism, from Marx to the First Five Years' Plan*, Oxford, 1934. — SHEED, F. J., *Communism and Man*, New York, 1940. — TRUMER, M., *Le matérialisme historique chez K. Marx et Fr. Engels*, Paris, 1934.

munist Manifesto. In 1848, after a vain attempt to organize the socialist party in Germany, he retired to London, where he wrote the following : *A Critique of Political Economy* (1859); *An Appeal to the Working Classes of Europe* (1864); and the celebrated, *Capital* (1867).

Throughout this time, Marx continued his revolutionary efforts under the slogan, " Proletariats of the world, Unite! ". In 1866, he founded the first *Socialist International* at London, an organization which continued until 1870. But the Franco-German war and the failure of the *La Commune* in Paris weakened his standing considerably. Internal dissensions also arose; in 1874, the Russian anarchist Bakounin founded a rival association, and, in Germany, Lassalle founded a non-Marxist party.

The social movement, however, continued, though it relied more and more on the organizations of syndicalism and other professional groups. In 1889, at the International Congress of Paris, the disciples of Marx[1] founded the *Second Socialist International*, having its headquarters at London, which continues until these days. The Soviets, masters of Russia since 1917, have a parallel organization, the *Third Communist International*, at Moscow.

Socialist doctrine has found its most perfect expression in *Marxism*, which had the preponderant influence both on socialist and on communist movements. Marx's work, *Capital*, was intended to be a work in economics rather than a philosophical work; this was one of the causes of its success with the thinkers of the nineteenth century, who were imbued with scientism. However, a real philosophical doctrine is found in the historical and dialectical materialism which this work inspired, and in atheistic communism which is its full realization.

1. **Fundamental Theory : Historical and Dialectical Materialism.** Lenin thought that the fundamental question of all philosophy, and especially of modern philosophy, was that of the relation of thought and being. What is the primordial element, spirit or nature? The idealists, as Hegel, voted for spirit, and from it they deduced all reality. Karl Marx resolutely chose nature : there is no other reality for him but matter and its forces, and their continual evolution explains the various aspects of the universe. But Marx did not insist on the inferior degrees of reality, but studied human history, mainly, which explains the title, " historical materialism ",

---

[1] Among his disciples are : the Germans, BEBEL and LIEBNECHT; the French, JULES GUÊDES and VAILLANT; the English EVELING and MORRIS; the Belgians, ANSEELE and DE POEPE; the Hollander, DOMELA NIEUWENHUIS; the Italians, COSTA and CIPRIANI; the Russian, LAWROFF; the Swiss, BRANDT — and many others; see J. WINTERER, *Le socialisme contemporain*, p. 88.

given to his doctrine. In his view, the development of the individual and of the social life of man depends totally on material and economic conditions. The degree of civilization is measured by the degree of wealth or of industrial and rural prosperity. He believed that the manner of production of material life conditions the process of social, political and intellectual life in general. It is not, he thought, men's consciousness which determines their being, but it is their social being which determines their consciousness.

As any other phenomenon, so the development of humanity is likewise subject to the *determinism* of nature and is ruled by the laws which science established. But these laws are no longer viewed, as in Comte's sociology, as specifically distinctive of the human realm. One must look into the conditions of economic life, for scientific, juridical and social life is but a sort of " superstructure ". Marx's central intuition is, then, that economic life realizes the law of becoming with the three periods of thesis, antithesis and synthesis proposed by Hegel [1]. This dialectic, which commanded the evolution of the Idea, keeps its necessary and creative urge in Marxism, but is applied to a world constituted of material and economic realities. This explains why his view is called *dialectical materialism*. Marx's view of the class-struggle is the actual manifestation of the dialectical law. Briefly, his basic view comprises the following :

Matter and its forces are the unique reality whose continual and progressive evolution finally engenders human societies and their civilizations; this evolution follows the Hegelian law of thesis, antithesis and synthesis, but for Marx the latter becomes a social expression manifested in the struggle of the classes. This view served Marx as director in all his studies. Marx believed that it could be shown true by a study of the economic life of his times.

2. **The Economic Life : Capital and Labor.** Marx's four most powerful deductions in his work, *Capital*, can be stated in four propositions.

a) The true value of all merchandise is equal to the quantity of work incorporated into it. This holds to such an extent that the worker, the unique source of this value, also has the incontestable right of appropriating it entirely. In order to understand this view, on which Marx's whole theory rests, it should be mentioned that work is measured precisely by the time given to its production

---

[1] See above, n. 428.

and by taking a mean, in order to balance off the individual variations of the workers. Thus, the value of a piece of merchandise will be equal to the number of working hours required to produce it, under normal conditions.

Other causes besides work, it is true, seem to constitute the value of an object, but Marx thought all others illegitimate, for they implicated some confusion between the *value of usage* and the *value of exchange*. The first expresses the utility which one derives from an object; the second, the role of merchandise in economic life. Thus, air has a great value of usage, but no value for exchange. The diamond has hardly any use, but it has a real exchange value because of the work involved in discovering and refining it. Now, according to the economic viewpoint in which one must place oneself here, Marx holds that the veritable value can only be the value of exchange, and this is identical with the work involved. Exchange requires a common property between two products making them equivalent; only the quantity of work involved in merchandise can realize this condition. For instance, if one exchanges wheat for iron, there can be physical or chemical qualities common to them, and such qualities do not generally enter into consideration as giving them any value of usage; in economic matters one makes abstraction of these qualities. Work alone constitutes the true value of merchandise.

b) *The second proposition* of Marx states that the capitalistic organization deprives the worker of a part of the value of his work. This is the *plus-value* of merchandise, and the owner makes it the unique source of his *profit*, and thus accumulates capital. Hence, *capital is a continuous theft of work*, and by its natural effect it becomes an instrument for domination to the owner and of oppression for the worker.

If a capitalist does not work but is content to supply labor and is willing to observe justice, he would get no benefits. For instance, if he sells wood at a just price (by paying for all the work of extraction and preparation), and transforms it into a commodity, the value of the latter is only that of the wood and whatever estimate was needed to ready it. Thus, the price of the commodity returns completely to those who extracted and transformed it, and there is no profit for the capitalist. The latter, in order to profit from the operation, sells the energy of the workers, not according to the value of their labor, but by paying them what is strictly necessary for them to live or, at least, if the worker will be content, by following the law of supply and demand [1]. A salary of this sort would correspond, for instance, to but a half-day of work. The capitalist appropriates the other half-day, and this plus-value increases his capital.

For these reasons, Marx believes that such an organization tends, of itself, through maintaining the same salaries, constantly to increase the profit from work, especially through the use of machines allowing for longer and quicker work, and for the use of women

---

[1] Marx looked upon this " law " of economics as an abuse and an injustice.

and children. Briefly, all industrial progress is but an increasingly efficacious means of exploiting the workers.

c) The antagonism between capital and labor becomes more violent and iniquitous through the use of machinery and its free and covetous use; this is Marx's *third proposition.* In this open and free process, the greater capitalists eliminate their weaker rivals so that the industrial life concludes with being a monopoly by a few omnipotent and immensely rich trusts, capable of thoroughly exploiting the worker. In addition, the more modest capitalists, the small bourgeois, or men of the middle class, will be reduced to the rank of the proletariat. The class of the proletariat becomes larger and remains the only class opposed to the capitalists. As time goes on, the working or proletariat class becomes more conscious of its interests and communal aspirations, of its rights and its strength [1].

d) This increasing and necessary antagonism between the two social classes led Marx to his *fourth proposition.* The working class, having right, number and force on its side, will necessarily be victorious in the struggle against the capitalists. The latter will be finally expropriated [2], and all their riches, lands, factories and means of production will become the *collective property* of all; then each will find in his work its proper fruit and the means of abundantly satisfying all his needs. Marx does not treat the organization nor the practical functioning of collectivism. He only concludes to the industrial progress which makes any return to private ownership impossible, and he saw as increasingly imminent the rise of the new collectivist society, founded on the ruins of capitalistic society.

The *struggle of classes* proposed by Marx is an application of Hegel's dialectic. Human society appears as the final manifestation of the evolution of material forces, developing according to the rhythm of thesis and antithesis in order to achieve a final synthesis of a classless society, perfectly socialized.

3. **Value of Marxist Economics.** Marxism has a twofold aspect: it appears as a scientific system, based on study, facts and statistics; it also is an interpretation of these facts in the light of historical and dialectical materialism.

With regard to *economic science*, it is as legitimate a field of inquiry as that of experimental psychology and sociology [3]. Whenever, in fact, an ensemble of facts, sufficiently distinct and capable of being studied by an experimental method adapted to them, is accumulated, nothing prevents one from setting up a special science. Economic facts are of this type; they are sufficiently

---

[1] These steps of the economic evolution were developed in great detail by Marx; he based his study on the English economics of his age. It can be admitted that the facts partly confirmed his predictions because of the accidental abuses which arose, as the working conditions of women and children. Social legislation corrected most of these abuses, however.

[2] In Marx's view, expropriation can be done legally and pacifically, by giving the capitalist a just compensation.

[3] See above, n. 469. Economics can also be viewed as a chapter in sociology.

dependent on matter to be subsumed to certain laws which, respecting human freedom, still possess a sufficient necessity to give them scientific value.

But a science of this sort can lose its legitimacy if one forgets that morality is founded on the philosophical knowledge of man and of God, and that economics cannot replace morality. Such was the common error of the liberal and socialist economists. The liberal school, starting with the fiction of a *homo economicus*, solely moved by interest, thought of discovering economic laws that were fully autonomous and whose application was beyond any moral regulation. Socialism got its force by beginning with the same premisses, though it arrived at different conclusions. One cannot deny that the capitalistic conception of free enterprise and the law of supply and demand has entrained numerous abuses [1]. Socialism presented itself as a remedy for these abuses. It was a remedy worse than the evil itself, for it ruthlessly denied any subordination of economics to morality. In contrast to such a view, it is true, instead, that any " positive " or particular science, as economics, is submitted to the direction of ethics as being a subalternate science. Economic facts, the proper object of economic science, form a portion of the wider object of moral science which includes all facts of human life and studies them from the broader and more inclusive view of the destiny of man's immortal soul.

The second aspect of socialism is its *materialistic* aspect; this is but a *gratuitous postulate*. Instead of using facts as a conclusion from legitimate induction, it predicts, by logic, the events which are to occur and which the facts contradict. This holds especially for the master-idea of the system, the progressive division of society into two inimical classes. This simplicist division in no wise corresponds to social reality, which is always made up of a complex group of professions, as in agriculture, industry, commerce, and even the great number of liberal professions. Far from tending fatally to a struggle, these professions, through mutual aid of employer and employee and in cooperating for the common good under the sovereign direction of political authority, are enjoying increasing prosperity.

In fact, Marxist materialism is a fruit of Kantian criticism and a reaction against the excesses of idealism; the better thoughts of the great spiritualist thinkers that have been presented thus far refute this view without difficulty. It was Marx, in fact, who inspired the ideal of an intellectualist, moral and religious life which began to spread in Russian Communism. The synthesis which he inspired will now be presented as viewed in the following works : F. ENGELS', *The Origin of the Family, of Property and of the State* (1893); LENIN'S, *Marx, Engels, Marxism* (1935); his *Infantile Malady*

---

[1] See the Encyclical letters of Pius XI, *Quadragesimo anno* and *Divini Redemptoris* for a statement and a denouncement of these abuses.

of Communism (1921), and his *The Proletariat Revolution* (1921); STALIN'S, *The Principles of Leninism.*

4. **Cultural Life : the Individual for Society.** In historical materialism, the highest forms of civilization are but an efflorescence or a superstructure of the evolution of economic laws and the progress of material forces as made known to consciousness. Communism does not deny reason; it rather exalts it as capable of dominating the universe and of securing the happiness of humanity. Reason is to pursue the modern sciences and their industrial applications. Its proper culturing lies in positive philosophy [1], and includes literature and the arts, capable of interpreting its scientific ideal. But inasmuch as reason is but the final fruit of material forces, it cannot surpass them and remains, as a result, encased in the sensible world.

Communism, nonetheless, made a remarkable effort, especially with Lenin, to construct a coherent, doctrinal basis for itself. It attempts to explain the evolution of things with the aid of three basic laws, which it also uses to explain the value of human knowledge and the stages of human history.

1. **The three fundamental laws.** These laws are those of dialectical materialism, which derive from Hegel's method.

a) The law of the unity of contraries. Every nature is constituted of contradictory elements or forces, as positive and negative electricity, discontinuous corpuscles and continuous waves, attractive and repulsive forces. The struggle of these forces determines, in each being, an internal evolution, as that of the vital cycle; but this evolution is in the interior only within certain limits. When these limits are surpassed, destruction eventuates, which produces other natures, similarly evolving.

b) The law of passage from quantity to quality. Evolution is primarily of the mechanical order, following the law of action and reaction, in which the amount of energy transformed remains constant. But at the moment when these natures break, change has gone beyond the limit and goes from one bond to another of the qualitative order; for instance, after water has been warmed to one hundred degrees, surpassing this limit causes a qualitative transformation into a gas. This law explains the meaning of the evolution in which living things, through abrupt mutation, are formed from chemical combinations which have arrived at their limits. Then, from vegetal matter, conscious beings and man are finally formed.

c) Law of the " negation of negation ". In the progress obtained by the struggle of contraries, the new termination suppresses the preceding in such a way that it retains all of the former's

---

[1] See n. 459 and n. 467, a above.

positive richness. Thus the grain is supplanted by the plant which derives from it, and the fruit, in its turn, negates the plant which it still contains germinally.

2. **Knowledge.** These same laws can explain the appearance and the nature of human knowledge.

As a reality, knowledge is primarily referred to the energies of the nervous system. Consciousness is but the internal face of the physiological, material fact, which makes up its total reality (epiphenomenalism). But, in applying the second law, a real, qualitative progress is achieved over merely physiological phenomena (just as the latter, in their turn, and according to the same law, surpass every physico-chemical phenomenon). Moreover, sensible knowledge, by developing itself in human consciousness, attains a new limit and thus gives rise, by a quick leap, to a qualitatively more perfect knowledge. This latter is the abstract concept, the source of our sciences and of the higher truths which clarify and direct human civilization. Dialectical materialism, thus understood, is close to spiritualism; while it is erroneous inasmuch as it refers thought to sensation, it still recognizes the superiority of thought.

But in order that knowledge be valuable and fertile, it must always remain in contact with the material energies from which it emanates. Sensation, for Lenin, is the direct liaison of ourselves with the exterior world; elaborating this figure, thought must also keep its indirect contact with the same world. Every knowledge, Lenin believes, is the reflection of nature by man. The fact that our scientific laws, which inspire modern technology, reunite to transform nature at man's wish, is a proof that our knowledge is a *veridical reflection* of reality. This, then, is the sole criterion valuable for determining the truth of our sciences and our thoughts : their aptitude to join us to the external world in order to transform it by work and technology, and to turn it to our profit. Every purely speculative theory which detaches us from these economic applications, as religious dogma, is but the fruit of the imagination, being an illusion and erroneous. In this sense, Lenin holds that the work which man produces to transform nature is the fundamental truth of nature, and that the criterion of truth is the activity of the worker, who transforms the exterior world. This is the " proletarian philosophy " which makes of work, in an economic sense, the source of all truth.

Now determinism rules as master throughout nature, both below and in man, as the success of technology shows. But in submitting to it, the worker dominates nature and leads it to his own ends. He possesses the true *liberty* which is the consciousness which we take of our necessitation. On the other hand, this domination of natural forces would be impossible to individual labor. It is the fruit of social interaction. It is, then, through society that man achieves himself, becomes fully man and perfectly free.

3. **The five stages of history.** Man is the fruit of an evolution which goes through five principal stages.

The first is long and slow, and sees humanity emerge from the ape, and witnesses instinct emerging towards the distinctive use of the bodily members. This is the age of a classless society, and thus of communism in a rudimentary stage.

The three following stages are characterized by the *struggle of the classes* which must be constituted in order to accelerate the movement towards perfection. In antiquity, there was the state of *slavery*, in which the rich possessed everything, even their servants. — In the Middle Ages, there arose the period of *feudalism*, in which the wealthy possessed the land to which the serfs were attached as workers. — During the present age of revolution, it is the age of *capitalism*, in which the rich possess the means of production and live at the cost of the worker.

The progress of history is leading to the fifth stage, that of *communism*, in which the classless[1] state of primitive society will be found, but now arrived at its perfection for the greatest happiness of humanity.

The true value of man in this final stage lies in being a worker, a " producer " worthy of being a part, the working class, which is the ruling group. At the termination of evolution, the individual, in the Communist view, is totally absorbed by the class. Educed by the class from infancy, he finds his happiness in serving it without any desire of solitude or of personal activity. From this viewpoint, woman is man's equal : the social organization will seek to free her as much as possible from the burdens of maternity, in order that she might realize the essential role of being a worker[2].

In this novel culture, everything points to the destruction of the family. The institution of monogamous marriage and of its indissolubility is considered the fruit of the capitalistic economics. Engels believed it was born of the great concentration of riches in the same hands, and of the desire of transmitting riches through heredity to one's own posterity and by excluding others. Once the means of production have become common property, the *individual family* ceases to be the economic unity of society. The care and education of infants becomes a public concern, and society cares for all children, whether natural or legitimate. Communism looks upon the union of man and woman as the result of an inferior, sexual instinct, as in animals. It is moral to satisfy this desire just as man eats or drinks. Marriage

---

[1] Certain communist philosophers have concluded that this fifth stage will be eternal, since there is no principle of disaggregation remaining. But this view is contrary to the very principle of evolution on which dialectical materialism is based.

[2] From this notion, the communists concluded to the legality of abortion; faced with the menacing flood of depopulation, Stalin recoiled from this view. He proclaimed the honor of maternity, though without re-establishing the rights of the family.

is a simple, individual contract which can be broken by reason of antipathy, argument, or, when a more attractive mate appears — this is the theory of *free-love*. A disagreeable result of this view is a fall in the birth rate, for a large number of children is a great social wealth as being able to renew the army of workers. Society solves this problem by organizing maternities and nurseries in which mothers and the newly-born enjoy care actually reserved for the rich; it also organizes places in which young children can be prepared for social life until they are ready for the socialized factories where work will make them happy. If their dispositions direct them towards higher studies, they can serve society by work of the spirit.

This ideal is radically opposed to the most profound aspirations of the human heart. From the communist viewpoint, for which there is nothing definitive, absolute or sacred, but merely an interrupted deployment of phenomena, the situation must necessarily evolve towards a social condition which will make this gregarious life natural and spontaneous, so that the individual will be totally absorbed into society.

5. **Moral Life : Egoism of the Classes.** Lenin believes that education and teaching and all formation of contemporary youth should be geared towards communist morality; the latter is entirely subordinated to the *interests* of the proletariat and to the demands of the struggle of the classes. This morality can be considered as the termination of evolution, or as it is in its present state.

As the terminus of evolution, society becomes a collectivity without any hierarchy but that of economic systems. Its sole mission is the production of goods by collective work; its unique goal is the enjoyment of these earthly goods in a life wherein each gives according to his energies and receives according to his needs. Society forms a *pyramid of soviets* or particular councils charged with pursuing their proper interest; these send delegates to the superior soviets, regional or national, leading to the highest supreme council, charged with establishing the general plan of production which is most favorable to the common good. The state thus becomes a vast cooperative association for production [1], and the actual forms of any other government will be abandoned as useless.

---

[1] According to Kaustky, Vandervelde and other socialists, this formula evades the difficulty of imposing on the state a task beyond its power, by giving it control over all economic life. This conception is a sort of " corporatism " defended by some Catholic sociologists. It insists, with good reason, that work is noble and not a merchandise but a means for man to assure his existence. But communism gives this economic organization the supreme authority of the state, for it reduces human life to economic life, and this is its source of error.

Then, the working class having absorbed all of humanity, all causes of antagonism and of war furnished by the differences of countries or of social conditions will disappear. This will be definitive peace, in which each will find his joy in devoting himself to his fellow workers, voluntarily giving whatever he can : the inventor gives his spirit and direction, the worker giving his muscular force — all of them sure of having their needs satisfied in age and sickness as in health and work. The heads of state assure the exercise of full, equalitarian justice and the subjects enjoy it by the exercise of mutual aid and universal charity. Thus, there shines forth the ideal of a " universal altruism " rising from the ruins of various egoisms; a true apocalyptic vision of paradise on earth.

But the times are still far from such an ideal. The morality of religious inspiration and the code of laws in force in capitalistic states are evidently decrepit, as is the institution of the family. The law of progress will bring about their ruin. But the communists also believe that they play a role in this evolution. " Insisting on the dialectical aspect of their materialism, the communists claim that the conflict which carries the world towards its final synthesis can be accelerated by man. Hence they endeavor to sharpen the antagonisms which arise between the various classes of society. Thus the class-struggle with its consequent violent hate and destruction takes on the aspect of a crusade for the progress of humanity " [1]. From their viewpoint, it is an act of devotion to the working class to foment strikes, revolutions and wars. If they join other groups in order to establish reforms it is not to stabilize a situation but to " begin " the total upheaval. As long as the transformation of the peasants and of the small bourgeois is not achieved, the struggle must continue. Stalin, having this aim in mind, set up a plan of warfare that follows a shrewd and methodic procedure. The immediate end is the downfall of the capitalistic state in order to set up the " dictatorship of the proletariat ", as in Soviet Russia. In the transitional stage, the principal role is played by the *Party*, a minority of convinced communists who pursue the education of the masses by progressively extirpating what remains of the bourgeois and capitalist spirit.

6. **Religious Life : Militant Atheism.** One of the obstacles that must be exterminated at all costs, in the communist view, is religion and the belief in God. Lenin states that

---

[1] Pius XI, *Divini Redemptoris*, § 9.

Marx's famous phrase, " religion is the opium of the people " [1], is the corner-stone of every Marxist conception of religious matters. Religion is an aspect of the spiritual oppression that has always lain heavily on the masses who have been crushed by perpetual work for another's profit and by misery and solitude. Faith in a better life beyond brings with it inevitably the powerlessness of the exploited classes to fight against their exploiters, as it was responsible for the powerlessness of the savage in his struggle against nature. Religion soothes those in poverty by promising a heavenly reward to those in suffering, and it allows the rich man to enjoy peace, despite his robbery, on condition that he do some simple acts of charity.

This religious conception involves, as does morality, the dual aspect of achievement and of preparation. In the fully evolved society, the idea of God will be absent, and the " comfort " obtained as the final goal will remove any wishes for cult or for religion. In the state of transition, however, one of the most rigorous requirements to be a pure Party member is to be a militant atheist; efforts of every sort are to be used in order to destroy the remains of belief in God in the proletariat masses. Preventing its inclusion in the education of the young is one of the best services that can be done to the working class.

CONCLUSION. The ideal of the convinced communist who devotes himself body and soul to the happiness of the working class and sacrifices every immediate and personal interest, colors the mediocrity of his materialistic goal with a certain nobility. In this sort of Epicurean " comfort " towards which he aspires, the vision of a universal peace reuniting all men in the exercise of justice and of charity lifts this earthbound level of terrestrial paradise [2] to a more noble level. It has been said that this ideal is a " faith " accepted without proof, and that its utopian vision glitters to the eye in opposition to the natural sentiments of mankind. It should be noted, however, that this faith is presented as a *conclusion* rigorously

---

[1] Taken from Marx 's critique of the Hegelian philosophy of law (1844).

[2] Certain socialists, as De Man, aim to surpass Marxism by giving the system a *spiritual aim*, which is not the pleasure of economic goods, but the noble and disinterested effort towards culture, or an effort towards a perfection and towards an absolute which cannot be realized in any social institution. See, on this matter, the explanation given of communism in J. T. PRINCE, *The Creative Revolution*, Milwaukee (Wis.), 1937.

deduced from a law which, in turn, claims scientific proof —
the economic law of progress. It is only by digging down
to this foundation that one can judge the system with some
efficacy. If historical and dialectical materialism is true,
one should not be amazed at the profound transformations
foreseen by the communist philosophy. But this " vision
of the world ", with its materialistic basis, ordinarily a sign
of an age of decadent thought, will always bump against the
great propositions of perennial philosophy : God, spiritual
beings and human souls exist; there are immutable principles
which rule our moral and social life, as there are principles
which rule the bodily world. The authentic inclinations of
reasonable human nature are not merely passing phenomena,
capable of radical changes, as is supposed in the Hegelian
dialectical, for they are reflections of the eternal law of
providence. The natural law is indestructible, and is the
basis for traditional morality with its propositions on the
family, on private property, liberty, personality, and man's
duties to God, His Creator and final End. The dream of
a " collectivist state " is not merely a utopia; it is a profound
error, misconstruing the most basic principles of metaphysics
and of psychology. The " mysticism " which inspires the
anti-religious crusade of the militant communists is irreducibly
opposed to the supernatural ideal of Catholicism, and even
to the rational ideal discoverable by philosophical thought.
The human person can never consent to be absorbed by
society, for human personality has an eternal value to whose
service society itself should be dedicated; nor can the human
soul be calmed down with an earthly happiness, for the urge
of its nature is to repose only in God.

SECTION TWO.
THE PSYCHOLOGICAL CURRENT.

483. The psychology of the nineteenth and of the twentieth
centuries had three outstanding traits which trace its origins
back through Comte and Kant to Descartes, and also make it an
authentic stream of the great positivist flood of thought.

1) The *fact of consciousness* is its object; this includes whatever
is internally observed, without distinguishing, as does Scholasticism, sensible from spiritual consciousness. The only classification
that has any precision is one which distinguishes the facts of
exterior observation, called *material* or *physical* objects, from
the facts of consciousness which are called, by opposition, *psychical*
facts; the latter belong to the ideal order, and are *spiritual*.

The facts of consciousness are universally distributed into three categories or faculties inherited from Descartes : representative facts or ideas, passive facts, as emotions and sentiments, and active facts or volitions [1].

2) Every metaphysical problem or solution is studiously avoided. This is due to the influence of Kant, whose criticism seemed to demonstrate the emptiness of metaphysical theories, and of Comte, who showed his disdain for any question of this sort by his practical method. Research on the nature of the soul and of its faculties is to be replaced by scientific hypotheses in the positivist sense [2], destined to unify the phenomena of the self.

3) Psychological method becomes more and more scientific and mathematical, and its sole aim is to establish laws explaining the origin and the development of the various states of consciousness. In 1878, Wundt founded the first psychophysiological laboratory in Leipzig, and these laboratories had already grown to the number of thirty in Europe and America by 1893.

With regard to the dominating theories, there are two schools which succeed each other in order of time.

a) The *associationist* school, which is content with applying the mechanist theory in psychology. It aims to explain everything by the " atoms " of consciousness and the laws of their combination, as everything is explained in physics by corporeal atoms and their laws. This school was dominant until the close of the nineteenth century. Its theoricians are especially found in England, where John Stuart Mill was its chief proponent, mainly in his logical works. It was transplanted in France by Taine, who incorporated it into his own system. In Germany it took on a more mathematical character.

b) In contrast, the *dynamist school*, which arose in France with Ribot, considered the facts of consciousness not as a synthesis decomposable into simple and unconscious facts, but as an original reality having its own individuality, its own evolution and proper laws.

This dynamist psychology also constituted a transitional phase towards pragmatism, especially as presented by William James and Henri Bergson. Under this view, the work of Fouillée will also be considered.

---

[1] See above, n. 328. The three faculties are intelligence, sensibility and will, taken in the positivist sense of an ensemble of facts of consciousness, endowed with similar qualities. Sensibility was raised to the dignity of a faculty by nineteenth century Romanticism.

[2] See above, n. 472.

This section will include the following four paragraphs:

 I. The English School: John Stuart Mill.

 II. The Synthesis of Taine.

 III. The German or Mathematical School (Wundt).

 IV. The French or Dynamic School (Ribot).

I. The english school: John Stuart Mill (1806-1873).

Special bibliography.

1° **Works :** *On Liberty*, London, 1929. — *Examination of Sir William Hamilton's Philosophy*, London, 1878. — *Philosophy of Scientific Method* (ed. E. Nagel), New York, 1950. — *Principles of Political Economy* (abbr. and annot. by C. T. Tang), Shanghai, 1931. — *System of Logic*, New York, 1930. — *Utilitarianism, Liberty and Representative Government*, (ed. J. Plamenatz), New York, 1949.

2° **Studies :** Anschutz, R. P., *Philosophy of J. S. Mill*, Oxford, 1953. — Courtney, W. L., *Life of John Stuart Mill*, New York, nd. — Crawford, I. F., *Relation of Inference to Fact in Mill's Logic*, Chicago, 1916. — Douglas, C., *J. Stuart Mill*, Edinburgh, 1895. — Hamilton, M. A., *John Stuart Mill*, London, 1933. — Jackson, R., *Examination of the Deductive Logic of John Stuart Mill*, Oxford, 1941. — Kubitz, O. A., *Development of John Stuart Mill's System of Logic*, Urbana (Ill.), 1932. — Morlan, G., *America's Heritage from John Stuart Mill*, London, 1936. — Neff, E. E., *Carlyle and Mill*, New York, 1926. — Street, C. L., *Individualism and Individuality in the Philosophy of John Stuart Mill*, Milwaukee (Wis.), 1926. — Thouverez, E., *Stuart Mill*, Paris, 1905. — Whittaker, T., *Comte and Mill*, New York, 1908.

483[bis]. English philosophy was always friendly to experiential facts and to individual realities, and this factor helps account for the great success positivism had in England in the nineteenth century. In addition to the syntheses inspired by mechanism[1], we find a large group of thinkers studying psychological facts by the experimental method, each of whom has some originality; they are the true founders of *experimental psychology*[2]. On the other hand, while the English genius is less coherent and less logical than the French, it is more rich and open. The sociological conclusions rigorously deduced

---

[1] See above, Darwin (n. 475 ff.) and Spencer (n. 479 ff.).

[2] They preserved, in a sense, the tradition of philosophers of the Cartesian era (Hobbes, Locke, Berkeley, Hume); but they used psychological analysis as a critical method for evaluating the sciences, whereas psychologists of the 19th century studied the acts of consciousness for their own sake, thus constituting a positive science.

through positivism by Comte found little favor in England; instead, the English studied economic laws in order to find the reference point for man's domination over nature, and the feeling of individual liberty remains quite alive and vivid.

This double trait is quite remarkably evident in the work of John Stuart Mill, the master of English philosophical thought in the nineteenth century. More than any other thinker, he is a partisan of the experimental method and is completely penetrated with positivism. At the same time, he stated that one of Comte's greatest faults was to leave no question open. Accordingly, while the center of Mill's philosophy is found in experimental psychology, he remains " open " to a large number of influences, and his thought is filled with questions which lie beyond the framework of phenomena of the soul. He is, above all, a psychologist, as is the large number of his predecessors, precursors and those who continue his thought.

I. *Initiators and Precursors.*

484. One can distinguish three groups of thinkers which had a greater or lesser influence on the thought and a formation of John Stuart Mill. At the lowest rung we have William Hamilton and his pupil, Mansel; then Bentham and the utilitarian school· finally, his own father, James Mill.

A) **William Hamilton** [1] (1788-1856).

Born at Glasgow, Hamilton studied at Oxford, and later was a professor at the University of Edinburgh, first holding a chair in civil law, and then one in logic and metaphysics. Many of his ideas were made known through articles in the *Edinburgh Review;* in addition, he wrote *Lectures on Metaphysics, Elements of the Philosophy of the Spirit,* and *Essay in Moral Philosophy;* the latter was edited after his death. Hamilton was greatly influenced by Thomas Reid and is attached to the Scottish school which was dominant in the England of the eighteenth century. He was also influenced strongly by Kant, as well as by Schelling and Cousin, whom he refutes. Living in a transitional age, his thought is drawn from these various influences, but his personal predilection was towards positivism. One finds this latter view influencing his notions on perception, on knowledge and on logic.

[1] **Works :** *Lectures on Metaphysics and Logic,* 4 vols., London, 1866.
Studies : MILL, J. S., *Examination of Sir William Hamilton's Philosophy,* London, 1878. — RASMUSSEN, S. V., *The Philosophy of Sir William Hamilton,* London, 1927. — VIETCH, J., *Hamilton,* Edinburgh, 1882.

1⁰ **Theory of Perception.** Hamilton's theory is presented in his refutation of THOMAS BROWN [1] (1778-1820), who held that perception reaches only the fact of consciousness. Hamilton returns to Reid's realism of common sense, admitting the value of our perception of the external world; the latter is grasped by intuition, as an object opposed to the self. " We have consciousness of the self and of the non-self in an indivisible act of knowledge which includes both of these; but we also are aware of them as being different in themselves, and exclusive of one another " [2]. Hamilton, however, introduces a remarkable precision here; the real object thus known is not that which is far from us, but the reality in immediate contact with our senses. Thus, we do not directly perceive the sun situated in thousands of places in space, but its effect, the light which is impressed on the eyes. In this way we have a " consciousness " [3] of the exterior world, by seizing it in the phenomenon which it produces upon our senses. This theory is perfectly in accord with a sound doctrine of knowledge, and is also a progression towards experimental psychology, in which one rightly distinguishes the object of pure sensation intuitively known [4], and that of perception, in which the education of the senses intervenes, and which is not immediately known.

2⁰ **Relativity of our Knowledge.** Hamilton is especially known for the vigor with which he refuted Schelling, by showing the impossibility of man's attainment of the absolute. He took recourse to psychological observation and synthesized the proper character of our knowledge in the law, *to think is to condition*. In other words, no object is accessible to our thought in a clear, positive and precise fashion, if it is not subsumed to certain *conditions* which make it necessarily *relative* and *limited*. Knowledge always supposes an object known and a knowing subject which mutually limit each other. It also supposes that the object known comes into us, is in contact with consciousness, and thus is related to it, and becomes relative. " Thought cannot transcend consciousness; consciousness is only possible under the antithesis of a subject and object of thought, known only in correlation, and mutually limiting each other; while, independently of this, all that we know either of subject or object, either of mind or matter, is only a knowledge in each of the particular, of the plural, of the different, of the modified, of the phenomenal " [5].

By adopting this theory, it was easy for Hamilton to prove that the Absolute and the Infinite are inconceivable for man.

---

[1] In psychology, Brown did some good research on aspects of the sense of touch; he distinguished touch as giving discontinuous sensations; he spoke of the muscular sense, whose impression is continuous, and also of the sense of pressure. Erasmus Darwin, Charles' father, had also spoken of the muscular sense.

[2] *Lectures on Metaphysics and Logic*, I, p. 288.

[3] Consciousness is not a special faculty for Hamilton, but more of a comprehensive term applicable to all the movements of the spirit which are awakened by an outward stimulus and have a certain degree of intensity.

[4] This is the so-called *nativist* theory, the only one defendable; see below, n. 506, 3.

[5] As cited by Herbert SPENCER, *First Principles*, § 24.

He showed, in fact, that the ideas of Absolute and of Infinite are contradictory, although many people invincibly identify them. The Infinite is defined as the " unconditionally un-limited ", while the Absolute is the " unconditionally limited ". This contradiction, he continues, arises from the fact that whatever is unconditioned is by that very fact freed from the conditions of thought itself; in construing such an object for thought, we necessarily throw irreconcilable elements together. In fact, the true definition of the unconditioned is wholly negative : it is the total absence of thought or of conceivability. With regard to Cousin, for whom the Absolute was first cause, Hamilton remarks that every cause is necessarily *relative* [1] to its effect, and that Cousin refers the principle of causality to his theory of the inconceivable Absolute. Hamilton explains the belief in causality not as showing a power but an impoverishment of the mind; that is, by the law of the conditioned, or by the incapacity of comprehending an absolute beginning " [2].

Even though our scientific knowledge is restricted to the relative, we can go beyond this stage by the help of *belief*. " And by a wonderful revelation, we are thus, in the very consciousness of our inability to conceive aught above the relative and finite, inspired with a belief in the existence of something unconditioned beyond the sphere of all comprehensible reality " [3].

HENRY LONGUEVILLE MANSEL (1820-1871), a disciple of Hamilton and a professor at Oxford, and, later, Dean of St. Paul, adhered strongly to this last mentioned view of Hamilton's. In his, *The Limits of Religious Thought*, he gathers all the proofs for the inconceivability of the Absolute and of the Infinite, and from this concludes to the emptiness of rationalistic objections against Christian dogmas, as that of the Trinity or the Incarnation. The contradictions which reason discovers in them do not in any way hinder their acceptance through belief [4].

However, it was not through this aspect of his thought that Hamilton prepared the way for Mill, but through his affirmation, so conformable to positivism, that every object of science is but a relative phenomenon, and through his works in logic.

3⁰ **Logical Theories.** Since the time of Descartes, the logicians attempted to add some precision to the methodology of the positive sciences, and they unanimously denounced the abuse of the syllogism by the ancient thinkers. Hamilton, who had read Aristotle and the Scholastics, bore witness to the value of ancient work in logic, and profited much from their ideas. He hoped to perfect their work by his theory of the QUANTIFICATION OF THE PREDICATE. Aristotle distinguished three species of

---

[1] St. Thomas would distinguish, and state that the Creator has only a *relation of reason* with the creature.

[2] See Janet and Séailles, *Histoire de la Philosophie*, p. 165.

[3] As quoted in Herbert Spencer, *op. cit., ibid.*

[4] The main difficulty of this doctrine is that it gives as an object of belief that which is *totally incomprehensible*. The doctrine of analogy, on the contrary, maintains that there is nothing absurd in Christian mysteries; see above, n. 244.

propositions, universal — particular and singular — according to the extension of the *subject*. Hamilton thought this classification insufficient, believing that one must also take into account the quantity of the predicate. For, in saying, " every man is reasonable " or, " every man is living ", the mind applies the subject differently. All men, in reality, are all reasonable being, but all men are not *all* living being. In making these nuances of thought explicit, one can distinguish four forms[1] of propositions : the toto-total, as in definition; the toto-partial, as, " some living thing is some man "; parti-total, as, " some of living being is all men "; the parti-partial, as, " some equilateral figures are some triangles ". If one adopts this classification, every true proposition expresses the *equality* between two groups of individuals which respectively designate the subject and the predicate. The judgment becomes a sort of mathematical equation, and even the rules of formal logic are simplified or modified; thus, all propositions are subject to simple conversion, and all laws of the syllogism become one law, that of the substitution of similarities.

But this classification of Hamilton's can be readily contested. The judgment expressed by the proposition is not a simple equation between *two groups* of facts or of individuals; it is an identity thought through between two manners of conceiving the same *universal nature*, and as long as one respects the originality of this action of the mind, it is sufficient to follow Aristotle's quantification of the subject. That of the subject or attribute involved is then determined according to the quality of propositions (affirmative or negative), as is their necessary or contingent matter. Through this hope for a reform, Hamilton shows his positivist tendency : he conceived thought as attaining only individuals and the facts of experience, of which concepts represent various groupings; he viewed judgment as a mathematical equation. This notion is quite close to the one which will be the basis of John Stuart Mill's logic[2].

B) The Utilitarianism of Jeremy Bentham[3] (1748-1832).

Bentham's originality lies more in the school of thought which he founded to propagate his ideas and to obtain the reform of

---

[1] Four negative and four affirmative; eight species in all.

[2] John Stuart Mill, however, also criticizes Hamilton's position.

[3] **Works :** *Deontology*, London, 1834. — *Introduction to the Principles of Morals and Legislation*, New York, 1948. — *Limits of Jurisprudence Defined*, New York, 1945. — *Theory of Legislation* (ed. C. K. Ogden), New York, 1953. — *Economic Writings* (critical ed., ed. by W. Stark), 3 vols., London, 1952-53.
   Studies : BAUMGARDT, D., *Bentham and the Ethics of Today*, Princeton (N. J.), 1952. — HALÉVY, E., *La formation du radicalisme philosophique*, 3 vols., 1901-1904. — KEETON, G. W., and SCHWARZENBERGER, G. (eds.), *Jeremy Bentham and the Law*, London, 1948. — LUNDIN, H. G., *Influence of Jeremy Bentham on English Democratic Development*, Iowa City (Ia.), 1920. — MILL, J. S., *On Bentham and Coleridge*, New York, 1951. — OGDEN, C. K., *Jeremy Bentham*, 1832-2032, London, 1932. — STOCKS, J. L., *Jeremy Bentham*, 1748-1832, Manchester, 1933. — WISDOM, J., *Interpretation and Analysis, in Relation to Bentham's Theory of Definition*, London, nd.

laws. With James Mill he founded, in 1824, the *Westminster Review*, in order to achieve these ends. His system of thought is contained in *An Introduction to the Principles of Moral and Legislation*, and in his *Deontology*, published in 1834, after his death. Many of his works were translated into French by one of his pupils who also redacted his master's notes; among them is *The Rationale of Punishment* and *The Rationale of Reward*.

In all his decisions, man's unique and determining motive is the pleasure or the pain which attends his actions. Bentham supposes this as a certified fact, and on it he builds the supreme rule of morality : *every act which is capable of assuring us of the greatest sum of happiness is morally good; the good is that which is useful to us and the evil that which is harmful*. Such is the foundational principle of UTILITARIANISM. It should also be noted that the good concerned here is that of the economic order, or sensible goods, as riches, and the commodities of life. As in Epicureanism, happiness is defined as the greatest possible sum of pleasures. Following Hobbes and Helvetius, Bentham establishes his morality on a positive basis.

Nevertheless, man does not go towards his good as an animal towards immediate pleasure. By reason, he can foresee and calculate the result of his actions. Even if all pleasures are goods, they are not such to the same extent. Morality teaches us to choose, always, that which will *in reality* procure for us the greatest summation of advantages. Bentham called this science " moral arithmetic ", for he wished to determine a scale of pleasures with a rigor similar to that of mathematics. In the meantime, his reflections fell into a quite complex calculus, for he distinguished a triple aspect : that of the object, the subject, and society.

a) The object. Here we find circumstances extrinsic to the pleasure pursued. In order to determine their value, one must consider the *intensity* of pleasure, its *duration*, its *certitude* and *proximity*, its *fruitfulness*, or power of producing other pleasures, and its *purity*, or the fact of not being troubled by any mixture of pain.

b) But in order that we can choose a pleasure, it must not only exist, but it must appear to us *(subjectively)* as the greatest. This is why reflection must consider the psychological dispositions and circumstances which modify it : climate, temperament, age, sex, character, habits, the development of the mind and all those causes which modify sensibility and really change the nature of pleasure in our eyes. They enter as items given with the problems of moral arithmetic.

c) Finally, the *social* viewpoint is most important, for individual interest gets mixed up with general interest, since the latter is but the sum of individual interests[1]. General interest contains them all, and consequently surpasses all of them in importance. For instance, to appreciate a theft, it is not sufficient to consider the harm done to a person or to a family, but the general alarm

---

[1] This conception is quite superficial; the common good is the goal of every society and is of another order than the individual goods of its members.

caused by the crime, the evil of bad example and the social
disorganization which tends to produce infraction of laws. The
ideal which determines true moral goodness is not the greatest
sum of individual pleasures, but the *greatest happiness of the
greatest number*.

Bentham, interested in law, was especially concerned in applying
these principles to the reform of legislation. In his view, the
justice of a law was due to its *utility* or its aptitude for procuring
the greatest happiness of all. A good *penal code* is an efficacious
means of obtaining this happiness. No doubt every punishment
is evil, but the function of punishment is to enter into the
calculation of the pleasures and pains of a possible delinquent
and cause an equilibrium to the pleasures resulting from the
crime, and thus to force a delinquent to follow the rules which
the legislator believes useful to the greatest number. Bentham
did not believe that laws can repress all faults or abuses; he counted
on legal sanctions, and on such natural sanctions as the troublesome consequences of indulgence, popular sanction or the morality
of public opinion and especially on religious sanctions. Taken
together, these penalties help one to identify personal with the
general interest and assure a reign of true happiness [1].

The utilitarian point of view is one to which the ECONOMISTS
are attached; since the time of Adam Smith, they tried to make
the laws of man's material life more precise, by supposing that
man acts uniquely from economic motives; that is, for riches
or interest. Among the contemporaries of John Stuart Mill,
mention should be made of MALTHUS, mentioned earlier [2], and
of DAVID RICARDO, the author of *Principles of Political Economy
and Taxation* (1817). Ricardo makes much of Marx's iron law
of wages, whereby salaries tend to be as low as possible and profits
accruing to employers tend to be concentrated in the hands of
an increasingly small number of men.

C) The Associationism of James Mill [3] (1773-1836).

The father of John Stuart Mill, James, who was of Scottish
origins, sought his fortune in London whither he accompanied
Lord Stuart, a member of Parliament. A remarkable work,
The History of the India Companies (1818), got him a job in this
company, wherein he held important positions until his death.
At the same time, quite curious about the movement of ideas,
he detached himself from traditional doctrines in order to enter

[1] Influenced by James Mill, Bentham was inclined towards democracy in
politics; he thought that the best means of obtaining legal reform was by
appealing to the people through universal suffrage.
[2] See n. 475, above.
[3] **Work :** *Essay on Government* (intro. E. Barker), Cambridge, 1937.
Studies : BAIN, A., *James Mill. A Biography*, London, 1882. — BOWER, J.,
Hartley and James Mill, London, 1881. — ROBINSON, E. S., *Association Theory
Today*, New York, 1932. — WARREN, H. C., *History of the Association Psychology*, New York, 1921.

openly into democracy in politics, and into positivism in philosophy. A collaborator of Bentham's, and a friend of Ricardo[1], he is especially known by his *Analysis of the Phenomena of the Human Mind* (1829), a treatise of experimental psychology in which there is contained a systematic exposition of his theory of ASSOCIATIONISM[2].

The fundamental principle of this theory states that one can reduce all the phenomena of consciousness into simple elements, which, by being diversely combined according to the laws of association, explain all psychological functions. This is similar to chemistry explaining all bodily combinations by union of simple ones. Mill believed that *sensation* was the primitive fact, along with its well known species. The *idea* is but a *copy of sensation;* it is its image or permanent trace. But as long as we are passive in sensation, our ideas have the property of associating and of thus creating new facts of consciousness. The fundamental law involved is that our ideas are born or exist in the order in which the sensations of which they are a copy exist. All forms of association, then, can be reduced to one, that of *association by contiguity* in space and in time[3]. " When sensations are produced simultaneously, the ideas are also awakened simultaneously; when sensations are successive, ideas are born successively "[4]. The strength of the bond between ideas depends, above all, on the vividness of the sentiments associated thereto and on the frequency of association.

With the help of only these three elements, sensations, ideas and the law of association, Mill reconstructs all the aspects of conscious life. He does not consider the formation and evolution of man's functions as did Spencer, but is concerned with the psychology of the civilized adult and explains his imagination, memory and reason.

Imagination is the simplest instance of association of ideas. Consciousness is the name given to our sentiments taken one by one, while imagination is the name of a series of sentiments or ideas. These groups take various forms, depending on the occupation of each man : " They are different in the merchant, occupied with purchase and sale, than in the lawyer occupied with judges, witnesses and clients, and different in the physician than the man of state, different in the soldier than in the metaphysician "[5].

Memory at first seems similar to imagination; it is a series of ideas which are born and developed by the laws of association.

---

[1] James Mill owes his work, *Principles of Political Economy*, to the inspiration of Adam Smith and Ricardo.

[2] Here he was influenced especially by David HARTLEY; see above, n. 369.

[3] Hume would also admit association by *resemblance* and by *causality* (see n. 381); James Mill refers them to contiguity : an attempt at simplification which, in Stuart Mill's opinion, is the least happy of the whole work.

[4] T. RIBOT, *op. cit.*, p. 50.

[5] *Ibid.*, p. 55.

But its distinctive trait is the *recognition* placing this series in a determined moment of the past. Recognition is a quite complex notion, consisting of three elements : 1° a state of actual consciousness, which we call the self remembering; 2° a state of consciousness, which we call the self which has perceived or known; 3° the states of successive consciousness, which fill the interval between these two points. Thus, by thought we run through with rapidity the series of states of consciousness which are intermediary between the moment of remembrance and the moment in which the event was produced, and it is this rapid movement which makes a fact appear as past; it is in this way that memory differs from imagination[1]. This is a rather ingenious explanation offered by Mill, but it is more systematic than psychological[2].

Mill also attempts to explain the activities of *reason* by sensations, ideas and association. *Classification* is the source of our general ideas. The word, " man ", for instance, is first applied to an individual; it is first associated with this individual, and acquires the power of stimulating the idea of that individual. Then it is applied to another individual, and acquires power to stimulate that idea, and so on until it has acquired the power to stimulate an infinite number of these ideas, indifferently. To classify, then, is to name; everything depends on the common name associated with an indefinite and indistinct aggregate of concrete and similar individuals, and the general idea is thus explained without recourse to the mechanics of abstraction. Mill was acquainted with abstraction, and viewed it as the act of separating a part of that which is contained in a complex idea in order to make an object which is considered in itself. Inasmuch as this abstractive procedure was not in line with association, he considered it as secondary. General ideas, once they are formed, become associated in judgments. The certitude of judgments, or belief in them, is explained by the firmness of the bond associating subject and predicate.

Ideas in themselves are intellectual facts; considered as stirring one to action, they form *affective facts* which are explained in a similar way. Here the primitive facts are pain and pleasure, from which all other sentiments flow. " When an agreeable sensation is conceived as future but without one's being certain of it, the state of consciousness is called *hope;* if one is certain of it, it is called *joy;* in the same circumstances, a disagreeable sensation engenders either *fear* or *sorrow.* The idea of a pleasure is called *desire,* that of a sorrow, *aversion.* An agreeable sensation or the idea of this sensation, joined to the idea of the cause which can produce it, engenders *affection* or love for this cause. The disagreeable sensation joined to the idea of its cause, engenders *antipathy* or hate for this cause "[3]. Mill made an analysis of these causes, especially on future causes, and showed that their

---

[1] *Ibid.*, p. 57.

[2] We do not often find ourselves obliged to run through such intermediary stages in order to remember; this is but a special aspect of memory, localization in the past, which Mill did not clearly distinguish.

[3] These quotations and presentation are from T. RIBOT, *op. cit.*, p. 58, ff.

efficacy depends on association[1]. Finally, he made a study of moral sentiments and of the will; but this study is quite inadequate in many ways.

Despite its omissions and its excessive systematization, Mill's treatise gives an excellent notion of the object and method of English experimental psychology in the nineteenth century, and he had a great influence on his son, John Stuart Mill.

2. *John Stuart Mill* (1806-1873).

485. John Stuart Mill had no other teacher than his own father, James Mill; by the age of fourteen, he had finished his classical studies and was initiated into philosophy. Already as a young man, he collaborated with his father in a critical analysis of Condillac, Helvetius and Hartley. He read Bentham's views on legislation and became enthusiastic for utilitarianism, which he later modified. In 1823, he entered the East India Company, where his father worked. This did not in any way slow up his philosophical activity. He wrote for the *Westminster Review*, of which his father was editor, and, with a number of friends, he founded a Utilitarian Society in Bentham's home to propagate the ideas of the school.

About the age of twenty, he had a crisis of intellectual scepticism and moral discouragements, due, he believed, to excessive mental work. He had the idea that Bentham's calculus of pleasures could give him no happiness, and believed that he could find surcease only in sentiment and in the love of friends. During the French Revolution, in 1830, he went to Paris to visit Lafayette, Enfantin and Bazard; the great ardor for social reform overwhelmed him, and he returned to London exalting the revolution in a way which pointedly showed his new, sentimental orientation. He read deeply in romantic[2] literature, and was associated for a short while with Carlyle. His interest in and marriage to Mrs. Taylor, which began about 1832, accentuated this sentimental aspect; he explained this friendship by the element of sentiment and pity which began to appear more openly in his writings, leading

---

[1] The distant causes are most important, for they have a vast field of action and associate themselves with more pleasures than the nearer causes. Besides, Mill believes that those which do not associate any agreeable idea with sounds or colors, cannot " sense " beauty.

[2] The romantic movement in literature was, in philosophy, a reaction against positivism; it exalted sentiment. COLERIDGE (1772-1834) was a thinker and writer in the Platonic strain, as was Carlyle (1793-1881), a lover of intuition, who played up the notion of heroics.

him more and more from economic liberalism to the protect-ionist and effeminate views of state socialism [1].

Nevertheless, he never became completely dominated by sentiment. Mental equilibrium became re-established by his reading of Comte, especially of the first two volumes of the *Positive Philosophy*, which he obtained in 1837. He was ravished by Comte, and wrote his admiration to the author [2]; later, however, he separated from him with regard to the legitimacy of psychology as a science, and on the function of the individual and his liberty in sociology. While staying faithful to essentials in positivism, he still developed his own originality.

His thought is expressed especially in his two main works, *A System of Logic*, begun in 1828 and completed in 1843, which was widely successful in Europe [3], and his *Principles of Political Economy* (1848), which " expresses, in relation to the previous works of Malthus and Ricardo, a reaction based on sentiment and on moral optimism " [4]. After the death of his wife, he involved himself in moral and political studies in order to defend the ideal of liberty so dear to Mrs. Taylor. He wrote the following : *On Liberty* (1859); *Thoughts on Representative Government* (1859); *Utilitarianism* (1861), which corrects Bentham's views. He gathered his articles from the *Westminster Review* in *Dissertations and Discussions*, and, in 1865, he wrote two critical works : *An Examination of Sir William Hamilton's Philosophy*, and *Auguste Comte and Positivism;* in the latter work he rejects every form of mysticism or religious spirit [5]. His final work, *The Subjection of Women*, appeared in 1869. Mill also wrote an *Autobiography* and some *Essays on Religion*, published posthumously.

A) General Characteristics and Fundamental Theory.

485 bis. The value of Mill's work lies rather in its richness, originality and suggested solutions rather than in any well

---

[1] E. Thouverez, *Stuart Mill*, p. 13. In 1851, Mrs Taylor became a widow, and shortly afterwards married Mill; she died seven years later.

[2] In 1844, Mill and the English positivists sent a subsidy of 6000 francs to Comte.

[3] Through this work Mill, in Taine's expression, " became the master who advanced and spoke amidst the silence of Europe "; E. Thouverez, *ibid.*, p. 14.

[4] *Ibid.*

[5] In 1865, he was elected to the House of Commons; but since he defended his political convictions as against the views of his constituents, he was not re-elected.

defined speculative propositions whose applications are logically pursued into various domains. Nevertheless, his work has a certain unity by being concerned completely with man in his psychological, moral, social and political life, dealt with by positivist methods and oriented towards the defence of personality. In order to understand his *fundamental proposition*, one can state the following :

Vital spontaneity is essential to man's existence; it is to be conceived, not as a substance or a spiritual principle, but as a fact of experience, seizable in itself by consciousness, and known in others by external observation.

This proposition is supposed throughout his thought, though never explicitly; it is an effort at conciliating two theories which logically exclude each other, positivism and liberalism. This explains why Mill has left many questions open, without offering a definitive solution for them. It is also an explanation of his life, in which his first formation, exclusively speculative and empirical at first, was followed by a reaction towards personal independence and sentimentality of life [1].

Mill applied these basic notions to the various domains of human life : first to logic, where his main work contains a totally positive psychology, and then to moral life with utilitarianism, and finally to studies on social and religious life. This triple domain makes up the whole of philosophy on Mill's views, for he believes it to be the science of man as an intelligent, moral and social being [2].

B) Logic : Psychological Applications.

486. Preoccupied with emphasizing the value of human personality, Mill, without having written a systematic treatise in psychology, still showed himself a great psychologist. He won back the title of science for psychology, and also wished to revivify logic. He made a remarkable attempt to submit the life of the spirit to positivism in its three acts of ideation, judgment and reasoning [3].

1o **Experimental psychology as a positive science.** Comte denied the possibility of a special science of conscious facts, and placed

---

[1] E. THOUVEREZ explains the influence of Mrs. Taylor on Mill's ideas (see p. 12 and pp. 17-20).

[2] See T. BOTI, *op. cit.*, p. 91.

[3] Mill did not clearly distinguish logic from psychology; the above treatment will also unite them.

its study between physiology and sociology[1]. Mill could not
admit this attitude, but separated himself from Comte though
remaining faithful to his spirit, and thus complemented his views.

Mill distinguishes two types of positive science. The first are
exact, since all the details of their object are subjected to precise
measures and are handled with the mathematical calculus, as
astronomy since Newton's time. The others are *approximative*,
since they have a quite complex object, part of which escapes
the predictions founded on precise laws, as the science of the tides.
One can determine, for the latter, their major causes (attraction
of the sun and moon), but the role of secondary causes (direction
of the wind, local circumstances), while theoretically subject
to fixed laws, escape prediction of any precise sort. Experimental
psychology belongs to this latter class. " It is quite distant from
the exactitude of astronomy, but there is no reason why it cannot
be a science as the science of the tides " [2]. It has an object, laws,
and a method.

Its proper *object* is the facts of consciousness, as the thoughts,
sentiments and actions of men. We know its fundamental
laws, and the ideal in applying these laws would be to know
certainly how an individual thinks, feels or acts in the course
of his life. We would never have all the given material needed
for such a deduction [3], but what is improbable when asserted
of individuals taken at random, is certain when affirmed of the
character and the conduct of groups. In this sense, psychology
establishes true laws.

It has its own *method*, internal observation or introspection.
To Comte's objections, Mill gives a twofold answer. First, he
refers him to " the experience as well as to the writings of
psychologists as a proof that the mind can not only have
consciousness of several impressions but can also give attention
to them ". Then, he remarks that " it is possible, in fact, to
study them through the intermediary of memory, not at the very
instant in which we perceive them, but in the moment after;
and this is, in reality, the mode according to which we acquire
the best part of the science of intellectual activity " [4]. This
method, then, permits one to set up psychology as a science.

2⁰ **The Idea and the Theory of Substance.** Mill begins, here,
with associationism, according to which the primitive elements
are sensations whose object embraces all the phenomena or
facts of experience studied in our sciences. For this reason,
all the operations of the mind in constructing science are
referable to sensations diversely associated. This is the
case first with the idea, for " psychologically, the universal

---

[1] See above, n. 460.

[2] *A System of Logic*, VI, Ch. III.

[3] In order to approach this ideal, Mill proposed to complete general psychology
by ETHOLOGY or the science of character; see T. RIBOT, *op. cit.*, pp. 103-106.

[4] *Ibid.*, p. 96.

concept is nothing ". Introspection proves this, for no one can represent a general nature to himself in the pure state. How can one have the idea of a man who will be neither great nor small, neither fat nor thin, neither white nor black, neither male nor female, neither young nor old, but at once all of these and none of these? One thinks of nothing when one believes he is thinking of such things, and each time one thinks something, concrete images are present to the mind[1]. In turn, Mill demonstrates the mechanism of general ideas in order to show their wholly empirical value. In an object of complex experience, the mind fixes its attention on a restricted group of properties. It adopts this habit spontaneously under the impression of exterior objects, in which, despite individual divergences, the same group of traits is always found in order to impressionate the senses[2]. Then we give this habit all its efficacy by artificially associating with this group of properties a *common name* which permits one easily to evoke a plausible sum of qualities for any individual of the group. Thus, the general idea is but an abstract word with the stereotyped meaning given by Condillac; it is the name which synthesizes a group of sensations in memory, so that its richness can vary. However, the name does not go beyond the concrete; man does not think by universal concepts but by concrete images[3].

What value do our ideas of *matter* and the *self* have in such a theory? In order to explain them, Mill first mentions two principles of explanation. The first is the *law of association* which is capable, in his eyes, of clarifying, little by little, all the facts of consciousness. Completing the views of his father, James, he mentions three aspects. 1) We have a tendency to think by grouping similar phenomena, and similar ideas tend to awake each other. 2) We have a tendency to think by grouping facts perceived as contiguous in space and in time, and the idea of one of these facts tends to evoke the other. 3) Repetition makes these associations most certain and most rapid[4] even to making them practically indissoluble so that even the phenomena appear equally inseparable in

---

[1] *An Examination of Sir William Hamilton's Philosophy*, Ch. XVII.

[2] This explains how Mill distinguishes between *primary* and *secondary* qualities; primary are those which manifest themselves most often in bodies. With regard to their reality, both types of qualities have the same value.

[3] See above, n. 374, for a critique of nominalism.

[4] A very great force of impression is equivalent to a repetition.

existence. — The second principle is that the human spirit is *capable of attention;* in other words, after having had actual sensations, we are capable of forming a conception of possible sensations. This power is admitted as a fact by Mill, who does not examine its value or its significance [1].

If, in the light of these principles, one examines the belief in external objects or an external world, one finds either actual sensations or possibilities of sensation. For instance, we believe in the existence of Rome, because if we transport ourselves to the banks of the Tiber, we bring ourselves to the *vision* of this city. Now, actual sensations are fugitive, although the possibility of rediscovering them is stable and permanent; this possibility then becomes a principal element in our conception. The independence we recognize in the fact of our subjective phenomena suggests to us the idea of *exteriority*, or of an object outside of ourselves, and existing in itself.

Moreover, association comes in from all sides to re-enforce this stability, for it is not only one sensation which manifests itself as constantly possible, but a group of qualities affecting the various senses. They are, in fact, so well joined that the presence of the one ordinarily announces the possible presence, at the same moment, of all the rest [2]. Not only are these groups fixed, but they impose themselves on us in an *order of fixed succession* which strengthens their cohesion. Finally, we see that other men have the same sensations and the same possibility of sensations as ourselves; all of this helps explain the force and the universality of belief in the exterior world. Briefly, our whole idea of matter arises from possible sensations, groups of sensations, an order between these groups and an accord between our belief and that of those similar to us. Matter can be defined as the permanent possibility of sensations. Thus, Mill adopts Hume's phenomenalism for the external world.

Logically, he should have applied the same theory to consciousness; as a matter of fact, he judged the soul, as a *substratum* of phenomena of the interior life, to be just as useless as matter. In his view, if one retains these phenomena and their groupings by uniting them simply by an internal

---

[1] The notion of "possibility" is beyond mere empiricism; it supposes the action of spiritual reason, and raises the problem of its value in expressing reality.

[2] T. RIBOT, *op. cit.*, p. 136. It is this grouping which distinguishes the idea of substance from the idea of a simple, possible sensation.

law, one arrives, without substance, at the result in view of which substance was supposed to exist. But there is an objection which he declares insoluble. " If, therefore, we speak of the Mind as a series of feelings, we are obliged to complete the statement by calling it a series of feelings which is aware of itself as past and future " [1]. In other words, we see clearly that our self constitutes a permanent LINK, imposing unity on facts, as a girl who does not leave her pearls in the state of separation, but forms a necklace of them. We meet again, here, the basic idea of Mill : the intuition of our personal spontaneity. Before this reality, which Mill considers the most excellent, the logic of pure empiricism must bend. He holds it as beyond doubt that the self is something as real as sensation and that it is not a simple product of the laws of thought. How do we know it? Mill does not answer this question, but leaves it open [2]; it does seem, however, that the intuition of the self is beyond pure phenomenalism for Mill.

3° **Logic and Truth.** Logic is radically changed when it meets with this empirical psychology which resolutely denies any universal idea. For Kant and Hamilton, logic was a purely *formal* science. It did not consider things or known truths, but merely the laws of mental functioning in combining abstract concepts in judgments and reasoning processes; this was the " logic of conclusions ". Mill was looking, in contrast, for a " logic of truth ", useful for knowing reality. Not that logic was to be identified with the other sciences, but it should indicate the method of setting them up. Logic is properly defined as *the science of proof*. Now, it is by interpreting the ancient logical theories in conformity with empirical psychology that one can, in Mill's view, achieve this transformation.

If there is a question of concepts and universal terms, these lose their importance, for we think through concrete images. Hence, Mill replaced the theory of comprehension and extension of ideas by the notions of connotation and denotation. Connotation simply expresses the fact that a subject possesses certain attributes; denotation designates the subjects which possess the same attributes. For instance, the name " man " *connotes* the group of properties common to all men, and it *denotes* all the individuals which possess them. One can easily see that the concept interpreted in this way designates nothing abstract, but gives to logic as object the selfsame object of the sciences, or the concrete phenomenon. The same result is obtained by a like interpretation of judgment and of reasoning.

---

[1] *An Examination of Sir William Hamilton's Philosophy*, Ch. XII.

[2] " I think, by far the wisest thing we can do, is to accept the inexplicable fact, without any theory of how it takes place... " *(Ibid.)*.

4° The Judgment and its Empirical Value.

Every judgment, even a purely ideal one, is based on experience, whether real or imaginary, and is but a generalization of experience.

This proposition causes no difficulty for judgments of experience, certifying, for instance, that " this wall is white ". But the positivist postulate, according to which no knowledge can surpass experience, clashes with the existence of a judgment of the ideal order or of necessary truth, whose value is uniquely based on the analysis of the predicate and of the subject; as, for example, if one states, " every event which occurs has a cause ", or, " two and two are four ". In order to establish his solution, Mill advances two proofs, one negative, and the other positive.

a) The negative proof consists in refuting the main argument of his opponents. The judgment of the ideal order, they say, expresses *that which must be,* and consequently is beyond experience, which only states *that which is.* But this necessity, Mill replies, has no other meaning but that of *non-conceivability* of the *contradictory* [1]. The latter is a result of experience and is explained by the law of association of ideas, which has become an inveterate and hereditary habit and thus made certain empirical relations indestructible in appearance. The proof of it is that a change in the subjective conditions of the brain, due to new experiences, can break these relations. Thus, the ancients could not conceive of the antipodes, while it is very easy to the moderns.

b) The positive proof is based on the role of experience. One grants that any truth, even of the ideal order, is not fully independent of an experience either actual or at least imaginary. For it is impossible to form a clear idea without recourse to an image. Then one certifies that this experience, always necessary, suffices, in all rigor, to give value to the judgment, since the most abstract principles, as those of mathematics, receive a real confirmation from experience. Mill views this as a truth of fact; thus, the result of an addition appears more clear after its verification by the aid of stones or sticks. The negative proof having shown that no other explanation is possible, it must be admitted that only experience and the laws of association of ideas are

---

[1] *A System of Logic,* Book II, Ch. VII, § 2 and 3.

responsible for the value of every judgment, even of the ideal order.

487. The apparent force of this convincing presentation comes from the fact that it lights up an essential trait of all intellection expressed in the old adage, " no intellection occurs without conversion to phantasms ". This dependence on the sensible order extends to judgments as well as ideas. The discovery of new relations and even of abstract ones (for example, those which contain new geometrical theorems) seems to require, first, the sensible perception or the images of these relations realized in concrete objects [1].

But the alleged proofs are not decisive :

a) The confirmation which experience gives to principles of the ideal order is explained by the fact that we necessarily read the idea in the image, but this necessity has nothing to do with the value of our judgments. The value of our judgment is due to evidence, or the clear view of the identity between subject and attribute by reason.

b) Furthermore, two sorts of inconceivability can be distinguished. *The one, negative* and relative, comes from the fact that reason lacks the images or necessary notions to conceive the contradictory; thus, the ancients, ignorant of terrestrial attraction, affirmed the antipodes inconceivable. *The other, positive* and absolute, comes from the fact that by granting the contradictory, one would destroy the object itself by conceiving it without an essential element; this type is invariable and is proper to axioms that possess even analytic evidence. For this reason, the variations in non-conceivability cannot be realized except for complex propositions, in which the given materials of judgment can change.

5° **Reasoning and Causality.** If every universal proposition lacks empirical value, the Aristotelian syllogism lacks any efficacy in leading us to new truths. For, if the major of the syllogism is but a collection of facts, one cannot assert it without knowing and affirming, already, the special fact envisaged in the conclusion. The judgment " every man is mortal ", for instance, is true only if all particular cases are also true; one cannot, without a " begging of the principle ", invoke one of these cases as proof [2]. The syllogism, for Mill, keeps its usefulness as a procedure of verification; in generalizing, it keeps us from being precipitate.

---

[1] This view is held by Cajetan : " Habitus principiorum præexigit experimentum non solum ratione cognitionis terminorum, sed etiam ratione complexionis eorumdem " (*Commentarium in Posteriorum Analyticorum*, II, Ch. XIII).

[2] This critique is valid on the *hypothesis of empiricism;* but the latter is untenable.

The only type of valuable reasoning is *induction*, and the syllogism is but a mode of presenting this form. For this authentic type of reasoning, the universal major proposition is totally useless, for induction is an inference from one particular to another, founded on the association of ideas. If, for instance, one wishes to prove that Socrates is mortal, the starting point is the ensemble of experiences which have shown us death as effective in many men. The assertion that these men are mortal is evidently *particular*, but it does not contain the special case of Socrates who is still full of life. How does one get to the certain conclusion that Socrates is mortal? This is done by association of similitude : Socrates has so many points in common with men already dead that our mind irresistibly recognizes this property in him. Thus we proceed, too, in establishing scientific laws : by virtue of association we assert that this antecedent will necessarily be followed by this consequent.

However, in order to authorize the establishment of a general law in such a way that deduction can be made from it without allowing all future, similar cases to deceive us, associationism must maintain the practically indissoluble solidity of *causality*. The latter is the basis of all induction and of all valuable reasoning. Faithful to positivism, Mill explains it by empiricism. The notion of cause, he says, reveals to analysis an antecedent and a consequent which follow each other *invariably*. In general, it is not one phenomenon which produces an effect, but a *group*. Cause, then, is the sum of positive and negative conditions taken together; it is the totality of contingencies of every nature which the consequent invariably follows when they are realized. There are invariable successions which no one considers to be a case of causality, as the succession of day and night. This succession is conditional : the production of the day is surmised on a condition which is not the anteriority of the night, but the presence of the sun. It is to this type of connection that the *necessity of the causal bond* is reduced by Mill; it is not subjected to any condition [1]. One can thus define cause as *the antecedent, or the union of antecedents of which the phenomenon is invariably and unconditionally the consequent* [2].

---

[1] One can more clearly say that a true cause *communicates* a perfection to its effect; see n. 473, above.

[2] T. RIBOT, *op. cit.*, p. 117.

It is in order to disclose the meaning of this causal bond that Mill proposed his famous four methods. The first is the *method of concordances*, in which the phenomenon to be explained is always realized after the same antecedent, while the other circumstances vary and are thus eliminated. *The method of differences* is the second; in it, the suppression of one fact of explanation entrains the suppression of an antecedent, which thus reveals itself as cause. The third method is the *method of concomitant variations*, in which changing the phenomenon for explanation entrains similar changes in the antecedent-cause. Fourthly, the *method of residues*, in which the unexplained part of a phenomenon is recognized as an effect of the circumstance which remains in the antecedent after the elimination of the circumstances whose influence is known [1].

These methods are a completion of the tables of Francis Bacon, and have been very successful in the positive sciences. But they are independent of the empirical theory of causality and are adapted, without difficulty, to the Thomistic doctrine on induction.

6⁰ **Corollary. Theory of Liberty.** In order to construct psychology in positive science, one must evidently apply the notion of cause to the facts of consciousness. Each of these has an antecedent which explains it, because it is indissolubly joined to it according to certain laws, whose main one is that of association. For, " that which the law of gravitation is to astronomy, and that which the elementary properties of tissues are to physiology, the laws of associations of ideas are to psychology " [2].

Our volitions, as all other facts of consciousness, are subsumed to this law. Nevertheless, Mill believes that this causal bond is fully compatible with our *liberty*, for invariable, certain, and unconditional succession can be had without the antecedent exercising on the consequent a necessary and irresistible constraint. Mill believes that we have certainty in all our volitions that there is no mysterious constraint; we know that we are not forced, as by a magic charm, to obey for a particular motive [3]. Here again, positivist logic throws itself back on its basic theory of personal spontaneity : without abandoning

---

[1] Thus, by the method of residues, Le Verrier, looking for the cause of some perturbations (unexplained phenomenon) which he could not attribute to the attraction of a known body, discovered the planet Neptune.

[2] John Stuart Mill, *Auguste Comte et le positivisme*, p. 53.

[3] T. Ribot, *op. cit.*, p. 127.

the first, it does not wish to sacrifice the second. In its view, even if one accepts fatalism, the chastisements and recompenses can be justified just as one accepts the internment of madmen. But our action is not fatal; we are capable of working towards our moral perfectioning. If one were, however, to ask Mill the precise nature of this spontaneity or of this power of directing ourselves, Mill would leave the question " open " [1].

C) Moral Applications : Utilitarianism.

487 [bis]. Faithful to his early formation, Mill always defended utilitarianism. But by the aid of psychological analysis, wherein the human person is revealed as often having high aspirations, he corrected the down-to-earth nature of the theory and impressed a more noble direction upon it.

I. His starting point is the same as Bentham's : the goal of life is the greatest happiness of the greatest number. Mill added precision to the notion of happiness in this principle, and insisted on its social characteristics.

Actions are good, Mill believes, in the measure that they give happiness; bad, if they produce the opposite of happiness. Happiness means pleasure or the absence of suffering; unhappiness is suffering and the absence of happiness. This definition is openly a positivistic one, and Mill never abandons it completely. He always interprets happiness through pleasure, by placing the latter in the *sensible order*, since his empiricism prevents him from admitting functions of another order within us.

In the meantime, he introduces an important correction which strongly seeks to surpass empiricism. One cannot, as did Bentham, classify all pleasures as being of the same species, but their QUALITY must be considered. The utilitarian principle is in accord with this fact, that certain species of pleasures, if one considers their *quality* alone, are most desirable and have more value than others [2]. What means can be used to discern these qualitative differences? There is but one for the positivist : *experience*, along with consultation

---

[1] Mill objected to the proof of liberty drawn from consciousness, for he said that one would have to be aware, before deciding, that he could decide in one or another way. Further, consciousness tells me what I feel or do, but it does not tell me what I could do, for it is not the gift of prophecy. — One could reply that an *intellectual* consciousness can also appreciate and estimate the fact, and indicate its causes and its free or necessary character.

[2] *Utilitarianism*, Ch. II.

of *competent men*. Now, only those men who have experienced various pleasures can teach us their comparative value; they tell us that the " best " are those which satisfy our most noble faculties or those which are most elevated above animal life. It is certainly most difficult to satisfy these high aspirations, but Mill says " it is more worthwhile to be a malcontented man than a satisfied pig, to be an unhappy Socrates than a contented imbecile; and if the imbecile and the pig are of another view, it is because they know only one side of the question. Others know both sides " [1].

Happiness, the supreme rule of morality, is not only the happiness of the agent, but of all his interests. Bentham had already stated this, and Mill insists on it in order to correct false interpretations. Between one's own proper happiness and that of others, utilitarianism requires that the individual show an impartiality equal to that of a benevolent and disinterested spectator. Do unto others what you would have them do unto you, Mill states, and love your neighbor as yourself — these are the two rules of the ideal perfection of utilitarian morality [2]. Mill does not acknowledge sacrifice, for its aim is not to increase the sum of happiness. The only renunciation he allowed was devotion to another's happiness, to that of humanity or of individuals; this holds within the limits imposed by the collective interests of humanity. Within these limits, utilitarianism believes it has founded disinterestedness as a function of the common good.

This may seem an exorbitant pretence for an empiricist. Mill justifies his views by an appeal to experience. He does not believe that a man is necessarily an egoist who occupies himself only with his own, miserable individuality; even in his own age, he found men of superior nature, and quite numerous, who would give one an inkling of what might happen to humanity through change. Adopting the view of Comte on the constant progression of altruistic sentiments, Mill looked for a social state in which each would find his happiness in realizing this fine, positivist device : live for others. In waiting for the day in which utilitarianism would be synonymous

---

[1] *Ibid.* This view on the quality of pleasures joins traditional morality, if one recognizes spiritual faculties with their absolute demands in man, and the supreme joy or " pleasure " of happiness in God alone. This interpretation, however, is contrary to the positivist spirit.

[2] Mill says that these are the golden rules of Jesus of Nazareth (*Utilitarianism, ibid.*).

with devoted disinterestedness, Mill proposed two means
for obtaining the result sooner. The first was *legal sanction,*
which would attach individual penalties to mistakes concerning
the happiness of all, so that the interest of each would become
harmonious with the general interest. Secondly, *education,*
aided by public opinion, could create in the spirit of each man
an indissoluble association between his own happiness and
that of others, particularly between his own happiness and
the practice of rules prescribed for the general interest.

2. Once the utilitarian principle has been made precise, it
should be demonstrated. But inasmuch as it is the starting point
of all moral deduction, it cannot be given a strict demonstration,
which would suppose a principle above it. One must have
recourse to experience and show that it is an immediately evident
and incontestable fact that all men desire happiness and that
they have no other aim in all their actions. Now, taking happiness
in the sense explained above — whatever gives pleasure, including
the highest forms of intellectual and artistic pleasure — it is
clear that all our desires tend towards happiness. Mill says it
is a physical and metaphysical impossibility to desire something
without this desire being proportionate to the idea of pleasure
involved [1].

But does man have no other end in the activities of his life?
Mill examines two possibilities : the practice of virtue for itself,
and the performance of duty in the inverse sense of pleasure.
He interprets both by utilitarianism, and with the psychological
laws of association and habit. *Virtue* is but a means of attaining
happiness. By the force of practice and perseverance, so strong
a bond is established between virtue and happiness that psychologically one concludes with identifying them. It is similar to
avarice; money is desirable only for the pleasure it gives. In the
avaricious spirit, it has taken the place of the goal and is sought
for itself. Thus the virtuous man loves virtue for itself. Now,
utilitarianism considers this psychological disposition as useful
and necessary for procuring the common good.

With regard to the voluntary act which pursues a task without
pleasure, it is explained by the force of habit. At the beginning,
the will is unsteady and decides only for attractive motives.
Once it is rooted in its choice by habit, it is moved to the act
itself, in the absence of all pleasure [2]. But the will is the original
daughter of pleasure and its activity; just as virtue, so the will
is very useful for the happiness of all.

3. Through the same psychological procedure, Mill interpreted
all the fundamental notions of morality, especially the idea of
justice and of obligation.

---

[1] *Utilitarianism,* Ch. iv.
[2] *Ibid.* This explanation does not account for all voluntary acts, especially
those which dispose of certain habits in order to create new ones.

The love of justice imposes itself at our own expense, and does not seem to be referable to utilitarianism. But analysis reveals two elements in it, the first being a rule of conduct called " duty " and this rule must be supposed as common to humanity and established for its good; it is but a variant of the utilitarian principle. The second is the aspect of sentiment, or the desire to punish the person who has done evil and the belief that one or several determined individuals have suffered from this evil [1]. This sentiment is not the result of utilitarianism; it arises from the double natural instinct of legitimate defense and of the sympathy which makes us test the desire of avenging a harm done to those similar to ourselves. But there is no morality in this sympathy, and one acquires it only when exercising himself for society's good. Thus, far from opposing the love of justice, the utilitarian principle adopts it as one of its integral parts in order to give it a moral interpretation.

Moral obligation is also explainable by a sentiment which psychological experience finds in each man. A man who says, " I should ", expresses a sentiment which he does not analyze; it is the sentiment of a menace. Such a man has seen the evident consequences of an act; in thinking on this action, unconsciously, he thinks of the evident consequences and expresses this sentiment by the words, " I should not ". This association persists indefinitely, and the sentiment with it. The same situation holds for the sentiment of responsibility; to feel responsible is to feel punishable [2]. If every moral obligation is referred to this subjective disposition [3], then whatever be the supreme principle of morality — duty for duty's sake, the will of God, or the utility of all — particular precepts can always be supported with this sanction. If one finds men psychologically deprived of these sentiments, Mill concludes, no moral system can make them obey; there remains only the external sanction of laws in order to make them cooperate for the common good.

D) Social and Religious Applications.

488. In this final realm, Mill, still guided by his fundamental principle, separates himself from Comte and seems impatient to avoid the narrow limits of positivism. And yet he remains completely faithful to the essential propositions of positivism. He believed that human life, in the economic and social orders, is subject to laws. Besides experimental psychology, the unique science of mankind is *sociology*, in which, by the aid of personal observations and history, and using the statistical method, the phenomena proper to man can be explained. Even as Comte [4],

---

[1] *Ibid.*, Chap. v. The sentiment of justice, for Mill, is manifested most vividly in the case of an injured right.

[2] *Ibid.*, Ch. iii.

[3] But this is the very problem at hand; this individual basis for morality does not account for the absolute nature of duty, as Kant saw (see above, n. 411); God is needed to explain this aspect.

[4] See above, nn. 464-466.

he distinguished the two parts of this science : *static* sociology, which indicates the conditions of existence of societies, and establishes the laws for the coexistence of social facts; *dynamic* sociology, which studies the formation and the evolution of societies, and searches for the laws of the succession and the subordination of events.

But what characterizes his doctrine especially is the primordial role which he assigns to spontaneity and to individual liberty. The latter is the most important fact to account for, and the prerogative which must be maintained and favored by social institutions.

For this reason, Mill points up the influence of qualitative factors, as science, the will of man, and the spirit of order and work on *economics*. He defends the rights of the workers, and does not hold to the iron law of wages arising from the law of supply and demand. The wage depends on qualitative consider- ations and on the confidence which varies with persons. He admits the thesis of Malthus on overpopulation and accepts the remedy he proposes for the limitation of births, through intellectual foresight and moral restraint [1]. He is favorable to the division of large properties and to the views of social agrarianism, but is far from accepting anything like the class-struggle theory. If Mill was interested in abolishing the subjection of the working to the " directing " class, it was only to establish more fully the reciprocal relations of rights and of duties in all classes of which society is composed [2].

In *politics*, liberalism was Mill's ideal. The state should allow all religions to exist and permit all men to express their opinions. The freedom to err, he held, was a necessary condition of science, and autonomy a necessary condition for social virtues. He looked, in consequence, for legal guarantees in order to protect the weak from the strong, and individual thought from the collective will. He was partisan to representative government, and he wanted the minority to be proportionately represented. He also defended the function of the elite class, and held to a plurality vote in favor of propertied citizens and those eminent by their moral and intellectual qualities.

Throughout the entirety of social life, he proclaimed the *emancipation of woman*, who should enjoy the same rights as man in the civil, and even in the political order. Examining the objection that the natural function of woman confines her to the family, and that her physical and psychical dispositions are adapted for this same goal, he attributes this fact " not to nature, but to the prolonged education of previous generations; education is to correct this atavistic error and re-establish psychical identity between the two sexes " [3].

---

[1] Neither Malthus nor Mill counselled immoral practices to limit births; but their views in this regard had no efficacy in maintaining virtue in human weakness.

[2] E. THOUVEREZ, *op. cit.*, p. 54.

[3] This objection is full of good sense, and was originally made by Comte; see n. 465, above.

Faithful to positivism, Mill sees the full flowering of man's vital spontaneity only in this life. He believes the immortality of the soul to be scientifically indemonstrable. However, the " thinking self ", which unifies the phenomena of consciousness and distinguishes itself from them, seemed capable of continuing life in another order of experiences than the one in which it depends on body. One can admit its passage to immortality, then, as long as one does not see this as a quick change. The soul must pass from the present to the future life in the state of virtue and of vice, with the ensemble of tendencies which animate it at the moment of death.

The final problem of God and religion was also taken up by Mill. He gave a positivist interpretation to the role of religion in human life, and especially in social life. Its great benefit is that it sanctions the rule of morality with its undisputed authority. Its greatest harm is that it arrests the urge of thought by the fixity of its dogmas. In order to keep its benefits, and be freed from its defects, the form of religion most adapted to our nature is the religion of humanity [1].

But there is another aspect of the religious problem which opens other perspectives : the existence of so well-ordered a universe. In order to explain this world, the hypothesis of God must be considered, even though the existence of evil imposes restrictions on this view. Mill believes that there is in the works of nature, and especially in the tendencies of the soul, a sufficient trace of goodness favoring the greater probability that a good God exists. But there is also enough evil in the world for the counter admission that the goodness of God is limited by his lack of complete power.

CONCLUSION. While Mill's thought, so rich and complex, is not a logically interconnected system, it has a true unity by its spirit and constant tendency; it is similar to Locke's system, but in an inverse sense and with greater originality. Locke began with the traditional truths on God and the soul; from them he descended towards the positivist negations, and stopped half way through his spirit of tolerance. Mill began with a more profound ignorance of God than that of the pagans; his father had abandoned all belief in God, and brought him up in pure positivist doctrine and in a spirit of complete irreligiousness. The science of phenomena was made to be the sole source of truth, and utilitarianism the sole rule of goodness. His personal reaction, powerful and persevering, was to remount and to elevate himself farther away from materialism towards the spiritual world for which he seemed nostalgic. His noble soul seemed always ill at ease in the narrow world of sensible experience.

---

[1] See above, n. 468.

Sadly enough, his early formation rooted him in empiricism. Like Spencer, he admitted no truly scientific knowledge beyond the positive sciences. His most essential philosophical principles preserved him from the metaphysical realm which so attracted him. In this domain, he approached truth only in the measure in which he freed himself from the laws of logic. This explains the obscurity of his greatest doctrines and the weakness of the proofs with which he supported them.

He admitted a soul in order to unify internal facts, and even considered its possible immortality. He did so only by placing the notion of causality surreptitiously into his thought, for his logic admitted only associationism as an explicative cause. For, instead of a necessary antecedent joined by determinism to a consequent, as in Mill's explanation, the soul is a substance, the efficient source and the formal cause of its properties according to the Scholastic axiom, " activity is rooted in being ". Mill had sufficient reasons for appealing to an intuition of the " self ", and it became, at his hands, a solid proof and a fertile source of higher truths. His empiricism kept this intuition within the framework of positivism, but his spiritual insight made him reach the domain of substance and of ontological causality, allowing him to leave the realm of pure phenomena. However, empiricism prevented him from profiting from any further insight into these matters; for instance, when he speaks of God as the cause of the universe, he concludes with a divinity similar to the inferior gods of the pagans, who had only limited powers.

When Mill tries to make man's destiny more clear by correcting utilitarianism, it is the intuition of the personal self which again directs him towards a solution close to that of spiritualism. Here he has marked similarities to the Socratic utilitarianism [1], from which the morality of Aristotle and St. Thomas was derived. Mill must be credited, in this connection, for having given the human person its preponderant place in social life. Here again, he failed to achieve the balance of full truth, because he based his doctrines exclusively on experience in the positivist interpretation. One cannot scientifically [2] establish the final destiny of each man nor the nature of the common social good unless one places the

---

[1] See above, n. 32.
[2] This means " science " in the Thomistic sense; see above, n. 264.

glory of God, the Provident Creator, at the summit of things and as the supreme good to be attained.

Finally, Mill's genius flowered especially in psychology. In this domain, the intuition of the self, of which he had so vivid and deep a sentiment, gave him an authentic object for the positive sciences. His role was decisive in creating a science of the facts of consciousness, and he gave a vigorous impulse to research in this direction. His best title to glory was to have been the chief thinker of the English school of Experimental Psychology in the nineteenth century.

3. The Continuators of Experimental Psychology [1].

489. The push given by Mill to the associationist school continued in England in the work of many psychologists. The preferred and most remarkable disciple of Mill's was ALEXANDER BAIN (1818-1903), a professor at the University of Aberdeen, his native city. His principal works are: *The Senses and the Intellect* (1855); *The Emotions and the Will* (1859); *Mind and Body* (1873), *Logic, Deductive and Inductive* [2] (1875), and others.

1. Bain's *directive idea* is fully in conformity with that of Mill. He wanted to set up a science of conscious facts by applying the *method* of the other positive sciences, especially of natural history and of physiology. Bain attempted to describe the facts of consciousness exactly, whether known by introspection or by observation, and especially those of the mentally ill; then he classified them and explained them through unifying laws. Two traits mark his treatment, the first being the continual use of physiology. Bain believed that physiology and psychology are two aspects of conscious facts so closely united, especially in primitive facts, that they form an indissoluble whole. Secondly, the basic law which explains our interior life is that of *association*. Using his law, Bain shows its richness and applicability in explaining the two portions of conscious life, knowledge and sentiment.

2. The order of *knowledge or of intelligence* begins with sensation. Bain shows that the seat of intelligence is not only the brain but the whole nervous system. He analyzed the humblest manifestation of intelligence down to the least physiological facts. For instance, he shows the double aspect of the *organic sense.* First, the muscular sensations, which make us aware of our movements and make us know resistance and effort; then, the general organic sense [3], which makes us know the good or bad status of digestion, circulation, respiration, and so on. The latter activities are quiet

---

[1] On these authors, see R. METZ, *A Hundred Years of British Philosophy*, New York, 1938, Chs. II-IV, and T. RIBOT, *La psychologie anglaise contemporaine,* pp. 221-411.

[2] Bain collaborated in writing Mill's *Logic*.

[3] Later this was called the kinesthetic sense.

and obscure, but exercise a continual influence on our psychological life. In the study of the other senses, as touch, sight and hearing, he resorted to the role of education, which allows binocular vision to suggest the idea of volume to man [1].

Knowledge does not arise in this first stage. Taking up an idea of Spencer's, Bain distinguishes three degrees in conscious life. The first is *simple sensation*, in which the subject passively receives an impression [2], and in which there is no consciousness. In the second stage, there is the passage of one sensation to another which is sufficiently distinct; the mind grasps this difference, and with this *act of discrimination* knowledge or consciousness properly appears [3]. It follows, then, that all knowledge is relative and that the metaphysical dream of attaining an absolute must be abandoned. The third stage relates new sensations to this known object, constituting classifications, the source of all intellectual progress; here the law of association plays a large part.

Association, for Bain, is exercised in three ways, by contiguity, by resemblance and by contrast or difference. This last form makes up the very essence of knowledge. Association by contiguity reproduces the ensemble of facts which are neighboring in space and time; it unifies them more and more closely and leads to their *fusion*. Ideas here follow the law of nervous currents, which, in meeting, compenetrate each other. The bond which they have with nervous excitation explains why the idea of a movement, when it is quite vivid, spontaneously entrains the movement itself without the intervention of our will [4].

Association by resemblance states that actions, sensations, thoughts or emotions, when present, tend to revive those which resemble them from previous impressions and states. This law is first applied to memory and explains its mechanism. It is especially the source of the higher functions of reason : it accounts for classification, which assembles objects of the same order; it accounts for the operations of abstraction, generalization, definition and reasoning, for which Bain adopts the empiricist view of Mill's logic. Finally, there are some derived forms of this type of association; when it joins not simple ideas but syntheses previously associated (*composite* association), or when the mind joins ideas in a spontaneous and new fashion, as in the work of creative imagination (*constructive* association).

3. The world of *sentiments* is not as well unified, in Bain, as that of ideas. Analysis and many particular laws abound. Basically, there are nine simple emotions which appear to introspection

---

[1] Bain resolved the problem of how the reversed images on the retina can appear upright; our ideas of above and below are due to our sense of movement and not to optical images.

[2] The object of this impression, for Bain, is a fact of consciousness; but he does not hold out for this idealism.

[3] This doctrine can be questioned; it points up *differential sensibility*, but does not account for fundamental sensation.

[4] See the theory of *idea-forces* of Fouillée, n. 511, below.

as irreducible among themselves [1]; their combinations give us composite emotions as sympathy, imitation, the moral sentiment and the esthetic emotion. They are governed in their entirety by the *law of diffusion*. When an impression is accompanied by sentiment or by any consciousness, the currents aroused spread freely into the brain and conduct a general agitation of the motor organs, and affect the viscera. This law applies to the various emotions with small differences. Thus, the states of pleasure are joined with an increase, while those of pain with a diminution of all the vital functions or of some of them.

Emotions, as a tendency toward action, comprise both instinctive activities and also the first elements of the will. Bain refuses to consider the will as a decision coming from without and inserted into the stream of consciousness; he thinks it is a complex phenomenon made up of sentiments and actions which the law of association can explain. Analysis reveals two phases in it. The first is a conflict of motives, which are always reducible to the attraction for pleasure or repulsion from pain. In the higher states of the soul, it can propose a great number of motives to the soul, some of which are favorable to the proposed act, while others are opposed to it; this is deliberation. But, following the law of pleasure and of pain, it always arrives at a moment in which one of the alternatives triumphs; then, by the law of fusion, the idea of the act is identified with the nervous current, and this act must then be realized. Briefly, " various motives concur in pushing me towards action; the result of the conflict shows that one group is stronger than the other : this is the whole and complete case " [2].

In this psychological fact, can one speak of *liberty ?* In answering this question, Bain underscores the spontaneity of the self, which reacts before motives according to its instincts and temperament. If one means by liberty the fact that the action comes from the spontaneity of the self without any exterior impediment, Bain would defend this view. But if one defines it as the power of dominating one's actions so that though acting in one way one can act in another, he excludes this view because it supposes the substantial self to be distinct from the series of phenomena, and his positivism makes him reject this notion.

In the interpretation of moral sentiments, Bain also follows Mill. The notion of obligation is explained by the feeling of fear before sanctions, as that of public opinion or of legislative measures. The universality of laws is the fruit of the consent of all men to certain modes of action recognized as useful or necessary. When this accord does not exist, one takes as the moral criterion the law promulgated by existing society, or those coming from a man who has been invested with the authority of a moral legislator.

---

[1] They are : pleasure and pain; the emotions of relation, astonishment and surprise; terror; the tender emotions; the personal emotions; the feeling of power; cholera; emotions which result from action; those which come from the use of mind.

[2] T. RIBOT, *op. cit.*, p. 292.

These theories openly tend to give morality a properly human slant, and to found its efficacy without recourse to God or any metaphysical principle. This fear of any absolutes remains the greatest weakness of the positivist thinkers. But Bain also ventured beyond the outposts of experimental psychology on these matters, and followed Mill's spiritualistic directions.

4. Among the lesser members of the school is GEORGE LEWES (1817-1878), a physiologist and author of several philosophical works, among which are *The History of Philosophy* (1845), and *Problems of Life and Mind* (1874-79). He takes his place enthusiastically with positivism, but keeps a place among the sciences for psychology. As Bain, he also insists on the phenomena closest to physiology, as reflex movements and primitive sensations. He defends the view that consciousness is not uniquely seated in the brain, but also in the other centers of the nervous system, as in the external organs and in the ganglions of the spinal cord. In order to explain the relations between physiology and psychology, he adopts *epiphenomenalism* [1] *;* the physical and the mental processes are two aspects of the same reality, the nervous fact. — SAMUEL BAYLET is another member of the school, who wrote *Letters on the Philosophy of the Human Mind* (published in 3 volumes, 1855-1863), and *The Theory of Reasoning*. He also treats the study of conscious facts by the positivist method, but insists less on the physiological phenomena. He adopts the Scottish school on the value it attributes to the perception of the external world as a valuable belief. He explains the voluntary act by the influence of motives which permit of prediction, as did Bain, and agrees that liberty is not thereby destroyed. — JOHN DANIEL MORELL is the author of *An Introduction to Mental Philosophy on the Inductive Method* (1862), and of *The Philosophy of Religion*. He also wished to submit psychology to the inductive method, but by giving greater importance to religious facts which make us see the Unknowable beyond phenomena. He pointed out the interaction of the various functions of life. He showed the ascending transformation of vital action over nervous activity; the highest functions are those of reason, which is the faculty coordinating all our conscious facts in order to adapt them to a most complex environment [2]. — M. MURPHY, the author of *Habit and Intelligence in their Connection with the Laws of Matter and Force* (2 vols., 1869), refers all phenomena of life to two primitive facts, mind and habit. Mind in general is the knowledge capable of adapting our action to its environment, but it is at first unconscious in the inferior realm of life in which it explains the construction of organs and the wonders of instinct. It becomes fully conscious in the brain of man in which it has developed the sciences. The law of habit is that in virtue of which actions and characteristics of living beings tend to repeat and to perpetuate themselves, not only in individuals, but in their descendants. Habit applies to all the facts of life, so that association is but

---

[1] On this theory, see above, n. 494 and n. 506.
[2] This theory was inspired by Herbert Spencer; see above, n. 480.

an aspect of it. " Just as the law of habit is the law of all life, so the law of mental habit or of association is the law of every mind "[1].

II. THE SYNTHESIS OF TAINE.

(1828-1893).

SPECIAL BIBLIOGRAPHY.

1° **Works :** *Sa vie et sa correspondance*, 4 vols., Paris, 1904-1907. — *Works*, 4 vols., New York, nd. — *Origins of Contemporary France* (tr. J. Durand), 6 vols., New York, 1931. — *Les Philosophes classiques du XIXᵉ siècle en France*, Paris, 1855. — *La Fontaine et ses Fables*, Paris, 1861. — *Histoire de la Littérature Anglaise*, Paris, 1864. — *L'Intelligence*, 2 vols., Paris, 1906. — *Philosophie de l'art*, Paris, 1882.

2° **Studies :** CHEVRILLON, A., *Taine, Formation de sa pensée*, Paris, 1928. — DE MARGERIE, A., *H. Taine*, Paris, 1895. — EUSTIS, A. A., *Hippolyte Taine and the Classical Genius*, Berkeley (Calif.), 1951. — GIRAUD, V., *Essai sur Taine, son Œuvre et son Influence*, Paris, 1903. — *Bibliographie critique de Taine*, Paris, 1904. — *H. Taine, Etudes et Documents*, Paris, 1928. — KAHN, S. J., *Science and Æsthetic Judgment*, New York, 1953. — LABORDE-MILAÀ, A., *H. Taine, Essai d'une biographie intellectuelle*, Paris, 1909. — NÈVE, P., *La Philosophie de Taine, Essai critique*, Paris, 1908. — ROUX, L. H., *Taine*, Paris, 1904. — SALOMON, M., *Taine*, Paris, 1907.

490. Hippolyte Taine was born at Vouziers. After a primary Catholic education, he went to continue his studies in Paris; there he lost his faith when about fifteen years of age, under the pressure, it seems, of positivistic science, which always seemed to him as in radical opposition to revelation. During his attendance at normal school (1849-50), he found a definite orientation for his positivism by reading Spinoza and Hegel. But his philosophical ideas opposed the official teaching and won him the disfavor of his teachers. He was not able to graduate or to obtain a teaching position at the university. He turned to literature and art then, and was granted a doctorate in letters in 1853, for his dissertation on " La Fontaine and his Fables ". At the same time, he kept up his philosophical studies, publishing them in various books and articles. He was especially interested in English philosophy, and he visited England a number of times. He gave his full approval to the logic of John Stuart Mill. In 1865, his

---

[1] T. RIBOT, *op. cit.*, pp. 401 and 410.

remarkable criticisms of art got him a chair in the school of *Beaux-Arts*, where he taught for twenty years.

Taine was a discreet and modest man with an unrelenting fidelity to intellectual labor, and a man of complete sincerity. He had but one weak side : he vowed, with some pride of spirit, to keep absolute faith with positivist science, which he judged alone capable of resolving all problems of man and the universe, without the help of revelation. This gives a neat and firm unity to his system. But he pursued his thought in the abstract, as if in a speculative dream, without being preoccupied with the rules of conduct which could be deduced from them; he was quite surprised when Paul Bourget, in his novel, *Le Disciple,* showed the disastrous consequences of his views [1].

The evils of the war of 1870 and of the Paris Commune led him to renounce pure speculation, in order to look into history for a scientific basis capable of helping a social regeneration. He consecrated the last twenty years of his life to composing his great work, *The Origins of Contemporary France.* This work shows his good qualities of mind, his ability to write, and even some show of a systematic philosophy; his contact with Catholicism in his research gave him a little more respect for its views.

Taine's main works in philosophy are the following :

The Classical Philosophers of the Nineteenth Century in France — *History of English Literature* (5 vols.) — *Concerning Intelligence* (2 vols.) — *The Philosophy of Art* (2 vols.) — *The Origins of Contemporary France* (12 vols.).

Fundamental Theory.

491. Taine is fascinated both by positivistic science and by the need for unity pushed even to pantheism. The principle which synthesizes this double tendency and the key to all his philosophy can be stated as follows :

Given that the only object proportionated to our intelligence is the fact of sensible experience, the ideal of the savant is to

---

[1] Taine proposes a morality with Stoic tendencies (see below, n. 500); but he treats this matter only incidentally, and by supposing the value of a *scientific morality* in which the obligation to tend to the good has no more function. Bourget, on the contrary, drew out the consequences of his principles according to the common idea of morality.

disengage, by abstraction, the unifying and explanatory law of the group of facts constituting each science, in order finally to attain the unique and supreme law which unifies all the sciences.

This principle is but an affirmation of two postulates whose proof lies in the totality of Taine's philosophy. The first postulate is that of positivism, that we attain only the experiential fact; Taine proposes to justify it by analyzing the various phases of our knowledge. The second is that each science has a unifying law, and Taine tried to discover this law for the principal cases, and then to show its necessity for all.

APPLICATIONS. **492.** The applications, proofs of the basic theory, are reducible to four objects : God, nature, man and society. The individual man and society have special importance, as the proper object of all positivistic philosophy.

I. God.

1. It is necessary to admit, as a principle of supreme unity, a unique being of whom the multiple phenomena of nature are but a manifestation.

2. This being is God, Who is to be conceived — in order to be accessible to science — not as substance, but as one supreme law. God is the *Eternal Axiom* [1] Who predominates over all things and irradiates Himself to the confines of the universe by applying Himself to each particular law.

The first part of Taine's view, affirming the pantheistic unity of being, is demonstrated, Taine maintains, by the a priori proof of Spinoza : it is evident that non-being cannot exist and the imperfect, being sheer privation and limited, that is, a non-being, has no reason for existence and cannot exist; consequently, only the absolutely perfect being exists, and such a Being is evidently unique.

With regard to his second statement, it can be viewed as a positivistic interpretation of pantheism. God conceived as a law becomes a general fact, the fact endowed with supreme generality, and its existence is proved by induction. As a matter of fact, we hold that there is always in reality a unifying law to answer to the need for unity expressed by our mind. Now our reason itself needs such a law, dominating all science. Here, too, it must be presumed that there is a response in facts, and that the supreme law exists.

---

[1] H. TAINE, *Les philosophes classiques du XIXe siècle en France*, pp. 370-1.

II. Nature.

493. The universe is but an assemblage of facts, reunited by laws, whose series is harmoniously arranged and is the manifestation of the divine being. These facts or phenomena of nature have for their common trait a referability to local movement, so that their supreme law is basically one of mechanics.

From this fact three consequences follow; they give some idea of Taine's metaphysics.

1. All things in the world, even the rocks of the mineral order, are living and animated, endowed with at least an obscure consciousness (panvitalism); each thing is but a parcelling out of the supreme life of God.

2. *Substance*, in the ordinary sense of a *thing in itself*, is but an illusion. Each essence is one hierarchy of observable laws, and substance is the permanent possibility of sensations through which we observe these laws.

3. For these reasons, the *cause* with which science is occupied is not, as in its traditional sense, the pre-existing substance which communicates its perfection to others [1], but the *a priori or concomitant fact whose quantitative relation with another consequent fact is measured*, to which it is indissolubly bound by nature's determinism.

The study of these latter causes and of the supreme substance, in the sense indicated, is the only metaphysics whose possibility Taine admits [2].

III. Man.

494. The various operations and activities whose assemblage constitutes man in positivism are grouped around two faculties, mind and will. Taine, after he has given his most important philosophical labor to the mind, wished to complete his work

---

[1] This metaphysical definition comes from traditional philosophy; see above, n. 75.

[2] This pantheism clashes with the remarks proposed above on Spinoza (n. 348 and n. 355), and on the positivistic postulate which arbitrarily restrains our knowledge to the facts of sensible experience (n. 473). Taine's originality is to reunite two points of view which naturally exclude each other; this also explains his weakness. The Eternal Axiom is but a poetically personified abstraction.

by a similar study of the will; of this work, though, only some important fragments remain.

A) The Intelligence.

Faced with intellectual life, positivism has the following tasks : to define it and to explain its activity of ideas, judgments and reasonings, and to determine the objective value of these actions. Taine proposed a positivistic view on each of these points.

I. *Definition of Intelligence : the Function of Sensation.*

The object of psychology, evidently, cannot be the substance of the soul or the nature of its faculties [1], but only the facts of consciousness and their laws. Since these facts are subject to measurement, they are observable with the same scientific precision as any others.

Moreover, applying the same positivistic postulate, every fact of intellectual consciousness (that is, every act of knowledge), is constituted of sensation alone, more or less elaborated. While sensation might at first seem to be a special phenomenon, it must be identified, according to Taine, with the nervous phenomenon which is its necessary accompaniment. Only the hypothesis of a fact having a double aspect, the one physiological and the other psychological, explains this intimate union of two phenomena without recourse to a cause outside of nature; that is, a supernatural or anti-scientific cause.

In order to illustrate his theory, Taine compares the double series of phenomena to a book in which the original is accompanied with an interlineary translation [2], in such a way that the two texts are incomplete. At first, that which represents unconscious life is not seen, and is but the series of physical facts. But at the end, these facts are gradually shaded off and blurred, until the text representing consciousness becomes most clear. Since the essential aspect of the event is, for Taine, the physical fact, this view has been called EPIPHENOMENALISM. The latter is definable as " the theory which holds that consciousness is an accessory phenomenon, whose presence or absence has nothing to do with the production of the essential phenomenon " [3], which is the physiological fact. In order that the physiological fact can be clarified from within and be accompanied by consciousness, certain conditions are required which do not always occur.

---

[1] This follows from the positivistic principle; see above, n. 471.

[2] H. TAINE, *De l'Intelligence*, I, Book IV, Ch. II, 5, pp. 331-5.

[3] A. LALANDE, *Vocabulaire technique de la philosophie*, under " Epiphenomene ".

As a result, the two series have gaps — and this distinguishes epiphenomenalism from psychophysical parallelism, since the latter presupposes a one-to-one correspondence between the psychological and physiological facts. Taine's view approaches parallelism, for he holds that when the two series exist, they exactly correspond, " Phrase to phrase, word to word, the physical event as we represent it translates the moral event " [1].

In itself, sensation appears as a subjective fact and thus distinct from the exterior object. But it always produces a representation (or image), in the consciousness, of this external object. This distinguishes sensation from the pure nervous phenomenon. Sensation always corresponds to actual experience, real or possible, being the most simple element of the intellectual life.

All the other acts of intelligence follow from this element in uniform fashion. *Substitution* is an act by which a most complex and rich sensation becomes the *sign* evoking a certain number of more simple sensations. Thus, the image replaces elementary sensation; it is signified by a proper name, the proper names by common names, and the latter by laws. In this hierarchy, two stages are of great importance : that in which is found the theory of the common name, and the theory of abstraction.

2.   *The Universal Idea : Theory of the Common Name.*

495.   The properties of the universal idea are explained by that of the *common name* conceived as a *sign* endowed with a double property : *a*) that of being evoked by each individual of the class; *b*) that of evoking in us the sensation proper to the individuals of this class alone.

Taine begins by distinguishing the *general idea* from the *image*. These two are opposed, first, with regard to clarity and precision. For instance, the idea of a *myriagon* has an exact definition though its image is blurred [2]. They are also opposed in richness : the image applies to but one sensation, while the idea embraces a great number of them.

Now the properties of a sign can be completely explained with recourse to a soul or to a spiritual faculty. In fact, the sign is an actual sensation to which it is proper that it awake

---

[1] *De l'Intelligence, ibid.*, p. 334.

[2] Taine is speaking of a thousand-sided polygon, which he calls *myriagon;* see *De l'Intelligence*, Book I, Ch. II, 2, pp. 37-8.

the remembrance of past sensations, and suggest new ones. But if one analyzes the conscious fact called " general idea ", one always finds therein the actual sensation of a name, either in the state of tendency, expressing itself by a movement, or in the perfect state of an articulated word. This quite simple sensation explains the *clarity* of the idea.

It also explains its richness, not only because it is a sign evocative of sensations which it brings forth and of similar sensations (as the word *tree* evokes an oak or a fir), but also because the mind forms its common names by combining simpler names in a more complex definition. As a result, the definite object does not correspond to any immediate experience, and is connected with the fact only indirectly and through its elements. Thus, to the definition of triangle there cannot correspond any reality or precise image, and only its elements (sides, angles) are directly observable.

These assemblages are not arbitrary, but imposed by the analogy of sensations, the source of association of ideas. One meets this mental operation in animals, but in a restricted number. Man can multiply them infinitely through the invention of the common name, which can reassemble the most distant analogies and become a sign that is more and more universal. Nevertheless, the procedure remains essentially the same : between man and animal there is no difference of natures [1].

496. This nominalism is the most ingenious attempt yet made by a positivistic psychology. It has the merit of showing the radical difference between the universal and abstract idea and the concrete and singular image. But the explanation proposed, the theory of the sign, is manifestly insufficient. For a *sensible* sign, since it is sensible, can designate only a concrete object circumscribed by time and determined place. The clarity and richness of the general idea — its universality, its cohesion or internal necessity — require a sign of an immaterial order, a spiritual concept.

What makes this theory specious is that it states as *proper* to the common name the qualities which it possesses only *by participation;* the common name is an immediate sign of the *idea* and, through the idea, of concrete realities. Only the idea possesses, properly, clarity and richness together. By suppressing the idea, Taine removes the source of these properties and his theory of the name as the sign of concrete objects is inadequate.

---

[1] Taine holds that whatever distinguishes man from animal is referable to this faculty which grasps the most exact analogies (*De l'Intelligence*, ii, p. 265).

3. *Judgment and Reasoning : Theory of Abstraction.*

497. Ideas or common names have another property, that of uniting themselves in indissoluble couples in order to constitute a law or universal and necessary judgment. This association is not only the result of habit (John Stuart Mill) nor an a priori form of the spirit (Kant), but the fruit of natural connections of observed facts. Thus, for the most simple laws, observation alone suffices to bring them forth.

But the most universal laws, as the most common and general names, require the work of *abstraction*. This is a logical operation determining the common quality by extracting a most simple and general fact from a most complex and particular one. In the most difficult cases, the movement of the abstractive mind is called reasoning, which, under the form of induction and deduction, is needed to constitute science.

Induction is the mental effort of isolating, in the complex fact, the most simple fact (called causal fact) by means of the various methods outlined by Mill. One mounts, thus, towards increasingly general laws, towards the supreme law, the Eternal Axiom. The theory of abstraction thus becomes the means for Taine to join his pantheism with his positivism.

Deduction is the inverse movement of the spirit, beginning with the most general fact (the cause), in order to refer all particular efforts to it. It is the great means of systematization and unification, setting up a science as a pyramid of laws.

4. *The Value of Knowledge : Theory of True Hallucination.*

498. Since all forms of knowledge are made up of sensations, the critical problem is simply one of finding the objective value of sensation. Taine resolves this in a realistic sense through his theory of true hallucination.

At first, every sensation is an *hallucination* [1], since the object immediately known is never the exterior object, but an internal image which we instinctively, though illusorily, project to the exterior thing. As proof of this, Taine states that we thus explain the fact that a diseased hallucination is identical

---

[1] " The perception awakened by an individual, or quite rarely by a group of individuals, of a sensible object which is not really present or of a phenomenon which is not real " (A. LALANDE, *op. cit.*, under " Hallucination ").

with ordinary sensation; the difference is uniquely due to the absence or the presence of the object.

In the normal man, sensation is regularly produced in the presence of reality, so that the object projected on the outside coincides, by a sort of naturally pre-established harmony, with the exterior object. This explains the terminology, " true hallucination ". As proof Taine states that the concordance between scientific laws and experience can be explained in this way.

But the definitive reason which legitimizes an absolute faith in the value of science is, for Taine, his Spinozistic pantheism. For, the unity of this manifest source fully explains and requires the correspondence of the two series of manifestations which are sciences in us, *psychologically*, and which are things, *physically*.

It follows that the weakness of pantheism entails the ruin of this realism, leaving but a positivistic psychology, incapable of leaving the self. In misunderstanding the value of *sensible intuition*, Taine should logically conclude with the absolute idealism of Hume. If the sole source of truth is sensible experience, the latter is evidently incapable of ever demonstrating the presence of the exterior object, since, by hypothesis, it can never be attained. But as a positivist, Taine did not search out the critical problem too deeply. By setting up philosophy through the sensible evidence of the sciences, he supposed, with good sense, its objective value.

B) The Will.

I. *Definition and Laws : Liberty.*

499. In positivistic psychology, the only facts accessible are those of voluntary decisions; their originative and developmental laws are to be determined. The will is not a faculty, but the *permanent possibility of decisions*. These decisions are explainable by the laws of tendencies.

Now it is evident that each idea is accompanied by a tendency to action, and is subject to a double law. At first, the force of this tendency varies in inverse ratio to the degree of abstraction of the idea, and in direct ratio to the interest bearing on the object of the idea. Besides, with or without a struggle between the various tendencies, the strongest has the property of *fixating itself*, or of becoming transferred into action excluding the others. This fixation constitutes decision, or the act of will.

In consequence, the liberty of our decisions is but an illusion arising from the multiplicity of our tendencies. When one of them becomes fixed, we believe that another could, in the same set of circumstances, be fixed likewise; but this is impossible. Taine confirms this essential point by two proofs. First, experience shows that either men are dominated by their passions or only the strongest tendency is translated into action. Secondly, and a priori, liberty is meaningless, for if the act produced could equally have been not produced, there is no explanation of previous events; the act is a fact without any reason for being, which is meaningless and impossible.

This latter reason is a decisive one for positivism, in which the sole reason for being assignable to a fact is a prior or concomitant fact. But one can look for the reason of a free act in the very perfection of the soul and its spiritual faculties, which sufficiently dominate action in order to produce it without it being thereby necessitated. It is true that the determinism of the psychological laws of ideas or of tendencies is necessary in order to set up psychology as a strictly positivistic science. This necessity rules in the sensible life, as in the physiological and mineral realms. But the spiritual part of man escapes it. One can, instead, consider experimental psychology as a special science, in the same way as sociology, without denying our liberty [1].

2. *Morality.*

500. Since our voluntary acts are subject to determinism, morality cannot state that which should be done or avoided, but merely studies that which has been done by men with the aim of discovering the laws of voluntary activity and of foreseeing their application. Morality must, therefore, be founded on the historical and inductive method, as every other positive science.

Taine does not believe that determinism destroys responsibility; in fact, he requires it to show how we are the *true causes* of our actions, which are, as a result, imputable to us. Liberty, on the contrary, by supposing actions without a cause, would make man irresponsible. This is a logical conclusion if one admits the positivistic prejudice which reserves the name of true cause only for that antecedent phenomenon from which another phenomenon necessarily flows; but this is an arbitrary denial of liberty, as has already been pointed out.

Taine deduces several rules of conduct from these principles :

a) **The Rule of Relativism,** applying to the estimation of goodness and of honesty. It follows directly from the historical method.

---

[1] See above, n. 469 and n. 486, 1⁰.

Moral good, which is proper to man as such, for it is most favorable to social life, must necessarily vary (according to sociological laws) with times, places and peoples. One must thus conform to the spirit of his age and seek to consolidate himself with his contemporaries by returning the goodness which one has received from them.

b) **The Rule of Moderation** in the plan of action. It is useless to look for heroic efforts, since nature necessarily directs us towards the good.

c) **The Rule of Stoic Resignation** as an ideal in adversity, for determinism only allows one to make a *virtue out of necessity*. This makes Marcus Aurelius the moralist preferred by Taine.

These attempts at positive morality, which need many rectifications, are drawn from scattered remarks in Taine's works. The attempt to organize morality into a science will be taken up later under the sociological school [1].

3. *The Self : Theory of the Master Faculty.*

501. According to the general theory of the hierarchy and unification of laws concerning the same object, there must exist in each man a deep-seated tendency which will be the most general fact on which all other facts of a man's life depend. This is similar to the way in which the universe depends on the Eternal Axiom. This unifying and explicative tendency is called the master or ruling faculty.

Now, the law of dependency, which unites all the facts of consciousness, explains the feeling of identity which we have, and it constitutes the *self* or personality. The substantial self or the spiritual soul thus vanishes, for it is but a pure abstraction or a simple, common name obtained by the customary process. Nothing corresponds to it in reality, except the ordered and unified series of our psychic events.

One can see that this theory is based on that of the common name, and has no solidity at all. Furthermore, it neglects an important fact, that of our internal experience, which grasps the existence of our own, proper personality. Our mind can know its own activity and, through it, the soul which is its source; we know its existence, and can even know its nature [2]. But Taine's positivistic prejudice prevents him from certifying this fact of intuition and of intellectual reflection.

It should be added that by rejecting personality and liberty, and the immortal soul and God, Taine makes the notions of obligation, responsibility, and duty meaningless, and destroys the whole basis of morality in the ordinary sense of the word.

---

[1] See below, Durkheim's theory; n. 516.
[2] See above, n. 262 and n. 327.

4. *Esthetics.*

502. One can place Taine's views on art under morality. For, to judge positively of beauty, as of the good, Taine believes in the use of historical method and not in a priori analysis. The method is that of induction, based on the examination of the main works. This method leads him to a definition and a law of the good.

a) The beautiful, Taine holds, is the work capable of stimulating an agreeable sensation in us which is noble and useful; that is, it increases our power of activity.

b) The law of the artistic work is that a work is all the more beautiful in proportion as it expresses a subject that is more important, benevolent and unified. *Importance* derives from that which is fundamental and constitutive of man, though not in a passing way, but with regard to that which remains imprinted from one generation to another; or, even better, that which is the very basis of the human race. In a general way, importance is the characteristic of a force dominating nature.

Benevolence strengthens importance, for it supposes in the object a fulness such that its good expands outside of itself. Thus, the fulness of an act of charity or of heroism is, of itself, more beautiful than that of a criminal act. Finally, *unity* assures one of brilliance and power of expression to the measure in which most of the possible traits are best coordinated to bring out the common character (in a man, the master faculty), which synthesizes the whole work.

One can say that observation led Taine to a quite exact analysis of art and of beauty.

IV. Society.

503. Like all positive science, that of society must be synthesized in a basic law which will explain the social institutions and their function.

1) **The Law of Primordial Facts.** Every form of social life is definitively explained by three factors.

a) *Race*, which is the great force from within society. It brings a group of stable modifications to life, obtained by the continuous effort of past generations, and transmitted through heredity.

b) *Environment*, the great force from without, is formed by physical climate, the social status and the daily occupations of life.

c) The *moment* is the synthesis of unstable and variable modifications, due to the action of the immediately preceding generations. It combines with race and environment to produce a manner of thinking, a " ruling idea ", which varies with centuries and places.

The action of these factors, according to Taine, produces the social state of an age with the same necessity that affinity produces a chemical combination; this was Taine's extension of positivistic science to man. History is also treated in this naturalistic way. Taine defends himself from any blame for his view, which really necessitates human events; at the same time, he fails to understand their intrinsic value.

2) **The Institutions** of which Taine speaks are, mainly, religion and government.

Religions have their origin in response to the general need of the race in a determined epoch. The founder is followed because he carries the " unique word ", universally expected. Religion becomes a social force as soon as it has undergone some secular experience; then it is transformed into an " hereditary prejudice ", or the general persuasion that it possesses the best solutions for the happiness of societies and individuals. Thus, the birth of Christianity answers the need of the noble souls who wished to react against the pagan disorders; its benevolent action has been prolonged even to us.

Governments, such as one encounters in various countries, are the necessary result of the three primordial factors. Nonetheless, history shows that all are not of equal value. This leads to the law that a society will be the better governed the more the state renounces extreme centralization and interventionism, and thus remains within the limits of its mission.

Now, history shows us that states are not uniquely formed with the aim of protecting peace and social prosperity against neighboring, enemy societies, or internal enemies, as thieves and criminals. This " protective " mission requires an army, a constabulary, a police, tribunals and taxes. But all the other social functions, as religion, instruction, teaching, industry and the exploitation of capital, should be exercised by private initiative and particular societies; in this respect, the state should encourage as much activity as possible. Any direct intervention on its part, as history shows, has a disorganizing effect and is beyond the competence of the state [1].

---

[1] One could call this view that of the " Police-State ". As a matter of fact, the state has a much broader mission. Ordered to aid the citizens in the pursuit of their destiny and in the conquest of a better human life, it accomplishes these functions not only by protecting rights, but also by a positive action of control, of supplying things and even of initiative in the domain of the public good. The condemnation of excessive centralization is quite justifiable.

Thus, for Taine, there are essentially two types of government. The first is based on decentralization and is good; the other centralizes, and is bad. The form of this government is a secondary matter. From this point of view, the democratic form, based solely on number, is most unjust. It misunderstands the two most important social forms, that of heredity, which guards traditions, especially through the royal family, and that of perpetuating riches and public positions for the nobility. Thus, the better government will realize the synthesis of these three forces, adapting them to the degree of civilization possible.

Here we find the same weakness as in Comte's sociology : the doctrine of absolute determinism and of agnosticism [1]. If it is true that the great historical events are prepared by previous events, one must account for human liberty and divine providence, without excluding miracles. In particular, the explanation of the origin of Christianity, in Taine, is wholly inadequate, as is shown in Catholic apologetics : the Church is a true, moral miracle.

Besides, the personal influence of certain men, and especially of the saints, escapes the law of primordial factors. Taine himself seemed to see this gap in his theory, by holding that these factors do not create great men; Taine supposes that nature has given them their greatness germinally, but these factors are necessary to explain the birth of geniuses and to permit their full development.

With these reservations, Taine's political theory is one of the better portions of his system, and had a real influence on many sociologists.

Summary and Conclusion.

504. As Spencer was for England, so, for France, Taine is the *metaphysician of positivism*. He was so fascinated by the modern sciences of fact and mathematical law, that he condemned, prior to examination, any other source of truth, including supernatural faith. But he was also dominated by an intense desire towards unity and towards organizing a well coordinated system unifying all forms of knowledge. His main ambition was to place a general and dominating law in the foreground in each science, through his master faculty in the individual and primordial factors in society, and, in the universe, through his Eternal Axiom.

Without knowing much of Comte, and without being directly a disciple of his, Taine is close to him in thought and completes his views. His most original views are those of the common name; though they are inadequate, they are among the better attempts of positivistic psychology. His laws of sociology, if taken as true only in most cases, and if human liberty be sufficiently accounted for, are quite exact.

---

[1] See above, n. 469.

His influence was increased by his literary presentation, which is rich in detail and well unified by the dominating influence of his general theories.

His philosophical efforts succeeded in causing the downfall of eclecticism, but he had no disciples, since unlimited confidence in science soon began to wane. His literary, artistic, historical and social work, however, made him influential even into the twentieth century.

III. GERMANY: THE MATHEMATICAL SCHOOL. (WUNDT).

SPECIAL BIBLIOGRAPHY.

BORING, E, G., *A History of Experimental Psychology*, New York, 1929. — CROCE, B., *Germany and Europe*, New York, 1944. — JONES, W. T., *Contemporary Thought of Germany*, 2 vols., New York, 1931. — RIBOT, T., *La psychologie allemande contemporaine*, Paris, 1879.

505. Positivistic psychology, built up by the associationistic method, was born in England with John Stuart Mill and his disciple Bain, and implanted into France by Taine. It had its apogee, however, in Germany, where the psycho-physical studies were inaugurated with the hope of discovering the mathematical formulas for psychological laws. The initiator of this school was Herbart; his ideas were more fully exploited by Lotze and Fechner. The outstanding member of this school, however, is Wundt.

A) **J. F. Herbart** [1] (1776-1841).

A professor at the University of Göttingen, and then at Königsberg, Herbart connects positivistic psychology to Kant and even to Leibniz. The aim of philosophy is to explain reality which is revealed by appearances, the only items directly perceived. But, inasmuch as being is, of itself, a unity, and appearances are multiple and varied, the problem of their correspondence arises. Herbart believes that what is real is each of the simple qualities (as *whiteness*); they are fully existent, and are fully independent and infinite in their own order, like Leibniz's monads. That their union constitutes a special object (as the color, form, weight of an apple), is the work of our intelligence and has nothing more than purely subjective value.

---

[1] **Works :** *Sämmtliche Werke* (ed. by Hartenstein), 12 vols., Leipzig, 1850-52.
Studies : COLE, P. R., *Herbart and Froebel*, New York, 1907. — DE GARMO, C., *Herbart and the Herbartians*, New York, n. d. — HAYWARD, F. H., *Meaning of Education as Interpreted by Herbart*, London, n. d. — KINKEL, W., *Herbart, sein Leben und seine Philosophie*, Giessen, 1903. — RIBOT, T., *German Psychology of Today*, New York, n. d.

In applying this theory, Herbart fell into a mathematicized psychology. Our soul is one of these simple realities whose basic activity is to conserve and defend itself against all others. The variety of conscious facts is due to the struggle against the many blocks and attractions from without. Since every conscious fact, in his view, is a *representation*, the latter is but an effort of the soul to conceive itself. In other words, " our sensations, our ideas and remembrances, and all that makes up our psychological life, exists within us, only as an effort of the conservation-tendency which is determined and specified by relationship with other beings " [1].

Now, all these interior phenomena show themselves " as coming and going, oscillating and fluctuating, or as something which becomes stronger or weaker " [2]. This entitles them with a quantitative aspect, so that they can be studied by mathematical means. Psychologists have not previously attempted this method, because the extreme variability of facts escaped measurement by their indetermination. Since the discovery of the infinitesimal calculus, which subsumes movement and even its variation to number without it being necessary to have absolute precision on the variable quantities, it has become possible to study the variations of consciousness mathematically without having a fixed unity which would directly measure our representations. It is sufficient to consider them as *forces* endowed with a certain intensity and as struggling among themselves. If two representations are of equal force, they are equilibrated and reduced to a state of tendency : this is a state of rest or passage from the conscious to the unconscious. But if one of them gets more force, it appears in consciousness, and in this sense, is put in motion. The calculation of this equilibrium and of this movement of representations is the object of the statics and the dynamics of the spirit [3].

Herbart was not content with merely outlining a program to be followed; he realized it through the publication of his *Psychology as Science*, in which he bases psychology on experience, metaphysics and mathematics. His other important work is *Manual of Psychology* [4]. He did not, however, succeed in creating a durable psychology. Though he avoided the difficulty of looking for a direct measurement of conscious facts, he mixed a large number of hypotheses with his equations; since the hypotheses were often contradicted by facts, the calculations based on them lost their value. He was, however, quite influential, and founded a school [5]. Two of his ideas brought forth many consequent

---

[1] T. RIBOT, *La psychologie allemande contemporaine*, p. 3.

[2] *Psychologie als Wissenschaft*, Introduction. — [3] T. RIBOT, *op. cit.*, p. 13.

[4] The German titles of these works are : *Psychologie als Wissenschaft, neu gegründet auf Erfahrung, Metaphysik und Mathematik* (1824-25) and, *Lehrbuch zur Psychologie* (1815).

[5] Some of his disciples developed the psychology of peoples, or folk-psychology; these " Herbartians " include DROBISCH, the author of *Erste Grundlehren der mathematischen Psychologie* (1850); CORNELIUS, who wrote *Theorie des Sehens und räumlichen Vorstellen* (1861); NARLOWSKI, the author of *Gefühlsleben;* J. MULLER, and others.

reflections : 1) the exterior world does not act on the soul except through transforming itself into representation; 2) because of their quantitative character, psychical facts can be treated by the calculus; this view was taken over by Weber and Wundt.

B) Lotze [1] (1817-1881).

505 bis. Rudolph Herman Lotze, like many a positivist, joined a taste for philosophy with that of the sciences. He obtained a doctorate in philosophy and also in medicine at the University of Leipzig; he taught at Göttingen and then at Berlin. In addition to his medical works, as *A Treatise on Pathology and General Therapeutics* (1842) and *Physiology of the Corporeal Life* (1851), he wrote the following : *Metaphysics* (1841), *Logic* (1843), *Medical Psychology* (1852) and *Microcosmus* (2 vols., 1856-1864). In the latter he studies body, soul, life, man, mind, the course of the world, history, progress, the connectivity of things, and so on. His final work was his *System of Philosophy* (1874-79).

1. **General Philosophy.** Lotze has his own way of interpreting things; his position is intermediary between the realism of Leibniz and Herbart, and the idealism of Schelling or Hegel. He asserts equally both the importance of the idea and the function of mind, as well as the existence of experiential facts and of exterior things. In order to explain the universe, he held to three realities, or three superimposed kingdoms, through which one must pass in order to achieve full truth. The first is the kingdom of universal and necessary laws, the condition for all possible reality. The theory of the Kantian categories applies here; through them one can establish the remote conditions and the deepest basis for the sciences, but one cannot explain the apparition of any phenomenon. — The ensemble of experiential facts makes up the second order of realities; we attain these through perception. — The action of the external world on consciousness brings up a difficult problem whose resolution is found in the third order of realities, the *kingdom of values*, by which our intuition of the world finds its unity. In this realm, which Lotze calls " teleological idealism ", one affirms the unity of substance as being the Good towards which everything converges. " Pluralism must be achieved by a monism, by means of which apparently transitive action is changed into immanent action.. This action is but an appearance between two finite beings; in truth, it is the absolute which acts on itself " [2]. The interaction of soul and body is thus interpreted as an illusion; corporeal realities tend to be reduced to phenomena and even,

---

[1] **Works :** *Logic*, (tr. by B. Bosanquet), 2 vols., Oxford, n. d. — *Metaphysics* (tr. by B. Bosanquet), 2 vols., Oxford, n. d.

Studies : BORING, E., *A History of Experimental Psychology*, New York, 1929, pp. 250-9. — HALL, G. S., *Founders of Modern Psychology*, New York, 1912, pp. 65-121. — MOORE, V. F., *Ethical Aspects of Lotze's Metaphysics*, Ithaca (N. Y.), n. d. — RIBOT, T., *German Psychology of Today*, New York, 1912. — ROBINS, E. P., *Some Problems of Lotze's Theory of Knowledge*, Ithaca (N. Y.), n. d. — THOMAS, E. E., *Lotze's Theory of Reality*, New York, 1921. — WENTSCHER, M., *Fechner und Lotze*, München, 1925.

[2] *Psychologie médicale.*

as in Berkeley, to external perceptions experienced in our souls. The soul, in turn, is less a substance than an emanation from the unique, cosmic substance.

Nevertheless, Lotze's thought is not too sure on this latter point; in other places, he speaks of the unity of the self grasped by intuition as a substance. He demonstrates its spirituality and defends it against materialistic objections. Beginning with the value of the aspirations of the soul, he concludes that the supreme Spirit, ordering all things to the Good, must be a person distinct from man. " That which is veritably real, which is and must be, is not matter nor the Hegelian idea, but the living and personal Spirit of God, and the world of personal spirits He created; this is the true place of the Good and of goods " [1]. At the same time, he held to the reality of experiential facts as the object of the positivistic sciences, and hoped to conciliate this notion with idealism [2]. The problem of the relations between the physical and the mental is thus opened; in order to shed light on it, he presented a theory of local signs.

2. **Local Signs.** In itself, this theory has a restrained meaning; it is concerned only with the perception of space through the two external senses of sight and touch. But it opens the most fundamental problem of psychology, that of knowledge, and is in the direction towards a correct solution. For modern psychologists, the perception of extension supposes that there is in man, in the order of knowledge, an image equally endowed with extension, so that there is one-to-one correspondence between image and objective extension. This is the theory of tableau-ideas of Descartes, which has some affinity to the εἴδωλα of Democritus [3]. Lotze begins by criticizing this conception, believing that perceptions as such do not have any extension. " Our visual and tactile impressions *cannot be perceived but under the form of intensive states*. What each point that is touched or seen transmits to the soul is not an extended image of this point, but an intensive modification varying according to the nature and energy of the impression " [4]. It is by means of these given materials that the soul reconstructs extension in itself, transforming anew the intensive into the extensive. The theory of local signs is nothing else but a hypothesis for explaining the manner in which this reconstruction occurs.

Lotze believes that only sight and touch perceive extension, and that other sensations, those of smell, hearing and taste are purely qualitative [5]. He further admits, as a doctrine common since Descartes, that sensible perception, being a fact of conscious-

---

[1] *Mikrokosmus*, Vol. III, p. 519 and p. 616.

[2] One could perhaps say that distinction and plurality hold for the inferior degrees, while the supreme degree of intuition attains the unity of the cosmos; but this is an interpretation of a doctrine with vague contours, difficult to systematize (see T. RIBOT, *op. cit.*, p. 68).

[3] See above, n. 20 and n. 323.

[4] T. RIBOT, *op. cit.*, p. 73.

[5] This point is contested by William James, who, quite rightfully, argued for the extensive character of *all* our sensations; see below, n. 526.

ness, is produced in the sensorial center of the brain, and not in the peripheral organ; the latter simply receives the impressions in order to transmit them to the central organ. Now, the impressions thus received through touch and the eye, not only have an intensive character, but they are also localized and different from each other by their positions. For instance, when several points equally red are impressed at the same time on various rods of the retina, they do not fuse upon their arrival at consciousness. They are coordinated, but retain their relation of reciprocal distance; the same holds for touch. Each point of the retina or skin has its own proper manner of being impressionated, and each impression is presented to consciousness with its distinctive mark. This mark is the *local sign*.

Concretely, this sign consists either in the muscular sensations associated with each tactual or visual impression, or more probably in the *system of movements* or tendencies to movement released by each excitation. Thus, in vision, as soon as the luminous stimulus is received in any point of the retina, it tends spontaneously to transport itself to the yellow spot of the retina; it is clear that this movement is necessarily distinct for each of the points which surround the yellow spot; each of these signs thus possesses its distinctive, local sign. For touch, the " sign " is constituted by the diversity of the corpuscules of touch, by the muscular movements accompanying each impression, and especially by the " wave of accessory sensations ". Each excitation of the skin involves tension, pressure, displacement, and so on, in the neighboring portions; this gives precise localization to the impression in the body. Accordingly, consciousness receiving each excitation fortified by its local sign, would have the elements required for reconstructing extension of one or two dimensions in the psychological order, corresponding to the exterior excitation. This interpretation of local signs is sometimes conscious, when we are aware of a tactile sensation at a point of our body, but often it remains unconscious and is produced by a sort of reflex, the fruit of habit and the education of the senses. Accordingly, the localization of objects seen seems immediate and intuitive, but it was acquired from infancy with the aid of numberless experiences.

3. **Value of this Solution.** This theory is a remarkable attempt to explain the passage from the physical to the psychical, but Lotze criticized only a part of the current idealistic conception. He admitted, with idealism, that the object on which our perception bears is a fact of consciousness, or what he calls the " intensive impression ". He did not understand how visual or tactual intuition, while remaining *subjectively* a psychical fact (intensive) could *objectively* terminate in an extended physical reality[1]. It remains true, though, that knowledge is a sort of transposition of the physical to the psychical order, though not with regard to the *thing known*, but rather with regard to its *mode of existence*. The object seen, for instance, which is material in

---

[1] This is a partial statement of how Thomistic realism solves this problem.

itself and endowed with quantity, is the same which is also in
consciousness; however, considered *precisely to the extent of being
seen*, it is nothing other than the vision of this object. It also
exists under a psychological form which escapes all conditions
of matter; its mode of being, which was extensive (quantitative),
has become intensive (qualitative). This Lotze saw well. He
also placed in relief among our conscious facts, the very real
aspect by which they seem to escape mathematical measurement.
This idea, originally from Herbart, is not forgotten, and Fechner
will analyze it much more successfully.

C) Fechner [1] (1801-1887).

506.   Gustav Theodore Fechner, a professor at Leipzig,
published a large number of works in which metaphysics is
given an honorable position.   Among these are *Nanna or the
soul-life of Plants* and *Zend-Avesta or the Things of Heaven
and Beyond*.   He is especially known for his *Elements of Psychophysics*, in which this new science is founded, and which he
was later forced to defend against objections.   These two
groups of works, metaphysical and psychological, quite different
in themselves, were inspired by the same experimental method.
Fechner proposes an inductive metaphysics and it is by his
precise observations that he created psychophysics.

1. Inductive Metaphysics. Fechner rises to a general conception
of the world by beginning with internal observation, and continues
with a great amount of boldness.   Certifying that a great variety
of thoughts and of images are born in his soul, he conceives of
nature as being of the same type and teaches *panpsychism*.
In his view, the entire universe possesses a soul which deploys
its richness in all substances, in the stars, which are the " angels
of heaven ", as well as in plants, animals and men.   Each of these
particular souls is a manifestation of the soul of the world, as each
of our thoughts is but a manifestation of our soul.   His theory
is quite similar to that of Plotinus [2], but is obtained by an *induction*
or comparison with man's interior life.   One of the most striking
traits of our conscious life is the law of unity.   " Is it not an active

[1] **Works :** *Das büchlein vom Leben nach dem Tode* (1836). — *Über das höchste
Gut* (1846). — *Nanna oder über das Seelenleben der Pflanzen* (1848). — *Zendavesta
oder die Dinge der Himmels und der Jenseits* (1851). — *Die physikalische und
philosophische Atomenlehre* (1855). — *Die Elemente der Psychophysik* (1860). —
Über die Seelenfrage (1861). — *Die drie Motive und Grunde des Glaubens* (1863).
— *Vorschule der Aesthetik* (1876). — *In Sachen der Psychophysik* (1877). —
Die Tagesansicht gegenüber der Nachtansicht (1879). — *Revision der Hauptpunkte
der Psychophysik* (1882). — *Life after Death*, New York, 1943. — Lowrie, W.
(ed.), *Religion of a Scientist*, New York, 1946.

Studies : Boring, E., *A History of Experimental Psychology*, New York,
1929, pp. 265-287. — Laszwitz, K., *G. T. Fechner*, 3rd ed., Stuttgart, 1910. —
Wentscher, M., *Fechner und Lotze*, München, 1925.

[2] See above, n. 131.

progress from the past to the present and to the future? Does
it not join the distant and the near? Does it not include in itself
a thousand diversities in an indecomposed unity? Now the law
of the world is a unity endowed with the same properties, except
that they pertain to the world in an unlimited manner " [1]. It is
proper, then, to conceive of the universal soul, which is God,
as the unique consciousness of the universe. Our souls are distinct
from one another, since each is " characterized by a threshold
beyond which there is but a portion which coincides with the
divine consciousness " [2]. Consciousness is fully realized in God
without limit. When we flee the threshold of our own consciousness,
we find ourselves wholly identical, through the unconscious,
with Divinity itself.

Whatever value Fechner may have accorded to these views,
they are pure hypotheses and far from being demonstrated
inductively. The subconscious will be found as an hypothesis
with William James [3], but psychophysical research is founded,
more solidly, on actual facts.

2. **Psychophysics.** Fechner was fond of imputing the
honor of founding this science to the physiologist, E. H. WEBER
who, in 1846, published a series of experimental researches in
the *Handwörterbuch der Physiologie* (under the word, *Tastsinn*).
He stated the following law as synthesizing his research :
" The increase of the stimulus which should engender a further
and appreciable modification of sensation is in constant
relationship with the quantity of the stimulus to which it
refers ". It was Fechner himself, however, who published
the first methodical treatise of psychophysics based on
mathematics.

" By psychophysics I understand an exact theory of the
relations between soul and body, and, in a more general
manner, between the physical and the psychical worlds " [4].
There is question here, however, only of the phenomena and
their laws, abstracting from the substantiality of the body
or of the soul. It is, thus, an *experimental science*, similar to
the physical sciences.

However, as a positive science, its hypotheses are not always
legitimate; at the beginning, Fechner supposed that the
opposition between spirit and body is but a difference of
viewpoint. " That which appears to you as your spirit from
an interior viewpoint, from an exterior viewpoint appears to
you as the corporeal substrate of this spirit " [5]. This hypothesis

---

[1] *Zend-Avesta*, 2nd ed., p. 167. — [2] E. BRÉHIER, *op. cit.*, II, p. 994.
[3] See below, n. 527.
[4] T. RIBOT, *op. cit.*, p. 149.
[5] *Elemente der Psychophysik*, Introduction.

has been called *psychophysical parallelism*, which can be defined as " the hypothesis according to which the physical and the psychical are in point to point correspondence so that there is between them the same correspondence as between a text and its translation, or as between two translations of the same text " [1]. Fechner seems to have been the first to use this expression, although a similar doctrine is found in Leibniz and Spinoza [2]. In these latter two men, however, psychology was deduced a priori from metaphysics, while in Fechner it is presented as an independent science, and parallelism is viewed as a scientific hypothesis and as an instrument for research. From this viewpoint, there is nothing to prevent its being used, if one watches whether experience confirms or reverses its validity.

One of the first effects of this hypothesis was to favor the creation of psychophysics. For, in order to introduce measure into experiential facts, some artifice had to be found which would allow for the application of a quantitative unity, since the conscious fact, through its qualitative, " intensive " character, escapes every direct measurement. But if it can be viewed as identical with the *nervous phenomenon* whose internal aspect it is, it becomes possible to attain it indirectly and submit it to calculation. This is especially true of a sensation in which the nervous movement depends on a physical stimulus whose strength can be determined exactly. This stimulus can serve to measure sensations, just as one measures variations in intensity of heat by the displacement of a column of mercury expanding within a thermometer. The only difference is that in place of measuring the cause by the effect, one here measures the effect (sensation) by its cause (the stimulus); but this does not affect the value of the procedure. Thus, Fechner concludes, interior sensation is measured by an exterior instrument.

Here, however, a difficulty arises. What is thus measured is not an isolated sensation, but their variations or relations. For instance, it is known that vision in moonlight is *less* than at full day, and one aims to determine the difference. Now,

---

[1] A. LALANDE, *op. cit.*, under " Parallelism "; see also *Zend-Avesta*, Book III, Ch. XIX. One often confuses this hypothesis with Taine's epiphenomenalism (see n. 494, above); in the latter view, however, the two series are not parallel, for the series of conscious facts admits of interruptions.

[2] See above, n. 352 and n. 362.

it does not suffice to compare the stimuli, for numerous facts show that sensation is neither increased nor diminished in the same rhythm as the stimulus. If one adds ten lamps to a light of ten lamps equal in intensity, the sensation of vision is not twice as strong. These facts impressed Weber, who embodied them in the law cited above. Accordingly, in order to introduce measurement into conscious facts, the first task of psychophysics was to determine, with mathematical precision, the relation between the increase of sensation and that of the stimulus.

Fechner at first set up three methods of experimentation [1] in order to measure the differences of intensity of sensations. 1) *The method of the smallest perceptible differences;* one looks for the smallest measure which must be added to other measures so that the difference of pressure will be perceptible. 2) *The method of true and false cases;* given a number of experiences to distinguish, for example, the difference of two weights, one looks for the relationship of right or erroneous weights : if seventy over a hundred would be right, one then looks for another weight and the difference that would have to be added to get the same relationship of 70/100. 3) *The method of erroneous means*, according to which one begins with a precise weight (as 10 grams), and seeks to determine by sensation the most different weight which would seem equal. Then, after quite a number of attempts, one divides the number of errors by the number of experiments, and obtains the mean error, which serves as the standard, as in the second method.

In applying these methods by long and patient research, Fechner was prepared to give Weber's law its mathematical formulation. He began by establishing this exactitude : in order that the sensation increase for the slightest perceptible difference, the increase of the stimulus must be, for muscular effort, as 1/17; for touch, temperature and sound, as 1/3; for light, as 1/100. Then, having determined the *threshold of excitation* for each sense, he set up two series of progressions; one was for the stimuli, the other for the sensations. The progress of the stimulus was clearly measured and resulted, as has just been shown, in a constant relation. It is sufficient to suppose that each perceptible increase of sensation represents a *unity always equal* (a hypothesis suggested by the constancy of the relation between the increase and the stimulus), in

---

[1] See E. Boring, *A History of Experimental Psychology*, pp. 284-285.

order to obtain two progressive series which can be mathematically compared. In submitting the two series thus constituted to the rules of algebraic and integral calculus [1], Fechner showed that " the stimulus must increase following a geometric progression (as that of 1, 2, 4, 8... or 1, 3, 9...) in order that the sensation increase following an arithmetic progression (as that of 1, 2, 3, 4...). This yields the celebrated formula of the psychophysical law : sensation increases as the logarithm of the stimulus [2].

Fechner's work stimulated a lively interest and occasioned numerous controversies among psychologists. Some, with Wundt, saw in it the first step towards a truly scientific psychology. Others, as Hering, Delbœuf, and others, brought forth various objections. The most serious was the application of calculation to conscious facts. This application was based on the hypothesis that all perceptible increases of sensations have an equal quantitative value; this allowed the formation of two series, stimuli and sensations, numerically comparable. In order that this comparison be legitimate, each series had to have its own unit of measurement; and just as one ordered the various sound stimuli by the number of vibrations, one could order various auditory sensations by repeating the same unit of auditory sensation previously determined. The hypothesis of Fechner supposes, despite everything, that sensation is directly measurable, though this is impossible. Sensation, in itself, is a pure, vital quality whose variations are witnessed to by consciousness without their being capable of mathematical measurement. The two series have a mutual dependence, and Weber's law retains its value; but one can hardly accept the purely mathematical formula of Fechner.

3. However, Fechner's example stirred a great movement of experimental research which aimed at scientific and even at mathematical precision in the solution of psychological problems. Two of these will be mentioned here : that of the duration of psychic states, and that of the perception of space.

The fact of consciousness is a complex " totality " whose various aspects must be analyzed by scientific method in order to submit them, if possible, to measurement. One of these aspects most accessible to measurement is that of *time*. When HELMHOLTZ (1821-1894) had determined, in 1850, the time necessary for a nervous influx to be propagated, it became possible to isolate the psychical fact quite closely in order to study its duration. For instance, in requiring of a subject that he respond with his arm when he receives an electrical stimulus at his foot, it is sufficient to record the two extremities of the experience and to deduce from the time elapsed the duration of nervous influx. One then has the exact duration of an act of consciousness inserted

[1] See T. Ribot, *op. cit.*, pp. 185-187.
[2] See E. Boring, *A History of Experimental Psychology*, pp. 274-286.

between the excitation and the response. About 1871, DONDERS was quite successful in this line of research for the most simple actions, those of visual and auditory sensations. These studies were continued by HELMHOLTZ, MACH, VIERORDT, BAXT and EXNER in a memoir entitled, " Experimental Research on the most simple Psychic Processes "[1] (1873). A few years later, WUNDT at Leipzig and BUCCOLA at Milan, studied the duration of more complex actions, as associations, judgments, volitions, choice, and so forth.

The problem of the *perception of space* was studied with less care than emotion. Psychologists separated into two opposed camps. The *nativists*, as JEAN MÜLLER and WEBER endowed man with a natural intuitive power of seizing the notion of space of three dimensions by touch, and at least surface extension by sight [2]. In this group also were TOURTUAL (1827), VOLKMANN (1836), DONDERS and NAGEL, who defended the *hypothesis of projection* [3]. PANUM and HERING even granted to sight the immediate intuition of three dimensions. — Opposing this view was the *empiricist* notion held that every sensation is qualitative and that experience alone explains the origin of the notion of space (from which it also derives the name of *geneticism*). Helmholtz defended this position in various works. Using his theory of local signs, he proposed that one first acquires the idea of exteriority, for these signs appear as effects requiring a cause outside of us; then, by associating visual, muscular, and tactual sensations, one slowly determines, with the help of habit and education of the senses, the precise localizations of perceptions. Finally, STUMPF, in a work entitled *On the Psychological Origin of the Notion of Space* (1873), summarizing these various theories, harmonizes them by the principle that " the notion of space is based on direct sensation with regard to its elements, and on association with regard to its development "[4]. This is quite correct, as has been pointed out [5], and it is to the credit of the empiricists that they gave evidence for this fact.

D) **William Wundt** [6] (1832-1920).

507. Wundt, a professor at the University of Leipzig, outreached the particular research of Fechner. He is allied

---

[1] T. RIBOT, *op. cit.*, p. 308.

[2] This group concentrated its attention on touch and sight.

[3] " It consists in admitting that the retina has the innate power of transporting its impressions outwardly in a determined direction, which is that of the lines of direction or the lines of vision " (T. RIBOT, *op. cit.*, p. 121).

[4] *Ibid.*, p. 126. — [5] See above, n. 377.

[6] **Works :** *Elements of Folk Psychology* (tr. E. L. Schaub), New York, 1916. — *Facts of the Moral Life*, 3 vols., New York, 1901. — *Human and Animal Psychology*, New York, n. d. — *Introduction to Psychology* (tr. R. Pintner), New York, 1912. — *Outlines of Psychology*, 3rd ed., New York, 1917. — *Principles of Physiological Psychology* (tr. E. B. Titchener), vol. 1, New York, 1902. — *Logik*, 4th ed., Münster, 1919-21. — *System der Philosophie*, 4th ed., Münster, 1919.

Studies : BORING, E., *A History of Experimental Psychology*, New York, 1929, pp. 310-344. — NEF, W., *Die Philosophie W. Wundts*, Leipzig, 1923.

to him in thought, however, by maintaining the positivistic viewpoint and in giving a choice position to psychological problems.

1) **Fundamental Principle.** According to Wundt, *philosophy is an effort at interpreting the authentic facts of experience by explaining and unifying them through the principle of sufficient reason.*

In order to establish this principle, Wundt indicates 1) what is authentically given in experience; 2) the nature and value of the principle of sufficient reason; 3) the results of its application.

1. **The Authentic Materials of Experience.** The fact of primitive consciousness is the authentic material. It is not a static representation or an objective idea, but at first only a vital event whose primordial element is the *subjective aspect;* the consciousness of the self as sensing. The objective image, though more apparent, is but a secondary aspect. Thus, what is primarily given is the synthesis of subject and object, of action and " passion ". The work of *understanding*, which must explain experience by its concepts, is to separate these two aspects by abstraction. This done, it will have distinguished psychology, as the study of the subjective and active aspect from the other sciences, which study the various objective aspects. Unification is the work of metaphysical reason aided by the principle of sufficient reason.

This distinction of understanding *(Verstand)* and reason *(Vernunft)* harks back to Kant. Wundt, however, rejects idealism and asserts that every concept or elaborated idea attains external reality. While understanding constructs the positive sciences within the limits of experience, reason looks for the final and total unification of facts by going beyond experience with the help of the principle of sufficient reason.

2. **Meaning and Value of the Principle of Sufficient Reason.** This principle is the expression of the law of unity governing all scientific research. It states that all the parts of human knowledge, in order to be fully intelligible, must be bound to each other so as to constitute a totality exempted from contradictions.

Since this effort at unification is universal, it must surpass experience (which is particular). This can occur in one of two ways. First, one may give as sufficient reason a phenomenon of the same order, and by following a series towards infinity; here the cause is again real and observable, and transcendence is had only in the infinity of the series. — Secondly, one may attain an explanation of another order, qualitatively different, which supposedly is incapable of direct observation. Here the transcendence is that of an imaginary object and results only in pure hypothesis.

The latter hypotheses, however, are legitimate and have a scientific value in the measure that they are based on experience and are content to explain experience. This is positivistic metaphysics [1].

3. **Applications.** With the principle of sufficient reason, one has to explain and unify the authentic materials of consciousness under two aspects.

a) Taken *subjectively*, the fact of consciousness is characterized by *activity* and that which is best expressive of activity, appetition or volition. The sufficient and unifying reason will then be a profound, primitive volition. In order that this volition synthesize all conscious acts, it must be conceived as a voluntariness, empty and without any determined object.

b) Since the fact of consciousness, taken *objectively*, is characterized by *passivity* and variety, the exterior object will be active and multiple. The sufficient reason for these objects, accordingly, will be a totality of volitive unities.

In Wundt's view, this volition (and here Wundt is faithful to the positivistic principle) is a purely phenomenal activity. It does not require a substantial subject [2]; in this way his theory is opposed to the monadology of Leibniz and Herbart.

Accordingly, everything is explicable by but one reality, voluntary activity. Even intellectual life is explained in this way, since it is the action on the soul of external " volitive unities " transformed into representation.

But to satisfy man's need for unity, as expressed in the principle of sufficient reason, there is still a plurality which must be explained : the plurality of individual souls. Experience, which shows us a hierarchy of wills in society (the family, tribe, corporation, nation), must be completed by the transcendental application of sufficient reason. This is done by conceiving of a *spiritual totality* [3], or an ideal humanity in which all particular wills will be united in the pursuit of their goal. This totality must serve as the end and the rule for individuals, and also be the basis of morality.

---

[1] See above, n. 472, for the second essential principle of positivism.

[2] Wundt calls his doctrine the *theory of actuality* in opposition to ancient psychology, or the *theory of substantiality*. In his view, substances do not fall under the immediate seizure of consciousness, and the psychologist should neither affirm nor deny them. Psychology is a science of *immediate experience*, and " metaphysical hypotheses " are estranged from its consideration. It can be seen that Wundt's theory is but a restatement of *phenomenalism*.

[3] This is the source of Durkheim's *social realism;* see below, n. 523.

But this humanity itself remains limited in space and in time. Thus, it cannot be the sufficient reason of our will, which has an infinite capacity. Humanity requires completion by the idea of a perfect and infinite God on Whom it is necessarily dependent.

2) The Positivistic Psychology of Wundt.

508. It should not be forgotten that this metaphysics has only the value of an hypothesis for Wundt, even though it is quite legitimate as explaining and fully unifying the facts. But what must be considered as definitive and scientific is the positivistic thesis : the multiple facts constituting reality are diverse forms of a volition subsumed by experience, or, of the sensible order, and that our various psychological functions, including judgment and reasoning, are but a fuller development of sensation.

I.   **Physiological Psychology.**   Faithful to the spirit of Herbart and Fechner, Wundt believes that psychology can become scientific only by the use of experimentation. The latter must be accompanied by *measurement*. " To measure and to weigh — these are the great means of experimental research whose usage leads to precise laws " [1]. Measurement helps find the *constants* in nature, or the fixed laws which rule phenomena. Its results must be given in numbers, which alone can reveal law. Wundt is thus a convinced partisan of psychophysics. He defended Fechner's logarithmic law, believing that the psychical fact is truly, though indirectly, subject to measurement by its effect. But, in enlarging the quite narrow domain of psychophysics, he attempted to measure not merely sensations by their stimuli, but all phenomena by their *physiological correspondents*.

The soul can be looked upon as a " spiritual organization " which is but the " living body itself ". In virtue of this hypothesis, which is psychophysical parallelism [2], the group of experiential facts which constitute man have, by their unique mode of reality, a twofold aspect. One aspect, internal, is the conscious fact; the other, external, is the physiological function, and especially that of the nervous system. Since the latter domain is increasingly subject to experimentation and measure, it becomes possible to set up a science of the

---

[1] T. RIBOT, *op. cit.*, p. 223.
[2] See above, n. 506, 2; see also D. J. MERCIER, *The Origins of Contemporary Psychology*, pp. 160-215.

soul which Wundt called *physiological psychology*. With this aim in mind, he founded a *laboratory of psychology* at Leipzig. Among his researches there, he especially studied psychometry, showing that the reaction time of a given stimulus varies with one's interior state (attention, distraction, emotion). Besides many detailed results, he established many laws on knowledge and feeling.

2. **Knowledge.** In the study of sensation, Wundt emphasizes physiological conditions and especially examines [1] the theory of specific nerve energy and the localization of perceptions.

Many thinkers, among them J. Müller in his *Manual of Physiology*, taught that the diversity of sensible qualities (color, sound, heat, and so on) is not the result of the difference of stimulus but is due to the physiological nature of the stimulated nerve. Now, since these authors give the external organs the role of merely recording, and since the conducting nerve was universally considered as a simple transmitter, this theory of " specific nerve energy " granted the special power of transformation [2] to each cerebral center. Wundt criticized this doctrine. He showed that there are reasons for extending the functional indifference granted to other nerves to the brain itself, and he preferred to explain the various qualities sensed by the diverse aspects of the stimuli. He admitted, though, that the brain or consciousness played an active part, for the stimuli ordinarily are vibrations transmitted to us under the form of sensible qualities.

This part of the activity is most apparent in the localization of objects outside of ourselves. Wundt defended a middle solution. In his view, experience gives to the senses the *elements* of localization, and these he explains by the local signs of Lotze. " Each point of the skin (for touch) and each point of the retina (for sight) possesses its own local sign, its proper and particular manner of sensing impressions; this is what produces a beginning of localization. — Moreover, these various impressions are accompanied by movements and, consequently, by a certain feeling of innervation, which varies with the member and the affected place " [3]. These, then, are the two elements given by experience. But the cerebral center in which they are transmitted possesses the innate power of uniting them into a *psychical synthesis* and of thus constructing an arrangement of sensations in space. This arrangement, imperfect at first, is made more precise by education and habit.

The more complex psychological forms are derived from simple perceptions. At first, " general notions " and " concepts " arise;

---

[1] According to the nature of the stimulus, the senses are classed into mechanical and chemical; sight is placed in the mechanical.

[2] Müller recalls the proof of the " inadequate stimulus "; if one directly applies an electric current to the optic nerve and then to the auditory nerve, the same stimulus is at first transmitted as a blink of light and then as a sound. But experience can interpret this as a case of hallucination.

[3] T. RIBOT, *op. cit.*, pp. 234-35.

these two are quite distinct. General notions are formed by the repetition of similar sensations; the analogous parts impress themselves most strongly on the brain and, by the law of habit, acquire a powerful force of reproduction. This accounts for schematic notions, which are a simple resume of particular, multiple perceptions. But the concept is something more : it expresses the *law* of phenomena and pertains to scientific knowledge. It is, consequently, not resolvable into precise experience. In the sensible order its only substitute is the *word*. Of such a sort is the concept of sufficient reason, which unifies all knowledge. Briefly, it is a *postulate*, the fruit of the activity of our consciousness.

In order to explain the stages of knowledge, Wundt presented two different theories. He taught, at first, that *reasoning* is man's basic activity; its various forms are arranged serially from sensation up to scientific demonstrations. For, in the hypothesis of psycho-physical parallelism, one can define reasoning as the series of cerebral impressions joined by psychological laws; the judgments associated in induction or in the syllogism are but conscious reflections of these impressions. Sometimes, however, the premisses remain in the unconscious, and we have a case of pure sensation; sometimes they are conscious facts, and we have a case of reasoning.

In the second edition of his work on physiological psychology, he recognized that the hypothesis of unconscious reasoning went beyond facts. In order to explain the origin and the evolution of our knowledge, he believed it sufficient to have recourse to *apperception*. The latter is a *sui generis* psychical act, accompanied by a feeling of tension, and producing a very great distinction in our representations. Quite similar to attention, it is also looked upon as active or passive, depending on whether it is exercised under a powerful impression or under our personal effort in an attempt to clarify a point in our state of complex consciousness. It is, accordingly, an expression of the spontaneity of the self; it is another name for " will " or the very reality of all our conscious facts. Thus, apperception unifies all theories of experimental psychology; it is exercised in the psychical synthesis of sensations; it constructs the concept-postulates; it is deployed in scientific reasoning; it is the explanation of feeling.

3. **Feeling.** In its most simple form, feeling is attached to most sensations in which one distinguishes, beyond the specific quality and the measured intensity of the stimulus, a subjective aspect of pleasure or pain, which is its *affective tone* or feeling. Despite this subjective aspect, which seems to make it passive, feeling is the true source of external activities called " facts of the will ". To describe what we experience in the state of pleasure or of pain, the best procedure would be to call pleasure an aspiration or a tendency towards an object, and pain, a repugnance or a repulsion from the object. Between these two opposed poles, feeling is spontaneously moved by passing from a state of *neutral* sensation, so that its intensity depends both on the force of the stimulus and on the dispositions of the subject. All of these characteristics are explained by defining them as " the mode

of reaction exercised by the activity of apperception against the sensorial stimulus " [1].

Just as simple sensations are developed by judgments and reasonings in order to attain scientific *ideas*, so sentiments evolve towards that which is called an *ideal*, whose two main types are the object of esthetics and morality. But while the intellectual development is conscious, that which creates the ideal remains entirely unconscious. This gives obscurity and indecision to the ideal, which, for these reasons, is called " infinite ". The task of the thinker is to refer the ideal to a scientific idea by explaining its content and the stages of its formation. In the esthetic order, this work amounts to giving the rules of the beautiful founded on the mathematical relations of the elements employed in the arts, as the relations of lines in architecture, sonorous vibrations in music, and so forth.

In *morality* the method of reducing an ideal to an idea does not consist, Wundt thinks, in analyzing the actual conscience of civilized, adult man. This latter doubtlessly is his rule of life, but it is an *effect;* in order to explain it one must study people and their morals, especially among the primitives in order to get back to the formation of morality in its origins. Ethnology is the study competent for this, and Wundt contributed much to it. The conclusion of his search is that " the conscience of peoples, as that of individuals, in all the periods of its development calls every act moral which is useful to the agent himself or to others, so that he and they could live conformably to their proper nature and exercise their faculties " [2]. Wundt thus falls into a utilitarianism tainted with evolutionism, quite similar to that of Spencer and John Stuart Mill [3]. At the beginning of humanity, when physical force alone was dominant, people followed the morality of conquest; with the progress of civilization, society organized itself and the good finally began to lie in working for the common utility.

Voluntary activity, under its form of apperception, constitutes the great portion of psychological facts; as such, it brings up the difficult question of human *liberty*. Wundt does not deny that we are conscious of having the power of acting without external or internal constraint. But he does not believe it follows that this free action is without a cause. The laws which govern marriages, suicides and other social facts which are highly voluntary, show that all these actions are subjected to causes. But while the sociologist retains only general influences in stating his laws, the psychologist finds in each individual decision the intervention of a personal, decisive factor. This factor is *character*. It is the sole, immediate cause of voluntary activity, motives having but

---

[1] T. RIBOT, *op. cit.*, p. 268.

[2] Imbued with the positivistic prejudice, Wundt interprets revealed religions in a rationalistic way, considering *Jahweh* as a simple god of the Jews and holding that the cult of Catholic saints is similar to the cult of pagan gods. See his *Menschen und Thierseele*, II, 37 and 41; see also T. RIBOT, *op. cit.*, pp. 272-281.

[3] See above, n. 481 and n. 489.

a mediate influence. But " between the motives and the causality of character there is this great difference that motives are either conscious or can easily become conscious, whereas character always remains *absolutely unconscious*. This personal fact thus remains as a dark point in the brilliant light of the causes " [1]. One can, in the meantime, attempt to explain character. It is either an original creation in each man, or the result of preceding generations [2]. The problem of liberty is thus reduced to that of psychological heredity.

4. **Folk-Psychology.** Through this last view, Wundt's doctrine is close to a study which also suggests the notion of moral feeling, that of the *psychology of peoples* or genetic psychology. In this domain, he had for precursors the disciples of Herbart, especially THEODOR WAITZ (1821-1864), who wrote *The Anthropology of People in the State of Nature*. In this work he shows, experimentally, that men are specifically distinguished from other animals, and that the various races do not break the unity of their species. LAZARUS, STEINTHAL, DELBRÜCK, COHEN and others, the founders (1860) and collaborators of *Zeitschrift für Völker Psychologie und Sprachwissenschaft*, defended the existence in each people of a " Folk-Spirit " or a sort of " objective spirit " expressive of social life. This spirit was supported by the ordinary individual and was cut off from geniuses as well as from backward individuals or children.

Wundt also wrote a work on Folk-Psychology, in which he treats of the great permanent classes manifestative of collective life, as language, art, myths and religion, society, law and civilization [3]. The aim of this science, for Wundt, lies in describing the formation of conscious life, from the most primitive to the most civilized epoch. It constitutes a true synthesis of all the positivistic sciences dealing with mankind.

CONCLUSION. Wundt, like Spencer, Mill and Taine, is a novel example of the unsuppressible tendency of reason to evade the pure phenomenon in which it is imprisoned by the positivistic prejudice. Explicitly, he recognized only the fundamental *fact* of volition as something legitimately given in the sciences, but he discovered a profundity and a richness in this activity which is strongly reminiscent of the substantial self. Besides, the decisive intervention of character in the free act can be interpreted in a sense that is close to the Thomistic solution of liberty; the latter holds that it lies in the domination of the spiritual soul over all finite goods. The theory of the concept-postulate gives evidence as to how the spiritual fact of thought imposes itself with evidence

---

[1] See T. RIBOT, *op. cit.*, p. 295.
[2] The first explanation falls with the theory of the fixity of species; the second, with that of evolution.
[3] E. BRÉHIER, *op. cit.*, Vol. II, p. 953.

to all sincere introspective activity. That which Wundt calls a postulate is but the power of reason to grasp things under the aspect of being or intelligible essence. These evasive attempts towards the absolute are but forerunners of the great revolt of pragmatism, and Wundt also announces its coming through his voluntarism. His doctrine, however, still falls under the psychological current of open positivism.

IV. FRANCE : THE DYNAMIST SCHOOL. (RIBOT).

(1839-1916).

SPECIAL BIBLIOGRAPHY.

1o **Works :** *Maladies de la Mémoire*, Paris, 1881. — *Evolution des idées générales*, Paris, 1897. — *La logique des sentiments*, Paris, 1905. — *Problèmes de psychologie affective*, Paris, 1910. — *La Vie Inconsciente et les mouvements*, Paris, 1914. — *Diseases of Personality* (tr. P. W. Shedd), New York, 1909. — *Diseases of the Will* (tr. Snell, M. and Marie), Chicago, 1894. — *Heredity*, New York, 1895. — *Psychology of the Emotions*, New York, n. d. — *Psychology of Attention*, New York, 1946. — *English Psychology*, New York, nd. — *German Psychology of Today*, New York, nd. — *Essay on the Creative Imagination*, Chicago, 1912.

2o **Studies :** BENRUBI, I., *Contemporary Thought of France*, New York, 1926. — DWELSHAUVERS, G., *La psychologie française contemporaine*, Paris, 1920. — GUNN, J. A., *Modern French Philosophy*, New York, 1922. — LEVY-BRUHL, L., *History of Modern Philosophy in France*, Chicago, 1899. — PARODI, D., *La philosophie contemporaine en France*, Paris, 1919.

509. In adopting the mathematical point of view, German psychology tended to construct psychology into an objective science, independent of individuality. In contrast, the French psychologists emphasized the individual life or what came to be called the *personal equation;* the laws of this psychology did not express measured relationships but the quality and the order of conscious facts. Theodule Ribot was the founder of this school, and many psychologists grouped themselves around him. Among them, one man is prominent as a most metaphysical philosopher, even though his basic principle was psychological; this man was A. Fouillée.

A. **Theodule Ribot** (1839-1916) unreservedly adopted the positivistic psychology of John Stuart Mill and of Taine, and thus continued the reaction against eclecticism. After he had completed his studies in medicine, which furnished him with many experimental facts, he took a professorship at the College of France in 1889. Prior to this time, in 1886, he founded the magazine, *Revue Philosophique*.

Ribot's *general position* can be stated as follows :

Psychology is a positivistic science whose object is the conscious fact studied in its individuality by the experimental method, in order to establish a system of dynamic laws.

Three elements of this proposition will be explained : the object, the method and the laws.

1) **The object** to be studied is the fact of concrete consciousness; it is not the soul and its faculties considered in themselves separately from the facts, which was the practice of the eclectics. Loyal to his positivistic prejudice, Ribot rejects as anti-scientific any so-called " supernatural " explanation which surpasses experience, as that of substance, a spiritual soul, or God.

At the same time, he was strongly opposed to the mathematical and to the associationist school by taking the fact of consciousness in its individuality, and not as a composite whose elements (simple facts of consciousness) were to be re-discovered and studied. He replaced mental atomism by *dynamism*.

2) **The method** employed was to be an harmonious union of three procedures : the subjective, the objective and the experimental.

a) The subjective method is that of introspection, the witness of consciousness of our interior life. At first, in an exaggerated reaction against eclecticism, Ribot had fully condemned and excluded this method. In 1908, he recognized its utility if it were tempered by the two other methods, both of which were more positive.

b) The objective method is the observation of psychological facts in other men. It is made up of oral and written investigations, the former being more restrained but more certain; it includes the reading of autobiographies or similar writings, and the use of *tests*. The latter are prepared and graduated exercises (for instance, a series of easy questions for a five year old child, and more difficult questions for older groups) which aim to determine the capacities and circumstances of psychological activity.

c) The experimental method consists in provoking psychological states in order to verify an hypothesis. The psycho-physical and psycho-physiological experiences studied in the German laboratories are an application of this method. But Ribot thought these experiences involved too much calculation with too little results, and preferred pathological experiences instead. These were obtained by considering the phenomena produced in mental illness, or by stimulating them through hypnosis.

3) **The laws.** Ribot's studies led him to three main conclusions; the latter also serve to mark off three periods of his life.

The first period is mainly *combative.* In refuting his opponents, Ribot established the following view. Inasmuch as psychological facts are of the sensible order and endowed with vital spontaneity, they are not referable to a self and to immutable faculties (in the eclectic sense), but they follow biological and dynamic laws.

This view can be found in his works, *Psychologie anglaise contemporaine* and *Psychologie allemande contemporaine,* but more especially in his work, *L'Hérédité.* The latter writing shows the dependence of conscious life on material conditions, which, in Ribot's view, are opposed to spirituality and lead us to explain everything by physiological laws. He thus favors the hypothesis of *psychophysical parallelism.* He writes that " Physiology has shown through observations and repeated experiences that every psychic state is invariably associated with a nervous state whose reflex act is of the most simple type. This principle is incontestable for most cases, and probable to a high degree for others ". In this fashion, psychology, losing its interest in the soul, becomes " the study of two phenomena which are in such constant connection that it would be most exact to call them a phenomenon with a double face " [1].

The second period is *constructive.* Going beyond the superficial analysis of association of ideas, Ribot established that mental life develops through superimposed levels of consciousness from the unconscious, which is of the psychological order, up to thought, which is a representative fact; the latter is not the basis, but the crown of life. Taken in this meaning, the profound principle of unity explaining the person must be sought in the organism rather than in consciousness. These levels of consciousness are entwined in a stable order,

---

[1] T. Ribot, *La Psychologie allemande contemporaine,* Introduction, p. ix and p. xi.

so that the law of regression — when a sickness destroys psychological life — is exactly the inverse of the law of acquisition; for example, the memories of childhood are acquired first, and disappear last.

This second proposition is proved by studies on the illnesses of memory, of the will, of personality, and studies on attention. Observation shows, for the most part, the persistence of the most material and simple facts, and the instability of the most complex and intellectual states. Observation also shows the importance of motor elements for grasping and retaining an impression, for regulating its evolution, or for the best retention and reproduction of an impression. The function of the word as a motor element retentive of the idea illustrates this view.

The third period is devoted to the study of affective psychology. Here, too, Ribot arrived at his own conclusions.

Ribot maintained that the affective state is a primordial one of consciousness. It evolves according to a law of successive enrichment, going from the simple to the composed and concluding with the representative fact. The affective state, however, does not surpass the sensible order of things. Ribot tried to prove these views by seeking to establish the origin, development and goal of affective states through a factual analysis.

a) The *origin* of primitive appetition lies in a group of unconscious movements and tendencies due to physiological reactions, which constitutes the basis of the various temperaments.

b) Thus, in Ribot's [1] view, emotion is a fortified tendency which begins before consciousness; it awakens consciousness by fixing attention on the object. This explains the function of sentiment or feeling in the evolution and association of ideas. Moreover, sentiments and emotions have their own logic, differing from abstract logic; this logic is not governed by objective truth, but is wholly subordinated to subjective interest.

c) At the peak of conscious life, intelligence transforms the image which is impregnated with emotion into schematisms and clear words which are stabilized and capable of combining

---

[1] This theory on the physiological origin of emotions is also that of William James and C. Lange; see below, n. 526.

themselves according to their own laws. Ribot held that there are no ideas without images, and explained ideas as the *substitution* of a most simple sign (word or concept) for a most concrete image [1]. His positivism, however, kept him from admitting a soul or a spiritual faculty.

Ribot's works are full of correct and meaningful observations on mental life, but his interpretation of these facts is often falsified by arbitrary restrictions arising from his positivistic viewpoint. He was unaware of the precise distinction between three degrees of tendency which St. Thomas Aquinas had clarified : a natural appetite, independent of knowledge and preceding consciousness; a sensible appetite or " passion " (emotion), which follows sensible knowledge; an intellectual appetite, or the will, which depends on the judgment of reason and is the seat of liberty in man.

Ribot could have restrained his views to experimental psychology, which he helped to set up as a true, special science. But he should have recognized the scientific value of conclusions on the spirituality of man's higher activities, as well as on the nature and destiny of the human soul.

B. The Paris School. 510. Inspired by Ribot's influence, a group of psychologists became associated in Paris and applied his method to various domains.

1) **Alfred Binet** [2] (1857-1911) specialized in the use of the objective method, giving particular attention to psychological tests. His work led him to establish the law of independence of thought from an image in the strict sense, though not from all sensation : it is often sufficient to have a quick or a vague sign to awaken a precise thought. Binet also established some conclusions useful to pedagogy in his research on the psychology of children.

2) **Pierre Janet** [3] continued the application of the pathological method. He held that it is value which constitutes personality.

---

[1] See above, n. 494, Taine's theory of substitution.

[2] **Works :** *Les Altérations de la personnalité*, Paris, 1892. — *La psychologie des grands calculateurs et joueurs d'échecs*, Paris, 1894. — *La Suggestibilité*, Paris, 1900. — *L'Étude expérimentale de l'intelligence*, Paris, 1903. — *L'âme et le corps*, Paris, 1905. — *Les Révélations de l'écriture*, Paris, 1906. — *Les idées modernes sur les enfants*, Paris, n. d. — *On Double Consciousness*, Chicago, 1890, — **Study :** E. J. Varon, *Development of Alfred Binet's Psychology*, Columbus (O), 1935.

[3] **Works :** *L'Automatisme psychologique*, Paris, 1889. — *L'état mental des hystériques*, Paris, 1894. — *Névroses et idées fixes*, Paris, 1898. — *Les obsessions et les psychasténies*, Paris, 1903. — *De l'angoisse à l'extase*, t. 1 : *Un délire religieux; La Croyance;* t. 11 : *Les sentiments fondamentaux*, Paris, 1926-28. — *Major Symptoms of Hysteria*, New York, n. d. — *Principles of Psychotherapy* (tr. Guthrie, H. M. and E. R.), New York, 1924. — *Psychological Healing* (tr. Paul, E. and C.), 2 vols., New York, 1925. — **Study :** E. Mayo, *Psychology of Pierre Janet*, London, 1952.

By this he meant the power of synthesis which unifies the numerous and varied facts of consciousness, making the person capable of submitting to exterior influences and of acting on others. He held that two common traits can be found in the multiplicity of mental troubles (in obsessions, compulsions, phobias, manias and so forth) : the first is the feeling of *incompletion*, which stems from the weakening of the power of synthesis; the second is the *lack of adaptation to reality*, which is due to a diminution of the active power of personality.

These observations are quite exact. Janet, however, used this view to explain certain pathological states which he called " ecstasy "; he made these similar to the ecstasies of the saints, holding that the only difference lay in the fact that mental illnesses did not have the same philosophy or religion as ecstasies. Ecstasy is the effect of *introversion*, which makes all activity retire from exteriority to be carried on in an interior, imaginary world which is better and more adapted to the real world. This causes a sentiment of happiness, of triumphant liberty and of the love of inactivity. It is, of course, easy to see how true mystics surpass these naturalistic explanations [1].

3) **Paulhan** [2] continued the study of affective states which Ribot had begun. He held to an unconscious sentiment as the basis of psychological life; its predominant tendency founded the *character* of each man. He explained consciousness by the struggle of the diverse tendencies which seek to realize themselves. He referred the laws of association of ideas not to objective representations, but to relations of affective agreement or exclusion lying deeply in personality.

4) Two Austrian psychologists can be included under the Paris school. FRANZ BRENTANO (1838-1917) is the first; he founded a school of dynamist psychology at Vienna. Sigmund FREUD [3] (1856-1939) founded a school of *psychoanalysis* at Vienna, and specialized in the study of the subconscious. Freud formulated a rather arbitrary systematization which tried to explain all psychological life by the suppression of a lower desire called *libido*. Freud did much experimentation with the laws of dreams and reveries; in these states, he held, man's profoundest desires — often unconscious and held in check by conscious life — are liberated, and often have meaning.

---

[1] See H. BERGSON, *Les deux sources de la morale et de la religion*, p. 244, for a decisive refutation of this assimilation of ecstasy to a disease. Also, see below, n. 550.

[2] **Work** : *Laws of Feeling*, (tr. C. K. Ogden), New York, 1930.

[3] **Works** : *Standard Edition of the Complete Psychological Works* (ed. J. Strachey), 24 vols., New York, 1953. — **Studies :** BAKER, R. M., *Sigmund Freud*, New York, 1952. — DALBIEZ, R., *Psychoanalytic Method and the Doctrine of Freud*, 2 vols., New York, 1941. — PUNER, H. W., *Freud, His Life and Mind*, New York, 1948. — VANDERVELDT, J. H., and ODENWALD, R. P., *Psychiatry and Catholicism*, New York, 1952. — WITTELS, F., *Freud and His Times*, New York, 1948.

Alfred Fouillée [1] (1838-1912). **511.** Though he does not strictly belong to Ribot's school of thought, Fouillée's views are not completely estranged from those of Ribot. By his theory of *idea-forces* he referred everything to psychology; like Ribot, he was inspired by Spencer, whom he wished to complete by reducing to perfect unity the basic difference that Spencer had left between the physical and psychological worlds, and between the phenomenon and the absolute Unknowable.

Basic Principle : *Each reality is constituted, basically, of the idea-force, whose primitive form is appetition or the mute desire to live; this idea-force develops itself, through evolution, from the subconscious mineral element up to the clear consciousness of intelligence, though without leaving the sensible order.*

By *idea* Fouillée means every fact of consciousness, similar to the " thought " of Descartes; for, every conscious event is accompanied with some representation.

In order to establish this view, Fouillée 1) showed the mark of force that each idea possesses, 2) how it is extended to the universe, and 3) how it absorbs the absolute Unknowable.

1. It is not possible to look upon the idea as being a pure light accidentally added to the fact of consciousness (epiphenomenon) [2], for such a function does not enter at all into the current of life, and would soon be eliminated as useless. Attentive observation shows, instead, that every idea is basically made up of a force or an activity which makes it capable of producing other facts in consciousness. This notion of force is the very trait which characterizes psychological facts and opposes them to the *object* studied by science, in which one measures quantities, movements and their succession, without considering the energy which unites them. At the same time, we can readily and directly observe that every conscious fact is made up of this force.

2. Moreover, it is possible to refer every form of energy, even that which makes up physical realities, to the varieties

---

[1] **Works :** *Philosophie de Platon*, 4 vols., Paris, 1888-89. — *L'Avenir de la métaphysique*, Paris, 1889. — *L'Evolution des Idées-forces*, Paris, 1890. — *La Psychologie des Idées-forces*, Paris, 1893. — *Tempérament et caractère*, Paris, 1895. — *Morale des Idées-forces*, Paris, 1907. — *Esquisse d'une interprétation du monde*, Paris, 1913. — *Modern French Legal Philosophy* (trs. Scott, Mrs. F. W., and Chamberlain, J. P.), New York, 1921.

[2] This theory was widely accepted among the positivist psychologists; it was held by Taine and even by Ribot.

of idea-forces or conscious facts, on the condition of noting
a gradation in consciousness. One can begin with ideas which
have distinct objects, then descend to states of soul which
are appetitions for vague objects, then to simple sensations
of well-being or discomfort and then to a pure desire of being
or of living which one can rediscover spread throughout the
principle of action [1].

3. Having thus unified reality, the idea-force also allows
one to achieve a synthesis by explaining the absolute Unknowable of Spencer. Fouillée, faithful to the positivistic prejudice [2],
considers the absolute to be an illusion that is, however,
explainable by the idea-force, which, in its higher form of
activity, is creative of its object. Thus, the idea of unity and
of desirable harmony in our lives concludes with the affirmation
of a personal self. Similarly, the idea and the desire of God
as the final explanation of all things and as the supreme ideal
of morality leads to the affirmation of His existence.

A systematic view of this sort does not lack grandeur and
is strongly unified, but it is turned towards idealism by referring
every reality to the *idea*. This view is also imprisoned in
positivism by its denial of substance and of an absolute.
In its essential outlook, Fouillée's view is classifiable under
the current of positivistic psychology, whose vigorous research
continues even to our day; it tends, however, to enlarge its
own narrow limits and to be a new orientation towards
contemporary pragmatism.

Conclusion : The Status of Experimental Psychology.

511. I. The psychological current is the most original
aspect of positivism. However, despite the combined efforts
of numerous psychologists, who were patient, persevering,
and often eminent, to detach their " science " from philosophy
and make of it an autonomous science comparable to physics
and astronomy, failure marked all attempts. " Psychology
without a soul " is still in a preliminary stage, and the treatises
on it await the architect who will be capable of erecting them

---

[1] This obscure force at the bottom of the soul seems to designate the natural
appetite. But it lacks, for Fouillée as for Ribot,
the precise distinctions furnished by a sound metaphysics : the essential
distinctions between the various degrees of activity and life, to which correspond
the different kinds of appetite : natural, elicited, and voluntary.

[2] This prejudice asserts that the only object of science is the fact of sensible
observation. See above, n. 471.

into a science. Among the philosophers, one can distinguish those who oppose, and those who favor this sort of psychology.

Among the *opposition*, the most indomitable were the Scholastics, who saw in the new science only the error of phenomenalism which needed refutation. But the recent orientation of Neo-Thomism, more open to modern views, was inaugurated by Cardinal Mercier, and brilliantly continued by the universities of Louvain and Milan, the Catholic Institute of Paris, and others. Their combined efforts slowly turned the opposition into collaboration. The notion of a relatively autonomous subject of experimental psychology gained ground. For many, however, the study of " conscious facts " remained joined to philosophy either by borrowing its unifying propositions from it, or by being either a preparation or a complement to rational psychology.

On the other side, the convinced *partisans* were quite numerous. They were not truly in accord, however, on one point : they could not proclaim the full independence of experimental psychology from so-called " metaphysical " principles, so that it could be elevated to the rank of science like other modern sciences [1]. Various tendencies and divergent views can be distinguished in this group.

a) *The school of introspection* continued the investigations begun by the Cartesians [2], believing, with this latter group, that the best way of being informed on internal phenomena was to observe them in oneself from within. This attitude, however, took two divergent forms. Some, as William James and Henri Bergson, adopted this method more as a reaction against the hope of submitting interior life itself to measurement. They thus placed in relief the personal and dynamic side of consciousness, with a tendency towards metaphysics. — Others proposed to submit introspection to experimental control. They adopted the method of *stimulated introspection*, and worked on various problems with the laboratory method. O. KÜLPE (1862-1915) used this method, as did SIMON, TOULOUSE and PIÉRON, the successors to Binet. DWELSHAUVERS employed it at the Catholic Institute of Paris, and MICHOTTE, DE MONTPELLIER and others at the University of Louvain. The procedure of this group is to gather a large number of facts on some determined subject; statistical method, is then employed in order to establish precise laws. This is somewhat similar to the method of the German mathematical school of psychology.

b) *The school of purely external observation* is the other view. It denies all validity to introspection, and attempts to set up a psychology without a soul and a psychology without consciousness. The main representative of this view is the American, JOHN

---

[1] In other words, they ignored the problem of natures or of the substance of the soul, considered insoluble since the time of Kant, and examined instead the problem of the classifications and laws of psychic phenomena. This position, however, may be used as a *method*.

[2] That is, by men such as Locke, Berkeley, Condillac, Hume, etc.

WATSON, founder of the psychology of behavior, or BEHAVIORISM [1];
under this latter heading we can place H. C. WARREN in America,
and PIÉRON and GUILLAUME in France. Holding out for external
observation alone, these thinkers defined the psychological phenomenon through *behavior*, or as a mode of reaction to an external
stimulant in which there intervene all the functions of an individual.
The influence of a light upon a plant towards which the plant
turns, or upon an eye which is dazzled and closes, is but a simple
reflex; the light produces an object of psychological study if,
for instance, it determines the bee to look for flowers. This method
was first applied to animals [2] and then extended to man. Three
main types of behavior are distinguished : instincts, emotions and
habits. *Thought* is classified under implicit habits. It is internal
behavior, and can be studied by three methods : observing the
reaction of a subject in the presence of every sort of external
stimulus; verbal reactions and responses; the method of tests
used as a measure of intelligence and of professional aptitudes.

Under this view one can classify some similar research, especially
that of the *Objective Psychology* of BECHTEREW [3] and the Russian
school. Their aim is to study the higher mental activities
(association of ideas, reasonings, and so forth), not in themselves,
but in the physiological conditions to which they are joined.
These mental activities are complicated reflexes which are not
the work of nature, but of diverse associations created by instinct,
education, and, in man, by will — which explains their multiplicity
and variety. Classified under this type are the so-called conditioned
reflexes, the study of which is pursued by experimental method.

c) Between these two opposed views there lies a view which
is called *the school of Integral Psychology*. It holds that in order
to set up experimental psychology as a new science, it is necessary
to use all the methods, whether introspective, experimental,
psychophysical or statistical, stressing one or another according to
the needs of the problem under consideration. GEORGES DUMAS
is one of the main representatives; he wrote *Traité de psychologie*,
with the help of the following psychologists : L. LAPICQUE,
H. PIÉRON, PIAGET, C. BLONDEL, É. CLAPARÈDE, P. JANET,
H. DELACROIX, A. MEYER, A. LALANDE, A. OMBREDANE, B. BOUR-
DON, and others. Inasmuch as each of these men retains the freedom
of his own interpretations, the result is a vast assemblage of materials which is not synthesized but is inspired by the same notion :

---

[1] On this subject, see the following : DIEHL, F., *Historical and Critical Study
of Radical Behaviorism as a Philosophical Doctrine*, Baltimore (Md.), 1934. —
KANTOR, J. R., *Psychology and Logic*, 2 vols., Bloomington (Ind.), 1945-50. —
LEARY, D. B., *Modern Psychology, Normal and Abnormal*, Philadelphia (Pa.),
1928. — ROBACK, A. A., *Behaviorism and Psychology*, Cambridge (Mass.), n. d.
— WATSON, J. B., *Behaviorism*, New York, 1925. — WEISS, A. P., *Theoretical
Basis of Human Behavior*, Columbus (O.), 1929.

[2] In this field, it should be mentioned, THORNDIKE applied the test method
to animals, and MAC DOUGALL specialized in the study of instinct.

[3] See his *General Principles of Human Reflexology* (tr. Murphy, E. and M.)
New York, 1933.

the desire of treating psychological problems from the scientific viewpoint.

Various tendencies within the school of Integral Psychology can be noted. Some, as BAUDIN, insist on introspection; his treatise on psychology adopts the classical division of three faculties, intelligence, sensibility and will. — Others show a more marked tendency towards experimentation. Among them are DWELS-HAUVERS, who made a remarkable effort to establish a provisory synthesis. His treatise points out the *main directions* of mental life : its tendency towards synthesis, its aptitude for self-activity and its dynamic personal reaction. He considers these three to be similar to general laws, under which other tendencies are classifiable as applications. The latter are then studied, so that one can ascend from elementary facts of conscious life to the higher structures of thought. A similar tendency is found in CUVILLIER'S *Traité de psychologie*, LINDWORSKY'S *Experimentele Psychologie*, and FROEBES' *Lehrbuch der experimentele Psychologie*, and others.

Others of this group insist on *physiological explanations* which point out the influence of the nervous system on mental life. This group frequently appeals to pathology and to the study of mental illness. Following in the line of Janet and Ribot is DUMAS, who shows a special predilection for all those problems in which the psychical is closely allied to the physical. Towards the close of the nineteenth, and at the beginning of the twentieth century, quite a large number of " physiologists " put their hopes in the methods of hypnotism and suggestion. This work was begun especially by CHARCOT, and continued by RICHET, BERNHEIM [1], AZAM [2], and others, in France. Worthy of mention, here, are the studies on somnambulism by GURNEY [3] and MYERS in England, by HEIDENHAIN in Breslau, and by MORTON PRINCE [4] in the United States. Psychologists, however, gradually began to believe that too great a suggestibility in the subject took away a large part of the scientific value of these experiences.

A final group emphasized the influence of society even on individual psychology. Prominent in this group is C. BLONDEL, in his *Introduction à la psychologie collective*, LEBON, in his *Psychologie des foules*, DELACROIX, and others. This last group is closely allied to the sociological current which will be treated below.

---

[1] **Works :** *De la suggestion dans l'état hypnotique et dans l'état de veille*, Paris 1884. — *Hypnotisme, suggestion, psychothérapie*, Paris, 1891.

[2] Azam described the now classic Felida case (successive redoubling of personality).

[3] See his *Phantasms of the Living*, London, 1888.

[4] A professor at Boston, Morton Prince wrote up the case of Miss Beauchamps, a student at the University, who presented a plurality of personalities, both successive and simultaneous. The psychologists cited above, e. g. Binet, Paulhan, Ribot, and William James, based their hypotheses concerning the variations of personality on these observations. See the following : CASEY, D. M., *La théorie du subconscient de Morton Prince*, Paris, 1945. — ROBACK, A., *History of American Psychology*, New York, 1952.

In Summary, experimental psychology appears as a new conquest proposed to the positivistic spirit : its methods have been sufficiently clarified, research is being done, and materials are being accumulated. A Thomistic philosopher has no objection to this gigantic effort towards the scientific organization of the phenomena of consciousness. He would, however, ask that scientific status also be given to the philosophical propositions on the nature of the soul and its faculties, and their solid foundation for morality. He would encourage the persevering efforts to erect experimental psychology as a true science.

SECTION THREE.
THE SOCIOLOGICAL CURRENT.

SPECIAL BIBLIOGRAPHY.

1º **Works :** BOUGLÉ, J., *Les idées égalitaires*, Paris, 1899. — *Essai sur le régime des castes*, Paris, 1908. — CASTELL, A., and KUYPERS, M. J. S. (eds.), *Selected Readings in Social Criticism from Adam Smith to Karl Marx*, St. Paul (Minn.), 1946. — DAVY, G., *La foi jurée*, Paris, 1922. — *Le Droit, l'Idéalisme et l'Expérience*, Paris, 1923. — DURKHEIM, E., *Education et sociologie*, Paris, 1925. — *Sociologie et philosophie*, Paris, 1925. — *L'éducation morale*, Paris, 1925. — *Elementary Forms of the Religious Life*, (tr. J. W. Swain), Chicago, 1947. — *Division of Labor in Society* (tr. G. Simpson), Chicago, 1947. — *Rules of Sociological Method* (tr. Solovay, S. A., and Mueller, J. H.; ed. by G. E. G. Catlin), Chicago, 1950. — *Suicide, A Study in Sociology* (tr. Spaulding, J. A., and Simpson, G.), Chicago, 1951. — FAUCONNET, A., *La responsabilité*, Paris, 1920. — HALBWACHS, M., *La classe ouvrière et les niveaux de vie*, Paris, 1912. — *Les cadres sociaux de la mémoire*, Paris, 1925. — *Les causes du suicide*, Paris, 1930. — LEVY-BRUHL, L., *La morale et la science des mœurs*, Paris, 1927. — *History of Modern Philosophy in France*, Chicago, 1899. — *How Natives Think* (tr. L. A. Clare), New York, 1926. — *Primitive Mentality* (tr. L. A. Clare), New York, 1923. — *Soul of the Primitive* (tr. L. A. Clare), New York, 1928. — *Primitives and the Supernatural* (tr. L. A. Clare), New York, 1935. — MAUSS, M., *Essai sur la nature et la fonction du sacrifice*, Paris, 1897-98. — *Esquisse d'une théorie générale de la magie*, 1902-03. — SÉMIAND, A., *Le salaire, l'évolution sociale et la monnaie*, 3 vols., Paris, 1932. — SOROKIN, P. A., *Social Dynamics*, 4 vols., New York, 1937-41. — WEBER, M., *Theory of Social and Economic Organization* (tr. Henderson, A. M., and Parsons, T.), Oxford, 1947.

2º **Studies :** ALPERT, H., *Emile Durkheim and his Sociology*, New York, 1939. — DEHOVE, H., *Mélanges sociologiques*, Lille, 1931. — DEPLOIGE, S., *Le conflit de la morale et de la sociologie*,

Paris, 1923. — FURFEY, P. H., *Scope and Method of Sociology*, New York, 1953. — GEHLKE, C. E., *Emile Durkheim's Contributions to Sociological Theory*, New York, 1915. — MIHANOVICH, C. S. (ed.), *Social Theorists*, Milwaukee (Wis.), 1953. — TIMASHEFF, N. S., and FACEY, P. W., *Sociology*, Milwaukee (Wis.), 1949.

512. All the great positivists, as Spencer, Taine and John Stuart Mill, granted a significant place in their syntheses for sociology. Towards the close of the nineteenth century, however, there arose, in France, a school of thought exclusively dedicated to the study of society by positivistic method. This school attempted to establish morality with the help of sociology, and it prolonged and renewed one of the most original points of Comte.

There are a number of men who can be viewed as precursors to the sociological current.

E. RENAN [1] (1823-1892) was a dilettante who had an amateurish taste for every sort of philosophical system. His main influence is as a litterateur and exegete. His works, however, are dominated by two ideas which place him within social positivism. The first is the a priori exclusion of any supernatural influence in the name of science; the second is the predilection for the positivistic historical sciences (paleontology, exegesis, and so forth), which, he believed, were destined to replace all others [2].

GABRIEL TARDE [3] is a unifying link between the psychologists and the sociologists. He made a special study of the psychology of crowds or groups in which he laid emphasis on the function of imitation.

Emile Durkheim (1858-1917). Durkheim was born in Epinal, spent most of his life as a university professor, and is the founder of the Sociological school.

The foundation of the school can definitely be dated to the publication of Durkheim's *Rules of Sociological Method* in 1895, and to 1896, when the periodical *L'Année sociologique* was begun; the latter is a summary of original studies and analyses made by sociologists during each year. Durkheim associated himself with a group of thinkers who had the same

---

[1] **Works :** *Les sciences de la nature et les sciences historiques*, and *L'avenir de la science*, (selections and introduction by I. O. Wade), Princeton (N. J.), 1944. — *La réforme intellectuelle et morale* (ed. P. E. Charvet), Cambridge, 1950.

Studies : LAGRANGE, M. J., *Christ and Renan*, New York, n. d. — LASSERRE, P., *La jeunesse d'E. Renan*, 2 vols., Paris, 1925. — POMMIER, J., *La pensée religieuse de Renan*, Paris, 1925. — *Renan et Strasbourg*, Paris, 1926.

[2] Thus, he exalted the historical sciences, because through them, apparently, he hoped to justify his apostasy.

[3] **Works :** *Les lois de l'imitation*, Paris, 1890. — *La logique sociale*, Paris, 1893. — *L'opposition universelle*, Paris, 1897. — *Les lois sociales*, Paris, 1898.

fundamental principles, the main ones being L. Lévy-Bruhl, Marcel Maus, Henri Hubert, Paul Fauconnet, Bouglé, Simiand, G. Davy and Maurice Halbwachs.

Durkheim's main works are the following : *The Division of Labor in Society*, *The Rules of Sociological Method*, *Suicide*, *Elementary Forms of Religious Life* (dealing with the Totemic system in Australia), *Education and Sociology*, *Sociology and Philosophy*, and *Moral Education*.

Durkheim's writings are similar to various works of other sociologists, as those of the Englishmen, Smith and Spencer, or the Germans, Schaeffle, Wagner, Schmoller, Wundt, and others. The idea of " social realism " was common to all of them. At the same time, their efforts are the final episode of the opposition which continued throughout the nineteenth century against the theory of an individualistic natural law. This effort was begun by Rousseau, and was applied to a radical reform of society in the French Revolution; it was taken up again by Cousin and the eclectic school, but then applied to the defense of the traditional social order. But the scientific minds were a bit demanding, and were not satisfied with a method which pretended to deduce in a priori fashion and only from an analysis of the individual, a whole code of morality and of politics; they opposed this view with the social fact and the affirmation of observable, social, scientific laws.

This reaction was especially strong after the war of 1870. In 1872, Littré founded a " society for sociology " which lasted only two years, but stimulated many interesting studies, especially that of ESPINAS (1844-1922) on " animal societies ".

One can view Durkheim's school as resuscitating and continuing this social view.

Circumstances imposed a double task on the new school. Their first work was to establish sociology as a special positivistic science; up to this time it had been neglected in official teaching, though it was, evidently, necessary for any sound politics. Their second task was to found morality as a positivist science. There are, accordingly, two parts to Durkheim's work, the first being sociology, and the second, morality. These two parts are but two aspects of the same solution, for he believed that he could find the basis for morality in sociology. Both parts of his work can be clarified by presenting an analysis of his basic proposition.

I. Fundamental Proposition.

513. *The study of the activity proper to man, that is, of moral and social life, constitutes a special positivistic science whose* *object is a reality distinct from all others : it is a being " sui generis ".*

This proposition is not a unity, but is subdivided into two independent principles, that of social realism and that of absolute positivism.

1) **Principle of Social Realism.** Society is specifically distinct from the individuals who compose it; it is a new reality, endowed with proper qualities, with its own life and activity and governed by special laws.

Durkheim presents this view as a throwback to the thought of Comte, for whom the true being was humanity, and thus considers his own view as easily acceptable. He offered an a priori proof, or proof by analogy. The whole is not identical with its parts. A compound obtained through chemical synthesis has properties which each of the composing bodies do not possess alone. Durkheim illustrates this view with water, bronze and the living cell. He then argues that the association of individuals in order to constitute society is not a matter of pure juxtaposition, but is more comparable to a chemical synthesis. Society, therefore, is a unique reality.

2) **Principle of Absolute Positivism.** There is no other legitimate or fruitful means of studying man than that of scientific observation, which is objective and external, and has already been applied to other domains. This is the function of *sociology*, the final and supreme positive science.

This principle is easily justified as an application of the positivistic doctrine that only sensible phenomena and their laws can be known scientifically [1]. From the viewpoint of sensible observation (especially if, with Comte, one wishes it to be mainly external), everything which is proper to man can be referred to social activity, and even morality is a part of it.

Without being explicitly demonstrated, this principle engenders a double position for a positivist. The first is the sterility of subjective or metaphysical morality, which attempts, in Rousseau's style, to deduce all scientific knowledge of individual or social human life by an a priori analysis of the individual nature, independently of experience. The second position is the fruitfulness of positivistic science in all other domains, a fact which invites them to extend the method to man himself.

---

[1] See above, n. 471, the basic principle of positivism.

Two corollaries immediately complete this principle. *a*) The determinism of the laws of nature should be extended to the facts of social life, for the latter is the necessary basis or the basic postulate of all positivistic science. *b*) One can refer the study of society neither to biology (which is the study of man's corporeal organs) nor to psychology (which is the study of conscious facts); sociology has its own object, laws and proper methods.

This latter corollary could unify the two principles, or that the proper object of sociology would be the *sui generis* reality of social being. But in order that the synthesis be real, this being would have to be an *observational fact* (as was Humanity for Comte and the Supreme Law for Taine). Durkheim, however, gave it an a priori position as a mysterious thing, drawing many conclusions from it which surpassed experience. His fundamental proposition, accordingly, has a double face, giving his system a somewhat incoherent dualism, and marking it with hesitation and occasional contradictions. However, one can sufficiently refer most of his theories to this basic position, whether in sociology or in morality.

II. Sociology.

514. In Sociology, Durkheim's main concern was with methodology, which he treated in detail, giving only a few rather loosely applicable examples .

A) Method of Sociology.

The method deduced from the basic position can be stated as four rules.

1) **The Rule of Preparation,** which is either negative or positive. The sociologist must begin by freeing himself of every preconceived notion of man; he must not begin with any a priori theory concerning man. He must practice methodic doubt and place himself in the presence of his object as before a fact about which he wishes to ascertain its existence and characteristics. Then he can establish a preliminary definition by the aid of some *external* and *distinctive* characteristics which are chosen so as to determine an object of study (for instance, the family or suicide). He need not indicate necessarily the most essential characteristic, for it is often hidden and found only at the conclusion of research.

This rule is a consequence of the second principle and should assure sociology a place in the realm of experimental or positivistic science.

2) **Rule of Specificity.** The sociologist must make every effort to consider facts from a slant in which they show themselves as isolated from their individual manifestations [1]; and, in order to establish laws, he must seek the explanation or the cause of a fact which is exclusively social in another social fact. For example, in order to study the family, one should not base his study on personal memories, but on the customs, morals and the law which have made of the family an " objective " institution, independent of individuals. The origin of the family is not to be sought in the aspirations of the individual nature, but in religion, which is another social fact.

This rule is deduced a priori from " social realism "; it is the indispensable condition for attaining the " special being " of society. But it is not always coterminous with experience; one can see that it is often difficult to apply, especially because the social fact, as isolated from individual facts, is almost unintelligible. In addition, the influence of individual causes on the explanation of social facts is sometimes so evident to observation that Durkheim himself, despite his own rule, conceded this influence. For instance, in his view, the instinct of conservation, which is an individual fact, has an important role in the development of the division of work, which is a social fact [2].

3) **Rule of Adaptation** of the experimental method to society. The best method of discovering the cause of a social fact is that of *concomitant variations*. If one grants that the same fact always has the same cause, then if two unified facts apparently vary from one another, they are evidently joined as cause and effect in the positivistic sense; that is, they are joined as antecedent and consequent and are governed by the law of determinism.

In order to discover the origin of social facts by this method, it seems necessary to study their history in all the various peoples. This study is not always possible; hence there must first be established a classification of societies which would permit one to choose but one fact of experience from each

---

[1] S. DEPLOIGE, *The Conflict Between Ethics and Sociology*, p. 52.
[2] *Ibid.* p. 72.

class. This classification is a complex problem, not as yet resolved. Durkheim proposed that the most simple society is the *horde* or *mob* which is the free union of consanguine people. Various types of society are distinguished according to the more or less complex combinations of the simple elements of the horde, thus becoming the family, the state, and so forth.

This rule is also a logical application of absolute positivism. But it also runs against the fact of liberty, which does not always give the same cause for the same event (for example, in suicide).

4) **Rule of Specialization.** The program of the sociologist is immense; he must explain the actual nature of many social institutions, and their origin and laws. Consequently, one must renounce the hope of establishing universal laws for the present (in the manner of Comte, Spencer or Taine), and devote himself to *monographs* or detailed studies. Sociology must, for some time, remain but a *method* which directs various particular works towards the same goal, and it must wait for the time when general conclusions can be reached.

This rule helped Durkheim explain the failure of his predecessors in sociology; they were guilty of too much generalization. He was content with some special applications only.

B) **Attempts at Application.**

515. 1) The main attempt has for its goal the *definition of the social fact*. Durkheim looked upon it as every manner of activity (action, feeling, thought, and so forth) capable of exercising an exterior constraint on an individual. This exterior sign of *constraint* seemed to him the clearest sign distinguishing the special being of society, with the help of social realism.

This constraint can be fixated in a text of law, in a custom or in similar ways; or, it can remain free, as in such *social tendencies* as the enthusiasm of a mob or the rate of suicide. In these latter cases, constraint is directly exercised. Constraint is less apparent in other cases, as in an economic organization. This leads to another definition of the social fact as every manner of *general* activity in a society having its own, independent existence apart from its individual manifestations; this, of course, is social realism. In an even more general view, a social fact is every manner of activity which is capable of being an *institution* or the fruit of social activity, which the individual finds completely made and of which he must take account in his own life.

The traits of the social fact, then, are that it is an institution, an objective reality, that it imposes itself from without and is, consequently, general.

This definition, however, stated with merely positivistic traits, is somewhat obscure. Without doubt, the social fact is that which is the concern of society and not of the individual. But what is society? It is not, as Durkheim believes, a physical being but rather a *moral being*, possessing simply the *unity of order* between several wills pursuing the *same goal*. By relinquishing the study of natures and of goals through his positivism, Durkheim has also given up any possibility of giving a clear definition to the social fact.

2) Among the monographs of Durkheim, the following are worthy of mention. *a*) His studies on the division of labor and the origin of civilization; he gives the growing density of population as cause for these. *b*) His studies on suicide are statistically explained by the existence of *suicide tendencies* in society. *c*) His study on the origin of prohibiting incest holds that it is attributable to a pre-historic custom preventing the members of a clan from having sexual intercourse among themselves.

Durkheim believes that the mentality or the logic of primitive peoples is different from that of the civilized [1]. He undertook, as a result, the explanation of the origin of man's categories or fundamental ideas, as those of space, time, causality, genus, species, and so forth. Their origin is due to the influence of society, since these ideas, to the extent that athey re universal and necessary, surpass the individual. From this it follows that the action of society penetrates deeply into psychology [2].

III. **Morality.**

516. Durkheim's views on morality are quite complex. In order to present his views as clearly as possible, there will be presented, first, his *positivistic moral science* as related to the logic of his fundamental proposition; this moral science has a method and an object, is related to sociology and is completed by a moral art. Other points of view, less logically connected with his morality, will also be pointed out.

A) **The Method** that alone is capable of setting up a true moral science is *objective* and *sociological*.

a) *Objective;* it does not consider what should be, but what is. Morality is not to deduce from the analysis of human nature and its relations with God a code of duties, but it should rather

---

[1] This view has been especially developed by Lévy-Bruhl, but it has been weakened by further observations on the part of sociologists; see G. Boas, in his *Culture et race* (Paris, 1922), J. DE HOVRE in his *Essai de philosophie pédagogique* (p. 267), and H. BERGSON in his *Les deux sources de la moralite et de la religion* (pp. 159-169).

[2] See C. BLONDEL, *Introduction à la psychologie collective*, Ch. III.

observe the actual moral activity of present or past humanity in order to establish the definition and the laws of moral science. This, of course, is the substitution of the scientific method for the subjective method of philosophers, who have had such notorious failure in this regard.

b) Sociological; the best method is to consider the moral fact as eminently social and to assign causes to it that are exclusively social, according to the four rules mentioned above [1]. The reason justifying this view is not explicitly given, but it is sufficiently implied : the moral fact belongs to man as such, to the exclusion of other beings, and must therefore be treated by sociology, which, among the positivistic sciences, is concerned with specifically human activity.

An immediate corollary of this view is the *relativity* of morality, which is no longer an absolute rule imposing itself immutably on all men, but a relative property which varies with the various states of humanity. An act which is morally good for a primitive could be morally bad for us today, and vice versa.

B) The Characteristics of Morality. 517.

By applying simultaneously the two aspects of his method — which also correspond to the two sides of his basic proposition — Durkheim discovered three basic elements of morality : a spirit of discipline, attachment to the group, and the autonomy of will.

1) The Spirit of Discipline.

An act is considered moral when it is determined by an external rule or law which predetermines it and makes it habitual and stable. One can easily see that these rules are not rigid and universal, as the Kantian imperative, but are rather special and variable, having their own independent life, so that one can disappear without the others disappearing also.

Moreover, since no one (in Durkheim's view) would believe an act done spontaneously to be *moral*, rules, in order to be moral, must be imposed with authority as from an exterior power which constrains mankind.

These two notions of *regularity* and *obligation*, which are certified by experience, are summed up in the *spirit of discipline*, which is the form of every moral act. The exterior sign of obligation is sanction, enabling one to define the moral fact as a rule of sanctioned conduct. The good acts which are not sanctioned pertain to the " esthetic " or moral life.

2) Attachment to the Group.

It is easy to show that every egoistic action is reputedly immoral; accordingly, the second

---

[1] See above, n. 514.

trait of every moral act is to be altruistic. An act is called egoistic because it is related to one's own personality. But if one refuses morality to such an action for a reason of that sort, the same can be said of an act done for another personality; the latter is worth no more than our own, and even a group of individuals, as such, has no more worth, for addition adds nothing to their value. Hence, in order that an act be truly disinterested and moral, its object should be *society*, which, by the principle of social realism, is a new being, more noble than the individual.

If common sense, Durkheim adds, admits the morality of devotion to an individual, it is because it sees there the sentiment of self-forgetfulness, which is a disposition or a participation in the truly moral fact by attachment to the group.

3) **Autonomy of the Will.** Finally, observation confirms the view that everything which violates personal conscience and the free disposition of the self is reputed immoral. Accordingly, the third element of morality is the sacred trait of the individual, or the autonomy of his will.

This third element seems to contradict the other two, but is harmonizable with them if one sees how we guard and increase our own independence of action due to positivistic science. Physical science, for example, without removing anything from the forces of natural laws, allows us to dominate them. Similarly, a scientific study of society will leave intact the dominative authority of moral laws; it will teach us to obey while keeping the autonomy of our own will. We will obey these laws by fully consenting to them, with the aim of using them.

C) **The Role of Society. 518.** Society is not only necessary in order that activity, losing its egoism, can become morally good, but it also helps to explain a trait of the moral fact which is quite difficult to interpret in positivism, that of *obligation*. Durkheim gives an indirect proof of obligation, using religion as a detour.

One admits readily that obligation and duty are universally referred to the religious fact. They are interpreted as a submission to the will of a sovereign God Who is Good and Just, and Who sanctions His law by rewarding the faithful and punishing the transgressors.

Society, however, is a sufficient and scientific (that is, experimental science) explanation of religion.

a) At first, the application of the sociological method obliges one to explain religious facts through society. These facts possess the characteristics of the social fact in a very high degree : a constrainin; authority, obligatio.1 and sanction, and the independent existence of individuals.

b) Then it can be seen that society can play the role assigne 1 to the Divinity in religion. Like the Divinity, society is a distinct and superior being, the source of all good for its members and having the capability of punishing them.

c) Finally, historical observation agrees with this transformation of society into the Divinity. Primitive religion, in Durkheim's view, is a cult of the *Totem*, an animal or a plant, as for example, a pelican, whose name was attributed to a clan. This cult was not addressed to one plant or animal, but to the whole species, which was thereby accounted sacred and which could not be used without very precise rubrics. This respect, unexplainable by the natural qualities of these beings, demonstrates that the primitives honored a symbol of society in their *Totem*. Having proved the special force which society holds over their assemblies and its mysterious domination over individuals, these primitives associated with it the presence of a certain animal species which became the symbol of their clan. This substitution is further explained by the logic of society, which is different from our individual logic.

Somewhat in this way, society explains both religion and moral obligation.

D) **The Art of Morality.** As every positivistic science, moral science has a practical aim. Just as physics or chemistry concludes with industrial applications, moral science leads to educative applications which can teach the child, newly entered into society, or allow men to live their lives fully by conforming to the best known laws of their existence.

But these practical applications are but a hope, for, as an actual fact, there are very few conclusions of positivistic morality which have been scientifically demonstrated.

519. Durkheim's system is certainly the most complete effort yet made to constitute moral science on positivistic principles. But it is the very conception of *positivistic morality* which involves a contradiction. From one point of view, positivism wishes to consider human and social life as being but a unique assemblage of facts governed by necessary laws. From this view it follows that everything which is done by men is legitimate, and that it is a vain hope to look for some ideal destined to correct human life, just as it would be useless to wish to correct a chemical reaction.

From another point of view, morality is a *practical science* for common sense and for any true philosophy. It is destined to direct human life by making precise what is man's supreme good as the object of his natural aspirations, and it should point out the means of leading man to his good. Morality thus arranges a program of life, classifying acts as good or bad by relation to their goal. Moreover, this program is not merely an ideal proposed to good will (an esthetic, pagan morality), but it is an *order* imposed on man's liberty by the Creator Who inscribed it within man's nature, and Who Himself sanctions its execution. Thus, true morality is founded on God, the final end of man, and on the freedom of man as dependent on the Creator. The positivistic view, denying substances and causes, makes meaningless these essential notions of right and duty, of good and bad.

Durkheim himself explained obligation through social realism, which is beyond experience, and which is insufficient as a replacement for God; only the Infinite Good is the final goal legitimate for man. Quite often, in fact, Durkheim abandons the strict view of positivistic morality, in order to consider the ideal to be sought for, and the means that are best suited for attaining it. He called this ideal, moral or social *sanctity*, distinguishing the action of the *normal fact* favorable to sanctity from the *pathological fact*, contrary to this sanctity. He thus supposes that the final goal of individuals is to live for society and that society is essentially constituted by order, peace, justice, harmony and solidarity. From this viewpoint, suicide is a pathological fact. The same holds for the excessive liberty granted to the modern states, and the great remedy proposed is the re-establishment of corporations. Furthermore, in order to lead individuals to accept constraints and social duties, Durkheim appealed to their own interest as properly understood, and to their sentiment of gratitude for the benefits of society.

These views are not, of course, sufficiently demonstrated. Other sociologists of the school no longer accept them and they merely increase the complexity of Durkheim's system. They do show, however, a return towards the morality of good sense, and underscore the inevitable weakness of every positivistic morality.

The Morality of Solidarity. 520. This view of morality was proposed by LÉON BOURGEOIS, and has much affinity with the sociological morality of Durkheim. It is founded on observation of the fact of general inter-dependence of all the beings in the universe, of the physical and living order of things, as well as in the moral society of men. This fact is then raised to the fundamental law of morality; it is the source of all duties, for every law imposes it. Moreover, in accepting the advantages of society, we are bound, as it were, contractually, to repay our benefits. Finally, inasmuch as each has received, he should, in justice, return a similar good.

From this principle our individual duties are first drawn out. In order that we might return to others what they have given us, we must perfect ourselves. Having received advantages from the state or civil society, and especially from our family, there arise special duties to these groups which are proportionately more numerous and obligatory.

Without denying the fact of solidarity, it can be said that this rule is insufficient, for it does not take into account the proper value of the human person. The latter finds itself totally subsumed to the general society of beings, while, on the other hand, by reason and liberty, it refers to God alone.

Conclusion : Catholic Sociology [1].

521. The sociology of Durkheim and of his school does not form a complete philosophy. One of the best portions of it is its method, which is capable of furnishing some of the elements towards a solid, scientific construction. But its great weakness is the lack of a truly unifying principle which would embrace all details.

This principle is supplied by the Catholic faith, since it has a precise doctrine on the nature and goal of society, especially as regards social and individual morality. Moreover, throughout the nineteenth century, alongside of the positivistic reaction, there arose a vigorous *Catholic* reaction against the revolutionary morality of Rousseau and the rationalistic morality of Cousin. But this aspect is of interest to the history of the Church rather than to the philosopher. One group of Catholics in this realm emphasize the principles of sociology and keep close to their faith, as in the traditionalist school (of which De Bonald is an example) and, more especially, the publicists (for instance, L. Veuillot). Others are more concerned with the realm of direct action, as those who were concerned in the campaign for freedom of teaching in France, or the foundation of social measures through Ketteler (1811-1877) in Germany, and, after 1870, the workers' unions of A. De Mun, and so forth.

An effort worthy of mention is that of Frédéric LE PLAY [2] (1806-1882). He attempted a philosophical or scientific study

---

[1] CASSERLY, J. V. L., *Morals and Man in the Social Sciences*, New York, 1951. — DAWSON, C. H., *Religion and the Modern State*, New York, 1935. — FURFEY, P. H., *Scope and Method of Sociology*, New York, 1953. — HUTCHINSON, J. A. (ed.), *Christian Faith and Social Action*, New York, 1953. — MARITAIN, J., *Scholasticism and Politics*, New York, 1952. — TIMASHEFF, N. S., and FACEY, P. W., *Sociology*, Milwaukee (Wis.), 1949. — WILLIAMS, M. J., *Catholic Social Thought*, New York, 1950.

[2] He based his conclusions on extensive research, conducted with perseverance, according to a scientific method on *monographs of working families*, the results of which are embodied in his great **work** : *Les ouvriers européens*, 6 vols., Paris, 1855-1879. Other **works :** *La méthode sociale*, Paris, 1879; — *Les ouvriers des deux mondes*, 1858-79. — *La réforme sociale en France*, 1864-78; — *L'organisation de la famille*, 1870-75. **Study :** F. L. D. R. HERBERTSON, *Life of Frederic Le Play*, Ledbury (Herefordshire, England), 1951.

of society and its laws by observing European society, and established that the basic condition for social prosperity is the observation of the decalogue. Another effort in this direction is that of LA TOUR DU PIN [1] († 1924), who tried to set up a cooperative plan of organization in order to tend towards a *Christian social order*.

CHAPTER FIVE.

PRAGMATISM [2].

(20th century.)

The Antipositivistic Reaction.

522. For the most part, the nineteenth century held on to the negative conclusions of the Kantian criticism. Both idealists and positivists completely abandoned any study of the *thing-in-itself*, which Kant had excluded from the domain of science. They reduced philosophy to a simple exercise of general synthesis made of the materials given by science. The great idealistic systems were nothing more than this, and, even more explicitly, the positivistic philosophy itself did not wish to be defined in any other way.

Towards the close of the nineteenth century, and especially at the opening of the twentieth, there arose a reaction, even among the modern philosophers [3]. Moved by the natural desire of the human mind, a good number of thinkers attempted to surpass the sensible phenomenon and its laws, wherein " science " had encamped, and turned towards substance and spiritual reality. Sadly enough, they remained imprisoned

[1] **Works :** *Aphorismes de politique sociale*, Paris, 1929. — *Vers un ordre social chrétien*, Paris, 1929. — **Study :** C. BAUSSAN, *La Tour du Pin*, Paris, 1931.

[2] BROWNE, S. S. S., *Pragmatic Theory of Truth and Reality*, Princeton (N. J.), 1930. — CALDWELL, W., *Pragmatism and Idealism*, New York, 1913. — DRISCOLL, J. T., *Pragmatism and the Problem of the Idea*, New York, 1915. — HOOK, S., *Metaphysics of Pragmatism*, Chicago, 1927. — MORRIS, C. W., *Logical Positivism, Pragmatism, and Scientific Empiricism*, Paris, 1937. — LEISEGANG, H. *Deutsche Philosophie im XXsten Jahrhundert*, Breslau, 1928. — MUIRHEAD, J., *Contemporary British Philosophy*, London, 1924. — PARODI, D., *La philosophie contemporaine en France*, Paris, 1926. — PERRY, R. B., *Present Philosophical Tendencies*, New York, 1919. — RUGGIERO, G. De, *La filosofia contemporanea*, 2 vols., Bari, 1920. — WIENER, P. P., *Evolution and the Founders of Pragmatism*, Cambridge, (Mass.), 1949.

[3] Scholastic philosophy remains unswervingly realist; see the following chapter.

in the Kantian and positivistic negations; while they somewhat inaugurated a " resurrection of metaphysics ", it was by appealing to some other faculty in man than to his intelligence. While being explicitly opposed to Kant, they but developed the third portion of Kantianism by taking up, though in an original fashion, the thesis of the primacy of practical reason and of a moral metaphysics.

From the doctrinal point of view, this philosophical school, pragmatism, can be characterized by three basic propositions.

1⁰ **Absolute Agnosticism :** *human intelligence* [1] *is radically and totally incapable of knowing reality.*

This proposition is the unanimous point of departure for all of these thinkers. In this way, they accept as definitive the conclusions of Kant's critique and of the positivistic principle. The " intellectualism " which wishes to construct metaphysics with the concepts of reason is but an outmoded system. They do not deny the fact of intellectual knowledge, but they give it a totally new significance; this is done in their second proposition.

2⁰ **Utilitarian Truth :** *intellectual conceptions have value only in the measure in which they favor life and its progress.*

In other words, the truth expressed by man's judgments and in his sciences has no *objective* property as an immutable reflection of eternal truths and as sharing in the absolute truth of God Himself. Truth has a totally *relative* property which depends on the actual status of humanity and varies with it. This, of course, is a corollary of agnosticism; having deprived the intelligence of its proper function of conquering truth, this function is given to the will, which is to attain the good and the useful. However, inasmuch as common sense preserves the notion of ontological truth, this school, through a paradoxical transposition, charges the will with the task of giving man this truth.

3⁰ **Sentimental Knowledge :** *the sole means of attaining objective truth is sentiment or action.* This third trait especially marks the " new philosophy ", which does not wish to be constituted of knowledge supplied by a passive faculty subjected to the action of the object, but rather by man's *active* powers, as the subconscious, experience, life, intuition and action. The

---

[1] We use this term here in the ordinary sense (without the systematic distinctions of Kantianism) as designating the faculty of spiritual knowledge, also called reason or understanding.

latter, this school holds, are the only powers of man adapted to the actual needs of humanity. In this sense, one can classify all of these philosophers under the common title of *pragmatists* or philosophers of action.

The doctrinal movement characterized above is, at the beginning of the twentieth century, the most powerful reaction against positivism. Le Roy has saluted it as the " new philosophy ". It has officially taken on the title of pragmatism along with the American philosophers, chief of whom is William James. This current of pragmatism, of course, is not the only one alive. In an age where each philosopher makes up his own system, one finds a great number of them, many quite diverse, and some even quite far removed from pragmatism. But they can all be gathered together by their common effort of reaching *beyond positivism*. The most famous and the most profound representative of this latter view is Henri Bergson, who tried to set up a complete system. Three articles will present this material :

Article   I. American Pragmatism.   (William James).

Article II. Beyond Positivism.

Article III. Henri Bergson.

ARTICLE ONE.

AMERICAN PRAGMATISM.

WILLIAM JAMES.

(1842-1910).

SPECIAL BIBLIOGRAPHY.

1º **Works :** DEWEY, J., *Studies in Logical Theory*, Chicago, 1909. — *How We Think*, Boston, 1910. — *The Influence of Darwin on Philosophy*, New York, 1910. — *Essays in Experimental Logic*, New York, 1910. — *The Quest for Certainty*, New York, 1921. — *Logic, the Theory of Enquiry*, New York, 1938. — JAMES, W., *Essays in Pragmatism* (ed. A. Castell), New York, 1948. — *Principles of Psychology*, 2 vols., New York, 1950. — *Varieties of Religious Experience*, New York, 1952. — *Essays in Radical Empiricism* and *A Pluralistic Universe* (ed. R. B. Perry), 2 vols., New York, 1943. — *Essays on Faith and Morals* (sel. R. B. Perry), New York, 1943. — *Pragmatism* and four related essays (sel. R. B. Perry), New York, 1943. — *Some Problems of Philosophy*, New York, 1940. — *Talks to Teachers on Psychology*, New York, 1939. — *Will to Believe*, and other Essays, New York, 1937. — *Meaning of Truth*, New York, 1928. — *Memories and Studies*,

New York, 1928. — *Human Immortality*, New York, 1898. — *Letters* (ed. by his son H. James), 2 vols., Boston, 1926. — SCHILLER, F., *Humanism*, London, 1903. — *Studies in Humanism*, London, 1907.

2º **Studies :** BERTHELOT, R., *Un Romanticisme utilitaire ; le Pragmatisme religieux*, Paris, 1913. — BRODBECK, M., *Philosophy in America*, 1900-1950, Chicago, 1952. — BOUTROUX, E., *William James* (tr. A. and B. Henderson), New York, 1912. — *La pensée américaine et la pensée française*, Paris, 1913. — BUSWELL, O., *The Philosophies of F. R. Tennant and J. Dewey*, New York, 1950. — FARBER, M., *Philosophic Thought in France and the United States*, Buffalo (N. Y.), 1950. — FISCH, M. H. (ed.), *Classic American Philosophies*, New York, 1951. — FLOURNEY, T., *Philosophy of William James*, New York, 1917. — GRATTAN, C. H., *Three Jameses*, New York, 1932. — HÉBERT, L., *Le Pragmatisme*, Paris, 1909. — *In Commemoration of William James*, 1842-1942, New York, 1942. — JONES, A. L., *Early American Philosophers*, New York, n. d. — KALLEN, H. M., *William James and Henri Bergson*, Chicago, 1914. — LECLÈRE, A., *Pragmatisme, Modernisme, Protestantisme*, Paris, 1909. — MAIRE, G., *W. James et le pragmatisme religieux*, Paris, 1933. — MICHELET, G., *Dieu et l'agnosticisme contemporain*, Paris, 1909. — MOORE, A. W., *Pragmatism and Its Critics*, Chicago, 1910. — MORRIS, L. R., *William James*, New York, 1950. — MUELDER, W. G., and SEARS, L. (eds.), *Development of American Philosophy*, New York, 1940. — NATHAN-SON, J., *John Dewey*, New York, 1951. — PARRINGTON, V. L., *Main Currents in American Thought*, 3 vols., New York, 1939. — PERRY, R. B., *Thought and Character of William James*, 2 vols., Cambridge (Mass.), 1948. — RILEY, W., *American Thought from Puritanism to Pragmatism and Beyond*, New York, 1941. — ROBACK, A. A., *William James, His Marginalia, Personality, and Contribution*, Cambridge (Mass.), 1942. — SABIN, E., *W. James and Pragmatism*, London, 1916. — SCHILPP, P. A., *The Philosophy of John Dewey*, New York, 1951. — SCHNEIDER, H. W., *History of American Philosophy*, New York, 1946. — SPIRITO, U., *Il pragmatismo nella filosofia contemporanea*, Florence, 1920. — THAYER, H. S., *The Logic of Pragmatism. An Examination of John Dewey's Logic*, New York, 1952. — THOMPSON, M. H., *Pragmatic Philosophy of C. S. Peirce*, Chicago, 1953. — TOKSVIG, L., *E. Swedenborg, Scientist and Mystic*, New Haven (Conn.), 1948. — TOWNSEND, H. G. *Philosophical Ideas in the United States*, New York, 1934. — WAHL, J. A., *Pluralist Philosophies of England and America*, Chicago, 1925. — WERKMEISTER, W. H., *History of Philosophical Ideas in America*, New York, 1949.

523. William James was born in New York. His father, Henry, was a minister and a disciple of SWEDENBORG [1],

---

[1] In his *Arcana cælestia* (8 vols.), Swedenborg held to the existence of mysterious relations between this world and the next and indicated the way to establish communication through a new religion; he also pretended to possess doubling of personality.

a Swedish spiritualist. Henry injected a taste for mystery into his son's mind, but gave him a rather disorganized and poorly formed education. William completed his studies while taking various journeys, frequenting schools and universities in Europe and in the United States. He finally settled at Harvard, where he first held a professorship in the sciences, then in philosophy, and finally in psychology. His main works are : *The Principles of Psychology* (1890); *The Varieties of Religious Experience* (1902); *Pragmatism* (1907).

William James' pragmatism is also held by F. C. S. Schiller, the author of *Humanism* and a professor at Oxford, by John Dewey, and others.

The doctrine of James himself will be presented here, since he is the incontested chief of this school of thought. His views, a reflection of his half-completed education and of his mobile personality, do not possess the unity of a completed system. The center of attraction, however, is his theory of *pragmatism;* it helped him establish a rule of truth which he was able to use in his psychological research. It enabled him to propose his famous view of the subconscious, and to offer an immanentist metaphysics which was a precursor of modernism and of the movement that involves contemporary philosophy in looking *beyond positivism.* Two paragraphs will present James' philosophy :

    I. The Theory of Pragmatism.

    II. Experimental Psychology and Immanentist Metaphysics.

I. The Theory of Pragmatism.

524. The theory of pragmatism, which transformed the notion of truth, is, basically, a new attempt at solving the critical problem. James was led to it by a twofold preoccupation. The first was his hope to establish empiricism [1] in order to appreciate properly the value of man's knowledge. Mulling over the current objections on the impossibility of our abstract ideas being identified with the concrete object exterior to us, James concluded, without much depth, that Kant was in the right : the intelligence is deceived in believing that its ideas reflect the *thing-in-itself;* only that which comes from experience can be accepted as valuable.

---

[1] On the meaning of this word see above, n. 356.

Consequently, James proclaims himself a pluralist [1]; that is, in encountering the monistic explanation of the universe (as in Spinoza, Hegel, and others), which refers everything to a unique principle discovered by intelligence, James holds, instead, that there is primitively given a plurality of hetero-geneous elements perceivable by the senses, dispersed by chance, and forming some sort of assemblage.

However, James had a second preoccupation : he wished to do scientific work. Not content with counting and classifying facts, he wished to express " judgments of value " on these facts. In order to do so, he needed a *rule of appreciation;* this had to be sought beyond the speculation which had deformed reality by imposing itself on it in a priori fashion. There remained only the alternative of seeking this rule in the practical order. In his view, *a doctrine is true in the measure that it is useful or profitable* [2].

In this way, James contended, human intelligence finds its true function, which is not to be static and passive, but dynamic and active; to think is to resolve problems. We are all aware that occasionally we resolve a problem in daily life by contact with experience. In winter, for instance, we might be suffering from cold. It is then and only then that there is really produced the phenomenon called thought in order to resolve this difficulty; it is only then that we judge with truth, " fire warms me ". Before this time the judgment had no sense, since it had no reason for being; it was neither true nor false. This same argument holds for a great number of purely speculative questions.

In this way, truth is appreciated without our leaving empiri-cism. For we judge a doctrine by concrete facts which are its consequence and which, thereby, make it useful and profitable for ourselves. James is not thinking only of material profit, or of riches or sensible pleasure, but of all those things which favor progress, civilization, social life, and even moral and intellectual life. For example, an absurdity could never be true, for it can inject nothing but trouble into our habits and thoughts. Moreover, if truth is measured, in final analysis, by the profit which accrues, this profit is not for humanity

---

[1] For the definition of pluralism, see footnote to n. 361, A.

[2] " The truth of a proposition consists in the fact that it is useful ", that is " has good results ", that it " gives satisfaction " (A. LALANDE, *Vocabulaire technique de la philosophie,* under " Pragmatism ", meaning, " B ").

(which is an abstraction), but for each individual man. At the same time, the community of nature among men assures a certain stability to a large number of truths. For example, " Two things equal to the same, third thing, are equal to each other " is true always and for all men, for its practical utility is universal. On the other hand, the fact that society is indispensable for the perfect good of each man, guarantees truth against individual arbitrariness.

Pragmatic truth, nonetheless, has no absolute value but is wholly relative to man, and variable with him. James did not fear to draw out the consequences of his view whether in theodicy [1] or in morality. He believes that the speculative notions of a supreme good, of duty, of merit and of freedom itself do not, as such, have any meaning. They are true only in the measure that they suggest to us a route to be taken which is worth the effort, because of the advantages we seek. In this sense, it is true that man is free and that the good should be done, for these affirmations are such that they will develop our personality, whose whole push is towards disinterestedness, goodness and devotion.

525. This rule of practical appreciation includes all three basic principles of pragmatism, because it grapples with the very notion of truth itself, removing it from the speculative order and inserting it into the practical realm. What gives it its appearance of value is that a true doctrine, as a matter of fact, cannot, as true, have any bad result. That is why the " profits " [2], which we find there, can be a *sign* or a consequence capable of demonstrating, at least probably, that a certain doctrine is true. But the pragmatists conclude that truth is *intrinsically* [3] constituted by utility so that a judgment has no usefulness because it is true in itself, but it is or becomes true at the moment that it is or becomes profitable; and this is the pragmatist error.

Furthermore, if pragmatism is taken literally, all the sciences and morality are ruined in their very roots. They have no more stability than was given them by Hume's phenomenalism, for their truth depends on individual utility [4]. In addition, it seems impossible to grasp " what is our profit " if one totally ignores

---

[1] See below, n. 528.

[2] This word is taken in a broad sense, as James himself used it.

[3] The pragmatists make utility the *formal cause* (constitutive) of truth, while it can be no more than a mere sign *(logical cause)* or manifestation.

[4] As LALANDE remarks (*op. cit.*, under " Pragmatism "), the formulas defining pragmatism are somewhat equivocal. " One could understand by *that which is useful* every personal profit, and then what is error for one is, with the same basis, truth for another "; this is *scepticism*. " If one understands this expression as meaning *succeeds well*, or the spontaneous accord of minds on that which objective facts verify when taken in common ", one is closer to *rationalism*.

what is human nature. It is impossible to judge truly what is profitable to us without implicitly affirming that man is, in himself, his own final goal, as a function of which the value of all his actions is to be measured. This is a purely speculative, and an erroneous principle, since it is equal to denying any reason for being extrinsic to our finite and contingent nature. Thus, pragmatism is self-destructive when stated; its basic principle — there is no speculative truth — cannot be proposed without at least affirming one speculative truth.

One is tempted to compare this incoherence with the unshakable firmness of Thomism, which, faithful to good sense, is content to philosophize with the intelligence. Thomism, by searching deeply through the truths of common sense, can resolve all the antinomies which perplex the modern thinkers [1] and which led James to his paradoxical positions.

James was more fortunate in his psychological research.

II. Experimental Psychology and immanentist Metaphysics.

526. William James is one of the foremost representatives of experimental psychology, and his book, *Principles of Psychology*, became the standard manual for teaching this branch of learning in the schools of the United States. In this work he first analyzes *conscious facts*, and proposes a number of original theories in explaining them. Then he conducts a wide investigation of religious sentiment, explaining it by his hypothesis of the *subconscious;* onto this is grafted his *immanentist metaphysics*.

A) Conscious Life.

The psychological analyses of James are not inspired by a very unified system; they merely follow experience [2], just dealing with conscious life in a general way, and then concluding with some special points.

1) **In general,** consciousness, in the view of the positivists [3], was simply a series of internal facts joined by the laws of association; its total reality was that of physiological phenomena. James, as well as Bergson, protested against this epiphenomenalism. Under the banner of psychological intuition, they asserted that

---

[1] In particular, moderate realism safeguards everything which is true in James' empiricism, and, at the same time, establishes a rule of speculative appreciation as is demanded by truth.

[2] In psychological method, James is in accord with Ribot (see above, n. 509); he conducted investigations and tests, and used introspection.

[3] For example, Taine (n. 495), and Ribot (n. 509).

consciousness is a reality of the physical order. Its essential trait is to be a living, uninterrupted current, unexpressible in concepts, having a unity that must be determined. With this aim in mind, James distinguishes two types of conscious states. The first, and the more basic, are the *transitive states*, constituting the current of interior life. The *substantial states* are the second; they signify rests or points of reference in the experiences of the transitive current, thus allowing for natural divisions. It is in this sense alone that one can speak of such various faculties as intelligence, sensibility and will.

Once the proper nature of psychological facts is known, their relationship to the body can be made precise. The interdependence of consciousness with physiological phenomena, especially with those of the brain, is a certain law; *perfect parallelism*, however, has not been demonstrated. Experience is better explained, James believes, by considering the brain as an instrument of transmission which binds the essentially distinct activities of consciousness to the corporeal organism [1].

The most universal law in psychology is the *law of interest;* the spontaneous reactions of the interior world of consciousness are ordered, by nature, towards the general good of the person. Moreover, the higher centers of the brain are especially adapted to respond to stimuli of the higher psychological order, with the evident goal of concern for one's life.

2) **Special Points.** *a*) Education alone distinguishes perception from sensation; it teaches one to distinguish precise objects in the field of experience. Both sensation and perception are, originally, but an *intuition* of the exterior world and of *qualities* grasped as objectively endowed with extension [2] (nativism).

Weber's law, accordingly, has a foundation on the part of the stimulus, from which it gets its real value; the mathematical distinctions of Fechner, however, have no significance.

b) The *abstract concept* is explained with the aid of the laws of attention. Attention is governed by the law of selection, according to which attentive perception grasps, in an object, only that which is of interest, and omits the rest. When the common residue of several acts of attention is fixed in memory, a general idea is formed which is then put to full use by the verbal symbol (nominalism) [3].

c) Finally, James held to the *physiological origin of the emotions*. Ordinarily, one looks for the cause of emotions and passions in the good or bad object brought to our knowledge, with its resultant

---

[1] These notions are quite in accord with Thomistic psychology, which defends the independence of the soul in its spiritual activities, and the necessity of the soul's seeking the material for its activity in the sensible order, according to the axiom, " there is nothing in the intellect which was not first in the senses ". But James, imprisoned by empiricism, did not admit to the existence of the substantial soul or to spiritual reason.

[2] James speaks of a volume of sound and a volume of odor.

[3] See above, the similar theory of Taine and the observations which arise therefrom, nn. 495 and 496.

movements of attraction and search or repulsion and flight which
follow, and which are considered as effects. William James,
along with Lange, reversed this order. Instead of having the
known object — emotion — reaction, they proposed the known
object — reaction — emotion. Emotion thus becomes merely
the conscious sentiment which we have of our visceral, circulatory,
muscular and motor reactions that follow perception of the object.
Thus, at sight of a wolf, we do not flee because we have fear of
it, but we have fear because we flee. James offered as proof of
this the fact that one stops the passion by dominating its reactions,
and if one withdraws all concomitant reactions from an emotion,
both exterior and interior, hardly anything remains [1].

With the aid of the general law of interest, a relationship can
be set up between James' psychology and his pragmatism; for,
in considering that to be true which is profitable, one can apply
this rule even to the speculative order. James himself used it
in this way. In 1870, in the midst of a neurasthenic crisis, he
found help by accepting as true a belief in divine help and in
his own liberty as capable of ameliorating his condition.

B) The Subconscious.

527. The notion of an unconscious or a subconscious had
been known since Leibniz. With the help of some research
in experimental psychology, James added precision to this
notion. This research, James believed, demonstrated the
necessity of a threshold, or a minimum level of excitation
below which the sensible quality, though existent, is not
known. A similar result holds for the existence of a horizon,
beyond which there are, for example, visible objects removed
from sight. By analogy with this threshold and field of vision,
consciousness is conceived as a vast field of observation in
which objects must be possessed of a minimum intensity in
order to strike against the interior eye. It is at this interior
point that our actual personality is constituted by the aid
of the law of association, which groups our ideas, feelings and
other psychological facts about a dominant tendency.

But below this clear consciousness, there is the subliminal
consciousness or the subconscious, in which several kinds of
consciousness or secondary personalities exist [2]. This view,
of course, is merely an hypothesis, since it escapes experimental
observation, but it is legitimate, since it furnishes a good

---

[1] These proofs, however, are not decisive against the common sense theory;
see A. BAUDIN, *Cours de Psychologie*, pp. 506-510.

[2] According to James, plurality is the primitive fact; according to other
psychologists, consciousness is obtained by the break-up of the primitive
consciousness.

explanation for a number of psychological facts, as the narrowing of consciousness when one reflects on a certain point, somnambulism, the pathological states involving a change of habit, memory and character (the doubling of personality), and so forth.

In the same way, James explained the mechanism of *conversions*, whether slow or sudden. They result, in his view, from the simple fact that a consciousness was hidden until a certain time; under favorable circumstances, it appears in the full light of day and succeeds, sometimes at once and sometimes after a long or short struggle, in imposing itself and in driving back the preceding personality into the subconscious.

The hypothesis of the subconscious has its place in a positivistic science as experimental psychology. There is nothing to prevent one from holding that certain external or internal sensations which are capable of being perceived by consciousness, exist for a time without being the object of actual introspection. The act of taking consciousness is a special function which normally accompanies the other interior facts, but can be separated [1] from them, and the facts seem to indicate the legitimacy of the subconscious.

But this does not imply that everything is explained, nor does it make useless the notion of human personality in the sense of a substantial reality endowed with a spiritual soul. Many other psychological facts require this notion, as the awareness of permanent identity and of personal responsibility. Briefly, while the positive observations of James are rich and profound, his denials, as a positivist, are quite arbitrary.

C) Immanentist Metaphysics.

528. To this purely psychological theory, James added an important complement with the hope of explaining the transcendental character of religious feeling. He holds that all the religious experiences of conversion, despite diversities, have a dual state of the soul in common. At first, the same inquietude or feeling that there is something which is not going well; then, the deliverance from this state, or the feeling of being saved from this evil by a *Superior Power*. The real activity of this power is guaranteed by the beneficial results

[1] In the sensible order, St. Thomas called this faculty *common sense;* the intelligence can also act as consciousness, and is thus distinguishable from interior sensible life, which can develop without the control of intelligence, as in dreams. However, with regard to the extent of the subconscious, and how much of intellectual activity it can include, there is no certainty.

it produces in the life of human souls. Everything can be explained, James holds, if one admits that through the sub-conscious we identify ourselves with a Being or a Self much greater than our own conscious self, a Being Who can be called God or the Divine.

Applying the pragmatist principle here, James asserts the truth of this belief, for it produces such beneficial results in converts. But to the conception of an infinite and unchangeable being, James prefers one of a finite God; this latter view more readily explains evil and greatly favors the free desire for the good, in order to help God work more efficaciously for the destiny of the universe. It follows from this view that the purely speculative attributes of God, as His " aseity ", immateriality and simplicity, must be discarded as having no sense. Only moral attributes are to be retained, or such as are useful for life. For example, God is holy, just and all-knowing, for these attributes arouse us to fear; He is all-powerful and good, for these awake hope.

Briefly, for pragmatism, the proofs for God's existence which were attacked by the Kantian critique are defunct. God's existence is not demonstrated, but religious experience leads us to this notion as to a profitable belief and, consequently, a true belief. In this very point of an *internal experience of the Divine* there exists, in a state of tendency, the materials which are systematized by the modernists.

ARTICLE TWO. — BEYOND POSITIVISM [1].

529. In order to mark off the great currents of contemporary philosophy, two points must be born in mind. On the one hand, the positivistic mentality remains quite powerful, especially in psychology and sociology, as was already pointed out in the preceding chapter. On the other hand, the awaken-ing of Catholic thought under the heading of Neo-Thomism has brought forth a movement full of richness and of hope in the metaphysical, psychological and critical orders, as will be shown in the following chapter. Between these two and preceded by American pragmatism, there lies a group of thinkers unified by the common hope of removing the prohibitions placed on thought by positivism. Two different routes are

---

[1] Brock, W., *An Introduction to Contemporary German Philosophy*, Cambridge, 1935. — Laird, J., *Recent Philosophy*, London, 1936.

being taken to accomplish this goal. The one group adopts the *way of the spirit*, returning to the sources of idealism and Kantian criticism in order to correct and surpass them and hoping to find the *thing-in-itself*. The other group, more narrowly classifiable under pragmatism, adopts the *way of sentiment* or feeling. In this latter class we find the group of religious thinkers who found the last great heresy of modern times, that of *modernism*. Consequently, without emphasizing each of the philosophers, for their writings are as yet often incompleted, we will give a sketch of the main streams of current ideas under the following three paragraphs :

    I. The Way of the Spirit.

    II. The Way of Feeling.

    III. Modernism.

I. The Way of the Spirit.

530. The dissociation of Kant's doctrine, in the nineteenth century, brought forth the great systems of idealistic pantheism which were opposed to positivism. Among these systems, that of Hegel was influential, continuing even to our day. It was the first form of the reaction of the *way of the spirit* against positivism. But inasmuch as Hegelianism imposed arbitrary restrictions on human knowledge by holding there is no science accessible to man beyond that of phenomena, a large number of thinkers, while remaining convinced of the philosophical value of the intelligence, took positions diametrically opposed to these pretensions. *Critical idealism* is one of these views; it undertook a critical examination of human knowledge in the Kantian manner. *A critique of the sciences* also arose by adopting a severe reflection on truth as given by the positivistic sciences. The view of *phenomenology* arose by bringing up anew the problem of the possibility of philosophy and of its object.

A) Hegelian Idealism.

Hegel's influence was powerful in the nineteenth century, especially in the Anglo-Saxon world, though it also was strong in Italy and France.

In accepting idealism, the Anglo-Saxon thinkers became subjected to an attraction for the concrete. The *universal spirit* of pantheism was, for them, a reality which experience should not despair of attaining. In addition, Hegelian monism tended slowly to dissolve into pluralism. Hegel was revived in England through the efforts of J. H. Stirling, who wrote *The Secret of Hegel* (1865). Thomas Hill Green was the main nineteenth century representative. In the twentieth century, Francis Herbert Bradley (1846-1924), Bernard Bosanquet (1848-1923), John Mac Taggart

(1866-1925), and the American JOSIAH ROYCE (1855-1917) are the main representatives.

T. H. GREEN[1] emphasizes the role of the spirit as binding various sensations together, thereby making of them a genuine scientific knowledge. It is in this way that the spirit shows it has not derived from the evolution of mechanical forces; it is an immaterial reality, beyond space and time. In its very root, spirit is the very consciousness of God, for each consciousness is but a limited participation in God, whose thoughts constitute all the beings of the universe. This view, then, concludes with idealistic pantheism, in the same way as Fichte and Hegel.

BRADLEY[2] believes that the given sensible experience, taken in its totality, contains the infinite " Absolute " and that our individualities are but fragmentary manifestations of this " Absolute ". Such an object remains an undescribable and unexplainable fact in sensible experience, but through scientific judgments some of its partial attributes are determined. The latter are true, however, only to the extent that they suggest the total reality, which seems to be alive at the basis of everything, similar to Hegel's notion of spirit which was both universal and concrete. — BOSANQUET[3] emphasizes the experimental confirmations for this idealism, be they from social life or from the realm of art and religion. In these latter domains the resolution of contradictions is not obtained by intellectual work, but through the presence of a reality in which everything is coherent. — This dominance

[1] **Works :** *Lectures on the Principles of Political Obligation*, New York, 1942. — *English Revolution*, New York, n. d. — *Prolegomena to Ethics* (ed. A. C. Bradley), Oxford, n. d.
Studies : FAIRBROTHER, W. H., *The Philosophy of Hill Green*, London, 1896. — LAMONT, W. D., *Introduction to Green's Moral Philosophy*, New York, 1935. — LELAND, A. P., *Educational Theory and Practice of T. H. Green*, New York, 1911. — NETTLESHIP, R. L., *Memoir of Thomas Hill Green*, New York, 1906. — PARODI, J., *Du positivisme à l'idéalisme*, Paris, 1930. — SASSEN, F., *Wijsbegeerte van onzen Tijd*, Brussels, 1938. — TOWNSEND, H. G., *Principle of Individuality in the Philosophy of Thomas Hill Green*, Ithaca (N. Y.), 1914.

[2] **Works :** *Ethical Studies* (Selected Essays ed. by R. G. Ross), Oxford, 1927. — *Collected Essays*, 2 vols., Oxford, 1935. — *Aphorisms*, Oxford, 1930. — *Appearance and Reality*, Oxford, 1930.
Studies : LOFTHOUSE, W. F., *F. H. Bradley*, London, 1949. — LOOMBA, R. M., *Bradley and Bergson*, London, 1937. — ROSS, R. G., *Scepticism and Dogma. A Study in the Philosophy of F. H. Bradley*, New York, 1949. — SEGERSTEDT, T. T., *Value and Reality in Bradley's Philosophy*, Lund (Sweden), 1934.

[3] **Works :** *History of Æsthetic*, New York, 1917. — *Logic, or the Morphology of Knowledge*, 2 vols., Oxford, 1932. — *Meeting of Extremes in Contemporary Philosophy*, New York, 1921. — *Philosophical Theory of the State*, New York, 1920. — *Science and Philosophy and other essays*, New York, 1927. — *Social and International Ideals*, New York, 1917. — *Some Suggestions in Ethics*, New York, 1918. — *Three Chapters on the Nature of Mind*, New York, 1923. — *Three Lectures on Aesthetic*, New York, 1915. — *Value and Destiny of the Individual*, New York, n. d.
Studies : BOSANQUET, H., *Bernard Bosanquet*, New York, 1924. — BRADLEY, A. C., and HALDANE, R. B. H., *Bernard Bosanquet*, 1848-1923, Oxford, 1924. — PFANNENSTALL, B., *Bernard Bosanquet's Philosophy of the State*, Lund (Sweden), 1936.

of the universal spirit in Hegelian idealism always threatens absorption of the individual into monism. ROYCE [1] tried to conciliate these two aspects. He affirmed the existence of an absolute " self " whose unity possesses all the objects of thought and guarantees the validity of human science. But this " self " is manifested only in a plurality of free individuals who are the artisans of their own destiny. — MAC TAGGART [2] retains only the dialectical method of Hegelianism. He grants reality only to the finite and multiple " selves " which are variously grouped; among them, God Himself is a finite being possessing limited power. This view is close to the pluralism of James.

In Italy, Hegelianism kept its monistic character. It was studied there as the principle of interpreting history and even as the inspiration for political activity. Its two main representatives, BENEDETTO CROCE (1866-1952) and GIOVANNI GENTILE (1875-1945) were ministers of public instruction, the first named from 1920-21, while the second from 1922-24. B. CROCE [3] adopted the dialectical method of Hegel. He held that the contraries are opposed to each other, but they are not opposed to unity,

[1] **Works :** *Logical Essays* (ed. D. S. Robinson), Dubuque (Ia.), 1951. *Religious Philosophy of Josiah Royce* (ed. S. G. Brown), Syracuse (N. Y.), 1952. — *Social Philosophy of Josiah Royce* (ed. S. G. Brown), Syracuse (N. Y.), 1950. — *Conception of Immortality*, New York, n. d. — *Fugitive Essays*, Cambridge (Mass.), 1920. — *Lectures on Modern Idealism* (ed. J. Loeevenberg), New Haven (Conn.), 1919. — *Philosophy of Loyalty*, New York, 1908. — *Religious Aspect of Philosophy*, New York, 1885. — *Sources of Religious Insight*, New York, 1912. — *Spirit of Modern Philosophy*, New York, n. d. — *World and the Individual*, 2 pts., New York, n. d.
Studies : LEIDECKER, K. F., *Josiah Royce and Indian Thought*, New York, 1931. — MARCEL, G., *La métaphysique de Royce*, Paris, 1945. — SMITH, J. E., *Royce's Social Infinite*, New York, 1950.
[2] **Works :** *Philosophical Studies* (ed. S. V. Keeling), New York, 1934. — *Commentary on Hegel's Logic*, New York, 1932. — *Nature of Existence*, 2 vols., New York, 1921-27. — *Some Dogmas of Religion*, New York, 1930.
Studies : BROAD, C. D., *Examination of McTaggart's Philosophy*, 2 vols., New York, 1933-38. — *John McTaggart Ellis McTaggart*, 1866-1925, Oxford, 1928. — DICKINSON, G. L., *J. McT. E. McTaggart*, New York, 1932.
[3] **Works :** *Aesthetic, as Science of Expression and General Linguistic* (tr. D. Ainslee), New York, 1953. — *Germany and Europe* (tr. V. Sheean), New York, 1944. — *Politics and Morals* (tr. S. J. Castiglione), New York, 1945. — *Theory and History of Historiography*, New York, 1933. — *Conduct of Life* (tr. A. Livingston), New York, 1924. — *Historical Materialism and the Economics of Karl Marx* (tr. C. M. Meredith), New York, 1914. — *History, Its Theory and Practice* (tr. D. Ainslee), New York, 1921. — *Logic as the Science of the Pure Concept* (tr. D. Ainslee), New York, 1917. — *Philosophy of Giambattista Vico* (tr. R. G. Collingwood), New York, 1913. — *Philosophy of the Practical : Economic and Ethic* (tr. D. Ainslee), New York, 1913. — *Freedom, Its Meaning* (ed. R. N. Anshen), New York, 1940. — *Benedetto Croce, An Autobiography* (tr. R. G. Collingwood), Oxford, 1927.
Studies : CARR, H. W., *The Philosophy of Benedetto Croce*, New York, 1927. — CHIOCCHETTI, E., *La filosofia di B. Croce*, Milan, 1924. — CRESPI, A., *Contemporary Thought of Italy*, New York, 1926. — ROMANELLI, P., *Croce versus Gentile*, New York, 1947. — SPRIGGE, C. J., *Benedetto Croce*, New Haven (Conn.), 1952.

since true and concrete unity is nothing but the unity or synthesis of contraries. With the aid of this method, he considered spirit as the basic reality, and from it he deduced his esthetics, logic and ethics. In the latter, he gave laws the function of being merely helpful to real volitions, and held to the necessity, especially for a government, of adapting decisions to concrete realities. Following his example, GENTILE [1] viewed the Absolute as a creative act of the spirit who is immanent to all reality. He looked upon history as the expression of his doctrine.

Mention can also be made of the Hegelian GERARD BOLLAND [2] (1854-1922) from the Netherlands. In various writings, he developed the various evolutions of the Absolute Spirit, which concludes with the full flowering of philosophy. — In France, Hegel also influenced the views of V. Cousin [3]; but French idealism was more influenced by Kantian criticism.

B) Critical Idealism.

Docile to the conclusions of Kant, positivism resigned itself to the impossibility of ever going beyond phenomena. The philosophers who revived criticism in the latter part of the nineteenth century, tried to correct this attitude by attaining the *thing-in-itself*. The movement began with French Neo-Criticism, begun by JULES LEQUIER (1814-1862), and advanced with its main representative, CHARLES RENOUVIER [4] (1815-1903). Renouvier held that science deals especially with phenomena and that it is conditioned by the a priori forms; however, he gives a revised list of the latter. He also wished to respond to the demands of moral life, which involve man in the problem of his destiny and the question of God; these were mere speculative probabilities in Kant's view. Accordingly, he adopted the *postulate of liberty* as his point of departure, and attributed to the latter the definite formation of truths. He did not believe that evidence constrained us to accept anything, and that we are always free to suspend our assent; we find the truth by freely accepting the most probable as being truth. Applying his method, Renouvier arrived at the

---

[1] **Works:** *Reform of Education* (tr. D. Bigongiari), New York, 1922. — *Theory of Mind as Pure Act* (tr. H. W. Carr), New York, 1922.

Studies: BOYER, C., *L'idéalisme de M. G. Gentile*, Paris, 1932. — CHIOCCHETTI, E., *La filosofia di G. Gentile*, Milan, 1925. — CRESPI, A., *Contemporary Thought of Italy*, New York, 1926. — HOLMES, R. W., *Idealism of Giovanni Gentile*, New York, 1937. — LION, A., *Idealistic Conception of Religion : Vico, Hegel, Gentile*, Oxford, 1932. — ROMANELLI, P., *Croce versus Gentile*, New York, 1947. — *Gentile*, New York, 1938. — THOMPSON, M. M., *Educational Philosophy of Giovanni Gentile*, Los Angeles (Cal.) 1934.

[2] B. WIGERSMA, *Bolland*, Amsterdam, 1927. — [3] See above, n. 443.

[4] **Works:** *Essais de critique générale*, 4 vols., Paris, 1851-64. — *Science de la morale*, Paris, 1869. — *Esquisse de classification systématique de doctrines philosophiques*, Paris, 1885-86. — *Philosophie analytique de l'histoire*, 4 vols., Paris, 1896-98. — *Nouvelle monadologie*, Paris, 1899. — *Les dilemmes de la métaphysique pure*, Paris, 1901. — *Le personalisme*, Paris, 1903.

Studies: HAMELIN, O., *Le système de Renouvier*, Paris, 1927. — SÉAILLES, G., *La philosophie de Ch. Renouvier*, Paris, 1905. — VERNEAU, R., *L'idéalisme de Renouvier*, Paris, 1945.

conviction that the universe is formed of a certain number of realities, living and personal, which one can call "monads" in the manner of Leibniz. These are ruled by laws discovered in the sciences. They are governed by a one supreme Being [1], God, Who is good and powerful as the guarantee of the moral order, but finite and limited in action, as is shown by evil, which he could not avoid. — OCTAVE HAMELIN [2] (1856-1907) wrote Essai sur les éléments principaux de la représentation. In this work, he adopts the categories of Renouvier without much change, and conceives of the universe under the form of associated individuals. He tried to present his doctrine as a completed system, and, at its summit, he placed a personal God Who is free, Who is the Creator and is providential.

But it was especially in Germany that Neo-Kantianism spread most widely as a reaction against the a priori systems of idealistic pantheism and against the narrow vision of positivism. The movement was inaugurated by O. LIEBMANN (1840-1912); in his work, Kant und die Epigonen (1865), he proclaimed that a return to Kant is necessary. Neo-Kantianism was continued even into the twentieth century by the school of Marbourg and of Bade, each of which developed different aspects of Kantianism.

The school of Marbourg [3] was faithful to the "way of the spirit" and looked for truth in the work of the intelligence. Kant, however, required the collaboration of sensible intuition and the concepts of the understanding (Verstand) for constructing science; this school rejected this duality. It held that the spirit, by its own activity of thought produces the object itself, not as creating it in the ideal order, as in Fichte's pantheism, but insofar as the constructive effort of our conception and judgments constitutes the scientific object itself. The two main representatives of the school are HERMANN COHEN [4] (1842-1918) and PAUL NATORP [5]

---

[1] Renouvier asked himself, at the beginning of his reflections, whether it would not be better to adopt polytheism; but monotheism seemed more compatible with the regular connectivity of scientific laws.

[2] L. J. BECK, La méthode synthétique d'Hamelin, Paris, 1935.

[3] NATORP, P., Kant und die Marburger Schule, Berlin, 1912. — STERIAD, A., L'interprétation de la doctrine de Kant par l'école de Marbourg, Paris, 1913.

[4] Works : Kants Theorie der Erfahrung, Berlin, 1871. — Kants Begründung der Ethik, Berlin, 1877. — Kants Begrundung der Aesthetik, Berlin, 1889. — System der Philosophie, 3 pts., Berlin, 1902-12. — Der Begriff der Religion, Berlin, 1915. — Die Religion der Vernunft aus den Quellen des Judentums, Berlin, 1919.
Studies : NATORP, P., H. Cohen als Mensch, Lehrer und Forscher, Marburg, 1918. — ROSMARIN, T. W., Religion of Reason, New York, 1936. — VAART SMIT, H. W. van der, H. Cohen en de Marburgsche Schule, Baarn, 1924.

[5] Works : Descartes' Erkenntnistheorie, Berlin, 1882. — Forschungen zur Geschichte des Erkenntnisproblems in Altertum, Berlin, 1884. — Die Religion innerhalb der Grenzen der Humanität, Berlin, 1894. — Sozialpädagogik, Berlin, 1899. — Die logischen Grundlagen der exakten Wissenschaften, Berlin, 1910. — Allgemeine Psychologie nach kritischer Methode, Berlin, 1912. — Sozialidealismus, Berlin, 1920. — Genossenschaftliche Erziehung, Berlin, 1920. — Vorlesungen über praktische Philosophie, Berlin, 1925.
Study : E. WECK, Der Erkenntnisbegriff bei P. Natorp, Bonn, 1914.

(1854-1924), both university professors at Marbourg. They believed that one of the best realizations of their doctrine was the elaboration of higher mathematics, as in infinitesimal calculus; the formulas of this type of mathematics are fruitful and exact, and make up the very reality of movement and extension. — HANS VAIHINGER [1] (1852-1933) should also be mentioned here, as well as ERNST CASSIRER [2] (born in 1874), two renowned followers and commentators on Kant. — ALBERT GÖRLAND (born in 1869) and K. VERLÄNDER (1860-1928), are authors of several historical studies.

The school of Bade, for its part, emphasized the concluding portion of Kantianism, in which the primacy of practical reason is asserted. This school concluded with a " philosophy of values ", which will be treated below [3].

One of the rather recent and influential representatives of critical idealism is LÉON BRUNSCHVICG [4] (1869-1944), who held a professorship at the Sorbonne. An heir of Descartes and Kant, he does not hold with common sense testimony on the substantial reality of things. Without denying the existence of the exterior world, he declared it unknowable, for experience presupposes the work of reason on the brute fact; the object of the sciences is a construction of the spirit. He defends idealism, but it is a *critical* type, which means, subject to verification. The supreme criterion by which each doctrine should be measured is the *mathematical judgment;* it alone can always be perfectly verified by analysis which rediscovers the simple elements from which one originally began. From the mathematical sciences, as from a center, all other philosophical knowledge flows. By reflecting on its own creative power in independence of all else, the spirit

---

[1] Vaihinger's chief work is *The Philosophy of As If* (tr. C. K. Ogden), New York, 1945; it is pragmatic in tone, measuring the value of judgments according to their usefulness for life.

[2] **Works :** *Philosophy of Symbolic Forms* (tr. R. Manheim), 3 vols.; Vol. I, *Language*, New Haven (Conn.), 1953. — *Substance and Function and Einstein's Theory of Relativity* (tr. Swabey, W. C., and M. C.), 2 vols., New York, 1953. — *Language and Myth* (tr. S. K. Langer), New York, 1953. — *Philosophy of the Enlightenment* (tr. Koelin, F. C. A., and Pettegrove, J. P.), Princeton (N. J.), 1951. — *Problem of Knowledge; Philosophy, Science and History since Hegel* (tr. Woglom, W. H., and Hendel, C. W.), New Haven (Conn.), 1950. — *Essay on Man*, New Haven (Conn.), 1944. — *Myth of the State* (ed. C. W. Hendel), New Haven (Conn.), 1944. — *Rousseau, Kant, Goethe* (tr. J. Gutmann et al), Princeton (N. J.), 1945.

Studies : SCHILPP, P. A. (ed.), *Philosophy of Ernst Cassirer*, New York, 1949. — KIBLANSKY, R., and PATON, H. J. (eds.), *Philosophy and History* (Essays presented to Ernst Cassirer), Oxford, 1936.

[3] See below, n. 531, A.

[4] **Works :** *Introduction à la vie de l'esprit*, Paris, 1900. — *Les étapes de la philosophie mathématique*, Paris, 1912. — *L'expérience humaine et la causalité physique*, Paris, 1922. — *Les progrès de la conscience dans la philosophie occidentale*, Paris, 1927. — *De la connaissance de soi*, Paris, 1931. — *Les âges de l'intelligence*, Paris, 1947.

Studies : CARBONARA, L., *L. Brunschvicg*, Naples, 1931. — MESSAUT, J., *La philosophie de Léon Brunschvicg*, Paris, 1938.

creates not only its scientific and esthetic values, but its moral values as well; the universality of science gives reasons why one should renounce egoism in order to achieve the love of humanity. Briefly, in Brunschvicg's view, man is the modern savant who identifies his spirit with universal science and becomes unto himself the proper rule of truth and morality.

C) Critique of the Sciences.

One of the forms which the anti-positivistic reaction takes in contemporary times is the rigorous criticism often exercised by the savants themselves on the value of the results of modern science. These sciences were the positivistic ideal of science; they were the great light capable of definitively satisfying human reason. But along with the renaissance of metaphysical aspirations, the powerlessness of positivism to resolve the basic problems of life became evident.

The French precursors to this movement were A. COURNOT (1801-1877) and E. BOUTROUX (1845-1921). COURNOT [1] engaged in research on chance and the laws of probability; he concluded that human knowledge, though remaining incapable of breaking the barriers of the relative in order fully to attain the absolute, can approach to the latter quite closely. There are degrees in relativity, he said, and man is able to raise himself from an order of relative and phenomenal realities to an order of superior realities, thus penetrating gradually into the intelligence, which is the very basis of the reality of phenomena themselves. In order to go to a new order of science, Cournot proposed the adoption of a new, basic idea not reducible to the preceding science; the value of this new notion is to be gaged by its aptitude to unify the facts and to explain them with the most logic and the greatest simplicity. At the summit of knowledge there even exists a domain of " trans-rational " realities to correspond to the religious feeling in man. — BOUTROUX [2] already questioned the value of scientific laws

---

[1] **Works :** *Exposition de la théorie des chances et des probabilités*, Paris, 1843. — *Matérialisme, Vitalisme et Rationalisme*, Paris, 1875. — *Traité de l'enchaînement des idées fondamentales dans la science et dans l'histoire*, Paris, 1881. — *Researches into the Mathematical Principles of the Theory of Wealth* (tr. N. T. Bacon), New York, 1927. — *An Essay on the Foundations of Our Knowledge*, New York, 1953.
Studies : BOTTINELLI, J., *Cournot, métaphysicien de la connaissance*, Paris, 1913. — DARBON, A., *Le concept de hasard dans la philosophie de Cournot*, Paris, 1911. — FLOSS, S. W., *Outline of the Philosophy of Antoine-Augustin Cournot*, Philadelphia (Pa.), 1941. — MENTRE, F., *A. Cournot*, Paris, 1907. — *Cournot et la renaissance du probabilisme au XIXᵉ siècle*, Paris, 1908; — *Pour qu'on lise Cournot*, Paris, 1927.

[2] **Works :** *Certitude et Vérité*, Oxford, 1915. — *Contingency of the Laws of Nature* (tr. F. R. Rothwell), Chicago, 1916. — *Historical Studies in Philosophy* (tr. F. Rothwell), New York, 1912. — *Pages choisies*, Oxford, 1916. — *Relation between Thought and Action from the German and from the Classical Point of View*, Oxford, 1918. — *William James* (tr. Henderson, A. and B.), New York, 1912.
Studies : ARCHAMBAULT, P. E., *Boutroux*, Paris, 1910. — CRAWFORD, L. S., *Philosophy of Emile Boutroux*, New York, 1924.

in his basic work, *De la contingence des lois de la nature* (1874). He studied determinism in the physical, mechanical, and psychological orders, and held that the higher one lifts himself in the scale of beings, the wider becomes the margin of contingency which requires a creative source as the explanation of nature. God is the being Whose creative action we feel in the profoundest depths of ourselves, and in the very efforts we take to get close to Him. The whole hierarchy of beings is but the means and the condition for finding a liberty which believes, less and less, in physical fatalism.

Without referring to God, a group of thinkers crowned their scientific study with philosophical reflections on the sciences. The chief of this movement was HENRI POINCARÉ [1] (1854-1912), famous for his work, *Science and Hypothesis;* he completed and extended his ideas in *The Value of Science* (1905), in *Science and Method* (1909), and in *Final Thoughts* (1913). In these works he showed that scientific theories cannot possess the absolute value which positivism had conferred on them; in their application, especially to future phenomena, there is always the possibility of variation and there always remains a certain inequality which permits of another explanation. Briefly, there is always some hypothesis connected with science. His critique concluded that theories are called *true* when they are *most commodious* as simplifying the work of the thinker and giving him a most beautiful picture of the universe. — PIERRE DUHEM [2] (1861-1916), in his *The Aim and Structure of Physical Theory*, held that scientific theories have a value which is, in large part, merely symbolical, though based on reality. — EMILE MEYERSON [3] (1859-1933) wrote *Identité et réalité* (1908), *De l'explication dans les sciences* (1921) and *Du cheminement de la pensée* (1931). His works continue the critical examination and tend towards realism. In his view, scientific thought is in no wise concerned with exploring phenomena and irresistibly tends towards explaining them in terms of their real causes. In his *La déduction relativiste*, he gives an illustration of his views through the theory of general relativity as proposed

---

[1] **Works :** *Foundations of Science, Science and Hypothesis, the Value of Science, Science and Method* (auth. tr. G. B. Halsted), Lancaster (Pa.), 1929. — *Mémoires* (tr. Sir G. Arthur), 4 vols., New York, n. d.
Studies : LANGEVIN, P., *Henri Poincaré, l'œuvre scientifique, l'œuvre philosophique*, Paris, 1914. — TANNERY, J., *La philosophie de H. Poincaré*, Paris, 1912.
[2] **Works :** *Le Système du Monde, Histoire des doctrines cosmologiques de Platon à Copernic*, 5 vols., Paris, 1913-17. — *The Aim and Structure of Physical Theory* (tr. P. Wiener), New York, 1953.
Study : LOWINGER, A., *The Methodology of Pierre Duhem*, New York, 1941.
[3] **Work :** *Identity and Reality* (tr. K. Loeuenberg), New York, 1930.
Studies : Boss, G., *Critical Analysis of the Philosophy of Emile Meyerson*, Baltimore (Md.), 1930. — GILLET, M., *La philosophie de M. Meyerson*, Paris, 1931. — GUNN, A., *Modern French Philosophy*, London, 1922. — HESS, G., *Französische Philosophie der Gegenwart*, Berlin, 1933. — KELLY, T. R., *Explanation and Reality in the Philosophy of Emile Meyerson*, Princeton (N. J.), 1937. — SEE, H., *Science et philosophie d'après la théorie de M. Emile Meyerson*, Paris, 1932.

by EINSTEIN [1]. This latter theory has exercised the talents of many philosophers, as the works of Maritain, Bergson, and others, testify. Einstein's work is, above all, a work of higher mathematics in which all the laws of modern physics are unified. From the philosophical viewpoint, it is difficult to admit his basic proposition as an expression of physical fact; it states that two physical events simultaneous for one observer can be successive for another observer placed in different conditions. Einstein himself seems to give his view an idealistic twist, holding that truth is diversified according to various intelligences. A Thomist might conclude, with Maritain, that while Einstein's theory has a great mathematical value, it has only a symbolic meaning as an interpretation of reality.

Two spiritualistic philosophers should be included here, FÉLIX RAVAISSON (1813-1900) and JULES LACHELIER [2] (1832-1918). While they are not directly concerned with the critique of science, these two men bring out in relief one aspect of the anti-positivistic reaction whose main directions are here being outlined. They emphasize the need of a *spiritual reality* capable of satisfying the intelligence much better than the sensible phenomenon. RAVAISSON recommends a realism or spiritual positivism which takes as its principle the consciousness which the spirit has in itself, of an existence on which it recognizes every other existence to depend and from which it derives; this is none other than its own action. In his dissertation, *De l'habitude* (1838), he finds a proof for his view by analyzing the phenomenon of intellectual work; the latter becomes more quick and spontaneous, and finally becomes a *real* intuition in which the real and the ideal, thought and being are fused. This intuition, by taking the form of a desire for an ideal, lifts itself upward to grasping the very existence of God Himself. — LACHELIER is the inspirer of the *reflexive method*, as it was called by his pupil, J. LAGNEAU (1851-1894); the latter applied this method to psychology. The method consists in decomposing a representation in order to discover all the conditions of its existence on the objective as well as on the subjective side. By the use of this method, Lachelier was led to hold an identity between the laws of the spirit and the laws of being, and he held

---

[1] **Works:** *Cosmic Religion*, New York, 1931. — *Sidelights on Relativity;* *1 Ether and Relativity, 2 Geometry and Experience* (tr. Jeffrey, G. B., and Perrett, W.), New York, 1923. — *World as I See It* (tr. A. Harris), New York, 1949. — *Out of My Later Years*, New York, 1950. — *Meaning of Relativity* (tr. E. P. Adams et al), Princeton (N. J.), 1953.

Studies: BERGMANN, P. G., *Introduction to the Theory of Relativity*, New York, 1942. — BIRKHOFF, G. D., *Origin, Nature, and Influence of Relativity*, New York, 1925. — BORN, M., *Einstein's Theory of Relativity* (tr. H. L. Brose), London, 1924. — BROWN, M. M., *Historic Approach to the Theory of Relativity*, 2 vols., Locust Valley (N. Y.), 1948-50. — FRANK, P. G., *Einstein : His Life and Times*, New York, 1953. — INFELD, L., *Albert Einstein*, New York, 1953. — LANGDON-DAVIES, J., *Man and His Universe*, New York, 1934. — LEVINGER, E. C. E., *Albert Einstein*, New York, 1949. — MOLIER, C., *Theory of Relativity*, Oxford, 1952. — NORDMANN, C., *Einstein and the Universe*, New York, 1922. — SCHILPP, P. A. (ed.), *Albert Einstein, Philosopher-Scientist*, New York, 1952. — WEYL, H., *Space-Time-Matter*, New York, 1951.

[2] G. SÉAILLES, *La philosophie de J. Lachelier*, Paris, 1935.

that the final condition of all thought is the existence of God. Lachelier held that the highest question of philosophy, more religious than philosophy itself, is how to go from the formal absolute to the real and living absolute, from the idea of God to God.

D) Phenomenology [1].

This new theory was founded by EDMUND HUSSERL [2] (1859-1938), a pupil of F. BRENTANO [3]. Husserl taught at Göttingen, and then at Fribourg, and had a great number of disciples, the main one being MARTIN HEIDEGGER [4] (born in 1889). Among these decided partisans of realism, should be mentioned MAX SCHELER [5] (1874-1928) and NICOLAÏ HARTMANN [6] (born in 1882). This movement is rather new, and has not as yet uncovered its full development or clearly established its own way of thought. All the members of the school, however, are agreed on the *phenomenological method*, though they diverge on points of doctrine.

As is the case with many modern thinkers, Husserl entered philosophy through mathematics. Struck by the solidity and

---

[1] FARBER, M., *Foundation of Phenomenology*, Cambridge (Mass.), 1943. — GURVITCH, G., *Les tendances actuelles de la philosophie allemande*, Paris, 1930. — JONES, W. T., *Contemporary Thought in Germany*, London, 1930.

[2] **Works :** *Philosophie der Arithmetik*, Berlin, 1891. — *Logische Untersuchungen*, 3 vols., Berlin, 1900-1920. — *Ideen zu einer reinen Phänomenologie und phänomenologische Philosophie*, Berlin, 1913. — *Formale und transzendentale Logik*, Berlin, 1929. — *Méditations cartésiennes*, Berlin, 1931. — *Ideas ; General Introduction to Pure Phenomenology* (tr. W. R. B. Gibson), New York, 1952.

Studies : BERGER, C., *Le " cogito " dans la philosophie de Husserl*, Paris, 1950. — FARBER, M. (ed.), *Philosophical Essays in Memory of Edmund Husserl*, Cambridge (Mass.), 1940. — LEVINAS, E., *La théorie de l'intuition dans la phénoménologie de Husserl*, Paris, 1930. — OSBORN, A. D., *Edmund Husserl and His Logical Investigations*, Ann Arbor (Mich.), 1949. — WELCH, E. P., *Edmund Husserl's Phenomenology*, Berkeley (Cal.), 1939. — *Philosophy of Edmund Husserl*, New York, 1941.

[3] See above, n. 510.

[4] **Works :** *Sein und Zeit*, Berlin, 1926. — *Vom Wesen des Grundes*, Berlin, 1929. — *Was ist Metaphysik*, Berlin, 1928. — *Kant und das Problem des Metaphysik*, Berlin, 1929. — *Existence and Being* (tr. D. Scott et al), Chicago, 1949.

Studies : KRAFT, J., *Von Husserl zu Heidegger*, Leipzig, 1932. — WAELHENS, A., *La philosophie de Martin Heidegger*, Louvain, 1942.

[5] **Works :** *Der Formalismus in der Ethik und die materiale Wertethik*, Berlin, 1913. — *Der Genius des Krieges und der deutsche Krieg*, Berlin, 1915. — *Vom Umsturz der Werte*, Berlin, 1919. — *Vom Ewigen im Menschen*, Berlin, 1921. — *Die Wissensformen und die Gesellschaft*, Berlin, 1926. — *Die Stellung des Menschen im Kosmos*, Berlin, 1928. — *Philosophische Weltanschauung*, Berlin, 1929. — *Phaenomenologie der Religion ; nach ihrem Wesentlichsten allgemein verständlich dargestellt und beurtheilt von Joseph Geyser*, St. Louis (Mo.), 1924.

Studies : L. de RAEYMAEKER, *De philosophie van Scheler*, Malines, n. d.

[6] **Works :** *Grundzüge einer Metaphysik des Erkenntnis*, Berlin, 1921. — *Die Philosophie des deutschen Idealismus*, Berlin, 1923-29. — *Zum Problem der Realitätsgegebenheit*, Berlin, 1931. — *Das Problem des geistigen Seins*, Berlin, 1933. — *Systematische Selbstdarstellung*, Berlin, 1933. — *Zur Grundlegung der Ontologie*, Berlin, 1934. — *New Ways of Ontology* (tr. R. C. Kuhn), Chicago, 1953. — *Ethics* (tr. S. Colt), 3 vols., New York, 1932.

Study : P. V. S. NARAYANA, *Critique on Nicolai Hartmann's Ethics*, Madras (India), 1937.

precision of the exact sciences in comparison to the fluctuations of philosophy [1], he hoped to give the latter a foundation for infallible truth which would allow philosophy to be set up as a *true science*. The phenomenological method is, therefore, a new kind of criteriology, seeking for more rigor than that of Descartes or Kant. It is based on two principles, one negative, and the other, positive.

a) Negative principle. One must first be rid of any presupposition and consider as meaningless whatever has not been demonstrated apodictically. The state of soul here required resembles the universal doubt of Descartes, but is not based, as is the latter, on positive reasons [2]. In the expression of Husserl, it is " placed in parentheses "; it is an *Einklammerung;* it is an effort to hold the glance of the spirit pure when faced with the object, grasping it in all its extent, but without any deforming intermediary.

b) Positive Principle. This principle indicates what the object is. One must go to things themselves, and the things which manifest themselves with such a fulness of unimpeachable evidence are the PHENOMENA. This term is not used, however, in the idealistic sense of Hume or Kant, nor in the positivistic sense of Comte or Taine. Husserl believed that he had shown that these doctrines mutilate the object of philosophy by introducing arbitrary presuppositions. The phenomenon is the *fact immediately attainable in all its aspects.* Two points should be stressed. At first, the phenomenon appears to these philosophers as a *very rich synthesis;* it is an object known and, at the same time, the knowledge of this object (the fact of consciousness). This essential relationship to the object which the phenomenological school, following Brentano [3], calls " intentional being ", constitutes the very nature of knowledge. — Finally, the object known must be taken in the concrete and seized at the same time by the various internal and external senses, as in perception; moreover, it must be endowed with the intelligible aspects which refer it to reason. Thus, the first task of phenomenology, according to its defenders, is to describe, with exactitude, the scientific phenomena through proceeding methodically; this should be done especially for fundamental concepts. The efforts of this school have renewed the exposition of central ideas in morality, psychology and physical science. Finally, this descriptive effort must be, above all, intellectual and intuitive. If it penetrates the most profound aspects of reality, it is not in order to deduce some from others, but in order to make them explicit and to define them exactly. What is thus attained is not pure appearance, but *essences* themselves with their stable properties, capable of being the foundation of true sciences.

Does such a method lead to *realism?* The members of the school are not in accord on this question. Heidegger empha-

---

[1] Here we are speaking of modern philosophy as Husserl sees it, with its many contradictory theories.

[2] This refers to the *negative doubt* recognized in Thomistic criteriology; see above, n. 318 and 321.

[3] Brentano borrowed this terminology from the Scholastics.

sizes the concrete and real traits of the phenomenon. In his work, *Sein und Zeit*, he teaches an open realism, though he views time and limitation as essential to real beings. Husserl, on the contrary, following the rigorous application of his method, puts all real existence " in parentheses ". He does not believe that the pure essence grasped by consciousness, which opposes itself to an object while possessing it, is something given as absolutely evident. Continuing in the high degree of abstraction which he calls the " transcendental phenomenon ", he attempts to analyze the foundation of the sciences from this point of view. He thus falls into what has been called " transcendental phenomenological idealism " which is distinguished from ordinary idealism, for it does not exclude the reality of the soul and of external things from the realm of psychology and physics.

It is evident that phenomenology constitutes a reaction against positivism and idealism, and its method seems capable of leading to a truly realistic philosophy.

E) **Existentialism** [1].

This movement was born in Germany about 1925. SOREN KIERKEGAARD [2] and MARTIN HEIDEGGER were its precursors.

---

[1] ALLEN, E. L., *Existentialism from Within*, New York, 1953. — BEAUVOIR, S. de, *Ethics of Ambiguity*, New York, 1948. — BLACKHAM, H. J., *Six Existentialist Thinkers*, New York, 1952. — BOBBIO, N., *Philosophy of Decadentism*, New York, 1948. — COLLINS, J. D., *Existentialists : A Critical Study*, Chicago, 1952. — FOULQUIÉ, P., *Existentialism*, New York, 1950. — GRENE, M. G., *Dreadful Freedom*, Chicago, 1948. — HARPER, R., *Existentialism : A Theory of Man*, Cambridge (Mass.), 1948. — HAWTON, H., *Feast of Unreason*, London, 1952. — HEINEMANN, F., *Existentialism and the Modern Predicament*, New York, 1953. — KEAN, C. D., *Meaning of Existence*, New York, 1947. — KUHN, H., *Encounter With Nothingness*, Chicago, 1949. — MARITAIN, J., *Existence and the Existent*, New York, 1948. — MASCALL, E. L., *Existence and Analogy*, New York, 1949. — MOUNIER, E., *Existentialist Philosophies*, New York, 1949. — REINHARDT, K. F., *Existentialist Revolt*, Milwaukee (Wis.), 1952. — RUGGIERO, G. de, *Existentialism ; Disintegration of Man's Soul* (tr. E. M. Cocks) New York, 1948. — TROISFONTAINES, R., *Existentialisme et pensée chrétienne*, Louvain, 1946. — WAHL, J. A., *Short History of Existentialism*, New York, 1949.

[2] **Works :** *Christian Discourses ;* and *The Lilies of the Field* and *the Birds of the Air ;* and *Three Discourses at the Communion on Friday* (tr. W. Lowrie), Oxford, 1940. — *Journals* (ed. and tr. A. Dree), Oxford, 1951. — *Attack upon Christendom* (tr. W. Lowrie), Princeton (N. J.), 1944. — *Concept of Dread* (tr. W. Lowrie), Princeton (N. J.), 1944. — *Edifying Discourses* (tr. Swenson, D. F., and L. M.), 4 vols., Minneapolis (Minn.), 1943-46. — *Either Or ; A Fragment of Life*, 2 vols., (vol. 1 tr. Swenson, D. F. and L. M.; vol. 2 tr. W. Lowrie), Princeton (N. J.), 1944. — *For Self-Examination* and *Judge For Yourselves* and three *Discourses*, 1851 (tr. W. Lowrie), Princeton (N. J.), 1944. — *Gospel of Suffering* and *The Lilies of the Field* (tr. Swenson, D. F., and L. M.), Minneapolis (Minn.), 1947. — *Training in Christianity* and *Accompanying Edifying Discourse* (tr. W. Lowrie), Princeton (N. J.), 1944. — *Works of Love* (tr. Swenson, D. F., and L. M.), Princeton (N. J.), 1946. — *Concluding Unscientific Postscript* (tr. D. F. Swenson), Princeton (N. J.), 1941. — *Fear and Trembling* (tr. R. Payne), Oxford, 1939. — *Point of View*, etc. (tr. W. Lowrie), Oxford, 1939. — *Repetition ; an Essay in Experimental Psychology* (tr.

It spread to France, where a number of idealists, as LOUIS LAVELLE [1] and RENÉ LESENNE [2], adapted their doctrine to these new perspectives. Existentialism has become more and more in favor since the war of 1939 among men of letters, as A. Camus, Jeanne Hersch, M. Merleau-Ponty, and also among the historians, as J. Wahl and M. Souriau. The Russians, Berdiaeff [3], Chestov, W. Jankelevitch, and the Czech, Kafka, also belong to this school. Other important names include KARL JASPERS [4], in

W. Lowrie), Princeton (N. J.), 1941. — *Sickness Unto Death* (tr. W. Lowrie). Princeton (N. J.), 1941. — *Stages On Life's Way* (tr. W. Lowrie), Princeton, 1940. — *Thoughts On Crucial Situations In Human Life* (tr. D. F. Swenson; ed. L. M. Swenson), Minneapolis (Minn.), 1941. — *Philosophical Fragments;* or, *A Fragment of Philosophy* (tr. D. F. Swenson), Princeton (N. J.), 1936.

Studies : ALLEN, E. L., *Kierkegaard : His Life and Thought*, New York, 1936. — BONIFAZI, C., *Christendom Attacked : A Comparison of Kierkegaard and Nietzsche*, London, 1953. — CHANING-PEARCE, M., *Soren Kierkegaard*, New York, 1947. — CHESTOV, L., *Kierkegaard et la philosophie existentielle*, Paris, 1937. — COLLINS, J. D., *Mind of Kierkegaard*, Chicago, 1953. — CROXALL, T. H., *Kierkegaard Studies*, London, 1948. — FRIEDMANN, R., *Kierkegaard*, New York, 1950. — HAECKER, T., *Soren Kierkegaard*, Oxford, 1937. — *Kierkegaard, the Cripple* (tr. C. van O. Bruyn), New York, 1950. — HUBBEN, W., *Four Prophets of Our Destiny* (Dostoievsky, Nietzsche, Kafka, Kierkegaard), New York, 1952. — JOLIVET, R., *Introduction to Kierkegaard*, New York, 1951. — KOCH, L., *Soeren Kierkegaard*, Issy-les-Moulineaux, 1934. — LOWRIE, W., *Kierkegaard*, Oxford, 1938. — *Short Life of Kierkegaard*, Princeton (N. J.), 1942. — MARTIN, H. V., *Kierkegaard, the Melancholy Dane*, New York, 1950. — MESNARD, P., *Le vrai visage de Kierkegaard*, Paris, 1948. — PATRICK, D. G. M., *Pascal and Kierkegaard*, 2 vols., Chicago, 1948. — SWENSON, D. F., *Something About Kierkegaard*, Minneapolis (Minn.), 1945. — THOMTE, R., *Kierkegaard's Philosophy of Religion*, Princeton (N. J.), 1948. — WAHL, J., *Etudes kierkegaardiennes*, Paris, 1938.

[1] **Works :** *La conscience de soi*, Paris, 1933. — *De l'être*, Paris, 1935. — *De l'acte*, Paris, 1937. — *La présence totale*, Paris, n. d. — *Le moi et son destin*, Paris, n. d. — *Du temps et de l'éternité*, Paris, 1945. — *La dialectique du monde sensible*, Oxford, 1922. — *La perception visuelle de la profondeur*, Oxford, n. d.

[2] **Works :** *Le devoir*, Paris, 1930. — *Le mensonge et le caractère*, Paris, 1937. — *La morale générale*, Paris, 1942. — *Introduction à la philosophie*, Paris, n. d. — *Obstacle et valeur*, Paris, n. d. — *Traité de caractériologie*, Paris, 1946.

[3] **Works :** *The Destiny of Man*, London, 1937. — *Divine and the Human* (tr. R. M. French), New York, 1949. — *Dream and Reality* (tr. K. Lampert), New York, 1950. — *Realm of Spirit and Realm of Caesar* (tr. D. A. Lowrie), London, 1952. — *Slavery and Freedom* (tr. R. M. French), New York, 1944. **Studies :** CLARKE, O. F., *Introduction to Berdiaef*, London, 1950. — LAMPERT, E., *Nicolas Berdijaev and the New Middle Ages*, London, 1945.

[4] **Works :** *Origin and Goal of History* (tr. M. Bullock), New Haven (Conn.), 1953. — *Existentialism and Humanism* (ed. H. E. Fischer; tr. E. B. Ashton), New York, 1952. — *Tragedy is Not Enough* (tr. H. A. T. Reiche et al), Boston, 1953. — *European Spirit* (tr. R. G. Smith), New York, 1949. — *Man In the Modern Age* (tr. E. and C. Paul), London, 1951. — *Perennial Scope of Philosophy* (tr. R. Manheim), New York, 1949. — *Reason and Anti-Reason in Our Time* (tr. S. Godman), New Haven (Conn.), 1952. — *Way to Wisdom : An Introduction to Philosophy* (tr. R. Manheim), New Haven (Conn.), 1951. — *Question of German Guilt* (tr. E. B. Ashton), New York, 1947. **Studies :** BROCK, W., *Karl Jaspers*, Cambridge, n. d. — TONQUÉDEC, J. de, *L'existence selon K. Jaspers*, Paris, 1945.

Germany, GABRIEL MARCEL [1] and JEAN-PAUL SARTRE [2] in France.

Existentialism can be defined as *the philosophy of the personal existence of man, synthesized in the free choice of his own destiny*.

Every philosophy is an effort at reflection in order to discover the profound causes of the universe. It is proper to philosophy to consider *existence* as an integrating part of its object, in opposition to the abstract essence which is the exclusive domain of the classical philosophers from Plato to Leibniz. The first trait common to all existentialists is their reaction against the " perennial philosophy ".

Moreover, existentialism is concerned mainly with the *existence of the human person* as immediately grasped through introspection. There is no open denial that other realities exist, but these " beings-in-themselves " are like strange lumps with which one collides; in themselves they remain inaccessible, unintelligible and absurd. Thus the subjective and human point of view is strongly affirmed.

What " creates " our personality is the *free choice of a destiny*. This is the primordial, given fact of existentialism [3]; everything else is judged by relationship to this basic choice in such a way that this subjective dialectic seems to realize the final explanation of things. For, everything becomes intelligible only by taking one's place in this universe which springs forth from human liberty [4]. In this sense, existentialism is a humanistic point of view.

In order to attain and study this existence, existentialism adopts the *phenomenological method*. The phenomenon of the personal self, however, now appears with all its attachments to the external world, along with its multiple, subjective aspects.

---

[1] **Works :** *Man of God* (tr. M. Gabain); *Ariadne, The Funeral Pyre* (tr. R. Heywood), London, 1952. — *Man Against Humanity* (tr. G. S. Fraser), London, 1948. — *Philosophy of Existence* (tr. M. Harari), New York, 1949. — *Being and Having* (tr. K. Farrer), London, 1949. — *Homo Viator : An Introduction to a Metaphysic of Hope* (tr. E. Craufurd), Chicago, 1951. — *Metaphysical Journal* (tr. B. Wall), Chicago, 1952. — *Mystery of Being*, 2 vols. : *Reflection and Mystery* (tr. G. S. Fraser); *Faith and Reality* (tr. R. Hague), London, 1950-51.

Study : R. TROISFONTAINES, *De l'existence à l'être, d'après G. Marcel. Synthèse doctrinale*, 2 vols., Louvain, 1952.

[2] **Works :** *Existential Psychoanalysis* (tr. H. E. Barnes), New York, 1953. — *Nausea* (tr. L. Alexander), New York, 1949. — *Psychology of Imagination*, New York, 1948. — *What Is Literature?* (tr. B. Frechtman), New York, 1949. — *Age of Reason* (tr. E. Sutton), London, 1947. — *Emotions, Outline of a Theory* (tr. B. Frechtman), New York, 1948. — *Existentialism* (tr. B. Frechtman), New York, 1947.

Study : P. J. R. DEMPSEY, *Psychology of Sartre*, Westminster (Md.), 1951.

[3] In this sense, " existence *precedes* essence ", since one " creates himself " by this fundamental choice, on which depends whatever one is as a human person.

[4] Furthermore, this existence languishes in an atmosphere of anxiety, due to the formidable problem of destiny, always resolved in favor of liberty, and often without one being sure what good will be accomplished.

Starting from this center, which is in communication with the entire universe, each thinker can undertake to explain everything. Despite common resemblances, and a common predilection for psychological analysis, each existentialist develops his experiences in his own way. Some of them, as Kierkegaard, who are poets as well as philosophers, simply aim to awake in their readers an experience similar to their own, which has revealed to them the meaning of life. Others offer more general views.

Among the latter, there are two opposed currents. The first, represented by Sartre, follows Heidegger, accepting human existence as a brute fact, as an absolute beginning and a pure contingency which cannot be explained. It is but " a being, thrown thither ", the *Dasein*, or the self, condemned to the liberty of choosing a destiny though it knows it will lead nowhere. In this view, the sentiment which is most revelatory of existence is that of *nausea*. Despite all of this, the true philosopher will be sincere. Without avoiding bad faith, which is so frequent (since one seeks a goal which he knows to be basically impossible of attainment), he will openly accept his tragic situation. His happiness will lie in affirming himself while choosing anything at all, though he must remain faithful to his choice [1].

This direction towards despair, however, is not the only one possible. An authentic type of existentialism, as that of G. Marcel, who follows Kierkegaard and Jaspers, can remain " vertically " open towards the side of God. For Marcel, the first choice which is constitutive of our personality, is the acceptance of the self as created by God, in Whom it will find its repose and happiness. The basic free act, in his view, is to say " yes " to grace. The weakness of our liberty fills this " yes " with humble and fearful anguish, but also with confident hope. The goal of life, then, is to render testimony to God by faithfulness to one's interior voice.

Whatever doctrinal form existentialism may take, a basic question arises : Will it find in its own method the means of criticizing its point of departure? The primordial choice, which gives a meaning to our existence by fixing a precise goal for it, is the first duty of moral life. It must ordinarily be clarified in order to be stated with prudence and in the complete surety of conscience. A philosophy such as Thomism finds in its psychology and theodicy a firm rule for orienting this first direction of moral life. But if one adopts free choice as a basis, one is condemned to an indifferent reception of all experience, whether it be that of an atheist, as Sartre, or that of a Christian, as Marcel. Both could be equally authentic and, consequently, legitimate. It seems that, in order to retain its precious wealth of psychological materials, existentialism should renounce any attempt to be set up as a separate system, and remain what it could most excellently be, a general introduction to philosophy.

---

[1] See, on the other hand, *L'existentialisme est un humanisme*, a conference given by Sartre in 1946, in which he proposes a more human morality which takes into account social contingencies.

II. The Way of Feeling.

531. In turning towards feeling or sentiment in order to go beyond positivism, philosophers, sometimes knowingly and sometimes unknowingly, have continued the final portion of Kantianism, which proclaimed the primacy of practical reason. This is the position of the school of Bade which led to a *philosophy of values*. This idea of value, concentrated by Nietzsche in his own personality, inspired his *philosophy of the Superman*, which is a vigorous protestation of sentiment against the scientific culture of ruling positivism. This same type of protestation takes a less offensive form in current *religious philosophy*, which, since the nineteenth century, has attempted to reunite with the divine reality by intuition. The same preoccupation is evident in the *philosophy of action* currently proposed by Blondel.

A) The Philosophy of Values[1].

The fundamental principle of the philosophy of values can be proposed as follows. Just as in morality, the good is that which should be willed (Kant says it is duty for duty's sake), so in the realm of speculation, *truth is that which should be thought;* that is, that which has some value for us. This view, evidently, is quite close to pragmatism. But, instead of placing the criterion of truth in that which is useful to man, it looks for this criterion in that which ennobles, elevates and " civilizes " man. It is a philosophy of culture, implying, as does the German philosophy of value, that " civilization " and " culture " are opposed. The first, civilization, is but material and industrial progress, *useful* in the deprecatory sense of the word. Culture, on the other hand, represents everything which gives value to human life. This cultural value, according to these thinkers, is not relativistic as is the scientific phenomenon; it is an *absolute* which philosophy must discover and make precise in order to apply it to the different domains of the sciences and morality.

Among the Neo-Kantians of the school of Bade, who defend this view, Wilhelm Windelbandt [2] (1848-1915) is worthy of mention; he found the system of values in the " normal conscientiousness " in which humanity expresses its culture. — Heinrich

---

[1] Messer, A., *Deutsche Wertphilosophie der Gegenwart*, Leipzig, 1926. — Osborne, H., *Foundations of the Philosophy of Value*, New York, 1933.

[2] **Works :** *Geschichte und Naturwissenschaft*, Berlin, n. d. — *Einleitung in die Philosophie*, Berlin, n. d. — *Das Heilige*, Berlin, nd.

Studies : Picard, M., *Values, Immediate and Contributory, and their Interrelation*, New York, 1920. — Rickert, H., *Wilhelm Windelband*, Tubingen, 1916. — Vaart Smit, H. V., van der, *Windelband*, Baarn, 1922.

RICKERT [1] (1863-1936), applied this principle to history, wherein, he held, one must choose the facts which have a value for culture. — BRUNO BAUCH (born in 1877) applied this view to morality and concluded that the legitimate political view is that of force at the service of values. — HUGO MUNSTERBERG [2] (1803-1916) wrote *Philosophie der Werte* (1906), in which he finds the principle of the philosophy of values in an original action which lends meaning to our existence, in the will that there is a world and that our impressions do not have value only for ourselves as impressions but assert themselves independently [3]. — OSWALD SPENGLER [4] (1880-1936), wrote *The Decline of the West*, in which he harshly criticizes our present culture.

One can refer to the philosophy of values the theory of RACISM [5] invented by J. A. GOBINEAU [6] (1818-1882); this theory was enthusiastically received in Germany where it was propagated by Houston STEWART CHAMBERLAIN [7] (1855-1927). Though an Englishman by birth, Chamberlain became an apostle of Pan-Germanism. This theory holds that there exists a privileged race, the *Aryan race*, which alone and with full right possesses the ideal of human values; thereby this race is destined to dominate all other races, which are inferior. All the rules of esthetics, morality and politics can be summarized in but one, " to preserve and promote the purity of Aryan blood ". Ethnologists almost

---

[1] See J. FISCHER, *Die Philosophie der Werte bei W. Windelband und H. Rickert*, Münster, 1913.

[2] **Works :** *On the Witness Stand ; Essays on Psychology and Crime*, New York, 1927. — *Eternal Life*, New York, 1905. — *Eternal Values*, New York, 1909. — *Psychology and Industrial Efficiency*, New York, 1913. — *Psychology and the Teacher*, New York, 1909. — *Psychology, General and Applied*, New York, 1914. — *Science and Idealism*, New York, 1906.
Study : M. A. A. MUNSTERBERG, *Hugo Munsterberg, His Life and Work*, New York, 1922.

[3] See E. BRÉHIER, *Histoire de la philosophie*, II, p. 1083.

[4] **Works :** *Decline of the West*, (tr. C. F. Atkinson), 2 vols., New York, 1945. — *Man and Technics ; A Contribution to a Philosophy of Life* (tr. C. F. Atkinson), New York, 1932.
Studies : GODDARD, E. H., and GIBBONS, P. A., *Civilisation or Civilisations*, New York 1926. — HUGUES, H. S., *Oswald Spengler : A Critical Esimate* New York, 1952.

[5] HIRSCHFIELD, M., *Racism* (tr. and ed. E. and C. Paul), London, 1938. — SOPER, E. D., *Racism, A World Issue*, New York, 1947.

[6] **Works :** *Essai sur l'inégalité des races humaines*, 4 vols., Paris, 1853-55. — *Histoire des Perses*, 2 vols., Paris, 1869.
Studies : DREYFUS, R., *La vie et les prophètes du comte de Gobineau*, Paris, 1905. — KRETZER, E., *J. A. Graf von Gobineau, sein Leben und sein Werk*, Leipzig, 1902. — LANGE, M., *Le comte Arthur de Gobineau*, Oxford, 1924. — SPRING, G. M., *Vitalism of Count de Gobineau*, New York, 1932.

[7] **Works :** *Die Grundlagen des XIXen Jahrhunderts*, Munich, 1942. — *Arische Weltanschauung*, Munich, 1938. — *Goethe*, Munich, 1939. — *Deutsches Wesen*, Munich, 1942. — *Lebenswege meines Denkens*, Munich, 1942.
Study : H. MEYER, *Houston Stewart Chamberlain als volkischer Denker*, Munich, 1939.

unanimously teach that all men are equal in nature [1], and that there does not actually exist a human group of pure race. However, the racist doctrine was explained by ROSENBERG in his *Mythe du XXe siècle*, and became the religious and political *credo* of the Third Reich. In this way, Hitler conferred authority on this view from without, and it was able to exert, through his power, an influence which its scientific and philosophical defects hardly warranted.

B) The Philosophy of Superman.

FRÉDÉRICK NIETZSCHE [2] (1844-1900).

This rather famous thinker also presented a philosophy of values. However, instead of looking for the principle in human blood or race, he placed it in the "self". The son of a Protestant minister, Nietzsche spent his youth in the faithful practice of his religion. But when he chose his career, he separated himself from all belief in order to follow the bent of his powerful personality. He studied, and later taught philology at Bâle (1869-79), though he was quite happy when sickness enabled him to give up his teaching position and devote himself completely to his philosophical

---

[1] This is also the doctrine of the Catholic Church, fully in accord with true science. See BRIÈRE, Y. de la, et al, *Racisme et Christianisme*, Paris, 1939; — BRESSOLES, J., et al, *Racisme et Catholicisme*, Tournai, 1939. See also the 8 propositions issued by the Sacred Congregation of Religious (Acta Catholicae Sedis, April 13, 1938).

[2] **Works:** *Complete Works* (ed. O. Levy), 18 vols., New York, 1925. — *Philosophy of Nietzsche: Thus Spake Zarathustra, Beyond Good and Evil, The Genealogy of Morals, Ecce Homo, The Birth of Tragedy* (ed. W. H. Wright), New York, 1937. — *Anti-Christ* (tr. H. L. Mencken), New York, 1931.
Studies: ABRAHAM, G. E. H., *Nietzsche*, New York, 1933. — ANDLER, C., I. *Les précurseurs de Nietzsche*, Paris, 1920. — II. *La Jeunesse de Nietzsche*, Paris, n. d. — III. *Le pessimisme de Nietzsche*, Paris, 1921. — IV. *Nietzsche et le transformisme intellectuel*, Paris, 1922. — V. *La maturité de Nietzsche* Paris, 1928. — VI. *La dernière philosophie de Nietzsche*, Paris, 1930. — BENTLEY, E. R., *Century of Hero-Worship;* study of Carlisle, Nietzsche and others, New York, 1944. — CHALLAYE, F., *Nietzsche*, Paris, n. d. — CROOKSHANK, F. G., *Individual Psychology and Nietzsche*, London, 1933. — DWELSHAUVERS, G., *La philosophie de Nietzsche*, Paris, 1909. — FOSTER, G. B., *Friedrich Nietzsche*, New York, 1931. — KAUFFMAN, W. A., *Nietzsche: Philosopher, Psychologist, Antichrist*, Princeton (N. J.), 1950. — KNIGHT, G. W., *Christ and Nietzsche*, London, 1949. — LEFEBVRE, H., *Nietzsche*, Paris, 1939. — LICHTENBERGER, H., *Gospel of Superman*, New York, 1926. — LUBACK, H. de, *Le drame de l'humanisme athée*, Paris, 1945. — MANN, H., *L'œuvre immortelle de Nietzsche*, Paris, 1909. — MENCKEN, H. L., *Philosophy of Friedrich Nietzsche*, Boston, 1908. — MORGAN, G. A., *What Nietzsche Means*, Cambridge (Mass.), 1941. — MÜGGE, M. A., *Friedrich Nietzsche*, Chicago, n. d. — NICOLAS, M. P., *From Nietzsche Down to Hitler*, London, 1939. — REYBURN, H. A., et al, *Nietzsche*, New York, 1948. — ROMER, H., *Nietzsche*, Leipzig, 1911. — SALTER, W. M., *Nietzsche the Thinker*, New York, 1917. — THOMPSON, R. M., *Nietzsche and Christian Ethics*, New York, 1952. — VAIHINGER, H., *Nietzsche als Philosoph*, Langensulze, 1930. — WILLIAMS, W. D., *Nietzsche and the French*, New York, 1953. — WOLF, A., *Philosophy of Nietzsche*, New York, 1925.

" mission ". Constantly struggling against his illness, he was able to have a few years of respite. During this period, he produced a large number of writings, but was interrupted by a severe mental illness that occurred in 1889. Nietzsche never recovered the use of reason and died in this condition in 1900.

Nietzsche's philosophy is essentially *individualistic;* it is like a reflection of his personality and like the history of his interior life. His aim, in writing, is not to convince the reader, but to lead him to the same discoveries of himself. If he can be viewed as having a basic principle, it would be somewhat as follows : " be yourself, without weakness, logically, and remain such until the end ". It was in obedience to this principle that Nietzsche changed his first enthusiasm for Schopenhauer to an acerb criticism, and broke his friendship with the musician, Wagner, without any hesitation; he saw that his ideals and theirs did not match. Now the experience which Nietzsche recounts for us in his writings is one of pitiable grandeur; it gives us the portrait of the insane pride of a man of genius who consciously puts himself in the place of God. He tells how he restored meaning to his existence by the aid of his own instinct to live, after he had " killed God " in his heart. His presentation is completely unsystematic, though it is literary, lyrical, alive, imaginative, harmonious and dramatic as a work of art. Furthermore, his views change quite a number of times throughout his writings; at first he praises Schopenhauer and Wagner, and attacks them bitterly in his later writings. At the same time, there are a few master ideas which appear throughout his works and give some unity to his doctrine. Two aspects can be distinguished in his works, a negative and a positive one.

1. *The negative side* is a quite radical criticism of the culture and civilization of the nineteenth century, which Nietzsche summarizes in the expression, " European nihilism ". Every culture supposes a *table of values* or a certain number of goods considered as the best, and towards which the social organization tends as towards an ideal. In Nietzsche's view, the determination of this scale of values is but a reflection of character or of the physical temperament of the people who adopt it. From this notion he gets two categories : the first is a culture of degenerate and servile people; the other is that of masters full of health and vitality. In his view, all the values adopted by his civilization are marks of the degenerate culture, and owe their origin to the Jewish people, a servile race. These values were renewed in the triumph of Christianity especially through its assertion of a life beyond, which leads to forgetfulness of this life, which alone is real. The dogmas of God the Creator and Judge, and of the immortal soul are anti-scientific, and conjured up in order to found hope in another world. The Christian doctrine of sin is the work of the illusory notion of a free will[1], which is declared responsible so that one can require patience, resignation, humility and obedience

---

[1] Nietzsche believes that one should blindly obey his vital instinct and that liberty is but an illusion.

to a God-Messiah. All of this, Nietzsche believes, is but a manifestation of weakness and of a degenerate state; the priesthood
transforms this into virtue in order to maintain its domination
over the people by making them accept present misery in the
hope of a future equalization of all ills.

Nietzsche's writings contain pages upon pages of accusations
against Christianity, and especially against the Catholic Church
and priesthood; they are of an unparalleled violence and are
profoundly unjust. He does not attack the priesthood as it is,
but as it exists in his imagination. He gratuitously asserts that
the great truths established by the philosophy of good sense on
God and the soul, are but illusions or dogmas invented with more
or less astuteness by a priesthood thirsty for power. He declares,
it is true, that his own opinions are probably no more true than
those he is combatting, for what is important is not objective
truth but the victory of his " self ". At the same time, he also
speaks of his doctrine as if it were the infallible truth.

On the other hand, he is no more just nor less tender when he
considers the efforts at civilization of the modern savants. These
men, it seems, as imbued with positivism, are inimical to the
Christian ideal. But in Nietzsche's view, they are either inspired
by the same ideal, placing " science " in God's place, or they
are but mediocre men, incapable of renovating the scale of values.
For, even in rejecting Christianity, these men easily set themselves
up in a society founded on democracy, liberalism, the search
for ease and riches — all of these being symptoms of degeneracy
equally as bad as religious faith.

2. The *positive part* of Nietzsche's doctrine consists in a proposal
to break this scale of values and return to the culture of the masters.
This doctrine is proclaimed by Nietzsche's counterpart, Zarathustra,
" I will teach you of Superman " (Übermensch). It should be
noted that this new lineup of values is not addressed to all, but
to some exceptional beings in whom humanity finds its goal and
best expression, and whose appearance demands the labor of
countless men in an inferior condition who are weak, inferior,
slaves, and, consequently, unhappy. These men must have the
consolations of a religious morality. Above this common crowd,
the superior men must take account of their situation in a culture
of degenerate people. The best way for them to surmount their
disgust is to live freely and fully in order to prepare for the coming
of *Superman*.

The *Superman* does not seem to be a being of a new essence.
" One can define the Superman as the actual state which will
surround man when he will renounce the actual hierarchy of
values of the Christian, democratic or ascetic ideals which is
current in modern Europe, in order to return to the table of values
held among noble races or among those Masters who create the
values which they themselves recognize, in place of receiving
them from without " [1]. Prior to the decadence current in Europe,

---

[1] H. LICHTENBERGER, *La philosophie de Nietzsche*, p. 149.

there existed such a state among the conquering and dominating races of antiquity, as the Greeks, the Romans and the Germans. The future *Superman* will profit from all the conquests of science in order to dominate nature itself.

There is a radical distinction between *Superman* and inferior men; their rules of morality are completely different. Superman has realized the *transvaluation* of all values *(Umwertung aller Werthe)*. His unique goal is the expansion of his will-to-power; the latter is a vital instinct which, in every sane and vigorous being, irresistibly inclines him to dominate another as much as possible. Whatever favors this vital force is true and good. In order to follow this route, one must expect great sorrows and an unending struggle against the crowd, which he uses as his instrument. For the small men, by their number and trickery, could quite often conquer the heroes who attempt the adventure of *Superman;* the right motto, then, is " live dangerously ". Since the unique goal of such a man is victory, he will regard any pity for the unhappy as a weakness. Since humanity is recapitulated in himself, he will dominate without remorse, and find his supreme joy in triumph. Finally, such a man will forever fix his destiny by accepting to relive his heroic life endlessly, according to the doctrine of the " eternal return ". Nietzsche at first faced this hypothesis with terror. But he saw therein the necessary consequence of the great complexity of events in this world — which he could not fathom, and which needed to be based on scientific study. Then, fascinated by his grandiose perspectives, he accepted himself as the only one worthy of responding to the will-to-live of *Superman.*

It is difficult to give a philosophical appreciation of a doctrine which offers itself as some sort of special " message " or revelation. To the extent that he places all the value of our judgments and theories on their aptitude to favor our vitality, Nietzsche is a pragmatist and cannot surpass their intellectual level, which is already mediocre. To the extent that he proclaims the unconditioned morality of *Superman*, Nietzsche illustrates, by his very excess, the tendency of modern philosophy[1] to put the human person in God's position by granting man all the rights of the Supreme Being. An hypothesis of this type cannot overcome the first reflections of common sense, which obstinately refuses to identify our little, human conscience with the incomparable Wisdom of God. The literary style of Nietzsche's works may somewhat mask, but can never destroy this irremediable contradiction.

Similar to Nietzsche is the thought of JEAN-MARIE GUYAU[2] (1854-1888). In his two main works, *Esquisse d'une morale sans obligation ni sanction* (1885), and *L'irreligion d'avenir* (1887), he believes that it is our power or living potentiality which measures our duty and constitutes the rule of morality.

---

[1] See above, n. 313.
[2] See his *Education and Heredity; A Study in Sociology* (tr. W. J. Longstreet), New York, 1897.

C) The Philosophy of Religion [1].

We are not concerned here with theories interpreting religious phenomena, but rather with those thinkers who sought in religious faith the source of the truth which they despaired of finding by reason. This makes them give to their belief a value of feeling, intuition or of instinct, and thus they belong under pragmatism. C. SECRÉTAN (1815-1895), a Swiss philosopher, and the author of *La Philosophie de la liberté* (1849), gave reason the task of defending and justifying the truths which it could not discover itself, but which had been furnished by faith. He believed that the only way of avoiding pantheism was to assert the absolute liberty of God as the explanatory source of all things. — SOREN KIERKEGAARD (1813-1855), a Danish philosopher, is the author of many works, among them *Either-Or* (1843), and *Stages on Life's Way*. He placed truth in the individual subject, who discovers it fully by accepting faith through an act of trust, despite the paradoxes and even the absurdities of faith itself [2].

RUDOLF EUCKEN [3] (1846-1926) especially looked for the basis of his *philosophy of life* in religion. He believed that the world of sensible experience, even after the brilliant success of modern culture, leaves us unsatisfied, for each act of knowledge affirms a *life of the spirit* which has most profound needs. The act of knowledge presupposes a new world, peopled with eternal and unchangeable realities and endowed with infinite possibilities. But this superior world is inaccessible to conceptual reason; one attains it by what Eucken calls the *noölogical method*. This method is not that of positivistic psychology, which deals with pure phenomena of consciousness, nor that of abstractive metaphysics, which allows reality to escape it. It is, instead, a sort of intuitive reflection on the fact of our own mental life, and Eucken, in recommending it, becomes completely engaged in the *way of*

---

[1] BASKFIELD, G. T., *Idea of God in British and American Personal Idealism*, Washington (D. C.), 1933. — BECKER, C. L., *Heavenly City of the Eighteenth-Century Philosophers*, New Haven (Conn.), 1932. — BURTT, E. A., *Types of Religious Philosophy*, New York, 1951. — GILSON, E. H., *God and Philosophy*, New Haven (Conn.), 1941. — PRZYWARA, P. E., *Polarity* (tr. A. C. Bouquet), Oxford, 1935. — SHEEN, F. J., *God and Intelligence in Modern Philosophy*, New York, 1935. — *Philosophy of Religion*, New York, 1948. — WATKIN, E. I., *Balance of Truth*, London, 1943.

[2] He felt, for example, that the mystery of the Incarnation is absurd; Catholic theology, on the other hand, shows that dogma is never absurd. For a list of his works see p. 938, fn. 2.

[3] **Works :** *Christianity and the New Idealism* (tr. Gibson, L. J., and W. R. B.), New York, 1912. — *Ethics and Modern Thought*, New York, n. d. — *Life's Basis and Life's Ideal* (tr. A. G. Widgery), New York, n. d. — *Meaning and Value of Life* (tr. Gibson, L. J., and W. R. B.), New York, n. d. — *Problem of Human Life* (tr. Hough, W. S., and Gibson, W. R. B.), New York, 1914. — *Socialism, An Analysis* (tr. J. McCabe), New York, 1922. — *Truth of Religion* (tr. W. T. Jones), New York, 1911.

Studies : BÉCHER, E., *Eucken und seine Philosophie*, Leipzig, 1927. — GIBSON, W. R. B., *Rudolph Eucken's Philosophy of Life*, New York, n. d. — JONES, T. W., *Rudolph Eucken*, New York, 1915. — SIÉBERT, R., *Euckens Welt und Lebensanschauung*, Langensalza, 1926.

feeling in order to discover that which gives meaning and value to life.

Now, the eternal world found by this method is precisely the one which all religion asserts, so that the very meaning and function of religious sentiment is to be in correspondence to the highest aspirations of our intellectual life. One should not be content, however, with *common religion*, which merely affirms a suprasensible " beyond " in a vague way; an ideal of this sort stands in risk of being snuffed out by the attractions of material culture. One should become attached to the *characteristic religions*, that is, to the great historical religions. The founders of these latter religions, among whom Christ holds first place, had a most rich and high experience of the life of the spirit, and knew how to fix the meaning of the eternal realities. Through these intermediaries, and not through reason, man can obtain the conviction of God's existence.

Eucken looked upon himself as being more than a philosopher, for he believed he was a guide for his contemporaries who were deeply immersed in the need of an absolute. He tried to lead them in the direction towards the true God, but his thought remains tinged with rationalism. All religions, he held, are explainable without supernatural revelation, and their value is measured by their ability to respond to the needs of the life of the spirit. The situation was different for another thinker who was also attracted by the religious problem but who was faithful to grace and became a convert to Catholicism.

JOHN HENRY NEWMAN [1] (1801-1890) is the most celebrated of the protagonists of the " Oxford Movement ", which, beginning in 1833, became a powerful stimulus on the fervor of the Protestant Church in England. Newman followed the logic of his thoughts, converted to Catholicism in 1845, and consecrated the remainder of his life and all of his talents to the defense of Catholicism. His writings are extremely personal, and are inspired by a religious philosophy which is close to pragmatism and to the philosophy of action proposed by Blondel.

---

[1] **Works :** *University Sketches* (ed. M. Tierney), Westminster (Md.), 1953. — *Apologia Pro Vita Sua*, New York, 1950. — *Essay on the Development of Christian Doctrine* (ed. C. F. Harrold), New York, 1949. — *Christianity and Science* (ed. R. J. McHugh), Dublin, 1945. — *Christianity and the Sceptic* (ed. R. J. McHugh), Dublin, 1945. — *Essay in Aid of a Grammar of Assent* (ed. C. F. Harrold), New York, 1948. — *Idea of a University* (ed. C. F. Harrold), New York, 1948. — *Newman Synthesis* (arr. E. Przywara), New York, 1945. — *Present Position of Catholics in England*, New York, 1942. — *Discussions and Arguments on Various Subjects*, New York, 1907. — *Essays, Critical and Historical*, 2 vols., New York, 1895. — *Historical Sketches*, 3 vols., New York, n. d.

Studies : FOLGHERA, J. D., *Newman's Apologetic*, St. Louis (Mo.), 1929. — HARROLD, C. F., *John Henry Newman*, New York, 1945. — *John Henry Newman : Centenary Essays*, Westminster (Md.), 1945. — KARL, A., *Die Glaubensphilosophie Newmans*, Bonn, 1941. — MAY, J. L., *Cardinal Newman*, Westminster (Md.), 1951. — MOODY, J., *John Henry Newman*, New York, 1945. — NÉDONCELLE, M., *La philosophie religieuse en Grande-Bretagne de 1850 à nos jours*, Paris, 1934. — WARD, W. P., *Life of John Henry, Cardinal Newman*, 2 vols., New York, 1934.

One of the main things written up by Newman is the history of his own religious experience; he believed it was capable of clarifying the views of his contemporaries and of leading them to the truth. Born into a Christian society and having early acquired a kind of experiential conviction of God's existence — that is, of the God and supernatural faith as revealed in the Gospel — Newman held that if one seeks for the religious society which has actually conserved a life authentically inspired by the gospel message, one will find the Roman Catholic Church itself.

Accordingly, the criterion of truth which guides Newman is not of the intellectual order. It presupposes the " primacy of conscience ", which is " the divine law, the supreme rule of morality apprehended by each individual soul " [1]. Newman believes that a religious doctrine is not true or worthy of our assent unless it fully answers this voice of conscience. But there are two types of assent, discussed by Newman in his *Grammar of Assent*. The first refers to abstract knowledge, the fruit of the reasoning of speculative intelligence; the knowledge which it yields is like an outward veneer, unreal and lacking efficacy for conduct. The other is *real assent* or an " experienced " adhesion to the truth, encompassing one's whole existence; it is an experiencing of the doctrine which is proposed, and a conviction according to which one has decided to live. Religious faith is of this second type. Since this experience and real assent conformable to the Gospel is realized fully only in the Catholic Church, this Church alone is the true Church of Christ.

One could not, by means of this criterion and method, propose a philosophical explanation of the universe without adopting an untenable and anti-intellectual pragmatism in which the criterion of truth is not objective evidence, but the aptitude of the doctrine to be favorable to human life. But Newman never held anything similar to this. He only wished, as a concrete thinker, to indicate a way which was his own, and which might be capable of leading others to the full religious truth. Moreover, for many of the moderns who aspire to go beyond positivism by the *way of feeling*, Newman's views are most heartening. His view is continued through the much more rigorous philosophical thought of Blondel.

D) The Philosophy of Action.

Alongside of Anglo-Saxon pragmatism there was formed a *philosophy of action* in France which could also be called pragmatism, but in a different sense. It is more a foreshadowing of the groups yet to be treated, for it uses the *method* of immanence as will the modernists, and it seeks to attain reality, as will Bergson.

One of its precursors is GRATRY [2] (1805-1872), who speaks of a " sense of the Infinite " as alone capable of giving knowledge

---

[1] H. BREMOND, *Newman* (Paris, 1906), p. 395.

[2] **Works :** *Logic* (tr. Singer, H. and M.), La Salle (Ill.), 1944. — *Well-Springs* (tr. S. J. Brown), London, 1931.

Studies : AUBIN, A., *Le P. Gratry, essai de biographie psychologique*, Paris, 1912. — GUILLEMONT, B. P., *Essai sur la philosophie de Gratry*, Paris, 1918. — PERRAUD, A., *Le P. Gratry, sa vie et ses œuvres*, Paris, 1900.

of God. Léon Ollé-Laprune [1] (1839-1899), the teacher of Blondel, is the author of *La certitude morale* (1880). In this work he speaks of the necessary collaboration of the will with reason in order to attain truth.

Maurice Blondel [2] (1861-1949) is the theorist of this system of thought. He proposed it in his dissertation, *L'Action* (1893), a work which stirred a lively polemic. Then, after long reflection, which resulted in some magazine articles, he published a large number of works containing his definitive thought.

The basic principle of his system can be formulated as follows :

In its full sense, truth requires the perfect adequation between object known and the knowing soul in such a way that on the part of the object, every being should be grasped in an exhaustive view of the ensemble and, for man's part, the union to this object must be immediate and intuitive.

From this principle, most often taken as an axiom though never explicitly demonstrated, Blondel concludes that man possesses two subordinate and necessary means of knowing beyond sensible knowledge. The first is *notional knowledge*, which proceeds by abstract concepts, while the second is *real knowledge*, which alone, though aided by action, attains the object intuitively. Intellectualism in the Thomistic sense [3] is viewed as insufficient, since the concept, in Blondel's view, only functions as a filter or screen, and thus cannot immediately attain that which reality is. Moreover, the concept can grasp only a part of reality at one time, and thus is incapable of adequation to the totality of being which is required for truth. In the meantime, our conceptual sciences have *their truth*, inasmuch as they are a useful road thereto, and even necessary in order to attain real knowledge. Abstractive activity is needed to awake and orientate the need of intuition, and, even after the latter is attained, abstraction is necessary to safeguard the

---

[1] **Works :** *De la certitude morale*, Paris, 1880. — *La philosophie et le temps présent*, Paris, 1890. — *Le prix de la vie*, Paris, 1894.
   Study : J. Zeiler, *Léon Ollé-Laprune*, Paris, 1932.
[2] **Works :** *L'action, essai d'une critique de la vie et d'une science de la pratique*, Paris, 1893. — *Le problème de la philosophie catholique*, Paris, 1932. — *La pensée*, 2 vols., Paris, n. d. — *L'être et les êtres*, Paris, 1935. — *L'action*, 2 vols., Paris, 1936. — *La philosophie et l'esprit chrétien*, 2 vols., n. d.
   Studies : Archambault, P., *Vers un réalisme intégral : l'œuvre philosophique de M. Blondel*, Paris, 1928. — Eypernont, T. d', *Le Blondélisme*, Louvain, 1933. — Gilbert, K. E., *Maurice Blondel's Philosophy of Action*, Chapel Hill (N. C.), 1924. — Hurtin, H., *Vers une science du réel*, Paris, 1931. — Lefèbvre, F., *L'itinéraire philosophique de M. Blondel*, Paris, 1928. — Maes, J., *De godsdienstphilosophie van Blondel*, Malines, 1934. — Paliard, J., *Maurice Blondel ou le dépassement chrétien*, Paris, 1950. — Romeyer, B., *La philosophie religieuse de M. Blondel*, Paris, 1945. — Seaby, A. W., *Blondel, the Minstrel*, London, 1951. — Tonquédec, J. de, *Immanence, Essai critique sur la doctrine de M. Blondel*, Paris, 1908. — Valensin, A., and Montcheuil, Y. de, *Maurice Blondel*, Paris, 1934.
[3] See above, n. 259.

distinction between the knower and the known. Thus the truth of notional knowledge is quite similar to pragmatic truth.

But it is *real knowledge* which properly attains truth. It consists in an intuition of the totality of being, obtained by the help of a sort of connaturality with being which it procures by *action*. Taken in the complete sense of the total activity of the soul, and especially of the soul's vital activity which pushes it towards the absolute good and truth, action has the advantage of being placed in the concrete order, of adapting itself and uniting to this order without any sort of intermediary. The *real* thus achieved, respond-ing to our aspirations for the infinite, is soon revealed as the Infinite Being Himself; from Him all other created realities flow as from their fully explicative cause. In this way, and in agreement with the basic principle, all the needs of truth are realized, leading to the definition of truth as the *adequation of our internal tendencies with life*.

Thus, the theory of real knowledge is completed by a mysticism and a totally immanentist apologetics similar to the view of the modernists. From this same point of view, mention can be made of two other Catholics who were avid defenders of immanentist apologetics, L. LABERTHONNIÈRE [1], and DE BROGLIE.

One can accuse Blondel of an exaggerated defiance towards our abstractive intelligence, making him minimize the value of the conceptual edifice of the sciences constructed by human reason. Blondel concedes a certain share of truth to abstractive intelligence, it is true, but it is subordinated and incomplete, even in the rational order itself. He thus returns to the viewpoint of the Augustinians [2] of the Middle Ages, who did not succeed in distin-guishing philosophy and theology clearly because they lacked a precise criterion of the notion of distinct formal objects.

Nevertheless, by his desire to assert the transcendental and supernatural characteristics of revelation, Blondel correctly con-ceived of the relationship between faith and reason. Through his apologetic writings, he achieved a doctrinal resurrection of the notion of a Christian philosophy [3]. Despite all, however, his views are still a compromise between the modern spirit imbued with rationalism [4], and the realistic aspirations of traditional philosophy.

---

[1] He is the author of two works : *Essais de philosophie religieuse* (Paris, 1905) and *Le réalisme chrétien et l'idéalisme grec* (Paris, n. d.), in which he combats intellectualism and holds to a philosophy of action similar to that of Blondel. As director of the *Annales de Philosophie chrétienne* (beginning in 1905), he was, at first, even favorable to the modernists.

[2] See above, n. 247, and the doctrine of Saint Bonaventure, nn. 279-281.

[3] See above, n. 244.

[4] The influence of idealism is evident in Blondel's interpretation of the concept, insofar as he makes it an *object* of knowledge. In the realist doctrine of St. Thomas, on the contrary, the concept is purely a *means* of knowing which we place in direct communication with existent (or trans-subjective) reality (see above, n. 409), although it does not attain it in its individual aspect. Also, *notional knowledge* is sufficient for attaining complete truth.

III. Modernism.

Special bibliography.

1° **Works** : Fogazzaro, A., *Il Santo,* Milan, 1905. — Harnack, A., *Das Wesen des Christentums,* Leipzig, 1900. — *Il programma dei modernisti,* Rome, 1907. — Loisy, A., *L'Evangile et l'Eglise,* Paris, 1902. — *Autour d'un petit livre,* Paris, 1903. — *Simples réflexions sur le décret " Lamentabili " et sur l'Encyclique " Pascendi ",* Paris, 1908. — Réville, J., *Le Protestantisme libéral, ses origines, sa nature, sa mission,* Paris, 1903. — Sabatier, A., *Esquisse d'une philosophie de la religion d'après la psychologie et l'histoire,* Paris, 1897. — *Les Religions de l'autorité et la religion de l'esprit,* Paris, 1904. — Tyrrell, J., *Religion as a Factor of Life,* Exeter, 1902. — *Lex orandi,* London, 1903. — *Lex credendi,* London, 1906. — *Through Scylla and Charybdis,* London, 1907. — *Mediaevalism,* London, 1908.

2° **Studies** : Bessner, J., *Philosophie und Theologie des Modernismus,* Fribourg (Belgium), 1912. — Gisier, A., *Der Modernismus,* Cologne, 1912. — Mercier, D., *Le Modernisme,* Brussels, 1908. — Perrotta, A., *Modernist Movement in Italy and Its Relation to the Spread of Protestant Christianity,* New York, 1929. — Pius X, Encyclical, *Pascendi,* Sept. 8, 1907. — Rivière, J., *Le modernisme dans l'Eglise,* Paris, 1929. — Rosa, E., *L'encyclica " Pascendi " e il modernismo,* Rome, 1909. — Rickaby, J., *The Modernist,* London, 1908.

532. At the beginning of the twentieth century, a certain number of theologians, most of them Catholic, took upon themselves the task of adapting the dogmas of the Church to the modern mentality. They were led in France by A. Loisy, Turmel, E. Le Roy, Wilbois, and the Protestants, A. Sabatier and J. Réville. In Germany, the liberal Protestants were led mainly by A. Harnack. The leader of the movement in England was J. Tyrrell, and, in Italy, A. Fogazzaro. These men wished to remain within the fold of Christianity in the hope of transforming it; they proceeded quite cleverly in their expositions, though they avoided any presentation of the ensemble of belief and insisted on the difficulties in belief arising from modern science. In the encyclical letter *Pascendi,* Pius X gave an exposition of their system in a fine synthetic view; he pointed out their philosophical principles and from them logically deduced all the consequences of their system which were completely destructive of the Catholic faith.

The modernists developed the metaphysical portion of their hypothesis with the notion of William James' theory on the subconscious. As theologians, they wished to make the nature of God and of religion more precise. They used the " new "

philosophy, however, for their theological synthesis, for they
agreed that the human mind had a basic incapacity to know
truth. They wished to save religion from the crisis into which
a Scholastic intellectualism had imprisoned it, by founding
it on sentimental knowledge, or the *way of feeling*, believing
that the latter domain was completely separated from science
and metaphysics and would thus be free from attack. This
absolute agnosticism is the hidden resort of modernism, as was
shown by Pius X, being based philosophically on the critiques
of Kant and Bergson. At the same time, the modernists
were not looking for a complete philosophy; their primary
aim was to set forth the nature of man's knowledge of God
and the value of the dogmas of faith.

A) Sentimental Knowledge of God.

533. The knowledge of God lies at the base of every religion
and theology. It is of great importance, accordingly, to
establish its nature and to seek the method which yields this
knowledge.

I. **Nature.** Since God is present to the very basis of our
soul, it is not necessary to have recourse to the intelligence
and to valueless concepts to attain Him. It is sufficient to
become recollected, for it is impossible that God should not
manifest Himself through His operations. We thus have
consciousness of the Divine by immediate contact, or a knowledge of the sentimental type. This is the foundation of all
true religion.

This primordial knowledge of God, in place of being the
fruit of the work of reason on God (which would make it
decadent), is more the product of intelligence working under
pressure from the heart. " It is primarily and principally
the work of God within man and with man " [1]. This knowledge, then, has the value of a fact or of an energizing feeling
through which God acts, and " this action of God is light and
grace, it is truth and power for the good " [2]. Its salient
characteristics are its vagueness and lack of precision which
leads us to dogmatic elaboration; but it also possesses the
stability and universality needed to found a Catholic religion,
since one can find it in every human consciousness.

---

[1] A. LOISY, *Autour d'un petit livre*, p. 198.
[2] A. LOISY, *Quelques Lettres*, p. 234; see also A. MICHELET, *Dieu et l'agnosticisme
contemporain*, pp. 198-9.

Two main proofs seem to justify this doctrine of immanence or experience of the Divine. *a*) *A proof of fact* in that all men, if well prepared, validate this direct contact of a God living within them; the modernists acknowledge it in themselves, and confirm their view by the *mystics*, who often speak of a direct and quasi-experimental knowledge of God. *b*) *A proof from reason*, in the fact that the Creator, as St. Paul[1] and St. Thomas Aquinas[2] teach, is most intimate to the soul, since everything depends on God for its being and its life.

It is difficult to use the testimony of mystics[3] in philosophy, for their case is quite rare and unique. In the ordinary order of things, our knowledge of spiritual things, as of God and the soul, is wholly founded on analogy with sensible things, and is obtained by reasoning and not by a direct and intuitive method. One could, perhaps, concede the possibility of an intuition of God's existence, analogous to the act of perfect reflection through which the soul immediately grasps its own existence; for God, pure spirit and intelligible in Himself, is present to the deepest interiority of the soul[4] as the soul is present to itself. Granting this possibility, such an idea of God could not be very clear, and it will always be necessary to have recourse to metaphysics in order to establish a scientific theodicy.

This possibility, however, joined in a Christian soul with the intensity of faith and the supernatural presence of God by grace and charity, explains how we could have the sentiment and quasi-experience of God living within us. But the immediate contact with God in the modernist sense, that is, without the precision offered by Scholastic theology, leads directly to *pantheism*. The intimate union between the self and the Divine which it offers inclines one to believe that we are identified with God in the subconscious, according to the hypothesis of William James. If God remains transcendent, it is only in the manner of a universal consciousness which envelops all particular forms of consciousness[5].

2. **Method. 534.** While it is true that God is immanent to man's soul, He cannot be found there without preparation, for distractions and bad dispositions have relegated Him to the subconscious. This is why so many people are ignorant of that which they bear about within them. The method of

---

[1] *Acts of the Apostles*, xvii, 28.

[2] *Summa Theologica*, i, q. viii.

[3] Bergson used this method with a remarkable finesse; see below, n. 550 and n. 554 (criticism).

[4] This was St. Bonaventure's view; see above, n. 279. It should be mentioned that God is present to the soul as *Creative Cause* more than as *object of knowledge;* for this reason, the ordinary way of even knowing of His existence is from effects to cause, or *a posteriori* demonstration.

[5] A. MICHELET, *op. cit.*, pp. 295-8.

immanence aims at making God emerge into consciousness, at first and especially through asceticism, by sanctifying life; then the method shows, by analysis of human life, that this divine element is, despite everything, implicated in all our actions. Accordingly, a human action, with all the conditions, desires and items of knowledge it presupposes, logically leads to God and to the revealed mysteries of the Catholic faith as the course of a river leads to the ocean.

It is easily seen that this method is perfectly adapted to the doctrine of immanence, which suppresses the distinction between the natural and supernatural orders, and even between God and man. It is thus the pantheistic portion of modernism. One can, however, separate the method from the doctrine, and give the method a legitimate meaning, for every man elevated to the supernatural order can discover in his life the need of revelation, based on supernatural grace, which is never refused even to the sinner or unbeliever, and which is necessary for salvation [1].

But these notions take us out of the philosophical realm, and, when one passes through apologetics into the theological domain, it is necessary to admit the authority of the supernatural revelation which has been confined to the Catholic Church as the source of truth. The modernists refused to accept this authority and transformed the meaning of dogmas into the meanings of a pragmatist philosophy.

B) Pragmatist Dogma.

535. For the modernists, *religious experience* or the sentimental knowledge of God is the first fruit and the solid basis of all religion. From this knowledge they tried to derive the whole of Catholicism, keeping the Catholic terminology, but changing whatever it originally signified.

Revelation becomes this very experience which each man carries within himself. The only difference is that some souls are privileged and have been favored with a greater intensity, and have taken stock of their wealth more carefully; these men are the prophets, among whom Christ was the greatest.

Dogmas in theodicy and the mysteries of faith have no absolute value, but their truth lies in their being useful for religious life whether individual or social. The *individual*, wishing to have his life conform to his faith and to exteriorize his religious sentiment, feels the need of dissipating the vagueness which envelops him, since clear formulas, and even somewhat rigid ones are needed to direct practical life. The intelligence, then, reacts on the immanent data and constructs a theodicy.

---

[1] Admitting the method of immanence as a legitimate possibility does not destroy the value of the other apologetic proofs. In fact, the method of immanence alone is insufficient even though it might, as a matter of face, best lead certain souls to God or satisfy them.

From the *social* viewpoint, men feel within themselves particularly rich experiences which they wish to share with others; to accomplish this, formulas are indispensable. Among these formulas, religious society sanctions the best, approves those which are most fruitful for practical life and those which are most favorable to the conservation and development of the religious sentiment — in this way, dogmas are formed. Every religion which arises is true, and most true to the extent that the interior life of its believers is intense. Old dogmas must be renewed, since their value and all of their truth lies in their agreement with the living religious sentiment, living and progressing in the mass of the believers. It is from the believers that the impulse for reforms arises. Authority, faithful to its function of conservation, at first challenges and fights reforms, but finally accepts them and sanctions them as new dogmas [1]. This sketch shows how modern philosophy helped bring forth the most recent heresy.

CONCLUSION. Under the combined pressure of idealism, positivism, and of Bergson, modernism accepts absolute agnosticism of the intelligence as the foundation of philosophy. Then it discovers a unique, valuable knowledge in the religious experience as the vague sentiment of the Divine and of an interior life joined to God and logically identifiable with the Life of God. All forms of intellectual activity, as theodicy and dogmas, are destined only to conserve, exteriorize and perfect this sentiment in which the whole treasure of human knowledge finds its refuge. This is a bold and rash application of the modern mentality of *pragmatism* to religious doctrine.

The movement, though born in Catholicism, was checked and then halted by the clear and vigorous action of the great Pope, Pius X (1903-14).

In the philosophical order, modernism had only a limited influence on some problems concerning the value of truth and of our knowledge of God.

Completely different is the work of Bergson, which is wholly in the philosophical order and which constitutes a universal system by itself.

---

[1] The Encyclical *Pascendi* points out the manner in which the modernists deduce their conclusions on cult, the Bible, the history of the Church, its relations with the State, and so forth.

ARTICLE THREE.

HENRI BERGSON (1859-1941).

Special bibliography.

1° **Works :** *Matter and Memory* (tr. Paul, N. M., and Palmer, W. S.), New York, 1950. — *Selections* (ed. H. A. Larrabec), New York, 1949. — *Time and Free Will* (tr. F. L. Pogson), New York, 1950. — *Creative Evolution* (tr. A. Mitchell), New York, 1944. — *Creative Mind* (tr. M. L. Andison), New York, 1945. — *The Two Sources of Morality* (tr. Audra, R. A., and Brereton, C.), New York, 1935. — *Dreams* (tr. E. E. Slosson), New York, 1914. — *Introduction to Metaphysics* (tr. T. E. Hulme), New York, 1912. — *Mind-Energy* (ed. H. W. Carr), New York, 1920.

2° **Studies :** Berthelot, R., *Un romantisme utilitaire. Le pragmatisme chez Bergson*, Paris, 1913. — Carr, H. W., *Philosophy of Change*, New York, 1914. — Challaye, F., *Bergson*, Paris, 1947. — Chevalier, J., *Henri Bergson*, New York, 1928. — Cunningham, G. W., *Study in the Philosophy of Bergson*, New York, 1916. — Dehove, J., *La théorie bergsonienne de la morale et de la religion*, Lille, 1933. — Dodson, G. R., *Bergson and the Modern Spirit*, Boston, 1913. — Elliot, H. S. R., *Modern Science and the Illusions of Professor Bergson*, New York, 1912. — Farges, A., *La philosophie de M. Bergson*, Paris, 1912. — Fénart, M., *Les assertions bergsoniennes*, Paris, 1936. — Flewelling, R. T., *Bergson and Personal Realism*, New York, 1920. — Höffding, H., *La philosophie de Bergson*, Paris, 1916. — Jankelevitch, V., *Bergson*, Paris, 1930. — Jolivet, R., *Essai sur le bergsonisme*, Paris, 1931. — Kallen, H. M., *William James and Henri Bergson*, Chicago, 1914. — Le Roy, E., *New Philosophy of Henri Bergson*, (tr. V. Benson), New York, 1913. — Loomba, R. M., *Bradley and Bergson*, London, 1937. — Mac Williams, J., *Criticism of the Philosophy of Bergson*, New York, 1929. — Maire, G., *Bergson, mon maître*, Paris, 1935. — Maritain, J., *La philosophie bergsonienne*, Paris, 1948. — Miller, L. H., *Bergson and Religion*, New York, 1916. — Penido, M., *Dieu dans le bergsonisme*, Paris, 1934. — Rideau, E., *Le Dieu de Bergson*, Paris, 1932. — *Les rapports de la matière et de l'esprit dans le bergsonisme*, Paris, 1932. — *Descartes, Pascal, Bergson*, Paris, 1946. — Sait, U. M., *Ethical Implications of Bergson's Philosophy*, New York, 1914. — Scharfstein, B., *Roots of Bergson's Philosophy*, New York, 1943. — Segon, J., *L'intuition bergsonienne*, Paris, 1913. — Stalknecht, N. P., *Studies in the Philosophy of Creation*, with special reference to Bergson and Whitehead, Princeton (N. J.), 1944. — Stephen, K., *Misuse of Mind*, New York, 1922. — Stewart, J. M., *Critical Exposition of Bergson's Philosophy*, New York, 1911. — Thibaudet, A., *Le bergsonisme*, 2 vols., Paris, 1924. — Tonquédec, J. de, *Sur la philosophie bergsonienne*, Paris, 1938. — Wheeler, O. A., *Bergson and Education*, New York, 1922. — Wilm, E. C., *Henri Bergson*, New York, n. d.

536. Henri Bergson was born in Paris on October 18, 1859 of a Jewish family of foreign origin. After brilliant studies which showed his exceptional talents for the sciences, he turned to philosophy. For teachers he had Ollé-Laprune and Boutroux. He got his doctorate in philosophy in 1881, and taught at Angers and Clermont until 1888. It was during these years of reflection that he discovered the central idea of his system through a deep reading of Herbert Spencer.

He then taught at Paris, and soon became famous. His lectures at the Collège de France, beginning in 1901, attracted numerous listeners and enthusiastic followers, both by their literary perfection and by their doctrine, which freed the minds of those caught up in positivistic science and Kantian idealism. When the League of Nations named a commission of twelve for intellectual cooperation, Bergson was elected their president, and held this post until 1925. He died in January, 1941.

Bergson's system is contained in four basic works, the fruit of long and conscientious reflection, each work marking an important doctrinal progress. The first is his *Essai sur les données immédiates de la conscience,* of 1889, his doctorate thesis, which contains his intuitive method. *Matière et Mémoire,* published in 1896, explains the union of soul with body. *L'évolution créatrice* (1907) extends his theory of life to the whole universe. *Les deux sources de la morale et de la religion* (1932) establishes the existence of God by the aid of mystical intuition. Some other, secondary works can be mentioned : *Le Rire* (1900); *Durée et simultanéité* (1922); a large number of articles and conferences which have been edited in book form, as *L'énergie spirituelle* (1919) and *La pensée et le mouvant* (1933).

Foundational Principle and Division.

537. Bergsonianism is the last great system of modern philosophy. It is fully unified by an original principle, capable of setting up a sufficiently complete philosophy. It can be characterized as follows :

The real, the object of philosophical science, is not the stable being known through intellectual concepts, bu: PURE BECOMING, *in which intuition discovers the universal explanation of things.*

Evidently, this principle is incapable of inductive or deductive proof in the Thomistic sense; it itself is the object of a basic intuition. The primary trait of Bergson's system is that of being an INTUITIONISM. In order to understand it better, its historical genesis will be given.

1. Like most modern thinkers, Bergson was struck by the stability and progress of the physico-mathematical sciences as contrasted with the fluctuations and contradictions of philosophy. He looked upon the experimenta method as the cause of this progress, for it was careful to proportionate the certitude of its conclusions to the observation of incontestable facts, so that the results are readily accepted by all men. Bergson decided to transport this method into philosophy. " In a general way, we believe that an object which exists is an object which is perceived or which could exist " [1]; every object of a concept is thus of an ideal order. Hence Bergsonianism is a radical EMPIRICISM.

2. However, the eminent value of the experimental method had already been proclaimed by Kantianism and positivism; these latter doctrines were prominent in the official teaching to which Bergson was submitted, and neither had thought that the experimental method was possible for metaphysics. The best method, and the infallible truth in the proper sense, for these men, was the monopoly of the modern sciences; one could not go beyond the world of phenomena or of the relative. Bergson, following the profound instinct of human nature, believed that the absolute could not be so inaccessible. He looked for it under the relative, and found, in physics, *movement* itself and real time, which mathematical formulas could not encompass. In psychology, he found consciousness as the life with an active bent which the associationism of his time neglected. From this he concluded with these four words, *becoming, time, vital urge* and *consciousness,* as designating the unique reality and the object of his philosophy — which thus can be called a REALISM.

3. At the same time, Bergson realized that this unique reality wholly escaped mathematics, until then held to be the only valuable science. Bergson considered this powerlessness essential to all abstractive intellectual activity. He looked for another faculty besides intelligence with which to philosophize, and found it in *intuition.* Hence his doctrine is an unrestricted ANTI-INTELLECTUALISM.

Briefly, this new philosophy, like all previous ones, wished to explain reality completely even in its very foundations;

---

[1] *Les Deux Sources.* p. 257.

it concluded that the real coincided with pure becoming. This central viewpoint suggested a new method which had to be applied to the universe under its multiple aspects. Historically speaking, Bergson, a good psychologist, begins by introspection of his own proper self. But in his systematic exposition, man is but a portion of the total universe which must be treated. His whole edifice is finally crowned with God. Four paragraphs will treat his views :

I. The Method : Intelligence and Intuition.

II. Biological Intuition : the Universe.

III. Psychological Intuition : the Self.

IV. Mystical Intuition : God.

I. The method : Intelligence and Intuition.

538. The foundational principle of Bergson harks back to the doctrine of Heraclitus [1], but while this ancient system of the fifth century, B. C., asserts pure becoming through ignorance of our abstractive intelligence, Bergson, in the twentieth century, consciously opposed himself to the accepted rational and scientific methods with which he was well acquainted. Accordingly, before establishing his new method, he criticizes human intelligence in its very roots.

A) Critique of Intelligence.

Bergson clearly stated what he meant by " intelligence ", which he accuses of a basic incapacity for philosophy; he gives a complete explanation of his position.

I. **Definition.** It is not Bergson's custom to give fixed definitions, but one can quite exactly summarize his various descriptions by stating that the intelligence is the faculty of analytically or abstractively grasping exterior objects. It includes all the different activities of knowledge which modern experimental psychology classifies under the rubric, " intelligence ".

Sensation comes first. It is an analytical knowledge of the external senses whose object, in Bergson's view, is truly a sensible quality, immediately grasped as exterior and essentially extended. This view is fully in accord with the view of Thomism.

---

[1] See above, n. 8.

Perception then grasps the individual as a totality distinct from others, and it is normally endowed with the same quality of objectivity.

Under intelligence there comes next the whole apparatus of the physico-mathematical sciences with their precise notions and definitions, their laws and rigorous reasoning processes and their coronal of broad theories.

Finally, Bergson puts under this heading all the *general knowledge* pertaining to common sense, to religious dogmas, and to the various tracts of philosophy. One sees that all these types of knowledge are turned towards *exteriority*. Bergson does not deny that there is also an intellectualist psychology which uses introspection. He states that the interior life, in this latter view, becomes a sort of spatialized consciousness, in which everything takes place as it does in the physical world, and which, thereby, is exterior to true consciousness.

2. **Critique.** The intelligence thus comprised, taken in all its amplitude, is *declared basically incapable of knowing reality*. According to the basic principle, reality is pure becoming; its two properties, simple and indivisible continuity and mobile fluidity, are opposed to the two characteristics of all intellectual knowledge. These latter traits are the precise delimitation of the objects of thought as well separated from each other, and the stability of defined essences which remain eternally, immutably and necessarily what they are.

Bergson more often directs his criticisms to the *abstract concept*, which is the masterpiece of the intelligence. He finds therein two congenital faults which he calls, in opposition to the image of pure becoming as the sole reality, the *dissection* of reality. " Every division of matter into independent bodies with absolutely determined contours is an artificial division " [1]. The *solidification* of fluidity is the second fault, for it makes a monism out of life and crystallizes becoming. The intellectual method used for defining life is similar to that of a film which recomposes movement by a rapid succession of stable views.

3. **Explanation.** This natural incapacity of our intelligence would be inadmissible if one could not explain it. The theory of evolution [2] helps to understand it best. It should be mentioned here that, for Bergson, the intelligence was not

---

[1] *Matière et Mémoire*, p. 218.
[2] See below, n. 532.

made for speculation but for action. Intelligence is *con-natural with matter;* nature, however, has not allowed us to know the essence of this matter [1], but to dominate it by breaking or overcoming the obstacle which it opposes to life.

For these reasons, the intelligence is molded exactly according to matter, which has the property of extension divisible into determined figures (from which arises the dissection) and of dead and stable inertia (from which arises the solidification of fluidity). Thus, the two traits of the concept which are defects for speculation are marvelously adapted for action, as is shown by the great success of modern science applied to the conquest of the world. Furthermore, these defects have permitted the rise of language with its multiple and well defined words perfectly corresponding to dissected and stable concepts. This has led to social interaction and the transmission of progress to new generations, increasing the chances for further success.

Thus, the intelligence, by this very speculative weakness, is a faculty which is by nature quite precise. In this sense Bergson recognized that Aristotle's metaphysics constitutes the natural structure of human intelligence.

B) **Intuition.**

539. Although Bergson admitted, with Kant and Comte, that every intellectualist metaphysics is illusory, he did not renounce metaphysics. He discovered another faculty of philosophical method, that of intuition. Despite the difficulty of speaking about it in conceptual phrases, he described it, tried to prove its existence, and indicate its methodology.

I. **Description of Intuition.** The clearest way of understanding intuition is to oppose it to abstractive knowledge with regard to both activity and the object known.

In itself, intuition excludes all mediation of the concept [2]; it is a *coincidence* between the knower and the known. Thus

---

[1] In *La pensée et le mouvant* (p. 45), Bergson wrote : " We do not see why the science of matter has not attained an absolute. It attributes this talent to itself instinctively, and thus every natural belief must be taken as true, every appearance for reality, so that no one has established its illusory character... The articulations of intelligence come to apply exactly to those of matter, just as intuition is performed in order to grasp the spirit in ourselves and in the universe as it is mobile and real time ".

[2] In Scholastic terms one could say that Bergson's intuition excludes all *species*, both the impressed and expressed.

it pertains to psychology in an eminent manner, for there the identity of the self as known and as knowing is indisputable.

But it can be applied to other objects. Then it consists in taking oneself into the interior of the thing by a sort of divinatory sympathy, analogous to the artistic sense.

Both cases above are situations of immediate contact, excluding any combination of ideas or any reasoning; with one glance, intuition lifts us to the insight of reality in all its fulness. In his own words, " one calls intuition that species of intellectual sympathy by which one transposes himself to the interior of an object in order to be coincident with that which is unique in it, and, consequently, inexpressible " [1].

Intuition grasps the *simple*, or the indivisible, which contains, without distinction, all the riches of the multiple aspects distinguished by concepts. Thus, the contradictory antinomies, into which intelligence falls on almost every problem [2], are easily resolved by mounting, through intuition, to the common and simple root which is fluid reality itself.

Intuition attains this reality from within, and in itself, through that which the thing is, and not, as in analysis, by referring it to a pre-existing concept, which is to explain the thing by what it is not. In a word, intuition attains the *absolute* and not the relative.

But this fully independent absolute seems to be the totality, the unique and the infinite. This conclusion would follow logically, but Bergson, held back by the experience of his own fragmentary and progressive intuition, carefully asserts that our intuition of the real is *limited*, though not relative. He adds that it could be indefinitely drawn away [3]. Bergson's thought here is rather unstable and susceptible of precise rectification [4], or of sliding into pantheism.

2. **Existence of Intuition.** Is so perfect a method, even though it does not attain the infinite at one glance, possible for mankind? Bergson believed that it was, for he found traces of it in instinct and even in intelligence.

---

[1] See A. LALANDE, *Vocabulaire technique de la philosophie*, " Intuition ", Meaning " D ".

[2] The reference is to the antinomies of Kant; see above, n. 408.

[3] A. LALANDE, *op. cit.*, under " Unknowable ", Bergson's remarks on p. 358.

[4] J. CHEVALIER remarks (see his *Bergson*, p. 78) : " The absolute which we cannot grasp in this way, is not the Absolute in itself... one could say it was an absolute *secundum quid*, to use an expression of St. Thomas (*Summa Theologica*, I, q. LXX, art. 2) ".

The instinct of animals, especially of the more evolved branches (as the bees) is seen at once to be so marvelously adapted for action and thus for living, that this is evidently an instance of perfect intuition. Sadly enough, it exteriorizes itself entirely in action; it is a sleeping consciousness which has the answer to the great problems of origin, of essence, of the aim of life — but asks no questions. Intelligence, more disengaged from matter, brings up these problems, but cannot resolve them. Since the basic principle shows that instinct and intelligence are but complementary manifestations of the same reality, it is possible for man to remount the current and to penetrate into the interior of instinct, there to discover, intuitively, the secrets of reality.

On the other hand, much closer to man and around the nucleus of his intelligence, there exists a vague and fluid fringe which is a true intuition, although vague and quite discontinuous. Bergson enumerates the objects which it clarifies now and then, and, in some cases, hardly does so at all : " Our personality, our liberty, the place which we occupy in the totality of nature, our origin, and, perhaps, our destiny " [1].

3. **The Method of Intuition.** These " vanishing intuitions " must now be recovered in order to draw up a philosophy. Since this method is not very natural to man, he must prepare for it by a slow and conscientious analysis which will familiarize him with all the documents dealing with the object of his study.

By an effort which Bergson calls " dolorous " one must reverse the ordinary course of our spirit and deprive ourselves of the inveterate habits of thinking through concepts. Then our vision can coincide with life (reality), which, above all else, is action and volition. This essential stage leads to defining intuition as " the faculty of seeing, immanent in the faculty of acting, which springs from a kind of turning of the will upon itself " [2].

Finally, since each intuition is but fragmentary, Bergson approves of the method of *checking results,* by which a number of philosophers, finding reality through various aspects, confirm and mutually complete each other. Their accord on one point, for instance, on the immortality of the soul, is practically equivalent to certitude.

---

[1] *Evolution créatrice,* p. 290.
[2] *Ibid.,* p. 272.

How can the philosophers communicate their results, since they can only use words made for intellectual concepts? This can be done by looking for concepts which are fluid and malleable, and by correcting the rigidity of abstract terms by concrete images. This accounts for the rich style and brilliant metaphors at which Bergson is a master, and which he methodically uses to explain his intuitions.

C) Value of the Intuitive Method.

540. In order to give a thorough appreciation of this method, it would be necessary to gather together various propositions from psychology and epistemology. Only some essential points will be mentioned here.

1. The appeal to intuition as the basis for metaphysical truth is fully justified. The Thomistic method also bases all science on the double intuition of the concrete by the external senses, and that of being and the first principles by the intelligence[1]. Criteriology recognizes and fully justifies the value of this first intuitive stage of our knowledge.

2. Moreover, Bergson's criticism of the intelligence is efficacious with regard to the physico-mathematical sciences which are incapable of expressing substances, the reality of movement, and even less so, life and consciousness, in mathematical formulas. The scholars themselves, as Duhem and Poincaré, grant that scientific theories have a value that is mainly symbolic[2].

3. Nevertheless, it cannot be denied that Bergson has not only condemned and rejected the abuse of intellectualism, but has condemned all intellectual knowledge in general. He denied to sense perception and to all abstract notions the capacity of expressing reality as it is. *His basic error was to look beyond the concept for a reliable philosophical intuition.* Such an intuition is nonexistent. Moreover, a right grasp of the abstract concept can serve as the basis for an infallibly true metaphysics, with an intuitive basis.

The notion of intuition is quite complex. In order to separate the true from the false in Bergson's thought, several distinctions are required.

A knowledge is called *intuitive* when it is joined with existent reality without any intermediary, or is immediate, and when it is related to concrete or existent reality.

These two conditions are fully realized in *external sense knowledge*. This is a case of intuition in the strict sense, though it is not scientific, for it grasps the object only in its concrete aspect, without giving it any reason for being.

---

[1] See above, n. 262.

[2] See above, n. 529. It should be noted that a Thomistic critique might tend to grant a *true, objective value* to scientific affirmations, though indirect, and as transmitted in mathematical symbols; see, for instance J. MARITAIN. *Les degrés du Savoir*, pp. 269, ff.

In the same pre-scientific order, there is a sort of *intuition-divination* in a broad sense. This is the power of forming an exact judgment, an appreciation or a required solution at one glance, without looking or reflecting further. It is, then, immediate, and ordinarily deals with concrete events. The existence of this sort of intuition is a fact; examples of it are abundant in the realm of poetry, art, and even in the mother's knowledge of her child. But intuition is not a special faculty, but is merely the spontaneous exercise of the intelligence, closely collaborating with sensible activity (perception, creative imagination) in order to know the same *material and concrete object* [1]. It is not infallible and requires the active control of discursive reason; it cannot, consequently, be the basis of a valid philosophy. It should rather be looked upon as knowledge through affective sympathy or through *connaturality* [2].

Do we have an *intellectual intuition?* In the strict sense, we do have such an intuition of the existence of our own, thinking self, but not of the essence of the self. Nor is there an intellectual intuition for every other external object; the existence of God presupposes analogy with sensible reality, and the existence of the latter, inseparable from matter, is left to one side by our abstract concepts. Even if one does not admit that a reasoning process is necessary to make an intellectual judgment of existence that is truly valid [3], one must at least refuse to all our concepts the *direct* knowledge of the singular material thing, and the immediate character of intuition is not fully retained in this case.

But if there be question of an intuition in the broad sense, the concept is wholly filled with this notion. It expresses a nature (for instance, the concept of the plant expresses the nature of vegetative life) which is not a subjective image considered as merely similar to reality, but is, through identity, reality itself. In the concept, the vegetative life of all plants (actual or possible) is had. This identity, of course, is of the spiritual or intentional order, which safeguards the real distinction of the known and the knower in the physical order. This identity does not exclude the subjective intermediary of the *impressed species;* the latter, however, is merely a means of knowing, and in no wise the object directly known. Hence, there is *intuition*, or immediate contâct with the real in a broad sense only, for the concrete existence is absent from the direct content of the concept, which is of the abstract and ideal order.

Bergson was ignorant of this profound view of St. Thomas, and all his criticisms of this view are defective. Bergson himself,

---

[1] That is, the *same reality* known under various aspects by intelligence and by sense.

[2] Thus, the perfect possession of a virtue inclines the intelligence spontaneously, and without reasoning, to make a right judgment on the things falling under this virtue; see St. Thomas Aquinas, *Summa Theologica*, i, q. i, art. 6, ad 3 and J. MARITAIN, *La philosophie bergsonienne*, pp. 175-188.

[3] Cardinal Mercier believes it is possible for man to affirm, with certitude, the existence of one or several extramental realities without using the principle of causality; see his *Critériologie générale*, p. 360.

when speaking of coincidence, without distinguishing whether it is of the physical or *intentional* order, leaves his notion of intuition at the level of dangerous ambiguity. For, in the intuition of the infinite, physical coincidence is the assertion of pantheism.

At the summit of science one also finds a sort of intuition in the contemplation of the conclusions which have become evident through demonstration. But its value rests on that of the concepts concerned.

Finally, there is mystical intuition which is certainly able to surpass the concept and lead man to discover ineffable secrets; it is of the supernatural order, however, and cannot be the basis of pure philosophy [1].

In the meantime, one can say that in recognizing a *fringe of intuition* around intelligence, Bergson concedes the validity of intuition in this broad sense. This explains the portion of truth, often quite striking, which he finds in applying his method to the various aspects of reality.

II. BIOLOGICAL INTUITION : THE UNIVERSE.

541. In his explanation of the universe, Bergson holds that everything occurs as if a great stream of consciousness or a *living urge* had been unleashed on all matter in order to give it organization. One can thus speak, here, of a *biological* intuition.

But it is important that one does not forget what this intuition is really stating through its brilliant metaphors. In order to grasp their meaning, the following order will be followed : a precise statement of the problem to be solved; the meaning of Bergson's *elan vital*, and the corollaries which follow for man and matter.

A) **The Problem.**

How can intuition explain the actual universe as it has been described by the astronomical, physical, chemical, biological and even psychological sciences? That is the problem. There is no question of knowing the origin of the world, whether it is self explanatory or if it comes from a distinct Creator. That is another problem which metaphysics has to resolve, and which is reserved for another effort at intuition [2].

Now, in Bergson's view, everything is explained in the universe by admitting *life* as the unique reality, not as stopped

---

[1] See below, n. 550 and n. 554, for the way in which Bergson uses this supernatural intuition, and the value of this method.

[2] It is resolved through the help of mystical intuition; see below, n. 553.

up in a species, but as progressive, and as advancing through creative succession : it is a vital urge *(élan vital)*. It is true that one portion of the universe, and even the greater part, seems deprived of life. But Bergson does not believe that life is reserved to our little earth. It most probably flourishes on analogous planets in all the stellar systems, perhaps even better than on this earth. Moreover, through a final deepening, the intuition of the vital urge permits one to come in through the back door, as it were, and to comprehend matter and its astronomical and physical laws.

Thus, the problem was at first limited to grasp the meaning of life on our planet. Bergson, encountering the mechanistic and evolutionistic explanations which Spencer's system gave of the universe [1], refutes them and puts the vital urge in their place. The vital urge, then, has both a negative and a positive meaning.

B) Significance of the Vital Urge.

542. Through a happy analysis of some well chosen facts, Bergson first shows that life cannot be referred to any physico-chemical activity, and that the development of species cannot be due to exterior influences (environment, struggle for life, and so on). This impossibility follows due to the fact that these influences exert themselves slowly, and that their proponents generally admit quick variations retained through heredity. This critique of Darwinism is excellently done by Bergson.

Bergson also rejects finalism, according to which the germ *totally* contains the perfection of the new species, though only in a virtual fashion, as the artist's sketch contains his work. The evolution of life, Bergson holds, contains a richness that is always new and that gushes forth in an unpredictable fashion — as a creation which does not exist in the preceding degrees. Bergson's assertion of a vital urge at first, then, summarizes these various refutations.

Positively, the notion of a vital urge answers the question of the problem of life and resolves the difficulties if it be taken as an absolute, the object of intuition. One can then see it as a simple act, a force that is at once synthetic, unique, and opposed.

---

[1] See above, n. 480.

Synthetic, for all the perfections of living species are contained in the vital urge, not as parts forming a totality, but in the state of reciprocal implication, and as constitutive of a simple thing. Later, they become complementary aspects after they have been sorted out from the unforeseeable riches which are truly new [1].

Unique, or the trait which explains the similarity of functions and of organs in living things which are otherwise independent.

Opposed or at cross-purposes, for in viewing matter as an obstacle, the many details whose arrangement appear so complicated from without, are taken together in one glance. The situation is similar to that of plunging one's hand into a group of iron filings; at one blow, the multiple arrangements of the small pieces finds a new equilibrium.

Thus, the extraordinary variety of vital forms is manifested, if viewed from without, as a great tree whose root is the vital urge seeking to develop itself, as we see in ourselves, in the fulness of the spiritual life. But the unstable equilibrium of tendencies which this urge synthesizes in its simplicity, and the resistance of matter, have required it to unfold as a dispersion. The many species represent varied attempts of *life* to progress. Some of these turned out to be impasses; *consciousness* could not pass beyond and hence turned around in its place — this explains the fixity of species. But in a number of directions which Bergson ingeniously set up, progress arose beyond the torpor of vegetative life towards the greater activity of animal life by conquering for itself a nervous system which is most perfect. Thus, the species do not follow a straight line, but are often complementary, and often go two by two, representing various solutions to the same problem.

Without emphasizing the inferior degrees, it can be noted that at the summit, the two that are most perfectly joined are instinct in the animals towards social life (as in bees and ants) and intelligence in man. *Instinct* is the power of using and even of constructing organized instruments, which explains why it is perfectly organized at once; it is, however, essentially specialized and cannot surpass a group of closed activities. *Intelligence* is the power of making inorganic implements, distinct from our members. At the beginning, its success is quite imperfect, and each instrument made fulfills needs

---

[1] *Les Deux Sources de la moralité et de la religion*, p. 119.

and new activities. It also remains open to indefinite progress, and its superiority stands out when it has invented machines to make instruments.

Between instinct and intelligence there is a difference not only of degree, but of *nature*, as between the closed and the open. Nevertheless, the two are complementary, so that instinct has traces of intelligence, and about the luminous center of human intelligence there is a fringe of instinct which makes the intuitive method possible for man.

C) Matter.

543. With the aid of his basic principle that the only reality is *pure becoming*, Bergson had to explain matter itself by the vital urge. He did so with some success by taking life from a *negative point of view*. Thus the three properties of matter, inertia, extension and necessity can be fully explained.

If one *denies* vital movement by halting its progress, one is in the presence of an inertia in which activity cedes to passivity.

In taking the direction opposed to the simplicity of the vital urge, one obtains a composition of parts which, by spreading itself outwards, forms geometrical space.

Since the vital push is creative, unforeseeable and thus free, its suppression will produce the necessity of the laws of nature, in which the antecedents allow one infallibly to foresee the consequents.

But this explanation is due to an *inexpressible intuition;* in order to stimulate it, Bergson makes use of multiple images. He defines matter through a kind of descent, and descent through an interruption of rising; matter is a psychic reversal of the vital urge in regression. Matter is, then, a relaxation of the inextensive into the extensive, and, in this way, a relaxation of liberty to necessity [1]. Briefly, it is the negative of all of that which is positive in life.

D) Monism or Pluralism.

544. It is impossible to appreciate Bergson's thought without being precise as to what he means in advance, for he refused to express himself in concepts, our natural mode of thinking. The theory of the vital urge is capable of two contradictory completions between which there lies an unstable equilibrium which is a bit abstract or indecisive, like a genus between its two species.

---

[1] See, for instance, *Evolution créatrice*, p. 217, 237, etc.

1. **Monistic Interpretation.** In this view, the vital urge is viewed as a unique *substance*, rigorously absolute, and thereby infinite and necessary, explainable in itself as is God. One cannot avoid evolutionary pantheism, and the theory is nothing more than an unintelligible scheme of contradictions which do not hold together except through the mirage of metaphors, for one adopts in principle that *what is*, is equivalent to *what is not*, but is becoming. The very title of *creative evolution* is an absurdity, asserting that the *lesser* of itself produces the greater.

Bergson protested against this interpretation [1]. He maintained that the theory of creative evolution was most favorable to the distinction between the world and God, especially since this problem has not yet been solved. It should be recognized that the monistic explanation, although hardly avoidable, *adds* to Bergson's thought, and that it is possible to complete his thought in a manner more favorable to the truth.

2. **Pluralistic Interpretation.** The living urge can be understood as coming from a Source, really distinct, and which would be the infinite and free activity of the Creator. In this view, the evolution of species expresses the plan of the Creator, which the philosopher discovers by looking at the facts from below. The inferior degrees appear, in retrospection, as joined to the higher as a preparation for them, but without containing them. There is newness in Creation which is explained by the Creator being immanent to His work, while matter represents the negative side, functioning as a limit, as the source of multiplicity and of necessity, analogous to the role of prime matter in Thomism. This interpretation is quite legitimate, even though some details of Bergson's view remain disputable, as the presence of life on other planets; these details can be looked upon as hypotheses and not as certitudes.

But this explanation also *completes* Bergson's thought to the extent that it affirms God to be an unchangeable substance, and the world as formed of individual substances obeying their immanent law of evolution by acting upon each other. These are intellectual notions, which are estranged from intuition. The latter recognizes only the straight line of vital evolution, whose simple eruption is neither the unique, pantheistic substance, nor the multiple created substances, emanating from God according to the old laws of causality.

It should be added that this position of Bergson's is not merely incomplete, but also erroneous, since it upholds the impossibility of knowing anything besides mobile reality with metaphysical certitude.

III. Psychological intuition : the Self.

545. Since man carries an emanation of the vital urge within himself, intuition should help us clarify our personal

---

[1] See Bergson's letters to J. de Tonquédec, published in *Etudes*, February 20, 1912. See also J. Farges, *La philosophie de M. Bergson*, pp. 462-5.

life. In order to understand Bergson's proposals, the problem which they attempt to answer must be stated.

A) **The Problem.** When Bergson was writing his first works, the philosophers were applying the procedures used in the study of the external world to the world of consciousness. The substance of the soul was believed inaccessible, as was any other absolute (in agreement with Kantianism and positivism), and the object of psychology was the phenomenon or fact of consciousness *(phenomenalism)*.

The concern of psychologists, at this time, was the hope of discovering the primitive elements and laws of evolution *(associationism)*. Moreover, moved by the desire for unity, many referred consciousness to a simple aspect of the physiological fact, so that to each internal fact there corresponded a cerebral modification, the consciousness of which was an epiphenomenon *(psychophysical parallelism)*.

Is this claim of science to explain our intimate life legitimate? Is it forbidden to discover our absolute and spiritual self, studied through a metaphysical psychology? This is the problem which Bergson resolves by denouncing the malpractice of the intellectualist method, and requiring intuition to answer the problem by furnishing the proper object of psychology, thus explaining the union of soul and body and the nature of the body itself.

B) **Solution.**

I. **Object of Psychology. 546.** *The reality of the self, of our interior life, the object of psychology, is not a series of phenomena, but* DURATION *or real time as a participation in the living urge which constitutes the unique reality.*

We have here a particular instance of the intuitive method, and one which everyone can easily experience. It is sufficient for us to lead our introspection beyond divisions and conceptual schematisms to what is *immediately given* in consciousness. There we will encounter the flow of duration with its three properties by which it is opposed to matter.

a) Continuity. Like that of the living urge, our duration is essentially simple. In it are embodied the phenomena which are considered as distinct and successive by intelligence. They are stored there as in their source wherein they are identified through their duration. Consciousness is a continuous current. This shows that associationism and phenomenalism are but artificial theories.

b) Heterogeneity. This simplicity is not that of an immobile point or a uniform current, but of a creative progress. In man as well as in the universe, the new living manifestations possess a superior perfection that is not contained in the preceding; thus, perception and images follow sensation, and the former lead to ideas and the sciences. This property of continually enriching consciousness with qualities that are always new is called *heterogeneity*, since it opposes human life to homogeneous matter. In matter homogeneity prevails and movement is but repetition without progress.

The notion of heterogeneity refutes the evolutionistic theory of Spencer, Taine, and others, for they sought to explain the increasing richness of human life by referring it to the inferior degree of physiological facts.

This property further distinguishes duration or the real time of the self from the time studied in the physico-mathematical sciences. The latter type of time is but a void and stable receptacle exterior to movement, with the result that by reducing, say, the unity of time to a half, the laws and predictions of astronomy remain true; though one cannot diminish real time in man without consciousness being aware of a diminution of enrichment.

c) Liberty. Our duration, like that of the vital urge, is an *absolute*, and constitutes our personality. The activity in which personality is expressed is thus fully independent and unpredictable, and therefore *free*. " If it be proper to call free every act which emanates from the self and the self alone, the act which bears the mark of our person is veritably free, for the self alone vindicates its paternity " [1].

This resolves, in Bergson's mind, all the deterministic objections which presuppose distinct and successive parts in consciousness, as well as thoughts and sentiments which are conditioned as the cause conditions its effect. But for the same reason, Bergson likewise rejects the intellectualist defenders of liberty, and holds that the intuitive affirmation of consciousness grasps liberty as an aspect of the self or of real duration.

Since this duration is identifiable with pure becoming, the sole reality (following the basic principle), one can consider

---

[1] *Essai sur les données immédiates de la conscience*, p. 132.

liberty a property of every living thing. There are degrees of manifestation of the vital urge, however, and, in its proper sense, liberty pertains only to the summit of life. Instinct itself remains imprisoned by the mechanisms which it has set up; man alone has succeeded in breaking bondage [1].

Just as the three properties which characterize duration and give psychology a proper object opposed to matter, spring from the vital urge, so Bergson proclaims the immateriality of life in general, though it is only in man that spirituality has realized itself successfully. Having conquered liberty, the self, held up by the powerful push of the vital urge, is capable of overcoming other obstacles, " perhaps, even, death itself " [2].

This raises the question of the *immortality of the soul*. Bergson refuses to resolve it by accepting the definition of the soul as a spiritual substance. He takes refuge in intuitive experience, whether psychological or mystical. The first certifies the independence of vital activity from the body, and concludes with the possibility of survival, at least of temporal survival. The mystical intuition which shows that some privileged souls have been joined with the eternal activity of God through a sharing in the Divine Essence, is a more exact indication of immortality. But new intuitions must be indulged in to make the solution to this problem precise, and " the problem must remain open " [3].

2. **Union of soul and body. 547.** Intuition not only establishes the radical distinction between body and soul, it also grasps their union. Since the self is *duration*, it is through memory that there is best manifested both the independence and the solidarity of spiritual activity as related to the brain.

Bergson at first distinguishes two sorts of memory which are quite different :

a) The Memory-habit (or motor-memory) is the aptitude of reproducing a text or an action learned by heart. It has all the characteristics of corporeal habit (habit in the modern sense) : it is acquired slowly through repetition, it tends towards unconsciousness, and consists in a series of movements involved

---

[1] See *L'Evolution créatrice*, pp. 286-87; see also, A. FARGES, *La philosophie de M. Bergson*, pp. 249-250.

[2] *L'Evolution créatrice*, p. 294. See also A. FARGES, *op. cit.*, p. 259.

[3] *Les Deux Sources de la morale et de la religion*, pp. 283-84.

in a fixed order. This memory is seated in the body, especially in the head, whose motor centers direct the performance of actions. It *recalls* or exactly reproduces the same action in the present.

b) *Pure-memory*, on the contrary, or (remembrance-memory) is situated directly in the past; it preserves the event in its totality, without dividing it. It consists in *recalling to oneself;* that is, in recognizing a past fact as pertaining to ourselves, since we actually continue to live.

Now, both normal and pathological facts show that remembrances are conserved independently of the brain. Thus, certain injured people, despite the loss of one portion of the brain, have recovered all their remembrances [1]. Consequently, Bergson holds that pure memory is of the spiritual order, and not an organic faculty, localized in the body. Pure memory is in the soul.

Nevertheless, facts show the *solidarity* of every memory within the brain. This is due to the fact that pure memories remain in a virtual state, unconscious, as it were, in the duration which holds all of them in its own simplicity. They tend to exteriorize themselves in the repetition of an event in order to become present to clear consciousness. There they encounter memory-habit, which they use in order to express themselves.

This is the point of contact between soul and body. The existence of remembrances refutes psychophysical parallelism. The fact of consciousness is not on the reverse side of the cerebral fact, but the soul is related to body as the worker to his instrument.

Bergson compares this dependence to that of clothing to the nail on which it hangs or to various scenes placed within the same frame. Thus, the most diverse memories can be expressed by the same cerebral mechanism which conditions them and yet respects their spirituality.

The explanation of this lies in the function of our soul as a part of the living urge. Since life in us can attain its fulness, it must act upon matter in order to overcome the resistance of matter, and the body is its necessary means. The body is the point in which the soul inserts its action upon the world. Our soul, for Bergson, is not a spiritual substance, but a duration, a life, and the most perfect spreading out of pure becoming on this earth.

---

[1] See J. Chevalier, *Bergson*, pp. 171-172.

3. **Nature of Body. 548.** Since becoming is the unique reality, it must explain body itself. This Bergson does by explaining the activities of the soul. He distinguishes four states, going from the most material to the most spiritual : pure perception, conscious perception, the memory-remembrance and the pure memory.

Below, there lies *sensation* or pure perception, which is absolute sensible intuition constituted by immediate contact and total identity between the knower and the matter known. It exists, inasmuch as matter is " psychically inverted ", but in the pure state it remains unconscious, and does not awaken until the second stage. This is the stage of *conscious perception,* which is that of a choice made spontaneously by the nervous system through the great intuition of matter in general, with the view of permitting and directing our activity. The procedures of division and schematization proper to sense already constitute the beginning of intellectual work, the aim of which is to allow man to conquer the universe.

On the other hand, *pure memory* would be the perfect, intuitive possession of our duration, which would make us relive our whole past at every moment. But, in its turn, such a memory would make adaptation to present life impossible. This explains the usefulness of forgetting and the necessity of letting the pure memory drop into unconsciousness towards the remembrance-image which is the expression of a particular event of the past, ready for repetition or for aiding us in the line of action.

It is clear that conscious perception and the remembrance-image mutually open and close the mechanism of the memory-habit and of the external carrying out of active life. Accordingly, there must lie, between these two extremities of matter and spirit, an uninterrupted series of intermediaries, among which the life of the soul amounts to a ceaseless coming and going, with the result that our duration or the reality of the self is this very movement, or equilibrium between body and soul. Just as the unique vital urge explains life by its creative effort and matter by regression, the unique duration explains the soul by its ascension towards liberty and the remembrance, and our body by its descent towards spatial perception of exteriority [1].

----

[1] On the notion of memory in Bergson, see J. MARITAIN, *La Philosophie bergsonienne,* pp. 255-281.

C) **A Dual Interpretation.**

549. Here again, a double interpretation is necessary and possible as an explanation of Bergson's thought.

1. In the *pluralistic sense*, Bergson has rediscovered the great truths of the spirituality and freedom of the soul, and of its partial dependence on the body, whose negative role, like that of matter, is rightly asserted.

Nevertheless, the choice of memory as the activity characteristic of the spirit is not a happy one. One needs to distinguish memory of *ideas*, which alone is properly spiritual, from sensible memory, whose object is concrete, and it seems that Bergson more often refers to the latter. It is true that the immateriality of remembering, even concretely, can lead to the Thomistic assertion that immateriality is at the root of all knowledge [1].

Could one hold that Bergson's views on these propositions of Christian philosophy on the nature and prerogatives of the soul are an authentic prolongation of Bergson's thought, with the latter as their true source? It does not seem that they are positively excluded by the affirmations which Bergson himself certainly held. But they do not flow from his thought necessarily, and here, at the basis of his system, the opposed interpretation arises.

2. In the *monistic sense*, our personality disappears by identification of our duration with the unique becoming which is God Himself. In memory, the past is identified with the present without ceasing to be past, and our body, identical with the sleeping consciousness of matter, is opposed to the soul, though identifying itself with soul in the unique duration. Completed in this way, all of Bergson's formulas are nothing more than unintelligible contradictions.

IV. MYSTICAL INTUITION : GOD.

550. Having considered pure becoming in its manifestations in the universe and in man, Bergson takes up the problem of its origin. He does this by examining a new problem to which he adapts his intuitive method. The problem is that of moral and religious life, which leads to God.

I. **The Problem and the Method.**

Besides life dispersed in the multiple species of the world and psychological life concentrated in the personal self, there is the life of humanity characterized by society. Instinct

---

[1] In all sensible knowledge (especially in memory) there is an activity higher than that of the physical or physiological orders, and thereby *immaterial*, though in an imperfect mode, remaining subject to various material conditions. Independence is not fully realized but in intelligence and in will.

has already realized social life among certain animals, as among bees and ants, but human society has three characteristic traits. It is *moral*, based on obligatory laws; it is *religious*, possessing an organized cult; it is *progressive*, capable of varying its institutions. This new problem has to be explained by the intuition of pure becoming.

The method which first presented itself to Bergson was to take up the study of the vital urge or of duration through his own means of investigation, since his intuitive method carried with it, so to speak, the very notion of society in itself. Without neglecting this attempt, Bergson appealed to another source of intuition which he believed more profound and more informed than his own — it was that of the founders of society and of religion, namely the heroes, saints and *mystics*. He was pressed, of course, to justify this enlargement of his own method in order to show its strictly philosophical value.

At first he refuted the psychologists who, with Pierre Janet, considered mystical phenomena only a form of hysteria or other mental illness [1]. The mystics, Bergson believes, manifest their intellectual sanctity by " the taste for action, by their power of adapting and readapting themselves to circumstances; they show firmness allied to suppleness, a spirit of simplicity which triumphs over complications, and, finally, a superior good sense " [2].

Then Bergson shows that their testimony has more than a strictly personal value and can serve as the basis of a universal science. Their utterances awaken a resonance within us, and engender a sympathy which permits us to view their statements as probable or as an object of possible experience. This is due to the fact that the method of checking their results with other philosophical intuitions leads, through the converging of the lines of facts, to certain conclusions. The intuition of the vital urge suggests the possibility of contact with the principle of life; this contact is precisely that of mystical intuition, as long as the latter furnishes answers which marvelously complete the points acquired by the other ways.

But the mysticism endowed with this philosophical value pertains, according to Bergson, only to *Christian mystics*. Surpassing the stage of intellectual ecstasy, in which Neo-

---

[1] See above, n. 510.
[2] *Les Deux Sources de la morale et de la religion*, p. 244.

Platonism voluntarily halted, and the total detachment of the Hindu nirvana, which contemplates without leading to action, the Christian mystics went so far as to identify their wills with God's. Ecstasy, for them, is a provisory affair; across the obscure night, they feel a transformation of their being which elevates them to the rank of *divine helpers*, a role which gives them an extraordinary power of action. This explains the works of St. Paul, St. Therese, St. Francis, St. Joan of Arc, and others, and of Christ Himself, of Whom all these others are but a participation. Only the Christian mystics possess the complete mysticism which Bergson defines as " a grip of contact and a consequent partial coincidence with the creative effort which manifests life " [1].

It should be pointed out that Bergson remains faithful to his radical anti-intellectualism. He uses mysticism only to the extent that it agrees with his basic principle, and abstracts from all historical fact or dogmatic assertion. He takes it in its purely intuitive form, for he sees in it a procedure analogous to his philosophical intuition which alone is capable of penetrating the secrets of pure becoming, or the unique reality of the vital urge.

This intuitive method is quite synthetic. One can resolve moral and religious problems without any appeal to God Whose docile instruments the mystics declared themselves. Nevertheless, Bergson's philosophical propositions on the existence and nature of God are also a conclusion suggested by the fact of human society.

II. **The Dual Morality.**

551. The facts of moral life involve contrasts which require, according to Bergson, two distinct moralities, one *closed*, and the other *open*. Without doubt, they are not found separated, but it is convenient to isolate them in order to give a clear and satisfying solution to the moral problem.

A) **Closed Morality** is the group of prescriptions and defenses imposed on the individual by society in order to make life in common possible and useful for all. It has a triple trait; it is obligatory, instinctive and closed.

I. **Obligatory.** Bergson clearly recognized the two aspects of obligation : " It is the very form itself which necessity takes

---

[1] *Ibid.*, p. 235.

in the domain of life when intelligence, choice, and, consequently, liberty are required in order to realize a certain goal " [1].
In closed morality, the dominant aspect is that of necessity,
whose source is the force of habit which we have contracted
by obeying the demands of society. These habits, the fruit
of education, form such a portion of the self that we even
bear them in solitude and they direct our personal progress
as well as our relations with others.

Their necessity is not absolute, as in the case of the animal.
Only obligation in general, without which society would be
impossible, is absolute. Each obligation in particular is
variable, permitting dispensations and infractions, and thereby
safeguarding liberty.

2. **Instinctive.** This explanation refers obligation to instinct
and shows the impossibility of deducing any purely rational
system from it. The purely scientific morality of the positivist
or the esthetic morality of the pagan will always be without
obligation and sanction [2].

There is no question, however, of instinct in the strict sense,
since man has received the social urge with intelligence and
reflection. It is, Bergson says, a *virtual* instinct, or a disposition
willed by nature, playing the same role as instinct in animal
society; it assures life in common, but adapts itself to the
conditions of intelligence.

Intelligence exercises itself on social prescriptions, pruning
the useless, inserting a logical order in them, and finding their
motives. These intellectual representations are a great help
in halting the egoistic tendencies which dissolve society. But
their efficacy rests on the force of the social habit, which
constitutes obligation.

3. **Closed.** Finally, the prescriptions of social morality
do not go beyond the narrow framework of the city or of
a limited country; other moralities are foreign to these limited
ones. It seems logical to go from the duties among citizens
to the duties among all men. But this cannot be done, and
one can prove this position by realizing that the philosophers,
for example, the Stoics, who attempted to do so concluded
with an inefficacious ideal. The pagan rule, " the welfare
of the people is the supreme law ", is accepted by all men only

---

[1] *Ibid.*, p. 24.

[2] This is the formula suggested by the work of GUYAU which is entitled
Esquisse d'une morale sans obligation ni sanction; see above, n. 891.

in case of declaration of war; in practice, it denies all rights to enemies. In this way, morality is similar to instinct and keeps a certain stability in humanity.

B) **Open Morality,** on the contrary, is constituted by the simple and fertile impulse of charity which takes its sources in the Creative Love of God of which it is a participation. From then it pours out over all humanity and every creature. It has three characteristics opposed to those of closed morality; it is spontaneous, intuitive, and progressive.

1. **Spontaneous.** Open morality also has a form of obligation, but it is the aspect of liberty which dominates it. Instead of being a social bent, it is essentially a spontaneity which goes on forward; it is properly the trait of the privileged individual, a hero or a saint. The latter, far from being forced in following this attraction, feel themselves free. They joyously give up all terrestrial goods in order to be wholly dedicated to God and to the work to which they are absolutely devoted. All that remains of necessity, here, is the total absence of resistance.

From these privileged souls, this morality overflows onto the crowd, whose conduct it enobles. But instead of commanding and punishing, it attracts and converts through the force of example and heroism.

2. **Intuitive.** This type of morality gets its extraordinary efficacy from a *creative emotion*, a kind of affective or mystic intuition through which one is co-incident with the creative effort, as was mentioned above. It is also an affective morality, though not sentimental, for the emotion which is its basis is not of an inferior, sensible and infra-rational order, but highly *supra-rational*. It does not follow representation of ideas or images; it precedes them and adopts them, similar to the initial emotion of the artistic which his master work transmits, though without emptying it out completely. Thus, intelligence will also translate this open morality into a code of laws and counsels, but its efficacy is not intellectual but intuitive. And, since Christian mysticism alone is complete, open morality is the morality of the gospel.

3. **Progressive.** Through this intuition, human life in privileged souls really takes a great step forward; it breaks the circle in which society is enclosed, and renews its creative urge. Instead of mounting by degrees from society to humanity

and then to God, it attains a tie-up of immediate contact with God through *charity*, the fusion of the human will with that of God; this is the very essence of mysticism. In its higher forms, it includes, even without effort, both humanity itself and every creature. Open morality, consequently, defends the sacredness of the human person, for it makes one practice love and devotion to all, even towards one's enemies.

C) **Unification.** Between these two views of morality considered in their pure state, there is not only a difference of degree, but also of nature. In the meantime, since both are addressed to the same humanity, the practical work of codification undertaken by intelligence has made them quite close to each other as if they were fused, and existing systems of morality are a composite of the two in varying proportions. Thus, in Bergson's view, the inspiration of open morality is seen in the declaration of the rights of man, and the regulations of ecclesiastical discipline are inspired by closed morality.

This mutual influence of these two moralities is for their mutual good. Social obligation, which is most rigorous, by communicating with the laws of universal charity, holds up their execution for the weak. Charity, by spreading its perfume over society, sweetens the harshness of its egoism.

The final explanation of this unification lies in the unity of pure becoming which, by the basic principle, characterizes the whole reality of social life, as well as that of individual and universal life. These two moralities, so basically opposed, then appear, if looked at from within, as two complementary solutions found by the vital urge which seeks to deploy its virtuality to the negative resistance of matter. If the common multitudes plunge the very roots of their being into the torrent of life in which the mystics become entirely renewed, there is nothing surprising in the fact that these privileged souls should found a school, and, by their example, complete their lives by training all of humanity. But, in order to obtain this result, they leaned on the authority of religion.

III. **The Dual Religion.**

552. The view of a dual morality makes clear what Bergson means by religion. If the vital urge, arrived, in free and intelligent man, at the summit of its terrestrial expansion, has need of moral obligation to make social human life essentially possible, this obligation is insufficient. Certain dangers inherent in intelligence require a group of other means of life, which constitutes the first form of religion, *static religion*, parallel to closed morality. On the other side, the soul of the great mystic finds at once the solution of all difficulties. Thus arises a new and superior religion for the good of humanity, *dynamic religion*, parallel to open morality.

Between these two religions there is the same radical distinction of nature and the same mutual influence as between the two types of morality; this justifies usage of the same word to designate both. Considering what is common to both, Bergson defines religion as " a system of convictions and of practices destined to maintain the attachment of humanity to life in all its amplitude ". But this system is quite different, depending on whether it is static or dynamic. In order to make clear what existing religions owe to one or the other, the nature of these two religions in their pure state can be explained.

A) Static Religion.

By pointing out the dangers that should be avoided, Bergson shows the function of belief and religious cult, and tries, in addition, to explain their psychological origin.

1. In the framework of society, a double danger menaces human life through the use of intelligence : egoism and fear.

With regard to *egoism*, there are many cases in which reflection makes us aware of social requirements that are opposed to our own personal interests.

Now, man does not have the blind instinct of animals, who unconsciously sacrifice themselves for the common good. As a result, and because other obligation is insufficient, religion intervenes by its defenses and its commands. By speaking in the name of God, whose sovereign authority is incontested, it increases the force of obligation, and conquers egoism by its sanctions, threats and promises.

A most grave difficulty, especially at the beginning of humanity, arises from the *aptitude for prediction* which is proper to intelligence. When science did not as yet exist as a means of teaching the usage of nature, man did not act with the surety of instinct, and often became dubious of the results of his action. Between the act and its results, between the sowing and the harvesting or between the hunt and the captured game, man perceived a margin of discouraging incertitude. The most important of these fears is that of inevitable

death, which seems to destroy or make useless human enterprises. Here religion intervenes. In order to keep the taste
for action alive, it gives credence to immortality, to the
influence of death and to the supernatural forces which aid
us in difficult or .n hazardous circumstances, teaching the
cult of ancestors and of the gods.

2. These beliefs and practices, for Bergson, have a *natural
origin*, useful and valuable in its own realm. He attributes
them to *fiction*, that is, to the imagination as creative of fables
necessary for social life. This function is not proper to the
primitive mentality as opposed to our own psychology, but
one finds it among men today in its essential manifestations;
for instance, a man playing roulette objectivizes " chance "
into a beneficent semi-personality, as if to supply for the
lack of efficacy in his own physical action. The primitives
acted in the same manner, the only difference being that
the physical means which they knew and used were more
restrained, and the realm of fiction more ample.

Finally, there comes the work of organization by intelligence.
In this indecisive state into which nature places man, intelligence develops the *impersonal side :* this explains magic and
sorcery founded on the belief in an impersonal force diffused
throughout, but being at the service of mankind. The *personal
side* is also developed with its many anonymous spirits and
its well-defined God. Reason places some order among these,
and elevates itself to the idea of a supreme and unique being.
But progress in this domain remains static, since it is incapable
of going beyond the limits of social religion, a national cult
and a national god.

B) Dynamic Religion.

Instead of counterbalancing intelligence by remedies of the
same order — that is, by representations whose object has
no reality and is but practical in aim — the soul of the great
mystics finds a solution which is most profound and fruitful,
contact with the vital urge itself. The extension and value
of this religion will be pointed out.

1. **Extension.** The national framework is henceforth
broken. Dynamic religion is a universal religion addressed
to all men, for it speaks in the name of the only true God,
the Creator of all peoples. This religion is the Christian religion,
whose universal expansion demonstrates the incontestable
value of its initial impulse.

Other great mystics are but a prolongation of the action of Christ, embracing all of humanity in their vision and zeal, as did He. But they could not attain this of themselves, and consequently founded works, as religious orders, destined to perpetuate the living urge by attracting the greatest possible number to follow in their wake.

2. **Value.** But it is clear, after what has been said about the intuitive method, that the essential value of this religion lies uniquely in emotion, the initial creative force which is prior to any intellectual exactness and any social organization. These latter two conditions, however, are necessary for this religion to express itself, to expand, and to attract the multitudes. It ordinarily makes use, therefore, of existing habits by infusing a new spirit into national religions, purifying their exercise and adapting them to its own end.

In order to be more precise, let us take the example of Christianity, as viewed by Bergson. He did not give a detailed statement of what he thought decadent in it, but it seems that everything which concerns revealed dogmas, as that of the Trinity and Incarnation, as well as everything concerning the social organization of the Church, its hierarchy, sacraments, and so forth, had but one of two origins. They are either the remains of static religion, a fictional work, or they are creations of intelligence, seeking to find the best possible expression of the rich emotion of primitive charity. Only in the latter is the whole value of Christianity contained. Somewhat as in modernism, with its sentimental knowledge of God [1], though much more clearly, does Bergson resolve the meaning of his intuition of God.

IV. God.

553. In the living light of the great mystics Bergson rediscovers the existence and the principle attributes of the true God.

A) Existence of God.

Faithful to the end in his radical anti-intellectualism, Bergson begins by denying value to the classical proofs for God's existence. In his view, the God of the intellectualistic philosophers, the Ideal God of Plato or the Pure Actuality

---

[1] See above, n. 532.

of Aristotle, obtained by reasoning, have but a logical role as the supreme abstraction unifying the sciences. One neither adores nor loves this sort of God. In contrast, God, the object of all religions, is a personal being, entering into communion with man, and is real and living as man himself. Thus, as for any reality, God's existence can be known only through experience.

Accordingly it is only mystical intuition which, as has been shown, possesses real philosophical value, that gives this experience to Bergson. God exists; He is the object of dynamic religion and it is with Him that the mystics were in immediate contact. He is the God of Christianity.

B) Attributes of God.

Evidently, the metaphysical attributes of God as His Pure Actuality, or His Subsisting Being are without value, for they are the result of intellectual work. After studying the mystics, however, Bergson proposed some formulas whose meaning can be intuitively grasped by comparing them to our own psychology.

1. **God is Love.** Love here means a supra-rational emotion, analogous to the intuition which lies at the basis of open morality and dynamic religion, but carried up to its highest degree. This " love " is not something of God, but it is God Himself [1], constituting His Essence so completely that all other attributes flow from this one.

2. **God is Personal.** Bergson's views on this point are quite precise. The artist can testify that all his personality is expressed and contained in the loving intuition from which his work was produced. This, though realized fully, holds for the Person of God-Love.

3. **God is Free.** It has been shown that the self, by expressing itself completely in an act, manifests its independent spontaneity and liberty [2]. In a similar though absolute way, the activity of Love, conceived as intuitive emotion, is so perfect that it is self-sufficient and does not require an object to be defined : it is the *Absolute, Liberty* itself.

4. **God is the Creator.** He is acting, a vital urge, analogous to that which we experience in ourselves and in the universe.

---

[1] *Les Deux Sources de la religion et de la morale*, p. 270.
[2] See above, n. 546.

For " it is difficult to conceive of a love which is acting but is not addressed to anything " [1]. In a complete sense, God is *Creative Emotion*, whose work of artistry is the unfolding of universes. Bergson believes, for this reason, that creation is not at all mysterious, for we experience it ourselves every time that we create a work of art.

5. **Creation is a Work of Love.** It can be viewed as " an enterprise of God to create creators and to join to Himself beings worthy of His Love " [2]. In this sense, God has need of us in order to love us, and confers on man the noble goal of partaking in His benevolent action, which is an effusion of Love.

The distinction between God and man, and the reason for the universe is expressed as follows : " There are beings called to existence who are destined to love and to be loved, the Creative Energy needs to define itself by love. Distinct from God, Who is this very Energy, they could not arise but in the universe, and that is why the universe has arisen " [3]. This interpretation of creation — though the word is not Bergson's — can be called Divine Providence.

6. The Existence of Evil does not destroy this conception, since all objections which are drawn from it are due to an a priori definition of God. The true method, inversely, is based on the existence of the world *as it is*, in order to conclude to God. For instance, one can say that God, being All-Powerful, if He existed as Love, would not tolerate evil. But one should rather conclude that the notion of Almightiness must be corrected; it must be harmonized with the fact of evil and designate the fulness of the creative spontaneity as an " energy without determinable limits " [4].

554. In this final stage, as in the others, it is impossible to think in Bergson's manner without *completing* his view with the aid of common sense and Christian philosophy. This complementation, again, is possible in two different ways.

1. The mysticism which he invokes and interrogates is, as a matter of fact, of the *supernatural* order, for it is based on the Catholic faith and depends, solely, on a freely given grace of God. It is, then, essentially distinct from all philosophical knowledge. By considering it from his own viewpoint, without dogmas, Bergson

---

[1] *Les Deux Sources de la morale et de la religion*, p. 273.
[2] *Ibid.*
[3] *Ibid.*, p. 276.
[4] *Ibid.*, p. 281.

does not refer to such a distinction, and his view can be interpreted as holding an identification between philosophical and mystical intuition. This would then be the rationalistic error which lowers the value of supernatural revelation to the measure of natural reason.

2. In morality and in religion, one meets the doctrine of the vital urge. If one adopts the favorable pluralistic interpretation [1], one could say that Bergson expresses, on one side, the natural function which God assigned to society with regard to moral and religious life [2], and that he re-established, on the other, the value of the human person, who refers immediately to God in his rights and his destiny [3]. — But many corrections are necessary to adopt this view. For, in morality, Bergson's view justifies certain forms of social egoism, contrary to the eternal law, and it does not concede to charity the strict obligatory character which it possesses. In religion, besides the notion of superstition, which he takes legitimately to task, Bergson unduly restrains the domain of true religion, attributing rites, beliefs and dogmas — which have their rightful place in natural religion or in a religion divinely instituted — to superstition or symbolism.

3. Finally, in *theodicy*, despite the clear statements of Bergson, the basic principle which he maintained to the end did not keep him from *evolutionistic pantheism*. If pure becoming is the unique reality and if its evolution constitutes various universes, God being but the center of this emanation, it is impossible, without adding to his system, to uphold a substantial and personal distinction between God and the world. That is why all the forms of his philosophy are compatible with pantheism.

Moreover, Bergson lacks a clear idea of analogy. His comparisons between the divine attributes and human experience are vague. For instance, when he represents the Personality of God as the Creative Emotion of the artist in its highest meaning, the result is not pure anthropomorphism (which Bergson excluded), nor perfect univocity. But this could be a case of what is called *distended univocity* [4], occurring when the one essence has varying degrees of perfection, as that of animality, which goes from microbes to vertebrates, or as heat increasing in intensity. This would be the *same specific essence*, (the unique reality of Life), realized in various degrees. But a God possessing the same essence as creatures, even in the supreme degree, is no longer the true God.

However, if one looks for the strict meaning of Bergson's formulas, it seems as though they are not pantheistic, since he only gave them the value of *intuition* — that is, a value placed beyond that of conceptual exactness as at a point of bifurcation from which they can be turned towards pantheism, as well as toward dualism and Thomistic analogy, without losing any of

---

[1] Here, as above (n. 544), his system can also be interpreted in a pantheistic sense, making Bergsonianism a kind of realist Hegelianism.

[2] This is *static* religion and morality.

[3] This is *dynamic* religion and morality.

[4] See A. PENIDO, *Dieu dans le bergsonisme*, p. 45.

their content.   One could add that the answers which Bergson
got from the Christian mystics incline towards this favorable view,
although the actual words which he uses lead to the opposite view.

Considered from every point of view, however, the essence of
Bergson's thought as concentrated in his basic principle, bears
with it an element of exclusion.   It does not admit any other
valuable manner of knowing than intuition, nor any other reality
accessible to philosophy than pure becoming.   And, in this way,
it will always remain anti-Thomistic and anti-Catholic, irreducible
to Christian philosophy.

CONCLUSION.

555.   Bergson's system is the last great effort of modern
thought to liberate itself from the shackles of Kantianism
and of positivism in order to reconquer the metaphysical science
of absolute reality.   But he also pulled on his chain and only
succeeded in making it longer.   He was, as a matter of fact,
imprisoned by the dual prejudice of idealism and scientism.
Fascinated by the experimental method of modern science,
he hoped for the same method in metaphysics.   Supposing
that every object of a concept is of the ideal order, a pure
possibility or subjective construction, he was no longer able
to attain reality.

Bergson is not a pragmatist in the sense of referring every
truth to an affirmation useful for action.   His ideal, on the
contrary, was that of a perfect, disinterested vision of the
absolute totality.   One finds the three traits of the pragmatist
period in his thought : absolute agnosticism of the intelligence;
purely utilitarian value in order to dominate matter of conceptual knowledge, and the transformation of truth to a power
of the sentimental order of things, to the intuition which is
also the creative emotion.

He went much farther than the other pragmatists towards
truth, and he expressed his discoveries in magnificent language.
These factors help explain his wide influence on many contemporary thinkers, as on Le Roy, Wilbois, Chevalier, and others.
But he himself did not achieve his goal : he is like an urge
filled with promises which comes to break on imaginary walls
where his modern prejudices have shut him up.

For these reasons, Maritain has distinguished two " Bergson-
ianisms " [1], one of fact and the other of intention.   The first
is erroneous and anti-Catholic, justifying the decree of the

---

[1] See his *La philosophie bergsonienne*, Part III, " Les deux bergsonismes ".

Church which has placed the first great works of Bergson on the Roman Index. The other is the effort to rediscover the basic truths of Christian philosophy on God and on the soul, and one does find, though somewhat transformed and somewhat sketchy, various Thomistic propositions, as that on the proper formal object of the intelligence in his theory of its connaturality with matter. The solution of the problem of evil, looked at from the divine point of view by Bergson, reveals the fathomless care of God's infinite and loving wisdom.

Accordingly, Bergsonianism can be viewed as placed by Providence as an appeal to modern thought, and as a road toward the direction of truth. But it is only a road for those who are held back and embarrassed by the errors of modern philosophy. For Catholics to engage in his views would be a retardation, for they possess the true wisdom, and, in order fully to discover it, they need only listen to the voice of their leaders who call them to the study of Thomism.

CHAPTER SIX.

NEO-THOMISM.

SPECIAL BIBLIOGRAPHY.

1⁰ **Works :** Some representative works will be mentioned in footnotes.

2⁰ **Studies :** BLANC, E., *Histoire de la philosophie*, III, Ch. XLI, Paris, 1896. — BRUNI, G., *Progressive Scholasticism*, St. Louis (Mo.), 1929. — DE WULF, M., *Scholasticism Old and New*, Dublin, 1907. — GONZALÈS, A., *Histoire de la philosophie*, IV, Paris, 1891. — HART, C. A. (ed.), *Aspects of the New Scholastic Philosophy*, New York, 1932. — LEO XIII, Encyclical, *Æterni Patris*, Aug. 4, 1879. — MARITAIN, J., *The Angelic Doctor*, New York, 1937. — SERTILLANGES, A. D., *Le Christianisme et les philosophes*, t. II, Paris, 1941. — VAN RIET, G., *L'épistémologie thomiste*, Louvain, 1946. — ZYBARA, J. S., *Present-Day Thinkers and the New Scholasticism*, St. Louis (Mo.), 1928.

556. In the 18th century, Scholastic philosophy seemed to be quite dead; its proponents, because of the two factors already mentioned [1], their distaste for metaphysics and their

---

[1] See above, n. 312.

lack of understanding in regard to the advances of modern science, were carried along by the flood of new ideas which, impregnated as they were with liberalism and rationalistic laicism, were coming into conflict with Christian thought. Decadent Scholasticism had clearly lost the fight. Although Suarezism had managed to survive in Spain[1], and though in Italy[2], Roselli, O. P., had edited a *Summa philosophica ad mentem Angelici Doctoris*, towards the end of the 18th century, everywhere else, especially in France, Scholasticism was forgotten. Even in the seminaries the doctrines of Descartes and Malebranche were taught. During the nineteenth century a vague eclecticism was prevalent, Cartesian in principle and inspired by such men as Reid, Cousin, and Hegel, but modified sufficiently to bring it into agreement with revealed doctrine. Not infrequently we find men of ability : Taine, Renan, Jouffroy, Charles Maurras, and others, losing their faith and accepting rationalism in the course of their philosophical studies. Only the theologians, as Gotti (1664-1742), St. Alphonse of Liguori (1696-1787), and Billuart (1685-1757), kept the influence of Thomism alive during the 18th and 19th centuries. And in Protestant countries, in England and Germany, there was lacking even this last bulwark against the encroachments of the modern spirit, which, with its ferment of new ideas as rich in promise of progress as they were in errors, was imposing itself everywhere.

We have already seen how, during the 19th century, a noteworthy movement was in progress among Catholic philosophers, a movement of defense and of assimilation. Men of importance, such as Lamennais, De Bonald, Gerbet, Rosmini, Gunther, and others, tried to renovate Christian philosophy and to adapt it to the problems of their times. But these attempts, too far removed from authentic tradition, were unable to control or subdue modern thought. The systems that were proposed — Christian idealism, tradition-alism, ontologism, and so forth — were but compromises that

---

[1] A total of 22 works written by the Jesuits between 1542 and 1726 on all aspects of philosophy make up what is known as *Philosophy of Coimbre*. Then, too, the *Cursus philosophiæ complutensis*, and the extensive Course of Theology of the *Salmanticenses*, both of which works were produced by Spanish Carmelites in the 17th century, are Thomistic. The works of John of St. Thomas and of Goudin have been mentioned previously. (n. 310).

[2] Two Jesuits in the 17th century deserve mention : Come Alamanni (1559-1634), author of a *Summa philosophiæ* after the manner of St. Thomas, and Silvester Maure, a commentator on Aristotle.

retained a part of the rationalist errors; accordingly, all suffered the condemnations of the Church.

But not content merely with detecting errors, the Church also, through the voice of its Popes, redirected Catholic thought towards the source of true philosophy. Already on several occasions Pius IX had encouraged attempts to return to Scholasticism; and Leo XIII in particular became the real originator of the new movement. He gave Neo-Scholasticism the double characteristic that has been its strength : respect for *tradition* and a spirit of *progress*. This will be discussed in three paragraphs :

    I.   The Beginning : The Encyclical " Æterni Patris ".

    II. The Traditional Element.

    III. The Progressive Element : Cardinal D. Mercier.

I. The beginning : the Encyclical " Æterni Patris " by Leo XIII.

(Aug. 4, 1879).

557. One of the outstanding objectives of the pontificate of Leo XIII (1878-1903) was to guide modern thought, misled into so many errors, back to the light of revealed truth adjusted to present day needs. Therefore, we have a series of doctrinal encyclicals on the problems of the modern world : liberalism [1], Christian society and its relation to the Church [2], the family [3], the condition of the working man [4], Holy Scripture and exegesis [5], and so on. But realizing that the source of the intellectual confusion among the moderns lay in their false philosophy, the Pope began with the bold proposal that Christian philosophy be restored : in the second year of his pontificate, he published the Encyclical *Æterni Patris.* It may be remarked that by this noble act the Holy Father addressed both laity and clergy with the purpose of leading them back to St. Thomas.

   i. **To the Clergy.** Leo XIII speaks first of all in a general way of Scholastic philosophy. He recalls its basic merit for

---

[1] Encycl., *Libertas,* June 20, 1888.

[2] Encycl., *Diuturnum,* June 29, 1881, and *Immortale Dei,* Nov. 1, 1885.

[3] Encycl., *Arcanum divinæ Sapientiæ,* Feb. 10, 1886.

[4] Encycl., *Rerum Novarum,* May 16, 1891.

[5] Encycl., *Providentissimus Deus,* Nov. 18, 1893.

the Christian, its perfect accord with the Catholic faith and, therefore, its ability to explain and to defend the faith in apologetics and in theology. He also shows, from history, that when philosophy respectfully accepted the assistance of faith, it was, far from being weakened, enabled rather to expand to the fullest, so long as it avoided error, without loss to its legitimate independence.

It was rash, therefore, the Pope concluded, to have abandoned Scholastic philosophy; and it is the duty of Christian philosophers, especially those who are preparing for theology, to return to it. Supporting his teaching by action, he demanded of the Catholic universities and of the Institutes which had arisen in France, at Paris, Lille, Toulouse, among others, and of the University of Louvain, that they adopt Scholastic philosophy.

Thus, the first object of the encyclical was to restore Catholic philosophy to its traditional status, and to return to the clergy this rich and solid doctrine which afforded so admirable an instrument for theology.

2. **To the Laity.** But Leo XIII desired also that the light of Scholastic doctrine be extended outside the confines of the clergy and even of the Church, so that its broad influence might be felt not only among the laity but even among the learned and thinking men who are not of the faith. For this reason he insisted upon two fundamental points. First, the *necessity of choosing* among the doctrines that are to be restored : " If there are included in the Scholastic doctrines ", he says, " any overly subtle questions, any unverified affirmations, or anything which is not in agreement with doctrines established in later times or which is, in a word, divested of all probability, we have no intention of proposing these to our age for imitation ". Secondly, the *necessity of properly acknowledging the progress of science* by keeping up to date with whatever of value is accomplished : " We proclaim ", the Pope adds, " that we must accept with good grace and with due acknowledgment every worthwhile contribution to thought and every useful discovery, from whatever source it comes ".

These two objectives are complementary and mutually connected, since it was by their exaggerated attachment to the outmoded parts of their systems that the later Scholastics remained stubbornly opposed to all scientific progress and showed themselves incapable of controlling modern thought or of absorbing whatever good it possessed. It was the task of Leo XIII to propose Neo-Scholasticism, and by destroying the twofold cause of its decay, he restored its vitality and its prestige.

3. **Back to St. Thomas.** Among the Scholastic Doctors, Leo XIII singled out St. Thomas Aquinas, " the prince and master of all ". He pays him magnificent tribute, pointing out that he excells all the other philosophers, and concluded that " reason, borne on the wings of St. Thomas to the pinnacle of human knowledge, can hardly rise higher, and faith can hardly expect more or greater assistance from reason than that offered to it by St. Thomas ". For this reason, observing that most religious orders have already chosen him as their Master — Dominicans, Benedictines, Carmelites, Augustinians, Jesuits — and that the Sovereign Pontiffs have always recommended him in a special manner, he insists that we return to the teaching of pure Thomism in the higher education of youth, with particular concern " for · what the wisdom of St. Thomas drew from its own sources or at least from those from which it was immediately derived ".

The selection of St. Thomas was not, therefore, arbitrary, but was justified historically and doctrinally; the Holy Father saw in him a sure means of avoiding the useless discussions which burdened Scholastic thought; and also, by rallying minds to a unified system, a remedy for one of the evils of the period of decadence : the crumbling of systems due to their sterile polemics. In a word, according to the wish of Leo XIII, the rebirth of Scholasticism should be, in truth, a *Neo-Thomism*.

This movement towards unification is still more accentuated in the successors of Leo XIII. Pius X pointed to Thomism as the sole effective bulwark against modernism. One of his last acts was the approbation of the 24 Thomistic theses, an official summary of the philosophy of the Angelic Doctor. And in his *Motu Proprio* of June 29, 1914, he points out that if any other doctrine " has been recommended by the Roman Pontiffs with particular praise, in such a way that to the praise is added an invitation and a command to spread and defend it, this was only insofar as it was in accord with the principles of St. Thomas, or was not opposed to them in any manner ".

Pope Benedict XV resumed the same attitude when he affirmed that the Church has proclaimed the doctrine of

St. Thomas to be her very own [1]. In the Code of Canon Law, likewise, it is the philosophy and theology of St. Thomas alone that the Church chooses and imposes upon her clergy, both regular and secular [2].

However, we must not exaggerate the import of these directions. From the viewpoint of apologetics, it is undeniable that the Catholic faith, in its strictest orthodoxy, is compatible with other systems than Thomism. The decree which closed the sessions of the famous congregation, *De Auxiliis* (1598-1607), forbade Thomists and Molinists to treat one another as heretics [3]; the decree of the Holy Office, issued by Paul V, declaring that Scotism is free from theological censure, and other similar acts, remain in force to this day. Within Thomism itself there are regions open to further investigation and to difference of opinion. In addition to the 24 theses which are unanimously accepted, there are others, even in philosophy (as that dealing with the constituents of personality) and especially in theology, that are freely controverted [4].

But from an historical point of view, it is evident that the efforts of Leo XIII and his successors towards a restoration of Scholasticism, were primarily directed to a reflourishing of Thomistic philosophy. It should also be noted that this desire, far from limiting the universality of Catholic doctrine, simply paid homage to the universal spirit of him whom the Middle Ages spoke of as the " Common Doctor ". As has been previously observed [5], the viewpoint of Thomistic philosophy is the same as that of common sense; that is, the most objective and the most impersonal, so that it is eminently suitable for adaptation to all mentalities and can assimilate to itself any elements of truth which modern thought might contain.

To unite Catholic thinkers for the conquest of modern thought, such seems to be the objective of the Church in reviving Thomism, and history has already shown us the beginning of its realization.

---

[1] Encycl., *Fausto appetente*, June 29, 1921.

[2] *Codex Juris Canonici*, cc. 589, 1366.

[3] Decision of Pope Paul V, April 28, 1607, confirmed by a decree of Benedict XIV, July 13, 1748.

[4] See D'ALÈS, *Thomism* (in the *Dict. Apol.* col. 1667-1712); the papal decisions leave to reason its legitimate liberty : see col. 1672, the response of Benedict XV to P. Ledochowski, leaving the followers of Suarez at liberty on the question of the distinction between essence and existence; see also the comments by MARITAIN in his *The Angelic Doctor*, pp. 118-122. — [5] See above, n. 258.

II. The traditional element.

A) The Forerunners.

558. By its praise and encouragement, the Encyclical *Æterni Patris* acknowledged the value of several partial attempts to revive Thomism. Among these forerunners, two names deserve special mention :

1° James Balmès [1] (1810-1848) is the principal Spanish philosopher of the 19th century. His works, in particular the *Filosofia fundamental* (4 volumes), and *El criterio*, prolonged his influence, quite decidedly, as a result of their determined opposition to modern errors. He is not a Thomist in the strict sense of the word, it is true, for he rejects several of the essential theses, as the real distinction between essence and existence, the psychology of the impressed species, and so on. But though his eclectic system shows the influence of Suarez, and even of Descartes and several of the moderns, he still gives first place to Saint Thomas, whose excellence he extolls above all others.

Balmès also took up the task of adapting Christian philosophy to the needs of the time; he effectively opposed Kantianism and German pantheism. Recognizing the importance of the critical problem, he examined thoroughly the various criteria of truth which had been proposed up to his day, then developed a vigorous refutation of idealism. Nevertheless, his work is only an elementary and imperfect attempt at criteriology. He is still overly dogmatic, as were most of the early Scholastics; according to him, we must accept, as the starting point of all certitude, three fundamental principles that support the three great orders of truth that we possess : truths of the *subjective* order based upon the fact of *consciousness;* truths of the *objective* order, such as necessary scientific judgments, based on *evidence* and on the principle of *contradiction;* and, finally, the truths of *common sense*, those which one needs no time to examine in order to see their evidence and which, independent of consciousness, are universally necessary, based as they are on *intellectual instinct*, a natural and irresistible inclination to accept them as true. The principal truth of this kind is the affirmation of the objective validity of our ideas. It is evident that Balmès, little accustomed to the subtle viewpoint of the new critique, did not have a comprehensive grasp of the new science, such as Kant had inaugurated.

Balmès had some successors in Spain, the most important of whom was Cardinal Gonzalès (1831-1892), whose large history of philosophy (4 volumes) expounds and criticizes every system from the viewpoint of pure Thomism. Also, there were followers in Italy, where Tongiorgi and Palmieri, in their *Institutiones*

---

[1] See D. Mercier, *Critériologie générale*, Louvain, 1911, p. 91. See also Blanche-Raffin, *Balmès*, Paris, 1849.

Philosophiae, restated the theory of the three fundamental truths.

2º Also in Italy we find the second important forerunner : SANSEVERINO († 1870), who clearly demonstrates his Thomism in his principal work, *Philosophia christiana cum antiqua et nova comparata* (7 volumes), completed, with the encouragement of Pius IX, by his nephew Signoriello. The work is somewhat deficient in arrangement and sometimes over emphasizes secondary questions, but it achieves its main purpose : to show that the doctrine of Saint Augustine and of Saint Thomas resolves all the problems and refutes all the errors of the modern age.

Mention must also be made of the work of LIBERATORE (1810-1892), who in the same Thomistic vein wrote, besides an *Institutiones Philosophicae,* several works in Italian : their content can be indicated by their English titles, as *On Intellectual Knowledge* (1857), *On the Human Composite, The Composition of Bodies* (1878), and *Principles of Political Economy* (1894).

B) Early Supporters.

559. Again, it was in Italy that the instructions of Leo XIII were first carried out. The chairs of the Roman Universities, closest to his influence, were most prompt in following his directions.

Cardinal ZIGLIARA (1833-1893), whose two principal works are a *Summa Philosophica* (3 volumes) and *De lumine intellectuali* (a critical examination of ontologism and its sources), knew how to emphasize the essential points of Thomism without insisting upon the secondary opinions. He maintained its metaphysical purity against its many corruptions, especially through his refutation of ontologism. Leo XIII named him Cardinal and President of the Academy of Saint Thomas, which Leo XIII founded to promote Neo-Thomism.

With Zigliara, one should mention also Father CORNOLDI, S. J., founder of a similar, Thomistic academy at Bologna; the Jesuit professors of the Roman College, Fathers Schiffini, Urraburu, Mazella, and so forth, and the Dominican professors of the Angelicum after Zigliara, as Fathers Lepidi, Gatti, and others.

From Rome and Italy, the movement soon spread into the entire Catholic world. In Spain, as we have seen, it developed under the influence of Cardinal Gonzalès. In Germany, J. KLEUTGEN, S. J. (1811-1883), in his work *Die Philosophie der Vorzeit,* expounded the principal theses of Thomism, insisting particularly upon the theory of truth and error for the principal purpose of refuting the errors of certain German philosophers, namely Gunther and Hermès. To the same end, A. STOECKL wrote his *Geschichte der Philosophie des Mittelalters;* an active group of Jesuit professors edited the *Philosophia lacensis,* a comprehensive course, and also the manual, *Cursus Philosophiae* by FRICK. Finally, the encyclopedic dictionary of theology by Father Ehrle deserves mention. Not all these writters were as faithful to Thomism as Kleutgen; it may be said that their general tendency is towards Suarez.

In Holland, on the other hand, we find a rebirth of pure Thomism, with Father DE GROOT († 1922), and even more so in Belgium and France, where the revival was more complete and more vigorous and adopted the progressive outlook about which more will be said later. Among the early contributors we find VALLET, who wrote a manual of Thomistic philosophy as early as 1879, and especially his successor, Msgr. FARGES, who in a series of *Etudes philosophiques* attempted to popularize Thomistic doctrines. Each of the nine volumes develops clearly and extensively one essential point, later explained in logical and summary fashion in his *Cours de philosophie*. This last work was adopted as a textbook by a number of seminaries.

The list of French Dominicans (many of whom were professors at the Angelicum in Rome) is no less remarkable. Besides Father Lacordaire (1802-1863), the Dominicans of Notre-Dame de Paris — Father Monsabré († 1906) and Father Janvier (and before him Msgr. d'Hulst, 1841-1896) — brought Thomistic doctrines to the attention of the public. Father COCONNIER († 1918) founded the *Revue Thomiste;* Father PÈGUES wrote an extensive literal commentary on the *Summa Theologica* in French; Father HUGON wrote a *Cursus philosophicus completus* and explained in a number of popular works the principal philosophical and theological questions of Thomism; Father GARRIGOU-LAGRANGE, in his monumental work on " God ", delves into the metaphysical foundations of religion; and Father GARDEIL, in *Revelation and Theology*, determines in the spirit of Saint Thomas, the relations between philosophy and faith.

E. BLANC must be mentioned for his course in philosophy and his *History of Philosophy* (3 volumes); also C. PIAT († 1918), a Thomist with a shade of eclecticism towards modern philosophy; Father DE RÉGNON, S. J., a Thomist with Suarezian leanings, GARDAIR (1846-1911), who opened a free course at the Sorbonne for the exposition of St. Thomas and later edited his lectures; DOMET DE VORGES (1829-1910), Father PEILLAUBE, Msgr. SAUVÉ (1817-1896), Msgr. CHOLLET, and others, all of whom, on particular points, sought to revive Scholastic and Thomistic doctrine. Finally, Cardinal BILLOT, S. J., for many years a professor at the Gregorianum, deserves special consideration, even though his work is primarily theological, because of his tendency away from Suarez towards a more complete agreement with St. Thomas, especially in philosophical questions, and also because of the clarity and comprehensiveness of his exposition.

C) Traditional Characteristic.

560. All these varied and valuable efforts have in common a twofold characteristic : respect for tradition, and opposition to modern errors — for it was most expedient first to regain contact with the firm doctrines whose restoration was desired. This task was undertaken principally by Italian and French writers, who generally were content, in the bulk of their works, to expound Thomistic doctrine without attempting to develop it. Their purpose was to make known the eternal and unchanging truths that Thomism contains, that is, its strictly philosophical and especially its metaphysical parts; and, furthermore, to throw into relief its opportuneness, its depth, and its breadth.

Often, it is true, the reformers were not content with this *calm exposition* of Thomistic doctrine. They compared it with modern thought, but only to bring out its *opposition* and to defend it against error. This polemical trait is also an outstanding characteristic of philosophy in Spain, where one of the Neo-Scholastic magazines was entitled *Defense of Society*. The German philosophers were similarly engaged, in fact, ever alerted to oppose the errors they found about them; but their learning was rather restricted, for they were little acquainted with modern thought outside that of German philosophy. Criticisms and refutations by other Scholastics show a broader understanding, but all of them were characterized by an attitude of defense and opposition. In short, the Neo-Thomists looked upon modern thought primarily as a source of errors to be refuted, and their attitude is still one of defiance.

In a word, the first phase consists in a *traditional element*, with the objective of reforging the broken chain of Scholastic philosophy. It is characterized by respect for tradition both in content and in form. As a matter of fact, a good number of works, especially refutations, were written in the vernacular; but just as many retained Latin as the most appropriate means of expressing Thomistic thought, for it also remained, with good reason, the official language of Catholic seminaries of the Latin rite and of the Roman universities, where Neo-Thomism first flourished.

This respect for tradition is, of course, necessary for anyone who wishes to be a disciple of St. Thomas. It presents, however, a danger of falling back into the errors of the decadent Scholastics, who became sterile and without influence upon their own times, because in restricting themselves to their traditional point of view, they condemned themselves to total ignorance of all progress and of new problems. Leo XIII had explicitly urged that this pitfall be avoided, and it is due to his approbation that we find a second group of Neo-Thomists resolutely engaged in a new orientation — that of progress.

III. The progressive element : Cardinal D. Mercier.

(1851-1926).

561. In this phase, we no longer find merely a revival of the ancient Thomistic doctrines, but a vigorous effort to assimilate everything good that modern thought has been able to discover. This effort implies, as a result, a more benevolent attitude towards the moderns, still severe where definite error is concerned, but with greater emphasis on the elements of truth contained in every important system, and thus without fear of acknowledging that even Thomism may profit therefrom.

The leader of this aggressive phase of Neo-Thomism was Cardinal Mercier [1] (1851-1926), Archbishop of Malines after 1906. In 1880, when Leo XIII requested of Cardinal Dechamps, then Archbishop of Malines, that he found a chair of Thomism at the University of Louvain, the Archbishop selected Father Mercier, who, since 1877, had taught Thomistic philosophy at the Minor Seminary of Malines. In 1880, he began his assignment as titulary of the Chair of Philosophy, which, in the University's syllabus, is called an " Advanced Course in the Philosophy of St. Thomas ". During his vacation in 1881 the new professor went to Rome to learn personally the directives of Leo XIII. In order to become better able to reconcile modern science with philosophy, he followed for some time, at Paris, a course in physiology offered by the celebrated Charcot.

From the very start, Father Mercier's teaching was characterized by a threefold innovation, which marks him as the true initiator of the progressive phase of Neo-Thomism. It is concerned with the sciences, with modern philosophy, and with the methodology of teaching.

A) Thomism and Science.

562. It is in the domain of the positive sciences that modern thought has made the greatest progress and the most

---

[1] **Works :** *Manual of Modern Scholastic Philosophy* (tr. Parker, T. L., and S. A.), 2 vols., St. Louis (Mo.). 1950. — *Origins of Contemporary Psychology* (tr. W. H. Mitchell), New York, 1918. — **Studies :** DUBLY, H. L., *Life of Cardinal Mercier* (tr. H. Wilson), Cork (Ireland), n. d. — GADE, J. A., *Life of Cardinal Mercier*, New York, 1934. — GOYAU, G., *Cardinal Mercier*, New York, 1926. — KELLOG, C., *Mercier, The Fighting Cardinal of Belgium*, New York, 1920. — LA VEILLE, A. P., *Life of Cardinal Mercier*, New York, 1928.

amazing discoveries; and one of the greatest defects of decadent Scholasticism was that it ignored the special sciences. Msgr. Mercier, on the other hand, looked upon them as the auxiliaries of philosophy. " Philosophy ", he states, " is by definition the knowledge of all things through their ultimate causes; but is it not evident that before we arrive at the ultimate causes, we must pass through the more proximate causes examined by the particular sciences? " Not that he would make the validity of philosophy dependent on the status of the sciences : " The advances of philosophy ", he also states, " are not always in direct proportion to the sum total of the material that experience has accumulated " [1], and he recognizes that Thomistic metaphysics is founded upon our most common experiences, which are independent of learned research and thereby retain an enduring validity.

But there is in philosophy an entire department which is immediately concerned with the facts observed by the particular sciences : that is, " Natural Philosophy ", which studies the nature of corporeal beings, minerals, animate substances and especially man; or, in other words, the science which has been called, since Descartes and Kant, Cosmology and Psychology. Following the great Scholastics of the thirteenth century, and the example of St. Thomas and St. Albert the Great, Msgr. Mercier assumed the difficult task of reviving these two areas of Thomism, by taking into account the progress made in physics, in chemistry, in biology, in psychology, and in the other experimental sciences : a project of great dimensions, of which he above all was the initiator. Later, he directed one of his students to explore the mineral world : D. Nys († 1929) has given us the results of these researches in his *Cosmology* and his two studies on " Time " and " Space ".

Msgr. Mercier himself specialized in psychology. He showed that while Cartesianism was utterly incapable of explaining the facts, the psychology and anthropology of Aristotle and St. Thomas, in which the soul is the substantial form of the body, proves to be, on the other hand, in marvelous harmony with every observation of science and furnishes the basis for a truly " *scientific philosophy* ". Thus he was inspired to bring about the establishment at the University of Louvain of a laboratory for psycho-physiology and psycho-physics, at which certain conscious acts were studied according to the

---

[1] *The Origins of Contemporary Psychology*, 2nd ed., p. 336.

methods of modern science with the resulting observation that if the operations of the sense order are, from one point of view, of a quality superior to that of chemical phenomena, they still remain dependent upon matter and quantity. According to St. Thomas, " sensatio est actus conjuncti ", and not, according to the assumption of Descartes, a simple and spiritual act. And so it is possible to study scientifically quantitative conditions; and even if such studies are not philosophy, they still afford it a valuable assistance.

B) Criteriology.

563. Even if it were possible for a follower of St. Thomas to adopt a favorable attitude towards all the scientific endeavors of the moderns, the same could not be said for their work in philosophy, infested as it is with serious errors : idealism, positivism, agnosticism, and pantheism. However, from all their efforts there does arise, quite definitely, one new philosophical idea which is both legitimate and fruitful : the necessity of raising and solving, in a strict and scientific way, *the critical problem* of the value of our knowledge in general or of the basis for scientific knowledge (epistemology).

In the Middle Ages, this science was unknown; the quarrel over universals had remained a logical and psychological question. The naturally realistic attitude of the human mind in relation to things known was admitted by all, and thus no one thought of establishing it scientifically. But in the face of the denials of modern idealism, and the critical requirements evoked by the work of Descartes and Kant, Thomistic doctrine had no chance of being accepted unless it underwent a critical proof. A good number of Neo-Scholastics, however, were quite opposed to such efforts, content with Balmès to appeal to common sense and our natural trust in reason. Others, like Zigliara, while they insisted on establishing the criteria of truth, treated this point as if it were merely a question of logic.

Here again Msgr. Mercier was resolutely determined to improve the situation. Thomism contained only the principles of the solution. These he organized in a special scientific treatise. And though he corrected the Cartesian doubt, he did not hesitate to state the critical problem in all its universality, and just as radically as did Descartes. With Kant, he instituted a reflexive examination of true judgments, but brought out better than Kant the passive as well as the active nature of the judicial synthesis and pointed to the moderate realism of St. Thomas as the true solution to the problem. *Criteriology* is the most original work by Cardinal Mercier and the one wherein he contributed most to the progress of Thomism.

C) Use of the Vernacular.

564. Finally, in one other way, admittedly secondary, but sensational nevertheless, Msgr. Mercier was an innovator. He abandoned Latin, the traditional language of Scholasticism, and expounded Thomism in the vernacular, in French. Certainly, he never denied the advantages of an international language; he preferred that Latin remain the language of the seminaries, and as Archbishop he maintained it for his diocese. Nevertheless, at the University of Louvain, where the elite of Belgian Catholicism were gathered, most of whom were laics (not to mention the many foreigners), Thomism was to transcend the narrow circle of ecclesiastics and to become the basis not only for the training of priests, but also of magistrates, politicians, historians, directors of social work, in a word, of the leaders in every department of life. The first means of attaining that objective was to bring it within reach of all by using the vernacular. In this way, Msgr. Mercier succeeded in gathering about his chair a rather large number of faithful disciples.

Before long, to spread his ideas and to defend his positions, he founded the *Revue Néoscolastique* and edited his principal works : *La psychologie,* in which he stresses experimental psychology; *Les origines de la psychologie contemporaine,* in which he singles out Descartes as the leader of modern philosophy, his influence in psychology being felt even to the present time. He also wrote *La Logique, L'Ontologie,* and finally *La Critériologie générale,* which was to have been completed by a *Critériologie spéciale ;* but episcopal duties permitted him only to revise and reedit the other works.

Cardinal Mercier never lost interest in philosophy; it was the inspiration of his retreats and his pastoral letters. At the request of Pius X he wrote a small work on *Modernism;* during and after the war of 1914, he endeavored to solve, in the light of St. Thomas, the grave social problems that arose. We may say that his last philosophical work was the active part which he played in the redaction of the " Christian Social Code ", drawn up by sociologists of the International Union of Social Studies, an association founded in 1921 under his presidency.

The pupils trained in his school rapidly became his co-laborers; first of all, D. NYS, the author of *Cosmology;* Msgr. DEPLOIGE, who wrote *The Conflict Between Ethics and Sociology,* a refutation of Durkheim by way of St. Thomas; Maurice DE WULF, who revived interest in the history of medieval philosophy; Msgr. SENTROUL, author of *Kant and Aristotle* and professor at Sao Paulo (Brazil), and others. From 1888 to 1894, in accord with the wishes of Leo XIII, steps were taken in an effort to transform the Chair of Philosophy into a Superior Institute; in 1889 the goal was realized with the naming of Msgr. Mercier as President of the Institute. Then, in 1892, he also established a Seminary for ecclesiastical students, called the Seminary of Leo XIII. That great pope, in a brief dated March 7, 1894, recognized the two new institutions (the Superior Institute and the Seminary) and granted them legal status.

D) **Struggle and Victory.**

565. But though the work of Msgr. Mercier was not without achievement, neither was it free from contention; his courageous position was subject to a great deal of prejudice, to say nothing of opposition. He wanted a " philosophy friendly to science " and modern philosophers objected that Scholasticism was essentially opposed to modern science [1]. On the other hand, a good number of Catholics were alarmed at his concessions to modern thought. They feared that by embracing experimental psychology, Thomism would be infected with positivism; or, that in constructing its criteriology it would compromise with Kantianism; or, finally, certain strict partisans of tradition pretended that the vernacular could not express Thomistic thought exactly, and in their eyes the epithets " Neo-Scholastic " and " Neo-Thomist ", the boast of the school of Louvain, had a pejorative connotation. Their criticism was so persistent that they finally succeeded in impressing even Rome [2]. The faculty of granting degrees in Scholastic philosophy, given to the Superior Institute of Louvain, was withdrawn for a time, and, in 1896, Msgr. Mercier was summoned to Rome to defend himself. But he refused to abandon his work, and continued courageously without changing its character, which he knew was in accord with the desires of Leo XIII. Pope Leo very soon indicated his complete agreement, and history must recognize that the philosophy of Cardinal Mercier, even in its innovations, is faithful to all the principles of Thomism.

---

[1] *Ibid.*, p. 335 ff.

[2] Objections of a doctrinal nature were raised by a number of Catholics who were so established in the old school of Cartesian spiritualism or else were so conservative that they had an instinctive fear for anything new; but their views were not taken into consideration by the authorities. M. Van Steenberghen remarks, " Critics are making their appearance at Louvain and at Rome, against arrangements for a program of studies containing a dosage of new material, against the use of French in teaching, against, even, a legally established Institute in the midst of the University ". (*Revue Néoscolastique*, Feb., 1938, p. 170).

This powerful impulse towards progress is still bearing fruit in our own day, and demonstrates the vitality of Neo-Thomism. The historical studies begun by M. de Wulf have found successors; they have drawn attention to the great Scholastic systems and have destroyed the unjust misconceptions about the philosophy of the Middle Ages.

At the same time, Scholastic doctrine not only reigns supreme once more in the teaching of the Church, but already it is demanding the attention of all thoughtful men. With the passage of time, the new Scholasticism tends more and more to identify itself with Thomism. However, there are shades of difference among the Thomists. They can be grouped into three schools :

a) *The historical school*, which investigates the system in itself, as a notable event in history. Among these are many non-Catholics, as G. TRUC, who wrote *Le retour à la Scolastique* (1919) and *La pensée de St. Thomas* (1924). This is also the attitude of the group of historians already mentioned, who apply the methods of modern criticism to the study of Thomistic thought, and generally to all medieval philosophy. The most notable are, after M. DE WULF[1], Ehrle, Grabmann (director of the vast collection of historical research in philosophy and theology of the Middle Ages, organized at Munster in 1891, by Baeumker), Baumgartner, Pelster, Endrès, Geyer, Koch, in Germany; — Mandonnet (founder of the *Bibliothèque thomiste*), Gilson (director of Studies in Medieval Philosophy), Thèry, in France; — C. Webb, Little, Carlyle, in England; — Miquel Asin y Palacios et Xiberta, in Spain; — Haskins, Lacombe, Paetow, in America; — Pelzer, Lottin, and de Ghellink, in Belgium; — Birkenmajer and Michalski, in Poland; — Longpré, and the groups at Quaracchi, Masnovo and the school of Milan, in Italy.

b) *The critical school* tends to bring out the weak points of Thomism, and to look upon some of the twenty-four theses as only probable opinions. Such are the contributors to the *Archives de philosophie*, P. DESCOQS, the author of *Institutiones metaphysicæ generalis* (1925), and *Prælectiones theologicæ* (1932). In his *Essai critique sur l'hylémorphisme*, he questions the thesis on the unity of form; and that of the real distinction between essence and existence in *Thomisme et Scolastique*[2] (1927). Others worthy of mention are P. ROUSSELOT, A. D'ALÈS, director of the *Dictionnaire Apologétique*, Y. DE LA BRIÈRE, ROMEYER, R. DE SINÈTY, G. PICARD and J. DE LA VAISSIÈRE.

c) *The progressive school* holds that, fully to appreciate Thomism, we must render due tribute to its inherent strength and fecundity by emphasizing its adaptability to new problems. This school

---

[1] *History of Medieval Philosophy*, I, p. 12. The work of Haureau, of Denifle and of Baeumker at the end of the 19th century, also deserves mention. The principal works by these men will be found listed above in the various bibliographies for medieval philosophy.

[2] His work is a reply to ROUGIER's *La scolastique et le thomisme* (1925), which subsumes Scholasticism under Thomism in order to attack its basic principles from the idealistic viewpoint.

proposes to enrich Thomism from its environment and to renovate it " by effecting an assimilation of all the nutritive substance that the ages have since elaborated ". So speaks Father Sertillanges at the conclusion of his *St. Thomas*, in which he makes a notable contribution to this work, as well as in his other books : *Les sources de la croyance en Dieu*, the contents of which are restated in *Dieu ou Rien* (2 volumes); also *Les grandes thèses de la Philosophie Thomiste, St. Thomas, Art et Apologétique*.

The promising labors of J. MARITAIN [1] must also be mentioned : *Bergsonian Philosophy, Theonas, Anti-Moderne, Art and Scholasticism, Reflections on Intelligence and Life, Three Reformers, Primacy of the Spiritual, The Angelic Doctor, Course of Philosophy;* and extensive work in criteriology; *The Degrees of Knowledge, A Preface to Metaphysics, The Philosophy of Nature,* and several studies on the " Disputed Questions " of St. Thomas. *(Religion and Culture, Christian Philosophy, Temporal Rule and Liberty)*.

Having embraced Catholicism after adhering to Bergsonianism, Maritain had a thorough understanding of the evils of the modernistic spirit, rooted in idealism and scientism, and he never tired of showing how pure Thomism is its providential remedy. He took up the idea of a Thomistic criteriology and indicated its clear distinction from formal, and even from material logic. He considered it as the first division of metaphysics, since it pertains to wisdom or philosophy to justify and defend its own principles and those of the other sciences, by taking up the general problem of truth. He is particularly fond of delineating the true value of modern sciences, and showing their accord with Thomism. He clearly fixes their place : as sciences they are " subalterns of the second degree of abstraction " and they are " materially physical and formally mathematical ". He has wisely suggested that these sciences be reserved for the study of non-living beings, in which their absolute determinism permits these quantitative relations to be realized rigorously, whereas in the study of living beings, in which the mathematical ideal is not realized, it is more proper to subordinate the natural sciences once again to the principles and viewpoints of philosophical physics.

The twofold problem of a Thomistic critique of knowledge, and of the assimilation of the modern sciences, is becoming more and more the field of action of the progressive school. In this group are numbered the disciples of Cardinal Mercier, Kremer († 1934), Noel, and others, Y. Simon, and J. de Tonquédec. Of special importance is Maréchal, whose five-volume work, *Le Point de départ de la métaphysique*, leads to an attempt at Thomistic criteriology according to the method of Kant [1]. Then, too, we should mention the Dominican followers of Sertillanges, P. Gillet (who wrote on education), Wébert, Allo, Barbado *(Introduction to Experimental Psychology)*, and so forth.

---

[1] See C. A. FECHER, *The Philosophy of Jacques Maritain*, Westminster (Md.), 1953.

[2] See above, n. 389.

Italian Neo-Scholasticism of the *School of Milan* [1] also comprises a very active group. Its labors date from 1909, with the founding of the *Rivista di filosofia neoscolastica* by Father A. GEMELLI, the acting rector of the Catholic University of the Sacred Heart in Milan, where he devoted himself to establishing a faculty of philosophy [2].

Two factors encouraged this group of philosophers to devote themselves to the renewal of Thomism : first, the example of Cardinal Mercier, whom they loved to regard as their leader. That is why they openly supported the program of the *progressive school*, making their aim to rethink the " eternal philosophy " of St. Thomas in order to answer the problems of the day. Secondly, they wanted to counteract the modern errors that were withdrawing souls from the faith.

At first it was especially *scientific positivism* that was emphasized in teaching, and, to counteract this, Father Gemelli distinguished himself by his studies in *experimental psychology* [3], which he undertook in the university laboratory of biology and psychology, with the aid of A. GALLI, G. PASTORI, A. GATTI, A. ZAMA, among others.

But soon, in reaction to the prevalent Hegelian idealism under B. Croce and G. Gentile, the Italian Neo-Scholastics opened a further investigation of the problem of knowledge [4]. G. MATTIUSSI [5] still held to absolute dogmatism founded on common sense; but others, like G. CANELLA and Msgr. TREDICI, adopted the criteriology of Cardinal Mercier and used it to oppose idealism. Some even undertook a more profound investigation of the problem and criticized Cardinal Mercier on some points : thus F. OLGIATI [6], E. CHIOCHETTI [7], and G. ZAMBONI [8]. The latter, in his pure gnoseology draws a sharp distinction between the phenomenal and ontological real, and bases the validity of the idea of being on the experience of the self. A. MASNOVO [9], who, abandoning

---

[1] See *Indirizzi e conquista della filosofia neoscolastica italiana*, Milan, 1934, a publication by a group of professors from the University of the Sacred Heart at Milan, retracing the activity of the review and of the Neo-Scholastics over a period of 25 years.

[2] *Ibid.*, p. 19.

[3] Of these works we mention the following : *Il mio contributo alla filosofia neoscolastica*, and, from the numerous articles in the fourth series of *Contributi del laboratoria di biologia e psicologia* (to which his collaborators also contributed), his research on perception, manual skills, character, and so on.

[4] See *Indirizzi e conquiste...*, pp. 43-161.

[5] He helped to compile the catalogue of the 24 Thomistic theses, on which he wrote a commentary.

[6] Works include : *L'anima di S. Tomaso ; — L'anima dell' Umanesimo e del Rinascimento ; — Il significato storico di Leibniz ; — L'idealismo di G. Berkeley ; — Cartesio*, and others.

[7] Works include : *La filosofia di B. Croce*, 1920; — *La filosofia di G. Gentile*, 1925, etc.

[8] Works include : *La gnoseologia del atto ; — Introduzione al corso di gnoseologia pura*, etc.

[9] Works include : *Problemi di metafisica e di criteriologia*, Milan, 1930, wherein he has collected his critiques of Cardinal Mercier; and *Il neotomismo in Italia ; — Da G. d'Auvergne a S. Tomaso d'Aquino*, 2 volumes, and so on.

the viewpoint of Cardinal Mercier that one must first establish the validity of judgments in the ideal world before one can justify statements of the real order, takes, on the contrary, as his point of departure these very judgments about the real order[1] in order to avoid an illegitimate passage from the logical order to the real.

One of the particular characteristics of Italian Neo-Thomism is the impetus it gave to the study of the history of philosophy. Since Hegelian idealism sought to prove its theories on the development of the mind by pointing to their realization in history, to refute them effectively it was necessary to show that the facts contradicted their hypothesis.

But the labors that have sprung from the undertakings of Cardinal Mercier are immense, and have enlisted the persevering cooperation of a large number of workers. Just as the preparations of the 11th and 12th centuries were necessary to enable St. Thomas to construct his synthesis, so also the labors of the Neo-Thomists of today are but the remote but necessary preparation of the new synthesis in which modern science and philosophy will be completely harmonized.

Finally, we must refer to the dawning of a rebirth of *Augustinian Philosophy*. Alongside the Thomistic literature there is also a growing *Augustinian literature*, under the direction of P. Fulbert CAYRÉ, A. A., author of *Augustinian Contemplation* and *The Sources of Divine Love* according to St. Augustine, and so on.

The celebration of the centenary of this great Doctor (1930) has occasioned a number of studies, a task to which even E. Gilson, R. Jolivet, Boyer, C. Combès, and others, made notable contributions.

It does not seem impossible to construct a truly Augustinian philosophy " which will not be identified with Thomistic philosophy, and yet not at variance with it "[2], and its existence will be a new proof of the fertile vitality of Christian thinkers, and another indication of the legitimate liberty which the Church permits her children in the domain of reason.

---

[1] Masnovo calls the position of Cardinal Mercier, " idealist subordinationism ", and his own, " realist subordinationism "; to resolve both problems at the same time, one would have a kind of " criteriological parallelism ", which he also rejected. See *Indirizzi e conquiste...*, p. 94.

[2] F. CAYRÉ, *Revue de Philosophie*, Aug., 1936, p. 308; the author points out in this article that " the point of departure of Augustinian philosophy was the noological proof for the existence of God ". See above, n. 177.

GENERAL CONCLUSION.

566. At first glance, the history of philosophy leaves a rather deceptive impression. In spite of the undeniable grandeur of the giants in the realm of thought who demand recognition by all, no system of reasoned doctrine has ever been able to endure without eclipse. If we consider particular questions, even, for example, those as important as the question of God, His existence and His nature, or of the human soul, its immortality and its destiny, even there we find the same fluctuations. This aura of confusion is particularly evident in the face of the many theories of the modern era. One is tempted to conclude with Descartes that, in philosophy, "there is not one thing which is undisputed and, therefore, beyond doubt " [1]. The contradictions of philosophers constitute one of the most formidable arguments in favor of scepticism.

This view, however, is quite superficial. By striving to penetrate to the meaning of the various systems and to draw out the elements of truth which are always in some degree present, we have truly found throughout, " that heritage of truths which all men deserving of the name ' wise ' possess in common ", as was described in the Introduction to this book.

By realizing that this common heritage remains the same in spite of external differences, we preserve it more securely, and the mind is even improved and expanded by striving to encompass all these various points of view, all legitimate, but differing from its own.

But this heritage has not been perpetuated with the same fidelity by all philosophers, nor has it been utilized by all with the same fecundity. We see it developing little by little into two systems which are actually complementary, though often in conflict. The one, springing from Plato, is predominantly idealistic; the other, coming from Aristotle, is predominantly scientific. Each system, in its own way, experiences the misfortune of decadence : materialism envelops the commentators on Aristotle, and the lofty spiritualism of Plato fades off into pantheism.

It seems that the reason of man is incapable of preserving the treasure of truth over any length of time. In fact, Platonism

---

[1] *Discourse de la méthode*, Part I (Durand edit., p. 28); see above, n. 318.

as well as Aristotelianism has attained its most glorious fulfillment in the light of the Catholic faith; the first, in
St. Augustine, the second, in St. Thomas Aquinas.

It is in these great doctrines, primarily, that we find the
greatest number of teachings in conformity with common
sense and, therefore, most expressive of the *perennial philosophy*.

On the other hand, turning to modern times, it is difficult
to discern a continuity in the currents of philosophical thought.
We are offered such systems as the phenomenalism of Hume
and the pantheist idealism of Hegel, in which the particle
of truth is so small, that we might turn as a last resort to the
depths of scepticism. In spite of all, even in these radical
positions, we find some legitimate principles, be it only the
affirmation that our mind is able to know its own existence,
and, following on this, the affirmation of the principle of identity
with its unlimited applicability. In the opposite extreme,
the absolute materialism of a Hobbes or of a La Mettrie contains
a proper recognition of the value of our sense experience.
And in our own day, after the excesses of critical idealism,
as in an earlier day after the excesses of sophistry, reason
is resuming its flight towards reality and towards the affirmations of that enduring common sense which is so abundantly
utilized in Scholasticism.

Thus, the movement of human thought down through the
ages seems to be marked with a profound network of unity,
in the center of which stands Christian philosophy and Thomism.
This very fact supplies valuable instruction. The great lesson
that it gives is a lesson of humility for purely natural reason,
an impelling demand to acknowledge its own impotence, and
a vivid demonstration of the apologetic thesis invoked at the
beginning of this book : the moral necessity of revelation
in order that the truths, even those in the natural order, which
are necessary for a moral life, may be known " by all, easily,
with firm certitude, and without admixture of error ".

It is remarkable that the errors of the modern age should
reiterate those of the pagan era, and for a similar reason,
in spite of preventative opposition. Paganism, as we have
noted [1], because it was not yet favored with the light of
revelation, never arrived at a firm and precise conception
of a personal God, a Creator, a Legislator and Rewarder, who

---

[1] See above, Conclusion to pagan philosophy, n. 141.

is at the peak of natural wisdom. This explains its hesitancy with regard to the nature of man, whose spiritual and immortal soul must be immediately created by God, and with regard to the value of morality, the imperative character of which has no other foundation but the divine law. On the other hand, modern thought, having rejected the light of revelation with a proud misunderstanding, has often displayed a similar impotence.

Among the ancients, however, there is a genuine development from the *Nous* of Anaxagoras to the " One " of Plotinus; the latter can be viewed as a synthesis and clarification of the perfections of Plato's Demiurge contemplating the Ideal world, of Aristotle's pure Act, transcendent and independent, and of the Stoic *Logos*, omniscient and providential. Among the moderns, on the other hand, there is a constant decline, from the God of Descartes, whose doctrine, as to essentials, remains faithful in the area of the Catholic faith, to the numerous forms of pantheism — conceptualist with Spinoza, idealist with Hegel, materialist with Comte, immanentist with Loisy, evolutionist with Bergson [1] — and to the varieties of agnosticism — critical with Kant, scientific with Spencer and positivism, and anti-intellectual with the modernists. Similar consequences are to be found in morality : the human soul as a spiritual substance, free and immortal, is as often mis-interpreted as is God. Various preconceptions become the principles of morality, as in the egoism of Hobbes, the notion of interest in Hume and Stuart Mill. The categorical imper-ative of Kant remains in a vacuum, and modern sociologists, following Durkheim, seek to establish a moral science, which, to them, is still non-existent.

The source of this lamentable return to paganism is easily found : the modern mind was dumbfounded by the sudden advances made by the natural sciences in the seventeeth century due to mathematical interpretation of experience. It attributed to these new sciences, which it truly considers as " Science ", a monopoly on truth, and hoped to find in them, in complete independence, the answer to all the problems which reason must face. Reason was from then on supreme, and it eventually abandoned the assistance of faith. Thus, modern philosophy was born from a desire to replace the old Scholastic method by a twofold method, one of the clear and intuitive idea,

---

[1] According to one possible interpretation of his anti-intellectualism.

prevalent in mathematics, the other that of experience, which dominates the area of physics. But by making a *tabula rasa* of everything in the past, modern philosophers were forced to posit, in all its implications, the critical problem : " How do we know truth? " Then, deprived of the metaphysical and psychological insights accumulated in centuries gone by, particularly by the profound analysis of St. Thomas, they found themselves unable fully to resolve the great question which they had brought up. The scientific method failed to rebuild the structure of philosophy. Either it sacrificed experience by using the clear idea as its point of departure, as in *idealism*, or else, what is still less desirable, *positivism* sacrificed speculative knowledge, leaving only a reason enslaved to sense experience. But since it is impossible to philosophize without intellectual ideas, these men found themselves back in fundamental postulates and scientific hypotheses, with the result that all positivist constructions fell back into the grips of idealism and crumbled under its criticism. As a last resort, *pragmatism* sacrificed both the clear idea and experience, transferring truth to sentiment, and resigning itself to absolute agnosticism. By presuming on its own capacities, reason has ended by doubting itself and sinking into *scepticism* [1].

It is Neo-Thomism, as we know it today, which will restore to reason its life and its productivity, just as it was the revelation of the Evangelists which regenerated the declining philosophy of the pagans. In spite of its grievous errors, modern philosophy is pregnant with new and valuable doctrinal riches; critical science, legitimate in itself, though better employed on other questions; and, especially, the particular sciences of reason in their full development. Now, Thomism possesses in its metaphysical principles a foundation all ready to support these new sciences, by way of explaining and maintaining their validity, better even than do their inventors. It also possesses in its psychology and its ontology, theories sufficiently precise fully to solve the problem of truth in conformity with common sense and, at the same time, in conformity with all the demands of the new critical science.

Thus, the controlling universality of its fundamental principle allows Thomism to reconcile what other systems oppose. In it, the divorce between " Philosophy " and " Science ",

---

[1] " It is knowledge destroying itself ", writes Brehier to characterize philosophy at the turn of the century; *Histoire de la philosophie*, II, p. 1024.

so often proclaimed by the moderns, is resolved in a harmony wherein each science finds its determined place. All evident conclusions, in chemistry, physics, or history as much as in psychology, metaphysics, or morality, constitute the unchangeable and definitively acquired sciences, which are completed by an assemblage of probable opinions, still subject to development. In this way, the rule of evidence justifies all sciences of the natural order, as also it justifies, by way of the motives of credibility, the doctrinal riches provided by supernatural faith. Thomism thus supplies to our minds a magnificent unification in which theology, a higher wisdom which synthesizes faith and reason, governs and directs all the other sciences, respecting, nevertheless, the independence relative to their frames of reference. Through Thomism, reason, properly subordinated to faith, will find again the needed confidence in its own power to encompass, under the light of divine assistance, the entirety of natural truth within philosophy.

INDEX OF PROPER NAMES[1].

---

[1] This is not a list of authors cited, but of the *philosophers* studied or mentioned in the book. Names printed in bold face indicate the most important philosophers, whose doctrines are treated in more detail. Numbers given refer to *pages*.

DOCTRINAL TABLE [1].

I. — INTRODUCTION TO PHILOSOPHY.

1. **PHILOSOPHY. A) Definition and Extension.** Pythagorean origin of the name, 12. — Real definition, 1. Conception of an autonomous universal science, 40, 66 (Plato); 68, 95 (Aristotle); 261-266 (St. Thomas); subordinate to faith, see *Relation to faith and religion*, n. 3. — Conception limited — *a*) to the nature of the physical world, 5 (first philosophers); — *b*) to sensible phenomena, 459-461 (A. Comte), 480 (H. Spencer), see *Positivism*, n. 12; — *c*) to invisible reality, 537 (Bergson); — *d*) to the problem of morality, 28 (Socrates) 96, 98 (Stoics), 106 (Epicurus); — *e*) to the problem of knowledge, 114 (Scepticism).

B) **History of Philosophy.** Notion, 1; — method, 2; — usefulness, 2· — Aristotle, the first historian of philosophy, 69; — Thomistic doctrine on the history of philosophy, 257; doctrine of Hegel, 428; of A. Comte, 457. — Relation to eclecticism, 442.

2. **Relation between Philosophy and the Sciences.** Philosophy encompasses the sciences, 21 (Atomists), 77, 78, 80 and 82 (Aristotle), 234 (St. Albert the Great), 265 (St. Thomas); — it is subservient to the sciences, 31 (Descartes), 404 (Kant), 479 (Spencer), 530, B) (Brunschvicg, p. 880), 530, C) (Poincaré); — It is totally distinct from the sciences, 164 (St. Augustine), 538 (Bergson); — mutual assistance and harmony, 556 (Leo XIII), 562 (Card. Mercier), see 82 and 265 (Thomistic doctrine).

3. **Relation of Philosophy to Faith and Religion.** *a*) Philosophy dominates religion and faith, 93, 4° (Aristotle), 110 (Epicurus), 121 (Gnostics), 191 (Averroes), 249 (Siger of Brabant), 368bis, D), 4° (Hobbes), 369, B) (English Deists), 370 (encyclopedists), 416 (Kant), 428 (Hegel), 457, 458 (A. Comte), 535 (Modernists); — *b*) it exercises or demands a *rather hostile independence*, 121 (Philo), 185 (Avicenna), 203 (J. Scotus Eriugena), 213 (Abelard), 311 (Renaissance), 313 (characteristics of modern philosophy), 336 (Descartes), 346 (Malebranche), 347 (Spinoza), 435 (Lamennais), 442 (Cousin), 531, B) (Nietzsche); — *c*) it *collaborates amicably*, 178 (characteristics of Scholasticism); — with explicit distinction, 234 (St. Albert the Great), 244 (St. Thomas), 557 (Neo-Thomists); — without clear distinction, 146, 177 (St. Augustine), 216 (St. Anselm), 250 (Augustinians), 280 (St. Bonaventure), 531 (Blondel); — *d*) it is *to some extent dependent*, upon religion, 51 (Platonic myth), 120 (mystic philosophy), 531, C) (Eucken, Newman); upon Christian faith, 273 (Raymond Lull), 284, 291, 298 (Duns Scotus), 303 (Ockham), 306 (Suarez); — *e*) it is a *totally subordinate servant*, 187 (Algazel), 227 (intransigent theologians); — *f*) *Moral necessity of Revelation*, 2, 141, 436, 2°, 566.

GREAT SCHOOLS OF PHILOSOPHY.

4. **Platonism.** The founder, Plato, 39; fundamental principle, 40 (the ideal world); good and bad points, 66; — Neo-Platonists, who continued the system : 123 (Plotinus), 197 (Dionysius the Areopagite), 200 (J. Scotus Eriugena), 337, a) (Platonic school of Cambridge), 378bis (Berkeley). — *Influence* on Scholasticism, 209 (school of Chartres); on the Renaissance, 311, 1. — Augustinian Platonism, see *Augustinianism*, n. 6. — Decadent followers of the system, 113 (Academician probabilists).

5. **Peripateticism.** The founder, Aristotle, 68; fundamental theories, 69-70 (act and potency; analogy); value of the system, 95; — disciples, writers of commentaries, 118; — the Arabs, who distorted the system, 181, 190 (Averroes), 248 (Latin Averroists), 311, 2 (Averroists of the Renaissance); — Scholastic Peripateticism, 192, 2; see 232 (translations of Aristotle); — Catholic opposition to Peripateticism, 227 (theologians, twelfth century), 232 (condemnation by the popes, thirteenth century), 250 (Augustinians); — opposition of Moderns, 312; of Bergson, 538, 553. — Catholic assimilation, see *Thomism*, n. 7; *Scotism*, n. 8.

6. **Augustinianism.** The founder, St. Augustine, 144; fundamental theory, 146, 161 (explanation of everything in terms of God); true philosophy, 177; — followers, 216-221 (St. Anselm), 275-281 (St. Bonaventure), 565 (Neo-Augustinianism). — Partial influence, 255 (upon St. Thomas); — questionable or erroneous interpretation, 250-251 (Augustinians), 341 (Malebranche : vision in God), 437 (Ontologists).

7. **Thomism.** The precursor, St. Albert the Great, 233-234 (Christian Aristotelianism); the founder, St. Thomas, 239, ff.; fundamental principle, 258-260 (analogous being); characteristics of Thomism, 256 (analytic and synthetic), 261-265 (universal), 270 (philosophy of common sense); — followers, 282, II (first disciples), 304 (Thomists of the fourteenth and fifteenth century), 310 (sixteenth and seventeenth century), 556 (eighteenth century), 557, ff. (Neo-Thomism); — modified Thomism, 305-309 (Suarez). — Opposition to Thomism : 250 (Augustinians), 251 (condemnation of 1277), 282 (correctorium), 284, ff. (Duns Scotus), 312 (moderns).

8. **Scotism.** The founder, Duns Scotus, 283; fundamental theory, 285 (voluntarism) and 286 (formalism); value of the system, 287, 298; — followers, 316 (sixteenth century); — influence on Ockhamism, 301, 303; on Suarez, 306, 309.

9. **Christian Philosophy.** Theoretical notion, 244; it is less a school than a group of schools, 3; see 142 (characteristics of the patristic and medieval period); — its principal representatives, see *Relation of philosophy to faith and religion*, n. 3, c); amicable collaboration, 298 (Duns Scotus). — Opposed to modern philosophy, 313; Descartes, 336, Malebranche, 346, Pascal, 338.

10. **Cartesianism.** The founder, Descartes, 317; fundamental principe, 319 (cogito, ergo sum) and 320 (the clear idea); value of the system, 321 criticism of its method), 336 (rational). — *Influence* : a) moderated by faith, 337, (Bossuet, Fénelon), 338 (Pascal, 339 (Malebranche), 556 (Catholic school of the nineteenth century); — b) by its

rationalist principle, 347, 355 (Spinoza), 358 (Leibniz); — c) by its critical method, see n. 14, a); — d) by its psychology, 483 (general survey), 374 (Locke), 443 (Cousin), 558 (Balmès); — e) by its mechanism, 368bis (Hobbes), 369, A) (Newton), 370 (philosophy of the eighteenth century), 480 (Spencer); see *Evolutionism*, n. 42, a) and b).

11. **Kantianism.** The founder, Kant, 388, ff.; general characteristics, 396; value of the system, for science, 404, for metaphysics, 419, in general, 420; — followers, 530, B) (neo-criticism, Renouvier, school of Marbourg, commentators). *Influence*, — a) with progress in idealism, 422 (idealistic pantheism), and particularly, 425 (Fichte); 530, B) (Brunschvicg); — through Hegelianism, 427 (Hegel), 482-III, 1 (Karl Marx), 530, A) (Hegelian idealism of the nineteenth century); — b) with progress in agnosticism, 471 (positivism in general), 480-II, 2 (Spencer), 522 (pragmatism in general), 524 (William James), 532 (Modernists); — c) with a reaction toward realism, 438-439 (Rosmini and other Catholics), 530, D) (phenomenology), 537 (Bergson).

12. **Positivism.** Definition, 356, 2; 444. Precursors, 21 (early Atomists), 95 (Aristotle), 101-102 (Stoics); modern origins, 315-316 (Francis Bacon), 333 (Cartesian mechanism), 370, 379 (philosophers of the eighteenth century), 368, 369, 374, 382 (English empiricism), 404 (Kant). — The founder, Auguste Comte, 456, ff.; fundamental principles, 471-472; value of the system, 473; followers, 470. *Influence*, — a) in the sciences, 476 (Darwin), see *Evolutionism*, n. 42, a), b), d); — b) in psychology, see *Empiricism*, n. 52; — c) in sociology, 488 (St. Mill), 503 (Taine), 513-514 (Durkheim), 521 (Le Play), 551, A) (Bergson). Realist positivism, 530, C) (Ravaisson). — d) *Anti-positivist reaction* in the nineteenth and twentieth centuries, 529 (general survey), 530 (idealism), 531, A) (Value philosophy), 531, B) (Nietzsche), 531, C) (Religious philosophy), 536 (Bergson).

II. — EPISTEMOLOGY [1].

A) GENERAL SOLUTION.

13. **Nature of the Critical Problem.** a) *In itself*, 562 (D. Mercier), 321 (explained along with correction of Descartes). — b) *In fact :* the problem arose from contradictions among philosophers, 23 (ancient Sophists), 113 (Sceptics), 318 (Descartes); or from the objections of sceptics, 144, 4 (St. Augustine), 388 (Kant), 432 (traditionalists). — c) Truth and error, see *Truth and falsity*, n. 75 c). — d) The *threefold data* of the problem : 1) incontestable value of conscious acts, 114 (Sceptics); 2) existence of an indubitable certitude, 149 (St. Augustine), 319 (Descartes), 391 (Kant); 3) faculty of reflection, 395 (Kant).

14. **The Critical Methods.** a) *Method of psychological analysis :* universal doubt and the clear idea, 318-322 (Descartes), 321, 323 (value); direct and explicit use, 373, 375 (Locke), 380, 383-384 (Hume); indirect use to develop a coherent system, 358, ff. (Leibniz), 347, ff.

---

[1] Investigation of the value of knowledge and science.

(Spinoza); with restriction, 339, ff. (Malebranche). — *b) Method of critical or transcendental reflection :* explained, 394 (Kant); explicit use, 398, ff. (Kant), 563 (D. Mercier), 565 (Maritain); — limited use : refutation of Sceptics by reduction to absurdity, 10 (Aristotle), 148 (St. Augustine). — Phenomenological method, 530 D). — *c) Implicit method of metaphysical exposition,* 41-42 (Plato), 69-70 (Aristotle), 259, 1 (St. Thomas).

15. **Criteria of Truth.** *a) Extrinsic criteria :* authority, 12 (Pythagoras); faith, 337 (Huet), 338 (Pascal); fideistic tendency, 203 (J. Scotus Eriugena), 217 (St. Anselm); tradition, 433-434 (De Bonald), general reason, 435 (Lamennais). — *b) Subjective intrinsic criteria :* common sense, 386 (Scottish school); sentiment, 386, p. 650 (Jacobi); blind instinct, 443 (Jouffroy); conformity to action and to life), 522, 524 (pragmatists), 531 (Blondel), 532 (modernists), primacy of consciousness, 531, C) (Newman). — *c) Mixed criteria :* sensible clarity and moral conformity, 108 (Epicurus); subjective clarity and divine truth, 320 (Descartes). — *d) Criteria of Objective Evidence :* implicitly, 397 (Kant), 530, D) (phenomenologists); explicitly, 563, 565 (Neo-Thomists); see 321, 3; — its necessity, 436. — *e) Secondary Criteria :* universal consent, 404, III (Kant), 436, 3 (traditionalists).

16. **Scepticism.** *a)* Definition of universal philosophical scepticism, 114; arguments, 24 (ancient Sophists) and especially 115; — refutations, 116; see 148 (St. Augustine). — Principal representatives, 24 (Sophists), 113 (Phyrrho, etc.), 311, 3 (Renaissance), 188 (Algazel). Partial scepticism in *Positivism,* see n. 12; and *Idealism,* see n. 17; and 356 (general account). — *b) Relativity of Knowledge,* 484, A), 2 (Hamilton), 480-II, 2 (Spencer). — *c)* Sceptical tendencies; 297, 298 (Duns Scotus), 303 (Ockham).

17. **Idealism.** Definition, 356, 1. Cartesian origin, 332, 333, 1. — Various forms of idealism : *a) Provisory Idealism,* at the beginning of a critique, 332 (Descartes), 362 (Leibniz); — *b) Definitive Idealism,* in regard to secondary qualities, 333 (Descartes), 375, 3° (Locke); in regard to all corporeal substance, 377 (Berkeley); in regard to any substance whatever, 384bis (Hume), 421 (total idealism or pantheism, Fichte, etc.), 530 (contemporary idealism); — *c)* transcendental idealism, 404 (Kant), transcendental phenomenological idealism, 530, D) (Husserl), teleological idealism, 505 bis I, (Lotze). — *d)* Platonic idealism, see *Exaggerated realism,* n. 19. — *e) Phenomenalism,* definition, 356; (see p. 553); principal representatives, 384bis (Hume), 486 (St. Mill), 493 (Taine), 507, 3 (Wundt), 509 (Th. Ribot); criticism of the system by Bergson, 545-546.

18. **Realism in General.** Natural position of common sense, 46, *a* 206, B); 316, A) (Bacon). — Realist systems : not explicitly critical, see *Platonism,* n. 4, *Peripateticism,* n. 5, *Augustinianism,* n. 6, *Thomism,* n. 7, *Scotism,* n. 8; *Positivism,* n. 12; — critical realism : *a)* based on divine truth, 320, *d,* 331 (Descartes), 378 (Berkeley's spiritual realism); — *b)* based on faith, 342 (Malebranche); — *c)* on pre-established harmony, 363 (Leibniz); — *d)* on pantheism, 347, ff. (Spinoza), 498 (Taine); — on the clear idea, 320, 321, 3 (Descartes), 375 (Locke); — *e)* on intuition, 537, ff. (Bergson); — *f)* on critical demonstration, 563, 565 (Neo-Thomists) ; see also 409.— Forms of realism : naive realism, 108 (Epicurus); transfigured realism, 480 II, 2 (Spencer); phenomenological realism, 530, D) (Heidegger); see nn. 19 and 20.

B) THE PROBLEM OF UNIVERSALS.

19. **Exaggerated Realism.** Definition, 46, *a*. First theoretical solution of the problem of universals, 206, 1. — *Absolute forms :* Plato's world of Ideas, 41-43; first solution by William of Champeaux, 208. — *Modified forms*, the School of Chartres, 209; the formalism of Scotus, 286; tendency to exaggerated realism in St. Anselm, 220, in Bergson, 537, 2.

20. **Moderate Realism.** Fourth theoretical solution of the problem of universals, 206, 4; expounded, 69 (Aristotle), 214 (12th century), 235 (St. Albert the Great), 259 (St. Thomas); includes whatever truth is contained in Plato's exaggerated realism, 46, *a;* or in the formalism of Scotus, 287; or in Kantian conceptualism, 403, 409; or in nominalism, 374, (see p. 604), 382, 496; — *Imperfect form*, 213, 1 (Abelard); *equivalent form*, the psychological realism of St. Augustine, 149, 151, 1°, 166, *b*, 4.

21. **Conceptualism.** Third theoretical solution of the problem of universals, 206, 3; pure conceptualism mixed with *idealism*, see n. 17; — Kantian conceptualism, 403, positivist conceptualism, 508, 2 (Wundt); — conceptualism with realist tendencies, 213 (Abelard).

22. **Nominalism.** Second theoretical solution of the problem of universals, 206, 2. — *Forms of nominalism :* — *a*) logical, 212 (Roscelin), 302 (the terminism of Ockham); — *b*) materialistic, 101 (Stoics), 368 bis, B) (Hobbes); — *c*) positivistic, 375, 3° (Locke), 379 (Condillac), 382 (Hume), 486 (St. Mill), 495-496 (Taine, theory of the sign), 508, 2 (Wundt).

III. — LOGIC.

23. **Logic in General.** *a*) Definition, 71 (Aristotle); principal works : the Organon of Aristotle, 67, 71-73; translated into Latin, by Boethius, 198, by William of Moerbeke, 232; commentary by Porphyry, 122 (Introduction or Isagoge), by St. Albert the Great, 233, by St. Thomas, 242, etc. *Novum Organum* by F. Bacon, 315; — nominalist logic, of the Stoics, 101, of Hobbes, 368bis, B); idealist logic, 427 (Hegel); — logic of truth, 386, 3° (St. Mill). — Study of logic popular in the Middle Ages, 199, 2; in the Ockhamist school, 303. — *b*) *Logistic :* the great art of Raymond Lull, 273; Leibniz's object of study, 357. — *c*) *Sophistry :* origin, 23; classification of sophisms, 73, 3 (Aristotle); — utilized by the Sceptics, see n. 16; — tendency to sophistry, see Abuse of the Syllogism, n. 26, *d*), — social logic, 518, C) (Durkheim).

24. **Logical Categories.** *a*) Definition and classification by Aristotle, 72, 1°. Origin of the categories, see *Abstraction*, n. 51, *a*); and *Moderate Realism*, n. 20; — sociological origin, 515; — nominalist interpretation, see n. 22. — *b*) Definition and classification according to Kant, 401, 402; legitimate use, 404 (for science); illegitimate, 406 (in regard to *numina*) and 408. — *c*) Classification of *Ideas*, according to Plato, 48 (realism); according to Kant, 407 (idealism); in Cartesianism, representative acts of consciousness, 328 (Descartes), 374 (Locke), 377 (Berkeley), 381 (Hume).

25. **Judgment.** Definition and classification according to Aristotle, 72, 2. — Stoical interpretation, 101, *b* (an attempt at agreement); —

positivist interpretation, 368bis, B) (Hobbes), 486, 4º (St. Mill), 497 (Taine). — Kant's classification, 392; function of *a priori* synthetic judgment, 401, 3; judgment with respect to finality, 417; — classification according to quantity of the predicate, 484, A), 3º (Hamilton). — Judgment the sole depository of logical truth, according to St. Thomas, 321, 3, *b*, and according to Kant, 392.

26. **The Syllogism.** *a*) Definition and theory, 72, *b* (Aristotle). — *b*) *Kinds :* demonstrative syllogism, 73, 1 (Aristotle), 264 (St. Thomas); — dialectical syllogism, 73, 2 (Aristotle), see n. 29; — classification according to Kant, 407. — *c*) *Legitimate use*, 234 (St. Albert the Great), 256, *b* (St. Thomas). — *d*) *Abuse of the syllogism*, 209, 3 (Adam du Petit Pont), 212 (Roscelin), 213 (Abelard), 299, 2, 303 (decadent Scholastics); — objections against the syllogism and dialectic, 227 (intransigent theologians), 272 (R. Bacon), 315bis, B) (F. Bacon), 338, *a* (Pascal), 408 (Kant's critique), 487 (St. Mill). — *e*) *Deduction :* identical to the syllogism, 73 (Aristotle); series of intuitions, 322 (Descartes), applied to induction, 487, 5º (St. Mill), 497 (Taine), applied to calculus, 368bis, B) (Hobbes).

27. **Induction.** Origin with Socrates, 29, B). — Definition and forms according to Aristotle, 72, and St. Thomas, 263; method of St. Albert the Great, 234, of R. Bacon, 276. — Development of rules of induction, 315, (Francis Bacon), 487 (St. Mill), 497 (Taine). — Induction according to Descartes, 322, 4; according to Kant, 477; according to Spencer, 480-II, 2; according to Wundt, 508, 2.

28. **Science.** *a*) Definition in the strict sense, 73, 1 (Aristotle), 264 (St. Thomas); — distinction between philosophical and theological science according to formal objects, 234 (St. Albert the Great), 244 (St. Thomas); according to their complementary functions, 280 (St. Bonaventure); see n. 2. — *b*) Cartesian science, 323. — *c*) *Science in the modern sense :* the forerunner, 273, 3 (R. Bacon); the founder, 315bis, A) (F. Bacon); true notion, 82; see 562, 565 (Neo-Thomists); — Kantian interpretation, 404; — positivist interpretation, 368bis, B) (Hobbes), 461 (A. Comte), 498 (Taine), see n. 12; — pragmatist interpretation, 524 (W. James), 538, 3 (Bergson); — particular sciences according to the ancients, 77, 78, 81, 82 (Aristotle); see n. 2. — *d*) Classification of the sciences : according to F. Bacon, 315bis, C); according to A. Comte, 461-462; according to Aristotle, 73; (see p. 102); according to the idealists, 428 (Hegel). — *e*) *Scientism :* 311, 3 (Renaissance), 420; see *Positivism*, n. 12; influence on Bergson, 555. — *f*) *Critique of the sciences*, 530, C) (Boutroux, Poincaré), 531, B), 1 (Nietzsche), 538, A), 2 (Bergson).

29. **Dialectic.** *a*) According to Plato, 40, 44 (science in the strict sense); — *b*) according to Aristotle and the Scholastics, 73, 2, 265 (domain of opinion and of probable systems); dialectical syllogisms and Aristotle's *Topics*, 73. — *c*) Dialectic in the general sense meaning logic, 199, 1, 227, 1. — *d*) Transcendental dialectics of Kant, 406.

30. **Methodology.** The various philosophical methods : *a*) Socratic method, 26-30. — *b*) Platonic method, 44, 45 (Plato), 123 (Plotinus), 139 (degrees of purification) ; 144, 6, 159, 4 and 166, 5 (Augustinian method). — *c*) Peripatetic method : the application of logic, see n. 23; deductive method, n. 26; — inductive method, n. 27. — *d*) Cartesian method, 322; see n. 14 : *Critical methods. — e*) Method of immanence, 534; — intuitive

method, see n. 55, *Intuition.* — *f*) Historical and sociological method, 463 (rules of A. Comte), 514 (rules of Durkheim); the method of moral science, see n. 104, *Systems of Morality.* — *g*) Eclectic method, explained, 306 (Suarez), 442 (Cousin); pagan eclecticism, 117 (Cicero), 118 (commentators).

IV. — NATURAL PHILOSOPHY.

A) THE STUDY OF MINERALS : COSMOLOGY.

31. **The Problem of Motion.** *a*) How the problem arises for philosophers, 5 and 69. — *b*) *Solutions :* everything is real motion, 8-9 (Heraclitus), 368bis, A) (Hobbes), 537, ff. (Bergson); — everything is ideal motion, 427 (Hegel); — there is no motion, 14 (Parmenides), 16 (arguments of Zeno of Elea); — mobile being is a shadow of the immutable, 51 (Plato), 123 (Plotinus); — it is a simple mode, 350 (Spinoza); — moderate solution : motion and rest are real, 74 (Aristotle); motion defined in terms of actuality and potentiality, 74. — *c*) *Laws* of motion, see *Evolutionism*, n. 42. — *d*) *Palingenesis* or the periodic return of evolution, 99, 4 (Stoics), 249, *c* (Averroists), 480, (Spencer), 531, B), 2 (Nietzsche).

32. **Cause and Transmission of Motion.** *a*) *Matter,* condition and source of all motion, 52 (Plato), 133 (Plotinus), 170 (St. Augustine), 209 (School of Chartres); — condition of change in spiritual beings, see n. 33, *d*) *Universal hylomorphism.* — *b*) *Efficient cause* of motion : its necessity, 75 (Aristotle); God, source of all motion, as first Mover, 55, 20 (Plato), 92 (Aristotle), 248, (Averroists), 369, A) (Newton); as Creator of motion, 333, 3 (Descartes); — God alone, see *Occasionalism*, n. 98, *f*); — the soul, with respect to the body, see *Union of Soul and Body*, n. 70. — *c*) *Mechanism :* definition, 333, 2; — principal adherents, 18 (Atomists), 333 (Descartes), 339 (Malebranche), 368bis, A) (Hobbes), 369, A) (Newton), 370 (philosophers of the 18th century), 479 (Spencer).

33. **The Nature of Bodies.** *a*) Atomism. Explanation of pure philosophical atomism, 19; first adherents, 18 (School of Abdera); continuators, 109 (Epicureans), 337 (Gassendi). — Value of the system and relation to scientific atomism, 21. — *b*) Dynamism. Theory of Leibniz, 359 (dynamistic atomism); theory of Fouillée, 511 (idea-forces); theory of Bergson, 541-543 *(Elan vital).* — Psychological dynamism, 509 (Ribot). — *c*) Hylomorphism. Various meanings : prime matter, pure potentiality, 77 (Aristotle), 235 (St. Albert the Great, 268 (St. Thomas); — prime matter, incomplete act, 232bis (Neo-Platonic eclectics), 276, 1 (St. Bonaventure), 289 (Scotus), 308, *b* (Suarez), 273, 1 (Rog. Bacon : plurality of prime matters); — Platonic interpretation, 52 (Plato), 133 and 134, 2 (Plotinus : objections against hylomorphism), 170 (St. Augustine); — denial of matter, 377 (Berkeley). — *d*) Universal hylomorphism. Theory of spiritual matter, 161, 170, 4 (St. Augustine, hesitantly), 192 (Avicebron), 232bis (Neo-Platonic eclectics), 250 (Augustinians), 276, 2 (St. Bonaventure), 288 (Scotus). — *e*) denial of the reality of bodies and of matter, see *Phenomenalism*, n. 17, *e*).

34. **Materialism.** Definition, 356, 2; doctrine of decadence, 97, 1 and 370. (see p. 591). Ancient adherents, 99-100 (Stoics), 107, 109,

112 (Epicureans), 144, 3 (Manicheism); — in the Middle Ages, 210, 2 (David of Dinant); — among the moderns, see *Positivism*, n. 12 and especially 368[bis], A) (Hobbes), 478 (Buchner, etc.), 482 (Spencer), 482-III, 1 (Karl Marx); — combatted by Berkeley, 376-378, and by spiritualism, see n. 73.

35. **Origin of the World.** *a) Eternity of the world*, defended explicitly as necessary, 79 (Aristotle), 190 (Averroes), 248 (Averroists); — admitted implicitly, 5 (first philosophers) and by the *pantheists*, see n. 96; admitted with respect to space and time, 369, A) (Newton); — admitted as merely possible, 158 (St. Augustine), 194 (Maimonides), 267 (St. Thomas); — combatted by the Augustinians, 250, (see p. 373), by St. Bonaventure, 275-III. — *b)* Creation of the world, see *God the Creator*, n. 98. — *c) Order of the world*, 11 (Pythagoras, the first to speak of a κόσμος), 54 (Plato); see *Demiurge*, n. 100.

36. **Quantity.** *a)* Constitutes the *essence of bodies*, as number, 11 (Pythagoras); as extension, 333 (Descartes), 343, *b* (Malebranche). *b) A proper accident of bodies*, 78 (Aristotle), 170, 4⁰ (St. Augustine), 268 (St. Thomas), 308, B) (Suarez). — *c)* Extension, an attribute of God, 341 (Malebranche), 349 (Spinoza). — *d)* Quantity of sensations, 505, A) (Herbart), 506, 2 (Fechner), 508, 1 (Wundt), 526, A), 2 (W. James). — *e)* Quantity, the object of *modern science*, see n. 28, *c)*.

37. **Corporeal Qualities.** Quality, one of the ten categories, 78 (Aristotle); its importance, 21, 80; — distinction between primary and secondary qualities, 333 (Descartes), 374, 1⁰ (Locke); 377 (Berkeley); — denial of quality, see *Mechanism*, n. 32, *c)*.

38. **Position and Space.** Identical with matter, 52 (Plato), 133 (Plotinus); — distinct properties of quantity, 78 (Aristotle), 308 (Suarez, but in a different sense); — absolute space of Newton, 369, A); — space an a priori form of sensibility, 398, 2 (Kant).

39. **Time.** One of the ten categories, 78 (Aristotle); — a property of matter, 133 (Plotinus); 170 (St. Augustine); — an a priori form of sensibility, 398, 2 (Kant). — Real time, identical to the self, 546, *b* (Bergson). — The creation of time, 158, 2 (St. Augustine); eternity of time, see *Eternity of the world*, n. 35, *a)*.

40. **The Individual.** *a) Principle of individuation*: numerical multiplicity due to matter, 52 (Plato), 133 (Plotinus), 209 (School of Chartres); — due to matter quantified, 268 (St. Thomas); — due to matter informed, 276, 2 (St. Bonaventure); true even of spiritual beings); — due to *haecceitas*, 290 (Duns Scotus); — absence of matter brings about a specific distinction for every angel, 268 (St. Thomas); also, there is a specific distinction between atoms or monads, 361 (Leibniz). — Individual excluded by monism or *pantheism*, see n. 96. — *b) Pluralism*. Definition, see p. 560, note; — fundamental postulate of Leibniz, 361, 1; defended by pragmatism, 524; pluralist tendency, 530, A), (English idealists, 19th century), pluralist interpretation of Bergson, 544, 549, 554. — *c) Knowledge of the individual*. The proper object of the senses, 213 (Abelard), 262, *a*, 265 (St. Thomas); — not the object of science, 30 (Socrates), see *Abstraction*, n. 51, *a*); but only of probable knowledge, 51 (Plato), 265 (St. Thomas); — the proper object of the sciences according to *nominalism*, see n. 22; — is known directly by the intellect, 293 (Scotus), 309 (Suarez); indirectly, according to St. Thomas, 403.

B) THE STUDY OF LIVING BEINGS.

41. Life in General. a) Principle of life : the vegetative soul, 80 (Aristotle); nature or ψύσις, 100 (Stoics). — b) *Panpsychism* or *panvitalism:* theory of universal life, 6 (hylozoism of the first philosophers); — explained in terms of a World-Soul, 22 (Anaxagoras), 37, b (Socrates), 55, 2° (Plato), 100 (Stoics), 131, ff. (Plotinus); 153 (St. Augustine denies the theory); — in terms of dynamism, 362 (Leibniz); — in terms of pantheism, 493 (Taine), see n. 96; — in terms of the subconscious, 506, 1 (Fechner), see *The Unconscious*, n. 43, c). — c) Life the only reality, 541, ff. (Bergson). Mechanist interpretation of life, 333, 2 (Descartes), 480-I (Spencer). — d) Unconscious vital activities, 80 (Aristotle); see *The Unconscious*, n. 43, c).

42. Evolutionism. Definition of evolution, 480. — a) Universal form, 9, b (Heraclitus), 427 (Hegel), 480, ff. (H. Spencer), 542 (Bergson and *Elan vital*), see *Evolutionist pantheism*, n. 96, b). — b) *Transformism* or modified evolutionism, 476-477 (Darwin), 482 (Huxley, etc.). — c) *Seminal reasons* or Augustinian transformism, 171 (explanation and evaluation); — origin of the theory, 99, A) (the Stoic Logos), 131 (the World-Soul of Plotinus); — influence on the Middle Ages, 232bis (Neo-Platonic eclectics); 250 (Augustinians); 272 (R. Bacon), 276, 3 (St. Bonaventure). d) The evolution of man, 370 (see p. 590 : Condorcet), see *Dynamic sociology*, n. 119, c), d).

C) CONSCIOUS VITAL ACTIVITY : EXPERIMENTAL PSYCHOLOGY.

43. Consciousness. a) A property : in God, 93, 2°, c (Aristotle), 125, a (Plotinus), 423-424 (idealistic pantheists), see *A Personal God*, n. 97; in man, 149, 3, 152 (St. Augustine), 262, b (St. Thomas), 279 (St. Bonaventure), 324, ff. (Descartes), 505bis, 1 (Lotze); see *The Object of experimental psychology*, n. 44, b). — b) *Epiphenomenal* consciousness, 430 (Schopenhauer), 495 (Taine), 511 (Fouillée); criticism by W. James, 526, A), 1; by Bergson, 545-546. — c) *The Unconscious :* its presence in God, 126 (Plotinus), 209 (Scotus Eriugena); universal source of being, 431 (Hartmann), 423, ff. (idealistic pantheism); — in us, 430 (Schopenhauer), 441 (Maine de Biran), 505 (Herbart), 506, 1 (Fechner), 508 (Wundt); — the subconscious, 362 (Leibniz, indistinct perceptions), 511 (Fouillée), 527 (W. James), 534 (modernists).

44. Experimental Psychology. a) General view of the field, 483. — b) *Object* : the conscious act, or thought, 324 (Descartes), 328 (classification according to Descartes), 374 (Locke, *ideas* and classification), 377 (Berkeley), 381 (Hume, *perceptions* and their classification), 480-II, 1 (Spencer), 486 (St. Mill), 494, 499 (Taine), 505 (Herbart, representations), 508 (Wundt), 509 (Th. Ribot), 526 (W. James), 546 (Bergson, immediate data of consciousness). — c) *Method*, combined psychological and critical, 320, 324 (Descartes), 373 (Locke), 377 (Berkeley), 381 (Hume), 386 (common sense method, Scottish School), restored by eclecticism, 443; — purely psychological and positive : combined objective and subjective, 509 (Th. Ribot), see p. 922, note 2, same method used by W James,

511-I, c (contemporary psychologists); — method of introspection, 373 (Locke), 441 (Maine de Biran), 486, 1° (St. Mill), 511-I, a (school of Wurzbourg, provoked introspection), 539 (Bergson); — purely objective method, 506, 2 (Fechner), 489, 1 (Bain), 510 (Binet), 511-I, b (Watson, Bechterew). — d) *Laws :* mechanistic, see *Mechanist School,* n. 44bis, a); — mathematical, 505 (Herbart), 506, 2 (Fechner), 508, 1 (Wundt); — dynamistic, see *Dynamist school,* n. 44bis, b). — e) *Psychology as positive science :* first contributions, 81 (Aristotle); principal modern representatives, see b) *Object* of experimental psychology and 486 (St. Mill), 489 (English psychologists), 509 (Ribot), 511-I (contemporary psychologists), 562 (Mercier), 565 (Gemelli, etc.); objections and rejection by A. Comte, 460. — f) *Special psychological sciences :* Psychophysics, 506, 2 (Fechner), see p. 1008 (Gemelli); — Psycho-physiology, 508, 1 (Wundt), 511-I, c (Dumas); — Folk-Psychology, 508, 4 (Wundt), 511-I (see p. 901, Lebon, etc.), 512 (Tarde). — Psychological laboratories, 483 (their prevalence in Europe).

44bis. **Important Schools and Theories.** a) *Mechanist school,* 368bis, C) (Hobbes), 480-II, 1 (Spencer), 505, A) (Herbart), see *Association of images,* n. 49, b) and c); — b) *Dynamist school,* 362 (Leibniz), 430 (Schopenhauer), 441 (Maine de Biran), 485-I (St. Mill), 507, 3 (Wundt), 509 (Ribot), 511 (Fouillée), 526 (W. James), 545 (Bergson). — c) *School of integral psychology,* 509 (Ribot), 511-I, c (the movement itself). — d) *Behaviorism* or psychology of *behavior,* 511-I, b (Watson and Bechterew, objective psychology). — e) *Associationism :* 483, a ; — proponents, see *Imagination,* n. 49, b) and c). — f) *Epiphenomenalism :* definition, 494; — proponents, 486, 2 (St. Mill, hesitantly), 489, 4 (Lewes), 494, A) (Taine), 507, 3 (Wundt), 509, 1 (Ribot); combatted by Bergson, 545. — g) *Psychophysical Parallelism :* definition, 506, 2; proponents, 352 (Spinoza, parallelism of modes), 506, 2 (Fechner), 508, 1 (Wundt); — imperfect parallelism, 494, A) (Taine), 526, A), 1 (W. James); — combatted by Bergson, 545.

Personality. 45. a) In the Scholastic sense, 290 (Duns Scotus), 308, B) (Suarez). — b) In the modern sense, the conscious self : as a substance, 325 (Descartes), 441 (Maine de Biran), 486, 2° (St. Mill, hesitantly) ; — as the sole reality or pure becoming, 546-548 (Bergson) ; — as a mode of God : real, 350, B) (Spinoza); ideal, or a distinct consciousness, 423, ff. (idealistic pantheists), 430 (Schopenhauer); — as a critical subject or phenomenal self, 401 (Kant), 428 (Fichte); — c) as a *series of* associated subjective *phenomena,* 372 (Locke), 383 (Hume), 501 (Taine), 507, 3, b (Wundt), 509 (Th. Ribot), 526 (W. James). — d) Splitting of personality, 527 (W. James). — Correct theory, 327.

D) PSYCHOLOGY OF THE SENSES.

46. **Knowledge in General.** a) Atomist theory, 20 (Democritus); — Aristotelian theory, in terms of actuality and potentiality, 81; see 268 (St. Thomas); — Stoic theory, in terms of effort, 101; — intuitive theory, see n. 55; — idealist theory, see n. 17; — Kantian theory, 398; materialist explanation of thought, 369, B) (Toland, Priestley), 375, 3° (Locke), 482 (the mental matter of Clifford). — b) the stages of knowledge, 101 (Stoics), 261-265 (St. Thomas), 379 (Condillac), 438 (Rosmini), 480-II, 1 (Spencer).

47. **Sense Knowledge.** *a*) An activity of the soul alone : by simple reaction, 60 (Plato); by spiritual reaction or thought, 328 (Descartes); as creative of matter, 136 B) 2 (Plotinus); as creative of an image of the world, 163 (St. Augustine). — *b*) An activity of the composite, or of the soul informing the body, 81 (Aristotle). — *c*) Kantian theory, 398; — Theory of Wundt, 508, 2 (product of unconscious reasoning). — *d*) Value of sensation : valueless, 344 (Malebranche); valuable insofar as controlled by reason, 81 (Aristotle), 149, 163 (St. Augustine); or by common sense, 386, B) (Reid); — unlimited value, 108 (Epicurus). — Is our only knowledge, see *Nominalism*, n. 22 and *Empiricism*, n. 52. Intuition of external senses, see n. 55, *d*). — *e*) *Division of the senses :* the external senses, 81 (Aristotle); internal senses, 82 (Aristotle), 151, 2 and 163, 3 (St. Augustine); the fundamental sense, 438 (Rosmini); moral sense, 386, A) (Shaftesbury, Hutcheson), 386, B) (Reid); — sensation and perception, 526, 2, *a* (W. James), pure perception and conscious perception, 548 (Bergson). — *f*) *Perception of space :* nativist theory, 484, A), 1 (Hamilton), 506, 3 (Muller, etc.), 526, 2, *a* (W. James), 548 (Bergson); — empiricist theory, 377 (Berkeley), 489, 2 (Bain), 506, 3 (Helmholz, etc.); — attempt at harmonization, 484, 1° (Hamilton), 508, 2 (Wundt); — correct theory, 377. — *g*) *Training of senses* in general : 379 (Condillac), 480-II, 1 (Spencer), 484, A), 1 (Hamilton), 489 (Bain), 508 (Wundt); — law of sensations, 506, 2 (law of Weber, stated precisely by Fechner), 526, 2, *a* (W. James); — calculation of the *time* of sensations, 506, 3 (Helmholz, etc.). — *h*) *Theory of local signs*, 505 bis, 2 (Lotze), 508, 2 (Wundt). — *i*) *Apperception and sense perception*, 362, *b* (Leibniz), 398, 3 (Kant), 508, 2 (Wundt).

48. **Memory.** *a*) As source of all our knowledge (theory of *reminiscence*) : because of a previous life, 45 (Plato), because of divine illumination, 166 (St. Augustine), (see p. 244). — *b*) As a sense faculty, 81 (Aristotle), 163, 3 (St. Augustine); lost after death, 85 (Aristotle); relation to sensation and imagination, 368bis, 1 (Hobbes), 380-II, 1 (Spencer), 484, C) (James Mill), 489 (Bain). — Habitual memory and pure memory, 509 (Th. Ribot).

49. **Imagination.** *a*) The faculty, 81 (Aristotle), 379 (Condillac). — *b*) *Laws of association*, 368 bis, C), 1 (Hobbes), 381 (Hume), 480-II, 1 (Spencer), 484, C) (James Mill), 486, 2° (St. Mill), 489, 2 (Bain), 509 (Th. Ribot), 510, 3 (Paulhan); — law of substitution of images, 494 (Taine) ; — law of interest, 526 (W. James). — *c*) *Associationism :* influence in the 19th century, 483, *a ;* — criticism by Bergson, 545-546; — proponents, see *Laws of association*, *b*).

E) INTELLECTUAL PSYCHOLOGY.

50. **Intellectual Knowledge.** *a*) Affirmed implicitly by the first philosophers, 7; clarified by Socrates, 30, 38, II. — *b*) *Intelligence*, a spiritual faculty, 60, 3 (Plato), 83 (Aristotle), 136, B) (Plotinus), 164 (St. Augustine), 183 (Avicenna), 190 (Averroes), 268 (St. Thomas), 278 (St. Bonaventure), 293 (Duns Scotus). — *c*) A faculty connatural to matter, 538, 3 (Bergson) ; — intelligent fire (Logos), 9 (Heraclitus), 99, 3 (Stoics). — *d*) Double faculty : active and passive intellect, 83 (Aristotle), 235 (St. Albert the Great), 249 (see p. 367, St. Thomas' refutation of Siger

of Brabant), 278 *a* (St. Bonaventure), 293 (Duns Scotus). — Separate agent intellect, see n. 68, *f*). The five degrees of intelligence, according to Avicenna, 183. — *e*) *Object* of intelligence : being, see n. 74; the abstracted essence, see n. 51, *a*) : *Abstraction ;* — the individual, see *Knowledge of the individual*, n. 40, *c*) ; — God, see *Ontologism*, n. 51, *c*). — *f*) *Intellectualism :* characteristic of St. Augustine, 173, 177; of St. Thomas, 259, 2; — anti-intellectualism : 9, *d* (Heraclitus), 455 (Rousseau), 522 (pragmatists), 537, 3 (Bergson).

51.   **Origin of Ideas.** *a*) **Abstraction.** Incomplete theory, 29, 30 (Socratic induction), 209, 2 (Gilbert de la Porrée), 213 (Abelard). Complete theory, 69, 84 (Aristotle : theory of the agent intellect), 214 (12th century); — insufficient theory, 165, 2 (inexact interpretation of St. Augustine), 278, *a* (St. Bonaventure : inferior knowledge), 293 (Duns Scotus). — Nominalist explanation, 382 (Hume), 497 (Taine), see n. 22. — *b*) **Illumination** from God : 164-167 (St. Augustine, moderate intuitionism), 220 (St. Anselm), 278, *b*, 279 (St. Bonaventure, contuition or more emphasized intuitionism), 232bis (Neo-Platonic eclecticism); 250 (Augustinians, exaggerated intuitionism). — *c*) **Ontologism** or vision in God, the theory of Malebranche, 341; followers, 437, 2° (Gioberti, etc.); — 166, 3 (falsely attributed to St. Augustine). — *d*) **Innatism.** Definition, 46, *b ;* — by the pre-existence of souls, 45 (Plato) ; — by divine creation, 165 (first held, then later rejected by St. Augustine), 320, *d* (Descartes), 362 (Leibniz). — *e*) The sole source of ideas is sense experience, see *Empiricism*, n. 52.

52.   **Empiricism or Sensualism.** *a*) Definition of the two terms, 356, 2. Empiricism in the loose sense, see *Abstraction*, n. 51, *a*). — *b*) Empiricism in the strict sense (*sensualist empiricism* or positivist psychology) : ancient empiricism, 21 (Atomists), 101 (Stoics), 108 (Epicureans) ; — Modern empiricists, 316, B) (Fr. Bacon), 368 bis, C), 1 (Hobbes), 370 (philosophers of the 18th century), and especially, 379 (Condillac), 374 (Locke), 377 (Berkeley), 380 (Hume), 460 (empiricist method of positivism), 480-II, 1 (Spencer), 482 (Huxley, etc.), 484, C) (James Mill), 495 (St. Mill), 489 (Bain), 495 (Taine), 507 (Wundt), 509 (Th. Ribot), 524 (point of departure of W. James and of pragmatism). — *c*) Intuitionist Empiricism, 272 (R. Bacon), with divine illumination, 537, 1 (Bergson). See also *Nominalism*, n. 22.

53.   **Origin of the First Principles.** Innatism, 279 (St. Bonaventure), see p. 598 (School of Cambridge) and note (Herbart of Cherbury); illumination, 232 bis (Neo-Platonic eclecticism); 250 (Augustinians), modified intuition, 262, *c* (St. Thomas), intuition involving a voluntary effort, 441 (Maine de Biran); experience alone, see *Empiricism*, n. 52, *b*).

54.   **Extension of Knowledge.** *a*) *Analogy :* nature and proof, 70 (Aristotle), 259, 3; 286, *b* (St. Thomas) ; — analogy of attribution, 309, A) (Suarez). Origin in Plato, 50, 2; tendency to analogy, 481, 3 (Spencer) ; — Means of knowing God, 125 (positive theology of Plotinus), 267 (St. Thomas), 275-II (St. Bonaventure) ; — see 127, critique of Plotinus, 194, critique of Maimonides, 348, critique of Spinoza, 482, critique of Spencer. — *b*) *Universal Univocity*, 286 (Duns Scotus); distended univocity, 554, 3 (Bergson) ; — *c*) Intellectual knowledge of the concrete object, see n. 40, *c*) ; — limited knowledge of the sensible, see *Positivism*, n. 12 and *Empiricism*, n. 52, *b*).

55. **Intuition.** *a)* Definition and possible forms, 540, 3. *b)* Platonic intuitive method, 44-45 (Plato), 123 (Plotinus), 144, 6, *b* (St. Augustine), 279 (St. Bonaventure), 273, 2 (R. Bacon). — *c)* Bergsonian intuition, 539. Cartesian intuition, 320, *b ;* see *Method of the clear idea,* n. 14, *a*); intuition of the spiritual life or the noological method, 531, C) (Eucken); — *d) Sense intuition :* of the external senses, 81 (Aristotle), 262, *a* (St. Thomas), 358, 1 (Kant); denial of all other intuition, see *Empiricism,* n. 52, *b*). — *e) Intellectual intuition of the self,* 262, *b* (St. Thomas), 279, *a* (St. Bonaventure), 324-327 (Descartes), 378bis, (Berkeley), 441 (Maine de Biran), 486, 2° (St. Mill); — *f) Intuition of God,* 139 (Plotinus, 2nd degree), 151, 3, 173 (St. Augustine), 279, *b* (St. Bonaventure), 329, *b,* 330 (Descartes), 533 (modernists); see *Vision in God,* n. 51, *c*). — *g)* Mystic intuition, see *Mysticism,* n. 57. — *h)* Intuition of common sense, 262, *c* (St. Thomas). — *i)* Intuition in the loose sense or abstractive intuition, see *Abstraction,* n. 51, *a*).

56. **Rationalism.** Definition, 313, Characteristic of pagan Hellenism, 141, and especially so of modern philosophy, 313. Principle examples, 93, 4° (religion of Aristotle), 97, 3 (naturalism of the decadent period), 140 (rationalist piety of Plotinus), 191 (Avicenna), 196 (Maimonides), 213, 2 (Abelard); with restriction, 202 (Scotus Eriugena). Among the *moderns,* 336 (Descartes); see n. 10, *Cartesianism ;* — 416, 420 (Kant), see n. 11, *Kantianism ;* — 490 (Taine); see n. 12, *Positivism ;* — 443 (Cousin and eclecticism), 447, C) (Montesquieu). — Inexact interpretation of St. Anselm, 217.

57. **Mysticism.** *a)* Definition as a system of philosophy, 120. Principal schools : Platonic mysticism, 66; — Alexandrian or Neo-Platonic, 120 (its three characteristics), 121 (principal representatives among the pagans) 123, ff. (Plotinus), 197 (Dionysius the Areopagite), 201 (Scotus Eriugena) ; — *Augustinian,* or Catholic, *mysticism,* 155, 177; 227 (School of St. Victor), 232 bis (Neo-Platonic eclecticism) ; 250 (Augustinians), 279 (St. Bonaventure). — *b)* Mystic intuition according to Bergson, 550. — *c) Ecstasy,* mystic intuition par excellence, 139, 3rd degree (Plotinus), 173 (beatific vision according to St. Augustine) ; — rationalist interpretation of mystic phenomena, 510, 2 (Pierre Janet).

58. **Agnosticism.** With regard to God, 127 (Plotinus, negative theology), 194 (Maimonides, in regard to positive attributes), 384 bis, 3° (Hume), 468 (A. Comte), 481, 3 (the Unknowable of H. Spencer) ; — with regard to every substance and every absolute, see *Positivism,* n. 12 and 552 (2nd thesis of pragmatism) ; 532 (modernists).

59. **Pragmatism.** Definition, 522 (the three essential theses). Kantian origin, 419, 1, 420, *c ;* precursors, 430 (Schopenhauer), 455 (Rousseau) ; — the theorist, 524 (W. James) ; — influence, 535 (modernism), 538, 3, 552, B), 2 (Bergson) ; 531, C) (inexact interpretation of Newman). — 531, D), Philosophy of action (Blondel).

60. **Language.** Had supernatural origin, 434 (De Bonald). Functions in relation to intelligence : replaces it, see *Nominalism,* n. 22; — is the sign of concepts, 72 (Aristotle); is insufficient as a sign, 164 (St. Augustine) ; — retains the idea, as motive element, 509 (Th. Ribot); as a social intellectual capital, 464, 3 (Comte).

F) PSYCHOLOGY OF ACTION AND EMOTIONS.

61. **Appetite in General.** *a*) Definition and classification, 87 (Aristotle), 269 (St. Thomas), 328, *b* (Descartes). — *b*) *Natural appetite :* in the form of desire, 137 (Plotinus), 362, *c* (Leibniz), of vague desire, 511 (Fouillée); of love of God, 172 (St. Augustine). 354 (Spinoza); as simple affection, 441 (Maine de Biran); — laws of the affective states, 509, 3 (Th. Ribot). — *c*) *Sensibility*, one of the three principle faculties in positive psychology, 483. — *d*) *Higher Sentiment*, love of God, basis of life, 172 (St. Augustine); possession of God, see n. 105 and especially 106, *Beatitude;* — altruism and egoism, 466, 4 (A. Comte); Feeling or moral sense, 386; see n. 104, *Systems of Morality, i*).

62. **Passions and Emotions.** *a*) Definition and classification, 60 (Plato), 87 (Aristotle), 104 (Stoics), 107, 3 (Epicurus), 335, 2 (Descartes), 368bis, C) 2 (Hobbes), 484, C) (James Mill), 386, B) (Reid). — *b*) Physiological origin of the emotions, 526, 2, *c* (W. James, Lange); — logic of passion, 509, 3 (Ribot). — *c*) Supra-rational emotion, 551, B), 2 (Bergson). — *d*) Passions in the moral order, see n. 111.

63. **Will.** Defined as the intellectual appetite, 60 (Plato), 87 (Aristotle); — as illuminated by God, 280 (St. Bonaventure); — as an autonomous faculty, 292 (Duns Scotus), 309, B) (Suarez); — principle of all things, 430 (Schopenhauer), 507 (Wundt); — principle of the philosophy of values, 531, A) (Munsterberg); — positivist definition, 499 (Taine). — The voluntary effort, 441 (Maine de Biran); — the will to power, 531, B) (Nietzsche).

64. **Freedom.** Recognized as *a reality:* admitted implicitly, 34 (Socrates), 63 (Plato); — clearly demonstrated, 87 (Aristotle), 168 (St. Augustine), 221 (St. Anselm), 235 (St. Albert the Great), 269 (St. Thomas), 280 (St. Bonaventure), 292 (Duns Scotus), 412 (Kant); admitted as useful, 526, 1 (W. James). Essential to man, 449, 450, II (Rousseau); — essential to life, 546, *c* (Bergson); — reconciled with determinism, 487, 6⁰ (St. Mill); see 469, *b;* 508, 3 (Wundt); — is merely an illusion, 248, *b* (Latin Averroists), 252 (Spinoza), 368bis, C), 2 (Hobbes), 480-II, 1 (Spencer), 489 (Bain), 499 (Taine), 531, B), 1 (Nietzsche).

65. **Determinism.** Origin of the theory, 19 (Atomists : the pagan notion of *fate*); — determinism combined with pantheism, 102 (Stoics), 352 (Spinoza); — with the necessary causality of God, 248 (Averroists). A postulate in positivism, 368bis, C), 2 (Hobbes), 461 (A. Comte), 500 (Taine); extended to sociology, 469 (A. Comte), 480-III (Spencer), 482-III, 1 (K. Marx), 503 (Taine), 513 (Durkheim). — Psychological determinism, 366 (Leibniz), 303 (see p. 457, Buridan).

66. **Voluntarism.** Definition, 287; philosophical characteristic : 173 (St. Augustine), 189 (Algazel), 232bis (Neo-Platonic eclecticism); 250 (Augustinians), 285 (Duns Scotus), 331 (Descartes), 508 (Wundt); see *The Good, Summit of all things*, n. 75, *d*).

67. **Habit.** Definition of Aristotle, 88, 2⁰; — physical function, 100 (Stoics); — psychological function, 384 (Hume), 486, 2 (St. Mill), 489, 4 (Murphy), — critical function, 530, C) (Ravaisson). — Moral function of habit, see *Moral virtues*, n. 110.

67 bis. **Instinct.** *a) Specific difference of animals,* 81, 2 (Aristotle), see p. 900, note 2, (Mac Dougall). — *b) Origin of instinct :* mechanist theory, 476 bis, 2 (Darwin), 480-II, 1 (Spencer) ; — intellectualist theory, 482 (Romanes) ; — vitalist theory, 542 (Bergson). — *c)* In man : blind instinct, criterion of truth, 443 (Jouffroy) ; — instinct, the foundation of morality, 384 bis, 4º (Hume) : see n. 104bis).

G) THE HUMAN SOUL : RATIONAL PSYCHOLOGY.

68. **Nature of the Soul.** *a)* A *spirit,* 36 (Socrates), 58 (Plato), 85 (Aristotle) : see *Immortality of the Soul,* n. 72. — *b)* A *material* being, 19, *b* (Atomists), 109, 2 (Epicurus), 100 (Stoics : notion of a subtle fire), 368 bis, C), 1 (Hobbes), 370 (Philosophers of the 18th century). — *c)* Is an association of conscious acts : see n. 45, *c).* — *d)* A universal soul, or *Panpsychism,* see n. 41, *b).* — *e) Faculties of the soul:* in general, 60 (Plato), 136 (Plotinus) ; in particular, see n. 47, the senses, n. 48, memory, n. 49, imagination, n. 50, intellect, n. 61, appetite, n. 63, will. — *f) Separate agent intellect,* 86 (a possible interpretation of Aristotle), 118 (Alexander of Aphrodisias), 183 (Avicenna), 190 (Averroes), 248, *c)* (Latin Averroists). 311, 2 (Averroists of the Renaissance) ; — 273, 2 (identical with God, according to R. Bacon).

69. **Origin of the Soul.** *a)* Is eternal and pre-existent, 45, 58 (Plato), 136 (Plotinus), 413 (Kant) ; — comes from without, 85 (Aristotle) ; emanates from the World-Soul, 37, 1, *b* (Socrates), 136 (Plotinus) ; — from God, see *Pantheism,* n. 96. — *b) Traducianism :* 169, F) (St. Augustine), 438 (Rosmini). — *c) Generationism,* see *material soul,* n. 68, *b).* — *d) Creationism,* 169, F) (Sts. Augustine and Thomas), 218 (St. Anselm). — *e)* Origin of the soul ignored, 384 (Hume) ; see *Agnosticism,* n. 58. — *f) Metempsychosis,* 11 (Pythagoras), 65, 2º (Plato), 139 (Plotinus).

70. **Union of Soul and Body.** *a) Accidental* union, 45, 58 (Plato), 327, 334 (Descartes), 344 (Malebranche), 352 (Spinoza, parallelism of modes), 363 (Leibniz, pre-established harmony). — *b)* Union *through their functions,* 183 (Avicenna), 235 (St. Albert the Great), 547 (Bergson). — *c) Natural* union, 162 (St. Augustine). — *d) Soul the form of the body,* 85 (Aristotle), 250, 268 (St. Thomas).

71. **Unity of Form.** *a)* Proponents, 85 (Aristotle), 250, 268 (St. Thomas). — *b) Plurality of forms* or of souls, 60 (Plato), 136 (Plotinus), 235 (St. Albert the Great : in compounds), 247 (Augustinians), 273, 1 (R. Bacon), 276, 4 (St. Bonaventure), 282 (Olivi), 291 (Duns Scotus).

72. **The Immortality of the Soul.** *a) Proofs,* of Socrates, 36; of Plato, 58, 3; of Aristotle, 83-85; of Plotinus, 136; of Augustine, 169; of St. Anselm, 219; of St. Thomas, 268; of St. Bonaventure, 276, 2; of Descartes, 326; of Berkeley, 378; of Kant, 414; of Bergson, 546. — *b)* Known by faith, 188 (Algazel), 294 (Duns Scotus), 303 (Ockham) ; — or by tradition, 379 (Condillac), 368 (Reid), 451, 3 (Rousseau) ; — doubtfully, 375 (Locke), 488 (St. Mill) ; — temporary immortality, 100 (Stoics); partial, 195 (Maimonides), see *Separate agent intellect,* n. 68, *f).* *c) Denial of immortality,* see n. 68, *b) Material soul,* and 45, *c) The self, association of conscious acts.*

73. **Spiritualism.** *a)* A system which asserts the existence of spiritual beings : the soul, see n. 68, *a)* and 72 *a)* ; — God, see n. 81-86. Eclectic

spiritualism, 442 (Cousin), 556 (Catholics of the 19th century). —
b) *Angels or pure forms :* their existence, 27, 37 (*daimon* of Socrates),
56, 3° (inferior gods in Plato's system), 93, 4 (movers of the celestial
spheres, according to Aristotle); see *Polytheism,* n. 90. — Nature of the
angels, 121 (Philo : messengers of God), 161 (St. Augustine), 235
(St. Albert the Great), 268 (St. Thomas).

V. — METAPHYSICS.

74. **Metaphysics in General.** *a)* Its existence as the philosophy
of being, 14 (Parmenides, discovery of being), 48 (Plato), 69-70 (Aristotle),
124 (Plotinus), 260 (St. Thomas); — its three parts according to the
moderns : cosmology, psychology, theodicy, 391 (Kant). — Moral metaphysics, 415 (Kant); immanentist metaphysics, 528 (W. James); see
Pantheism, n. 96. — *b) Metaphysical characteristics :* of Platonism, 66
(Plato), 134, 141 (Plotinus), 177 (St. Augustine); — of Thomism, 253;
— of Cartesianism, 317, 336; — of Taine, 504; — of Bergson, 555; —
metaphysical tendencies of H. Spencer, 481; of St. Mill, 488, concl.;
of Wundt, 508, concl.; of contemporary philosophy, 529. — *c)* Condemnation of metaphysics as a science, 408 (Kant), 444 (positivism), 460
(A. Comte), see *Positivism,* n. 22.

75. **The Transcendentals.** *a)* As arrived at by deduction, 14, *b*
(Parmenides), 70 (Aristotle), 260 (St. Thomas). — *b)* **The One and the
Many.** Problem of the one and the many, 286 (Duns Scotus and
St. Thomas); — the unity of God, 12 (see p. 19, note 4, Pythagoras),
125 (Plotinus); — unity according to Plotinus, in the *Nous,* 129; in
the Soul, 131. The unity of composites through incomplete beings,
275, 4 (St. Bonaventure); the unity of form, see n. 71. — Plurality,
a property of matter, 133 (Plotinus); divisibility *ad infinitum,* 16 (Zeno
of Elea); infinite multitude, 19 (Atomists), 361 (Leibniz). — Various
distinctions : 286 (according to Duns Scotus, formal distinction *a parte
rei*); 301 (according to Ockham), 307 (according to Suarez), 325 (according
to Descartes). — *c)* **Truth and Falsity.** Definition of Truth, 220
(St. Anselm). Truth according to pragmatism, 524 (W. James); according
to Blondel, 531, D). — Truth, the summit of all things, 146 (St. Augustine);
according to Plotinus, possessed essentially by the *Nous,* 129; imperfectly
by the Soul, 131. — Logical truth is in the idea, according to Descartes,
319, *c ;* — in the judgment, according to St. Thomas, 321, 3, and Kant,
392. — Impossibility of attaining truth, see *Scepticism,* n. 16. — Error,
explained in terms of non-being, 48 (Plato), in terms of matter, 133
(Plotinus); — see *Criteria of truth,* n. 15. — *d)* **Good and Evil.** The Good,
summit of all things, 49 (Plato), 123 (Plotinus). — The Good according
to Plotinus, participated in by the *Nous,* 129, and by the Soul, 131. —
Natural goodness of man, 450 (Rousseau). — Moral good, see n. 104, ff. —
The Principle : Good is diffusive of itself, 124 (Plotinus). The problem
of evil : optimism and pessimism, see n. 102. — *e)* **The Beautiful and
Esthetics.** Definition of the beautiful, 417 (Kant). Beauty of God
participated in by the *Nous,* according to Plotinus, 229, B), 2. — Esthetics
of Aristotle, 91; of Taine, 402. — Pure ugliness in terms of matter, 133
(Plotinus). — Transcendental esthetics of Kant, 398. — Esthetics of the
moral life, 517, 1 (Durkheim).

76. **General Divisions of Being.** *a)* **Actuality and Potentiality.** The theory, 70, 2 (Aristotle), 260 (St. Thomas); — as applied to bodies, see *Hylomorphism*, n. 33, *c*); to knowledge, see n. 50, *d*). — *b)* **Essence and Existence.** Distinction imperfectly grasped by Aristotle, 76; minimized by Duns Scotus, 288; precisely demonstrated, 267 (St. Thomas), 282, II (Giles of Rome); — denied, 250 (Godfrey of Fontaines), 301 (Ockham), 306 (Suarez). — *c)* **Substance and Accident.** An application of actuality and potentiality, 76 (Aristotle), 267 (St. Thomas); — distinction attenuated, 162 (St. Augustine), 232 bis (Neo-Platonic eclecticism), 277 (St. Bonaventure); — distinction denied, 325 (Descartes). — Denial of substances, see *Phenomenalism*, n. 17, *e*); *Positivism*, n. 12; *Pragmatism*, n. 59.

77. **Possibles.** Their foundation in God, 297 (Scotus), 331 (Descartes); in the Divine Ideas, see *Exemplarism*, n. 93, *c*). Proof of the existence of God through possibles, 364, 2 (Leibniz).

78. **The Principle of Causality.** *a)* Its validity : as the foundation of philosophy, 124 (principle of the perfect cause, Plotinus), 146 (St. Augustine); — as the foundation for the proof of God's existence, see n. 81, 83, ff. — Absolute validity, but for phenomena only, 401, 404 (Kant); — accepted without criticism, 374, 2°, *b* (Locke); — merely the value of psychological habit, 384 (Hume); based on experience and association, 487, 5° (St. Mill).— *b)* *Principle of sufficient reason :* its twofold formula, 360; — foundation of Thomism, 258-259 (principle of universal intelligibility); — basis of the real order, 359, 364 (Leibniz); — foundation of substances and of God, 507 (Wundt).

79. **Theory of the Four Causes.** *a)* Explained, 75 (Aristotle). — *b)* *Efficient cause :* vague notion, 6 (first philosophers); — cause of movement, 75, 92 (Aristotle), see *God, the First Mover*, n. 84, *a*); — Efficient cause in the modern sense (necessary antecedent), 316, B) (origin with F. Bacon), 368 bis, C) (Hobbes), 384 (Hume), 472 (positivism), 493 (Taine). — *c)* *Physical law :* 461 (A. Comte), 491 (Taine), 513 (Durkheim); — criticism of the positivist interpretation, 473.— *d)* *Material and Formal Cause*, see *Hylomorphism*, n. 33, *c*), *d*). — *e)* *Final Causes :* their existence, 37 (Socrates), 75 (Aristotle), 417 (Kant). Criticized by Bergson, 542. Denial of final causes in favor of chance, 109 (Epicurus); excluded from science, in favor of *mechanism*, see n. 32, *c*) and 333, 3 (Descartes). — Foundation of a proof for the existence of God, see n. 83.

80. **Participation.** (Platonic theory of causality). The principle of participation, 151, 3° (St. Augustine). — Participation among the Ideas, which are real according to Plato, 48; — between the Ideas and the world, 53 (Plato); — between substances, 128, 131, 133 (Plotinus); — between God and the world, 161 (St. Augustine), 201 (Scotus Eriugena), 378 bis, (Berkeley); see *Exemplarism*, n. 93, *c*). — In the pantheistic sense, 351 (Spinoza); see *Pantheism*, n. 96.

VI. — THEODICY.

A) EXISTENCE OF GOD.

81. Possibility of Proof. *a)* Affirmed, 267 (St. Thomas), 295 (Duns Scotus); denied, 408, III (Kant); considered as useless, 124 (Plotinus), 201, B) (Scotus Eriugena); — or quite unnecessary, 275-I (St. Bonaventure), 340 (Malebranche), impossible for our intellect, 553, A) (Bergson). See *Our knowledge of God*, n. 86. — *b) Atheism*, 482-III, 6 (communists), 531, B) (Nietzsche); see *Agnosticism*, n. 58.

82. A Priori or Ontological Proof. Proponents, 223 (St. Anselm), 275-I (St. Bonaventure), 295, 3 (Duns Scotus), 329, *b* (Descartes), 364, 2 (Leibniz), 348 (Spinoza), 492 (Taine), 530, C) (Lagneau). — Criticized by Gaunilon and by St. Thomas, 223; and by Kant, 408, III.

83. Proof from Final Causality. Proposed as valid, 22 (Anaxagoras), 37 (Socrates), 55, 1° (Plato), 92 (Aristotle); 99 (Stoics), 369, A) (Newton), 369, B) (Deists), 370 (Voltaire), 530, C) (Boutroux). — Accredited with imperfect validity, 408, III (Kant), 488 (St. Mill).

84. Physical Proofs. *a) From motion :* 55, 2° (Plato), 92, 2 (Aristotle), 194 (Maimonides); — criticism of Scotus, 295, 3. — *b) From contingency*, 185 (Avicenna), 194 (Maimonides), 295, 3 (Duns Scotus), 364, 1 (Leibniz), 375, 3° (Locke). — *c) From degrees of perfection*, 222 (St. Anselm), 275-I (St. Bonaventure), 152, 2° (abbreviated proof of St. Augustine).

85. Psychological and Moral Proofs. *a)* From the eternal truths, 151 (complete Augustinian proof), 152 (shortened form). — *b)* Proof from the idea of infinity, 329, *a* (Descartes), 340 (Malebranche). — *c)* God needed as the basis of our ideas, 481, I (H. Spencer); as the basis of our will acts, 507, 3 (Wundt); of our interior life, 533 (modernists). — *d)* Proof founded on moral obligation, 414 (Kant); — on the usefulness of a superior being (pragmatic truth), 528 (W. James); on life, 531, C) (Eucken, noological method); — on the testimony of mystics, 553 (Bergson). — *e)* proof from *universal consent*, 150 (St. Augustine), 435 (Lamennais); — from history, 481, 2 (H. Spencer). — *f)* Proof from faith, 303 (Ockham). — *g)* Proof for the existence of the gods from tradition, 109, 3 (Epicurus).

86. Our Knowledge of God. *a)* Impossible, see *Agnosticism*, n. 58; — *b)* possible, but very limited, 155 (St. Augustine, by purification of all our ideas); — more negative than positive, 126 (Plotinus), 194 (Maimonides), 203 (Scotus Eriugena), 481, 3 (H. Spencer); — by way of analogy, see n. 54, *a)*; — univocally, 295 (Duns Scotus). — *e)* Knowledge through clear ideas, 329, 330 (Descartes), 349, 352 (Spinoza); — through mystic intuition, 127, 139, 3° (Plotinus), 550, 553 (Bergson).

B) NATURE AND ATTRIBUTES OF GOD.

87. Essence of God or His Fundamental Attribute. God is the Logos, intelligent Fire, 9 (Heraclitus), 99 (Stoics); spiritual Intelligence, 22 (the *Nous* of Anaxagoras), 37 (the Demiurge of Socrates); the regal Soul, 55 (Plato); — immobile Being, 14 (Parmenides); supreme Being,

451 (Rousseau); necessary Being, 185 (Avicenna); pure Existence : *Ipsum Esse subsistens*, 267 (St. Thomas); — pure Actuality, 92 (Aristotle), 235 (St. Albert the Great); — the One, 125 (Plotinus), 364 (Leibniz); — Truth, 154 (St. Augustine), 275-I (St. Bonaventure); — Goodness, 222 (St. Anselm) or the Good, according to one interpretation of Plato, 49, 55, 3; — Love, 553, B), 1 (Bergson); — the Infinite, 296 (Duns Scotus), 329 (Descartes); the sovereign Nature, 201 (Scotus Eriugena); the unique Substance, 348 (Spinoza); the Divine, 533 (modernists), 528 (W. James); — the supreme Legislator, 414, b (Kant); the eternal Axiom, 492 (Taine); — Spirit, 428, 2 (Hegel); the Unconscious, 431 (Hartmann); the Unknowable, 481 (H. Spencer). — Humanity, 468 (A. Comte).

88. **Distinction of Divine Attributes.** *a*) Their real identity, 154 (St. Augustine). — *b*) Distinction of reason without foundation, 301 (Ockham); — virtual distinction or distinction of reason with foundation, 57, 3 and 267 (St. Thomas); — formal distinction « a parte rei », 295 (Duns Scotus); — distinction through clear ideas, 349 (Spinoza). — *c*) Distinction between speculative attributes (rejected) and practical (granted), 528 (W. James).

89. **Unity of God.** *a*) the attribute of unicity, 125 (Plotinus), 37, 2 (Socrates), 56, 3 (Plato), 93, 1°, *d* (Aristotle), 154 (St. Augustine), 348, 3 (Spinoza). — *b*) *Simplicity* of God : essential characteristic, 57, 3 (criticism of Plato); doctrine of Aristotle, 93; of St. Augustine, 154, 1. — *c*) *Immateriality* or spirituality of God, 22 (Anaxagoras), 93, 1 (Aristotle); A material God, 99, 3 (Stoics), 368 bis, A) (Hobbes), 369, D) (Toland). — *d*) *Transendence* of God, 120 (a doctrine common to mystic philosophy), 121 (Philo), 126 (Plotinus), 197 (Dionysius the Areopagite), 201, 1 (Scotus Eriugena).

90. **Polytheism.** *a*) Ridiculed by Xenophon, 13; defended by Epicurus, 109, 3 (material gods). — *b*) *Explanation*, in terms of inferior gods, 37, 2° (Socrates), 56, 3 (Plato); in terms of movers of the celestial spheres, 93, 4° (Aristotle), 131, A) 3 (Plotinus). — *c*) *Destiny :* blind force, 19, A) 3 (Atomists). — Rationalized destiny, 55, 3 (Plato); — denial of destiny, 109 (Epicurus).

91. **Eternity and Immutability.** Doctrine of Aristotle, 93, 2; of Plotinus, 131; of St. Augustine, 154, B), 3°, 4°; relation to absolute time, 369, A) (Newton, Clarke). — God, the necessary Being, 185 (Avicenna), 225 (St. Anselm). Eleatic immobilism, 14.

92. **Immensity of God.** *a*) Doctrine of St. Augustine, 154, B), 5; of St. Anselm, 225; — an attribute known by faith, according to Duns Scotus, 298. Relation to absolute space, 369, A) (Newton, Clarke).— *b*) the *Infinity* of God, 296 (Duns Scotus), 329 (Descartes), 340 (Malebranche), 348, 2 (Spinoza); the absolute and infinite God, 423 (idealistic pantheists). — A *finite* God, 488 (St. Mill), 528 (W. James), 530, A) (Mac Taggart).

93. **The Divine Knowledge.** *a*) God knows Himself and the world perfectly, 22 (Anaxagoras), 56, 1 (Plato), 267 (St. Thomas, see 94, correction of Aristotle), 160 (St. Augustine), 248, *b* (Siger of Brabant); 275-III (St. Bonaventure). — *b*) God knows Himself perfectly but is ignorant of the world, 93, 2 and 3 (Aristotle); He has only general knowledge of the world, 185 (Avicenna); has no foreknowledge of free acts,

117 (Cicero). — c) *Exemplarism :* analysis, 159, 275-II; — exemplarism by way of separate Ideas, 42, 43, 53 (Plato); by way of Ideas of the Intellect, which is an effect of God, 121 (Philo), 129 (Plotinus), 201, 2 (Scotus Eriugena); —by way of the Divine Ideas, 159 (St. Augustine), 209 (School of Chartres), 275, II and III (St. Bonaventure). — *d)* God the guarantor of our knowledge, 331 (Descartes); — sources of our ideas, especially from sensations, 378 (Berkeley).

94. **The Goodness and Perfection of God.** God just and holy, 56, 2 (Plato); God perfect, 125 (Plotinus), 154 (St. Augustine), 225 (St. Anselm), 275-III (St. Bonaventure); God is without defect, 331 (Descartes). God, the perfect Ideal, 407 (Kant).

95. **Love and Beatitude.** God is happy, 56, 1 (Plato), 93, 2 (Aristotle), 125 (Plotinus). — God is Love, 553, B), 1 (Bergson). — Creation, a work of love, 152, 2 (St. Augustine), 553, B), 5 (Bergson).

C) RELATIONS BETWEEN GOD AND THE WORLD.

96. **Pantheism.** *a)* Definition, 134, *b*, 3. — *b) Its forms :* realistic pantheism, *evolutionism,* 9 (Heraclitus : *pure material becoming*), 544 and 554, 3 (a possible interpretation of Bergson : *Pure Becoming,* a combination of matter and spirit), 99 (the Stoic *Logos,* materialistic), 492 (Taine); — *static pantheism,* totally, 13 (Xenophon), 14 (Parmenides); partially, 348 (Spinoza : evolution only of modes); pure materialistic pantheism, 210, 2 (David of Dinant), 369, B) (Toland). — *Idealist* pantheism, 210, 1 (Amalric of Bene); evolutionist pantheism, 422, 423 (German idealists) especially 427 (Hegel : *pure* ideal *Becoming*); — pantheism in terms of the unconscious self, 425 (Fichte), 426 (Schelling), 430 (Schopenhauer), 431 (Hartmann). — *c) Panentheism,* 429 (Krause). — *d)* pantheist tendencies, 435 (Lamennais), 200, 202 (Scotus Eriugena); but falling short of pantheism, 134, *b*, 3 (Plotinus), 341, 344 (Malebranche), 287 (Duns Scotus); — exclusion of pantheism, 160, *d* (St. Augustine); absurdity of the system, 355. — *e) Monism,* expressive of the same doctrine as that of pantheism. See 478, materialistic monism of Haeckel.

97. **A Personal God.** *a)* Little known to the Hellenistic age, 141; — *b)* Clearly affirmed, 154 (St. Augustine); see Christian philosophers, n. 9 and n. 3, *c), Collaboration between faith and reason; —* doctrine of Bergson, 553, 2. — *c)* An impersonal God, 423-424 (the Unconsciousness of idealistic pantheism), 425 (Fichte), 431 (Hartmann), 528 (W. James), 533 (modernists).

98. **God the Creator.** *a)* Doctrine not discussed by the pagans, 57, 1 (Plato), 94 (Aristotle). — *b)* Theory of creation, 158 (St. Augustine), 224 (St. Anselm), 248, *b* (Siger of Brabant), 134 and 267 (St. Thomas), 275-III (St. Bonaventure); — theories approaching the notion of creation : the perfect cause according to Plotinus, 124; emanation according to Avicenna, 184; see *Participation,* n. 80. — *c)* God the Creator of motion, 333, *c* (Descartes). — Creation known by faith, 342 (Malebranche). — *d)* Pantheist interpretation, 351 (Spinoza), 423 (idealists); — psychological explanation, 443 (Cousin), 553, 4 (Bergson). — *e) Conservation* or continued creation, 158, 3 (St. Augustine), 224 (St. Anselm), 267 (St. Thomas), 329 (Descartes); — known by faith, 298 (Duns Scotus). — *f) Occasionalism* or the all-encompassing causality of God, 189, *b* (Algazel),

343 (Malebranche). — *g*) Physical premotion and simultaneous concurrence, 309, B) (Suarez), see p. 468, note 2; Banez and Molina.

99. **The Freedom of God.** *a*) At the summit of all things, 285 (Duns Scotus), 331 (Descartes), 531, C) (Secretan). — *b*) Attributable to the act of Creation, 158, 2 (St. Augustine), 189 (Algazel), 285, 297 (Duns Scotus), 553, 3 (Bergson). — *c*) *Necessary* action of God : as mover of the world, 93, 3 (Aristotle), 190 (Averroes), 248 (Latin Averroists); — as source of emanation, 128, *b* (Plotinus), 201 (Scotus Eriugena); see *Pantheism*, n. 96.

100. **God as Demiurge and Soul of the World.** Theory of Anaxagoras, 22; of Socrates, 37, 1; the more probable interpretation of Plato, 55. — The World Soul, third substance according to Plotinus, 131; cautious attitude of St. Augustine, 153. — The Platonic Trinity, 55 (see p. 71, note 1 : Plato), 132 (Plotinus).

101. **Providence.** *a*) Its existence in God, 22 (Anaxagoras), 37, 2 (Socrates), 56, 2 (Plato), 160 (St. Augustine), 267 (St. Thomas), 275-III (St. Bonaventure), 343, C) (Malebranche, law of the simplicity of Providence), 553, 5 (Bergson). — *b*) Providence in the loose sense, 93, 2 (Aristotle), 99, 2 (Stoics). Providence in terms of the World Soul, 131, B), 3° (Plotinus).

102. **The Problem of Evil and Providence.** *a*) Moderate solution, 160, 3 (St. Augustine), 553, 6 (Bergson). — *b*) Predestination to the good, 201 (Scotus Eriugena); suppression of evil, 353 (Spinoza). — *c*) *Optimism* or the victory of the good : moderate, 56, 2° (Plato), 160, 3°, *d* (St. Augustine), 189, *a* (Algazel), 553, 6 (Bergson); — absolute, 365 (Leibniz). — *d*) *Pessimism*, 430 (Schopenhauer).

103. **Duty of Man towards God.** *a*) In general, 37, 2 (Socrates). Love of God, the fundamental virtue, 172 (St. Augustine). — *b*) *Religion :* of the wise and of the common man, 65 (Plato), 93, 4 (Aristotle); — rational and non-supernatural religion, 368[bis], D), 4 (Hobbes, religion subject to State control), 369, B) (Deists), 375[bis], 1° (Locke), 384[bis], 3° (Hume), 416 (Kant), 428, 3 (Hegel), 451, 4 (Rousseau), 481, 2 (Spencer), 531, C) (Eucken); — positive religion, 468 (A. Comte). Religion, a relation of friendship with the gods, 109, 3° (Epicurus); submission to the will of God, 105 (Stoics, equivocal pantheists). — *c*) Condemnation of *superstitions*, 109, 3 (Epicurus); their useful function, 552, A) (Bergson); — primitive religion, cult of *Totem*, according to Durkheim, 518, *c*. — *d*) Attack and defense of the *religious* life, 241, 246 (St Thomas and the seculars); anticlericalism, 369, B) (Deists), 482-III, 6 (Communists), 531, B), 1 (Nietzsche).

VII. — MORALITY.

A) GENERAL ETHICS.

104. **Systems of Morality.** *a*) *Spiritualist morality* or morality of good *(traditional morality)* : pagan origin, 32 (Socrates), 61 (Plato), 88 (Aristotle); — among the Christians, 172 (St. Augustine, 269 (St. Thomas), 280 (St. Bonaventure), 297 (Scotus), 345 (Malebranche). — *b*) *Ascetic and mystic* morality, 135-139 (Plotinus), 172 (St. Augustine),

551, B) (Bergson : open morality). — c) *Stoicism :* Origin, 97 (see p. 141, the Cynics). Definition and pagan Stoics, 98; — other Stoics, 311, 4 (Renaissance), 500, c (stoic tendency of Taine), and even of Descartes, 335. — d) *Epicureanism* or *hedonism :* origin, 97 (see p. 141, the Cyrenaics). Definition and pagan Epicureans, 114; 480-III (Spencer), characteristics of the ideal Communist, 582-III, concl. — e) *Utilitarianism :* individual, 369, C) (B. de Mandeville), 370 (Helvetius), 384bis (Hume), 484, B) (Bentham); — social, 487-I (St. Mill), 480-III (Spencer), 508-III (Wundt). In the improper sense, 32 (Socrates), utilitarian tendency, 316, D) (Fr. Bacon). — f) *Scientific* or *sociological morality :* first attempts, 335 (Descartes), 466, 4 (A. Comte), 480-III (Spencer), 500 (Taine); — complete theory, 516-518 (Durkheim), 551, A) (closed morality, according to Bergson). — g) *Kantian morality* or *formal* morality, 410, ff. — h) Pantheist or *normative* morality, 353 (Spinoza), 354 (morality of joy). — i) Morality of *sympathy,* 369 (A. Smith), 384bis, A) (Hume); of *solidarity,* 520 (L. Bourgeois). — k) Morality of *pessimism,* 430 (Schopenhauer). — i) Morality of *nature,* 452 (Rousseau). — Evolutionist morality, 480-III (Spencer), 530, A) (Gentile). — Morality of *racism,* 531, A) (Gobineau, Rosenberg); morality of the superman, 531, B) (Nietzsche).

105. **The Ultimate End or Beatitude in the Present Life.** a) Through habitual contemplation of God, 88 (Aristotle); through union with God or creative emotion, 551, B), 2 (open morality according to Bergson); — b) through the harmony of goods, 31 (Socrates), 61 (Plato); — c) through absence of trouble, due to pleasure, 106 (Epicurus), due to tension of the will, 98 (Stoics), by avoiding judgment, 114 (Sceptics); — d) through peace, 368 (Hobbes); or through complete individual liberty, 449 (Rousseau); — e) through social perfection, 480-III (Spencer), 482-III, 4 (Communists), 487-I (St. Mill), 519 (Durkheim), 551, A), 3 (closed morality according to Bergson). — f) *Possibility of attaining Beatitude in this life :* perfectly, 104, 3 (Stoics); — imperfectly, 88, 3 (Aristotle); — not possible, 173 (St. Augustine), 90 (St. Thomas), 414 (Kant).

106. **The Ultimate End or Beatitude in the Future Life.** The true doctrine, 90. It consists in — a) contemplation of the Ideas, 65, 2 (Plato), or ecstasy, 139, 3 (Plotinus); — b) loving vision of God, 173 (St. Augustine); with priority of the will, 247, 1 (Augustinians), 292 (Duns Scotus); with priority of the intellect, 269, 2 (St. Thomas); — c) intellectual love of God, 354 (Spinoza); — d) sovereign good, or absolute moral perfection, 414 (Kant).

107. **The Moral Law.** a) Complete theory, 175 (St. Augustine), 269, 4 (St. Thomas), 280 (St. Bonaventure). — b) Imperfect theory, 63 (Plato); 88, 3 (Aristotle). — c) False theories : expression of the general will, 453, 3, c (Rousseau); — or of the order of the State, see *Statism,* n. 116, c). — d) The laws of desire, according to Plotinus, 137, B); — e) Natural law and positive laws, 64, 3 (Plato), 117 (Cicero), 175 and 176, 3 (St. Augustine), 269, 4, 4 (St. Thomas), 368bis, D), 2⁰ (Hobbes), 447, D) (Montesquieu). The distinction depends on the Free Will of God, according to Scotus, 297. The Mosaic law as interpreted by Maimonides, 196. — Relativity of moral laws, 375 bis, 1 (Locke), 384 bis, 4 (Hume). Positive law, the foundation of morality, 370 (D'Holbach), 489, 3 (Bain).

108. **Moral Obligation.** *a*) Definition, 175, 2. — *b*) Established as a reality, 35 (Socrates), 88, 3 (Aristotle); as the foundation of morality, 411 (Kant). — *c*) *Imperfect explanations :* in terms of utility, 35 (Socrates), 487-I (St. Mill); in terms of the attraction of the Good, 63 (Plato); — in terms of the necessity of the natural law, 88, 3 (Aristotle); — in terms of sanctions, 489, 3 (Bain); — in terms of pantheistic determinism, 353 (Spinoza); in terms of the Categorical Imperative, 411 (Kant); — in terms of society, 518 (Durkheim), 551, A), 1 (in closed morality, according to Bergson); — in terms of the law of altruistic progress, definition of duty according to A. Comte, 466. — *d*) *True explanation :* in terms of the divine Eternal Law, 175, 2 (St. Augustine), 344, 4 (St. Thomas); — in terms of the Divine Will, 345 (Malebranche). — *e*) Morality with neither obligation nor sanction, 531, B), 2 (Guyau).

109. **Sanctions.** *a*) Their necessity, 65 (Plato); 375 bis, 1 (Locke), 484, B) (Bentham), 487-I (St. Mill); essential to the moral act, 517, 1 (Durkheim); — excluded, 411 (Kant : duty for the sake of duty). — *b*) Sanctions in the present life, through the joy which accompanies virtue, 35 (Socrates), 196 (Maimonides); — *c*) in the future life, see n. 106. — *d*) Positive sanctions : the *pain of death*, rejected, 176, 3 (St. Augustine), admitted, 428, 1 (Hegel).

110. **The Moral Virtues.** *a*) Virtue equated with knowledge (the *Socratic paradox*) : 33, 34 (Socrates), 62, 1 (Plato, for perfect virtue). — *b*) Virtues are *acquired* habits, 62, 2º (Plato, common virtue), 88, 2 (Aristotle), 269, 4 (St. Thomas); or the order of reason, 174 (St. Augustine). — *c*) Stoic definition, 103; Epicurean, 111. — *d*) Unity of virtue, 104, 2 (Stoics) unification through love, 174 (St. Augustine). — *e*) Their *classification :* perfect and imperfect virtue, 62 (Plato); the four cardinal virtues, 62, 2 (Plato), 88, 2 (Aristotle), 111 (Epicurus), 280 (St. Bonaventure); — Specification through formal objects, 269, 3 (St. Thomas). — Love of virtue, explained through utilitarianism, 487-I (St. Mill). — *f*) *Wisdom*, supreme virtue, 31, 4º (Socrates), 61 (Plato), 103 (Stoics), 111 (in the form of prudence : Epicureans). — *g*) Exclusion of virtues, 451, 1 (Rousseau); — denial of vices, 353 (Spinoza).

111. **The Passions in the Moral Order.** *a*) Total condemnation, 104, 1 (Stoics), 137, 3, 139 (Plotinus); — partial condemnation, 111, 2 (Epicurus); — *b*) moderation necessary, 316, D) (Fr. Bacon), 335 (Descartes), 354 (Spinoza).

112. **Specific Virtues.** *a*) *Prudence :* supreme virtue according to Epicurus, 111, 1. — *b*) *Fortitude :* the virtue of soldiers, 64, *b* (Plato); Stoic impassibility, 104, 1. — *c*) *Temperance*, virtue of laborers, 64, *a* (Plato); — its Epicurean form, 111, 2. — *d*) *Moral purification :* 137, 3 (Plotinus), 174 (St. Augustine), 534 (modernists); — its degrees according to Plotinus, 139; — Self-control or Socratic mortification, 31, 3º and 32, *a*. — *e*) Work; reserved for slaves, 89, 2º, *b* (Aristotle); basis of the right of property, see n. 119 bis, *c*). — *f*) *Justice*, 64, *c* (Plato), 111, 3 (Epicurus), 368, D), 2 (Hobbes), 375 bis, 3º (Locke). Equality, the natural state, 449 (Rousseau, see 450, III, critique). Love of justice, explained in terms of utilitarianism, 487-I (St. Mill). — *g*) *Religion*, see *Duty of Man towards God*, n. 103. — *h*) *Friendship*, 88, 2º, *b* (Aristotle), 111, 4 (Epicurus).

B) SPECIAL ETHICS.

113. **Individual Duties.** *a*) Towards God, see n. 103. — *b*) Duties to oneself : suicide permitted, 98 (Stoics); — social trends causing suicides, 515, 2 (Durkheim); suicide, a social evil, 519 (Durkheim). — *c*) Duties towards others to the exclusion of all rights, 466 (A. Comte); duties of solidarity, 520 (L. Bourgeois); tolerance, 375 bis (Locke), 380-III (Spencer); sympathy, the foundation of morality, 369, C) (A. Smith); see n. 104, *i*).

114. **Society in General.** *a*) Is a natural right, 384 bis (Hume); for the purpose of attaining beatitude, 64 (Plato), 89 (Aristotle), 176 (St. Augustine), 269, 5 (St. Thomas), 464 (A. Comte). — Is contrary to nature, 368 (Hobbes), 449 (Rousseau). — *b*) *Socialism :* definition, 482-I, 3; see p. 810, note 2; — directive principles, 482-I, 3; — forms of socialism : *Saint-Simonism,* 482-II, 1 (Saint-Simon, Enfantin); *La Phalange,* 482-II, 2 (Fourrier, Considerant); *mutualism,* 482-II, 3 (Proudhon); the *right to work,* 482-II, 4 (L. Blanc); *Marxism,* 482-III, 1-3 (K. Marx); *atheistic Communism,* 482-III, 4-6; — *rational communism,* 64 (Plato). — *c*) *Social contract,* 368 bis, D) (Hobbes), 385 bis, 4° (Locke), 453 (Rousseau); — criticized by Hume, 384 bis; — Catholic theory, 309 bis (Suarez). — *d*) *Civilization,* end of society, 480-III (Spencer), 482-III, 4 (Communists); — an effect of the Decalogue, 521 (Le Play); — civilization and culture, 531, A).

115. **Familial Morality.** *a*) The family an institution by natural right, 64 (Plato, in the Laws), 89 (Aristotle), family, the social cell, 464, 2 (A. Comte). — *b*) the family wage, 467, *d* (A. Comte). — *c*) *Husband and Wife :* their mutual obligations, 89, 1 (Aristotle); emancipation of woman, 482-III, 4 (Communists), 487-I (St. Mill); indissolubility of marriage, 467, *e* (A. Comte); theory of free union, 482-III, 4 (Communists); prohibition of incest, its origin, according to Durkheim, 515, 2, *c*. — *d*) *Children :* their duties, 89, 1 (Aristotle); their education, 64, 2 (Plato), 89, 2 (Aristotle), 375 bis, 2° (Locke), 451 (Rousseau), 480-III (Spencer), 487-I (St. Mill). — *e*) *Slavery :* a necessary evil, 64, *d* (Plato); — a natural institution, 89, 2°, (Aristotle), 305 (Sepulveda); — fruit of civilization, 449, 2, *c* (Rousseau). — *f*) Family sacrificed to the State, see *Statism,* n. 116, *c*).

116. **The City or State.** *a*) Its extension limited by the ancients, 64 (Plato), 89, 2 (Aristotle). — *b*) The City of God according to St. Augustine, 176. — *c*) *Statism :* totalitarian form, 311, 4 (Machiavelli), 354, 2 (Spinoza), 368 bis (Hobbes), 418 (Kant), 428, 2 (Hegel), 453, 3 (Rousseau); — in education, 64, 2 (Plato), 89, 2 (Aristotle). — *d*) *Relations with the Church :* independence and submission, 176, 5 (St. Augustine), 305 (Vittoria), 467 (in the theological age, according to A. Comte), see A. Comte. the distinction between spiritual and temporal power, 465, 2, the Church replaced by sociology in the positive age, 467; the State governs the Church, 368 bis, 4° (Hobbes), 375 bis, 4° (Locke), 482-III, 5 (Communists); — *e*) decentralized State, or police State, 480-III (Spencer), 503, 2 (Taine).

117. **Authority.** *a*) Necessity, see *Society, a natural right,* n. 114, *a*). — *b*) *Origin :* comes from God, immediately according to the Protestants,

309[bis], mediately through social institutions, 176, 2 (St. Augustine); — through the people, 245 (St. Thomas), 309[bis] (Suarez), 375[bis], 4° (Locke). — c) Comes from man through a *contract*, 368 (Hobbes), 453 (Rousseau). — d) Comes from nature : due to the germ of wisdom, 64, c (Plato), due to the germ of a capacity to be exercised, 176, 2° (St. Augustine, Cicero), 465, 2 (A. Comte).

118. Forms of Government. a) Harmonizing theory of the three fundamental forms (monarchy, aristocracy, democracy), 64, 3° (Plato, aristocratic tendency), 89, 2 (Aristotle), 245 (St. Thomas), 447 (Montesquieu), 503 (Taine). — Their similarity (according to St. Augustine), 176, 2°. — b) Proponents of the democratic system, 354, 2 (Spinoza), 449, 453 (Rousseau), 482-III, 5 (dictatorship of the proletariat : Communists); — c) Proponents of the despotic system, 368[bis], D), 4° (Hobbes).

119. Sociology. a) Definition, 463; legitimacy of the study, 469, c. — b) *Sociological method*, 463 (A. Comte), 514 (Durkheim). — c) *Object :* definition of the social act, 515, 1 (Durkheim); division into two parts : static and dynamic sociology, 464-467 (A. Comte), 488 (St. Mill). — d) *Social laws :* law of progress, 370 (see p. 590, Condorcet), 466 (A. Comte); law of primordial factors, 503 (Taine). — e) Social realism, 507, 3 (Wundt), 513 (Durkheim).

119[bis]. Social and Political Economics. a) *Definition and legitimacy,* 283-III, 3. — b) Principal proponents : liberals, 369, C) (A. Smith and the physiocrats), 375[bis], 3° (Locke), 484, B) (Ricardo), 488 (St. Mill); — socialists, see *Socialism,* n. 114, b). — c) *Work, the origin of the right to property,* 375[bis], 3° (Locke), 482-II, 3 (Proudhon), 482-II, 4 (Blanc), 482-III, 2 (K. Marx). — d) Capital and capitalism, 369, C) (A. Smith), 482-III, 2 (criticism by K. Marx); see b) *liberal proponents.* — e) *Law of supply and demand,* 369, C) (A. Smith), 484, B) (Ricardo); criticism of this law by K. Marx, 482-III, 2, b ; and by St. Mill, 488.

120. International Morality. Existence of international rights, 117 (Cicero), 269, 5 (St. Thomas). The colonial problem, 305 (Vittoria). — Society of nations, 418 (Kant).

121. War. Conditions for a just war and the causes of war, 176, 4 (St. Augustine). The absurdity of war, 418 (Kant). Justified by success, according to Hegel, 482, 2 and Cousin, 443.

VIII. — ALPHABETIC INDEX
TO THE DOCTRINAL TABLE[1].

---

[1] Numbers after the titles refer to *topic numbers* in the preceding *doctrinal table* and not to pages, unless otherwise indicated.

TABLE OF CONTENTS.

PART ONE.

GREEK AND ROMAN ERAS.

PAGAN PHILOSOPHY.

(From 6th century B. C. to 6th century A. D.).

FIRST PERIOD.

DAWN OF PHILOSOPHICAL HELLENISM.

(6th and 5th centuries B. C.).

SECOND PERIOD.

GOLDEN AGE OF PHILOSOPHICAL HELLENISM.

From 470 : birth of Socrates, to 322, death of Aristotle
(5th and 4th centuries B. C.).

THIRD PERIOD.

DECLINE AND TRANSITION.

From 322 : death of Aristotle, to 270; death of Plotinus (3rd Century
B. C. — 3rd Century A. D.) — 529 : Close of the School at Athens.

PART TWO.

PATRISTIC AND MEDIEVAL ERAS.

CHRISTIAN PHILOSOPHY.
(2nd-16th century).

FIRST PERIOD.

PREPARATION, FATHERS OF THE CHURCH.
(2nd-7th century).

SECOND PERIOD.

THE SCHOLASTIC SYNTHESIS.

(7th-13th century).

THIRD PERIOD.

DECADENCE.

(14th-17th centuries).

PART THREE.

MODERN ERA.

MODERN AND NEO-THOMIST PHILOSOPHY.

(17th-20th centuries).

FIRST PERIOD.

THE CARTESIAN SPIRIT.

(17th-18th centuries).

SECOND PERIOD.

THE KANTIAN SPIRIT.

(19th-20th centuries).

TABLES.

Printed in Belgium by DESCLÉE & Cie, ÉDITEURS, S. A. Tournai. — 10.088